☆ *PETER H. ODEGARD'S* **THE AMERICAN REPUBLIC**

With **HANS H. BAERWALD**

UNIVERSITY OF CALIFORNIA, LOS ANGELES

and **WILLIAM C. HAVARD**

UNIVERSITY OF MASSACHUSETTS

SECOND EDITION

☆ *PETER H. ODEGARD'S* # THE

AMERICAN REPUBLIC

ITS GOVERNMENT AND POLITICS

HARPER & ROW, PUBLISHERS   NEW YORK · EVANSTON · LONDON

CONTENTS

PREFACE

WHEN ONE STUDIES the government and politics of any society, certain basic questions inevitably and invariably arise. Among those suggested by Professor Robert Dahl are the following: (1) What is politics and what is it all about? (2) What do political systems have in common and how do they differ? (3) What is the role of power, authority, and influence in political systems? (4) What conditions make for political stability, orderly change, or revolution? (5) What factors determine or influence political behavior? (6) What norms or standards are available to evaluate various political systems? That is, what political system is best for a particular area, people or time?

In summary, for any particular political system one might ask, Who governs? How? Why? and To what ends? This book represents an effort to answer these questions for the political system called the American Republic. Part I we have called "Political Life in America," in which we explore the nature and environmental conditions of political power and power structures. Part II has to do with "The American Political Process," in which we attempt to examine some of the dynamic forces which shape government and political behavior in the American political system, that is, the operation of that system. Part III, titled "Public Policy in American Democracy," is an analysis of certain basic policies of the American Republic, that is, the policy produced by the system.

This prefatory description of the Second Edition of *The American Republic* was completed by Professor Peter Odegard shortly before his death. The major part of the last year of his life had been taken up with the thorough reorganization and extensive rewriting of the materials for this edition. We are pleased to be participants in this renewal of *The American Republic* for students of American politics.

HANS H. BAERWALD
WILLIAM C. HAVARD

☆ *PETER H. ODEGARD'S* THE
AMERICAN
REPUBLIC

PART I

POLITICAL LIFE IN AMERICA

1

ANALYSIS OF POLITICAL SYSTEMS

☆ *POWER IN SOCIETY AND GOVERNMENT*

Whenever one speaks of government, one speaks of power, for without power government is meaningless. When it is said that "politics is the study of influence and the influential . . . [and that] the influential are those who get the most of what there is to get," only part of the story is told. For what there is to get is power and the fruits of power, which may well be, as Professor Lasswell says, "income, deference and safety."

But power itself is an ambiguous term. In general one may say that any individual or group able to control the behavior of other individuals or groups has power. Or put another way, power is the capacity in any individual or group to make and enforce decisions (rules and regulations) affecting the behavior of other individuals or groups. The exercise of power, therefore, involves the application of sanctions—penalties—of some kind to behavior that deviates from what is required under decisions that have been made. Without this ability to enforce decisions, one cannot speak realistically of power or for that matter of government.

Power, in this sense, is widely diffused in society, and government and politics are attributes of every type of organized activity. The trade union leader, the business executive, the teacher, the priest, even the father or mother in the family—as well as prime ministers, presidents, governors, and mayors—exercise power and consequently are involved in the process of government. For all of these, in varying degrees, may command and control human behavior by applying sanctions of some kind to enforce decisions that have been made. The process of government, in these general terms, cuts a wide swath and includes the making and enforcement of decisions in virtually all types of organizations, including trade unions, churches, corporations, and colleges, as well as towns and cities, states, and nations.

Although it may be argued that the political state represents but one of many kinds of government, there are important attributes that distinguish it from other organizations. Among these are the extent of its jurisdiction and the degree and nature of its power. Historically the political state has claimed jurisdiction over all persons residing within more or less clearly defined geographical limits, as in the Greek city-state, the Roman Empire, and the modern national state. Within these limits the state has claimed supremacy over individuals, groups, and associations. Even where the jurisdiction of these subordinate associations may extend beyond the territorial limits of the state, as in the case of certain churches, corporations, and labor organizations, the state claims supremacy and expects loyalty and obedience from all those living within its borders. Moreover, for those living within its territorial limits, membership is compulsory. In general, this is not true of other organizations.

But there is another and perhaps more important respect in which the political state differs from other social organizations, namely in the nature of the sanctions by which its decisions may be enforced. The working man who defies the commands—that is, does not abide by the decisions—of his trade union may be fined, suspended, or even expelled from the union. Employees of business corporations, members of churches, college students and their faculties may be dismissed or in other ways disciplined when they "get out of line." But in none of these may they be punished by imprisonment or death. Only the state may legitimately use physical coercion to carry into effect the decisions made by its constituted authorities.

It is this claim to compulsory jurisdiction over all its citizens or subjects, and this monopoly of coercive power, that makes control of the state of such transcendent importance. Indeed, it is this state monopoly of violence that Thomas Hobbes, in his great book, *The Leviathan,* described as a *sine qua non of* civilization itself. For, he argued, it is only by giving up the private exercise of force and violence that we can insure the peace, security, and freedom upon which civilization depends.

If, as Hobbes argues, a monopoly of coercive power in the state is a necessary condition of internal peace and of civilization itself, it may also be a weapon by which ruling elites promote their private interests at the expense of the common good. It is this aspect of political power that throughout history has engendered fear of the tyrant. For political power, like atomic energy, can be a force for good or evil. It may be used to promote the security, freedom, and welfare of the individual and the community or to exalt and enrich those who command at the expense of those who are forced to comply. In one guise political power is embodied in the public health officer, the reclamation engineer, the schoolteacher, or the policeman directing the orderly flow of traffic; in another it appears in the tyrant of varying dimensions, from the petty, selfish, and corrupt ward boss to Hitler or Stalin. Its symbols are, on the one hand, the public highway, hospital, or schoolhouse—and on the other hand, the prison or concentration camp. The history of politics is in large measure the story of the unremitting struggle to make coercive power the servant rather than the master of the community.

Political power, unlike political influence, carries with it the threat of violence. In its naked form its symbols are the sword, the bombing plane, and the stockpile of atomic weapons. It operates, moreover, as some scholars have argued, in one direction only. Once a decision has been made, once a law or decree has been proclaimed, the full force of the state's coercive power stands ready to enforce it. Political power, it is said, is asymmetrical: the state commands and the citizen obeys under the ultimate penalty of fine, imprisonment, or even death. Influence, on the other hand, is a two-way street, that is, a symmetrical or reciprocal relation of argument and response, promise and performance, of conduct governed by *quid pro quo*. One may argue with the butcher or the baker, one may even tell his boss to "go to," but one does not, with any prospect of success, argue with the cop on the corner, the state trooper, or the soldier under orders. And so too in the external relations of sovereign states, once negotiations have concluded and a decision has been reached affecting the vital interests of the nation, defiance may bring swift and terrible retribution. For negotiation among nations, like debate among individuals, is a process of more or less formalized influence, of give and take, of conflict, concession, and compromise. But in the internal government and external relations of political states—unlike those of private associations—there looms in the background of all negotiations the possibility that in the end, force may be the arbiter.

The Ethical Basis of Power

This description of political power in the state as an organized monopoly of coercive force is but a first step to an understanding of power in society, or of government and politics. For compliance with the commands, the laws, the rules, and regulations of the state requires the use of force only in rare instances. Whether in the organization of the public services, the enforcement of the criminal code, or in providing for national security, voluntary compliance is the rule. Indeed, disobedience of the political state is probably less frequent and less widespread than disobedience of other forms of social control in the family, the trade union, or the church. Obviously, custom and tradition, education and indoctrination play a prominent part in developing habits of compliance. How far, for example, are the formal attributes of power—the pomp and pageantry of kings, the charisma of presidents and premiers—necessary to the exercise of effective political power? In his classic essay on the English

Constitution, Walter Bagehot emphasized the importance of the pageantry and panoply of power to effective government. The mace and the scepter, the orb and crown are more than the childish baubles of kings. They are the essential symbols of the "power and glory" of the state. Without these, government becomes a mean and common thing, ripe for defiance and rebellion—without order and stability. These symbols and ceremonies sheath the naked sword of power and make compliance palatable and even pleasant.

Republics, according to Bagehot, that fail to invest power with appropriate symbols of authority and legitimacy tend to be weak and unstable. The loyalty that makes for greatness in a state, that evokes not sullen obedience but service beyond the call of duty, is not won by threat of force alone. For, as the English political philosopher Thomas Hill Green observed, it is *will*, not force, that furnishes the only enduring basis for political power. On one occasion, when urged to forego a certain course, Napoleon is said to have shouted angrily, "let the decree issue— my dragoons will see to it that the people obey." To which his worldly wise foreign minister, Talleyrand, is reported to have replied: "Sire! You can do much with bayonets except to sit comfortably enthroned upon them."

Political Authority and Legitimacy

One may indeed ask how long effective power can endure in the absence of *authority* which rests on a deep-grained consensus that the existing power structure is legitimate. Without authority, political power lies exposed as naked force without support in reason, sentiment, or will. To say that power, as distinguished from influence, is asymmetrical, operating only in one direction—from sovereign to subject and never from subject to sovereign—and that authority serves to rationalize or legitimize both does no more than state the problem. To invest political power with authority, that is, to make it legitimate, becomes a central goal of all government and politics.

For nearly everywhere today political authority has its roots in the consent of the governed. To review the development of this so-called social contract theory would be to write a political history of Western civilization. Out of the rich heritage of classical Greek and Roman political history and philosophy, out of the struggles of artisans and merchants against the landed gentry in the seventeenth and eighteenth centuries, out of the religious struggles of the Protestant Reformation, out of the Enlightenment and the Heavenly City of eighteenth-century philosophy, and out of the impact of science and technology upon nearly every social institution, the idea grew that neither force alone—nor divine right— could furnish a proper ethical basis for political power. In their attack upon the established church and the divinely established political order, of which the church was deemed a necessary part, the leaders of the Puritan Revolution sought a new foundation for the political state. It is, they said, "an undeniable maxim of government . . . that all government is in the assent of the people."[1]

Thus the secularization of the state went hand in hand with a demand that all legitimate power and authority must rest on the consent of the governed. Even those philosophers, like Thomas Hobbes, who sought to uphold and strengthen the monarchy, based their claims upon a social contract by which, in return for law and order, the people gave up their freedom to avenge their own wrongs and redress their own grievances to the monarch who henceforth ruled in their behalf. To John Locke, in seventeenth-century England, this social contract theory became the ethical foundation, not for the absolute monarch of Hobbes, but for the constitutional monarchy of William and Mary and their successors. In France, J. J. Rousseau extended the doctrine to place all legitimate power in the people, blasting in the process the ethical foundations of all governments not based on the consent of the governed, or what he called the "general will." And he did not hesitate to say that "the most general will is always the most just, and the voice of the people is, in fact, the voice of God."

In its American version, the social contract theory has been most eloquently expressed by Thomas Jefferson in the Preamble to the Declaration of Independence.

> We hold these truths to be self-evident, that all men are created equal,
> that they are endowed by their Creator with certain unalienable Rights,
> that among these are Life, Liberty and the pursuit of Happiness.—That
> to secure these rights, Governments are instituted among Men, deriving
> their just powers from the consent of the governed,—That whenever any
> Form of Government becomes destructive of these ends, it is the Right of
> the People to alter or to abolish it, and to institute new Government,
> laying its foundation on such principles and organizing its powers in such
> form, as to them shall seem most likely to effect their Safety and Happiness.

It is these words, not those of Hobbes or Locke or Rousseau, which have encircled the globe and which even today play a major role in the development of democratic institutions on the ruins of undemocratic regimes, many more ancient than the Declaration itself. And it is in the tradition of the Declaration that American government and politics have evolved, with no little conflict and confusion as to the proper relation of the people to the government or of so-called ruling elites to the masses. Nor are we quite certain how far the power of government should be used to determine the basic direction and purpose of our national life.

[1] A. D. Lindsay, *The Modern Democratic State* (New York: Oxford University Press, 1943) , p. 118.

☆ *THE STRUCTURE OF POWER*

The power structure of any society presents an almost infinitely complex and shifting pattern of interpersonal relations arranged in a variety of hierarchical orders of leaders and followers. The pattern is reminiscent of the well-known couplet:

> There never was a tiny flea but had a flea to bite him,
> And on that flea another flea, and so ad infinitum.

Leaders and elites, as everyone knows, come in all sorts and sizes, from the president of the PTA to the President of the United States. The real power elite, however, according to C. Wright Mills, "is composed of men whose positions enable them to . . . make decisions having major consequences."[2]

The relation of leaders and followers, of elite and mass to each other, however, is so integral as to make such distinctions in many organizations more formal than real. As a general rule those at the lower levels are to be distinguished from those at the top, not only by varying degrees of power, as measured by the number of people subject to their jurisdiction, but by the nature and effectiveness of the sanctions by which their decisions are enforced. There is, for example, a difference in the power status of a teacher who may keep a child after school, the principal who may discipline the teacher, the superintendent who may dismiss the principal, the school board which may dismiss the superintendent, and the voters who may, on election day, defeat the school board. One measure of power might be the extent or intensity of the effects within the organization of decisions that are made and enforced. In general those decisions made at the top of the pyramid, if enforced, have greater, more widespread, effect than those made at lower levels. Hence an individual's formal position in the hierarchy of any organization is a crude measure of his power and prestige, since in most societies prestige is a function of power. Branch managers normally have greater power and prestige than local managers, district managers than branch managers, and so on up the pyramid to the president of the organization. As a rule the intensity and significance of the power struggle in any organization is likely to increase as one moves from lower to higher levels of authority.

These observations apply to interpersonal power relations in any organized group or community. And since, as we have seen, power in its broadest sense is widely diffused, a comprehensive description of the total power structure in any society would require an examination of social and economic interrelationships as well as those of the political state. Professor Mills, for example, says that "within American society major

---

[2] *The Power Elite* (New York: Oxford University Press, 1956) , p. 4.

national power now resides in the economic, the political, and the military domains." Other parts of the total power structure, in the great families, churches, schools, and colleges are, he argues, peripheral to the central core of the major power elites. In any case, the interrelations of the many power elites in America are so intimate, continuous, and significant that no one power elite can be fully understood in isolation. One would find that within the 500 largest corporations, for example, the hierarchies of power and authority, the decision-making process, and the struggle for control of governing boards and offices are not too dissimilar from what goes on in the government of city, state, and nation.[3]

Bearing all this in mind, however, there remain important respects in which the power elite known as the American government differs from other so-called power elites. They differ first of all in the scope of their jurisdiction. Only the government of the city, state, or nation can claim jurisdiction over all persons within prescribed territorial limits. And sanctions available to the government are both more extensive and intensive. No private corporation, religious body, or trade union, however powerful, may legitimately employ physical coercion against its rivals or subordinates. Even the military elite, as an integral part of the total political power structure, is not a law unto itself, but in our system subject to civilian control.

Military, economic, and other power elites may, and do, exercise great influence on political or governmental elites—as they in turn are profoundly influenced by government. But when all is said and done, only the government may legitimately employ physical coercion. It is well to remember, too, that the basic structure of other power systems, and even their internal governance, are either specifically defined by the political state or operate at all times under laws made and enforced by state authorities. It is, therefore, without apology that we look more closely at the structure of political power in the political state.

Classifications of Governments

Political systems have been described in a number of ways since Aristotle offered the first systematic analysis in terms of the number of persons who participate in making basic decisions. A second system classifies governments according to the manner in which power is organized within the government itself, that is, the power relations of legislative, executive, and judicial officers or elites. Another system classifies governments according to what may be called the geographical structure of power. A fourth system looks at governments in terms of their party systems on the

---

[3] See, for example, A. Berle, *Power Without Property: A New Development in American Political Economy* (New York: Harcourt, Brace & World, 1959). Also, R. A. Dahl, "Business and Politics: A Critical Appraisal of Political Science," *American Political Science Review* (March, 1959).

theory that it is to the political parties and/or pressure groups that one must look for the key to power relations in any political system. And finally, governments have been classified according to the extent or scope of power which they possess vis-à-vis individuals and other groups or institutions within the society. We may look briefly at these various systems.

ARISTOTLE'S CLASSIFICATION. In making his analysis of governments, Aristotle makes two basic assumptions. First, he says that in every society there will be different social and economic classes with interests of their own, often in conflict with the common good of all. "In all states," he says, "there may be distinguished three parts or classes . . . the very rich; the very poor; and the middle class. . . ." The best and most stable government, in Aristotle's view, would be one in which a fair equilibrium among these classes was maintained—but with the middle class firmly in the saddle, since they are likely to be the best guardians of the common good. "It is clear," he says, "that the best form of political society is one where power is vested in the middle class." For the middle class, he argues, by holding the balance of power in the community, can prevent the rich on the one hand or the poor on the other from subverting the government to their own interest. Hence, he says, "good government is attainable in those states where there is a large middle class . . . large enough . . . at any rate . . . to prevent either of the opposing extremes from becoming dominant."[4]

Second, he says that whatever may be the formal structure in the state, only those governments that promote the interest of the community as a whole can be regarded as legitimate. Those in which political power is used, not for the common good, but for the special interest of the ruling class, he regards as corrupt or perverted. "All those governments," he says, "which have a common good in view are rightly established and strictly just, but those who have in view only the good of the rulers are all founded on wrong principles and are widely different from what a government ought to be, for they are a tyranny over slaves, whereas a city (a just state) is a community of free men."[5]

In classifying governments, Aristotle's formal principle is the number of persons who share in the decision-making process. Thus, "a state which is governed by one person for the common good" is a *monarchy*. "One that is governed by . . . a few, an *aristocracy*." And finally, "when the citizens at large govern for the common good, it is called a *polity*." Against these legitimate forms he sets those corrupt or perverted forms in which power is exercised not for the common good but for the special interest of the power elite. Thus, he says, a *tyranny* is "a monarchy where

[4] *The Politics of Aristotle*, trans. Ernest Barker (Oxford: Clarendon Press, 1948), p. 182.

[5] Aristotle, *Politics*, Everyman's Edition, Book III, chap. VI.

Who Governs?	Government in Whose Interest	
	Legitimate Government In the Interest of the Whole Community	Perverted Government In the Interest of the Rulers Themslves
One Man	Kingship (Monarchy)	Tyranny
A Few Men	Aristocracy	Oligarchy
The Majority	Polity	Democracy

Figure 1–1   Aristotle's Classification of Governments.

the good of one man only is the object of government," an *oligarchy* is where the supreme power is lodged in a few, that is, the rich, who govern in their own interest, and a *democracy* where the multitude, that is, the poor, govern without regard for the interests of other classes in the community.

Schematically, Aristotle's classification[6] may be shown as in Figure 1–1.

As a practical man, Aristotle knew that these formal distinctions in terms of the number who govern were by no means sharp ones, nor were the various categories mutually exclusive. "The factor of number," he said, "is an accidental attribute, due to the simple fact that the rich are generally few and the poor are generally numerous."

Although the basic principles of Aristotle's classification remain as valid today as when he first taught them to his students, there are gaps and weaknesses in his system when applied to contemporary political systems. *Monarchy*, for example, as a form of government, has become virtually extinct, and where it does survive, it serves mainly to provide a ceremonial setting for governments that are essentially democratic. Kings have in fact become the servants of their ministers rather than the other way around. One is reminded in this connection of Charles I's remark when he found the following note tacked to his bedchamber door:

> *Here lies our sovereign lord the King,*
> *Whose word no man relies on.*
> *He never says a stupid thing,*
> *He never does a wise one.*

"To be sure," said Charles, "for whereas my thoughts are my own, my deeds are those of my ministers." And *tyranny*, the corrupt form of monarchy, has been transformed into a kind of totalitarian democracy, in which the tyrant is less likely to be one man than the chairman of a ruling monolithic political party. Nor can *aristocracy*, in the Aristotelian

6 From Andrew Hacker, *Political Theory* (New York: Macmillan, 1961) , p. 82.

sense, be said to be a very common form of government in our modern world. Every ruling elite fancies itself an aristocracy—that is, an elite of quality as well as of power—but in fact is more likely to resemble Aristotle's corrupt form of aristocracy—that is, *oligarchy.*

Indeed, oligarchy is probably the most common form of government in the world, for as R. Michels has said, "who says organization, says oligarchy." The few, of course, always govern; although the few who do are not always the rich, as Aristotle thought, nor are they free from popular and other controls. But the basic problem today, as in Aristotle's time, is to compel those who govern to do so for the common good and not for the selfish interests of the power elite itself. Although Aristotle regarded democracy as a corrupt or perverted form of government, it is doubtful that he would take this view toward modern representative democracies. Unfortunately, Aristotle confined his analysis of democracy almost exclusively to the system of direct democracy in which the multitude of citizens participate not only in the selection of public officials but also in the actual processes of legislation and administration. Had Aristotle been familiar with modern systems of constitutional government, representation, separation of powers, and federalism, he might well have regarded modern democracy as a form of government "rightly established" if not "strictly just."

CLASSIFICATION ACCORDING TO THE INTERNAL OR FUNCTIONAL STRUCTURE OF POWER. Under our second system of classification according to the internal or functional structure of power, two main systems are usually described: the *parliamentary* and the *presidential.* Parliamentary government is essentially a power structure in which (1) the legislative and executive branches of government are closely integrated, interdependent, and responsible to the mass electorate; (2) the titular head of state is often, if not always, distinguished from the active head of the government; (3) the effective government, or executive, is able to initiate an appeal to the electorate prior to the expiration of its constitutional term; and (4) the courts are independent of political control but do not presume to pass upon the constitutional validity of acts of the legislature.

The prototype of the parliamentary system is the government of England, where, as Walter Bagehot put it, the government is "possessed of two parts," the dignified parts and the efficient parts. The queen and the royal establishment, serving as the titular head of state, provide the dignified—or as Bagehot said elsewhere, the "theatrical"—elements. The efficient parts of the system are provided by the prime minister and his Cabinet, all of whom, although formally appointed by the queen, are members of Parliament. Indeed the Cabinet members derive whatever power they have, not from their designation by the queen but from their membership in Parliament. The prime minister, in fact, is selected not because of his loyalty to the crown or because of his own talents, but because he is the leader of the majority party in Parliament.

The Cabinet, or as it is known in England, the "Government," is thus, to use Bagehot's words, a "combining committee—a hyphen which joins, a buckle which fastens the legislative part of the state to the executive part of the state." Theoretically, whenever the Cabinet loses the confidence of Parliament, it must resign so that the queen may appoint a new "Government" more in harmony with the legislative will. In practice, however, this rarely occurs, since the prime minister and his Cabinet, as leaders of the majority party in Parliament, control that body with an iron hand. Indeed, it is not the Parliament which normally destroys the Cabinet, but the Cabinet which can destroy the Parliament. This it does by asking the queen to dissolve Parliament even before the expiration of its full constitutional term. And the time selected for such dissolution is calculated to serve the interests of the Cabinet and the ruling party. Thus the Cabinet, though a creature of the legislature, can destroy its own creator. It is small wonder that one hears talk about the "Cabinet dictatorship" in England.

In contrast to the parliamentary system is the so-called *presidential* system, of which the government of the United States is the prototype. Instead of an integration or fusion of the executive and legislative branches, there is a strict separation. Not only are the President and Vice-President outside and independent of the Congress, they are elected from different constituencies for different terms. Moreover, the Constitution expressly provides that "no Senator or Representative shall, during the time for which he was elected, be appointed to any civil office under the authority of the United States, which shall have been created or the emoluments of which have been increased during such time." And there is a like prohibition that "no person holding any office under the United States shall be a member of either House during his continuance in office." Both the President and the Congress are elected for fixed and staggered terms—and the President has no power to dissolve the legislature prior to the expiration of its term.

To make this separation of powers clear and as unambiguous as possible, the Constitution, in separate articles, provides that "all legislative powers herein granted shall be vested in a Congress of the United States" and that "the executive power shall be vested in a President of the United States of America." In theory, therefore, neither the President nor the Congress may exercise powers assigned by the Constitution to the other. No small amount of controversy has occurred concerning the extent to which Congress may constitutionally invade the powers of the President, and the President may exercise the legislative powers of Congress. To maintain this strict separation of powers, the Constitution and political custom have assigned to the Supreme Court—itself independent of both the executive and legislative branches—responsibility for resolving conflicts of power and jurisdiction.

We shall take a much closer look at this principle of separation of powers later on. At this point one may remark only that neither the fusion of executive and legislative powers in the parliamentary system nor the separation of powers in the presidential system is as complete in practice as it is sometimes represented to be in theory. Proponents of the parliamentary system praise it as a formula for effective and responsible government, and proponents of the separation of powers urge that system as a necessary safeguard against usurpation and tyranny. Both may be right!

CLASSIFICATION ACCORDING TO THE GEOGRAPHICAL STRUCTURE OF POWER. Since the political state claims plenary jurisdiction over all people in a given territory, the geographical structure of power within that territory serves as a convenient basis for another system of classification. Forms of political organization in these terms vary from loose unions of sovereign states to the most highly centralized states. On one end of the scale one might place what Professor Jellinek calls "unorganized unions," in which there is no central legislature, executive, or system of courts, but simply a general agreement on common ends and purposes. Personal unions of ruling monarchs, loose alliances of independent states, and agreements of a temporary nature are examples. At the other end of the scale are those *unitary* states in which all power is concentrated in the central government, except as it may delegate limited powers to local or provincial authorities. France, England, and Italy are examples.

Between these two extremes are many types of "organized unions" varying from the leagues of independent sovereign states such as the United Nations to *federal unions* such as the United States, Australia, and Canada. There are, of course, many intermediate types, such as the Organization of American States (OAS), the North Atlantic Treaty Organization (NATO), and our own Articles of Confederation, which we shall examine in more detail later on. In all cases "confederal unions" are bound together more or less permanently by juridical (legal or constitutional) ties and have some central legislative, executive, and judicial organs. Powers of these central authorities, however, are delegated by the constituent member states and are usually strictly limited both in scope and in procedures. Jurisdiction of the central authorities does not normally extend to individual persons but only to the member states as such.

Federal unions, however, such as the United States, Canada, and Australia, have much closer bonds of unity—with more power in the central government. Usually the allocation of powers between the central government and the constituent states is made in the constitution of the federation and cannot be altered, at least formally, without the consent of both the central and constituent state authorities. Most important is that both central and constituent governments, within constitutionally prescribed limits, exercise jurisdiction over individual persons, groups, and organizations found within their territorial limits. Moreover, both governments normally have their own independent legislative, executive, administrative, and judicial organs. Thus, as we shall see, in the United States the same individual in New York may be taxed by both the state of New York and the federal government. He may be tried for crimes under the laws of both—even, indeed, for the same crime if proscribed by both.

Intergovernmental relations in a federal system can become extraordinarily complex. Consider, for example, that in the United States there are more than 90,000 different governmental units, nearly all of which have power to collect taxes. Of these, the federal government is but one unit. In addition there are 50 state governments, over 3,000 counties, 17,000 municipalities, 17,000 townships, just under 35,000 school districts, and over 18,000 special districts.

This formal structure of power in a federal system does not, of course, tell the whole story. In a dynamic society, centripetal and centrifugal forces continue to operate to shift power now in one direction, now in another. Moreover, the formal constitutional federalism of the law books often takes on quite a different form in the face of technological, economic, and social change unanticipated by the founding fathers. But the essential structure remains as one of the most ingenious and creative political inventions for the government of large, heterogeneous states.

CLASSIFICATION ACCORDING TO THE PARTY SYSTEM. The formal structure of power as seen in Aristotle's classification of states, in the parliamentary and presidential forms, and in unitary, confederal, or federal systems, may fail to give an accurate account of the real power structure, unless one takes account of political parties and so-called interest groups as they exist in these various systems. Indeed, the formal system itself may be transformed by the operation of these informal power structures. For example, Montesquieu and our own founding fathers believed that the fusion of executive and legislative powers in the same person was "the very definition of tyranny." If this were true, then the prime minister of Great Britain would be a dictator and the liberties of every Englishman would be in jeopardy. That this is not the case may be due not to any formal structure of political power but to the operation of the English party system. For in Parliament the majority party is forever compelled to fight for its policies, if not for its life, against Her Majesty's Loyal *Opposition,* that is, the minority party. Day in and day out the Opposition searches for weaknesses in the Government—for every sign of corruption or betrayal of the public interest. And although the Cabinet may choose its own time to dissolve Parliament and "go to the country" at some time, at or before the expiration of its established term, it must face the Opposition before the sovereign voters who in the end make or unmake governments.

To understand the government of England without reference to its party system would be like playing Hamlet without his father's ghost. And what is true of England is equally true of France or Italy or, for that matter, the USSR. In a word, the structure of power in any society must include the system of parties and interest groups through which the struggle for power and the decision-making process itself are carried on.

CLASSIFICATION ACCORDING TO THE SCOPE OF POWER.   When one attempts to classify governments according to the scope of political power, certain difficulties immediately arise. The extent to which any government may control the economic and social life of its people will depend less on its formal structure than on its values and traditions and the economic and social system of the country. Traditionally, political systems have been classified in this way by placing them on a continuum ranging from *anarchy* on one end to *totalitarian communism* on the other. To the anarchist, all coercive power—and hence all political power—is evil. The life of a nation and its people, he would argue, should be left to voluntary action by its citizens without the need for any government beyond that generated through voluntary cooperative effort. To the totalitarian, on the other hand, every aspect of life is properly subject to control by the political state. The national economy, education, communication, the family, the church, recreation, all the practical and the fine arts, science and technology are regarded as legitimate subjects for state intervention and control. To the anarchist, the state should disappear and only society should remain; under the totalitarian, society itself would disappear and only the state would remain.

Between these extremes will be found most modern states with policies varying, in theory if not in practice, from a strict adherence to laissez faire, under which state intervention is minimal, to state socialism, under which government regulation, ownership, and operation of the economy are extensive. As we shall see, the trend in most governments has been away from laissez faire, but without embracing socialism, into what both its friends and critics characterize as the *welfare state*. Whether this trend will continue and at what pace is a theme for endless discussion and a major source of conflict in every democratic state. Our concern here is not to resolve this issue but to suggest that the structure of power in any society may have an important bearing on how it is resolved.

Traditionally, democratic governments have reflected a distaste for and a distrust of political power. "The most serious weakness in American life," says William S. White, "is . . . [that] a majority of this country is in headlong flight, morally, literally, from Power. We have rejected it not simply as it may be ill-used or over-used, we have rejected Power simply as a concept."[7]

The whole development of constitutionalism and the incorporation into most constitutions of bills of rights and other limitations upon the scope of political power are evidence of this distrust. On the other hand, the extension of the suffrage and the progressive democratization of governments nearly everywhere in the world has inevitably led to increasing demands upon the political state for social and other services previously left to private, voluntary effort. How are we to reconcile this deep distrust of political power with the increasing pressure for state intervention in our economic and social life? Should we say with Wilhelm Humboldt that the state should "abstain from all solicitude for the positive welfare of the citizens and ought not to proceed a step farther than is necessary for their mutual security and protection against foreign enemies"?

Do we agree with John Stuart Mill that "the sole end for which mankind are warranted . . . in interfering with the liberty of any of their number is self-protection . . . [or] to prevent harm to others. His own good, either physical or moral, is not sufficient warrant . . ."? Or do we believe, with Aristotle, that whereas society exists to make life possible, "government exists to make life good"?

☆ *GEOPOLITICS AND THE AMERICAN REPUBLIC*

The political life and institutions of any country are profoundly influenced by the physical environment in which they develop. Yet as Ellen Semple has observed in her study of the *Influences of Geographic Environment:* "Man has been so noisy about the way in which he has conquered nature and nature has been so silent in her influence over man that the geographical factor in the human equation is frequently overlooked."

One need not be a geographic determinist to admit the importance of geographic influences upon the political life and institutions of mankind. To be sure, a good deal of nonsense has been written about this subject. Democracy and dictatorship, monogamy and polygamy, monotheism and polytheism, even the details of a nation's artistic, economic, political, and religious life have been attributed to geographic influences. Statistical correlations have been established between climate and variations in the distribution of health and disease, literacy, industrial efficiency, and economic enterprise. Even the origin of "men of distinction," the ownership of automobiles, the incidence of crime, and many other aspects of human behavior have been attributed to variable climatic conditions.

Fairly elaborate theories of history and politics have been written in

[7] *Saturday Review* (August, 1960).

similar terms. The English historian Henry Buckle, flatly denying the "metaphysical dogma of free will," asserted that climate, food, soil, and the general aspect of nature were the decisive factors in history.[8]

Others have sought to explain more particular policies in geographic terms. The late Professor Spykman argued that *"size* affects the relative strength of a state in the struggle for power. *Natural resources* influence population density and economic structure, which in themselves are factors in the formulation of policy. . . . *Topography* affects strength because of its influence on unity and internal coherence. *Climate,* affecting transportation and setting limits to the possibility of agricultural production, conditions the economic structure of the state. . . ." And the "shape and topography of a state" will have a direct influence on internal communication and administration and thus affect political institutions and policies. "States that are long and narrow in shape," he said, "tend inevitably to disintegrate. . . . Mountain distribution, the chief cause of the present *ethnic* distribution, has exercised on Switzerland a definitely decentralizing effect. . . ." A network of rivers makes Paris "the inevitable center of France. . . ."[9]

One needs to be cautious in making generalizations of this kind. Human nature is not an inert plaything of the so-called forces of nature. History and contemporary life afford many illustrations of various peoples living in substantially similar geographic environments—but with strikingly different political and social institutions. The Europeans who settled in North America developed a culture in sharp contrast to that of the Indians, although both lived in the same geographic setting.[10]

Quite as important as the physical environment itself is the way in which people perceive their environment. As R. G. Collingwood says, "the fact that certain people live, for example, on an island has in itself no effect on their history; what has an effect is the way they conceive of that position."[11] And how they conceive of their position will depend not alone upon their geographic conditioning but upon numerous and complex factors that enter into their biological and social heritage. At the same time, one cannot ignore the influences of geography upon political institutions and behavior. Among the major geographic factors that have helped to shape American government and politics we may note the following: (1) location, (2) size, (3) climate, (4) topography, and (5) land and other resources.

8 See H. T. Buckle, *History of Civilization in England* (London, 1863) , Vol. I, pp. 14–15 and 29–30. See also Admiral Alfred T. Mahan, *Influence of Sea Power upon History* (New York: Sagamore Press, 1957) ; and Halford J. Mackinder, *Democratic Ideals and Reality: A Study in the Politics of Reconstruction* (New York: Holt, Rinehart and Winston, 1942) .

9 See "Geography and Foreign Policy," *American Political Science Review* (February, 1938) .

10 Robert H. Lowie, *Culture and Ethnology* (New York: P. Smith, 1929) , pp. 58–59.

11 *The Idea of History* (Oxford: Clarendon Press, 1946) , p. 200.

The location of the United States, facing Europe on one side and Asia on the other, has made it inevitable that we should become a power both in the Atlantic Community and on the Pacific rim. It was our relative proximity to Europe during the great age of exploration—from the sixteenth century on—that determined the conditions of our early settlement and development. It would be interesting to speculate on what the history of the modern world might have been had the American continent been settled from Asia instead of from Europe.

☆ THE AMERICAN GEOPOLITICAL PARADOX

Although we have been primarily a member of the Atlantic Community, the United States until recently has been relatively remote from the major centers of Atlantic power. We have been cousins to our European neighbors—but rather distant cousins geographically. Distance, more-over, has fostered in us a sense of security and isolation, as well as quali-ties of self-reliance and independence. "The last cause of this disobedient spirit in the [American] colonies," Edmund Burke told Parliament at the time of the American Revolution, "is deep laid in the natural consti-tution of things. Three thousand miles of ocean lie between you and them." The policy of "splendid isolation" outlined by Washington and Jefferson, and reaffirmed if not followed in nearly every major interna-tional crisis during much of our history, was due in considerable measure to our geographic isolation.

Our physical isolation from Europe and our cultural ties with Euro-pean peoples have resulted in what can only be described as an American geopolitical paradox. We have combined a proclaimed policy of isolation with an actual practice of participation in world affairs. Except for the Crimean and Franco-Prussian wars, we have been deeply involved in virtually every major European war. Even during our colonial days we participated in the War of the Palatinate, the War of the Spanish Succes-sion, the War of the Austrian Succession, and the Seven Years' War—although we knew them as King William's War, Queen Anne's War, King George's War, and the French and Indian War.

In recent years this gap between theory and practice has been nar-rowed. The doctrine of isolation has become a casualty of instantaneous communication and supersonic transportation which have made mill-ponds of oceans and all but banished barriers of time and space. Our fellowship in the Atlantic Community which, in spite of isolationists, has always been a fact, has now been given formal recognition by our mem-bership in the North Atlantic Treaty Organization. When Secretary of State Olney in 1894 blandly announced that, in the Western Hemis-phere, the interests of the United States were paramount, he was giving voice to what seemed to him the logical implication of our geographical location. So, too, was the earlier Monroe Doctrine, which continues today as a sort of official-unofficial policy defining our relations with Latin America. And just as our geographic position as a member of the Atlantic Community has been formalized in NATO, so our position in the Western Hemisphere has been formalized in the OAS.

Geography has made the United States a power not only in the Atlantic and the Caribbean, it has also thrust us deep into the politics of the vast Pacific area. Beginning with the voyage of the *Empress of China* in 1784, commercial vessels bearing the American flag carried on an active trade with the Orient. The continent of Asia and the islands of the Pacific were thus brought within the orbit of American interest even before the American flag had been firmly planted on our Pacific coast. The "rounding out" of our continental empire, with the incorporation of California and the Oregon territory, made it inevitable that the United States should play an important role in the Pacific. And when Hawaii, the Philippines, and Guam became our territorial outposts in those waters, science and technology combined with politics to end an isolation that geography alone had imposed.

For the United States World War II was in a very special sense a global conflict, because no other great power was so deeply involved in both the Atlantic and Pacific battlefronts. Although in recent years we have turned increasingly to Asia and even to Africa and the Middle East, our closest ties remain primarily in Europe.

Modern techniques of communication and transportation—not to mention recent achievements in the art of mutual annihilation—have reduced the strategic significance of geographic location. Moreover, the isolation that characterized much of our history has given place to increasing involvement in nearly every corner of the globe, an illustration of how culture can transcend geography.

Yet the influence of geographic location upon the political history of America can scarcely be exaggerated. For one thing the great oceans served for over two centuries not only as a bridge but as a kind of moat around us. With the Atlantic in our own hands, or controlled by a friendly power, we were able to devote our major energies to internal expansion. For at the doorstep of the original colonies was a fabulously rich and virgin territory to be conquered and cultivated, and this became our manifest destiny.

☆   *THE FRONTIER IN AMERICAN*
     HISTORY AND POLITICS

Except for the early possessions of England, France, and Spain, there were no serious political obstacles to our expansion. As population pushed ever westward and southward, even these were swept aside. In the process we were prepared to make whatever alliances seemed necessary, as when, in 1803, President Jefferson wrote to Robert Livingston, saying, "There is on the globe one single spot the possessor of which is our natural and habitual enemy. It is New Orleans through which the produce of three-eighths of our territory must pass to market. . . . The day that France takes possession of New Orleans . . . From that moment we must marry ourselves to the British fleet and nation." The fact is of course that the colonies of European powers were our natural prey, and when the time came they dropped like ripe fruit into our lap.

This conquest of the continent has left ineffaceable marks upon the government and politics of this country and upon the character and quality of the American people. The development of America was like a living panorama of human history from the Stone Age to the highest level of Western culture. In other parts of the world these various stages of cultural evolution had occurred very slowly through hundreds and even thousands of years. Like geological strata one culture was laid upon another in a time-bound sequence ranging from the most primitive to the most advanced. But in America these cultural strata become a spectrum of social evolution in which the various stages occurred simultaneously.

The first two centuries and a half of American history is essentially a record of the conquest of a wilderness mainly by adventurers, immigrants, and refugees of various kinds from Europe. Just as the original colonies were frontier outposts of European civilization, so with each succeeding advance the margin of settlement becomes a frontier of a new American civilization—a product of the interplay of geography and culture.

☆ **WIDE-OPEN SPACES**

The total land mass now included within the fifty states embraces an area of more than 3 million square miles, or approximately 2 billion acres. Except for Canada, the USSR, and Brazil, the continental area is the largest contiguous land mass under a single government.

In area the continental United States is greater than France, Spain, prewar Germany, Great Britain, Italy, Poland, and Hungary combined. California alone has nearly twice the land area of Great Britain. Texas, California, and Montana combined could swallow up four countries the size of Poland, two and one-half Germanys, six Great Britains, or five Italys. With a population approximately four times that of Great Britain, this country has a territorial area over thirty times as great.

The United States is a land of magnificent distances. The air distance from San Francisco to New York is greater than from London to Israel. From London to Paris is about the same (205 miles) as from Boston to Bangor, Maine. And from Boston to San Diego is about the same distance as from Madrid to Leningrad. America is a country of wide-open spaces. And this fact has not only affected American cultural development, it has conditioned our government and politics in numerous ways.

The sheer geographical magnitude of the country has required the multiplication of governmental units until today there are about 90,000 in the continental United States. Some of these local units are themselves of imperial dimensions. Los Angeles County, for example, covers over 4,000 square miles, an area as large as the state of Connecticut and ten times the size of New York City. San Bernardino County, with an area of 20,000 square miles, is as large as Massachusetts, Connecticut, and New Hampshire combined. This one county in California is larger than the Netherlands, nearly as large as Lithuania, and has nearly twice the area of Albania.

The sheer size of the country has had both centrifugal and centripetal effects in American politics and has posed administrative problems unknown to countries of smaller dimensions. It has given transportation and communication a high priority not only in our economic but in our political life as well. No small part of the energies of the American people have gone into the conquest of space. The building of roads, canals, railways, automobiles, superhighways, and air-transport lines has not only absorbed a large proportion of our labor and private capital resources—it has also required large subventions from government. It is not surprising that some of the earliest steps in government regulation and planning came in the field of transportation. Equally significant has been the development of a vast communications network of post offices and post roads, of telegraph and telephone lines, of radio and television.

According to Stuart Chase, "We whoop it up for railroads, motor cars, and speed."[12] This may also account for the exceptional mobility of the American people. With literally hundreds of millions of acres in which to move around, and with space machines galore in which to move, we have been from the beginning a nation on the march. This physical mobility has been accompanied by a *social* mobility characterized by a ceaseless movement up and down the social ladder—from one job or one social class to another. The time-bound pattern of European culture where generation has followed generation in the same location, occupation, and social class is, if not wholly alien to America, the exception and not the rule.

This dual mobility affects our politics in a direct and often disturbing fashion. For one thing, the migrants, moving from the East into the North Central area, or from the Old South into the new Southwest, or from everywhere into the Far West, have carried their political loyalties and traditions with them. The result has been to establish in the new

12 *Rich Land, Poor Land* (New York: McGraw-Hill, 1946).

areas enclaves of Republicans or Democrats whose partisanship has its roots in the older areas from which the migrants came.[13] The all but continuous movement from one community to another within a single state often results in a loss of voting rights to many and a change in the composition of the electorate, often unforeseen and unpredictable. Not infrequently a candidate for public office may find himself facing a substantially different body of voters from one election to the next. And the constant shifting of voters makes it difficult to maintain stable party organizations.

☆ PEOPLE OF PLENTY

Fortunately, the American people have been blessed by nature with natural resources beyond the dreams of avarice. With few exceptions—as, for example, natural rubber, tin, manganese, and metal alloys—practically everything needed for the development of an industrial civilization and a high standard of living is to be found within the continental limits of the United States. This fabulous natural wealth may have helped to make us appear to the rest of the world as independent, complacent, and without proper understanding of the economic and social problems of less fortunate peoples. On the other hand, the extraordinary mobility of Americans, blessed beyond belief with natural resources, has fostered ideas of individual liberty, initiative and opportunity, social and political equality, and human perfectibility that have seemed downright utopian to observers from abroad. We are, as David Potter has suggested, a *People of Plenty* with supreme "confidence that our abundance will suffice for the attainment of all the goals of social justice."[14] It was that same confidence that made possible the Marshall Plan and other programs of foreign aid since World War II. No more dramatic illustration can be cited of the American belief in an economy of welfare, if not of abundance, as a necessary condition for the survival of democratic values.

The American economy of abundance, however, has not been without its seamy side. For one thing, we have been plagued by a surplus problem—with surpluses not only of raw materials but in recent years of manufactured and capital goods as well. Historically we have relied on our exports of raw materials to pay for our imports of capital and to sustain a price structure that might otherwise collapse if these surpluses were dumped on our own domestic market. For generations, for example, America was an important source of food and fiber for Europe—and if British textile mills were dependent on American cotton, American

---

13 Viva Booth, *The Political Party as a Social Process,* Ph.D. thesis (Philadelphia: University of Pennsylvania, 1923) .

14 D. M. Potter, *People of Plenty* (Chicago: University of Chicago Press, 1954) , p. 119.

cotton growers were by the same token dependent on these British mills. This reciprocal interdependence has been profoundly disturbed since World War I, and our own burgeoning economy has sought outlets not alone for surplus raw materials but also for investment capital and manufactured goods. The chronic problem of farm surpluses, and the recent crisis in our international balance of payments, are symptoms of these underlying trends.

On the other hand, our "surplus" economy has made possible the programs of foreign economic aid which have been a central pillar of American foreign policy since 1945. That they helped not only to restore a war-ravaged Europe but also to maintain high employment at home made them a double blessing. But foreign aid has brought other problems, not the least of which is a growing concern over the rate at which our natural resources are being consumed. The United States, with only 6 percent of the world's population, consumes nearly half of the world's steel, more than half of its crude petroleum, and nine-tenths of its natural gas. As a recent study points out, the United States

> is the leading consumer of nearly every industrial raw material, and, with some notable exceptions, is also the leading producer. . . .
> Some observers of this remarkable performance point with alarm to the denuding of the soil and the depletion of key minerals. They foresee for the United States—and not far off—the fate of those Old World nations which retrogressed after gaining first rank. . . .[15]

In recent years the United States has become a major importer of raw materials, not only of rare metals but also of such formerly abundant resources as wool, copper, lead, zinc, bauxite, crude petroleum, and even iron. In view of these developments it is not surprising that the resources problem has moved from the wings to the center of the American political stage.

☆   CLIMATE, CHARACTER, AND CONDUCT

"Everybody complains about the weather," says an old aphorism, "but nobody ever does anything about it." Politicians running for office, especially in rural districts, farmers anxiously reading the weather bulletins, baseball managers praying for sunny days, and everybody hoping for good weather on holidays know that climate is important. But does climate affect human character and conduct in ways that are politically important? According to Professor Ellsworth Huntington, human energy, efficiency, and even intelligence are intimately related to climate. For best results, he says, we should live where the mean temperature is 40° F. in winter and 61° F. in summer, where relative humidity is about 60

[15] See J. Frederic Dewhurst and Associates, *America's Needs and Resources* (New York: Twentieth Century Fund, 1955).

percent at noon and high enough at night so that dew is precipitated, and where changes in the weather are frequent but not extreme.[16] The development of an advanced civilization with free democratic institutions will depend upon how closely the human habitat approximates these "ideal" conditions. By this test much of the United States is ideal. For this, if we believe Professor Huntington,[17] we should be grateful.

But how relevant is climate to the study of American government and politics? This becomes immediately obvious if we focus briefly on differences of rainfall in various areas of the United States. The fact, for example, that two-thirds of the annual rainfall falls east of the Great Plains means that the states to the west are generally less concerned with floods than with drought and irrigation. Pressure for storage dams and great reclamation projects comes almost entirely from the states of this arid West. The federal water shortage and the multipurpose projects of the Bureau of Reclamation are almost wholly confined to 17 states, the so-called Western Reclamation States. Even within a smaller region variations in rainfall can have far-reaching political effects. Southern California, with more than half of the state's population, receives less than a third of the state's annual rainfall. Without access to water from the Colorado and various rivers beyond the Sierras or from northern counties within the state, "the populous southern three-fourths (of California) would be a semi-desert."[18] It is not surprising, therefore, that the allocation of water resources has become a major political issue in California.

Rainfall, or melting snow, is the ultimate source of every river—and rivers have played an important role in American government and politics. Try to think of New York without the Hudson River; St. Louis and New Orleans without the Mississippi; or Portland, Oregon, without the Willamette and the Columbia. Approximately 160 different streams, with their tributaries, comprise the major river basins upon which the American people depend for their water for domestic use, for industry and transportation, for irrigation, sanitation, electric power, and recreation. To make most effective use of these rivers is a problem confronting governments at all levels: federal, state, and local.

But rivers, at least in their natural state, are not an unmixed blessing. Every year floods take their toll of life and property. When disaster of this kind strikes, the resources of private philanthropy, local, state, and even federal, government are called upon. Unfortunately, like the lazy man with the leaky roof, once the crisis has passed, we fail to follow through with measures adequate to provide permanent protection. But some measure of our efforts to do so is the fact that since 1936 federal,

---

16 W. S. and E. S. Woytinsky, *World Population and Production* (New York: Twentieth Century Fund, 1953), pp. 20–31.

17 See *Civilization and Climate* (3d ed.; New Haven, Conn.: Yale University Press, 1939).

18 Robert A. Walker and Floyd Cave, *How California Is Governed* (New York: Holt, Rinehart and Winston, 1953), p. 25.

state, and local expenditures on flood control projects have exceeded $10 billion.

Flood control, and its related problems of deforestation and soil erosion, is but one sample of "river politics." No less important has become the progressive pollution of surface waters as we make greater demands on these precious resources.[19] Many rivers and lakes in densely populated areas have become useless or dangerous for domestic, recreational, or even commercial use. To control or abate these evils has become a major problem requiring the joint and cooperative efforts of governments at every level, for the waterways of the country are no respecters of political boundary lines. Few cities or states acting alone are able to deal effectively with these problems. Only a comprehensive program on a statewide, regional, or national basis will be adequate. How to meet these problems and conserve a healthy balance between local, state, regional, and federal authorities will call for political imagination and daring.

The most dramatic effort to accomplish this thus far attempted has been the establishment under federal auspices of the Tennessee Valley Authority. For the first time a new government agency—the valley authority—was set up to provide for the integrated development of a major river basin embracing over 40,000 square miles in seven states and with a total population of more than 6 million. Whether the pattern of the TVA can be applied to other major river basins is by no means clear. But it is along some such lines that future public policy must proceed.

"How to meet nature's requirements" has become a basic problem of American government and politics. How can we adapt our political institutions and policies to the facts of geography, not only in domestic affairs but in foreign policy? Upon our answer to this problem may depend the future security and welfare of the American nation.[20]

---

[19] "Expenditures for flood control by the Federal Government alone in the years up to 1950 totaled about $2.4 billion, exclusive of expenditures for operation and maintenance of completed projects. Approximately 80 percent of the outlay had been made since 1936 and about one-quarter of it had been for works and structures in the lower Mississippi valley." If one adds to these outlays the expenditures of state and local governments, "the total public investment in flood control . . . approached $3 billion. . . . It is estimated that upwards of $15 billion of government funds will be required during the next generation or so to provide reasonably adequate flood protection for the American people." See Dewhurst and Associates, *op. cit.,* p. 546. Between 1940 and 1963 expenditures on Federal Reclamation projects increased from $84 million to more than $350 million. Cumulative appropriations in 1963 amounted to more than $5 billion.

[20] It is not without some significance that the TVA has become a symbol around the world of what a democratic people can do deliberately to shape its own future. Without dictatorship, without sacrificing freedom or responsible government, TVA has demonstrated the superiority of democratic planning to totalitarian control. In China, India, Africa, and the Middle East, the TVA is already providing an answer to the Communist canard that Western democracy cannot plan for prosperity and freedom. See David Lilienthal, *TVA: Democracy on the March* (New York: Harper & Row, 1944), chap. 19.

☆ THE GEOGRAPHY OF AMERICAN POLITICS

The rivers and lakes of America, her valleys, mountains, and plains have a deeper significance, however, than to require a regional approach to our resources problems. For the shape of the land has marked off geographic regions or sections from one another. And these regions, with their differing resources, climatic conditions, and economic interests, have developed political interests and loyalties that have been among the major dynamic factors in American politics.

Everyone who examines the government and politics of the United States is impressed with the central significance of sectional conflicts in our political history. North and South, East and West, in the political terminology of the United States, are more than points on a compass. They represent symbols which, in the context of American politics, evoke loyalties of varying intensity. They affect the way votes are cast, public policy determined, and administrative organization and procedures developed. Just where these great sections begin and end is and must always be a bit hazy. The Mason and Dixon Line on the boundary between Maryland and Pennsylvania has traditionally marked off North and South. The line between East and West, however, has shifted with every generation as the frontier of settlement moved from the Atlantic to the Pacific. In the beginning it was the "fall line" in the seaboard states. Later on it was the Cumberland Gap and then the Tennessee and Ohio. Still later it was the Mississippi and the Missouri. And today it would be rash indeed to locate any clear line between East and West.

More refined analysis distinguishes subsections or regions as having greater political cohesion and hence greater political significance. The Northeast, the Middle Atlantic, South Atlantic, North Central, South Central, Southern, Far Western and Pacific sections are often used. And within these are many subregions, until progressive refinement ultimately robs sectionalism of its significance. That it has significance, however, is attested by every analysis of voting behavior, of administrative areas or regional authorities.[21]

In final analysis, sectionalism can probably best be defined as a state of mind, reflecting the influence of geography and culture, of climate, racial or ethnic origin, natural resources, and even differences of dialect and diet. To a man of the South or of the North, of the East or of the West, of New England or the Middle West, the terms have meaning, however vague and varied. And however much it may trouble the scholar

---

[21] The late Professor V. O. Key used Midwest, Northeast, Far West, and South as meaningful regions or sections in his survey of political attitudes. See *Public Opinion and American Democracy* (New York: Knopf, 1961), chap. 5.

or the scientist to define them, experienced politicians, like the voters to whom they appeal, understand and use them to good effect.

Sharp differences within most such areas serve to emphasize the difficulties and dangers in any strictly geographic interpretation of government and politics. Nevertheless, as Frederick Jackson Turner put it:

> We in America are really a federation of sections rather than of states. . . . In political matters the states act as groups rather than as individual members of the Union. They act as sections and are responsible to the respective interests and ideals of these sections.[22]

It is in the precise definition or delimitation of these sections that difficulties appear. For some purposes, the terms New England and the Southwest have significance, but for other purposes they are of little use. The United States Bureau of the Census uses a variety of sections or regions for various purposes. Population statistics are reported state by state, but with the states grouped under four major regions—the Northeast, North Central, South, and West—and nine subsections or regions. Some seventy agencies of the federal government employ over 100 different regional arrangements as administrative areas. The National Resources Committee proposed a new grouping into ten or twelve major regions for purposes of resources planning and administration, while professor Arthur Holcombe based his penetrating study of political parties upon alliances among twelve geographic regions. "National parties," he said, "as the history of national politics clearly demonstrates, can be formed only on the basis of durable combinations of sectional interests." And Donald Hecock, using Holcombe's sections, found a significant degree of cohesion among the Senators and Representatives of these areas. Indeed, in the Senate, "there was a higher degree of cohesion [within] geographical division than [within] party divisions."[23]

Public opinion polls have used still other sections or regions in seeking representative samples of the population. The George Gallup organization in 1948 used seven regions but more recently reduced them to five. The Elmo Roper poll used four major areas.[24] The Michigan Survey Center, in its studies of presidential elections, samples four geo-

[22] See "Sections and Nation," *Yale Review*, XII (October, 1922), 1–21; also, *The Significance of Sections in American History* (New York: Holt, Rinehart and Winston, 1932).

[23] See *Regional Factors in National Planning*, a report of the National Resources Committee, 1935. Also Howard Odum and H. E. Moore, *American Regionalism* (New York: Holt, Rinehart and Winston, 1938); esp. chaps. VIII, X.

See Holcombe, *The Political Parties of Today* (New York: Harper & Row, 1924); Hecock, *Political and Geographical Cohesion in Congress* (1931).

[24] See *The Gallup Political Almanac* (Princeton, N.J., 1962 [compiled by the American Institute of Public Opinion]); and Gallup and Roper releases, 1956.

graphic areas.[25] Although differences do emerge on the basis of these regional groupings, it is significant that differences within the various regions are often as great as differences between them.

It is obvious that no single plan of sectional classification can answer all of the questions that arise in seeking to adapt our political institutions to the geographic facts of life. Nor can we place too much confidence in sweeping generalizations like the "Mind of the South" or the "Spirit of the West." Such terms may be useful to the poet and the campaigning politician, but we ought not to expect too much of them.

It may be, as Professor Holcombe has argued, that sectional politics in America are giving way to class politics.[26] The influence of the automobile and the airplane, of radio and television, the growth of cities and of large-scale industry, may tend to reduce geographic distinctions and undermine sectional loyalties. But the influence of geography upon the political institutions and behavior of the American people will continue.

---

[25] No explanation is offered by the polling groups of why particular geographic areas were used. Presumably these decisions were the result of a combination of circumstances including tradition, convenience, population distribution, and composition. See Angus Campbell, and others, *The Voter Decides* (New York: Harper & Row, 1954).

[26] See Holcombe, *The Political Parties of Today, op. cit.; The New Party Politics* (New York: Norton, 1933); and *The Middle Classes in American Politics* (Cambridge, Mass.: Harvard University Press, 1940).

DEMOCRATIC
GOVERNMENT IN THEORY
AND PRACTICE

☆ *DEMOCRACY'S COAT OF MANY COLORS*

In today's world *Democracy* wears a coat of many colors. We speak of American democracy and of the other democratic nations of the free world. We speak of the cold war as a contest between democratic and nondemocratic ideologies. And yet in the Soviet Union and its satellites they too speak of "People's Democracies." Indeed, nowhere is the term more frequently used than in Poland, Hungary, Czechoslovakia, and in China. In Indonesia, Pakistan, and Ghana; in Egypt, Turkey, and the Congo, we hear of "directed" democracy. Nor does the confusion end with these varied and often contradictory uses of the term. Within the "free democratic nations" we hear of "social democracy," "Christian democracy," "economic democracy"—until the term itself is qualified almost to death. How can one account for all this semantic confusion in the use of a term so ancient and so honorable?

One needs to remember, of course, that in politics, as in religion or ethics, we are concerned with values—and value terms are notoriously ambiguous. Love and mercy, freedom and justice, right and wrong, good and bad, cannot be defined with the same precision as the terms employed in mathematics or chemistry. Political terms are so highly ambiguous that politics might well be defined as a continuous exercise in the logic of ambiguity.

But the universal—if conflicting—use of "democracy" as a term of praise for political systems as different as those of the USA and the USSR is something new. "Seventy years ago," wrote Viscount Bryce in 1920, "the word Democracy awakened dislike and fear. Now it is a word of praise. . . ."[1] The democratic implications of the American and French revolutions gave a bad name to democracy in nearly every country of Europe. Catherine the Great of Russia withheld official recognition of the United States for many years because its political principles were regarded as subversive of the legitimate authority of every reigning monarch. After the Napoleonic "wars of liberation," the so-called Holy Alliance became a symbol of the union of legitimate regimes against the spreading virus of democratic revolution.

Many of the framers of the American Constitution themselves took a dim view of democracy. Madison feared it because, he said, it "can admit of no cure for the mischiefs of faction. . . . Hence it is that democracies have ever been spectacles of turbulence and contention; have ever been found incompatible with personal security or the rights of property; and have been as short in their lives as they have been violent in their deaths." And Alexander Hamilton, in a speech to the New York ratifying convention, argued that the "ancient democracies, in which the people themselves deliberated, never possessed one feature of good government. Their very character was tyranny: their figure deformity. When they assembled, the field of debate presented an ungovernable mob, not only incapable of deliberation but prepared for every enormity."[2] Few of the framers or of their contemporaries would have described the United States as a democracy. They preferred to call it a republic and to refer to themselves as republicans.

Nevertheless, the spread of democratic ideas during the nineteenth and early twentieth centuries had reached a point where President Wilson did not hesitate to proclaim our basic purpose in World War I to be to "make the world safe for democracy." Since 1920—with temporary setbacks in Fascist countries—the sweep of democracy as a symbol to be praised has been virtually worldwide. So universal was the acceptance of democracy that even Communist dictatorships are represented as "true democracies" or as "people's democracies" to distinguish them from the "false" or "capitalistic" democracies of the West. This triumph of the democratic idea constitutes a major revolution in the intellectual and political history of mankind. In Africa, Asia, and the Middle East, as in Latin America, revolutions, whether from the right, left, or center, are fought in the name of democracy. To explain this triumph of the democratic idea is beyond the scope of this discussion. It may help, however, to understand what is meant by democracy in America if we seek out a few of the more stable guideposts in its long history.

1 James Bryce, *Modern Democracies* (New York: Macmillan, 1921), Vol. I, p. 4.
2 Quoted in Richard B. Morris (ed.), *Basic Ideas of Alexander Hamilton* (New York: Pocket Books, 1957), p. 106.

☆ HUMAN NATURE AND THE FOUNDING FATHERS

Basic to all theories of government and politics are some assumptions concerning human nature. In general, we may say that America's founding fathers were neither optimists nor pessimists in their views of human nature. Few of the leaders of American thought, however, believed with Rousseau that "man is a being naturally good, loving justice and order; that there is no perversity in the human heart and that the first movements of nature are always right." Not all of them, on the other hand, agreed with Hamilton when he described the people as a "great beast." Nor would they have endorsed Horace White's remark that the Constitution of the United States "assumes that the natural state of mankind is a state of war and that the carnal mind is at enmity with God."[3] Most of the founding fathers took a more moderate, intermediate view. By nature, they believed, human beings are selfish and aggressive, given to passionate outbursts of temper and to nonrational behavior. But they are also "political animals," who, to survive, must live in organized society. Hence their aggressions and their passions are tempered by innate capacities for rationality, cooperation, justice, and mercy.

It was in terms of this ambivalent nature of man that the founding fathers sought to build the political institutions of this country. They believed that only a strong government could curb the antisocial, aggressive, brutish impulses in man and allow his better nature to assert itself. They also believed that no ruling elite has a monopoly of rationality, nor of concern for the common good. Rulers, no less than the people who are ruled, are capable of aggression and avarice. Unless rulers are restrained by constitutional and other limitations they may themselves become wolves to prey upon the flock over which they are appointed to keep watch. Because the founding fathers preferred reason to instinct, and because they feared passionate, impulsive behavior on the part of both rulers and people, they sought to minimize the possibilities of hasty action. By limitations upon the scope of political power, and by an elaborate division of powers, they hoped to maximize opportunities for full inquiry, discussion, and debate as the best guarantee that reason, in the end, would prevail.

> If [wrote John Adams] reason is . . . supreme in man . . . it would be
> most suitable . . . to have no civil or political government at all. The
> moral government of God . . . [would] be sufficient. . . . But the nature
> of mankind is one thing and the reason of mankind another. . . .
> The passions and appetites are part of human nature as well as reason
> and the moral sense. In the institution of government it must be

[3] Quoted in Richard Hofstadter, *The American Political Tradition and the Men Who Made It* (New York: Knopf, 1948) , p. 4.

remembered that, although reason ought always to govern individuals, it certainly never did . . . and human nature must be taken as it is . . . and will be. . . . It is however weakness rather than wickedness which renders men unfit to be trusted with unlimited power. . . . [Men] were intended by nature to live together in society and in this way to restrain one another; but they know each other's imbecility so well that they ought never to lead one another into temptation [that is, by giving them too much power].[4]

It was this view, shared by most of the architects of American political institutions, that made them skeptical not only of the claims of unlimited monarchy, but of democracy as well. For when they talked about democracy, the image they had in mind was strikingly different from democracy as it is so variously understood in our contemporary world. Democracy to them meant the democracy of ancient Athens.

☆ THE FOUNDING FATHERS AND THE ATHENIAN MODEL

The Athenian model to which the founding fathers referred was a government in which the people themselves—the whole body of citizens—made all major political decisions, and in committees, chosen by lot, performed both judicial and administrative tasks as well. "In a democracy," said Madison, "the people meet and exercise the government in person. . . ." The prospect of 30,000 to 40,000 citizens of Athens meeting together in an assembly to deliberate and debate, to legislate, and, by casting lots, to judge and to administer must have seemed to Madison an invitation to anarchy and mob rule. This was all the more likely, since in Athens no clear distinction was made between the political state and society, and consequently no limit was imposed upon the scope of political power. The founding fathers looked upon the assembly which condemned Socrates to death, and could not see it as a safe repository of freedom. They saw in colonial and in revolutionary America examples of intolerance and political tyranny on the part of popular assemblies. They saw the trials for witchcraft in Salem and mob violence and popular assaults upon private property and the established institutions of church and state, and their natural skepticism concerning human nature and democracy was reinforced.

The framers were also aware of the limitations which the Athenian model would impose upon the expansion of the American nation. A democracy, said Madison, "will be confined to a small spot . . . [since] the natural limit of a democracy is that distance from the central point which will just permit the most remote citizens to assemble as often as

[4] John Adams, *The Works of John Adams, Second President of the U.S.,* C. F. Adams (ed.) (Boston: Little, Brown, 1857), Vol. IV, pp. 402 ff.

their public functions demand, and will include no greater number than can join in those functions."[5] Besides, the framers could see in pure (direct) democracy no sure defense against the natural propensity of selfish factions to push their own interests at the expense of the common good. "Men will pursue their interests," said Hamilton. "It is as easy to change human nature as to oppose the strong current of selfish passions. A wise legislator will gently divert the channel and direct it, if possible, to the public good." How could this be done in a democracy where crowds of ill-assorted men—some illiterate and ignorant of the first principles of law and justice—meet to transact the public business? Inflamed by clever demagogues, the people in assembly could more easily be deceived to serve a selfish interest under the impression that they were protecting their own.

All this but helps to show that democracy in America, as we think of it today, was not a conscious creation of the founding fathers. On the contrary, they saw themselves as the authors, not of a democracy, but of a republic, by which they meant something quite different from the Athenian model. A republic differed from a democracy in a number of important ways. First and most important, whereas in a democracy the people "assemble and administer the government in person," in a republic "they assemble and administer it by their representatives and agents." This simple difference put democracies and republics poles apart. It made possible a government in which the leaders of the people—a more or less natural elite—would represent and speak for them. However crude the selection process might be, it could not but improve upon an assembly composed of all citizens regardless of character or capacity. Because the representative assembly would be smaller and more select, opportunities for deliberation would be improved. A representative assembly would be less likely to yield to passion and prejudice, less likely to be swayed by demagogues, and consequently more likely to resist the appeals of selfish interests masquerading as patriots. By the same token, power would be checked, since representatives would work under the constant surveillance of their constituents, knowing that if they betrayed the public interest they could be replaced.

There was the further advantage that a representative republic could govern an expanding population, since it would require only the representatives of the people, rather than the people themselves, "to meet as often as may be necessary for the administration of public affairs." Envisioning a united country of continental dimensions, this was most important. Indeed, the "most immediate object of the federal Constitution," said Madison, "is to secure the union of the thirteen primitive states . . . and to add to them such other states as may arise."[6] A fatal

[5] H. B. Dawson (ed.), *The Federalist, A Collection of Essays,* No. 14 (New York: Scribner, 1863).
[6] *Ibid.*

weakness in the popular governments of antiquity had been their failure
to discover and apply "the great principle of representation," and they
were consequently unable to incorporate new territories and populations
without sacrificing the principle of popular control.

There were other features that distinguished the new Constitution
from classical democracy. The inner checks against hasty and ill-considered action embodied in the principles of bicameralism, the separation of
powers, and the federal system were emphasized. The different systems of
election and representation for the House of Representatives, the Senate,
and the President were a further safeguard against the "turbulence and
folly of democracy." And the limited powers delegated to the central
government gave added protection against the tendency of democracies to
acknowledge no limit or restraint upon their power.

Athenian democracy acknowledged no formal restraint upon the
power of the political state, and distinctions between state and society
were often shadowy. Athenian democracy, wrote Ernest Barker, "is a
small intimate society: it is a church as well as a state; it makes no
distinction between the province of the state and that of society: it is, in a
word, an integrated system of social ethics, which realizes to the full the
capacity of its members and therefore deserves their full allegiance."[7]
This failure to distinguish between the state and society brought all
aspects of social life—the family, education, religion, economics, etc.—
under state control. It is small wonder that such a political system should
excite fear rather than enthusiasm among our own founding fathers, to
whom freedom from state control was a major goal. But there is another
side to the story, for, if Pericles is to be believed, Athenian democracy did
in practice acknowledge a distinction between state and society.

> The freedom which we enjoy in our government [he says] extends also
> to our ordinary life. There, far from exercising a jealous surveillance over
> each other, we do not feel called upon to be angry with our neighbor
> for doing what he likes. . . . Our public men have, besides politics,
> their private affairs to attend to, and our ordinary citizens, though
> occupied with the pursuits of industry, are still fair judges of public
> matters. . . .[8]

There are other features of the Athenian model of democracy that
the framers might have emphasized had they been disposed to describe
the American government under the Constitution as a democracy. They
might, for example, have pointed out that the principle of direct government by all the citizens was tempered somewhat by at least the germ of a
representative system in the Athenian Council of 500, the magistrates,

[7] Sir Ernest Barker, *The Political Thought of Plato and Aristotle* (New York:
Russell & Russell, 1959) ; also see his *Greek Political Theory: Plato and His Predecessors*
(New York: Barnes & Noble, 1960) .

[8] Thucydides, *History of the Peloponnesian War,* Everyman's ed. (New York:
Dutton, 1926) , chap. VI, p. 123.

and the juries, which carried on the government between the sessions of the popular Assembly. The Council, for example, was an elected body composed of 50 members from each of the ten Athenian tribes. The juries, too, were representative, in that they were chosen by lot from a panel of several thousand citizens elected each year. "The juries," says Professor Mayo, "even more than the Council, were large samples of the citizens acting in the name of all, and it is not far-fetched to see in this a form of representation, since the panels of candidates were for convenience, presented from what might roughly be called wards . . . of the city-state."[9]

In addition to these features of Athenian democracy—that is, the distinction between state and society and the principle of representation—there were others that have come to be accepted as essential to the modern democratic state. According to Professor Mayo, they are "(1) the direct control or making of the political decisions by the assembled citizens, (2) the political equality of all citizens, (3) the liberties, including the freedom to oppose, and (4) the taking of decisions by a majority vote."[10] To these, one might also add: (5) the principle of constitutionalism, or a "higher law," to impose limitations upon political power, (6) a distinction between state and society, although this was not too clear in the Athenian model, and (7) the democratization of the administrative and judicial processes. The only one of these principles to which the framers of the Constitution strongly objected was the first. Instead of making decisions "by the assembled citizens," they preferred decision making by "representatives of the people."

In the more complex modern democracies, the task of insuring full compliance with these basic principles is by no means easy—and it requires continuous vigilance and widespread, active participation in political affairs by the people. Although this was fully implied in Athens, participation in practice was by no means universal. Out of a total adult population of 30,000 to 40,000 citizens in fifth-century Athens, maximum attendance at the Assembly probably never exceeded one-third. For the rest, preoccupation with their private affairs, ignorance, and plain apathy kept them from any active participation. This indifference was deplored then, as it is today. "Unlike other nations," said Pericles, "[we regard] him who takes no part in these [civic] duties, not as unambitious, but as useless, [for] we Athenians are able to judge at all events [even] if we cannot originate, and instead of looking on discussion as a stumbling block in the way of action, we think it an indispensable preliminary to any wise action at all."[11]

---

[9] Henry Mayo, *An Introduction to Democratic Theory* (New York: Oxford University Press, 1960), p. 39.

[10] *Ibid.*, p. 41. See also Thomas L. Thorson, *The Logic of Democracy* (New York: Holt, Rinehart and Winston, 1962).

[11] Thucydides, *op. cit.*, p. 123.

If, then, we view democracy as a process, we may say that it places a high value on equality and freedom. It strives for universal accessibility of all citizens to the ruling or power elite and seeks to prevent the rise of an official or ruling class recruited from a "closed-status" group. It seeks to minimize the authority of the power elite and to expand the influence of a public opinion formed and expressed through free discussion, a free press and communications system, and freedom of political association. It is to be distinguished from a totalitarian society not only by these features but also by maintaining a distinction between state and society and thus limiting the scope of political power. That is, a democracy is an open, pluralistic society as against a closed, monolithic one. In the decision-making process, democracy prefers an empirical, experimental method to dogma, doctrine, ideology, or revelation.[12]

☆ FOUNDATIONS OF DEMOCRACY IN AMERICA

It is unlikely in any case that American political institutions could have followed the Athenian model. This is so not only because the framers were skeptical of democracy, but because any political system must strike roots in its own soil, whatever model it may accept or reject. And the roots of the American Republic are to be found mainly in our own experience. Some of the implications of our geographic environment have been discussed. At this point, we might cite a few illustrations of how our colonial experience contributed to the development of democracy in America.

It is well to remember that democratic (or republican) government did not come to America as a gift from abroad, although we inherited a thousand years of European history that contributed to this end. During our colonial period, democracies or republics were, for practical purposes, unknown in the civilized world. Many of the historic "rights of Englishmen" were won both in England and America during this very period, and we profited from that struggle. The Petition of Right (1628) provided, among other things, for taxation only by and with the consent of Parliament, for protection against arbitrary imprisonment and also against the quartering of troops on householders without their consent. The Habeas Corpus Act of 1679, the Bill of Rights of 1689, and the Toleration Act of that same year, strengthened the rights of Englishmen in America as at home. But no one could argue that England was either a republic or a democracy. Neither were the political institutions by which its colonies were governed. Virginia, at the outset, was, for all practical purposes, a despotism, and not always an enlightened one. The governor

12 See Marie Swabey, *Theory of the Democratic State* (Cambridge, Mass.: Harvard University Press, 1937), p. 32. See also Edward Albert Shils, *The Torment of Secrecy* (New York: Free Press, 1956).

and other officials, with plenary power to govern, were appointed by the company in London and responsible only to it. The proprietors of New York, the Carolinas, and Georgia were, to all intents and purposes, feudal lords. In Massachusetts, where a charter of 1628 provided for a government of "one governor, one deputy governor, and eighteen assistants to be from tyme to tyme . . . chosen out of the free men of the said company" designated in the charter, democracy was in bad odor. Cotton Mather made no bones about saying that democracy "was never ordained of God" as were monarchy, aristocracy, and theocracy.

But a nondemocratic society in the environment of the new world could not endure. In 1618 a "great charter of privileges" was signed in Virginia; and in 1619 the first representative assembly in any English colony was summoned.[13] Even in Massachusetts Bay, where only members of approved Puritan churches could be freemen and participate in the General Court, demands for a more democratic regime were effectively made. By 1691 provision was made for a "General Court of Assembly," composed of the governor and his council, plus two representatives from each town or other place of habitation. Although property qualifications for voting were imposed, the new government was an important advance toward a more representative republic.

In the meantime, even more important changes were being made elsewhere to democratize colonial governments. When Thomas Hooker took his flock to Connecticut in 1635, he made provision for a government of the combined settlements of Hartford, Windsor, and Wethersfield. The Fundamental Orders of Connecticut became the first written constitution in America—if not in the world—to establish a representative republic, or as they called it, a "Publik State or Commonwealth." Each town was authorized to elect four representative freemen "as their deputies to every General Court." The General Court, in turn, was to meet twice a year to elect a governor and other officers and to transact the usual business of a legislative assembly.

Hooker's contemporary, Roger Williams, established a new colony, named The Providence Plantations, whose charter was another giant step toward the development of responsible representative government. To the "inhabitants of the towns . . ." was granted "a free and absolute charter of incorporation. . . . Together with full power and authority to rule themselves . . . by such form of civil government, *as by voluntary consent of all, or the greater part of them, they shall find most suitable.*"

Steps in the development of republican (democratic) government

---

[13] This was confirmed by an ordinance in 1621, which provided for "Two Supreme Councils." One, "Council of State," to advise the governor, was "chosen, nominated, placed and displaced . . . by us, the said Treasurer, Council and Company and our successors." The second council, "The General Assembly, shall consist . . . of the Council of State and two Burgesses out of every Town, Hundred or other particular Plantation to be respectively chosen by the Inhabitants. . . ."

were taken in other colonies. When William Penn purchased West Jersey from Lord Berkeley in 1692, he drew up a plan of government that has been described as the most democratic in the world at that time. "We lay a foundation," Penn said, "for after ages to understand their liberty as men and Christians, that they may be brought in bondage [only] by their own consent, for we put the power in the people." Specifically, the plan called for a unicameral legislature, elected by all the inhabitants by secret ballot. Unfortunately, this bold experiment died when both East and West Jersey passed to the crown in 1702.

When religious nonconformists insisted upon freedom of religious belief and the separation of church and state, it was only a step to a further demand for full civil liberties. And the principle of self-government expressed in the right of the church congregation to choose its own clergy and define its own religious doctrine early became, by extension, the right of self-government in civil affairs. The church congregation thus became the prototype of the town meeting and the representative assembly.

> The ideal of local self-government [says Ernest S. Bates] was brought to America by the Pilgrims; the separation of church and state was derived from the Baptists; the right of free speech was a development of the right to freedom of conscience established by Roger Williams and William Penn; the equality spoken of in the Declaration of Independence was an outgrowth of the equality practiced by the Quakers. Democracy was envisaged in religious terms long before it assumed a political terminology.[14]

Some religious leaders did not hesitate to defend democracy as the most desirable form of government. Contrast Cotton Mather, to whom democracy was anathema, with John Wise, a Congregational minister of Ipswich, Massachusetts. In his *Vindication of the Government of New England Churches* in 1772, Wise said: "The end of all good government is to cultivate humanity and promote the happiness of all and the good of every man in all his rights . . . without injury or abuse to any. . . . And it is as plain as day light, there is no species of government like a democracy to attain this end."

When John Wise's *Vindication* appeared, the democratic tide was running strong. The right to vote and hold office, although limited by property qualifications—and in a few places by religious tests—had nevertheless been gradually extended. Representative assemblies were provided for in every colony, although the basis of apportionment was by no means equitable. These assemblies had gradually acquired more and more power at the expense of the royal governor and council. In Rhode Island and Connecticut, where the governor was himself an elected official, a full-fledged representative democracy was already in being.

14 E. S. Bates, *The American Faith* (New York: Norton, 1940), p. 9.

Religious freedom, freedom of association and of speech were perhaps more widely enjoyed than anywhere else in the world. These and other democratic ideas germinating in the colonies were dramatically affirmed and extended in the struggle for independence and during the so-called critical period between the Treaty of Peace and the Constitutional Convention.

As we shall see, it was against this democratic tide, against these "excesses of democracy," that the founding fathers sought to erect safeguards. How this was done we shall see. We shall also see how, in the course of time, the Constitution itself has been democratized. The extension of the suffrage, the secret ballot, the transformation of the electoral college into an instrument for the popular election of the President, the direct election of United States Senators, the expansion of civil and political rights by constitutional amendment, statute, and judicial interpretation, and the development of political parties as the vehicles for popular control of both Congress and the President are some of the results of this process. In the states there have been even more democratic innovations, such as the popular initiative and referendum, the direct primary, and the popular election of most statewide officials, including judges. Someone has said that democracy in America has developed from a continuous struggle between the spirit of the Declaration of Independence and the spirit and structure of the Constitution. It is also said that it is the Declaration that in the end must triumph. The fact is that there is no serious conflict between these two great charters. The Preamble to the Declaration sets forth the basic assumptions of the American Republic: freedom and equality in the pursuit of happiness under a government whose just powers rest on the consent of the governed. The Constitution reaffirms these goals and creates a government designed to achieve them.

☆   *AN OPEN SOCIETY*

Political institutions[15] are shaped not only by their geographic environment or their political history but by the kind and character of the people who compose the political community.

For most people who came to America the New World was not only a haven from religious and political persecution, it was an avenue of escape from poverty, frustration, and loss of social status in a rigidly stratified society. The United States held out hope for a better life in material terms, for opportunity to "get ahead." "America," someone has said, "was promises."

---

[15] We use the word "institution" here, not as some fixed or firm physical or structural entity but as a pattern of human behavior that persists, within reasonable margins of change, through time.

In general, those who migrated were economically and socially vulnerable at home. They were poor people, peasants, laborers, and lower-middle-class merchants or artisans. Some few were prosperous, but they were exceptional. The rich and wellborn, those who enjoyed status and security at home, remained behind.[16] So too did the hopeless and the derelict, those lacking in the imagination or the initiative required to migrate.

Some few of the immigrants had substantial resources to "tide them over." Many others, although poor, could pay for their own passage. Still others were assisted by friends and voluntary organizations established to encourage imigration. For many thousands, however, even these resources were unavailable; for them the most common arrangement was the laborer's contract, under which the immigrant, in return for his transportation, subsistence, and sometimes equipment, agreed to work for a term of years for his patron or sponsor. Among the inducements offered were (1) freedom after from four to seven years; (2) a grant of land, usually 50 acres in the back country after expiration of the contract; (3) the right to vote on becoming a freeman; and, of course, (4) religious and civil liberties. Literally hundreds of thousands of such indentured servants came, until the importation of contract labor was suppressed.

The fact that economic motives loomed large has had important consequences. The vast majority of the 40 million immigrants were laborers, peasants or small farmers, mechanics, miners, or small merchants. They brought to this country their brawn and their brains, not potentially as children but as adult men and women. The United States has thus been the beneficiary of an unearned increment of skill and ingenuity, an asset few other nations have had.[17]

Because the immigrants were generally of humble origin, the social stratification of the Old World, in which status was based as much on birth, class, race, or religion as on income or occupation, had no exact counterpart in this country. The character of the immigrants and the mobility characteristic of life in America were not conducive to rigid lines of caste or class. When children of penniless immigrants could

16 "Men of position and power," wrote W. J. Cash, "men who are adjusted to their environment, men who find life bearable in their accustomed place, such men do not embark on frail ships for a dismal frontier where savages prowl and slay, and living is a grim and laborious ordeal. The laborer, faced with starvation; the debtor anxious to get out of jail; the apprentice, reckless, eager for a fling at adventure, and even more eager to escape his mother; the peasant, weary of the exactions of milord; the small landowner and shopkeeper, faced with bankruptcy . . . all these will go." See W. J. Cash, *The Mind of the South* (New York: Knopf, 1941) , pp. 17, 18.

17 The eighth census of the United States, for example, reported the following occupational distribution of immigrants in 1860:

Laborers	827,317	Merchants	231,852
Farmers	764,837	Miners	39,967
Mechanics	407,524		

become leaders in church and state, notions of fixed classes, of rights and privileges rooted irrevocably in birth or class, had to give way. In the rough-and-ready, almost rambunctious, social atmosphere of the New World, men—and women too—moved up and down the social ladder almost as easily as they moved physically from place to place. Efforts to transfer to the New World the stratified society of Europe, as in the semifeudal patroon system of New York, were not conspicuously successful. Even where large plantations and a slave economy produced many of the outward signs of such a society, it was on the whole a pretty fragile structure, constantly challenged by the small independent farmers and by a pervading consciousness among the southern "gentlemen" themselves of their own humble origin.[18] Outside the South, and even in large areas of that section, America was an "open society."

☆ THE POLITICS OF EQUALITY AND FREEDOM

Not the least important by-product of this "open society" has been the development of egalitarian sentiments among the American people to a degree unknown elsewhere. In the absence of "artificial" distinctions of class or creed, the idea that one man is inherently as good as the next one seemed but a logical inference from the conditions of life as it was lived. The American people, wrote the French expatriate Crèvecoeur in 1793, "is not composed, as in Europe, of great lords who possess everything, and of a herd of people who have nothing. Here are no aristocratical families, no courts, no kings . . . no ecclesiastical dominion. . . . The rich and the poor are not so far removed from each other as they are in Europe."[19] The immigrants who came, he said, from whatever political or religious background, quickly became Americans with a pride in country which most of them had never known. For, wrote Crèvecoeur, "two-thirds of them had *no* country. Can a wretch who wanders about, who works and slaves, whose life is a continual source of sore affliction or punishing penury; can that man call England or any other kingdom, his country?" By contrast America could say to the immigrant: "Welcome to my shores, distressed European; . . . if thou wilt work, I have bread for thee; if

---

18 See W. J. Cash, *The Mind of the South, op. cit.*, where the myth of the southern planter as a descendant of Cavaliers and hereditary aristocrats is effectively exposed. In spite of his pride and his addiction to the romantics of Sir Walter Scott, says Cash, "the Southerner's primary approach to his world was not through the idea of class. He never really . . . [thought] of himself as being before all else a member of a caste . . . The reasons why the idea of a society of rigid caste and class did not take hold even of the southern "gentlemen," says Cash, were ". . . the tradition of the back country, and the . . . remembrance of the community of origins, factors operating . . . for the preservation of the old basic democratic feeling. . . ." (pp. 48–52).

19 Hector St. John de Crèvecoeur, *Letters from an American Farmer* (Philadelphia: Mathew Carey, 1793), quoted in L. Hacker, *The Shaping of the American Tradition* (New York: Columbia University Press, 1947), p. 161.

thou wilt be honest, sober and industrious, I have greater rewards to confer on thee—ease and independence. . . . I shall endow thee besides with the immunities of a free man."

No one can pretend that these glowing sentiments were a completely accurate description of life in America even in 1793. But that they expressed a widely shared view of the relations that should prevail among men cannot be denied. It is significant that other observers—Franklin, Jefferson, Charles Pinckney, Alexis de Tocqueville, Walt Whitman—saw American society in similar terms. It would be most inadvisable, said Franklin, "for a person to go [to America] who has no other quality to recommend him but his birth. In Europe it has . . . its value; but it is a commodity that cannot be carried to a worse market than to . . . America, where people do not inquire concerning a stranger: What is he? but: What can he do?" Because of the classless nature of American society, said Charles Pinckney, "a greater equality arises than is to be found among the people of any other country." It is, however, an equality of opportunity, not of economic condition or even social status. It is an equality where industry and competence will be rewarded and where "every member of the society almost, will enjoy an equal power of arriving at the supreme offices and . . . of directing the strength and sentiments of the whole community."[20]

Americans have not confused equality with *identity*, either of competence and character or of industry and achievement. On the contrary, the egalitarian tradition in the United States assumes that the individual, given as nearly as possible equal access to education and to opportunity, will achieve his own status in society. Equality, in a phrase, implies an equal right to achieve distinction. As Tocqueville put the matter, after identifying equality as a basic value of American democracy, "I do not mean that there is any lack of wealthy individuals in the United States: I know of no country, indeed, . . . where a profounder contempt is expressed for the theory of the permanent equality of property. But wealth circulates with inconceivable rapidity, and experience shows that it is rare to find two succeeding generations in the full enjoyment of it."[21]

This also helps to explain why Americans regard liberty and equality not as contradictions but as corollaries. In the mobile, fluid, "open society" of the United States, individuals were more likely to be on their own than in the comparatively "closed," immobile societies from which most immigrants came. The individual farmer and his family were largely dependent on their own efforts and in the city the individual worker was left pretty much to his own devices in seeking a job and in

---

[20] J. Johnson (ed.), *The Works of Benjamin Franklin* (London, 1806), Vol. III, p. 399. Also Pinckney in *The Records of the Federal Convention of 1787*, quoted in Hans Morgenthau, *The Purpose of American Politics* (New York: Knopf, 1960), chap. I.

[21] *Democracy in America* (New York: Knopf, 1945), Vol. II, chap. III.

bargaining for his wages and general conditions of employment. If he prospered, he took pride in being a self-made man. If he failed, he suffered the agony of feeling that his failure was condign punishment for defects in his own character or conduct; or he rationalized it as due to hard luck or to some evil force or forces over which he had no control. Thus the Protestant emphasis on individual responsibility for salvation was reinforced by the conditions of economic and social life. The stern discipline of this Protestant ethic not only helped to account for the spectacular economic growth of the United States, it also developed embarrassing contrasts of affluence and poverty—or what Henry George called Progress and Poverty. It was inevitable that in time the American sense of social responsibility (what Tocqueville called "self-interest rightly understood") would seek to mitigate or to eradicate these inequalities through welfare legislation of various kinds. The goal, however, has never been equality of status or income but always greater equality of opportunity to achieve both higher income and higher status.

☆   INDIVIDUALISM AND SOCIAL DEMOCRACY

The politics of freedom and equality in America has not been a mere game of verbal charades or a kind of empty political ritual. It has always involved not only tangible *political* rights like the suffrage, eligibility for public office, civil liberties like freedom of speech, of the press, assembly, and religious worship, and constitutional rights of due process and equal protection of the laws; latterly it has also implied certain specific *social* rights as well. Among these are access to education, to employment, to some measure of security against the hazards of unemployment, sickness, and old age, and, as nearly as possible, to equal opportunity without regard to ethnic origin, religion, or social status.[22]

It may be well to look briefly at American achievement in the field of these so-called social rights. Basic to all such analyses are the twin values of individualism and social responsibility. American individualism has a variety of meanings, two of which are of special importance. On the one hand, individualism serves to place the individual human being at the center of the stage in the struggle for political freedom and equality. This, of course, is part and parcel of the whole Judeo-Christian tradition, which asserts the supreme value of each individual human being in the divine scheme of things. Hence it regards the individual as an *end* and not as a *means*. Only on this assumption do ideas of freedom and equality have any significance. Expressions like the "common good" and the "general welfare" are, consequently, to be interpreted in terms of the

22 T. H. Marshall, *Citizenship and Social Class* (London: Cambridge University Press, 1950), pp. 14–65.

common good or the general welfare of the individuals in the community and not of some abstraction like the State or the Group.

Individualism in this sense has also involved a radical change from the theory of human depravity or original sin. The notion that man is essentially a beast of prey is in the long run incompatible with democratic values. At the very least, democracy assumes that the weaknesses of human nature can be overcome in an environment that is just and free. Hence democracy assumes, as Tocqueville has said, that:

> In proportion as castes disappear and the classes of society draw together, as manners, customs, and laws vary . . . as new facts arise . . . as ancient opinions are dissipated and new truths brought to light, the image of an ideal but always fugitive perfection presents itself to the human mind.[23]

This idea of human perfectibility remains as a central assumption of most democracies.

A second meaning of individualism has to do with the means by which individual welfare and salvation, if not individual perfection, can be attained. Individualism in this sense places the basic responsibility upon the individual himself. The influence of the Protestant principle of "every man his own priest" and the so-called Protestant ethic, which placed individual industry, frugality, and thrift high in its scheme of values, helped to strengthen individualism as a *means*. But as we have also seen, individualism in this sense has been modified by a sense of social responsibility.

Although major responsibility for the achievement of social values remains with the individual, public policies and democracy itself as a process and as a "way of life," are being increasingly tested by the degree to which they contribute to these ends. It is in these terms that the vast public expenditures in the United States on public works, education, recreation, housing, health, and welfare are to be understood. Fair labor standards legislation, workmen's compensation and disability insurance laws, aid to dependent children, aid to the blind and the physically handicapped, unemployment compensation are other aspects of the contemporary emphasis upon social democracy.

Social Mobility

To examine in detail how far the theory of social democracy corresponds to the facts of American life is beyond the scope of our present inquiry. One measure of this, however, may be examined—that is, the extent to which *upward* social mobility has been a characteristic of American society.

The most striking indication of social mobility in the United States has been the massive movement of population from the farm to the city.

---

[23] *Democracy in America* (New York: Knopf, 1945) , Vol. II, book I, chap. VIII.

In 1880 nearly 80 percent of those gainfully employed were farmers or farm workers. By 1960 less than 6 percent of the "civilian labor force" was employed in agriculture.[24] For the vast majority this change meant a substantial improvement in standard of living and social status. Many became owners and managers of business enterprises; others became skilled or semiskilled workers with higher incomes than they had had as farmers.

It is significant that in recording the shift from farm to nonfarm occupations, the Bureau of the Census, up to 1930, took account of all "persons 10 years old or over," whereas after 1930 the figures show only "persons 14 years old and over." This shift alone reflects a substantial change in the social status of American youth. The progressive rise in "school leaving age" from 10 to 12 to 14, and now generally 16 or 18, indicates not only a rising standard of living for the population as a whole, but, since formal education is a factor in producing social mobility, it may represent a further acceleration in this process for the future. As the Bureau of the Census has observed, "the social-economic status of the nation's labor force [has been] definitely upward—definitely away from heavy, arduous, unskilled manual labor, and . . . toward more highly skilled manual . . . and intellectual pursuits."[25]

> The transition from blue-collar to white-collar work [says Elbridge Sibley] can be taken as a rough index of upward occupational movement. Considering only transfers between these two broad categories and disregarding vertical mobility within each one, changes in the national economy between 1870 and 1930 produced a very marked shift in the center of occupational gravity. . . . On the average, about 150,000 workers per year ascended from blue collar [manual labor] to white collar jobs.[26]

In 1910 unskilled laborers comprised 36 percent of those gainfully employed; by 1965 they represented less than 10 percent. During these years there has been a spectacular increase in the percentage of professional, technical, clerical, sales, and service workers in the total labor force. By 1965 these occupation groups accounted for more than 40 percent of the total labor force as against barely 30 percent as recently as 1950. Managers and proprietors made up some 15 percent in 1965, about the same proportion as in 1950. Farm families had declined to less than 18 percent.[27]

The shift in occupation and social status appears also from one

24 See U.S. Bureau of the Census, *Statistical Abstract of the United States: 1966* (Washington, D.C.: U.S. Government Printing Office) , p. 219.

25 U.S. Bureau of the Census, *Comparative Occupation Statistics for the U.S., 1870–1940*, p. 184.

26 Elbridge Sibley, "Some Demographic Clues to Stratification," *American Sociological Review*, VII (June, 1942) , 322–330.

27 See U.S. Bureau of the Census *Reports* and the *Wall Street Journal* (March 30, 1961) .

generation to the next. Thus in 1946, only 23 percent of a sample of professional workers had fathers who were also professional workers. Some 24 percent were children of businessmen, 10 percent of white-collar workers, 18 percent were children of skilled or semiskilled workers, and 5 percent had parents-who were domestic or personal servants.[28]

Another sign of social mobility in the United States is the changing pattern of individual and family income. Real wages (that is, in terms of purchasing power) of workers in all nonfarm industries increased approximately 38 percent between 1890 and 1926.[29] Between 1926 and 1955 there was a further advance of more than 60 percent. Between 1955 and 1963 median family income, stated in constant dollars, rose from $5,074 to $6,249, an increase of some 20 percent. Moreover, labor's share of the total national income had increased substantially, thus reducing the distance between various income groups.[30] In recent years there has been a further trend toward reducing the gap.

As a corollary to these shifts in family income is the fact that many of the material goods and services formerly available only to a few at the top have now become accessible to the vast majority of American families. Thus over 60 percent of American families either own or are buying the houses in which they live. Over 75 percent own an automobile, and 10 percent have two or more; radio sets are universal, and over 86 percent have television sets. Over three-fourths of American families have telephones, and virtually all have electricity in their homes, with mechanical refrigerators, washing machines, and other "gadgets" and comforts of our technological age.

Many of the material attributes of the social elite have become so nearly universal among the American people that they are no longer reliable guides to social status. It is not easy to distinguish the merchant

[28] That nonfarm occupations afford greater mobility is seen in the fact, as revealed in this study, that 84 percent of the farmers or farm workers were children of farmers or farm workers. In no other occupation was there anything approaching this degree of stability or immobility. Only 31 percent of the businessmen had businessmen as fathers; in the case of white-collar workers, it was only 15 percent; of skilled workers only 30 percent; semiskilled workers 19 percent; domestic servants only 8 percent; and nonfarm laborers only 19 percent.

These figures are from a study of the National Opinion Research Center on "Jobs and Occupations: A Popular Evaluation" (1946), p. 12, adapted in Leonard Broom and Philip Selznick, *Sociology: A Text with Adapted Readings* (New York: Harper & Row, 1958), Table VI: 5, p. 198.

[29] See Paul H. Douglas, *Real Wages in the United States, 1890–1926* (Boston: Houghton Mifflin, 1930).

[30] The average hourly earnings of workers in all industries increased from 21 cents in 1890 to over 71 cents in 1926, a gross increase of nearly 240 percent. When these figures are adjusted for changes in prices, one arrives at Douglas' more modest increase of 38 percent. The average hourly earnings of workers in manufacturing increased from 19 cents in 1909 to $2.29 in 1960. Average weekly earnings rose from $9.84 in 1909 to $90.91 in 1960. Even when these figures are adjusted for price change, they show a striking increase in the earnings of American workers. See U.S. Bureau of the Census, *Statistical Abstract of the United States: 1960* (Washington, D.C.: U.S. Government Printing Office), Historical Statistics of the United States, p. 320.

prince from one of his clerks by the clothes he wears, the automobile he drives, or the mechanical contrivances with which he surrounds himself. Moreover, mass communications, universal free education, and cultural activities of wide variety have made available to nearly every family some of the best in science and literature, music, and art. Access to these treasures has largely ceased to be a criterion of social and economic status.

Of course these are not uniquely American phenomena, nor are they due solely to the influence of social democracy. Similar trends are to be found in other parts of the world.[31] But the social mobility characteristic of American society is due to a unique system of values. American egalitarianism "has not denied or even challenged existing differences in rank and authority. It has, however, insisted that such differences are only justified as a reward for demonstrated ability. . . . While family background and inherited social position play a role . . . eminent businessmen . . . and other upper-class leaders point in self-justification to the humble youthful origins from which they have risen." In Europe and Asia, this has not generally been the case. Hereditary rights and privileges have been more generally accepted. In America, on the contrary, even those enjoying the highest social status have never felt they had "a permanent and irrevocable place in the upper class."[32]

Social mobility is not incompatible with a stratified society. In the absence of some stratification, social mobility would have little significance. It is not, therefore, surprising that the American people too may be grouped into various social strata or classes, and a considerable literature has appeared to make this clear. But stratification may be *more* or *less* rigid, characterized by *more* or *less* mobility.[33]

[31] See Seymour Martin Lipset and Natalie Rogoff, "Class and Opportunity in Europe and the U.S.," *Commentary*, XVIII and XIX (December, 1954, and January, 1955), 562–568 and 86–88. [Reprint No. 161 of the Bureau of Applied Social Research, Columbia University.] Also see S. M. Lipset, "The Changing Class Structure and Contemporary European Politics," in *Daedalus, Journal of American Academy of Arts and Sciences* (1963).

[32] Lipset and Rogoff, *op. cit.*

[33] See, for example, Charles A. Beard, *An Economic Interpretation of the Constitution of the U.S.* (New York: Macmillan, 1954); also his *Economic Origins of Jeffersonian Democracy* (New York: Macmillan, 1915), and his *The Economic Basis of Politics* (New York: Knopf, 1945). See also Thorstein Veblen, *Theory of the Leisure Class* (New York: Macmillan, 1899); O. G. Libby, (Geographical Distribution of the) *Vote of the Thirteen States on the Federal Constitution, 1787–88* (Madison, Wis.: University of Wisconsin, 1894); A. M. Schlesinger, Sr., *The Colonial Merchants and the American Revolution, 1763–1776* (New York: Columbia University Press, 1918); J. F. Jameson, *The American Revolution Considered as a Social Movement* (Princeton, N.J.: Princeton University Press, 1940); Hinton R. Helper, *The Impending Crisis of the South* (New York: Burdick Bros., 1857); W. J. Cash, *The Mind of the South* (New York: Knopf, 1941). These are but a few examples of historical, political, or social analysis in terms of stratification and class conflict.

More systematic studies of stratification would include: Reinhard Bendix and Seymour Martin Lipset (eds.), *Class, Status and Power: A Reader in Social Stratification* (New York: Free Press, 1953); W. Lloyd Warner and others, *Social Class in*

Some critics of American democracy have argued that our social system is becoming *more*, not *less* rigidly stratified. Class lines, they say, are beginning to harden, and the "good old days" of the Horatio Alger myth have gone. "The strata are becoming more rigid," says J. O. Hertzler, "the holes in the seine are becoming smaller."[34] As this process continues, so runs the argument, class lines will harden and the spirit of American government and politics will change.[35]

The frontier is now closed, it is said—the endless acres of free land that meant freedom and opportunity are gone. Business opportunities that appeared on every hand in the nineteenth and early twentieth centuries are now few and far between. The giant corporation has displaced thousands of small businessmen, and administrative regulations, trade-union practices, and confiscatory taxes, have made it more and more difficult for a man to "get ahead," that is, to move from one social class to another.

The facts, however, would indicate no noticeable decline in social mobility. After a careful study of occupational mobility in Indianapolis during two periods, 1910 and 1940, one student found no evidence to support "the notion that the social structure has grown more rigid . . . (and) the likelihood of a son being in an occupational class different from that of his father was about the same in 1910 and 1940."[36] Another inquiry, by W. Lloyd Warner and James Abegglen, compares mobility rates for occupational groups in the United States in 1900, 1920, 1930, and 1950. Their conclusions, in summary, were that

> American society is not becoming more castelike: the recruitment of
> business leaders from the bottom is taking place now and seems to
> be increasing. . . . In spite of the pessimistic predictions about an
> immobilized society, this evidence shows that our society, although much
> like what it has been in past generations, is more flexible than it was;

America (Chicago: Science Research Associates, 1949) ; *The Social Life of a Modern Community* (New Haven, Conn.: Yale University Press, 1941) ; *Democracy in Jonesville* (New York: Harper & Row, 1949) ; *The Status System of a Modern Community* (New Haven, Conn.: Yale University Press, 1942) . Also, see Robert S. and Helen M. Lynd, *Middletown* (New York: Harcourt, Brace & World, 1929) and *Middletown in Transition* (New York: Harcourt, Brace & World, 1939) , Richard Centers, *The Psychology of Social Classes* (Princeton, N.J.: Princeton University Press, 1949) ; John Dollard, *Caste and Class in a Southern Town* (New York: Harper & Row, 1949) ; C. Wright Mills, *The Power Elite* (New York: Oxford University Press, 1956) ; W. Lloyd Warner and James C. Abegglen, *Big Business Leaders in America* (New York: Harper & Row, 1955) ; and Bernard Barber, *Social Stratification* (New York: Harcourt, Brace & World, 1957) .

[34] See J. O. Hertzler, "Some Tendencies Toward a Closed Class System in the United States," *Social Forces*, XXX (March, 1952) , 313–318.

[35] For other reports of the increasing rigidity of class lines in America, see W. Lloyd Warner and J. O. Low, *The Social System of the Modern Factory* (New Haven, Conn.: Yale University Press, 1947) ; Elbridge Sibley, *op. cit.*, 322–323; and others cited in Bernard Barber, *Social Stratification* (New York: Harcourt, Brace & World, 1957) , p. 429.

[36] Natalie Rogoff, *Recent Trends in Occupational Mobility* (New York: Free Press, 1953) .

more men and their families are in social motion; pessimism about
decreased flexibility and mobility is not warranted.[37]

Other studies of stratification and mobility in the United States tend to
confirm these conclusions.[38]

Although America is still an "open society," it would be a mistake to
deny that it is also stratified. In any stable society, this must be the case.
The nice balance between permanence and change which characterizes a
stable yet dynamic culture is not easy to define. A "closed" or rigidly
stratified order, in which there is little or no mobility, may appear to be
more stable than one in which class lines are less rigid and less clearly
defined. But by sacrificing the possibility of peaceful and orderly change,
it runs a greater risk of radical or even violent revolution. The general
persistence of social classes from one generation to another, together with
a comparatively high degree of social mobility, has combined to create in
the United States a stable yet dynamic society. This combination of
permanence and change is to be seen in the continuing vitality of political and economic institutions whose external forms and procedures have
remained substantially unchanged for nearly two hundred years.

The substantial growth of both political and social democracy in
America does not, however, justify complacency. Recent studies show that
even in our affluent society millions of families do not have access to the
"good things of life." Our Negro population, hundreds of thousands of
Mexican-Americans, Puerto Ricans, and other minorities, the growing
array of the dependent aged, migratory farm laborers, and unskilled
workers in general, continue to live on the level of poverty or deprivation.[39]

Terms like "poverty" and "deprivation" are, of course, ambiguous
and relative both as to time and place. A standard of living in the United
States in 1968, described in current articles as one of "poverty" or "deprivation," would be regarded in most underdeveloped countries as one
of prosperity or even affluence. Only by measuring incomes in constant
dollars and standards of living in terms comparable at various times and
places, can one arrive at any reliable estimate of general trends in
poverty or deprivation. For our present purpose it will suffice to point out

[37] W. Lloyd Warner and James C. Abegglen, *Occupational Mobility in American
Business and Industry, 1928–1952* (Minneapolis, Minn.: University of Minnesota Press,
1955) , p. 36.

[38] See Bernard Barber, *Social Stratification* (New York: Harcourt, Brace & World,
1957) , p. 468. Students interested in more intensive study of this important problem
might well begin with this volume and the extensive bibliography cited by the author.

[39] See Michael Harrington, *The Other America: Poverty in the United States*
(New York: Macmillan, 1962) . Gabriel Kolko, *Wealth and Power in America: An
Analysis of Social Class and Income Distribution* (New York: Praeger, 1962) . Morgan,
Jones, *et al.*, *Income and Welfare in the U.S.* (New York: McGraw-Hill, 1962) . T.
Arnold, L. Kaperline, *et al.*, *Poverty and Deprivation in the U.S.* (Conference on
Economic Progress, 1962) . See also Dwight MacDonald, *The New Yorker* (January 19,
1963) , pp. 82 ff.

that although 10.5 million families in 1960 were described as living in poverty (that is, with annual incomes under $4,000 before taxes), this number represented 23 percent of the total number of families as compared with over 68 percent living in poverty in 1935–36, 37 percent in 1947, and over 27 percent in 1953. These figures would indicate that the growth of social democracy in the United States as measured in these terms has continued, although at a somewhat slower rate.[40]

The U.S. Bureau of the Census reported a total of 8,800,000 poor families in 1963, that is, families with incomes of less than $3,000. This represents approximately 20 percent of all families.

☆ ALIENS AND AMERICANS

The American people have their roots in a tidal wave of immigration that came to North America during a period of more than 250 years. Statistics for the earliest years are unreliable, but it is estimated that before 1700 more than 250,000 people left the British Isles for America, and that during the eighteenth century 10,000 to 15,000 from England and elsewhere crossed the Atlantic every year. By 1800 total net immigration from Europe exceeded 2 million, not including more than 200,000 slaves who came as involuntary immigrants.

But even these figures seem modest when compared with the exodus that took place in the next century and a half. From 1800 to 1963 over 60 million emigrants left Europe, of whom nearly 43 million came to the United States. In addition, over 6 million more came from Canada, the West Indies, Mexico, Central and South America. Asia in turn contributed another million. From a tiny stream during the first decade of the eighteenth century, the volume grew to 300,000 in 1850, nearly 700,000 in 1881, and over a million in each of six years between 1900 and 1920.

In the early years the vast majority of the immigrants were of English origin. During the first half of the nineteenth century, the British, Irish, and Germans accounted for a large majority. After the Civil War these groups were supplemented, and later outnumbered, by immigrants from Norway and Sweden, Italy, Austria-Hungary, Russia, Poland, Mex-

---

[40] See *Survey of Current Business* (May, 1961). Also, "Size Distribution of Income Since the Mid-Thirties," by S. Goldsmith, *et al.*, in *Review of Economics and Statistics* (February, 1954). Also, U.S. Bureau of the Census, *Current Population Report*, Consumer Income, Series P–60, No. 37 (January, 1962).

"During the three decades 1929–1960, the total number of Americans living in poverty was reduced at an average rate of 2.2 percent. From 1935–36 to 1947, [however] the annual rate of reduction was 4.8 percent, due to the permanent economic reforms of the 1930s . . . [and] the great economic expansion of the World War II era." See Conference on Economic Progress, *Poverty and Deprivation in the U.S.* (Washington, D.C., April, 1962), p. 3.

ico, and more recently by a kind of intramural migration from other countries in the Western Hemisphere. Since World War II hundreds of thousands of refugees displaced from countries ravaged by war, revolution, or despotism have clamored for admission.

No small part of the American "miracle" has been the absorption of these diverse human beings and their transformation from aliens into Americans. For whatever may be the American "type"—if indeed there is an American type—it is by no means uniform, although Americans are united by a common language and by common social values. Under the circumstances, our national motto, *E Pluribus Unum* (one composed of many), would seem appropriate not only as a description of our federal system of government, but of our ethnic and cultural composition as well. For in the American scheme of things, diversity has been as important as uniformity in achieving national unity.

Fanlike, the Anglo-Puritan culture of New England and Virginia—Protestant, English-speaking, individualistic, generally rural, moralistic, and bearing the traditions of English law and politics—spread over the rest of the nation. In the process, it became the hallmark of Americanism and the standard image by which Americans were distinguished from "foreigners" or aliens. When the mighty torrent of immigration began to flow after 1800, it was by this Anglo-Puritan standard that the newcomers were measured and to which they were expected to conform. By education and indoctrination most of them, in a generation or two, came to resemble this model. To the degree that they did, they were said to be "assimilated" or "Americanized." When they departed from the model, they were regarded as "aliens." Thus, although all were aliens in the beginning, some remained more alien than others.

It would be a mistake, however, to assume that the process of "assimilation" operated in only one direction. The Anglo-Puritan model furnished the basic matrix of American character and conduct, but it was by no means a rigid, inflexible one. It has been modified and enriched by contributions from virtually every culture and from every corner of the globe. So numerous and diverse were the various cultural groups in colonial America that the years preceding the Revolution have been called the "Age of the Foreigner." By a process of intermarriage, crosscultural fertilization, and education, the new American was an ethnic and cultural hybrid. "I could point out to you," wrote Crèvecoeur in 1793, "a family whose grandfather was an Englishman, whose wife was Dutch, whose son married a French woman, and whose present four sons have now four wives of different nations. *He* is an American. . . ."[41]

How important these ethnic "minorities" can be even after a century and a half of assimilation is known to every practical politician. None would be so rash as to ignore the Irish in Massachusetts or New York, the

---

[41] *Letters of an American Farmer* (Philadelphia: Mathew Carey, 1793).

Scandinavians in Minnesota or the Dakotas, the Dutch in Pennsylvania, the Germans in Wisconsin, or the German, Russian, and Polish Jews in New York City. Some 40 percent of the population of New York, Massachusetts, Connecticut, North Dakota, and Rhode Island are classified as foreign born or of foreign or mixed parentage.[42]

Yet even where some cultural autonomy has persisted from one generation to the next, *political* adaptation proceeded at a rapid pace. "Aliens" became voters long before they became "Americanized," and in some places even before they became citizens. Democratic political institutions, free elections, free public schools, and a large measure of freedom and equality facilitated the process of assimilation.

☆ THE GOLDEN DOOR

At the base of the Statue of Liberty, this inscription appears:

> . . . "Give me your tired, your poor,
> "Your huddled masses, yearning to breathe free,
> "The wretched refuse of your teeming shore.
> "Send these, the homeless, the tempest-tossed, to me;
> "I lift my lamp beside the golden door."

These lines by Emma Lazarus are a fair poetic expression of America's traditional immigration policy. For nearly 150 years following the Revolution, the "welcome mat" was out for immigrants. What laws or regulations did exist were designed to encourage and protect the immigrant rather than to discourage him from coming. Nevertheless, during the century from 1820 to 1920 there were recurrent campaigns to discourage or prohibit the admission or more "aliens" from abroad. Our immigration laws, indeed, are largely a response to these campaigns.

Some antialien agitation followed the French Revolution because Americans feared infiltration and subversion by revolutionary sympathizers. However, this died out with more settled conditions in Europe, the expansion of the country, and the tolerant governments of Jefferson, Madison, and Monroe. But equally important was the fact that the volume of immigration remained comparatively small between 1800 and 1830—a period of extraordinary territorial expansion.

Reliable figures on immigration prior to 1820 are not available.

---

[42] The ethnic composition of cities is often revealed in the frequency with which certain surnames occur in official directories. In New York, for example, the Cohens rival the Smiths for first place, and among the leading names are Friedman, Goldberg, Goldstein, Schultz. Almost equally prominent are the Murphys, Kelleys, and Sullivans. These and other Irish names are among those most frequently encountered in Boston also. In Milwaukee, on the other hand, seven of the ten leading names were Schmidt, Mueller, Schroeder, Schneider, Schultz, Wagner, and Weber.

See H. F. Barker, "The Racial Composition of American Cities," *American Mercury* (October, 1932) .

Beginning in 1820 the official figures decade by decade are as shown in Figure 2–1.

In general, as immigration increased, tension mounted. Antialien agitation, with its demands for restrictive legislation, seemed to follow the ebb and flow of the immigrant tide.

The volume of immigration, however, was only one factor in outbursts of xenophobia (fear of strangers or foreigners). Equally important were the ups and downs of the business cycle. During good times the immigrants were more easily absorbed and were generally welcomed as an economic asset. With bad times, however, the immigrants were regarded by workers and small businessmen as competitors, or, when unemployed, as a drag on the economy.

These factors help to explain the agitation as such. But they do not account for the direction it took. In general, it was the Irish, Italian, and Polish Catholics, and the German, Polish, and Russian Jews who suffered most. That is to say, those who seemed to deviate most from the Anglo-Puritan model of what an American should be. The Italians and Poles had "three strikes on them," language, religion, and "race"—that is, being of south European origin. And the Jews suffered not only the disabilities of language, ethnic origin, and political tradition, but were non-Christian as well. Most of these minorities lived in ghettolike en-

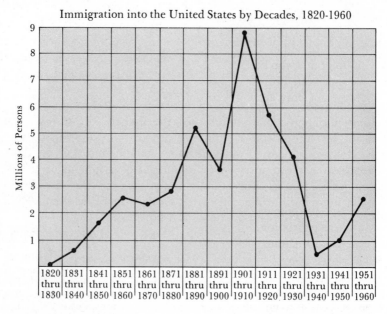

Figure 2–1   Based on data from U.S. Bureau of the Census, *Statistical Abstract of the United States: 1967*. (88th edition.) Washington, D.C., 1967, p. 95.

claves of the cities. As city-dwellers, they not only aroused the suspicion of a rural agrarian culture, but by sheer concentration of numbers they invited the attention of all those seeking to rationalize their own discontents by attributing them to some scapegoat called the "stranger," the "alien," the "foreigner," or the "infidel."

The most intensive antialien agitation occurred during and immediately following years of large-scale immigration and in periods of war or economic recession. And the chief victims were the groups which seemed to differ most from the Anglo-Puritan model, or which in time of war were identified with the enemy. Equally important were the economic conditions under which these minorities lived. They were poor and economically insecure; many knew little or no English and hence were unable to communicate effectively outside their own groups.

This is no place to recount, except in most general terms, the major antialien crusades that have occurred. Members of the Know-Nothing party (founded in 1837) pledged themselves not to "vote . . . for any man . . . unless he be an American-born citizen . . . nor if he be a Roman Catholic." In 1854 the Know-Nothing party could boast of over one-fourth of the vote in New York; two-fifths in Pennsylvania; and nearly two-thirds in Massachusetts, where it claimed to have elected every statewide official and nearly every member of the state legislature. By 1856 it claimed a hundred Congressmen and confidently hoped to elect a Know-Nothing President in 1860. Although mob violence was no part of its official program, anti-Catholic riots were frequent, during one of which, for example, the Ursuline Convent in Charlestown, Massachusetts, was burned, and other Catholic institutions were raided by "nativist" gangs (immigrants who had arrived earlier).

The American Protective Association (APA) agitation of the 1880s was directed not only against Irish Catholics, but against the great wave of immigration then pouring in from southern and eastern Europe.[43] And during this period, one began to hear, for the first time, about the "new immigration," which was represented as "un-assimilable" and therefore "alien" and "un-American," as compared with the "old immigration" from the British Isles and northwestern Europe, which was said to be "assimilable" and hence less "alien" and more truly American. Central to the purpose of the APA was more restrictive immigration and naturalization legislation, which, it was said, would put an end to the flood of "steerage slime" that was undermining the virtue and vigor of the American nation.

During World War I the volume of immigration fell off sharply, and

43 In the years 1905–1914 when over a million immigrants came to the United States in each of six separate years, over 70 percent (73.4) came from southern and eastern Europe as against 13.4 percent from northern and western Europe. Richard Morris (ed.), *Encyclopedia of American History* (New York: Harper & Row, 1953), p. 448.

the antialien crusade declined, except for the anti-German and anti-Irish agitation that accompanied the preparedness campaigns—the Germans, because of their identification with the enemy; and the Irish, as usual, because of their religion but aggravated in this period by their sworn hostility to England, our Ally. Popular reaction to all things German went to absurd lengths. Hamburgers became "liberty steaks," towns bearing German names were rechristened with English, French, Indian, or "native-American" ones, and the teaching of the German language was dropped or discouraged. German literature, music, and art were suspect; and Beethoven, Bach, and Brahms disappeared from concert programs. Atrocity stories fanned the flames of anti-German sentiment, and during Liberty Bond drives men and women of German origin were rounded up and held in stockades until they bought their quota. Although the Germans were the chief victims, the years 1915–1920 were filled with outcries against all forms of hyphenated Americanism. Polish, French, and Italian-Americans, however, suffered less, since they were identified with our wartime Allies.

As the stream of immigration began to rise in the postwar years,[44] antialien agitation took a new lease on life. Intensified by the postwar recession and reaction to the Russian Revolution, fears of unemployment and business failure were compounded with campaigns against "Bolshevism," "Anarchism," "Communism," and "Socialism." Labor unrest, class conflict, and other evils of the time were attributed to "foreign elements," especially to the so-called "new immigration." Moving into this volatile environment was a revived and redirected Ku Klux Klan. Directing its fire at all so-called "alien" elements, as well as against birth control, pacifism, internationalism, evolution, and pro-wet (antiprohibition) propaganda, the Klan and its influence spread like a prairie fire. By 1924 it was said to have over 5 million members and had become a powerful political pressure group in states where nativist sentiment was strong. In the 1924 Democratic Convention a proposal to denounce the Klan by name deadlocked the proceedings and no doubt was a major factor in the defeat of both Al Smith and William McAdoo and in the final nomination of John W. Davis.

Giving important aid to these antialien campaigns were not only the major patriotic societies, conservative religious and business leaders, but also labor leaders, intellectuals, and prominent educators. In an address to the workingmen of New England in 1832, Seth Luther, secretary of the Boston General Trades Convention, said: "If Congress have power to protect the owners [of factories] against foreign competition . . . of goods, they have the same right to protect the operative [worker] from foreign competition . . . of [imported] foreign mechanics and laborers

---

[44] The number of immigrants grew from 110,000 in 1918 to nearly 500,000 in 1920 and over 800,000 in 1921.

to cut down wages of our citizens." From the beginning of an organized labor movement in the United States, labor leaders have been in the forefront of those seeking to restrict immigration—a position which, with a few exceptions, they still maintain.

In this they have been in "good" company. Samuel F. B. Morse, for example—artist, inventor of the telegraph, and contemporary of Seth Luther—warned the country about the "imminent" dangers to the free institutions of the United States through foreign immigration. . . ." The distinguished attorney, Chauncey Depew, argued most eloquently against the "new immigration" from southern and eastern Europe, as a menace to American institutions. "Foreigners" in our midst, he professed to believe, were out "to destroy our government . . . and to divide our property."

No one should be surprised if Congress, through the years, yielded to these antialien crusades and in the course of time abandoned the policy of unrestricted immigration. The Supreme Court's decision in the so-called *Passenger Cases* in 1849 established the exclusive control of immigration by the federal government, leaving the states only such power as was necessary for local health and quarantine regulations. When the Office of Commissioner of Immigration was established in 1864, it was mainly to protect, not prohibit, immigration. At first only minor restrictions were imposed. For against the antialien pressures there were counterpressures from employers who wanted "cheap and docile" labor, from steamship lines who found the immigrant traffic profitable, and from railroads who wanted workers and families to settle on their land grants in the West.

The first general immigration act was passed in 1882, imposing a head tax on all immigrants and providing for the exclusion of lunatics, idiots, convicts, and persons likely to become a public charge. A law of 1885 forbidding the importation of contract labor was followed in 1891 by a law forbidding agents of American employers to solicit labor abroad. At the same time the list of excluded groups was extended to include persons having certain diseases or physical defects, and persons believing in polygamy. Bills to impose a literacy test were passed in 1896 and 1913, but were vetoed by Presidents Cleveland and Taft as inconsistent with the tradition of America as a land of opportunity. President Wilson vetoed similar legislation, but in 1917 a literacy test was passed over his veto, requiring all aliens over 16 years of age to demonstrate an ability to read "not less than 30 nor more than 80 words in ordinary use" in English or some other language.

The Quota System

With each upsurge in the number of immigrants, and with each outburst of antialien feeling, restrictions on the right to enter multiplied. By 1920 the number of excluded classes had grown to more than thirty, including contract laborers, convicts, paupers, insane persons, those suffering from various diseases, illiterates, polygamists, anarchists, persons advocating the overthrow of the government, and persons guilty of moral turpitude. In the Immigration Act of 1921 a new principle of admission on the basis of race or ethnic origin was applied to all immigrants. A "quota" for each nationality was established equal to 3 percent of the total number of that nationality already in the country in 1910. In no case was the quota to be less than 100, but the total number to be admitted from all groups was not to exceed 357,000.

This quota system, although changed in detail, has remained the basis of American immigration policy to the present time. In 1924 the law was amended to limit immigration from any country to 2 percent of the number of such persons in the United States in 1890. In 1929 the "national origins" basis was shifted from 1890 to the census of 1920, and the total number to be admitted in any year was reduced to 150,000, and in 1924 raised to 156,000.

At every step this legislation has been not only to impose an overall limitation on immigration but to give preference to immigrants from the United Kingdom and the countries of northern Europe as against those from southern and eastern Europe. For example, some 85 percent of all white persons in the United States in 1920 traced their "national origin" to the United Kingdom or some other country in northwestern Europe. Thus 85 percent of the total number allowed was assigned to these nationalities, and only 15 percent to those from eastern or southern Europe. Over 70 percent of the total number allowed have been customarily allocated to three countries—Great Britain, Germany, and Ireland. (See Figure 2–2.)

This policy was continued in the so-called McCarran-Walter Act of 1952. This act, while continuing a revised quota system, tempered earlier Oriental Exclusion Acts by putting immigrants from Japan, China, India, and other Asia-Pacific countries on the same basis as those from Europe. Persons from Canada, Mexico, and independent countries of the Caribbean and Central and South America were admitted as nonquota immigrants, subject only to the personal and political limitations which apply to all immigrants. Communists and other "subversives" were added to the excluded list, and the Attorney General was given power to deport immigrants for "Communist or Communist-front affiliations," even after they had acquired citizenship.

Unhappily, since World War II the greatest pressure has come from countries in eastern and southern Europe with the smallest allowable quotas. Italy, for example, with a quota of 5,666, had over 130,000 applicants on the waiting list in December, 1952; Greece had over 100,000 applicants for a quota of 308; and Russia (that is, refugees from Russia, for the most part) over 36,000 applicants for a quota of 2,697. On the

Immigration Quotas, 1966

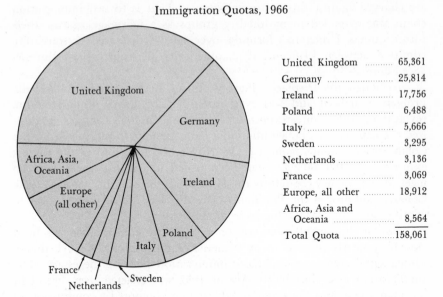

United Kingdom	65,361
Germany	25,814
Ireland	17,756
Poland	6,488
Italy	5,666
Sweden	3,295
Netherlands	3,136
France	3,069
Europe, all other	18,912
Africa, Asia and Oceania	8,564
Total Quota	158,061

Figure 2–2 Based on data from U.S. Bureau of the Census, *Statistical Abstract of the United States: 1967*. (88th edition.) Washington, D.C., 1967, p. 94.

other hand, Great Britain, with a quota of more than 65,000, had no applicants on its waiting list. These inequities might be mitigated if in any given year the unused quota of one country could be used for other countries with an excess of applicants over the quota. However, since 1924 it has not been possible to assign the surplus quota of one country to another, nor can surplus quotas be pooled for reallocation to those countries having long waiting lists. It is not surprising therefore that the total number of quota immigrants admitted has fallen considerably short of the maximum number allowed under the law. This number was set at 159,000, or one-sixth of 1 percent of our total population in 1920.

The limitations in the law and its inflexibility became evident in the years following World War II. Thousands of political refugees and persons rendered homeless and often stateless by war (the so-called displaced persons) sought asylum here. The vast majority were from countries of eastern and southeastern Europe—Hungary, Poland, Czechoslovakia, Russia, Latvia, Esthonia—whose quotas were hopelessly inadequate to accommodate more than a few applicants. And since the surplus quotas of other countries could not be pooled for this purpose, emergency legislation was required if the United States was to respond to this cry of mass distress.

Accordingly, an emergency Displaced Persons Act was passed in 1948 to authorize the entry of displaced persons and refugees without reference to established quotas. All persons admitted under this act, however, are charged against future annual quotas. That is to say, immigration credit was extended to nationality groups as a mortgage against their future quotas. Under this formula, over 350,000 displaced persons were admitted between 1948 and 1952, practically all from eastern Europe. (See Figure 2–3.)

Although the Displaced Persons Act of 1948 expired in 1951, the problem remained and was even intensified by waves of persecution, revolution, and counterrevolution. Therefore, in 1953 Congress authorized the issuance of 214,000 nonquota entry permits to refugees from the Communist-dominated countries. By November, 1956, just before the act expired, over 166,000 visas had been issued under this legislation. To meet the emergency created by the Hungarian uprising in October, 1956, Congress authorized the President to use the balance of unused visas to admit more than 20,000 refugees from Hungary.

But in the overall immigration picture the golden door has been closed, or nearly so, and many students of the problem believe that a fundamental change in our basic immigration policy is necessary. The Immigration and Nationality Act of 1952 was enacted over President Truman's veto, and the President thereupon appointed a commission to investigate the basic policy and administration of the new law. After

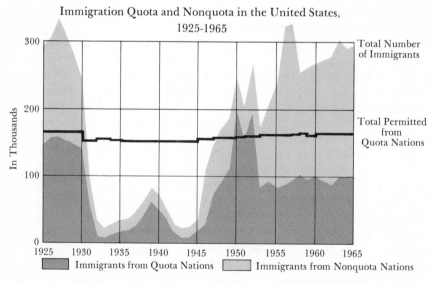

Figure 2–3 Based on data from the following sources: 1952–1957—U.S. Bureau of the Census, *Historical Statistics of the United States, Colonial Times to 1957,* Washington, D.C., p. 63; 1958–1961—U.S. Bureau of the Census, *Statistical Abstract of the United States: 1962.* (83rd edition.) Washington, D.C., 1962, pp. 318, 331; 1962–1965, *Statistical Abstract of the United States: 1967.* (88th edition.) Washington, D.C., 1967, p. 95.

extensive study, the commission submitted its report and recommendations in January, 1953. In summary, it concluded that:

1. The Immigration and Nationality Law embodies policies and principles that are unwise and injurious to the nation.
2. It rests upon an attitude of hostility and distrust against all aliens.
3. It applies discriminations against human beings on account of national origin, race, creed, and color.
4. It ignores the needs of the United States.
5. It contains unnecessary and unreasonable restrictions and penalties against individuals. . . .
6. It should be reconsidered and revised from beginning to end.

Specifically, the commission attacked the national origins quota system, which, it was argued, was based on theories of racial superiority or ethnic purity that are scientifically indefensible and politically unwise. Such discrimination, it was said, is offensive to the very peoples whose support the United States must seek in its effort to check the spread of communism. The commission also objected to a policy which limits total immigration to 154,000 persons each year. Admitting that some overall limitation is necessary, it argued that the total number should more nearly "reflect the needs and capacity for absorption of the United States."

This was a sweeping indictment. To remedy present immigration policies, the commission proposed that:

1. The national origins quota system be abolished.
2. There should be a unified quota system which would allocate visas without regard to national origin, race, creed, or color.
3. The maximum annual quota immigration should be one-sixth of one percent of the population of the United States as determined by the most recent census. Quota immigration would be open to 251,162 immigrants annually instead of 154,887 now authorized.
4. All immigration and naturalization functions . . . should be consolidated in a new agency to be headed by a Commission on Immigration and Naturalization . . . appointed by the President and confirmed by the Senate.
5. This Commission should distribute the total annual quota on the basis of the following five categories:
   The Right of Asylum
   Reunion of Families
   Needs of the United States
   Special Needs in the Free World
   General Immigration

Presidents Kennedy and Johnson, in their turn, followed the recommendations of President Truman's commission to abandon the quota system and increase, however slightly, the total number of admissible immigrants. The most recent legislation proposed by President Johnson in a special message to Congress, January 13, 1965, and enacted into law October 3, 1965, increased the total number of admissible immigrants from 158,000 to 170,000 and replaced the country-by-country quotas with a blanket prohibition against any discrimination "in the issuance of an immigrant visa because of race, sex, nationality, place of birth or place of residence."[45] Limited preferences, however, are to be given to the husbands or wives and the unmarried children of citizens of the United States or of aliens "lawfully admitted for permanent residence," to brothers and sisters of citizens of the United States, to immigrants where professional training or skills "will substantially benefit the national economy, cultural interests, or welfare of the United States," and to others seeking asylum from racial, religious, or political persecution. It remains true, under the new law as under the old, that immigrants from Canada, Puerto Rico, and Central and South America are not included in the global limitation of 170,000 established in 1965.

Underlying the new legislation was the uneasy sense that we had failed to resolve the basic contradiction in our Alien-American paradox. As a nation, our whole history has involved a continuous reception and absorption of aliens. Our language, literature, fine arts and music, science and technology, agriculture and industry, education, law and politics— all are marked at nearly every point by contributions from practically every race, nationality, class, and creed in the world. The basic purpose of our government and politics is to insure freedom and equality without reference to such "artificial" distinctions as race or religion, language or nationality. Yet we are uncertain as to how far we should continue to welcome the alien, the stranger, the foreigner. Although many of us, and all of our progenitors, were immigrants, we have no sure sense of direction even in our present immigration policies.

The world being what it is, we shall probably never open the golden door again, nor hold out a welcome to the world's "huddled masses yearning to breathe free." But our readiness to mitigate the worst inequities of the quota system and provide asylum for the victims of tyranny and disaster would indicate a deep-seated desire to find a way back to the more indulgent and confident policies of the past.

[45] See *Hearings Senate Judiciary Committee; Immigration Subcommittee* (February 10, 1965) . See also *The New York Times*, February 11, 26, 1965.

The Johnson proposals, like those of Presidents Truman and Kennedy, were assailed in Congress by those who have consistently defended the quota system. Senator Eastland of Mississippi, chairman of both the parent Judiciary Committee and the Subcommittee on Immigration strongly opposed the bill. So too did Senator Sam Ervin of North Carolina, who became a major spokesman for the opposition. The proposed bill, he said, would not increase substantially the number of immigrants with special skills needed by the country. The present system, he said, makes provision for immigrants having such skills—yet in 1965 only 2,475 aliens in the special-skills category were admitted out of a total of about 158,000 immigrants. Echoes of earlier arguments were heard in Senator Ervin's charge that while Congress was appropriating millions of dollars to train unemployed American youths, the proposed bill would admit nearly 66,000 more immigrants each year "to compete with Americans for available jobs."

☆ *NATURALIZATION*

The formal transformation of an alien into an American citizen is accomplished through the process of naturalization.[46] Prior to the Revolution, the inhabitants of the colonies in America were British subjects. With independence they became citizens of the several states and remained so under the Articles of Confederation. But among the powers conferred on the Congress by the Constitution in 1787 was the power to "establish a Uniform Rule of Naturalization."[47]

The first Naturalization Law of 1790 was a model of brevity. It simply authorized the courts to confer citizenship upon all unindentured white males who had lived in the United States two years. In 1795 this original act was changed to require a term of residence of five years; and the Alien Acts of 1798 increased the term to fourteen years. Following Jefferson's inauguration in 1801 a new naturalization law was adopted providing for five years' residence, some demonstration of "attachment to the principles of the Constitution," good moral character, supported by the testimony of witnesses, and a formal oath of allegiance. The law also provided that foreign-born children of aliens should become citizens on the naturalization of their parents. There were no educational requirements, nor was there any notion of "illegal entry" as a bar to naturalization.

For over a hundred years this naturalization process was administered by the courts, federal and state, with little or no central control. The result was a great lack of uniformity in the procedures followed, the records kept, and the documents issued. As the number of immigrants increased, chaos was confounded by corruption. Certain courts made a political football of their power and naturalized large numbers of aliens immediately before elections.[48] Although the candidates were supposed to understand and to speak English, this requirement was often satisfied by an ability to answer "yes" or "no" when told to do so. One judge, when asked if a candidate for naturalization before him could speak and understand English, is said to have answered, "Oh, yes! He nods his head in English!" Mass naturalization just before elections played into the hands of local political machines who, in return for minor favors of one kind or another, were able to control the immigrant vote. This was made

---

[46] See Ruth Z. Murphy, "Government Agencies Working with the Foreign Born," *The Annals of the American Academy of Political and Social Science* (March, 1949), p. 134. The present procedure of naturalization is described in Rollin B. Posey, *American Government: National, State, Local* (4th ed.; Paterson, N.J.: Littlefield, Adams, 1960), pp. 48–49.

[47] Constitution of the United States, Art. I, Sec. 8.

[48] See Murphy, *op. cit.,* p. 135.

easier in a good many states where citizenship was not a requirement for voting.[49]

In 1906, following the report of a special commission of inquiry appointed by President Theodore Roosevelt, a new Naturalization Act was passed. To the requirements provided for in the old law, the new act added certain education requirements. Henceforth applicants were required to read and write the English language and to show some knowledge of the history and principles of American government. The new law also established a Bureau of Immigration and Naturalization. Although the actual process of naturalization remains with the courts, the new agency is able to enforce a certain degree of uniformity in standards and procedures.

One important amendment to the law of 1906 was adopted in 1922. This provided for separate naturalization of married women. Prior to this, the citizenship of the husband had determined the citizenship of his wife. Under the new act, women now stand on substantially the same basis as men in acquiring or losing American citizenship. Marriage to an alien does not cancel a woman's citizenship, nor does an alien woman become a citizen simply by marrying an American, although the period of residence required for naturalization in such mixed marriages is reduced to three years.

In the uncertain world of the 1930s, with economic paralysis, rival dictatorships in Russia, Germany, and Italy, and impending revolution elsewhere, the Alien Registration Act was born. This act, designed primarily to check subversive activity, required all aliens to be registered and fingerprinted, and provided for the deportation of those aliens advocating the overthrow or destruction of government in the United States. Aliens must report their current addresses annually between January 1 and January 31. Naturalization procedures have also been tightened, so that although the formal requirements remain substantially the same, the road to citizenship has become a bit more steep and hazardous.[50]

☆ *CITIZENSHIP*

It is, of course, only the alien who must traverse the naturalization route to become a citizen. For most of us, citizenship is a matter of birth. If we

[49] "Alien" voting in the United States did not really end until 1926 when it was finally abolished by constitutional amendment in Arkansas. Up to 1875 over half the states allowed aliens to vote if they met certain other requirements, like residence. By 1900 the number of states in which aliens could vote had been reduced from a high of 22 to 11, and by 1926 to zero. [See L. E. Aylsworth, "The Passing of Alien Suffrage," *American Political Science Review*, XXV (1931), 114–116.]

[50] See J. C. Bruce, *The Golden Door: The Irony of Our Immigration Policy* (New York: Random House, 1954).

are born in the United States or in territory subject to its jurisdiction, we become citizens by virtue of this fact even if our parents are aliens. If we are born of American parents in a foreign country we become citizens because our parents are citizens, or because at least one of them is. This is the meaning of Section I of the Fourteenth Amendment, which provides that "All persons born or naturalized in the United States, and subject to the jurisdiction thereof, are citizens of the United States and of the states wherein they reside."

Or as Professor Corwin has said, some people are born citizens, some achieve citizenship (by naturalization), and some have citizenship thrust upon them. This last has been true of the inhabitants of territories annexed by the United States. When Louisiana, Florida, Alaska, Texas, Hawaii, and the Virgin Islands were annexed, their inhabitants were granted citizenship by special act of Congress. In the case of Puerto Rico and the Philippines, however, citizenship was withheld, and Puerto Ricans and Filipinos were thenceforth known as "nationals" of the United States—an ambiguous status hovering between that of alien and that of citizen. In 1917 Puerto Ricans were made full citizens by law, and Filipinos of course became citizens of the Republic of the Philippines when that territory achieved its independence on July 4, 1946.

Much has been said about the rights and privileges of citizens of the United States. What are these rights and privileges? Only citizens of the United States may become members of the House of Representatives or the United States Senate. To become President or Vice-President, one must be a natural-born citizen—no naturalized citizen need apply. Other rights and privileges attach to citizenship, such as the right to vote *and* the right to the protection of the United States while traveling abroad. Many employers, both public and private, hire only citizens, and in a good many cases this is required by law. But as we shall see, there are other rights and privileges of citizenship that are by no means clear. For example, Article IV of the Constitution provides that "citizens of each state shall be entitled to all the *privileges and immunities* of citizens of the several states." And the Fourteenth Amendment says that "no state shall . . . abridge the privileges and immunities of citizens of the United States." But just what these privileges and immunities of citizens are, no one can definitely say. One thing, however, is clear: the Constitution knows no difference between the rights and the privileges and immunities of citizens, no matter what the color of their skin, their ethnic origin, their social status, or their religion.[51]

51 Some other provisions of the Constitution in which the word "citizen" is used are Article III, which gives jurisdiction to the federal courts of cases "between a State and citizens of different States, between citizens of the same state claiming lands under grants of different states, and between a state or the *citizens* thereof and foreign states, *citizens*, or subjects." The term occurs again in the Eleventh Amendment, which denies jurisdiction of the federal courts to cases "against one of the United States by citizens of another state, or by citizens or subjects of any Foreign State." The Fourteenth Amend-

However, it is most important to remember that the basic rights of life, liberty, property, and the pursuit of happiness are not confined to citizens. Freedom of speech, of the press, of assembly, and of religious worship; freedom from bills of attainder and ex post facto laws; freedom to move from place to place; a right to trial by jury, to a writ of habeas corpus, to due process of law; access to public education; and other rights and privileges of our welfare state—extend to all persons, whether citizens or not. When the Fourteenth Amendment says, "nor shall any state deprive any *person* of life, liberty or property, without due process of law; nor deny to any *person* within its jurisdiction the equal protection of the laws," it makes no distinction between aliens and citizens. Both are *persons* within the meaning of the Constitution.

☆ WE, THE PEOPLE—SOME PROBLEMS OF GROWTH

From a tiny handful of settlers at Jamestown and Plymouth, the American people have become a mighty nation. Our growth has been due to a combination of immigration and natural increase. Just how much our phenomenal increase has been due to immigration, it is not easy to say. It seems doubtful that natural increase alone would have multiplied the original colonial population of some 4 million over fifty times, to 200 million, by 1965.

No other country in the Western world has grown so rapidly. The greatest rate of increase came in the colonial period. In spite of an excess of males in the population,[52] and in spite of the harsh conditions of life, population multiplied seventy-fivefold from 52,000 in 1650 to 4 million in 1780. Between 1790 and 1820 population again increased by more than 100 percent, an average of 35 percent each decade or 3.5 percent per year. This rate of increase, with minor variations, was maintained until the Civil War, when in spite of massive immigration it gradually de-

---

ment provides further that "when the right to vote . . . [at any state or national election] is denied to any of the male inhabitants of such state, being twenty-one years of age and *citizens* of the United States," the states so denying the suffrage shall have their representation in Congress reduced in the proportion which the number of such male citizens (who are denied the right to vote) shall bear to the whole number of male citizens twenty-one years of age in such state. Again the Fifteenth Amendment says, "the right of *citizens* of the United States to vote shall not be denied or abridged . . . on account of race, color, or previous condition of servitude," as the Nineteenth provides that "the right of citizens of the United States to vote shall not be denied . . . on account of sex."

[52] In 1635 there were six men to every woman, and even in 1774 just before the Revolution, men outnumbered women three to one. As Professor Eggleston has observed, "a colony of bachelors can never found a state." Or as a Virginia colonist in 1618 said, "a plantation can never flourish till families be planted and the respect of wives and children fix the people on the soil."

In this respect the New England settlements had the advantage over Virginia, since from the outset they were communities of families.

TABLE 2–1
Population of the United States Since 1790

Year	Population	Percent Increase over Preceding Census
1790	3,929,000	—
1800	5,308,000	35.1
1810	7,240,000	36.4
1820	9,638,000	33.1
1830	12,866,000	33.5
1840	17,069,000	32.7
1850	23,192,000	35.9
1860	31,443,000	35.6
1870	39,818,000	26.6
1880	50,156,000	30.1
1890	62,948,000	25.5
1900	75,995,000	20.7
1910	91,972,000	21.0
1920	105,711,000	14.9
1930	122,775,000	16.1
1940	131,669,000	7.2
1950	150,697,000	14.5
1960	178,464,000	18.4
1965[a]	194,000,000	8.6

[a] Five-year period.
SOURCE: U.S. Bureau of the census, *Statistical Abstract of the United States: 1967*, p. 5.

clined until after World War II. Table 2–1 shows population growth by decades in actual numbers and percentages. That the rapid increase from 1790 to 1860 was made possible only by immigration is evident from the fact that the average decennial increase of nearly 35 percent was maintained in spite of a falling birth rate after 1820, a rate sustained in part by an even faster decline in the death rate.[53] In each decade prior to 1920, immigration contributed from 26 percent to 55 percent of the total population increase.

Important as immigration has been, however, except for the decade 1900–1910, it has at all times been exceeded by natural increase. (See Figure 2–4, p. 68.) Up to 1920 the death rate has declined more rapidly than the birth rate, and it was this combination of natural increase plus a declining birth rate plus massive immigration that made possible the American population explosion. Between 1920 and 1940, however, a sharp decline in immigration was accompanied by a decline in the rate of

[53] See "The Demographic Revolution in the United States," *The Annals of the American Academy of Political and Social Science* (March, 1949), p. 62.

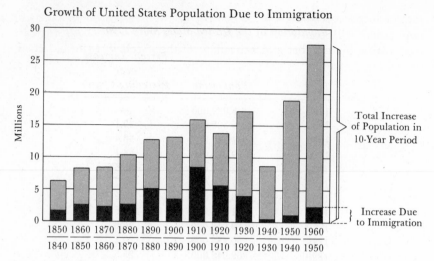

Growth of United States Population Due to Immigration

Figure 2–4 Based on data from U.S. Bureau of the Census, *Statistical Abstract of the United States: 1967*. (88th edition.) Washington, D.C., 1967, pp. 5, 95.

natural increase, and there was a corresponding slump in our rate of population growth. Since World War II a spectacular 23 percent increase in the birth rate, plus a phenomenal 10 percent decline in the death rate, has set off another minor population explosion. What, then, of the future?

Only a seer would presume to predict the future pattern of America's population growth.[54] Population forecasting is by no means an exact science, and even the best of demographers occasionally go astray. For example, in 1938 Warren Thompson and P. K. Whelpton, of the Scripps Foundation for Research on Population Problems, prepared careful estimates of the total population in the United States, up to and including 1980, on the basis of various assumptions concerning mortality, fertility, and immigration. They came up with a minimum estimate of 133,000,000 by 1980, a medium estimate of 158,000,000, and a maximum estimate of 174,000,000. The 1965 figure has already passed the maximum figure by 21,000,000, with fifteen years yet to go.

Recognizing that population, like the weather, is hard to predict, it is safe to assume that the so-called population explosion of recent years will continue for some time. At the turn of the century there were about 76,000,000 people in the United States. Today, there are more than 200,000,000—an increase of more than two and one-half times. And the

[54] Census estimates of population growth are continuously being made and it is not easy to arrive at any great degree of certainty in the matter. In February, 1965, for example, the Bureau of the Census forecast a population for the United States, of 265,575,000 by 1985. At that time California, with an estimated 32,000,000, would have 10,000,000 more people than New York, whose population in 1985 would be over 22,000,000. See *New York Times,* February 27, 1965.

rate of increase is going up, not down. What is the outlook? Our own population will continue to grow, and life expectancy will increase, multiplying the number and percentage of the so-called senior citizens in the total population. Males will probably continue to be outnumbered by females, with a resulting increase in the number and percentage of women in the labor force.

Population will probably continue to move northward, westward, and cityward, but at a slower rate. With automation in both industry and agriculture, there will be a continued shift in the way Americans earn a living. There will be fewer manual or unskilled workers, both actually and relatively, and more skilled workers, more white-collar jobs, and probably more blue-collar jobs as well; and there will be a sharp increase in craftsmen and foremen, operatives, technicians, and quasi-professionals. In 1900, 17 percent of Americans gainfully employed were white-collar workers; today nearly 50 percent are so classified. Significantly, the newer jobs are more stable and better paid—less subject to radical fluctuations of the business cycle. But it is not clear whether the new jobs generated by technology and automation will make up for the decline in employment which these changes are even now producing.

The possible dimensions of technological unemployment are difficult to estimate. In agriculture, over 4,000,000 workers have left the farm for the city since 1940, yet agricultural production is today greater than ever. With 30 percent fewer workers, American farms are turning out over 30 percent more food and fiber. If anything like this were to occur in industry, we should face an unemployment problem of staggering proportions. The effects of automation in the steel and automobile industries have already reduced employment, and at the same time caused an increase rather than a decline in production. We do not know what all this may portend in shorter hours and more leisure time, in increasing government control of the economy, and in patterns of education and recreation.

One thing is sure. These economic changes will reflect and be reflected in a change in the general educational level of our population. High school is now universal; college is rapidly becoming so. Science and technology will loom larger in the educational pattern of the future. Although everyone will talk about the importance of the social sciences and the humanities, the natural sciences and technology will occupy the center of the stage. Increased educational demands will raise ticklish political questions as school budgets balloon and the teacher shortage becomes more acute. We can expect more, not less state aid, and vastly more federal aid to education at all levels. And this will raise real problems of educational policy and administration. Moreover, the political implications of rising educational standards—more stable employment at higher pay—are bound to give politicians, both Republican and Democratic, something to think about.

Perhaps the most radical shift of our population has been from farm to city. Although total population has increased by about 450 percent, the number of farm workers today (about 5,000,000) is less than in 1870. Yet farm production continues to increase until in America we face a Malthusian problem in reverse. Not too many people for too little food and fiber, but too much food and fiber for too few people. And to save the farmer from a catastrophic fall in prices and consequent bankruptcy, government has had to buy his surpluses. It is to be hoped that some day we may find a way to deal with this agricultural abundance by public policies more equitable and intelligent than continuing subsidies and the piling up of increased surpluses.

As farm population goes down, our cities multiply and magnify. By 1960 nearly 70 percent of our population was classified as urban, and over half of us lived in some 225 great metropolitan areas. These metropolitan areas often extend not only beyond the borders of a single city or county, but beyond the limits of a single state. Many, if not most, of the urgent problems of metropolitan areas—problems of sanitation, transportation, public health, air and water pollution, police protection, garbage and sewage disposal—are beyond the powers of existing political units to deal with. The automobile alone may cause either urban strangulation by traffic congestion, or urban starvation as people move to the fringes, and freeways take them *away* from and not into the central city. In our desperation, we may deal with this problem with piecemeal, step-by-step, *ad hoc* measures and thus create new problems almost as difficult as those we seek to solve.

The population drift from South to North may be arrested if and when the southern states begin to feel the full impact of the industrial revolution. The Supreme Court decisions outlawing racial segregation in public schools, and recent civil rights legislation may play a decisive role in both directions. The Deep South, since the Civil War, has suffered from arrested economic development; for all practical purposes the American South has been properly classified as an underdeveloped area. The availability of an abundant, illiterate, servile, cheap, and inefficient labor force has deprived the southern states of the initiative, energy, and drive that have characterized their northern and western neighbors.

In the South there are to be heard voices that realize the magnitude and significance of this problem. On December 11, 1958, for example, Ralph McGill, editor of *The Atlantic Constitution,* had this to say in a leading editorial. After describing the political isolation of the South, he said:

> And the deep South, most unhappily, again has been maneuvered by its leadership into a position of being on the wrong side of a moral question as it was in defending slavery in 1860. Once again there is a hard and fast coalition of the West and North in defense of the Union and its processes

of law, which provide civil rights to all citizens. This is the essence of the classic Greek tragedy and there is no lightness in it.

Recent decisions of the Supreme Court and recent Civil Rights Acts of Congress, in response to the so-called Negro Revolt of the 1960s, are bound to accelerate the process of putting an end to racial segregation, and lifting the American Negro to a position of full civic equality. The significance of this domestic racial problem for our foreign policy is obvious. A large and increasing majority of the world's mounting population are people of color. It is not easy to convince them that we sincerely believe all men are created equal and that we will treat with them as equals; what we do speaks louder than what we say. Nothing could add more strength to our position among the uncommitted colored peoples than a major victory in the present struggle to lift our Negro citizens to full equality in the exercise of their constitutional rights. Perhaps such a victory can be won in the 1960s; let us hope it is not too late.

FOUNDATIONS
OF CONSTITUTIONAL
GOVERNMENT

☆ *THE MEANING OF CONSTITUTIONAL GOVERNMENT*

When the founding fathers rejected democracy, as they understood that term, to establish what they were pleased to call a republic, they had something more in mind than government by representatives of the people as distinguished from government directly by the people. They had in mind a system which would impose limitations upon the scope of political power and prescribe certain procedures in the exercise of power. That is to say, it was their intention to establish not merely a representative republic, but also a constitutional government. For constitutionalism as a principle, whatever the form of the constitution itself, implies (1) a "higher" or fundamental law, to which all other laws are subject and subordinate; (2) a government of limited powers; (3) some idea of personal rights and freedom for individuals and private groups and associations; and (4) certain established procedures by which the limitations on the government may be enforced and the personal rights of individuals and groups secured.

The idea of a higher law can be more easily stated than understood. As defined by Professor Corwin, it assumes that there are:

> Certain principles of right and justice which are entitled to prevail of their own intrinsic excellence . . . regardless of those who wield the physical resources of the community. Such principles were made by no human hands; indeed if they do not antedate deity itself, they still so express its nature as to bind and control it. . . . They are eternal and immutable. In relation

to such principles, human laws are . . . an act not of will or power but one of discovery and declaration.[1]

This idea of a law to which government, no less than private persons, is subject is almost as old as recorded history. It reaches back to the ancient codes of Hammurabi and Moses, to the fundamental "laws" of Solon and Lycurgus, in which rules of conduct are laid down as universal principles of justice, having their origin in what were called the laws of reason, of nature, or of God, and applicable alike to rulers and ruled, to the sovereign in the state as well as to its citizens or subjects. It is, as we have seen, reflected in the distinction, however vague and shadowy, that is made in ancient law between the state and society, between the rights of the community and of the individual. It is to be seen in embryo in Antigone's defiance of the tyrant Creon and his decree, which had no "binding force," because it was in conflict with the "unchangeable unwritten code of Heaven."[2]

Every citizen of Athens swore an oath to ". . . slay by word and deed, by my vote and by my hand, whomever shall suppress the democracy of Athens." When illegal, that is, unconstitutional, proposals were made or adopted, there was a special procedure or indictment by which such violations of the fundamental law of the constitution could be corrected through revision or repeal. One can find intimations of a higher law in Aristotle's distinction between laws and decrees, and between forms of government that are rightly established and those that are corrupt or perverse. One finds more than an intimation of a higher law in Plato's statement that a "state in which the law is subject and has no authority [is] . . . on the highway to ruin, but . . . the state in which the law is above the rulers and the rulers are the inferiors of the law, has salvation, and every blessing which the gods can confer."[3]

The doctrine of a higher law, shadowy and fugitive among the Greeks, becomes more precise—although still vague and ambiguous—among the Romans. It is the "true law" of which Cicero speaks and to which the Roman legal writers always defer.

> True law [says Cicero] is right reason, harmonious with nature, diffused among all, constant, eternal. . . . It is a sacred obligation [of government] not to . . . legislate in contradiction to this law; nor may it be derogated from nor abrogated. . . . [By] neither the Senate nor the people can we

1 Edward Samuel Corwin, *The "Higher Law" Background of American Constitutional Law* (Ithaca, N.Y.: Cornell University Press, 1955) , p. 4. See also Charles Howard McIlwain, *Constitutionalism, Ancient and Modern* (Ithaca, N.Y.: Cornell University Press, 1940) .

2 See Sophocles, *Antigone*, trans. Sir George Young (Everyman's Ed.; New York: Dutton, 1925) , p. 14.

3 See "The Laws," *The Dialogues of Plato,* trans. Benjamin Jowett (Oxford: Clarendon Press, 1892) , Vol. 5, p. 715. See also Francis Dunham Wormuth, *The Origins of Modern Constitutionalism* (New York: Harper & Row, 1949) .

be released from this law. . . . Nor is it one law at Rome and another at Athens; one now and another at a later time; but one eternal and unchangeable law binding all nations through all time. . . .[4]

One striking difference between the Roman doctrine and its expression among the Greeks is that Cicero, for example, bases his theory of a higher law on the natural equality of all men. All are capable of virtue, and it is not human nature but vice and injustice that produce inequality. To establish justice, therefore, it is necessary to return to the first principles of nature, and it is these that should guide and control not only individuals but governments as well. Moreover, since men existed prior to the state, they have *natural* rights that the state may not lawfully infringe or impair. These ideas of human equality and of natural rights, according to Professor McIlwain, are "the profoundest contribution of the Stoics to political thought," and in the words of Professor Carlyle, mark the "dividing line between ancient and modern political theory." With these principles, we are "at the beginning of a theory of human nature and society of which the 'Liberty, Equality and Fraternity' of the French Revolution is only the present-day expression."[5]

The Roman-Stoic doctrines of a higher law and of natural rights were extended and elaborated during the Middle Ages, but modified, at least in the early Middle Ages, by the Christian doctrine of original sin. Fundamental or higher law is identified as the law of nature, and this in turn with the law of God. The new doctrine assumed that only in a state of innocence were all men free and equal. Once sin had entered the world, inequality entered too. It was sin, therefore, which made government necessary in order to curb man's evil nature and thus let the good in him shine through. "Let every soul" therefore says Paul, "be subject unto the higher powers. For there is no power but of God; the powers that be are ordained of God. Whosoever therefore resisteth the power, resisteth the ordinance of God: and they that resist shall receive to themselves damnation."[6] But this language was not intended to provide a blanket absolution for everything the "powers that be" should take a fancy to decree. Although all legitimate political power was "ordained of God," not every exercise of power had divine sanction. "It is one thing," said Peter Abelard in the twelfth century, "to resist the tyranny of an evil ruler, it is another to resist his just power which he has received from God."

Statements of this kind were common among both religious and lay

[4] Marcus Tullius Cicero, *De Republica, De Legibus,* trans. Clinton Walker Keys (New York: Putnam, 1928) quoted in Corwin, *op. cit.,* p. 10; and quoted also in Charles Howard McIlwain, *The Growth of Political Thought in the West* (New York: Macmillan, 1932) , p. 111.

[5] Sir Robert Warrand Carlyle, *A History of Medieval Political Theory in the West* (London: William Blackwood & Sons, 1936) , Vol. I, p. 9.

[6] Romans 13:1–2, King James Version.

leaders seeking a moral and religious basis for resistance to injustice and tyranny. Obedience to the "powers that be" was a Christian duty—obedience even to rulers who were themselves evil, for they, it was often said, were sent by God to punish men for their sinful ways. But in final analysis, the Christian citizen was enjoined to "obey God rather than man," and this could, and often did, require him to resist unjust, immoral laws in conflict with God's law or the universal laws of nature.[7]

These laws of nature in the course of time came to be identified with the fundamental law to which governments no less than citizens were subject. In substance, they were thought to consist of all those rules of right conduct which reasonable men everywhere and at all times understood and observed—a sort of universal common law, in which even the alien subject could find some safe refuge from arbitrary power.[8] To the devout these laws were equated with the moral principles of the Christian religion. To the Christian, all men are brothers, children of one father, and endowed with a moral sense that enables even those outside the Christian faith to distinguish right from wrong and hence to judge the laws to which they were subject. "When the gentiles," wrote Paul, "which have not the law, *do by nature the things contained in the laws,* those having not the law are a law unto themselves *which show the work of the law written in their hearts.*"

It was no long step to assert the supremacy of this natural law over any man-made laws in conflict with it. The difficulty was that the laws of rulers were usually clear and explicit by comparison with the laws of nature, which were at best vague and diffuse. It was one thing to say that all legitimate law was subordinate to this higher law, and something else again to know how, in case of conflict, the higher law was to take precedence. And whatever supremacy the higher law might have in theory, some practical means by which the *natural* rights embodied in it could be secured against invasion by governments or private persons was essential. Otherwise, a man's *natural* rights would remain empty rights, and the higher law little more than an abstraction, a "brooding omnipresence in the sky." In the absence of effective procedures for the enforcement of natural rights under the higher law, their only sanction would be a right of revolution, or a return to private retribution, in cases where one's natural rights were violated by private persons or agencies. In either case, the remedy might prove more costly than the disease.

---

[7] See R. W. Carlyle, *op. cit.* Also see McIlwain, *The Growth of Political Thought in the West,* chaps. V and VI.

[8] "Whatever any people itself has established as law for it," said the great Roman jurist Gaius, "this is confined to it alone and is called *jus civile,* as a kind of law peculiar to the state; *whatever, on the other hand, natural reason has established among all men, this is observed uniformly among all peoples and is called jus gentium, as a kind of law which all races employ.*" (Quoted in McIlwain, *ibid.,* p. 122.) The distinction between *jus gentium* and *jus naturale* came to be more and more attenuated.

☆ CONSTITUTIONALISM—MAGNA CHARTA TO THE DECLARATION OF INDEPENDENCE

To give more specific substance to the higher law, it came to be identified with certain types of interpersonal behavior, rights, and relationships which through long-established custom were regarded as natural and for all practical purposes immutable. These customary patterns of behavior, and the rights and obligations associated with them in the family, the church, the economic order, and the state, took on all the authority, all the mystique of natural law. In England, this pattern of rights and obligations and what was called the "common law of the realm" were so related that for centuries royal laws and decrees in conflict with them were open to challenge, either by direct action in a quasi-revolutionary refusal to comply, or later on in the courts.[9]

The classic example of a direct challenge to the state's authority is, of course, the successful resistance of the English barons at Runnymede in 1215, where King John signed the Magna Charta. This rebellion was not against the king's legitimate authority, but against his continual illegal invasion of the customary rights and obligations of his feudal lords. Whether one regards the Magna Charta as a great charter of human liberties or a reactionary document designed only to protect the privileges of a feudal aristocracy, it has an important place in both English and American constitutional history. It was a dramatic appeal to a higher law against the powers and pretensions of the state, and as a written document it gave to the higher law a tangible content and form. Moreover, its guarantees leave no doubt that there are customary or natural laws protecting the natural rights of citizens which the state (in this case the king) is bound to respect on pain of open rebellion. Like other great constitutional charters, the language in many of its 70 chapters was vague and ambiguous, allowing later generations to read into it guarantees that more specific language would not have allowed. Chapter 39, for example, says that:

> No free man shall be taken or imprisoned or deprived of his freehold or of his liberties or free customs, or outlawed or exiled, or in any manner destroyed, nor shall we send upon him, except by a legal judgment of his peers or by the law of the land.

9 This identification of customary rights and privileges with natural law is made plain in Henry of Bracton's thirteenth-century *Treatise on the Laws and Customs of the Realm of England (Tractatus de Legibus et Consuetudinibus Regni Angliae)*. "While . . . they use *leges* and a written law in almost all lands, in England alone there has been used within its boundaries an unwritten law which usage has approved. . . . For the English hold many things by customary law which they do not hold by *lex*." [Quoted in McIlwain, *ibid.*, p. 192.] Bracton, says McIlwain, was in error only in assuming that England was an exception, "for such statements are to be found all over the feudal world."

What such phrases as "liberties," "customs," and "the law of the land" mean in specific cases remains uncertain. The method of enforcing the rights guaranteed in the Magna Charta—by a committee of twenty-five—proved to be ineffective. Civil war broke out when King John repudiated the charter as having been signed under duress and was formally supported in this action by Pope Innocent III. But the memory of the Great Charter remained, and under John's successors it was renewed again and again until it became, in legend if not in law, the great palladium of English liberties and an important factor in the development of constitutional government in both England and America.

It was not enough, however, to give substance and content to the higher law unless some more effective procedure for its enforcement than open rebellion could be developed. In words attributed to Bracton in his *Treatise on the Laws and Customs of England*:

> The King has a master, namely God. Likewise his curia, to wit, the earls and barons: for the earls are . . . a kind of associates of the King, and one who has an associate, has a master; and so if the King is without a bridle, that is, without law, they ought to put a bridle on him.[10]

But the bridle which the earls could put upon the king proved effective in the long run only as it became part of those restraints imposed by Parliament and the courts. In the conflict between the rights of Parliament and the royal prerogative, the idea of a higher law and of the natural rights of Englishmen play an important role. As the "High Court of Parliament" (which nominally it is even today), it served as a court of last resort for many cases and was also empowered to consider complaints and petitions for redress of grievances. With its power to control taxation, which it had won in 1340 from Edward III, Parliament thus came into possession of a powerful sanction for the protection of the "natural rights of Englishmen."

The idea that the High Court of Parliament could impose restraints upon the power of the state (that is, the king) marked an important step in the discovery of an effective instrument for the enforcement of natural or higher law against the claims of kings and commoners alike. To extend this idea to the courts of law in general and to look to the judges for the defense of natural rights even against Parliament itself was a long but by no means an illogical development. Under Sir John Fortescue, Chief Justice of the King's Bench from 1442 to 1460, and Sir Edward Coke (1552–1634), the supremacy of the common law (that is, as higher or natural law) as applied in the courts—if necessary against the will of both king and Parliament—was established.

[10] These words, which Professor Maitland says are "no part of the original text" of Bracton's book, serve nevertheless to illustrate the emerging doctrine of a higher law imposing constitutional restraints upon the state. See Charles McIlwain, "The Fundamental Law Behind the Constitution of the United States," *The Constitution Reconsidered,* ed. Conyers Read (New York: Columbia University Press, 1938).

In his most important book, his *Institutes,* Coke bases his arguments clearly on the Magna Charta, which he says had been confirmed and reconfirmed more than thirty times. And giving the language of the great charter a liberal interpretation, he found in it the basic principles of due process of law, habeas corpus, indictment by grand jury, trial by the "law of the land," defense against monopoly, and taxation only by consent of Parliament.

In his famous decision in the so-called Bonham Case in 1610, Justice Coke said:

> And it appears in our books, that in many cases the common law will control acts of Parliament . . . and sometimes adjudge them to be utterly void: *for when an act of Parliament is against common right and reason . . . the common law will control it and adjudge such an act to be void.*[11]

Important as the contributions of these great lawgivers, statesmen, and philosophers have been, it is to authorities closer to our time that the founding fathers looked for their theories of constitutional government. Not the least among these was the English philosopher John Locke, who wrote among other things a model constitution for the colony of what later became North and South Carolina. His model constitution, however (which was never put into effect), was the least of his contributions to the growth of constitutionalism in America. Most important were the doctrines he set forth mainly in his *Second Treatise of Civil Government,* first published in 1690.

According to Locke, men in a state of nature were in "a state of perfect freedom [and equality] to order their actions and dispose of their possessions and persons as they think fit *within the bounds of the law of nature* without asking leave or depending upon the will of any other man." All legitimate political power, therefore, must rest upon the consent of the governed. "The liberty of man in society is to be under no other legislative power but that established by consent in the commonwealth, nor under the dominion of any will or restraint of any law, but what that legislature shall enact according to the trust put in it." But government, even when based on the consent of the governed, is itself limited by the law of nature and the natural rights of man. No legitimate governmental power, therefore, can "extend further than the common good" and the preservation of these natural rights. No legislative body

---

[11] The Bonham Case involved an act of Parliament which authorized the London College of Physicians to license and control the practice of medicine and to punish persons for practicing medicine without a license. It was against this act that Dr. Bonham was protesting—a protest sustained by Coke's decision. The ruling in the Bonham Case became moot (of no legal effect) with the establishment of the supremacy of Parliament. But the power of the courts—including the High Court of Parliament, i.e., the House of Lords acting as a court—to "construe" the language and meaning of Parliamentary acts so as to save the natural rights of citizens remains. See, for example, Sir David Lindsay Keir and F. H. Lawson, *Cases in Constitutional Law* (New York: Oxford University Press, 1954), chap. I.

can "assume to itself power to rule by extemporary, arbitrary decrees . . . [or] take from any man [his life, or liberty, or] part of his property without his own consent . . . [or] transfer the power of making laws to any other hands. . . ." These, he says, are the bounds "which the trust that is put in them by the society and the law of God and nature have set to the legislative power of every commonwealth in all forms of government."[12]

Locke's ideas found an echo in the American colonies and furnished an arsenal for the war of words that led in the end to independence. "British liberties," wrote John Adams, "are not the grants of privies [King's Councils] or parliaments, but original rights, conditions of original contracts . . . coeval with government. . . . Many of our rights are inherent and essential, agreed on as maxims . . . even before parliament existed . . . [they are] rooted in the constitutions of the intellectual and moral world."[13] James Otis, in his outline of the *Rights of British Colonies Asserted and Proved,* based his argument squarely on the doctrine of a natural or higher law. "Should an act of Parliament," he said, "be against any of his natural laws, which are immutably true, their declaration would be contrary to eternal truth, equity and justice and consequently void." Even the empirical and at times almost cynical Alexander Hamilton spoke of "the sacred rights of mankind [which] are . . . written as with a sunbeam in the whole volume of human nature, by the hand of Divinity itself, and can never be erased or obscured by mortal power. . . ."[14]

Nowhere in the long history of constitutional government have its basic assumptions of a higher law and natural rights been more clearly set forth than in the Declaration of Independence. In the opening sentence reference is made to "the Laws of Nature and of Nature's God." And there follows the simple assertion that certain truths are "self-evident," namely, that "all men are created equal . . . [and] are endowed by their Creator with certain unalienable Rights . . . [among which] are Life, Liberty, and the pursuit of Happiness." It is the sole purpose of government "to secure these [God-given or eternal] rights." And whenever "any Form of Government becomes destructive to these ends, it is the Right of the People to alter or abolish it. . . ." In the catalogue of grievances that follow, not the least of them has to do with the alleged violation by the king of Great Britain [and Parliament] of the constitutional rights of the colonists.

So important were these constitutional issues, that Professor McIlwain has argued that the American Revolution itself may be best

[12] John Locke, "The Second Treatise of Civil Government," *Two Treatises of Government,* ed. Sir Robert Filmer (New York: Hafner, 1947), chap. XI.

[13] John Adams, "The Common and the Feudal Law," *The Life and Works of John Adams,* quoted in E. S. Corwin, *op. cit.,* ftn. 1, p. 79.

[14] Quoted in Charles Edward Merriam, *A History of American Political Theories* (New York: Macmillan, 1951), p. 48.

understood as a part of the general movement for constitutional government in both England and the colonies. The arguments used were
essentially constitutional arguments based on the alleged violation not
only of the natural rights of man but more specifically of the constitutional rights of Englishmen. "Taxation without representation" was, in
the beginning, the central issue—an issue rooted in over 500 years of
English constitutional history. Thus as Professor Boorstin has argued, the
Americans' "loyalty to British institutions was itself a cause of the
Revolution." However farfetched this may be, the terms in which the
Revolution was rationalized among the colonial leaders had an important bearing on the development of our political institutions.

Because the Revolution in "political theory and practice . . . drew
its inspiration from the parliamentary [constitutional] struggle of the
seventeenth century," it failed to develop the kind of ideological overtones that characterized the French Revolution. Whereas the American
leaders talked of their grievances as arising from violation of the constitutional rights of Englishmen, the French leaders talked of the universal
rights of man—of Liberty, Equality, and Fraternity. "By [thus] seeming
to tend rather to the regeneration of the human race than to the reform of
France alone, [the French Revolution] roused passions such as the most
violent political revolutions had been incapable of awakening. It . . .
became a sort of new religion . . . without God, worship or future life,
but still able, like Islam, to cover the earth with its soldiers, its apostles,
and its martyrs."[15] There were ideological aspects to the American
Revolution, especially in the arguments of Thomas Paine and Samuel
Adams, but even these drew their inspiration not from the French
philosophers, such as Rousseau, but from John Locke.

The chief permanent achievement of the French Revolution, according to Tocqueville, "was the suppression of those political institutions,
commonly described as feudal, which for many centuries had held
unquestioned sway in most European countries."[16] The American Revolution had no entrenched feudal system to sweep aside, no kings, no
hereditary aristocracy. Hence the Revolution did not become in any
significant sense a class war, and the struggle for independence did not
become a war for the liberation of mankind from the bonds of an
anachronistic social order. It was instead a struggle for the reform or
restoration of our own domestic institutions to conform to our own
model of a constitutional government and to our own conception of the
traditional rights of Englishmen.

[15] Alexis de Tocqueville, *The Ancient Regime and the French Revolution*, trans.
Joseph Bonner [as *The Old Regime and the Revolution*] (New York: Harper & Row,
1876) , pp. 26 ff., quoted in Daniel Joseph Boorstin, *The Americans; the Colonial
Experience* (New York: Random House, 1958) , p. 83. See also the more recent edition
of this work, *The Old Regime and the French Revolution*, trans. Stuart Gilbert
(Garden City, N.Y.: Doubleday, 1955) , pp. 13 ff.

[16] Stuart Gilbert, *ibid.*, p. 19.

☆ CONSTITUTIONAL GOVERNMENT— THE COLONIAL PATTERN

"The fate of every democracy," wrote Lord Acton, "of every government based on the sovereignty of the people, depends on the choice it makes between . . . absolute power on the one hand, and on the other, the restraints of legality and the authority of tradition. . . ."[17] For the founders of the American Republic, this was never a serious issue. The basic principles of democracy, of popular sovereignty, of government by consent, of majority rule were generally assumed. But the idea of absolute or unlimited power, even in the people themselves, was never assumed or accepted. That is to say, the most distinctive feature of the American political tradition has been its dedication to the principles of constitutional government—of government limited by a higher law, and restrained in its exercise of power by the natural or unalienable rights of man, and the principles of due process of law.

It has been part of the unique experience of the American people that these principles have not been expressed solely in high-order abstractions from the works of legal scholars and political philosophers or passed from one generation to another by word of mouth. They have, on the whole, been committed to writing with the same care and caution that a prudent man observes in the making of a contract. Indeed, the social contract theory, which through Hobbes, Locke, and Rousseau has furnished the ethical foundation for political power in every modern democratic state, was not merely a theory but a condition of political life in America from the Mayflower Compact to the Constitution. The colonial charters became for all practical purposes the written constitutions or social contracts in terms of which the basis, the structure, and the scope of political power were defined.

By 1776 all the colonies except Rhode Island and Connecticut were governed as royal colonies under charter from the king. The pattern varied somewhat from one colony to another, but the similarities were, on the whole, greater than the differences. All except Rhode Island and Connecticut had a royal governor and council appointed by the crown and serving during the king's pleasure, a colonial assembly elected by qualified electors for a limited term, and a system of courts based on the justices of the peace and a number of county courts. Appeals from the county courts were normally to the governor (or chancellor) in council, except in Massachusetts and Pennsylvania, where they were supreme courts appointed by the governor. From these high courts, appeals could be taken in some cases to the Privy Council in London.

[17] John Edward Acton (First Baron), "Political Causes of the American Revolution," *Essays on Freedom and Power* (New York: Meridian, 1955), p. 171.

Under the prevailing plan of constitutional government in the colonies, the royal governor was the main sign and symbol of political power. Holding office at the pleasure of the king, he was largely independent of the popularly elected assembly. The governor's council was a creature of the governor and hence no great threat to his power. The governor was the chief executive and administrative officer, and head of the armed services with authority to levy troops and assume command. He had power to appoint and to remove all important officials, civil and military, and could, on occasion, create new offices. His power to pardon extended to all cases except those involving treason or felony, and even in these he could grant a reprieve pending final decision in England. The governor had important powers to propose legislation to the assembly, to issue executive orders and decrees often having the force of law, and to veto acts of the legislature. In addition, he could charter towns and cities, license markets and fairs, censor the press, and of course conduct the foreign relations of the colony, including negotiations with the Indians. In his independence of the legislature, the scope of his powers, and the symbolic and ceremonial significance of his office, the royal governor was a model, on a small scale, of what the President was to be under the Constitution.

The major threat to the governor's power came from the colonial assembly. This body was elected by the people, although both the size of the electorate and eligibility were limited by property and other qualifications. The powers of the assembly were not always carefully defined, and there was more or less constant tension between the assembly on the one side and the governor and his council on the other.

In this respect the contest for power between the crown and Parliament was re-enacted on a smaller scale in the colonies. Most important of the powers which accrued to the assembly was its control over taxation and appropriations. With its control of the purse, the assembly could bargain with the governor and often bring him to heel, very much as Parliament bargained with the king of England. In Rhode Island and Connecticut the popularly elected assembly was the supreme power in the colony, since it was not only a legislative body but also elected the governor and his council for one-year terms. In practice, legislative and executive powers were thus merged, although not quite in the parliamentary manner.

Throughout the colonial period, the contest for power between the governor and the assembly continued. The external struggle of the colonies with the king and Parliament in London was matched by a struggle between the assembly and the royal governor in the colonies. There were also sporadic protests, especially from the workers and artisans of the towns and the small farmers of the back country, against the apportionment of representation in the assembly and the high qualifications for voting and for holding office. These contests were part and parcel of the wider struggle for responsible constitutional government in England and America.

☆ CONSTITUTION MAKING DURING THE REVOLUTION

The combination of forces that led to the Declaration of Independence also produced an irresistible demand for more democratic political institutions in the colonies themselves. The result was that during the Revolution every charter was not only transformed into a state constitution but, except in Rhode Island and Connecticut, was rewritten to provide a greater measure of democracy. Since those two so-called charter colonies were already fully self-governing, with the popularly elected assembly in the saddle, it was only necessary for them to omit the king's name from legal documents to become full-fledged independent states. In the other "free and independent states," the Revolution set in motion an unprecedented period of constitution making.

On May 10, 1776, about two months before the Declaration of Independence, the Continental Congress urged all the colonies to revise their charters or constitutions to meet the new situation. Although the Congress emphasized the desirability of a "full and free representation of the people" in the process of constitutional revision, only Massachusetts saw fit to call a specially elected constitutional convention for this purpose. In most states, however, special elections were held for the colonial legislatures, whose task it was to frame the new constitutions.[18] In most cases the prerevolutionary qualifications for eligibility and for the suffrage were retained, but in a good many these too were liberalized.

Since the revolutionary legislatures had other work to do, the job of drafting the constitution was normally left to a special committee. Once the committee's work had been approved by the legislature, the new constitution was put into effect without a special vote of the people, except in six states where the new draft was submitted for ratification by popular vote. Only in Massachusetts and New Hampshire was ratification by the voters made mandatory. In this and other respects, the framing and ratification of the Massachusetts constitution of 1780 marks the beginning of modern state constitution making. That is to say, the draft constitution was the work of a specially elected constitutional convention with ratification by popular vote required before the new plan was put into effect.

Except in North Carolina and Pennsylvania, there were no very serious conflicts in the framing and adoption of the new state constitutions, and, although there were some important differences among the

[18] In South Carolina, Virginia, and New Jersey not even this concession to any special procedure was made.

states, the new fundamental laws had much in common. All reflected the revolutionary principle of popular sovereignty, but all showed an equally widespread distrust of political power. Reflecting this distrust, the new constitutions put an end to any semblance of executive prerogative and confined the legislature to certain delegated powers. As a further safeguard for the natural rights of all citizens, the new constitutions contained more or less extensive bills of rights. So important were these guarantees regarded that in seven states they appeared as the first section of the new constitution. No substantial changes were made, however, in qualifications for voting or eligibility for public office. On the whole, the new constitutions were liberal and democratic as measured by the standards of the late eighteenth century, but in no case did they depart from the principles of a constitutional and representative republic, as distinguished from pure or direct democracy. Nor did they resemble in any way the so-called people's democracies of today.

Because these revolutionary constitutions did contain important features which the founding fathers thought admirable—and others for which they had an ill-concealed dislike—it may be well to take a closer look. In the first place, all were written constitutions. In this respect they established a practice of committing constitutional principles to writing which has become all but universal in the modern world. Not so widely copied, although enthusiastically adopted at Philadelphia, was their support of the principle of separation of powers. This principle was as much honored in the breach as in practice, but nowhere was it more widely extolled than in the revolutionary constitutions. Although the new constitutions provided for three branches of government—executive, legislative, and judicial—the allocation of powers among them was anything but equal.

The new state chief executive was but a pale shadow of the powerful, independent royal governor. The accumulated grievances of the colonial assemblies against the royal governors took their toll at the expense of the new state executives. In nine states the governor was to be elected by the legislature for a limited term. Only in New Hampshire, Vermont, Massachusetts, and New York was he to be elected by the people. In ten states his term was limited to one year.[19] Only in Massachusetts did he retain his veto power (although one may note that by 1800 four other states had returned this power to him), and this could be overcome by a two-thirds vote in both branches of the legislature. In New York the veto power was shared by the governor with his council. The governor's appointing power was severely limited and in many important cases was shared with the council (Senate) or the Assembly. His legislative powers, as well as his term of office, were curbed. The general theory of the executive embodied in the revolutionary constitutions was

19 In New York and Delaware the term was three years; in South Carolina, it was to be two years.

expressed in Maryland, where it was said that "a long continuance in the first executive department of power or trust, is dangerous to liberty." Except for the governors of New York and Massachusetts, the prevailing model of the chief executive provided for in these constitutions proved singularly unattractive to the founding fathers when they came to provide for a President of the United States.

The theory of the revolutionary constitutions was that the safest repository of political power was the popularly elected legislature. It was for this reason, presumably, that a majority of the states not only stripped the governor of his powers but provided for his election not by the people directly but by the legislature. This body, in all but three states, was bicameral.[20] The lower house, or House of Representatives, in most states was popularly elected for a one-year term. The apportionment of representation varied widely from state to state and was in no case a model of equity. In New England, the town was the usual representative district; in other states, the county. There was accordingly only a coincidental correspondence of population and representation. Eligibility for office was limited by property qualifications—as, for example, in New Jersey and Maryland £500; in Georgia £250; and in North Carolina 100 acres of land.

The upper chamber, called the Senate, was in most cases an enlarged and reformed governor's council. Except in Maryland, where a rather complicated electoral college was used, election to the Senate was by popular vote. The term of office, however, was longer—from two to five years—and the representative districts were larger in size and population. Eligibility for the Senate was also limited by somewhat higher property qualifications. In Massachusetts, only citizens owning £600 or more of property were eligible, and in South Carolina the requirement was £2,000. In some states the right to vote for members of the Senate was limited by higher property qualifications than those required in the case of representatives to the lower house. New York, for example, limited the right to vote for members of the Senate to those having a freehold of £100 or more. It has been estimated that only about 1,200 persons out of a total population of 30,000 could meet this test.[21] In general, suffrage requirements were but little changed from prerevolutionary days, although there was some broadening of the base.

Not only the governor but the courts also were made subordinate to the legislature. In the colonies, most of the judges, from the justices of the peace to the courts of appeal, were appointed, usually by the governor or by the governor and his council. Except in Pennsylvania, Delaware, and

---

[20] Pennsylvania used a unicameral legislature until 1789, and Georgia, which adopted the unicameral plan in 1777, gave it up in 1790. In Vermont the unicameral system survived from 1777 to 1836.

[21] See Oliver Douglas Weeks, *Two Legislative Houses or One* (Dallas, Texas: Southern Methodist University, 1938).

New Jersey—where they held office for seven years—judges served during good behavior. Under the revolutionary constitutions—except in Massachusetts, Maryland, Vermont, and New Hampshire—judges were elected by the state legislatures, and in six states they could be removed by the governor on an address from both branches of the legislature. The powers and jurisdiction of the courts were not radically changed. There was no recognition of judicial review of legislation in the new constitutions, and it was generally assumed that the legislature would be the judge of its own powers, subject to the limitations in the constitution itself. The Massachusetts constitution of 1780 provided for the calling of a convention in 1795 to "correct those violations [of the constitution] which by any means may [have been] made." Massachusetts also provided for advisory opinions from the supreme court on legislation, assuming, however, that the legislature would have the final say. In Pennsylvania, New York, and New Hampshire, councils of revision or of censors were provided "to inquire whether the Constitution has been preserved inviolate in every part." What they were to do about unconstitutional acts, however, was not clear.

This review of the main features of the revolutionary state constitutions shows again and again how deeply the basic principles of constitutionalism, as they had evolved through the centuries, had penetrated the theory and practice of American government. It shows also that the major features of the Constitution of the United States were not innovations but adaptations of institutions and procedures already familiar in the states. Many features of the revolutionary state constitutions were heartily approved. Bicameral legislatures, the strong chief executive on the New York or Massachusetts model, the principle of a government with only delegated powers, the germ of judicial review in the councils of revision or censors, and the universal endorsement, at least in theory, of the principle of separation of powers—all found favor in the eyes of the framers.

A major source of concern, however, was the extent to which the revolutionary constitutions violated this latter principle in practice. Instead of a nice balance of power among executive, legislative, and judicial branches, the state constitutions, with one or two exceptions, operated to make the legislature supreme. Governors and even courts of law were made subject to the will of the legislature. And because the legislative branch was directly elected by the people, it became the instrument through which the tyranny of popular majorities threatened the security and stability of the social order and the freedom and constitutional rights of minorities. "This," wrote Paul Leicester Ford, "was the almost universal defect of the state governments prior to the adoption of the Federal Constitution, and led Madison to assert that 'in our Government the real power lies in the majority of the community and the invasion of . . . rights is chiefly to be apprehended, not from the acts of government contrary to the sense of its constituents, but from the acts in which the Government is the mere instrument of the major number of constituents.'" In spite of elaborate bills of rights and in spite of the theory that only delegated powers could be exercised, conservative critics pointed to acts of the new state governments, both during and after the Revolution, that violated fundamental law and natural rights. They cited, for example, how the Virginia legislature suspended the sitting of courts, limited the suffrage, enacted legal tender and other ex post facto laws, and even "attainted a man of high treason and declared his life forfeit without process of law."[22] In Massachusetts, Rhode Island, New Hampshire, and other states, examples of "legislative usurpation" were cited to show the dangers of a "tyranny of the majority" flowing from the "excesses of democracy."

☆ "EXCESSES OF DEMOCRACY"—THE CRITICAL PERIOD

The legislative behavior most loudly complained of was, in part at least, both cause and effect of other factors at work in the colonies during and following the Revolution. During the struggle for independence some of the states played fast and loose with long-established rights and privileges. They confiscated loyalist estates, usually without compensation of any kind; they abolished quit rents owed to proprietors; they abolished the ancient rights of primogeniture and entail, and decreed the equal distribution of intestate property. They refused to recognize the "legitimate" debts and other property rights of loyalist merchants, both during and after the Revolution, notwithstanding Article V in the Treaty of Peace which recommended that the states "provide for the restitution, rights, and properties, which have been confiscated." Loyalists were expelled from all offices, banned from all professions, and forced to pay double or even treble taxes. Due process of law was denied to British subjects (that is, loyalists); and Georgia, according to one complaint, "declared that no suit shall be proceeded on, if brought by a British subject; while on the other hand, they allowed British subjects to be sued by their creditors."[23] They did away with established churches and provided that "no man should be obliged to pay any church rate, or attend any religious service, save according to his own free and unhampered will."[24]

[22] Paul L. Ford (ed.), *The Federalist* (New York: Holt, Rinehart and Winston, 1898), p. 55 n.

[23] Allan Nevins, *American States During and After the Revolution, 1775–1789* (New York: Macmillan, 1924), p. 649.

[24] John Fiske, *The Critical Period of American History, 1783–1789* (Boston: Houghton Mifflin, 1899), p. 28.

The property confiscated during the Revolution included lands worth some $3,500,000 in New York, $2,000,000 in Maryland, and over $2,000,000 in Pennsylvania. The De Lancy estate alone in New York was sold to 275 different persons; the Roger

All such acts, which under normal conditions would have disturbed men of status and property, might have been tolerated and even approved as a necessary, if evil, consequence of the war. Revolutions have a way of releasing pent-up aggressions and setting in motion unpleasant leveling tendencies. But popular outcries against speculation, profiteering, and other abuses during the Revolution often assumed a dangerously radical tone. "Throughout the war [the Revolution]," wrote Charles Beard, "a desperate struggle was waged in Virginia between planters and small farmers of the interior. . . . A kindred spirit flamed out in South Carolina where slave owners of the lowlands and merchants of the towns engaged in almost daily contests with mechanics from the shops and farmers from the back country. . . . Across the border in Georgia, the social battle between conservatives and radicals was carried to such a pitch that in a moment of bitter rivalry the patriot party could boast of two legislatures and two executives."[25]

Men of wealth and status, including not only avowed Tories but many leaders of the Revolution, looked upon these radical outbursts with fear and misgiving. Although they welcomed the fiery pen of Thomas Paine in the cause of independence, some of Paine's ideas were disturbing to men of conservative temper. They were not too unhappy when he said that the idea of hereditary government and "hereditary legislators is as inconsistent as hereditary judges or hereditary juries; and as absurd as an hereditary mathematician, or an hereditary . . . poet laureate." But they were worried by his argument that wealth was "no proof of good character, nor poverty of want of it." Although, said Paine, the distribution of property "will ever be unequal," it was an obligation of government to promote equality, to protect the weak against the strong, because, he said, "protection of a man's person is more sacred than the protection of property."[26]

During the course of the Revolution, there were signs of an uneasy sense of insecurity among the more economically affluent and politically conservative, whether Tory or Patriot. "Between the radicals and conservatives," says the historian Van Tyne, "the chasm was widening . . . [and] in one sense the American revolution was a social and economic rebellion of the lower classes against the domination of the colonial

---

Morris estate went to 250 persons. New Hampshire confiscated 28 estates, and Massachusetts confiscated all the property of everyone who had fought against the United States or had retired into places under British authority without permission of the United States. The loyalists who fled to Canada and to London (about 100,000) claimed damages from the British government (in lieu of compensation in America) of some £8,000,000. The British, by 1790, had reimbursed them in the amount of £3,400,000.

25 Charles A. Beard and Mary R. Beard, *The Rise of American Civilization* (New York: Macmillan, 1927), Vol. I, p. 266.

26 Carl Van Doren (ed.), [*Selections from*] *The Writings of Thomas Paine* (New York: Modern Library, 1922); esp. pp. 166–84.

aristocracy."[27] Even so redoubtable a Patriot as James Otis was alarmed at the radical notions widely expressed and the untoward conduct of the lower classes. "When the pot boils the scum will arise," he said. In Pennsylvania, the "cursed spirit of leveling" was condemned, and demands were made to curb the tradesmen "[who] take too much upon them. They ought not to intermeddle in state affairs. . . . They will become too powerful."[28]

The revolutionary state constitutions, by making the popularly elected legislatures virtually supreme, provided an official channel through which the "radicals" could operate. Had the radical sentiments and acts ceased when victory was won, this system of legislative supremacy might have been tolerable. But when the war was over and peace restored, the populistic acts of "tyrannical" legislative majorities continued.

The internal conflicts among Whigs and Tories, radicals and conservatives, between small farmers, artisans, and tradesmen against the large landowners, wealthy merchants, and professional classes were considerably tempered by a variety of circumstances during the Revolution. There was first of all the need for unity among Patriots of all classes in their struggle for independence. There were also substantial tangible rewards arising from revolutionary legislation and from wartime "prosperity." Royal restrictions on the acquisition and use of land and forests were wiped out. The general harassment of Tories helped to satisfy leveling egalitarian demands among the people. Moreover, wartime prosperity helped to dull the edges of social conflict. Although there were some disadvantages, such as the closing of British ports to American vessels, there were compensations, even for these, in the profits to be made from privateering and war-inflated trade and shipping. On the whole, business was good. Even the farmers "experienced a wave of prosperity as unexpected and unaccustomed as it was alluring. There was an unusually heavy demand for foodstuffs, and with a good market, prices steadily rose."[29] The market for other commodities—for uniforms and ordnance for the army; for land, food, clothing and shelter—was also steady and strong. The costs of the war were met, not primarily out of taxes, but from loans and Continental currency. In addition, there was a ready and abundant flow of British gold for supplies and services of all kinds. The resulting inflation was reflected in high prices, high wages, and high profits for merchants, artisans, and entrepreneurs. Some of the

[27] Claude Halstead Van Tyne, *The War of Independence; American Phase* (Boston: Houghton Mifflin, 1929) , pp. 22–37.

[28] See John Chester Miller, *Origins of the American Revolution* (Boston: Little, Brown, 1943) , pp. 491–505.

[29] John Franklin Jameson, *The American Revolution Considered as a Social Movement* (Princeton, N.J.: Princeton University Press, 1940) , p. 51.

more prudent paid off their debts in inflated currency and came out of the war stronger and more solvent than before. Others plunged into one speculation after another, and when the war was over not a few found themselves more deeply in debt than ever.

With the coming of peace and independence, there came also the inevitable economic slump. The British withdrew, and the flow of British gold dwindled. The army was disbanded, and the wartime demand for goods and services slacked off. In the absence of a commercial treaty, American access to fishing grounds and to trade with Britain and her other possessions was under a cloud. Foreign trade languished, and the balance of payments turned strongly against the new nation.

Prices sagged, and the burden of the indebted farmers correspondingly increased. In Massachusetts, where the conservatives were in control, "heavy taxes were levied to pay the revolutionary debt of the state, a large part of which had passed into the hands of speculators. And just when this burden fell on the people, private creditors . . . deluged the local courts with lawsuits and foreclosures of farm mortgages."[30] According to the historian J. B. McMaster, half the community in Vermont was bankrupt; and in New Hampshire, if the laws against debtors had been rigorously enforced in 1785, "it is probable that not far from two-thirds of the community would have been in the prisons."[31] Unemployment in the cities and bankruptcy or threat of bankruptcy in the country were widespread. Even Washington was moved to say: "Nothing could be a more melancholy and depressing sight than to behold those who have shed their blood . . . in the service of their country, without shelter, without a friend, and without the means of obtaining any of the necessaries, or comforts of life, compelled to beg their daily bread from door to door."[32]

There is, of course, another side to this story. One writer in New Jersey was of the opinion that in spite of distress in some areas no other 3 million people on the earth were as prosperous as the Americans. He invited comparison with any other people in Europe. Another satirical pamphlet on "Proof of the Scarcity of Money" said that money was so scarce that an unprecedented £2,000 had been paid to winning horses at ten turfs in Virginia. Great crowds, he said, in fine clothes, could be seen almost any day betting on the races, and there were five times as many four-wheeled carriages as ten years before. Governor Trumbull of Connecticut, in 1782, said that most of the talk about bad times was nonsense and that if people would only work hard, stop spending, and save their money, all would be well.

30 See Beard, *op. cit.*, p. 307.
31 John Bach McMaster, *A History of the People of the United States During Lincoln's Administration* (New York: Appleton-Century-Crofts, 1927), Vol. I, p. 302.
32 John Marshall, *The Life of George Washington* (New York: Walton, 1930), Vol. II, p. 87.

Whatever may be the true picture of conditions during this so-called "critical period," the demand for legislation to relieve debtors and others suffering from economic depression was widespread. The demands for relief included new issues of paper money to restore prices, wages, and profits, if not to wartime heights, at least to prewar levels.[33] To support the new currency and insure its acceptance, legal tender acts were proposed. There were demands for "stay laws" and other restrictions upon the courts to postpone foreclosures, for lower taxes, and for legislation against speculative land monopolies. The pressure for relief measures of this kind was often intense. At Exeter, New Hampshire, in 1786, a mob gathered outside the meetinghouse and threatened violence against the legislators unless something was done. There were tax strikes and mass picketing of courthouses to suspend foreclosure proceedings. In Massachusetts, twelve hundred angry citizens under Daniel Shays, a veteran of the Revolution, marched against the arsenal at Springfield in their effort to force the government in Boston to pass remedial measures. The unrest—which spread to Worcester, Berkshire, Bristol, and Middlesex counties—was put down only when Governor Bowdoin sent the militia against the Shaysites. This "Shays' Rebellion" became a kind of sign or symbol of the revolutionary forces at work in the states during these years. It became also a major factor in the demand for constitutional reform.

Under pressure and even threats of violence from the embattled forces of discontent, legislatures in state after state responded with "radical" legislation for the relief of those suffering from economic distress. "Unchecked by the balance usually supplied by manufacturing or commercial interests," wrote Paul Leicester Ford, "the land-holding [agrarian] classes [in control of the legislatures] ran riot. Paper money and tender laws robbed the creditor, regrating [quantity purchase for retail at a profit] and anti-monopoly acts ruined the trader. When the weak courts . . . sought to protect the minority, the legislatures suspended their sitting or turned the judges out of office."[34] Nor could the national government under the Articles of Confederation offer any substantial protection against these "excesses of democracy" in the states, or even against sharp trade practices of foreign shippers and importers.

American manufacturers, overwhelmed with a flood of British goods after the Revolution, found little protection from the predominantly

---

[33] Recent historical scholarship has given a somewhat different interpretation to the extent and severity of economic distress and social conflict during this period. See, for example, Merrill Jensen, *The Articles of Confederation: An Interpretation of the Social and Constitutional History of the American Revolution, 1774–1781* (Madison, Wis.: University of Wisconsin Press, 1940). Also see Merrill Jensen, *The New Nations: A History of the United States During the Confederation, 1781–1789* (New York: Knopf, 1950). For an excellent review of the more recent literature on this problem, see "The Founding Fathers: Young Men of the Revolution," by Stanley Elkins and Eric McKittrick, in *Political Science Quarterly* (June, 1961), pp. 181–216.

[34] P. L. Ford, *op. cit.*, Introduction, p. x.

agrarian state legislatures, or the Congress. Businessmen were harassed by state restrictions on the free flow of trade and commerce. There was no uniform currency, and the paper currency of the Continental Congress and the states was all but worthless. Under agrarian pressure, state legislatures had impaired the obligation of contracts by "stay laws" and other legislation hostile to creditors. The lack of adequate tax revenues made it impossible for either Congress or the states to pay their debts, and government securities steadily depreciated. Not even the rich western lands in the possession of the central government could be adequately developed or exploited without better facilities for transportation and communication than could be provided. Against the threat of rebellion from within, of Indian attacks on the frontier, and from enemies, real and potential, in the outer world, neither the states nor the Congress could offer substantial protection.

☆ THE ARTICLES OF CONFEDERATION

Conservative critics of the state constitutions and the Articles of Confederation painted a discouraging if not a desperate picture. How much the evils of the day were due to an "excess of democracy" and how much to postwar conditions of depression and deflation that would have occurred under any form of government, it would be difficult to say. The weaknesses of the central government might have been tolerable or at least remediable had the economic and social environment in which it functioned been more auspicious. In any case, we have heard so much about the weaknesses of the central government before the Constitution that we tend to forget its achievements. We forget that for seven years (1774–1781) the "United States" were governed by a wholly extralegal, nonconstitutional body known as the Continental Congress. We tend to forget that by the time this body was legalized and constitutionalized as the Congress of the Confederation it had adopted the Declaration of Independence, made defensive and offensive alliances with foreign powers, raised and organized a continental army, borrowed millions of dollars on its own credit, issued currency, granted letters of marque and reprisal, and built a navy. The need to formalize this revolutionary body was recognized from the outset, and in June, 1776, the Continental Congress appointed two committees: one to formulate a Declaration of Independence, the second to propose a "form of confederation." The second committee's report was approved in November, 1777, and submitted to the states for their unanimous ratification. This proved to be a painful process, because Maryland refused to approve the new constitution until the states claiming western lands agreed to cede their claims to the new Confederation. When in January, 1781, Virginia finally agreed to this condition, Maryland ratified, and the Articles of Confederation, after a final ratification by the Congress, went into effect.

For eight years (1781–1789) the Congress of the Confederation governed the country under a constitution that vested all powers in the legislature in an even more marked degree than had the revolutionary state constitutions. The Congress was authorized to appoint an executive Committee of States "to execute in the recess of Congress such of the powers of Congress, as the United States in Congress assembled, by the consent of nine states, shall . . . think expedient to vest them with." This Committee of States was authorized to "appoint one of their number to preside [as president] provided that no person be allowed to serve in the office of president more than one year in any term of three." The Congress was authorized to appoint such other committees and "civil officers as may be necessary for managing the general affairs of the United States." In addition to its legislative and executive powers, the Congress of the Confederation was also authorized to serve as "the last resort on appeal in all disputes and differences, now subsisting or that hereafter may arise between two or more States. . . ." To discharge this responsibility, an elaborate system of committees and subcommittees was outlined in the Articles. Neither the Congress, however, nor any other agency of the central government had any jurisdiction over disputes among private persons or between officers of the central government and private persons, except "controversies concerning the private right of soil claimed under different grants of two or more States." In such cases the procedure was to be the same, that is, by committees of Congress, as in the case of disputes between the states. Thus the Articles of Confederation united legislative, executive, and judicial powers in a single body—the Congress. In this respect, the Congress under the Confederation was not unlike the Assembly through which government was carried on in what we have called the Athenian model of democracy. It differed, of course, in its composition and in the limited scope of its powers.

In spite of its weaknesses, it was the Confederation Congress that enacted the Northwest Ordinance of 1787, which established the basic policy for the government of territories and the procedure by which these territories might become states—"on an equal footing with the original states, in all respects whatever." In this Northwest Ordinance, moreover, the Confederation Congress set forth a bill of rights that became a model for the Bill of Rights in the Constitution. Among the rights guaranteed in this epochal piece of legislation were those to religious liberty, to a writ of habeas corpus and trial by jury, and to protection against "cruel and unusual punishments." It was also provided that "no man shall be deprived of his liberty or property but by . . . the law of the land . . . [and with] . . . full compensation." Moreover, the wisdom and vision of the Confederation Congress is reflected in Article III of this Northwest

Ordinance, which provided that "religion, morality, and knowledge being necessary to good government and the happiness of mankind, schools and the means of education shall forever be encouraged." Nor should we forget that it was the Congress of the Confederation, belatedly and reluctantly, to be sure, which in February, 1787, issued a call for a convention to revise the Articles and which instead drafted a new Constitution.

"With all its imperfections," said Thomas Jefferson, "our present government [under the Articles of Confederation] is without comparison the best existing or that ever did exist." Even John Marshall, a severe critic of the Confederation, admitted that by providing us with our first national constitution and by keeping alive the idea of a "perpetual union" among the states during most turbulent times, "this service alone entitles that instrument to the respectful recollection of the American people." Finally, it is well to remember that it was under the Articles of Confederation that "the United States of America" was born.

The weaknesses of the Confederation are familiar. Except for the Committee of States, it lacked any effective central executive establishment with its own machinery for the enforcement of the laws of Congress. All government was, in effect, in commission, with all the weaknesses that go with rule by committees.[35] The weaknesses of committee government were compounded under the Articles by the fact that every state had an equal vote, and most important legislation, and most important administrative acts, required the consent of nine of the thirteen states. The Confederation had no courts of its own to enforce the laws and had to rely on state courts for this. And, of course, Congress had no power to regulate commerce, to enforce the validity of contracts, and—most important—no independent power to collect taxes.

The major weakness of the Confederation, however, was not its lack of powers, but rather its lack of power to enforce its powers. The paper powers of the Congress were extensive. They included (1) exclusive powers over foreign relations and over war and peace; (2) coinage, weight, and measures; (3) the establishment of post offices and the appointment of all officers of the Confederation's land and naval forces. Congress, moreover, had (4) power to issue bills of credit and to borrow on the credit of the United States. Although no national citizenship was defined or established, (5) citizens of each state were guaranteed the privileges and immunities of citizens in the several states, and a citizen of one state, when in another state, was to enjoy all the rights of citizens in that state. (6) The right to free ingress and egress into and from all the states was assured, and (7) full faith and credit was to be given in each

---

[35] One is reminded of Clemenceau's remark that "if the good Lord had relied on a committee to create the world, chaos would still reign." There is also the well-known definition of a camel—"a horse designed by a committee."

state to the records, acts, and judicial proceedings of courts and magistrates in every other state.

Never before had a central government in America been vested with such extensive powers. The fatal defect in the Articles of Confederation was that all the extensive powers of the Confederation were dependent for enforcement upon the states. Without an independent source of revenue, and with no executive machinery to enforce its laws directly upon individuals, the Congress of the Confederation was a pawn and creature of the states. It was almost superfluous under these circumstances for the Articles to say that "each State retains its sovereignty, freedom and independence, and every power, jurisdiction and right, which is not by this Confederation expressly delegated to the United States in Congress assembled."

In reciting the weaknesses of the Articles, we ought not to forget that they were designed for a *confederation* (a loose union of states) and not for a *federation* (a union in which legitimate powers are divided between a central government and the governments of constituent territorial units, both operating directly on the people). As the Preamble and Article I of the Articles make clear, it was a "confederacy," a "union between the states"—unlike the Constitution, which in the words of its Preamble was "ordained and established" by "we the People of the United States."

☆ CENTRIFUGAL VERSUS CENTRIPETAL FORCES

No instrument of government operates in a vacuum, but in response to dynamic economic and social forces at work within the community for which it is designed. Some of these forces may be described as centrifugal —tending toward disunity and diversity, decentralization rather than centralization. Others at work exert a centripetal force tending toward greater unity and conformity, centralization rather than decentralization. A brief summary of some of the centrifugal and centripetal forces at work in the years before the Constitutional Convention met in 1787 may help to explain the spirit and structure of American political institutions during this period.

On the whole, it was a period in which centrifugal forces were in the ascendancy. In the first place, there were intense sentimental tensions rooted in religious, political, economic, and cultural factors tending to produce interstate conflict and rivalry. One writer in 1760 declared that "such is the difference of character, of manners, of religion . . . that I think . . . were [the states] left to themselves, there would be civil war from one end of the continent to the other." James Otis, a militant exponent of American constitutional rights against the British government, deplored all talk of independence in 1765, because, he said, "were these colonies left to themselves . . . America would be a shambles of blood and confusion." During the Revolution interstate and sectional tensions complicated General Washington's problem in creating an effective fighting force. Soldiers from the South found it hard to go along with those from New England. Even Pennsylvanians found it difficult. The Yankees were described as "a set of dirty, griping, cowardly, lying rascals." One brigadier said that the "Pennsylvania and New England troops would as soon fight each other" as the British. In the first flush of revolutionary enthusiasm, following the Declaration of Independence, men were heard to say: "Virginia is no more, Massachusetts is no more. . . . We are now one nation of brethren. We must bury local interests and distinctions." But as James Wilson later observed, no sooner were the new state governments formed "than their jealousy and ambition began to display themselves. Each endeavored to cut a slice from the common loaf to add to his morsel till at length the Confederation became frittered down to the impotent condition in which it now stands."

There were boundary disputes that often reached the point of armed conflict. Communication and transportation were primitive at best. In 1783 the journey from Boston to New York by stagecoach consumed a full week. Mail, which moved at a faster pace, required as little as 6 days—although Paul Revere made the round trip from Boston to Philadelphia in 11 days. Roads were bad, often little better than trails, and in bad weather often impassable. Bridges were few and not always safe, and ferries were uncertain. There were innumerable interstate disputes over trade and commerce. An internal tariff system existed, with New York, Baltimore, Philadelphia, Providence, and Boston collecting customs on imports intended for sale throughout the country. Entrance and clearance fees were common on ships and other vessels moving between the states. There was no uniform coinage or currency until 1785, and none really effective prior to 1790. English, French, Spanish, and German coins were in circulation with no assurance that an English pound would be worth the same weight in silver or gold from one state to another. There were complaints and recriminations about the differential distribution of war burdens, and many of the states received in payments from the Congress more than they contributed to its support. In some states a fearful burden of debt was piled up during the war, which caused bitter complaints at the heavy taxes needed to service it. Until the Revolution, there was, of course, no stable unified military force, and even the revolutionary army was a kind of loose confederation of state-recruited troops.

Against these centrifugal forces there were centripetal forces also at work. Throughout the period the fear of Indian attacks on frontier settlements was a force for unity among the colonies. Even more important was the influence of a common language, and, except in the Spanish settlements of Florida and Louisiana, a common legal and political tradition. Trial by jury, habeas corpus, the common law, were all but universally recognized. Aided and abetted by committees of correspondence, a more or less common public opinion developed on the major policies at issue between the colonies and the mother country.[36] Lexington and Concord, the Continental Congress, the Declaration of Independence, and the establishment of a Continental army under Washington helped to unite the people in a common cause. The western lands, which had been a source of bitter conflict, became a force for union when these were ceded to the central government. For this not only gave to Congress plenary power over an extensive territory, but gave to it a modest source of revenue from land sales. Finally, there was the burgeoning economy, which, long before the Constitutional Convention, was reaching dimensions incompatible with any political system less extensive than the nation.

If one may say that time and circumstances, plus geography and economic interests, made the Continental Congress and the Articles of Confederation inevitable, so one may say that changing times and new circumstances, an expanding territory and new and growing economic interests made the Constitutional Convention at Philadelphia in 1787 inevitable. That convention, however, did more than create the charter for a new government better adapted to the needs of the nation in the late eighteenth century. It translated into new terms and into a new structure of power constitutional principles reaching back to the Athens of Pericles, and embodied in one form or another in Magna Charta, the colonial charters, the revolutionary state constitutions, and the Articles of Confederation.

[36] Not the least of these grievances was the Quebec Act of 1774, which extended the boundaries of Canada to the Ohio River and thus threatened the land claims in this area of Virginia, Connecticut, and Massachusetts. And adding insult to injury, it provided for a highly centralized system of government for this vast area, with rights of taxation reserved for the British Parliament, civil trials without jury, and special privileges for the Catholic Church.

FRAMING
AND RATIFICATION OF
THE AMERICAN CONSTITUTION

The basic purpose of the Constitution was to establish a nation with a government not only adequate to the exigencies of the time but capable of growing and adapting itself to changing circumstances. The goal, in short, was to provide for that nice balance of order and liberty, power and restraint, permanence and change that is essential if a free political society is to survive and grow.

A constitution in its broadest sense is a way of life. Ours may not, in and of itself, be synonymous with our way of life; but it provides the framework within which that way of life is lived. Every nation has its own way of life, but not every one has a constitutional way of life. For a constitutional way of life implies a number of things not necessarily found in every political state. As we have seen, it implies first of all a belief in a higher law or of human rights that lie beyond the reach of legitimate political power. Thus a constitution not only limits political power; it guides the power of the State toward certain ends. If it is to achieve these ends, it must endow the State not merely with powers but with *power* adequate to the needs of the community it serves. The Articles of Confederation failed not because it failed to give great *powers* to the Congress. The Confederation failed because it failed to give Congress *power* to put its powers to work. It had, as it were, no bite.

☆ **THE FRAMING OF THE CONSTITUTION**

Before the Convention met at Philadelphia, there had been a number of efforts to strengthen the Articles of Confederation. Specific suggestions had been made (1) to give Congress power to tax, (2) to grant it power to regulate commerce, and (3) to use coercion against delinquent states.

There were also some ambitious proposals. In 1782, under Hamilton's influence, New York had proposed the calling of a convention to amend or revise the Articles, but nothing came of it. On February 16, 1783, there appeared a prophetic pamphlet by Pelatiah Webster titled "A Dissertation on the Political Union and Constitution of the thirteen United States of America." As outlined in Hannis Taylor's *Origin and Growth of the American Constitution,* Webster's plan called for:

1. A Federal Government with independent power to tax.
2. Separation of powers among executive, legislative, and judicial branches.
3. A legislature of two houses.
4. A central government of delegated powers operating directly on the citizens, with powers reserved to the states.

The air was full of ideas and proposals for radical revision of the Articles. "According to the system of policy, the states shall adopt at this moment," said Washington, in a letter to the governors of the several states in June, 1783, "they will stand or fall [and will decide] whether the revolution is to be considered a blessing or a curse." And Noah Webster sounded an equally ominous note in 1785. "So long," he said, "as any individual state has power to defeat the measures of the other twelve, our pretended union is but a cobweb." In the same year the General Court of Massachusetts passed a resolution calling for a general convention. But the Massachusetts representative in Congress did not urge it upon that body. A year later a Committee of the Congress did propose seven amendments, but they, too, died aborning.

☆ THE ANNAPOLIS CONVENTION

In the meantime discussions were going forward between Virginia and Maryland covering navigation on the Potomac. As early as 1773, in fact, three commissioners had met to discuss this problem, but to no avail. Finally, in 1785 commissioners representing the two states met at Mount Vernon. Since the issues, including rival claims to western lands, involved Pennsylvania and Delaware as well as Virginia and Maryland, it was decided to call another meeting of the four states. When this was proposed in the Virginia legislature, it seemed best to extend the invitation to all of the states "to consider how far a uniform system in their commercial relations may be necessary to their common interest and permanent harmony." A resolution to this effect was adopted in January, 1786, and a call for such a general meeting was issued to assemble in September at Annapolis. However, delegates from only five states showed up. Nine states had voted to participate, but the delegates from New Hampshire, Rhode Island, Massachusetts, and North Carolina failed to reach Annapolis in time.

The Annapolis Convention, like earlier meetings of the kind, seemed destined to be merely another futile gesture. Although the slender attendance precluded any significant action, the delegates decided to raise the issue of a general convention with a broader mandate, so a committee was appointed to draft another appeal to the states. The report of this committee, written by Alexander Hamilton, proposed a convention of delegates from all states to meet at Philadelphia on the second Monday in May, 1787, "to take into consideration the situation of the United States, to devise such further provisions as shall appear to them necessary to render the Constitution of the Federal Government adequate to the exigencies of the Union . . . [which] when agreed to by [Congress] and afterwards confirmed by the legislatures of every state, will effectively provide for the same."

☆ THE CONSTITUTIONAL CONVENTION

This report went to Congress and, on February 21, 1786, that body, with no mention of the Annapolis report, issued the call for a convention "for the sole and express purpose of revising the articles of confederation . . . and to report such alterations as should render the federal constitution adequate to the exigencies of government and the preservation of the Union." It was in response to this call that every state except Rhode Island appointed delegates to the Philadelphia Convention.

It was hot in Philadelphia during the summer of 1787, but on May 14, the day set for the opening of the Convention, bad weather had delayed the arrival of many delegates and the opening was deferred until May 25.

Although it was over ten days after the official opening date that enough delegations arrived to make a quorum, on May 25 seven states (Virginia, Pennsylvania, New York, North Carolina, Delaware, New Jersey, and South Carolina) were on hand and business began at the State House. Later these were joined by delegations from Massachusetts, New Hampshire, Connecticut, Maryland, and Georgia; all states were represented except Rhode Island, which boycotted the Convention from beginning to end.

On nomination by Robert Morris, Washington was unanimously elected to preside. Major William Jackson (not a delegate) became Secretary on Hamilton's nomination. Washington then appointed a committee composed of Hamilton, George Wythe of Virginia, and

Charles Pinckney of South Carolina to draw up rules of procedure. These provided that everything was to be done in executive session and mostly in Committee of the Whole. There were no reporters, and only the sketchiest official record. Major Jackson's notes were meager, and it was not until 1840 (four years after his death) that Madison's notes were published and the inside story of what transpired could be told.

As much as possible, decisions were to be taken by consensus. Voting on issues was to be avoided until all minor or preliminary points were disposed of. Under these circumstances, a man could change his mind and not lose face, and rigid factions on minor issues were minimized. Hence, discussion was frank and free. The delegates spoke to one another, not to the galleries, the Philadelphia crowds, or their constituents at home.

Altogether, 74 delegates were elected, and 55 actually participated. They included men of great learning, experience, and wisdom. But they were also men of affairs, identified not only with the new nation but with particular states. And within these states they were identified with certain social, political, and economic interests arising from their own heritage and their own occupational or professional pursuits. To think of them otherwise is to create an image of a Constitutional Convention composed not of great men but of masks in a pageant. For many years this *was* the popular image of the founding fathers. Washington and Franklin, George Mason and James Wilson, Madison and Randolph appeared not as great statesmen but as heroic, classic figures moving in a long lost Golden Age.

It was inevitable, history and politics being what they are, that this imagery would in time produce a reaction. And beginning with J. Allen Smith's *Spirit of American Government* in 1907, a quite different picture of the founding fathers began to emerge. In a wave of what passed for realism, scholars began to examine the men behind the masks. Before long a new image was born—an image of the framers as self-interested members of the "propertied classes" erecting safeguards for their own interests. "It was," wrote Smith, "the property owning class that framed and secured the adoption of the Constitution." Even more extreme was A. M. Simon in a book he called *Social Forces in American History* (1912). "The organic law of this nation," he wrote, "was formulated in secret session by a body called into existence through a . . . trick, and was forced upon a disfranchised people by means of dishonest apportionment in order that the interests of a small body of wealthy rulers might be served."

The facts are, of course, that neither theory is wholly accurate. The delegates were not demigods. Neither were they eighteenth-century hucksters intent only on protecting their own interests. What kind of men were they? In terms of age, they were young, although ages varied from Franklin, who was 81, to Jonathan Dayton of New Jersey, who was only

26.[1] Hamilton was 30, Pinckney, only 29, and the average, skewed somewhat by Franklin's advanced age, was around 50. Over half were lawyers, 9 were planters, 11 were in shipping or manufacturing, 6 qualified as financiers, 4 as physicians, and an indeterminate few as college professors or presidents. Four held public office at the time. As men of property, they included 15 slaveholders and 40 who owned government securities in varying amounts. Twenty-four were said to be the chief creditors of their local communities.

In terms of education, all but a small minority were college-trained or had an equivalent education; 26 of the 55 delegates had attended one of 6 colleges—Harvard, Yale, Princeton, William and Mary, Kings (Columbia), and Pennsylvania. Eleven had attended British universities, 7 had studied with private tutors, and the schooling of an equal number had stopped with grammar school. Most were church members, including 15 Episcopalians, 10 Presbyterians, 9 Congregationalists, 3 Quakers, 2 Catholics, 1 Methodist, and 1 Huguenot. Although, so far as anyone knows, there were no atheists, 14 acknowledged no formal religious affiliation.

Virtually all of the delegates were men of experience in public affairs: 26 of them had served in their state legislatures, 14 had been judges, 7 had been governors, and 13 had participated in earlier constitutional assemblies. Most significant was the fact that nearly 80 percent (41) had served in Congress, and 20 were veterans of the Revolution, thus identifying themselves formally and actively with the new nation. This identification may help to explain why a large majority were committed to the establishment of a stronger central government.

In this gallery of great men there were some notable gaps. Jefferson was in France and hence not a delegate. Neither was Patrick Henry of Virginia nor John Hancock of Massachusetts. It would be easy to use the absence of these leaders to confirm the theory that the Convention was a kind of conspiracy against the principles of the Declaration of Independence. Henry, it is said, declined to be a delegate, saying "I smell a rat." But, as we shall see, both Jefferson and Hancock finally joined in supporting the Constitution during the fight for ratification.

The best evidence indicates that the delegates were on the whole a moderately conservative group, and the Constitution reflects this moderation. However, by the standards prevailing in England and on the Continent, the founding fathers were liberals or even radicals of rather advanced political ideas. At the same time they were men of substance and experience—an elite of education, knowledge, and social status.

---

[1] Dayton, it is reported, attended as a substitute for his father. The son, so ran the rumor, was something of a gay blade, who was sent to Philadelphia to keep him from bad company at home.

They were well-fed, well-clothed, affluent men who loved the good things of life, and they found a good deal in Philadelphia society to satisfy their love of life.

The framers were aware of the importance of what they had been called to do. "After the lapse of 6,000 years since the creation of the world," said James Wilson, "America now presents the first instance of a people assembled to weigh deliberately and calmly and to decide leisurely and peaceably upon the form of government by which they will bind themselves and their posterity." Washington, too, emphasized the gravity of what they were to do. "It is probable," he said, "that no plan we propose will be adopted. Perhaps another dreadful conflict is to be sustained. If to please the people we offer what we ourselves disapprove, how can we afterward defend our work? Let us raise a standard to which the wise and the honest can repair. The event is in the hand of God."

As men of wide knowledge and experience, the framers could draw upon over 150 years of American political history in the development of constitutional government. They knew at first hand the constitutions of the several states and how they worked. They were familiar with the unicameral legislature of Pennsylvania, the Councils of Censors in Pennsylvania and Vermont, and the Council of Revision in New York. They knew the arguments for and against the weak governors in most of the states and the relatively strong governors of New York and Massachusetts. They had firsthand experience with bicameral legislatures and with the electoral college system used to choose the upper house in Maryland. They knew all about an independent judiciary's effort to sustain the fundamental law against unconstitutional legislation. And they had detailed knowledge of the Confederation and its weaknesses. In addition they were widely read in the classical works of political philosophy as well as in more recent materials, including the seventeenth-century English liberals such as Harrington and Locke and the eighteenth-century Enlightenment thinkers.

Rarely in history have so many well-qualified men assembled to frame a government out of the accumulated wisdom and experience of mankind. It is a tribute to this wisdom that nearly every feature of the new Constitution had already been tested in the laboratory of actual government. The new instrument was distinguished not so much by the novelty of its separate parts as by the ingenious combination of tried and proved principles and practices.

The Virginia Plan

Drawing upon this accumulated knowledge and experience, Governor Edmund Randolph of Virginia on May 29 presented 15 resolutions to the Convention. Developed no doubt largely by James Madison, these resolutions as debated and amended became the Constitution of the United States.

The basic framework proposed in this Virginia Plan called for radical amendment of the Articles of Confederation. Instead of a unicameral Congress as provided for in the Articles, the new plan called for a bicameral legislature with one house to be elected by the people and apportioned according to population, and a second to be chosen by the first "out of a proper number of persons nominated by the individual legislatures." The right to vote in the national legislature was to be in proportion "to the quotas of contribution or to the number of free inhabitants, as the one or the other rule may seem best in different cases." An executive, chosen by the legislature, was to have "general authority to execute the national laws" and to "enjoy the executive rights vested in Congress by the Confederation." The plan called for a national judiciary "of one or more supreme tribunals, and of inferior tribunals to be chosen by the national legislature, to hold their offices during good behavior." And, finally, there was to be a Council of Revision, to include the executive and a "convenient number of the judiciary . . . with authority to examine every act of the national legislature before it shall operate, and every act of a particular legislature before a negative thereon shall be final." But the national legislature could by a suitable majority override the Council of Revision.

The central government, under this plan, was to have power "to legislate in all cases to which the separate states are incompetent . . . [and] to negative all laws passed by the several states contravening, in the opinion of the national legislature, the Articles of Union, and to call forth the force of the Union against any member of the Union failing to fulfill its duty under the Articles thereof." The central government was also to guarantee to each state a "republican government," and provision was to be made for admission of new states "lawfully arising within the limits of the United States." Amendments to the new Articles of Union were not to require "the assent of the national legislature." Officials of the central government were to receive compensation for their services and to be paid by the nation, not by the states as under the Articles of Confederation.

In summary, the Virginia Plan laid the basis for a central government of extensive powers, operating directly on individuals and with a veto power over state laws. Although the national executive was to be chosen by the legislature, it was assumed that there would be a more or less strict separation of powers between the executive, legislative, and judicial branches.

The Virginia Plan became the basis for the most extended debate in the Convention, with Hamilton, Madison, Mason, and Wilson leading the argument for the Plan, and Robert Yates and John Lansing of New York and Luther Martin of Maryland in opposition.

The New Jersey Plan

Two weeks after Randolph had proposed his Virginia Plan—a plan identified with the interests of the larger states—a second plan was offered by William Paterson of New Jersey. This plan, probably the work of Paterson, Roger Sherman of Connecticut, and Luther Martin of Maryland, came to be known as the Small State Plan. In nine resolutions, it proposed to revise the Articles of Confederation "so as to render the federal Constitution adequate to the exigencies of government and the preservation of the Union." Specifically, it would increase the powers of Congress to include, in addition to other powers granted under the Articles of Confederation, power to tax and power to regulate trade and commerce. Congress, to remain as under the Confederation, was to choose an executive with general executive power including executive appointments and power as commander in chief. The federal executive was also to have power to use force to compel obedience to federal acts and treaties. There was to be a Supreme Court appointed by the executive to hold office during good behavior. And, most significantly, it was provided that "all acts of the United States shall be the supreme law of the respective states . . . and that the judiciary of the several states shall be bound thereby . . . anything in the respective law of the individual states to the contrary notwithstanding." There were also provisions for the admission of new states and for a uniform national rule of naturalization.

☆ THE "BUNDLE OF COMPROMISES"

Limited space forbids a detailed review of the debate on these proposals. On certain fundamentals there was general agreement. Most important was the agreement on the need for a strong central government based on the federal principle but acting directly on individuals. "Under the existing Confederacy," said George Mason, "Congress represents the states, not the people of the states: their acts operate on the states, not on individuals. The case will be changed in the new government."[2] On May 30, following the introduction of the Virginia Plan, the Convention approved a resolution "that a [central] government ought to be established consisting of a supreme legislature, executive, and judiciary."

More specifically, it was agreed that the central government should have power (1) over foreign policy, (2) to lay and collect taxes, (3) to

---

[2] Hamilton, as is well known, would have gone very far toward a unitary state. "The general power," he said, "must swallow up the state powers. Otherwise it will be swallowed up by them. Two sovereignties cannot coexist within the same limits." He went on to say that in his opinion "the British Government was the best in the world" and he doubted that "anything short of it would do in America."

regulate commerce, (4) to pay debts of the Confederation, (5) to provide for a uniform currency, (6) to protect contracts, and (7) to exercise all powers necessary and proper to carry these into effect.

The major points of disagreement concerned (1) the basis of representation in Congress, including the question of whether slaves should be counted in estimating population, (2) the power of Congress over the slave trade, and (3) the President's powers and the method of electing him. Other minor issues involved the qualifications and terms of office for legislators, qualifications for the suffrage, the power to initiate money bills, the purpose and method for apportionment of taxes, especially of direct taxes, and judicial review.

An important difference between the Virginia and New Jersey Plans was the basis of representation in Congress. The Virginia Plan would have based representation in both houses on population, thus giving to the large states a paramount voice in legislation. The New Jersey Plan proposed to give each state equal representation in Congress, thus continuing a central feature of the existing Articles of Confederation. This obviously would give the smaller states a better break in the legislature. Under this Plan Georgia's 25,000 people would have had equal representation with Virginia's 400,000 or Pennsylvania's 350,000. On the other hand, if representation were apportioned according to population, five large states (Virginia, Massachusetts, New York, Pennsylvania, and Maryland) with over half the total population, could, if they acted together, control the legislature.

The debate over this issue waxed long and bitter. It was said that some of the small states would "sooner submit to a foreign power than . . . to be deprived of an equality of suffrage" in Congress.[3] At times it seemed that no settlement of the issue was possible and that the Convention would be destroyed on the rock of representation. In the end a compromise was reached; representation in the lower house was to be apportioned according to population, whereas in the upper house each state was to have an equal vote. As a further concession to the small states, the provision for equal suffrage in the Senate was made unchangeable even by Constitutional amendment. As a compensation to the large states, money bills were to originate in the lower house, where their larger population would presumably give them control.

A sectional cleavage also emerged in this debate over representation. Should slaves be counted in the apportionment, or only free persons? To southern slaveholders, it seemed obvious and just that all persons, includ-

---

[3] "Shall I submit the welfare of New Jersey with five votes," said Paterson, "in a council where Virginia has sixteen? I shall never consent to the proposed plan. Neither my state nor myself will ever submit to tyranny." Governor Bedford of New Jersey was even more blunt. "Gentlemen," he said, addressing himself to the delegates from New York and Pennsylvania, "I do not trust you. If you possess the power the abuse of it could not be checked . . . sooner than be ruined, there are foreign powers that will take us by the hand."

ing slaves, should be counted. To northerners it was equally obvious that since slaves had no voice in public affairs, they ought not to be counted for purposes of representation. To do so would be to base representation not only on population but on property (that is, slaves) as well. If the property of slaveholders was to be counted, why not other forms of property? Again, a compromise was reached by which only three-fifths of the slaves were to be counted. To further reassure the southerners, it was agreed that although Congress was to have plenary power to regulate foreign commerce, no legislation to prohibit the importation of slaves would be enacted prior to 1808.

Since representation in the lower house was to be based on population, and since money bills were to originate in the lower house, there was some fear that taxes might impose an inequitable burden on the small states. To guard against this the Convention provided that direct taxes, like representation in the lower house, be apportioned among the states according to population.

Both the Virginia Plan and the New Jersey Plan called for the election of the President by the Congress, and this proposal had twice been approved by the Convention. There was something of a paradox in this, since both Plans and the most influential delegates were resolved to create a strong executive in the new government. Experience with state executives chosen by state legislatures was not reassuring to those who wanted a vigorous and independent executive establishment. Not only would an executive dependent on the legislature for his election be a violation of the principle of the separation of powers, but it would produce a weakling where a strong hand was needed. There was some talk of having the President elected directly by the people, but no one seriously believed this to be possible or desirable. In the end, another compromise was arrived at in the complicated plan for an electoral college. This was considered an almost ideal solution, since it combined equal suffrage for the states with representation according to population.

Debate on qualifications for the suffrage was ardent and revealed strikingly different attitudes concerning popular participation in the government. Elbridge Gerry of Massachusetts took a dim view of universal suffrage. In Massachusetts, he said, "the worst men get into the legislature. . . . Men of indigence, ignorance, and baseness spare no pains, however dirty to carry their point. . . ." The suffrage, he argued, ought to be so regulated as to secure more effectively "a just preference of merit." Gouverneur Morris of Pennsylvania was even more emphatic. "Give the votes to the people who have no property," he said, "and they will sell them to the rich who will be able to buy them."

Colonel Mason, James Wilson, and Franklin, on the other hand, expressed more confidence in the people. "Every man," said Mason, "having evidence of attachment to and permanent common interest with the society, ought to share in all its rights and privileges." The legislature, argued Wilson, ought to be an exact transcript of the whole society —and to protect property is by no means the sole end of government. "The cultivation and improvement of the human mind [was] the most noble object." The aged Franklin expressed strong dislike of everything calculated "to debase the spirit of the common people. . . . If honesty is often the companion of wealth and if poverty is exposed to peculiar temptations, it is not less true that . . . some of the greatest rogues are the richest rogues. . . . The Constitution will be much read and attended to in Europe, and if it should betray a great partiality to the rich, it will not only hurt us in the esteem of the most liberal and enlightened men . . . but discourage the common people from [coming] to this country."

To avoid a multitude of doctrinal conflicts as well as to avoid state resentment at interference with their control over suffrage qualifications, this matter was resolved by leaving well enough alone. "Electors in each state," reads Section 2 of Article I, "shall have the qualifications requisite for Electors of the most numerous branch of the state legislature." That is to say, the right to vote in national elections will be determined by the states. This was a compromise that we must still live with, but which, except for the Negro, has not seriously compromised the principle of universal suffrage.

These issues, both major and minor, having been resolved, the Constitution—that "bundle of compromises," as it was called—was ready for a preliminary draft. On July 26, after two solid months of discussion, the Convention adjourned until August 6 to enable the committee on detail to prepare such a draft for further consideration. The Convention resumed again on August 7, and debate continued until September 10, when Gouverneur Morris was assigned the task of preparing a final draft. Two days later he reported back to the Convention, and for three days the finished document was read, clause by clause. Even at that stage some minor changes were made.

On September 17, the 42 delegates remaining in Philadelphia assembled in final session to sign the letter transmitting the new Constitution to Congress for submission to the states. Three of the 42 present refused to sign—Gerry of Massachusetts, and Randolph and Mason of Virginia—so only 39 of the original 55 actually signed.

No one was wholly satisfied, and even those who signed had reservations about certain features of the new Constitution. The prevailing sentiment was, perhaps, best expressed by the venerable Dr. Franklin. "I confess," he said, "that there are several parts of this Constitution which I do not at present approve, but I am not sure I shall never approve them. For . . . I have experienced many instances of being obliged by better information . . . to change opinions even on important subjects which I once thought right but found to be otherwise. . . . I agreed to this Constitution with all its faults . . . because I think a general government necessary for us, and there is no form of government but what may be a blessing to the people if well administered. . . . I doubt, too, that any other Convention we can obtain may be able to make a better Constitution. . . ."

Others expressed similar sentiments, signing not because they believed the document to be perfect but rather because they believed, with all its faults, that it was better than the Articles of Confederation. Besides, they pointed out, the faults could be cured by amendment and experience.

As the last signatures were being added, Dr. Franklin pointed to a rising sun painted on the back of the President's chair. Observing that artists had found it difficult to distinguish a rising from a setting sun, he went on to say: "I have often in the course of the session, and the vicissitudes of my hopes and fears as to its issue, looked at that [sun] behind the President without being able to tell whether it was rising or setting. But now at length I have the happiness to know that it is a rising and not a setting sun."

☆ RATIFICATION

Having surmounted the often bitter conflicts of the Convention, there still remained the hurdles of the state-ratifying process before the new Constitution could take effect.

Although the twelve states represented unanimously agreed to recommend the Constitution to the states, not all of the individual delegates did so. Governor Randolph, whose Virginia Plan was the basis for the new Constitution, refused in the end to sign. Hoping to prevent the Constitution from going to the states for ratification, he proposed that a second general convention be called—a motion unanimously rejected by the Convention. George Mason, also of Virginia, withheld his signature because he professed to see in the new government an incipient "monarchy or a tyrannical aristocracy." Elbridge Gerry of Massachusetts refused to sign, his reasons being (1) the six-year term for Senators, (2) the absence of any protection against monopolies, (3) the counting of three-fifths of the slaves in apportioning representation, and (4) the absence of any bill of rights in the Constitution.

Governor Charles Pinckney of South Carolina pointed out that he, too, had reservations, but that the only way to avoid an "ultimate decision by the sword" was to give the new plan his support. These non-signers and the numerous reservations of those who did sign seemed to indicate that the ratifying process might be a long and tough one.

The process of ratification and the terms on which the new Constitution was to take effect were set forth in Article VII of the draft instrument. It reads: "The ratification of the *Conventions* of nine states, shall be sufficient for the establishment of this Constitution between the states so ratifying the same."

Two things are of particular significance in this: (1) Ratification was to be by conventions specially chosen for this purpose and not by the state legislatures. (2) The Constitution was to take effect upon its approval by nine out of thirteen states.

It was thus proposed to go over the heads of existing legislatures to assemblies called into being by the legislatures but independent of them. While amendments to the Articles of Confederation had required the consent of all thirteen states, the Constitution was to take effect when ratified by only nine.

Did the Constitutional Convention in this way also go over the head of the Congress? Formally, at least, the Congress had not only called on the states to appoint delegates to the Convention, but now, without expressing any opinion of its own, it unanimously voted to transmit the new Constitution to the state legislature for submission to specially elected conventions. By this slender thread the forms of legality were observed. But, in fact, was not the whole proceeding unconstitutional—at least under the only Constitution then in force, the Articles of Confederation? Professor Burgess, in his *Political Science and Comparative Constitutional Law,* has argued that what the Convention "actually did . . . was to assume constituent powers, ordain a constitution . . . and demand a *plebiscite* thereon over the heads of all existing legally organized powers. Had Julius (Caesar) or Napoleon committed these acts, they would have been pronounced *coups d'états.*"

Constitutional lawyers might point out that in issuing the call to the Philadelphia Convention, Congress declared it was "for the sole and express purpose of revising the Articles of Confederation . . .," revisions which presumably could become effective only when ratified by all the states.

Going beyond these instructions, the Convention had scrapped the Articles and substituted a new Constitution. Did the formal action of the enfeebled Congress provide a firm constitutional basis for the new Constitution, or was it merely a thin transparent gloss for what was in fact a Second American Revolution?

In Article XL of the *Federalist,* Madison discusses this whole problem of "The Right of the Convention to Frame Such A Constitution." If the proceeding is unconstitutional, he says, what then about (a) the 12 states that sent delegates, (b) the Congress that recommended its appointment, and (c) the State of New York that made the first suggestion for a convention. Suppose the argument against legality is admitted? "Does it follow that the Constitution should be rejected? If it . . . be lawful to accept good advice even from an enemy, shall we [refuse] . . . such advice even when it is offered by our friends?"

By now this issue is, as they say, "purely academic." Even during the contests for ratification the question of the legality of the Constitution was a minor issue. The major issues were more substantial, and involved both the structure and the scope of power to be established under the Constitution.

During the campaigns for the election of delegates to the ratifying conventions, voters and delegates were aligned as friends or foes of the proposed Constitution, that is, as Federalists or Anti-Federalists. Although the economic, social, and political interests that lay behind this bipolar alignment varied considerably from state to state, a more or less consistent pattern did emerge. The Federalists represented the clergy and the commercial, manufacturing, financial, and creditor interests; the Anti-Federalists spoke for the back country farmers and, to a lesser extent, the urban workers. But even these generalizations admit of so many exceptions as to make them dubious at best.

From the bitter controversies in the Convention between delegates from the small states and the large states, one might have expected this alignment to continue into the ratification campaign, with the small states in the Anti-Federalist camp and the large states strongly Federalist. In fact, no such alignment appeared. Among the first to ratify were small states—Delaware, New Jersey, Connecticut, and Maryland, whose representative in the Convention had most bitterly attacked the *national* plan when it was first proposed by Governor Randolph. Among the early ratifiers, also, were the large states, Massachusetts and Pennsylvania; although among the last to ratify were other large states, Virginia and New York. North Carolina, a medium-large state, and Rhode Island, a small state, failed to ratify until after the new government was established. In North Carolina, the Convention adjourned without taking action, and in Rhode Island, where the Constitution was submitted to a direct vote of the people, it was rejected by a 10–1 margin in an election which was systematically boycotted by Federalist voters.[4]

The decision of the framers to ask ratification by specially elected conventions proved wise in the end. In this way they avoided a head-on fight with the entrenched incumbents in the legislature; and instead of having to fight their way through two legislative chambers, they had only one to deal with. The campaign for delegates, moreover, provided an excellent forum in which to carry on a program of propaganda in support of the Constitution.

The contest between friends and foes of the new Constitution was an uneven one in most states. Since most of the leaders of public opinion were Federalists—the clergy, the lawyers, newspaper publishers, the financial and business leaders, and the great planters in the South—they

---

[4] North Carolina ratified in 1789 at a second convention by a vote of 194–77 after Congress had submitted a Bill of Rights of 12 amendments. Rhode Island ratified May 29, 1790, at a state convention called for this purpose. The result was very close: 34 to 32 votes.

had a great advantage over the Anti-Federalists. They had more money, were better organized, and they knew what they wanted. The Anti-Federalists by comparison suffered from a poverty of leadership and intellect, of money, organization, and purpose. They were essentially an *anti* party, having no constructive alternative to propose beyond a continuation of the Articles. Besides, the Federalists had Washington on their side. Even then he had become the father of his country—a soldier-statesman of heroic proportions, of legendary virtue and prowess. In Virginia, where the contest was a close one, not even Anti-Federalist names like Henry, Randolph, and Mason were a match for Washington, Madison, and Jefferson.

Jefferson, incidentally, although he was to become leader of the Anti-Federalists, was not to be counted in their ranks during the ratification campaign. In a letter to James Madison from Paris in December, 1787, he had expressed some reservations concerning the new Constitution. He disliked the omission of a bill of rights; he also objected to the unlimited re-eligibility of the President and said that, in general, he was "not a friend to a very energetic government." Nevertheless, he later (March 13, 1789) wrote to Francis Hopkinson: "I am not a Federalist. . . . But I am much farther from that of the Anti-Federalists. I approve . . . of the . . . new Constitution . . . from the first moment."

The Federalist case was a simple one based on (1) the general need for a strong government and specifically to get the treaty of peace observed by Britain, (2) the possibilities of growth under a government that could weld the nation together, and (3) the need for internal order maintained by a stronger hand—the shadow of Daniel Shays was a great ally for the Federalists.

In a majority of the states, both at the polls and in the conventions, ratification had a fairly easy time. In Delaware, the first state to ratify, the vote was unanimous. In Pennsylvania, the second to approve, more opposition appeared, but the final vote was 46 to 23, just 2 to 1.[5] In New Jersey, there was no opposition; nor was there in Georgia. Connecticut showed only token Anti-Federalist strength by its vote of 128 to 40. And Maryland ratified by the overwhelming vote of 63 to 11. In South Carolina, only a single vote was cast against the Constitution.

In the large states of Massachusetts, New York, and Virginia, however, the result was by no means clear. In Massachusetts, although Federalist sentiment was widespread, the Anti-Federalists looked to Sam Adams and John Hancock to block ratification. If a vote had been taken on January 9, 1788, the day the Convention met, the Constitution would

---

[5] Without awaiting action by Congress, the Federalists in the Pennsylvania Assembly voted to call a state convention. In protest, 19 Anti-Federalists absented themselves from the Assembly to break a quorum. No appeals were effective, so a Federalist mob dragged two absentees to the Assembly to make a quorum. They then passed a resolution to provide for election to the ratifying convention.

probably have been rejected. Fortunately the vote was delayed for nearly a month and both Adams and Hancock were apparently much impressed by pro-Federalist demonstrations among the mechanics and artisans of Boston.[6] Moreover, although conditional ratification was impossible, the Anti-Federalist leaders were apparently reassured by promises of Federalist support for a number of amendments, including a Bill of Rights to be proposed by the first Congress. Accordingly, on February 9, by a vote of 187 to 168, "in the name and in behalf of the people of the Commonwealth of Massachusetts [the Convention did] assent to and ratify the said Constitution for the United States of America."

The precedent established by Massachusetts of recommending amendments to the Constitution—not as a condition of ratification but as proposals to the Congress—was followed by Virginia and New York, where ratification won by a slender margin.

Before Virginia and New York got around to voting, in June and July, 1788, the required nine states had already ratified. But both Federalist and Anti-Federalist leaders realized that without New York and Virginia the new Union would be weak if not worthless.

In Virginia the debate was heated and opinion closely divided. Anti-Federalists Patrick Henry, Richard Henry Lee, and George Mason were able antagonists, even against Federalists like Madison and John Marshall. Jefferson, from Paris, in spite of some reservations, added weight to the Federalist case. And the news that New Hampshire had ratified, thus completing the number required, was not without some effect. After three weeks of discussion and debate, Virginia ratified by the close vote of 89 to 79. And, again, a number of amendments were recommended, including a bill of rights.

The contest in New York was memorable for a number of reasons:

1. An Anti-Federalist majority of nearly two-thirds, after more than a month of debate, was transformed into a Federalist majority of three (30 to 27).
2. Both sides were ably led—the Anti-Federalists by John Lansing, Robert Yates, and George Clinton; the Federalists by Hamilton, John Jay, and Robert Livingston, with strong on-the-spot assistance from James Madison.
3. News that ten states including Virginia had ratified enabled the Federalists to argue that the issue was now "union or disunion" with telling effect. So important was Virginia's ratification considered that Madison and Hamilton had arranged for a fast relay team on horseback to bring the news to Albany.
4. The campaign in New York called forth a series of published papers in defense of the Constitution composed mostly by Madison and Hamilton that Jefferson characterized as "the best commentary on the principles of government which ever was written." Known as the *Federalist Papers,*

---

[6] Hancock (the governor), who was to preside, didn't attend. He gave gout as the reason—gout no doubt complicated by politics.

they remain the best analysis of the Constitution as it came from the Convention.[7]

Essentially the *Federalist Papers* made four points:

1. The need for a stronger central government to preserve the Union.
2. The need for a vigorous executive and judicial establishment independent of the legislature.
3. The necessity for a system of countervailing powers or checks and balances to check the "violence of faction" and at the same time preserve the spirit and structure of republican government.
4. The need for a representative republic as against a democracy in a country of large territory and a great variety of interests.

In the outpouring of articles on both sides, the *Federalist Papers* stand as monuments to a kind of political discourse unhappily long vanished from American public life. In 85 articles, every detail of the Constitution was put under scrutiny. Nothing quite comparable in quality appeared among Anti-Federalist literature except perhaps Richard Henry Lee's *Letters from a Federal Farmer*. As the protagonist of a losing cause, these letters have suffered a quite undeserved neglect. Temperate in tone and of high literary quality, they argue the Anti-Federalist case with dignity and conviction. In some respects they are less polemical than *The Federalist* and also less persuasive.

The burden of Lee's argument was that the proposed Constitution was undemocratic. It put the majority under control of the minority, and did not reflect the sober judgment of the people. He also argued that the proposal was unconstitutional. The Convention, he said, was called to revise, not to destroy, the Articles. "Not one man in ten thousand in the United States, within ten or twelve days, had an idea that the old ship was to be destroyed and put to the alternative of embarking in the new ship . . . or of being left in danger of sinking."

Whether the *Federalist Papers* or the *Farmer's Letters* had any influence on the outcome, no one knows. Most scholars believe it to have been small in any case. No doubt the march of events, especially ratification by Virginia, was more important. In any event, on July 26, 1788, the New York Convention voted to approve the Constitution by a vote of 30 to 27. At the same time it recommended not only a number of specific amendments but that a second general convention be called to consider all the amendments that had been proposed.

Although the belated action of Virginia and New York had no legal effect on the launching of the new Constitution, it had immense psychological and political effect. Without these states, the new Government would have begun its career a cripple, limping upon the stage and, who knows, dying even in being born.

---

[7] Written in reply to articles attacking the Constitution by George Clinton which he signed, *Cato,* these Federalist Papers by Madison and Hamilton bore the classic signatures of *Caesar* or *Publius.*

☆ *"THE MOST WONDERFUL WORK"*

William Gladstone once described the American Constitution as "the most wonderful work ever struck off at a given time by the brain and purpose of man." One need not disagree with Gladstone to point out that this wonderful work as we know it was not struck off at a given time, but has evolved through time to become the oldest written constitution in the world.

There are those who claim that the Constitution of 1787 is by no means the Constitution of today. According to P. L. Ford, ". . . most of the men who framed the Constitution would have refused to sign it could they have foreseen its eventual development." But this is to look at superficial things. For the spirit and the structure remain pretty much the same from generation to generation.

As we have seen, J. Allen Smith, in his *Spirit of American Government* (1907), published the first critical re-examination of the origin and development of the Constitution and of the spirit and structure of American government. Caught up in the Progressive tide of the early years of this century, Professor Smith was shocked to discover that the framers were not democrats and that the Constitution was not a charter of democracy. "Democracy," wrote Smith, "was not the object which the framers of the American Constitution had in view, but the very thing they wished to avoid. . . . The efforts of the Constitutional Convention were directed to the task of devising a system of government which was just popular enough not to excite popular opposition and which at the same time gave the people as little as possible of the substance of power."

This is, in fact, a fairly accurate description of what the framers had in mind in establishing not a democracy but what they preferred to call a *representative republic.* They were by no means enamored of direct democracy as in the Athenian model. In a republic they saw an answer (1) to the "turbulence and folly" of direct democracy, (2) to the problem of government over a vast and expanding territory, and (3) to the problem of reconciling majority rule with minority rights. The framers most likely would not have denied Smith's allegation; they would only have been surprised that he was surprised.

When, however, critics go beyond description and characterize the Constitution as reactionary and illiberal, the framers might well cry out in protest from the shades. Madison, Hamilton, Washington, or Franklin, reactionaries! Surely not by the standards of their own time or even by those of our own day.

If liberalism implies unlimited power in numerical majorities, then of course the Constitution was and is not liberal. But if liberalism requires a nice but difficult balance between numerical and concurrent majorities and a respect for minority rights, then the American Constitution was and is a triumph of liberalism. Catherine the Great of Russia knew this when she described the new Constitution as so radical, so subversive of legitimate authority that for many years she withheld recognition of the new government.

But Smith was not the only critic who saw the Constitution as something less than a charter of democracy. Professor Charles Beard in 1913 argued that the Constitution was "essentially an economic document based upon the concept that the fundamental private rights of property are anterior to government and morally beyond the reach of popular majorities." More specifically, he said that the framers themselves "were immediately, directly and personally interested in and derived economic advantages from the establishment of the new system." According to Professor Beard's *Economic Interpretation of the Constitution,* the same interests that were responsible for framing the Constitution were also responsible for its ratification. These interests were (1) those who held public securities, (2) those who were speculators in land, (3) those interested in finance, that is, creditor interests, (4) those interested in trade, manufacturing, and shipping, and (5) those interested in slaves and the slave trade.

These same interests, according to Beard, led the fight for ratification and controlled the new government during the first twelve years of its life. It was they who stood to gain most under the new Constitution. The whole process of ratification, according to this theory, reveals a clear line of cleavage between these so-called *personality* interests and the small farming and debtor interest—the Federalist being the former and the Anti-Federalists being the latter.

It is pointed out that although the small farmers and debtors were a majority of the people, they were not a majority among the voters because many were disqualified by property and other qualifications. It has been estimated that only about 160,000 persons (about 5 percent of the population) actually voted in the elections to choose delegates to the ratifying conventions.

However, assuming that there were 500,000 qualified voters, the turnout of 160,000 on very short notice under primitive conditions of travel was not too bad. And one might ask where else in the civilized world of the late eighteenth century was a Constitution submitted to a direct vote of the people?

In spite of the small turnout, runs the argument, the vote shows widespread opposition to the new Constitution among the people. In Rhode Island, for example, the Constitution lost by a 10 to 1 vote. An analysis by Dr. O. G. Libby in the *Geographical Distribution of the Vote in the Thirteen States on the Federal Constitution* shows that "the Constitution was carried . . . by the influence of those classes along the great highways of commerce, the seacoast, the Connecticut River, the Shenandoah Valley, and the Ohio River; and in proportion as the material interests along these arteries of intercourse were advanced and strengthened, the Constitution was most . . . heartily supported." The bitter fight in the ratifying conventions of New York, Virginia, and Massachusetts is said to reveal a clear alignment of agrarian-debtor interests against personalty-creditor interests.

In Pennsylvania, it appears, delegates from Philadelphia and other commercial centers were Federalist, while those from purely agricultural areas, especially in the West, were Anti-Federalist. In Massachusetts, according to a letter from General Knox to Washington in 1788, "there were three parties. . . .

1. . . . the commercial part of the state to which are added all the men of considerable property, the clergy, the lawyers . . . the judges . . . officers of the late army, [and] . . . the neighborhood of all the great towns . . . 3/7 of the state. . . . This party are for vigorous government . . . many of them would have been more pleased with the new Constitution had it been more analagous to the British Constitution. . . .

2. The second party are the eastern part of the state lying beyond New Hampshire forming the province of Maine. This party are chiefly looking towards the erection of a new state and the majority of them will adopt or reject the new Constitution as it may facilitate or retard these designs—this party 2/7. . . .

3. The third party are the Insurgents . . . the great majority of whom are for an annihilation of debts public and private and therefore they will not approve the new Constitution—this party 2/7th.

The vote in the Massachusetts ratifying convention shows that the 4 commercial counties on the Coast gave 100 votes for the Constitution and 19 against, while the interior counties were strongly against.

In Virginia the eastern "tidewater," that is, the great slave plantation and commercial centers, were strongly Federalist, while the western counties, an area of small farmers, were strongly Anti-Federalist. In New York, the City of New York and its environs was strongly Federalist, but the upstate agrarians were strongly Anti-Federalist. In New Hampshire, according to a letter to Washington on June, 1788, "The opposition here [is] composed of men . . . involved in debt and of a consequence . . . averse to any government which was likely to abolish their tender laws. . . ."

Elsewhere the pattern was similar, indicating a fairly clear cleavage of economic, political, and social interests in the vote on the Constitution. These analyses simply tend to confirm what Hamilton had said immediately after the Philadelphia Convention. Those who were for the Constitution, he said, were the commercial interests; most men of property who wanted a government

to protect them against domestic violence; the . . . creditors of the United States [who hope] that a general government possessing the means of doing it will pay the debt of the Union; and people [who believe] the present confederation [unable] to preserve the existence of the Union . . . and . . . their safety and prosperity.

Those against the Constitution, he said, included the officeholders of the States "who fear loss of their power, considerable men in office with great talent who like to fish in troubled waters; those who fear that a strong government will mean higher taxes; and all men in debt who will not wish to see a government established which will keep them from cheating their creditors. . . ."[8]

In spite of all these efforts to see in the Constitution and the ratifying process a clear cleavage between agrarian-debtor and commercial-creditor interests, a closer look reveals a much more complex pattern.

Robert Brown, in his book, *Charles Beard and The Constitution,* concludes that there is no correlation between the property holdings of the framers and their attitude on the Constitution. And "it is not true," he says, "that large numbers of adult males were disfranchised: the suffrage was remarkably liberal everywhere." Moreover, most farmers were not chronic debtors; many were creditors. Nor were the security holders united in favor of the Constitution. They did not know that the debts of the Confederation would be paid at par; otherwise, Robert Morris, for example, would not "have speculated in Western lands with the thought of paying for them in depreciated paper."

Professor Forrest McDonald's searching analysis exposes the inadequacy of Beard's argument that the major alignment was between large security holders and agrarian-debtor interests. Such a theory is not consistent with the facts. In three states, for example—Delaware, New Jersey, Georgia—there were no votes against the Constitution and hence no comparison of interests *pro* and *con* can be made. In New Hampshire and North Carolina the number of security holders among the delegates was very small and not significant either way. In Rhode Island, Maryland, and Virginia, where there were contests and a considerable number of security holders, the *pros* and *cons* on ratification included approximately the same percentages of security holders—a situation that clearly contradicts Beard's thesis. In two states, however—Massachusetts and Connecticut—the *pro* ratification delegates included a considerably

---

[8] Richard Henry Lee, in his "Essay in Opposition to the Constitution," said he could see three major groups contending:

"One party is composed of little insurgents, men in debt, who want no law, and who want a share of the property of others; these are called Levellers, Shaysites, etc."

"The other [extreme] party is composed of a few but more dangerous men, with their servile dependents; these avariciously grasp at all power and property; you may discover in all the actions of these men an evident dislike to free and equal government . . . these are called aristocrats, [monarchists], etc."

"Between these two parties is the weight of the community; the men of middling property, men not in debt, and men . . . content with republican governments and not aiming at immense fortunes, offices and power."

larger percentage of security holders than those opposed. In summary, one may say that here and there the Beard thesis holds up; but in general it is an oversimplification of a complex social and political event.

The fact is that from state to state the alignment varied, and in some states the major drive for or against had little to do with the economic interests of the founding fathers. In Delaware, for example, which ratified unanimously, only 5 of the 30 delegates held securities and a majority were small farmers who, according to the Beard thesis, should have opposed ratification. Delaware probably ratified in the hope that a new government would assume some of her financial obligations; over 72 percent of Delaware's tax revenue went for obligations which it was hoped the new government would assume. New Jersey's situation was comparable, and no doubt the delegates anticipated financial relief from the new government. Georgia, on the other hand, with only one security holder among the delegates, was economically prosperous and virtually debt free. But she looked to the new government for more effective defense against Indian attacks—a service which Congress was unable to provide under the Articles of Confederation.

And so in the other states there were special circumstances having little relation to the theory of class cleavage advanced by Smith, Beard, and others of that school. But this does not mean that no pattern at all emerged. In a recent re-examination of the problem, Professors Elkins and McKittrick say: "The States where ratification was achieved most readily were those that were convinced, for one reason or another, that they could not survive and prosper as independent entities; those holding out the longest were the ones most convinced that they could go it alone."

The particular reasons vary from state to state. The search for impersonal factors to explain social and political movements often blinds us to the importance of those personal influences we associate with effective leadership. Not the least important factor in the adoption of the Constitution was the character of the Federalist and Anti-Federalist leaders.

The Federalists were nationalists who believed the Revolution to be the birth of a new nation. Merrill Jensen, in his book *The New Nation,* was impressed by their sheer force and determination. These Federalist leaders were not any more aristocratic than the Anti-Federalists—probably less so in fact. The Federalists had been reluctant revolutionaries, fearful lest a break with England release centrifugal forces that would keep the American people from becoming a nation. But once they were committed to independence, they identified strongly with the Army and the Congress, that is, with the continental-national-centripetal forces at work in the Revolution. Washington, Robert Morris, John Jay, James Wilson, Hamilton, Knox, Gouverneur Morris—Federalists all, identified more with the new nation than with their own states. Anti-Federalist leaders were more state-centered. Federalist leaders, on the whole, were younger by 10 to 12 years than the major Anti-Federalists. Nearly half of them had seen their careers launched in the Revolution. Whereas most of the Anti-Federalists had grown to maturity and leadership in the states, the Federalist leaders saw their future in the new nation.

As is so often true in the great crises of history, the framing and adoption of the Constitution was a struggle between those who were committed to the *status quo ante,* those who looked to the past, and those who believed in a new future for America. In this sense Gladstone was right and the Constitution was "the most wonderful work ever struck off at a given time . . . by the mind of man."

But there was something more involved than can be accounted for by any behavioral analysis of the age, education, experience and interests of the contending parties. There was, as Franklin put it, "the example of changing a Constitution by assembling the wise men of the state instead of assembling armies. . . ." There was, in effect, the peaceful re-enactment of the Social Compact itself. As the Massachusetts ratifying convention put it:

> Acknowledging with grateful hearts the goodness of the Supreme Ruler
> of the universe in affording the people of the United States . . . an
> opportunity, deliberately and peaceably, without fraud or surprise of enter-
> ing into an explicit and solemn compact with each other . . . do in the
> name and in behalf of the people of the Commonwealth of Massachusetts
> assent to and ratify the said Constitution for the United States of America.

☆ *ECONOMIC GOALS OF THE NEW CONSTITUTION*

The American Revolution, the Declaration of Independence, and the Constitution were all part of a revolt against a social system based on hereditary rights and privileges, and on a political system based on the divine right of kings and feudal lords. Most social and political feudal usages never took root on this continent, and those that did—like an established church or primogeniture and entail—we pretty well got rid of in the Revolution. Our Revolution was also a revolt against the stifling effects of the merchantilist economic .policies of the British government. These policies, represented in the Trade and Navigation Acts, and in the laws regulating and even prohibiting certain kinds of manufacturing and commerce in the colonies, were downright evils to an American economy ready to burst at the seams. We fought, in a word, for a free economy as against a controlled mercantilist economy. It was significant that Adam Smith's great tract against mercantilism, *The Wealth of Nations,* Jeremy Bentham's *Fragment on Government,* and our own Declaration of Independence appeared in the same year. And Bentham's treatise on utilitarian principles of government appeared in 1789 simultaneously with the establishment of the new government under the Constitution.

In our struggle against the mercantilists and their elaborate system of state-sponsored monopolies, we had powerful allies in England and on the Continent. And it is significant that although the Constitution was imbued with the spirit of a free economy, some of those who opposed it did so because it omitted any express prohibition against monopolies. On the other hand, the Federalist defenders of the Constitution made clear that a basic goal was to free commerce and manufacturing from the burdens under which they limped along, confined to the limited markets of the separate states. To create a free economy and a national common market was a basic reason for giving Congress power to regulate commerce.

This was not the only power conferred by the Constitution to promote a free economy. A uniform and stable currency and a uniform system of weights and measures are also essential. Accordingly the Constitution gives to Congress power to "coin money, regulate the value thereof, and of foreign coin, and fix the standard of weights and measures." And having in mind the disorders of the so-called critical period—the passion for paper money with the resulting inflation, bankruptcy, and collapse of credit—the Constitution in Section 10 of Article I provides that "No state shall . . . coin money; emit bills of credit; make anything but gold and silver coin a tender in payment of debts. . . ." With this restraint upon the power of the state governments and the affirmative power given to the Congress, the way was open for a uniform system of coinage and currency without which a free economy is impossible.

To put an end to the multiple state-imposed trade barriers that threatened to strangle commerce, the Constitution provides that

> No state shall without the consent of [the] Congress, lay any imposts or duties on imports or exports, except what may be absolutely necessary for executing its inspection laws; and the net produce of all duties and imposts laid by any state on imports or exports shall be for the use of the Treasury of the United States.
> And: No state shall, without the consent of Congress, lay any duty on tonnage. . . .

Thus did the framers seek to prevent burdensome and discriminatory tariffs and taxes. At the same time in Section 8 of Article I, it conferred upon the central government powers "to lay and collect taxes, duties, imposts and excises, to pay the debts and provide for the common defence and general welfare of the United States." Thus the Constitution repaired a major defect of the Articles of Confederation and endowed the central government with the broad power to tax.

But it does more, for the power to lay duties on imports includes as a corollary power to use such duties not merely for revenue but to protect the American economy from foreign competition. And if this seems inconsistent with the framers' goal of a free economy, one need only remember that they were not doctrinaires or ideologues but empiricists and realists. To encourage manufacturing and insure a free internal market they were not unwilling to break with Adam Smith's model of a free economy and a free market for the world.

In vesting the Congress with this power, however, the Constitution also requires that "all duties, imposts and excises shall be uniform throughout the United States"; that "no tax or duty shall be laid on articles exported from any state" and that "no preference shall be given by any regulation of commerce or revenue to the ports of one state over those of another." Other provisions contribute to this goal of an economy free from state impediments and barriers. Congress has power to enact bankruptcy laws that are uniform throughout the United States; to establish post offices and post-roads; and to promote the progress of science and the useful arts "by granting exclusive copyright and patent privileges for limited times" to authors and inventors.

The preoccupation of the founding fathers with economic goals is revealed in other provisions of the Constitution. In Section 8 of Article I, Congress is given power to borrow money on the credit of the United States. But to do so it was necessary first to establish the credit of the United States; the credit of the government was impaired because, having no independent source of revenue, the Confederation was unable to redeem its bonds. To establish the credit of the United States, the framers gave to the central government an independent "power to lay and collect taxes [and] to pay the debts . . . of the United States."

But this alone they thought was not enough to put a solid base under any debts to be incurred in future years. As successor to the Confederation, said the framers, the new government must assume the debts of the old Congress under the Confederation. This debt had been incurred in the cause of independence and was a legitimate obligation of the nation as a whole, whatever the form of government. Accordingly the Constitution provides in Article VI that "All Debts contracted and engagements entered into, before the Adoption of the Constitution, shall be as valid against the United States under this Constitution as under the Confederation." It was under this provision that Congress, on the initiative of Hamilton, as Secretary of the Treasury, provided for the funding of the old Confederation debt. Whatever one may think of all this as public policy, the *goal* was clear: to establish the credit of the United States, not only at home but in the money markets of the world.

Both public and private credit had suffered during the difficult years following the Revolution under state laws affecting private contracts—especially mortgage contracts. To relieve farmers desperately in debt, and to protect them against foreclosure, state legislatures extended the terms of the mortgage contracts through "stay laws" and in other ways sought to help the debtor hold out against his creditor. Regarding this as an evil practice, dangerous alike to public and private credit, the framers wrote into the Constitution a so-called "contract clause," providing in Section 10 of Article I that "No state shall . . . make . . . any . . . law impairing the obligation of contracts."

☆ **SOCIAL AND POLITICAL GOALS**

If we have emphasized the economic goals of the Constitution, it is because they were high on the priority list of the framers. But these were by no means their sole or even major concern. In the *Federalist Papers,* four articles by John Jay emphasized the necessity for a stronger union in the conduct of foreign relations. The prospect of thirteen separate states or even a smaller number of independent confederacies did not augur well for the continued independence of the American people.

We need to remember that in 1787 the nation had less than 4 million people, scattered over a vast territory. We faced powerful and ambitious rivals in Britain, France, and Spain, each ready to move in on the slightest provocation.

> Leave America divided [Jay wrote] [or weak] . . . what armies could [we] raise, what fleets could [we] ever hope to have? On the other hand, as a nation we have made peace and war, as a nation we have vanquished our common enemies, as a nation we have formed alliances and made treaties . . . with foreign states. Only as a united nation [he argued] could we continue to face the world with hope and confidence.

If a strong union was conceived to be necessary to the security and independence of the nation, so, too, argued the framers, only a strong central government could be proof against "domestic faction and insurrection."

"It is impossible," wrote Hamilton, "to read the history of the petty republics of Greece and Italy without . . . horror and disgust at the . . . rapid succession of revolutions by which they were kept in a state of perpetual vibration between the extremes of tyranny and anarchy." The surest guarantee against a similar fate for America is a *united* America resting on a "broad foundation" of popular consent and republican institutions.

To this end the Constitution in Section 4 of Article IV provides that

> The United States shall guarantee to every State in this Union a republican form of government, and *shall protect them against invasion;* and on application of the legislature, or of the Executive (when the legislature cannot be convened) *against domestic violence.*

To insure domestic peace and security from external attack, the Constitution placed in the central government sole power to maintain armies and navies, and to declare war.

No state shall, without the consent of Congress . . . keep troops, or ships of war in time of peace . . . or engage in war unless actually invaded. . . .

That the armed force of the nation may be subject to a single civilian command, Article II provides that "The President shall be Commander in Chief of the Army and Navy of the United States."

Not least among the basic goals of the framers is the protection of those unalienable individual rights and liberties to which the Declaration of Independence refers. One major objection to the Constitution, as it came from the Convention, was that it contained no formal bill of rights, although there were, to be sure, some important guarantees. Section 9 of Article I, for example, provides that "The Privilege of the Writ of Habeas Corpus shall not be suspended unless in cases of rebellion or invasion the public safety may require it" and that "No Bill of Attainder or ex-post facto law shall be passed."

But many people were unhappy that the document drawn up at Philadelphia did not include the full panoply of civil liberties guaranteed in most of the state constitutions. Accordingly, in ratifying the Constitution, Massachusetts, New York, and Virginia insisted that such a bill of rights be added, and in due course this was done (December 15, 1791). Freedom of religious worship, of speech, of the press, of assembly and petition are guaranteed. So, too, are the rights of trial by jury, protection against illegal searches and seizures, and against self-incrimination.

The American passion for equality as well as liberty also found expression in the Constitution, although in somewhat muted tones. Section 9 of Article I provides that "No title of nobility shall be granted by the United States." And "no person holding any office of profit or trust under them shall, without the consent of Congress accept any present, emolument, office or title of any kind whatever from any King, Prince, or foreign state." But the major guarantees of equality, aside from those in the Bill of Rights, were implied from the "general welfare" clause of Article I and the Preamble, until the more specific provisions of the Thirteenth, Fourteenth, Fifteenth, and Nineteenth Amendments were added.

No complete statement of the goals of the American Constitution can be made from the text of the Constitution itself, even as amended. Nevertheless, the Constitution of the United States holds up for the American people goals which, even after nearly two hundred years, can challenge our best endeavors. Nowhere are these more eloquently summarized than in the Preamble.

We the People of the United States [it reads], in Order to form a more perfect Union, establish Justice, insure domestic Tranquility, provide for the common defense, promote the general Welfare, and secure the Blessings of Liberty to ourselves and our Posterity, do ordain and establish this Constitution for the United States of America.

Cynics, of course, will point scornfully to phrases so vague and ambiguous. But to those who cannot tolerate ambiguities one may say that there is something more to the human mind than can be measured in a mechanical computer. Something that is at the same time both sublime and a bit ridiculous—a kind of merger of the irrational and the wise, this is the language of the Preamble.

☆ BASIC STRUCTURE: MEANS AND ENDS

The purposes for which the Constitution of the United States was established have been clearly stated in the Preamble and the text of the Constitution itself. But aspirations, goals, and purposes—however grand and universal—require for their fulfillment a nice correlation of means and ends. It is to the means—the structure and machinery which the Constitution provides for the realization of its basic goals—that we must now turn.

The Constitution was a product of the *Age of Reason*—of that period known as the Enlightenment—when men of intellect and good will all over the Western world thought of human reason as a royal road to what Carl Becker has called the Heavenly City of the eighteenth century. Faith in reason was essential to the very notion of government by consent of the governed. Jefferson was much impressed by this aspect of the Constitutional Convention. "We are yet able," he said, "to send our wise and good men together to talk over our form of government. . . . with the same *sang froid* as they would a subject of agriculture. The example we have given the world is [unique], that of changing our form of government under the authority of reason only, without bloodshed."

The founding fathers were men of the Enlightenment who shared the eighteenth-century faith in human reason. But unlike some of the more extreme philosophers like Rousseau and Condillac, they knew that in man reason is more often than not tempered with emotion and biased by self-interest. They knew that humans could act on impulse as well as reason—on the spur of the moment as well as after due diliberation. They knew, too, that reason unattended by experience could lead a man astray, could make him a stargazer, so intent on Heaven that he falls into a ditch. Reason enlightened by experience and transformed into common sense they thought of as a better guide.

In creating a Constitution to govern men rather than angels, therefore, they sought a structure, a decision-making process, that would give reason, experience, and common sense as large a role as possible. They sought to curb impulse and to give freer rein to deliberation and reflection. It was to this end that they preferred a representative republic to a direct democracy. They were fearful of decisions made by ill-informed masses of men under the influence of passion or prejudice inflamed by demagogues and the special pleading of selfish interests. They were pretty generally agreed that the "superior will of the people" must prevail. But it should be a "reasonable not a distracted will."

The best safeguard for the rights of man, said John Dickinson, is not "obtained by a bill of rights," important as that may be. "They . . . must be preserved by soundness of sense and honesty of heart. Compared with these what are a bill of rights or any characters drawn upon paper or parchment, those frail remembrances."

"It is an axiom of my mind," said Jefferson, "that our liberty can never be safe but in the hands of the people themselves, and that, too, of people with a certain degree of instruction." It was to give the people this "certain degree of instruction" that the American people have always given a high priority to public education and to freedom of thought and expression.

It is significant that Jefferson, the great protagonist of the people, expressed serious doubt about the wisdom of having the House of Representatives directly elected by the people. "I think," he wrote to Madison, "a House so chosen will be far inferior to the present Congress [of the Confederation], a body chosen not directly by the people but by the state legislatures."

The provision in the Constitution that "the House of Representatives shall be composed of members chosen every second year by the People of the several states" was the only major concession made by the founding fathers to direct participation of the people in the operation of the new government. To this they added the requirement that "All Bills for raising revenue shall originate in the House of Representatives" as another concession to the principle of popular control. But these concessions were tempered by (1) making the apportionment of representation depend partly upon the basis of property—in the provision for counting three-fifths of the slaves, and (2) the absence of any provision for universal suffrage. Unable to agree upon property or other qualifications, the Convention left these to be determined by the states.

Thus it turned out that although "We the People" ordained and established the Constitution through the direct election of delegates to the ratifying conventions, direct participation of the people in the operation of the new government was greatly limited. And only those could participate who could surmount the numerous qualifications which the states imposed upon the right to vote.

In other respects the formal structure of the government as outlined in the Constitution seemed to follow the views which Roger Sherman of Connecticut expressed in the Convention that "the people . . . immediately should have as little to do as may be about the government. They want information and are constantly liable to be misled."

The Senate, of course, was designed not to represent people directly, but the states—not the numerical majority but the concurrent majority. And the election of Senators was left to the state legislatures, thus insulating the process from the follies and foibles of the people. The staggered terms of Senators and Representatives had the same end in view.

As for the President, his election was also to be removed from the people. As originally planned, the electoral college was thought of as a body of men of great wisdom and virtue, selected "in such manner as the state legislature might direct" and free, after due deliberation, to choose a President. To insure that they would be disinterested and objective in this process, no Senator or Representative in Congress or any person holding office under the United States could be an elector. Singularly enough, this plan, perhaps the least successful of the basic features of the original Constitution, called forth little criticism. "The mode of appointment of the Chief Magistrate," wrote Hamilton, "is almost the only part of the system of any consequence which has escaped without severe censure, or which has received the slightest mark of approbation from its opponents."

Because this system has not worked as the framers intended, we ought not to lose sight of the theory underlying its adoption. Even if the electors were, in time, to be chosen by the people, the framers had arranged to provide against excessive direct influence of the people in the process. An absolute majority of the electors was (and is) required to elect a President. Since the electors were to meet separately in their respective states, the framers assumed that only on very rare occasions would a clear majority agree on any person. In this contingency the election was to go to the House of Representatives, which was to choose a President from the five highest on the list, with each state having only one vote regardless of its size. This, they thought, would be the normal procedure, thus removing the election of the President still further from the people. In point of fact, this highly undemocratic process was employed on only two unhappy occasions: in 1801 in the election of Jefferson, and in 1825 in the election of John Q. Adams.

The third branch of the central government—the Supreme Court—was made even less directly dependent upon the people. Appointed by the President with the advice and consent of the Senate, the Constitution provides that "the judges, both of the Supreme and inferior Courts shall hold their offices during good behavior." To remove a judge, moreover, requires his impeachment before the Senate for high crimes and misdemeanors, and conviction by a two-thirds vote.

Thus the basic structure of government was designed to insulate the election of decision makers and the decision-making process itself from any considerable participation by the people. With the passage of time, the process has been democratized (1) through the extension of the suffrage, (2) by the Seventeenth Amendment providing for the direct election of United States Senators, (3) through the direct election of presidential electors as the chosen instruments of major political parties, and (4) through the increasing influence of public opinion upon public policy.

As we have seen, the power structure established in the Constitution was designed to insulate decision makers—except for Representatives in Congress—from immediate dependence upon the people. To attribute this, as some critics have done, solely to a class bias among the framers, is superficial and at best a half truth. Equally important was their desire to bring into the decision-making process men whose reputation, experience, education, and common sense would make them less likely to be swayed by transitory gusts of popular passion and prejudice.

This is clearly revealed in the debates on the suffrage and the basis of representation. Elbridge Gerry spoke warmly in favor of the proposition that the people directly should choose one branch of the legislature "in order to inspire them with the necessary confidence." But in the election of the Senate he wanted this principle modified so "as to seem more effectively a just preference for merit."

John Dickinson referred to the indirect election of Senators as a "refining process." And in the debate on the suffrage there were frequent references to the ease with which poor and ignorant voters could be victimized and controlled by "the rich," "their employers," or an "aristocracy" of opulence and ambition." To dismiss all of these reservations as mere rationalizations of class interest is to do less than justice to the framers, who desired a political community in which reason and common sense would prevail. To maximize the role of reason and deliberation was an important reason for establishing a bicameral legislature. Not only did this afford opportunity for the representation of different interests, but it interposed an element of delay that would enable Congress to give more careful consideration to important decisions.

". . . All single and numerous assemblies," said Hamilton, have a propensity "to yield to the impulse of sudden and violent passions, and to be seduced by factious leaders into intemperate and pernicious revolutions. . . . A second branch [he said] . . . must [therefore] be . . . a salutary check on the government." Moreover, argued Hamilton, the smaller size and indirect election of the Senate are more likely to bring "greater knowledge and more extensive information [to] the national councils" and such a body is "less apt to be tainted by the spirit of faction, and more out of reach of those occasional ill humors or temporary prejudices . . . which beget injustice and oppression. . . ."

If a bicameral legislature was conceived as necessary to encourage greater deliberation and rationality in the legislature, a similar line of reasoning lay behind the separation of powers—a cardinal principle of American government. We shall take a close look at this principle later on. For the present it is enough to say that it, too, grew out of the desire of the framers to increase the role of reason in the process of government.

States and the Central Government

If the separation of powers is one cardinal feature of the American government, the federal System is another. Whatever may be true today, it is clear that at the time of the Constitutional Convention and for over one hundred years thereafter "the question of the relation of the states to the Federal government [was] the cardinal question of our constitutional system." It is the question that lay behind the Civil War and reconstruction, and it is the question that in a variety of ways continues to plague American politics today.

"Among the first sentiments expressed in the first Congress," said James Wilson, "was that Virginia is no more, Massachusetts is no more. . . . We are now one nation of brethren. We must bury local interests and distinctions. . . ." But with independence the old rivalries and ambitions "began to display themselves. Each endeavored to cut a slice from the common loaf to add to his morsel, till at length the Confederation became frittered down to the impotent condition in which it now stands."

We know how rivalry between the large and small states over representation in the new government almost destroyed the Constitutional Convention. We know also how this was solved in the federal compromise by giving each state equal representation in the Senate. But the basic conflict was between those who saw in the new Constitution the birth of a new nation and those who continued to speak of the "sovereign" states and to maintain and enlarge the scope of state authority.

Exponents of the so-called States' rights school find their constitutional base in the theory of state sovereignty, and in the principles of *delegated* power in the nation and powers *reserved* to the states. They recall that the Articles of Confederation had provided that "Each state retains its sovereignty, freedom and independence and every power jurisdiction and right, which is not by this Confederation *expressly* delegated to the United States in Congress assembled." They pointed to a similar provision in the Tenth Amendment, reading: "The Powers not delegated to the United States by the Constitution, nor prohibited by it to the States, are reserved to the States respectively, or to the people."

What is often overlooked is that while the Articles of Confederation refers to powers not *expressly* delegated to the United States, this word is omitted from the Tenth Amendment. Does this change the meaning of this reservation? Obviously had the word *expressly* been retained, the scope of power delegated to the nation would have had to be most strictly construed. If the central government need not look for authority in a specific grant of power, but only for a *general* grant of power, a more liberal construction may be given to the power of the United States as against the separate states.

On many occasions the exercise of power by the central government has been challenged as an unconstitutional invasion of the powers reserved to the states in the Tenth Amendment. The prevailing view, however, would seem to support the Supreme Court's opinion in the case of *U.S.* v. *Sprague* 282 U.S. 716 (1931) that the Tenth Amendment "added nothing to the [Constitution] as originally ratified." It merely declared what was obvious, that powers not delegated were not delegated. But it shed no light on the nature or scope of the powers conferred.

The relation between the central government and the states under the Constitution is radically different from what it was under the Articles of Confederation. The new Constitution established a federation, not a confederation—that is, a central government with its own independent powers and its own executive, administrative, and judicial machinery. On the issue of federal supremacy, few reservations were expressed in the Constitutional Convention. Both the Virginia and the New Jersey Plans included provisions to give to the central government power to use force if necessary to compel the states to comply with a legitimate exercise of federal power. If under the Constitution no such power was conferred, it is because no such power was necessary. The government of the United States does not act on or through the state governments but directly on all individuals living within the territorial limits of the United States.

The importance of this constitutional principle was dramatically illustrated in the Civil War and the theory in terms of which that bitter conflict was carried on. When federal property was seized in Charleston, and when armed forces fired on Fort Sumter, Lincoln had to decide on what authority he, as Commander in Chief, could dispatch troops to protect federal property and reinforce a federal fortification. Did he have this authority under an implied power in the central government to coerce a sovereign state? In the Virginia Plan the United States was to have express power to "call forth the force of the Union against any member of the Union failing to fulfill its duty . . ." and a similar provision was in the New Jersey Plan. But no such power was expressly conferred in the Constitution. Could the President, then, under some implied power, use force against a state? President Buchanan had decided he had no such power. Lincoln, too, seemed to agree with this ruling. How, then, could he justify the use of force in South Carolina and later against the Confederacy? This he did by relying upon his oath to "defend the Constitution" . . . and his Constitutional duty to "take care that the laws be faithfully executed. . . ." Force, said Lincoln, could be used not against a state as such but against any individual, including officers of a state, who disobeyed or defied the laws of the United States. And it

was on this theory, that the United States could act directly upon individuals and not indirectly as under the Articles of Confederation through
the states, that the war was fought.

It was on this same theory that Lincoln had planned to base his
reconstruction policy. He rejected the argument that by their rebellion
the Confederate States had committed suicide, and also the argument
that the rebellious states could be treated as conquered provinces. The
states, argued Lincoln, had not committed suicide; they had never been
out of the Union and could not therefore be treated as conquered
provinces. Rather, he said, certain individuals had defied the law and
had been in rebellion. Once this rebellion had been put down, and these
individuals punished, the Confederate States would resume their proper
place as members of the federal union of which they had continued to be
members.

Had Lincoln's theory prevailed, the nation might have been spared
much of the agony of the tragic Reconstruction era. Unfortunately, other
counsel prevailed, counsel which by a curious paradox sought to maintain federal supremacy by impliedly admitting the possibility of state
sovereignty and secession. The constitutional issue has now been resolved
as Lincoln would have had it resolved. The issue of centralization or
decentralization within the federal system under the Constitution remains. But it has become an issue largely of policy and not of conflict
between two equally sovereign powers.

These, then, are the main outlines of the basic power structure
provided for in the Constitution.

☆ THE LAW AND CUSTOM OF THE CONSTITUTION

Constitutional government is often described as a government of laws
and not of men. An English statesman, knowing that laws as such do not
govern but that men do, once said, "Away with this cant about a government of laws and not of men. Away with the silly notion that it is the
harness and not the horse that pulls the load." Nevertheless, Mr. Can-
ning knew that without the harness he would have no horse to pull a
load. For the law is the harness men must wear to preserve order, and as
law is a harness for men, so the Constitution is a harness not only for men
but for the law itself.

Constitutional lawyers like to distinguish between statute law and
constitutional or fundamental law. This distinction is often made in
terms of the process by which each is enacted. Ordinary or statute law is
enacted by the legislature and duly signed by the chief executive. Or it
grows out of the accumulated judgments of courts—like the common law.
A constitutional law is a provision either of the original Constitution or
of one of its amendments adopted according to the special procedures

outlined in the Constitution. Such a distinction would not hold in England, since no special procedure is required for amending the English Constitution. An ordinary act of Parliament is sufficient.

A procedural distinction is thus not too useful; and we must look therefore to the substance of the law itself. In these terms a constitutional law is one which significantly affects the basis, the structure, or the scope of power in the government. Laws outlining the powers of Congress or the President or the courts, or defining the terms on which they are to be elected or removed from office may properly be called constitutional, whether adopted as part of the formal constitution or merely as acts of legislation.[9] A statute, on the other hand, is a rule of law enacted by Congress (or a state legislature) or developed by the courts which defines or regulates the rights or conduct of individuals or groups in their relations with one another or with the state.

But distinctions between constitutional and ordinary law tend to break down, and so too do the common distinctions between *written* and *unwritten, rigid* and *flexible* constitutions. It has been customary, for example, to describe the Constitution of the United States as both *written* and *rigid* to distinguish it from the English Constitution, which is described as *unwritten* and *flexible.* To a considerable degree, these distinctions are meaningful and significant. The Constitution of the United States is in fact a written document of roughly 8,000 words comprising a Preamble, seven major articles, and twenty-five amendments.[10]

[9] In these terms a statute like the Judiciary Act of 1789 setting up our system of federal courts may properly be regarded as a constitutional law.

[10] Article I outlines the structure, organization, and powers of Congress.

Article II provides for the executive power, including the qualifications, methods of election, and powers of the President.

Article III establishes a Supreme Court, defines its powers and jurisdiction, and authorizes Congress to create inferior federal courts and to define their powers and jurisdiction.

Article IV outlines in some detail the relations that shall prevail among the several states and between the territories and states on the one hand and the United States on the other.

Article V outlines the process by which amendments may be added to the Constitution and imposes a limitation of the scope of the amending power itself.

Article VI guarantees the payment of the debts of the Confederation, establishes the supremacy of the United States, and forbids any religious qualification for federal office.

Article VII outlines the procedure for securing ratification of the Constitution.

Amendments numbered I through X are referred to as the Bill of Rights.

The Eleventh Amendment imposes a limitation on the judicial power of the United States. The Twelfth Amendment prescribes a new procedure for voting in the Electoral College. The Thirteenth outlaws slavery. The Fourteenth defines citizenship, provides penalties against state limitations on the right to vote, guarantees due process and equal protection of the laws, and denies any federal liability for the debts of the Confederacy. The Fifteenth forbids states to deny the right to vote on grounds of race. The Sixteenth gives Congress power to tax incomes without apportionment according to population. The Seventeenth provides for the direct election of United States Senators. The Eighteenth outlaws the manufacture and sale of intoxicating liquor. The Nineteenth forbids the states to deny the suffrage on grounds of sex. The Twentieth changes

Certainly one will search in vain for any similar comprehensive document setting forth the structure and powers of the government of England. According to the late Viscount Bryce, the British Constitution "is a mass of precedents carried in men's minds or recorded in understandings and beliefs, a number of statutes mixed up with customs, and all covered with a parasitic growth of legal decisions and political habits." It is, he said, formless, dateless, and elusive.

A. V. Dicey, in his book *The Law of the Constitution,* distinguished between what he called the *law* and the *custom* of the English Constitution. The *law* he defined as those rules which could be enforced in the courts. The *custom* of the Constitution are those rules and procedures unknown to the law and not enforceable in the courts. If custom is breached, only a political remedy is available. Many of the most hallowed parts of the English Constitution are unknown to written or even to the common law. The queen must give her consent to laws passed by Parliament. The queen must dissolve Parliament when asked to do so by the prime minister. But what if she declines to sign or to dissolve? The prime minister and his Cabinet are members of Parliament and come from the majority party in the House of Commons. But suppose the queen chose her prime minister from outside the House of Commons? She is amenable to no court, to no law. There is no legal remedy against this; and though Parliament would most likely find a remedy, that too would be constitutional.

Nowhere are the civil rights and liberties of citizens more secure than in the United Kingdom. But suppose Parliament were to pass a law to impair freedom of speech, or of the press, no one could challenge it in the courts directly. No one could declare an Act of Parliament unconstitutional. Nowhere is the maxim that the best safeguard of civil liberties is in the hearts and habits of the people better illustrated than in the British Isles.

On the other hand, some of the most important parts of the English Constitution are in fact written. Magna Charta is surely as much a part of the English Constitution as are the conventions, the King Can Do No Wrong, and the prime minister is entitled to a dissolution when he loses his firm grip on the House of Commons.

---

the dates for the assembling of Congress and the inauguration of the President and gives Congress power to provide for cases in which death may intervene to affect the choice of a President. The Twenty-first repeals the Eighteenth Amendment. The Twenty-second prohibits a President from serving more than two terms. The Twenty-third gives citizens of the District of Columbia the right to choose electors for President and Vice-President. The Twenty-fourth Amendment outlaws the poll tax as a qualification for voting in elections for President, United States Senator or Representative. The Twenty-fifth Amendment provides for succession to the Presidency in case of the death or disability of the President.

In Section 9 of Article I, no less than in the first fifteen amendments, there is an extensive catalogue of limitations upon the powers of both state and federal governments.

The Unwritten Constitution

If the unwritten Constitution of England is in fact partly written, so the written Constitution of the United States is, to a very considerable extent, unwritten. Custom and convention have played their part in America as in Britain. One will search the written Constitution in vain for any mention of the President's Cabinet. The great executive departments, represented in the Cabinet, have been established by Acts of Congress, but there is no written law which entitles them to a place in the Cabinet. Nor is there any written law that requires or authorizes the President to have a cabinet at àll. This institution has developed from the President's power to "require the Opinion in writing, of the principal officer in each of the executive Departments, upon any subject relating to the duties of their respective Departments."

POLITICAL PARTIES.   Members of the electoral college have become little more than messengers for the political parties whose agents they are in fact, if not in law. And what has happened to the electoral college points up the importance of another unwritten feature of the American Constitution, our party system. The framers were intent on preventing the growth of political parties, yet without political parties the government of the United States could probably not function at all. In the organization of Congress and, the state legislatures, in the determination of public policies, in the appointment of official personnel, and even in the administrative process the influence of political parties is as pervasive as the atmosphere. Yet these critically important institutions are unknown to the Constitution.

THE COMMITTEE SYSTEM.   The Constitution, in Article I, describes in considerable detail the composition, organization, and procedure of the House of Representatives and the Senate. It provides that the Vice-President shall preside over the Senate; and when he is not in the chair, a President pro tempore, who is to be chosen by the Senate itself, shall preside. "The House of Representatives," says the Constitution, "shall chuse their Speaker and other Officers." Also, that "Each House may determine the Rules of its Proceedings."

But nowhere does the written Constitution recognize those prime movers of all legislative proceedings, the congressional committees. No word about the Ways and Means Committee of the House, or the Senate Finance Committee, or about Committees on Appropriations, Foreign Affairs, and the other areas of public policy which have made congressional government the wonder and despair of both practical politicians and scholars. Nor does the Constitution present any indication of the real character and powers of the Speaker of the House.

RESIDENCE OF REPRESENTATIVES.   In describing the qualifications required of a member of the House of Representatives, Article I provides that he must be 25 years of age, a citizen of the United States of 7 years' standing, and an inhabitant of the *state* in which he seeks election. But nowhere does it say that a Representative must be an inhabitant of the *district* he seeks to represent. This, too, is a convention of our Constitution, a convention incidentally unknown in Great Britain.

SENATORIAL COURTESY. Article II of the written Constitution says that the President "shall nominate and by and with the advice and consent of the Senate, shall appoint Ambassadors, other public Ministers and Consuls, Judges of the Supreme Court, and all other Officers of the United States whose appointments are not herein otherwise provided for, and which shall be established by law; but the Congress may by law vest the Appointment of such inferior Officers as they think proper, in the President alone, in the courts of law, or in the Heads of Departments."

There is nothing in the language of this provision to require the President to consult the individual Senators or Representatives of his own party concerning appointments which he proposes to make in the particular states from which they come. Yet for the President to make a nomination for any one of half a hundred federal offices that fall to him to fill, without prior approval by the Senators from that state of the President's own party, would be to court almost certain defeat when the nomination came before a committee or to the whole Senate for approval.

JUDICIAL REVIEW.   Among the most unique features of the American Constitution, none is more important than the principle of judicial review. Yet this, too, rests more on custom than on any clear language of the Constitution. Article III, which makes provision for the judicial branch of the government, says nothing about the power of any court to declare acts of Congress or of the states unconstitutional.

"Law," said Aaron Burr, "is that which is boldly asserted and plausibly maintained." Nowhere is the truth of this more evident than in the development of this unwritten custom of the American Constitution. Its roots, to be sure, lie deep in our legal and political culture. Sir Edward Coke and Blackstone would have understood it, for they came close to asserting the same right for the English courts. And it was perhaps only by accident that Parliament itself, or at least the House of Lords, was the Highest Court in the realm that stayed the development of judicial review in England. James Otis's argument in the Parsons Case in effect asserted the right of courts to pass judgment upon legislation challenged as in violation of the Constitution.

The courts of Rhode Island had, in fact, declared an act of the legislature to be unconstitutional in 1786; and Councils of Censors or of Revision functioned in Pennsylvania, Vermont, and New York. Chief

Justice Marshall was therefore asserting no revolutionary right when, in *Marbury* v. *Madison,* he held an act of Congress to be beyond its powers under the Constitution. But the doctrine of judicial review is neverthe-less an implied power and not one expressly conferred. Yet this doctrine has become a part of the *mystique* which envelops the Constitution of the United States and gives it the quality of a higher law.

Constitutional Change

So important is the Court's role in our constitutional system that a Chief Justice, Charles Evans Hughes, once said that the "Constitution is what the judges say it is." And since what they say it is differs from time to time, and even from case to case, the judges of the Supreme Court have exerted a powerful influence for change in an otherwise *rigid* Constitu-tion. For it is said of our Constitution not only that it is written—and this we have seen is not wholly true—but also that it is a rigid, inflexible instrument. If one has regard for the formal amending process, this is true. A process that involves a resolution passed by two-thirds of both houses of Congress or by two-thirds of the state legislatures and ratifica-tion by three-fourths of the states cannot be described as flexible. For this would seem to create an all but impossible course to run.

For many years, in fact, the Constitution was regarded as virtually unamendable. From September, 1804, until February, 1913, over one hundred years, no amendment was added except as the result of Civil War. But between February, 1913, and August, 1920, three amendments were added, as were six more between 1920 and February, 1967.[11]

Formal amendment is but one of the means by which the Constitu-tion has evolved. It has grown by a kind of glacial accretion, adding customs and traditions having all the weight and substance of formal amendments. These unwritten conventions are themselves subject to change. During a century and a half, since both Washington and Jeffer-son had declined to run for a third term, it had come to be regarded as part of the unwritten code of the Constitution that no President could be elected to a third term. But Franklin Roosevelt proved this to be no effective bar to his re-election for a third term in 1940, and a fourth term in 1944. To reduce this unwritten provision against a third term to writing, the Twenty-second Amendment was added in 1951.

A constitution grows also by judicial interpretation. The commerce clause, the taxing powers of Congress, and the general welfare clause have given Congress, with the Court's blessing, a wider and wider field in

---

11 It is worth noting that in the formal amending process, the most difficult hurdle has been Congress, not the states, in the initiation not in the ratification process. Literally hundreds of amendments have been introduced only to fall before the barrier of a two-thirds vote in Congress. Of thirty that have been submitted by Congress, twenty-five have been ratified, the most recent (Twenty-fifth) in February, 1967.

which to maneuver. Congress, too, has contributed to constitutional change. Many acts of legislation have had as great or greater effect upon the structure and scope of power under the Constitution than provisions of the written Constitution itself.

The Judiciary Act of 1789, the Northwest Ordinance as Re-enacted in 1791, the Homestead Act of 1861, and the acts creating the Budget Bureau and other administrative agencies are among acts of legislation that are part of our Constitution in substance if not in form. The Constitution has also changed through action of the President in defining the all but illimitable powers of his office. He has become, in fact, the chief source of legislation, the nation's chief economic planner, and in many ways the sign and symbol of the American republic before all the world.

A constitution is, as we have said, a way of life. Men look to a constitution and find what they seek, especially a constitution couched in language as ambiguous as that to be found in the Constitution of the United States. Moreover, a constitution through time takes on a symbolic, almost a mystical, quality to represent what men think of as fundamental and, as such, immutable and beyond reproach. Industry and frugality, goodness and virtue, loyalty and courage—all the values that lie deep in the American soul are identified with the Constitution. And evil, simple and compound, is unconstitutional.

THE SEPARATION
OF POWERS

On March 21, 1955, two officials of the Foreign Operations Administration appeared before the Senate Permanent Subcommittee on Investigations for questioning concerning the work of their agency. Acting under instructions from their chief, Harold Stassen, both declined to respond to the committee's questions. Mr. Stassen's instructions were that employees of the FOA were not to submit to interviews by staff members of the subcommittee except when he (Mr. Stassen) or his attorneys were present.

Aroused by this refusal of administrative officers to submit to questioning, the subcommittee voted to subpoena Mr. Stassen himself to appear and bring with him "every record, every document" in which the subcommittee was interested. The Senators regarded Mr. Stassen's position in this matter as a challenge to the legitimate investigative powers of the Senate. On the other hand, the issuance of a subpoena by a Senate subcommittee to the administrative chief of a major executive agency raised a serious question concerning the independence of the executive branch of our government. As Russell Baker of *The New York Times* observed, the decision to issue the subpoena "raised the Constitutional question whether Congress had the right to subpoena officers of the Executive Branch despite the separation of powers doctrine."[1] If committees of the Congress could compel the attendance and testimony of executive officers, what becomes of the theory that such officers are responsible not to Congress but to the President, who in turn is responsible directly to the people? If, on the other hand, executive officers may thus defy committees of the Congress and refuse to answer questions except upon

[1] *The New York Times*, March 1, 1955.

their own terms, how is Congress to obtain the information so essential in the enactment of legislation?

This Stassen incident thus poses a fundamental issue of constitutional government in the United States. It is not likely that such an issue could arise in Great Britain, where the chief executive officers (the prime minister and his Cabinet) are not only the queen's chief ministers but as such are also members of Parliament. But in the United States, where the principle of separation of powers is embodied in the Constitution and hallowed by the custom and usage of 150 years, conflicts between the executive, legislative, and judicial branches are frequent.

American history is filled with "incidents" in which the President and Congress, the Supreme Court and the President, Congress and the Court, even the House of Representatives and the Senate, have been arrayed against one another. Although conflicts of this kind have never involved resort to violence, they have nevertheless played a significant and dynamic role in American government.

☆ TO SECURE THE PUBLIC GOOD AND PRIVATE RIGHTS

Everyone knows that the government of the United States—like ancient Gaul—is divided into three parts. There is an *executive* branch headed by the President, a *legislative* branch called Congress, made up of the House of Representatives and the Senate, and a *judicial* branch headed by the Supreme Court. It is the function of Congress, we are told, to "make" the laws, of the President to "enforce" the laws, and of the Supreme Court to "interpret" the laws. As a corollary and necessary consequence of this separation of powers, the three branches of government are designed to check and balance one another. The President has a veto with which he can check Congress, but Congress can check the President by passing a law over his veto by a two-thirds vote or by refusing to pass laws which the president wants, and even by removing him from office through impeachment for high crimes and misdemeanors. And, of course, the Supreme Court can check both Congress and the President, when in the Court's judgment they have exceeded or abused the powers granted to them in the Constitution.

The separation of powers and the system of checks and balances are nowhere explicitly outlined in the Constitution, although they were very much in the minds of the framers at Philadelphia in 1787. As in the case of so many features of American government, the doctrines of separation of powers and checks and balances arise rather by logical inference from the debates in the Constitutional Convention, the arguments of Hamilton and Madison in *The Federalist,* and from the language of the Constitution itself. Article I provides that "All legislative Powers herein granted shall be vested in a Congress of the United States, which shall consist of a Senate and a House of Representatives." Article II provides that "The executive Power shall be vested in a President of the United States of America." And Article III provides that "The judicial Power of the United States, shall be vested in one supreme Court, and in such inferior Courts as the Congress may from time to time ordain and establish."

Having thus established three distinct agencies of government in three separate Articles of the Constitution, it may be reasonably assumed that the framers intended the principle of separation of powers to be a cardinal principle of the Constitution. This assumption is further supported by the differing terms of office, methods of selection, internal organization, and procedures of the three branches of government. The President is elected for a four-year term by an electoral college, which in the contemplation of the framers was itself to be selected by the state legislatures and thus one step removed from popular control. Within Congress, an internal system of checks and balances was provided by the bicameral system. The Senate and the House of Representatives are not only elected from different constituencies, for different terms, but differ in their powers, internal organization, and procedures. Finally, the Constitution provides that judges of the Supreme Court and other inferior federal courts shall be appointed by the President "by and with the advice and consent of the Senate," and that they "shall hold their offices during good behavior," that is, for life.

These complex arrangements are further complicated by a fourth power—the People of the United States. For, in final analysis, the people, acting formally as voters and informally as citizens, have the last word on what the government can or should do. As citizens individually, and as members of countless groups and associations, they can bring pressure to bear on their public servants, letting them know what they want and what they will not tolerate. As voters they can hire and fire their elected public officials, including in most states the judges of the highest courts.

Although members of the United States Supreme Court and other federal judges are not elected but appointed by the President to serve "during good behavior," even they and their decisions can be influenced by the people as voters and as citizens. Their qualifications as judges are subject to review and approval by elected officers—the President and the Senate. They can even be removed from office by Congress, an elected body, through impeachment. And although their decisions are independent of "political" (that is, popular) influence or control, even these can be revised or reversed by the people or their elected representatives through the normal legislative process or by constitutional amendment. And although its original jurisdiction is protected by the Constitution, its appellate jurisdiction (the power to hear cases on appeal) is determined by legislation. Thus even the most distinctive feature of our American courts—the power to set aside acts of both the executive and the legislature as unconstitutional—is ultimately subject to final review by the fourth power in the great court of public opinion. Judges in deciding cases involving acts of Congress or the President are not unaware of this fact. No court likes to be reversed by a higher tribunal; and the Supreme Court is no exception, even though the "court of review" in these cases is the American people.

Notwithstanding these controls by the ultimate power of the people, the judicial branch of our government occupies a special position in our constitutional system. It is the immediate arbiter of conflicts between the President and Congress, between the Congress and the states, and between any branch of the government and individual citizens. If it is to judge these conflicts fairly and impartially, the judiciary must be independent of the other branches of government and of popular clamor and control. It is for this reason that federal judges are appointed to serve "during good behavior" rather than for a limited term of years.

One may well ask why judges should enjoy this special status. Why should the Supreme Court—often a mere majority of that Court—be able to nullify an act of the people's elected representatives in Congress and the White House? Isn't this a flagrant violation of the principle of majority rule? And since the Court itself is relatively immune from control either directly by the people or indirectly by the President and Congress, isn't this practice of judicial review a violation of the separation of powers and the system of checks and balances?

This is not the place to resolve that controversy. The point to be emphasized here is that the Supreme Court occupies a special position in our system of separation of powers. For it is in the courts that conflicts concerning the constitutional powers of Congress and the President—and as we shall see between the federal government and the states—are resolved, pending their final settlement in the great court of public opinion. The Court is alert to see that the President does not unconstitutionally invade or impair the powers of Congress, and that Congress in turn does not invade or usurp the powers of the President, or that both of them together do not impair the constitutional rights of the states or private persons. It is equally alert to protect its own independence of Congress and the President.

How can one explain or justify a system of government so complex and unwieldy? How can the President carry out his tremendous responsibilities if at every turn he must fight a rear-guard guerrilla campaign with over 500 members of Congress and the many political factions to which they belong? How can Congress, on the other hand, exercise "all legislative powers herein granted" if it is hampered by executive resistance to congressional requests for information and its legislation is threatened by presidential veto and judicial nullification? Does such a system increase the power and influence of special interests at the expense of the public interest, by multiplying their avenues of access to decision makers? How can a government plan for the orderly development of its human and natural resources where competing interests are able to play Congress against the President or the President against Congress or rival factions within the Senate and the House of Representatives against each other? How can a republic engaged in a cold war for survival make decisions with speed and efficiency if its decision-making process is divided against itself by a system that invites deadlock and stalemate? Does this system put the United States at a marked disadvantage when dealing with the streamlined governments of the Communist powers or even with democratic parliamentary states in which executive and legislative powers are closely integrated?

These and other questions have been raised by thoughtful students of political science, and we shall comment briefly upon some of them later on. Before doing so, however, we need to know why the wise men of 1787 deliberately incorporated in the Constitution of the United States the principle of separation of powers and its corollary system of checks and balances. Fortunately, in the debates at Philadelphia, in the *Federalist,* and elsewhere they have told us why.

We may say at the outset that the separation of powers as outlined in the Constitution was not the product of some whimsical theorist's mental aberrations. It was, on the contrary, conceived as a practical answer to one of the most perplexing of all the problems confronting democratic or republican governments. Briefly, the problem may be stated as follows: How, on the one hand, can a government based on the consent of the governed, according to the principle of majority rule, make sure that the majority will not ride roughshod over the civil and political rights of minorities and end, as so many democracies have ended, in dictatorship and a denial of individual liberty? And as a corollary question: How can a government based on majority rule make sure that its policies represent the "real" or mature will of the majority and not a transitory, ephemeral impulse of the moment behind which some special interest or interests masquerade as the majority will?

No one has stated the problem more clearly or cogently than James Madison in Paper No. X of the *Federalist.* Factions (special interests) , he says, of all kinds grow up in every civilized society. "Those who hold and those who are without property have ever formed distinct interests in society. Those who are creditors, and those who are debtors . . . a landed interest, a manufacturing interest . . . a moneyed interest, with many lesser interests . . ." appear and divide people into different classes, "actuated by different sentiments and views." Indeed, says Madison, "the regulation of these various and interfering interests forms the principal task of modern legislation and involves the spirit of party and faction in the necessary and ordinary operations of the government." In popular governments, factions of this kind can neither be prevented nor suppressed without sacrificing the freedom such governments are sworn to protect. For, says Madison, "liberty is to faction what air is to fire." Since this is the case, the evils of faction can be cured not by "removing its causes" but "by controlling its effects."

If, then, a faction "consists of less than a majority, relief is supplied by the republican principle, which enables the majority to defeat its sinister views by regular vote." Such a minority faction or interest "may clog the administration, it may [even] convulse the society [that is, Shays' rebellion]; but it will be unable to execute and mask its violence under the forms of the Constitution." But when "a majority is included in a faction, the form of popular government [majority rule] . . . enables it to sacrifice to its ruling passion or interest both the public good and the rights of other citizens. *To secure the public good and private rights against . . . such a faction, and at the same time to preserve the spirit and the form of popular government,* [our italics] is . . . the great object to which our inquiries are directed." To solve this problem, the framers hit upon two major devices: (1) the *geographical division* of power between the central government and the states in the federal system, and (2) the *functional division* or separation of powers among the legislative, executive, and judicial departments of government.

As to the first method, Madison said: "Extend the sphere [of the government, that is, its territorial extent] and you take in a greater variety of parties and interests; you make it less probable that a majority of the whole will have a common motive to invade the rights of the citizens. . . . A rage for paper money, for an abolition of debts, for an equal division of property, or for any other improper or wicked project, will be less apt to pervade the whole body of the Union than a particular member of it; in the same proportion as such a malady is more likely to taint a particular county or district than an entire State."

☆ THE DEFINITION OF TYRANNY

As to the second method for reconciling majority rule with minority rights—a *functional division* or *separation of powers*—Madison said: "The accumulation of all powers, legislative, executive, and judiciary, in the same hands, whether of one, a few, or many, and whether hereditary, self-appointed, or elective, may justly be pronounced the very definition of tyranny." One of the most ancient maxims of constitutional government is that no man, or body of men, should be a judge in his own cause, and no man, or body of men, should be the final judge of the extent of his own power. If the same man, or body of men, which makes the laws, is also charged with their execution, that is, with their application to particular cases, both of these principles are in jeopardy. If the President, for example, were not only the nation's chief executive but also had full power to legislate, without restraint from Congress or the courts, his power, for all practical purposes, would be unlimited. He himself could determine the scope of his own power, notwithstanding any limitations that might be inscribed in the written Constitution. As we shall see, it is precisely this monopoly of legislative and executive powers—without restraint from courts, congresses, or people—that has characterized the government of tyrants and dictators from Pisistratus in ancient Athens and Julius Caesar in Rome, to Mussolini, Hitler, Stalin, and lesser lights in more recent days.

The pattern of dictatorship varies considerably from place to place and time to time. The bloody regime of the Roman dictator Sulla differed from the relatively benevolent and progressive dictatorship of Julius Caesar; the Fascist dictatorship in Italy was by no means identical with the Nazi dictatorship in Germany; the dictatorship of Stalin and Khrushchev (or as they would say, the dictatorship of the proletariat) differs in many ways from the dictatorships of Franco in Spain or Salazar in Portugal. But all have in common the consolidation of legislative and executive powers in one man or body of men, no constitutional limitations or judicial review, and no accountability to the people or to their representatives. It was against this threat to constitutional government that the framers sought safeguards in the separation of powers and the system of checks and balances.

> The great security against a gradual concentration of the several powers in the same department [wrote Madison] consists in giving to those who administer each department the necessary constitutional means and personal motives to resist encroachments of the others. . . . Ambition must be made to counteract ambition. The interest of the man must be connected with the constitutional rights of place. . . . In framing a government which is to be administered by men over men, the great difficulty lies in this: *you must first enable the government to control the governed; and in the next place oblige it to control itself.* A dependence on the people is no doubt the primary control . . . but experience has taught mankind the necessity of auxiliary precautions. . . . [Among these precautions is] the constant aim to divide and arrange the several offices in such a manner as that each may be a check on the other—that the private interest of every individual may be a sentinel over the public rights. . . .[2]

☆ COUNTERVAILING POWERS—BULWARK OF FREEDOM

No one would pretend that quasi-mechanical devices, like the separation of powers, checks and balances, or even constitutional limitations enforceable in the courts, can under all circumstances withstand revolutionary forces that may be at work in any society during times of economic or social crisis. The constitutional powers of the Roman Senate

[2] *The Federalist*, No. LI, printed in the *New York Packet*, February 6, 1788.

and the executive powers of the consuls proved to be no firm bulwark against the military power of a Sulla or a Caesar. The nice balance of power and responsibility among the king, the Italian Senate, the Chamber of Deputies, and the Ministry, fortified by constitutional guarantees of civil and political rights, failed to withstand the force of Fascist Blackshirts and Mussolini's ruthless drive for supreme power. Yet even that frail structure might have stood had the Italian economy and social system not been alternating between paralysis and revolutionary upheaval. The Weimar Constitution—with its built-in path to dictatorship in Article 48—might have saved the German republic had it not been for the punitive provisions of the Versailles Treaty, mass unemployment, widespread bankruptcy, and general economic depression during the early 1930s. Even these hazards might have been surmounted had it not been for the fragmentation of political power by a multiple-party system, aggravated by proportional representation, and a progressive polarization of anticonstitutional ideology between the Nazis on the right and the Communists on the left.

Political institutions, in brief, and the constitutional power structure which they embody, do not operate and cannot be understood apart from the structure of economic power and social status in the society to which they relate. Nor can one reasonably expect institutional arrangements—including the separation of powers—to provide for those checks and balances essential to the maintenance of constitutional government without a general agreement or consensus among the major factional interests concerning basic values, decision-making procedures, and modes of political conduct. As Madison observed, these factional interests—organized labor and agriculture, business and industry, banking and finance, and so forth—are the dynamic factors in any democratic political system. It is they, operating independently and through competing political parties, which furnish the countervailing forces that make for compromise, moderation, and consensus without which the formal separation of powers or institutional checks and balances cannot function effectively. It is, however, not essential that these countervailing forces themselves be institutionalized in such a system. An effective system of checks and balances does not require, for example, that different economic and social factions be in control of the different branches of government, although historically this has often been the case, as, for example, in the unreformed British House of Lords and House of Commons. For the same factional interests, working both independently and through organized political parties, operate to set up a system of countervailing forces or checks and balances that make possible the reconciliation of majority rule with minority rights.

The framers of the Constitution were aware of this, although in general they assumed that substantially different political, economic, and social interests would predominate in the House of Representatives, the

Senate, the Presidency, and the Supreme Court. But they also assumed that the process of compromise and moderation in the search for consensus would go on *within the Congress* as well as *between* Congress and the President.

> What [asked Madison] are many of the most important acts of legislation but so many judicial determinations . . . concerning the rights of large bodies of citizens? And what are the different classes of legislators but advocates and parties to the causes which they determine? Is a law proposed concerning private debts? It is a question to which the creditors are parties on one side and the debtors on the other. Justice ought to hold the balance between them.

In establishing a government based on a separation of powers, the framers counted not only on the checks and balances among rival factions within the various branches of the government, but also upon the conflict of interest between Congress, the Presidency, and the Court. Indeed, it was assumed that whatever factional interests might be represented in the different branches of government, the institutional rivalry between them would in itself prove to be an effective check against hasty, intemperate, intolerant, or unjust laws. "Ambition [would] be made to counteract ambition" by associating the interest of congressmen and Presidents as men "with the constitutional rights of . . . place." It would thus not only promote more rational policies by facilitating extended debate and deliberation, but also would provide protection of the minority from the tyranny of an unfettered, unchecked majority.

Although the separation of powers was plainly a central feature of the Constitution, some critics demanded sharper lines of demarcation among the three branches. They complained, for example, of the "mixture" of executive, judicial, and legislative powers in the President's power to pardon, to veto, and to recommend measures to Congress. They pointed to the Senate's participation in the appointment of certain executive officers, in the ratification of treaties, and in the essentially judicial process of trial on impeachment. Were not these violations of the separation of powers as outlined by Montesquieu? Madison devoted two articles of *The Federalist* in replying to these critics. "The British constitution," he wrote, "was to Montesquieu what Homer has been to the didactic writers on epic poetry. . . . [Yet] on the slightest view of the British constitution, we must perceive that the legislative, executive, and judiciary departments are by no means totally separate and distinct from each other."

When Montesquieu wrote that "there can be no liberty where the legislative and executive powers are united in the same person or body of magistrates," or "if the power of judging be not separated from the legislative and executive powers," he did not mean that they should have no relation to each other. What he meant, argued Madison, was that "where the *whole* [our italics] power of one department is exercised by the same hands which possess the *whole* [our italics] power of another department, the fundamental principles of a free Constitution are subverted." The separation of powers as provided in the Constitution, he said, represents not a doctrinaire but a practical solution of the problem. "Unless these departments be so far connected and blended as to give to each a constitutional control over the others, the degree of separation which the nation requires, as essential to free government, can never in practice be duly maintained." This connection and blending, he maintained, is happily provided for in the Constitution.

☆ THEORY AND PRACTICE—CONFLICT AND CONSENSUS

The blending or mixture of powers offers a constant temptation for each branch of government to expand its own power at the expense of the other branches. And the ambiguous terms in which the constitutional grants of power are made invite controversy not only concerning their meaning but concerning the extent of power conferred. Article II of the Constitution places "the executive Power" of the United States in the President, as Article III clearly vests "the judicial Power . . . in one supreme Court, and in such inferior Courts as the Congress may from time to time ordain and establish." What, then, is the meaning and extent of the "executive" and the "judicial" power? May the Congress, as the legislative branch, ask the courts to perform executive or administrative functions? May Congress authorize an executive to review and veto decisions of a court without unconstitutionally invading the judicial power? May the President's power to pardon nullify the courts' power to punish?

Some of these questions arose very early in our history. In 1792 Congress provided that veterans of the Revolution seeking pensions should apply to the federal courts. If the court approved an application, it was "to certify the claim to the Secretary of War." The Secretary of War, however, could refuse to pay the claim if on review he found evidence of "imposition or mistake." That is to say, he was given power to overrule a decision of a federal court. The validity of this act was challenged in the case of a veteran named Hayburn. In asking the courts to make administrative decisions involving pensions, and in making these decisions subject to review by an administrative officer—the Secretary of War—it was argued, the Congress had violated the separation of powers in the Constitution. "Neither the legislative nor the executive branches," said the court, "can constitutionally assign to the judicial [branch] any duties but such as are properly judicial, and to be performed in a judicial manner . . . [and] neither the Secretary of War, nor any other executive officer nor even the legislature, are authorized to sit as a court of errors on the judicial acts or opinions of this court."[3]

Decisions of this kind raise almost as many problems as they solve. Congress, says the Court, cannot impose nonjudicial functions on the courts, but may it not impose judicial functions on legislative or executive officers. What is a judicial function? Isn't the President's power to pardon "for offenses against the United States" a judicial power granted by the Constitution itself and not subject to judicial review? On the other hand, since the power to pardon has been an attribute of chief executive officers for centuries, may it not therefore be regarded as an executive as well as a judicial power? Whatever one may say to these questions, it is clear that in general the President's power to pardon may nullify the courts' power to punish. But does the President's power to pardon extend to persons who have been found guilty of "contempt of court," even though the power of a court to punish a person for contempt is almost the only legal means it has to protect its own dignity and to enforce its own decisions?

In creating the inferior federal courts by the Judiciary Act of 1789, Congress had conferred power on all courts of the United States "to punish by fine or imprisonment, at the discretion of said courts, all contempts of authority in any cause or hearing before the same." Does this act imply that Congress might have withheld this power from the courts, or is the power to commit for contempt "inherent" in the courts without any special grant from Congress? In 1831 Congress limited the contempt powers of federal courts to misbehavior in the presence of the court or "so near thereto as to obstruct the administration of justice," to misbehavior of officers of the court, and to disobedience or resistance to any lawful writ, process, or order of the court. Although the Supreme Court upheld this act in 1874, Justice Field took careful pains to say that "the power to punish for contempt is inherent in all courts. . . . The moment the courts of the United States were called into existence . . . they became possessed of this power." But how far may this power extend? And may the President nullify it by his power to "grant reprieves and pardons"? If he may, does this not impair the independence, power, and dignity of the judicial branch of the government? In 1925 the Supreme Court said "no" to this question by upholding the power of the

---

[3] Actually, the Supreme Court never decided the case, because while it was pending the law was changed. But other similar cases had already come up in other federal courts "on which the Supreme Court justices then sat as trial judges." The decisions in the lower court cases were accordingly collected by the Supreme Court Reporter and printed as *Hayburn's Case*, 2 Dallas 409 (1792). Even before a final decision could be reached, Congress had changed the law to meet the Court's objections.

President to pardon a person sentenced by a federal court for contempt.[4] Does this decision not vest in the President power to review (and to set aside) a decision of a court? Can it then be reconciled with the decision in Hayburn's Case?

If Congress may not delegate executive powers to the courts, may it confer legislative or judicial powers upon the executive beyond those specified in the Constitution? When executive officers and tribunals hold hearings, and after deliberation make decisions affecting the rights and duties of other agencies or private persons, are they exercising a judicial function? Nearly every executive officer in the government, and a dozen or more great federal commissions (Interstate Commerce Commission, National Labor Relations Board, Securities and Exchange Commission, Federal Trade Commission, Federal Communications Commission, and so forth) make decisions in cases and controversies of almost infinite variety. Are they then exercising a judicial function?

And when executive officers and administrative tribunals issue rules and regulations having the force of law, are they exercising a legislative function? If so, can Congress delegate legislative power of this kind to the President or other executive officers? The answer, of course, is that it can and does delegate such powers to administrative officers, calling them *quasi-judicial* and *quasi-legislative.* Thus numerous officers and agencies of the federal government exercise not only executive power to enforce laws but quasi-judicial power to interpret the law and quasi-legislative power to make the law.

The fact is that the lines between the legislative, executive, and judicial departments of government have become increasingly thin. With a lavish hand Congress has delegated rule-making (legislative) powers to judicial, executive, and administrative agencies. The practice began very early with an act of Congress giving the federal courts power to establish rules of practice, provided only that such rules were not repugnant to the laws of the United States. When this was attacked as an unconstitutional delegation of legislative power, Chief Justice John Marshall upheld the law, saying:

> It will not be contended that Congress can delegate to the courts, or to any other tribunals, powers which are strictly and exclusively legislative. But Congress may delegate to others powers which the legislature may rightfully exercise itself. . . . The line has not been exactly drawn . . . [but it includes those laws] in which a general provision may be made, and power

4 See Ex parte *Robinson,* 19 Wallace 505 (1874) ; also Ex parte *Grossman,* 267 U.S. 87 (1925). Grossman had been sentenced for contempt in violating a court order enjoining him from selling liquor in violation of the prohibition law. The President pardoned Grossman, and the district judge refused to recognize the pardon on the ground that the President's power to pardon extends only to "offenses against the United States." A contempt of court, it was argued, is not an offense "against the United States," but against an order of the court. In upholding the President's pardon of Grossman, the Supreme Court in effect rejected this argument.

given to those who are to act under such general provisions, to fill up the details.[5]

This delegated power to "fill up the details" has been supplemented by another which gives to executive, administrative, or judicial agencies power to "determine the particular facts or the particular occasion to bring a declared general policy of Congress into operation."

Under one or the other of these theories, Congress has delegated to the President, administrative officials, or independent boards and commissions, power to determine tariff rates; to fix prices, wages, and hours; to formulate codes of fair competition for business and industry; to regulate and if necessary prohibit the transportation of oil in interstate commerce; to determine "excessive profits"; to renegotiate war contracts; and so forth. "In such instances," said the Court in an early case, "Congress declares the public policy . . . and charges an administrative body with the duty of ascertaining . . . from time to time, the facts which bring into play the principles established by Congress. . . . [Thus] it converts legislation from a static into a dynamic condition."[6] The general provisions or "principles established by Congress" are often so vague and ambiguous as to impose only the most general limitations upon the legislative powers of executive agencies. Such phrases as "fair competition," "the public interest," "fair and reasonable rates," the "public interest, convenience and necessity" have served as the general legislative policies for which delegated legislation is to "fill in the details" or "ascertain the facts which bring into play the principles established by Congress."

Delegation of legislative power in the United States has not gone so far as it has in England. Nor has the Supreme Court been wholly compliant in approving the transfer of legislative power from Congress to the executive. "Recognition of the necessity and validity of such provisions," the Court has said, "and the wide range of administrative authority which has developed by means of them, cannot be allowed to obscure the limitations of the authority to delegate, if our constitutional system is to be maintained." Accordingly, the Court held the code-making authority delegated to the President by the National Industrial Recovery Act to be "an unconstitutional delegation of legislative power."[7]

In spite of an occasional setback of this kind, the process of delega-

---

5 *Wayman* v. *Southard*, 10 Wheaton 1 (1825).

6 See *Sears and Co.* v. *Federal Trade Commission*, 258 Federal 307. See also *Field* v. *Clark*, 143 U.S. 649 (1892); *Hampton and Co.* v. *United States*, 276 U.S. 394 (1928); *Schechter* v. *United States*, 295 U.S. 495 (1935); *Panama Refining Co.* v. *Ryan*, 293 U.S. 388 (1935); *Lichter* v. *United States*, 334 U.S. 742 (1948); *Yakus* v. *United States*, 321 U.S. 414 (1944).

7 *Schechter Poultry Corp.* v. *United States*, 295 U.S. 495 (1935). One justice characterized this code-making authority as "delegation run riot." The Court had previously held the oil control provisions of the same act to be unconstitutional in the case of *Panama Refining Co.* v. *Ryan*, 293 U.S. 388 (1935).

tion has continued, until, as Professor Haines has observed, "among the chief law making agencies in both England and the United States . . . are administrative officers, boards and commissions."[8] In both the United States and England, delegated legislation has long since outstripped the formal legislative acts of Congress and Parliament—both in volume and in impact on the people.

How can all this be reconciled with the principles of separation of powers and checks and balances? And what shall we say of the expanding role of the President not only as chief executive but as chief legislative officer? The Constitution requires the President to recommend to the Congress "such measures as he shall judge necessary and expedient." This has come to mean not only general recommendations but, as is increasingly the case, detailed legislative proposals in the form of special messages and draft bills. Nearly half of the legislation before Congress and most of the important bills come from the executive. How are we to reconcile this with the constitutional provision that reads: "All legislative Powers herein granted shall be vested in a Congress of the United States"?

These are troublesome questions and have caused no end of tension between the White House and "the Hill" (Congress). Time and again, members of both the House of Representatives and the Senate have raised the cry of executive usurpation and have protested against the alleged Presidential inclination to make Congress a "mere rubber stamp." "Congress may [as well] go home," said Senator McClay in the very first Congress to meet under the Constitution. "Mr. Hamilton is all powerful and fails in nothing he attempts."

During the debate on the Pure Food and Drug Act in June, 1906, Senator Isidor Raynor, with biting sarcasm, commented on the steady encroachment of President Theodore Roosevelt upon the legitimate powers of Congress.

> Here we are [said he] day after day struggling with questions of constitutional law, as if we really had anything to do with their settlement, laboring under the vain illusion that we had the right to legislate; that we are an independent branch of the government . . . and the Executive another, each with its separate and well defined distinctions . . . while [all the time] the President was at work dominating the legislative will . . . assuming legislative rights to a greater extent than he could possibly do if he were sitting here as a member of this body; dismembering the Constitution . . . [and] adopting a system that practically blends and unites legislative and executive functions.[9]

8 See Charles G. Haines in *American Political Science Review* (October, 1932). One example from England will suffice. The Rating and Valuation Act of 1925 provided that any administrative order issued under the act "may modify the provisions of this Act, so far as may appear to the Minister necessary or expedient. . . ."

9 Quoted in Edward S. Corwin, *The President: Office and Powers*, 1787–1957 (New York: New York University Press, 1957), p. 426 n.

The tug of war between Congress, the President, and the courts has by no means always resulted in the expansion of presidential power. Congress too has sought to enlarge the sphere of its own authority at the expense of the President, as the framers of the Constitution feared that it would.

From Madison to Jackson, the Presidency functioned under the shadow—almost under the thumb—of the congressional caucus by which successive Presidents were nominated and virtually elected. "For twenty years," says Professor Corwin, "the plan rejected by the framers of having the President chosen by Congress was substantially in operation. . . ." Even after the power of the congressional caucus was broken, congressional interference in executive affairs continued. A congressional Committee on the Conduct of the War sought to tell Lincoln what generals he was to appoint, what military strategy he should employ, and in general how he should carry on the war to preserve the Union. In 1876, through the appointment of an extraconstitutional Electoral Commission, Congress went behind the electoral vote in the Hayes–Tilden contest and actually excluded from office the presidential candidate who had received a majority of the votes.

Congress has used its control of the purse strings not only to share in the determination of basic public policy, but to determine details of personnel policy and administrative organization and procedure, which should more properly be left to the President. Several congressional committees and subcommittees have used their powers of investigation and surveillance to become virtually management committees for various executive agencies. Through the custom of senatorial courtesy, and by special riders on appropriation bills, Congress has encroached upon the President's power of appointment.

Shall we say, then, that the separation of powers and the check and balance system have failed? First of all, it would seem clear that under the jealous eye and the restraining hand of Congress and the Court, it is not likely that an American President will become a tyrant after the manner of Mussolini, Hitler, or Stalin. Nor can Congress transform itself into an omnipotent oligarchy so long as the President and the Supreme Court retain their independence and their powers. According to its protagonists, the separation of powers does something more than this. It interposes a salutary delay in the process of government that facilitates debate and thus helps to increase the role of reason in the determination of policy, and to increase the probability that legislation will represent a more stable consensus of the national will and purpose.

Critics of the system see it in a somewhat different light, as a cumbersome, unnecessarily complex and unwieldy form of government. The system invites unnecessary delay, deadlock, and impotence. Nor does it promote debate and deliberation. On the contrary, they say, it promotes intrigue, political pressure, backscratching, wirepulling, and logrolling by private factional interests at the expense of the general welfare. The separation of powers and checks and balances, it is said, make responsible government virtually impossible.

> We arbitrarily separate the legislature and the executive [said Henry Hazlitt]. We choose each in such a way that there is no assurance that they will want the same policies—indeed often in such a way that it is almost certain that they will want different policies. Congress can prevent the President from doing what he wishes but cannot make him do what it wishes unless its desired policy is almost unanimous. . . . The result is hopelessly to confuse the public regarding whom it can hold responsible for a policy or for failure to adopt a policy.[10]

And these evils are compounded when rival parties are in control of different branches of the government. Even when both Congress and the Presidency are controlled by the same party, one can never be sure that policies agreed to by large legislative majorities and approved by the President will pass muster with the Supreme Court.

The traditional tension and rivalry between the various branches of government is a source of embarrassment and uncertainty, not only in the formulation of domestic policy but in the delicate field of foreign relations. The President may negotiate a treaty, or agree with friendly powers upon a given policy, only to have the Senate refuse its approval or the Congress withhold the funds necessary to carry the policy into effect. Chairmen of congressional committees—with the immunity born of their independent status—can badger and bully Secretaries of State and other members of the Cabinet, issue statements on matters for which they cannot be held responsible, and generally present a picture of chaos and confusion to the world.

Finally, it is said, the separation of powers is an ideal instrument of reactionaries seeking to prevent orderly social change. "There is no enthusiasm for checks and balances among those who are impatient to create a new social order," said Professor Finer. It is not surprising, therefore, that the principle of separation of powers has not been widely adopted in other countries. Most of the constitutions adopted in the last century have taken as their model not the government of the United States but the government of Great Britain, which is distinguished not by a *separation of powers* but by an *integration of powers*.

The cabinet system, it is said, with its integration of legislative and executive powers, provides a more flexible, efficient, and democratic form of government than one based on the separation of powers. The direct confrontation of executive and legislative officers in Parliament facilitates discussion, raises the quality of debate, and makes for greater rationality in the process of government. It thus strengthens the democratic principle of majority rule and political responsibility.

[10] Henry Hazlitt, *A New Constitution Now* (New York: McGraw-Hill, 1942), p. 277.

Many distinguished American scholars and statesmen, for whom Woodrow Wilson was a major spokesman, had these misgivings about the American system. In his classic analysis of what he called our *Congressional Government*, he argued strongly for something like the British cabinet system. The President would choose his Cabinet from Congress and they would continue to participate in the legislative process. If any major part of the President's program were defeated in Congress, he and his Cabinet would resign. A less drastic reform is the proposal to give members of the President's cabinet seats in Congress, not as voting members but as participants in debate.[11] Professor Corwin has suggested a joint legislative-executive cabinet to bridge the gap created by the principle of separation of powers.

It is worth noting that none of these proposals, short of the adoption of a cabinet government, would materially affect the system. To bring members of the Cabinet into Congress as nonvoting visitors would accomplish little. Even now they appear before congressional committees where the real work of Congress is done. It is not likely that the President would welcome strong, wise, and eloquent subordinates in Congress competing with him for public attention and support. And unless they were strong, wise, and eloquent, their appearance in Congress might be a source of weakness, not strength. As for a joint legislative-executive Cabinet, this in effect is now operative in the almost continuous conferences between the President and the Big Four in Congress—the speaker of the House, the Vice-President, the majority leader of the House and the majority leader of the Senate. Finally, it is worth pointing out that the President's Cabinet has ceased to be a major factor in determining policy and has lost a good deal of its luster and power to other executive agencies.

Short of a cabinet system, more drastic reforms might include (1) the abolition of judicial review to remove the threat of a Supreme Court veto on legislative or executive acts; (2) the election of the House of Representatives for four-year terms corresponding to the term of the President, to make Congress more responsive to presidential leadership; (3) a constitutional amendment to enable the President to dissolve the House of Representatives when his program was defeated in Congress, and in such a contingency, the President, too, would run for re-election to a new term; and (4) the development of a more unified, disciplined, and responsible two-party system to bridge the gap between Congress and

11 There is some precedent for this in the early practice of Jefferson, Hamilton, and Knox, as members of Washington's Cabinet, appearing in Congress to "report . . . explain . . . [and] give information." Even today the Secretary of the Treasury is required by the organic act of that Department to "give information to either branch of the legislature, in person or in writing, as may be required." His annual report is addressed not only to the President but also to the Speaker of the House of Representatives and the President pro tempore of the Senate.

the Presidency. All but the last of these measures would require constitutional amendments; and discussion of them had best be deferred.

Whatever may be its weaknesses, it is well to remember that under our present system the American nation has grown from a tiny outpost on the edge of a great wilderness to become the most powerful nation on earth. Except for the signal failure of the Civil War, the Constitution, with all its built-in sources of indecision and conflict, has served the American people well. If it has delayed orderly social change and hampered the development of great leadership, it cannot be said to have prevented either the one or the other. Speed in decision making is often a virtue, and when the three branches of our government "move in concert"—as in emergency they almost invariably do—the Constitution makes this possible. But wisdom and a basic consensus upon major public policies are also important factors in a well-governed community, and these are often purchased at the price of speed.

Conflict is inherent in the process of democratic government—conflict among rival factions and interests concerning what is best for them and what will best promote the public good. Are we sure that the separation of powers in the structure of a state which serves a pluralistic society does not contribute substantially to social change in an orderly transition from conflict to consensus?

The *power to govern* is the power to determine the basic conditions of our common life. "Power," said Lord Acton, "tends to corrupt; absolute power corrupts absolutely." How to use the *power to govern* and at the same time *govern power* to make sure that it remains *man's servant and not his master,* is the basic problem.

THE FEDERAL SYSTEM

☆ *FEDERALISM, AN AMERICAN INVENTION*

Had the framers of the Constitution been asked to name the most important feature of the new government established under that document, they would no doubt have pointed to the federal system. For it was to provide against centrifugal forces at work in the country under the Articles of Confederation that they had come together in Philadelphia.

One need not accept the gloomy picture of those times drawn by John Marshall or the historian John Fiske to agree that the framers of the Constitution had in mind, not primarily a reaffirmation of the rights of the several states, but of a new and vigorous central government against what they saw as forces of dissension, if not disintegration in the new nation. "It is the State systems," said Henry Knox in 1787, "that will prevent our being a nation."

Not everyone shared these sentiments, but all, without exception, agreed on the urgent need for "a more perfect Union," if the new nation was not to decline and die, or become the victim of the imperial ambitions of France, Spain, and Great Britain. The problem was a familiar one: how to organize political power to govern effectively a vast and expanding territory. Without a strong central authority, the separate states and territories might fall away, one by one, becoming independent petty nations, easy prey to the great powers even then seeking to extend their dominion in the new world. And without local self-government in the constituent states, not only might resentment breed rebellion but centralized rule might sacrifice the freedom and flexibility indispensable to an expanding and dynamic society.

They knew that however feasible a strong unitary system might be in a state of small area and population, it would not fit the needs of a nation of continental dimensions with the then existing means of transportation and communication.

The framers knew what they were doing. The major theme of the debates at Philadelphia, in the ratifying conventions, and in the *Federalist* papers was precisely the reconciliation of a strong centralized authority in the Union with the greatest possible freedom for decision making in the constituent states. Nearly 40 of the 85 *Federalist* papers are devoted to this problem. The framers knew the history of the great empires and confederacies of the past. In *Federalist* paper *No. 18,* Hamilton and Madison discussed the empires, leagues and confederacies of Ancient Greece and Rome. In *No. 19,* they recounted the examples of Germany, Poland, and the Swiss Confederacy. And in *No. 20,* they analyzed the structure of power in the United Netherlands.

They understood that on the record, these confederacies had all succumbed to one of two fatal maladies: either they dissolved into a number of separate and independent political sovereignties, or they developed into highly centralized, unitary states, often too top-heavy—at least with the available means of transportation and communication—to administer their far-flung provinces.

How alert the framers were to the problems involved can be indicated by the briefest mention of some of the topics to which they gave extended time and attention: the relation of geographical and ethnic homogeneity to national union; the advantages of a centralized control over foreign relations, national defense, trade, and commerce; the enforcement of public and private contracts, taxation, and economic growth. They also looked upon a federal union as a necessary check on faction—particularly in a nation of great territorial extent. In a smaller society, Madison argued, with a unitary government political conflicts would become polarized between the few and the many, the rich and the poor. Inevitably this class conflict would result in alternating periods of anarchy and tyranny as civil war gave way to the human hunger for order and authority.

A federal system could also help to reconcile republican government by majority rule with the rights of minorities. In short, the framers sought what Calhoun later more systematically described: a government in which numerical majorities as represented in the House of Representatives would combine with concurrent majorities of states as represented in the United States Senate to insure "the public good and private rights" which they conceived to be the goals of all well-constructed political communities.

Or, to put it another way, the countervailing powers of President and Congress would be matched by the countervailing powers of the states and the central government. Ambition would be set against ambition to insure a free pluralistic and dynamic society. The peaceful arbiters of the system would be the Supreme Court and the rather complex process of constitutional amendment in which both numerical and concurrent majorities would participate.

The framers knew, as the writings of Madison so clearly indicate, that particular factions or interests would fix upon one or more of these countervailing powers—now to promote, now to oppose, particular public policies. To be sure, Congress and the President, the central government, and the states would generate their own interest in the power struggle. These conflicts themselves would in most cases also reflect conflicts between rival economic and social interests which used these instruments of political power for their own ends. Thus it is that in contests over the allocation of powers between the central government and the states, before the Supreme Court, the parties in conflict are only rarely state and federal governments, but rather private parties themselves or private parties and a state or federal agency.

In discussing federalism, we need to keep this always in mind, or we shall miss the full significance of the power struggle in its modern dress. The pattern changes not because the formal allocation of powers in the Constitution has changed, but because the parties and interests at issue both in the Congress, the states, and in the Court have changed. When, for example, in 1886 the Wabash, St. Louis and Pacific Railway Co. protested against the regulation of its rates by the State of Illinois, on the ground that such regulation was an unconstitutional burden on interstate commerce, it was not because the Wabash Railway wanted the central government to regulate its rates rather than the State of Illinois, but because it did not want its rates to be regulated at all.

Contests in which problems of federalism are thus involved are frequently not contests over whether the state or the federal government should have jurisdiction, but whether any government, federal or state, should act. For example, those who argued against the constitutionality of state laws establishing maximum hours and minimum wages for labor argued just as strenuously against federal legislation of this kind.

There are occasions, of course, when, for a variety of reasons, individuals, corporations, or other interests prefer to be subject to one jurisdiction rather than to another—now preferring the state and at another time the federal government. Much depends upon the policy being prepared and its differential effect upon the individuals and groups to which it applies. To some it will represent an act of indulgence, lucrative contracts, subsidies or subventions; to others it will mean deprivation, new taxes, new regulatory burdens. These factors rather than abstract questions of political theory—of centralization versus decentralization—are more likely to affect the posture that people take toward the exercise of power by the states or the central government.

This is not to say that abstract questions of political theory are of negligible importance in the study of federalism. On the contrary, they are of central concern to all who believe that the greatest possible decentralization of decision making in government is essential to a free pluralistic society. The practical problem then becomes one of deciding what kind of decisions, affecting what kind of interests or behavior, can or should be made, and at what level of government.

The answers to questions of this kind will vary with time and circumstance. They will not be the same in an age of jet propulsion and instantaneous communication as in an age of the canal boat and the pony express. That is why, as Woodrow Wilson said, "The question of the relations of the States to the Federal Government . . . cannot be settled by the opinion of any one generation. . . ." That is why the ideas of John C. Calhoun or Jefferson Davis or Thomas Jefferson, however reasonable they may have been in the nineteenth century, are not necessarily a sure guide to public policy in the late twentieth century.

However the pattern of decision making may change with time and circumstance, the central problem remains, that is, the reconciliation of centralized authority with the greatest possible freedom of decision making at the state and local level. This is the central problem for which a federal system offers a better solution than does a unitary state, a league, or a confederation.

This is not to say that a federal system is a better structure at all times and under all circumstances. A small state with a homogeneous population, without historic regional or sectional loyalties, and with a well-developed system of transportation and communication might well find a unitary government to be a better instrument for maintaining its national security and independence and promoting the welfare and freedom of its people.

Even a small state however torn by linguistic, religious, or cultural differences may find federalism a more viable system for making and enforcing political decisions than one more highly centralized. Switzerland, with its variety of languages and religions, comes to mind. Large states having extensive territories and certain well-defined regions with which a variety of political, religious, or cultural traditions have been historically associated will find the road to union long, rough, and hard. In these circumstances political federation or confederation is likely to be a condition of survival. One thinks, for example, of Canada, the United States, the USSR, and Australia.

It is circumstances such as these that explain the long and painful struggle of Central Europe to achieve some measure of political unity. The idea of a unified or federated Europe is an old one. Roman emperors and Holy Roman Emperors, kings of France and Germany, conquering heroes like Napoleon, philosophers like Immanuel Kant, and many others have dreamed of a European federation. But the uneven distribution of resources and population, and historic religious and cultural conflicts with deeply ingrained, and even blood-drenched political loyalties, have conspired against it—even when, with the advent of the Industrial Revolution, it became clear that the full utilization of science and technology in production and distribution required mass markets, uniform or at least stable currencies, and free and equitable access to the natural resources of the Continent.

Since 1945, partly as a result of the Marshall Plan, but also in response to external pressures from the USSR and the Communist states of Eastern Europe and under the wise leadership of men like Robert Schumann, Jean Monnet in France, Paul-Henri Spaak in Belgium, and other statesmen in West Germany, Italy, and the Netherlands, there has begun to emerge the outline of what may become a federal union of European states which can transform the face of that Continent and profoundly affect the history of the world. If the Treaty of Rome of March, 1957, and the formal establishment of the European Economic Community in January, 1958, are not to be compared with our own Annapolis Convention and the subsequent Constitutional Convention in Philadelphia, at least they represent steps in that direction.

☆ FEDERALISM IN TRANSITION

The Federal Model

The federal system, which in its modern form is largely an American invention, has been the only feature of our Constitution that has been widely copied. Separation of powers, checks and balances, and those other distinctively American institutions, the Presidency and judicial review, have not commended themselves to other countries to anything like the same extent. In Europe—Austria, the USSR, Switzerland, West Germany, and Yugoslavia; in Asia—Australia, India, Pakistan; in Africa— the Congo, Ethiopia, Nigeria, and South Africa; in South America— Argentina, Brazil, Venezuela; and in North America—Canada and Mexico, all have governments that in form, at least, are federal. And now even the sovereign states of Central Europe have taken the first steps toward a European federation. Nor is this the whole story. In the West Indies, and among the new states of Asia and Africa, numerous plans for federation are under discussion, including a federal union of all African states.[1] Within the United States itself some form of federation is being urged as the most viable form of political organization for the great metropolitan areas in which a majority of the American people now live. It may not be wholly romantic to assume, or at least to hope, that an inter-American federation of the Western Hemisphere, tied closely to a

[1] See *Federalism and Economic Growth in Underdeveloped Countries, a Symposium* (New York: Oxford University Press, 1961).

European federation, and perhaps to other great regional federations, may offer a stronger basis for a revised and renewed United Nations than the hundred or more separate, sovereign, and independent states that now make up its membership.

No one can pretend that every experiment in federal government has been an unqualified success. In Indonesia, Malaysia, Vietnam, and Pakistan, federalism has thus far been more of a dream than a reality; and in Brazil and Argentina, "American federalism, in an alien environment, quickly gave way to centralization and dictatorship." Even the American system, under the harsh pressures of irreconcilable interests, had to go through the fires of civil war to survive. What then are the conditions and attributes of a federal system as distinguished from unitary or confederal systems?

A confederal system implies a rather loose union of more or less independent political units, in which even the limited powers of the central government are dependent upon the member states for their origin and exercise. Our own Articles of Confederation was a model. By unitary systems we refer, of course, to those in which power is highly centralized and in which other political subdivisions are subordinate to, derive their power from, and in large measure depend upon, the central government for their existence. The United Kingdom, France, and Italy are examples. So, too, are the American state governments in their relation to counties, cities, and other political subdivisions.

Professor Kenneth Wheare has outlined six factors that have been important in the development of federal systems. These include:

1. A feeling of insecurity [among the states concerned] arising from outside threat or pressure.
2. The desire to be independent of foreign [or colonial] powers.
3. The hope of some general economic advantage.
4. Some form of political association [among the participating states] . . . prior to federal union. . . .
5. Geographical neighborhood [proximity] of the federating states.
6. Similarity of political institutions of the federating states.[2]

Among other important factors one should, of course, mention a considerable degree of economic or functional interdependence, vigorous and intelligent political leadership, and a fair degree of consensus on basic political values. These conditions have impelled independent states to join together; other conditions have impelled them to retain a considerable measure of independence and hence to prefer a federal to a unitary system. Among these one may note a tradition of political independence, important differences of economic resources or interests, geographical obstacles to centralized decision making, and differences of

2 Kenneth S. Wheare, *Federal Government* (3rd ed.; London: Oxford University Press, 1953) , ch. III. See also *Federalism and Economic Growth, op. cit.,* p. 23.

culture, race, ethnic origin, religion, nationality, and social institutions.

If these are some of the conditions out of which federalism may be said to emerge, what then are the attributes of a viable federal system? Among these, the following would seem to be important if not in every case essential.

1. An allocation of political power between the central government and the constituent governments which cannot be changed by either the central or the constituent governments acting alone.
2. The powers allocated to the central and the constituent governments must be substantial and significant, and not merely "trivial."
3. Both the central government and the constituent governments must be able, each within its own jurisdiction, to make and enforce its own laws upon the inhabitants.
4. Considerable freedom must remain both with the central government and the constituent governments to modify their own political institutions, policies, and procedures.
5. The constituent governments must be regarded as legally and politically equal, vis-à-vis each other and in their legal relations with the central government.[3]

In summary, federalism is a system contrived to reconcile the need for centralized control of certain functions with the desire for local, state, or regional control of other functions.

As in other models, not all the features of a model federal system are always found in the federal governments of the world. Consider, for example, the first principle: the allocation of power between the central government and the constituent governments cannot be changed by either acting alone. In Canada this is not the case, for the Dominion government may, in fact, and does, change the allocation of powers without the formal consent of the provincial governments. Moreover, Canadian provincial governments have only those powers delegated to them. That is, Canadian federalism is a kind of inverted American federalism. In Canada the central government and not the state has all powers not delegated. Nevertheless, the powers delegated or contracted are real and substantial.

A similar situation exists in other federal systems such as South Africa, the Federal Republic of West Germany, India, and Indonesia. Even, as in the United States, where theoretically the allocation of powers in the Constitution can be changed only by formal amendment with the federal government and the states acting together, the dynamics of change often disregard these formal procedures. Indeed, formal amendment has been the least important force for change. It is, in fact, the President and Congress—subject, only when challenged, to review by the Supreme Court—that have been the major instruments of change.

[3] See Arthur Macmahon (ed.), *Federalism—Mature and Emergent* (Garden City, N.Y.: Doubleday, 1955).

The respective powers of the state and central governments have changed, not so much by formal amendment as by acts of Congress and by judicial interpretation. Since the Supreme Court itself is a branch of the central government, it is not an exaggeration to say that the federal government, acting alone, can change the formal allocation of power between itself and the states. "Whatever is enacted by Congress," said the late Howard Lee McBain, "and approved by the Supreme Court is valid. . . . There is no limitation imposed on the national government which Congress, the President and the Supreme Court, acting [together] . . . may not legally override . . . the [central] government as a whole is clearly a government of unlimited powers; for by [judicial] interpretation it stakes out its own boundaries."[4]

The fact that the allocation of power between the federal government and the states is, in fact, made by the federal government itself— that is, by Congress and the President and a majority of Supreme Court judges—would seem at first glance to make the government of the United States, in effect, a unitary state. But to assume this would be to confuse form with substance. The centrifugal force of the fifty states in our system, and their continued strength and vitality, depend not alone on the formal provisions of the Constitution. Equally important at least is the jealous regard for their own power and independence on the part of state governments, state-oriented political parties, and hundreds of state-centered farm organizations, and business, professional, labor, social, educational, and cultural interests. Even Congressmen and Senators, although officers of the central government and dependent on the central government for their pay and perquisites, have their roots, and more often than not their basic loyalties, in the states or the districts they represent.[5]

---

[4] See Howard Lee McBain, *The Living Constitution* (New York: Macmillan, 1941) .

[5] The following table indicates the extent of these local roots for congressional leaders prior to their transfer to Washington:

Offices Held	Percent of Congressional Leaders	
	1903	*1963*
Any state or local office	75	64
Elective local offices	55	46
State legislature	47	30
Appointive state office	12	10
Governor	16	9

SOURCE: Adapted from Samuel P. Huntington, "Congressional Responses to the Twentieth Century," in D. B. Truman, ed., *The Congress and America's Future* (American Assembly; Englewood Cliffs, N.J.: Prentice-Hall, © 1965), p. 14. Used by permission of Prentice-Hall, Inc.

Since the Civil War every President, except Grant and Hoover, and a large majority of Supreme Court judges have served an apprenticeship in state or local government.

Not even Supreme Court judges and Presidents are immune from the influence of a cultural heritage that gives high priority to state and local self-government. By the time they reach the high eminence of the Presidency or the Court they have been quite thoroughly indoctrinated in the philosophy of a federalism in which centralized power is suspect and decentralization almost a synonym for political wisdom and virtue. It is a combination of these built-in, informal restraints rather than the formal structure of power that enables federalism to function so effectively in American society.

The second principle, that the powers allocated must be substantial and not trivial, admits of wide differences as to what these terms mean. Certainly in the American system the powers of both the central government and the states are substantial, as we shall see.

The third principle, that both central and constituent governments must be able to make and enforce laws directly upon the inhabitants who reside within their territorial limits, is less ambiguous. As Justice Waite said in *United States* v. *Cruikshank* (1876) :

> The people of the United States resident within any state are subject to two governments. One State and one National. . . . They are established for different purposes and have separate jurisdictions. . . . It may sometimes happen that a person is amenable to both jurisdictions for one and the same act. . . . [But this] is the natural consequence of a citizenship which owes allegiance to two sovereignties and claims protection from both. . . .

Freedom of both state and central governments to determine the form and structure of their own political institutions and policies is another component of our federal model. The value of a federal system, it is argued, in allowing for political experimentation is likely to be sacrificed if all members are forced into a single institutional mold. Not every state will want to have the same kind of school system, public health and recreation programs, penal institution, or marriage and divorce laws. Not all will want, or need, the same system of courts or of state and local government. Within broad limits consistent with basic human values, and given minimum uniform policies to which the whole society is dedicated, there should be ample scope for experimentation.

In the American system this principle is recognized in the wide variety of political institutions and public policies that exist side by side, from Mississippi to New York and from Maine to California. The provision in Section 4 of Article IV that "The United States shall guarantee to every state . . . a Republican Form of Government . . ." imposes no serious restraint upon the freedom of the states to adopt and to change their own constitutions and laws. Although the Constitution, especially the commerce clause, and the Fourteenth Amendment as interpreted by the Supreme Court, imposes limitations upon the states, even these restraints have been relaxed to expand the states' "police powers" to provide for the health, welfare, and safety of their inhabitants.

The final criterion of a model federal state, namely legal equality among the constituent members of the union, is recognized in the American system in a number of ways of which equal representation in the United States Senate is the most obvious. Moreover, this feature of the Constitution is presumably unamendable, since the amending clause itself provides that "no State without its consent shall be deprived of its equal suffrage in the Senate." To insure equality among the states vis-à-vis each other, Article IV requires each state to give "Full Faith and Credit to the Acts, Records, and judicial Proceedings of every other State," and requires each state to render up fugitives from justice upon demand of the state from which they fled. Moreover, once a state has been admitted to the Union, it enjoys full legal equality with every other state, including the original thirteen states. As the Court said in *Texas* v. *White,* ours is "an indestructible union of indestructible states."[6] Hence the Constitution provides that no "new States shall be formed . . . within the Jurisdiction of any other State; nor any State be formed by the Junction of two or more States, or Parts of States" without the consent of the states concerned.

Although states are legally equal, they are not politically equal; nor are they equal in terms of population, natural resources, or political power. Indeed it is precisely these differences, together with differences of culture and tradition, that give the American federal system many of its most fascinating and dynamic qualities. These differences also create problems of mounting dimensions in a society committed as America is to the basic goals of freedom and equality. It is at this point—where the freedom of each state to go its own way conflicts with the overriding goals of the nation—that much of the tension and conflict within our federal system occurs. It is at this point also that the so-called supremacy clause of Article VI has its greatest significance. For although the states are legally and constitutionally equal vis-à-vis one another, they cannot be said to stand on a plane of equality with the government of the United States.

"This Constitution," says Article VI, "and the Laws of the United States which shall be made in Pursuance thereof; and all Treaties made, or which shall be made, under the Authority of the United States, shall be the supreme Law of the Land; and the Judges in every State shall be bound thereby, any Thing in the Constitution or Laws of any State to the Contrary notwithstanding."

Where the constitutionally legitimate powers of the central government come in conflict with powers claimed by a state, it is the state and

6 *Texas* v. *White,* 7 Wall. 700 (1869).

not the central government that must yield. The nub of the problem of federal versus state power in the United States lies in determining the nature and extent of the powers delegated to the United States by the Constitution, since in the language of the Tenth Amendment all powers not so delegated are "reserved to the States respectively, or to the people," except, of course, for those powers forbidden to the states by the Constitution itself. In determining this allocation of powers, incidentally, the Tenth Amendment itself is of no help, since it merely asserts the obvious principle that what is not delegated is reserved or denied. It is important to note, however, that under the Constitution these residual powers are reserved not only to the states as political entities but to the people.

The Constitutional Allocation of Powers

It is easy enough to outline the distribution of powers between federal and state governments as set forth in the Constitution. A standard classification runs something like this:

I. *Powers falling within the exclusive jurisdiction of the federal government*
   A. To declare war and presumably to make peace.
   B. To make treaties, appoint ambassadors, and otherwise carry on the foreign relations of the United States.
   C. To provide, and to command, the Army and Navy of the United States and the State militia when "called into the actual service of the United States."
   D. To establish uniform rules of Bankruptcy and Naturalization "throughout the United States."
   E. "To regulate Commerce with foreign Nations and among the several States," including the right to lay and collect duties on imports.
   F. "To Coin Money, regulate the Value thereof, and of foreign Coin, and fix the Standard of Weights and Measures."
II. *Powers reserved for the exclusive jurisdiction of the states (that is, not delegated to the federal government)*
   A. Power to determine the form and structure of state and local units of government and their powers, subject only to the limitations set forth in the Constitution.
   B. To enact laws relating to wills, torts (personal wrongs arising under the Constitution and laws of the state), domestic relations, contracts concerning transactions based on the state constitution or laws, trusts, etc., affecting property, real and personal, and other transactions of a purely intrastate character.

C. To enact laws for the health, safety, and morals of the people living within the state, that is, the police powers.[7]

D. To make laws to license or otherwise regulate purely intrastate business and commerce.

E. To borrow money on the credit of the state.

III. *Powers that may be exercised by both the federal government and the states (that is, concurrent powers)*

A. To lay and collect taxes on property, income, sales and other transactions, except on imports and exports which may be imposed only by or with the consent of the federal government.

B. To enact laws for the suppression, prevention, and punishment of crimes.

C. To enact laws providing for inspection and quarantine of persons and property—to protect the health and security of the state and the United States.

IV. *Powers denied to the federal government*

A. To lay a tax "on Articles exported from any State."

B. To give preference "by any Regulation of Commerce or Revenue" to the ports of one state over those of another.

C. To suspend the writ of habeas corpus "unless when in Cases of Rebellion or Invasion the public Safety may require it."

D. To make any law "respecting an establishment of religion, or prohibiting the free exercise thereof; or abridging the freedom of speech, or of the press; or the right of the people peaceably to assemble, and to petition the Government for a redress of grievances." Other restraints are set forth in the Bill of Rights.

V. *Powers denied to the states by the Constitution of the United States*

A. To "enter into any Treaty, Alliance, or Confederation; grant Letters of Marque and Reprisal; coin Money; emit Bills of Credit; make any Thing but gold and silver Coin a Tender in Payment of Debts; pass any Bill of Attainder; ex post facto Law, or Law impairing the obligation of Contracts, or grant any Title of Nobility."

B. To "keep Troops or Ships of War in Time of Peace, enter into any Agreement or Compact with another State, or with a foreign Power, or engage in War unless actually invaded, or in such imminent Danger as will not admit of delay."

C. To make or "enforce any law which shall abridge the privileges or immunities of citizens of the United States . . . [or] deprive

---

[7] Theoretically the central government under the Constitution has no "police powers" in this sense—except in the District of Columbia, the territories of the United States, and other areas subject to the exclusive jurisdiction of the United States. In fact, however, it exercises extensive "police powers" arising from its power to tax, pay the debts of the United States, regulate commerce, and enact laws "necessary and proper" to carry out other powers granted in the Constitution.

any person of life, liberty, or property without due process of law; nor deny to *any person* within its jurisdiction the equal protection of the laws."

    D. To deny any citizen the right to vote because of race or sex.

    E. By judicial interpretation the states are also restrained by all the provisions of the First Amendment in the same manner as is the Congress.

VI. *Powers denied to both the federal and the state governments*

    A. To enact bills of attainder or ex post facto laws.

    B. To abridge freedom of religious worship, speech, press, or assembly.

    C. To deprive any person of life, liberty, or property, without due process of law, or take property without just compensation.

    D. To grant titles of nobility.

In addition to the powers conferred and denied, the Constitution sets forth certain duties and obligations which the federal government and the states are required to respect and to perform.

For the states these duties and obligations are:

    1. To grant full faith and credit "to the Public Acts, Records, and judicial Proceedings of every other State."

    2. To insure to citizens of each state "all Privileges and Immunities of Citizens in the several States."

    3. To deliver up, "on Demand of the executive Authority of the State from which he fled" a person "charged in any State with Treason, Felony or other Crime."

For the federal government these duties and obligations are:

To guarantee "to every State . . . a Republican Form of Government, and . . . protect each of them against Invasion; and on Application of the Legislature, or of the Executive (when the Legislature cannot be convened) against domestic Violence."

Such a catalogue of powers, however, is of limited utility. Scarcely a word or phrase of the language used is so clear and unambiguous as to require no further elaboration or interpretation. Most of the conflicts arising in our federal system grow out of conflicting interpretations of the words and phrases of the Constitution. It is easy enough to say that Congress has power to "regulate Commerce with foreign Nations and among the several States." But what does "commerce" mean and what does it mean to "regulate"? Both the federal government and the states are forbidden to deprive any person of "life, liberty, or property, without due process of law." What is "due process of law"? Congress has the power to lay and collect taxes, but direct taxes must be apportioned according to population. What is a direct tax?

These and countless other questions have created a kind of "twilight zone" or semantic wilderness, in which rival power structures, both public and private, joust for power and position. Some of the conflicts arising in this zone are resolved by the Supreme Court; others are determined by the President and Congress under the impact of pressure from competing interest groups and political parties. Only a tiny fraction of them are resolved by formal amendments to the Constitution.

The Doctrine of Implied Powers

"Each state," said the Articles of Confederation, "retains its sovereignty, freedom and independence, and every power . . . etc., which is not by this Confederation *expressly delegated* to the United States." Except for a few words like "state sovereignty" and "expressly," this is substantially the language of the Tenth Amendment to the Constitution. Omission of the word *expressly* in referring to the powers delegated to the United States is of more than semantic interest, since the most important powers conferred on the federal government are not *expressly* described, but are granted in general terms. To be sure, some powers are *expressly* granted, that is, in fairly specific and unambiguous terms. Congress has power to enact patent and copyright laws, uniform statutes on naturalization and bankruptcy, to coin money and determine uniform weights and measures, to lay and collect taxes, imports, and excises, to raise and maintain an army and navy, to declare war, to make treaties, to borrow money, to establish post offices and post roads, to establish federal courts inferior to the United States Supreme Court, to enact all laws for the government of the District of Columbia and the territories of the United States. But there is no *express* grant of power to establish a postal savings system or the parcel post. Nor is Congress *expressly* authorized to grant subsidies to steamship lines and railroads, or loans to tottering banks and factories. Congress has no *express* power to establish a social security system or the TVA, or to outlaw trusts and combinations in restraint of trade, or to establish an Atomic Energy Commission. Whence comes the authority for the central government to engage in these and hundreds of other activities for which the Constitution makes no *express* provision? Part of the answer is to be found in the broad or liberal definition that Congress and the President—supported, where challenged, by the Supreme Court—have given to the ambiguous language of the Constitution. And in this process of constitutional interpretation they have relied upon still another ambiguous phrase. At the tag end of Section 8 of Article I, an omnibus article in which the powers delegated to Congress are set forth, occurs the following language: "The Congress shall have the Power . . . to make all Laws which shall be *necessary and proper* for carrying into Execution the foregoing Powers, and all other Powers vested by this Constitution in the Government of the United States, or in any Department or Officer thereof." It remains then for the central government and, where challenged, the Supreme Court to decide what laws are "necessary and proper" to carry into effect its delegated powers.

In 1791 Congress, on the recommendation of President Washington and Alexander Hamilton, his Secretary of the Treasury, established a central Bank of the United States with an initial capital of $10 million ($2 million of which was subscribed by the federal government itself). Its initial charter was to run for twenty years (until 1811), and it was authorized to issue notes, make loans and hold deposits of both private and public funds. "It handled payments on the public debt for the Treasury, received subscriptions for new issues of government securities and paid the salaries of public officials." With headquarters in Philadelphia, the Bank operated through branches in eight of the more important commercial centers. Although the establishment of the Bank was assailed—by Jefferson, among others—as an unconstitutional usurpation of power by the central government, it was never challenged in the courts during the term of its initial charter. The Bank was rechartered in 1816, when financial conditions in the country, following the War of 1812, made some central bank necessary. "Almost immediately," says Professor Cushman, "it incurred the bitter odium of large sections of the Country. . . . The Bank was largely under the control of the Federalists, who were accused of using it as a political machine . . . [and] its stock was largely held by British and foreign investors." A period of inefficient and even corrupt management, resulting in a high degree of inflation and heavy losses to many investors, was attributed to the Bank, which was "accused of being responsible for a period of depression which brought ruin to thousands." The Baltimore branch of the Bank failed, with losses to Maryland investors estimated as high as $3 million. New management and new policies, however, put the Bank on "a financial course as conservative as it had hitherto been headlong. It refused to accept bank notes of imprudent state banks . . . ," and one after another of these institutions failed, bringing ruin to hundreds of honest investors as well as reckless speculators.

Responding to demands for stricter regulation of the central bank, a Maryland statute "forbade all banks not chartered by the state . . . to issue bank notes save upon special stamped paper, obtainable upon the payment of a very heavy tax." James McCulloch, cashier of the Baltimore branch of the Bank of the United States, issued notes on unstamped paper, without payment of the $15,000 tax, in violation of the state law. Action was brought on behalf of the State of Maryland to recover penalties for this violation. McCulloch, for the Bank, argued that the state law was invalid, as imposing an unconstitutional burden upon a legitimate agency of the central government. To which the State of Maryland replied that the act of Congress establishing the Bank was itself unconstitutional, since no power to establish such a central bank could be found in the Constitution. The case came on appeal to the Supreme Court and was decided on March 19, 1819. Chief Justice John Marshall, speaking for the Court, recognized that the Constitution contained no *express* grant of power to Congress to charter a central bank, but that its power to do so was nevertheless clear as a necessary and proper measure "for carrying into execution" other powers delegated to the central government in the Constitution. In his opinion, the Chief Justice gave the broadest possible construction to the language of this so-called necessary and proper clause. "Let the end be legitimate," he said, "let it be within the scope of the Constitution, and all means which are appropriate, which are plainly adapted to that end, which are not prohibited, but consistent with the letter and spirit of the Constitution are constitutional. . . ."[8]

What Marshall was saying was no more than common sense, namely that for the Congress to have power to lay and collect taxes or to regulate commerce or to promote science and the useful arts without the means to make the power effective would be to grant the shadow without the substance. And, he was saying, it is up to Congress and the President to decide upon the "means which are appropriate." But he was also saying something more: that not only must the end be legitimate but the means must be "appropriate" and "plainly adapted to that end." In short, Congress cannot use unconstitutional means to accomplish a constitutional end—nor constitutional means to further an unconstitutional end.

While the Bank of the United States involved no conflict between means and ends, other cases in the Court's opinion did present such a problem. When, for example, Congress sought to outlaw child labor in industry, first by excluding the products of child labor from interstate commerce, and later by a discriminatory tax on the products of child labor, the Court struck down both laws.[9] In these cases the *means* were legitimate, for Congress indubitably had power to tax and to regulate, and in some cases to prohibit, interstate commerce. Unfortunately, said the Court, the end for which these means were to be used, namely the prohibition of child labor, was not within the legitimate (that is, necessary and proper constitutional) powers of Congress.

We are not now concerned with whether the reasoning of the Court in these cases was logical or constitutional. (The fact is the decisions have now been reversed.) But they illustrate the Court's insistence, in cases where the power of Congress is challenged, upon the constitutionality not only of the end sought but of the means by which it is to be accomplished. In these, as in other cases, the Supreme Court echoes again and again the words of Marshall, that the end must be legitimate and the means "plainly [and constitutionally] adapted to that end." There is no warrant in American constitutional law that the end justifies the means.

[8] *McCulloch* v. *Maryland*, 4 Wheaton 316 (1819).
[9] *Bailey* v. *Drexel Furniture Company*, 259 U.S. 20 (1922).

Questions of Power and Policy

In thinking about these and other issues arising in our federal system, it is important to distinguish questions of power and authority from questions of policy or purpose. The fact that an act of Congress or of a state legislature may seem to us *good* or *bad* as a matter of public policy is, in our system, subordinate to the question of whether Congress or the state has *power* under the Constitution to enact such legislation. The Supreme Court, in deciding cases or controversies concerning the respective roles of federal and state governments, is primarily concerned with questions of *power* to act, and not with the wisdom or unwisdom of a given policy. After all, as Justice Brandeis once said, "Many foolish laws are nevertheless quite Constitutional."

And while we think of the Supreme Court as an arbiter of the allocation of power in our federal system, we ought not to forget that the vast bulk of legislation enacted by Congress and the states raises no question of constitutional power, however bitter the battle may be over their wisdom or necessity. Conflicts over constitutional issues of power are the exception and not the rule. Were it otherwise, the government would break down. The American federal union is not a family of delinquents, nor a married couple on the verge of divorce. The powers of the United States to provide for the common defense, to raise and support armies, to provide and maintain a navy, to establish post offices and post roads, to conduct foreign relations, and to declare war are relatively unambiguous and generally uncontested. No one pretends that the states have any jurisdiction in these matters, which account for more than 80 percent of federal expenditures and civilian employment.

On the other hand, the constitutional powers of the states over local government, domestic relations, police and fire protection, the licensing and control of common callings and occupations are almost equally free of ambiguity and conflict. Even in the vague area known as the police power to legislate for the health, welfare, public safety, and public morals of its citizens, the power of the state to act is no longer seriously challenged. And it is well to remember that these matters account for a high proportion of state and local governmental expenditures and employment.

Commerce Among the States

Although relatively few acts in our federal system raise serious constitutional questions, there is scarcely an act that goes uncontested on the issue of public policy. We ought not, however, to minimize the importance of constitutional issues or the frequency with which they arise. The literature of politics and the official reports of the Supreme Court are filled with conflicts of this kind. In general, constitutional issues arise from the ambiguous language in which the allocation of power between the central government and the states is made in the Constitution. Among the more important of these ambiguities is the grant of power to Congress "to regulate Commerce with foreign Nations and among the several States, and with the Indian tribes." In deciding the nature and scope of this power, one is bound to ask, What is "commerce," and when is it "among the states"? What does it mean to "regulate"? And does "regulate" include power to exclude or to prohibit?

It was thirty-five years before these questions were faced squarely by the Supreme Court in the case of *Gibbons* v. *Ogden,* decided in March, 1824.[10] The steamboat was just beginning to appear as an important means of transportation, and the State of New York had granted to Robert Fulton and his associates (and by assignment from them to Aaron Ogden) "exclusive navigation of all waters within the jurisdiction of that state." Others, notably Thomas Gibbons, who sought to enter this potentially lucrative business, argued that such a grant was in violation of the Constitution of the United States in that it placed a burden on interstate commerce, and thus transgressed the jurisdiction of the United States.

In deciding against the grant, Marshall took the occasion to define commerce and indicate the scope of congressional power in this field. "Commerce," he said, "is traffic, but it is something more—it is all kinds of intercourse," including navigation, among the states and with foreign nations. The word "among," he said, "means 'intermingled with.' " It follows, therefore, that "commerce *among* the states cannot stop at the external boundary line of each state but may be introduced into the interior . . . ," although it does not extend to activities that are "completely internal" and hence do not affect other states. Yet, even when commerce was wholly internal to a state, it nevertheless might come under the power of Congress if it had an effect on the commerce of other states. Moreover the power "to regulate [to prescribe the rule by which commerce is to be governed] is complete in itself, may be exercised to its utmost extent, and acknowledges no limitations other than are prescribed in the Constitution." This power to regulate commerce among the states, he continued "is vested in Congress as absolutely as it would be in a single government, having in its constitution, the same restrictions on the exercise of the power as are found in the Constitution of the United States." The power of the Congress over commerce, Marshall insisted, was *exclusive,* and, within the limits of other constitutional restraints, was absolute. The sole restraint on this power, he said, is "the wisdom and discretion of Congress, their identity with the people, and the influence which their constituents possess at elections."

[10] *Gibbons* v. *Ogden,* 9 Wheaton 1 (1824).

Marshall's definition of "commerce" provided ample scope for the federal government to regulate virtually all phases of American economic life which, either directly or indirectly, might affect "commerce *among* the states." It should be noted that the Court refers to "commerce *among* the states" and not merely to commerce *between* the states. And, as Professor Crosskey has shown, in the eighteenth and early nineteenth centuries the word *among* was commonly taken to mean "within."[11] "The 18th Century," said Walton Hamilton, "did not separate by artificial lines aspects of culture which are inseparable. . . . Commerce was then more than we imply now by business or industry. It was a name for the economic order, the [whole] domain of political economy. . . . This usage is reflected in Marshall's statement that "commerce *among* the states cannot stop at the external boundary of each state, but may be introduced into the interior."[12]

Indeed, three yeas before *Gibbons* v. *Ogden,* Chief Justice Marshall, speaking for the Supreme Court, had said that

> The United States form, for many, and for most important purposes, a single nation. In war we are one people. In making peace we are one people. In all commercial regulations we are one and the same people and in many other respects the American people are one. The Government which is alone capable of controlling and managing their interests in all these respects is the Government of the Union.[13]

From the decisions in *Gibbons* v. *Ogden* and *Cohens* v. *Virginia* to the present time, the commerce clause of the Constitution has been a major source of federal power in the broad field of economic, commercial, and social regulation and control. To be sure, not all decisions of the Court have sustained federal intervention, and there have been occasions when both federal and state authorities have been denied power to legislate. But the general thrust of both public and private power structures has been toward centralization of decision making. Indeed, centralization and concentration of power in the modern corporation, accelerated by improved communication and transportation, have been major factors in the expanding role played by the federal government in the American economy.

The progressive integration of the American continent in a single market, not only for business but for agriculture and labor as well, has led to a corresponding increase in demands for federal legislation and control. How our federal system, as interpreted by the Congress and the Court, has responded to these demands may be illustrated by a few examples. In 1890, in an effort to control private monopoly, Congress had

11 William W. Crosskey, *Politics and the Constitution* (Chicago: University of Chicago Press, 1953) , Vol. I, ch. IX.

12 See Peter Odegard and Victor Rosenblum (eds.) , *The Power to Govern* (White Plains, N.Y.: Fund for Adult Education, 1957) .

13 *Cohens* v. *Virginia,* 6 Wheaton 413 (1821) .

enacted a Federal Antitrust Law which declared that: "Every contract, combination in the form of trust or otherwise, or conspiracy, in restraint of trade or commerce among the several states or with foreign nations, is hereby declared to be illegal." Violations were punishable by fine and/or imprisonment. By 1895 the American Sugar Refining Co. had secured control of approximately 98 percent of sugar refining in the United States. It was accordingly prosecuted by the National government as a "combination in restraint of trade" under the Sherman Antitrust Act. In an 8 to 1 decision, the Supreme Court ruled against the government. "Commerce among the states," the Court held, does not include manufacturing and even though 98 percent of the refined sugar consumed in the United States was supplied by this combine, the combine itself, being engaged in manufacturing and not in commerce, was not subject to congressional regulation. Regulation of manufacturing, as such, was a function reserved to the states. This decision, had it been allowed to stand, would have been a serious, if not fatal, blow not only to the Antitrust Act but to the commerce power of Congress.

Again in 1908 the Court undertook to limit the power of Congress over "commerce." Interstate railroads had customarily required, as a condition of employment, that workers agree not to join a labor union. In 1898, by the Erdmann Act, Congress outlawed these so-called yellow dog contracts on interstate railroads. This law, under attack by the railroads, was declared to be unconstitutional because, said the Court, labor contracts or the conditions of employment in private interstate industries were not interstate commerce.

As recently as 1935, in *Schechter Bros. Poultry Co.* v. *United States* and *Carter* v. *Carter Coal Co.*, the Court held that Congress could not, under the guise of regulating commerce, control manufacturing or the conditions of employment in manufacturing industries operating within a state.

Had these and similar decisions been allowed to stand, the extensive power of Congress under the commerce clause of the Constitution would have been severely impaired. The Supreme Court, however, responding to insistent demands in the country and in the Congress, had, by World War II, returned to the general principles laid down by Marshall in *Cohens* v. *Virginia* and *Gibbons* v. *Ogden*. As early as 1905, in a case involving the so-called "beef trust," the Court changed its mind as to the relation of manufacturing and "commerce among the states." The constitutional phrase, the Court said, is a dynamic, not a static one and may refer to a continuous process that begins on the cattle ranges of Wyoming, passes through the manufacturing process in Chicago, and ends on the dinner tables of millions of Americans located in every state in the Union. And in 1922 Chief Justice Taft, following the lead established in the "beef trust" case, said that in interpreting the commerce clause the rule should be that

Whatever amounts to a more or less constant practice and threatens to obstruct or unduly burden the freedom of interstate commerce is within the regulatory power of Congress . . . and it is primarily for Congress to consider and decide the fact of the danger and to meet it. The Court will certainly not substitute its judgment for that of Congress in such a matter unless the relation of the subject to interstate commerce and the effects upon it are clearly non-existent.[14]

By 1967 the power of the central government to regulate "commerce among the states" had come to embrace virtually all forms of commerce, trade, transportation, and communication among the states, and also many aspects of manufacturing and trade within the states themselves. Federal laws outlawing "yellow dog" contracts, establishing a system of workmen's compensation, limiting the use of injunctions in labor disputes, guaranteeing to workers the right of collective bargaining, and establishing minimum wages and maximum hours of employment have been upheld as a legitimate exercise of congressional power to regulate "commerce among the states." And the power to "regulate" has been expanded to include the power to *prohibit* commerce in lottery tickets, stolen automobiles, false and misleading advertising, impure or dangerous foods and drugs, liquor, and women for immoral purposes. Racial discrimination by restaurants, motels, hotels, or any other establishment "which provides lodging to transient guests" is prohibited by Title II of the Civil Rights Act of 1964 on the assumption that all such establishments "affect commerce" among the states. Kidnappers have been brought within the jurisdiction of the central government under the commerce clause by a statute declaring that a victim not released within 48 hours is "presumed" to have been transported in interstate commerce; and so, too, have farmers who produce crops subject to federal quota controls, even when the grain they raise never leaves their own farms but is consumed by their own livestock on the premises. The Supreme Court may have seemed to wobble a good deal over the years, but it has recognized that concepts like "commerce among the states" change with time and circumstance.

The Power to Tax

Second only to its power to regulate commerce among the states has been the central government's power to "lay and collect Taxes, Duties, Imposts and Excises, to pay the Debts and provide for the common Defence and general Welfare of the United States." Not only has this power to tax been a vital factor in the growth of the central government, but it has on occasion been a source of tension and conflict with the states, which also enjoy a broad power to lay and collect taxes. One source of conflict has

14 *Swift & Co.* v. *United States,* 196 U.S. 375 (1905) ; *Stafford* v. *Wallace,* 258 U.S. 495 (1922).

been the imposition of state taxes that lay an unconstitutional burden on interstate commerce.[15] For example, in 1827 the Court was called upon to decide the validity of a license tax levied by the State of Maryland on "all importers of foreign articles as commodities." This Maryland law, said the Court, was an unconstitutional burden on interstate and foreign commerce. So long as the imported goods were in their "original package," the Court held, they were part of "commerce with foreign nations" and immune from taxation or regulation by the states. Only when the importer "mixes them with the general property of the State by breaking up his packages" do they come within the jurisdiction of the state.

This so-called original package doctrine, says Professor Corwin, "still remains the law on the subject [and is accordingly] a unique instance of longevity in [a] field, which may be described as a graveyard of discarded concepts." Although the general principle of the original package doctrine still applies, it has been applied less consistently and with less force to commerce *among* the states than to "commerce with foreign nations."

The whole problem of state taxation as a burden on interstate commerce is too complex for extended discussion here. The United States will obviously be unable to maintain a common free trade market of continental dimensions if state governments are free to impose whatever taxes they choose on the interstate exchange of goods and services among the American people. State-imposed taxes, fees, or licenses on persons, goods, or services moving in interstate commerce could become, to all intents and purposes, an internal tariff system that could destroy the national market that the framers of the Constitution sought to create. How to reconcile the states' growing need for revenue with the immunity of "commerce among the states" from state taxation is a key problem of the American federal system. As matters now stand, the following generalizations would seem to be valid:

1. Goods and persons in transit in interstate commerce may not be taxed by the states through which they are passing.
2. Nondiscriminating state taxes, however, on goods produced for sale in interstate commerce are allowed if levied before the goods are shipped.
3. Goods coming into the state from outside may be taxed if and when they have come to rest in the state, even though they are still in the original package—except, of course, for foreign imports.
4. Sales within a state, by mail or salesmen, of goods manufactured outside the state and shipped in interstate commerce directly to the customer are not subject to state sales taxes within the state of sale and delivery. They may, however, be subject to "use" and property taxes after they have "come to rest" in the state.

[15] E. L. Bassett Jr., "State Taxation of Interstate Commerce," *Vanderbilt Law Review* (April, 1951).

5. State-imposed fees or licenses on interstate trucks and buslines which are not discriminatory and which may be said to make a reasonable contribution to the maintenance of the state highways are valid.

These are relatively simple problems compared with the complex problems involved in the licensing and taxation of corporations chartered in one state but doing business in other states. The apportionment among the states, for tax purposes, of the property and income of railroads, chain stores, or commuters who reside in one state and work in another has generated mountains of litigation.

In 1946 Justice Frankfurter, speaking for the Court, said:

> The power of the states to tax, and limitations upon that power imposed by the commerce clause, have necessitated a long and continuous process of judicial adjustment. The need for such adjustment is inherent in a Federal Government like ours . . . where the same transaction . . . may . . . involve the authority of both the Central Government, and the constituent states. The history of this problem is spread over hundreds of volumes of our Reports. To attempt to harmonize all that has been said in the past would neither clarify what has been done before nor guide the future. Suffice it to say . . . in this field opinions must be read in the setting of the particular cases and as the product of preoccupation with their special facts.[16]

Reciprocal Tax Immunity

Among the most bewildering aspects of federal-state tax relations has been the effort of the Court to work its way out of the confusion arising from the so-called doctrine of reciprocal tax immunity. According to this doctrine, neither the federal government nor the states can tax the instrumentalities of the other. As we have seen in the case of *McCulloch v. Maryland* (1819), John Marshall, speaking for the Court, had held that the State of Maryland could not tax a branch of the Bank of the United States. "The power to tax," Marshall had said, "is the power to destroy." Since the Bank of the United States was an instrumentality of the national government, to allow the states to tax it would enable the states to destroy it. Presumably, if this were allowed, the state taxing power could be used to destroy the government itself. Fifty years later, however, in 1869, the Supreme Court held that a federal tax on the notes of state banks, even though it drove them out of circulation, was within the constitutional taxing power of the central government.[17] The power of the central government in cases of this kind could be found not only in the necessary and proper clause, but also in the so-called supremacy clause. That is to say, when the legitimate powers of the state and central

---

16 *Freeman* v. *Hewit*, 329, U.S. 251 (1946).
17 *Veazie Bank* v. *Fenno*, 8 Wall. 533 (1869).

governments collide, the latter must prevail and the state must yield under Article VI of the Constitution which declares:

> This Constitution and the Laws of the United States which shall be made in Pursuance thereof . . . shall be the supreme Law of the Land; and the Judges in every State shall be bound thereby, any Thing in the Constitution or Laws of any State to the Contrary notwithstanding.

In 1871, however, when a federal income tax was levied against the salaries of certain state officials (in this case state judges), the Supreme Court held such a tax, however valid when applied to private persons, could not be applied to officers or agencies of the state governments. In the case of *Collector* v. *Day* (1871), the Court laid down a rule of reciprocal tax immunity which forbade taxation of state officials and agencies by the central government and of federal agencies and officials by the states. Justice Nelson said:

> In respect to its reserved powers, the state is as sovereign and independent as the general Government. And if the means and instrumentalities employed [by the general government] are . . . exempt from taxation by the states, why are not those of the states . . . equally exempt from Federal taxation? Their unimpaired existence in the one case is as essential as in the other.[18]

In subsequent cases this rule of reciprocal immunity was applied to a federal tax on income received from investments by a municipality and income of private persons and corporations received from state or municipal bonds, a ruling which still stands.[19]

Since 1900, however, this doctrine of reciprocal immunity has had a checkered career. The immunity of federal instrumentalities from state taxation, established in *McCulloch* v. *Maryland,* has never been seriously challenged, although private income from federal bonds is now taxed by both federal and state governments. The immunity of state activities from federal taxation is by no means clear. To be sure, the federal government continues to respect the immunity of income from state and municipal bonds from federal income taxes, although its power to tax such income would seem to be as clear as its power to tax income from its own securities, which it does. State bonds, even now, may be taxed by the federal government when they are part of an estate subject to a federal inheritance tax. Confusion concerning the scope of reciprocal immunity also developed with reference to taxes other than those on income or inheritance. As early as 1905 a federal excise tax on state-owned and -operated liquor stores was upheld, but in 1931 a federal excise tax on motorcycles sold to a municipal government for its police force was

---

[18] *Collector* v. *Day,* 11 Wall. 113 (1871).

[19] *United States* v. *Baltimore and Ohio R.R. Co.,* 11 Wall. 322 (1873); *Pollock* v. *Farmers Loan and Trust Co.,* 17 U.S. 429 (1899).

declared unconstitutional. But in 1933 federal customs duties on scientific equipment were upheld, even though the importer was the University of Illinois, an instrumentality of the government of that state. And in 1946 the Court upheld a federal excise tax on mineral waters taken from property owned and operated by the State of New York.[20]

In deciding these and similar cases the Court has tried to distinguish between strictly *governmental* activities of state and local governments and what have been called nongovernmental, or *proprietary,* activities. Thus a police force was held to be a governmental activity; hence a federal excise tax on motorcycles sold to a municipality for its police force was not allowed. But federal taxes on the South Carolina state-owned liquor business and the New York state-owned business of bottling and selling mineral waters were upheld.

In the New York case the Court divided sharply on the issue, with Justices Douglas and Black—on the rather shaky ground of the Tenth Amendment—protesting that the majority's decision placed "the sovereign states on the same plane as private citizens" and made them "pay the Federal Government for the privilege of exercising powers . . . guaranteed them by the Constitution." As matters now stand, the immunity of the states from federal taxation on a wide variety of activities has been steadily narrowed, although the immunity of the federal government from state taxes stands virtually unimpaired.

In the field of personal income taxation, however, the doctrine of reciprocal tax immunity has been abandoned. For some years the Court tried to maintain the doctrine, even in this field, by making a distinction between the income of employees engaged in *governmental* activities and that of those engaged in *proprietary* activities. Income of the former only was held to be immune. Thus the income of employees of a state-owned transit system was said to be taxable by the federal government on the ground that transportation was a nongovernmental, or proprietory, activity, whereas the income of the employees of a metropolitan water department was held to be nontaxable by the central government because they were engaged in a governmental activity. Obviously such hairline distinctions could not long be made as the functions of state and local governments increased.

Finally, in 1939 the Court overruled most of these earlier cases, including *Collector* v. *Day,* "as far as they recognize an implied constitutional immunity from income taxation of the salaries of officers or employees of the national or state government or their instrumentalities."[21] Thus ended the doctrine of reciprocal tax immunity as applied to the personal income of state and federal officers and employees. In one

20 *South Carolina* v. *United States,* 199 U.S. 437 (1905) ; *Indian Motorcycle Co.* v. *United States,* 283 U.S. 520 (1931) ; *University of Illinois* v. *United States,* 289 U.S. 48 (1933) ; *New York* v. *United States,* 326 U.S. 572 (1946) .

21 *Graves* v. *New York,* 306 U.S. 466 (1939) .

of his most felicitous dissenting opinions, the late Justice Oliver Wendell Holmes, commenting on Chief Justice Marshall's statement in *McCulloch* v. *Maryland* that the "power to tax is the power to destroy," said:

> In those days it was not recognized that most of the distinctions of the law are distinctions of degree. If states had any power it was assumed they had all powers, and that the necessary alternative was to deny it altogether. But this Court, which has so often defeated the attempt to tax in certain ways, can defeat an attempt to discriminate or otherwise go too far without wholly abolishing the power to tax. The power to tax is *not* the power to destroy while this Court sits.[22]

What Justice Holmes was saying is that notwithstanding legal doctrines the best safeguard of the federal system is not only in the Supreme Court, but in the sense of mutual respect and self-restraint which state and federal governments observe in their relations with one another.

Regulation by Taxation

As Justice Holmes has said, the "power to tax" is not the power to destroy so long as the Supreme Court sits. We have seen how, in a long line of decisions, the Court has struck down both federal and state taxes that might undermine the allocation of power in our federal system. We have also seen that under the supremacy clause of the Constitution, where the otherwise legitimate process of state and federal governments collide, the federal power must prevail. But may the central government, through its power to "lay and collect Taxes . . . to pay the Debts and provide for the common Defence and general Welfare of the United States," accomplish purposes for which it has no other constitutional authority?

In 1922 the Supreme Court held that a discriminatory federal tax on the products of child labor was unconstitutional, on the ground that the taxing power of Congress could not be used to accomplish an unconstitutional end: the regulation or abolition of child labor in industry.[23] And again in 1936, in *United States* v. *Butler* (297 U.S. 1), the Court held that a federal tax levied on flour mills and other processors of agricultural products in order to raise funds to make adjustment payments to farmers was an unconstitutional effort to regulate activities beyond the legitimate scope of the central government.

These cases, however, are exceptions to the prevailing doctrine. In 1934 the Court said:

> From the beginning of our government, the Courts have sustained taxes . . . imposed with the . . . intent of effecting ulterior ends, which were beyond

---

[22] *Panhandle Act Co.* v. *Mississippi* ex rel. *Knox,* 277 U.S. 218 (1928).
[23] *Bailey* v. *Drexel Furniture Company, op. cit.*

the constitutional power of [Congress]. . . . A tax does not cease to be valid because it regulates, discourages or even definitely deters the activities taxed. The principle applies even though the revenue obtained is obviously negligible . . . or the revenue purpose of the tax . . . secondary.[24]

In line with this theory, Congress has used its taxing power to develop a kind of federal "police power" to legislate for the safety, health, welfare, and public morals of the United States. Customs duties have been used not only to raise revenues but to protect American business and industry from foreign competition. Federal excise taxes have been imposed on oleomargarine to discourage its sale and thus protect the dairy industry from competition, and on tobacco and intoxicating liquor not merely for revenue purposes but to promote public health and sobriety. Federal license fees have been imposed on the sale of narcotic drugs, not for revenue but to prescribe regulations as to how and under what conditions they can be sold, with heavy penalties for violations of these regulations (*United States* v. *Doremus,* 1919). In *United States* v. *Butler* (1936) the Court held that Congress could not use tax money to buy the compliance of farmers with regulations over matters (agricultural production) beyond the control of the central government. Yet in 1937 the Court upheld a special federal tax on employers to provide unemployment benefits—with a 90 percent credit allowed to any state having an unemployment insurance plan,[25] thus using the federal taxing power to "encourage," "induce," or, as critics say, "bribe" and "coerce" the states to pass such laws.

Grants-in-Aid

Money raised by taxation has also been used to make conditional grants-in-aid to the states for activities over which the national government would otherwise have no power. Nothing characterizes the cooperative federalism of the American system so completely as this expanding program from 1955 to 1968.[26] Federal aid to state and local governments has more than quadrupled. (See Table 6–1, Figure 6–1, below.) Federal grants-in-aid have been used to support education, public health and welfare, the building of highways, local airports, hospitals and medical facilities, housing and urban renewal projects, as well as public works of great variety and magnitude. Grants-in-aid have also been used for control of outdoor advertising, and of water and air pollution, for

[24] *Magano Co.* v. *Hamilton,* 292 U.S. 40 (1934).

[25] *Steward Machine Co.* v. *Davis,* 301 U.S. 548 (1937).

[26] Federal grants to the states are not a recent invention. The use of federal funds to finance internal improvements of great variety was common as early as the 1830s. "Indeed," says a recent writer, "Federal aids may have been more important during the 19th century than they have been since World War II." See Charles Adrian and Charles Press, *The American Political Process* (New York: McGraw-Hill, 1965), p. 143.

conservation of human and natural resources, and for landscaping and scenic improvement. By 1967 such grants amounted to upwards of $14 billion and accounted for about 20 percent of all state revenue. Theoretically and normally, federal grants-in-aid are matched in whole or part by the states, although the degree of this sharing varies greatly from program to program. In some cases federal grants are matched dollar for dollar by the states; in others the respective shares may be as disproportionate as 90 percent federal and 10 percent state and local. The total amount granted also varies from state to state, from as much as $250 per capita in Alaska to less than $50 in Wisconsin, Illinois, and Connecticut. Even the largest of present grants, as a proportion of state revenues, are small compared to the days of depression in the 1930s, when in many states federal aid exceeded total state revenues from all other sources.

New dimensions are being introduced into this system of cooperative federalism by the development of more regional authorities, composed of groups of states, and by a spectacular increase in direct financial and administrative relations between the federal government and local—especially metropolitan—authorities. The first is symbolized by the TVA, the second by the establishment of the new Department of Housing and Urban Affairs. As existing programs of cooperation expand and new ones emerge, the American federal system is being transformed beyond anything that might have been anticipated in 1900, let alone by the framers of the Constitution.[27]

Critics of the federal system of grants-in-aid have claimed the following: (1) It is an unconstitutional use of the federal taxing power to invade the reserved powers of the states. (2) It is a further step on the road to a centralized governmental system at the expense of state and local self-government. By attaching conditions to its grants, the central government, it is said, has made the states "vassals" of a centralized bureaucracy. (3) It has been used to induce, seduce, bribe, or coerce the states and municipalities into embarking upon dubious projects of welfare which they would otherwise avoid and has made the federal government the arbiter of the domestic policies of the states. (4) It has pushed us farther and farther toward a welfare state.

Concerning the constitutionality of federal grants-in-aid, the Supreme Court has repeatedly upheld the system as within the legitimate powers of Congress to collect taxes and to spend money for the common defense and general welfare. In the leading cases of *Massachusetts* v. *Mellon*, 262 U.S. 447 (1923) and *Frothingham* v. *Mellon*, 262 U.S. 447

[27] "The Federal Government is now administering over 40 separate programs of financial aid for urban development. . . . Increasing national awareness of urbanization's accelerated pace during the past decade and a half is reflected in the fact that more than half of these grants-in-aid . . . were enacted subsequent to 1950." See *Impact of Federal Urban Development Programs on Local Government Organization and Planning*. A report of the Advisory Commission on Intergovernmental Relations, 1966.

TABLE 6–1
How States Rank

The redistributive effect of federal grants is shown by dividing each state's share of total grants (Column 1) by its share of the 1963 federal tax burden (Column 2), yielding a "benefit-to-burden" ratio or index (Column 3) according to which 34 states (and the District of Columbia) received *relatively* more in grants than they paid in taxes, while 16 states received *relatively* less. States are ranked according to this index.

Rank	State	1	2	3
1.	Alaska	.57%	.12%	4.75
2.	Wyoming	.65	.16	4.06
3.	North Dakota	.71	.19	3.73
4.	South Dakota	.68	.22	3.09
5.	Mississippi	1.46	.48	3.04
6.	Montana	.77	.27	2.85
7.	Arkansas	1.33	.47	2.82
8.	New Mexico	.99	.36	2.75
9.	Idaho	.63	.26	2.42
10.	Louisiana	2.65	1.16	2.28
11.	Oklahoma	2.09	.94	2.22
12.	Utah	.83	.39	2.12
13.	Vermont	.35	.17	2.05
14.	Alabama	1.98	.98	2.02
15.	Tennessee	2.30	1.21	1.90
16.	Kentucky	1.85	1.04	1.77
17.	Georgia	2.30	1.36	1.69
18.	Oregon	1.51	.91	1.65
19.	Hawaii	.60	.37	1.62
20.	South Carolina	1.04	.64	1.62
21.	Arizona	.98	.65	1.50
22.	West Virginia	1.01	.68	1.48
23.	Colorado	1.49	1.01	1.47
24.	D.C.	.98	.69	1.42
25.	Nebraska	.91	.67	1.35
26.	Maine	.55	.41	1.34
27.	Nevada	.31	.23	1.34
28.	North Carolina	1.91	1.47	1.29
29.	Washington	1.88	1.58	1.18
30.	Kansas	1.16	1.00	1.16
31.	Minnesota	1.94	1.68	1.15
32.	Texas	5.01	4.37	1.14
33.	Missouri	2.46	2.31	1.06
34.	Iowa	1.29	1.23	1.04
35.	Virginia	1.87	1.79	1.04

TABLE 6-1 (Continued)

Rank	State	1	2	3
36.	New Hampshire	.32	.34	0.94
37.	Rhode Island	.47	.50	0.94
38.	Florida	2.31	2.48	0.93
39.	California	9.08	11.23	0.80
40.	Wisconsin	1.69	2.09	0.80
41.	Massachusetts	2.79	3.57	0.78
42.	Michigan	3.36	4.39	0.76
43.	Maryland	1.45	1.97	0.73
44.	Indiana	1.68	2.33	0.72
45.	Pennsylvania	4.78	6.55	0.72
46.	Ohio	4.03	5.64	0.71
47.	Illinois	4.36	7.04	0.61
48.	Delaware	.29	.50	0.58
49.	New York	7.12	13.39	0.53
50.	Connecticut	1.11	2.21	0.50
51.	New Jersey	1.94	4.30	0.45

SOURCE: Reprinted by permission from *Congress and the Nation, 1945–1964* (Washington, D.C.: Congressional Quarterly Service, 1965), p. 1387.

(1923), the system was attacked on the ground that it took money in federal taxes from private citizens of some states to make payments for the benefit of citizens of other states. It was argued that Massachusetts paid more in taxes to the federal government than it received in federal aid, while other states received more from the federal government than they paid in federal taxes. The Court was not impressed by this argument, noting that there was nothing in the Constitution to require the allocation of federal expenditures among the states in strict proportion to the federal taxes paid in each state.[28] Moreover, federal taxes collected from corporations in New York, California, Massachusetts, and North Carolina are paid out of income derived from the entire nation. As for the intrusion of the federal government into areas reserved to the states by the Tenth Amendment, any state could avoid this "invasion" of its legitimate jurisdiction by simply declining to participate in the system. As for the power of Congress to appropriate funds for welfare and other essentially local purposes, the Court has found ample authority in the Constitution. As Justice Roberts again observed in 1936, "the power of Congress to authorize expenditure of public moneys for public purposes

[28] In 1963, for example, some 34 states received relatively more in federal aid than they paid in federal taxes, while 16 states paid more in federal taxes than they received in federal grants. In 2 states—Wyoming and Alaska—the ratio was 4 to 1; in 3 states—North Dakota, South Dakota, and Mississippi—the ratio was 3 to 1; in 9 states it was over 2 to 1; in 20 states it was more than 1 to 1; and in 16 states it was less than 1 to 1. See *Congress and the Nation, 1945–1964* (Washington, D.C.: Congressional Quarterly Service, 1965), p. 1387.

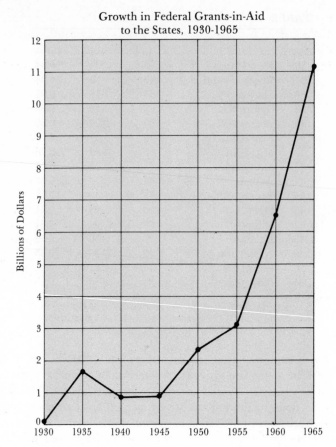

Growth in Federal Grants-in-Aid
to the States, 1930-1965

Figure 6–1 Adapted from U.S. Department of Commerce, *The National Income and Product Accounts of the United States, 1929–1965,* Table 3.3, pp. 54–55.

is not limited by the direct grants of legislative power found in the Constitution." Nor is this a wholly novel doctrine.

"The phrase 'general welfare' [as used in the taxing power]," wrote Alexander Hamilton,

> is as comprehensive as any that could have been used. . . . It is therefore . . . left to the discretion of the national legislature to pronounce upon the objects which concern the general welfare. . . . And there seems no room for doubt that whatever concerns the general interests of learning, of agriculture, of manufactures and of commerce are within the sphere of the national councils, as far as regards the application of money.

It has been argued also that the federal system of grants-in-aid constitute coercion upon the states, compelling them to embark upon programs that they would not otherwise adopt. A classic example, as we have seen, is the Federal Social Security Act, under which 90 percent of the revenue from a federal payroll tax is returned to the states on condition that they establish suitable systems of unemployment insurance. Such a system, said its critics, gave the central government "weapons of coercion, destroying or impairing the autonomy of the States." The Court, however, rejected this argument, holding that federal expenditures for the relief of unemployment under such a cooperative plan with the states was a legitimate combination of means and ends under the constitutional power of Congress to promote the general welfare. No state was compelled to cooperate if it was willing to forego its share of the payroll tax collected by the federal government. The same or a similar argument has been used to justify other federal grants-in-aid.

Federal grants-in-aid are conditional grants. Normally the states are not only required to match federal funds in some agreed ratio, but to conform to certain standards of organization and administration prescribed by the federal government. Such conditions, it is said, impair the freedom and independence of the states and make them "vassals of the Federal Government." In 1947, for example, a grant of federal highway funds was denied the State of Oklahoma because a member of the state's Highway Commission was found to be actively engaged in partisan politics, in violation of a condition laid down by the federal government as prerequisite for such grants-in-aid. "While the United States," said the Supreme Court,

> is not concerned with and has no power to regulate local political activities . . . of State officials, it does have power to fix the terms upon which its money allotments to the State shall be disbursed. The end sought by Congress . . . is better public services by requiring those who administer funds for national needs to abstain from active political partisanship. Even though such action taken by Congress does have effect upon certain activities within the State, it has never been thought that such effect made the federal Act invalid.[29]

Other conditions, including proper systems of accounting, administration, engineering and other technical standards, may be similarly justified.

Among the more controversial conditions now being attached to federal grants-in-aid is state compliance with federal civil rights legislation. Withholding grants-in-aid from states that fail to observe these laws may prove to be the most effective of all sanctions against racial discrimination.[30]

Whatever else may be said about federal grants-in-aid, they have ceased to raise any serious constitutional issues. Although political at-

29 *Oklahoma* v. *United States Civil Service Comm.*, 330 U.S. 127 (1947).

30 "U.S. Counts on Cutoff of Funds to Stimulate Compliance with Rights Act," *The New York Times*, January 18, 1965.

tacks upon the system continue to be made, it has continued to expand with the willing, if not enthusiastic, support of state and local governments. Those who say federal grants-in-aid "make the states vassals of the Federal Government," are a "giant step toward a centralized dictatorship," or "have transformed the American Republic into a welfare, if not a Socialist State" are less concerned with questions of constitutional power than with questions of public policy. It is not merely federal support of education, housing, urban rehabilitation, and so forth, that these critics find offensive, but, except perhaps for education, support of such activities by state and local governments as well. The core of the political argument in support of the system is that the greater taxing power of the federal government may thus be used to "equalize," or at least provide a minimum of access to such services and opportunities as education, health and recreation, child welfare, and decent highways for people everywhere in the nation, and not merely for those fortunate enough to live in the more affluent states. (See Figures 6–2 and 6–3.)

Percent Changes From 1957 to 1963 in Total Allocated Federal Expenditures

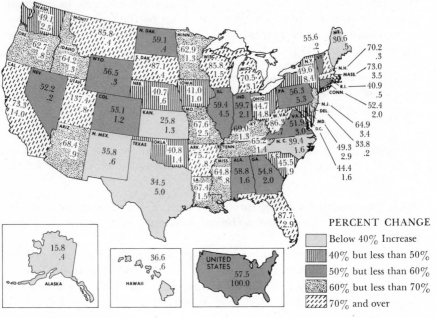

Figure 6–2   After Senate Committee on Government Operations—Subcommittee on Intergovernmental Relations, *Federal Expenditures to States and Regions, 1966*, p. 29.

Percent Distribution of Total Allocated Federal Expenditures Within
The States, By Regions, 1957, 1960 and 1963

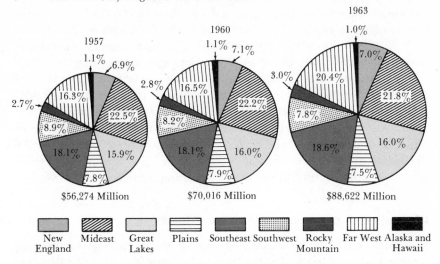

New   Mideast   Great   Plains   Southeast Southwest Rocky   Far West Alaska and
England   Lakes   Mountain   Hawaii

Figure 6–3   After Senate Committee on Government Operations—Subcommittee
on Intergovernmental Relations, *Federal Expenditures to States and Regions,
1966*, p. 31.

"Unless we get help from the Federal Government," said a resident of
South Dakota in 1939, "we in the dust bowl must watch our babies die
for lack of care." In a nation committed to the basic goals of freedom and
equality of opportunity, this is a hard argument to answer.

Some criticisms, however, are not so easily disposed of, such as the
charge that conditional grants of federal funds bring with them an increase of centralized bureaucratic controls that may undermine the flexibility of our federal system. Other complaints are that some federal aid
programs are often too narrowly functional and pay too little heed to the
needs, customs, and procedures of state and local organizations and that
the federal standards imposed are too narrow and rigid.

Commission on Intergovernmental Relations

Systematic studies of the problem have multiplied since the Hoover Commission, in 1951, reported that improvement in intergovernmental relations was essential to the maintenance of the federal system. In 1953
President Eisenhower appointed a Commission on Intergovernmental
Relations, which recommended creation of a continuing advisory body to
provide a "permanent center for overall attention to the problems of
interlevel relationships." Finally, in September, 1959, Congress established a permanent Advisory Commission on Intergovernmental Rela-

tions, composed of three representatives from the executive branch of the federal government, six from Congress (three Representatives and three Senators), four governors, four mayors, three state legislators, three county officials; and three private citizens. The Commission also consults with business and labor organizations, taxpayers' leagues, bureaus of governmental research, and other civic groups and organizations.[31]

The record of this Commission while not spectacular is nevertheless impressive. By providing a continuing review of problems arising under the grants-in-aid program, by conducting research and providing technical assistance in the preparation and review of relevant legislation at all levels of government, and by providing a representative forum for the discussion of intergovernmental relations, the new agency has already made substantial contributions to strengthening the federal system.[32]

Governmental Expansion at the Grass Roots

Preoccupation with the expanding role of the central government in American society has had a tendency to obscure the corresponding expansion of both state and local governments. It is well to remember that the growth of federal activities and expenditures has been primarily in the fields of national defense and foreign relations, over which the Constitution unambiguously grants exclusive power to the central government. In other areas of most intimate concern to the average citizen, state and local governments continue to carry from 50 to over 90 percent of the burden. These include such vital services as education, roads and highways, sanitation, police and fire protection, crime and correction, parks and recreation, domestic relations, the licensing and control of common callings of all kinds, including trade and commerce, agriculture and the professions, and legislation to promote the public health, safety, welfare, and morals of the community.

If one excludes expenditures for national security and foreign affairs, state and local government expenditures have expanded more rapidly than those of the federal government. Joseph Loftus wrote:

[31] The representatives of the federal government are appointed by the President and Congress, respectively; representatives of state and local governments are appointed by the Governors' Conference, the Council of State Governments, the U.S. Conference of Mayors, the National League of Cities, and the National Association of Counties; the citizen members are appointed by the President.

[32] By 1965, the Commission had held over 20 meetings and adopted 26 policy reports and 7 information reports prepared by its staff and consulting experts. The policy reports contained 18 recommendations concerning intergovernmental taxation and finance, the structure of state governments, metropolitan problems, local government, personnel, and grants-in-aid. An impressive majority of these recommendations was approved by the relevant organizations of state and local governments. See "Five Year Record of the Advisory Commission on Intergovernmental Relations," in Report of the Senate Subcommittee on Intergovernmental Relations, Washington, D.C., 1966.

> A myth that defies time . . . says that the Federal Government is a swollen
> ever-growing bureaucracy, . . . demanding fatter budgets and greater
> power. The complement of this myth says that state and local governments
> practice ascetic restraint, contentedly munching along on the same old lean
> fare. Yet the opposite falls closer to the truth. Federal (civilian)
> employment has been almost level for 10 years, while state, county and
> municipal employment, spending and debt have been soaring and will
> continue to soar.[33]

Federal grants-in-aid, to be sure, have made possible some of this expansion, and now account for about 20 percent of state expenditures and slightly more than 10 percent of state and local government expenditures combined. It is no doubt also true that without federal grants-in-aid, some of the present activities of state and local governments would not be undertaken.

It would, however, be a mistake to assume that state and local governments have been reluctant partners in this process. On the contrary, intergovernmental relations in the United States, have been, on the whole, happy relations. American federalism has been a cooperative rather than a competitive venture. And this has been true not only in the case of federal grants-in-aid, but in other areas as well. Time and again, federal action is taken to assist state and local governments in dealing with problems they would be powerless to control without federal cooperation.

When, for example, in 1895 Congress prohibited the transportation of lottery tickets in interstate commerce, it did so not to pre-empt powers of the states, but to support them. At the time the federal law was passed, every state had outlawed lotteries, laws which were easily circumvented by gamblers operating across state lines in interstate commerce. The federal law brought the power of the central government to the aid of the states. The National Motor Vehicle Theft Act of 1919 was passed to supplement already existing laws on this subject in every state. The Sherman Antitrust Act of 1890 followed the enactment of similar state legislation by 27 states. The Pure Food and Drug Act of 1906 was enacted to supplement, not to supplant, state legislation. When the Lindbergh Act, against kidnapping, was enacted in 1932, only 4 states had laws less severe than the federal act. The so-called Federal Mann Act, prohibiting the transportation of women in interstate commerce for an immoral purpose, was passed only after two-thirds of the states had enacted laws against the white slave trade. When, in 1902, Congress imposed a tax of 10 cents a pound on colored oleomargarine, more than 30 states had already prohibited the manufacture and sale of oleomargarine colored to look like butter. The Federal Narcotic Act was passed in 1914, after 40 states had already outlawed the sale of narcotic drugs except on a doctor's

[33] *The New York Times,* February 1, 1965.

prescription. And the Webb-Kenyon Law of 1913, forbidding the shipment in interstate commerce of liquor consigned to purchasers in dry states, was enacted at the earnest solicitation of states already having prohibition laws. In upholding state-imposed "use" taxes on goods purchased in interstate commerce, in allowing state regulation of interstate activities not in conflict with federal standards, and in many other ways, both the Supreme Court and the Congress have sought to strengthen, not weaken, the state's police powers.

Decentralization of Decision Making

In the administration of federal projects and in the enforcement of federal laws, the central government has generally sought to cooperate rather than to compete with state and local authorities. The devolution of decision making, through the establishment of local, state, and regional offices of federal agencies, has not only made the central government more accessible to the average citizen, but has made possible more effective cooperation with state and local governments. Even the Tennessee Valley Authority and other federally sponsored regional projects tend to decentralize decision making and make such agencies more responsive to state and local governments and their inhabitants. Indeed, one writer has criticized the TVA on precisely this ground, namely that it makes the federal agency too responsive to state and local interests.[34]

However harmonious federal-state relations may be, tensions remain and new sources of conflict will continue to develop. The permanent Advisory Commission on Intergovernmental Relations can help to ease these tensions and resolve conflicts as they occur. Of overriding importance for the future will be a continuing search for reasonable answers to two basic questions: (1) What functions, performed in whole or in part by the federal government, are state and local governments ready to assume entirely on their own? (2) What financial aid is the federal government willing to provide, or what sources of tax revenue is it willing to relinquish, and on what terms, to enable state and local authorities to meet these expanding obligations? Unconditional and unearmarked grants may do no more than relieve local taxpayers at the expense of services regarded as essential to the general welfare now being supported by grants-in-aid.

Interstate Cooperation

When one turns from vertical intergovernmental relations —that is, between the federal government and state and local governments—to

---

[34] See Philip Selznick, *T.V.A. at the Grass Roots* (Berkeley, Calif.: University of California Press, 1949). See also David Lilienthal, *T.V.A.: Democracy on the March* (New York: Harper & Row, 1944).

horizontal intergovernmental relations—that is, among the states themselves—a similar pattern of competition and cooperation appears. States,
of course, compete with one another for population, industry, research
and development grants, and public works and defense contracts of the
federal government. Much of this competition is conditioned by differences of natural and human resources, traditional skills and technological "know how." Also important in this interstate rivalry are public
policies relating to taxation, labor-management relations, welfare, scientific research, and education. A state with high minimum wage laws,
liberal welfare and labor policies, and high property or inheritance taxes
may find it difficult to compete in the race for economic growth and
development with states in which business and industry are left largely
free of such burdens. No small part of the drive for federal legislation in
these fields comes from a desire for greater equality among the states in
this competition.

The states, however, have not left this drive for equality of competitive conditions wholly to the federal government. The Council of State
Governments, the Conference of Commissioners on Uniform State Legislation, the National Legislative Conference, the National Association of
State Budget Officers, and the National Association of Tax Administrators are but a few of some twenty or more organizations engaged in the
promotion of interstate cooperation on a wide variety of problems.

Article I, Section 10, of the Constitution provides that

> No State shall without the Consent of Congress, . . . enter into any
> Agreement or Compact with another State, without the consent of the
> United States in Congress assembled, specifying accurately the purposes for
> which the same is to be entered into, and how long it shall continue.

Although this language is negative in tone, Congress has, in fact,
been most liberal in authorizing and even encouraging interstate compacts, as they are commonly called. Best known of these, perhaps, is the
compact between New York and New Jersey that established the Port of
New York Authority to build and operate a common port, transit, and
other facilities for the two states. Other interstate compacts relate to
interstate boundaries, water supply and sanitation, air and water pollution, marine fisheries, forest fire protection, juvenile delinquency, higher
education, parole policies, mental health, regional planning, and dozens
of other problems.[35]

In two other important respects, the Constitution makes provision
for cooperation and mutual respect among the states. The full faith and
credit clause enjoins each state to give "Full Faith and Credit . . . to the
Public Acts, Records and judicial Proceedings of every other State," and

---

[35] Between 1961 and 1965 thirteen interstate compacts that were ratified involved a
total of nineteen states and on subjects as varied as interstate parks, air pollution,
public welfare, and metropolitan transit. See *The Book of the States, 1966–67* (Chicago,
Ill.: The Council of State Governments) , p. 242.

the so-called privileges and immunities clause provides that in order to secure "mutual friendship and intercourse among the people of the different states . . . the free inhabitants of each of these states shall be entitled to all privileges and immunities of free citizens in the several states . . . free ingress and egress to and from any other state and . . . all privileges of trade and commerce. . . ." To be sure, this language is replete with ambiguities, but both provisions are nevertheless vital to the success of our federal system. In general, the Courts have taken a narrow view of the "privileges and immunities" to which citizens of each state are entitled in every other state. Every state, it is agreed, may reserve certain privileges to its own citizens which are not available to citizens of other states on the same terms. Access to state-supported colleges and universities, hospitals, and other health and recreation facilities may be limited to its own citizens or to citizens of other states only on payment of special discriminatory fees. "The right to hunt or fish . . . to work for the state or local government, to obtain public assistance, are other examples of special . . . privileges restricted to the citizens or residents of the state."[36] The "privileges and immunities" enjoyed by all citizens without discrimination were summarized by the Washington, D.C., Circuit Court as early as 1825. These include, said the court, "the right of a citizen of one state to pass through or reside in any other state for purposes of trade, agriculture, professional pursuits or otherwise; to claim the benefit of the writ of habeas corpus; to institute and maintain actions of any kind in the courts of the state, to take, hold and dispose of property. . . ."[37] In more recent decisions of the Supreme Court, moreover, the guarantees of the federal Bill of Rights of the federal Constitution have been progressively extended to residents of all the states.

Not even the full faith and credit clause is free of ambiguity. Although in general the laws, records, and judicial decisions of one state will be respected by all other states, they carry only such weight "as they have by law or usage in the courts of the state . . . from which they are taken."[38] Thus a resident of California cannot escape his debts or other legal obligations by moving to New York, since his creditors in California may bring action in the New York courts. In other respects, however, where state laws differ, or where contracts made in one state are to be enforced in another, a "conflict of laws" may arise, the resolution of which is by no means automatically provided for by the full faith and credit clause of the Constitution. For example, differences in state laws concerning marriage and divorce create a tangle of conflict and confusion under which a couple may be legally married in one state, divorced in another, and, where one or both have remarried even be subject to the

[36] William Anderson *et al.*, *Government in the Fifty States* (New York: Holt, Rinehart and Winston, 1960) , p. 90.
[37] *Corfield* v. *Coryell*, 4 Wash., D.C. 371 (1825) .
[38] 28 U.S. Code, 1946 ed., 1949 Supp.

indictment for bigamy. The point is that a state is not required to respect marriages performed or divorces granted in other states in which the requirements differ substantially from its own.[39] By and large, interstate "comity" prevails even in these troublesome areas. However, the variety of customs and traditions in the various states being what they are, it is not likely that this kind of "conflict of laws" will soon be resolved, although proposals for uniform state laws, interstate compacts, and even federal legislation are becoming more frequent with each passing year.

One final clause of the federal Constitution bears directly on the relations of the several states with one another. "A Person," says Section 2 of Article IV, "charged in any State with Treason, Felony, or other Crime, who shall flee from Justice, and be found in another State, shall on Demand of the executive Authority of the State from which he fled, be delivered of, to be removed to the State having Jurisdiction of the Crime." Although this provision of the Constitution would seem to impose a clear duty upon each state to refuse sanctuary to persons accused of crimes in other states, it is by no means wholly automatic. If a governor believes that the fugitive will not receive a fair trial in the state from which he has fled, or for any other reason declines to deliver him up, there is no way in which his discretion may be limited or controlled, except by the Constitution or laws of his own state. Nevertheless the interstate extradition of fugitives of this kind works smoothly in the vast majority of cases. Once the proper papers showing the arrest and/or indictment of the fugitive have been presented to the governor a favorable response is in most cases virtually automatic. Moreover, since a majority of the states have uniform laws on this subject, it is not a major source of interstate conflict or tension.[40]

The Increase of Centripetal Forces

An important part of the American political tradition is an avowed fear of centralized power. It was this tradition that dictated the loose union of states under the Articles of Confederation and led the framers of the Constitution to prefer a federal to a centralized unitary system. It is this tradition that is repeatedly invoked in political campaigns, legislative debates, presidential speeches, and litigation in the courts. And it is to this tradition that business and labor, along with countless other pressure

[39] *Haddock* v. *Haddock,* 201 U.S. 562 (1906); *Atherton* v. *Atherton,* 181 U.S. 155 (1901); *Davis* v. *Davis,* 305 U.S. 32 (1938); *Williams* v. *North Carolina,* 317 U.S. 287 (1942); *Williams, et al.* v. *North Carolina,* 325 U.S. 226 (1945); *Sherrer* v. *Sherrer,* 334 U.S. 343 (1948); *Estin* v. *Estin,* 334 U.S. 541 (1948). See also Monrad Paulsen, "Migratory Divorce," *Indiana Law Journal,* Vol. 24 (1948), p. 25.

[40] The most frequent reason for a governor to deny extradition is his belief that the fugitive, if returned, will not receive a fair trial according to due process of law. This applies quite often in the case of Negroes fleeing from states in which racial discrimination is an accepted or even an official policy.

groups, appeal when opposing federal policies deemed unfriendly to their interests.

Yet, in a kind of perverse fashion, our professions of faith in small business and small government, in decentralized decision making, and in local self-government have been accompanied by an almost steady growth in big business, big labor, and big government. In the interplay of centripetal and centrifugal forces in our society, the centripetal forces would seem to be in the ascendancy.

Whereas fifty years ago the vast bulk of taxes were collected and spent at the state or local level, by 1960 approximately two-thirds of all taxes were collected and disbursed by the federal government. Why this trend toward a centralized government in a nation so profoundly dedicated to state and local government? To attribute this solely to the influence of greedy bureaucrats in Washington or to the propaganda of so-called do-gooders, welfare workers, and socialistically inclined politicians is to indulge in self-deception. No doubt the ambitions of enterprising bureaucrats and politicians have played a part. No doubt, too, an increasing sense of social responsibility at all levels of government has had its effect in expansion at the federal level. But more important than these are centripetal forces at work in American economic and social life. Not least among these have been the meteoric growth of the American economy and the increasing scale of commercial and industrial operations.

In 1789 the American economy was agrarian; trade and commerce and manufacturing and heavy industry played a minor role. Both supply and demand were generated and satisfied at a state or local level. Yet even at that time, regional and national markets, and even world markets, for American goods and services had expanded to a point where the framers of the Constitution insisted upon giving to the central government power to regulate commerce among the several states and with foreign nations. As these markets grew and as the scale of American business and industry increased, state and local controls became more and more irksome. Business enterprise itself demanded their elimination. It was, indeed, business enterprise, aided and abetted by the Supreme Court, that made this initial assault upon States' rights in the process of creating a united nation and a common continental market out of 13 separate states. The centralization of power in government was a logical and inevitable reaction to the centralization of power in the world of business and industry. It would be an exaggeration to call this change a "revolution": it evolved too slowly for that, for centralization in the public power structure lagged behind centralization in the private power structure. In 1938 Senator O'Mahoney, speaking to the New York Board of Trade, said that there were "thirty corporations in the United States, each with assets in excess of one billion dollars . . . [with combined assets of] more than 50 billion dollars." The assets of these thirty corporations exceeded the value of all property in 22 states. "No state," he pointed out, "can exercise the slightest power beyond its own boundaries, but each of these corporations has an influence that is national and even international in its scope."

By 1930 nearly 90 percent of the installed capacity in the electric light and power industry was controlled by 19 holding companies or financial groups. One company alone controlled more wealth than the total value of all other property in 24 states and the Dominion of Canada. In 1957 Adolph Berle wrote:

> In terms of power, not only do 500 corporations control two-thirds of the nonfarm economy [of the United States] but within each of that 500, a still smaller group has the ultimate decision-making power. This is, I think, the highest concentration of economic power in recorded history. . . . Many of these corporations have budgets, and some of them have payrolls, which, with their customers, affect a greater number of people than most of the ninety-odd sovereign countries of the world.[41]

By 1960 state and local business enterprises and their markets had given way to national, and even international, concerns doing business in national or international markets. Technological developments in transportation and communication and a revolution in organization and managerial skills accelerated this process.

Whatever else may be said of this trend, it created a private power structure to which no government, and least of all the federal government, could be indifferent. Under pressure from a hundred directions—farm organizations, organized labor, consumers' associations, small businessmen, political parties—the central government has been impelled to intervene to establish policies compatible with this new scale of economic operations. The wonder is not that the central government has intervened so much, but that its intervention has, on the whole, been so meager and so mild. For the most part it has left the incorporation, licensing, and control of business enterprise, the professions, and agriculture to the states in a cooperative and highly flexible federal system.

Greater even than the growth of an American national economy as a centripetal force in the American polity have been the impact of war and rumors of war. It was the search for a government able to maintain order at home and security and independence in its external relations that, as much as anything else, led to the adoption of the federal Constitution. And whenever our national security is threatened or challenged by wars—hot or cold—the power and influence of the central government grows at a spectacular rate to levels to which it rarely returns when the war or crisis is past. What is true of war-induced crises is also true, although in more modest dimensions, of other crises arising from eco-

---

[41] *Economic Power and the Free Society* (New York: Fund for the Republic, 1957).

nomic depression or other forces of national disaster. The Great Depression of the 1930s and World War II resulted in a major and permanent expansion of federal power and responsibility.

These are by no means the only centripetal forces at work in American society. Others include a highly mobile population, a common culture and a common language, sustained and developed by the world's most impressive system of mass communications and entertainment, and a system of free education reaching from kindergarten to graduate and professional schools, in which normative instruction and indoctrination lay special emphasis upon national patriotism and national values. Only in the southern states is there any comparable emphasis on state or local loyalties.

Against these centripetal forces, which during most of our history have been of increasing importance, there are strong centrifugal forces that have helped to maintain the American federal system: the dimensions and shape of the country itself; the diversity of climate, topography, and natural resources, with corresponding regional or sectional interests; a population unique for its ethnic, religious, racial, political, and linguistic variety; and the long tradition of local government—all have exerted persistent pressures against the concentration and centralization of power. Even in these latter days of the so-called administrative state and the organization man, and the apparently triumphant trend toward large-scale enterprise, there are strong forces at work toward the devolution of political power and the decentralization of decision making. We may indeed be on the threshold of a new period in which our system of cooperative federalism will give increasing attention to state, metropolitan, and regional governments as counterweights to centralized authority. In any case, the American federal system will continue to provide the world with a workable, if not an ideal, model for the adaptation of political power to geographic, economic, and social reality and to the centripetal and centralized forces that they generate.

PART II
THE AMERICAN POLITICAL PROCESS

PUBLIC OPINION
AND SUFFRAGE

The Declaration of Independence says that "all governments derive their just powers from the *consent* of the governed." It does not say, nor can it be interpreted to mean, that government—to be just and legitimate—must also be government directly by the people. When Lincoln spoke at Gettysburg about "government by the people," he had in mind, not the direct democracy of a New England town meeting, or even a modern system of popular initiative and referendum, but rather the representative democracy of the American Constitution. The distinction is important, since it raises a significant issue as to how far, and in what way, government by "consent of the people" or "by the people" is to be understood as government by what is commonly called public opinion. It is confusion concerning this problem that has caused, in Walter Lippmann's words, a "functional derangement" in the United States between the masses of the people and the government. "The people," he says, "have acquired power which they are incapable of exercising and the governments they elect have lost powers which they must recover if they are to govern."[1] Vital matters of public policy and administration, he argues, are determined, not on the basis of careful research, discussion, and informed judgment but on the basis of guesses as to what the so-called public, or public opinion, wants or will tolerate.

In his concern over what he regards as an excessive intervention of the people, or as the saying is, of "public opinion," in the decision-making process of government, Lippmann has many worthy predecessors.

[1] See Walter Lippmann, *The Public Philosophy* (Boston: Little, Brown, 1955); Mentor Book ed., p. 19.

☆ PUBLIC OPINION

It was the uninformed, unstable, fickle character of public opinion that led the founding fathers of the American republic to distrust *democracy,* which they identified as government by public opinion. Hamilton bluntly called the public a "great beast which seldom judges or determines right." Aristotle and Plato had similar misgivings. So too, if we can believe Shakespeare, did the Romans. Note, for example, the contempt in which Coriolanus holds the Roman electorate and the ease with which Marc Anthony transforms a Roman crowd into something little better than a lynching mob.

Public opinion, it is said, is not only ignorant, fickle and unstable, it is often cruel and unjust. The condemnation of Socrates, the Salem witch hunts, the Ku Klux Klan raids, and other examples of public intolerance and persecution, all exhibit the same compound of fear and hate, ignorance and insecurity. The crowd, hissing or shouting down an unpopular leader or idea differs only in degree from a lynching mob.

And there is a certain kinship, too close for comfort, between the lynching mob and the mass adulation of popular idols or heroes. For the same crowds that cry Hail! today, may cry Havoc! tomorrow. Public opinion can almost literally destroy in an hour what it takes years and even generations to build. As Mark Twain once said, "A lie can go around the world while the truth is putting on her shoes."

Public opinion, not infrequently, is a compound of gossip and rumor, born of fear, ignorance, or misinformation. The National Opinion Research Center on October 6, 1946, asked a random sample of people: "What do you know about the Bill of Rights? Do you know anything it says? Have you ever heard of it?" The results were a bit startling. Thirty-one percent said they had never heard of the Bill of Rights. Thirty-six percent had heard of it but knew nothing about it; 12 percent thought they knew but were misinformed. Only 21 percent had any accurate information at all.

Other examples might be cited. Only a few months before he was nominated for the Presidency in 1952 Adlai Stevenson was unknown to 66 percent of the public. In August, 1952, after the national conventions, 55 percent did not know the name of the Republican vice-presidential candidate. Also in 1952 some 30 percent of the public had never heard of the Taft-Hartley Act, which had been widely discussed, bitterly contested in Congress, and finally passed over the veto of President Truman.[2]

Most studies of this kind indicate a significant relation between a lack of education and information on the one hand and a susceptibility

[2] See R. E. Lane and D. O. Sears, *Public Opinion* (Englewood Cliffs, N.J.: Prentice-Hall, 1964), p. 58.

to rumor and gossip, fear, and mass hysteria, on the other. Education and information enable one to check rumor against reality, and the habit of doing so helps to produce a suspended judgment where information is lacking. It is the suspended judgment "until the facts are in," the courage to say, "I don't know," or "I'm not so sure," that characterizes the rational citizen from the mass man, the wise man from the fool. And it is the process of checking rumor against reality that is the heart of rational deliberation, a process that takes both time and effort. It was to insure this process of rational deliberation that the founding fathers contrived our complex system of checks and balances. They knew how important it is that the people, and especially their representatives, have as accurate a picture as possible of the world of reality—that they see the world as it is, not as imagination would have it. They knew, as Professor Lasswell has said, that, "As the factual face of the world is dimmed, anxiety increases and the pressure of the fantasy-drives grows increasingly intense and successful."

All governments, as David Hume once said, rest on public opinion since public opinion, in the long run will determine the limits of public toleration and consequently the nature and orientation of public policy. This is, of course, particularly true of democratic political communities. It is important, therefore, that public opinion be an informed opinion, for only informed opinion is proof against rumor, gossip, fantasy, and hysteria, seduction, and subversion. How to bring informed opinion to bear on public issues is a major problem of democratic government.

"The public has," wrote Tocqueville, ". . . among a democratic people a singular power of which aristocratic nations could never so much as conceive . . . In the U.S. the majority undertakes to supply a multitude of ready-made opinions for the use of individuals who are thus relieved from the necessity of forming opinions of their own."

Hence, in a democracy, says Tocqueville, "it may be foreseen that faith in public opinion will become a species of religion and the majority its ministering prophet."

But Tocqueville was quick to note the hazards in government by public opinion. "In the principle of equality," he said, "I very clearly discern two tendencies, the one leading the mind of every man to untried thoughts, the other inclined to prohibit him from thinking at all. . . ."

If we merely substitute the absolute power of majority opinion for the absolute power of a privileged class over individual minds, "the evil would only have changed its symptoms. Men would not have found the means of independent life; they would simply have invented a new dress for servitude."

How to reconcile government by public opinion with the freedom and energy of individual minds thus becomes a central problem of political science.

Much of the discussion about government by public opinion is obscured by the variety of meanings with which the term is used. Public opinion is often used as synonymous with *culture,* the common body of attitudes, beliefs, opinions, and behavior which holds the community together. Culture it is said is "the sum of all the patterns of behavior impressed from the cradle which keep the group from flying into a thousand fragments." Most writers on the subject give public opinion a more restricted meaning although most agree that it is composed of ideas, attitudes, beliefs, and behavior patterns hard to define or discover. It has been said that public opinion is like the atmosphere—you can't see it but you know it is there.

Nor is the relation between opinion and overt behavior as clear as one might wish. Behavior, as Walter Bagehot observed, shapes opinion quite as often as opinion shapes behavior. A man's religious or political opinions are as often determined by the church into which he is born or at which he worships and by the party with which he votes as by more formal ideological influences. Many opinions serve mainly to rationalize interests or behavior patterns in a relationship of cause and effect without indicating, however, which is cause and which is effect. It is this integral relation between opinion and behavior that makes the study of public opinion so important. To study voting behavior without regard for the voter's political opinions is to deprive voting behavior of meaning—and to study political opinion without regard for overt political behavior is to deprive political opinion of its main significance.

The relation between opinion and behavior may be clarified by distinguishing attitudes and opinions. An attitude may be defined as the pre*disposition* of an individual to behave in a certain way in response to certain conditions. An opinion may or may not be the *verbal* expression of an attitude. If it is, it may be a fairly reliable indication of how an individual may behave. But mere verbal reactions unrelated to basic attitudes may tell us little or nothing about behavior. Hence it is that verbal response to political questions may be misleading unless they reflect basic attitudes. Not all public opinion polls are equally reliable or significant. Many of them merely report opinions made public through an interview. Not all opinions made public represent a true public opinion, since they may be unrelated in any significant way to underlying attitudes on significant issues.

The late Viscount Bryce once defined public opinion as "the aggregate of views men hold regarding matters that affect or interest the community." To Walter Lippmann public opinion is the prevailing or aggregate opinion of the "interested spectators to action." That is, it is the opinion of those whose support rival factions seek to win, as nations in the cold war seek to win the uncommitted. According to Harold Lasswell public opinion is developed and mobilized about "debatable demands for action." Where there is no issue, no demand for action on a public question, one cannot speak of public opinion. Wilhelm Bauer makes a similar point in his distinction between *dynamic* and *static* opinions—the former being opinions on issues in controversy, the latter on matters already resolved or noncontroversial. It is with *dynamic* opinion that the political scientist is mainly concerned. Other definitions and distinctions might be cited to clarify (or perhaps to confuse) the meaning of the term "public opinion"—a term so vague that Walter Lippmann once referred to it as a "phantom."

To find this phantom public opinion, to measure its direction, magnitude, intensity, and composition is a major problem, perhaps *the* major problem of every responsible government. Among the more tangible evidences of public opinion are the thousands of organized groups which exist in every mature society and which express themselves on issues of public policy. The American Medical Association, the AFL–CIO, the Farm Bureau Federation, the National Association of Manufacturers, the League of Women Voters, the NAACP and hundreds more—compose a chorus of political voices that makes up in volume and intensity what it lacks in harmony. Where the vital interests, that is, the basic attitudes of such groups are engaged, they may become a major factor in the molding and mobilization of public opinion.

But public opinion—like the public interest—is something more than the sum total of the "opinions" of special interest groups. There is, in a word, a public opinion above and beyond the opinions of organized groups, a public opinion which includes millions who are unattached to any of the contesting factions. Public opinion in this wider sense is a product of education, indoctrination, self-interest, and other "conditioning" as complex as life itself. It is not to be discovered solely by listening to the clamorous voices of pressure groups but by listening to or watching interactions or transactions among individuals in an almost infinitely complex pattern of verbal expression and overt behavior.

To be meaningful and significant public opinion must represent something more than verbal responses to hypothetical or trivial questions. It ought to give some reliable indication of how "the public" and especially the voting public will behave in actual situations where they are called upon to choose, that is, to vote. Verbal reactions to the various propositions with which the public is confronted are meaningful and significant mainly when they indicate how the individuals who compose the public will behave when called upon to choose. That is when they represent or rationalize basic attitudes.

The gap between professions of moral and religious belief and actual conduct is well known, and some cynics say that only overt behavior, not opinion, is of any significance to the political scientist. What the cynic forgets, of course, is not only that opinions are in themselves a form of political behavior, but that they *can* help us understand and even to predict overt behavior.

Although verbal reactions do not *always* correspond to underlying attitudes or behavior, they frequently do. Indeed it is only because human beings customarily do what they say they will do that organized society can function at all. That is why the study of public opinion is a legitimate and important branch of political science.

Whether, like Rousseau, one regards public opinion as the voice of God—or, like Alexander Hamilton, as a great beast, all will agree upon the importance of discovering it, whether to obey, change, placate, or evade it. That is why devices for the discovery of public opinion have become increasingly important in both private and public government. Nearly every major industry not only has its advertising and public relations staff, but it also has a staff of public opinion analysts or employs professional organizations engaged in public opinion research. Public opinion or survey research centers have become important adjuncts to social science departments in major universities, to government agencies, and to political parties. If public opinion has not become the "mistress of the world" as Tocqueville predicted, it has become a major preoccupation of decision makers everywhere. It behooves the student of political science, therefore, to become familiar with the arts of programming, sampling, interviewing, coding, and analysis—essential to the study of public opinion and political behavior.

Some critics regard this trend as subversive of representative democracy. Excessive concern for public opinion, they believe, undermines the independence of elected representatives and substitutes the opinions of transient majorities for the judgment of legislators and executives. The "polling craze," it is said, makes robots of representatives, and a mockery of the deliberative process. When the founding fathers insisted that governments derive their just powers from the consent of the governed, they did not envisage government by public opinion, but by responsible representatives of the people. Government of the people does not require that public officials (the President or the Congress) act in response to the latest public opinion poll or the demands of organized interest groups or even the views expressed by leading editors, commentators, preachers or pundits. Conscientious legislators and executives will take all such opinions into account—but they will not be governed by them. It is well to remember that public opinion *governs* not by defining issues or, as a rule, making decisions on particular alternatives of policy and administration. It governs mainly by expressing preferences among general systems of goals or values identified with political parties and candidates for public office. As George Bancroft said, government of the people "maintains not that the people can make right but that the people can discern right," that is, can judge between alternative goals presented to them. The nature of the alternative goals and the manner in which they are presented for public scrutiny and choice will be the measure of political leadership in any community. Where leadership is lacking, public opinion will be confused and confusing. It will indicate not preferences concerning the direction in which the state should move, but merely the limits of what the people will endure.

☆ **THE RIGHT TO VOTE**

The ultimate weapon by which the people rule is the ballot. If governments derive their just powers from the consent of the governed, some formal, legal means must be devised by which consent is given or withheld. To be sure, even without the right to vote, citizens of a free society enjoying other civil liberties might still play a role in decision making. Through speeches, books, pamphlets, parades, demonstrations, letters and petitions they could exert considerable influence, but without free elections such expressions of public opinion would lack their cutting edge, the right to make and unmake governments. Hence a fair index of the growth of democratic government is the gradual extension of the suffrage.

The terms upon which persons are allowed to vote, the conditions and manner of voting have been of great variety. Where voting is by voice (*vive voce*), or by "show of hands," or by division (the "ayes" on one side, the "nays" on the other), or by colored ball or *ballotta,* the voter makes his choice in public so that all may see. Under such circumstances voters vulnerable to bribery or pressure can be held accountable to those who seek to corrupt them and the voting process is less likely to reflect the free choice of the voter than where he casts his vote in secret. Notwithstanding the ease with which elections could be corrupted under these circumstances, many defended "open" voting on the theory that a man ought to "stand up and be counted," and "voters, like officials, ought to be held responsible for the way they vote." But this argument misconceives the role of voters and elected representatives in the decision-making process. It is the representative who is to be held responsible to the voters and not the other way around. For this reason open voting in legislative assemblies and in executive and administrative agencies is essential if elected officials are to be held to account for what they do.

Persuaded by arguments of this kind, most democratic governments have adopted what is called the Australian ballot system of voting. Having its origin in Australia in the 1880s this system is commonly characterized by:

1. Elections conducted under public auspices and control and at public expense.
2. Only duly qualified (or registered) voters are allowed to participate.
3. Printed ballots, provided at public expense, containing the names of candidates and propositions to be voted on and instructions to the voter on how to mark and cast his ballot.

4. Closed alcoves or booths within which the voter may mark his ballot in secret.

The Australian ballot system also normally includes provision for a careful check by "watchers" and election officials, to see that the secrecy and integrity of the ballot is maintained with safeguards against plural voting, breaches of secrecy, and fraudulent counting. In many places the official paper ballot is being replaced by voting machines which automatically record and count the votes as they are cast, but which embody in all essentials the foregoing characteristics of the Australian ballot.

Who May Vote

No electoral system allows everyone to vote—but only those who meet certain qualifications usually defined by law. Against the theory that the right to vote should be restricted to certain privileged classes, the democrats of the eighteenth century claimed the suffrage as one of the natural rights of man. Thomas Paine, the great pamphleteer of the American Revolution, ridiculed property qualifications. "Wealth," he said, "is no proof of moral character; nor poverty of the want of it; on the contrary, wealth is often the presumptive evidence of dishonesty." When a man must own a mule in order to vote "in whom does . . . such a right exist? Is it in the man or in the mule?"

But radical notions of the suffrage as a natural right have never been widely accepted. The prevailing theory has regarded the right to vote as a privilege conferred by the State on those only who possess certain qualifications. Without tests of property or education or status it was argued that the voter would have no real stake in the community. Moreover, it was said, votes of propertyless, illiterate citizens could easily be controlled by the more prosperous, educated and powerful members of the community. "Give votes to the people who have no property," said Gouverneur Morris, "and they will sell them to the rich who will be able to buy them." To these arguments was added the fear that the poor, who in every society outnumber the rich, would use their political power to advance their own interests at the expense of their more affluent neighbors.

Such misgivings were candidly expressed by James Madison in the Constitutional Convention. During the debates, Charles Pinckney had argued that universal suffrage in America would present no great danger, since with vast areas of free land available, substantial equality would prevail. To this argument Madison replied:

We cannot be regarded even at this time as one homogeneous mass . . . In framing a system which we wish to last for ages, we should not lose sight of the changes which ages will produce. An increase in population will of necessity increase the proportion of those who labor under all the hardships

of life and secretly sigh for a more equal distribution of its blessings. These
may in time outnumber those who are placed above the feelings of indigence.
According to the equal laws of suffrage the power will slide into the hands
of the former.[3]

In spite of Madison's misgivings, however, the right to vote was
progressively extended until the United States became one of the first
great powers to achieve universal suffrage. Prior to the Revolution, age,
residence, sex, property, taxpaying, and religious qualifications were
practically universal. The right to vote, in the colonies and under the
Articles of Confederation, was determined not by the central government
but by the several colonies or states. Suffrage qualifications therefore
reflected the particular prejudices of the ruling elites in each state, and
there was considerable variation from state to state.

During the Constitutional Convention a plan to extend the suffrage
to all adult male citizens was proposed but not seriously considered.
There was, moreover, no very extensive support for uniform qualifications for the suffrage. "If the interests of the several parts of the commonwealth were identical," said Judge Upshur, "it would be safe and
proper that a [numerical] majority . . . should give the rule of political
power. But our interests are not identical and the difference arises from
property alone. . . ."

In the end the Convention simply incorporated the prevailing state
suffrage qualifications into the Constitution and made them the basis for
voting in federal elections. "The Electors (voters) in each state," says
Section 2 of Article I, "shall have the Qualifications requisite for Electors
of the most numerous Branch of the State Legislature," and this remains
the basic constitutional provision on the suffrage. This, said Hamilton,
was the only practicable solution since it would have been unwise to give
Congress power to establish uniform qualifications for state elections and
equally unwise to let the states determine qualifications for federal office.
By making suffrage qualifications the same for both, the Constitution
recognizes the need both for state autonomy and for some uniform
federal rule.

The first major test of this system came in the elections for delegates
to the state conventions called to consider ratification of the Constitution
itself. In a total population of nearly 4 million probably not more than
500,000 were qualified to vote—the excluded classes being mainly
women, slaves, and indentured servants. Not many free adult males, even
at that time, were excluded by property, taxpaying, or religious qualifications. The chief hazards were requirements of age, residence and registration, plus apathy and indifference. In any case, it is estimated that only

---

[3] Madison proved to be a good prophet. Universal suffrage has brought with it free
public education, vast programs of public housing, health, and welfare summed up in
what is called the "welfare state."

some 160,000 out of the 500,000 eligible voters actually participated in these important elections.

With the establishment of the new government under the Constitution, agitation against limitations on the suffrage was intensified. New Jersey in 1807 and Maryland in 1810 moved toward universal suffrage for free white males and in other states pressure for more liberal qualifications increased. The democratic trend was most notable in the new states that were admitted to the Union after 1800.[4] Indiana in 1816, Illinois in 1818, Alabama in 1819, and Maine in 1820 provided for universal suffrage for free white males.[5] Partly in self-defense, partly under pressure of the same democratic trend, the older states fell into line. By 1850 white manhood suffrage had been adopted in all but a few states and by the end of the Civil War had been extended to these also. Extension did not come without a struggle and in one case a threat of civil war.[6]

The full scope of congressional power over the right to vote in federal elections has never been systematically explored either in Congress or before the Supreme Court. As we have seen, the basic power to determine suffrage qualifications was left with the states by Section 2 of Article I of the Constitution. But the powers of Congress in this area are not without ambiguity. Section 4 of Article I provides that although the "times, places, and manner of holding elections for Senators and Representatives, shall be prescribed in each state by the Legislature thereof," it also says, "but the Congress may at any time by law make or alter such regulations, except as to the place of choosing Senators." One might argue that the "manner of holding elections for Senators and Representatives" could include the power to prescribe suffrage qualifications and that congressional power to "make or alter such regulations" would include power to determine the qualifications of voters in federal elections. But no such argument has been seriously advanced in the face of Section 2 of Article IV, which expressly gives this power to the states. Section 4 of Article I has been held to apply not to the qualifications for the suffrage but, as the Constitution makes clear, to the *time, place,* and *manner* of holding elections for Representatives in Congress. Even this power is

---

[4] It is worth noting that in establishing qualifications for membership in the House of Representatives and the Senate, and for President and Vice-President, the Convention imposed *no* property qualifications.

[5] Incidentally, by 1828, in only 2 out of the 24 states were presidential electors chosen by the state legislature. In all others they were directly elected.

[6] In what was called Dorr's rebellion in Rhode Island in 1841 the central cause was whether a government which limited suffrage to property holders was a "republican form of government" which, under the Constitution, Congress was bound to guarantee to the states. The issue reached the Supreme Court in 1849, and the Court avoided it by saying it was a "political question" and not therefore "justiciable." See *Luther* v. *Borden,* 7 Howard 1 (1849). In recent cases dealing with representation and reapportionment, the Supreme Court has not relied on the constitutional provision that "the United States shall guarantee to every State . . . a Republican form of government." It has preferred to rely on the equal protection clause of the Fourteenth Amendment.

expressly denied to Congress "as to the place of choosing Senators" which is fixed by the Constitution in the state and cannot therefore be changed. However, congressional power over the "manner of holding elections for Senators and Representatives" has been held to include all legislation necessary "to insure a fair and honest conduct of an election at which a member of Congress is elected" including an honest count and report of the election and the preservation of returns. It also includes, as Professor Corwin says, congressional power to "protect the act of voting, the place where it is done, and the man who votes, from personal violence or intimidation and the election itself from corruption and fraud." As we shall see, this gives to Congress a significant power to protect citizens in their right to vote.[7]

Congressional power to regulate the suffrage has been further extended by formal constitutional amendment and by judicial interpretation. Section 2 of the Fourteenth Amendment, ratified in 1868, provides that "when the right to vote at any election for the choice of electors for President and Vice-President . . . Representatives in Congress, the Executive and Judicial officers of a state, or members of the Legislature thereof is denied to any of the male inhabitants of such State, being twenty-one years of age, and citizens of the United States, or in any way abridged except for participation in rebellion, or other crime, the basis of representation . . . [for such state] shall be reduced in the proportion which the number of such male citizens shall bear to the whole number of male citizens, twenty-one years of age in such State." Congress, however, has never seen fit to apply this provision of the Constitution in apportioning representation among the states.

Moreover, the Fifteenth Amendment ratified two years later (1870) expressly prohibits the states from imposing any racial qualification for the suffrage. Section 1 of this amendment reads, "The right of citizens of the United States to vote shall not be denied or abridged on account of race, color, or previous condition of servitude." And Section 2 provides that "Congress shall have power to enforce this article by appropriate legislation." Only in recent years has Congress acted under this section, notably in the Voting Rights Act of 1965.

Alien Voting

In their zeal to attract settlers some of the new states extended the suffrage even to aliens, and by 1875 at least 22 states allowed aliens to vote. One by one, however, these states returned to the common requirement of citizenship as a qualification to vote. When in 1926 Arkansas abolished alien voting, citizenship became a uniform requirement.

---

[7] See Ex Parte *Siebold*, 100 U.S. 371 (1880) ; Ex Parte *Yarborough*, 110 U.S. 651 (1884) .

The achievement of universal manhood suffrage left two major groups outside the community of voting citizens: women and Negroes.

Woman Suffrage

During our early history women were uniformly excluded from the suffrage, being classed for this purpose with idiots, criminals, and Indians not taxed. But not all women were willing to resign themselves in silence to this kind of sexual servitude. Writing to her husband, John Adams, at the Continental Congress in 1776, Abigail Adams urged him to "remember the ladies" in the new code of laws, and to "be more generous and favorable to them than your ancestors. Remember all men would be tyrants if they could." Hannah Lee Corbin, sister of General Henry Lee, in 1778 protested against the taxation of women without representation and in 1792, Mary Wollstonecraft's *Vindication of the Rights of Women* gave voice to a demand for Women's Rights. By 1844 a woman's suffrage movement was under way. The arguments, both pro and con, were compounds of sense and nonsense. For example, in the *New York Herald*, September 12, 1852, the editor wrote, "How did women first become subject to man as she now is all over the world? By her nature, her sex, just as the Negro is and always will be to the end of time inferior to the white race, and therefore doomed to subjection, but she is happier than she would be in any other condition, just because it is the law of her nature."

On the other hand, Ralph Waldo Emerson, writing to the Massachusetts Woman's Rights Convention in Boston in 1856, said that when women voted, "polling places would be no more in barber shops and up back alleys, but in beautiful halls, decorated with paintings and noble statuary and fragrant with fresh flowers." They would elevate politics, produce better candidates, improve the laws, and produce more support for education and human welfare.

The claim of the right to vote as one of the unalienable, or natural rights of man was advanced on behalf of woman suffrage. It was also claimed as one of the "privileges and immunities of citizens of the U.S." under the Constitution, a claim rejected by the Supreme Court.[8]

But the constitutional arguments were less important in the campaign for woman suffrage than other forces at work in American society. In our expanding frontier society, men soon came to outnumber women in the population, and this operated in two ways to advance the cause of equal suffrage. As a minority—even if one assumed that women would vote as a bloc—they could scarcely hope to outvote the men. Furthermore, since women were a minority, they were in short supply and men were consequently more inclined to make concessions to them. This was particularly true in the western states, which took the lead in extending

8 See *Minor* v. *Happersett*, 21 Wall. 162 (1875).

the suffrage to women. Although a limited right to vote—as, for example, in school elections—came early in some 20 states, Wyoming in 1890 pioneered in extending the right to women on equal terms with men. Utah and Washington as territories and later as states followed the lead of Wyoming. So too did California in 1911. When, in 1917, the United States declared war on Germany, a number of circumstances combined to accelerate the drive for full woman suffrage. During the preparedness campaign preceding our entry into World War I, and even more so during the conflict itself, women were drawn, in increasing numbers, into agriculture, business, and industry. Pictures of women harvesting crops and even driving farm machinery as "farmerettes" appeared in the popular press and it became fairly common to see women factory workers, street car conductors, stenographers, clerks, railway maintenance employees, and even industrial workers in occupations formerly reserved for men. If women could be called on to do men's work, the national Women's Party argued, they surely could be trusted with the ballot. Militant "suffragette" leaders picketed the White House, had themselves arrested and, as they said, "jailed for freedom." Nor were they backward in pointing to the apparent contradiction between President Wilson's eloquent plea for a war "to make the world safe for democracy" and his steadfast opposition to a constitutional amendment extending full suffrage to women.

By 1918 twenty-nine states had given women the right to vote, although in only six Wyoming, Colorado, Idaho, Utah, Washington, and California—were they granted equal suffrage with men. Under the impact of the war and the intensive pressure politics of equal suffrage organizations, Congress finally in 1919 submitted a constitutional amendment prohibiting the states henceforth from imposing a sexual qualification for the suffrage. This amendment, called the Susan B. Anthony Amendment, after a pioneer leader of the American Women's Suffrage Association, was promptly ratified by the states and in August, 1920, became the Nineteenth Amendment to the Constitution. It reads:

> The right of citizens of the United States to vote shall not be denied or abridged by the United States or by any state on account of sex.
> Congress shall have power to enforce this article by appropriate legislation.

Since 1920, therefore, women have enjoyed full suffrage rights with men. In this respect the United States has blazed a trail which other democratic states, some most reluctantly and belatedly, have since followed. What women have done with the ballot is another story.

Negro Suffrage

Notwithstanding the express language of the Fourteenth and Fifteenth Amendments and the plenary powers granted to Congress under these provisions of the Constitution, Negro citizens in the United States have been denied the right to vote in many states. How this has been accomplished and how, especially since World War I, the barriers have been slowly removed is too long and complex a tale to tell here. Only the barest outline can be indicated.

In early colonial times free Negroes who could satisfy other qualifications of age, sex, property, and religion were customarily allowed to vote except in Georgia and South Carolina. Slaves, of course, were everywhere excluded from the suffrage. As slavery was extended and the number of free Negroes multiplied, racial discrimination increased until by 1860 only five states, all in New England, were without racial qualifications for the suffrage. Nor was this situation radically changed by the Civil War itself. There was no great enthusiasm for Negro suffrage even in the victorious northern states, where racial discrimination continued during the war and for many years thereafter. The Emancipation Proclamation made no provision for extending the right to vote to Negroes; Lincoln himself was cold to the idea, nor did the Republican party in 1864 officially commend it. It was only the triumph within the party of the so-called Radical Republicans that made Negro suffrage an issue of practical politics and legislation. In 1867 Congress extended the vote to otherwise qualified Negroes in the District of Columbia—over President Johnson's veto. "Hardly yet capable of forming correct judgments upon the important questions that often make the issue of a political contest," said the President, "they [the newly emancipated Negroes] could readily be made subservient to the purposes of designing persons."[9]

Congress, however, in a militant mood pushed through the Reconstruction Act of 1867, calling for conventions to be elected in the erstwhile Confederate States to frame new constitutions with "all male citizens," except those who had been in rebellion, qualified to vote. All of the so-called Reconstruction Constitutions, moreover, provided for universal manhood suffrage, without racial discrimination of any kind. And, as we have seen, Congress, in the Fourteenth and Fifteenth Amendments, moved both directly and indirectly toward full Negro suffrage: directly, through the sanction of reduced representation against any state denying the suffrage to male citizens and the prohibition in the Fifteenth Amendment against any discrimination on grounds of race; indirectly (at least so some Republican leaders reasoned), through the guarantees in the Fourteenth Amendment of "equal protection of the laws" and "privileges and immunities" of citizens of the United States.

The guarantees of the Fourteenth and Fifteenth Amendments were fortified by federal civil rights acts designed primarily to protect Negroes

_____

[9] This argument, obviously, was not calculated to support racial discrimination but to emphasize the importance of other qualifications for the suffrage. Indeed President Johnson had suggested giving the vote to literate Negroes with property valued at $250 or more.

in their right to vote in the newly reconstructed Southern states. Under this legislation, enforced mainly by military occupation, male Negro citizens in the states of the Confederacy voted in considerable numbers during the Reconstruction period.

During this period of Reconstruction and to some extent thereafter, southern opposition to wholesale Negro enfranchisement was carried on by intimidation and violence—precisely the "crimes" against which the civil rights acts were directed. The law proved to be a fragile shield against such organized resistance as was carried on by the Ku Klux Klan, the Knights of the White Camelia, and a white population made sullen and vindictive by military defeat.[10] Moreover the Civil Rights Acts were narrowly and often adversely construed by the Supreme Court in a number of decisions.[11] In any case, as the Reconstruction period came to an end and with it federal military occupation, southern leaders turned to new and more genteel devices for keeping Negro citizens from the polls.

It should, in fairness, be said that some southern leaders, resented what to them seemed the hypocrisy of the North in imposing Negro suffrage on the South without enforcing it in their own states. In 1867, for example, the very year of the Reconstruction Act, Kansas, Michigan, Minnesota, and Ohio rejected amendments to their own constitutions designed to extend the suffrage to Negroes. Still another source of resentment was the disfranchisement of many southern whites for participation in the rebellion, at the time Negroes were being admitted to the suffrage. By 1890 the political disabilities imposed on southern leaders were removed and they proceeded upon a broad campaign to disfranchise the Negro. So effective was this campaign that in 1899 Governor Johnson of Alabama could boast that "There is not a negro in all the commonwealth of Alabama holding a public office . . ."

The devices used to keep Negro citizens from the polls were numerous and various. Laws against bigamy, larceny, vagrancy, and other offenses were enforced with particular zeal against Negroes. In seven southern states payment of poll taxes was made a qualification and poll tax receipts were required as evidence before a citizen could register. In some places the poll tax liability was cumulative, so that failure to pay during several years could create a heavy obligation for defaulters who later sought to register and vote. Educational and literacy tests were often enforced against Negroes more zealously than against whites. And where the literacy test included a requirement not only to read a section of the Constitution but also to "give a reasonable interpretation thereof"

---

[10] Under an act of April 20, 1871, the President was authorized to use military force against organized conspiracies to deprive citizens of their rights. Known as the Ku Klux Klan or Anti-Lynching Act it defied the evil but made little headway against it.

[11] See for example the *Slaughter-House Cases*, 16 Wallace 36 (1876); *U.S.* v. *Cruikshank*, 92 U.S. 542 (1875); and the *Civil Rights Cases*, 109 U.S. 3 (1883).

vast discretion was given to officials in deciding what constituted a "reasonable interpretation," so that few Negroes could meet this test.

Because the suffrage qualifications operated to disfranchise not only Negroes but also many whites, several states adopted what came to be called a "Grandfather" clause, as an "escape hatch" for whites. Those citizens whose fathers or grandfathers were qualified to vote prior to 1866 or 1867 were declared exempt from other qualifications, notably literacy tests. Since no Negroes were qualified to vote prior to Reconstruction, none could qualify.

But the Grandfather clause as a formal device for imposing a racial qualification on the right to vote was at best a temporary expedient. In 1915 the Supreme Court held it to be unconstitutional as a violation of the Fifteenth Amendment.[12] Denied this "escape hatch" white citizens as well as Negroes were required to meet the literacy and other legal qualifications imposed on the right to vote. To keep Negroes from the polls without disqualifying or discouraging the whites has been the settled policy of many southern states since Reconstruction days.

In addition to devices already mentioned, one of the most effective was the so-called White Primary. In 1921 the Supreme Court in the case of *Newberry* v. *U.S.* held that primary elections "are in no sense elections for an office, but merely methods by which party adherents agree upon candidates whom they intend to support for ultimate choice by the qualified voters." Presumably under this decision qualifications for voting in primary elections would not be subject to the constitutional guarantees of the Fourteenth, Fifteenth, or even the Nineteenth Amendments. Acting upon this assumption the Texas legislature took the lead in 1923 in excluding Negroes by law from participation in *primary* elections. "In no event," said the law, "shall a Negro be eligible to participate in a Democratic party primary election held in the state of Texas . . ." In most southern states from the Reconstruction period until recent years the Democratic nomination for public office has been equivalent to election, since the Republican candidates have presented only token opposition. To exclude Negroes from participation in Democratic primary elections was therefore equivalent to denying them the right to vote in the only election that really mattered.

However, the Supreme Court ruled the Texas white primary law to be unconstitutional as a violation of that section of the Fourteenth Amendment providing that "no state . . . shall . . . deny to any person within its jurisdiction the equal protection of the laws."[13] Bound by its

12 See *Guinn* v. *U.S.*, 238 U.S. 347. The case involved a provision in the Oklahoma constitution of 1910 which was struck down by the Supreme Court. This provided that any person "who was, on January 1, 1866, or at any time prior thereto, entitled to vote . . . and any lineal descendant of such person" need not meet the literacy test imposed by law.

13 *Nixon* v. *Herndon,* 273 U.S. 536 (1927) .

earlier decision that a primary election was not an election within the meaning of the Constitution, the Court felt compelled to base its decision on the equal protection clause of the Fourteenth Amendment rather than the Fifteenth Amendment, which forbids any state to deny or abridge the right to vote "on account of race, color or previous condition of servitude."

Unable to exclude Negroes from the primary by direct legislation, the Texas legislature sought to do so by delegating the power to determine qualifications for voting in the primary to the State Executive Committee of the party, which promptly did so by executive rule. This subterfuge was also thrown out by the Court on the ground that action by the State Executive Committee of the party was equivalent to action by the state itself.[14] Whereupon the state legislature remained silent, while the state Democratic Convention, without any formal legal authority, proceeded to rule that only whites could participate in Democratic primary elections. The Court now felt constrained to sustain this ruling on the shaky ground that the Democratic party was a purely voluntary organization and as such was free to determine the qualifications for participation in its primary contests. This decision in effect gave judicial sanction to the Democratic white primary which accordingly became a major device for the disfranchisement of Negroes in southern states.[15]

It was not until 1941 that the Supreme Court moved toward a revision of the doctrine of *Newberry* v. *U.S.* and held in the case of *U.S.* v. *Classic* that "the primary is by law an integral part of the election machinery." That is to say, it recognized that a state sponsored and supported primary election *is* an election under the Constitution, which gives Congress power to regulate the "manner of holding elections for Senators and Representatives including the right of a citizen to have his vote counted in such a primary election." Three years later in the case of *Smith* v. *Allwright* (1944) the Court finally threw its full weight against the white primary by holding that the "right to vote in such a primary for the nomination of candidates without discrimination by the state, like the right to vote in a general election, is a right secured by the Constitution. . . . Under our Constitution the great privilege of the ballot may not be denied a man by the state because of his color."

Since 1944, therefore, although there has been some abortive maneuvering in several states to preserve it, the white primary has ceased to be a major factor. As a consequence Negro voters in the South increased from 595,000 in 1947 to more than a million in 1956. Notwithstanding this impressive increase only approximately 25 percent of the Negroes of voting age were able to qualify in the erstwhile solid South prior to the 1964 and 1965 Civil Rights Acts. Racial discrimination continued under

14 *Nixon* v. *Condon,* 286 U.S. 73 (1932) .
15 *Grovey* v. *Townsend,* 295 U.S. 45 (1933) .

inequitable, even dishonest, election administration, and massive community pressure or intimidation of Negroes who sought to vote. The 1957 and 1960 Acts authorized the Attorney General to initiate actions for injunctions to put a stop to discrimination and intimidation in voting. The intricate legal proceedings involved, however, with their customary delays, reduced the laws' effectiveness. By 1965, for example, some 70 suits had been filed under the 1957–1960 legislation, of which 53 had been tried, and 30 concluded successfully. The net effect of these laws had not been impressive, although some progress had been made.

Since World War I the large-scale migration of Negroes to northern cities where their right to vote is normally unchallenged, at least on racial grounds, has given new force to the drive for full Negro suffrage. Politicians from districts with significant blocs of Negro voters have been constrained to join in what has become something of a crusade to protect the American Negro in his right to vote. Presidential candidates have been sensitive not only to the moral and constitutional issues involved, but also to the electoral weight of the Negro vote in critical states. Federal intervention has taken the form of new civil rights laws in 1957, 1960, 1964, and 1965, the establishment of a federal Civil Rights Commission, and renewed vigor by the Department of Justice in enforcing federal laws to protect the Negroes' right to vote.

After searching investigations the Civil Rights Commission, aided by such organizations as the Southern Regional Council and the NAACP, indicated something of the scope of the problem and suggested a program for doing something about it. While there were bright spots, the overall picture was of continued and widespread discrimination. Although some 60 percent of southern whites were registered in 1959, only 25 percent of the South's 5 million Negroes were qualified to vote. (See Table 7–1.) Discrimination was more widespread and effective in rural than in urban areas, and in those areas in which Negroes comprised 50 percent or so of the total population.[16]

To remedy this situation the Commission recommended a program including:

1. A directive to the Bureau of the Census to make a compilation of registration voting statistics by race, color, and national origin—to provide accurate information on voting behavior and discrimination.

[16] "Of the 158 counties . . . where Negroes are a majority of the population, (almost all rural counties), 16 have not a single Negro voter and in 49 others fewer than 5 percent of voting age Negroes are registered." Actually as many Negroes were registered in New York City alone as were on the rolls in South Carolina, Georgia, Alabama, Mississippi, and Louisiana, combined. See Report of *Civil Rights Commission*, 1959.

"In April, 1964, only 21.6 percent of voting age Negroes in Alabama were registered; in Louisiana only 31.6 percent; in Mississippi 6.7 percent; in Virginia 27.7 percent." E. W. Kenworthy, in *The New York Times*, March 16, 1965.

TABLE 7-1
Voter Registration in the South, Winter-Spring 1968

State	White VAP[a]	Negro VAP	White Regis-tered	% White VAP Regis-tered	Negro Regis-tered	% Negro VAP Regis-tered	% Black
Alabama	1,353,058	481,320	1,119,000	82.7	271,000	56.3	19.5
Arkansas	850,643	192,626	616,000	72.4	121,000	62.8	16.4
Florida	2,617,438	470,261	2,194,000	83.8	293,000	62.3	11.8
Georgia	1,797,062	612,910	1,450,000	80.6	334,000	54.5	19.1
Louisiana	1,289,216	514,589	1,122,000	87.0	301,000	58.5	21.1
Mississippi	748,266	422,256	655,000	88.9	264,000	62.5	28.4
North Carolina	2,005,955	550,929	1,555,000	77.5	293,000	53.2	15.8
South Carolina	895,147	371,873	567,000	63.3	183,000	49.3	24.4
Tennessee	1,779,018	313,873	1,434,000	80.6	225,000	71.7	13.6
Texas	4,884,765	649,512	3,532,000	72.3	540,000	83.1	13.2
Virginia	1,876,167	436,720	1,200,000	63.9	247,000	56.6	17.1
TOTALS	20,096,735	5,016,100	15,454,000	76.9	3,072,000	61.2	16.6[b]

a VAP = Voting Age Population.
b 1960—10.7.

SOURCE: Voter Education Project, Southern Regional Council, 5 Forsyth Street, N.W., Atlanta, Georgia 30303. (404) 522–8764. Reprinted by permission.

2. That Congress enact legislation to declare that suffrage qualifications other than those of age, residence, and noncriminal status be regarded as *prima facie* evidence of racial discrimination, and hence unconstitutional. This would outlaw poll tax, property and other "artificial" tests.

3. Legislation to provide that where "literacy" or so-called "understand" tests are given a citizen may qualify if he has completed six grades in school, i.e., that a sixth grade education be made conclusive evidence of literacy for voting purposes.

4. Legislation by Congress to penalize arbitrary inaction by election officials, where such inaction works to deprive any citizen of the right to register, to vote, and to have his vote counted.

Parts of this program have been adopted or have reached the stage of formal legislative proposals. A constitutional amendment has been ratified to outlaw the poll tax in federal elections.[17] The Civil Rights Act of 1964 prohibited state registrars from discriminating against Negroes in

---

17 "Although the 24th Amendment prohibits the poll tax as a qualification for voting in national elections, a three-judge federal court in Virginia in November, 1964, upheld a state law requiring payment of a poll tax as a qualification for voting at state and local elections. The issue involved only the Virginia poll tax, but it would seem to apply, unless upset by the Supreme Court, to similar laws in Oklahoma, Mississippi and Texas." See *The New York Times*, November, 13, 1964.
On appeal to the Supreme Court, however, in March, 1966, the lower court's decision was reversed. A state poll tax was unconstitutional, said the Court, as a denial of equal protection of the laws. See *Annie E. Harper et al.* v. *Virginia State Board of Elections*, 383 U.S. 663 (1966).

reviewing application forms and "interpretations" of legal texts and also prohibited them from disqualifying applicants for minor or inconsequential errors or omissions.[18] In 1965 a new Voting Rights Act was adopted to enable the federal government to move more directly and effectively in protecting Negroes from discrimination at the polls. The law is filled with technical complexities to guard against unnecessary interference by federal authorities with the power of the states to determine voting qualifications. Its affirmative provisions, however, authorize the Attorney General of the United States to appoint examiners to "prepare and maintain" lists of eligible voters in any political subdivision in which 20 or more persons complain that they have been denied the right to vote "under color of law by reason of race or color." Such complaints may arise, and such action may be taken in any state or political division in which "the Director of the Census determines that . . . less than 50% of the persons of voting age . . . were registered on November 1, 1964, or that less than 50% of such persons voted in the Presidential election of November, 1964."

The federal examiners are to inquire into the qualifications of all applicants to determine if, in fact, there has been racial discrimination in the administration of such voting tests as education, literacy, understanding, or interpretation of any matter, or of the applicant's good moral character. "Any person whom the examiner finds to have the qualifications prescribed by state law . . . shall promptly be placed on a list of eligible voters." Provision is made for state and local officials to challenge such lists before hearing officers, appointed by the U.S. Civil Service Commission, with a right of appeal to the appropriate U.S. Circuit Court of Appeals. However, "Any person listed shall be entitled . . . to vote pending final determination by the hearing officer, and by the Court."

In his address to the Congress proposing the Voting Rights Act of 1965 President Johnson denied any attempt by the federal government to usurp, or interfere with, the legitimate powers of the states. "To those," he said, "who seek to avoid action by their National Government in their communities—who seek to maintain purely local control over elections—the answer is simple: Open your polling places to all your people. Allow men and women to register and vote, whatever the color of their skins. . . . There is no Constitutional issue here. . . . There is no issue of

---

[18] As the Congress prepared to remove barriers to Negro suffrage, state legislatures in the South moved to erect new ones. To "get around" Court decisions enjoining certain discriminatory procedures, the Mississippi legislature moved to provide that when an applicant for registration was denied, no reason at all should be given for the denial. The theory was that such "reasons" might constitute illegal assistance to the applicant in a subsequent constitutional interpretation test. Another law added a requirement of "good moral character;" still another provided for a "third party" challenge to good moral character at a hearing before a registrar. Louisiana amended its registration law to require "perfect completion" of the application form. It also added a "citizenship" test. See *The New York Times*, March 16, 1965.

State Rights or national rights. There is only the struggle for human rights."[19]

The Supreme Court, in a number of significant decisions, has sustained the Voting Rights Act and helped to break down the barriers to full Negro suffrage.[20] The Acts of 1964 and 1965 also gave impetus to civil rights leaders to organize extensive voter registration drives throughout the South.[21] The results were dramatic. Of just over 5 million Negroes of voting age in the South, approximately 1,345,000 (less than 27 percent) were registered to vote in 1962. By the election of 1964 the figure had risen to more than 2 million (about 41 percent of the population of voting age); and by the election of 1966 more than 2,600,000 southern Negroes were registered (over 52 percent). The southern population is roughly 20 percent Negro; by 1966 Negroes constituted 15.4 percent of the voters in that section. Only in Georgia, Louisiana, Virginia, and Mississippi were less than half of the Negroes of voting age registered, and even in the last-named state the number of registered Negro voters increased from 24,000 in 1962 to 139,000 in 1966 (from 5.3 percent of voting age population to 36.1 percent).

It is said that racial discrimination at the polls will end only when racial discrimination in housing, transportation, education, recreation, employment, and even in religious worship ends. When American Negroes receive equal opportunities to these social and civic rights, then and only then will they become first-class citizens. There is, of course, much truth in all this. But it is also true that the right to vote itself can be a

19 See *The New York Times,* March 14, 1965.

20 For example, in March, 1965, the Court upheld the power of the Justice Department to sue the State of Mississippi in order to enforce Negro voting rights. The complaint of the Justice Department had been dismissed by a three-judge U.S. District Court in Jackson, Mississippi, on the ground that the U.S. Department of Justice could not sue a state. In revising this decision the Supreme Court said: "We have no doubt . . . that it was error to dismiss the complaint without a trial. . . . The complaint charged that the State of Mississippi and its officials for the past three quarters of a century have been writing and adopting Constitutional provisions, statutes, rules, and regulations . . . all designed to keep the number of white voters at the highest possible figure and the number of colored voters at the lowest. . . . The allegations of this complaint are too serious, the right to vote . . . is too precious . . . for this complaint to have been dismissed." *U.S.* v. *Mississippi,* 380 U.S. 128 (1965).

In another case a lower court's decision was upheld, maintaining that a Louisiana vote registration test requiring a citizen to interpret a section of the state constitution or of the federal Constitution to the satisfaction of the voting registrar, had been administered in such a way as to discriminate against Negroes and hence was unconstitutional. "This," said the Supreme Court, "is not a test but a trap, sufficient to stop even the most brilliant man on his way to the voting booth. The . . . right . . . to vote cannot be obliterated by the use of laws like this, which leave the voting fate of a citizen to the passing whim or impulse of an individual registrar." *Louisiana* v. *U.S.,* 380 U.S. 145 (1965).

21 The story is most dramatically told in Pat Watters and Reese Cleghorn, *Climbing Jacob's Ladder, The Arrival of Negroes in Southern Politics* (New York: Harcourt, Brace & World, 1967).

formidable weapon in winning other civil rights. Where the vote is denied, public services will be poor or lacking altogether. Housing will be substandard, streets, sewers, and fire fighting equipment inadequate, schools will be poor, public recreation facilities will be lacking or of poor quality, and police protection will become police harassment. The fact is that where the vote is denied, civil rights will be denied, for a voteless people is a voiceless people, and a voiceless people is a defenseless people. In any case a voteless people in a democratic republic is a contradiction in terms.

To be effective, of course, the right to vote must be exercised. To win the suffrage and then through apathy, ignorance, or inertia, to neglect it by not voting, is to win an empty victory. And America's Negro citizens, even where they enjoy equal suffrage, notoriously neglect its use. Nearly everywhere the turnout of qualified Negro voters falls lamentably short of what it might be and considerably below the turnout of qualified white voters. Among Negro voters the percentage of actual participation in elections varies with age, sex, education, income, and social status in substantially the same pattern as among white voters—except that for each category the Negro turnout is lower. No doubt this can be explained in terms of their comparatively recent enfranchisement, and the disadvantages they have suffered in their struggle for equality. What behavioral scientists call a sense of civic opportunity and responsibility, an awareness of the efficacy of voting as a means for their own advancement, appears to be less characteristic of qualified Negro voters than of whites. As evidence in the next section of this chapter will indicate, the Negro population suffers a larger share of social disabilities contributing to voter apathy than does the white population in general. However, under the impact of the current thrust for equality, it is apparent that Negroes are rapidly learning about the power of the ballot as a lever for prying other rights out of American society.

☆ PEOPLE WHO DON'T VOTE

But, it will be said, is the Negro voter's apathy not simply a special case of a general civic apathy that characterizes all Americans? Critics of American politics point to the generally low rate of voter participation at all elections in this country. Even in the sharply contested presidential election of 1960, they argue, less than 70 million voters went to the polls out of 110 million who might have voted. Studies of voting behavior indicate, as Table 7–2 shows, a high correlation between turnout rates and such factors as education, occupation, and social status. Voting participation in the United States compares unfavorably with other democratic nations (see Table 7–3). And participation in other than presidential elections makes the picture even more discouraging.

TABLE 7-2
Turnout, 1960

Social-Economic Status	Percentage Voting
College educated	90
Professional, managerial occupation	88
Other white-collar workers	84
Metropolitan area residents	82
High school educated	81
Nonunion members	80
Town and city dwellers	78
Skilled and semiskilled workers	78
Union members	77
Rural area residents	77
Farm operators	77
Unskilled workers	68
Grade school educated	67
Negroes	54

SOURCE: Adapted from data from a national survey conducted in 1960 by Survey Research Center, University of Michigan. Philip Converse of the Survey Research Center kindly made these findings available to Fred I. Greenstein, *The American Party System and the American People* (Englewood Cliffs, N.J.: Prentice-Hall, 1963), p. 19. Used by permission of the Survey Research Center and Prentice-Hall, Inc.

TABLE 7-3
Voting Turnout as a Percentage
of Age-Eligible Population

Country	Date	Percent Turnout
Australia	1961	95
Belgium	1962	93
Canada	1962	79
France	1962	72
West Germany	1961	88
India	1962	53
Israel	1961	81
Norway	1964	79
United Kingdom	1964	77
United States	1964	61

SOURCE: Adapted from *The Governing of Men*, Revised Edition, by Austin Ranney. Copyright © 1958, 1966 by Holt, Rinehart and Winston, Inc. Reprinted by permission of Holt, Rinehart and Winston, Inc.

From the record it would appear that in practice the American people take their civic rights and responsibilities rather lightly.

But to indict the American voter for apathy on the basis of comparative turnout rates can be misleading and unfair. One might, for example, dismiss the charge on the ground that in a truly free society with universal suffrage a low rate of voter participation may be evidence not of apathy but of civic contentment—or consensus. Where basic conflicts of public policy or of class interest divide the people one may expect a large turnout. The relative absence of such conflicts in the United States, our pervasive spirit of equality, our deep-rooted pride in the Constitution and in our political institutions—all conspire to create a confidence, if not complacency that militates against a high turnout at election time. Where major and widespread conflicts of interest are at stake, where issues are clearly defined, and where the margin of strength between competing candidates or issues is narrow, voter turnout in the United States, as in other countries, is high.

Comparative figures, however, even under these circumstances, can be misleading unless one takes into account those factors, peculiar to the United States, that tend to reduce the rate of voter participation. Unlike all the other countries included in the Gallup table, with the possible exception of Canada, the United States is a federal, not a unitary system of government. In most other democratic states suffrage qualifications, registration procedures, ballot forms, and election administration are uniform throughout the country. In the United States, except for the limitations imposed by the Fourteenth, Fifteenth, Seventeenth, and Nineteenth Amendments, each of the fifty states is free to establish its own rules concerning these matters. Thus we have in fact virtually fifty different electoral systems. Suffrage qualifications based on property, taxes, age, residence, and education vary, often greatly, from one state to another. To compare turnout rates without taking account of these differences is unfair and misleading. The rate of voter participation in the southern states, for example, will be only from one-third to two-thirds the rate in northern states.[22] This differential is due primarily to the systematic disfranchisement of the southern Negro. But it is also due to other special factors. Where a large part of the population is disfran-

[22] The following figures illustrate this differential rate of turnout for the presidential election of 1960 as percentages of population of voting age:

Southern States	Rate	Northern States	Rate
Mississippi	25.5	New York	67.1
Georgia	30.4	California	67.3
South Carolina	30.5	Pennsylvania	70.5
Alabama	31.1	Michigan	72.6
Virginia	33.4	Wisconsin	73.1
Arkansas	41.0	Delaware	73.7
Texas	41.8	Rhode Island	75.0
Louisiana	44.8	Illinois	75.8
Tennessee	50.4	Iowa	76.6
North Carolina	53.6	Massachusetts	77.0
Kentucky	59.3	North Dakota	78.9

chised, the habit of nonvoting may spread to those who have the right to vote. In many southern communities, *the* dominant issues of racial relations are "solved" by community consensus and not at the polls. There is the further fact that the one-party system, which until recent years prevailed in most southern states, removed the important political conflicts from the general election to the Democratic primary election. In a good many southern states voter turnout in primaries was higher than in general elections.

In studying voter turnout rates the American Heritage Foundation estimated that of the 40 or more million adults in America who fail to vote in presidential elections, some could be accounted for in these terms:[23]

1.	Insufficient residence in voting district	6,000,000
2.	Traveling on business on election day	2,600,000
3.	Illness	5,000,000
4.	Noncitizens	2,500,000
5.	Illiterate (not able to meet literacy test)	800,000
6.	Residents of the District of Columbia	500,000
7.	Voting contrary to religion	115,000
		17,515,000

To these one should also add some 2 million Negroes still denied registration in southern states, perhaps a million or more other adults who failed to meet rigid voter registration requirements, and upwards of another million in the armed services who failed to vote for reasons other than ignorance or apathy. Altogether it may well be that legal and bureaucratic regulations rather than apathy or inertia are the major factors in the comparatively low rate of voter turnout in the United States. Although residence requirements may be essential to avoid fraudulent multiple voting, surely a full year or more is excessive for this purpose. A citizen ought not to be denied the right to vote for governor or United States Senator because he has recently moved from one county or city or precinct within the state to another. Similarly one ought not to be denied the right to vote for President and Vice-President because he cannot satisfy the residence requirement for a particular state. Rigid residence requirements are especially onerous for a highly mobile people—and Americans are the most mobile people in the world.

One might also suggest other reforms that would facilitate voting. Among these would be permanent registration, which is not only less onerous to the voter but less expensive to administer and virtually fraud-proof. The initiative for voter registration might also be shifted from the voter by a periodic house-to-house canvass by mobile registrars. Better facilities for the registration and voting of the aged and the infirm might

[23] See *The New York Times*, November 28, 1956.

help to improve the turnout. A short simplified ballot, wider use of voting machines and improved methods of absentee voting, are other reforms that suggest themselves.

Some countries make voting compulsory and impose a fine for failure to register and vote. The arguments pro and con on this subject have been long and heated. To vote, say the proponents, is a citizen's major civic responsibility and it is absurd to fine him for negligence in not properly maintaining his property, and at the same time to allow him, without penalty, to neglect his duty in helping to maintain the community upon which the whole value of his property depends. A fine for nonvoting would spur many otherwise indifferent citizens to take a greater interest in public affairs. After all, say the advocates of compulsory voting, people learn by doing, and one can learn to take part in self-government only by active participation. Moreover civic interest, like other attitudes and behavior patterns, increases with participation and what may be a burden today will become a privilege tomorrow.

It is nonsense, say the opponents of compulsory voting, to compel a man to vote if he lacks the interest to do so without compulsion. To drive voters to the polls by threat of a fine will bring out the indifferent, the ignorant, and the resentful. Moreover a citizen lacking in interest does not deserve to participate in making the critical decisions of his community. Besides, voting is but one form of such participation. An aroused citizen can often be more effective in shaping public policy through trade unions, chamber of commerce, or other pressure groups to which he may belong. Contributing to campaign funds, working at headquarters for a political party or candidate, or attending political rallies are other forms of political participation as important—sometimes more important— than voting.

And so the argument proceeds. Compulsory voting in Belgium and Australia has produced few if any of the evils which its opponents predict. Neither has it contributed significantly to the general level of civic life. It is a reform with which we might well experiment in one or more of our fifty states.

☆ MAJORITY RULE AND MINORITY RIGHT

A basic principle of democratic government is majority rule. In electing the President and Vice-President, representatives in Congress and the Senate, the majority candidate is by law and custom the victor. In choosing their own officers and in passing laws and resolutions, Congress, state legislatures, city councils, local town meetings and the governing boards of private organizations usually abide by the will of the majority. Even the Supreme Court of the United States decides cases by majority vote.

Although there are 9 judges, 5 to 4 decisions are as binding as those agreed to by unanimous vote.

Why has this rule enjoyed such universal currency? Men abide by the will of the majority, says the cynic, simply because in numbers there is strength, and a majority vote shows on which side power lies. In primitive society the majority could outfight the minority, and in submitting to a majority vote the minority was doing the only thing it could. Hence, it is said, the minority wisely bides its time until, by fair means or foul, it can itself become a majority with power on its side. Law and right are on the side of the strongest battalions, and during most of human history the strongest battalions have been the largest.

A less cynical theory holds that wisdom and right reason are on the side of the many as against the few. To John Milton, as to Justice Holmes, the test of an idea is to get itself accepted in the market place. Majority rule is justified on the theory that the majority is more likely to be right, since it draws upon the wisdom and experience of more people. "Truth," said George Bancroft, "emerges from the contradictions of personal opinions . . . Thus the opinion . . . we respect is not the opinion of one or of a few, but the sagacity of the many. . . ." Thus majority rule implies a built-in mode for the correction of error.

Some people flatly reject this notion and argue as Hendrick Ibsen did in *An Enemy of the People*. The majority is always wrong, he said, because it lives by the truth of yesterday, "Truths so decadent, so senile, so old and decrepit, they are in a fair way to become lies." In a world of expanding knowledge and constant change, it is argued, the average life of an idea is a generation. By the time an idea wins acceptance by the majority, it is likely to have been displaced by new ideas based on new knowledge. Hence, the majority opinion always lags behind the frontiers of science and scholarship—and is likely, therefore, to be false.

The most common defense of majority rule is, however, not that the majority is necessarily right or wise or just but that since governments derive their just powers from the consent of the governed, the best way to measure consent or dissent is by a simple count. Majority rule implies, not that the majority is right, but simply that a majority vote furnishes a more stable basis for power than a minority vote because it more accurately represents the consent of the governed. The best indication of consent, or of the will of the people, would be a unanimous vote of the citizens or a "consensus" which approximates unanimity.

But to require unanimous consent or consensus on every issue would impose impossible limits upon what a government might do, and would give the minority a veto on any proposed action. To avoid this, one more than half has come to justify collective action. In some cases, as where several candidates compete for a single office, the one receiving the highest vote can win even where this is not a clear majority of the total vote cast. Other issues, on the contrary, are regarded of such importance that more than a simple majority is required. The Constitution, for example, requires a two-thirds vote for the ratification of treaties, for passing a law over the President's veto, and to remove a President or a federal judge from office by impeachment. And formal amendments to the Constitution itself require a two-thirds vote of both Houses of Congress, plus ratification by the legislatures of three-fourths of the states. Extraordinary majorities of this kind are often required to amend state constitutions or city charters. And some people believe that a two-thirds vote of the Supreme Court should be required to declare an act of Congress or a state legislature unconstitutional. Such provisions reflect a distrust of simple numerical majorities and a feeling that the larger majority will not only prevent hasty, ill-considered, action but will more clearly indicate the general will because it more closely approximates consensus or unanimity.

All of which suggests that the doctrine of majority rule is not as simple as it seems at first sight. When someone says therefore that the majority should rule, it is proper to ask, "what majority, a majority of whom, of how many, and for what?" The United States is not a consolidated, monolithic society, in which people are represented only in proportion to their numbers, but a pluralistic society in which they are represented also as members of communities called states. Decisions in the Congress are made by representatives not only of numerical majorities as in the House of Representatives, but by representatives of what John C. Calhoun called *concurrent* majorities of states, as in the Senate. The electoral college represents both numerical and concurrent majorities, since each state has as many votes as it has representatives in the House of Representatives and the Senate. And in the amending process the Constitution requires approval by both numerical and concurrent majorities.

The principle of representation by concurrent majorities might be extended to include not only majorities of political communities like states, but also majorities of voluntary interest groups. As Calhoun put the matter, there

> are two different modes in which the sense of the community may be taken, one, simply by the right of suffrage unaided . . . which regards numbers only and considers the whole community as a unit . . . the other . . . regards interests as well as numbers—considering the community as made up of different and conflicting interests as far as the action of government is concerned. . . . The former of these I shall call the numerical or absolute majority, and the latter, the concurrent or constitutional majority.

In Calhoun's view only policies based on unanimity or a consensus of numbers *and* interests could be legitimate. Carried to its logical conclusion this would provide each state and each major interest with a veto on political decisions. Calhoun's theory became the basis for the Ordinance of Nullification, adopted by a special convention and endorsed by the South Carolina legislature in 1832, which declared the tariff acts of 1828 and 1832 to be null and void and forbade the collection of federal customs duties within South Carolina. In this form the principle of the concurrent majority was an invitation to anarchy, since its implied *liberum veto* would make government virtually impossible. It was small wonder, therefore, that President Jackson characterized the doctrine as an "impractical absurdity."

Nevertheless it is well to remember that the framers of the Constitution were fearful of numerical majorities. According to Madison, the major task of the Constitutional Convention was "to secure the public good and private rights against the rule of factions . . . whether of a minority or a majority and at the same time . . . preserve the spirit and form of popular government. . . ."

The framers therefore devised a system of representation and decision making based on both popular numerical and concurrent majorities. Both, however, were limited by constitutional restraints, of which the Bill of Rights was most important. It was assumed that such a system would reflect the enduring will of the people—not merely the consent of a majority but a consensus of the community. This system would, in the words of Madison, "secure the public good and the private rights . . . and at the same time preserve the spirit and form of popular government . . ." The basic purpose has been to reconcile majority rule with minority rights.

Direct Democracy

Since 1789 the Constitution has been progressively democratized, as direct participation of the people in the process of government has increased. The selection of presidential electors by state legislature has been replaced by direct election until the electoral college has become little more than a rubber stamp for recording a popular verdict. From 1789 to 1963 the right to vote has been steadily extended. Limitations of property, sex, race, education, and even age and residence, have been abandoned or radically reduced. This trend has not yet run its course but it is unmistakable and probably irresistible. Distrust of faction-controlled state legislatures has led to the adoption of the popular initiative and referendum for both constitutional amendments and legislation. Although the town meeting has declined, direct participation in legislation has nevertheless increased. Increased reliance on popular referenda, plebiscites, and even public opinion polls, has led some scholars to question again the proper role for the electorate and mass opinion in the American Republic.

"The voter," says Walter Lippmann in *The Public Philosophy,* cannot be relied upon to represent the People . . . the voters . . . have never been and can never be, more than a fraction of the total population . . . [they] have no title to consider themselves the proprietors of the commonwealth and to claim that their interests are identical with the public interest. A prevailing plurality of the voters are not The People. The claim that they are is a bogus title invoked to justify the usurpation of the executive power by representative assemblies and the intimidation of public men by demagogic politicians. In fact demagoguery can be described as the sleight of hand by which a fraction of the people as voters are invested with the authority of The People. That is why so many crimes are committed in the people's names.

These are strong and intemperate words and require more analysis than we can give to them here. One may, however, observe that not even the most romantic of majoritarian democrats would claim that a plurality or even a majority of voters could speak with finality for all the People. The voters' task has always been the limited and relatively simple one of saying *yes* or *no* to candidates or propositions put before them. What is done after the election, the decisions made, the public deeds that are done or left undone, may or may not be in the public interest, and may or may not represent the will of all, or even a majority, of the people. Elections, at least, serve to indicate what a majority of those citizens qualified and willing to vote approve or disapprove, or tolerate as compatible with the common good.

The propositions posed or the candidates presented may be wise or foolish, depending on the leadership of those who propose the men or measures on which the voter is asked to say *yes* or *no*. The voters' verdict also may be wise or foolish, but such as it is, it remains for the time, at least, the decision upon which subsequent decisions depend. In the American system, under virtually universal suffrage, the chances are pretty good that through the years public policy, disciplined but not determined at elections, will represent the nation's underlying will and purpose. Who can say that through the years this system has not succeeded in promoting the common good, protecting individual freedom and reconciling majority rule with minority rights while preserving "the spirit and form of popular government?"

THE AMERICAN
PARTY SYSTEM

☆ *POLITICAL PARTIES AND THE FOUNDING FATHERS*

The framers of the Constitution had a deep and abiding suspicion of political parties, which they called alternately "factions" or "parties." In his farewell address Washington warned the country against the "danger of Parties in the State. . . . They serve," he said, "to organize faction . . . and by cunning ambitious and unprincipled men . . . to subvert the Power of the People and to usurp for themselves the reins of government. . . . The alternate dominion of one faction over another, sharpened by the spirit of revenge natural to party discussion . . . is itself a frightful despotism. . . ."

Political geniuses though they were, the founding fathers never quite understood the difference between parties and factions, or what we would call pressure groups. But they knew that conflicts of interest, such as debtors against creditors or workers against employers were inevitable in any civilized society. They knew also that finding some suitable basis on which those warring groups can live together in reasonable tranquility is the central problem of any responsible government.

They also wanted a government that would not only provide for the common good but also protect private rights, which they regarded as an indispensable component of the "common good." To do so they sought a system in which no single special interest or faction, whether a minority or a majority, could control the government and sacrifice the public good or private rights to its own special interest. By basing the system on both numerical and concurrent majorities, they sought to reconcile majority rule with minority rights.

They were, as we have seen, especially afraid of majority factions. A minority, they assumed, could never control the state since it could be outvoted by the majority. But in a government based on majority rule, only its own sense of self-restraint would keep the majority from sacrificing both liberty and the public good to its own interest.

To prevent this they set up a government in which power is both limited and divided. A majority faction might get control of the House of Representatives, since this body is elected in its entirety every two years by popular vote. But they thought it unlikely that a majority faction could, at the same time, control the Senate, since Senators were to be chosen by state legislatures for staggered terms of six years, only one-third being elected every two years.

Even if a majority faction could gain control of both the House of Representatives and the Senate, the President would remain free, since he was to be selected by an electoral college, chosen by state legislatures, for a term of four years. The idea that any majority faction could get control of the House of Representatives, serving for two years, the Senate, for six years, and the President, serving for four years, seemed unlikely. But, they reasoned, even if this unlikely event did happen, there was always the Supreme Court, chosen for life by the President and the Senate, to prevent the majority from betraying the public good or unconstitutionally invading private rights. Moreover, the limited powers granted in the Constitution, plus the positive prohibitions contained in the Bill of Rights, would help to insure against the tyranny of a majority. The centrifugal force of state and sectional interests, too, they thought would also check faction by isolating it.

Finally, to change the system, to expand the limited powers of the government by amending the Constitution, would be extremely difficult, since it would require a two-thirds vote in Congress (or in state conventions) to propose amendments and ratification not by the people directly but by three-fourths of the state legislatures. Moreover equal representation of the states in the Senate was unamendable. "No state," reads Article V, "without its consent, shall be deprived of its equal suffrage in the Senate."

What the founding fathers failed to understand was the role of parties, not only in overcoming these safeguards but also in the mobilization of minority factions in the public interest. For an American political party is not just another special interest group, or rather, if it is, its "interest" is in power, not to promote the narrow interest of any single minority faction, but the public interest as that appears to the various and often conflicting interests of which the party is composed.

☆ *PARTIES AND FACTIONS*

The politician who wants to win an election must attract to his standard the votes of a majority or at least a plurality in the constituency he seeks to represent. The wider that constituency and the greater its population the more numerous are its special interest groups or factions. We speak loosely of farm districts, or labor districts, or Catholic, Protestant, or Jewish districts, and there are districts in which the prevailing interests may be so defined. But it is a rare constituency in which a candidate can win by appealing to one faction alone.

Moreover, the politician cannot win simply by mobilizing the members of organized factions, by adding together the trade union vote, the farm vote, or the chamber of commerce vote. Millions of voters do not belong to any of these organizations. It is rare for any organization to include over 50 percent of its "potential" membership. The 18 million members of organized labor, for example, include less than one-third of the total work force. A majority of farmers belong to no farm organization. The politician must therefore reach those whose formal affiliations do not extend beyond their families, a small circle of friends, and perhaps their church.

Every politician soon finds also that not all the members of labor unions, chambers of commerce, or farm organizations think alike on political issues. After all, individuals have many interests. Not even the most redoubtable labor leader can deliver the votes of *all* his members to any candidate. The politician thus becomes a broker, a broker of consent. He picks up votes, the symbols of consent, from groups of organized voters where possible, but also from individual voters whenever he can.

Since no single politician can do this alone, particularly in large districts, he enlists the help of other politicians at the level of the precinct, ward, city, county, assembly district, congressional district, state, and nation. Together they create a new kind of faction, the political party, whose interest is not merely to influence decision makers, as do the so-called pressure groups, but to *control* power and the decision-making process itself. To this end the party strives to elect its own candidates to public office, from the county coroner to the President of the United States. This it does by soliciting the votes of individuals, and groups of individuals already organized in minority factions of one kind or another.

Where leaders of an organized minority faction or a majority of its members are enlisted by the party, the faction becomes a satellite of the party. Only rarely does a pressure group as such, whether it be the American Legion or the AFL–CIO, put its own candidates in the field, and rarely too is it organized on the basis of political subdivisions as is the party.

The platform of the party, the ideas, policies and programs with which it appeals for votes, reflects the kinds of interest of which it is composed, and the interplay of individual, group, or factional pressures within it. Consequently, the wider and more heterogeneous its constituency the more comprehensive and often vague its platform is likely to be—the more it is likely to avoid extreme positions on the left or right in favor of more moderate policies of the center.

To succeed and endure, the party as a state or national organization must not become a captive of any one of its constituent pressure groups, since no single interest can normally command enough votes to win. On the contrary, the party must discipline its factional satellites to subordinate their own special interests to the more general public interest with which the party is identified. This task of *faction control* becomes an essential feature of party government, since without it no party can hope to govern for long.

Political parties in most democratic states thus become instruments for the discovery of the public interest and the common good. A party, said Edmund Burke, "is a body of men united, for promoting by their joint endeavors the national interest, upon some particular principle in which they are all agreed." When rival parties compete for power they become the major instruments by which a democratic society, in Madison's words, seeks "to secure the public good and private rights" against factional interests and at the same time "preserve the spirit and form of popular government." This they do by offering alternatives of leadership and policies among which voters may choose.

We are thus confronted with a paradox, for a successful political party *is* a faction, but one that in the very process of enlisting the majority on which its power depends must control and discipline the minority factions of which it is composed. Where party is strong, therefore, faction is weak. The majority faction that Madison *most feared* thus becomes a major instrument for achieving the goal that Madison and the founding fathers *most desired*.

As the late Professor Franz Neumann put it: "The single most important instrument for the translation of social power [factional interest] into political power is the political party. . . . The party permits the presentation of [selfish] interests as national interests. At the same time . . . it prevents the . . . domination of national interests by particular [selfish] interests. The function of the political party in a democracy is ambiguous. The democratic process compels each social group [faction] to strive for mass support. Each group therefore must present its selfish interests as universal. . . . The very need [to do this] and to appeal to social groups larger than the immediate interest group compels adjustment of various interests" in the public interest. This function of the party is often described as its *aggregative* role.

There is another facet to this paradox. The founding fathers sought to prevent rule by a majority faction, by limiting and dividing power between the President and Congress and between the central government and the states. What they did not anticipate was that such a government might not work at all. With the President set against Congress, and Congress not only set against the President but divided against itself in House and Senate, the new government was almost ideally planned for inaction and inertia. For unless all of these counteracting powers moved together they could not move at all.

Paradoxically, it is the party system that this division of power was designed to checkmate that has furnished the means to make it work. For it is when the President and both houses of Congress are controlled by the same party, as has been the case during most of our history, that the American government moves with vigor and dispatch.[1] Without party politics working within this complex structure, government would waste itself in friction, frustration, and deadlock, as indeed it does when the White House and the Congress are in politically hostile hands. Or it breaks down in civil war, as it did in 1860. The party thus plays an *articulative* as well as an *aggregative* role.

It is not surprising that the founding fathers did not fully understand the role of political parties, for parties as we know them are fairly recent inventions, their origin being almost contemporaneous with the adoption of our own Constitution. Democracy, growing out of the Industrial and Commercial Revolution, the Protestant Reformation, and the Age of Enlightenment, had shattered the old framework of society. It had destroyed the old "hierarchy of classes and their internal cohesion, and the time-honored social ties which bound the individual to the community." Government could no longer rest on an exclusive set of landlords, high churchmen, soldiers, and royal retainers. Dozens, hundreds, even thousands of new interests, with millions of individuals, organized and unorganized, clamored for recognition and participation in the process of government.

The advent of democracy *involved a broadening of the basis of consent.* As old ties dissolved and new interests multiplied, the path to power was opened to large masses of men who were united by no common ideal or interest as had been the case under the Old Unity of the Old Regime. Under these circumstances, if government was not to degenerate into chaos and anarchy, it became necessary to mold this inchoate mass into some semblance of unity.

Factional organization was not enough, because the obstacle of mass consent was now interposed between the desire for power and the control of power. And no faction alone was big enough to command the necessary majority. Out of such conditions, political parties were born. The problem, as Disraeli put it, was "how are the [diverse] elements of the nation to be welded together?"

☆ PARTY SYSTEMS

Although the soil from which they grew was similar, it was not identical, and the party systems that emerged in different countries were not the same. In some states, Great Britain, Canada, Australia, and the United

---

[1] From 1789 to 1968 all 3 branches were under the same party in 106 out of 179 years.

States, for example, voters and factional interests were mobilized under the banners of two major parties, with minor splinter parties sulking in impotence, or as satellites of the major parties. In others, as in France, Italy, or the German Republic, multiple party systems developed. In still others, notably the USSR, Fascist Italy, and Nazi Germany, one party dominates the political scene.

We cannot now examine these various systems in detail or inquire into the reasons why they developed as they did. A few general observations, however, can be made.

A multiple party system has the advantage of corresponding more closely to the underlying pattern of factional interests in the community. Ideally one can have a Farmers' party, a Workers' party, a Merchants' party, a Catholic party, and so forth, with each major interest (each component of Calhoun's concurrent majority) having its own party, candidates, and organization reaching from the capital to the election precinct.

But this advantage is more than offset by several fatal defects. If majority rule is to govern decision making, the only way a majority can be composed is by a coalition of such parties. And this is true not only at the polls but in the legislature as well. The result of this is to substitute partisan maneuvering for party responsibility. Another defect is that a multiple party system tends to weaken the party's role in what we have called *faction control,* that is, the internal discipline of factional interests. In general, wherever party lines correspond closely to factional interests, as in a multiple party system, it becomes extremely difficult to construct a stable majority base for the exercise of power. The result is that in such systems governments are unstable or impotent or both. Moreover the organization of electoral contests on the basis of factional interests tends to intensify conflict in the community. By confronting the voter with not two, but three, four, or more alternatives, a multiple party system makes for complexity and confusion.

In a two-party system, factional interests must yield to the larger interest of a more comprehensive party in search of a majority. They must yield not only at the polls but, after the election, in the government. By the same token the policies and platform of the party must strive to reconcile and transcend the interests of the various factions in the community, and particularly those to which it makes its special appeal. A two-party system thus provides a better means for *faction control* and discipline, and thus contributes to stability in the government. It tends also to blunt the edges of party conflict by compelling major parties to move toward moderate positions ideologically, leaving ideological purity and political impotence to the extremists on both right and left.

A two-party system moreover, by presenting the voter with a relatively simple choice between two alternatives, makes the voter's job easier and translates complex political issues into terms the rank and file can understand and appreciate.

A one-party system has in recent years come to be regarded as the hallmark of a totalitarian, undemocratic society. The Communist party of the USSR, for example, is by definition and by constitutional provision *the* vehicle for maintaining the so-called dictatorship of the proletariat. Similarly in Mussolini's Italy the Fascists and in Hitler's Germany the Nazis were by law the exclusive instruments for mobilizing support and disciplining the population. In all such cases the party system becomes not an instrument of democracy but of dictatorship. The people as voters are unable to hold government responsible. Where they are dissatisfied, they cannot transfer power from one ruling elite to another without resort to violence.

Josef Stalin, in discussing the monopoly of power held by the Communist party in the USSR, argued that two-party and multiple-party systems reflect the existence of social classes in capitalistic democratic states. In the Soviet Union, he said, since there are no social classes, only one party is necessary to represent the only remaining class, the workers.

If this is true, one might ask, if parties reflect social classes, and all except the working class have been eliminated in the USSR, why is it necessary to outlaw all parties except the Communist party and to maintain its monopoly by force? One might ask also, if all political parties are simply instruments for carrying on the class struggle, and if classes have been eliminated, why is any party necessary? The fact is of course that in Communist countries as in Nazi Germany and Fascist Italy, the single ruling party is an arm of the state to control the people and not an instrument of the people to control the state.

A one-party system, however, is not necessarily synonymous with dictatorship or a totalitarian regime. Recent studies indicate that in Mexico's one-party system factional conflicts are fought out within the party, in a manner not too different from the democratic procedures which characterize a two-party or a multiple-party system. In many of our own states, a single party has had a monopoly of political power for extended periods. Yet no one could say that the situation in these states was comparable to the one-party systems of the USSR, Fascist Italy, or Nazi Germany. However tight the control, a free press, and freedom of assembly remained, and even channels for opposition to the ruling oligarchy were open in the primary elections. In fact, in many southern states the monopoly of the Democratic party simply moved the real battle into the primary election, where rival Democratic factions comparable to rival parties fought for control. As the pattern of economic and social life changes in the one-party states of both the South and the North, a two-party system will emerge. Indeed the number of one-party states has steadily declined in recent years.

If we define a one-party state as one in which 80 percent or more of the election results in major statewide contests favored one political party, and a two-party state as one in which neither party won more than 60 percent of the elections, between 1897 and 1921 there were 17 one-party Republican states and 13 one-party Democratic states. Because ours is an open society, however, party alignments are likely to shift from one period of history to another, and even from one election to another. Thus in presidential elections the number of one-party Republican states declined from 19 to 5 between 1929 and 1964 and the number of one-party Democratic states from 11 to 6. In senatorial elections, however, Republican one-party states declined during this period while Democratic one-party states increased. And in gubernatorial elections, while the number of Democratic one-party states remained constant at 13 during this period, Republican one-party states declined from 15 to 4. "A generation ago," writes one authority, "the one-party states controlled over seven-eighths of the electoral college vote; recently they have controlled less than one-third of it."[2]

Just why two-party, multiple-party or one-party systems should develop in the several states or in various countries is a problem too complex for any brief analysis. Some of the major factors involved, however, would include the structure and intensity of regional, religious, ethnic, or class conflicts and the degree of social mobility, that is, the extent to which there is a genuine circulation of elites or a more or less rigid system of social stratification. The factional parochialism and ideological rigidity which characterize closed societies tend also to produce faction-oriented parties. Other more formal institutional factors that shape a community's party system are (1) The structure of political power, that is, whether there is a presidential or parliamentary, unitary or federal, system of government. (2) The representative and electoral system. Single-member districts and majority rule contribute to a two-party system. Proportional representation, multiple-member districts, preferential voting without a plurality necessary to win, all encourage multiplication of parties.

Other factors are, of course, involved, both fundamental and frivolous. The two-party system, it has been said, results from the fact that (1) there are two sides to every question, (2) that a nation addicted to competitive team sports is more likely to favor a two-party system than is a nation given to individual sports competition. It has even been suggested that there are basic character traits that separate human beings into two main categories: liberal and conservative, Democratic and Republican.

More important perhaps are such factors as (1) Absence of any serious religious conflicts and the early separation of church and state,

2 See Paul David *et al.*, *The Politics of National Party Conventions* (Washington, D.C.: Brookings Institution, 1960) , p. 42.

thus removing religion as a political issue. (2) A general consensus on basic political values, leaving to the party battle issues of *means* rather than ends. (3) A strong tendency toward the empirical and the pragmatic and disinclination toward ideology. (4) An open society in which individuals can move from one class or faction to another with relative ease. We might also note as a corollary of this the absence of any widespread sense of class consciousness and conflict. (5) The election of a single executive, the President, by the nation as a whole. (6) A system of single member districts with a strong bias against plurality elections. (7) A system of nominations which places a high value on the resolution of intraparty conflicts, prior to the final interparty battle at the polls.

Even the architecture of public buildings can influence the structure and pattern of party organization. In commenting on the shape of the new House of Commons, in 1943, Winston Churchill said:

> We shape our buildings and afterward our buildings shape us. . . . [The new chambers] should be oblong and not semi-circular. Here is a very potent factor in our political life. The semi-circular assembly which appeals to political theorists enables every individual or every group to move around the center, adopting various shades of pink according to the weather changes. . . . The two party system is much favored by an oblong form of chamber . . . the act of crossing the floor [from the Government side to the Opposition] is one which requires serious consideration.

The upshot of what has been said may be briefly summarized:

1. Party systems have become major instruments for the discipline and control of minority factions in order "to secure the public good and private rights" and at the same time to "preserve the spirit and form of popular government." And most important, the party system offers a means for the peaceful transfer of power from one ruling elite to another.
2. A two-party system offers not only effective *faction control* (an aggregative role), but also simple alternatives of leadership and policy among which voters may choose.
3. The American two-party system, which our constitutional system was designed to smother, has been the means to make that system work. Party politics, in short, have become so indispensable that without them the American constitutional system would fade and pass away. That is, American parties play an indispensable role in the articulation of our complex political system.

☆ THE MYTH OF TWEEDLEDUM AND TWEEDLEDEE

We boast of a two-party system, but we might rather speak of two party systems. For within both Democratic and Republican parties are many subparties, reflecting the great variety of interests and sectional pride in this far-flung and variegated empire and its mobile, polyglot people. It is, of course, in Congress that this variety is most evident.

Of the 537 elected officers of the central government, the President and Vice-President alone are chosen by all the voters from coast to coast and border to border. Senators and Congressmen are responsible to the voters of a single state or congressional district. Only once in four years do members of the House of Representatives and the President "go to the country" together, and even then only one-third of the Senators go with them. At the so-called mid-term elections, both Representatives and Senators must "go it alone." To a large extent they win or lose by presenting national issues in terms of state and local interests. The tariff, for example, is seen not only as it affects our total economy, but also as it affects the wool growers of Montana, the beet sugar interests of Utah and Idaho, or the cutlery and watchmakers of Connecticut. Some candidates for Congress or for state elective offices are often more dependent upon powerful nonpolitical pressure groups than upon the party of which they are nominal members. There are many congressional districts in which support of organized labor or the Farm Bureau Federation or the American Legion or the CIO is more important than the support of the regular Republican or Democratic organization.

Economic factionalism is compounded by diverse ethnic, religious, and sectional loyalties. What pleases the Democratic Irish voters of Boston and New York may not please the nativist Protestant voters of the South and the Middle West. The Democratic Negro voters of the northern cities have only strained relations at best with the traditionally "lily white" Democratic voters of the South. Moreover, tribal memories of ancient battles won or lost between North and South, East and West, may transcend in importance ethnic and economic interests. The Republican party of Oregon and Nebraska is not the same as the Republican party of Maine and Vermont. And the Democratic party of New York and New Jersey is in many ways different from its namesake in Georgia and South Carolina.

Obviously, such a system places a premium not on party unity (and discipline) but on diversity and independence. These differences and factional cleavages become incandescent at mid-term elections or before national conventions, but are usually submerged once in four years in support of the party's presidential candidate. But once the election is over they reappear, and it is often against parochial interests in his own party quite as much as against the opposition party that the President must contend.

Votes in Congress, accordingly, rarely show Republicans and Democrats lined up solidly on opposite sides. Conservatives of both parties join against liberals of both parties, or high-tariff men unite against low-tariff men of both parties. "Like dancers in a vast Virginia reel," says James Burns, "groups merge, break off, meet again, veer away to new combinations." There is an almost continuous crossing and recrossing of party lines, so that it is not unusual for a Democratic administration to rely on western and eastern Republican votes to save its program, or for a Republican administration to rely on southern Democrats. Obviously, under these circumstances it is difficult to know which party is really responsible for a given policy.

The separation of powers, the staggered terms of the President, the House of Representatives, and the Senate, the growth of powerful pressure groups outside the party system, all combine to prevent the kind of party unity and discipline characteristic, for example, of the English system. Conflicts within the major parties are likely to appear almost as important as conflicts between them.[3]

Some authorities have argued that the major dynamic force in American politics has been these battles *within* the major parties. "Except for relatively brief intervals," says Samuel Lubell, "the pattern of American politics has not been that of two evenly competitive parties but of a normal majority party, which held dominance until its elements split, with a second minority party whose strength rises and falls with the heat of the friction within the majority party—much as is the moon's relationship to the sun."[4]

American political history adds force to this theory. Jefferson's victory in 1800 was due as much to the bitter feud within Federalist ranks, between Hamilton and John Adams, as to the rise of the new Democratic-Republican party. Jackson's rise to power was a triumph not only over the divided and debilitated Whigs but over the conservative coalition in his own Democratic party. Lincoln's victory as candidate of the new Republican party in 1860 would have been impossible but for the open split in the Democratic party that year. Woodrow Wilson's election in 1912 was a by-product of the revolt within both major parties, but which in that year produced an open break between the Roosevelt and Taft factions of the GOP.

Rebel groups in the major parties, along with more or less permanent splinter groups of idealists and reformers outside, have appeared in almost all campaigns. The result has been a succession of third, fourth, or fifth parties, calling themselves Know-Nothing, Anti-Masonic, Free Soil, Liberty, Populist, Workingman's, Farmer-Labor, Socialist, Prohibition, or Progressive. They have cut across major party lines and not infrequently have had a decisive effect upon elections and on policy. The

[3] Out of 300 roll calls in both Houses of Congress in 1960, no less than 207, or 69 percent, were described by the *Congressional Quarterly* as bipartisan—i.e., with no clear party cleavage at all.

That this is not a constant figure is indicated by the fact that, out of 302 roll calls in 1959, only 83, or 27 percent, showed such a North-South split among Democratic members as to be called bipartisan. In 1965 this North-South split among Democrats occurred in 160 out of 459 roll calls, i.e., about 35 percent of the time.

[4] See Samuel Lubell, *The Future of American Politics* (Anchor, 1956).

antislavery agitation, the campaigns for the income tax, direct election of Senators, women suffrage, and prohibition amendments to the federal Constitution, all may be traced to these political mavericks.

So persistent and intense have the intraparty battles been that some critics say the battle *between* the major parties is of minor significance. Both major parties, they say, are compelled to appeal to the same body of voters, and must resolve internal conflicts among substantially similar factions.[5] The result is a compelling drift to the center until, it is argued, that for practical purposes the major parties are indistinguishable. There is much to support this view. An examination of party platforms will reveal a striking similarity on many important issues of public policy. Even the voting records of Democrats and Republicans in local, state, and national legislative bodies are often hard to distinguish. Not only is the vast bulk of legislation disposed of by unanimous or virtually unanimous consent, but on many issues there is no significant division as Republicans join with Democrats on both sides of the tally. Party alignments are never neat and clear—with all the "good guys" on the one side and all the "bad guys" on the other. While American politics have thus been filled with intraparty factionalism and innumerable splinter parties, the basic rivalry has been polarized between the Democratic and Republican parties, and it is they who have had major responsibility for defining the issues, providing the leadership, and determining the public policies of the country. In our preoccupation with their similarities we ought not to neglect their differences, which are considerable. A delicate balance of conflict and conformity has been maintained within and between them.

The mere survival of these two major parties and their alternation in power indicate that they have offered the American people something more than a choice between Tweedledum and Tweedledee. Had the major parties been identical it is likely that one or both would have vanished from the scene, as did the Federalist and the Whig parties before them. Had the differences between them been *less*, it is unlikely that they could have survived against a host of competitors which have sought to displace them. Had the differences within the major parties been less, both Republicans and Democrats would have lost the dynamic

[5] This effort to reconcile rival factions is revealed in the theory of the so-called balanced ticket—even in presidential years. In 1928 Al Smith, the Catholic, urban, Tammany Democrat is balanced with Joseph T. Robinson, the Protestant, rural southern Democrat as vice-presidential candidate. In 1940 the Republicans "balanced" their ticket with Wendell Wilkie, a conservative lawyer and lobbyist for the electric power industry as candidate for President, with Charles McNary of Oregon, liberal and staunch advocate of public power. Similarly balanced tickets are evident in the Kennedy-Johnson Democratic slate of 1960, the Eisenhower-Nixon Republican ticket of 1952, and so forth.

At the local level, it is not uncommon to find a balanced slate of candidates including liberals and conservatives, Catholics, Jews, and Protestants, Irish, Italians, Scandinavians—in an effort to weld all these factions into some semblance of unity.

force that has compelled them to "adapt or die" in response to the demands of social change. On the other hand, had these internal differences been more intense than they have been, one or both of the major parties would have been destroyed by political fission.

Even party platforms—those repositories of glib and glamorous generalizations—reflect differences of policy, points of view and emphasis between the major parties. To be sure, these are not revolutionary differences, but they do nevertheless offer a choice as significant as that offered by the Conservative and Labor parties of Great Britain.[6]

Analysis of roll call votes in legislative bodies also reveals significant differences in the voting behavior of Democrats and Republicans—notwithstanding the large measure of agreement on most legislation and the many issues on which no clear party alignment appears. "In eight modern sessions of Congress," says Julius Turner "party behavior would be significantly distinguished on 407 of the 455 roll calls recorded in the House of Representatives." Typical of this alignment was the overwhelming commitment of the Democrats to (1) repeal of the Taft-Hartley Act, (2) generous support of foreign aid, and (3) lower taxes on the lower income brackets. To all of these the Republicans by large majorities were opposed. Other issues on which a clear party alignment appeared included continuation of rent control, tax policy, agricultural price supports, and many aspects of foreign policy. Looking back through the years, one finds similarly clear-cut conflicts between the major parties over such matters as the establishment of the Tennessee Valley Authority, public housing legislation, federal regulation of wages and hours, the school lunch program, social security legislation, and many other issues. Professor Dahl, in his study of *Congress and Foreign Policy,* found 90 percent of the Democrats in the House of Representatives united on 68 issues, and 90 percent of the Republicans united on 36 issues. In the Senate, party cohesion for both parties was almost identical. In a study of 459 roll calls in 1965, twelve in the Senate and thirteen in the House offered a choice between a larger and smaller role for the federal government. In the Senate 52 percent of the Democrats and only 36 percent of the Republicans supported a larger federal role. In the House the vote was 79 percent for the Democrats and only 33 percent for the Republicans.[7] The brokerage character of American party politics results in a strong tendency for both major parties to assume a central or moderate position on most issues, with Democrats slightly to the left of center and Republicans to the right. If either party moves too far in either direction on a left-right scale, it runs the risk of massive defection

[6] Among the leaders of the three major parties today in England, there is so much common ground that, if they changed parties, the results would hardly be noticeable. See Samuel H. Beer, *British Politics in the Collectivist Age* (New York: Knopf, 1965), esp. Parts II and III.

[7] *Congressional Quarterly,* No. 49 (December 3, 1965).

and defeat. Essentially this is what happened to the Republicans in 1964.[8]

If one were to summarize the major differences between our major parties, one could say that Democrats, as a rule, take an affirmative view of government; Republicans, a negative view. Democrats talk about what government ought to do; Republicans, about what government ought *not* to do. On many specific issues the major party battles have been fought and the conflicts resolved. An issue that bitterly divides the parties today will find them in substantial agreement tomorrow. This has been the history of the great conflicts over slavery, public land policy, the income tax, social security legislation, and most issues of foreign policy. What arouses bitter controversy at one time will, when resolved by majority vote, be accepted as established policy and henceforth supported by large majorities of both parties. Thus the dynamics of American politics may be described as a progressive movement from conflict to consensus, with the two-party system serving as the vehicle for this transformation.

A model party system, it has been said, ought to (1) provide meaningful alternatives among which voters can choose, (2) provide a basis for working majorities on which a stable government can depend, (3) mobilize both popular majorities at the polls and in legislative assemblies, (4) help to impose the discipline of the public interest or the common good on special interest groups and factions, (5) help to inform public opinion and to hold government responsible to the people, and (6) contribute to freedom, equality, and national unity or consensus. On all of these counts the American party system, although falling far short of perfection, nevertheless scores well. If our major parties agree on most things, this is but a measure of our national consensus. And if they confine conflict within tolerable limits, blunting the sharp edges of ideology, this is our safeguard against civil war.

☆ *POLITICAL BEHAVIOR*

In recent years students of politics have tried to probe beneath party labels, to discover the deeper motives or conditions that cause people to vote as they do. Politics, like religion, or love, is a kind of behavior which involves an incredibly complex array of motives, influences, interests, and conditions. Like other forms of behavior, political behavior is goal directed. People seek satisfaction (1) for basic physical needs (food, clothing, shelter) and (2) for psychic needs or values.

W. I. Thomas, in his essay *The Person and His Wishes*, described the

8 See V. O. Key, Jr., *The Responsible Electorate* (Cambridge, Mass.: Harvard University Press, 1966). Also Anthony Downs, *An Economic Theory of Democracy* (New York: Harper & Row, 1957).

major human goals as four in number: (a) new experience; (b) security; (c) recognition; (d) response. Harold Lasswell has listed man's political goals as Income, Deference, and Safety, while Thomas Hobbes saw man primarily as a power-seeking animal. "I put in first place," he wrote, "a general inclination of all mankind, a perpetual and restless desire for power . . . that ceaseth only in Death."

If one were to establish a rank order among human goals, most authorities would put basic physical needs high on the list. Sigmund Freud saw sexual motives in most human behavior; others give highest priority to economic motives. To William James recognition and re-sponse, self-esteem, personal significance and prestige were central to most human conduct. Perhaps all could be summed up in a thirst for love and affection. And because man is a rational animal, he is driven by an insatiable hunger to understand and to be understood.

It would be impossible to establish an order of priority among these basic human goals, mainly because one cannot disentangle one from another. Behavior as the psychologist observes is *Molar* not *Molecular*. It is patterned, not fractured. Economic goals include psychic goals, not only food and shelter, but prestige, self-esteem, even power. Political goals include economic and psychic goals, income, deference, and safety. Power is usually not an end in itself, but a means to prestige, income, safety, love and affection. Even the tyrant seeks not naked power for its own sake but for the income and deference, the love and affection power can command.

Not only are goals interlaced with one another; so, too, are the means or behavior patterns by which men pursue these goals. Political behavior, economic behavior, religious behavior, and so forth, are not separate and distinct from one another, but are, rather, different facets of the same general pattern of behavior. A man may pursue political power by economic means, or economic goals by political means, and all for the ultimate salvation of his soul. Prestige and even power may be pursued by self-immolation and sacrifice. Political behavior is consequently a complex form of conduct, whose central goal may be power but whose peripheral goals are private needs and aspirations.

Political behavior as such is not only power oriented; it also has to do with *public* as distinguished from *private* affairs. Public affairs, according to John Dewey, are those affairs the "consequences of which are perceived to reach beyond the persons and associations directly concerned with them." But it is not enough that a labor dispute, a bond issue, or an editorial have consequences extending beyond those immedi-ately involved. These consequences must be perceived. Otherwise they remain essentially private.

Nor is it enough that such consequences be perceived. They must be perceived as having consequences that are important enough to require that something be done about them by the community. Public, that is, political, issues arise when partisans seek to encourage, restrict, regulate or prohibit the consequences of action taken or proposed.

Political behavior, then, is decision making in which individuals choose among alternatives posed by public issues, by voting for a Republican, a Democratic, or other candidate, or by saying *yes* or *no* to a pending proposition. And this is true whether the decision to be made has to do with ends (policy) or means (administration). Hence no sharp line can be made between policy and administration—both are the subject matter of politics.

Not all decision making is political, and not all voting is political behavior. Voting in a beauty contest or for one TV program as against others are forms of decision making. But they become political only when it is proposed that the organized community, city, state, or nation do something about them. Private decisions in the family, or in strictly interpersonal relations are of no concern to the student of political behavior unless they become, or are associated with *public* issues, or what Lasswell calls "debatable" demands for action.

What we want to know is, Why do some people vote Democratic and others Republican? Why do some vote more faithfully at primary and general elections than at others? Nobody really knows the answer to these questions. The best we can do is to find out what kind of people vote one way or another, and to speculate on the underlying causes, or motives, that induce this form of behavior.

One fact seems clear, namely that party loyalties of long standing exist among the majority of voters and these, more than anything else, determine voting behavior in any particular election. But back of these formal loyalties deeper and more subtle forces are at work.

Most students of political behavior make several assumptions. Political behavior, they assume, is a complex product of both rational and nonrational factors that operate not separately and in isolation but within what Kurt Lewin has called a psychological *field*. That is to say, political behavior is not a simple response to a simple stimulus, but a complex response to a complex pattern (or gestalt) of stimuli. "Instead of reacting to local stimuli by local and mutually independent events," says Wolfgang Kohler, "the organism responds to the pattern of stimuli to which it is exposed, and this . . . is a unitary process, a functional whole . . . rather than a mosaic of local sensations. . . ."

The way we perceive our environment and the meanings we attach to it are quite as important in understanding political behavior as an objective description of the environment itself. To understand political behavior, therefore, we need to ask what are some of the major factors that affect or "condition" the way in which voters perceive their political environment, as this environment comes to focus in candidates, issues, and parties. In a more general sense this process may be called political socialization.

The entire process has been described as occurring in what the University of Michigan's Survey Research Center has called a "funnel of causality," which includes everything that in any way may have influenced or conditioned the final voting behavior of any individual. Since the stream of life and the history of mankind is a seamless web reaching back to the beginning of time, the funnel of causality may include items as remote in time as the fall of Rome or the birth of Christ, and as recent as a crop failure in Nebraska or a message from the President of the United States. Obviously no study can take account of this total environment of voters. Hence students of political behavior seek to select those factors that seem most relevant to the act of voting at particular times and places.

Not all of the forces influencing a voter's decision will move in the same direction. There will be pressures impelling him in a number of different directions. When such *cross pressures* (a Republican father and a Democratic wife) are strong, the result may be indecision, delay, or failure to vote at all. Political apathy and nonvoting may be as much a product of such cross pressures as of ignorance or laziness. In any case it is these cross pressures that make the decision-making process complex and the outcome difficult to predict.

Where all or most relevant factors move in the same direction, voting behavior can be more easily understood and predicted. It will not be difficult to predict the voting behavior of a man with a Republican father and mother, a Republican wife, a high economic and social status, and a life dedicated to investment banking or high finance. Indeed, some students of voting behavior believe that if one knows the economic and social status of an individual, it is possible to predict his voting behavior with a fair degree of accuracy. The components of his economic and social status include among other things his sex, age, race or national origin, income, occupation, education, and religion. From these, it is said, one can calculate the voter's *Index of Political Predisposition,* that is, the probability of his voting at all, and if he does, in what degree of probability he will vote in a particular way.

But this is getting ahead of our story. We need first to ask what are some of the major factors operating in this vast funnel of causality, that are most relevant (important) in understanding and predicting voting behavior? Among the relevant factors usually mentioned are those which may be called *personal* and those which we may call *external* to the individual, although these are not separate and distinct, except for purposes of analysis.

Personal factors include those personality traits, ideas, habits, and attitudes, that can be shown to affect voting behavior, some of which, at least, may be conditioned by environmental factors *external* to the individual.

External factors are those institutional, demographic, economic, social, or cultural factors that can be shown to influence political attitudes and behavior. *External* factors are most important when they are *internalized by* the individual to become part of his personality, just as *personal* factors become important politically when they are *externalized* on public issues. Both *personal* and *external* factors interact upon one another to produce either a positive or negative effect upon voting behavior. That is, their net influence may result in an affirmative or negative response to a candidate, an issue, or a party.

In general, as Professor Lasswell has argued, an affirmative response is more likely where factors of *indulgence* predominate, such as physical well-being, high economic and social status, and personal security. A negative response is more likely where factors of *deprivation* predominate, such as illness, falling wages and prices, low economic and social status, and personal insecurity. Theoretically we should be able to develop a calculus of indulgence and deprivation to forecast elections. When factors of indulgence significantly outweigh those of deprivation, that is, when there are conditions of full employment, high wages, good crops, and so forth, voters will choose to support the party in power and the *status quo*. On the other hand, where factors of deprivation such as unemployment, drought, racial or ethnic tension prevail, voters will vote for a change.

Relevant Factors in Political Behavior

SEX.   Are there significant differences in the voting behavior of men and women? Although women have enjoyed equal suffrage since 1920, they have not yet developed the habit of voting to the same extent as have the male citizens. Gosnell's pioneer study of nonvoting reported nearly twice as many female as male nonvoters. An Ohio study in 1924 showed that 73 percent of the men and only 57 percent of the women voted. In both presidential and congressional elections the percentage of men voting normally exceeds that of women by a considerable margin.

Where sex-role differences are most marked, as in the South and generally in rural areas, one finds the greatest difference in turnout, and the lowest relative participation of women is found in these areas. In rural areas the difference was 28 percent, as compared with only 5 percent in metropolitan centers. Sex differences in political behavior are also greater among the poorly educated. In northern centers the difference was 14 percent for those with a grade school education, and only 3 percent for those with a high school or college education. In the South, these differences were 27 percent and 1 percent respectively.

It seems clear also that husbands influence the voting behavior of their wives more than the other way around. In a Michigan study of the 1956 election, 27 percent of the wives said they were influenced by their husbands and only 6 percent of husbands confessed to being influenced by their wives. In Erie County in 1940, 33 percent of women and only 14 percent of men admitted to being influenced by their mates. On matters of policy, it is commonly assumed that women are more likely to vote when issues of public morality, education, and welfare are involved. In 1928 an Ann Arbor study showed that actually more women than men voted, alarmed, no doubt, by lurid tales of Tammany control, intemperance, and even vice associated with the Democratic candidate of that year. There is some evidence also that women are more *candidate-*oriented, and more Republican, than men, although the margins are small and inconclusive.[9]

There is no very persuasive theory to account for these differences. A general sense of female inferiority, fortified by centuries of subjection to male domination, and by legal disabilities that denied them full civil rights, may help to explain the relatively low rate of turnout even for qualified women voters. There is probably no biological basis for this sense of inferiority and the correspondingly low appreciation that women have for the efficacy of political action. One may expect that as opportunities for education, employment, and political participation for women increase, their sense of political efficacy will grow and with it their participation in political affairs. There is a considerable body of data to support this assumption. Even today organizations like the League of Women Voters and the American Association of University Women are among the most intelligent, best informed, and most effective in American politics.[10]

AGE.   Age, it has long been assumed, is an important factor in political behavior, although its effects are not unambiguous. As men move through their middle years to old age, it is commonly assumed that they become more civic minded and hence more concerned with politics, and also more conservative in their political attitudes. Reliable objective data to support these assumptions, however, are scarce. Most scientific studies do, however, indicate that participation in political life is lowest for the younger age groups, 21 to 40 years, highest among those between 35 and 54, but declining somewhat in later years. And there is some, but by no means conclusive evidence, that older voters are more conservative. In the 1951 election in Bristol, England, for example, it was found that nearly 45 percent of working class voters under 50 years of age voted for Labour candidates as against less than 25 percent who were over 50. In half a dozen American presidential elections since 1932, careful analysis indicates that older voters, 54 years and above, generally preferred the Republican candidate, whereas the younger voters cast their ballots more

---

[9] Recent studies in England indicate that women are more likely to vote Conservative. See Richard Rose, *Politics in England* (London: Faber & Faber, 1965) , p. 62.

[10] See Gordon Allport, *Personality and the Social Encounter* (Boston: Beacon Press, 1960) .

frequently for the Democrat.[11] But there are notable exceptions to this, and in any case it is not clear how much of this Republican preference among older voters is due to age and how much to the higher economic and social status that usually comes with advancing age. In their pioneer study of Erie County during the 1940 presidential election, Professor Lazarsfeld and his associates found a significantly higher percentage of Democratic voters among Catholics 45 years of age and above, whereas Protestant voters in this age group showed a marked preference for the Republican candidate. On the other hand, in 1944 some 82 percent of Negro voters under 44 years of age voted Democratic, as against only 59 percent of those above 45. There is some evidence, particularly among organized oldsters or "senior citizens" that old age may indeed result in a more liberal or even "radical" voting pattern. Other studies indicate that party adherence also correlates with increasing age.

The problem of age is an important one since a significant change in the age distribution of the population could result in a significant change in the political orientation of the whole community. A younger population may demand more public services in the way of schools and colleges, child care centers, job opportunities, and recreation facilities. But an aging population may also clamor for higher old-age pensions, more liberal state-supported medical care, and better housing for the aged.

RACE AND NATIONALITY.   In the late nineteenth and early twentieth centuries, there developed an elaborate theory of history and politics that found the key to national character and behavior in what were called racial or ethnic traits. This racist theory of politics and culture assumed a close interdependence of physical traits (skin color, hair texture, cephalic index, and so forth) and cultural traits such as language, social institutions, religious and political values and behavior. More careful anthropological research has largely exposed this assumption as a myth. Nevertheless, most authorities recognize that racial and ethnic factors do influence political behavior, not as inherent biological differences but as traits associated with cultural growth and development. One has only to note, for example, the Pulaski Day Parade in New York or similar observances among citizens of Polish, Irish, German, Jewish, or Negro origin to reflect on the political implications of ethnic and racial factors.[12]

In American history there have been three major areas of such ethno-racial relations involving (1) whites and Indians, (2) whites, Negroes and other nonwhites, and (3) ethnic immigrant minorities. Important for the political scientist are the interrelations of whites and Negroes and of the various and numerous immigrant minorities that comprise the

[11] A similar pro-Conservative bias was found among the older English voters in 1964. See Richard Rose, op. cit., p. 63.

[12] See Raymond E. Wolfinger, "The Development and Persistence of Ethnic Voting," APSR (December, 1965) .

American people. The problem is essentially twofold, involving on the one hand what has been called *ethnocentrism* or a strong sense of ethnic or racial identity within the group—what Giddings once called a "Consciousness of kind"—and on the other hand an often intense *xenophobia* or fear of strangers, a dislike and distrust of groups with traits differing from one's own. The interaction of ethnocentrism and xenophobia in American culture has produced political tensions of considerable significance.

The political significance of particular groups may be said to vary with a number of factors. The *size* of the group is important if it is to exert any considerable influence at the polls. Also important is the intensity of its own "consciousness of kind," of its own sense of identity as a separate and distinct group, that is, with its degree of ethnocentrism or internal cohesion. To be politically effective a racial or ethnic group must not only be sizeable in total numbers but must be sufficiently concentrated in politically strategic areas—a state, city, congressional or assembly district—to be able to affect the outcome of an election by "bloc" voting. Where a racial or ethnic minority, however large, is diffused widely throughout the population, much of its political "leverage" is lost, because nowhere, under conditions of wide diffusion, could it hold the balance of power at the polls.[13]

Among the more politically important of the racial and ethnic groups in the United States are the Negroes. Not only are they large in numbers, representing approximately 10 percent of our total population; they are also intensely conscious of their racial identity. Indeed, there is no other such group of comparable size in which this "consciousness of kind" burns with such continuous intensity. "American Negroes," say some commentators, "are obsessed with their identity as Negroes. No topic of conversation among them, no other interest, economic, social, religious, or political, is free of this preoccupation with race and race relations." Nor is this surprising. As a group, American Negroes have suffered personal indignities on a scale greater and through a longer period of time than any other minority. They are only now beginning to win equal suffrage with the white population. In some ten northern states, however, to which they have migrated in substantial numbers, they have become a significant and in many places a decisive factor in both primary and general elections. In New York, Ohio, Michigan, Illinois, California, and Pennsylvania, Negroes constitute a large and militantly self-conscious bloc of votes. Moreover, they are concentrated in a relatively few cities, counties, congressional and assembly districts where they are sufficiently numerous to weigh heavily in any election. Although Negroes comprise

[13] Two of the most highly concentrated minority groups, the Negroes and Jews, show a marked preference for one party. Thus among Jewish voters Democrats outnumber Republicans about 5 to 1, and in 1960 and 1964 Democratic Negro voters outnumbered Republican Negro voters by 10 to 1.

only some 10 percent of the population of Illinois, they constitute more than 23 percent of the population of Chicago and are easily the predominant group in three congressional districts on the South Side of that city. So in New York, Detroit, Toledo, Cleveland, Los Angeles, and other cities segregation has concentrated the Negro vote in a relatively few districts, and by a curious paradox has thus increased the Negro's political "leverage." Thus the end of racial segregation, which is the Negro politician's chief stock-in-trade, may also mark the end, or the sharp reduction, of his political power. For as Negro voters are more widely and sparsely diffused throughout the general population, this "leverage" will decline.[14]

Other Ethnic and Religious Factors in Political Behavior

Nearly 20 percent of the population in the United States in 1960 was composed of persons who were foreign born or of mixed foreign and native parentage.[15] Literally millions of American voters feel a strong sense of ethnic identity and loyalty that profoundly affects their political behavior. They are often moved to vote for or against a particular party, candidate, or issue on the basis of appeals to these historic cultural, linguistic, or religious ties. The political significance of these factors depends, as we have said, on the size, internal cohesion, and concentration of the various groups. Of those which exert a noticeable influence, 80 percent are to be found in a dozen states and in about as many cities. Although the basic trend is toward greater diffusion and a corresponding decline in the intensity and political significance of ethnic and religious minorities, some of them continue to exercise an important, if not a decisive, influence on millions of American voters.[16] In terms of turnout, most ethnic minorities follow the general pattern of behavior characteristic of the population at large. But there are significant differences in partisan orientation. Irish, Italians, and Polish-Americans are more inclined to support Democratic candidates, whereas those of Scandinavian and German origin are more strongly inclined toward the Republicans. But since these ethnic alignments correspond roughly also to religious differences, it is not clear whether the ethnic or the religious factor is more important. The Irish, Italian, and Polish-Americans are overwhelmingly Roman Catholic, while the Scandinavian- and German-Americans —with some important exceptions among the Germans—tend to be just

[14] See James Wilson, *Negro Politics* (New York: Free Press, 1960).

[15] The major nationalities represented were: German-Austrian, over 6,000,000; Italian, more than 4,500,000; Irish, about 2,500,000; Russian-Polish, about 5,000,000 (including a large percentage of the Jewish faith); Mexicans, 1,300,000; Scandinavian, about 2,400,000; English-Welsh and English-Canadian, 3,000,000.

[16] See Robert A. Dahl, *Who Governs?* (New Haven: Yale University Press, 1961); Lucy S. Dawidowicz and Leon J. Goldstein, *Politics in a Pluralist Democracy* (New York: Institute of Human Relations Press, 1963).

as strongly Protestant in their church membership. Jewish voters, whether of Russian, German, or Polish origin, have been strongly Democratic in their partisan orientation—at least since 1932. In any case, *within* all of these groups, with the possible exception of the Jewish group, voting behavior tends to follow lines of economic and social status, as in the general population. In terms of partisan alignment Negroes, Jews, Irish, Polish, Italian Roman Catholics, and Southern Baptists tend to vote Democratic, while other Protestants tend just as strongly to vote Republican.[17] But racial, religious, and ethnic factors in voting behavior are often modified by social and economic status.

SOCIAL AND ECONOMIC STATUS AND POLITICAL BEHAVIOR.   Social and economic status as measured by income, occupation, education, and place of residence seems to exert a most powerful influence upon political behavior. With only minor exceptions, voting studies covering a generation or more of elections in every part of the country and at every level of government yield similar results. Both turnout (voting participation) and a pro-Republican orientation tend to increase as one moves from lower to higher income brackets, from elementary education only to graduation from high school and college, from unskilled to skilled labor, clerical and technical occupations to the professions of law, medicine, and engineering, and from the lower echelons of agriculture and business to the giant corporation's high managerial positions. That is to say, those with higher education, better incomes, and professional or managerial positions as a general rule have a higher sense of the efficacy of politics, fewer nonvoters, and more Republicans than other economic and social groups. Moreover, residents of the great central cities are more solidly Democratic in their partisan orientation than are residents of rural areas, exurbia, and suburbia. This is to be expected since the city is the home of most voters of lower economic and social status. In terms of turnout, however, as one moves from the big city to the rural areas, the proportion of nonvoters seems to increase.

All of these factors—sex, age, ethnic, and religious affiliation, economic, and social status—taken together but with widely different intensities—help to explain much that occurs in American political life. (See Table 8–1.) They are, however, by no means the whole story, nor do they operate upon all voters in the same way or in the same degree. In spite of the cynic who sees political behavior as wholly nonrational with the voter impelled to vote as he does through the more or less blind confluence of external *stimuli*, there remains a great deal that is unaccounted for in this way. The character of the candidates and the issues and the way in

---

[17] See P. H. Odegard, *Religion and Politics* (New York: Oceana Press, 1960) ; S. M. Lipset, "Religion and Politics in the American Past and Present," in Robert Lee and M. Marty (eds.) , *Religion and Social Conflict* (New York: Oxford University Press, 1964) . Also, on the role of religion in the 1928 election see *Race, Religion and Votes, 1928 Reexamined* (University Park, Pa.: Pennsylvania State University Press, 1962) .

TABLE 8-1
Political Behavior by Various Characteristics

Characteristic	Higher Turnout	Lower Turnout
Sex	Men	Women
Age	Middle-age voters	Younger voters
Religion	Jews	Non-Jews
Race	Whites	Negroes
Type of community	Metropolitan	Rural
Education	College	Noncollege
Labor affiliation	Union	Nonunion
Income	High	Low

which the voter perceives them in their relation to his own interest and the common good, also play an important role in political behavior. There is, in a word, more of reason and reflection in the political process, more rational calculation of the consequences of the alternatives proposed than the confirmed cynic or radical determinist will admit. Voters are not billiard balls compelled by external forces to follow predetermined lines. It is, after all, in the voter's mind in the secrecy of the voting booth that the various stimuli and the multiple cross pressures are given order and meaning. It is he who must make up his own mind.[18]

☆ PARTY ORGANIZATION

The Need for Organization

Any group of more than three people setting out to do anything at all must organize. Even a committee of three will normally have a chairman. Even in a tiny village governed by a town meeting whose inhabitants are on a first name basis, organization is essential to promote this man or that for town clerk or moderator, or to persuade the town meeting to vote for or against some item in the town warrant or agenda. In every community there will be clusters of voters who look to the local banker, to the postmaster, to a merchant, a preacher, or even a professor, for guidance on how to vote.

Whenever this happens, politicians are at work and a political organization of some kind exists, even though it may be as temporary and as fluid as a passing cloud. Expand the size of the community, increase the number and variety of eligible voters, multiply the number of officials to be elected or of issues to be resolved, and the need for organization

18 See V. O. Key, Jr., *The Responsible Electorate* (Cambridge, Mass.: Harvard University Press [Belknap Press], 1966) .

grows. It is perhaps sad but true that the larger the political community the more numerous and diverse the electorate, and the greater the number of elective officers the smaller will be the relative knowledge and influence of each individual voter. The fact is that the vast majority of voters are too busy, too ill informed, too indifferent, or too lazy to maintain an active and continuous interest in public affairs. And this is true not only in political units, but also in trade unions, churches, fraternal bodies, and corporations. The average member of these bodies probably knows little or nothing about how they are governed or by whom. He rarely attends meetings, reads official reports, or votes, unless somebody guides or goads him to do so.[19]

The people who do this guiding and goading are the politicians who in our two-party system usually identify with the Republican or Democratic parties. Those politicians who give all or most of their time to party business make up an oligarchy known to their friends as "the organization" and to their enemies as "the machine." The big shots are known as "leaders" or "bosses," depending on whether they are friends or foes.

In a modern democratic state the election of public officials and in some cases the decision of important matters of public policy are made by thousands or even millions of voters. The activation and education of these millions of voters is the responsibility of political parties and more directly the responsibility of the politicians who make up the party organization or machine. The organization or machine is thus a labor-saving device—it carries on the work of the party so that the rest of us can earn a living, play golf, and watch television. Farmers, workers, businessmen, by the millions make up the party following. It is the job of the party organization to see that they are registered and get to the polls to vote for the party's candidates on election day. When the election is over, the voters go their separate ways and the "party" in its wider sense dissolves, leaving the organization to carry on.

The voters and the interests they represent are concerned mainly about how the control of power by one party rather than another will affect their own self-esteem, income, or safety, which they tend to identify as the "public interest." The organization, the machine, at least in the United States, has only an incidental interest in policy. Its concern is with power, with control of the government and the jobs and privileges that go with it. Politics for the professionals is an end in itself. "In the beginning," said Oswald Spengler, "the leadership and the apparatus come into existence for the sake of the program. . . . [Gradually the needs of the organization become paramount] the program vanishes from memory and the organization works for its own sake alone." Many a

---

[19] One has only to watch the proxy battles that take place for control of great corporations to realize how close the analogy is between the politics of business and the politics of the nation-state.

reformer needs to learn this lesson if he is to avoid the disillusionment that often follows hard upon his initial success.

The party organization is held together by patronage, loyalty to leaders, desire for prestige and power. The particular pattern of party organization that emerges in any community will depend upon a number of interdependent variables. These will include the prevailing form of government, the size of the community both in terms of area and population, the ethnic, racial, and religious composition of the population, the degree of social and physical mobility, the nature of the prevailing economy and culture, and especially the underlying attitudes toward government and political power in general. Just as the British party system reflects a unitary, parliamentary form of government, so the American party system reflects our federal, check and balance, separation of powers Constitution. Party organization, however, whether in Great Britain or America, invariably resembles other forms of organization and other power structures, in being both *hierarchical* and *oligarchical*.

The formal organization of American parties is easily sketched and resembles the familiar pyramidal structure of trade unions, churches, and corporations. At the base of the pyramid are the precinct committeemen or leaders—300,000 or more of them for both parties. Above them are the leaders or chairmen of committees for wards, counties, and assembly districts, culminating in a state central committee, whose chairman may or may not be the state leader, or boss.

Above the state committee are the national committees, composed of two members from each state (a man and a woman), plus representatives from the Young Democrats and Young Republicans and in some cases the state central committees. National committeemen are formally ratified by the delegates to the national convention, but are actually selected by the state delegations to the national convention, by state conventions, by direct primary in the states, or by the state central committees. In the permanent structure of the party the national committees are less important, except perhaps in a presidential year, than those at the state and local levels. National committees bear a kind of symbiotic relation to these more important groups, their power being dissipated by congressional and senatorial campaign committees and by voluntary groups such as Citizens for Eisenhower—or for Kennedy or for Johnson—which function more or less independently of the national committee. Within the national committee power is concentrated in the executive committee and its chairman, who is the personal agent of the President or the presidential candidate. Even within his own state a national committeeman is generally less influential than the chairman of the state central committee except where, as sometimes happens, these are combined in the same person.

The model party organization in the states is a quasi-military structure in which responsibility is from the bottom up and power and authority from the top down. "I have always believed," said Tom Platt, "that a political organization should be as well disciplined as the Army and the Navy. . . . Merit and devotion should be rewarded. Demerit and treachery should be condemned and examples made of those guilty."

At each level—precinct, ward, county, assembly district, and state— there are individual leaders who exert more influence and wield more power than others. Leadership comes from faithful and effective service in (1) getting voters registered, (2) raising money for campaigns, (3) getting registered voters to the polls on election day, (4) running errands, staffing party headquarters and doing the other chores that have to be done throughout the year, and especially during campaigns, (5) being faithful in attendance at committee meetings. Seniority counts in all this, but normally it must be accompanied by real service to the party.

The party organization or machine, says Ostrogorski, is "composed of a number of smaller machines which form so many microcosms within it: . . . in a sort of expanding ladder. . . . The title and role of leader [or boss] do not belong exclusively to the man at the top." In the state, "the leader is the local boss in his own district; the person in charge of the precinct is himself a little boss." The American party organization is thus a rather loose confederation of leaders rather than a tightly disciplined hierarchy.

In the fifty states of the American federal union there are 100 state committees for the two major parties. They vary in size from 13 members in Indiana to over 900 in California, with an average of 100. In the larger committees an executive committee, and within the executive committee the chairman and the party's secretary have their hands on the throttle. It is they who give orders and make decisions, and the larger the committee the more urgent is the need for this ruling oligarchy.

It is the inner circle, the oligarchs who make politics their major concern, who control the party's funds, its communications system, its schedule of conferences and meetings, its recommendations on appointments to be made, and its public statements on policy. And the larger the organization, the more certain is this to be the case. That is why Robert Michels, in his classic treatment of political parties, has said: "Who says organization, says oligarchy."

The oligarchical nature of party organization and control is true at the local level quite as much as it is at the state and national level. In New York City's Borough of Manhattan, for example, the party voters in each precinct choose delegates to serve as members of an assembly district committee in each of the 23 assembly districts in the borough. The members of these 23 assembly districts' committees in turn make up a county committee of several thousand—a body that is obviously unwieldy and useless in either a legislative or executive capacity.

So each assembly district committee chooses a district leader and co-leader (man and woman) with power to appoint other leaders in the precincts. These 46 district leaders and co-leaders compose the county executive committee which selects the county chairman and the leader of the party. In the Democratic party the county chairman is usually, but not always, also the leader of historic Tammany Hall.

What the Leaders Do

At the top of the party pyramid is the President or, in the case of the opposition party, the candidate for President at the last election. But, as Mr. Nixon has observed and Mr. Goldwater has learned, national party leadership must be earned, and this is especially true for the opposition party whose latest candidate for the Presidency is known only as the "titular" leader. Leadership in his case is likely to be more formal than real. For the opposition party the chairman of the national committee, the party leaders in Congress and state elective officers, especially the governors, are actual or potential rivals of the "titular" leader.

But whether he is the President's man, as in the incumbent party, or a rival of the "titular" leader in the case of the opposition party, the national chairman is the custodian of the national party organization in the periods between presidential campaigns. To help him discharge this responsibility, he has a headquarters staff of between 100 and 150 persons, and an annual budget of a million dollars or so, which he must raise along with other millions to wipe out the inevitable deficit that follows a presidential campaign. Essentially the national chairman is a kind of business agent for his party—intent upon strengthening the central structure, recruiting new workers, smoothing the ruffled feathers of quarreling factions, and preparing the organization for the next campaign. Between presidential campaigns, he has powerful rivals in the campaign committees of the Senate and the House. For assuming these multiple burdens he receives a modest compensation, about half of what a similar post in private life would pay. In earlier days he served without compensation except, when in the incumbent party, the national chairman served also as postmaster general, or combined his job with an executive position in business.

Bosses and Machines

Among the most romantic characters in American culture have been the political "bosses" whose exploits have become standard fare for writers of both nonfiction and fiction. The term itself—"party boss"—is ambiguous and the line between a leader and a boss is often very thin. As a practical matter, one may say simply that a boss is a leader, able effectively to control his organization, and through it to control or decisively influence the public decision-making process. He may do this for good or evil ends. Judged by these standards, there have been "good" and "bad" bosses—

although in the mythology of politics a boss is often thought of as a corrupt leader.

Although American politics have produced many bosses, few have operated on a national scale. Mark Hanna, Republican National Chairman for McKinley, came close to being a national boss—one to whom the odor of corruption never attached. Tom Platt of New York aspired to be a national boss, but found the going tough against the redoubtable will of his political protegé, Theodore Roosevelt. Among Democrats perhaps only James Farley of New York, who combined the jobs of Postmaster General and National Democratic Chairman, came close. But even he was overshadowed by his own superlative boss, Franklin Roosevelt.

At the state level, bosses have been more numerous and the names of Penrose, Stanford, Roraback, Platt, Mashke, among Republicans, and Croker, Murphy, Olvany, De Sapio of New York, Harry Byrd of Virginia, and Huey Long of Louisiana, among Democrats, come readily to mind. Not infrequently a United States Senator or a governor combines his official position with that of a statewide party boss—as the names of Aldrich of Rhode Island, Lawrence of Pennsylvania, Curley of Massachusetts, or "Pa" Fergusen of Texas suggest.

For the most part "bossism" has been a local phenomenon and the most famous or notorious bosses have been mayors or "leaders" of city or county political machines. Frank Hague of Jersey City, William S. Vare of Philadelphia, "Big Bill" Thompson, "Jake" Arvey, and Richard J. Daley of Chicago, "Doc" Ames of Minneapolis, Tweed of New York, are but a few on a long roster. Many a state boss began his career and based his operations in a city machine. The golden era of bossism was also the golden age of the so-called Robber Barons of Big Business, and had its roots in a partnership between the two.

It also had roots in the "spoils system" of public personnel administration. Jobs in the public service were combined with positions of party leadership, thus giving the professional politician an income from public funds. As we have seen, many bosses combined their party jobs with official ones as postmaster general, U.S. Senator, governor, or mayor. At the lower levels even precinct and ward committeemen are often rewarded with public jobs as attorneys, bailiffs, clerks, secretaries, supervisors, and so forth. J. T. Salter's study of bossism found that 85 percent of Republican committeemen in Philadelphia were on the public payroll, and in Cleveland it was found that 27 of 33 ward leaders had city jobs. For many years the federal civil service was regarded as a legitimate source of patronage for rewarding party workers for faithful service.

It is easier to deplore this than it is to find more suitable rewards for those upon whom political parties depend for the work they have to do. A business corporation or private group usually has a salaried staff, but the financial resources of most party organizations are inadequate to hire the help they need. Salaried jobs on party payrolls are few and poorly paid. The national committees of both major parties operate with paid skeleton staffs that any respectable trade union or trade association would scorn. And at state and local levels, party budgets rarely support more than a half dozen full-time employees. It should not be surprising therefore that party organizations seek to combine public with party employment.

In the heyday of the "spoils system," employment in the civil service was regarded as a reward for faithful party service. The manifest evils of this system led to civil service reform and the adoption of merit systems under which public employees are recruited on the basis of tested competence and character rather than party loyalty. Nevertheless the spoils system remains a major source of strength for our major parties. At the national level, an impressive number of positions outside the competitive civil service are available for presidential appointment, ranging from those of cabinet rank, federal judgeships, and ambassadorial posts down to postmasterships and clerical positions of a confidential character. About 100,000 federal jobs are available to the President as party leader, acting usually on the advice of Senators and Congressmen, or other party officials. Without these "political" appointments, the President would be denied an important source of power and influence.[20]

At the state and local level, remnants of the old spoils system continue to thrive in varying degree from state to state, and political appointments represent an important source of party strength. Not only are department heads selected for party loyalty, but hundreds of their subordinates are as well. While civil service reform has reduced this in many state governments, the system continues in most county and in many city governments. Where this is true, the party organization is still able to combine public and party employment.

Jobs are not the only source of party patronage and favor. When President Cleveland spoke of the "cohesive power of public plunder," he referred to a much wider and more dubious source of rewards for party loyalty and services. Public contracts, franchises, licenses of many kinds, leases of public property for private use or of private property for public use, exemption from building, health, fire, and other regulations have been sources of political favoritism for centuries. Tax favors of various kinds including preferential assessments, refunds, and remission of penalties, fees and commissions from receiverships for "services" in the procurement of permits, favorable decisions by partisan public agencies are

[20] With the installation of a new administration in the White House, there is always intense interest in the appointments. In 1933, for example, a resolution sponsored by Senator McKellar of Tennessee called on the Civil Service Commission to furnish "a full and complete list of all offices, positions, places and employments . . . with the . . . salaries attached . . . not under Civil Service rules and regulations." The resulting report was a document of over 400 pages which became, as a kind of patronage catalogue, the "best thumbed book in Washington. . . ." A similar report was prepared in 1953 with the installation of the Eisenhower administration.

other favors. And for the less scrupulous or less fastidious, there are the various forms of what one Tammany leader called "dishonest graft" from gamblers, vice lords, race track bookies, and other underworld characters ready and willing to pay heavily for "protection" or immunity from the law.

But political patronage and graft, whether honest or dishonest, are not and perhaps never were, the major factors in holding a party organization together. In the old days the party machine served as a combination welfare and legal aid society for constituents in difficulty. The boss and his district leaders helped new immigrants to find homes, jobs, and friends, assisted them in getting registered as voters and saw to it that they voted. The boss knew his district and its people, and at the district club house he served as guide, counsellor, and friend to those in need. He helped parents to discipline wayward children and saw that delinquent boys and girls got a second chance when they got in trouble. He provided legal aid, small loans, food baskets, and clothing, even paid the rent for constituents fallen on evil days. He organized baseball and basketball leagues, bridge clubs, clam bakes, picnics, and excursions. He saw to it that his district was represented in civic ceremonies and at parades and other demonstrations to commemorate St. Patrick's Day, the Fourth of July, Labor Day, Thanksgiving, and Christmas. One May Day picnic of the Thomas Farley Club served some 28,000 adults and children.

The party boss and his machine, which may have appeared to reformers as something evil and sinister, not infrequently appeared to the less affluent members of the community as a kind of Robin Hood, Lady Bountiful, or Social Welfare Agency. Nor was the classic cartoon image of the "boss" as an ugly, fat, vulgar, ignorant, ruthless spoilsman of alien origin, wholly accurate. Some few corresponded to this image, but many did not. Of twenty city bosses studied by Harold Zink, fifteen were native Americans and of the five born abroad only three were born in Ireland. Tweed of New York was a Scotsman, Vare of Philadelphia was English, Abe Reuf of San Francisco was of French origin, and "Doc" Ames of Minneapolis was a New England Puritan. Although most were of humble origin, there were notable exceptions. Ames's father was a prosperous physician, Penrose of Philadelphia came from a "good" family, Mashke of Cleveland was the son of wealthy parents, and Abe Reuf's father was a "capitalist." Mark Hanna was himself a wealthy man, as distinguished in business as in politics. Some were fat and ugly, but many were not, and a few, such as Curley of Boston, Aldrich of Rhode Island, Crooke of New York, and Reuf of San Francisco were positively handsome. Although few were orators, they were by no means ignorant dumbbells. Most had only limited schooling, and over half did not get beyond grade school. But "Big" Bill Thompson of Chicago held an L.L.D. degree, Olvany of Tammany was a graduate of New York University Law School, Abe Reuf was an honor graduate of the University of California, Mashke graduated from Exeter and Harvard, and Penrose was trained at Harvard in history and political economy. Penrose wrote a substantial history of Philadelphia and read the classics for personal enjoyment. Another state boss was a student of Assyrian antiquities.

A more recent analysis of Republican and Democratic state chairmen showed that over 80 percent had gone to college. In terms of occupation they included lawyers, business executives, publishers, merchants and public officials including an attorney general, a United States district attorney, a state secretary of state, and a county attorney. In general the state chairmen of the major parties rank well above the average of the population in terms of education, economic, and social status, and will compare favorably with comparable leaders of business and the professions. This is also true of national committeemen—virtually all of whom are college graduates and "men of affairs" in business, government or the professions.[21] Political loyalty and personal ties to older types of "leaders" or "bosses" have given way to new types of organization and leadership.

Nor is political loyalty confined to reciprocal trust among party leaders. It extends to countless thousands of volunteer workers who are sincerely devoted to the party and the principles for which they believe it stands. Not all of the tens of thousands of Citizens for Eisenhower or for Stevenson or for Kennedy were inspired only by loyalty to those leaders. They were also strongly "issue oriented"—believing that the welfare of the nation would be best advanced by victory for their party. Increasingly effective party organization will have to depend upon this kind of loyalty and dedication. Civil service reform will continue to reduce the number of jobs in the public service available for partisan appointment. Opportunities for "honest graft," while considerable, may be expected to decline as the public becomes more alert to this type of political favoritism and as "conflict of interest laws become more reasonable and effective."[22] "Dishonest" graft will become increasingly risky as standards of police administration, public service, and morality improve. And with the emergence in recent years of the so-called welfare state, the role of the party organization as Robin Hood or Lady Bountiful has visibly declined. Moreover the rise of labor unions and a drastic reduction in the immigration of poor and illiterate aliens has cut off important sources of machine support.

Other straws are in the wind pointing to important changes in party organization. Among these is the increasing mobility of the American

[21] See Peter H. Odegard and E. Allen Helms, *American Politics: A Study in Political Dynamics* (2nd ed., New York: Harper & Row, 1947), pp. 285–290, 446–450.

[22] "During all his years as Tammany's boss," writes Leo Egan, "De Sapio has not had a single city franchise to sell. He hasn't licensed a single gambling establishment or brothel, as far as any records show. Nor have repeated investigations turned up a single instance in which he has shared the profits of a city or state construction or purchase contract."

people which makes it difficult to build a stable organization in a particular district. In Alameda County, California, as many as 100,000 voters or more will move in and out between one election and the next. To organize a population so mobile is like trying to capture mercury on a glass plate. This factor is not unrelated to the increasing role of mass communication and of professional public relations firms in party organization and campaigns. The neighborhood club, the house-to-house canvass, and the personal contact of leaders with the rank and file, are giving way to the canvass by direct mail, outdoor advertising, radio, and television.

The model of a party organization reaching downward and outward from the White House to the local precinct has always been pretty much of a myth and it is becoming more so. In 1948 the Executive Director of the Republican National Committee reported that in over 10 percent of the counties there was no Republican chairman or vice-chairman, and in approximately a fourth of the precincts there was no Republican leadership at all. In Oregon only 13 out of 36 counties had a Republican organization. In a recent "Dollars for Democrats" drive only about 250 out of several thousand precincts in northern California reported anyone willing to assume responsibility for the drive. Party organization in the United States has become federalized, fractionized, almost atomized, until today it is a moving and almost formless pattern of individuals, cliques, and temporary combines of pressure groups and factions.

Under these circumstances it is not surprising if candidates increasingly strive to build their own personal organizations, and rely less on the party as such, but on professional public relations and mass media specialists. To them candidates turn not only for advice but for active campaign management, including the raising of funds. As campaign costs rise, so too does the influence of large contributors and fund raisers, who under this new pattern often eclipse the regular party leaders. It is not unusual, therefore, to find that for the traditional "inner circle" or oligarchy of party bosses, a new oligarchy has emerged composed of public relations officers, media specialists, fund raisers and large contributors—with the "official" party leaders sitting in. However, the influence of the professional campaign manager, of the mass media specialist, and of the fund raisers is not likely to increase indefinitely. New legislation including more rigid control and accounting for contributions, tax credits for small contributions, and even public grants-in-aid, may help to free candidates from their dependence on the large contributors, the so-called fat cats. Free access to the mails, to radio, and to television for campaign purposes may also reduce the dependence of the candidate on the new "Madison Avenue—Fund Raising Oligarchy." Governmental reorganization to reduce the number of elective officials, produce a short ballot, and thus simplify the voters' task might bring the process more within the understanding of the rank and file, and thus reduce the power of the professionals. As new programs of civic information and education are developed, we may hope for a revival of grass-roots organization composed not of party heads and hangers-on but of politically literate citizens concerned not with patronage and graft, but with issues and effective leadership.

☆ NOMINATIONS

The major function of a political party is to nominate and elect its own candidates to public office. The formulation of platforms, the conduct of campaigns, the whole vast panoply of party organization come to focus on this. However efficient its organization, however exalted its platform, unless it can succeed at the polls it will fail as a party. Party bosses may make deals with one another, but a leader's bargaining power depends finally upon his ability to elect his candidates to office. Otherwise a party becomes another pressure group, or it dwindles and dies.

In the United States and in most modern democracies, the parties control the path to power. For without a party organization few aspirants for office can hope to win. There are some exceptions, but they are rare. To say, therefore, that in a democracy the path to power should be open to all on equal terms can, in practice, mean only that the right to run for office must not be limited by legal qualifications of race, religion, wealth, birth, or political belief.

Theoretically these qualifications have largely disappeared, and, subject to special age requirements, any citizen who can satisfy the ordinary qualifications for voting, can also seek any office, from precinct committeeman to President. This he may do by simply announcing his candidacy and asking voters to write his name on their ballots on election day. Once in a blue moon this happens. Or he may, in most places, file a petition with a legally prescribed number of signatures as an independent candidate, and have his name printed on the ballot. This, too, is done and on occasion such candidates succeed. But even such "independent" candidates, if they lack their own organizations, will find themselves ineffective "outsiders." The simple fact is that the right of equal access to public office must be qualified by the knowledge that the keepers of the gates to power are the political parties. This being so, the process by which party candidates are nominated lies close to the heart of any system of responsible government.

Caucus Clubs

Even before the rise of the party system, informal meetings were held at which candidates were agreed upon in advance of the election. The members then scurried about, doing what they could to get their man in.

This, of course, had the advantage of placing some organized support behind a particular candidate; it also helped to screen candidates and limit the number in the final contest. And by limiting the number of candidates, the danger of any candidate's winning by a mere plurality (less than a majority) was reduced.

One of the earliest of these informal nominating meetings was the famous Boston Caucus Club. In 1763 Samuel Adams wrote in his diary:

> This day [I] learned that the Caucus Club meets at certain times in the garret of Tom Dawes. . . . He has a large house. . . . The whole club meets in one room. There they smoke tobacco till you cannot see from one end of the garret to the other. There they drink flip . . . and selectmen, assessors, collectors, firewards and representatives are regularly chosen before they are chosen in the town. . . . They [then] send committees to wait on the merchants' club and to propose and join in the choice of men and measures. . . .

Sam Adams himself learned this nominating business from his father. For he, too, with 20 others

> . . . used to meet . . . and lay their plans for introducing certain persons into places of trust and power. When they had settled it, they separated and each used their influence within their own circle. He and his friends would furnish . . . ballots (slate cards) including the names of the parties (persons) agreed upon, which they distributed on the days of election. By acting in concert . . . they generally carried the elections . . . In like manner it was that Mr. Samuel Adams first became a representative from Boston.[23]

These informal meetings were the prototype of the delegate convention, except that (1) they were irregular in their composition, with no guarantee that they were truly representative, (2) their decisions were not binding even on those who attended, and (3) since there were no official ballots supplied by public authority, those furnished by these groups were often numerous and confusing.

The Legislative Caucus

A more stable form of nominating machinery developed in the legislature to supplant these local caucuses. Members of the same party or persuasion in both houses met semiofficially and agreed upon nominees for district, state, and even congressional offices. The names were then printed and distributed in a formal proclamation to the voters. By 1796 this procedure was common in all states and appeared in Congress as the Congressional Caucus. Federalist members met and nominated John Adams for the Presidency, while Republican (or Democratic-Republican) members nominated Thomas Jefferson.

[23] A. C. Gordon, *History of the American Revolution.*

For a generation legislative caucuses in the states and the Congressional Caucus at the national level dominated the nominating process. Candidates for state offices owed their nomination to these legislative cabals; John Adams, Jefferson, Madison, and Monroe owed their presidential nominations to the Congressional Caucus. After 1800, however, the Federalist Caucus passed from the scene, leaving the Democratic-Republican Caucus as virtually synonymous with the Congressional Caucus and its recommendations came to be binding.

But the Congressional Caucus, too, came under attack, especially during the era of factional politics from 1801 to 1824. As early as 1814 the Congressional Caucus was denounced as a "hideous deformity." Popular meetings condemned the caucus. "The only unexceptional (proper) source from which nominations can proceed is the people themselves . . ." said an assembly of citizens in Jefferson County, Ohio, in 1823. But how were the people to do this? In defiance of the Congressional Caucus, Jackson's nomination in 1824 was advanced by state legislative caucuses of Democrats in Tennessee and Alabama.

Death of King Caucus

Although the Congressional Caucus nominated candidates for President and Vice-President in 1824, it had lost much of its force and influence. After 1824 even presidential nominations were made by state legislative caucuses, local assemblies and conventions. Under the impact of Jacksonian demands to "let the people rule," the nominating process was thus brought closer to the grass roots. But there were difficulties in this, not the least of which was the selection and transportation of delegates. It was fairly easy to attend a local or county convention, but a state convention was another matter and the state legislative caucus seemed logical since the legislators were together at the capital anyway. But the state legislative caucus was denounced on the ground that it violated the principle of the separation of powers by allowing the legislature to choose the executive.

Moreover, said the critics, it was unrepresentative, since it included only those districts from which the party had representation in the legislature. To meet this criticism there emerged the "mixed" or "mongrel" caucus in which representatives from districts having no party representation in the legislature were included. But this failed to stem the tide of opposition. By 1828 a rash of state nominating conventions put up candidates for President, and it was obvious that some new agency was necessary to avoid chaos in presidential nominations. The first national delegate convention for this purpose was called by the Anti-Masonic party in September, 1830. In December, 1831, a convention of the National Republicans met in Baltimore and nominated Henry Clay for President and John Sergeant for Vice-President. This convention also adopted the first formal platform in a statement of ten resolutions on public issues put out after the convention had adjourned. In 1832 Jackson's managers, Martin Van Buren, Amos Kendall, and Major Lewis, promoted a "spontaneous" call for a national convention by a number of Jackson-controlled state legislatures. In due course this convention met in Baltimore in May, 1832, and duly nominated Jackson and Van Buren for President and Vice-President. Representation in this convention was based on one voting delegate for each electoral vote to which the state was entitled.

This Jackson convention not only laid the basis for the allocation of representation that has been followed ever since, but also adopted two rules which plagued Democratic conventions for a hundred years: the so-called unit rule, under which states cast their votes as units, and the two-thirds rule requiring a two-thirds vote to nominate candidates for President and Vice-President. Both rules were designed to reduce factionalism, but both gave to the Solid South and to the "regular" machine a decided advantage.

After 1832 nomination of presidential and vice-presidential candidates by delegate conventions became an article of faith with the Democrats, although there were rumblings of protest that the convention that year was little more than an assembly of Democratic officeholders under the thumb of Jackson, who dictated Van Buren's nomination. By formal resolution the Illinois legislature denounced the national convention idea itself as "destructive of freedom of voting, contrary to republican institutions and dangerous to popular liberties." And when the Whigs appeared on the scene, they denounced the Democrats for using a convention to nominate presidential candidates. By 1840, however, the delegate convention had become the accepted instrument for making nominations.

In spite of harsh criticism, the delegate convention system has certain obvious advantages. In the first place, it is more democratic than the irregular popular meeting or the legislative caucus, both of which were invariably controlled by a small clique. Delegates typically were elected by the party faithful in the precincts, to attend ward, town, and city conventions. These then normally chose delegates to county or assembly district conventions which, in turn, chose delegates to the state convention. A neat hierarchy of interdependent conventions thus emerged with "mass" participation at the grassroots filtered through a series of selective screens. By the time delegates to the state conventions met, it was said, the people's voice could scarcely be heard. Nevertheless, it was an improvement on the "spontaneous" mass meeting and the legislative caucus.

Convention representation could include all sections or factions of the party and the system provided opportunity for the discovery of new candidates in the testing ground of party service. Instead of wasting energy, money, and time in trying his wings on an election, an aspiring candidate could get a hearing in a forum of professionals who could appraise his qualities and his prospects. And because it is much cheaper to campaign for delegates to a state convention than for votes of the whole electorate, the convention system puts less of a premium on a large campaign chest. Another advantage is that nomination by convention brings the unified party strength behind a single candidate and thus minimizes the waste and risk of defeat involved when multiple candidates of the same party vie with one another. The convention also simplifies the job of the voter by limiting the number of candidates to those who can command the largest support in the organization. Instead of a dozen candidates, only two, a Republican and a Democrat, are normally presented. The convention also provides a deliberative body not only to nominate candidates but to determine party policy in a written platform.

Theory and Reality

These are impressive arguments for a convention system. But there is another side to the story. As Calhoun observed in 1844, conventions are not really democratic, since they are usually composed not of delegates fresh from the people but "delegates of delegates," three or four times removed from the people. Moreover, the times and places of holding meetings were usually known only to the machine and its friends. Such meetings were easily controlled by the "insiders." As a result, power was in the hands of the party oligarchy or machine. And in the convention itself, the machine chose the "credentials" committee which passed on the qualifications of delegates, thus forming an effective barrier against "outsiders." As the machine controlled the credentials committee, so it controlled other committees on permanent organization, platform, and nominations. Nor, said the critics, was convention procedure democratic. The chairman could recognize only friends of the oligarchy, and resolutions and even nominations were the product of factional logrolling and "back scratching" in "smoke-filled rooms." The result of all this "wheeling and dealing" was the nomination not of the best candidates nor even the most "electable," but the most subservient.

Analysis of the composition and procedure of conventions showed that much of what the critics said was true. Delegates were often under obligation to pressure groups or were a pretty low order of party hack. Not infrequently votes were bought covertly or even openly. Theodore Roosevelt, writing in The Century Magazine for November, 1886, said that out of 1,007 local caucuses in New York City, 663 were held in saloons. In the Cook County (Illinois) Convention in 1896, it was said that out of 723 delegates 265 were saloonkeepers and nearly a hundred were ex-jailbirds.

Although these examples were by no means typical, the image of the machine-controlled convention was widely held. "The right of popular government," wrote Theodore Roosevelt, "is incomplete unless it includes the right of voters not merely to choose between candidates . . . [after] they have been nominated, but also the right to determine who these candidates shall be."

This demand for a direct primary system of nomination was especially important in one-party states, where party nomination was equivalent to election. Consequently, in the wake of a Populist upheaval in the 1890s, South Carolina adopted a statewide primary system. In 1903 Wisconsin also adopted this system and by 1915 some thirty-eight states had followed suit. Today, direct primary elections for nominations are used in every state for some offices and usually for most. New York, Indiana, Connecticut, and Delaware still use the state convention for nominations to statewide offices, while Michigan uses conventions mainly for local offices. Even in states where the convention has been abandoned as a nominating device, it survives to formulate the party platform, to select delegates to national conventions, and sometimes to endorse candidates who subsequently must run in the primary anyway. In general, however, the direct primary is used not only to nominate candidates but also to elect party leaders. And in eighteen states the direct primary is used both in selecting presidential candidates by expressing a preference among aspirants and by electing delegates to the national convention "instructed" to vote for a particular candidate at the convention.

The Direct Primary System—General Features

The direct primary system is simplicity itself. Primary elections are party elections but conducted under public authority by regular election officers. Ballots are printed at public expense and marked under the usual safeguards to insure an honest vote and an honest count. They apply normally only to established political parties, to those whose candidates polled a certain percentage of the vote in a preceding election.[24] New parties may qualify to use the official primary by filing petitions signed by a certain percentage of the voters.[25] Others may use the convention system to nominate their candidates, but still must file a petition to get them on the ballot for the general election.

Normally, any candidate for an established party nomination can get his name on the official primary ballot by (1) filing a petition signed by a small number of qualified voters who are registered members of the

[24] From 1 percent in Maine and Vermont to 30 percent in Florida. In some states it is mandatory for parties polling, say, 100,000 votes, and optional for those polling less than 100,000.

[25] Three percent in California, 5 percent in Oregon, 10 percent in Idaho.

party, and (2) paying a modest filing fee.[26] Most states also allow voters in the primary to "write in" the name of a candidate not included by petition on the official ballot.

In California, until 1958, a candidate could file in both party primaries. That is to say, a Republican could seek the nomination of both his own party and of the Democrats. This system of cross-filing often resulted in the same man winning both party nominations, as in 1946, when Earl Warren won both nominations for governor, and as William Knowland did in 1952 in his campaign for United States Senator. To do this, however, a candidate had to win his own party's nomination. A Republican could not become the Democratic candidate without winning in his own party primary. For example, Republican Governor Rolph won the Democratic nomination but lost in the Republican primary and was thus disqualified altogether. The California law was amended in 1952 to require that the party affiliation of candidates in primaries be printed on the ballot after their names. In 1959 cross-filing was outlawed altogether.

CLOSED AND OPEN PRIMARIES.   Qualifications for voting in primary elections are usually the same as for a general election, plus, in most states, a test of party membership. In closed primaries only voters registered in an established party are allowed to vote in that party's primary. At the polls the voter's registration is checked and he is given a ballot only for his own party. Most states use this closed system.

In most "open" primaries, on the other hand, no test of party affiliation is applied. The qualified voter himself decides whether he wants to vote in the Republican or Democratic primary, and this he does by simply asking for the ballot of one party or another. In the State of Washington a blanket or wide-open primary imposes no limitations at all on the voter's choice. The names of all candidates of all parties for nomination are printed on a single blanket ballot with each man's party affiliation after his name. A voter in this system may thus vote a "split" primary ballot, that is, he may vote for a Republican gubernatorial candidate and for a Democratic candidate for nomination as lieutenant governor.

The open primary has been criticized on the ground that it permits "raiding." A Democrat, it is said, may cross over and vote for a Republican, and vice versa. Evidence of raiding is hard to come by, but such as there is indicates that voters cross over not, as is often supposed, to nominate "weak" candidates of the opposition party but rather to pick candidates more in sympathy with their own views. Democratic labor

26 Usually one-half of 1 percent of the annual salary of the office. To keep down the number of frivolous candidates, many people propose (1) an increase in the number of signatures, and (2) a larger filing fee, refundable if the candidate gets a certain percentage of the vote.

voters may cross over to vote in a Republican primary to help a pro-labor Republican win against a candidate deemed less friendly.

MINORITY CANDIDATES AND RUNOFFS. If the name of only one candidate for a given office appears on the primary ballot, he becomes the party nominee. When only two candidates appear, the nominee will win by a majority of the votes cast. When more than two candidates appear, the successful nominee may win by a mere plurality. In some southern states where the Democratic nomination has been the equivalent to election, a majority vote in the primary is required for nomination. If no candidate gets a majority, a runoff, or second primary, is held between the two highest candidates, in which the majority candidate wins. In other than one-party states no such runoffs are held. Hence the parties can avoid minority nominees by keeping down the number of candidates.[27] This they do in some states by a system of formal or informal preprimary endorsements. In California such endorsements have been made by the extralegal California Democratic Council and in other states (Connecticut, Colorado, Massachusetts) by official party conventions.

THE DIRECT PRIMARY UNDER FIRE. As with the convention system, so, too, with the direct primary there has been considerable disillusionment. The indictment usually includes the following allegations: (1) The direct primary undermines party unity and thus weakens the party system. (2) Participation at primary elections is low, and where several candidates compete, the successful candidate often represents a minority of a minority of the party voters. If, to remedy this, preprimary endorsing conventions are held, the primary system itself is imperiled. (3) Because of the small vote, the machine can still pick the candidates because it can control enough "faithful" party votes to win any primary. (4) The primary opens the road to "crackpot," "lunatic" candidates who would never "get to first base" under the convention system. (5) It imposes an intolerable expense on aspiring candidates by compelling them to conduct two campaigns, one in the primary and a second, at the general election. (6) The primary increases the burden on the voter by multiplying the number of candidates and elections.[28] (7) It affords no opportunity for deliberation, and no machinery for the formulation of party policy or platform.

To this indictment one might reply: How can the primary at the same time undermine party discipline and leave machine control undisturbed? As for internal conflict, one might argue that this is the "life

[27] See Leonard Rowe, *Pre-Primary Endorsements in California Politics* (Los Angeles: University of California, 1962). Also, "Pre-Primary Conventions and The People's Choice," *California Monthly* (March, 1962).

[28] In April, 1961, there were 71 candidates for the United States Senate from Texas for the Democratic nomination. To select the man he wanted, the voter had to cross out 70 names.

of the party." Moreover, intraparty factionalism is not a product of the direct primary, but is inherent in a two-party system. Factional feuds were common in the Federalist party of Hamilton and Adams, the Democratic-Republican party of Jefferson and Burr, and the Democratic party of Jackson and Calhoun long before the primary became a nominating device. The direct primary offers an opportunity for these battles for control of the party to be fought in the open. In open conflict there is strength; in hidden conflict, there is conniving, conspiracy, and weakness.

Does the direct primary impair party unity at the general election? During the bitter New York Democratic primary in September, 1961, Representative Charles Buckley, leader in the Bronx, and Joseph Sharkey, leader in Brooklyn, denounced Mayor Wagner and were denounced by him in turn. But after the primary, both announced their support of the winning Wagner ticket. The party normally does not suffer from primary contests. Moreover, the cost of avoiding a primary fight may be very great, as California Republicans learned in 1958, when Governor Knight was persuaded not to contest the gubernatorial nomination with Senator Knowland. The resulting "party harmony" left bitterness that may well have contributed to the Republicans' disastrous defeat at the general election.

PARTICIPATION. Participation in primary elections is low, but even at its lowest, it is higher than under the old convention system. In one-party states, as in the Democratic South, the primary vote is often higher than the vote at the general election. In general, a primary vote is higher where a real contest is involved; where no real contest occurs, voters quite naturally stay home.

QUALITY OF CANDIDATES. The direct primary, it is said, encourages crackpot and lunatic fringe candidates. This may be true, since the primary does make it easier for any qualified voter to seek his party's nomination. But just what is a crackpot candidate? To Hamilton, Jefferson was something of a crackpot. To the Whigs, Jackson was a madman, lunatic, adulterer, murderer. William J. Bryan was a crackpot to Mark Hanna, and to Tom Platt, the Republican boss of New York, Theodore Roosevelt was "that damned cowboy." The lunatics of today may become the luminaries of tomorrow.

The primary affords a channel for new forces, new faces, new ideas to challenge the old, not only in back rooms but at the polls. We do well to remember, too, that the convention system produced its share of crackpots, in addition to men like Webster and Calhoun and Nelson Aldrich. So, too, the primary has produced Hiram Johnson and Earl Warren in California, William E. Borah in Idaho, Woodrow Wilson in New Jersey, George Norris in Nebraska, La Follette in Wisconsin. Who, under these circumstances, should cast a stone?

BURDEN OF EXPENSE. The great expense involved in fighting one campaign for the nomination and another for the election is a substantial source of complaint against the primary system. But this is part of the general problem of campaign finance and is not unique to the primary. A statewide campaign for delegates to a state convention can be expensive, too, unless one is prepared to have the delegates handpicked. The direct primary, it is said, also increases the burden on the voter by forcing him to participate in two elections instead of one and confronting him with an impossible choice among multiple candidates. This, too, is more apparent than real. If delegates to conventions are to be elected by party voters and not handpicked by the machine, the voters would still have to choose them, and if candidates are to campaign for delegates as they now campaign directly for voters, their numbers might increase, not diminish. The problem of multiple candidates can be met in part by (1) increasing the number of signatures required on nominating petitions and/or (2) requiring a substantial electoral deposit to be refunded only if a candidate wins a certain percentage of the total vote cast. The problem of multiple candidates is larger and has its roots in sources other than the direct primary. The long ballot in America is not a product of the direct primary but of our insistence upon the popular election of an army of officials most of whom might better be appointed. The remedy here is to reduce the number of elective offices and thus produce a shorter ballot. With upwards of 1 million elective offices in the United States, and with elections coming with the frequency of summer storms, the burden on the voter is great. The direct primary cannot be said to be a major cause of this blight.

The direct primary, say its critics, makes no provision for the formulation of party policy or the adoption of a party platform, and this is generally true. In most states the delegate convention is still used for this purpose, and this may indeed prove to be its salvation. The point is that nominations by direct primary and a deliberative convention are not mutually exclusive. The primary system is not a cure-all, but it does temper the rule of the machine by presenting it with a constant threat of challenge and by giving political expression to voices that might otherwise be unheard. It puts into the hands of the people a weapon which, used wisely and well, can give new life to American politics and can protect the jugular vein of our Republic from being cut or controlled by an irresponsible and unrepresentative oligarchy.

THE POLITICS
OF POLITICAL PARTIES:
CHOOSING THE CANDIDATES

☆ *THE NATIONAL CONVENTION*

A presidential nominating convention is like nothing else in the civilized world: a combined circus, mob scene, revival meeting and deliberative assembly. "The position of the average delegate," says Herbert Agar, "has neither dignity nor sense." The convention, say its critics, is an anachronism. Nominations are made in an atmosphere of high-minded carousel. Certainly, says one observer, the best way to nominate a President is not to get drunk and ride through hotel lobbies on a donkey. The late Viscount Bryce, after years of study of the American government, wrote: "A European is astonished to see (a thousand or more) men (and women) prepare to transact the two most serious and difficult pieces of business an assembly can undertake, the solemn consideration of their policies and the selection of the person they wish to place at the head of the nation, in the sight and hearing of 12,000 or 14,000 other men and women." And since TV they do this in the sight of 50 million or more spectators.

What the critics tend to forget is that the national party convention is not the apex of a well-ordered hierarchy. It is not like the College of Cardinals or the House of Lords. It is not built on logic or ideology "but rather," as Professor Herring has said, "on the broad mud flats of popular desires and individual ambitions. The party convention is not better than the loose and undisciplined local and state organizations that send their delegates to bargain." And bargain is what they do.

What is overlooked by the superficial observer is that a convention *does* deliberate, *does* debate, and *does* think seriously about its responsibilities to the party and the country. But it does the hard spade work in committees and in executive sessions of the larger delegations. In this respect it is not strikingly different from Congress or the House of Commons where policy is hammered out not on the floor but in smoke-filled committee rooms, in hotel suites, at country clubs and even at dinner parties. The convention as a whole, like Congress, is essentially a ratifying body, to affirm or not to affirm policies and persons agreed upon in committees, conferences of leaders, at state primaries and conventions, and, for the incumbent party, in the White House.

Critics also tend to forget that while the main job is to nominate candidates for President and Vice-President, it also has other work to do. It must adopt a platform on policy, a more important job than is often supposed, and not infrequently the major battles in national conventions are over the platform, not the candidates. For only the convention can define the party's position on the major issues of the day. The convention decides also on the party's basic structure, chooses its national committee, and lays down the rules governing the basis of representation, qualifications of delegates, and procedures for nominating the candidates. It is one of the ironies of American politics that although our political parties are subject to more detailed legal regulations than any other party system in the world, the convention is pretty much a law unto itself.

A national convention, however, is more than the formal legislative and constitutional authority of a major party. Not the least of its functions is to provide a meeting ground for party leaders to get together and exchange experiences, to gain a sense of the national will as distinguished from the will of their own districts. It also serves as a rally for the party faithful, and gives several thousand party leaders firsthand contact with one another and with the candidates for whom they will have to campaign. In this respect a political convention is more like a revival meeting designed to build *esprit,* to release and to resolve the factional tensions that, as Madison said, are rooted in human nature.

The national convention, as we have said, is a representative body of the party and its final source of authority. The apportionment of representation, to be sure, leaves much to be desired. The basic formula for each major party is simple enough, although its refinements can seem complex. Essentially both major parties provide for a certain number of delegates at large from every state and a variable number from the Canal Zone, the District of Columbia, and the territories, with additional delegates for states having elected Democratic or Republican Congressmen, Senators or governors. Additional "bonus" delegates are allocated to states casting their electoral vote for the party's candidate in the last preceding presidential election. In 1968 the Republican national convention was composed of 1,333 voting delegates. Since the Democrats allow for multiple delegates with "split votes," the 1968 convention included over 5,000 delegates and alternates with a total of 2,622 votes. Thus the voting delegates with their alternates make for a large body. However representative of the party it may be, it is not an ideal, deliberative assembly. It is at best a crude system and does not result in a mathematically exact and equal representation of party strength—although it comes pretty close.

In 1964, for example, in the Democratic convention each voting delegate from Illinois represented some 21,000 Democratic voters in that state; the proportion was 18,000 in Indiana, 21,000 in California, and only 2,500 in Nevada, and 6,000 in New Mexico.

In the Republican convention the number of Republican voters represented by each convention vote varied from over 37,000 in New York to 8,000 in Nevada, 5,000 in Wyoming, 5,000 in Mississippi, and 11,000 in Alabama.[1] Southern and western states are overrepresented in both conventions.

How Delegates Are Selected

In most of the states delegates are formally chosen by state central committees or by state conventions. The individual delegates are usually selected informally by the county chairman, an informal committee, or by the "boss." In some cases delegates are pledged to support a particular candidate, in which case they are regarded as "instructed" delegates. Unless instructed, the delegates are free to vote as they choose at the convention. In eighteen states rival delegates are voted on in presidential primary elections. Some of these are "preference" primaries, in which the voters express a preference for a particular aspirant for the party's nomination. In most of these cases the preference expressed by the voters is binding upon the delegates, at least during the initial period of voting in the convention.

The presidential preference primaries are at the same time a monumental headache and a great opportunity for aspiring candidates. A headache in that they are an all but intolerable burden, requiring immense physical and nervous energy and financial resources which only a select few can command. To "fight it out" in every presidential primary state between March, when the first such election is held in New Hampshire, to June, when the last is held would be beyond the strength even of Superman. Nor is it necessary. In the first place many of the presidential primary states with small delegations are of minimal importance, while others have "favorite son" candidates, against whom it is regarded as improper for an "outsider" to contend. Hence the primary battle is normally confined to not more than a half dozen states. Rival contenders pick and choose their primary battlegrounds, not so much because of the number of delegates as for other reasons. The primaries furnish a laboratory in which to demonstrate a candidate's ability to win where it

[1] Figures are based on the 1960 presidential vote.

counts, at the polls. Or it may show his strength with a particular bloc of voters—the labor vote, or the Negro, farm, or "minority group" vote. The presidential primary battles can also test a candidate's talents as a TV personality, as a debater, and as a good "man in the street." And, of course, the primary battles afford a fair test of a candidate's organization—how his own friends and "handlers" stand up under fire.

The history of presidential primaries would indicate that only on rare occasions do they play a decisive role. Winners at the primaries have not necessarily, or even usually, been the winners at the convention. It has been argued that a nationwide presidential primary would remedy this and take the important business of choosing a party's candidate out of the hands of the convention professionals and put it where it belongs in the hands of the rank and file of the party voters. But the enormous burden of a nationwide presidential primary has dampened enthusiasm for this reform. In effect, it would require aspiring presidential candidates to fight two nationwide campaigns. However feasible this might be in a small country, it assumes truly monstrous proportions in a nation of 200 million spread over 3 million square miles, in addition to Alaska and Hawaii. Nor is it demonstrable that the rank and file will in the long run produce better candidates than those much maligned denizens of "smoke-filled rooms."

With television giving the whole nation a ringside seat at the half dozen presidential primaries now seriously contested, the significance of this form of "trial by battle" may increase.[2] As matters now stand, while success in the presidential primaries does not insure nomination, failure can blast a candidate's chances and remove him from further serious consideration.[3]

The Republican presidential primaries of 1964 again illustrate their unpredictable impact on the ultimate result in the convention. Except in Oregon and California, it cannot be said that the presidential primaries had any significant effect in selecting the Republican presidential candidate. In New Hampshire both Goldwater and Rockefeller—the leading contenders—lost to former Senator Lodge, who remained in Vietnam and could scarcely be called an active candidate. Although Goldwater faced

[2] As many as 28 states at one time have used the presidential primary in one form or another. But by 1959, 9 states had tried the system and abandoned it.

[3] This happened to Wendell Willkie in 1944 when, having lost to Dewey in the Wisconsin primary, he dropped like a plummet from the race. Similarly Harold Stassen's defeat in the Oregon primary in 1948 proved fatal to his ambition. On the other hand, John Kennedy's striking victories in the 1960 primaries, especially in Wisconsin and West Virginia, may well have made his nomination "inevitable." In Kennedy's case, the Wisconsin victory demonstrated that he could win in a farm state even against the farmers' friend, Senator Hubert Humphrey of the neighboring state of Minnesota. Wisconsin also showed that Catholic voters would move strongly into the Kennedy camp. West Virginia seemed to show that he could win in an overwhelmingly Protestant state, thus allaying the traditional taboo that "a Catholic cannot be elected President." See *Congress and the Nation, 1945–1964* (Washington, D.C.: Congressional Quarterly Service, 1965), p. 53.

no serious opposition in Indiana, Illinois, Nebraska, Massachusetts, Pennsylvania, and South Dakota, his primary vote was unimpressive by any standard. More exciting and promising was Rockefeller's victory in Oregon, where, in defiance of all pre-election polls, he polled 33 percent of the vote against 27.7 percent for Lodge and 17.6 percent for Goldwater. But the New York governor's hopes for the nomination were dashed when again in defiance of the pre-election polls in California—this time in his favor—he lost to Goldwater by a narrow margin.

Goldwater's success at the San Francisco convention was perhaps best explained by Goldwater himself in June, 1963, when he said, "You see, I have one advantage [over my opponents]. I've done my political home work. I've spent the last 5 1/2 years traipsing around the country helping precinct chairmen elect candidates and raise money. Neither Rockefeller nor Romney has done this. I have good working relations with party regulars all over the country." By convention time he had coralled virtually enough delegates to secure the nomination, which he won on the first ballot. His "home work" had paid off in spite of the poor image he presented in the presidential primaries.

The effects of the 1968 presidential primaries will be discussed for a long time to come. For the Republicans the outcome was much less dramatic than for the Democrats. Governor Romney of Michigan saw his hopes dashed when he lost decisively in New Hampshire. Governor Rockefeller remained aloof until it was too late to make an impressive show of popular strength; and former Vice-President Richard Nixon won five primaries virtually without opposition as part of his carefully planned strategy of mixing his sources of support by securing a display of popular strength while simultaneously gathering commitments from delegates selected by methods other than the primaries. His success in using these tactics was indicated by his nomination on the first ballot.

By contrast the Democratic primaries generated party splits whose effects may extend well beyond the electoral year of 1968. Senator Eugene McCarthy of Minnesota, running largely on the single issue of opposition to President Johnson's policy in Vietnam, won the New Hampshire primary handily. The display of support for McCarthy's position, along with the Tet offensive on the part of the Viet Cong and North Vietnamese troops in South Vietnam, was interpreted by many observers to be the major factors in Johnson's refusal to seek the nomination for another term as President and in encouraging Senator Robert Kennedy to enter the contest for the nomination. Although Senator McCarthy did outrun Senator Kennedy in the later Oregon primary, elsewhere Senator Kennedy demonstrated in the primaries a capacity to mobilize a general popular support that might well have led him to victory at the chaotic Democratic convention in Chicago in August, 1968. However, the tragedy of his assassination following a conclusive primary victory in California cut short his challenge to Vice-President Humphrey's candidacy, which was based on staying clear of the primaries and securing delegate votes through regular party organizational channels. Senator McCarthy, although subsequently falling far short of the votes necessary to stop Humphrey on the first ballot, did manage to divide the Democratic party sufficiently to produce what some regard as a permanent or semipermanent defection of a sizable number of voters from adherence to the party.

Character of the Delegates

Only in recent years have any reliable data been available concerning the character and qualifications of convention delegates. In general it may be said that national conventions are fairly representative of the American people and of the two major parties, with the customary biases to be found in any such selective body. The convention is not a random sample of the party voters or of the American people any more than is Congress or a state legislature.[4] In terms of age both party conventions would seem to follow a normal distribution, with the bulk of the delegates falling between 40 and 64 years of age. There are, of course, the inevitable "juveniles" in their early twenties, and the "party sages" in their eighties. Although women comprise nearly half the registered voters, they account for only 10 to 13 percent of the delegates. Nor do Negroes do much better; with nearly 10 percent of the population, Negroes comprise from 1 1/2 to 3 percent of the delegates at national party conventions, although national demand on Democratic party delegations from the South is changing this proportion upward. In religious and ethnic terms, most significant groups are represented, although not in any strict proportion to their total numbers in the population. In this respect too, the party conventions, taking account of the differences between the parties, are probably as representative as any similar gathering.

In terms of education, convention delegates, like Congressmen or state legislators, include a substantially larger share of college graduates than does the rank and file of party voters. In income, occupation, and general social status, they are also considerably above the general population. Delegates also tend to be professional, self-employed persons, and elective public officials, for these, after all, are the people who can afford the time and money involved, since most delegates must pay their own way. Wage earners and salaried personnel are less politically mobile and hence less available as delegates. Although there is a surprising rate of turnover from one convention to another, a significant percentage will have had prior experience, either as a delegate or as a party worker or public official. As might be expected, "the larger delegations usually

---

[4] See the chart in Paul David, *et al., The Politics of National Party Conventions* (Washington, D.C.: Brookings Institution, 1960), p. 326.

contained larger numbers, and often larger percentages of distinguished and experienced delegates than the smaller ones."

There is a rather striking similarity in the composition of Republican and Democratic conventions. Democratic delegates are slightly younger than Republicans, a slightly higher percentage are women, and an increasing percentage are Negroes; they have somewhat lower incomes and include fewer delegates from professional and business groups, and a somewhat higher percentage of public officials. The most significant differences are to be found in the representation of religious, labor, and managerial groups. Democratic conventions include a disproportionate percentage of Catholics, Jews, and Baptists, while Republican conventions contain a heavy disproportion of Protestants generally and Presbyterians, Episcopalians, and Congregationalists in particular. Approximately twice as many Democratic delegates are representatives of labor unions, or are public officials, and a proportionately larger number of farm delegates is found among Republicans.[5]

Ideologically the differences between Democratic and Republican convention delegates are greater than are the ideological differences between the rank and file of Democratic and Republican voters. On policies having to do with the regulation of business enterprise, public ownership of power and other utilities, taxation, social welfare, federal grants-in-aid, and trade policy, the differences between Republican and Democratic leaders are significant.[6]

Long before the delegates are selected the national committee has selected a convention site and issued its formal call for the convention. Cities vie with one another to play host without any discernible partisan bias. To support their invitations the businessmen and occasionally the local governments themselves pledge contributions to the major parties. Although the size of these bids is taken into account, the convention does not always go to the highest bidder. Accessibility, hotel accommodations, an adequate convention hall, and facilities to accommodate an army of radio, TV, and press agents are more likely to be decisive. Few cities, in fact, are able to make provision for from 10,000 to 20,000 delegates, alternates, party hangers-on, newspapermen, TV commentators, technical staffs, and literally thousands of spectators, both resident and non-resident.[7]

Although local city officials and chambers of commerce may bid for

5 See David et al., op. cit., chap. 14, pp. 25–355, for detailed analysis of the "characteristics of Delegates and Delegations."

6 H. McClosky, P. Hoffmann, and R. O'Hara, "Issue Conflict and Consensus Among Party Leaders and Followers," American Political Science Review (June, 1960).

7 It is mainly because of its geographic centrality, hotel accommodations, ground transportation and convention hall that Chicago is so frequently chosen. Of twenty-seven Republican conventions (1856–1960), fifteen were in Chicago, four in Pittsburgh, two in Cleveland, one in Baltimore, and one each in Cincinnati, Minneapolis, St. Louis, Philadelphia, and San Francisco.

conventions as good for business, with a sublime indifference to any partisan considerations, in selecting a site, the national committee cannot ignore the political overtones attendant upon choosing one city over another. Being politicians, the national committee has political antennae more sharply attuned to these overtones than does a chamber of commerce. In Lincoln's day, for example, the national committee knew how important it was for Lincoln that the Republican convention met in Chicago in 1860. Nor was the national committee indifferent to the importance of nominating Al Smith, an urban Roman Catholic Democrat, in Houston, Texas, which was a southern, Protestant, Democratic stronghold. There are occasions indeed when selection of the convention city may indicate, to those perceptive in such matters, which way the wind blows among the party's high command.

The gathering of delegates and alternates, with their staffs and hangers-on, accompanied by a mass immigration of communications personnel and spectators, is a spectacle which is not soon forgotten. Not even the coming together of the ancient Scottish clans could match it for color and excitement. There are bands to greet the incoming delegations playing "California Here I Come," "The Eyes of Texas Are Upon You," "The Sidewalks of New York," "Dixie," and even on one memorable occasion, "The Dark Town Strutters' Ball," to welcome a delegation from the deep South. And there is always some delegation marching in, as the Taft delegates did in 1952, to the martial strains of "Onward Christian Soldiers." Streets and hotel lobbies are festooned with banners, placards, and billboards. Badges, ash trays, fans, paper caps, and pennants are handed out by the tens of thousands. Inevitably, too, there will be a baby elephant for the Republicans and an army mule or donkey for the Democrats—to parade up and down the streets and in and out of public buildings.

Headquarters are opened for the rival candidates and an intricate ritualistic pattern of intervisitation begins, while private conferences, cocktail parties, breakfasts, luncheons, and dinners go on to supplement the public rallies that seem always to be in full swing. Deals are made, promises of support, threats of retaliation or even revolt are muttered, as the leaders strive to put together a platform and a ticket that can win. The convention itself is mainly a forum, not for debate, but for demonstrations and invocations, for a "viewing with alarm" or a "pointing with pride," and finally, of course, for a formal recording of votes, most of which have been agreed upon beforehand in quasi-public caucuses of the separate delegations.

To keep this vast machine moving is the responsibility mainly of the temporary and permanent chairmen and four committees. The temporary chairman's major task, aside from calling the convention to order, is to deliver what is called a "keynote" speech. He and his keynote speech can be of considerable importance as indicating the party line for the oncoming campaign and even the faction likely to prevail in the critical vote on the nomination. Elihu Root's election as temporary chairman of the Republican convention in 1912, for example, indicated that the conservatives were in control and would oppose former President Roosevelt or Senator LaFollette as the presidential nominee. Root's election meant that the conservatives would pick the permanent officers of the convention, including the crucial committees of rules and credentials. Occasionally the keynoter and the temporary chairman are different persons, as in 1952 when General MacArthur delivered the keynote speech but did not serve as temporary chairman.

The keynote speech is by custom and tradition expected to be a stemwinder to smite the opposition as an iniquitous combination bent upon the nation's ruin, and to extol the speaker's own party as the fount of wisdom and patriotism from which all blessings flow. Some keynote speeches reach high levels of perfervid eloquence, while others are simply vulgar and bathetic, too loudly intoned to qualify as soporific. Occasionally a keynote speaker will highlight a burning conflict within his own party. Governor Mark Hatfield of Oregon, for example, in his keynote speech at the 1964 Republican convention denounced by name the John Birch Society, along with the Ku Klux Klan and the Communist party, as " 'bigots' . . . who spew forth the venom of hate." In doing so he added fuel to a smouldering fire of conflict in the Republican party between the so-called extreme right, moderates, and liberals.

The Steam Rollers

While all this is going on, committees on credentials, resolutions, permanent organization, and rules are at work preparing an official roster of delegates, writing the party platform, selecting permanent convention officials, including a chairman, and developing the basic rules of procedure. This indispensable machinery is both a source of tension and a necessary device for resolving conflicts. Without them the convention might bog down in a mass of detail and interfactional quarrels that could make a shambles of the whole proceeding. To those whose interests are adversely affected, however, they appear as "steam rollers" having scant regard for interests adverse to the controlling oligarchy.[8]

As we have seen, the committee on permanent organization can exert considerable influence on the general tone of the convention by the permanent officials it selects. Even more important is the credentials committee which scans the temporary roll of the convention and resolves

---

[8] In 1964 Governor Scranton of Pennsylvania further embittered an already embittered convention when a letter bearing his signature was circulated which said that the Goldwater managers "feel that they have bought, beaten and compromised enough delegates . . . to make the result a foregone conclusion." Nor was the tension noticeably relieved when Governor Scranton said that he had not read the statement before authorizing its circulation over his signature.

conflicts among rival delegations. Although the selection of delegates is normally controlled by state law, the convention reserves to itself the right to decide who may participate as voting delegates. In the vast majority of cases this causes no difficulty and the names on the temporary roll become the permanent delegates. But in some states the laws are ambiguous and contests frequently arise. In the Republican convention of 1912, for example, it was not only the selection of a conservative permanent chairman but the adverse decisions of the credentials committee that drove Theodore Roosevelt and the Progressives to open revolt. Again in 1952 a bitter battle was fought between rival pro-Taft and pro-Eisenhower delegations. Delegations representing these rival factions were on hand from a number of states, each claiming the right to sit and vote as the official delegation of that state. Especially bitter and prolonged were the contests from Georgia and Texas. Said Senator Richard Nixon:

> The issue of which delegation from Texas is seated is bigger than the Taft-Eisenhower contest for the Presidential nomination. The real issue is whether the Republican party is to survive. It is whether the GOP is to be a closed corporation or open to all people who want a change of administration in Washington. It is whether the selection of the Republican candidate for President is to be determined by the will of the people or by a small clique of politicians who happen to control the party machinery.[9]

It was this contest that inspired the placards prominently displayed during the convention which read, "Thou shalt not steal."

Usually the credentials committee arranges a compromise by allocating a certain number of delegates to each faction. Like most compromises these leave both sides somewhat unhappy, but avoid an open break in the party. Occasionally all contesting delegates are seated, each with fractional votes, a solution which evades the main issue, increases the size of the convention, and shifts the burden of the battle to the larger body itself. In the Democratic convention of 1940, 54 delegates from Mississippi were seated to cast 2 votes, or one twenty-seventh of a vote, per delegate. Almost the only element of excitement in the Democratic convention of 1964 was furnished by the delegation of Negroes from Mississippi claiming to represent the "Mississippi Freedom Democratic Party," which challenged the right of the "regular" Mississippi Democratic delegation to its seats. After considerable turmoil the regular delegation was seated, provided they signed a pledge to support the convention nominees (a so-called loyalty pledge). The Freedom delegation was also accorded two seats, with a further pledge against racial discrimination in future conventions.

WRITING THE PLATFORM. The national convention is the highest authority on matters of party policy, and the convention's platform represents

[9] *The New York Times,* July 3, 1952.

the most authoritative statement of the party, not only on the pressing
issues of the day, but of its basic political philosophy. Responsibility for
this important document lies with the Committee on Resolutions. The
process resembles that of a congressional committee holding hearings on
controversial legislation, but without the congressional committee's
powers to compel testimony or to commit for contempt. Nor does the
Committee on Resolutions have the research personnel and facilities
available to its congressional counterpart. Recent experiments in both
parties with interim committees to develop "background materials" for
the Committee on Resolutions have given greater coherence to the final
platform. But the process and the platforms themselves have not been
radically changed, and they are still a far cry from the research papers of
a scientific institute.

Nowhere, perhaps, is the factional composition of the major parties
so clearly revealed as in the proceedings of the Committee on Resolutions. Here most of the major organized interest groups of the country
pass in review, with spokesmen claiming to represent labor and agriculture, business and industry, education and the professions, and patriotic,
civic, religious, ethnic, and racial groups galore. The committee is
inundated with draft platforms and "planks" on particular issues until
the simple job of cataloguing, reading and analyzing them assumes staggering dimensions. Nor do the organized factions confine their efforts to
formal statements of this kind. Members of the committee are button-
holed, badgered, and belabored in the lobbies and corridors, in their
rooms, at meal time and at cocktail parties, face to face, by telephone
calls, letters, telegrams and petitions, mass meetings, even by television,
motion pictures, and all the arts of professional pressure and propaganda.

In such an atmosphere and in the face of so bewildering an array of
disparate and often conflicting interests, the wonder is not that party
platforms are prolix, vague, ambiguous, and internally inconsistent, but
that they are, on the whole, so specific, sensible, coherent and admirably
adapted to the purpose they serve. If the platform indulges excessively in
high-level abstractions about "solvency and integrity," or "freedom and
prosperity," and if it portrays the opposition as "incompetent and corrupt," and "unworthy of the nation's trust," this is to be expected. But
there is more to party platforms than all this. There are statements of
policy, often surprising for their clarity and candor, and not always calculated to mollify and ensnare the marginal voter. It is customary to discount party platforms as having little or no significance in outlining a
party's principles. But a careful reading of Republican and Democratic
platforms, not to mention those of minor parties, will give one insights
into the basic spirit and purpose of our parties that can come from no
other source.

If on many issues the platforms are much alike, this in itself is a sign
of the extent to which a national consensus has been reached. But if one

attends not to the similarities but to the differences, a significant contrast appears. On most major issues of domestic policy—taxation, farm legislation, social welfare, government ownership, the regulation and control of private business—and at least on some issues of foreign policy—foreign trade, foreign aid, or the United Nations—the major parties offer the voters meaningful and strikingly different programs and policies. Moreover, platforms can exert an influence upon the outcome of an election. There is a marked correspondence between the spirit and substance of the principles outlined in these documents and the interests in the population from which the parties derive their major support. No one who reads Republican platforms will be surprised to find that it is the party of business and industry, banking and finance, just as no one who reads Democratic platforms will be surprised to learn that the Democratic party is the party of organized labor, professional intellectuals, and racial and ethnic minorities.

The significance of platforms, moreover, is attested by the many and bitter conflicts that are fought over particular statements of party policy. Men normally do not quarrel over matters upon which they agree or which they regard as of no consequence, but in 1860 and 1896, in 1912 and 1932, in 1948, 1956, 1964, and 1968, both Republican and Democratic conventions were torn by conflicts over policy quite as much as by conflicts over candidates.[10] The struggles over slavery, the tariff, monetary policy, internal improvements, welfare legislation, taxation, foreign policy, and civil rights, which have agitated American political life, have almost always come to verbal focus in party platforms. Refinements of wording and ambiguous abstractions may satisfy the hard core of party adherents, but not the militant, marginal minorities upon whose loyalty and support victory may depend. Pious platitudes about "equal rights" and the "American Way of Life" are not likely to satisfy leaders of the National Association for the Advancement of Colored People (NAACP), the Congress of Racial Equality (CORE), and the Student Non-Violent Coordinating Committee (SNCC), who want stronger meat in more specific terms. They want to know not how the party stands on "equality" in general, but "equality" in particular—equality of access to education, housing, recreation, employment, and the right to vote. And so with farmers, workers, businessmen, integrationists, segregationists, nationalists, or internationalists. At point after point they want commit-

[10] At the Republican convention of 1964 Governor Rockefeller was wildly booed when he tried to speak in favor of three amendments to the platform, proposed on the floor, by moderate Republicans. These amendments would (1) denounce the John Birch Society by name, (2) urge faithful enforcement of the Civil Rights Acts and (3) endorse the long-standing policy of leaving to the President exclusive control of the use of nuclear weapons. And at the Democratic convention in 1968, one of the most turbulent conventions in history, the battle over the question of peace in Vietnam was long and bitter and spilled over into virtually every other issue before the party delegates.

ments not only to an "American System," but to higher tariffs on particular products, lower taxes on particular groups, relief from particular regulations, or more or less foreign aid. A platform, in short, must strike a delicate balance between the general and the particular, between the spirit and the letter of the party's basic philosophy.

The platform, of course, is not the only vehicle for defining party policy. The views of its candidates for President and Vice-President are often more significant than the platform, and they do not always agree. Thus in 1928 the Democrats nominated a "wet" (anti-prohibition) presidential candidate, Alfred Smith, after approving a "dry" (pro-prohibition) party platform. And in 1964 candidate Goldwater sought to push his party considerably farther to the "right" than the conservative platform adopted at the San Francisco convention. The candidate's position on many important issues no doubt helped to alienate many moderates. Statements on policy by other prominent leaders also help to define party policy. Most significant of all is the record of its adherents in public office. Every President who seeks re-election must "run on his record," no matter what the platform says. And every politician seeking re-election will be judged not only on his own record but also on the record of his fellow partisans in the White House, in Congress, and in the several states. Because interests vary and candidates must somehow satisfy a majority of voters in various political subdivisions, there is often considerable disparity in statements of policy and voting records, even among candidates of the same party. What is good party doctrine in Maine may not be so good in Minnesota. Yet, as we have seen, if one puts together these bits and pieces of party policy for the country as a whole, something clearly definable as Democratic or Republican doctrine will emerge. It is to this task that the Committee on Resolutions of the national convention must devote its best endeavor.

That the process can be improved is obvious. The Glenn Frank Republican Committee on Policy of 1937, the Percy Committee of 1960, the Democratic Advisory Council, the increasing attention to intercampaign policy research by national party committees, and preconvention platform research have all contributed to more meaningful, literate, and coherent party platforms. Interim regional party conferences on policy also represent a constructive innovation. Perhaps both major parties will one day experiment with biennial national conventions devoted solely to matters of party policy. This would indicate that the major parties were as much concerned with policy and philosophy as with the nomination and election of candidates for public office.[11] Regional and biennial

11 It might alleviate the present condition under which no authoritative, up-to-date statement on party policy is made in terms of which the "off-year" congressional campaign can be fought. In 1941 Senator Robert Taft was asked what foreign policy was to guide Republican candidates in the forthcoming congressional elections. "Well," said Senator Taft, "no Republican convention can be held to make any binding

national conventions on policy, moreover, might prove to be important aids in the continuing political education of the American people.

NOMINATING THE CANDIDATES. However important party platform making may be, the main business of the quadrennial national convention is, and will continue to be, the nomination of candidates for President and Vice-President. As the convention turns to this all-important business, it quickly becomes clear that not everybody can hope to become President of the United States. To aspire to this high office one must be what politicians call "available," and availability is, as it were, a coat of many colors. The central question asked by the convention's king-makers is always "Can he win?" If a majority of delegates think he can't win, his prospects will approach zero. No matter what his other qualities may be, they must in the final analysis add up to that most mystical of all qualities, "electability."

For practical purposes, "availability" and "electability" are synonymous, and to be available a candidate must meet certain rigid tests. These are tests of age and physical stamina, for the strains of a campaign and of the Presidency thereafter are such that only the stong of mind and body can hope to meet them. There are tests of political geography. Candidates coming from doubtful states—states like New York, Ohio, Illinois, or California—have a decided advantage over candidates from small or one-party states like Vermont or Alabama. Normally a convention does not like to waste a presidential nomination on a state with few electoral votes or one that can be counted on to support, or to oppose, the party ticket no matter who the candidate may be. For this among other reasons, the "solid" Democratic South has been fallow ground for presidential aspirants of both parties since the Civil War.

Religion was a test of availability until John Kennedy in 1960 demonstrated that a Roman Catholic could be elected, notwithstanding a century-old tradition to the contrary. It remains to be seen whether the religious test will continue to make Jews or Moslems or atheists unavailable. Political experience and knowhow are tests of variable difficulty, although in general conventions prefer seasoned politicians with experience as governor at the state level, or as a member of Congress. Mayors, even of great cities, state legislators, or judges of state or federal courts who lack experience as governors or in Congress, are likely to have a low availability. The major exception is a distinguished military figure. Generals Zachary Taylor, John C. Frémont, Ulysses Grant, and Dwight Eisenhower proved that military experience may be a fair substitute for political knowhow. A career in business or the professions, even a brilliant one, will normally not suffice to meet this test. Wendell Willkie and

declarations regarding policy before next year's elections [1942] and the National Committee has no authority to make such declarations. I see no reason [therefore] why each Congressman and each Senator should not run on his own foreign policy."

Herbert Hoover might seem to be exceptions, although Mr. Hoover came to the nomination only after a distinguished career as an unofficial ambassador and member of the Cabinet. For many years it was believed that great wealth would be a handicap, and national conventions have certainly shown no tendency to make wealth a test of availability. But Washington, Hoover, the Roosevelts, and Kennedy, among successful candidates, have found that wealth and availability are not mutually exclusive.

Normally, conventions prefer candidates with an established reputation for party loyalty. The "independent" or the "mugwump" is held in low esteem. But there have been exceptions, such as Hoover, Willkie, and Eisenhower, none of whom could be regarded as loyal, dyed-in-the wool partisans. There are tests of family, personal character and habits on which conventions lay some emphasis. A married man with a family, all other things being equal, will be preferred to a bachelor, and it has yet to be shown that a divorce is not a fatal flaw in a candidate's availability. Personal honesty, a corruption-proof career, and high standards of personal morality are also tests of availability. But there are exceptions here too. James Garfield won the Republican nomination nowithstanding the exposure of his dubious relations with the Credit Mobilier scandal. Cleveland was twice nominated and elected, although he was accused of being the father of an illegitimate child, a charge which he did not deny. A similar rumor about Harding failed to stop his nomination in 1920. A candidate's friends and associates, his relations with special interests, may sometimes be used to block his nomination, although not always. Thus Garfield, who was accused of being Jay Gould's errand boy, was nevertheless nominated. So too were William Jennings Bryan and Franklin Roosevelt, who were accused of cavorting with radicals and even subversives. Bryan himself helped to prevent the nomination of Champ Clark in 1912 by implying that Clark was under obligation to "J. P. Morgan, Thomas F. Ryan, August Belmont [and] other members of the privilege-hunting and favor-seeking class." And in 1924 both Smith and McAdoo went down under a barrage of abuse accusing the one (Smith) of being in league with the big city forces of crime, and the other (McAdoo) of being the candidate favored by the Ku Klux Klan. Convention delegates do not like to take chances on candidates who can be assailed as "hirelings of special interests," or "captives of radical factionalists," or, as Wendell Willkie was described by Harold Ickes, the "barefoot boy of Wall Street." In the 1964 Republican convention Governor Scranton issued a dramatic challenge to Senator Goldwater to debate the issues that divided them as prospective nominees. This in itself was a novelty. But when he referred to "Goldwaterism" as a "crazyquilt collection of absurd and dangerous positions that would be soundly repudiated by the American people in November," he went beyond the limits of acceptable convention billingsgate.

In applying these tests, a national convention has, of course, the evidence of the presidential primaries. But, as we have seen, results of the primaries are regarded as advisory, and not binding on the delegates. In addition to the candidates who have survived the primaries, the convention will have to review the record of dozens more who, for reasons of their own, have eschewed the primaries altogether or have participated only in one or two selected states, including their own. There will be a host of "favorite sons," usually governors, with their own state's delegation pledged for at least the first ballot. There will be the spent steeds of earlier conventions and campaigns who want to try again; the abandoned leaders who hope always to reassert their leadership; the hardy perennials who every four years move in force upon the convention, often with lavish outlays on promotion and public relations, and who, like moths in a flame, are as regularly consumed by the convention; and there are of course the dark horses, most of whom are dark only because no one takes them seriously.

As the convention moves to its main business of choosing a candidate, the states' delegations are called in alphabetical order, with Alabama first and Wyoming last. As the roll is called, a spokesman for each delegation rises and either offers the name of a candidate or yields to some other state, which then proceeds to place a name in nomination. The nominating and seconding speeches are usually dreadful examples of oratory at its worst, more significant as part of an inflexible ritual than as rhetoric. Most nominating speeches are followed by demonstrations in which delegates parade up and down the aisles in ordered pandemonium.

Most of the oratory is wasted, but on occasion a speech will electrify the convention and even change the course of history. Such was Garfield's speech on behalf of John Sherman in 1880, a speech that failed to make Sherman the Republican nominee, but succeeded unintentionally in making Garfield himself the nominee. Garfield was perhaps the only genuine dark horse candidate to win a nomination. Not so unintentional was the effect of William Jennings Bryan's classic "cross of gold" speech to the Democratic convention in 1896. Bryan had no headquarters, no banners, no manager, but the fourteen carloads of ardent supporters and the speech itself would suggest that he was a dark horse running in a strong light. "We have begged," he said, "and they have mocked when our calamity came. We beg no longer, we entreat no more, we petition no more. We defy them. . . . We will answer their demands for a gold standard by saying to them: You shall not press down upon the brow of labor a crown of thorns. You shall not crucify mankind upon a cross of gold." As he finished, delegates, and spectators took up the cry of Bryan! Bryan! Bryan!, and in the end Bryan it was.

When the roll call is complete and the orators have temporarily subsided, the convention turns to the balloting. Again the roll is called by states in alphabetical order and again each delegation's spokesman announces the vote of the delegation, or, awaiting further conferences or more straws in the wind, it "passes" for the time being. During the balloting, tension mounts as the leading candidates emerge. An elaborate pattern of inter-visitation among the various delegations goes on as the roll is called. Delegations caucus on the floor and off to settle differences and try to reach agreement so that the delegation's vote cast as a unit may exert its maximum influence. To a surprising degree the delegations reach agreement, although a good many remain divided to the end. The unit rule, which required all delegations to vote as a unit, and which characterized Democratic conventions for many years, is no longer a requirement but remains the hope and desire of every delegation chairman.

As the balloting proceeds, the extent of division within the convention as a whole becomes clear. If no candidate polls a majority on the first ballot, another is taken, and if necessary a third and a fourth and more. The number of ballots required is a fair measure of the conflicts and dissension within the party. The more ballots required, the more likely is the nominee to have a tough time holding his party together in the campaign. Hence multiple ballots in the convention are said to spell defeat at the polls, although this is by no means always true. Much depends on the opposition and the candidates themselves.

Most nominations, in any case, are made either on the first ballot, as is usual when an incumbent President is seeking a second term, or at least by the fifth ballot. In 20 Democratic and 21 Republican conventions between 1832 and 1968, the presidential candidate was nominated on the first ballot. And in 26 Democratic and 27 Republican conventions the nomination was confirmed after 5 ballots or less. Multiple ballots have occurred more frequently in Democratic than in Republican conventions largely because, prior to 1936, a two-thirds vote of all the delegates was required for the nomination as against a simple majority in Republican conclaves. The two-thirds rule in Democratic conventions had kept the party under bondage to the Solid South for a hundred years. Although southerners were unable to nominate candidates of their own (there was no presidential candidate of either party resident in the South until Lyndon Johnson's nomination in 1964), they were able to veto any other candidate who failed to meet their terms. Abandoning the two-thirds rule for a simple majority vote in Democratic conventions has thus reduced both the likelihood of endless balloting and the power of the southern wing of the party.

THE VICE-PRESIDENTIAL NOMINATION.   With the selection of a presidential nominee the convention's work is done, except for the choice of a vice-presidential candidate. In most cases this choice is, for all practical purposes, left to the presidential nominee, who names his own running mate, subject to ratification by the convention as a whole. Where the nomination is left to the "free and untrammeled choice" of the convention, exciting contests often take place, as in 1956 when Senator Kefauver won the vice-presidential nomination by a slender margin over Senator John Kennedy.

In selecting a vice-presidential candidate, a major consideration is to produce a "balanced ticket," balanced if possible in terms of geography, policy, and factional interest. Thus most tickets represent a combination of East-West, North-South, liberal-conservative, and urban-rural interests in the party. Other considerations include an effort to build strength in a strategic doubtful state and to placate powerful factions within the party.

It has been said that vice-presidential nominations are made in a fit of absentmindedness, with the convention in disarray after the main event and the exhausted delegates anxious to have it over with. The result, it is said, has been to pick agreeable mediocrities. And, it is argued, this is lamentable, in view of the high probability of a Vice-President succeeding to the Presidency. How much of this argument we ought to accept we shall examine later in our discussion of the Vice-Presidency. By 1964 it had been pretty well established that the presidential nominee should be permitted, when he wished to do so, to name his running mate.

American national party conventions are unique among the political institutions of the world—there is nothing quite like them anywhere else. Like other ancient monuments, they have been assailed by critics of both right and left. National conventions, it is said, are "unwieldy, unrepresentative, and irresponsible . . . a combination camp meeting, Congress, and medicine show." It is a miracle, say the critics, that we have survived in spite of this political anachronism, a miracle to show that "God takes care of drunkards, little children and the United States of America."

Before we scrap the national conventions, however, we need to ask what process could function with better results. After all, conventions furnish a machinery of party government not otherwise provided for in our system. They also serve to subject party leaders and candidates to public scrutiny and appraisal, a process now vastly improved by television. They enable literally thousands of citizens to participate actively in the decision-making process where issues of great importance are resolved. And, of course, the national conventions are invaluable as launching pads for the presidential campaign. How these functions could be performed without national conventions or their equivalent, it is hard to say. The fact is that if the national conventions did not exist, it would be necessary to create them.

This is not to say that the present system is beyond criticism. Both major party conventions could be made more representative of the rank and file of party adherents. Both could develop better machinery for planning and scheduling their proceedings. Perhaps an executive committee for each convention might be set up to include the chairmen of at least the larger delegations. More continuous research on party policy, organization and finance would improve the convention as a deliberative and decision-making body. Regional interim conventions and biennial national conventions might serve to improve party morale and to strengthen our parties as significant factors in the political education of the American people.

In the final analysis the convention system will be judged by the quality of its product, and in these terms the record is not one of which either party need be ashamed. Every President since Andrew Jackson has been an alumnus of the national convention system. Among them there have been great men, near-great men, men of average and even less-than-average stature. But the ratio of the great and the near great to the average and below is probably as high as for any comparable number of national leaders in any other country in the world, however they may have been selected. And Vice-Presidents who have succeeded to the Presidency will bear comparison with comparable leaders selected in other ways. If conventions do not nominate the best men but rather the most electable, it should be said that electability is itself an indispensable attribute of great political leadership.

☆ THE CAMPAIGN

How accurately the delegates to a nominating convention or the party voters at a primary election have assessed the electability of the party's candidates is finally tested at the polls on election day. But prior to election day the candidates are tested in the fires of a political campaign that, in presidential years, involves the mass mobilization of tens of millions of voters. In many ways a presidential campaign is less a nationwide advertising or sales campaign than it is a quasi-religious crusade designed to hold the faithful and win the doubtful in a process succinctly described as the "engineering of consent."[12] As in the army, there is a general staff, with services of supply, finance, research, intelligence, propaganda and publicity. At the top as commander in chief is the chairman of the national committee working in close collaboration with the nominee by whom he is selected, and to whom, in theory at least, he is responsible. There are divisional commanders in charge of the work among the foreign-born, the Negroes, farmers, workers, veterans, and the professions. There is a women's division, an industrial division, and others corresponding to virtually every major interest group to which an appeal is made. Below these is a host of subalterns, state, congressional district, county, city, ward, and precinct committees and their chairmen, corresponding to the captains, lieutenants, sergeants, corporals, and

12 See Peter Odegard and Allen Helms, *American Politics* (New York: Harper & Row, 1938), chaps. XVII and XVIII.

privates of the army. How many active party workers there are during a campaign it is impossible to say, but a million or more for each of the major parties and other thousands for the minor messiahs would seem to be a fair estimate. There were volunteer workers galore mobilized not only in the official party organization but in auxiliary groups calling themselves "Citizens for Eisenhower-Nixon," or "Volunteers for Stevenson," or other such titles.

Millions of pamphlets, leaflets, books, and films are issued and distributed through these far-flung organizations. Posters by the tens of thousands appear on billboards and in shop windows, as bumper strips on automobiles, placards on telephone poles, and in forms designed for display on any available vacant space. The mass media—radio, newspapers, magazines, motion pictures, and television—are filled with claims and counterclaims on behalf of rival candidates. Indeed, in recent years the mass media have become the major avenue of communication between candidates and their constituents—between political parties and the people. But below the brooding omnipresence of the mass media are the workers in counties and cities, wards and precincts, upon whom the parties rely to get the candidates to the voters and the voters to the polls.

☆ CAMPAIGN COSTS

All of this vast expenditure of time and effort costs money, and the financing of campaigns for public office has become a major problem of American democracy. The heart of a democratic system lies in the capacity of the voters to choose among a variety of rival parties and candidates representing different policies and programs. If this choice is to be effective the people must, at the very least, have access to information about the candidates, parties, or issues at stake.

By the same token, the rival parties and candidates must have access to the voters. To the extent that one party or candidate can reach the voters through the channels of mass communication now available, to the exclusion, or virtual exclusion, of its rivals, democratic government is imperiled. Such a monopoly may be achieved not only by direct legal control, as in nondemocratic states, but also, in democratic countries, by such superior financial resources as to enable one candidate or party to purchase time, space, organization and professional skills far beyond the reach of any rival. To purchase a fair share of these facilities becomes, therefore, a major problem for any candidate or party hoping seriously to compete for the attention and support of the voters. If they turn exclusively or primarily to rich individuals or groups for these funds, there is grave danger that commitments will be made or obligations incurred that are against the public interest. This danger is compounded when large contributions are made secretly and without public knowledge. As Leonard Friedman, Deputy Attorney General of California, told a legislative committee in 1955, the "unrestricted use of hidden money in election campaigns . . . operates internally, secretly, like a malignant growth . . . as a medium for exerting unholy pressures on elected public officials."

The costs of political campaigning have vastly increased with the size of the electorate, the cost of mass communication, and the use of professional personnel. An educated estimate of campaign spending in 1964 places the total in the neighborhood of 200 million dollars, only a fraction of which was accounted for under existing legislation.[13]

Present laws on this critically important problem have been termed by the late Senator Hennings as "so inadequate, so antiquated and so riddled with loopholes that they invite evasion." Although they pay lip service to the principles of limitation and disclosure, they make no effective provision for either. So-called Corrupt Practices laws, both federal and state, are essentially negative in their approach to the problem. In summary and with minor variations existing legislation is confined to (1) imposing restrictions as to the sources of campaign funds, (2) limiting the size of individual contributions, (3) imposing a ceiling on total expenditures, and (4) requiring both candidates and parties to file public statements of their income and expenditures. Restrictions as to sources include a prohibition against the solicitation of public employees, as well as against direct contributions by corporations and labor unions. Limitations on the size of individual contributions vary from a high of $5,000 under the Federal Hatch Act to $500 in some states. Legal ceilings on total campaign expenditures vary from $25,000 for a senatorial candidate and $3,000,000 for national party committees under federal law to considerably less under the various state laws. Both federal and state legislation requires some kind of public report of campaign contributions and expenditures, although there is great variety in the effective publicity which these laws produce.[14] The goals are commendable and it would be unfair to say they had altogether failed. Neverless certain obvious weaknesses impair their effectiveness. These include a high

---

13 See Herbert E. Alexander, *Financing the 1964 Election* (Princeton, N.J.: Citizens Research Foundation, 1966) , p. 13.

14 For the most exhaustive study of this problem, see Alexander Heard, *The Costs of Democracy* (Chapel Hill: University of North Carolina, 1960) . Earlier studies include James Pollock, *Party Campaign Funds* (New York: Appleton-Century-Crofts, 1926) ; Louise Overacker, *Money in Elections* (New York: Macmillan, 1932) . An *Election Law Guidebook, 1965*, was published by the United States Government Printing Office in 1956 as a report of the United States Senate Sub-Committee on Privileges and Elections. The Council of State Governments, Chicago, published a report on *Corrupt Practices in the Forty-eight States,* by Sydney Minault in 1955.

See also Herbert E. Alexander, *Regulation of Political Finance* (Princeton, N.J.: Citizens Research Foundation, 1966) .

degree of ambiguity in the terms employed, notably in the definition of (1) what constitutes a political committee, (2) who is to be responsible for the collection and disbursement of funds, (3) who is to be responsible for the reception, analysis, and publication of financial reports from political committees and/or candidates. Unrealistic limitations on total allowable expenditures, failure to include primary election contributions and expenditures, and failure to provide adequately for enforcement of the law are other common weaknesses.

Any system of disclosure, to be effective, must result in full disclosure and not concealment, both of campaign contributions and expenses. Among the suggestions that have been made to accomplish this end are the following:

1. Full reporting and publicity of all receipts and expenditures of candidates for federal offices, whether made by the candidate himself or by other individuals, groups, or organizations in his behalf, both in primary and general elections.
2. The candidate, his personal or party agent, and the treasurer of every political organization should be legally responsible for receiving, disbursing, and reporting all money received or used. No contributions or expenditures except those made through such authorized agents should be allowed.
3. Full reports of contributions and expenses should be required every year and both before and after an election.
4. Definite responsibility should be imposed upon some officer—under the supervision of a nonpartisan or bipartisan committee—to call for, receive, scrutinize, summarize, and publicize these reports as they are submitted. Such reports should be made public not later than seven days prior to an election. Adequate staff and financial aid should be provided for this purpose.
5. Reasonable limitations should be imposed on the amount which may be contributed by any one individual. Present limitations on the total amount that may be spent ought to be repealed or drastically revised upward.
6. Suitable penalties should be imposed for violation or noncompliance, including not only fine and imprisonment but disqualification from public office.

An adequate disclosure act would require radical revision of existing legislation. It would have to define "political committees" to include not only those operating in two or more states, or as branches of federal, state, or local committees, as now, but also voluntary "citizens' committees," trade unions, business, professional, or civic groups which spend money on behalf of any candidate. The terms "contribution" and "expenditure" would have to include all transfers of funds between candidates and/or committees, and there should be some provision for prorating contributions and expenditures among candidates.

Other Steps

An effective disclosure act should be supplemented by positive measures to insure, insofar as possible, equitable access of rival candidates and parties to the voters. Some such measures could include an allowable tax deduction or credit for campaign contributions, the privilege of at least one free mailing during the primary campaign and another during the general election campaign, and publication and distribution at government expense of a voters' bulletin in which each candidate would be allowed, free of charge, a limited amount of space to state his case. Some action toward equalizing candidates' access to the mass media might include a limitation on the amount of time to be sold on radio or television during any given campaign.[15] Or an amendment to the Federal Communications Act might require television and radio stations, as a condition to their license, to make available without charge a limited amount of time to candidates for public office. The present requirement of equal time for all candidates should be amended to provide for variable time allowances to minor parties.

These proposals fall far short of the proposals made by Theodore Roosevelt and Woodrow Wilson to appropriate, on some equitable basis, public funds for the support of election campaigns, proposals which still had currency in 1967 in the form of a provision (defeated) to allow a taxpayer to designate one dollar of his income tax to the support of the party of his choice. They do, however, represent a more constructive approach than the measures thus far employed. Unless we can assure reasonably equal access to the voters by rival parties and candidates, we run grave danger of seriously impairing the democratic process.

☆ THE ELECTORAL COLLEGE

After the tumult and the shouting of the presidential campaign, after the massive verdict of the voters at the polls, the People's Choice is formally ratified by one of the most cumbersome pieces of political machinery in the world—the electoral college.

It is a commentary on the limited vision even of great men that the framers of the Constitution should have regarded the electoral college as one of their most notable achievements. In point of fact, it has never functioned as they fondly hoped and expected that it would, save perhaps in the election of President Washington.

As originally planned, it was a most ingenious invention. Each state

---

15 In England this is accomplished by the British Broadcasting Company policy of granting equal time to the Labour and Conservative parties, and allowing no other political broadcasts at all.

was to choose "in such manner as the legislature may direct" a number of electors equal to the number of Senators and Representatives to which it was entitled. These electors were to meet in their respective states and vote by ballot for two Persons, one of whom could *not* be an inhabitant of the same state as themselves. A list of all Persons voted for was to be certified to the President of the United States Senate. This officer was then to open and count all of the certificates in the presence of both the Senate and the House of Representatives in joint session. The Person having the largest number of votes, provided it was a clear majority of the whole, was to be President, and the Person receiving the next highest number, also provided it was a majority, was to be Vice-President.

In case of a tie vote, each having a majority, the House of Representatives was to choose one of them to be President. The Person next on the list was to be Vice-President. In case no Person on the list received a clear majority of the votes, then from the five highest on the list the House of Representatives (with each state having one vote) was to choose a President, the next in line to become Vice-President. If, however, after choosing a President, the next two or more in line had an equal number of votes, the Senate was to choose the Vice-President from among them.

It is significant to note that the framers fully expected the choice normally to devolve on the House of Representatives, in which case the small states would have had an effective veto on the larger ones, since each state would have had but one vote. As a matter of fact, of course, the development of political parties played hob with this arrangement. On only two occasions has the election been thrown into the House of Representatives—in 1801 and in 1825.

The first case arose because the well-disciplined electors of the Democratic party voted en bloc for their two candidates—Jefferson and Burr—so that both received not only a large majority but the same number of votes. It was, of course, informally understood that Jefferson was to be President and Burr Vice-President, and this was indeed the choice ratified by the House, but only after a dramatic struggle behind the scenes.[16]

[16] The electoral vote as recorded gave

> Jefferson—73 electoral votes
> Burr—73 electoral votes
> Adams—65 electoral votes
> Pinckney—64 electoral votes

When the choice thus devolved upon the House of Representatives, a Federalist caucus out of hatred for Jefferson sought to throw the election to Burr. John Adams and Alexander Hamilton successfully resisted this intrigue, not out of love for Jefferson but out of fear and mistrust of Burr. Hamilton described Burr as "bankrupt beyond redemption. . . . [He] . . . formed himself upon the model of Catiline [and is] too cold-blooded and too determined a conspirator ever to change his plan." Even before the election came formally before the House of Representatives, Hamilton had an-

It was to prevent a repetition of this kind of deadlock that the Twelfth Amendment was added in 1804 to require the electors to vote separately for President and Vice-President. But the possibility remained that no candidate would receive a majority of the electoral vote, in which case the choice would still devolve on the House of Representatives, with each state having but one vote. In fact this contingency did arise in 1825, when the electoral vote was divided 99 for Andrew Jackson, candidate of several state conventions, 84 for John Quincy Adams, nominee of a Boston rally, 41 for William Crawford, the last nominee of the Congressional Caucus, and 37 for Henry Clay, nominee of the Kentucky legislature. Since no candidate had a clear majority of the electoral college, the election was again thrown into the House of Representatives which proceeded to choose a President from among the three leading candidates as required by the Twelfth Amendment. In the wheeling and dealing that went on behind the scenes, Clay, who had been eliminated as a candidate, threw his support to Adams even to the extent of inducing the Kentucky Congressmen to vote for Adams notwithstanding formal instuctions from the Kentucky legislature to vote for Jackson. In the end, on February 9, 1825, Adams was elected as President with the votes of thirteen states against seven for Jackson and four for Crawford.

Jackson's friends were, of course, bitter at this "betrayal of the people's choice," and charged Adams with having made a "corrupt bargain" with Clay. In return for Clay's support in the presidential balloting, it was said, Adams promised to make Clay his Secretary of State. This Clay vehemently denied and the charge was never proved, although Clay did, in fact, become Secretary of State.

The Twelfth Amendment, by requiring the electors to vote separately for President and Vice-President, had, in this case, resolved any controversy over the Vice-Presidency. John Calhoun, the vice-presidential candidate on both the Jackson and the Adams tickets, was elected with an overwhelming majority in the electoral college.

On only one other occasion since 1825 has the election of a President devolved upon the Congress. Following the election of 1876, although Samuel Tilden of New York, the Democratic candidate for President, had won a popular majority of some 250,000, disputed returns from four states (Florida, Louisana, South Carolina, and Oregon) left him one vote short of a majority in the electoral college. With a total of 184 electoral votes, Tilden needed only one more from these four states to

---

nounced that he would support Jefferson. But the battle was nonetheless a long and bitter one. On February 11, 1801, the House of Representatives began to ballot and after nineteen ballots, eight states were recorded for Jefferson, six for Burr, and two divided so that neither candidate had a clear majority. On February 12, 13, 14, and 15, after fifteen more ballots, the result was the same. Finally, on February 17, with open threats of uprising in the air if Burr were chosen, and under pressure from both Hamilton and Adams, and after a total of 36 ballots, ten states finally voted for Jefferson and four for Burr, making Jefferson President and Burr the Vice-President.

win. His Republican rival, Rutherford Hayes, on the other hand, needed to win all of the votes from the four states where the returns were in dispute.

The Constitution provides that the "President of the Senate shall in the presence of the Senate and the House of Representatives, open all [electoral] certificates and the votes shall then be counted." Unfortunately, it does not say by whom the count is to be made. If the Senate were to count the votes in this case, Hayes would win, since the Republicans were in control of that House. If, on the other hand, the count were made by the Democratic House of Representatives, Tilden would win. To solve this problem the Congress hit upon a novel solution and one of doubtful constitutionality. An Electoral Commission of fifteen members was set up—five each from the House of Representatives, the Senate, and the Supreme Court. Reflecting the partisan composition of each body, the House selected three Democrats and two Republicans, and the Senate, three Republicans and two Democrats. Four of the justices were named in the bill—two Republicans and two Democrats, the fifth to be selected by these four. The key to this deadlock therefore was this fifth justice— and it was assumed that Justice David Davis of Illinois, an independent, would be selected. In the meantime, however, Justice Davis was elected, as a Democrat, to the Senate, by the Illinois legislature and was therefore disqualified. In his place the other justices selected Justice Joseph Bradley, a Republican. The Commission thus contained eight Republicans and seven Democrats.

On the theory that presidential electors are state and not federal officers, the Commission refused to "go behind the returns" as certified by the states, although it was generally admitted that gross irregularities had occurred. In any case, voting in the Commission was on strict party lines, and *all* of the electoral votes from the four states in dispute were awarded to Hayes, giving him the Presidency by a margin of one electoral vote— 185 to Tilden's 184.[17]

To avoid such shenanigans in the future, Congress in 1887 enacted an Electoral Count Act which made each state the judge of electoral appointments and required Congress to accept the returns as certified by the state. Only if the state fails to decide or does so irregularly may Congress intervene. When it does intervene, a concurrent vote of both houses is decisive. If the two houses of Congress cannot agree, those electors certified by the governor of the state are to be counted.

Notwithstanding these electoral crises, and except for the Twelfth

---

[17] The pressure on the Commission must have been intense, and the result might well have led to violence had not certain concessions been made to the Democrats in Congress. Presumably among these concessions were Republican promises (1) to withdraw federal troops from the South, (2) to appoint a southerner to the Cabinet, (3) to make substantial appropriations for internal improvements in the South. It was also urged by a powerful railroad lobby that construction of the Texas and Pacific Railroad depended on a Republican victory.

Amendment, the formal structure and procedure of this archaic system for ratifying the people's choice remains unchanged. Informally, however, it has undergone a profound transformation. No longer are the electors regarded, even in theory, as a body of independent elder statesmen handpicked to choose a President from the best leadership of the nation without regard to partisan affiliation, factional interest, or regional loyalty. In actual fact, the electors are not only not independent but they have virtually nothing to do with the election of a President except to record the verdict of the voters at the polls. A good many states, with what is called a "presidential short ballot," do not even print the electors' names on the official ballot.

On rare occasions, however, an elector may kick over the traces and vote for a candidate other than the one nominated by his party and for which he is assumed to be pledged. In 1960, for example, one Oklahoma Republican elector refused to vote for Mr. Nixon and instead cast his ballot for Senator Harry Byrd of Virginia. In that election, also in Alabama and Mississippi, electors unpledged to any candidate were chosen over both those pledged to Kennedy and those pledged to Nixon. They, too, cast their ballots for Senator Byrd, giving him a total of 15 electoral votes, although he was not a candidate.

But these are among the lesser vagaries which critics of the electoral college cite in their demand that the institution be mended or ended. Among other things the critics say that because each state is awarded two electoral votes for its two Senators regardless of its population, the system gives undue weight to the small states in electing a President. In 1964, for example, in Nevada and Mississippi each electoral vote represented less than 60,000 people, while in Michigan and Indiana each elector represented over 150,000 people. An elector in Alabama and South Carolina spoke for no more than 70,000 people, in California, for nearly 200,000, and in Illinois, for 300,000.

Because the electors are not apportioned strictly according to population or the vote cast, a majority in the electoral college, as required by the Constitution, does not always go to the candidate receiving a majority or even a plurality of the popular vote. Abraham Lincoln, in 1860, for example, with less than 40 percent of the popular vote (1,866,000 out of a total of 4,680,000) had nearly 60 percent of the electoral vote (180 out of 303). (See Table 9–1.) Woodrow Wilson, in 1912, with less than 42 percent of the popular vote received more than 80 percent in the electoral college. These are flagrant examples due mainly to multiple candidacies in these years, but since the Civil War one can count no less than ten times that Presidents were elected with clear majorities in the electoral college but with less than a majority of the popular vote.[18]

---

[18] They were Hayes (1876), Garfield (1880), Cleveland (1884 and 1892), Harrison (1888), Wilson (1912 and 1916), Truman (1948), Kennedy (1960), and Nixon (1968).

TABLE 9–1
A Century of Presidential Elections

Year	No. of States	Candidates DEM.	Candidates GOP	Electoral Vote DEM.	Electoral Vote GOP	Popular Vote DEM.	Popular Vote GOP
1856 (a)	31	James Buchanan / John C. Breckinridge	John C. Fremont / William L. Dayton	174 (59%)	114 (39%)	1,838,169 (45.3%)	1,341,264 (33.1%)
1860 (b)	33	Stephen A. Douglas / Herschel V. Johnson	Abraham Lincoln / Hannibal Hamlin	12 (4%)	180 (59%)	1,375,157 (29.5%)	1,866,452 (39.8%)
1864 (c)	36	George B. McClellan / George H. Pendelton	Abraham Lincoln / Andrew Johnson	21 (9%)	212 (91%)	1,805,237 (45.0%)	2,213,665 (55.0%)
1868 (d)	37	Horatio Seymour / Francis P. Blair, Jr.	Ulysses S. Grant / Schuyler Colfax	80 (27%)	214 (73%)	2,703,249 (47.3%)	3,012,833 (52.7%)
1872 (e)	37	Horace Greeley / Benjamin Gratz Brown	Ulysses S. Grant / Henry Wilson	(e)	286 (82%)	2,834,125 (44.0%)	3,597,132 (55.6%)
1876	38	Samuel J. Tilden / Thomas A. Hendricks	Rutherford B. Hayes / William A. Wheeler	184 (50%)	185 (50%)	4,300,590 (51.0%)	4,036,298 (48.0%)
1880	38	Winfield S. Hancock / William H. English	James A. Garfield / Chester A. Arthur	155 (42%)	214 (58%)	4,444,952 (48.1%)	4,454,416 (48.5%)
1884	38	Grover Cleveland / Thomas A. Hendricks	James G. Blaine / John A. Logan	219 (55%)	182 (45%)	4,874,986 (48.5%)	4,851,981 (48.2%)
1888	38	Grover Cleveland / Allen G. Thurman	Benjamin Harrison / Levi P. Morton	168 (42%)	233 (58%)	5,540,309 (48.7%)	5,439,853 (47.9%)
1892 (f)	44	Grover Cleveland / Adlai E. Stevenson	Benjamin Harrison / Whitelaw Reid	277 (62%)	145 (33%)	5,556,918 (46.1%)	5,176,108 (43.0%)
1896	45	William J. Bryan / Arthur Sewall	William McKinley / Garret A. Hobart	176 (39%)	271 (61%)	6,502,925 (46.7%)	7,104,779 (51.1%)

TABLE 9-1 (Continued)

Year	No. of States	Candidates DEM.	Candidates GOP	Electoral Vote DEM.	Electoral Vote GOP	Popular Vote DEM.	Popular Vote GOP
1900	45	William J. Bryan / *Adlai E. Stevenson*	William McKinley / *Theodore Roosevelt*	155 (35%)	292 (65%)	6,358,133 (45.5%)	7,207,923 (51.7%)
1904	45	Alton B. Parker / *Henry G. Davis*	Theodore Roosevelt / *Charles W. Fairbanks*	140 (29%)	336 (71%)	5,077,911 (37.6%)	7,623,486 (56.4%)
1908	46	William J. Bryan / *John W. Kern*	William H. Taft / *James S. Sherman*	162 (34%)	321 (66%)	6,409,104 (43.1%)	7,678,908 (51.6%)
1912 (g)	48	Woodrow Wilson / *Thomas R. Marshall*	William H. Taft / *James S. Sherman*	435 (82%)	8 (1%)	6,293,454 (41.9%)	3,484,980 (23.2%)
1916	48	Woodrow Wilson / *Thomas R. Marshall*	Charles E. Hughes / *Charles W. Fairbanks*	277 (52%)	254 (48%)	9,129,606 (49.4%)	8,538,221 (46.2%)
1920	48	James M. Cox / *Franklin D. Roosevelt*	Warren G. Harding / *Calvin Coolidge*	127 (24%)	404 (76%)	9,147,353 (34.2%)	16,152,200 (60.4%)
1924 (h)	48	John W. Davis / *Charles W. Bryan*	Calvin Coolidge / *Charles G. Dawes*	136 (26%)	382 (71%)	8,386,503 (28.8%)	15,725,016 (54.0%)
1928	48	Alfred E. Smith / *Joseph T. Robinson*	Herbert C. Hoover / *Charles Curtis*	87 (16%)	444 (84%)	15,016,443 (40.9%)	21,391,381 (58.2%)
1932	48	Franklin D. Roosevelt / *John N. Garner*	Herbert C. Hoover / *Charles Curtis*	472 (89%)	59 (11%)	22,821,857 (57.4%)	15,761,841 (39.7%)
1936	48	Franklin D. Roosevelt / *John N. Garner*	Alfred M. Landon / *Frank Knox*	523 (98%)	8 (2%)	27,751,597 (60.8%)	16,679,583 (36.5%)
1940	48	Franklin D. Roosevelt / *Henry A. Wallace*	Wendell L. Willkie / *Charles L. McNary*	449 (85%)	82 (15%)	27,244,160 (54.8%)	22,305,198 (44.8%)

Year	States	Democratic candidates	Republican candidates	Electoral (Dem.)	Electoral (Rep.)	Popular (Dem.)	Popular (Rep.)
1944	48	Franklin D. Roosevelt / Harry S. Truman	Thomas E. Dewey / John W. Bricker	432 (81%)	99 (19%)	25,602,504 (53.5%)	22,006,285 (46.0%)
1948 (i)	48	Harry S. Truman / Alben W. Barkley	Thomas E. Dewey / Earl Warren	303 (57%)	189 (36%)	24,104,030 (49.5%)	21,971,004 (45.1%)
1952	48	Adlai E. Stevenson / John J. Sparkman	Dwight D. Eisenhower / Richard M. Nixon	89 (16%)	442 (83%)	27,314,992 (44.4%)	33,778,963 (55.1%)
1956	48	Adlai E. Stevenson / Estes Kefauver	Dwight D. Eisenhower / Richard M. Nixon	74 (14%)	457 (86%)	26,027,983 (42.0%)	35,579,190 (57.4%)
1960 (j)	50	John F. Kennedy / Lyndon B. Johnson	Richard M. Nixon / Henry Cabot Lodge	303 (62%)	219 (36%)	34,221,349 (50.08%)*	34,108,546 (49.92%)*
1964	50	Lyndon B. Johnson / Hubert H. Humphrey	Barry Goldwater / William E. Miller	486 (90%)	52 (10%)	43,126,233 (61.1%)*	27,174,989 (38.5%)*
1968 (k)	50	Hubert H. Humphrey / Edmund S. Muskie	Richard M. Nixon / Spiro T. Agnew	191 (36%)	301 (56%)	30,602,908 (42.9%)†	30,957,072 (43.4%)†

(a) 1856: Millard Fillmore, American Party, polled 8 electoral votes.
(b) 1860: John C. Breckinridge, southern Democratic nominee, polled 72 electoral votes. John Bell, Constitutional Union, polled 39 electoral votes.
(c) 1864: 81 electoral votes were not cast.
(d) 1868: 23 electoral votes were not cast.
(e) 1872: Horace Greeley died after election; 63 Democratic electoral votes were scattered. 17 were not voted
(f) 1892: James B. Weaver, People's Party, polled 22 electoral votes.

(g) 1912: Theodore Roosevelt, Progressive, polled 88 electoral votes.
(h) 1924: Robert M. LaFollette, Progressive, polled 13 electoral votes.
(i) 1948: J. Strom Thurmond, States' Rights, polled 39 electoral votes.
(j) 1960: 15 electoral votes cast for Sen. Harry Flood Byrd (D Va.).
(k) 1968: George C. Wallace, American Independent, polled 46 electoral votes.

* Percentage of major party vote only.
† Percentage of total votes cast for Democratic, Republican, and American Independent parties.

SOURCE: Reprinted by permission from Congressional Quarterly *Special Report*, Revised Dec. 15, 1964 (Washington, D.C.: Congressional Quarterly, Inc., 1964), p. 14. [NOTE: 1968 data have been computed by the authors of the present book as reported in *The New York Times*, November 10, 1968, p. 69.]

Failure of the electoral vote to correspond to the popular vote is due not alone to the system of apportioning electors among the states; it is also due to the custom of assigning the entire electoral vote of a state to the candidate with the largest popular vote in that state. In effect this "winner take all" system means that if the popular vote divides 51 to 49 percent, the candidate receiving 51 percent at the polls receives 100 percent of the electors. The minority of 49 percent in the popular vote counts for nothing in the electoral college. Where more than two candidates are on the ballot, 100 percent of the electoral vote will go to a candidate with the largest vote even though it is a minority of the whole. It was this situation that produced the most flagrant cases of minority Presidents in 1860 and 1912.

To cap the case against the electoral college, its critics remind us that deadlocks comparable to those of 1825 and 1876 are still possible where no candidate receives a majority of the electoral vote. In such a case the choice of a President would again devolve upon the House of Representatives where, each state having an equal vote, the result could be determined by Congressmen representing a tiny minority of the population. This indeed was what the unpledged electors in Alabama and Mississippi hoped to accomplish in 1960. The threat of deadlock, the denial of fair representation based on population or popular vote, and the frustration of the people's free choice have brought repeated demands for the reform or the abolition of the electoral college.

The most radical of these proposals would abolish the electoral college altogether. Considering the nation as a single constituency for presidential elections, this reform would award the Presidency and the Vice-Presidency to whatever candidates of whatever party polled the largest popular vote. Since a majority would not be required for election, the result might be the multiplication of parties and candidates and the breakdown of our two-party system. In the event this did occur, the presidential ballot might be so cluttered with candidates as not only to burden and confuse the voters but to increase the likelihood of the successful candidate being a minority President. To avoid this contingency, a runoff election might be held between the two highest on the list in those cases when no candidate received a majority of the popular vote. This would operate not only to compel coalition or consolidation among the various parties contending in the first election but would make sure that the successful candidate did, in fact, represent the choice of a popular majority. Unfortunately the burden of two campaigns might prove too much to bear. Moreover, a system of direct election by popular vote would by-pass the states as political entities, consider only numerical and ignore concurrent majorities, and thus be another blow at our federal system.

Less radical are various proposals which would retain the electoral college but apportion the electors within each state in strict proportion to the popular vote. Thus if candidate A received 51 percent of the popular vote, he would receive 51 percent of the electors, while his opponent, assuming only two candidates, would receive the remaining 49 percent. In case of multiple candidacies, the same plan would apply. Candidate A, with 40 percent of the popular vote, candidate B, with 35 percent, and candidate C, with 25 percent, each would be credited with electors in strict proportion to his popular vote. For the nation as a whole the electoral votes of the several states, as apportioned among the various candidates, would be added together with victory going, as now, to the candidate receiving a majority in the electoral college. In case no candidate received an electoral majority, the choice would, as now, devolve on the House of Representatives.

Unfortunately this proportional plan would operate to increase the influence of one-party states in the election of the President. The dominant party in those states would stand to win a higher proportion of electors than in those states where the parties are more evenly matched. It is unlikely that the larger, more hotly contested two-party states—like New York, Ohio, Illinois, and California—would vote for a plan which in effect would increase the power of the Solid South in the electoral college. As the two-party system is extended, objection to the proportional plan will lose much of its appeal. The proportional plan has the advantage—if it be an advantage—of retaining the electoral college and thus continuing to recognize both numerical and concurrent majorities in the election of a President.

A less popular variant of the proportional plan would retain the electoral college but would allocate each state's electors to existing congressional districts or to special electoral districts, with only two electors in each state being chosen at large. This plan would add to the existing inequities of the electoral college, the inequities of gerrymandered electoral or congressional districts.

Since almost any plan for major surgery on the electoral college would require a constitutional amendment and would have a differential effect on the power of existing parties, states, and sections, none is likely to be adopted in the immediate future. Nor is Congress, now based on a nice balance of numerical and concurrent majorities, likely to upset that balance for a system of direct election which would substitute for the handiwork of the founding fathers a plebiscitary system for choosing a President. In the long run, however, some reform is inevitable.

In the meantime, two minor changes might be possible. One would forbid the election of electors unpledged to any candidate and require electors once elected to cast their ballots for the candidate for which they are pledged. This would remove any doubt concerning the legal as well as the moral obligation of an elector to vote in accordance with the voters' verdict.

A second reform might require, in those cases where the choice of a

President devolves upon the House of Representatives, that the Congress in joint session vote on the three candidates having the highest vote, with each Representative and each Senator having one vote. This reform would abolish the present constitutional provision which, in case of dead-lock, leaves the choice of President to the House alone, and gives each state an equal voice in the process. Meeting in joint session and with each member having a single vote, the Congress would thus resemble an enlarged electoral college with recognition given to both numerical and concurrent majorities.

The electoral college which the framers regarded as one of their best inventions has been described by its critics as their greatest failure. But when we recall the framers' skepticism of direct democracy and their devotion to a system of limited and divided power as an essential safeguard against tyranny, we may well ask whether even this contrivance with all its faults has not served the nation well—better, perhaps, than a system based solely on a mass plebiscite. On a review of the record, the electoral crises arising from the present system were, in fact, resolved without violence, without serious derogation of the people's choice, and perhaps even wisely.[19]

---

[19] See Lucius Wilmerding, Jr., *The Electoral College* (Boston: Beacon Press, 1958).

10
PARTY POLITICS
AND THE PROCESS
OF GOVERNMENT

☆ *INTERPRETING ELECTION RESULTS*

When one reflects on the vast expenditure of time, energy, and money that goes into a presidential campaign, the question at once occurs—why? and to what end? If one were to believe or seriously to consider the oratory, billingsgate, and innuendo of the campaign, he would conclude that nearly every election involves the fate of the Republic and the survival of civilization. And we know from experience that this is not so.

The obvious answer, of course, is to say that the campaign and the election are interrelated as cause and effect. Without the campaign, campaigners are bound to believe, the election result would have been different. Time and again, they might point out, elections have been won or lost by the narrowest of margins. In 1958, for example, there were 105 congressional districts in which less than 5 percentage points separated the winner from the loser and nine Representatives in Congress in that year won by margins of less than 1 percent. Senator Keating was elected in New York by a margin of less than 1 percent. So too were the governors of Nebraska, New Mexico, and Pennsylvania. Eleven Congressmen were elected by less than 1,000 votes. The change of a single vote per precinct in California in 1916 would have made Charles Evans Hughes President rather than Woodrow Wilson. And in 1960 Kennedy's margin over Nixon was a scant 112,000 votes out of a total turnout of nearly 69 million. But can one say that without the campaign the results would have been significantly different?

Even if the campaign does not affect the outcome it helps to increase participation in the election, compels an otherwise indifferent public to concern itself with important public issues and thus contributes to civic education. And it serves as a periodic reminder to public officials that they are in fact servants of the public and may be turned out for any serious betrayal of the public interest.

There is much to be said for this line of argument. But a cynic might point out, for example, that in contests won by 60 percent or more the campaign effort probably had no discernible effect upon the outcome. He would point out that there are only about 100 or so doubtful districts (that is, where 5 percent or less separate winner or loser), in which the campaign may sway enough votes to determine the result.

Even in close elections, the skeptic might say that the relation between the furious tub-thumping of the propagandists and the result is more likely to be coincidental than causal. There is no way to prove, even with public opinion polls, motivational analyses, and indices of political predisposition, that the tub-thumpers are responsible for the votes that turn the tide. All the huffing and puffing of the press and TV, of general outdoor advertising, all the grand and glorious ballyhoo of the image makers, it is said, is fun but futile. When the votes are counted, the press agents and the public relations officers of the winner claim victory, saying "Look what we did!" Their opposite numbers are discreetly silent, never claiming credit for defeat.

In 1942 the famous firm of Whitaker and Baxter of San Francisco managed Earl Warren's campaign for governor, and Warren won with 58 percent of the two-party vote. The Republican candidates for lieutenant governor and secretary of state won by smaller margins and the Republican candidate for attorney general lost. Whitaker and Baxter naturally claimed Warren's victory as their own. In 1946 the same firm managed Goodwin Knight's campaign for lieutenant governor and he won with 56 percent of the two-party vote. In the same campaign another public relations officer managed William Knowland's campaign and he too won with 55 percent. But the Republican candidate for attorney general, and Governor Warren, this time unaided by any professional public relations firm, won both Republican and Democratic primaries by votes of 52 and 69 percent respectively.

The fact is of course that most elections generate what we have called a "Chanticleer Effect"—Chanticleer in the fairy tale, you remember, was a cock who crowed when the sun came up and naturally assumed that he, and not the rotation of the earth, was the cause of the sunrise.

Our skeptic might conclude that elections where real issues are at stake are decided not by promotion and propaganda but by the candidate's personality, by events, or by the voter's own perception of the world and his relation to it. He makes his calculation not so much in terms of what he is told as by what he has experienced. The propaganda of the campaign may help him to rationalize and to express this calculation, but as for determining his vote, this is a grand illusion.[1]

[1] See V. O. Key, Jr., *The Responsible Electorate* (Cambridge, Mass.: Harvard University Press, 1966). Professor Key argues most persuasively from actual voting data

In elections where no great issues are at stake, voters will stay at home in great numbers, and those who do vote will vote to leave well enough alone, clinging to their traditional party labels, like totems kept to ward off evil days. But where the issues in a campaign concern matters remote from the voter's own experience, where he must piece together "the face of the age" from telecasts, press reports, and other mass media, these media will play a larger role, perhaps even a major role in his voting behavior.

If, however, campaign issues or candidates are identified with problems that cut close to the voter's central attitudes, his religion, ethnic origin, or racial pride, if they threaten his job security or his personal esteem, campaign propaganda except as it conforms to these attitudes, will have little or no effect. In any case it is not likely to be decisive. On the other hand, where the campaign concerns peripheral attitudes, that is, brand preferences, political style, the candidate's personality traits, age, clothing, education and so forth, propaganda may be effective or even decisive. That is to say, campaign propaganda is most effective where less is at stake, where the issues are important but remote from the voters' experience, and where they concern problems that do not cut close to deep-seated loyalties, interests, or attitudes. But most presidential campaigns are like icebergs—there is more below the surface than above. Beneath the ballyhoo lie many silent issues which normally exert more influence than all the tumult and shouting of the campaign. The cross pressures of rival loyalties and deep-seated psychic conflicts and anxieties may be more persuasive than a thousand speeches. Person-to-person interaction and communication no doubt exert more influence on voting behavior than the more visible and audible claims and counterclaims of candidates.

The 1960 presidential election was surely no clear choice between leaders and parties committed, as Mr. Nixon once implied, to policies which would move the country "in two fundamentally different directions both at home and abroad." The presidential vote for Mr. Kennedy showed no massive move from the Republican to Democratic column, of any particular class, creed, or section—except only for Catholic voters. The sharp Catholic shift to the Democratic candidate in 1960 was, no doubt, a response to the opportunity which Mr. Kennedy offered of breaking a long standing taboo which said, "No Catholic can be elected President," and a return to the normal preference of Catholic voters for the Democratic party. This preference of long standing was broken only by the almost cosmic pull of General Eisenhower in 1952 and 1956, when a substantial majority of Catholic voters continued to vote for other Democratic candidates. In fact, in 1952 more Democratic than Repub-

and public opinion polls that there is a marked correspondence between the voters' policy and party preferences.

lican votes were cast for congressional candidates, although the Republicans won a slender majority of seats in both the House of Representatives and the Senate. But with Eisenhower not on the ticket in 1954, the Democrats again swept the congressional elections and recovered control of both houses. In 1956, even with his re-election, the Democrats increased their hold on Congress, and again in 1958 the country expressed an overwhelming preference for Democrats in the congressional elections. In 1960 John F. Kennedy's narrow winning margin for the Presidency was accompanied by a Democratic loss of 20 seats in the House of Representatives and 2 in the Senate.

Under these circumstances one may well ask what elections mean in America? What kind of mandate did the Whigs' Zachary Taylor have in 1848 when the electorate chose him along with a solidly Democratic Congress? What kind of mandate did General Eisenhower have in 1956, or for that matter in 1954 and 1958, when the electorate chose Democratic majorities in both houses of Congress?

Even as in 1960 and 1964, when the electorate chose a President and a Congress of the same party, such is the nature of our party system, with its intraparty factional conflicts, that one needs to speak cautiously about mandates. This is especially true where, as in 1960, the popular margin was microscopic and the victorious Democrats, while capturing the White House, lost seats in Congress. "What the election of 1960 seems to indicate," says William Chamberlain writing in the *Wall Street Journal,* "is that there is no clear mandate for drastic action of any kind. . . . The small gap between the Kennedy and Nixon vote . . . should be a warning against any idea that the American people are in a mood for revolutionary change. . . ."[2]

Nor was the 1964 contest substantially different. To be sure, the Republican candidate, Senator Goldwater, promised a campaign in which basic issues would be more sharply defined, and which would offer the voters a real "choice and not merely an echo." But this, in the end, proved to be more rhetoric than reality. Neither the Republican nor the Democratic platform called for radical changes in public policy, although both illustrate again the strongly pro-business, pro-balanced-budget, anti-welfare state, generally nationalistic and conservative bias of the Republican party, and the pro-deficit financing, pro-labor, pro-minorities, pro-welfare, anti-isolationist, and generally liberal bias of the Democrats.

In his speeches Senator Goldwater now and again took what many Republicans and Democrats alike regarded as an extreme position, such as suggesting the sale of TVA to private investors, the use of atomic weapons to "defoliate" the jungles of South Vietnam, the use of federal police power to put an end to violence and disorder in city streets, and giving to field commanders greater discretion in the use of nuclear

2 *Wall Street Journal,* November 16, 1960.

weapons. But these suggestions were subsequently modified, explained away, or denied, as the Republican candidate affirmed his support of virtually all of the existing policies of the government, with a demand only for more honest, efficient, and economical administration.

In the meantime the Democratic candidate, Lyndon Johnson, re-affirmed his faith in democracy, his dedication to civil rights for all minorities including Negroes, his determination to maintain American military might at a level beyond the reach of any other power but at the same time to work for peace and disarmament, his support for an expanded program of welfare legislation, his promise of lower taxes, and his pledge to follow in the footsteps of his martyred predecessor, President Kennedy, in both domestic and foreign affairs. He declared war on poverty, inequality, and injustice, summing it all up in a new promise to lead the nation not only to New Frontiers but to a "Great Society." Only on occasion did he take note of his Republican antagonist, and then usually by indirection, in warning the nation against reactionary and reckless leadership.

In short, it was a fairly typical campaign with the "outs" under Senator Goldwater's leadership assuming a negative, critical, querulous, and quarrelsome posture toward the "ins," and the incumbents, with President Johnson as spokesman, taking an affirmative, friendly, and optimistic position on the burning issues of the day. It was a campaign, however, in which issues were less important than the candidates—with Johnson striving, and in large measure succeeding, to be a "father image," experienced, indulgent, cautious, and wise; and with Goldwater seeking to appear as the symbol of an America mishandled, misled, outraged, and betrayed.

What this suggests is that the 1960 and 1964 elections, like most presidential and congressional elections in this country, were not mandates for radical changes, but demands for leadership dealing with old familiar problems along more or less familiar lines. They were, in short, what the University of Michigan Survey Research Center has called "maintaining" elections. As such they are to be distinguished from 1952 and 1956, which have been called "deviating" elections, and from 1932, which may be described as a "re-aligning" election.

Superficially, the 1964 election has some of the attributes of a re-aligning election.[3] President Johnson was re-elected in a landslide, with a total popular vote of more than 43 million, and an electoral vote of 486 from 44 states, while Goldwater's popular vote was some 27 million, and his electoral vote a mere 52 from only 6 states. Both parties, and especially the Republicans, counted on winning substantial support from voters officially registered with the opposite party. Senator Goldwater talked hopefully about a strong "backlash" of conservative Democratic

[3] See Aaron Wildavsky, "The Goldwater Phenomenon: Purists, Politicians and the Free Party System," *The Review of Politics* (July, 1965).

voters, betrayed and disillusioned by the "leftist" policies of northern Democratic leaders, including Presidents Kennedy and Johnson, especially on civil rights. It was this hope that no doubt persuaded Senator Goldwater to vote against the Civil Rights Act of 1964 and to softpedal the issue during the campaign. The Democrats, on the other hand, spoke of an impending "frontlash" of moderate or liberal Republican voters who would vote for the Democratic candidate out of fear of what was described as the extremist, reactionary, and reckless leadership of Senator Goldwater.

Both hopes were in some measure realized, but with the Democrats profiting more from a massive Republican frontlash, than the Republicans gaining from a Democratic backlash. With the exception of his home state of Arizona, Senator Goldwater's electoral vote came from states in the old, traditionally Democratic South. Georgia cast its vote for a Republican presidential candidate for the first time in its history. Mississippi voted Republican for the first time since 1879, and South Carolina for the first time since 1876. In addition to these, Senator Goldwater carried Alabama and Louisiana in the Old South. Much if not most of this southern Republican vote may be attributed to the hoped-for Democratic backlash. Nowhere outside of the South, however, did it assume decisive, or even serious proportions.

The Republican frontlash, however, was widespread in the North and especially in New York, Rhode Island, Kansas, Vermont, Oklahoma, Washington, Wisconsin, Pennsylvania, Oregon, and California, and probably also in Illinois, Michigan, and Ohio. In Massachusetts, President Johnson won a plurality of 1,236,000, although the Negro Republican candidate for attorney-general won by 750,000 votes. Michigan re-elected Republican Governor Romney, but Johnson carried the state by more than a million votes. And while the Democratic presidential ticket carried California by a plurality of 1,260,000 votes, Republicans elected a United States Senator with a plurality of 200,000. All of which would indicate a massive shifting of presidential voters from one party to the other. If this shift were to prove reasonably permanent, 1964 might be a "re-aligning" election. Otherwise, it must be regarded as another "maintaining" election, in which the dominant position of the Democratic party had been temporarily reinforced by thousands of Republican voters who were disappointed by the nomination of Senator Goldwater as their party's standard bearer.

To a considerable extent the 1968 election bears out this judgment. The Democratic candidate, Vice-President Hubert H. Humphrey, started with what looked to be an impossible deficit to try to overcome. All the opinion polls showed him far behind. The left wing of his party was seemingly permanently disaffected by reason of dissatisfaction with the Vietnam policy and the events of the Chicago convention. The party's base in the South was certainly lost, and the third party candidacy of

George C. Wallace also threatened to pull sufficient blue-collar workers away from the Democrats to cause the loss of some of the northern industrial states. Yet, when the votes were in, former Vice-President Richard M. Nixon led Mr. Humphrey by only about one-half of one percent of the popular vote. Although the electoral vote was (as is usually the case) more unevenly divided (Nixon 301, Humphrey 191, Wallace 46), a shift of only 150,000 votes in strategic states could have swung the election to Humphrey. Furthermore, the congressional elections demonstrated the tenuous nature of the Nixon victory: both houses remained Democratic, with a net Republican gain of only four seats in the House and five in the Senate, and nearly 400 House incumbents were re-elected. The 1968 election could thus be called a narrowly deviating election.

It is nevertheless true that a long-term realignment is taking place not only in the South but elsewhere. But this realignment will, in the long run, reflect changing patterns of social and economic interests rather than episodic shifts of attachment or opposition to particular leaders or candidates. What the pattern will be can be dimly seen in the changing location and composition of the population, the labor force, and the private power structure at home, as it reacts to the changing pattern of international relations.

As one reviews the history of American politics certain more or less consistent patterns of behavior emerge. It seems clear that presidential elections and congressional elections are quite different from one another in turnout, tone, and temper, as both of these in turn differ from state and local elections. Different constituencies are involved: the whole nation for the President, entire states for Senators, and statewide executives, and still others for mayors, county supervisors, sheriffs, coroners, and so on. Different issues are at stake. Even the type of candidates differ. The attitude of the voter toward the Presidency has a mystical, almost reverential, quality lacking in his attitude toward other public offices. Voting for a President takes on something of the solemnity and high seriousness of a quasi-religious experience. Hence to compare presidential elections or election behavior with congressional, state, or local elections is like comparing the Taj Mahal with Mme. Tussaud's waxworks.

Nevertheless the interrelations of presidential with congressional and other elections are numerous and significant. The invariable "drop-off" of the presidential party's strength in Congress at the so-called off-year elections may not be wholly due to "battle fatigue" from the preceding presidential campaign. Nor is it wholly due to the isolation of Congressmen in the off years from national and international issues and from the presidential coattails. It also may indicate disenchantment not only with Congress but with the President who seemed so like Galahad two years before. President Johnson's sweeping victory in 1964 was followed by a great success in getting a legislative program through in 1965. But the decline set in rapidly thereafter as domestic and international issues became acute. Heavy congressional losses in 1966 reinforced this trend. Through time, congressional elections may point to underlying trends of a more basic character than the campaign itself would reveal. They also may indicate which party is, at the grass roots, the majority party.[4]

As one reviews presidential elections with at least a sidelong glance at these other trends, it appears that some are more significant than others. Some, as we have noted, may be called maintaining elections, or holding operations, in which the electorate reaffirms its confidence in the majority party. Others may be called deviating elections, in which the voters choose a President from the minority party while continuing the majority party in Congress and at the state and local levels. Most important are those which the Michigan Survey Center calls re-aligning elections—which "presage or reflect a critical re-alignment of partisan attachments"—elections in which the erstwhile minority party or a new party replaces the old majority party in the confidence of the electorate.

As we seek to discern in all this what an election really means, we may note that there are three main points around which a voter's interest may cluster: (1) candidates, (2) issues, and (3) parties. These are by no means mutually exclusive but rather symbols of the voters' central concern. When that concern is mainly with traditional party labels and loyalties, when factors of indulgence produce a general satisfaction with things as they are, the result is likely to be a *maintaining* election. When the voters' central concern is captured by a candidate, who for a variety of reasons serves to rationalize widespread but inarticulate discontent with the incumbent party—the result may well be a *deviating* election. When, finally, the voters' central concern is with issues—as in 1800, 1860, and 1932—growing out of an acute sense of deprivation, the result may be a *re-aligning* election.

This swing from maintaining to deviating to re-aligning elections reflects the cyclical nature of our political life. The American historian, Arthur Schlesinger, Sr., has described this as a swing from liberal to

[4] Until the congressional elections of 1960, and 1962, it seemed that there had been under way since 1920 a long-term decline in Republican representation in the House of Representatives. The 1960 and 1962 results, however, cast some doubt on the validity of this projected trend.

1920	303	1946	246
1922	225	1948	171
1924	247	1950	199
1926	237	1952	218
1928	267	1954	203
1930	214	1956	200
1932	117	1958	152
1934	103	1960	174
1936	89	1962	176
1938	164	1964	140
1940	162	1966	187
1942	208	1968	192
1944	190		

conservative regimes and back again with an average length for each period of sixteen years.[5] As one reviews this cycle it would appear that *liberal* periods are initiated by *re-aligning* elections, as in 1800, 1860, 1912, 1932—and conservative periods by maintaining elections. Deviating elections, as in 1828, 1840, 1848, 1912, 1952, 1956, 1968, reflect a general sense of "puzzlement" and indecision among the voters—yearning to have the best of both major parties—in a word, to have their cake and eat it too.

☆ PARTIES AND THE PROCESS OF GOVERNMENT

The election of the President in the nation as a single constituency, plus the majority requirement in the electoral college, has a number of important effects. For one thing it offers strong compulsion toward a two-party system. Any single-member district system does this, and in electing a President the United States is a single-member district.[6] Because a single executive position is at stake, a presidential campaign compels factions to unite and to moderate their demands in the interest of the common goals represented by the rival presidential candidates. Voters who may never have heard of congressional or even gubernatorial candidates are familiar with presidential aspirants.[7] Moreover, the constitutional requirement of a clear majority in the electoral college compels a coming together of otherwise disparate factions that would be most unlikely in the absence of the majority rule.

But the electoral college system of choosing a President is but one feature of our party system. Equally important is the federal system. The geographic division of power among the states and the central government serves to mitigate centripetal tendencies and to encourage political

[5] 1765–1789   Liberal—Revolutionary
    1789–1801   Conservative—Federalists
    1801–1816   Liberal (Jefferson, Madison)
    1816–1829   Conservative (Monroe, John Quincy Adams)
    1829–1841   Liberal (Jackson, Van Buren)
    1841–1861   Conservative (Harrison, Tyler, Taylor, Fillmore, Pierce, Buchanan)
    1861–1869   Liberal (Lincoln, Johnson)
    1869–1901   Conservative (Grant, Hayes, Garfield, Arthur, Cleveland, Harrison, McKinley)
    1901–1919   Liberal (Theodore Roosevelt, Taft, Wilson)
    1919–1931   Conservative (Harding, Coolidge, Hoover)
    1931–1947   Liberal (Franklin Roosevelt, Truman) *
    1953–1961   Conservative (Eisenhower)
   * This liberal cycle might well extend to 1953.

[6] A system of proportional representation, with multiple member districts and the allocation of representation in strict proportion to the size of each party's (or each candidate's) vote, may not be a major cause of multiple parties, but it certainly contributes to this end.

[7] In a Gallup poll in 1943, 50 percent couldn't name their Representative. In a National Opinion Research Center report in 1944, only 31 percent knew the names of both Senators.

contests over issues having state or regional significance. The fact that the
states have both power and responsibility for dealing with many of the
most important of our domestic problems such as education, health,
welfare, transportation, and domestic relations, tends to give to local
political arguments a vitality and variety not found in countries having a
unitary form of government.

The federal system which gives formal political recognition to these
parochial interests helps to federalize the parties, too, through an excessive fragmentation of power. The result is not highly centralized, ideologically unified parties but loose alliances of state and local parties with
only vague and ambiguous ideological foundations. It is, rather, the
unifying force of the struggle for the Presidency and the majority requirement in the electoral college plus the centripetal tendencies in
American economic and social life that holds our parties together as
national organizations.

Separation of Powers—President as Party Leader

Still another feature of our Constitution that helps to shape our party
system is the separation of powers, a system designed to check, not to
facilitate, rule by numerical majorities, and a system in which the executive and the legislative are almost as likely to be rivals as partners. The
prime minister in the United Kingdom stands in sharp contrast to the
President of the United States. The prime minister is not only a minister
of the crown, but a member of Parliament. So, too, is every member of his
Cabinet. The prime minister may derive his constitutional authority
from the crown and his formal appointment from the king or queen; but
his political power comes from his leadership of the majority party in
Parliament. This integration of executive and legislative branches insures control of the entire government by the same party—the party with
a majority in the House of Commons and presumably in the country.
Party unity and discipline are essential to the operation of this system.
Without such unity the government falls; with it, the prime minister and
his associates are in complete command of both branches.

Theoretically the prime minister and his Cabinet must resign when
they lose the confidence of Parliament. But Parliament is also at the
mercy of the prime minister, since, if his policies *are* defeated he may ask
the queen to dissolve the House of Commons before the expiration of its
term. Thus, the prime minister, "standing," as Professor McBain has
said, "at the apex of a disciplined party machine, holds the power of
political life and death over his followers." No wonder Ramsay Muir
described the office of the prime minister as a "dictatorship."

Contrast this with the position of an American President. He, too, is
the leader of his party. But the prime minister becomes head of the
government because he has already become leader of his party. Only

because he is leader of his party does the queen appoint him as her chief minister. The President becomes leader of his party only because he is nominated and elected as head of the government. It is because he is President that he becomes the leader, and not the other way around.

The prime minister and his Cabinet are members of Parliament; the President and his Cabinet are independent of Congress. Indeed, members of Congress are forbidden by the Constitution to hold "any office under the United States." Congress is also independent of the President, and his power rests much more lightly on Congress than does the prime minister's power in Parliament. Under the American system, the President and Congress are rivals who negotiate with one another, more or less as equals, from alternating positions of strength and weakness. This rivalry is aggravated by an internal rivalry between the House of Representatives and the Senate.

This built-in conflict is further compounded by the participation of Congress, to a degree unknown by the English Parliament, in the initiation of legislation, the appointment of the President's subordinates, and in the general administrative process. Watch-dog committees, investigating committees, and the chairmen of important standing committees not only maintain an almost day-by-day surveillance but actually participate in administrative decision making. Not even in his conduct of foreign affairs is the President free of congressional surveillance and "interference." A statement on foreign policy by the Chairman of the Senate Committee on Foreign Relations or the Speaker of the House or the majority leader may be as important as a pronouncement of the President or his Secretary of State. "It is this lack of power [in the President] to shape the entire policy of the Government," wrote J. Allen Smith, "which more than anything else has given form and character to the party system of the United States."

The localization or federalization of issues—aggravated by the separation of powers—have been major factors in shaping our party system. Although major parties reach into nearly every town and precinct, they function as effective national organizations only every four years when the White House is the grand prize, and local, regional, and sectional interests are temporarily submerged. Voting behavior in presidential elections may be quite different from state and local voting behavior—as when the voters elect a President of one party and a Congress of the opposition. Normally, however, the President's party wins control of both the White House and Congress, and during the first Congress of his administration a President can expect more cooperation than later on. At first, he enjoys the prestige that goes with victory, and his party organization, having successfully waged a nationwide campaign, is in good shape. With a majority in Congress, he can command greater unity on policy; and with thousands of jobs to fill, he has valuable patronage to use in bargaining for congressional support.

But the President's power as party leader during this honeymoon soon ebbs and falls away for many reasons. In the beginning it is enforced as much by judicious use of patronage as by agreement on policy.[8] As these jobs are exhausted, the President's "big stick" becomes less fearsome. There is a return to factional deals, and local interests emerge as Congressmen again begin to say, "I glory in the fact that men who come from Peachtree Creek have Peachtree Creek at heart."

A second reason for the falling away of the President's power as party leader is the American system of staggered elections. The terms of 435 Representatives and 33 or 34 Senators expire midway in the term of the President. Since at these off-year elections the President is not running and the national organization is not effectively mobilized, congressional, state, and local candidates must look to state and local leaders and to their own personal campaign organizations, which are likely to be independent, even of the regular local party. Even the issues are more likely to involve state and local problems rather than those of the nation as a whole. The result of all this, plus the lower turnout at mid-term elections, is a normal decline in the voting strength of the President's party in Congress during the second two years of his administration. It is a falling off that is not random but fairly consistent.

Our Four-Party System

The complex problems of the President as party leader and in his relations with Congress have led some observers to say that the American system is not a two-party but a four-party system.[9] There is, first of all, the Presidential party—which includes the executive establishment with several hundred thousand persons dependent upon the President's political favor and largesse. In the Presidential party, too, one might include a vast but not clearly identified body of supporters who look to the Presi-

---

[8] In 1952 it was estimated that President Eisenhower had over 150,000 jobs available. In 1954 Herbert Kaufman reported that there were about 315,000 positions outside civil service, of which about half were available as patronage. The following, although outside the regular civil service, are not normally disposed of on a partisan basis:

20,000	in the foreign service
75,000	defense employees abroad
30,000	doctors, dentists, nurses
20,000	TVA
13,000	FBI
7,000	atomic energy
145,000	*Total*

By 1966 it was estimated that no more than 25,000 civilian jobs were available to the President as patronage.

[9] Note that Professor James Burns has described our four-party system in somewhat different terms than those set forth here. His four parties are simply a presidential and a congressional party for each of the two major parties. James MacGregor Burns, *The Deadlock of Democracy* (Englewood Cliffs, N.J.: Prentice-Hall, 1963).

dent for guidance without too much regard to intermediaries or subordinates. There is, secondly, the Congressional party with only a vague relation to the official party organization on the outside and more or less independent of the President. Congress has an identity, an esprit, and a pride that sets it apart. Moreover, each Congressman and Senator, if he has been in office for more than a couple of years, will have his own local organization, quite distinguishable from that of the President or the official party. A third party is clearly discernible in what the British call a Constituency party. This is more than and different from the Congressman's local party, although it may be related to it or part of it. The Constituency party is a hydraheaded monster composed of (1) the official party committees, frequently an empty shell, (2) the inner circle of leaders, contributors, workers and hangers-on that one finds around each elective office from governor to county supervisor, (3) those who are "recruited" from time to time by this inner circle to run errands, raise funds, and do odd jobs, especially in campaigns. And, finally, one notes a Grass Roots party of those who help do the work in the precincts and at the polls. This Grass Roots party will also include a goodly company of intellectuals or idealists who believe in the principles of the party, those who ask not "what can the party do for me but what can I do for the party."

Party Organization in Congress

In any party system it is essential to distinguish between (1) the party as a device for nominating and electing candidates, and (2) the party as an instrument of government and public decision making. Failure to make this distinction in the United States can cause endless confusion and misunderstanding. For the elaborate machinery by which candidates are nominated and campaigns carried on has only an episodic relation to the party machinery as it operates within the government.

To understand the American party system we must take a closer look at the party as it is organized within the government, especially at what we have called the Congressional party. Most important is the *party caucus,* as it is called, in the House of Representatives or the *party conference,* as it is known in the Senate. Both, of course, are unknown to the Constitution, the law, or to any formal rules of Congress. In both houses each party has its caucus or conference. It is the caucus or conference that chooses the majority or minority leader. In the House of Representatives, the majority caucus chooses the speaker, who is then formally elected by the whole House. The caucus or conference also chooses the Committee on Committees or, in the case of the Democrats, the Democratic members of Ways and Means, who then serve as a committee on committees. Representation on these important committees is accorded to each state having a member in Congress of the particular party choosing the committees. Individual representatives of the states are chosen by the party delegation from that state. Assignments to other committees are made largely on the basis of seniority, by the party committee on committees, usually in consultation with the majority or minority leader. Seniority is important not only in determining assignments to committees, but also in determining status within the committee, including the chairman and ranking member who is next in line. In the assignment of members of committees, especially in the case of new members of Congress, the committee on committees and the party leadership have considerable discretion. Members can be rewarded for faithful service and loyalty to the party by appointment to important and prestigious committees or punished for disloyalty or neglect by assignment to committees of lesser importance and prestige. Normally disciplinary action is not taken to enforce party regularity on matters of policy. Within very broad limits a Congressman, and especially a Senator, is free to vote his own convictions or as he believes his own constituents would have him vote on policy matters, even though he has to vote with the opposition to do so. Obviously this reluctance to enforce discipline makes the caucus and the party organization in Congress a less effective instrument for the President as a party leader to get his program through.

Party disloyalty, however, *can* be punished, although in recent years both parties have been reluctant to do so. It was not always so. When in 1924 Senator Robert LaFollette, a Republican, ran for the Presidency as a Progressive candidate, with a Democratic Senator as his running mate, he was excluded from the Republican Conference on his return to the Senate. So, too, were those Congressmen and Senators who supported the Progressive ticket.[10] Again, in 1928, when Republican Senators Norris, Blaine, and LaFollette, Jr., supported Al Smith, the Democratic candidate for President, they, too, were excluded from the Republican Conference and denied important committee assignments. More recently Senator Wayne Morse of Oregon switched his party affiliation from Republican to Democratic when faced with similar disciplinary action following his defection from Eisenhower to Stevenson in 1952. The Democratic Congressional party has been more tolerant; and Southern Dixiecrats, who repeatedly bolted the Democratic party and even campaigned against its presidential candidates, have not only not been punished but have been rewarded with preferred positions on the basis of seniority alone. A recent exception to this more tolerant policy was the case of Senator Strom Thurmond of South Carolina in 1965. Confronted with what seemed an unavoidable exclusion from the Democratic Conference because of his defection to Senator Goldwater in 1964, Senator Thurmond, like Wayne Morse before him, switched his party affiliation—in Thurmond's case, from Democratic to Republican.

[10] All except LaFollette, who died in 1925, were readmitted in 1926.

Unlike the Speaker of the British House of Commons, the speaker of the House of Representatives is a partisan officer, chosen by the majority party caucus, and a leader of the majority party in the House. Although, by custom, he presides with a strict regard for parliamentary fairness and impartiality, he nevertheless uses his considerable influence to move his party's program through. His power to give or withhold recognition on the floor, to entertain or ignore strategic motions, to interpret and apply the rules to particular cases, to put questions to the vote, to assign bills to various committees, to appoint all special, select, and conference committees, to leave the chair and participate in debate, and to cast the deciding vote in case of a tie, all combine to make the Speaker one of the majority's "Lord Proprietors" in Congress. His importance in the power structure of the government is reflected also in his position next in line after the Vice-President to succeed to the Presidency. He also sits above the Chief Justice at official dinners.

Second only to the Speaker in the hierarchy of the Congressional party is the majority leader. Elected by the party caucus, he is the active spokesman, strategist, chief conniver, guide, counsellor, and friend of the majority party. Like a field marshal he keeps in constant touch with committee chairmen, presides over the party caucus, arranges the work schedule of the House or Senate, often in private consultation with the minority leaders. To win the trust of his colleagues, to guide the course of legislation, to strengthen the faithful, reassure the doubtful, and win back to the fold the wayward and the wavering, requires the talents of a politician, statesman, traffic cop, and philosopher. Few measure up to the high standards required for success—but some do. Robert Taft, William Knowland, Lyndon Johnson, and Mike Mansfield in the Senate are recent examples of astute and skillful leaders.

If the majority leader is the field marshal, the chief party whip is the top sergeant of the Congressional party. He and his assistant whips, representing every section of the country and every faction in the party, are the eyes, the ears, the legs, and often the voice of the Speaker and the majority leader. It is the chief whip's job to tell the rank-and-file members what the party leaders want, to keep members in line on matters of administration policy, and to maintain constant vigilance over the minutiae of the legislative process. He and his assistants almost literally whip their party colleagues into line to see that they are on the floor to vote and that they vote right.

These, then, are the leaders; this, the basic organization of the Congressional party. To them must, of course, be added the chairman of important committees. Ways and Means in the House of Representatives, Finance in the Senate, Foreign Affairs or Relations, Appropriations, Armed Services, Judiciary—these and their chairmen are giants in the party hierarchy and in the legislative process. But most important is the *Rules Committee* of the House. It and its chairman are unique, *sui generis,* without parallel or model in other legislative assemblies. Theoretically merely a traffic cop or court to see that the legislative process goes on smoothly and with a minimum of delay, *Rules* has become, for all practical purposes, a miniature legislature. By allowing or denying a "special rule," it can keep legislation bottled up almost forever; it can revise, amend, rewrite, approve, or reject legislation, and not even the speaker, the majority leader, or the President himself can gainsay its chairman if he has a tightly knit majority in his committee. Under cooperative leadership, *Rules* can become a powerful force for presidential leadership in Congress. In hostile or unfriendly hands, it can be an impassable barrier or a kind of Sargasso Sea, where legislation drifts and dies.[11]

As party leader, it is with these formal and informal party spokesmen that the President must deal. All of the weapons in his arsenal, his great prestige, his patronage, his access through mass communications to the people, are but auxiliary to his influence with the leaders of the Congressional party. Today he breakfasts with the Chairman of Ways and Means, tomorrow with the Chairman of Foreign Relations, and the next day, perhaps, with the speaker to chart a course for moving legislation through *Rules.* Repeatedly, almost daily, the President himself, members of his Cabinet, or his large staff of administrative and legislative assistants are in touch with committees of one or more of the Big Four— the Vice-President, the speaker, the majority leaders, and the chief whips. Dean Acheson reports that, as Secretary of State, he met with congressional leaders, members, or committees no less than 214 times in four years. Directly or indirectly, the President uses the weapons he has: friendly lobbyists who have influence with particular Congressmen, patronage to satisfy and ingratiate ethnic, racial, or religious minorities in a Congressman's district, promises of active support in his next campaign, and always a warm respect for the interests, the hopes, and the fears of those on Capitol Hill who can make or break a President.

Party government in the United States is still further complicated by our unique system of judicial review. Even when the Presidential and Congressional parties move in harmony, the Court may intervene, for in a very real sense the Supreme Court often makes policy. Hence no President or party can be indifferent to the politics of the Supreme Court. It is not merely, as Mr. Dooley once put it, that "the Supreme Court follows the election returns." Judges, like other men, have value systems which they apply to the many important issues that they must decide. It is with these values rather than with narrow partisanship that the President

[11] The power of the Rules Committee was temporarily limited by the so-called 21-day rule adopted in 1965. Under this rule the speaker could ask the chairman of any committee having a bill in charge to call it up for immediate consideration if it was not reported out by Rules within 21 days after reference to the Rules Committee. This rule was rescinded by the 90th Congress in its adoption of rules, on January 10, 1967.

must be concerned. It happens, therefore, that although presidential appointments to the Court are mainly drawn from members of the President's own party, there are exceptions. Taft appointed a Louisiana Democrat, Edward D. White, to be Chief Justice, and Franklin Roosevelt moved Harlan Stone, a Republican, into that high post to succeed another Republican, Charles Evans Hughes.[12]

Parties and Constitutional Change

One final point needs to be made about the effect of the structure of American government on the American party system. Formal provisions of the Constitution put many things beyond partisan conflict, and this has been at times a blessing and at times a bother. The First Amendment provides, for example, that "Congress shall make no law respecting the establishment of a religion, or prohibiting the free exercise thereof." The separation of church and state is here clearly provided for and the diversity of religious beliefs in the United States has operated to prevent the growth of a Church party, although Protestants generally vote Republican and Catholics and Jews, Democratic. The procedure for formal amendment of the Constitution puts formal constitutional change outside the limits of strictly partisan endeavor. A two-thirds vote in Congress plus ratification by three-fourths of the states makes a purely partisan amendment virtually impossible.

Except for the Thirteenth, Fourteenth, and Fifteenth Amendments, all have been nonpartisan, although not nonpolitical. Neither Federalists nor Anti-Federalists, Whigs, Republicans nor Democrats can claim credit or should receive blame for the Bill of Rights, the income tax, the direct election of Senators, prohibition or its repeal, or woman suffrage. These were issues bitterly contested, but the lines of cleavage cut across party lines.

In summary, one may say that as the American government has been profoundly shaped by our party system, the party system has also been determined in large measure by the power structure provided for in the Constitution. It is complex, cumbersome, and often frustrating beyond endurance; but in the end, consensus comes and with it a peaceful reconciliation of conflicts that rarely assume ideological patterns.

☆   TOWARD A MORE RESPONSIBLE PARTY SYSTEM

The American party system in recent years has come in for sharp criticism. In summary, say the critics, the system is too weak, too lacking in

12 On the other hand, Franklin Roosevelt's partisan appointments included Black, Reed, Murphy, Douglas, Frankfurter, Jackson, Byrnes, and Rutledge. With few exceptions, Truman and Eisenhower appointed members of their own party to the Court.

internal order and discipline, too torn by factional intrigue and conflict, and the two major parties are too much alike to offer meaningful alternatives to the electorate, and too irresponsible both to their own members and to the electorate as a whole. To remedy these multiple defects, a special committee of the American Political Science Association in 1950 offered a comprehensive program of reform.[13] The Committee's report was based on a number of basic assumptions. It assumed, in the first place, that political parties are indispensable if the people are to choose among alternative leaders and policies. In the second place, it assumed that party policies and programs should be clear and that parties, once in power, should be strong enough to carry these programs into effect. It also took for granted that a strong opposition party is indispensable in a free society. Party leaders, the Committee assumed, must be responsible to the party membership, as the parties in turn are responsible to the electorate as a whole. Finally, it assumed that internal party discipline is essential with a reasonably high degree of articulation among the various levels of the party hierarchy. Specifically, this would require some participation by the national party in the selection of congressional and other candidates.

Among the most obvious defects of American parties, the American Political Science Association Committee and others have specified the following factors.

Party membership is highly ambiguous. There are, it is said, few, if any, doctrinal or other standards for membership in either party and no assurance that party members from different states or sections will agree on party program or policies. At many places, even at the polling booth in primary elections, voters are not always required to establish party membership, so that Republicans may participate in Democratic primaries and vice versa. Even candidates for office are not always required to demonstrate membership in the party whose nomination they seek or under whose label they campaign.[14]

This absence of meaningful tests of party membership or loyalty reflects the absence of any central leadership—formal or informal—able to enforce discipline or to outline party policy or strategy. Theoretically the national party conventions do this when they adopt the party platform in presidential years. Unfortunately, says the American Political Science Association report, the conventions are too unrepresentative, unwieldy, and irresponsible to define party policy. Moreover, they meet only once in four years, leaving a policy vacuum during the critical "off-

[13] See E. E. Schattschneider *et al.*, *Towards A More Responsible Two-Party System* (New York: Holt, Rinehart and Winston, 1950).

[14] At the time of the American Political Science Association report, 10 states required an oath that the candidate is a member of the party. Five states (Kentucky, Nevada, Ohio, Oklahoma, and Utah) required a pledge to support the party. One state required support of the party platform, and 31 states required candidates to be members of the party whose nomination they were seeking.

year" election campaigns. As for the platforms, they were described as hastily contrived collections of ambiguous generalities.

Much the same, it was said, is true of the national committees. They are too large, too weak, and do not accurately represent party strength. Nor have they any authority to define party policy or to impose any discipline on state or local parties. And the state and local committees, in turn, it was said, are too large, too oligarchical, and too susceptible to boss rule or control by factional interests. State party platforms, moreover, are jerry-built bundles of inconsistent and often irrelevant clichés which differ markedly from state to state. The resulting confusion is worse confounded by the kind of "Sein Fein" (ourselves alone) attitude assumed by most candidates in the conduct of their campaigns. A typical campaign in a general election is not fought between two major party organizations, but by a multitude of campaign teams organized around each candidate, with only minimal cooperation or coordination.

If the major parties lack effective internally disciplined and closely articulated organization, they fail also to provide responsible leadership based on the active and widespread consent of the party members. Although state legislation strives to insure democratic procedures within the parties, the fact is they exhibit all those trends toward oligarchy that characterize most large-scale organizations. The day-by-day life of the party is dull and uninteresting and there is little active participation by the rank and file in party deliberation or management. Even at party primaries participation is low; rarely do half of the party members turn out. Without preprimary conventions or other democratic ways for "screening" candidates, the primary may become a Donnybrook of rival factions with the prize often going to the most bizarre and demagogic of the contenders. A slogan like "Pass the Biscuits, Pappy," a guitar and a collection of hillbilly songs may be more effective than rational discussion of public issues. And since, in most states, a mere plurality is enough to win the nomination, party candidates may represent a tiny minority of the party members.[15]

The major parties fail also, said the American Political Science Association report, to contribute significantly to the civic education of the people. The research facilities of the national committees are meager, and in the states, almost completely absent. Where a director of education is provided for in the party organization—a rare phenomenon in any case—he has little status, and less support from the party leaders. Almost nothing that can be called an educational program is carried on between campaigns. And in election years the major efforts are toward

15 In over 30 states a mere plurality is enough to win the nomination. In one state (South Dakota) the successful candidate must have at least 35 percent of all the votes cast. In Washington he need have only 10 percent. Eight states require a clear majority of the primary vote to nominate, with a runoff election to be held between the two highest where no one has a majority at the first poll.

publicity, sloganeering, name calling, and appeals to passion and prejudice. Moreover, since both parties lack an effective grass-roots organization to reach the individual at his home, they are increasingly compelled to rely on the mass media.

Finally, say the critics, the party plays only a minor role in the actual process of government. In Congress and in most state legislatures, the party is primarily concerned with patronage and exerts little influence upon legislation. Relations between the legislative party organization and the executive, whether the President or governor, are vague and tenuous, lacking both internal unity, and continuity of policy. Moreover, the relations between the Congressional party and the regular party organization outside the government are poorly defined, characterized as often by conflict and confusion as by singleness of plan and purpose.

To remedy these defects and to promote a more effective two-party system, the critics have made a number of specific proposals, including the following:

1. A *national convention* reduced in size and more accurately representative of party strength throughout the country. Such a convention of, say, 600 delegates should meet at least every two years to formulate policy statements for mid-term elections as well as for presidential contests.
2. A *national committee,* small enough to function as a deliberative and decision-making organ, but large enough to be fairly representative of party strength. It should meet at least once a year under a strong chairman. A small executive committee and an adequate central staff should plan carefully for these sessions.
3. A *new concept* of party membership based on more specific standards, to include adherence to the party platform, contributions to party funds, registration as a party member, faithful attendance at party meetings and support of party nominees in general elections. Failure to meet these standards should entail some penalty including, as an ultimate sanction, exclusion from party membership.
4. *Closer articulation* between national, state, and local party organs, including the development of regional organizations. Sanctions to punish those guilty of party disloyalty should be available to the national committee and other official party organs.
5. The *closed primary* for the nomination of party candidates should be strengthened and extended, cross-filing and the open primary abolished. Preprimary endorsements by official party conventions, councils, or committees should become part of the regular nominating procedure. And a state convention to endorse candidates, formulate a party platform, and select party officials should become part of the official party organization in every state.
6. An adequate *Headquarters staff* should be provided for all major party organs to maintain continuous year-round liaison with party members in official positions, both legislative and executive. A research and education staff should also function throughout the year.
7. All of this will require a radical change in the nature and scope of *party*

finances. Membership dues, party registration fees, tax credits for party contributions, and modest public assistance could broaden the base of party finance and provide for stronger parties, more independent than they now are from control by special interests or factions.

8. At the national level the reformers would establish a *National Party Council* of some fifty members to include five from the national committee, five from the party organization (caucus or conference) in the House of Representatives and the Senate, ten selected by the national convention from state committees on a regional basis, five governors of states to be chosen by all the governors of each party if there are more than five, and twenty members to represent other party organizations, like the Young Democrats and Young Republicans, to be chosen by the national convention on nomination of these organizations themselves. The Council would also include the President, the Vice-President, and Cabinet members selected by the President for the party in power, and the party nominees in the case of the opposition party.

The *National Party Council* would deal with problems of party organization and management, prepare a preliminary draft of a national platform, recommend nominees for party committees and for convention posts, and in some cases even recommend candidates for nomination to public offices. The Council might also serve to screen aspirants for presidential nominations and to deal with party disloyalty. It would maintain close liaison with its own partisans in official government positions.

To improve party organization in Congress we should expand the present *Big Four* Conference to include not only the speaker, the majority leaders, and the Vice-President, but also the chairmen of important committees like the Rules Committee and the Committee on Committees. A *Leadership Committee* for each party in each house would be chosen by the party caucus or conference for continuous consultation on questions of committee assignments and party policy and procedure. The existing party caucuses or conferences should be strengthened and used frequently to make binding decisions on questions of policy. Members who "kick over the traces" might then be disciplined, and if flagrantly disloyal, excluded from the caucus.

The *Seniority Principle* should be modified to allow greater freedom to the party leadership committees and the party caucuses or conferences in making committee assignments. The *Party Leadership Committee* should have greater control of the legislative calendar and rules governing debate, amendments, etc., with a corresponding reduction in the political powers of the Rules Committee. Rule 22 should be modified to allow a majority of members present and voting to close debate on all matters before the Senate, thus ending the filibuster.

Practically all of these reforms, it is argued, could be accomplished by the major parties themselves without formal legislation. One major reform proposed, however, would require a constitutional amendment. This would increase the term of Representatives in Congress from two years to four—the longer term to correspond with that of the President. This reform, proposed by President Johnson in 1966, would go far to eliminate the possibility of a President of one party confronting a House of Representatives controlled by the opposition during the last two years of his term. By insuring the Presidency and control of the House of Representatives to the same party, this would contribute not only to a more responsible party system but, by the same token, to a more effective government.[16]

No doubt the American party system needs reform, and in due course many of these reforms may be adopted. But in considering them we must remember the underlying theory of party government on which many of them are based. These proposals see the parties, ideally at least, as organizations dedicated to a more or less consistent body of principle. Back of the reformers' preoccupation with organization and procedure is their concern with party principle and policy.

"An effective party system," says the American Political Science Committee, "requires, first, that the parties are able to bring forth programs to which they commit themselves, and, second, that the parties possess sufficient internal cohesion to carry out these programs." The assumption here is that the organization is important only as it enables the party to develop, proclaim, and put into effect a program of action. That is, it assumes that organization and ideology are related as means and ends.

If we are to believe the critics, our parties are lacking in both ideology and organization. To those who believe that parties should be distinguished by clearly defined ideological principles and centralized organization, the American party system is most unsatisfactory.

What the critics overlook is that Republicans and Democrats, although torn by internal conflict and indistinguishable as parties on many basic issues, are nevertheless sufficiently different from one another to present the voters with meaningful alternatives of policy and leadership. It is true, as found in recent studies by the Michigan Survey Research Center and others, that in American voting behavior, ideology is muted. There is very little evidence that voters see our major parties as black and white, or as good and evil alternatives. Insofar as there is evidence of ideological sophistication, it bears a close relation to education and to the voters' economic and social status. Since high status in these respects is associated with Republican preferences, it is probably fair to say that more Republican voters than Democratic voters are ideologically sophisticated. In general, however, most American voters are pragmatists— asking not for adherence to any very clearly defined ideology, but to far more mundane, practical, bread-and-butter goals.

[16] Many Senators, however, are skeptical of this reform because, among other effects, it would enable Representatives to contest senatorial seats without sacrificing their own incumbency.

Nevertheless the evidence points to a high degree of rationality if rationality is taken to mean a calculation as to which party or candidate will best serve the voters' interest.[17] This pragmatic, calculating character of American politics is the despair of foreign scholars who like to think of political conflict in ideological terms with sharp distinctions between *liberalism* and *conservatism* or of *left* and *right*. Even some American observers lament the fact that our major parties do not fit nicely into any such neat categories. Northern Democrats like to think of their party as a liberal party and of the Republicans as conservative. And many Republicans agree with this description. But *liberalism* and *conservatism* are ambiguous terms, and their meaning may change with time and circumstance. The "liberal" party of Thomas Jefferson and Andrew Jackson was opposed to the use of centralized power, and under their leadership the Democratic party became a party of States' rights. But even as the party of States' rights, it demanded that the full force of the central government be used to enforce fugitive slave laws, although not to exclude slavery from the territories, and not to enact protective tariffs. The "conservative" Federalist party of Alexander Hamilton favored a strong central government to promote manufactures, a funded debt, and a national bank. But the conservative Federalist party by succession became the Liberal Republican party on the issue of slavery, internal improvement, and free land for settlers.

"Liberal" Democrats in Congress support a larger role for the federal government five times as often as do the Republicans. On federal aid to education and to depressed areas, public versus private power, housing, water pollution, and so forth, the average Democrat supports a larger federal role 76 percent of the time, the average Republican, only 15 percent of the time.

It would seem that on the issues of centralized power, of federal aid, and government control, Republicans and Democrats have changed places. But this, too, is an oversimplification of the problem. For among the Democrats there are many (from the South) who vote mainly against all of these measures, while many Republicans, usually from urban areas, vote with the liberal Democrats on these same issues. The point is that not all liberals are Democrats, nor are all conservatives Republicans.

It is characteristic of American political parties that liberals and conservatives, and even a tiny sprinkling of radicals and reactionaries, are found in both our major parties. It is to this situation, reflecting our vast and varied culture, that our party system owes both its dynamism and its stability. If this be Tweedledum and Tweedledee then there is great wisdom in it. For even in terms of organization, it has not been the highly articulated, ideologically pure parties that have been most successful in the United States. Socialist, Communist, Fascist, and other highly

[17] See V. O. Key, Jr., *The Responsible Electorate, op. cit.*

disciplined "ideological" parties have been little more than minor voices crying in the wilderness, while the loose-jointed, undisciplined, and often ideologically confused Republicans and Democrats have sat in the seats of power. Pragmatic politics and a free pluralistic society seem made for each other—at least in the United States.

11

INTEREST GROUPS
AND PRESSURE POLITICS

It is a commonplace among students of American government and politics that organized interest groups of great number and variety play a significant, if not dominant, role in what the late Arthur Bentley called the Process of Government. They bring to the formal structure and organization the living forces that transform political statics into political dynamics. From Aristotle to the most recent political analysts, organized groups have been recognized as one of the basic facts of life in the study of political systems.[1]

Aristotle spoke of the origin and development of political society, from the interdependence of kinship, or primary groups, beginning with the family, which had its origin in the division of labor between male and female. From primitive kinship groups, other groups soon emerged having their roots in other forms of specialization or division of labor. Earliest of these perhaps were groups of farmers or farm families, with a further division into product or commodity groups: the herdsman or shepherd, the husbandman or tiller of the soil, and gradually the sheepherder and the cattle grower, the orchardist, and the grower of small grains. As civilization developed, the number of specialized groups began to multiply from those rooted in kinship and the soil to those having their basis in a common calling or occupation. With towns and cities, markets appeared, and with markets, merchants, artisans, mechanics—even artists, poets and philosophers, and in the process, lawyers, politicians, and statesmen. As the division of labor among human groups became more complex, the groups became more and more interdepen-

1 See Grant McConnell, *Private Power and American Democracy* (New York: Knopf, 1966).

dent and more in need of the skills of leadership and management, which are essentially those of politicians and statesmen.

Plato saw the ideal political community as one in which the politicians and the statesmen were guardians (the men of gold) of a complex and interdependent society, in which each occupational group or class found its proper station and its duties. The manner in which this was to be done, and peace and justice achieved, was by no means clear to Plato nor is it clear to us today. Out of differences of occupation or function grow differences of interest and behavior which in turn breed interdependence and also conflict. Indeed the earliest conflict recorded in the Bible is that between the farmer Cain and the herdsman Abel. To reconcile such conflicts of interest, to encourage those deemed worthy, to discourage the unworthy, and to find in their mutual interdependence what Aristotle called the common good and we call the general welfare has always been the proper role of government in human society. And government itself may be described as a special kind of super-group that other interest groups seek to control or influence, but to which in the end they submit as the price of peace and order, without which they cannot survive.

☆   GROUPS AND THE POLITY: POLITICAL SOCIALIZATION

To examine in depth the role that groups play in human behavior is beyond the scope of this discussion. To say that man is a "social animal," or for that matter, a political animal, is in effect to say that he is a gregarious animal who cannot survive in isolation. Hence to examine the relation of groups to human behavior would be to probe the deepest and outermost limits of human life itself. Our concern is a much more limited one, namely the relation of organized interest groups to political behavior and more particularly to those aspects of political behavior called "pressure politics."

In summary, we know that interest groups play an important and even a decisive role in molding the character and personality of their individual members. Aggressive, authoritarian, submissive, other-directed, inner-directed, liberal, conservative, ethnocentric, xenophobic, and other familiar character or personality types are in large measure the products of kinship and other primary groups in which they are born and raised as children, and of innumerable other groups with which they become associated. Indeed it is in large measure through group affiliations or relationships that individuals acquire their identity. A man is known, or identified, by his name and the name of his family, that is, the kinship group or groups to which he belongs, and by his religion, occupation, social status, racial or ethnic origin. All of these are group centered, and as important for personality development as the more personal physical traits that distinguish him from others.

More particularly we know that in the process of political socialization or conditioning, the family, the school, the church, and other group relations based on shared ethnic, racial, social, or economic interests play the predominant role. It is not surprising, therefore, to find that most voters cast their ballots for the political party of their parents, or their co-religionists; or that one can speak of bloc voting in terms of income or educational levels, racial or ethnic, occupational or professional, identification. Nor is it surprising that trade union leaders, corporation executives, officers or representatives of professional, ethnic, racial, or religious groups often speak for millions of voters who might otherwise be voiceless. Not all of them can speak with the same authority, nor are all of them of equal importance in the complex process of pressure politics. But all play a major or minor part in the political socialization, education, identification, and expression of the political attitudes and opinions of their members or adherents.[2]

☆ SPECIAL INTERESTS AND THE PUBLIC INTERESTS

Because organized interest groups are specialized and therefore seem more concerned with their own welfare than with the general welfare, they have been suspect by those who think of government as dedicated to the public interest or common good. In the classical literature of political science, the so-called special interests have always been regarded as natural enemies of the public interest.[3] In the same spirit, it has been common, particularly in the United States, to speak of these special interest groups as constituting a kind of sinister "invisible government," against which we must be forever on guard.

On the whole this is good advice, although the problem it poses is by no means as simple as it once seemed. For not all private or special interests are incompatible with the public interest, even when we think we know which is which. This, we now know, is a distinction more easily stated than applied in practice, since the common good of all, or the public interest as such, is pretty much of a phantom, except as it is translated into the interest or welfare of individual persons or groups. Presumably the larger the number of such persons or groups whose "in-

---

[2] See Robert Lane, "Fathers and Sons: Foundations of Political Belief," *American Sociological Review* (August, 1951); H. McClosky and H. Dahlgren, "Primary Group Influence on Party Loyalty," *American Political Science Review* (September, 1959); Sidney Verba, *Small Groups and Political Behavior* (Princeton, N.J.: Princeton University Press, 1961).

[3] Aristotle, as we have seen, distinguished legitimate from illegitimate, or corrupt, governments by the degree to which they served "the common good" rather than the special or private interest of a power elite.

terests" are served by public policies the more may they be said to promote the public interest or the general welfare. Essentially this is another
way of stating the familiar utilitarian principle: the greatest good to the
greatest number.

Sharp, black and white distinctions between public and private interests are not easily made, although in some cases, such as crimes against
persons and property, the distinction is fairly clear. But who is to say that
legislative or administrative decisions that promote the interest of
farmers, or businessmen, or workers, do not also promote the public
interest? Hence it is by no means absurd, nor a sign of hypocrisy or
cynicism, to say, "What's good for General Motors," or "What's good for
the United Automobile Workers," or "What's good for the Farmers'
Union," is good for the nation. It may very well be. It is common for
virtually every interest group to identify its own interests with the public
interest. Indeed it would be surprising if this were not so, since, otherwise, the major groups who make up the basic structure of any free
society would perforce admit that their own interest or welfare was not in
the public interest. Moreover, identifying itself with the common good
compels an interest group to think about the common good.

A central problem of government is to determine how and to what
extent the private or special interests that press their claims upon public
decision makers correspond in fact to the public interest. It was this
problem that Madison had in mind when he said in Article 10 of *The
Federalist* that to render "these various and interfering interests . . .
subservient to the public good . . . forms the principal task of modern
legislation."[4]

Madison also noted that

> the latent causes of faction [special interests] are thus sown in the nature of
> man, and we see them everywhere brought into different degree of activity
> according to the different circumstances of civil society. . . . But [their]
> most common and durable source . . . has been the various and unequal
> distribution of property. Those who hold and those who are without
> property have ever formed distinct interests in society. Those who are
> creditors and those who are debtors . . . a landed interest, a manufacturing
> interest, a mercantile interest, a moneyed interest, with many lesser interests,
> grow up of necessity in civilized nations, and divide them into different
> classes, actuated by different sentiments and views.

Madison might have gone on to talk about other interests often as
important as those arising from the "various and unequal distribution of
property." Religious interests, racial and ethnic interests, cultural and
esthetic interests, civic and political interests could be mentioned. And
from having interests in common, men are led to form groups and orga-

---

[4] Ambrose Bierce, in his *Devil's Dictionary*, defined politics as "the strife of interest
masquerading as principle."

nizations to share these interests, to promote them, and to defend them against other interests deemed hostile or merely different. When these organized interest groups seek for any reason, to influence decision makers, we call them pressure groups, and their behavior we call pressure politics.

Pressure politics is a feature of decision making in any large organization. There are, for example, pressure groups in the Standard Oil Company and other giant corporations, in the Presbyterian, Methodist, Catholic, and other churches—and in colleges and universities.

Youth in Revolt: The Student as Political Activist

During the past few years a new momentum has been imparted to participation by the young in politics through the development of various activist movements on the college and university campuses in America. If the movement had been characterized only by the effort to arouse the political interest of the postadolescent in politics, and thus overcome the apparent voter apathy of those under thirty, it would have been no more than a repetition of the usual pattern of political recruitment in this country, and would hardly warrant our attention. But the events that grew out of the new student activism are so dramatic and the ideas expressed in the movement are often so radical as to suggest the development of an altogether new ideology in the college-age population and in some segments of precollege youth.

Campus demonstrations, and even spring riots among students, are not new to American college life. In the past, however, many campus demonstrations and riots have originated from ephemeral or trivial causes. But the new student militancy has been directed against failure to solve larger institutional, national, and even international, problems. The first major outburst occurred at the University of California campus at Berkeley and subsequently spread, with various ramifications, into virtually every type of institution of higher learning in the United States. A climax of a sort was reached in the spring of 1968 when Columbia University, one of the great, staid and prestigious ivy league institutions, was paralyzed by a student revolt in which administrative, classroom and library buildings were seized and occupied by rebel students, with subsequent bloody clashes between these students and the police and considerable damage to persons and property.

Even after an experience of several years with this new form of student activism it is not easy to discern clearly the motivating influences behind the movement, the dominant ideology among the more militant students, and the number of students who are actively involved or who might be attracted by the appeals to participate. At first, much of the protest was directed against the institutional conditions of the universities themselves. In the 1960s higher education was undergoing a great change. In addition to the enormous growth of student bodies generated by the demand to expand higher educational opportunities, the universities themselves were changing their characters in other ways. Research, particularly in the sciences and in the social sciences, and the promotion of graduate studies largely superseded undergraduate instruction as a central focus of attention of many, if not indeed the majority, of university faculties. American universities, especially public ones, had always had considerable involvement in public affairs, but a new relationship was developing in which both private corporations and public agencies were making more stringent demands on academic specialists for research and service and were supplying enormous sums of money to stimulate response to these demands. The early days of the student revolt were characterized by protests against the impersonality of the university insofar as the student was concerned, the neglect of undergraduate instruction, and the disregard on the part of university administrations and faculties of student wishes for more participation in matters related to patterns of university life. The term "student alienation" became the popular cliché for describing the lack of effective relation of students to the purposes and functions of the university.

As a new and more vociferous student leadership emerged, the issues began to be broadened, and competing ideologies developed to express the unrest. The university, a place in which criticism and dissent—in verbal form at least—is usually strongly encouraged, began to be the focal point at which youthful criticism and dissent was most forcefully directed. Increasingly, one heard the charge that universities were simply part of the larger establishment, run by an administrative and faculty hierarchy with little regard for either the critical problems confronting the university itself or the society at large. More and more was heard about the university's failure to provide educational experiences relevant to the world in which the students are currently living and have to live in the future, about the extent to which the universities were cooperating with the military and corporate structure in the promotion of activities destructive of democratic ideals and the morality of individual conscience, and about the neglect by the university of its responsibilities in the area of social problems such as poverty and race relations. Students argued also that a mature student generation which had largely rejected the middle-class, middle-aged morality of the establishment elite was being treated in a paternalistic fashion which denied the right to participate in decisions that directly affected the lives and careers of its members. Although the criticism and the proposed alternatives ranged over a broad spectrum, the more extreme groups began to clamor loudly for complete rejection of the entire structure of the university and the necessity for destruction of the system as a precondition for a new society.

The influences behind this range of criticism, protest, and activism are also quite diffuse. Student dissatisfaction with the insecurity of conditions which affect student life in both the institutional and general public senses seems to be the primary source of discontent. The intensification of the division over the war in Vietnam, the draft, and the plight of American cities and the black minority—all point up a moral resentment that approaches existential despair and frequently finds its outlets in attitudes that resemble those associated with late nineteenth-century nihilism and anarchism. Furthermore, many of the students who are leading this movement had earlier participated in off-campus political activities that provided them with substantial experience in organizing and directing movements of political protest. Many of the student leaders, for example, have been actively involved in civil rights and antiwar campaigns that involved the techniques of militant demonstration and civil disobedience. These experiences are easily transferable into campus demonstrations, sit-ins and student strikes, and ultimately into forcible occupation of university premises and physical detention of military and defense industry recruiters and academic administrators.

One of the most striking aspects of the student revolt is the fact that it has not been a purely national phenomenon. By the late 1960s student activism of a type similar to that in the United States had developed in Japan, France, Germany, Italy, and several Communist states of eastern Europe. Under the impact of student leaders of a demagogic bent, several of them in their middle or late twenties, a so-called new left ideology emerged. Its adherents repudiated both liberal capitalist democracy and communism as outmoded. Although far from clear in its details, the ideology called for a new politics which would be truly democratic in its efforts to draw all people affected by political decisions into the political process. Again at its most extreme, proponents of the new ideology called for the rejection of existing moral and political systems much more fervently than they advanced any specifications for new directions. Although advocating an identification with dispossessed persons everywhere —the workers, the poor, and the nonwhite (both within and outside the Western world) —it was never quite clear how this identity was to be translated into positive organizations and programs designed to reallocate either the material goods or the values of society. Paradoxically, while clamoring for peace the movement frequently erupted into violence; and the avowed heroes of the youth of the new left were perpetual revolutionaries such as Ernesto "Che" Guevara, Mao-Tse tung, and Ho Chi Minh. Similarly, the most popular theoretical source espoused by the student left has been Professor Herbert Marcuse, whose complex treatment of dialectics is more Hegelian than Marxist, with an emphasis on the constant flux of things resulting from the destructive self-contradictions contained in every emerging societal institution. The radical movement is characterized much more by its rejections than by its affirmations, and thus in part reflects the rapidity with which contemporary social change seems to move from crisis to crisis without any sign of stability.

Numerous explanations have been advanced to account for the student revolt. Some commentators, noting the increasing emphasis placed on youth throughout American society, tend to regard the movement as a manifestation in extreme form of the usual conflict between generations. Others interpret it as a pure power struggle which was enhanced by the rapidity with which people can be ideologically mobilized under the influence of communications systems that are able to make emotional slogans a part of a common language in the matter of a few hours. Furthermore, experience with disruptive tactics almost certainly gave encouragement to the idea that a relatively small number of persons can effectively generate social disorder having far-reaching effects in a very short space of time. Still others accept at face value the charges by the student militants that existing institutions have failed to fulfill their promises and do not deserve to survive unless they can be completely transformed.

Response to the student revolt has been as varied as the activities associated with the movement itself. In a good many cases the universities moved rapidly in the direction of internal reform, or at least the promise of reform. In other cases counterforce has been used to restore the minimum level of stability deemed necessary before any planned response can be made to student demands. In the case of an apparent majority of students with some (but less radical) inclinations to activism, the effort to influence the direction of change has taken a more orthodox form. Except for the most militant groups of student leftists, social engagement in national politics through support of emerging candidates such as Senator McCarthy and Governor Rockefeller, new commitments to civil rights activities, and more intensive engagement in organizations for social action such as Vista and the Peace Corps have been the primary directions. But, regardless of the proportion of students involved, the variety of directions taken by the student revolt, and the intensity of either the revolt or the responses to it, the new political involvement of the college generation has resulted in serious concern on the part of society for solutions to the problem. And that, after all, is the first aim of the leaders of most political movements which are regarded as innovative.

☆ THE GROUP EXPLOSION

As the United States has grown from an agrarian society in which kinship, religious, and soil-centered interests were predominant, the number and variety of organized interest groups have multiplied. Even before the Revolution there were, in addition to hundreds of religious groups, other organized interests including organizations of artisans and tradesmen, subscription libraries, academies, fire insurance companies, land companies, philosophical associations, the Masons, and so on. The colonial merchants became the spearhead of the Sons of Liberty and the Committees of Correspondence which played so vital a role in bringing on the Revolution. In the postrevolutionary period, and especially after the ratification of the Constitution, organized interest groups increased enormously.

In addition to groups based on shared economic interests there were hundreds of religious and missionary societies, temperance, antislavery, intellectual, professional, fraternal, political, and reform organizations. With the founding of the Ancient Order of Hibernians in 1836, and B'nai Brith in 1843, organized ethnic groups began to multiply as well as others whose purpose was to combat these hyphenated Americans, to restrict immigration, and to launch vigorous "Americanization programs." The Anti-Masonic party in the 1830s was but one of many of these, although a few developed beyond the pressure group stage as did the Anti-Masonic groups, to become political parties. Tocqueville commented on the American tendency to organize private associations, and Thoreau was struck by the same phenomenon.

The post–Civil War period saw a further development of what was called "organizationitis." A spectacular multiplication of organized interests, both in number and variety, was a natural outgrowth of a rapidly increasing population, improved transportation and communication facilities, a growing sense of nationality, not to say nationalism, the rise of great cities, and a fabulous growth in business and industry. Giant industrial and business combinations, matched by giant labor organizations, with agrarian interests fighting for survival in an urbanized, industrialized, and highly specialized society, produced a new and more intricate pattern of social and political pressures. Pressure politics emerged not only as a major feature of our political life, but as the sign and symbol of our pluralistic society. For the very definition of a pluralistic society is found in the existence of a multitude of groups or power centers intermediate between the citizen and the State.

A political party, on the other hand, is normally organized on the basis of geographic or political areas and seeks to mobilize persons, often of widely differing functional interests, horizontally as it were, in an effort to put together viable electoral majorities. A political party, moreover, seeks not merely to influence policy, but to control the policy-making process itself. This it does by the nomination and election of legislative and executive officers, more or less committed to the party's general program (platform). The line of distinction is often blurred, and a pressure group may become a political party by nominating candidates of its own and seeking through their election to control, or merely influence, the decision-making process. A political party, on the other hand, may become, in effect, a pressure group if it comes to be identified with a single issue or policy that it seeks to promote even at the cost of losing elections.

☆ PRESSURE POLITICS—MEANS AND ENDS

In summary, one may say that the central goal of pressure politics is *influence,* whereas the central goal of party politics is *political power,* although the line of distinction becomes quite obscure at many points. Since pressure groups are concerned primarily with policies relevant to their special interests, they seek to influence decision makers regardless of party identification. The party affiliation of a legislator is less important than his attitude on the particular issues in which the pressure group is interested. As Jay Gould, a famous lobbyist for the Erie railroad, once put it: "In a Republican district I was Republican, in a Democratic district I was Democratic, in a doubtful district I was doubtful—but I was always for the Erie railroad."

It should be said, however, that pressure groups usually find members of one party more responsive to their appeals than another, in which case they too may become partisan. As we shall see, organized labor, certain racial, ethnic, and religious groups have generally been pro-Democratic in the United States, whereas business, industrial, and professional organizations generally have been pro-Republican.

How many organized interest groups are there in the United States today? Although the Department of Commerce from time to time has issued lists of them, no complete census has been made. It is usual to list those which maintain offices in Washington, or in state capitals, a number which varies from 2,000 to 6,000, depending on one's basis of classification. But these are at best only partial estimates and include for the most part representatives of combinations of groups which themselves number many times this figure. If one were to begin with kinship groups, which are certainly interest groups if not pressure groups, the number would exceed 60 million. Indeed the Federal Reserve Board's figure for so-called spending groups is about that number. It is estimated that there are some 6,000 trade associations whose underlying membership of sub-associations and suborganizations will run to many thousands, not including individual corporations or business establishments, many of which constitute pressure groups in their own right.[5] For example, a recent study shows that 130 of the 200 largest corporations maintain their own full-time representatives in Washington.[6]

Approximately 150 national labor organizations include upwards of

[5] In 1949 the Department of Commerce put the number of trade, professional, and civic associations at 4,000. But if one includes major subgroups, this figure expands to 12,000 trade associations, 4,000 Chambers of Commerce, not to mention tens of thousands of corporations and business establishments which are interest groups in their own right.

[6] See P. W. Cherrington and R. L. Gillen, *The Business Representation in Washington* (Washington, D.C.: Brookings Institution, 1962).

50,000 locals, each of which has "interests" of its own. Similarly, the 250,000 religious congregations in the United States are represented in Washington by a dozen or so national religious organizations. Beyond and below the three giant farm organizations—the Farm Bureau Federation, the National Grange, and the Farmers' Union—are some 12,000 marketing associations, and hundreds of commodity organizations with thousands of subgroups throughout the country. There is a bewildering array of racial and ethnic groups, numbering, with their subgroups, several thousands. On the national level there are half a dozen Negro organizations, representing hundreds of state and local or regional organizations.[7]

Not all interest groups have an economic, religious, ethnic, or racial orientation. There are, for example, an estimated 100,000 or so women's organizations devoted to almost everything from the study of how to be charming and/or beautiful, to problems of population control. Among them are the League of Women Voters and the American Association of University Women, which maintain impressive research, study, and action programs on public affairs. The League, especially, with its state and local branches, has had an influence on public policy beyond what its modest membership would indicate. It is well to remember also that thousands of garden clubs, which campaign for more and better public parks and billboard-free highways, and hundreds of Parent-Teacher Associations, which maintain surveillance over public schools, are largely composed of women. Among the most impressive of interest groups is the giant National Education Association, with hundreds of thousands of members in dozens of affiliated teachers' organizations throughout the nation. Among other quasi-intellectual interest groups are writers' clubs, and associations of artists and composers. None of these, however, compares in influence with such bodies as the American Medical Association, the American Bar Association, and other professional interest groups.

Within the government itself are the specialized interests of various agencies and their officers and employees. A recent figure indicates that more than 500,000 federal employees are members of some ten labor unions composed exclusively of workers in the federal service. And not least are the official and semiofficial organizations of military or quasi-military interests including the Department of Defense itself, the National Guard in the various states, and such groups as the Air Force Association, the Army Association, the Navy League, the American Ordnance Association, the Aerospace Industries Association, and the National Security Industrial Association. Allied with these are the numer-

[7] The National Association for the Advancement of Colored People (NAACP) is generally regarded as the parent organization. But the Urban League, Congress of Racial Equality (CORE), the Student Non-Violent Coordinating Committee (SNCC), and the Southern Christian Leadership Conference have played a major role in the ongoing Negro Revolt against discrimination. See L. Lomax, *The Negro Revolt* (New York: Harper & Row, 1962).

ous patriotic organizations which more or less consistently call for more rather than less expenditures on national defense. In a class by themselves are several national associations of Veterans with suborganizations in nearly every state and community and an underlying membership of several million.

The political effectiveness of any given group or association may be said to depend on (1) the number of its members or adherents, (2) its inner cohesiveness as a group, (3) the degree to which its members or adherents are widely diffused in the total population, or concentrated in significantly strategic political areas, (4) its financial resources, and (5) the quality of its leadership. To these factors, it is common to add that of *access* to decision makers. But access is rather an effect of the other factors mentioned, and especially of the group's financial resources and the quality of its leadership.

Obviously, an organized interest group that can potentially speak for thousands or millions of voters is more likely to be politically effective than one that speaks only for hundreds. But the authority with which group leaders actually do speak is not only measured by numbers of members or adherents, but by their cohesiveness as a group (what the sociologist Giddings called group consciousness). Even when a group has a large membership with a high degree of inner cohesion, it may still be less effective if its membership is so widely diffused that at no point can it cast a significant or decisive proportion of the total vote. A smaller group with a high sense of inner cohesion, but concentrated in strategic states or districts, can, under effective leadership, exert greater political influence. Thus the so-called urban ghettoes, in which Negroes, Jews, Catholics, and other minority groups have been concentrated have been, paradoxically, a source of political strength. Finally, of course, one must not underrate the importance of a group's financial resources in estimating its political power or influence. Even a small group, widely diffused, can exert considerable political influence if it has the financial resources to help significantly in financing political campaigns, or carrying on the manifold operations that characterize pressure politics in the United States.

Among these operations, contributing to campaign funds is but one, although an important one. In many states and congressional districts the major source of campaign funds for Democratic candidates is organized labor with different unions playing a special role in different states or districts. Without the United Automobile Workers in Michigan, or the Steel Workers' Union in Pennsylvania, Illinois, and Ohio, or the Amalgamated Clothing Workers in New York, many a Democratic or Liberal candidate's campaign would suffer. Similarly, without contributions from business and professional interest groups nearly everywhere, Republican campaigns would be poorly financed. Although both labor unions and corporations as organizations are forbidden to make direct campaign contributions, both, in fact, do so in a variety of ways: for example, through labor's Committee on Political Education (COPE) and through large contributions from corporation executives and business leaders, or through various "educational" committees, financed by professional and business groups. Contributions of money, moreover, are often less important than contributions of services, including publicity and propaganda on behalf of a candidate or his party. House-to-house canvassing of voters, making sure that they are registered and do in fact "get to the polls" on election day, sponsoring meetings at which the issues of the campaign are discussed, printing and distributing slate cards, posters, and other campaign literature, paying for billboards, newspaper ads, television and radio programs are among the services that interest groups supply.[8]

Beyond contributions to the campaign of friendly candidates or parties, pressure groups engage in many other political activities. Not the least of these is the representation of their members and adherents before legislative committees of the Congress and state legislatures. Through their own officers or legislative counsel, they present arguments and "evidence" to support or to oppose pending legislation deemed friendly or hostile to their interests. Nor are these representations confined to formal hearings but extend to individual legislators in their offices, in the lobbies of the capitol, or wherever they may conveniently meet. Lobbying, as this type of activity is called, has become virtually synonymous with pressure politics. Many legislators come to rely upon these lobbyists, as practitioners of lobbying are known, for information about legislative proposals concerning which the lobbyist and his staff are presumably experts, and the legislator is very much of an amateur. Among the hundreds, and sometimes thousands, of proposals that come before members of legislative bodies, there are always a large number that involve expert knowledge of an industry, a region, a scientific process, which the legislator himself does not have. It is not surprising, therefore, that he should turn for guidance not only to experts in the executive branch, or to the legislative reference service, but also to the lobbyist who is paid by his client, the interest group, to provide just such information and guidance.

Representatives of interest groups do not confine their attention to legislators, but also appear before administrative and executive agencies in behalf of their clients. These appearances are particularly important before those agencies having jurisdiction over the affairs of particular interest groups. Thus counsel for organizations of railroads or bus lines, steamship companies or air lines, or radio and television stations or networks will be found before the Interstate Commerce Commission, the Maritime Commission, the Civil Aeronautics Board, or the Federal Communications Commission. Counsel for labor unions will be heard at

8 See Herbert Alexander, *Financing the 1964 Election, op. cit.;* esp. chap. VI.

sessions of the National Labor Relations Board or of the Wages and Hours Division of the Labor Department. And representatives of trade associations, advertising agencies, or individual corporations appear to give evidence and to argue on behalf of their clients before the FCC or the Anti-Trust Division of the Department of Justice.

At nearly every point in the complex process of government, lobbyists will be found to be active participants. Not infrequently they will draft legislation for legislators, or help in the formulation of administrative rules and regulations affecting the interests they represent. So close have the relations become between public decision makers on the one hand and lobbyists on the other that Professor Samuel Huntington has described them as a form of "clientalism" in which it is not easy to distinguish the regulator from those who presumably are being regulated.

Representatives of pressure groups do a good deal of entertaining, not only of legislators and administrative officials but of key persons in political parties and in other interest groups whose assistance or good will they need. The influence of this so-called social lobby has been greatly exaggerated, but it should by no means be ignored. Lurid stories are told of champagne banquets with dancing girls and games of chance at which the lobbyists always lose to those whom they seek to influence, and they may indeed occur, but they are no longer, if they ever were, part of the normal process of pressure politics.

More common are campaigns of education and propaganda financed by organized interest groups that seek to influence public opinion, not only of their own members, but of the general public as well. The "educational" campaigns of the Joint Committee of Public Utilities against the Public Utility Holding Company Act; of the Anti-Saloon League and the Methodist Board of Temperance, Prohibition, and Public Morals, in favor of Prohibition; of the American Medical Association against Medicare; and of organized labor against the Taft Hartley Act are but a few examples. In such campaigns virtually every channel of communication will be used, from special "workbooks" for school children, to elaborate radio and television programs. As one lobbyist said of such a campaign, "we employed every publicity and advertising device we know, from classified ads to skywriting." Apart from special campaigns of this kind most of the larger pressure groups maintain a public relations staff, whose job it is to issue a continuous flow of educational materials including research monographs and books, pamphlets, news releases, and radio and television spots. Indeed, no small part of the daily content of the so-called mass media has its origin within the public relations staffs of organized interest groups. Some go beyond this to provide special materials for schools and colleges and other key groups.

To translate opinion into pressure, or influence, organized interest groups strive to mobilize their own adherents and allies to flood legislators or administrative officials with petitions, memorials, letters and telegrams, urging support for, or opposition to, pending policy decisions. In some cases such communications will run into hundreds of thousands, signed, as in one case they were, simply by copying names from public directories or telephone books. And on occasion large numbers of people will be brought to a committee hearing to support the testimony of the lobbyists. The Anti-Saloon League used to call such mass appeals "petitions-in-boots." In a very real sense these demonstrations serve to "operationalize" the constitutional guarantee of the right of the people "peaceably to assemble and to petition the government for a redress of grievances."

The literature on pressure politics affords countless illustrations of the role played by interest groups in the decision-making process. Among the earliest were the great land companies seeking from Congress and state legislatures grants of lands in the public domain. The famous Yazoo Land Company was said to have bribed an entire legislature to ensure passage of land grant legislation. Alexander Hamilton's "Report on Manufactures" to the first Congress under the Constitution was supported both in and out of the Congress by organizations of merchants and manufacturers. The incessant, and often intemperate, pressure on Congress from both proslavery and antislavery organizations helped to bring on the tragic era of Civil War and Reconstruction. In its campaign for government aid in building a railroad to the Pacific, the Southern Pacific employed no less a figure than the "Pathfinder," John C. Frémont. And the notorious history of Crédit Mobilier is an example of pressure politics in the raw.[9] In the late nineties and even after the turn of the century many state legislatures were said to be "captives" of railroad lobbyists. A committee of the Massachusetts legislature in 1891 reported that "a body of professional lobbyists has for years formed a part of the machinery of legislation."

Congressional committees have repeatedly exposed the scope and method of pressure politics. The first of these was appointed in 1913 following disclosures of interest-group influence on Congress during passage of the Underwood Tariff Act. Among the highlights of these congressional hearings was the news that a manufacturers' organization, the so-called National Council for Industrial Defense, had spent $1,500,000 for legislative lobbying over a period of six years. Sugar interests spent $750,000 to fight the Cuban reciprocity treaty. Other investigations showed that from 1913 to 1918 the U.S. Brewers' Association raised nearly $4,500,000 to influence legislation. Over $900,000 had been spent on public relations and pressure politics by the Pennsylvania brewers alone during a period of four years.

Many state legislatures have also conducted extensive investigations

[9] In April, 1870, Henry Cooke wrote to his brother Jay Cooke that the railroad bill was in good hands. "Blaine," he said, "is doing us great service. We have the bill in such shape that all the business of the House is suspended until it passes."

of pressure politics. In 1905 a Joint Committee of the New York legislature, with Charles Evans Hughes as counsel, made a searching study of
the political activities of life insurance companies. It was the ten-volume
report of this so-called Armstrong Committee that not only revolutionized the insurance laws of New York but also helped to make Hughes
governor of that state. The famous Philbrick report of 1938 on lobbying
in the California legislature contains a fascinating report on Arthur
Samish, a "Prince of Lobbyists," or "Lobbyists' Lobbyist," as he was
called. This remarkable man had as his major clients the Brewers' Institute, the California Liquor Dealers' Association, and the California
Motor Carriers' Association. But he also represented other groups, including the Los Angeles Turf Club, a San Francisco Bank, the Film
Actors' Agents Association, the American Potash and Chemical Company. Between 1945 and 1951 the brewers alone contributed some $2
million, that is, four or five cents per barrel on all beer produced, for Mr.
Samish's political and educational work on their behalf.[10] Samish engaged in virtually all the activities we have described above, contributing
money and services to political campaigns, controlling the most desirable
billboards, entertaining legislators, drafting legislation, retaining influential legislators as counsel or consultants to his clients, carrying on
educational and public relations work, and of course appearing formally
before legislative committees and executive agencies. He was an extraordinarily thoughtful man, who kept a careful file on his legislative and
other friends, their children, wives, and mothers, to whom he regularly
sent remembrances on appropriate occasions. So influential was Mr.
Samish that he was often referred to as the "boss" of California politics.[11]

Revelations of investigating committees, often sensational when
made, have generated repeated demands for reform and regulation of
organized interest groups. From time to time bills and resolutions have
been passed by Congress and state legislatures to impose controls upon so-
called lobbying activities. The constitutions of both Georgia and California once declared lobbying to be a crime. In California the crime was
defined as any effort "to influence the vote of a member of the legislature
by bribery, promise of reward, intimidation, or other dishonest means"—
making it virtually impossible to enforce. Most laws stop short of such

10 This was well worth the price, since Samish was credited with keeping the
California beer tax to a mere 62 cents a barrel as against an average of three or four
times that in other states.

11 As a commentary on this title, at a San Francisco Press Club dinner at which
Samish was a guest, Aubrey composed this widely quoted limerick:

> Who runs the State? You're going to get the answer.
> Who runs the State? It's plain as it can be.
> Who runs the State? Is it really Arthur Samish?
> No!! It's the Southern Pacific, and the P.G.&E.

See Lester Velie, "The Secret Boss of California," Colliers Magazine, 1949. The P.G.&E.,
of course, refers to the giant Pacific Gas and Electric Co.

drastic and fruitless measures and merely require lobbyists to register and make periodic reports of their clients' resources and activities. Even Georgia and California now require legislative agents to register and report.

Congressional efforts to regulate lobbying have had a rocky road. In 1875 a House Resolution required "all persons or corporations, employing counsel or agents to represent their interests . . . before the House or any committee thereof to file his name and the name of his client or clients with the clerk of the House." Those failing to register were forbidden to appear thereafter. This gentle tap on the wrist had no discernible effect, and a Senate bill in 1913 to require similar legislation failed even in the face of the sensational disclosures of the Pujo Committee in 1912, of the so-called Money Trust, and the tariff lobby investigation of 1913. Following the elaborate lobby investigations of 1926, a lobby Registration Act was passed in 1927. But efforts of Senator Black and other liberal New Dealers to tighten the law in 1935 failed even after Black's committee had laid bare one of the most far-reaching, and expensive pressure group campaigns in history against the pending Public Utility Holding Company bill.[12] "Contrary to tradition," said Senator Black, "against the public morals, and hostile to good government, the lobby has reached such a position of power that it threatens the government itself. . . ."[13] But Congress was deaf to his appeal.

After passage of the Foreign Agents Registration Law in 1938, however, most Congressmen admitted that a new Lobby Registration law was needed. Accordingly, in 1946 a Federal Regulation of Lobbying Act was passed as Title III of the Legislative Reorganization Act of that year. In summary, the law requires any person (other than official representatives of a political party) to register, "who, by himself, or through any agent, or employee or other persons, in any manner whatsoever, directly or indirectly, solicits, . . . or receives money, or any other thing of value" to influence the passage or defeat of any legislation by the Congress. This registration with the clerk of the House and the secretary of the Senate must give his name and address and that of his employer, how much he is paid, how much he receives and spends to influence legislation, including the names of articles, books, and so forth, which he has caused to be published. He must give the name of every contributor of $500 or more, and account for all expenditures of $10 or more. Penalties for failure to comply with the law could be a fine up to $5,000 and imprisonment for up to a year, or both. Any one convicted under the act is forbidden to appear before Congress or its committees for three years.

[12] Black's efforts were not wholly without issue. The Public Utility Holding Company Act of 1935 made it unlawful for any one employed by a registered holding company to seek to influence Congress, the SEC or the FCC, on matters affecting the utility business, without filing a statement describing his activities, income and expenditures.

[13] See Karl Shriftgiesser, *The Lobbyists* (Boston: Little, Brown, 1951), p. 74.

In presenting this bill to the Senate the late Robert LaFollette, Jr., of Wisconsin, said, "In the last analysis Congress is the center of gravity under our form of government because it reflects and expresses the popular will in the making of national policy. Too often, however, the true attitude of public opinion is distorted and obscured by the pressures of special interest groups. . . . The public welfare suffers in the warfare of private groups and Congress becomes an arena for the rationalization of group and class interest."[14]

Registration or disclosure laws of this kind have had little effect on the political behavior of organized interest groups. Most of them, including the Federal Lobbying Act, suffer from multiple ambiguities in the terms used and from the lack of any effective means of enforcement. Louisiana and Texas laws, for example, define lobbying as "any personal solicitation of any member of the general assembly . . . not addressed solely to the judgment" of the legislator, thus providing a loophole as wide as a barn door. Several other states define the term as applying to persons who seek to promote or oppose legislation, "affecting the pecuniary interest of any individual, association, or corporation, as distinct from those of the whole people of the State." But, as we have seen, such distinctions are not easy to make. Most laws apply only to those engaged in lobbying for pay, and in some cases exempt churches, educational institutions, and civic groups. In some more recent legislation, however, some of these exemptions are eliminated. The New York law applies to "all representatives of groups interested in legislation except counsel or agents of localities or public agencies . . . whether or not they are compensated for legislative appearances."[15] The Federal law of 1946 applies to persons and expenditures whose "principal purpose" is to influence legislation. But when does lobbying become one's "principal purpose" and not merely incidental to other purposes? The National Association of Manufacturers, for example, reported only 1.97 percent of its $4.3 million budget as properly charged to legislative lobbying as defined in the act. "Yet this is the same NAM," said the House Select Committee on Lobbying, "whose president told a Senate Committee in 1946 that his organization had spent $395,850 . . . in its campaign to abolish OPA [Office of Price Administration]."[16]

Most lobby registration laws apply only to direct appearances before

---

[14] *Senate Report on Legislative Reorganization Act of 1946,* 79th Congress, Second Session, p. 83.

[15] See *Report,* N.Y. Joint Legislative Committee on Legislative Methods, Practices, Procedures, and Expenditures. Legislative Documents No. 31 (1946). Quoted in Belle Zeller, *American State Legislatures* (New York: Crowell-Collier, 1953).

[16] See *Interim Report,* House Select Committee on Lobbying Activities, 81st Congress, Second Session, 1950, pp. 1–50. "Many groups," said the Committee Chairman, "do not report at all, taking the position that they are exempted by the 'principal purpose' clause of the Lobbying Act." The grand total of 2,878 reports filed in the four-year period 1946–1949 incl., represented only 495 groups, a "fractional proportion" of the national organizations engaged in lobbying activities.

legislative bodies, or to personal appeals to individual legislators. Consequently, they fail to reach those elaborate programs of publicity, propaganda, or, as they are commonly called, education through which pressure groups seek to influence public opinion or induce their members and friends to write to public decision makers. Efforts to bring such activities within the scope of the registration laws have been rebuffed by the courts on the ground that they are not covered by the law, and if they are covered, then the law itself is invalid as an unconstitutional interference with rights guaranteed in the First Amendment.[17]

Although Lobby Registration laws have not been as effective as their sponsors had hoped, neither have they been wholly fruitless.[18] They have given to legislators and to the public continuing information concerning pressure politics which has always played and no doubt will continue to play a most important role in the process of government. One need not adopt the populist view that pressure politics necessarily represents a corrupt or sinister influence to demand that those who play the game of politics in this way should report from time to time on who they are, whom they represent, how much they spend, for what purposes, and with what effect. Certainly there is no logic in subjecting political parties to the detailed and excessive controls characteristic of most American election codes, and leaving organized interest groups free from any control whatever. We know from reports that have been filed under the Federal Lobbying Act that expenditures by organized interest groups to influence the decision-making process equal, and usually exceed, those made by political parties in their efforts to nominate and elect decision makers. We know too that the reported expenditures of organized interest groups on pressure politics represent only a fraction of their actual expenditures, although more than $75 million was reported by 495 groups during the first four years of the Federal Lobbying Act.

"If the full truth were ever known," said Chairman Buchanan of the House Select Committee on Lobbying in 1950,

> this committee has little doubt that lobbying in all its ramifications, will prove to be a billion dollar industry. This figure is not offered in an effort to shock the complacent but as a sober estimate. Consider the costs of letter and telegram campaigns; the thousands of pages of institutional advertising; the purchase and distribution of millions of highly charged books and pamphlets on public issues; the salaries of executives, lawyers and publicists; the operating budgets of all the thousands of organizations . . . whose central purpose is to influence what government does—all of these costs and many more are chargeable to lobbying whether we like the word or not.

[17] See: *U.S.* v. *U.S. Savings & Loan League* (1949) ; *U.S.* v. *Slaughter*, 89 Fed. Supp. 876 (1950) ; *U.S.* v. *Rumley*, 345 U.S. 41 (1953) .

[18] See the regular reports in the *Congressional Quarterly* which summarize and analyze the reports of lobbyists under the Federal Lobbying Act.

The Group Basis of Politics

So important are organized interest groups in what Professor David Truman calls the Governmental Process that a "group theory of politics" has developed which views pressure politics in all of its complex manifestations as the sum and substance of all political behavior. As the grandfather of this group theory, Arthur Bentley wrote in 1908, "Groups of people, pushing other groups and being pushed by them in turn—this is the process of government—this is the raw material of politics . . . when the groups are adequately stated everything is stated."[19]

We cannot examine here either the practical or theoretical implications of the so-called Group Theory of politics. A simplistic view of it assumes that political systems, at least in open pluralistic societies, operate on the basis of countervailing powers, composed of organized interest groups competing with one another to determine or to influence public policies. To save the system from the "corruption" that Aristotle attributed to governments in which public power is used for private ends, it is assumed that rival pressure groups tend to check one another to insure that no single special interest will triumph. Out of this elaborate system of countervailing forces, of checks and balances, it is said, emerge public policies based on compromises, which in the long run represent the public interest and ensure political equilibrium and stability.

One is bound to observe however, that interest groups do not always *compete* and thus compel compromise. They also *cooperate* to ensure that "everyone gets what he is after," in a process commonly known as logrolling. Essentially they say, "You support me in my demands, and I'll support you in your demands," thus avoiding the necessity for compromise.

Under these circumstances the public interest must find its protagonists among the decision makers themselves. For they too play an active, and not merely a passive, role in the political process, sometimes as advocates of special interests, but also as protagonists of a public interest that reaches beyond organized pressure groups to the larger community of district, state, or nation, for which interest groups do not, and often cannot, speak.

Millions of citizens and voters, representing every conceivable interest, do not in fact belong to any organized group claiming to represent that interest.[20] Legislators and elective executive officers must, if they are to survive, listen to these voices as well as to those who presume to speak

[19] A. R. Bentley, in *The Process of Government*, ed. Peter Odegard (John Harvard Library; Cambridge, Mass.: Harvard University Press, 1966) , p. 208.
[20] See Elmer Schattschneider, *The Semi-Sovereign Voter* (New York: Holt, Rinehart and Winston, 1960) . Also Grant McConnell, *Private Power and American Democracy* (New York: Knopf, 1966) .

for them through a trade union, a farm organization, a manufacturing association, or a chamber of commerce. Moreover, it is well to remember that within any very large organization—the AFL–CIO, the Farm Bureau Federation, the Methodist Church, or the American Legion, for example—there are literally hundreds of subgroups and organizations with special interests of their own. The Steel Workers' Union, or the Building Trades, or the Automobile Workers do not see eye to eye on every issue with the Electrical Workers, the Longshoremen, or the Locomotive Engineers. Within any of the three major national farm organizations one will find commodity subgroups—wheat farmers, cotton growers, stockmen, and so on—who have quite different, and even conflicting, interests. The search for majorities, or consensus, within the great pressure groups themselves can be quite as difficult as the quest for consensus or a majority will in the larger political community. A wise legislator will search for these majorities, or this consensus, before committing himself to a given policy.

Finally it is important to emphasize that the decision-making process is not a game of blind man's buff in which competing interest groups push decision makers now this way, now that. It is a process in which reason and reflection, deliberation and debate, more often than not based on careful research, play an ever-increasing role. Part of the so-called knowledge explosion may be the transformation of the decision-making process from one of political pressures to one of rational inquiries and judgment.

CONGRESS AND
THE COMMITTEE SYSTEM

☆ *CONGRESS: AN INTRODUCTION*

This chapter is essentially a functional analysis of the Congress in terms
of its fourfold role as a representative, legislative, deliberative, and investigative body. Our emphasis therefore is on what Congress is and does,
that is, on congressional behavior, rather than on its constitutional
powers or formal structure, important as these are. Our analysis looks at
Congress as a whole rather than as two separate bodies, except as differences in function, esprit, organization, and behavior require that special
attention be given to the House of Representatives or the Senate.

Elsewhere in this volume the reader will find more or less extended
treatment of the Congress in its relation to the Supreme Court, to the
President, and the federal bureaucracy, to political parties, pressure
groups and public opinion, and to the all-important role it has played in
the determination of public policy, both foreign and domestic. To
repeat, our focus here is on representation, deliberation, investigation,
and legislation as these are carried on in the Congress.

☆ *BICAMERALISM*

To begin with it is well to be reminded that Congress is a bicameral
body, with a House of Representatives of 435 members and a Senate of
100. In a bicameral legislature the framers of the Constitution found a
solution not only for the representation of the numerical and concurrent
majorities, as represented in the federal system, but for the equally important problem of maximizing rationality in decision making through

extended deliberation and critical review of public policy in two chambers rather than in one. They were familiar with a unicameral legislature in the Congress of the Confederation and on the whole they did not like it. Since they were committed to a representative government having its roots in public opinion and popular consent, they were equally concerned to protect the decision-making process from hasty, ill-considered action. To provide an appeal, as it were, from Philip drunk to Philip sober. That this was a wise precaution, is clear when one examines the history of the Congress.

"I have seen this body [the House of Representatives]," writes William S. White, "approve a bill to draft striking railroad workers at the behest of a President named Harry Truman who, understandably, sick with frustration at a threatening paralysis of transport in war time, had quite forgotten a document called the Constitution of the United States. The Senate put the matter right by simply refusing . . . to let the measure arise there at all. . . . I have seen the House . . . approve with a great hurrah manifestoes on foreign policy which were unbelievable in their lack of awareness of the world, and which might have all but destroyed some of our highest foreign enterprises. Again it was the Senate which came to the rescue."[1]

It might also be observed that it was the House which, under the passionate partisanship of the Radical Republicans, moved articles of impeachment against President Andrew Johnson, and the Senate which refused to convict, thus saving the constitutional system from what might have been irreparable injury. It is interesting, too, to note that it is only in the House that one finds a standing Committee on Un-American Activities.

Because of the overlapping terms of Senators, the Senate, unlike the House of Representatives, is regarded as a continuous body.[2] As such, it would seem to have a life independent of each separate Congress, since the life of a Congress is two years, the same as for a Representative. During each Congress there are two sessions, each beginning on January 3 of the odd-numbered years.

In many ways Congress is unique among the bicameral legislatures of the world. It is a comparatively small body, with a total of 535 mem-

---

[1] William S. White, *Home Place, The Story of the House of Representatives* (Boston: Houghton Mifflin, 1965) , pp. 47–48.

[2] The question of whether the Senate is or is not a continuous body has become a hotly debated issue. If it is, then the rules under which the Senate operates are also continuous, and can only be changed by procedures outlined in those rules. For example, no changes can be made in Rule XXII, limiting debate, except by the extraordinary vote provided in Rule XXII itself. If, on the other hand, Congress is not a continuous body, its rules, like those of the House of Representatives, expire with each Congress and can be changed by a simple majority. On one occasion at least, Vice-President Nixon held that for purposes of changing its rules, the Senate was not a continuous body. At this writing the issue is still being debated, so far without a final answer.

bers, as compared with over 1,500 members in both chambers of the British Parliament—929 in the House of Lords and 630 in the House of Commons—over 700 in both houses of the Japanese Parliament, 758 in the French Assembly and Senate, 951 in the Italian Parliament, and more than 1,400 in the two chambers of the USSR.

It is also unique in being the only legislative body among the great powers in which both chambers have, if not equal power and prestige, very nearly so. In parliamentary governments generally, the so-called upper chamber—the House of Lords in England, the Bundesrat in Germany, the Senate in Canada, Belgium, and Italy—is the weaker of the two. This must necessarily be so when the government, that is, the prime minister and his Cabinet are selected from Parliament and responsible to it. Since this responsibility could not realistically be divided between two chambers which by composition, term of office, and political orientation are likely to disagree, parliamentary governments everywhere hold themselves responsible to the *lower* or popularly elected chamber, which, as a result, becomes the more powerful branch.

In the United States it is the upper chamber, the Senate, that is the more powerful and prestigious body. Although this was not the case in the beginning, it very quickly became so, and since the Civil War has been admittedly so, even by members of the House of Representatives. In the beginning there was a tendency to regard the Senate as a successor to the colonial governor's council and hence somewhat suspect, as compared with the House of Representatives, elected directly by the people and independent of the executive. The Senate's role in advising and consenting to presidential appointments and treaties made by the President, in serving as a Court of Impeachment, and in having the Vice-President as its presiding officer, tended to confirm these suspicions. As it turned out, however, these responsibilities, originally a source of suspicion and weakness, became a source of power and prestige.

As the government grew in size, as executive departments multiplied —especially as questions of foreign policy loomed larger and larger—the participation of the Senate in major executive appointments and in the treaty-making process became ever greater sources of power. Moreover, a Senator's longer term of office and his role as representative of an entire state gave him a greater sense of security and independence. It added to his influence and the esteem in which he was held. When, after 1913, a Senator owed his office to a direct vote of the people, the Senate, even more than the House of Representatives, became the popular branch of the Congress.

Senators, elected at large, with constituencies embracing whole states, became the representatives and spokesmen often for millions of people rather than for thousands as in the case of Representatives. The broader and more complex constituency of the State as a whole focused the attention of not one or a few, but many pressure groups upon him. In a single congressional district, groups representing one or a few organized interests like labor, agriculture, trade and commerce, or at best, a few ethnic or religious groups, may be irresistible. In the larger constituency of the state special interests of this kind must compete with others on a wider stage, of which the Senator rather than the Representative is the political focus. He can thus become more independent of any one special interest, or any single newspaper or channel of communication, and give more time and attention to the general welfare than to serving more parochial interests. Senators have a higher political visibility than Representatives, are sought after by more people, and hence enjoy both greater prestige and greater power than do Representatives. The fact, too, that each Senator's vote (1 of 100) is mathematically more than four times as much as a Representative's vote (1 of 435) also enhances a Senator's political power.

The Senate as representative of what John C. Calhoun called the "concurrent majority" of the several states was thought to be, and for many years was in fact, the stronghold of agrarian and sectional interests. It was also regarded as the conservative body—"the most exclusive club in America"—holding the line against the more radical populistic forces represented in the House of Representatives. However true this may have been, it is no longer an accurate appraisal of the two bodies. As our population has become increasingly urbanized, with more than 70 percent currently living in cities, and since the Senate is now directly elected by the people, it is the upper chamber that paradoxically has come to represent numerical majorities in the several states. And because these majorities are now to be found in larger cities rather than on farms or in small towns, and because Senators are elected from the state as a whole, it is in the Senate that the urban masses are more likely to find their spokesman.[3]

The House of Representatives, coming from more than 400 relatively small districts, remains more parochial, more preoccupied with home affairs, and more representative of the select elites that tend to predominate in congressional districts. It is in the House that the "concurrent majority" of special economic, social, ethnic, and religious interests finds more direct representation. The search for consensus among these factional interests helps to explain the complex pattern of coalitions, which often defy analysis, in the voting behavior of the lower chamber. It is the House, therefore, not the Senate, that is the conservative body.[4]

The wider constituencies of the Senators, the direct and active par-

[3] See Donald R. Matthews, *U.S. Senators and Their World* (Chapel Hill: University of North Carolina Press, 1960).

[4] See Lewis A. Froman, Jr., *Congressmen and Their Constituencies* (Chicago: Rand McNally, 1963), esp. chap. 6, "Why the Senate Is More Liberal Than the House." See also William S. White, *op. cit.;* Grant McConnell, *Private Power and American Democracy* (New York: Knopf, 1966), esp. chap. 4.

ticipation of the upper chamber in shaping foreign policy, and its smaller size, all combine to give Senators a wider perspective and to make the Senate a more exciting and effective forum for the discussion of the great issues of American and world politics. Almost within a generation, says William S. White, the "House has lost something of its old public place." Its size, its essentially parochial roots in state-defined congressional districts, the necessary preoccupation of each Representative with the interests of his own constituents or the relatively limited elites who speak for them, all combine to make the lower house a poor place to discuss the great issues of national economic policy, war and peace, or a continuing cold war such as that which has shaped both American domestic and foreign policy since 1945. As one able and distinguished observer puts it, the weaknesses of the lower house, as compared with the Senate, lie in its "own inherent incapacity to deal effectively with the highly generalized, constitutional issues arising in a century which is both increasingly brutal and increasingly sophisticated in the complexity of the questions it poses."[5]

Nevertheless, and in spite of the more glamorous, prestigious, and powerful position of the Senate, the House of Representatives remains as an important and powerful participant in the decision-making process at the summit of the American public power structure. In the development of tax legislation, in its searching analysis of the appropriations upon which the whole government and all public policy, foreign and domestic, depend, in its continuous and critical review of executive and administrative agencies, and in its representation of the innumerable functional interests, ethnic, and religious groups that compose our pluralistic society, the lower chamber plays a crucial and often a decisive role.

The House is proud of its place, its power, and its traditions. It is also a bit envious and jealous of its more glamorous partner in the legislative process. One does not, for example, refer to the Senate as such, in the House, but rather to "the other place," although Senators have no compunction about referring to the House of Representatives in their own chamber. Leaders of the lower house do not hesitate to assert their equality with the Senate on matters of protocol as in 1962 when the chairman of the House and Senate appropriations committees "brought the whole appropriations process to a prolonged halt when they conducted a cold war of 'face' as to which body should defer to the other in . . . selecting a common meeting place for certain negotiations between the two."[6] Nevertheless it is still regarded as a promotion to move from the House of Representatives to the Senate—a kind of upward political mobility.

In spite of these intramural tensions there is no lack of respect in either house for the other. Each has its own pride of place, its own

5 See William S. White, *op. cit.*, p. 137.
6 William S. White, *op. cit.*, p. 121.

cherished traditions of process and protocol, and, in spite of factional or partisan differences, its own sense of community which each member feels. And above and beyond identification with his own house, each member identifies with, and is loyal to, the Congress as a whole, especially when faced with what to them may seem unseemly conduct or excessive ambition in the executive branch.

☆ CONGRESS AND THE PRESIDENCY

No small part of the criticism that has been heaped on Congress in recent years stems from the restraints which it has imposed upon the executive. Congressional criticism, amendment, delay, opposition, and obstruction have been interposed between presidential proposals and their final enactment into law. Even when both houses of Congress and the White House are controlled by the same party, congressional "obstructionist" behavior has been a source of frustration not only to the President, but to those members of the so-called Presidential party in Congress itself, who look to the White House for legislative leadership. Measure after measure on the presidential legislative program, it is said, is bottled up in committees, to emerge, only after long delay, altered beyond recognition, or to languish and die at the hands of a so-called Congressional party which follows its own star and its own leaders. Moreover, not content with obstructions to the President's legislative program, the Congressional party strives by strict surveillance, fiscal controls of various kinds, and personal interference by committee chairmen, to intervene in the administrative process for which the President is responsible. This type of legislative behavior, or misbehavior, according to its critics, has made Congress all but obsolete or at least in need of radical reorganization. Only by streamlining its internal organization and procedure to give the Presidential party greater control of the legislative process, they say, can Congress, as an institution, play its proper role in our jet-propelled, atomic age.

This is not the place to explore these criticisms in any detail; some comments, however, may be made at this point. So-called Presidential and Congressional parties in the Congress are more easily identified from outside than from inside Congress itself. On close analysis, their composition is much less stable than the critics appear to assume. If one looks at congressional behavior, one finds that members who appear at one time as ardent supporters of presidential policy and are therefore identified as members of a so-called Presidential party, appear at other times in opposition to a presidential program and hence are identified with a so-called Congressional party. Much depends on the issues, the constituency from which the member comes, the political ideology, or orientation of the member himself, the "state of the Nation" or of public opinion, and the

"Man in the White House." Congressional combinations assume quite different forms in times of crisis or of "normalcy," under strong or weak Presidents, Democratic or Republican administrations.

One may observe also that in denouncing the legislative branch for imposing restraints upon presidential power and leadership, the critics are scolding Congress for doing what it was supposed to do. Ours is not a parliamentary system in which the active executive is merged with the legislative branch and indeed, is an executive committee of parliament. Ours is a system based on a separation, not a merging of powers, and one in which checks and balances operate precisely for the purpose of imposing restraints and delay. "Ambition," said Madison, is thus made to "counteract ambition." On the record, moreover, the case is by no means clear that the American Republic, with what Woodrow Wilson once called its congressional system, has been less able to meet the demands of crisis government than have the more "streamlined" parliamentary systems so admired by the critics of Congress and its ways.[7]

Nevertheless, and however much one may differ with the critics, it is obvious that Congress as an institution, and more especially the House of Representatives, has lost ground in terms of prestige and power vis-à-vis the President as state legislatures have lost ground vis-à-vis the governors. Superficially, this may be attributed to an ancient grudge against those who merely *talk*, as against those who act or do. Criticism of Congress has always been a favorite indoor sport of Americans, and the critics of today are, if anything, less caustic than the critics of the past. Certainly in popular esteem the Congress of 1968 will outrank the Congresses of the turn of the century or of the middle 1920s. Contemporary criticism, however, takes on an added "bite" and an increased significance because the problems of crisis government have ceased to be merely periodic and have become continuous.

For one thing the meteoric increase in the size and scope of governmental activity in the twentieth century has increased the size and importance of the executive establishment. The complex problems of urban growth and development, scientific and technological change, revolutions in transportation and communication, agriculture and industry, business and the professions have also "revolutionized" the decision-making process. The complexity and urgency of the decisions that have to be made and carried out in the administration of public policies affecting nearly every aspect of contemporary life demand at the same time greater rationality and greater speed. In both respects the executive has advantages which the legislative branch cannot hope to match. No committee and certainly no legislative body of several hundred members can move with the dispatch of an executive officer with a job to do.

---

[7] See James M. Burns, *The Deadlock of Democracy: Four-party Politics in America* (Englewood Cliffs, N.J.: Prentice-Hall, 1963). For another view, see William S. White, *op. cit.*, chap. 21.

Besides, the manifold activities of the executive branch reach continuously into virtually every nook and cranny of the nation and hence command greater attention from citizens and communications media alike than the speeches of a Congressman, or the doings of Congress as a whole. The fact is that virtually all the "favors" that Congressmen do for their constituents, the errands they run for them, and the questions they answer have to do with executive or administrative agencies. Even the contracts awarded to local firms, or new public works to be undertaken in a Congressman's district, depend for the most part on executive, not legislative, "largesse."

Not least of the reasons for the "decline" of Congress vis-à-vis the executive is the expansion of the President's role in initiating legislation and the increasing discretion granted to executive officers and agencies. Delegation of legislative and judicial power has reached a point where Congress is content to shape only the bare outlines of policy, leaving to executive and administrative officers power to make rules and regulations and quasi-judicial decisions, which, as the saying is, "fill in the details." This is especially true in the vast area of national defense, where, as Richard Neustadt says, "the most critical government decisions, the war-or-peace decisions, have been snatched from Congress by technology, despite the plain words of the Constitution."[8] And what is true of national defense is also true of foreign policy in general. In most of these urgent, important, glamorous, and highly visible activities, Congress is at least in the public view a backstop, or a hanger-on. Here, as in most of the continuing activities of the government, it is the President and not the Congress which occupies the center of the stage.

Whether as cause or effect, these and other changes in American government and society have been accompanied by changes in the relation of Congress and the executive to the most important power centers, both public and private. Between 1861 and 1896, according to Professor Samuel Huntington, 37 percent of Cabinet members had served in the House or Senate. Between 1897 and 1940 this dropped to 19 percent, and between 1941 and 1963 to only 15 percent. One side effect of the seniority rule in Congress has been to block members from moving to power centers outside Congress. Congressmen are not only thus politically confined but are denied both the physical and social mobility characteristic of other elite groups in the United States. It is interesting, for example, to note that whereas over 40 percent of 1959 Senators were living in their original hometowns, only 12 percent of corporation executives were doing so. "Seventy percent of the [corporation] presidents had moved 100 miles or more from their hometowns but only 29 percent of the senators had done so." There is nothing terribly surprising about this

---

[8] See Richard Neustadt, "Politicians and Bureaucrats," chap. 5, in David B. Truman (ed.), *The Congress and America's Future* (American Assembly; Englewood Cliffs, N.J.: Prentice-Hall, 1965).

relative immobility of Senators. Men who commit themselves to elective political careers, if they expect to achieve "seniority" must "stay put" in their home state or district. Moreover, since members of the Cabinet and top executive personnel are increasingly recruited from among private or public executives rather than from Congress, their relations with elite groups in the private and public power structure of the country are more intimate, continuous, and effective. Congress, as Professor Huntington has said, is more and more insulated "from the interests which have emerged in the 20th Century's 'organizational revolution.' How can national interests be represented in a locally-elected legislature?" One result is that the executive, rather than the legislative branch has come to be the "natural point of access" to the government for 'national organizations.' "[9] It is against some such general background that our study of Congress and congressional behavior must proceed.

☆ CONGRESS IN AN AFFLUENT SOCIETY

If one were seeking a symbol of our affluent society, Congress might serve as well as any. No other legislative body in the world is so richly endowed with the material facilities necessary to do its job. In terms of office space, salaries and allowances for travel, mail, home offices, pension and insurance rights, health care, opportunities for foreign travel, plus minor items like discounts on stationery, free flowers, low-cost meals in congressional restaurants, cut-rate haircuts and free parking, our Congressmen are the envy of legislators around the world. At their beck and call are the resources of the Library of Congress with over 39,000,000 items in its collection, including 12,000,000 books and pamphlets, and 2,500,000 maps and photographs on every conceivable subject. Although this magnificent institution serves other governmental agencies and the public, too, its first responsibility is to Congress. Not a few congressional speeches, reports, and documents are the product of the Legislative Reference Service, which functions exclusively as a research agency for Senators and Representatives. In addition to the Library of Congress, there is an impressive special library in the Capitol itself for the convenience of members of Congress.

Each Senator and Representative is provided with a salary of $30,000 and some $35,000 to $100,000 a year to pay for an official staff. A typical Representative will employ from three to nine aides of one kind or another, and a Senator's staff will number up to 25 or 30. This staff is a Congressman's eyes and ears and legs, in handling correspondence, running multifarious errands for constituents, doing research, and, in gen-

---

[9] See Samuel P. Huntington, "Congressional Responses to the Twentieth Century," pp. 5–31, in David B. Truman (ed.), *op. cit.*

eral, running the routine office affairs.[10] And there are other perquisites or aids available to members of Congress, including mailing privileges, travel allowance, and liberal pensions on retirement.

We have mentioned these facilities which a generous nation has made available to Representatives and Senators, not to satisfy an idle curiosity nor to suggest that they are unnecessary or unwise. On the contrary, the American people, we believe, are well advised to be generous in support of these public servants. We cannot, of course, buy honor, dignity, or character, but we can, in a measure at least, buy competence and independence.

Congressmen are full-time public servants. Unless they are paid for full-time service only those with independent incomes or those whose living is made at something else can afford to serve. Even at best the risks involved are great. Representatives and even Senators have a limited tenure and the ups and downs of politics being what they are, their jobs are insecure. Not even an otherwise adequate salary plus allowances and pension rights can fully compensate for this insecurity. They can, however, contribute to that end. They can reduce the pressure and the temptation to seek other income from sources not always compatible with an independent and objective view on matters of public policy.

"Conflict of interest" legislation has been passed in an effort to separate the private interests of our chief executive officers from their public interests and responsibilities. It has been suggested that such legislation be extended to include members of the legislative branch, and an objective review of all such legislation is long overdue. But in such a review any revision or extension of conflict of interest laws ought to take account of the hazards faced by those who enter public service and of the special risks incurred by those who serve in Congress.

A living wage will not alone insure the kind of independence we look for in our Congressmen. Fiction to the contrary, and in spite of commentary that smacks more of fiction than of fact, Congressmen are an able and an honest lot. But not even integrity and ability can insure an independent, objective judgment on matters of public policy in the absence of knowledge and information. No Senator or Representative, with the best will in the world, can hope unaided to understand the meaning and significance of all, or even most, of the issues upon which he must decide. In a typical Congress half of the members in the House of Representatives and the Senate will have served ten years, and one can learn a lot in that time. To men like the late Sam Rayburn, Carl Vinson, or Carl Hayden, with over 35 years in Congress, there are few things about government they do not know. But modern science and technology and the

10 In 1959 Senator Javits of New York had 26 employees and a total office budget of $149,322. Senator Keating, also of New York, had 20 employees and a total of $141,000. Compare this with the British Member of Parliament. His pay is one-fifth of an American Congressman's. And the English M.P. has no office space and no office help.

expanding role of government have made the problems of competence and comprehension increasingly difficult. Confronted with claims and counterclaims of technical experts testifying for pressure groups or executive agencies, the average Congressman might have a difficult time to understand the issue, let alone to decide how he should vote.

Long service on special committees or subcommittees can give a Congressman knowledge equal and often superior to that of the experts whose testimony he must judge. But for the 50 to 80 new members, and in some cases for those of long tenure on a new committee assignment, reliable sources of information, independent of the interests involved, are essential to an informed judgment. It is to provide this knowledge that the Library of Congress, the Legislative Reference Service, the staff assistants of committees, and the personal aides of the Congressman are made available. Armed with this help, no Congressman need depend solely upon advice or evidence offered by rival parties having special interests in the decisions to be made.

☆ CONGRESS AS A REPRESENTATIVE BODY

Since Congress is above all else a representative assembly, what can be said about it in this capacity? As a cross section of the population, Congress will not satisfy the statistician's requirements for random sampling. Congress is not a random sample, but a highly select sample of American political leadership.[11]

For example, over three-fourths (76 percent) of United States Senators and 69 percent of Representatives in 1962 were professional men, and over half of the Senators (59 percent) and Representatives (57 percent) were lawyers, although less than 13 of the total American labor force was classified as professional and technical. "Officials, Proprietors, and Managers" of business enterprises made up only 15 percent of the total labor force, but they accounted for over 20 percent of United States Senators and Representatives. Nearly 90 percent (88) of the Senators and 83 percent of Representatives were college graduates as against less than 25 percent of the population. Nor are Congressmen a fair sample of the religious, racial, or ethnic groups in the total population. Protestants (especially Congregationalists, Presbyterians, Episcopalians, and Unitarians), whites, and those whose parents or grandparents were from Great Britain, Ireland, northern and central Europe, and in the middle- and upper-income brackets are overrepresented, while Catholics, Jews, Negroes, and those with eastern European ethnic backgrounds, and

[11] In Congress there are more lawyers than businessmen and labor leaders than farmers, more farmers than journalists, more journalists than preachers. Yet most members of Congress are probably best described as career politicians, since for the great majority, years have passed since they first entered politics.

workers in the lower-income brackets are underrepresented. Although a large majority of the American people live in cities, "a majority of the Senators (64 percent) holding office between 1947 and 1957 were born in rural areas." The pattern is by no means stable through time and may fluctuate wildly in the next few Congresses as the effects of Supreme Court decisions on congressional reapportionment are felt. But it is unlikely that Congress will ever "represent" a true cross section of the population.[12]

Article I of the Constitution sets forth the general theory of representation.

> The House of Representatives shall be composed of members chosen every second year by the People of the several states and the electors in each state shall have the Qualifications requisite for electors of the most numerous branch of the State legislature.
>
> [It further provides that Representatives] . . . shall be apportioned among the several states . . . according to their respective numbers [that is, their population] . . .

Furthermore, representation in the House shall be reapportioned after every decennial census—provided that "each state shall have at least one Representative."

As for the Senate, Article I, as changed by the Seventeenth Amendment provides that "The Senate of the United States shall be composed of two senators from each state, elected by the people thereof, for six years; and each senator have one vote." This provision, incidentally, is presumably the one part of the Constitution not subject to amendment, for Article V reads: ". . . that no State, without its consent, shall be deprived of its equal suffrage in the Senate."

Space forbids a detailed analysis of this scheme of representation, but some general observations may be made. Congress is a bicameral body not only to insure greater delay and deliberation in the legislative process, but also to provide for representation of the people both as individuals and as citizens of the several states.

With the direct election of Senators by the people, the Senate, too, has come to be representative of the people, not in terms of numbers but as residents of the states. In the Senate, the people no longer speak through their state governments but directly for themselves. This is by no means a splitting of semantic hairs. The direct election of Senators has made a profound difference in the fact as well as the theory of representation. It has made Senators more dependent upon public opinion than upon the opinion of legislative elites. Moreover, as urbanization has

[12] See Dewey Anderson, *The Occupations and Schooling of Congress, National Administration and Federal Judiciary* (Washington, D.C.: Public Affairs Institute, 1962). See also Donald R. Matthews, *The Social Background of Political Decision Makers* (Garden City, N.Y.: Doubleday, 1954); Samuel P. Huntington, "Congressional Responses to the Twentieth Century," in David B. Truman (ed.), *op. cit.,* chap. 1.

increased in every state, Senators have become increasingly dependent upon and responsive to urban voters.

Complaints that the basis of representation in the Senate is undemocratic and violates the principle of majority rule have a superficial plausibility. After all, it is said, how can one defend a system under which Alaska with barely more than 200,000 people has the same representation as New York with nearly 18,000,000 and California with over 18,000,000. The most obvious answer, of course, is that the Senate is not supposed to represent a numerical majority of people in the United States but only a numerical majority in each of the several states, that is, a more or less democratized version of Calhoun's "concurrent majority." The Senate, more than any agency except the electoral college, remains the visible legal embodiment of our federal system.

It has also been said that in letting the states determine qualifications for the suffrage (subject to the Fourteenth, Fifteenth, and Nineteenth Amendments), the Constitution introduced another source of sectional inequality. Where Negro citizens constitute a significant proportion of the population, and where they have been denied the suffrage, the white population has enjoyed a privileged position in representation in the House of Representatives.

To prevent this inequity, Section 2 of the Fourteenth Amendment provides that when the right to vote in national elections is denied for any reason to adult citizens, the representation of that state in Congress shall be reduced in proportion to the numbers so disfranchised. As we have seen, this provision has been a dead letter, and the white population in many southern states has continued to enjoy a larger representation than it would have if this provision were strictly enforced.

The Gerrymander

There are other anomalies in the apportionment of representation according to population. In apportioning representation to the states, Congress uses what is called a method of equal proportions. The method is based on a mathematical formula designed to secure as little deviation from equal shares in representation by the general population as possible. Upon the basis of equal proportions tables prepared by the Bureau of the Census, Congress assigns to each state the number of seats to which it is entitled.

Prior to 1929 federal law required that each state then proceed to apportion the representatives to single-member "districts composed of contiguous and compact territory, and containing as nearly as practicable an equal number of inhabitants." Although this law has not been re-enacted, the internal apportionment of representation among single-member districts is practically universal among the states. Some argue that the old law is still in effect anyway. And it is in this process that one facet of the great game of American politics is played, called "gerry-mandering."

Because Republican and Democratic voters are not distributed evenly throughout the state, it is possible, by a skillful drawing of district boundaries, to include disproportionate numbers of Democrats or Republicans in particular districts and thus make them "safe" for one party or the other. By concentrating as many of the opposition voters in as few districts as possible and by spreading one's own strength as widely as possible, the party in control of the legislature at the time of reapportionment can perpetuate itself in power, except of course for unforeseen shifts in population or public opinion. Hence, when Republicans control the legislature, congressional and state assembly districts will be drawn to favor Republicans, and when Democrats are in control, they will favor that party.

The classic illustration of the gerrymander comes from Massachusetts, where some of the districts defined by the Democratic legislature of 1812 assumed odd shapes. A map of them on the wall of the editor Benjamin Russell's office was noticed by the artist, Gilbert Stuart. Stuart amused himself by giving one of the districts a few pencil touches to make it look like a salamander. "No," said Russell, looking at it, "It is not a salamander, it is a gerrymander," taking the name from the Democratic Governor at the time, Elbridge Gerry. The name stuck and the process has ever since been called a "gerrymander." (See Figure 12-1.)

Examples from the 1960 reapportionment may be cited. The *Congressional Quarterly* for November 17, 1961, reports:

> Brushing aside Democratic cries of "gerrymander" and "political murder," the New York Legislature on November 10th . . . gave quick approval to a . . . Congressional redistricting plan which observers believed would cause the defeat of at least six incumbent Democratic Congressmen in the 1962 elections. (Reapportionment was a painful business in New York in 1960 since the state's delegation in the House of Representatives was reduced by two members) . Some of the districts have strange shapes. Brooklyn gained two odd creatures; one, the new 15th (Republican) with its rear quarters in the Narrows and its head near the East River; another, the new 16th (Democratic) with its head in Central Brooklyn and body on Staten Island. Congressman Celler (Democrat) of Brooklyn said the reapportionment act left United States Congressional districts looking like a "wash hanging on the line" or a "quaint abstract painting."

Although the recent court decisions compelling the state legislatures to draw both congressional and state legislative district lines in such a way as to minimize the variations of population from district to district, the lines may still be drawn to maximize the effectiveness of the party vote. Even though districts of radically varying populations have been eliminated, the gerrymander as such goes on, as shown in Figure 12-1.

Gerrymandering

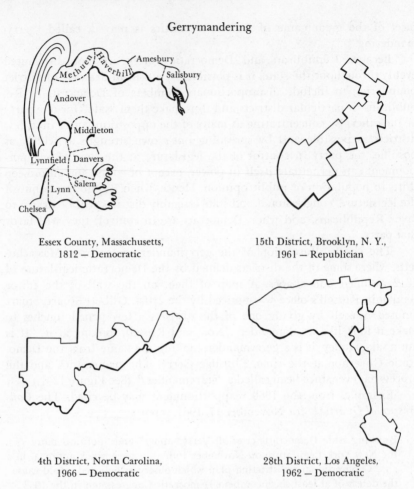

Essex County, Massachusetts,
1812 — Democratic

15th District, Brooklyn, N. Y.,
1961 — Republican

4th District, North Carolina,
1966 — Democratic

28th District, Los Angeles,
1962 — Democratic

Figure 12–1 Adapted from "Gerrymandering Lives On," *Congressional Quarterly Background Report* on *Representation and Apportionment,* August, 1966, p. 58. Used by permission.

One Man, One Vote

Prior to recent Court decisions compelling the equalization of populations within congressional districts, shifts in population, plus failure of the states to reapportion, plus the built-in vagaries of the gerrymander, often produced striking inequalities in the population of congressional districts. Tables 12–1 and 12–2 show some recent examples. It was usually urban districts that suffered from these inequalities. For many years proponents of numerical equality in representation tried to find a way to prevent such discrepancies.

In 1946 the issue was presented to the Supreme Court in the case of *Colegrove* v. *Green.* The facts in the case were that because there had

TABLE 12–1
Disparities in Congressional Districts (1962)

	District	Population	Variation
Arizona	Largest	663,510	over 3 to 1
	Smallest	198,236	
Colorado	Largest	653,954	over 3 to 1
	Smallest	195,551	
Connecticut	Largest	689,555	over 2 to 1
	Smallest	317,953	
Georgia	Largest	823,680	over 3 to 1
	Smallest	272,154	

SOURCE: Adapted from *Apportionment in the Nineteen Sixties* (August, 1967), Part II, p. "a" (New York: National Municipal League). Used by permission.

been no reapportionment in Illinois since 1901, glaring disparities had appeared among congressional districts. One district in Illinois had a population of 112,116 while another had a population of 914,056. Professor Kenneth Colegrove and others sought a declaratory judgment against the governor and other state officers on the state primary certifying board to declare the existing congressional reapportionment invalid and to require the election of all 26 Illinois Congressmen on a statewide ballot until the legislature should enact a valid reapportionment act. The argument was that under these circumstances people in some Illinois districts were being denied "equal protection of the laws" and their right to have their votes counted at full value. The district court dismissed the suit and an appeal was taken to the Supreme Court.

TABLE 12–2
Congruities in Congressional Districts (1968)

	Population	District	Deviation from Average (Percent)
Arizona	Largest	456,529	+ 5.18
	Smallest	405,217	− 1.47
Colorado	Largest	493,887	+12.63
	Smallest	405,889	− 7.43
Connecticut	Largest	482,135	+14.10
	Smallest	404,201	− 4.34
Georgia	Largest	455,575	+15.54
	Smallest	329,738	−16.38

SOURCE: Adapted from *Apportionment in the Nineteen Sixties* (August, 1967), Part II, pp. 1–3 (New York: National Municipal League). Used by permission.

By a vote of 4 to 3 the Supreme Court held the question to be "of peculiarly political nature" and therefore not a proper one for judicial determination. Justices Black, Douglas, and Murphy dissented, saying that "while the Constitution contains no express provision requiring that Congressional election districts . . . contain approximately equal populations, the constitutionally guaranteed right to vote and the right to have one's vote counted clearly imply the policy that state election systems, no matter what their form, should be designed to give approximately equal weight to each vote cast. . . . Legislation which . . . brings about glaringly unequal representation in Congress in favor of special classes and groups should be invalidated. . . ."

A number of other cases involving essentially the same issue have since been decided by the Supreme Court. The landmark decision which heralded a change in the Supreme Court's "political question" doctrine with respect to reapportionment cases was *Baker* v. *Carr* (1962), which had to do with the failure of the Tennessee legislature to reapportion itself. Not since 1901 had it reapportioned its own seats, although the state constitution requires reapportionment every ten years. No other method of apportionment was provided for, so that relief could not be found in a measure initiated by the people as can be done in many states when the initiative and referendum are available.

There had been a great shift in population from rural to urban areas, resulting in great inequalities in the population of representative districts. An interesting feature of the Tennessee case was that the state constitution requires that seats in the state legislature be apportioned on the basis of qualified voters, not population. City voters asked the Supreme Court to declare the 1901 redistricting act unconstitutional as in violation of the equal protection clause of the Fourteenth Amendment. Although the Court did not grant the relief prayed for, it did remand the case to the federal district court to inquire whether relief should not be granted.

In recent cases the Supreme Court has gone far beyond *Baker* v. *Carr* to order the reapportionment on the basis of population, not only of *both* houses of most state legislatures, but of congressional districts as well. As a guiding principle in these cases the Court has adopted the familiar rule of "one man, one vote" to test the constitutional validity of any particular apportionment. Where, through a system of apportionment, it requires half again as many votes, let alone two or three times as many, to elect a representative, the Court has said that voters residing in such districts are being denied equal protection of the laws. An apportionment of congressional districts, said the Court, that "contracts the value of some votes and expands that of others" is unconstitutional. "While it may not be possible to draw Congressional districts with mathematical precision, there is no excuse for ignoring our Constitution's plain objective of making equal representation for equal numbers of people the fundamental goal for the House of Representatives."[13] Following the Supreme Court's decisions more than half of the states, using a variety of methods, moved fairly quickly to reapportion their state and congressional districts and reapportionments have now been carried out in most of the remainder, in many instances following a series of cases in which the courts examined the reapportionment plans minutely to determine whether the equalization was as nearly complete as practicable. In general, this "reapportionment revolution" has increased urban and suburban representation at the expense of the rural areas.

What difference does it all make? One may well ask why such a fuss is made about the apportionment of representation. The most obvious reply is a mathematical one. A basic principle of our republican form of government is that one man's vote should count for one and only one, and that each vote should have as nearly equal weight as possible. If A lives in a district with only 200,000 people and B in a district with 400,000 people, A's vote mathematically is worth roughly twice that of B's, thus denying B an equal voice in choosing representatives.

But a more subtle question remains. Do these inequities make any difference in the *quality* of representation given to one body of voters as against another? As we have indicated, the major victims of malapportionment and gerrymandering are the cities, the metropolitan areas, and suburbia. If we classify congressional districts in terms of population density, we may identify four main types.

    I. Rural districts with no city of over 25,000
   II. Small town districts with no city over 50,000
  III. Mid-urban districts, including a city of 50,000–100,000
  IV. Metropolitan districts with cities of 200,000 or more

Does the voting behavior of representatives from these different kinds of districts vary significantly?

An interesting analysis has been made of the votes of both Republican and Democratic Congressmen from such districts on ten major issues of domestic policy, measures generally described as "liberal," having to do with social welfare, civil rights, and so forth. A score of 4 or more was taken to indicate a "liberal" voting record, one of 4 or less, as a conservative record. It is significant that the percentage of representatives with a "liberal" record increased markedly as one moved from rural to metropolitan districts.[14] V. O. Key, in his book, *Public Opinion,* has also examined the voting behavior of representatives coming from various types of districts. His analysis is summarized in Table 12–3.

These figures are by no means conclusive, but they would seem to confirm what is more or less common knowledge, that urban representa-

---

[13] See *Wesberry* v. *Sanders,* 376 U.S. 1, decided February 17, 1964; *Reynolds* v. *Sims,* 377 U.S. 533, June 15, 1964.
[14] See *New Republic,* October 15, 1956.

TABLE 12–3
Voting Behavior of Representatives

	Republican Representatives
District Types	*Percent of Republican Representatives with a score of 4 or more (i.e., liberal)*
i. Rural	22
ii. Small Town	24
iii. Midurban	43
iv. Metropolitan	57

	Nonsouthern Democratic Representatives
District Types	*Percent with a liberal score of 8 or more*
i. Rural	59
ii. Small Town	59
iii. Midurban	81
iv. Metropolitan	90

SOURCE: Based on data from V. O. Key, Jr., *Public Opinion and American Democracy* (New York: Knopf, 1961). Used by permission of Alfred A. Knopf, Inc.

tives tend (1) to be more Democratic than Republican, and (2) to be more "liberal" than conservative. To the extent therefore that gerrymandering favors urban as against nonurban districts, it will increase the Democratic liberal strength in Congress. As it tends to favor rural, nonurban districts, it will increase Republican conservative strength. Malapportionment and the gerrymander *do* make a difference.[15]

Who or What Does a Representative Represent?

These meager data illustrate the difficulty of knowing exactly what is meant by "representation." How does one evaluate a representative system? To *represent* must mean in some measure to reflect the image of the people. And, as we have seen, although Congress is by no means a random sample of the American people, it nevertheless is a fairly select sample of the kind of political leadership the American people seem to

15 Other recent studies make abundantly clear the not very surprising fact that the nature of a Congressman's constituency—whether it be urban or rural, with high or low population density, high or low percentage white or nonwhite, high or low in economic and social status—does make a significant difference in his voting behavior. See Lewis Froman, Jr., *Congressmen and Their Constituencies* (Chicago: Rand McNally, 1963), pp. 69–97.

want. It may thus be said to represent, that is, to reflect, the varied moods, interests, aspirations, and values of the people.

Most of our lives are lived in a twilight of uncertainty and ambiguity. Decisions are being forever made and regretted because the "right" answer isn't found. No doubt we prefer lawyers as representatives partly because lawyers are trained to make decisions in ambiguous situations, doing the best they can under the circumstances, even though one regrets the decision in the end. If the voters who elect representatives regret too many of these decisions, they may choose someone else to represent them.

What, then, is the proper relation between a Congressman and his constituency? Should he be a delegate or a representative? Is he a trustee or an agent of his constituents? Should he represent the interest of his district or his state, or the interest of the nation as a whole? These are questions on which endless erudition has been expended, and we cannot hope to give a definitive answer here. An idea or two, however, may be suggested. "The representative," said Edmund Burke, should be a pillar of state, "not a weathercock on the top of the edifice exalted for his levity and versatility and of no use but to indicate the shiftings of every fashionable gale. . . . Parliament is not a Congress of ambassadors from different and hostile interests. . . . Parliament is a deliberative assembly of one nation, with one interest, that of the whole—where not local purposes, not local prejudices ought to guide, but the general good, resulting from the general reason of the whole." But how is he to know what "the general good" is or what the "general reason of the whole" would require? Such is the nature of public opinion that a representative might not know, on any given issue, just what "the people" want—not even if he were to hang precariously on the coattails of every passing pollster.

In exploring this basic question we need to recognize the "facts of life" in the life of a Congressman. If he likes being a Congressman, his first concern is likely to center on his re-election. This is virtually a continuous preoccupation for members of the House of Representatives, who must face the voters every other year. He therefore must do what is necessary (or what he thinks is necessary) to this end. And this includes a lot of pedestrian things as well as a lot of high-level thinking.

He must be alert to what happens in his state or district, ranging from the wedding of a constituent's child to the proposed transfer of an air base from his community to another, or the building of a dam, a post office, or some other public works. And, of course, when action by any government agency promises to affect significantly his district, he must know about it, if only to lend encouragement or to lodge an appropriate protest. In all of this he is invariably assisted by communications and personal visits from individual constituents, organized committees, or interest groups.

Consider a day in the life of a Congressman as reported by Lubert St. Clair in December, 1943:

> Nine times out of ten when a member is not on the floor he is doing some other chore that is not half as easy as listening to debate. The chances are he either is doing committee duty which is a gruelling grind, or he is down at some department doing a job which an ordinary messenger could do if he just had the influence that goes with being a Congressman.
>
> 7 A.M. Leaped out of bed and, because we have no help, looked after the furnace, started breakfast while my wife was getting the kids ready for school, and dashed off to a breakfast meeting of a group of sightseers from my district.[16]
>
> 8 A.M. Met with twenty constituents, promised at least half of them to look after minor things they were interested in. Made brief address, and picked up the breakfast check, $17.50.
>
> 9 A.M. Read mail. Six demands from good friends for appointments to government jobs. Several letters from business groups insisting that I should do something to help them, but not saying what I should do.
>
> 10 A.M. A delegation calls to invite me to speak at a dinner, almost 1,000 miles from Washington and not in my district, on the occasion of something that neither concerns me directly or indirectly. They will be glad to pay my expenses and will assure me of splendid entertainment. I decline with thanks.
>
> 11 A.M. I arrive at a committee meeting only to find that an expert on acoustics has gotten before the committee and it takes thirty minutes to get him out of the way and start discussing the subject of the bill.
>
> 12 M. A visiting chaplain, to make the most of a rare opportunity for him, prays ten times as long as the regular chaplain usually does. The general consent calendar being up, only those with bills of personal interest to them and a few leaders remain. I go back to my office to try to catch up with my mail. Within ten minutes a group of my severest critics from back home barge in. They bawl me out for not being on the floor "doing my duty." I sigh and take them to lunch. Then since I am not on the floor anyhow, they decide it would be just too ducky if I would take them on a sight-seeing tour of Washington. I refuse, and, of course, make them madder at me than ever.
>
> 2–5 P.M. Visit departments, argue with bright young men who know all the answers except one: "How can I get this thing done?" Return to my office with a very tired pair of dogs. Find District of Columbia delegation waiting for me to tell them just why District people should not have the vote.
>
> 7 P.M. Home and into a hard-boiled shirt, eating a sandwich from the dresser the while. Just as I am ready to go, my heaviest financial backer back home calls by long distance and says his son is reported missing in Africa and I must get in touch with the War Department immediately. I start phoning, and my wife proceeds to the bridge alone, with the bridge of her nose raking the chandeliers.

16 This Spartan life has been considerably mitigated in recent years as congressional salaries and allowances have increased. It has rarely been "typical" in any case.

9 P.M. I get no information at the War Department, but I phone my friend telling him I will try again tomorrow. I arrive at the bridge and find that it really is being given to have me meet an uncle of the hostess who desires a government loan to help him locate some sunken Spanish treasure. Sandwiches, coffee. . . .

12 M. And so to bed.[17]

Every representative is under continuous pressure from his constituents. To explore how these pressures build up would be to explore the entire fabric of American politics.[18] With one in every six or eight persons in the total work force employed by a government agency or by a private employer working on government contract, government operations are a vital factor in the economic life of many states or congressional districts. Their installation, expansion, or contraction, location or relocation, can generate a head of steam that no Congressman can ignore if he wants to stay in Congress. But government employment is but one of many "interests" of which a Congressman must be aware. If he comes from a state or district in which agriculture or mining, wool or cattle growing, steel manufacturing, or automobiles, or aluminum, or glass or shoes is a major source of employment, he must perforce attend to its welfare as an integral part of the "general welfare."

Most Senators and Congressmen, in fact, are sufficiently attuned to the major interest of their constituencies that organized pressure to influence their votes is often unnecessary. Congressmen from the farm belt, it has been said, don't have to be told how to vote on farm legislation; they already know.

Congressmen are often criticized for these parochial loyalties, for assuming that what's good for Kalamazoo is good for the country. But we ought not to forget that parochial needs are by no means inconsistent with the needs of the nation. The general welfare of the nation is not something apart from the welfare of its regions, states, and local communities. The TVA, the Grand Coulee Dam on the Columbia River, the Central Valley development in California, the St. Lawrence Seaway, or the Argonne and Oak Ridge laboratories are national resources, even though their local operations constitute important resources for particular states or districts. Even a local post office adds to the wealth of the nation by increasing the value of the total postal system, just as every new phone installed adds to the value and efficiency of the total system. To forget this is to indulge in a kind of inverted parochialism that says: "What's good for the nation in general ought not to be good for any place or anyone in particular"—a manifest absurdity.

This is not to argue that every local project or parochial interest

[17] *N.A.D.A. Bulletin*, December, 1943, p. 8. See also C. Miller, *Member of the House, Letters of a Congressman*, John Baker, ed. (New York: Scribner, 1962) .

[18] S. Bailey and H. Samuel, *Congress at Work* (New York: Holt, Rinehart and Winston, 1952) , esp. pp. 97–135.

served by government contributes equally to the welfare of the nation. What we are saying is that the average Congressman who wishes to stay in Congress will strive to reconcile the interests of his constituents with the nation's interest and welfare. For the Congressman who too flagrantly serves special interests of a single group will sooner or later be labeled as a tool of this group—a label which no Senator or Congressman can wear for long and survive.

To say that a Congressman should represent the general welfare is easier said than done. He will be assailed by a hundred voices, no two of which may speak the same language or say the same things, but each of them will claim to represent the general welfare. Through their local, state, and national organizations they will inundate Senators and Representatives with letters and telegrams, resolutions, and proclamations, urging them to vote "right." A well organized campaign can flood the mails with hundreds of thousands of such "appeals." Through authorized spokesmen in Washington they will help a Congressman to understand a complex issue and why in the public interest he must vote *yes* or *no* on a pending bill, a bill incidentally which may have been drafted by special counsel for some organized pressure group. They will appear before committees singly or in groups, to argue the virtue or the inequity of a proposed line of public policy.

And every Congressman knows that through radio and TV, in pamphlets, books, and monographs, in press releases, inspired articles in magazines or other periodicals the great pressure groups are striving to crystallize public opinion to create an atmosphere friendly to their cause. In reading his mail, a Congressman will quickly learn to discriminate between letters and telegrams from his own constituents and those from residents of other states or districts. He will develop antennae that tell him when letters are from genuinely concerned constituents and when they are mass-produced epistles from organized interests generated by enterprising public relations officers. And he will know from past experience that the political bark of many a pressure group is worse than its bite. Few of them can actually control many votes, even of their own members. And he learns that the great body of unorganized farmers, businessmen and workers, not to mention a vast and silent army of consumers, may be voiceless except in the voting booth. The notion that Congressmen are puppets of these interest groups, voting *yes* or *no* in response to pressure from the AMA or the CIO, or a thousand and one other lobbies in Washington, is largely a myth.

But not wholly a myth, because many Congressmen are dependent upon factional interests for funds to finance their campaigns for re-election. This is a Congressman's Achilles' heel. The influence of these factions, as often as not, derives not from the votes they control but the money and services they can contribute to the process of mobilizing the votes of organized and unorganized citizens alike. Once Congressmen find reliable sources of campaign funds and services from the rank and file of their own party supporters, even these financial bonds that now tie them to special interest groups could be broken.

Thanks to facilities available to Congress, no Representative or Senator need depend for information on even the most complex questions of public policy upon the expert but biased testimony of organized special interests. Nor is he without what may be called an "independent audit" of contradicting "evidence" offered by rival lobbyists. In his own personal staff, in the Legislative Reference Service, in the experts employed by major congressional committees, and in the rich resources for research of the executive agencies, he has access to information and analyses as objective as it is humanly possible to be.

In suggesting that Congressmen be as free as possible from undue dependence upon organized interest groups, we are not suggesting that such groups be ignored. On the contrary, their testimony concerning the impact of public policies upon their own interests and upon the public interest as they see it is indispensable to any realistic discovery by Congress of what will best promote the welfare, not alone of particular groups, but of the whole nation. What we are suggesting is that each Representative and Senator in making up his own mind on these important matters should be as free as possible to exercise his own judgment in the light of the best information he can bring to bear upon the problem.

☆ ORGANIZATION AND RITUAL

If this seems an idealized version of the legislative process, so, too, is the notion that every congressional decision is a kind of Pavlovian reaction to the pressures and counterpressures of rival interest groups. If a member of Congress is not a mere puppet of pressure groups, if in casting his vote he consults not only his constituents but his own mind and conscience, he nevertheless does not function in a vacuum or in isolation. He is part and parcel of an organization with its own rules of procedure and its own customs and traditions. Every member of the Senate or the House of Representatives soon develops a loyalty to Congress as a whole and to his own house in particular. He becomes part of a group that, however much it may be divided and subdivided by parties, cliques, and factions, has its own sense of independence, integrity, and pride.

To the outsider and to the freshman member, the organization and procedure of Congress is a labyrinth of committees, caucuses, and conferences of "closed" rules and "open" rules, of "privileged questions" and "questions of privilege," of "filibusters" and "closure." Gradually the new member learns to distinguish the *Union Calendar* of the Committee of the Whole for revenue and appropriation bills, from the *House Calendar* for other public bills. He learns the great wisdom and significance of the *Consent Calendar* to which noncontroversial bills are referred for passage without debate on the first and third Mondays of each month, and he appreciates the value of a *Private Calendar* for bills involving private claims against the United States which can be passed without debate on the first and third Tuesdays of each month. And he will learn, too, that his motion to free a bill from a committee reluctant to report it will not get on the *Discharge Calendar* without 218 signatures—a high hurdle which few surmount.[19]

A new member of Congress will know that although the Constitution vests all legislative power in the House of Representatives and the Senate, it is a power that is shared with the President. Article II says that the President "shall from time to time give to the Congress information of the State of the Union, recommend to their consideration such measures as he shall judge necessary and expedient." Besides, every act of Congress and every joint resolution requires the President's signature, and his veto can, as a rule, kill any legislation of which he does not approve. So important has the legislative role of the President become that the late H. L. McBain once said:

> The prime function of the President is not executive at all. It is legislative. . . . Our presidential campaigns . . . are fought out normally upon the record of legislative achievement of the administration in power and proposals for constructive legislation ahead.

From Washington to Kennedy, the President and the major executive departments and agencies have been a major—and in recent years *the* major—source of federal legislation. Nevertheless, although the President proposes, Congress in the end disposes, for without congressional approval the President would be powerless both as a legislator and as chief executive.

In playing its legislative role, Congress has developed an elaborate ritual and a complex array of formal and informal patterns of organization and procedure.

In addition to the committee system there is a complex array of informal groups made up of members from the same state or region, or of similar ideological orientation, professional, or economic interest, ethnic or religious background among themselves or their constituencies. Easily discernible to the practiced eye are blocs, more or less cohesive, representing the California, New York, Nebraska, or other state delegations; the South, New England, the Southwest, the Middle West, or other regions; the medical profession, the oil and gas industry, labor or agriculture or special commodity interests; the Irish-American, Polish-American, Catholic, or Jewish constituencies; the "liberal" group, the "Conservative

---

[19] From the 61st (1909–1910) to the 88th Congress (1963–1964) only 22 out of 813 Petitions for Discharge were successful.

bloc," and so forth.[20] Not the least of these is the Congressional party or parties. Every freshman Representative or Senator from the beginning is a member of a party caucus or conference unless for disciplinary reasons he is excluded by his own party.

Self-discipline

The Constitution gives to each house the power to choose its own officers, determine its own rules, keep a journal of its proceedings, judge the qualifications of its own members, punish any of them for disorderly behavior, and, by a two-thirds vote, even expel a member. A nice constitutional issue might be raised about the power of each house to judge the qualifications of its own members. Their qualifications as set forth in the Constitution are: for the House, a Representative must be 25 years of age, 7 years a citizen, a resident of the state he represents, and duly elected by the voters; for the Senate, he must be 30 years of age, 9 years a citizen, a resident of the state he represents, and duly elected by the voters. He must also take an oath to defend the Constitution.

In judging the qualifications of its own members, may Congress add other requirements than those provided for in the Constitution? The answer would seem to be that Congress can do so, although the question is still at issue. In 1900 Brigham Roberts, duly elected to the House of Representatives from the State of Utah, was denied admission on the ground that, as a Mormon, he believed in polygamy, a practice outlawed in the United States.[21] In 1919 Victor Berger, a Socialist, was excluded because he had been convicted of violating the Espionage Act. Again, in 1927 William S. Vare of Pennsylvania and Frank L. Smith of Illinois, both duly elected to the Senate, were excluded because of excessive expenditures made in the primary campaigns at which they were nominated. How far the Congress may go in excluding duly elected persons from membership on grounds of this kind or for other reasons not mentioned in the Constitution remains a moot question.

On March, 1, 1967, Representative Adam Clayton Powell was denied his seat in the House for contempt of court and misuse of public funds. For the first time in a case of this type a remedy was sought through the courts. On March 8, 1967, Powell filed suit in the U.S. District Court challenging the constitutionality of his exclusion on the grounds that the House had based its reasons for exclusion on qualifications other than those in the Constitution. On April 7, the District Court dismissed the case. The case was then appealed to the Circuit Court of Appeals for the District of Columbia, which denied an immediate hearing. In the

[20] See Alan Fiellin, "The Functions of Informal Groups in Legislative Institutions: A Case Study," *The Journal of Politics*, February, 1962, pp. 72–91.

[21] Reed Smoot, elected to the Senate from Utah and challenged on the same ground as Mr. Roberts, was nevertheless seated.

meantime Powell was re-elected in a special election on April 11, 1967. Although the election returns were certified in the House of Representatives, Powell did not appear to be sworn in, apparently preferring to see the lawsuit through before attempting to resume his seat. In February, 1968, the Court of Appeals affirmed the District Court's dismissal of the case. Powell then appealed to the Supreme Court, and the case was scheduled for a hearing in late March, 1969. In January, 1969, his congressional colleagues reinstated Powell, but fined him $25,000 and stripped him of his 22-year seniority. Powell thus lost his post as chairman of the Education and Labor Committee. Although the idea that the issue was a political rather than a judicial one seemed to prevail, the Powell case evoked some strong legal and historical arguments in favor of restricting grounds for exclusion to strict constitutional criteria.

In some cases, time seems to heal the wounds. Both Brigham Roberts and Victor Berger were ultimately seated as members of the House, and it is doubted that the Senate would today exclude duly elected men for the relatively modest campaign expenditures made by William S. Vare and Frank L. Smith.

In any case, it is easier to *exclude* a prospective member than it is to expel him once he has been admitted. A member may be denied his seat by simple majority under the constitutional power of each House to "Judge . . . the Elections, Returns, and Qualifications of its own members." To *exclude* requires only a simple majority; to *expel* requires a two-thirds vote. In cases of bribery and corruption at the polls or other offenses against the purity of elections, the distinction between exclusion and expulsion may be a distinction without a real difference. Senator William Lorimer, for example, duly elected to the Senate from Illinois in 1909 and admitted to that body, was expelled (or excluded) in July, 1912, three years after taking the oath of office. The vote was 55 for exclusion to 28 against. In the early stages of this case, Senator Beveridge of Indiana had said "If Senators believe that he (Lorimer) knew and countenanced a single act of bribery, we need not conclude that we must *expel* him by a two-thirds vote. We need only to conclude that his election was invalid and so declare by a majority vote."[22]

The power to "judge . . . the elections, returns, and qualifications of members" may entail months or even years of investigation and debate. In the meantime, unless the seat is to remain vacant, the House may admit the member on the ground that so far as the official returns go, he had been "duly elected." In the case of Truman Newberry, elected

---

[22] Presumably this is a correct statement of the power of both houses to *exclude* by a majority vote members found guilty of bribery or fraud in their election, even though the erring member may in the meantime have taken the oath and been admitted to his seat. This would seem to arise from the power of either house to reconsider an earlier vote confirming the election of a member.

to the Senate from Michigan in 1918, and sworn in as a Senator on May 20, 1919, nearly two years elapsed before the Committee on Privileges and Elections, investigating charges of excessive expenditures in his campaign, finally reported, declaring him to be "a duly elected Senator from the State of Michigan."

The procedure followed in these contested election cases, although preserving many of the forms of an impartial, judicial proceeding, are more often than not decided on purely partisan grounds. Save in cases of flagrant fraud or misbehavior, or where the contest is between members of the same party, members of the Committees on Privileges and Elections normally divide on partisan lines with the majority having its way. Perhaps some less partisan procedures to resolve these contests would yield better results, but any move in this direction will have to come from within Congress itself, and Congress is a body jealous of its rights and prerogatives. Some reform to expedite the proceedings would not, however, impair congressional pride or prerogatives.[23]

"Each House," says Section 5 of Article I, "may . . . punish its members for disorderly behavior." "Disorderly behavior" may involve anything from a threatened assault with a deadly weapon by one member on another to conduct in derogation of the honor and dignity of the House. Punishment may be a mild rebuke, a resolution of censure or contempt, fine, imprisonment, or expulsion. When Senator Foote of Mississippi drew his pistol against Benton of Missouri during a bitter exchange on April 17, 1850, the matter was disposed of by a committee report deploring the conduct of both Senators as "discreditable to the Senate." This report, the committee hoped, would be "a sufficient rebuke and a warning" for the future. In May, 1856, following an intemperate and insulting speech by Senator Sumner of Massachusetts, Representative Preston Brooks of South Carolina entered the Senate Chamber and beat Sumner over the head with a thick walking stick, reducing him to insensibility. The Senate committee, appointed to investigate the matter, reported that although the assault was a breach of the privilege of the Senate, it could be punished only by the House of Representatives, of which Brooks was a member. The House committee denounced the assault as an attack on the privilege of the House and recommended that Brooks be expelled and that two members who had abetted him be censured. The vote, 121 to 95, in favor of this recommendation failed for lack of the requisite two-thirds vote necessary for expulsion. Brooks

[23] Speaking of the Senate, George H. Haynes has said: "There may be less menace in the presence of an occasional Newberry in the Senate than in its countenance of a method of dealing with contests which allows the challenged Senator to be sworn if his credentials are formally correct; secures his vote for party purposes for, it may be, three or four years; interposes delays in investigation; . . . and leaves the decision of the validity of his title to be upset at any time before the expiration of his six-year term when an adverse majority can be secured in the Senate." George H. Haynes, *The Senate of the United States* (Boston: Houghton Mifflin, 1938), vol. I, p. 143.

thereupon resigned, returned to South Carolina, where he was hailed as a hero, and was re-elected by a virtually unanimous vote. In February, 1902, following a fist fight on the floor between Senators McLaurin and Tillman of South Carolina, both men were declared to be in contempt of the Senate. Both thereupon humbly apologized and the Senate resolved:

> That . . . the Senators from South Carolina . . . for disorderly behavior and flagrant violation of the rules of the Senate . . . deserve the censure of the Senate, and they are hereby censured for their breach of the privileges and dignity of this body; and from and after the adoption of this resolution, the action adjudging them in contempt of the Senate shall be no longer in force and effect.[24]

In 1929 Senator Bingham of Connecticut was formally censured for appointing as a clerk, with access to executive sessions of the Senate Finance Committee, the assistant to the president of the Connecticut Manufacturing Association. Such conduct was censured as not merely injudicious but "disorderly." In 1954 Senator Joseph McCarthy of Wisconsin, after a stormy career in which he had shamefully abused the privileges of the Senate, was censured for conduct inconsistent with the honor and dignity of that body. And in June, 1967, Senator Thomas J. Dodd of Connecticut was censured for personal use of funds which had been raised for election expenses. The censure resolution followed a long investigation by a select committee which reported the results of its inquiry into several areas of alleged financial abuse on the part of Senator Dodd; however, the action of censure was directed only against the misuse of political funds.

☆ THE CONGRESSIONAL PARTY AND PARTY DISCIPLINE

Unlike the Speaker of the House of Commons, the Speaker of the House of Representatives is a partisan officer whose job it is to guide the party program through the House. His importance in the official hierarchy is reflected in the fact that after the Vice-President, the Speaker stands in line for succession to the Presidency.

The Speaker, unlike the Vice-President (who presides over the Senate) is a duly elected member of the House of Representatives and retains his right to vote. Upon leaving the chair temporarily, he may participate in debate. Although his powers today are pale beside those of his predecessors before 1910, he remains the central figure in the legislative struggle. Men like Reed and Cannon, Speakers before 1910, not only presided, but appointed committees—including the powerful Rules Com-

24 Quoted in Haynes, *op. cit.,* vol. I, p. 143.

mittee—and had an iron grip on the organization and procedure of the House.

There is no Czar Reed today, but the Speaker can exert an influence on legislation greater than any other officer of the government, often greater even than that of the President. The Speaker, the majority and minority leaders, and the party whips and deputy whips are not only officials of the House of Representatives and the Senate but of the Congressional parties. This creates a rival claim upon the loyalty of Congressmen and compels them to give high priority to both the general public interests which the party represents and to the more parochial claims of constituents and special interests or factions.[25] The President as chief executive and as a legislative leader must look to the Congressional party organization of his own party to see his program through.

Seventy percent of the Democratic members of both Houses of Congress supported President Kennedy's program in the Eighty-seventh Congress in 1961; and 66 percent of the Republican members supported President Eisenhower's program in the Eighty-sixth Congress. In the Eighty-ninth Congress (1965–1966) the Democratic support for President Johnson was 60 percent in the Senate and 69 percent in the House; in the first session of the Ninetieth Congress (1967) the rate remained at 69 percent in the House and increased to 61 percent in the Senate. Support for Mr. Kennedy from his own party was higher in the House of Representatives than in the Senate, whereas Mr. Eisenhower fared better in the Senate than in the House. In both cases the absence of anything approaching perfect party cohesion among his own partisans in support of the President or among the minority in opposition to his policies is simply further confirmation of the internal tensions which plague both major parties.

Party cohesion in Congress is a cohesion based mainly on conscience and conviction reinforced by patronage and personal loyalty rather than on discipline imposed by the party caucus or conference. It is rare for either the Republicans or Democrats to impose a party "line" on pending legislation. Under its rules the Democratic caucus may do so only by two-thirds vote and then not on constitutional questions and not contrary to pledges a member may have made to his constituents.

Fifty years ago the party caucus in Congress was a powerful instrument of party policy. Today—except for the election of officers and the assignment of committee posts—it exerts very little power directly on public policy. The Speaker and the majority leader play a larger role in mobilizing party support for legislation than the caucus or the conference. Decline in the importance of the caucus and the conference on legislation may be traced to a number of factors including the loss of

25 See Carl Friedrich, *Constitutional Government and Democracy* (4th ed.; Boston: Ginn, 1968) , esp. pp. 274–275, "The Dual Nature of Representation."

power in the Speaker, who used to dominate the Rules Committee. Another factor has been an increase in the importance of foreign policy where bipartisan agreements are more likely. A third factor in the decline of party discipline in Congress has been the deepening cleavage between southern Democrats and northern Democrats, and in both parties between liberals and conservatives.

If party discipline is to be increased, it will have to be done within Congress by the Congressional party itself. The Congressional party is not only jealous of the Presidential party, but also of what may be called the Constituency, or Grass Roots, party—outside the government. The effort of Paul Butler, when Chairman of the Democratic National Committee, to establish an Advisory Committee to provide outside support for the party inside Congress was not a conspicuous success and has been abandoned.

The difference between the Congressional party and the party outside is that the Congressional party is a part of the government with responsibility for making important decisions on public policy. The Constituency, or Grass Roots, party is an electoral party, primarily, if not exclusively, concerned with the nomination and election of candidates for public office. Even the party platform, although it can and should be a guide to decision makers, is not a body of policy decisions as such and is a vastly different thing from a legislative program on which Congressmen must vote *yes* or *no*. However desirable it may be to establish closer relations between the Congressional party and the outside party, the gap can never be closed. A Congressman, having in mind his oath of office, has a responsibility as a decision maker not only to his own party constituents but to all of the people in his district, his state, and the nation as a whole. Inevitably he will see matters from different perspectives as a candidate and as a member of Congress. Unless this were so, we might turn policy decisions over to party chairmen and campaigns over to Congressmen. Although members of Congress should and do attend carefully to the statements of platform and policy of their "grass roots" parties, they cannot without becoming robots place their votes at the disposal of any outside group, including their own constituency or electoral party.

This gap between the Electoral or Constituency party and the Legislative or governing party is by no means a unique feature of the American party system. The gap between the Parliamentary parties in England, for example, and the Constituency parties is often as great or greater than it is in the United States. And this is as it should be. For the party *outside* Parliament or Congress is more broadly based, more diffuse, more democratic, and in many ways more dynamic because it is less responsible than the Parliamentary or Congressional party. As the Congressional party's unique job is to make decisions, so the Electoral party's job is to goad and guide counsel and criticize its Congressional party, and to pass judgment upon it in the nominating and electoral process. This healthy relation of interdependence and independence is essential to the proper functioning of a responsible representative republic.[26]

☆ *CONGRESS AS A DELIBERATIVE BODY*

Congress is not only a representative and legislative body; it is also a *deliberative* assembly in which important issues of public policy are discussed for the enlightenment of its own members, their constituents, and the American people as a whole. Visitors to the galleries of Congress, especially to the House of Representatives, are often disappointed to discover the chamber empty or nearly so—with a member speaking to a thin scattering of colleagues who display a monumental indifference to what he is saying. If the visitor listens, he may be equally disappointed in the quality of what he hears. Nor will he be reassured if he reads the Congressional Record—that compendium of American wisdom, wit, and witlessness. But if he knows what he wants to hear, if he wants to read about a particular bill or a particular issue of public policy, and is willing to spend the time necessary, he can hear or read learned, if not eloquent, discussion and debate. He may have to pursue his interest in committee hearings or plow through technical reports prepared for members of Congress or their committees, and he may have to pick his day for attendance. But the opportunity is there—an opportunity too widely neglected by the American people.

The hope of the framers that the legislative process could involve a

[26] We have used the term *Congressional party* similarly to distinguish the organizations of the two major parties within Congress from the party organizations outside of Congress. In England, this distinction is the familiar one between what is called the Parliamentary party and the Constituency party. Professor James Burns and other critics of Congress have sought to distinguish between a Congressional party and a Presidential party within Congress. Within each of the major party organizations in Congress, it is said, one can identify those who look to the President for legislative leadership and those whose legislative behavior indicates a more or less consistent independence, or even opposition, to, the President and his program. The Congressional party or parties, it is argued, are more representative of concurrent majorities composed of states, and/or sections, powerful special interest groups in the several states, regions, or districts. Hence its legislative behavior is characterized as the politics of maneuver, coalition, and compromise, in which state, regional, and local interests are more influential than national interests, and domestic issues more important than those of foreign policy. The Presidential party or parties in Congress, on the other hand, are said to be more representative of the great urban, numerical majorities, as is the President, and hence less dependent on, and less representative of, state, regional, or local interests. By contrast with the politics of maneuver, compromise, or coalition, the Presidential parties are best characterized by the politics of majority rule.

We have commented on this earlier, but would say here again that this ingenious and imaginative analysis has much to commend it. The Presidential and Congressional parties, however, are no less coalitions than other congressional blocs, are no more stable, and although the terms may be used to describe a more or less continuous feature of congressional behavior, their composition varies even within a single Congress as issues, interests, personalities, and events change. See James M. Burns, *op. cit.* See also David B. Truman, *Congressional Party* (New York: Wiley, 1959).

large measure of rational deliberation and debate has by no means wholly failed. Indeed, one may argue that the decline of the great oratory of the past has improved the quality of deliberation and debate. Daniel Webster, in March, 1850, delivered his "Seventh of March Speech," to a Senate chamber so crowded by nonmembers, many of them female, that Senators could find no room to sit. By contrast, Senator George Norris defending the TVA or Brian McMahon arguing for Civilian Control of Atomic Energy may speak to empty seats and galleries and may sound dull and unexciting, but who can say they are less rational or shed less light on the problems under discussion.

Debate in the House of Representatives is severely limited. The very size of the House (435) and the nature of its organization and procedure make limitation essential. A House of Representatives in which debate was unlimited would require a radical change in function and in organization. As matters stand, there are no less than 30 questions or motions on which no debate at all is permitted. No member may speak more than an hour even on those matters which are open to debate on the floor, except with unanimous consent. Most debate on amendments to a pending bill is limited by the 5-minute rule (no member to speak more than 5 minutes). Even under a suspension of the rules, debate on amendments is limited to 40 minutes. No member may speak twice on the same subject without special permission of the House—unless he has moved or introduced the matter under discussion. Discussion must be relevant or germane to the subject under consideration except during general debate in Committee of the Whole House on the State of the Union. Even in Committee of the Whole, debate can be limited under a special rule of the Rules Committee. And of course to speak at all, one must be recognized by the chair. Thus is debate cabined and confined in the House of Representatives.

It is the Senate that provides the great *forum* for unlimited debate. Its basic rules impose no limitation, except by the very difficult process known as "closure." Discussion, moreover, does not have to be relevant or germane to the question at issue. Senators being fond of speaking, some device is necessary if the Senate is to get its work done. So it is customary to fix in advance by unanimous consent the time at which debate will stop and voting begin. This procedure—known in the House of Commons as the "guillotine"—makes it possible to curb the more garrulous members and get a decision on pending legislation.

The Filibuster

Unlimited debate in the Senate leads to a parliamentary maneuver called the "filibuster," by which opponents of a bill or a motion on the floor can delay or kill it by talking the matter to death, that is, by preventing the issue from coming to a vote. It may be used by the majority, but it is more often the weapon of a determined minority. It is most effective at the end of a congressional term, or near the end of a congressional session when Senators are anxious to get home for a rest and for general repair of their political fences and their own frayed nerves. But it can be used at other times.

There have been a number of historic filibusters. In 1863 the filibuster was used against a bill to suspend a writ of habeas corpus. During the closing days of the sixty-fourth Congress—ending March 4, 1917—a body of 12 Senators, "a wilful 12" as President Wilson said, talked to death the President's proposal to meet the German submarine threat by arming American merchant ships and instructing them to shoot if necessary. In the end he armed the ships anyway, under his general powers as chief executive and commander in chief. But the filibuster ran from February 28 until the end of the session on March 4, with members of the "wilful 12" dividing the time and the burden.

Senator Wayne Morse spoke vainly for 22 hours and 26 minutes on April 24, 1953, as one of a group opposing a bill to give the off-shore oil resources to the states. In 1957 Senator Strom Thurmond held the Senate floor for 24 hours and 18 minutes. Senator Paul Douglas spoke for three days against a bill to relax controls over natural gas. In recent years the filibuster has been used or its use threatened by southern Senators to delay or defeat civil rights legislation and in August, 1962, by liberal Democrats to delay but not defeat a bill to grant a private corporation control over the Telstar Space Communications System.

Opposition to the filibuster has alternated between conservatives and liberals, depending on whose "ox was being gored." Conservatives were indignant at the Norris and LaFollette filibuster against armed merchant ships in 1917, and at Wayne Morse in 1947 and 1953 when he filibustered against the Taft Hartley Act and the Tidelands Oil Bill. But the shoe is just as often on the other foot as liberals fight for civil rights legislation against southern Senators who use the filibuster against them.

Demands for Reform

"The filibuster," someone has said, "is like the weather—everybody talks about it but nobody does anything about it." But in 1917 the Senate amended its Rule XXII to provide that, upon the motion of sixteen Senators and a two-thirds vote of Senators present and voting, the pending measure "shall be the unfinished business to the exclusion of all other business until disposed of." And it provided that

> Thereafter no Senator shall be entitled to speak in all more than one hour on the pending measure, the amendments thereto, and motions affecting the same. . . . Except by unanimous consent, no amendments shall be in order after the vote to bring the debate to a close. . . . No dilatory motion . . . shall be in order. Point of order . . . shall be decided without debate.

In 1949 this was changed to require a two-thirds vote of all members, that is, 67 out of 96 instead of, as originally provided, two-thirds of those present and voting. But in 1959 the rule was again liberalized to require a two-thirds vote only of those present and voting.

The record would seem to indicate that the Senate does not like closure. Between 1917 and 1967, 37 petitions for closure had been filed with the Senate. Of these only 7 received the requisite two-thirds vote, and all but one of these occurred before 1928. In spite of almost continuous agitation for a more liberal closure rule, the old rule remains. But the debate on it goes on.

Those who favor a more liberal rule argue that closure will not interfere with free and full debate, since even after closure there would be ample room for debate—an hour for each Senator. Theoretically this would provide for one hundred hours of debate after closure had been voted. The filibuster, moreover, say its critics, permits a minority of Senators, as few as half a dozen, to thwart the will of the majority. Without a more liberal closure rule, they say, the Senate cannot do its work.

Friends of the filibuster who oppose a more liberal closure rule reply to all this by pointing to the language of Jefferson's *Manual of Parliamentary Procedure.* "The rules of the Senate," says the *Manual,* "which allows full freedom of debate are designed for protection of the minority, and this design is part of the ways and work of our Constitution. You cannot remove it without damaging the whole fabric." To this testimony they add that of Alexander Hamilton. "There are particular moments in public affairs when the people, stimulated by some irregular passion or some illicit advantage, or misled by artful misrepresentation of interested men, may call for measures which they themselves will afterward be the most ready to lament and condemn. In these critical moments, how salutary will be the interference of some temperate and respectable body of citizens—in order to check the misguided career . . . until reason, justice, and truth can regain their authority over the public mind?"

In any case, say those who oppose closure, the Senate can under present rules and by unanimous consent close debate by agreeing in advance to vote at a particular time on a particular measure—what in Parliament is called the "guillotine." Moreover, they say, there is nothing to indicate that the Senate is any less efficient than the House in getting through its share of the legislative load. And a free, untrammeled forum is indispensable to a responsible representative republic.

There are theoretical overtones in this ongoing debate over closure that raise again some basic questions about majority rule and minority rights. "Only the establishment of majority closure," said Vice-President Charles Dawes, "will enable the Senate to make itself a properly deliberative body. This is impossible when it must sit idly by and see time needed for deliberation frittered away in frivolous and irrelevant talk indulged in by individuals and minorities for ulterior purposes."

More recently Senator Morse, himself a veteran of several notable filibusters, has said: "Under the filibuster with all its insidious effrontery, the principle of rule by majority is denied the people in the determination of Congressional policy. I do not say the majority is always right, but I do say that under our form of representative government, a minority of Senators should not be permitted, by means of the filibuster, to block legislation favored by the majority." To which Senator Tydings retorted during a filibuster over a Fair Employment Practices bill, "The rule of the majority . . . the rule of votes! Majority to Hades! . . . Let us not fool ourselves with the silly thought that majorities are always right."

Ultimately, no doubt, there will be a more liberal closure rule. The pressure of business in the Senate will require some curtailment of the time-honored principle of unlimited debate. It is unlikely, however, that in the visible future the Senate will agree to what some of the reformers would like—closure by simple majority vote. Whatever may ultimately be agreed to, the Senate, in the meantime, will continue to be the world's freest forum governed only by the principle of *noblesse oblige* and a sense of personal self-restraint.[27]

☆ THE COMMITTEE SYSTEM

"It is not far from the truth to say," wrote Woodrow Wilson, "that Congress in session is Congress on exhibition, while Congress in its committee rooms is Congress at work." Debate on the floor, as everyone knows, is intended more often than not as much for the folks outside and especially for the member's constituents as for his colleagues in Congress. It is in the committee that real discussion and deliberation take place as Congress attempts to "get at the facts" on any proposed bill or resolution.

In his book *Congressional Government,* Woodrow Wilson took a dim view of this, saying that Congress, in becoming a work shop, was sacrificing its role as a talk shop—a Parle–ment. Even more lamentable was the sacrifice of its role as a primary force in public education. And all this had come about, said Wilson, because Congress was leaderless, uninformed, and poorly organized, hobbled by its own rules and by its own committees.[28] It was also Wilson's theory that Congress had not only failed in its more important responsibility as a "deliberative" body, but the volume of business which it had to transact had compelled it to work

[27] Efforts to change Rule XXII to put a curb on the filibuster were again made and again failed in the 89th Congress. Liberals had hoped that the threat of a southern filibuster against the then pending Voting Rights bill might induce the Senate leadership to modify the rule. These hopes were dashed when the Senate Rules Committee rejected the proposal and when no filibuster developed on the Voting Rights bill. See *The New York Times,* March 4, 1965.

[28] "Power is no where concentrated," said Wilson, "it is rather deliberately scattered amongst many small chiefs . . . these petty barons [the committee chairmen] . . . may at will exercise an almost despotic sway within their own shires, and sometimes threaten to convulse even the realm itself."

through committees which, in turn, had deprived both the House and the Senate of any effective leadership.

> On the opening day of a new Congress [James Reston wrote], the President will go to the Hill and define the state of the union in iambic pentameter. He will speak of continents and epochs and define the challenge of change. Then, after partisan applause of the soaring phrases . . . the Chinese Bandits will take over. The vast panorama of the nation in the world will be cut up into little pieces, each committee chairman will vanish into his privileged sanctuary with his special part of the picture and the vast Congressional machine will begin to grind.[29]

There is much to be said for Wilson's criticism (and Reston's commentary), but even they recognized that the volume of business Congress has to do compels some division of labor. In a given session from 8,000 to 10,000 or more bills and resolutions will be introduced. All a Congressman need do to get a bill moving through the mill is to drop it in the hopper by the Speaker's or Vice-President's desk, or hand it to the clerk. Although only a small fraction—5 percent or so—reach the stage of final passage, all must be classified and analyzed if the grain is to be separated from the chaff. Even when this is done, neither the House nor the Senate, acting as a Committee of the Whole, could handle the remaining volume of work.

The first step in the legislative process, therefore, after a bill is introduced is reference to a committee—a prerogative and responsibility of the Speaker in the House and the Vice-President or President pro tem in the Senate. (See Figure 12–2.) Thus the committees "take over" from the beginning. Even in 1789, when the volume of business was small and the House was a body of 65 and the Senate a body of 26, committees were used to consider legislative business. In the beginning every committee was a *select* committee; that is to say, every bill or resolution went to a special committee for consideration. As the volume of business increased, so did the number of these select committees until there were upwards of 350 of them. To bring some order into what threatened to be a chaos of select committees, these were at last grouped according to subject matter, and there was a notable decline in the number of subject areas. In the Thirteenth Congress (1813–1815) there were about 70; in the Twenty-third Congress (1833–1835) they had declined to some 35.

Toward the end of the nineteenth century, standing committees on specialized areas and problems were established; but these, too, multiplied as the government grew. By 1913 there were 61 in the House and 74 in the Senate on as many different subjects. The multiplication of standing committees, like the multiplication of select committees, raised serious questions of manpower if individual members were not to be

---

29 *New York Times*, January 8, 1963. See also Ralph K. Huitt, "The Congressional Committee: A Case Study," *APSR*, vol. 48, pp. 340–365.

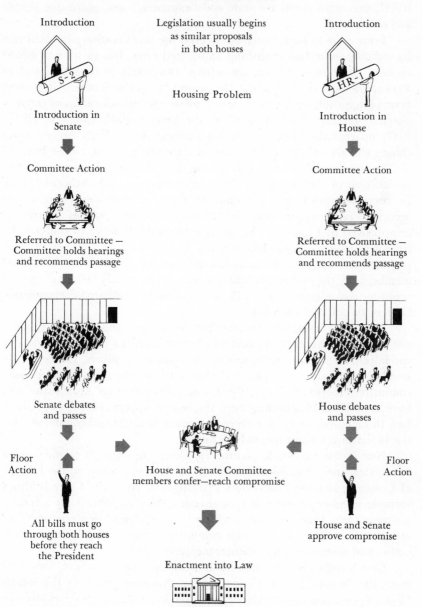

How a Bill Becomes a Law

Introduction

Legislation usually begins
as similar proposals
in both houses

Introduction

Housing Problem

Introduction in
Senate

Introduction in
House

Committee Action

Committee Action

Referred to Committee —
Committee holds hearings
and recommends passage

Referred to Committee —
Committee holds hearings
and recommends passage

Senate debates
and passes

House debates
and passes

Floor
Action

House and Senate Committee
members confer—reach compromise

Floor
Action

All bills must go
through both houses
before they reach
the President

House and Senate
approve compromise

Enactment into Law

President Signs
bill into law

Figure 12–2

overloaded with committee assignments. On the other hand, pressure for multiplication came not only from the volume of business but from the overloaded Congressmen themselves. After all, the more committees, the more chairmanships with all the perquisites that go with them, the more travel, the more funds for staff and "expenses," and patronage simple and unadorned.

From time to time, Congress checked the proliferation of committees by merging some and abolishing antiquated ones. But in spite of efforts to keep the number down, committees continued to multiply, and in 1945 there were still 48 in the House and 22 in the Senate. After many years of agitation for a general overhauling and simplification of congressional organization and procedure, the Seventy-ninth Congress (1945–1947) enacted the Legislative Reorganization Act of 1946. Among other things, the act reduced the number of committees in the House from 48 to 19, and in the Senate, from 38 to 15. The act also increased the jurisdiction of the remaining standing committees and authorized them to "exercise continuous oversight of the executive departments and agencies having responsibility for carrying into effect policies determined or approved by Congress." To increase the independence of Congress by increasing their independent sources of information, the Act of 1946 provided for larger staff assistance for committees and for individual members. By the end of 1952 there were approximately 600 employees of standing committees, about 315 of whom were professional economists, lawyers, or political scientists.

Although the number of standing committees was reduced, this did not reduce the total work load which continued to require progressive specialization among committees and committee members. Hence, as the number of standing committees declined, the number of specialized subcommittees increased. Thus, the House Committee on Agriculture will have as many as 16 subcommittees, the Senate Appropriations Committee had 10 or more. Altogether there are upwards of 200 subcommittees for the 34 standing committees in both houses.

Nor is this the whole picture, for there are some 25 or more *joint committees* including joint committees on Atomic Energy, on the Library of Congress, Defense Production, Printing, and so forth. There is also a variable number of select or special committees, appointed for a special purpose from time to time, and conference committees composed of members from House and Senate committees appointed to iron out difficulties and differences on particular measures.

Committees vary in both size and importance. As to size, they vary from the 50-man House Committee on Appropriations to the 9-man House Committee on Un-American Activities. There is also considerable difference in the power and prestige that attaches to membership, and especially to the chairmanship, of various committees. The Committee on Foreign Relations (on Foreign Affairs in the House) , on Armed Services, on Appropriations, on Banking and Currency, or on Government Operations in both House and Senate—the Committee on Finance in the Senate, the Ways and Means Committee and the Rules Committee in the House—rank high in any order of power and prestige. The chairmen often rival the President and Cabinet members in their influence on public policy.

Because committees are specialized as to subject matter, membership on them is coveted by Congressmen from those states or districts in which policies affecting these subjects are most important. Thus, the Senate Committee on Agriculture and Forestry is likely to be dominated by members from states in which agriculture and lumbering are important industries—states like Minnesota, Michigan, Ohio, Iowa, and Kansas. Interior and Insular Affairs will have members from Montana, New Mexico, Wyoming, Colorado, California, and Arizona, in which problems of grazing, rights on public lands, reclamation and irrigation projects are of particular interest. The House Committee on Merchant Marine and Fisheries will be composed, typically, of members from the states of Washington, Maryland, California, Massachusetts, New York, Louisiana, and others in which these interests are uppermost.

There is, of course, a certain logic in this, since members from these states are presumably most conversant with the problems of these economic interests and hence most competent to legislate for them. By the same token they are likely to be those members of Congress most easily influenced by these special interests to the neglect of the general public interest. It is not easy for a member from a farm state to vote against the wishes of powerful farm organizations. And so it is with other interests. Members of the Committee on Labor and Public Welfare coming from states like Michigan, Ohio, Pennsylvania, New Jersey, Illinois, and New York, where there are powerful labor organizations, are less likely to resist the demands of social agencies and labor leaders than members coming from states or districts where problems of employment and welfare are less urgent.

What is true of Senate committee members is likely to be even more so in the case of Representatives. A Senator representing a whole state is less likely to be dependent for support from a single interest, or a relatively few powerful interests, than is a Representative from a district in which such an interest or interests may be paramount. A Senator is normally subject to more cross pressures, or countervailing forces, than is a Representative. This, plus the security that comes with a longer term, makes for greater independence in a Senator than in a member of the House of Representatives.

This control of important committees by members from areas in which the subject jurisdiction of the committee corresponds to powerful local interests poses important theoretical as well as practical questions. Does this practice result in better legislation or simply legislation more to the liking of certain special interests? Does this aspect of the congressional committee system come close to distorting our principle of representation by area and population into a system of functional or interest representation? And to what extent does it violate a basic canon of justice that a man ought not to be a judge in his own cause? This control of standing committees by special interests has been mitigated somewhat since the 1946 reorganization by the wider jurisdiction of the new standing committees, but the same tendency continues to be manifest, especially in the numerous subcommittees.

Since membership on standing committees is allocated between the major parties, there is always some voice of opposition to the prevailing majority party, which always has a majority of the members of each committee. Moreover, the internal conflicts within the parties which appear in the voting pattern of both the House and the Senate floor also appear in voting within the committees. As a result the majority members on the various committees do not always have their way. It is the presence of internal strains and tensions of this kind that helps to mitigate not only the tyranny of the majority but the supremacy of private or parochial interests over the public interest.

Formally, each House determines the composition of its committees, including the appointment of the chairman. In practice, however, these matters are determined by the party caucuses or conferences through a Committee on Committees, or, in the case of the Democrats in the House of Representatives, the Democratic members of the Ways and Means Committee who serve as a Committee on Committees. In this complex process, however, the influence of the majority and minority leaders and other veteran members of each party is considerable. And, as we have seen, the assignment of committee posts and especially of committee chairmen is a major weapon for enforcing some measure of discipline on the free-wheeling Congressional parties. Rebels can be denied coveted offices or committee posts, and loyalty rewarded with preferred and prestigious assignments.[30]

Seniority

But even this source of party discipline is undermined by customs that virtually dictate to the party leadership *who* among its members gets *what*. Not the least of these customs is the "rule" (effective since 1846 in the Senate and 1910 in the House) that committee assignments—including chairmanships—are made on the basis of seniority. Rank within the

[30] "I attended a caucus at the beginning of this Congress," said the elder Senator La Follette in 1908. "I happened to look at my watch when we went into that caucus. We were in session three minutes and a half. . . . A motion was made that somebody preside. Then a motion was made that whoever presided should appoint a committee on committees, and a motion was made that we adjourn. Nobody said anything but the Senator who made the motion. Then and there the fate of all the legislation of this session was decided. . . . Mr. President, if you will scan the committees of this Senate, you will find that a little handful of men are in domination and control of the great legislative committees of this body, and that they are a very limited number." George H. Haynes, vol. I, *op. cit.*, p. 285.

committee, including the chairmanship, goes to the member of the majority party having the longest uninterrupted service on the particular committee. When a member loses his seat, he loses his seniority, even though he may be returned at the next election. If he moves from one committee to another, he also loses his seniority and must start at the bottom. When, for example, in 1961, Senator Fulbright moved from the Senate Committee on Banking and Finance, where he was chairman, to the Senate Finance Committee, he became low man on the new committee. His prestige, however, was not significantly diminished since, as senior member of the Foreign Relations Committee, he had become its chairman.[31] There are few exceptions to the seniority principle in the assignment of committee posts; but within the subcommittees chairmen and members, at least in the House, are as likely to be selected on the basis of ability, knowledge, and interest as on the basis of seniority. In the Senate, however, even in subcommittee assignments, the seniority principle operates.

The seniority system, say its critics, and they are numerous, flaunts established political principles, undermines party responsibility, and prevents the best use of the best-qualified members of Congress for the most appropriate tasks. The system favors Congressmen and Senators who come from "safe," or one-party, states or districts. Members who do not have to fight for election and hence are more or less automatically returned year after year are able to accumulate greater seniority than those who come from doubtful states or districts where the major parties may alternate in office. By the same token, it is said to favor age versus youth, the past versus the future, the conservatives versus the liberals. In the Democratic party it results in the control of Congress and its committees by conservative southerners, whose voting record more closely resembles that of their more conservative Republican colleagues than of their Democratic colleagues from the North. This has, in fact, been true for a century or more.

> You say you have a usage in the Senate [said Senator Pugh in December, 1859] first, never to displace a Senator from a committee without his own consent; and, second, never to promote anyone over him. . . . Your usage is intolerably bad. . . . It has operated to give to Senators from slave-holding states the chairmanship of every single committee that controls the public business of this government. There is not one exception.[32]

A similar situation prevails today as may be seen from a cursory glance at committee assignments. During the Second Session of the Eighty-ninth Congress (1965–1966), in which Democrats were in a majority in both Houses, the record was as follows: In the House of Repre-

---

[31] Was this done (1) to take Fulbright off a committee having to do with housing and segregation in view of his impending campaign for reelection in Arkansas, or (2) to keep Senator Proxmire of Wisconsin off the Finance Committee—at the behest of the oil and gas industry which feared him and preferred Fulbright as a friend at court?

[32] Quoted from the *Congressional Globe*, December 19, 1859.

TABLE 12–4
House Committee Chairmanships, Ninetieth Congress, First Session

	Number	South and Border	Elsewhere
Total chairmanships	20	14	6
Elected from "safe" districts	13	10	3
(by 70 percent or more majority)			

SOURCE: Adapted from *Congressional Directory*, 90th Congress, First Session, March, 1967.

sentatives, 14 of 20 committee chairmen were from the South. The 6 nonsoutherners came from California (1), Colorado (1), Illinois (1), New York (2), and Pennsylvania (1). In the Senate, 11 of 16 chairmen were from the South. Only Nevada, Washington, Arizona, and Michigan, from outside the South, could boast a committee chairman. Washington had 2. (Table 12–4 shows the House Committee Chairmanships, Ninetieth Congress, First Session.)

Such a system is bound to undermine party discipline and responsibility. "If committee chairmen," says George Galloway, "owe their places not to political parties but to the accident of tenure, then they can follow their own inclinations on legislative matters and disregard the platform pledges and legislative programs of party leaders. A majority of the House may come fresh from the people with a clear mandate for a program of social action, only to see . . . their bills whittled away or pigeonholed by a little group of committee chairmen who were first elected to Congress a generation ago on issues settled or forgotten. . . ." Seniority thus, it is said, makes a shambles of presidential and party leadership alike, since the veterans from safe states can defy both the President and their party.

Opposition to the seniority rule is of long standing. In January, 1923, Senator Medill McCormick, in a letter to Senator Henry Cabot Lodge, Sr., Republican majority leader, suggested "putting aside the rule under which the chairmen of the Senate committees are chosen by reason of their seniority . . . and for no other reason." The system, he said, had resulted in the selection of men "who were unfitted for their posts by reason of extreme old age, or of failing health, or because of great differences of opinion with the majority of their Republican associates. . . . The chairman of a committee acts not in his sole representative capacity but as the representative of the majority of that committee of the majority [party] to which he belongs. . . ." He ought, therefore, argued McCormick, to be a faithful and zealous champion of the policies of his party. Under the seniority rule, committee chairmen were mugwumps or rebels against the very party whose agent they are supposed to be.

The case against seniority rests essentially on three arguments.

1. The seniority principle attaches little or no significance to the special abilities and experience of an individual, but only to the duration of his service. It thus involves a serious misuse of Senate manpower and talent.
2. A committee chairman can never be removed even if the national interest is jeopardized by his continuance in that position. A good many examples of this could be cited.
3. Seniority rewards those states with one-party systems and . . . penalizes states in which two robust and equally matched parties fight it out at the ballot box. Moreover, it rewards with important committee chairmanships, Congressmen hopelessly out of sympathy with their own party leadership. By doing so, it undermines party discipline and makes a mockery of party responsibility.

Friends of the seniority rule are numerous and they are not without arguments for its defense.

1. Seniority insures leadership to men who know the ropes. In the complex pattern of rules, only a veteran can be at home. To give important committee chairmanships to recently elected members is a greater risk than assigning them to veterans. Seniority insures greater knowledge and experience. Younger, less experienced men could easily be victimized by the bureaucrats and lobbyists.[33]

Veteran Congressmen in Congress

Congress	Date	Representatives elected more than once Percent	Senators elected more than once Percent
42nd	1871	53	32
50th	1887	63	45
64th	1915	74	47
74th	1935	77	54
87th	1961	87	66

SOURCE: Samuel Huntington, "Congressional Responses to the Twentieth Century," in David B. Truman (ed.), *The Congress and America's Future* (American Assembly; Englewood Cliffs, N.J.: Prentice-Hall, © 1965), pp. 8–10. Reprinted by permission of Prentice-Hall, Inc.

The increasing number of veterans in Congress has no doubt increased rather than diminished the importance of seniority in committee assignments, although the argument from experience would seem less persuasive.

[33] It is interesting to note that the length of tenure in both the House of Representatives and the Senate has steadily increased through the years. "In 1900," says Professor Samuel Huntington, "only 9 percent of the members of the House . . . had served 5 terms or more and less than 1 percent had served ten terms or more. In 1957, 45 percent of the House had served five terms or more and 14 percent ten terms or more. In 1897, for each representative who had served ten terms or more in the House, there were 34 representatives who had served two terms or less. In 1961, for each ten-termer there were only 1.6 representatives who had served two terms or less." In 1961 nearly 90 percent of the House members were veterans. A similar trend is evident in the Senate as may be seen from the following table.

2. Young men of ability are even now eligible for chairmanships of sub-committees (at least in the House) where a great deal of the committees' most important work is done. But in this capacity they function under the guidance and good counsel of older men as chairmen.
3. Any other system "would involve vote-trading, fierce intraparty rivalry and general dissension." Besides, say the proponents of seniority, there is no effective, certainly no "fool proof," alternative.

Outside observers of Congress have proposed to let the party caucus choose committee chairmen freely from its membership. In this way the party caucus or the Committee on Committees could give due weight to seniority, experience, and knowledge without being hamstrung by the seniority rule.

The issue of seniority goes to the heart of the problem of power and leadership in Congress. The real rulers of both House and Senate are the committee chairmen. The committees over which they preside can amend or rewrite bills, report or pigeonhole bills indefinitely, secure under present rules against any effort to compel them to report; they can initiate measures they desire and bury or emasculate or stall others they do not like. In this power structure the chairman is at the top of the heap. It is he who arranges meetings, selects staff, appoints subcommittees, determines the order for the consideration of bills, holds public hearings or executive sessions, arranges the report on a bill, manages the floor debate, and serves on the conference committee to accommodate differences with the other chamber.

No small part of the so-called "obstructionist" behavior of Congress, according to its critics, arises from these very extensive powers of committee chairmen. Time and again, it is said, important legislation is smothered in committee by hostile chairmen and compliant committeemen, so that Congress is unable even to consider it. The situation is aggravated by the seniority rule, which places in these strategic positions Representatives and Senators who, coming from "safe" districts, are isolated from and indifferent to the dynamic forces of social change that are felt by members from competitive districts who are under constant challenge, but who, because of this, acquire less seniority. Thus, committee chairmen who are "out of step" not only with public opinion in the nation but in their own party are able to delay, mutilate, or "veto" legislation which a majority, given a chance to vote, would support.[34]

[34] This is true not only when the majority party rules with a slender margin. It is also true when the majority party has been returned by a popular vote of landslide proportions. Following the election of 1964, for example, nearly all of the Democratic committee chairmen in the 88th Congress were returned to the 89th, thus continuing in positions of great power conservatives whose interest in President Johnson's "Great Society" was mainly rhetorical. Even where change did occur through death, resignation, or retirement, the successors were of substantially the same views and vintage as their predecessors. For example, Representative Mahon of Texas succeeded the veteran Representative Cannon of Missouri, on Appropriations; Rivers of South Carolina replaced Vinson of Georgia, on Armed Services; Representative Fallon of Maryland replaced Representative Buckley of New York, on Public Works.

It is against this so-called "minority veto system" that the waves of reform alternately rise and fall. Most of the proposed reforms are calculated to mitigate rather than to eliminate the seniority rule, and to facilitate recall legislation from a hostile committee so that it may be debated and voted on by the whole House. Among recent proposals are those to allow the party caucus to choose committee chairmen freely from its membership with due regard to seniority, experience, and expertise in a particular field. Another would return to the Speaker, subject to caucus approval, power to nominate all committee chairmen. Still another would amend the so-called *Discharge Rule* to enable 218 members, as now, or 175 members and the Speaker, to bring any bill out of committee and before the House.

"For far too long," said Representative Richard Bolling, "conservative members of the Democratic party have been able to use their seniority to frustrate the plans and programs of the majority party."[35]

It should be said, of course, that a determined majority of either house of Congress can, if it has a mind to do so, circumvent even the most stubborn committee chairmen. In March, 1965, for example, when the voting rights bill was beginning its journey through the legislative mill, Senate Majority Leader Mansfield moved that the bill be referred to the Judiciary Committee with instructions to report it back by April 9. Senator James Eastland of Mississippi was outraged by a motion, which he described as "unheard of," which would limit his committee hearings to 15 days on a bill that "flies in the face of the Constitution." Other southern Senators joined Eastland in his opposition to the motion, but on a roll call, the Senate approved the motion by a vote of 67 to 13. The Senators, of both parties, who voted *aye* on this motion were not unmindful of the fact that "since 1953, the Senate had sent 122 civil rights bills to the Judiciary Committee, headed by Senator Eastland. Only once, in 1960, and then at the direction of the Senate, had a bill been reported back."[36]

The Rules Committee

Unique among the committees of Congress is the Rules Committee of the House of Representatives. Unlike other committees, it has no subject matter area to limit the scope of its interest and responsibility. It is the traffic cop of the House, able to give the "go" sign to legislation upon which it looks with a friendly eye, or a "slow down," "caution," or even "stop" sign to other bills less to its liking. As in most state legislative assemblies, upwards of 90 percent of the business of the House of Representatives is of a nonpartisan, noncontroversial nature and is disposed of by unanimous consent. From 10 to 15 percent—about a hundred or so

[35] See *The New York Times*, November 16, 1964.
[36] See E. W. Kenworthy, in *The New York Times*, March 19, 1965.

measures each session—are controversial. With the limited time available, some machinery is essential to establish an order of priority among these controversial measures as they come from their subject matter committees. It is this role of legislative traffic cop that the Rules Committee plays. Virtually all important (controversial) legislation, except appropriations, comes to the floor for debate and decision under a special rule of the Rules Committee. From fifty to eighty bills each session will be reported under special rules of this committee. Although it is possible, it is virtually unheard of for the House to reject such special rules.

Just as a traffic cop on a busy corner is not wholly neutral but will give priority to a police car, an ambulance, a fire engine, or the limousine of a VIP, so the Rules Committee is not wholly neutral toward the legislation that comes before it. For the powers of this committee extend not only to the timetable of the House but to other aspects of the legislative process. Among other things, its special rules can require a bill to be rewritten, limit the number and type of amendments that can be offered and specify to what sections of the bill they may apply, and it may even draft and report a bill of its own without reference to a subject matter committee. Moreover, its reports are privileged at any time except when a conference report is being considered or the House is in Committee of the Whole. And in its report, the Rules Committee may limit the time of debate—debate which its own members may dominate—and stipulate how the House shall vote on the measure—that is, by voice or teller. In addition to all this, the Rules Committee normally must pass on all resolutions to establish select committees and may determine their powers of subpoena, travel, and so forth.

The following special rule reported by the Rules Committee on July 25, 1956, will illustrate the sweeping nature of its powers.

> Resolved that upon the adoption of this resolution it shall be in order to move that the House resolve itself into the Committee of the Whole House on the State of the Union for the consideration of the bill (H.R. 11742) to extend and amend laws relating to the provision and improvement of housing. . . . After general debate which shall be confined to the bill, and shall continue not to exceed two hours . . . the bill shall be considered as having been read for amendment. No amendment shall be in order to the said bill except that it shall be in order for any member of the Committee on Banking and Currency to move to strike out all after the enacting clause of House of Representatives 11742 and insert as a substitute the text of the bill House of Representatives 12328 and such substitute shall be in order . . . but shall not be subject to amendment.[37]

It is inevitable that so powerful an engine of legislation should arouse opposition, and efforts to curb its powers have been frequent but largely futile. Everyone admits the necessity for some "traffic control," to expedite the important business of the House. But the critics say that the

[37] *Congressional Record,* July 25, 1956.

Rules Committee as it now operates goes beyond this to serve as a policy committee and almost as a super-legislature. They also question the existing tradition which makes the Rules Committee virtually immune from control by the House itself. It is almost never reversed, its special rules rarely rejected; and, under existing patterns of legislative behavior, it is difficult if not impossible to circumvent the Rules Committee or to use a Discharge Petition against it.

The reply to all this has always been that without something like the Rules Committee, chaos would reign in Congress. Moreover, this committee, or something like it, is necessary to screen legislation, eliminate screwball bills or spite legislation, smother proposals made by members not in earnest but solely to satisfy local constituents, downgrade bills designed to serve special interests, and upgrade those calculated to serve the public interest and general welfare. Besides, it is argued, the House itself can, if it wishes to do so, reject a special rule of the Rules Committee and deal directly with bills as they come from subject matter committees on Calendar Wednesdays, under suspension of the rules, by unanimous consent, or by scrapping the present system for a more flexible scheme. And there is always available against the Rules Committee, as against other committees, the Discharge Rule, by which any bill may be placed on the calendar of the House for debate and discussion if enough members (218) wish this to be done.

Critics reply that decisions concerning so-called screwball legislation, special interest legislation, "strike" bills or "accommodation" proposals ought not to be left to the uncontrolled discretion of a majority of this 15-man committee. As for the other remedies available, they say it is impossible, even dangerous, to propose rejection of a special rule and that Calendar Wednesday, suspension of the rules, unanimous consent, or even a Discharge Petition are unrealistic. On Calendar Wednesdays the chairmen of 19 or 20 committees are called upon in alphabetical order. To proceed with the legislation each reports would defeat any order of priority and make it physically and politically impossible for the House to legislate in an orderly fashion. To suspend the rules to consider a bill requires a two-thirds vote, and is as unrealistic as "unanimous consent" on controversial legislation. Moreover, so long as the seniority rule prevails, it is almost impossible to "reform" the committee from within.

☆ **HEARINGS AND INVESTIGATIONS**

To study and to investigate are certainly among the most important things Congress does. In discussing this aspect of congressional organization and procedure, however, we ought to distinguish between committee investigations and investigating committees. The former is what the standing committees do in their (1) hearings on pending legislation; (2)

their continuous inspection of executive agencies; (3) their review of appointments and treaties proposed by the President; and (4) their inquiries concerning the state of the Union. They are normally concerned with the needs and operation of government agencies, with new problems and proposed new agencies requiring legislative attention, and, in the case of the Senate, with presidential nominations for appointment, the ratification of treaties, and so forth.

Investigating committees, on the other hand, are usually select committees appointed for a special purpose or as subcommittees of other standing committees as, for example, the Subcommittee on Internal Security of the Senate Judiciary Committee. In a few cases such as the House Committee on Un-American Activities, originally a select committee, an investigating committee may become a standing committee.

Hearings before investigating committees tend to be adversary proceedings, a contest between committee members and reluctant or rebellious witnesses. They take on a quasi-judicial aspect rather than being strictly legislative. Investigating committees, moreover, are more likely to employ compulsory processes (subpoena) in bringing witnesses before them. Committee investigations have less of the adversary proceeding about them. Witnesses normally appear by invitation and a more generally friendly atmosphere of mutual respect is likely to prevail.

Congressional investigations are an essential part of the decision-making process, but generalizations about them are risky. They differ profoundly from one another, depending upon the purpose of the investigation, the composition of the committee, and the organization and procedures employed. They may resemble anything from an objective study of an important problem or a grand jury investigation to a cops and robbers melodrama. In atmosphere they will vary from a graduate seminar to a witch hunt. In terms of reference, the basic purpose of the investigation will have an important bearing on the spirit of the inquiry and the procedures employed. A committee appointed to investigate an executive agency and confined by its terms of reference to a narrow field of inquiry will differ from one appointed with the general assignment of investigating "government operations," "un-American activities," or "internal security."

The personnel of the committee will also have an effect upon the conduct of the investigation. A committee intent upon the facts, because investigations are essentially fact-finding projects, with a strong professional staff, will differ sharply from one primarily interested in achieving maximum publicity and in making political capital of the inquiry. In this respect much depends upon the character and ability of the chairman, for it is he who normally picks the staff, determines the procedure to be followed, and sets the tone of the investigation. The political capital that can come to a committee chairman from sensational disclosures of crime, corruption, and subversion is considerable, and an astute chairman will know how to make the most of it.

The built-in and traditional rivalry between Congress and the executive establishment will introduce political motives into almost any congressional investigation of an executive agency. And these motives will be intensified if the Congress and hence the committee and the White House are controlled by rival parties. Republican congressional committees investigating a Democratic administration, or vice versa, are more likely to resemble adversary proceedings than where both the committee and the White House are in the hands of the same party.

Committee Investigations

Each of the standing committees in both the House and the Senate has a multiple job: (1) to make sure that the agency under study is carrying out the purpose for which it was established; (2) to expose inefficiency, corruption, and waste in the administration of the law; and (3) to bring to light new needs and problems, or to seek more effective means for meeting old needs and problems. Senate committees, of course, have the additional responsibility of reviewing major diplomatic and executive appointments, and giving or withholding consent to treaties that may be submitted to them. But in these days, when foreign and domestic policies are so interrelated and when foreign aid programs, tariff and trade policies, defense appropriations, and intercultural relations are so vital to the free world, the House has also assumed a major role in the determination of foreign policy.

The formal organization of this extensive investigative machinery is simple enough. For each major agency or function of government, there is a corresponding standing committee, subcommittee, or joint committee. Specific areas include Agriculture, Forestry, Armed Services, Banking and Currency, Education and Labor, Merchant Marine and Fisheries, Interior and Insular Affairs, Judiciary, Post Office and Civil Service, Public Works, Science and Aeronautics, Veterans' Affairs, and, in the House, a Committee on Foreign Affairs, and, in the Senate, a Committee on Foreign Relations. In both houses there are committees with much more general frames of reference—Appropriations, Finance, or, as it is called in the House, Ways and Means, and Governmental Operations with a permanent Subcommittee on Investigations. Only the House of Representatives has a Standing Committee on Un-American Activities, which probably has the broadest mandate of all, although the Senate Judiciary Committee's Subcommittee on Internal Security comes close. Most standing committees have a number of subcommittees with jurisdiction over limited areas of the total field assigned to the standing committee.

Each committee and subcommittee in the course of its investigations normally holds hearings, some open to the public, others in closed or executive session.[38] Witnesses are heard, including in some cases hundreds of experts or interested individuals from the agencies under investigation, from interest groups, and from the general public. Special reports are made by the committee's own staff or under contract with unofficial research bodies, and by volunteer agencies interested in the problem. The published reports of the committees are often voluminous to the point of being unmanageable, but taken together they contain information and expert testimony on virtually every aspect of government and civilization in the United States.

The effectiveness of this mode of procedure, in giving to the committee and to Congress the information necessary for wise legislation, varies a good deal from committee to committee. Library shelves are burdened with congressional committee reports that are never read and accomplish little more than to gather dust and increase library appropriations. The theory seems to be, "Ye shall know the facts, but the facts shall be sufficient unto themselves." But alternatives to congressional committee investigations have not commended themselves to Congress.

Appraisal of the present system will depend a good deal on what one expects from it. Is it primarily to inform Congress and the public, or is it also a means by which Congress can control or direct executive agencies? Whatever the purpose, the process is difficult and complex.

Take, for example, the problem of congressional information and/or control of the federal budget, a gargantuan instrument that relates government expenditures to revenue. More than any other single document, the federal budget contains information concerning the present and proposed activities of our federal government. It is carefully put together by experts in every major department or agency, reviewed and revised by the Bureau of the Budget in the Executive Office of the President, and presented by the President to the Congress as the administration's program for the ensuing fiscal year. It will involve requests for appropriations and authorizations of more than $100 billion.

What can—or should—Congress do with the budget? No one is completely happy with present methods of congressional analysis and control through its Committees on Appropriations, Senate Finance, and House Ways and Means. Real control is in the subcommittees which study limited parts of the total budget rather than in the whole committee which puts the pieces together, usually accepting the subcommittees' recommendations. Nor is Congress as a whole able to scrutinize the product of committee deliberations under prevailing procedures. Between 1951 and 1966, in over 80 percent of the cases, less than a week

[38] Between 1953 and March, 1966, out of a total of 1,151 committee meetings, 399, or 35 percent, were closed to the public. See *Congressional Quarterly*, No. 20, May 20, 1966.

transpired between the report of the Appropriations Committee to the House and passage of the legislation recommended.[39] The subcommittees hear testimony of experts from the executive agencies, experts in the pay of special interest groups, governors, and other Congressmen and Senators who are by and large partisans of larger, not smaller, appropriations. Those who want reduced appropriations are less likely to appear and less well informed when they do.

Not all hearings are so one-sided. Occasionally a subcommittee will be flooded with mail and testimony, often well organized, not only in opposition to any increase in appropriations, but demanding radical cuts or even the elimination of a particular service or function entirely. Those activities of government lacking a large and articulate clientele, or lacking in projects that can be widely distributed among states and congressional districts, often suffer from underrepresentation at subcommittee hearings. Moreover, the environment of the hearings may be as important as the hearings themselves. A wave of public concern about education, public health, or scientific research may influence committee deliberations more than formal testimony. Sputnik, for example, was a major factor in the striking increase of congressional concern for education and scientific research.

But the job of analyzing and evaluating the testimony is difficult. It is to make this independent analysis and evaluation that Congress has provided professional staff assistance for its committees. And it is to assist in analyzing and controlling federal expenditures that the General Accounting Office was established in 1921 as an agency of Congress. Yet most of the committees complain that, confronted with the superior resources of the executive agencies and private interest groups, they are understaffed. What committees probably need, however, is not more staff but more effective and objective use of the staff now generously provided. Yet the cry for more help is constantly heard. "Congress," writes a recent chief of staff, for the Senate Committee on Banking and Currency, "does not now have access to nearly as much analytical data about the budget as does the Executive. . . . Even the Bureau of the Budget, which can acquire more information on programs for expenditures than any other governmental body, does not have sufficient staff . . . to exercise control except in terms of lump sums. . . ."

What we have said about the hearings of appropriations committees is more or less true of other standing committee investigations. The process is cumbersome and even clumsy. The appointment of committee chairmen on the basis of seniority, the partisan bias, plus the interest of committee members in the projects or activities under investigation, can and do distort the results. A further factor of distortion lies in the selec-

---

[39] See Richard R. Fenno, Jr., *The Power of the Purse: Appropriations Politics in Congress* (Boston: Little, Brown, 1966), p. 418. See also Aaron Wildavsky, *The Politics of the Budgetary Process* (Boston: Little, Brown, 1964).

tion of witnesses to support legislation already determined upon by the chairman and a majority of his committee. "If the committee chairman or other influential committee members . . ." writes Professor Cohen, "are already committed to the passage of a bill even prior to the hearings . . . then one of the major tasks of the staff is the delicate one of slanting the hearing in such a way that a previous commitment on a bill would be made to appear as a decision reached by rational detached deliberation. . . . If the previous commitment is to defeat or limit the proposal, the slanting of the hearing can be arranged in the other direction."[40]

Occasionally a hearing seems to have no other purpose than to exalt the chairman, give him national publicity beyond anything he might otherwise achieve. It thus becomes part of a more or less well-laid plan of political promotion. Or it can be used to allow representatives of certain pressure groups to reach headlines not otherwise available—as part of their general program of promotion and propaganda. Present procedures can also impose an almost impossible burden on executive agencies. Cabell Philips in *The New York Times*, February 15, 1959, described the anguish of "cabinet officers and other high functionaries of government . . . trooping in procession to Capitol Hill where . . . feeling like heretics called before the Inquisition . . . they are called on to account for their stewardship and to justify the program and policies they project for the year ahead." Day after day and week after week the Secretary for Defense or the Secretary of State will be called to testify before committees of Congress, whose chairmen are not always friendly.

There is, of course, no easy answer to all this. Government is not an easy business. Eternal vigilance is the price of liberty for Congress as for the individual citizen. A continuing review of the complex process of government is indispensable whether this is done by a Committee on Government Operations with a more or less roving commission, by subject matter committees corresponding roughly to the departments and agencies, or by investigating committees on special or general assignment.

Investigating Committees

As we have said, investigating committees may be distinguished from committee investigations. They are usually in the nature of adversary proceedings, summon witnesses under compulsion, and are more likely to be concerned with charges of inefficiency, corruption, crime, sedition and subversion, or other such breaches of the moral or legal code than they are with the normal needs and functions of government agencies. Special inquiries of one kind or another by congressional and state legislature

40 Professor Julius Cohen, 37 *Minnesota Law Review*, 34 (1952).

investigating committees have become almost a major industry—certainly a major factor in the congressional work load. During the 10-year period before World War II, there were 146 such investigations, but in the Eighty-second Congress alone (1951–1952) there were 236.

Congressional investigations have cut a wide swath and have embraced nearly every aspect of American government and life. According to George Galloway of the Legislative Reference Service, "almost as many investigations have been conducted by each Congress since 1950 as were carried on in the whole 19th century." Literally hundreds of problems have been subjected to congressional investigations during this period. Something of their nature and variety can be indicated by the following sample of topics studied between 1950 and 1967. In addition to more or less continuous investigations of so-called Un-American activities, there have been broad-scale inquiries into lobbying activities, the recall of General MacArthur, organized crime and labor racketeering, the Dixon-Yates contract fraud, corrupt practices and campaign expenditures, TV quiz shows, the munitions lobby, the U-2 flight and the Summit Conference, drug prices, the TFX Plane contract, government stockpiling of strategic materials, Bobby Baker's influence peddling while he was Secretary to the Senate Majority, Billie Sol Estes and his financial manipulations, economic concentration, automobile safety standards, birth control, water and air pollution, and urban development problems. Congressional investigations serve not only to inform Congress but the general public on important matters of which it may otherwise be only dimly aware. "The modern legislative committee," says one authority, "has become one of the most potent forces in American political life . . . in shaping public attitudes and influencing governmental and private action . . . during the past two decades."[41]

Although their number has multiplied and the scope of their inquiries has greatly expanded, congressional investigating committees are not new. As early as March, 1792, the House appointed a select committee to "inquire into the failure of the expedition under General St. Clair" against certain Indian tribes in the Ohio and Indiana wilderness. This first of all investigating committees raised many of the tough questions concerning their proper scope and methods that are still with us. How far, for example, may one branch of government (the Congress) go in prosecuting a full-fledged investigation of matters falling under the jurisdiction of another coordinate branch of government? Is a congressional investigation a proper way to determine questions of personal guilt or liability, or are such questions more appropriate for a grand jury or a court of law? How far can a congressional committee go in demanding from the President or the heads of executive agencies official reports,

---

[41] See Thomas Emerson and David Haber, *Political and Civil Rights in the United States* (Buffalo, N.Y.: Dennis, 1952). Quoted in *Congress and the Nation, 1945–1964* (Washington, D.C.: Congressional Quarterly Service, 1965), p. 1679.

documents, and other papers bearing on the subject under investigation? May the executive branch refuse to divulge information requested by a committee of Congress? May Congress request heads of executive departments to be present in the House or Senate when an investigating committee's report is to be considered? What rules of procedure should govern the calling and interrogation of witnesses?

Some of these questions were answered by President Washington's advisors in 1792 in terms that are still valid. Congress may conduct investigations of matters under the jurisdiction of the executive branch. Congress may call for relevant papers and documents. "The Executive ought to communicate such papers as the public good will permit and ought to refuse those the disclosure of which would endanger the public." Washington's advisors also told him that "neither the committee nor the House had a right to call on the Head of a department responsible to the President alone." The proper procedure, they said, was for the chairman to move the House to address the President. Department heads are responsible to the President and not to the Congress, and may be interrogated by congressional committees only with the President's permission.

For a hundred years or more after the St. Clair inquiry, congressional investigations were used primarily to investigate civil and military operations of the government. For the most part, they have been modest, even a bit dull and pedestrian, but some have generated bitter controversy and have yielded sensational headlines. After the outbreak of the Civil War, both House and Senate joined in establishing a Joint Committee "to inquire into the conduct of the War"—a committee that rode on Lincoln's back and made life even more miserable for him than it might otherwise have been during four long years.

The aftermath of the Civil War and the generally low level of both public and private morality during the Gilded Age brought many investigations. In 1876 a House Select Committee was set up to investigate the financial relations of Jay Cooke and Company, a banking firm, and a real estate pool in the District of Columbia. The company had financed much of the railroad building of the 1860s and 1870s, but had filed for bankruptcy, partly due to a European depression which caused withdrawal of funds from it. The manager of the pool, one Hallett Kilbourn, was subpoenaed, but refused to answer any questions or produce any requested documents on the ground that the House had no constitutional authority "to investigate private business in which nobody but me and my customers have any concern." After Kilbourn had been in jail for several weeks by order of the House, the controversy reached the Supreme Court in the case of *Kilbourn* v. *Thompson* (1880) in which the Court held that Kilbourn's imprisonment by Congress was unlawful. "The investigating function and contempt powers of Congress," said Justice Miller for the Court ". . . are subject to the limitations of the Constitution."[42] Moreover, matters which are more properly settled by the courts cannot be resolved by a congressional committee. This discussion is notable for imposing rather strict limits on the scope and powers of congressional investigating committees. According to Justice Field, speaking in 1887, "This case will stand for all time as a bulwark against the invasion of the right of the citizen to protection in his private affairs against the unlimited scrutiny of investigation by a Congressional committee."[43]

Undeterred by this temporary check, investigating committees continued to multiply. In 1892 both Houses investigated the use of Pinkerton detectives for strikebreaking, and in 1912, as an aftermath of the Progressive victories of 1910, came the sensational investigation of "The Money Trust." Nearly every leading financier in the country came under the withering examination of Samuel Untermeyer, a New York lawyer serving as special counsel to the committee, as he spelled out the concentration of economic power then under way.

One of the most sensational of all congressional investigations was launched in 1924 when the Senate directed its Committee on Public Lands to investigate the disposition of the naval oil reserves at Teapot Dome, Wyoming, and Elk Hills, California. It was revealed that these reserves, set aside for the Navy under Presidents Taft and Wilson, had been secretly leased to private oil operators by the Secretary of the Interior and the Secretary of the Navy in the Harding Cabinet. Under the direction of Senator Thomas Walsh of Montana, the Teapot Dome investigation took on many aspects of an old-time melodrama. There were bribes in the form of "loans," delivered mysteriously in a little black bag, secret meetings of conspirators, an alignment of good guys and bad guys that would do credit to a TV western. But the ending failed to fit the formula. Not all the bad guys were punished. While the Secretary of the Interior was convicted of bribery and sentenced to prison, the men who bribed him were acquitted on that charge and merely fined and imprisoned briefly for contempt of court.

Committees that cut so wide and dig so deep are bound to generate opposition. Commenting on the investigations of 1923–1924, the distinguished law dean, J. H. Wigmore, an outstanding authority on the law of evidence, referred to

> The senatorial debauch of investigations poking into political garbage
> cans and dragging the sewers of political intrigue, filled the winter of

42 "The House of Representatives," said the Court, "is not the final judge of its own power and privileges in cases in which the rights and liberties of the subject are concerned. . . . Its power to imprison for contempt . . . is limited to the cases expressly provided for in the Constitution, or to cases where the power is necessarily implied. . . . We must therefore hold . . . that the resolution of the House of Representatives finding Mr. Kilbourn guilty of contempt . . . [is] not conclusive, and in fact [is] no justification, because . . . the House was without authority in the matter."

43 In re: *Pacific Railway Commission,* 32 Fed. 241.

1923–1924 with a stench that has not yet passed away. Instead of employing the Constitutional, manly, fair procedures of impeachment, the Senate flung self-respect and fairness to the winds. As a prosecutor, the Senate presented a spectacle which cannot even be dignified by a comparison with the persecutive scoldings of Coke, Scroggs, and Jeffreys, but fell rather in popular estimate to the level of professional searchers of the municipal dunghills.

Without defending everything these investigating committees have done, one must say that the good Dean's outburst itself is scarcely the language of cool impartiality that most becomes exponents of the rule of law.

If the investigations of the 1920s revealed a carnival of political corruption, the investigations of the New Deal period were a kind of sociological cyclorama. There were investigations of the Stock Exchange, "unfair labor practices," organized lobbying, railroad reorganization and finance, public utility holding companies, the munitions industry and mass communications. Some of these resulted in important legislation including the National Industrial Recovery Act, the National Labor Relations Act, the Securities Exchange Act, the Public Utility Holding Company Act, amendments to the Federal Communications Act, and, ultimately in 1946, a Federal Regulation of Lobbying Act. Others, as it were, died on the vine.

Although investigating committees have cut a wide swath in more recent days, the most sensational and highly publicized have had to do with "un-American activities," "internal security," and Communist infiltration and subversion. Three committees have been mainly responsible for these investigations: the House Committee on Un-American Activities, the Permanent Sub-Committee of Investigations of the Committee on Governmental Operations, and the Subcommittee on Internal Security of the Senate Committee on the Judiciary. No other committees in our history have raised so much alarm, aroused so much controversy, or posed so many difficult questions.

In the search for Communist infiltration and subversion, the committees, their counsel and special staff of investigators, cast a wide net. Hollywood writers and actors have been subpoenaed and interrogated concerning un-American influences in the motion picture industry. Teachers, preachers, lawyers, doctors, merchants, and civil servants have been called; no profession or occupation has been immune from scrutiny and subpoena. When, for any reason, any witness declined to "cooperate" by answering questions, he ran the risk of arrest and imprisonment for being in contempt of the committee. The hearings themselves often resembled grand jury investigations rather than congressional hearings. Not infrequently the chairman of the committee was the only member present to conduct the hearing. Surrounded by TV and newsreel cameras and newspaper reporters, and with crowds of excited partisans and curiosity seekers looking on, the proceedings were not calculated to create the atmosphere of a calm judicious inquiry.

Nor is the interrogation itself always conducted in an impartial and objective manner. Questions are not only leading and tendentious but sometimes seriously prejudicial to the witness by none too subtle imputations of guilt. In his inquiry concerning the loyalty of a military dentist at Camp Kilmer, for example, Senator McCarthy implied that Brigadier General Zwicker, Commanding Officer of the Post, was indifferent to Communist infiltration and subversion. And because the General expressed confidence in the officers of his command, Senator McCarthy accused him of being "unfit to wear that uniform." It was in this final confrontation with Secretary of the Army Robert Stevens in 1954 that Senator McCarthy overreached himself and brought down the official censure of the Senate.

Commenting on the hearings, a leading authority has said:

> Disgusting the hearings often were; trivial they were not; for much was at
> stake . . . More than the individual fate of Senator McCarthy, [although]
> he was . . . the symbol and focus of the proceedings. . . . Utilizing the
> Senate's investigative power . . . he was openly threatening to upset the
> constitutional balance of power—to destroy the President's effective control
> of the Executive branch. . . . This is why a discussion of the investigative
> powers *vis à vis* the doctrine of separation of powers under the Constitution
> is no idle or academic exercise. Rather these concepts are the very stuff of
> today's political strife. . . .[44]

Not everyone will agree with this evaluation of the so-called era of McCarthyism. But no one can be indifferent to the problems raised by the use and the abuse of the investigative power of Congress under our Constitution.

No very firm conclusions can be offered about the proper scope and method of congressional investigations. A few benchmarks, however, may be indicated. The scope of the investigative power may not extend to every aspect of American life, but very nearly so. The limitations that have been imposed by Congress and the courts are mainly about the definition of the nature and purpose of the investigation, and the methods or procedures employed by investigating committees. It is well established that investigating committees may compel persons to appear and answer proper questions and may under some circumstances punish those who refuse to do so for contempt of the Congress. How far this power extends to officers of the executive or judicial branches of the government is, however, by no means clear.

In *Kilbourn* v. *Thompson*[45] the Supreme Court held that neither

[44] Telford Taylor, *Grand Inquest: The Story of Congressional Investigations* (New York: Simon and Schuster, 1955).

[45] 103 U.S. 168 (1881).

house of Congress has "a general power" to investigate the private affairs of citizens. Its power is limited to matters over which it has legislative jurisdiction under the Constitution. And if the matter concerns an offense for which relief or redress (or punishment) can be had only by a judicial process, it is beyond the power of a committee of Congress. That is to say, neither Congress nor its committees are proper agencies to determine the guilt or innocence of persons accused of crime. In most cases where the investigative power, that is, the power to compel testimony, has been challenged, the Courts have upheld the power of Congress.[46]

Besides the Kilbourn case, however, there are a few cases where the Court has imposed limits. In *Rumely* v. *United States,* decided in 1952, refusal to supply information to a committee investigating lobbying was upheld when the information demanded was not clearly within the scope of the information required by the law under which the committee acted. In *Watkins* v. *United States,* in 1957, the Court said, "Broad as is this power of inquiry, it is not unlimited. There is no general authority to expose the affairs of individuals without justification in terms of the functions of the Congress." Congress must "spell out" the committee's jurisdiction and the purpose of its investigation with sufficient particularity, so that a witness knows the nature and scope of the inquiry. The definition of "un-American activities" in the authorizing resolution of 1938, said the Court, does not meet this test. "Who," asked the Court, "can define the meaning of un-American?"

For the most part, however, the Court has taken an indulgent view of the investigating powers of Congress. In *McGrain* v. *Daugherty* in 1927 the Court upheld the investigating powers of congressional committees in language indicating little or no restraint. Even the limitation imposed in *Watkins* v. *United States* was very strictly construed in the case of *Barenblatt* v. *United States,* decided in 1959.[47]

In general the Supreme Court, no less than Congress itself, recognizes the importance of the investigative power. Without it, Congress and state legislatures would be deprived of a major means of acquiring indispensable information. It is a major weapon against incompetence, inefficiency, immorality, corruption, and subversion in the government itself. And as a means of arousing and educating an often apathetic public, congressional investigations can be extraordinarily effective.

But the excesses of some committees and their chairmen have shocked the public conscience and have led to numerous proposals for reform. One of these has been the delegation of more investigations to outside nonpartisan agencies or to special bodies acting under judicial

---

[46] *Anderson* v. *Dennes,* 1821; *McGrain* v. *Daugherty,* 1927; *Sinclair* v. *United States,* 1929.

[47] See *McGrain* v. *Daugherty,* 273 U.S. 135, *Watkins* v. *United States,* 354 U.S. 178, and *Barenblatt* v. *United States,* 360 U.S. 109.

auspices. The Carnegie, Rockefeller, and Ford Foundations, the Twentieth Century Fund, the National Bureau of Economic Research, the Social Science Research Council, the Brookings Institution, and the National Science Foundation are the kind of agencies that might be used. Even a Presidential Commission, or something comparable to an English Royal Commission, it has been suggested, would produce better results for certain purposes than a congressional investigating committee. It has also been suggested that *ad hoc* special investigating committees be abolished, leaving all congressional investigations under subcommittees of the regular standing committees of Congress. The mandate of present standing committees, it is argued, is already sufficiently broad to embrace virtually every type of legitimate congressional inquiry.

The most frequent proposal for reform would entail a somewhat stricter code of committee procedures, either as a voluntary act by each committee or as an act of legislation. Such a code would prohibit one-man hearings, impose stricter control on TV and radio publicity, would require disclosure of the nature and source of charges against a witness, and allow for confrontation of the accused and his accuser.

"At least," says Professor Chafee, "Committee proceedings should have the formality prevailing on the floor of the House and of the Senate. It is high time to throw out the klieg lights, the cameras, and the TV. They hinder calm determination of the fate of the accused person just as much as they would in a courtroom, and they destroy the dignity which ought to be displayed by the chosen representatives of the American people, sitting to discharge a grave public duty."[48] Perhaps an extension of the Administrative Procedures Act to congressional investigations would suffice. Perhaps Congress needs only to paraphrase the present language of the Sixth Amendment to say: "In all official investigations the witness shall enjoy the right (1) to a speedy and public hearing; (2) to be informed of the nature and cause of the inquiry; (3) to be confronted with witnesses against him; (4) to have compulsory process for obtaining witnesses in his favor; and (5) to have the assistance of counsel for his defense." As matters now stand, the major defenses of an individual witness against being compelled to testify before congressional committees are his right to counsel and his right to plead the Fifth Amendment against self-incrimination. The latter plea, however, may do him more harm than would the testimony.

---

[48] See his introduction to A. Barth, *The Loyalty of Free Men* (New York: Viking Press, 1951).

☆ THE PRESIDENTIAL OFFICE

In his book *The American Commonwealth,* the English scholar and diplomat James Bryce devoted a chapter to the problem of "Why Great Men Are Not Chosen President." The reasons, he said, were many and complex, but would include (1) the general downgrading of government in the United States, so that men of outstanding ability preferred to devote their talents to business or the learned professions; (2) the preference of nominating conventions for "safe" candidates, men who are not "controversial," rather than for strong-willed leaders of public opinion; (3) the exclusion of men of power and distinction because of religious, ethnic, racial, or national prejudice; (4) the selection of candidates of unalloyed party loyalty from populous, "doubtful" states; and (5) the tendency of party leaders to prefer good candidates to great men—usually assuming the two to be mutually exclusive. These and other reasons were repeated in laborious recitation by historians and political scientists for two generations or more. The obvious answer to Mr. Bryce of course is that great men are in fact elected to the Presidency. If it seems querulous to say so, nevertheless it should be said that the number of great men who have served as President will probably equal the number of great prime ministers during the same period. Indeed, a compatriot of Lord Bryce, the late Professor Harold Laski, in 1940, classified eleven of the thirty-one Presidents up to that time as "extraordinary men"—as high or higher a proportion as among English prime ministers.[1]

In 1948, fifty-five distinguished American historians and political

[1] See Harold Laski, *The American Presidency* (New York: Harper & Row, 1940).

scientists were asked to "rate" American Presidents as "great," "near-great," "average," "below average," and "failures." The results of this poll, in order of greatness,[2] are summarized below:

GREAT PRESIDENTS

1. Abraham Lincoln
2. George Washington
3. Franklin D. Roosevelt
4. Woodrow Wilson
5. Thomas Jefferson
6. Andrew Jackson

NEAR-GREAT PRESIDENTS

7. Theodore Roosevelt
8. Grover Cleveland
9. John Adams
10. James K. Polk

AVERAGE PRESIDENTS

11. John Q. Adams
12. James Monroe
13. Rutherford B. Hayes
14. James Madison
15. Martin Van Buren
16. William Howard Taft
17. Chester A. Arthur
18. William McKinley
19. Andrew Johnson
20. Herbert Hoover
21. Benjamin Harrison

BELOW AVERAGE PRESIDENTS

22. John Tyler
23. Calvin Coolidge
24. Millard Fillmore
25. Zachary Taylor
26. James Buchanan
27. Franklin Pierce

FAILURES AS PRESIDENTS

28. Ulysses S. Grant
29. Warren G. Harding

If to enjoy the esteem of one's own countrymen be a sign of greatness, then more than a third of these Presidents may be called great or at least near-great. But by what other standard can they be measured? According to Professor Allan Nevins, "the cardinal quality to be demanded is . . . imaginative leadership." A great President, or at least a "good" President, says George Kerman, causes people to reflect and to "ponder American society." Others call for "creative innovation," "unifier of the nation," "Ability to see into the future." "He doesn't have to be a father image," says Professor Kenneth Stampp, "but he has to be the kind of person . . . a majority of the American people have confidence in."[3] Obviously no single quality can account for the greatness of a Washington, an Andrew Jackson, an Abraham Lincoln, and a Woodrow

[2] See *Life Magazine,* November 1, 1948. See also A. M. Schlesinger, Sr., *Paths to the Present* (New York: Macmillan, 1949) , pp. 95–111.

Presidents William Henry Harrison, James A. Garfield, and Harry Truman were not included. The first two died after less than six months of service. Mr. Truman was excluded because his record was incomplete at the time of the poll. It is, of course, too early to appraise Presidents Eisenhower, Kennedy, and Johnson in these terms.

[3] These comments were solicited at a meeting of the American Historical Association and reported in *The New York Times,* January 3, 1960.

Wilson. In personality and behavior, the great and near-great Presidents, like others, have been as various as any group of men picked at random. Washington has been described as "austere"—showing an "icy aloofness, a quasi-regal character." Jackson, it is said, was "irascible" or "tempestuous." Franklin Roosevelt had about him an "airy sophistication." Woodrow Wilson was said to be "aloof," "suspicious," "reserved," and Lincoln was "somber," "witty," "homely," and "common." John Kennedy was called an "intellectual," and Lyndon Johnson an "anti-intellectual."

This easy indulgence in adjectives is a common manner of speaking where great men are concerned. Thus, while Woodrow Wilson seemed "arrogant" to some, to many others he was "affable," "most kindly, courteous, considerate." To his friends Jackson was "stalwart," "strong," "faithful"—to his enemies he was an "ignorant, reckless, vain, malignant tyrant." Even Washington and Lincoln were described by critics in less than complimentary terms. Tom Paine, in a pamphlet entitled "Letter to George Washington," in 1796, spoke of his "meanness and ingratitude" and described him as an "apostate or an imposter," "treacherous in private friendship . . . and a hypocrite in public life." Lincoln was ridiculed as "ignorant and vulgar," described as an "ape," and denounced as a "tyrant."[4]

All such terms tell us more about those who use them than about the men they purport to describe. Many people perceive Presidents, as they perceive other persons and events, from preconceived models of magnanimity or malignancy—models having their roots in interest, ignorance, or self-deception. The search for saints and saviors on the one hand, and for symbols of sin and satanism on the other, goes on in most of us, however unaware we may be of the process. Hence to zealous partisans the same President can appear to have different, if not wholly contradictory, traits of character depending on their party loyalties and frames of reference. This is doubly true of a President's contemporaries. In the appraisal of Presidents, as in the taste and bouquet of vintage wines— time tends to soften the sharp corners, purge the bitterness, and lend a luster that more often than not conceals the man within the myth. Washington, Lincoln, Jefferson have passed through this process of historic transmutation—Jackson is on his way—and Woodrow Wilson and Franklin Roosevelt lag behind. Perhaps this explains why great

[4] Quoted by Henry Wriston, "The Age of Revolution," *Foreign Affairs*, July, 1961, p. 537. See for other terms used above: John D. Hicks, *A Short History of American Democracy* (Boston: Houghton Mifflin, 1943); Claude G. Bowers, *Jefferson and Hamilton* (Boston: Houghton Mifflin, 1929); and also his *Party Battles of the Jackson Period* (Boston: Houghton Mifflin, 1922); Peter H. Odegard and E. Allen Helms, *American Politics: A Study in Political Dynamics* (2d ed.; New York: Harper & Row, 1947); Leonard D. White, *The Federalist* (New York: Macmillan, 1948); James Hart, *The American Presidency in Action, 1789; A Study in Constitutional History* (New York: Macmillan, 1948); Earl Latham (ed.), *The Philosophy and Politics of Woodrow Wilson* (Chicago: University of Chicago Press, 1958).

monuments to the first three and an heroic equestrian statue of the fourth are to be seen in Washington, while committees agitate for similar memorials of the other two among the great and Theodore Roosevelt among the near-great. Perhaps too it explains why twenty-nine states have named counties for Washington, twenty-six for Jefferson, twenty-four for Jackson—and only twelve for the runner-up, John Adams.[5] Herbert Hoover and Harry Truman are "too much with us" still to warrant appraisal, let alone canonization, although John Kennedy's tragic death has encouraged widespread efforts to appraise his years in office well before time has been able to lend appropriate perspective.

For some, as for Washington and Lincoln, political canonization comes quickly. The editor of the English satirical magazine *Punch,* who had held Lincoln up to ridicule and contempt, almost instantly recanted on hearing of his death. He wrote:

> Beside this corpse that bears for winding sheet
> The Stars and Stripes he lived to rear anew
> Between the mourners at his head and feet,
> Say, scurrile jester, is there room for you?
>
> Yes, he had lived to shame me from my sneer,
> To lame my pencil and confute my pen;
> To make me own this kind of print's peer,
> This rail-splitter a true-born king of men.[6]

"Objective" descriptions of what Americans look for in their Presidents are neither numerous nor very rewarding. To say he must be an "innovator," a "unifier," or a "seer" who can read the future tells little. When pollsters and behavioral analysts tell us that voters express a preference for "integrity," "honesty," "sense of duty," "sincere," "generally a good man"—more frequently than for any other personal traits—we come closer to the heart of the matter. Such reports in summary would describe an ideal President as "warm and decisive," with "an interesting personality," one who can "inspire confidence and command admiration," one who "has overcome personal difficulties (or handicaps)," with a "sense of humor," "free of all taint of sin"—although not "perfect," yet a "happy family man" who has "proved his capacity to get things done" and who is not "primarily a partisan politician."[7] No such paragon has

---

[5] See A. M. Schlesinger, Sr., *op. cit.* p. 291. Another "objective" evidence of greatness may be selection for the Hall of Fame at New York University—which now includes ten Presidents among its seventy-one notables (Washington, Lincoln, Jefferson, Jackson, Madison, John Adams, Monroe, John Quincy Adams, Cleveland, and even Ulysses S. Grant).

[6] See John Hicks, *op. cit.,* p. 407. Also see Lloyd Lewis, *Myths After Lincoln* (New York: Harcourt, Brace & World, 1929); and Roy P. Basler, *Enduring Lincoln* (Urbana: University of Illinois Press, 1959).

[7] See Eugene Burdick, "The Perfect President," in *This Week Magazine,* January 1, 1956.

ever occupied the White House, and it is doubtful that if one were to appear he would find the job of President rewarding or even tolerable. Certainly the American people have not insisted on any such model in the men they have elected to the Presidency, and lack of a good many of these traits has proved no great handicap to most aspirants for the job. All of these traits, we are told, add up to a "Father Image," a "Guardian, an Intimate Friend"—as the ideal President most Americans prefer. One can point to such phrases as "the father of his country" to describe Washington, or "father Abraham" as Lincoln was often called, as giving verisimilitude to this theory. Lloyd Lewis in his book *Myths After Lincoln* tells of the sense of personal loss felt by millions of Americans on hearing of Lincoln's death, and other millions who mourned the passing of Franklin Roosevelt as though he were the head of a great family. One small child, on being told of F.D.R.'s death, is said to have asked, "Who then will 'care' for us now?"

The universal sense of sorrow, outrage, and personal loss that followed the assassination of President Kennedy in November, 1963, has never been probed in depth or even adequately described. He had been the sign and symbol of a new generation of world leaders and of a new promise in American politics. To be cut down so early in his career was tragedy of a classic order.

No doubt some Presidents fulfill this Father Image. Some have that mystical quality called "charisma," once defined as a secular halo for heroes. But surely neither of these terms could describe Thomas Jefferson, Andrew Jackson, or Woodrow Wilson. It would seem therefore that something more is involved than a catalogue of Victorian virtues or Freudian "complexes." Studies of voter preferences among presidential traits during election campaigns are more likely to reveal what the voter looks for in a candidate, not what he regards as qualities of greatness in a President. Or they may be simply copybook attributes he has been told identify not only the ideal candidate but the preferences of all good citizens. Ideal candidates are not synonymous with ideal Presidents–nor are ideal Presidents synonymous with great Presidents.

The Presidency is of course greater than both the Office of the President and the individual Presidents who occupy the office. For the Presidency has mysteries and a mystique as profound and as important as "the mystery which doth surround a King." What part, if any, of the British monarch's royal prerogatives devolved upon the President one cannot and probably ought not to say or to argue. Yet it is obvious that the American Presidency by intention and design combines many features of the English Crown as it was known to the framers. If it be true that the English queen reigns but does not govern, it may well be argued that the American President does both. "The truth is," wrote Henry Jones Ford in 1898, "that in the Presidential Office . . . American democracy has revived the oldest political institution of the race, the elected kingship. . . ."[8]

The President as a Symbol

It is in the President—as in the Constitution itself—that the American people find themselves reflected, sometimes at twice or more their normal size, sometimes at less—sometimes in all their highest hopes, and sometimes in their less exalted moods of disillusionment and despair. In the Presidency they find not unity in the sense of agreement upon policy, but unity in a common cause above particular policies—a unity that agrees to disagree and to abide, for the time at least, by the result. It was in this sense that Jefferson could say in his first inaugural: "We are all Federalists, we are all Republicans." This is the *mythos* of the Presidency and of every President from Washington to Lyndon Johnson. Only as he operates within this *mythos* can we be sure that however bitter the battle over men and measures—the writ agreed upon even by a bare majority will serve until recalled.

The Presidency is the channel through which the will and power of the nation most clearly flows. This may be seen in the fact that his signature sets the final seal of approval upon the laws of Congress, and to withhold it will, save on rare occasions, kill the act. It is in his name that the official writs of all federal courts, including the Supreme Court, are issued. And his signature alone may set in motion vast armies of civil and military servants of the State on missions as far-flung and as various as human imagination can conceive. The President is the fount of honor and of mercy in his power to make appointments to high office, to award titles of honor or distinction, and to pardon for crimes committed against the United States. The Presidency, like the monarchy in England, is also a fount of fashion, culture, and taste. Does the President attend the opera or the symphony? Is he a jazz buff? Is he a patron of the arts, and does his taste include contemporary painting and modern music? Is the President's wife a collector? Is he? Does he say of the work of Picasso, "it's grand"; or does he say, as one President did of a widely admired painting by a contemporary artist—"if that's art, I'm a Hottentot!"? Would he, as President Coolidge is said to have done, reject six Cézannes that had been offered as a gift to the White House? A President who regularly occupies a box at the theater or the symphony, who not only praises poets but reads poetry, who is learned in languages and literature, and not wholly innocent of modern science—can have a profound effect upon the standards of public taste and on the cultural life of the nation. If he does these things easily and familiarly as one who knows what he's doing and

[8] H. J. Ford, *Rise and Growth of American Politics* (New York: Macmillan, 1898).

enjoys doing it, his influence will be greater than if his behavior is without zeal or zest, "simply a part of the job I have to do."

The President and His Wife

In his role as "taste-maker," the President's right arm is the President's wife, the First Lady of the land. Her taste in clothes, in furniture, art, food, recreation—her whole way of life becomes a matter of public interest, concern, or imitation. It has been reported that when Mrs. Kennedy moved into the White House, Washington had a revival of interest in period furniture, pillbox hats were in great demand, and small intimate dinner parties replaced the grand soirees of other days.

The role of the First Lady in all these matters has been important since Martha Washington moved into the presidential "palace" at 10 Cherry Street, New York, in April, 1789. For her first levee, as presidential receptions were known in those days, she "wore a white brocade gown, full-skirted and trimmed in silver. She flourished a fan, and wore a small white tulle hat, draped with an ostrich plume, on her powdered hair." Small wonder that ardent Republicans in Congress complained that the President and his lady were "assuming the trappings of royalty." But while the Republicans complained, the women of the country rejoiced, and the Presidency grew in dignity and prestige. The Washingtons were well aware of the importance of these aspects of the Presidency and deliberately set about to establish a pattern or "line of conduct" that would support "the dignity of the office"—always avoiding "the imputation of superciliousness or unnecessary reserve." President Washington cautioned Gouverneur Morris that in buying furnishings for the house on Cherry Street he should "avoid extravagance. . . . For extravagance would not comport with my own inclinations nor with the example which ought to be set." The presidential "style of life" from 1789 to the present time has been an important and at times a major factor in the political, social, and cultural life of the nation.

One is tempted to linger on these fascinating aspects of the Presidency, to recall the reports of Mary Todd Lincoln's extravagance—300 pairs of gloves in four months, $500 for a single point-laced shawl, $5,000 for three evening gowns. Or one might recall the influence of Mrs. Grant, who, in the words of a recent writer, "launched the White House, in 1869, upon a period of Victorian gaudiness that was to stretch the taste for tassels, hand-pressed paper ornaments, and heavy furniture into the nineteen hundreds," until the East Room resembled "the saloon of a sound steamer and the State Dining Room had the decor of a fashionable bar."[9] Mrs. Rutherford Hayes, the first college-trained First Lady, as her husband said, "may not have much influence with Congress but she

---

[9] See Daz and Richard Harkness, "The First Lady: A New Mood," in *The New York Times Magazine*, April 23, 1961.

does with me." Small wonder that her influence with Congress was not great, when as one Congressman ruefully remarked, at the nonalcoholic White House dinners, "buttermilk flowed like wine." The boisterous, not to say rambunctious family of Theodore Roosevelt not only brought a scholar to the Presidency, but a brood of children that translated some of the problems of the Presidency into a language every parent knew. As for the President, official duties at times seemed almost secondary to a campaign for simplified spelling, a war on "muckrakers," a crusade to restore the charm of rural life, and a match in the East Room of the White House between an American wrestler and a Japanese exponent of jujitsu to see which was superior. The Theodore Roosevelt style—which included literary teas and anthropological lectures with a continuous plea for the "strenuous life" of the cowboy—was continued, especially on the distaff side, by the Franklin Roosevelts a generation later. Mrs. Franklin Roosevelt made the job of First Lady a combination of research assistant, traveling ambassador-at-large, social worker, model housewife, and royal hostess. In her first year in the White House, it is said she traveled 40,000 miles, visiting farms, factories, mines, art galleries, schools and colleges—and writing memoranda to the President on nearly every conceivable subject. Mrs. Kennedy, in her own person and style of life, seemed to embody a new and more sophisticated generation. Her conduct as a young mother and gracious hostess again brought the Presidency into the lives of many otherwise indifferent citizens. The television tour of the White House which she narrated and conducted brought that monument and symbol of American culture to millions to whom it had been little more than a name. And "Lady Bird" Johnson continued in the style of Mrs. Kennedy, combined with energy and a straightforward simplicity that reminds one of Eleanor Roosevelt.

The Symbol and the Greatness

The title of "Mr. President" scarcely matches the grandeur of "Her Majesty, Elizabeth II, by the Grace of God, of the United Kingdom of Great Britain and Northern Ireland and of her realms and territories, Queen, Head of the Commonwealth, Defender of the Faith . . ." and so forth. But among the great ceremonial offices of the world, the American Presidency ranks high because it unites the symbol with the substance of power. There were those in the beginning who sought a title to match the unexplored dimensions of the office. "His Excellency" and "Elective Majesty" were suggested, ridiculed, and rejected. A Senate committee appointed to consider the matter recommended "His Highness the President of the United States of America and Protector of the Rights of the Same"—but this too died when a joint committee of both Houses reported against titles. Vice-President Adams was especially agitated over this matter, saying that the simple title of President was unbecoming and confusing. Every fire company, every cricket club, he remarked, had a president. "What will the common people of foreign countries," he asked, "what will the sailors and soldiers say, 'George Washington, President of the United States'? They will despise him to all eternity." Debate was spirited, with Congressman Tucker summing up the Republican case against titles by asking:

> Does the dignity of a nation consist in the distance between the first magistrate and his citizens? Does it consist in the exaltation of one man and the humiliation of the rest? If so, the most despotic government is the most dignified; and to make our dignity complete, we must give a high title, an embroidered robe, a princely equipage, and finally a crown and hereditary succession. . . .[10]

Fortunately, the matter was postponed. In the meantime, Washington appeared, took the oath, and was thereafter addressed as "President" or "Mr. President"—a title which neither Congress by law, nor the people by custom, have been able to improve.

It would be unfair to John Adams and those who shared his views, however, to assume that all of their concern for titles was foolish and misdirected. In those early spring days of 1789, newly elected Congressmen and the President and Vice-President-elect were acutely conscious of the importance of what they did for the future spirit and structure of American government. The debate on titles was by no means the only matter of presidential power and protocol with which they were concerned. The inaugural ceremony, the President's style of living, his compensation (Washington, incidentally, served without pay), the order of precedence of the President, Vice-President, and other federal and state officials when appearing on public occasions, the nature of the inaugural address, and the appropriate "replies" to be made to it, the President's power to issue "Proclamations," the proper role and demeanor of the President as head of state and when on tour, the relations of the President to Congress and more particularly to the Senate whose advice and consent were necessary for certain appointments and treaties —were some of the subjects discussed. Not a few of the informal or unwritten conventions of the Constitution were begun during Washington's first term and many during his first year in office. Not all the politicians of 1789 were philosophers—and none was a sociologist—but all knew the importance of symbolism and precedent in the lives of men. They knew also that among the most important symbols of government— second only to the Constitution itself—was the Presidency.[11]

[10] Quoted in Hart, *op. cit.*, p. 37. It was suggested that a title be conferred on Adams, more glamorous than the simple one of Vice-President. "Your Rotundity" was proposed.

[11] "Symbolism," says A. N. Whitehead, "is no mere idle fancy or corrupt degeneration; it is inherent in the very texture of human life. . . . However you reduce the functions of your government to their utmost simplicity, yet symbolism remains. . . . You abolish the etiquette of a royal court, with its suggestion of personal subordination, but at official receptions you ceremonially shake the hand of the Governor of your

To return, therefore, to the question with which we began—one measure of the greatness of a President is surely the degree to which he serves to symbolize the character, the way of life, and the values of the American people. Washington's greatness was due less to any qualities of charisma or Father Image than to the close correspondence of his own character, style of life, and values with those of his countrymen. When an English visitor was presented to the new President in May, 1795, he described him as follows:

> There are persons in whose appearance one looks in vain for the qualities they are known to possess, but the appearance of General Washington harmonized in a singular manner with the dignity and modesty of his public life. So completely did he look the great and good man he really was that I felt rather respect than awe in his presence. . . .[12]

In one way or another, and in varying degrees, all the great Presidents have had those qualities which inspire "rather respect than awe," for in them people like to see themselves reflected at twice or more their normal size. But however gifted a President may be in the qualities that make for greatness, he must somehow contrive to communicate them to the millions of people who never meet him in the flesh. This he can do by what he says and by what he does. General Washington had already become a symbol of the new nation, if not a legend, before his unanimous election as its first President. Jefferson, too, was well known before he became President, not so much as a doer of deeds, although he had been a legislator, governor, ambassador, and Secretary of State, as by his authorship of the Declaration of Independence. These and his other writings have become so much a part of the American political tradition that Jefferson and American democracy have merged in a single image.

Of all the great Presidents, Lincoln alone combined the politician, the statesman, the hero, and the martyr in a single image. It is consequently the most difficult to analyze or to appraise. "The Lincoln legend," says Richard Hofstadter, "has come to have a hold on the American imagination that defies comparison with anything else in political mythology. Here is a drama in which a great man shoulders the torment and moral burden of a blundering and sinful people, suffers for them, and redeems them with hallowed Christian virtues—'with malice toward none and charity for all'—and is destroyed at the peak of his success."[13]

State. Just as the feudal doctrine of subordination of classes . . . requires its symbolism; so does the doctrine of human equality obtain its symbolism. . . ." *Symbolism: Its Meaning and Effect* (New York: Macmillan, 1927) , pp. 60–88.

[12] Thomas Twining, *Travels in America 100 Years Ago* (New York: Harper & Row, 1902) , pp. 128–30.

[13] *The American Political Tradition and the Men Who Made It* (New York: Knopf, 1948) , p. 93. See also the interesting collection of personal comments on the Presidency by former Presidents, by Professor Henry F. Graft in *The New York Times Magazine,* April 12, 1964.

Washington and Jefferson and Lincoln are unique among the great men of this or any country. But Woodrow Wilson, Franklin Roosevelt, Andrew Jackson—and in only slightly lesser degree—Theodore Roosevelt, John Adams, and Grover Cleveland embody those qualities of character, style, doctrine, and deed that separate the great men from the not-so-great. But words alone do not make great men. Deeds are necessary too. The seminal acts of Washington's administration were in final analysis a better measure of his greatness than his words. The establishment of a firm financial basis for the new government, the organization of the executive departments, the funding of the debt, the chartering of the Bank of the United States, the admission of Vermont, Kentucky, and Tennessee to the Union, and even the show of force used to put down the so-called Whiskey Rebellion were major achievements at home—as the Jay and Pinckney Treaties with Great Britain and Spain, and the maintenance of neutrality in the face of Europe at war were in foreign affairs. Under Jefferson, the new capital on the Potomac, named for Washington, became a reality; the excise tax on whiskey and the Alien and Sedition Laws were allowed to lapse; the vast Louisiana Territory was acquired, and Lewis and Clark were dispatched to explore it; a new land law opened the new western lands in lots of 160 acres to any man with 50 dollars for a down payment; Ohio was admitted to the Union; and the Burr conspiracy was crushed. In foreign affairs, an American naval squadron put an end to the tribute exacted by the maritime state of Northern Africa.

The Civil War has so enveloped Lincoln that details of his domestic policies are all but forgotten. The upward thrust of the protective tariff, the National Banking Act of 1863, the Morrill Land Grant Act, which laid the foundation of many of our state colleges and universities, the legal tender acts, and a revolutionary land policy embodied in the Homestead Act of 1862 were among the policies with which Lincoln's name is linked.

Woodrow Wilson's name is so tied to his record as a war President, to his imperishable statement of American war aims, to his vision as the master builder of the League of Nations that the dramatic deeds of his first term are only dimly recalled. Yet between his inauguration March 4, 1913, and the Declaration of War on April 4, 1917, the United States, under Wilson's leadership, ratified the Sixteenth and Seventeenth Amendments; adopted the liberal Underwood Tariff, a radical revision of our traditional protectionist policy; established the Federal Reserve System; created a Federal Trade Commission; adopted Section 6 of the Clayton Antitrust Act, which organized labor hailed as its Magna Charta; set up a dozen Federal Farm Loan Banks; passed the Smith-Hughes Act and the Smith-Lever Act to provide federal grants-in-aid for agricultural extension and for education in commercial, industrial, and domestic science courses; and applied the same principle of grants-in-aid to road building under the Federal Highway Act of 1916.

Franklin Roosevelt is more vividly remembered as the architect of the "New Deal" than as leader of the "Free World" in World War II. Although time has still to soothe the bitter controversies that his name and policies aroused, few would deny the importance of his leadership during more than twelve critical years. Banking legislation, including the Federal Deposit Insurance Corporation, the Gold Reserve Act of January, 1934, and the Securities and Exchange Commission were steps taken toward fiscal and monetary reform. Also far-reaching in their effects were the National Labor Relations Act, the Tennessee Valley Authority, the Agricultural Adjustment Act, the Home Owners Loan Corporation, and the Social Security Act. In foreign policy his name is linked with American recognition of the USSR; a good-neighbor policy in Latin America; a policy of formal neutrality culminating in the Lend Lease Act of 1941; and a mammoth defense program, including a revived Selective Service Act.

Some of the factors that characterize the great Presidents identified in the poll of 1948 could, of course, be extended to those classified as near-great and even to some of those labeled "average." Indeed, it has been said that great events create great men, and that greatness is as much of an accident of time and circumstance as a product of the character and policies of particular men. Washington, it might be said, was a product of two revolutions—the War for Independence and the successful establishment of a new government under the Constitution. Jefferson was fortunate in being chosen to draft the Declaration of Independence and to be President at a time when Spanish ineptitude and Napoleonic necessity made possible his greatest achievement—the Louisiana Purchase. Jackson rode to greatness as the voice of the newly conscious West. In 1775 there were not over 5,000 white people in the whole Mississippi Valley outside New Orleans: by 1830 (Jackson came to power in 1829) there were nearly 3,000,000. By 1830, nine new states had been admitted from the West. Under these circumstances, leadership from the West was inevitable—and Jackson fortunately was on hand to serve. Without the Civil War, it has been said, Lincoln might never have risen to greatness. And Woodrow Wilson rode the crest of a Populistic-Progressive movement that had been burgeoning for twenty years—with leadership as various as William Jennings Bryan, Theodore Roosevelt, and Robert M. La Follette. Had it not been for the "accidental" split in the Republican party in 1912, Wilson might have lived out his days as a professor, not a practitioner, of politics, and certainly not as a "great" President. It was the Great Depression of the 1930s, and World War II, so it is said, that "made" Franklin Roosevelt a great President.

And so it may well be. Serendipity no doubt operates in politics as in science and invention. However, something more is needed. All of the great Presidents, in terms of character, style of life, capacity for communication, policies and basic values were distinguishable—even distinguished. Distinguished, not because they differed from the American people in these respects but precisely because they expressed these traits in clearer tones or to a higher degree.[14] All of them moved in the vanguard of events and social change, seeking to rationalize, guide, and in a measure to control them. And all of them were men of decision, however agonizing the process of decision making may have been for them.[15] What was true of them has been in varying degrees true of their successors, and only time will accord them the accolade of great, near-great, or less.

☆ *PRESIDENTIAL POWER: WHIG VERSUS FEDERAL IDEAS*

We have said that the Presidency is greater than the office of the President, as the office is greater than the man who occupies it. The full dimensions of the Presidency have never been explored, because some of the language of Article II of the Constitution is highly ambiguous. "The executive Power," says Section 1, "shall be vested in a President of the United States of America." But what is "the executive Power"? Sections 2 and 3 of Article II proceed to specify some of the powers of the President.

> He shall be Commander in Chief of the Army and Navy of the United States, and of the Militia of the several States, when called into the actual Service of the United States; he may require the Opinion, in writing, of the principal Officer in each of the executive Departments . . .; he shall have Power to grant Reprieves and Pardons for Offences against the

[14] Even the harshest critics of Franklin Roosevelt, for example, concede his capacity for expressing public opinion, and no doubt in expressing it—helping to mold and direct it. Thus Professor Edgar Robinson, who believed President Roosevelt did "incalculable harm" to the American nation, nevertheless says of him, "It is clear that the identification of the leader with the people had reaped its natural harvest. The level of national responsibility, of national life in general—was that of a majority of the American people." See Jonathan Daniels, "Appraisal of F.D.R." in *The New York Times,* April 10, 1955.

[15] Professor Richard Morris has listed what he calls "10 Fateful Decisions" of American Presidents. These include (1) Washington's decision to use armed force under his own command to put down the so-called Whiskey Rebellion in 1794; (2) Jefferson's decision to pay Napoleon $15 million for the whole of the Louisiana Territory, rather than pay only $5 million for a small part of it; (3) Monroe's decision to act unilaterally, rather than in concert with Great Britain, in warning European nations against further colonization or intervention in the Western Hemisphere; (4) Jackson's reply to Calhoun and to South Carolina's threat of nullification in 1830 in his toast, "Our Union, It Must Be Preserved," and his "Proclamation to the People of South Carolina"; (5) Lincoln's decision to call for volunteers to "suppress" rebellious "combinations"; (6) Theodore Roosevelt's decision to recognize and aid the government of Panama in its "war of independence" against Colombia, thus making possible the Panama Canal; (7) Wilson's fight for the League of Nations; (8) Truman's decision to use atomic weapons against Japan; (9) Truman's decision to commit American troops to battle in Korea; (10) Franklin D. Roosevelt's transfer of 50 overage destroyers to Great Britain on August 13, 1940. See *The New York Times Magazine,* December 4, 1960. Certainly one would now have to add President Kennedy's confrontation with the USSR on guided missiles in Cuba, and President Johnson's "commitment" to wage unofficial war in Vietnam.

United States, except in Cases of Impeachment. He shall have Power, by and with Advice and Consent of the Senate, to make Treaties, provided two thirds of the Senators present concur; and he shall nominate, and by and with the Advice and Consent of the Senate, shall appoint Ambassadors, other public Ministers and Consuls, Judges of the Supreme Court, and all other Officers of the United States, whose Appointments are not herein otherwise provided for. . . . He shall from time to time give to the Congress Information of the State of the Union, and recommend to their Consideration such Measures as he shall judge necessary and expedient; he may on extraordinary Occasions convene both Houses, or either of them, and in Case of Disagreement between them, with Respect to the Time of Adjournment, he may adjourn them to such Time as he shall think proper; he shall receive Ambassadors and other public Ministers; he shall take Care that the Laws be faithfully executed, and shall Commission all the Officers of the United States.

These are great powers in themselves. But do these enumerated powers taken together comprise the whole of "the executive Power"? It is worth noting that there is an important difference between the language of Article I establishing Congress and Article II establishing the Presidency. Article I reads: "All legislative Powers *herein granted* shall be vested in a Congress of the United States." Sections 4 through 9 specify in some detail the outer limits of the "legislative Powers herein granted." But Article II simply provides that "the executive Power shall be vested in a President." Not "the executive Power" herein granted—but "the executive Power." Presumably, therefore, it may be argued that the powers enumerated specify and illustrate but do not exhaust "the executive Power."

Are there other executive powers beyond those which are enumerated? Is there, in a word, "executive power" inherent in the Presidency but not enumerated in the Constitution? Upon the answer to this question and upon the full scope of the powers which are enumerated depends one's theory of the Presidency. In the course of our history as a nation, two main theories have emerged—one called the Federalist, or Hamiltonian, theory; the other generally known as the Whig theory.

The Hamiltonian Concept

With one or two doubtful exceptions, those Presidents who have been described as great or near-great have argued in both word and deed for the Federalist or Hamiltonian theory.

Energy in the executive [wrote Hamilton] is a leading character in the definition of good government. . . . A feeble executive implies a feeble execution of the government. A feeble executive is but another phrase for a bad executive; and a government ill executed, whatever it may be in theory, must be in practice a bad government. . . . The ingredients which constitute energy in the executive are first *unity;* secondly *duration;* thirdly an adequate *provision for its support;* fourthly *competent powers.* The ingredients which constitute safety in the republican sense are first a *due dependence* on the people, secondly a *due responsibility.*

The executive as provided for in the Constitution, Hamilton argued, meets all of these tests. Unity is secured in a single executive officer—the President. "Decision, activity, secrecy and dispatch" are possible with a single executive, and "in proportion as the number is increased these qualities will be diminished." Experience in Greece and Rome and in the American states teaches us not to be enamored of plurality in the executive. A plural executive invites dissension, intrigue and conflict, delay and indecision. But one of the weightiest objections to a plurality in the executive is that it tends to conceal faults or to destroy responsibility. A single executive provides two indispensable safeguards against the misuse and abuse of power—"first, the restraints of public opinion . . . and secondly, the opportunity of discovering with facility and clearness the misconduct of the powers they trust."

Duration in the executive, says Hamilton, is essential to "the personal firmness" and independence of the executive magistrate and "to the stability of the system of administration which may have been adopted under his auspices." A four-year term for the President who "is to be re-eligible as often as the people of the United States shall think him worthy of their confidence" will make reasonable provision for both executive independence and stability, although Hamilton himself believed "the longer the duration in office" the better. The "republican principle," he said, "demands that the deliberate sense of the community should govern the conduct" of the President, as of other officials, "but it does not require an unqualified complaisance to every sudden breeze of passion, or to every transient impulse which the people may receive from the acts of men who flatter their prejudices to betray their interests." Nor did Hamilton favor any limitations upon the re-eligibility of the President. Such limitations, he argued, would be to diminish "the inducements to good behavior, . . . [provide a] temptation to sordid views, to peculation, and in some instances, to usurpation . . . [and so deprive] the community of the advantage of experience gained in the exercise of his office . . . [and sacrifice] stability in the administration." Hamilton would not have approved the Twenty-second Amendment, which now limits the President to two terms. To make a President ineligible if the expiration of his term should correspond to "the breaking out of a war or . . . similar crisis," Hamilton thought unwise and even reckless.

The third principle of a proper executive—"adequate provision for its support"—was discussed only briefly by Hamilton. He thought the constitutional provision to be wise, although one suspects that even in this respect he would have preferred more independence of Congress. He was, however, reassured by the provision that the "President shall . . .

TABLE 13–1
Presidential Salaries

Effective Dates	Annual Salary	Annual Allowances	
1789–1873	$ 25,000	—	
1873–1909	50,000	$25,000	(travel) *a*
1909–1949	75,000	40,000	(travel) *b*
1949–1964	100,000	40,000	(travel)
		50,000	(official)

a Enacted in 1906.
b Increased to $40,000 in 1948.
NOTE: The President's annual salary always has been taxable. The $50,000 official allowance, which is enacted in 1949 was tax-free, was made taxable by a 1951 law effective Jan. 20, 1953. The $40,000 travel allowance remained tax-free.
SOURCE: Adapted from *Congress and the Nation, 1945–1964* (Washington, D.C.: Congressional Quarterly Service, 1965), p. 1435. Used by permission.

receive for his Services, a Compensation, *which shall neither be encreased nor diminished during the Period for which he shall have been elected. . . .*" (Hamilton's italics.) Without this safeguard Hamilton said, the legislature "with a discretionary power over the salary and emoluments of the Chief Magistrate, could render him as obsequious to their will as they might think proper to make him."[16] (See Table 13–1.)

In appraising the fourth requirement of a strong executive, "competent powers," Hamilton was obviously on the defensive.[17] He realized that within the language of Article II there were powers hidden that no literal reading of the words could reveal. He therefore expends most of his argument in reassuring the critics of the new Constitution that the Presidency was no monarchy and that the executive power was subject to all the controls essential to the safety of a republican form of government. The veto power, he describes as a "qualified veto" necessary to protect the executive from unconstitutional encroachments by the legislature. "It not only serves as a shield to the Executive," he says, "but it furnishes an additional security against the enactment of improper laws . . . against the effects of faction, precipitancy, or of any impulse unfriendly to the public good. . . ." It is not assumed, he says, that "a single man [will] possess more virtue and wisdom than a number of men . . . but upon the supposition that the legislature will not be infallible." To be sure, it might on occasion be used, as the critics say, to prevent the enactment of good laws. But this is unlikely, first because "every institution calculated to restrain the excess of lawmaking" is

16 *The Federalist, No. 73,* Ford.
17 In Articles 69, 73, 74, 75, 76, and 77 of *The Federalist,* Ford.

salutary, and secondly because if it is good and Congress is intent upon it, the veto can be overcome by a two-thirds vote. Moreover, the veto power in New York, where it is exercised in conjunction with an executive council, and in Massachusetts, where it resides solely in the governor and from which the framers copied it, has proved to be a blessing. So much has this been true that those who "were violent opposers of it [the veto] have from experience become its declared admirers."

In similar vein the powers conferred upon the President to pardon, to make appointments of ambassadors and other officers of the United States, to serve as Commander in Chief of the armed forces, and to make treaties are examined in some detail. In each case Hamilton is at pains to show that the power is essential to good government, is customary, and is compatible with the basic principles of republican institutions. His power as Commander in Chief "is so evident in itself . . . and so consonant to the precedents of the state constitutions . . . that little need be said to explain or enforce it. . . . The direction of war implies the direction of the common strength . . . [and] forms a usual and essential part in the definition of the executive authority." Just what expanse of power is to be implied in the phrase "the direction of the common strength" Hamilton does not say. The appointing power, he points out, is to be shared with the Senate and is thus both more limited and more stable than it would be without the Senate's participation. And in one so jealous of the executive's power and prerogatives, it is surprising to find Hamilton saying that "the consent of that body would be necessary to displace as well as to appoint"—a point on which time and tradition have proved him to be only partly correct. The power of the President to "require the Opinion in writing of the principal Officer in each of the executive Departments," Hamilton says, is "a mere redundancy" since such a right "would result of itself from the office." That is to say, such power is to be regarded as inherent in the executive without any special grant in the Constitution. One may ask, if this power is inherent in "the executive power," may there not be other powers which are also inherent?

On the treaty-making power and the President's general control over foreign policy, Hamilton stops short of John Locke, the great philosopher of republican government. Indeed, Hamilton's argument is largely designed to demonstrate the great wisdom of the framers in combining the Senate with the Presidency in this important field. And in the argument one finds such un-Hamiltonian sentiments as the following: "However proper or safe it may be in governments where the executive magistrate is an hereditary monarch, to commit to him the entire power of making treaties, it would be utterly unsafe and improper to intrust that power to an elective magistrate of four years duration." Such an executive, armed with this power, might be corrupted by a foreign power "to sacrifice his duty to his interest." The whole history "of human conduct," he says, "does not warrant that exalted opinion of human virtue which would make it wise in a nation to commit interests of so delicate and momentous a kind, as those which concern its intercourse with the rest of the world, to the sole disposal of a magistrate created and circumstanced as would be a President of the United States."[18] But Hamilton is equally emphatic in insisting that the House of Representatives ought not to participate in these delicate matters and that the President is the appropriate channel for negotiation with foreign powers. No servant of the Senate, he says, could "enjoy the confidence and respect of foreign powers . . . [nor could] act with an equal degree of weight or efficacy."

In this respect, Hamilton comes close to Locke, who declared, "The power of leagues and alliances, and all the transactions with all persons and communities without the commonwealth (even war and peace) . . . is much less capable to be directed by antecedent, standing positive laws . . . and so must . . . be left to the prudence and wisdom of those whose hands it is in to be managed for the public good. . . ." Although this power over foreign affairs which Locke calls the "federative" power is distinct from the executive power, "yet they are hardly to be separated and placed . . . in the hands of distinct persons. . . ."[19] To this Hamilton would most assuredly agree, as did the Supreme Court in the case of *United States* v. *Curtiss-Wright Export Corporation,* decided in 1936. What Locke was saying in effect was that in dealing with foreign affairs the executive power was necessarily less subject to legislative or judicial control or restraint than when it was concerned with domestic affairs.

Hamilton's analysis of the executive power in *The Federalist* must be read in the light of the campaign in New York for ratification of the Constitution. His analysis was a reply to those who opposed ratification because they said the Constitution vested too much power in the central government and especially in the President. He therefore sought to "play down" rather than to exalt the executive power. In speaking of the executive department he said, "the writers against the Constitution seem to have taken pains to signalize their talent of misrepresentation." Playing upon "the aversion of the people to monarchy, they have endeavored to enlist all their jealousies and apprehensions in opposition to the intended President of the United States. . . . He has been decorated with attributes superior in dignity and splendor to those of a king of Great Britain. . . . [Even] the images of Asiatic despotism . . . have scarcely been wanting to crown the exaggerated scene." To combat these arguments and to allay these fears, Hamilton proceeded to emphasize the constitutional limitations on the President and at the same time to make as good a case as possible for a strong, independent executive endowed by the Constitution with "competent powers" of his own.

18 *The Federalist,* No. 75.

19 John Locke, "The Second Treatise of Civil Government," *Two Treatises of Government,* ed. Sir Robert Filmer (New York: Hafner, 1947), p. 195.

The Whig-Buchanan Approach

Against this Hamiltonian model one may place what has been variously called the Whig or Buchanan model of the Presidency. Instead of a strong, independent executive, endowed by the Constitution with ample powers to make his will effective, the Whig model is a President whose powers derive mainly from legislation and who serves primarily as a servant of Congress in seeing that the laws "be faithfully executed." The Whig or Buchanan President takes a narrow, legalistic view of his office and its powers. To him, the job, apart from its ceremonial functions, is mainly one of administration or management, essentially nonpolitical in its structure and spirit. The Whig President eschews any hint of inherent powers, insisting that his authority can extend no farther than the powers enumerated in Article II of the Constitution, and that these must be narrowly construed. Thus President Buchanan, faced with secession and subversion, could find no warrant in the Constitution for presidential, or for that matter congressional action against the open defiance of federal laws, let alone authority to use force in putting down the rebellion.[20] With this view of his own office and its own powers, he was compelled by the logic of his own argument to stand helplessly by while the Union faced dismemberment and destruction. The Whig-Buchanan President has served as a model for a number of Presidents, including Taft, Coolidge, Hoover, and perhaps in a qualified sense even Dwight Eisenhower. Woodrow Wilson, who in later years as President radically revised his views, in his book *Congressional Government,* published in 1885, set forth the Buchanan theory:

> The business of the President, occasionally great, is usually not much above routine. Most of the time it is *mere* administration, mere obedience of directions from the masters of policy, the Standing Committees. Except in so far as his power of veto constitutes him a part of the legislature, the President might, not inconveniently, be a permanent officer; the first official of a carefully-graded . . . civil service system. . . . He is part of the official [administrative] rather than of the political machinery of the government, and his duties call rather for training [in administration] than for constructive genius. . . . [Hence, argued Wilson] for the sort of Presidents needed under the present arrangement of our federal governmnt, it is best to choose amongst the ablest and most experienced state governors.[21]

20 ". . . no such power," he said, "has been delegated to Congress nor to any other department of the federal government . . . it is not among the specific enumerated powers granted to Congress; and it is equally apparent that its exercise is not 'necessary and proper for carrying into execution' any one of those powers." See his Second Annual Message, December, 1860.

21 Woodrow Wilson, *Congressional Government: A Study in American Politics* (Boston: Houghton Mifflin, 1885) , pp. 254–256.

Abraham Lincoln, the prototype and model of the Federalist-Hamiltonian President, was challenged by those who held to the Whig-Buchanan theory of the presidential office. In the so-called Wade-Davis Manifesto of August 5, 1864, Congress formally declared that it was the President's proper role "to obey and execute, not to make the laws. . . ." And when Andrew Johnson succeeded to the Presidency, he found himself at war with a Congress committed to the Whig-Buchanan theory of the Presidency. Step by step the Republican leadership in Congress sought to strip the President of his powers on the theory that

> He [the President] is the servant of the people *as they shall speak through Congress.* . . . Andrew Johnson must learn that he is your servant and that as Congress shall order he must obey. There is no escape from it. God forbid that he should have one title of power except what he derives through Congress and the Constitution.[22]

It was on this theory that the Congress sought to humble and humiliate the President by the Tenure of Office Act, which took from him his power to remove disloyal subordinates even in his own Cabinet, and ultimately launched impeachment proceedings against him.

Early History of the Rival Concepts

The history of the Presidency and one important measure of the men who have occupied that office can be read in terms of whether the Federalist-Hamiltonian or the Whig-Buchanan model prevailed. The argument as to which is the "true" theory of the Presidency can, of course, never be resolved. Friends of both models may find in the Constitutional Convention statements to support their views. On the one hand, they can point to the fact that both the Virginia and the New Jersey plans, which furnished the basis for so much of the debate, proposed a President to be elected by and presumably responsible to Congress. Friends of the Whig-Buchanan theory can also point to the overwhelming rejection by the Convention on at least one occasion, of a proposal to provide for the popular election of the President without limit as to his re-eligibility. Indeed, it was only toward the end of the Convention that any other plan than election by Congress seemed to have significant support among the delegates. On the other hand, friends of the Federalist-Hamiltonian theory may cite the all but universal sentiment among the delegates in favor of a stronger executive than was then provided for by the Articles of Confederation and most of the state constitutions. As we have seen, the absence of a strong executive in the Confederation and in the states was regarded by many of the most influential delegates as a major cause of

---

[22] Author's italics. Excerpt quoted in Edward S. Corwin, *The President: Office and Powers* (New York: New York University Press, 1940), p. 27.

the "excess of democracy" from which the country suffered. And in the end, of course, although the Constitution did not provide for popular election of the President, it did provide in unmistakable language for a strong, independent executive.[23]

The two Federalist Presidents, Washington and John Adams, were clearly of the opinion that the President's powers and responsibilities were not limited to those of "mere administration," or even to those enumerated in Article II. Nor did they believe that the President was the "servant" of Congress and that "as Congress shall order he must obey." President Washington, with Hamilton at his side, was firm in maintaining the dignity, independence, and power of the Presidency. As we shall see, in the vast realm of foreign affairs he insisted on the independence of the President in selecting his ambassadors and in negotiations with foreign powers. He even used personal agents in these delicate matters without any formal confirmation by the Senate and on at least two issues, he successfully argued that the phrase "the executive Power" in Article II was itself a source of powers beyond those enumerated in Sections 2 and 3. In the first of these, the power of the President to remove executive officers without Senate approval was established, even in the case of those appointed "by and with the Advice and Consent of the Senate." In the second, he successfully asserted the power of the President to issue Proclamations—even the famous Proclamation of Neutrality in 1793— without congressional or senatorial approval. Moreover, the power of the President to participate actively in the legislative process was established. In his first inaugural President Washington refrained from "a recommendation of specific measures" out of "the tribute due to the talents, the rectitude and the patriotism" of Congress. Nevertheless, both he and members of his Cabinet were active in urging particular measures upon the legislature. Under the vigorous leadership of Alexander Hamilton, his Secretary of the Treasury, a legislative[24] program was pushed through the Congress as comprehensive and as far-reaching as any that

23 There is little doubt that the executive provided for in Article II comes closer to the model favored by most of the delegates—a model, incidentally, which came from New York, where a strong governor had been provided for. Gouverneur Morris' strong plea to the Convention on July 19, in favor of "an Executive with sufficient vigor to pervade every part" of the Union undoubtedly had some influence, although the Convention rejected his proposal for popular election. See Max Farrand (ed.), *The Records of the Federal Convention* (New Haven: Yale University Press, 1911), vol. I. See also Corwin, *op. cit.,* p. 13.

24 "Hamilton seems to the present writer," wrote Professor James Hart, "as he reads history backwards, to have endangered the position of the Presidency, as the necessary spearhead of a strong executive, when, as Secretary of the Treasury, he assumed a personal leadership of Congress, which tended to make a figure-head of the President, so far as policy initiation was concerned. If the function of Prime Minister is to be effectively assumed within the present framework of the American Government, it must be assumed, as Woodrow Wilson clearly saw, by the President." Hart, *op. cit.,* p. 238, note. See also Woodrow Wilson, *Constitutional Government in the United States* (New York: Columbia University Press, 1908), chap. 3; Wilfred E. Binkley, *The Powers of the President* (Garden City, N.Y.: Doubleday, 1937), chap. 2.

has since been proposed or enacted. Neither the President nor his chief Cabinet members hesitated to appear before Congress to "explain" and in the process to support specific legislative measures.

John Adams, Washington's successor, continued to maintain the Federalist theory of the Presidency. "In all great and essential measures," he wrote, "[the President] is bound by his honor and his conscience, by his oath to the Constitution, as well as his responsibility to the public opinion of the nation, to act upon his own mature and unbiased judgment, though unfortunately it may be in direct contradiction to the advice of all his ministers."[25] During the first year of the new government, 1789, Adams outlined his theory of the Presidency, saying:

> The duration of our president is . . . only for four years; but his power during those four years is much greater than that of . . . the King of Poland, nay, the King of Sparta. I know of no first magistrate in any republican government, excepting England and Neuchatel, who possesses a constitutional dignity, authority, and power comparable to his. . . . [But]in our Constitution, the legislative power, is greater than the executive; it will therefore encroach, because both aristocratical and democratical passions are insatiable. . . . I would therefore have given more power to the president and less to the senate. . . .[26]

Even Jefferson, who often spoke the language of the Whigs, was nevertheless an exponent of a strong, independent executive. He was critical of the "monarchical" tendencies which as a republican he professed to see in the conduct of the Presidency under Washington and Adams. He referred scornfully to the "trappings of monarchy" and he often spoke of the "supreme legislative power" as the best repository of republican principles. When elected to the Presidency, he dispensed with the usual inaugural folderol, and instead of a horse and carriage with postilion and outriders, he walked with a few friends up a muddy Washington street to the new Capitol to be "sworn in."[27] Instead of reading his first message to Congress, as Washington and Adams had done, in person—a custom all good republicans deplored as smacking of the "speech from the throne"—he sent the written speech by messenger to be read by a clerk. And in his first message to Congress, he said, "Nothing shall be wanting on my part to inform, as far as in my power, the legislative judgment, nor to carry that judgment into faithful execution." Ardent Federalists worried lest Jefferson's Whiggish republican theories reduce the Presidency to the level of a mere administrator—or worse still, a slavish suppliant and servant of the Congress. John Marshall, for

---

[25] "Letters to a Boston Patriot," 1809, quoted by Sidney Hyman in "The Presidency as Seen by Presidents," *The New York Times Magazine*, July 8, 1956.

[26] Quoted in Leonard White, *op. cit.*, p. 93.

[27] John Adams, incidentally, not only did not accompany his successor on this journey. He had already left Washington, refusing to dignify the "swearing in" with his presence.

example, was sure that Jefferson "would embody himself in the House of Representatives and by weakening the office of President increase his personal power. He will become the leader of that party which is about to constitute the majority of the legislature."[28]

This transformation of the President into a prime minister was not exactly what Jefferson did or hoped to do, although much of what Marshall said of him was true. As a party leader he did "embody himself" in the legislature and through his party's caucus succeeded largely in having his way with Congress. As John Quincy Adams said, Jefferson's "whole system of administration seems founded on the principle of carrying through the legislative measures by personal or official influence."[29]

But Jefferson was by no means a Whig-Buchanan President. Had he been, he might never have moved to buy Louisiana, or to defy the Supreme Court's attempt under John Marshall to subpoena the President as a witness in court. Nor could he have written the following:

> A strict observance of the written laws [he wrote to John Colvin in 1810] is doubtless *one* of the high duties of a good [officer], but it is not the *highest*. The laws of necessity, of self-preservation, of saving our country when in danger, are of higher obligation. To lose our country by a scrupulous adherence to written law would be to lose the law itself, with life, liberty, property and all those who are enjoying them with us; thus absurdly sacrificing the end to the means.[30]

Besides his record as President and his own words, we have the testimony of his ardent political foe, Alexander Hamilton, who served with Jefferson in Washington's first Cabinet.

> . . . It is not true, as is alleged, that he [Jefferson] is an enemy to the power of the executive, or that he is for compounding all the powers in the House of Representatives. . . . While we were in the Administration together he was generally for a large construction of the Executive Authority. . . .[31]

As President, through the party caucus Jefferson virtually controlled the Congress while seeming to subordinate himself to it. By thus creating the appearance of executive subordination to the legislative, Jefferson no doubt helped to prepare the way for that subordination in fact. Under Madison, Monroe, and John Quincy Adams the President became the creature if not the puppet of Congress. As Professor Corwin says, "for twenty years the plan rejected by the Framers, of having the President chosen by the Congress, was substantially in operation. During this

28 Albert J. Beveridge, *The Life of John Marshall* (Boston: Houghton Mifflin, 1911–1919) , vol. II, p. 537, quoted in Corwin, *op. cit.,* p. 19.

29 Quoted in Binkley, *op. cit.,* p. 52.

30 See Sidney Hyman, *loc. cit.*

31 *The Works of Alexander Hamilton,* ed. by Henry Cabot Lodge (New York: Putnam, 1904) , pp. x, 413.

period the practice grew up of each successive President continuing a considerable part of his predecessor's Cabinet in office; and when he convened them in council, the Chief Executive counted the votes of the heads of departments as of equal weight with his own. Hardly more than *primus inter pares* in his own right, he was glad if Congress accorded him that degree of deference. In short, the Presidency was in commission."[32]

The Jacksonian Revolution

With Andrew Jackson, the Presidency was not only revived, it was, in a very real sense, remade.

Jackson made the office a tribune of the people. This, as much as anything, is the main significance of the so-called Jacksonian revolution. As a candidate he defied and denounced the congressional caucus and brought about his own nomination by the more democratic institution— a national convention. It is not too much to say that with Jackson the people, for the first time, captured the Presidency.

> When Jackson arrived in Washington, he found that the frontier had moved to the Potomac with him. The place was jam-packed. Crowds overflowed the hotels and boarding houses into the streets, where men with coon-skin caps and buckskin shirts mixed with others in homespun and broadcloth. The "people," ardent Democrats said, had finally taken over from the monocrats and monopolists. "It was," said one observer, "like the inundation of Northern barbarians into Rome. Strange faces filled every public place and every face seemed to bear defiance on its brow."[33]

Where Jefferson had worked through the congressional caucus for his measures, Jackson appealed over the head of Congress to the people. Critics of both men might say that Jefferson connived with Congress, whereas Jackson used his great following among the people to coerce the legislative branch.

Jackson not only made the Presidency a tribune of the people, he reaffirmed the right of the President to participate actively in the legislative process. Not content to wait for Congress to tell him what to do, Jackson took an active part in the formulation of legislation and in exerting the not inconsiderable influence of the Presidency in getting it through the legislative mill. His war on the Whig proposal to recharter the Second Bank of the United States is a classic case of the use of the executive veto. In his annual message he told Congress that "both the constitutionality and the expediency of the law creating this bank are well questioned . . . and it must be admitted by all that it has failed in the great end of establishing a uniform and sound currency." When, after a bitter struggle between the President and the powerful forces

32 Corwin, *op. cit.*, p. 20.
33 Marquis James, *Andrew Jackson: Portrait of a President* (Indianapolis: Bobbs-Merrill, 1937) , p. 181.

arrayed on the side of the bank, Congress passed the bill to recharter, Jackson promptly vetoed the measure. He attacked the law on constitutional grounds and asserted that "It is as much the duty of the House of Representatives, of the Senate, and of the President to decide upon the constitutionality of any bill . . . as it is of the Supreme judges. *The opinion of the judges has no more authority over Congress than the opinion of Congress has over the judges, and on that point the President is independent of both.*" [Our italics]

Jackson asserted an inherent power in the President, not only to enforce the laws of Congress, but to preserve the Union against nullification and threats of secession. We cannot review here the dramatic conflict between Jackson and his own Vice-President, John C. Calhoun, over the proper procedures to follow in revising the Tariff Act of 1828. The southern states were outraged by the high rates imposed which they regarded as flagrantly discriminatory against their section. Calhoun took the lead in a campaign to nullify the law by state action. In 1826, even before the iniquitous Tariff Act, South Carolina, Virginia, and Georgia had adopted resolutions declaring a protective tariff to be "unconstitutional, unwise, unjust, unequal and oppressive." To provide a new rationale for nullification, Calhoun prepared the famous "South Carolina Exposition" in which he reasserted the essential principle of the Virginia and Kentucky resolutions. The federal government, he argued, with strictly delegated powers is not a sovereign state but a compact among sovereign states, and cannot therefore pass any legislation not expressly authorized by the Constitution. When it does pass such legislation, the states have a right to *interpose* against it and to declare it "null and void within the limits of the state." On the issue of "interposition" or nullification, however, Jackson regarded his oath to uphold the Constitution and laws of the nation as a higher obligation than his position on any particular policy.

Hence it was that on April 13, 1830, at a dinner to celebrate Jefferson's birthday, the President and Vice-President confronted each other in an atmosphere tense with emotion. The program of speeches had been carefully arranged to support the Vice-President's position. Jackson attended the dinner and agreed to offer the first "volunteer" toast following the formal speeches. These were preceded by no less than twenty-four "regular" toasts in which support for "interposition" if not "nullification" was carefully built up. When his turn came, he stood amidst guest applause and cheers. Waiting for the cheering to subside, he lifted his glass, and fixing his eyes on Calhoun boomed his toast: "Our Union. It must be preserved." According to reports of the time, the toast was received in utter silence. "A proclamation of martial law in South Carolina," said Isaac Hill, "and an order to arrest Calhoun where he sat could not have come with more blinding, staggering force." Calhoun's toast to "The Union, next to our liberty, most dear," was anticlimactic, especially when he followed this with a rather lame appeal for respect to "the rights of the states."

The significance of this incident is in the unequivocal assertion by Jackson of the President's inherent power and obligation to protect and preserve the Union. It was a theory of presidential power that Lincoln and other strong Presidents have reaffirmed. Had either Jackson or Lincoln, rather than Buchanan, been President in 1859–1860, secession might have been scotched at its birth. How far Jackson was prepared to go became clear in the months following the Jefferson dinner. When South Carolina issued a call for a special state convention to "interpose" against the tariff, Jackson acted at once. On September 11, 1832, he ordered the Secretary of the Navy to be ready for any show of resistance to federal customs men in Charleston harbor and ordered the garrison at Fort Moultrie, in Charleston, strengthened.

But South Carolina continued on its dangerous course and on November 24, an *Ordinance of Nullification* was passed. The state legislature at once passed legislation including provisions for military force to prevent federal officers from enforcing the tariff laws in South Carolina. Jackson replied with a firm reassertion of his intention to use all the force at his command to carry the laws of the United States into effect. It is said the President was prepared to put 40,000 soldiers into South Carolina if necessary. In January, Jackson asked for additional legislation to strengthen his hand and Congress responded by passing the so-called Force Bill. Fortunately, while the Force Bill was pending, revision of the Tariff Act was also in process and the date for nullification, February 1, 1833, was deferred pending tariff revision. Assured of a further tariff reduction the South Carolina Convention met March 11, 1833, and by a vote of 153 to 4 rescinded the Ordinance of Nullification. Both sides claimed victory—which is perhaps the happiest of all possible solutions for difficult political problems. The real victor, however, was clearly the President and the power and prestige of the great office he occupied.

Jackson added greatly to the power of the Presidency when he reasserted the right of the President to choose his own Cabinet and other personnel of the executive branch. In doing so he also asserted his rights and prerogatives as the leader of his party both in the country and in the government. Not only did he insist upon choosing his own Cabinet, but when members failed to recognize their subordination to the President— even in social affairs—he "reorganized" them out of his official family. As for administrative appointments, Jackson followed the pattern familiar to strong Presidents then as now; he insisted upon subordinates who were politically loyal to him as President and party leader. Following Washington's administration the custom grew up of continuing in office from one President to another not only minor administrative personnal but even men occupying, in Washington's phrase, "offices of consequence."

Jackson broke with this tradition and reasserted the principle of party loyalty. No doubt this principle was abused, but it is well to remember the political atmosphere of the time, the pressures upon Jackson, and his own egalitarian beliefs.

To those who saw the President as a servant of Congress, or at most as a chief administrator, the Jacksonian model was disturbing. Frightened by the prospect of presidential domination Chancellor Kent wrote in 1834, "I look upon Jackson as a detestable, reckless, vain and malignant tyrant. . . . This American elective monarchy frightens me." Daniel Webster protested in the Senate that "the President carries on the government, all the rest are sub-contractors." And Henry Clay talked about a "bloodless revolution." Under Jackson, he said, the country was "tending toward a total change of the pure republican character of the government, and to the concentration of all power in the hands of one man."

Later Presidents Define Their Office

These cries of alarm have been raised whenever a President, in the Hamiltonian tradition, seeks to explore the full dimensions of power conferred in Article II of the Constitution. To the Hamiltonian-Jacksonian Presidents the language of the Constitution, deliberately vague and ambiguous, offers a field for expansion of "the executive Power," to whatever dimensions seems necessary to the President. As Lincoln said in his first inaugural, addressing himself to the leaders of secession, "You have no oath registered in heaven to destroy the Government, while I have the most solemn one to 'preserve, protect and defend it.'" And, during the darkest days of the Civil War he wrote, "Was it possible to lose the Nation and yet preserve the Constitution? By general law, life and limb must be protected, yet often a limb must be amputated to save a life. . . . I felt that measures, otherwise unconstitutional, might become lawful by becoming indispensable to the preservation of the Constitution, through the preservation of the nation. Right or wrong, I assumed this ground and now avow it."[34]

Under this theory the President may become, in time of emergency, a dictator in the classic tradition—expanding his vast powers to protect the nation in time of great danger, and allowing them to contract again when the emergency is passed. It was under this theory that Jackson acted when he threatened to use force against nullification in South Carolina. It was under this theory that Lincoln "exercised more power during the early months of the Civil War than any other President in history."[35]

[34] See Hyman, *loc. cit.*
[35] Owen Stratton, "Presidential Power," *The New York Times Magazine,* January 20, 1957.

This was the theory on which Theodore Roosevelt acted and which with more candor than most Presidents he outlined as follows:

> The most important factor in getting the right spirit in my Administration . . . was my insistence upon the theory that the executive power was limited only by specific restrictions and prohibitions appearing in the Constitution or imposed by Congress under its constitutional powers. My view was that every executive officer . . . was a steward of the people bound actively and affirmatively to do all he could for the people. . . . I declined to adopt the view that what was imperatively necessary for the nation could not be done by the President unless he could find some specific authorization to do it.[36]

And it was a similar theory that guided Franklin Roosevelt through the hectic days of the New Deal and World War II. Even Henry Stimson, who was to become his Secretary of War, was appalled at the long reach of presidential powers during the days of the New Deal. "F.D.R.'s conduct," he wrote in April, 1937, "had the skeleton of dictatorship."[37] How far the Hamiltonian-Jacksonian model differs from the Whiggish model is revealed in President Taft's words. "The true view of the executive function is . . . that the President can exercise no powers which cannot reasonably . . . be traced to some specific grant of power, or justly implied or included within such express grant as necessary and proper to its exercise. Such specific grant must be either in the Constitution or in an act of Congress passed in pursuance thereof. There is no undefined residuum of power which he can exercise because it seems to him to be in the public interest."[38]

President Taft's theory, however, leaves the question of presidential power up in the air because even the so-called specific powers conferred are, as we shall see, themselves ambiguous. As Professor Neustadt has said in his penetrating study *Presidential Power,* the language of Article II is little more, and nothing less, than a "hunting license" for the incumbent President. Any President with a strong sense of mission, unafraid of power, and with those personal qualities which characterize great leadership, will be able to find within the language of the Constitution ample power. The President, as Woodrow Wilson once observed, can be as big a man as he wants to be and is capable of becoming.[39]

The ambiguity of presidential power and the various interpretations which different incumbents have given to it helps to account for its ebb

---

[36] *Autobiography of Theodore Roosevelt,* ed. by Wayne Andrews (New York: Scribner, 1958).

[37] See *The New York Times,* October 11, 1959, where this and other quotations from Stimson's unpublished diary are reported.

[38] William Howard Taft, *Our Chief Magistrate and His Powers* (New York: Columbia University Press, 1925).

[39] One is reminded of another Wilson witticism—"some men grow in high offices, others merely swell."

and flow from one administration to another. "The most defective part of the Constitution," wrote Abel Upshur in 1840, "is that which relates to the executive department. It is impossible to read that instrument without being struck with the loose, unguarded terms in which the powers and duties of the President are pointed out. So far as the Legislature is concerned, the limitations of the Constitution are, perhaps, as precise and strict as they could safely have been made; but in regard to the Executive, the Convention appears to have studiously selected such loose and general expressions, as would enable the President, by implication and construction, either to neglect his duties or to enlarge his powers."

So true is this that even as perceptive a student as Wilson moved full circle in his analysis of the Presidency. Writing in his classic treatise *Congressional Government,* in 1885, he said:

> Congress [is] the dominant, nay the irresistible power of the federal system, relegating some of the chief balances of the Constitution to an insignificant role. . . . [By contrast] the prestige of the Presidential office has declined with the character of the President . . .[and] the decline in the character of the Presidents is not the cause. . . . That high office has fallen from
> its first estate of dignity, because its power has waned; and its power
> has waned because the power of Congress has become predominant.[40]

Writing three years after Wilson, Viscount Bryce agreed. The powers of the President, he said, had declined because Congress had "succeeded in occupying nearly all the ground which the Constitution left debatable between the President and itself."[41]

However, in 1908, with the administration of Theodore Roosevelt coming to a close, Wilson offered a radically revised estimate of presidential powers. The President, he wrote, "is the only national voice in affairs. Let him once win the admiration and confidence of the country, and no other single force can withstand him. . . ."[42] During two terms as President he helped to confirm his own revised theory of the Presidency. So impressed was he by the scope of presidential power that H. C. Black, writing during his second term, said:

> The most portentous development in American political and constitutional history since 1865 is the change in the relations between the executive and legislative branches of Government, the one [i.e., the President] making enormous gains in . . . influence and actual power, the other suffering a corresponding decline in prestige, and in its control over the processes of government. *The President* of the United States occupies today a position of leadership and of command over the government of the country, so

40 Wilson, *op. cit., supra,* n. 21.

41 James Bryce, *The American Commonwealth* (New York: Macmillan, 1914; original, 1888).

42 *Constitutional Government in the United States* (New York: Columbia University Press 1908).

different from that which was intended by the framers of the Constitution, that if it were not the outcome of a natural process of evolution . . . it would bear the stigmata of revolution, and if it had been achieved in a single presidential term, it would have been denounced as a *coup d'état*.[43]

Presidential Power

As we have indicated above, the reaction of the framers to the virtually headless governments under the Articles of Confederation was one of unfeigned disillusionment, if not disgust. To be sure, few were willing to go so far as Hamilton in proposing a single executive for life with the power and dignity of the English monarch. But Gouverneur Morris, James Madison, James Wilson, and other outstanding leaders in the Convention shared Hamilton's desire for a strong, independent executive establishment. And it was with this goal in mind that they approved the language of Article II of the Constitution. We confine our present discussion to the so-called specific powers conferred in Sections 2 and 3 of Article II.

The first of these provides that the "President shall be Commander in Chief of the Army and Navy of the United States, and of the Militia of the several States, when called into the actual Service of the United States." The scope of power conveyed in these words has never been fully explored. Although Congress has power "to raise and support Armies" and ". . . to provide and maintain a Navy," once these are provided for they come under the command of the President. At the present time this language places at the command of the President armed forces numbering in the neighborhood of 3 million, not including members of state militia units which, in emergency, the President may call into national service under his command. Moreover it is within his discretion under the Selective Service and other laws passed by Congress to expand these military forces virtually without limit.

As Commander in Chief the President may, if he so desires, take personal command of the armed forces in the field. Indeed President Washington did precisely this during the so-called Whiskey Rebellion. Washington also dispatched troops against Indian tribes and in like manner President Hayes sent both arms and men into ten states during the railway strikes of 1877, with only the most vague and often dubious request from legislatures or governors of those states.

Under the Constitution, Congress has power to "make Rules for the Government and Regulation of the land and naval forces," and "to provide for calling forth the Militia to execute the Laws of the Union, suppress Insurrections and repel Invasions" and "to provide for organ-

[43] H. C. Black, *The Relation of the Executive Power to Legislation* (Princeton, N.J.: Princeton University Press, 1919) .

izing, arming, and disciplining the Militia, and for governing such part of them as may be employed in the Service of the United States." Most of these powers, however, have been delegated to the President as Commander in Chief.

Under the Constitution, Congress has the power to "guarantee to every State in this Union a Republican Form of Government, and shall protect each of them against Invasion; and on Application of the [state] Legislature, or of the Executive (when the Legislature cannot be convened) against domestic Violence." No request is required, of course, where the armed forces are used to carry into effect the laws of the United States, and it is under this theory that many Presidents have dispatched troops into various states without any formal request from the state itself. Indeed, during the bitter Pullman strike of 1894, President Cleveland sent troops to Chicago over vigorous protests from Governor Altgeld on the theory that the troops were being used, not to put down "insurrection" or "domestic violence" but to protect property of the United States and to "remove obstructions to the United States mails." Between 1917 and 1922 soldiers were ordered into various states no less than thirty times, mainly in cases involving labor disputes. To enforce the laws of the United States and, in this case, an order issued by a federal court, President Eisenhower in 1958 sent paratroopers to Little Rock, Arkansas, to protect Negro children in their right to attend a hitherto racially segregated high school. Presidents Kennedy and Johnson also dispatched federal troops and called state militia into service to protect Negro students in their right to attend the universities of Mississippi and Alabama and to protect civil rights demonstrators against violent assaults by hostile mobs.

If the President's powers as Commander in Chief are great in peacetime, they expand enormously in time of war or emergency. President Lincoln, faced with "combinations too powerful to be suppressed" by ordinary means, assumed that he could mobilize the entire might of the nation to put them down. Accordingly he called for volunteers, "embodied the militia into a volunteer army, added 23,000 men to the regular army and 18,000 to the navy, pledged the credit of the United States for a quarter of a billion dollars, paid out two millions from unappropriated funds in the Treasury, to persons unauthorized to receive it, closed the Post Office to 'treasonable correspondence,' proclaimed a blockade of southern ports, suspended the writ of habeas corpus in various places, caused the arrest and military detention of persons 'who were represented to him' as being engaged in or contemplating 'treasonable practices' and all this either without one whit of statutory authority or with the merest figment thereof."[44] In a message to Congress, later, Lincoln rather sardonically said that he had done nothing beyond the constitutional competency of Congress, had Congress been in session.

[44] Corwin, *op. cit.*, p. 157.

On June 9, 1941, six months before Pearl Harbor, but after a state of emergency had been declared, President Franklin Roosevelt as Commander in Chief directed Secretary of War Stimson to take over and operate the strike-bound North American Aviation Company plant. In May, 1942, he authorized the military commanders on the West Coast to round up and place in "relocation" camps over 100,000 persons of Japanese origin, two-thirds of whom were native-born citizens of the United States. In December, 1950, President Truman, in the midst of the Korean War, directed the Secretary of Commerce to take possession of the strike-bound steel industry and to operate it pending settlement of the strike. This action, although defended as necessary to keep the supply of munitions flowing to our armies in the field, was, as we shall see, disallowed by the Supreme Court.

The Korean War, and more recently the undeclared war in South Vietnam, serve to illustrate the vast power of the President as head of state to involve the nation in war, although the Constitution clearly gives Congress power to "declare War." Nor is it reasonable to argue that the President's power to involve American armed forces in this way is dependent on any formal resolution of the Congress. He is, however, dependent on Congress for appropriations to support any such action. The American expedition to China during the Boxer Rebellion, the bombardment of Vera Cruz, the invasion of Mexico in pursuit of Pancho Villa, President Eisenhower's dispatch of troops to Lebanon in July, 1958, and President Johnson's intervention in Santo Domingo in 1965 are other examples. Many months before Pearl Harbor, President Roosevelt supplied naval escorts for merchant ships carrying "lend-lease" materials to Great Britain, and there were repeated armed clashes between war vessels of the United States and German submarines. The President had also leased military and naval bases in the Caribbean from Great Britain in return for some fifty "overage" destroyers, without any special authorization from the Congress. In recent years American troops have been committed to battle in Europe, Asia, and the Middle East, under orders of the President and without prior action by the Congress.

How far the President's powers may extend without support from Congress no one can really say. The Constitution provides that the "United States shall guarantee to every state . . . a Republican Form of Government, and shall protect each of them against Invasion; and . . . against domestic Violence." The Constitution, however, is silent on what branch of the government is to decide what a republican government is and when such defense is necessary. The Supreme Court has said that "it rests with Congress to decide what government is the established one in a state . . . as well as its republican character."[45] Does Congress also decide where federal protection of a state "against Invasion and . . . domestic Violence" is necessary? Again the Supreme Court has given at

[45] See *Luther* v. *Borden*, 7 Howard 1 (1849).

least a partial answer when it held that in setting up the provisional governments in the Confederacy the President had acted within his power as Commander in Chief, but also held that such governments were to be provisional only until Congress shall decide upon a more permanent establishment.[46] At the time of the Whiskey Rebellion, Congress authorized the President to call out the militia in case of insurrection against the government of any state.[47] There is, however, no reason to believe that Washington might not have used troops even in the absence of such legislation. The President may also call upon all authorities—federal, state and local—and all citizens, if necessary, to aid in enforcing the "laws of the union." President Jefferson, in April, 1808, did precisely this in a proclamation directed against "sundry persons" in the region of Lake Champlain, who, he said, were combining and conspiring against the Embargo Act. President Fillmore, in 1851, called on this power in an effort to enforce the Fugitive Slave laws in Boston, and President Pierce, in 1856, placed the military forces of the United States at the disposal of federal marshals in Kansas to be used as a *posse comitatus* under his constitutional power as Commander in Chief and his obligation "to take care that the laws be faithfully executed."

Lincoln's call for volunteers to put down rebellion was later ratified by Congress in the Act of July 29, 1861.[48] It was under these acts of Congress as well as under Article II of the Constitution that Presidents Hayes and Cleveland sent troops into strike-bound states to "maintain order" and to "protect the property of the United States" and to enforce the laws of the United States. These actions were sustained by the Supreme Court in very broad terms. According to Justice Brewer, "the entire strength of the nation may be used [by the President] to enforce in any part of the land the full and free exercise of all national powers and the security of all rights entrusted by the Constitution to his care." And presumably he may do so with or without legislative authorizations by Congress.[49]

Nevertheless, by enacting legislation to authorize the President to use military force in certain cases, Congress sought to create a presump-

[46] See *Texas* v. *White,* 7 Wallace 700 (1869).

[47] This Act of 1792 is still in force and is often cited, at least *pro forma,* by the President in sending troops into a state. It reads in part: "Whenever the laws of the U.S. shall be opposed or the execution thereof obstructed in any state by combinations too powerful to be suppressed by the ordinary course of judicial proceedings or by the power vested in the marshals, the President may call forth the militia of the state involved or any *other state.*" This act was extended in 1807 to authorize the President to use not only the militia but "the land or naval force of the U.S."

[48] This law provided that "whenever by reason of unlawful obstructions it shall become impracticable, in the judgment of the President, to enforce by the ordinary course of judicial proceedings, the laws of the U.S. . . . it shall be lawful for him to call forth the militia of any or all the states, and to employ such parts of the land and naval forces of the U.S. as he shall deem necessary to enforce . . . the laws of the U.S."

[49] See In Re *Debs,* 158 U.S. 564 (1894).

tion that such congressional action may be necessary. On April 20, 1871, for example, Congress authorized the President to "take such measures," including military force, "as he may deem necessary" to put down unlawful combinations which deny to "any class . . . equal protection of its constitutional rights." On the other hand a provision of the Army Appropriation Act of 1878 undertook to impose limits upon the power of the President to use armed force to execute the laws of the United States. "From and after the passage of this Act," said Congress, "it shall not be lawful to employ any part of the army of the United States as a *posse comitatus* or otherwise, for the purpose of executing the laws, except in such cases and under such circumstances as such employment of said forces may be expressly authorized by the Constitution or by Act of Congress." In 1964 Congress, by resolution, approved and presumably authorized bombing of certain areas in North Vietnam following the so-called Tonkin Bay incident.

One may well ask whether these or other laws or resolutions have in any material degree enlarged or diminished the power of the President to direct the armed forces of the United States. The exercise of the vast powers of the President as Commander in Chief was not unanticipated by the framers of the Constitution. "The direction of war," wrote Hamilton in *The Federalist,* "implies the direction of the common strength, and the power of directing and employing the common strength forms a usual and essential part in the definition of the executive authority." What dimensions of power lie hidden in Hamilton's phrase "to employ the common strength," one can only conjecture. Do they include the mobilization, not alone of the armed forces, but of the total manpower and resources of the nation? And how far can the presidential power go in this direction without affirmative action by the Congress? President Wilson as Commander in Chief created a Committee on Public Information, and without any statutory authority he developed a program of public information and propaganda and exercised a censorship over cables, telephone, and telegraph lines. President Franklin Roosevelt, as Commander in Chief, seized a strike-bound aircraft plant, ordered the arrest and "relocation" (sequestration) of Japanese residents of the West Coast (citizens and noncitizens alike), and his authority to do so was sustained by the Supreme Court. President Truman sought to justify his seizure of the strike-bound steel industry under his power as Commander in Chief as well as under the general "inherent" powers of the chief executive. In this, however, he was rebuffed by the Supreme Court which, in the various opinions of the justices, examined the nature and scope of the executive power.[50] In ordering the Secretary of Commerce to seize the steel industry, President Truman cited his statutory authority but "invoked generally the powers vested in the President by the Constitu-

[50] *Youngstown Sheet and Tube Co., et al.* v. *Sawyer,* 343 U.S. 579 (1952).

tion." He also conceded the power in Congress to supersede his order. When the steel companies appealed against the order to the Supreme Court, that tribunal by a 6–3 vote declared that the President had exceeded the executive powers conferred on him by the Constitution and had invaded a field within the exclusive legislative process of Congress.

14

PRESIDENTIAL POLICY AND ADMINISTRATION

☆ THE PRESIDENT AS EXECUTIVE

Under his oath of office the President must "solemnly swear (or affirm)" that "I will faithfully execute the Office of President of the United States, and will to the best of my Ability, preserve, protect and defend the Constitution of the United States." He is also bound by a constitutional mandate which requires that "he shall take Care that the Laws be faithfully executed," and to this end he "shall Commission all the Officers of the United States." As in the old aphorism that "all roads lead to Rome," so in the government of the United States all roads seem to lead to the President. Congress may create the great Leviathan, but the Constitution puts the President in the driver's seat.

The Executive Power of the President

The complex structure of the federal bureaucracy and its relation to the President will be discussed in the next chapter. At this point we need do no more than to emphasize once again the central importance of the Presidency and the executive establishment over which he presides. Without executive and administrative officers the best-laid plans for promoting the common defense, insuring domestic tranquility, promoting the general welfare, and increasing the blessings of liberty to ourselves and our posterity would be stillborn. As the first Hoover Commission put it:

> The President, and under him his chief lieutenants, the department heads, must be held responsible and accountable to the people and [to] the Congress for the conduct of the executive branch. . . .

447

Yet it is obviously impossible for any President personally to "administer" a government whose official personnel includes over 2½ million and another 3 million in the armed services "organized" in some 2,000 departments, agencies and their subdivisions, and extending literally around the world. It is particularly difficult when this responsibility and the power that would go with it are not always clearly defined. "Responsibility and accountability are impossible," said the Hoover Commission, "without authority—the power to direct. The exercise of authority is impossible without a clear line of command from the top to the bottom, and a return line of responsibility and accountability from the bottom to the top."

The power and responsibility of the President is primarily a *political* power and a *political* responsibility. This, however, implies power to insure also the *administrative* responsibility of subordinate officers to their superiors; *legal* responsibility of administrative officers to act within the scope of the powers conferred on them; *professional* responsibility of administrators to high standards of competence and professional integrity; and *moral* responsibility to the highest moral and ethical standards of the society they serve. The *political* responsibility of the President, in a word, includes responsibility for the *administrative, legal, professional,* and *moral* standards of conduct throughout the federal service. For the vast majority of the executive officers of the United States, *political* responsibility is vicarious and not direct. For it is the President who, in final analysis, must "take the rap" for what is or is not done under his "Administration." It is at the President's desk, as President Truman once observed, that "the buck stops." For a President to say that he did not initiate, did not authorize, or did not know of an administrative act, under challenge, is a confession of weakness and an evasion of his constitutional responsibility to "take Care that the Laws be faithfully executed."

Because the white light of public responsibility focuses with such intensity upon the President, it is important that his power to control the operation of the federal bureaucracy be commensurate with this responsibility. If the President is held responsible for the deeds of incompetent civil servants, he must be able to discipline, and if necessary dismiss, such subordinates. Unfortunately this ideal union of political power and responsibility for administration is, in important ways, lacking in the United States. In establishing the major departments or other executive agencies of government, Congress has often interposed itself between the President and his subordinates, thus confusing the clear line of power and responsibility. For example, in establishing the Treasury Department, the Secretary is required "to make report and give information to either branch of the legislature, in person or in writing respecting all matters . . . which may appertain to his office." Although in a subsequent law of September 11, 1789, the Secretary of the Treasury was described as an "Executive Officer," both he and the Treasurer of the United States were nevertheless required to make annual reports to Congress. On at least one occasion this dual line of responsibility was a source of great embarrassment. In 1833 President Jackson ordered Secretary Duane to remove federal deposits from the Bank of the United States, although Congress had by formal resolution expressed its confidence in the Bank. When Duane chose to follow Congress rather than the President on this issue, Jackson replaced him with Roger Taney, who then carried out the order. Under a weaker President, Congress might have succeeded in this obvious invasion of the President's power as the chief executive.

Appointments and Removals

In March, 1869, Congress enacted a Tenure of Office Act that prohibited the President from removing officials appointed with the advice and consent of the Senate without Senate approval. This act, part of the congressional vendetta against President Johnson, was later used to block President Hayes from removing a collector of customs, and a port naval officer in New York. Hayes succeeded in getting rid of these subordinates only by suspending them from office after Congress had adjourned. This obnoxious legislation, of dubious constitutionality, was finally repealed in 1887 following repeated contests between Cleveland and the Senate over the presidential power to appoint and to remove. The President's sole and uncontrolled discretion in these matters has, however, never been fully established.

By another law in 1876 Congress provided that First, Second, and Third Class Postmasters be *appointed* and *removed* only by and with the consent of the Senate. This junior Tenure of Office Act went unchallenged until 1920, when President Wilson removed from office Frank Myers, a Postmaster at Portland, Oregon, without the advice and consent of the Senate. Myers' widow, her husband having passed away, challenged the legality of Wilson's removal order and sued for her husband's pay as Postmaster. In an opinion which is one of the great landmarks of American constitutional law, Chief Justice Taft speaking for the Supreme Court, held the Act of 1876 to be an unconstitutional invasion of the President's power to remove administrative officials.[1] This decision cleared the air and seemed to establish as a firm principle that the President's constitutional responsibility to "take Care that the Laws be faithfully executed" carried with it the necessary power to direct, discipline, or dismiss his administrative agents.

But the President's power in this important area has been obscured by more recent decisions of the Supreme Court. In 1933 President

[1] See *Myers* v. *United States,* 272 U.S. 52 (1926).

Franklin Roosevelt, having failed to induce William E. Humphrey to resign, removed him from the Federal Trade Commission. The law establishing this commission provided that members be appointed for seven-year terms with the advice and consent of the Senate and that they might be removed by the President for "inefficiency, neglect of duty, or malfeasance in office." President Roosevelt's reason for removing Humphrey was, however, none of these but solely because Commissioner Humphrey was opposed to the public policies of the President. Again the President's power to remove was challenged, and again by the displaced officer's widow (Mr. Humphrey having died in the meantime). But this time a unanimous Court held the President to be without power to remove members of the commission except for the reasons set forth by Congress. The Court had a good deal to say about the difference between this case and the Portland Postmaster. The Federal Trade Commission, it argued, was a nonpartisan, quasi-legislative and quasi-judicial agency "independent" of political control by the President.[2] If literally interpreted and applied, this decision would create a precedent, dangerous alike to the President's power and responsibility as chief executive. It would enable Congress to establish agencies, with vast executive, legislative, and judicial powers, independent of any effective control by the President. To justify this "independence" and hence political irresponsibility, by saying that these agencies in addition to their administrative power exercise quasi-legislative and quasi-judicial powers as well is to open the way to a creeping irresponsibility throughout the government. Any administrative officer, save the lowest man on the totem pole, exercises quasi-judicial and/or quasi-legislative powers. That is to say, these officers decide controversies, and issue rules and regulations as well as administrative orders.

A more recent decision of the Court has followed the line laid down in the Humphrey case. In 1953 President Eisenhower removed a Truman appointed member of the War Claims Commission, a Mr. Wiener, before the expiration of his term, and after he had refused the President's request that he resign. Although the Court of Claims upheld the President's right to dismiss Mr. Wiener, the Supreme Court in *Wiener* v. *United States* (1958) reversed the Court of Claims and applied the rule of the Humphrey case. Holding that the War Claims Commission was a quasi-judicial as well as a quasi-executive body, the Court decided that, in the absence of specific congressional authorization to do so, the President could not remove, in his own discretion, a member of such an agency.[3]

If the doctrine of the Humphrey and Wiener cases is followed and extended to other agencies, the President may be stripped of one of his

[2] *Rathbun* [Humphrey's Executor] v. *United States,* 295 U.S. 602 (1935).
[3] *Wiener* v. *United States,* 357 U.S. 349 (1958).

most effective powers for the control of agents for whose conduct he must assume responsibility.

But tenure of office legislation, and legislation making administrative agencies "independent" of the President are not the only ways in which the President's power has been impaired. Congress has created within major departments numerous bureaus and agencies over which particular committees of Congress and even particular Congressmen exercise more control than the department head or the President. Control over many detailed acts of administration are placed in congressional committees, and hence outside the control of the President. The long-standing rivalry between the Bureau of Reclamation in the Interior Department and the Corps of Engineers in the Department of the Army has its roots in the direct intervention of congressional committees in the administration of these important agencies, an intervention so powerful and persistent that it can ignore and even defy the President.[4]

Only strong leadership in the White House can cope with this problem. Otherwise the *power* of the President will be drained away, while his *responsibility* remains. And responsibility without power is as dangerous as power without responsibility. As matters now stand, the President is not only harassed by congressional impairment of his power, he is denied many of the powers essential to effective control of the vast administrative apparatus for which he is politically responsible. He lacks adequate power and authority to determine the organization and structure of the executive branch. Congress has continued to insist upon its own prerogative in this field. Although the Reorganization Act of 1959 gave the President power, within limits, to reorganize the government, any plan has to be submitted to Congress and becomes effective only if it is not vetoed by a simple majority of either house within sixty days after its submission. In 1961 President Kennedy was again given authority to "reorganize," subject to congressional veto within 60 days, but Congress

[4] See Inter-University Case Program, Arthur A. Maas, *The Kings River Project* (New York: Harcourt, Brace & World, 1952).

The Corps of Engineers is a classic example of congressional intervention and even control of administrative behavior. In general such controls involve one or more of the following: (1) control of personnel by requiring more or less formal committee "clearance" of certain administrative appointments, (2) budget control through the device of annual appropriations, not only for particular programs, but for the agencies themselves, (3) committee clearance of certain administrative acts before final action can be taken.

"Taken together," says Professor Neustadt, "these assertions seem to aim at giving legislative committees (and their members) a hold on bread-and-butter for home districts, site locations, purchase contracts, surplus sales."

Congressional clearances of the kind described are most commonly enforced by Committees on Agriculture, Armed Services, Interior, Public Works, and the Joint Committee on Atomic Energy.

See Richard Neustadt, "Politicians and Bureaucracy," in David B. Truman, ed., *The Congress and America's Future* (American Assembly; Englewood Cliffs, N.J.: Prentice-Hall, 1965), chap. 5, pp. 105–106.

refused to restrict its own veto power by requiring a constitutional majority of all members, rather than a simple majority of those present and voting to disapprove a proposed plan. Eleven of 41 reorganization plans submitted by President Truman, 3 of such plans out of 17 proposed by President Eisenhower, and 4 out of 10 submitted by President Kennedy were disapproved by Congress. President Johnson had somewhat better luck, although the final score remains to be recorded. Under the Humphrey decision a substantial number of administrative agencies are outside the President's effective control. Although his power to designate the chairman of some of these "independent" agencies has been established, a request to increase the power of the chairman—in this case, of the Federal Communications Commission, the Securities and Exchange Commission, the Civil Aeronautics Board, and the Federal Trade Commission—has been denied.[5]

Control of the federal budget is the key to control of the policy and administration of the government. Although the President's control of this important function has been greatly increased since the original Budget and Accounting Act was passed, he is still "handcuffed and hogtied" by line-by-line appropriations, and is denied an item veto. This last power to apply a selective or item veto to appropriations bills—a power possessed by most governors—would increase the President's control of administration by removing the power of factional interests in Congress to "blackmail" the administration into accepting unwelcome amendments on pain of losing or vetoing the whole bill.

☆ *THE PRESIDENCY AS AN INSTITUTION*

The President is many different men—yet only *one*. Perhaps it would be more accurate to say, the President plays many different roles—yet always the same one. He is Head of State, Chief Executive, Legislative Leader, Commander in Chief, Leader of his Party, Tribune of the People, and Father Image for 200 million people. To discharge these multiple responsibilities has always been beyond the capacity of a single individual, and yet the responsibilities are inescapably his and his alone. Obviously the President needs help, but help that will not intrude itself upon the public scene to a point where the image of the President is obscured by the image of his helper. It was this the President's Committee on Administrative Management had in mind when in 1937 they referred to the six presidential assistants they were proposing as men "with a passion for anonymity."

Among the President's major helpers are of course the members of his Cabinet and the directors of other major executive agencies. But these

5 See the *Wall Street Journal*, May 18, 1961, article by Louis M. Kohlmeier, "GOP will Fight to Block Agency Reorganization."

top officials have their own burdens in directing the work of twelve major departments and seventy or more major permanent agencies. They bring problems to the President, but rarely have the time or talent do do for him what it was once said the English monarch did for the prime minister, that is, to "consult, to advise, and to warn."

The Cabinet

Washington and many of his successors could rely for this upon the Cabinet—a body which existed only because the President might call the department heads together to "consult." As the creature of the President, the Cabinet has been used in a variety of ways. The lore of American government is full of stories to indicate that at times the President regarded his departmental secretaries as colleagues, even equals, in a common endeavor. Such Presidents held Cabinet meetings at which they were at best *primus inter pares* (first among equals). They listened and learned, and on rare occasions gave instructions or even orders. Other Presidents have used their Cabinet meetings very much as a commanding general uses his staff—to hear reports, protests, and petitions, and to give orders concerning major policy and strategy. Still others have regarded Cabinet meetings as little more than semisocial gatherings for the exchange of whatever gossip, wit, or wisdom the members could collectively recall. This kind of intelligence should not be underestimated. The heads of executive departments and agencies are the eyes and ears of the President.[6] Each member of the Cabinet normally has sources of information which reach beyond and below those that are otherwise accessible to the President, and collectively they can supply him with information indispensable to one or more of the many roles he has to play. Moreover, as is usually and quite properly the case, officers of Cabinet rank are appointed less for their administrative talents than for their political "know-how." A President who sacrifices this know-how for mere executive ability will misconceive the proper role of his major aides and advisers. President Kennedy, on several occasions, indicated impatience with the Cabinet as a high-level body to consult, to advise, and to warn. "I see all the cabinet officers every week . . . ," he is reported as saying, "but . . . general cabinet meetings . . . I feel to be unnecessary and involve a waste of time."[7] There isn't much point, he indicated, in discussing the Post Office budget with the Secretary of Agriculture who has his own special problems. This of course is not what Cabinet meetings, even in theory, are designed for.[8] Unless they can be used to discuss

---

[6] See Richard F. Fenno, Jr., *The President's Cabinet* (New York: Random House, 1960).

[7] *San Francisco Chronicle,* April 12, 1961.

[8] It is hard to believe that this news story accurately reflected President Kennedy's theory of Cabinet meetings. Any President who used his Cabinet meetings for this purpose would surely find them disappointing. President Johnson, by contrast with his

matters of major policy, and to inform the President and Cabinet colleagues of rough spots in the road ahead, Cabinet meetings *would* be a waste of time. Nevertheless the Cabinet as an institution has been fighting a more or less losing battle. The meteoric growth of the government has generated such a large number of major agencies that to include the chief officer of each in the Cabinet would make that body unwieldly and useless. On the other hand, to invite only a small number and thus conserve the consultative role of the Cabinet might be invidious and politically hazardous. The problem here is essentially that of organizing the executive branch in a manageable number of unmanageable departments or an unmanageable number of manageable departments. It is this problem that makes it especially urgent that the President be given greater freedom in determining the organization with which he can best operate.[9]

Counsel and Advice

The President has never relied solely upon members of his Cabinet, either collectively or as individuals, for the kind of help he needs most, that is, informed, wise and candid counsel, and help in using presidential and personal influence where it is most needed. Washington, as we have seen, had his unofficial counselors and representatives. So too have other Presidents. Most notable, perhaps, was the so-called "kitchen cabinet" of Andrew Jackson. The name, legend had it, derives from the fact that a small group of journalists and politicians, who had helped Jackson win the Presidency, chose to enter the White House through the kitchen door. Most Presidents have had their "kitchen cabinets"—small groups of trusted advisers with a passion for privacy if not for anonymity. But kitchen cabinets, like official Cabinets, have varied both in composition and in their methods of operation. Franklin Roosevelt's kitchen cabinet, at least after 1939, was made up of a few members of the official White House staff and "from men with 'Roosevelt's point of view' who held noncabinet posts elsewhere in the Government." The acknowledged, quasi-official head of this body was Harry Hopkins, the President's confidant and alter ego. President Truman's kitchen cabinet was something else again, drawn from old friends and political associates, included not so much because of their official position as because of their "know-how" and their loyalty to the President. Mr. Eisenhower's kitchen cabinet,

---

predecessor, resolved to "revitalize the cabinet as a dynamic and major instrument of government." How far he succeeded only time can tell. See *The New York Times,* January 16, 1965.

9 With something in the neighborhood of seventy federal agencies, which have, or perhaps should have, direct access to the President, the dimensions of the problem begin to emerge.

according to Sidney Hyman, with the exceptions of Secretaries Dulles and Humphrey, was "drawn from the staff of the White House proper. In theory they moved through a formal chain of command ruled by Sherman Adams, who held the title of The Assistant to the President." President Kennedy's kitchen cabinet was more like Franklin Roosevelt's than it was like either Jackson's or Eisenhower's. Its membership came mainly from the White House staff but included also "selected allies drawn from . . . 'Kennedy men' placed at strategic levels of power elsewhere in the Government." The Kennedy kitchen cabinet was also less highly formalized than its predecessor under President Eisenhower. "In its motions," said Sidney Hyman, "it is loose-jointed, enjoys a free interplay with an accessible President, subdivides its general areas of responsibility . . . but has no formal chain of command." Most of the members were general practitioners of government and politics, not specialists, nor professional administrators. President Kennedy found in this body a better vehicle than the Cabinet for the consultation, advice, and premonitory guidance every President needs. And it was within this group that major appointments and policy decisions were discussed before receiving the presidential imprimatur. As summarized by Mr. Hyman, this Kennedy kitchen cabinet functioned to see " (1) that the departments understand the implications of their own proposed policies, (2) that departmental proposals . . . reach the President in a coherent form [also the arguments against them], (3) that adequate means [political and administrative] are at hand to back up the final presidential decision, (4) that the final decision is gripped by the gears of the bureaucracy and faithfully executed, (5) that Congress and the people are brought into the process as each case warrants, (6) that the final decision is kept under review to see whether it actually attains the end for which it was framed."[10] One cannot be sure that this is not a highly idealized version of President Kennedy's inner council, but it will indicate how a kitchen cabinet under more or less ideal conditions probably ought to function.[11]

We have said that some members of President Kennedy's kitchen

[10] Sidney Hyman, "Inside the Kennedy Kitchen Cabinet," *The New York Times Magazine*, March 5, 1961. See also, "The President's Unknown Aides," *The New York Times Magazine*, March 31, 1957.

[11] The list of President Johnson's intimate advisers was a lengthening one as old faces were replaced or supplemented by new. Among the members of his kitchen cabinet at one time or another were an Associate Justice of the Supreme Court, a number of newspaper columnists, several friends and "cronies" from Texas, a couple of prominent, liberal Washington lawyers, including a former national chairman of Americans for Democratic Action, Governor John Connally of Texas, a few Cabinet officers on whose general counsel the President leaned heavily, a few key Senators and Congressmen, a number of key officials of the Democratic party, and, most important, Mrs. Johnson. See "The 'Inner Circle' Around Johnson," by Ben H. Bagdikian, in *The New York Times Magazine*, February 28, 1965. Also Tom Wicker, "Johnson and Johnson Men," in *The New York Times Magazine*, May 3, 1964.

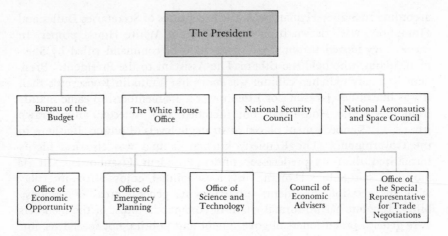

Figure 14–1 Executive Office of the President. (After *United States Government Organization Manual, 1966–67*, Washington, D.C., Revised June 1, 1966, p. 606.)

cabinet were members of the White House staff and this is likely to be true in any administration.

This White House staff is but one of ten more or less specialized agencies within the Executive Office of the President, created in 1937 following the report of the President's Committee on Administrative Management.[12] (See Figure 14–1.)

Lincoln operated his office with that indispensable team of secretaries, Nicolay and Hay—and a clerk or two. It is said that President Grant "ran the White House office" with 6 staff members on a budget of $13,800. Under McKinley this had grown to a staff of 27 and a budget of $44,000. President Coolidge spent over $93,000 on a staff of 46, and Franklin Roosevelt, prior to World War II, had 37 civilians and over 200 military personnel on his White House staff. In 1966 the Executive Office of the President had a budget in excess of $28 million and a staff of more than 1,500. Along with the White House staff, the Executive Office of the President includes the Bureau of the Budget, the Council of Economic Advisers, the National Security Council, the National Aeronautics and Space Council, the Office of Emergency Planning, the Office of Civil Defense Mobilization, the Office of Science and Technology, and the Office of Special Representative for Trade Negotiations. Each has a

12 The White House staff in 1965 included 10 Special Assistants to the President, having various assignments, 2 Administrative Assistants, a Press Secretary, a Special Counsel to the President, a Legislative Counsel, a Special Assistant for the Food for Peace program, and another Special Assistant for the Arts, an Advisor for National Capital Affairs, a Military Aide, a Physician to the President, a Personal Secretary to the President and another for the First Lady, a Social Secretary, an Executive Clerk, and a Chief Usher. Its budget expenditures for the fiscal year 1967 were nearly $3 million. See *U.S. Government Organization Manual, 1965–66*, p. 54.

special responsibility for informing the President, consulting with him on matters of policy and administration, and maintaining continuous liaison with the major executive agencies and with the Congress.

This institutionalization of the Presidency has no doubt helped to ease the burdens that rest upon the nation's Presidents. By a division of labor and by delegation of authority much has been done in this direction, and much more can be done. It has now been established that except for those few functions which he derives directly from the Constitution, the President may delegate to the Vice-President or to "any official in the Executive branch, whose appointment is subject to Senate confirmation," any statutory functions vested in his office. Recent Presidents, from Truman to Johnson, have issued executive orders delegating to subordinates dozens of functions that had formerly been performed by the President himself. The "issuance of regulations for Army hospitals, the wearing of uniforms by ex-servicemen, the award of the Legion of Merit, and the scheduling of leaves of absence for certain persons," were some. Other more important functions related to the Mutual Security Administration, emergency relief to India, and school construction in actual defense areas. Much of the paper work which through the years has devolved upon the President can be delegated.[13]

Fortunately or unfortunately, depending on one's point of view, the major burden of the Presidency cannot be delegated. For the responsibilities that lie most heavily on the mind and conscience of the President and that generate the greatest nervous tension, are not his administrative or managerial duties, nor even his ceremonial ones. In general it is his political responsibilities that create the greatest strains. By no managerial magic can he escape responsibility for the basic policies of his administration, for leadership to his party and to the nation, or for final decisions on matters that affect millions of people throughout the world. Paper work can be delegated, ceremonial responsibilities can be shared although not really delegated, managerial duties can be assigned, but the job of serving as Spokesman for the Free World and Head of State, this he cannot delegate or evade. No system of providing assistant or executive vice-presidents, or multiplying aides to give the President "time to think" can do more than mildly mitigate the literally awful and lonely responsibility that rests upon this "elective king," the President. "What is in shortest supply," wrote James Reston, "[in the Presidency as elsewhere in Government] is not time for thought but men of thought," men who in the words of Henri Bergson will "think as men of action and act as men of thought."[14]

There is another often unforeseen risk in the delegation of presidential power. The multiplication of subpresidents or agents, each

13 See Sidney Hyman, "To Ease the Burden of the Presidency," *The New York Times Magazine,* March 23, 1958.
14 See *The New York Times,* June 14, 1959.

exercising fragments of the executive power, ultimately leads to an increasing need for coordination of both policy and administration if the government is not to "ride off in all directions." Parkinson's law begins to operate. The multiplication of interagency committees creates a need for supercoordinators to coordinate the coordinators. Gradually, as the process continues, the President finds himself in communication not with officials having firsthand contact with, or even firsthand information about, major activities of the government, but with secondhand or third-hand surrogates of the operating agencies. By the time information gets to the President through this complex managerial sieve, it may bear only a coincidental relation to reality, and even if accurate may be both too little and too late.[15]

Most of the President's sources of information and advice are within the government itself. Occasionally, however, he turns to the outside for consultation, investigation, and recommendation. One example is the *ad hoc* consultant with some special knowledge or skill. Another is the more formal Presidential Commission. Unlike the Royal Commission of the British, the Presidential Commission is less likely to be regarded as an important oracle, immune from partisan attack, although many have achieved a comparable prestige. The President's purpose in using a commission may vary from a desire to test public reaction to a particular policy, to "build support for a policy already decided upon," to act as "soothsayers—to make believe that something is happening when in fact no action is contemplated," or to study a problem upon which the President is genuinely in need of advice. Not infrequently reports of Presidential Commissions have an important if not immediate effect on policy—as, for example, the President's Committee on Administrative Management, and the two Hoover Commissions on Organization of the Executive Branch of the Government. During 1965 and 1966 upwards of a dozen Presidential Commissions were appointed to explore problems as varied as law enforcement, juvenile delinquency, equal employment opportunity, equal opportunity in housing, heart disease and cancer, nuclear proliferation, and physical fitness. Although not all Presidential Commissions have an immediate or discernible effect upon public opinion or public policy, it is not quite true to say, as one writer does, that

15 It is noteworthy in this connection that President Kennedy, early in his administration, ordered the discontinuance of seventeen interdepartmental committees "that had been set up for high-level policy making. All but one had been established by the Eisenhower Administration." See Jack Raymond, *The New York Times*, March 12, 1961.

In April, 1961, the President abolished another forty-one interagency committees in what was described as a "continuing effort to abolish nonessential governmental agencies and place responsibility in specific individuals to the maximum extent possible." See article in *The New York Times,* April 9, 1961. Both Presidents Kennedy and Johnson, however, found it expedient to re-establish some of the old and to create some new interagencies.

"on the whole Presidential Commissions are probably better adapted to smothering problems with well-publicized inaction than to paving the way for novel action."[16]

☆ THE PRESIDENT AND FOREIGN POLICY

The presidential power as Commander in Chief is a major instrument of foreign policy. By calling up reserves in time of international tension, by deploying the armed forces in particular ways at particular times and places, and even committing American forces to combat, the President not only gives direction to American foreign policy but can, in effect, transcend or circumvent the express power of the Congress. The President as Commander in Chief may not only use armed forces in support of American diplomacy but may take the nation into a war *"de facto"* without formal action by the Congress. In doing so he may reduce to an empty formality the constitutional power of the Congress to declare war. Indeed such is the nature of modern world politics and of modern weapons that it is the President and not the Congress who will no doubt make the fateful decisions hereafter.

The President's powers in foreign policy, however, reach beyond those he exercises as Commander in Chief. Indeed, his powers as Commander in Chief are important primarily as a corollary to his powers over foreign relations. So important is the conduct of foreign relations that John Locke, in his Second Treatise of Government, classified it as a special kind of power—which he called *federative* to distinguish it from the usual executive, legislative, and judicial powers. And Locke did not hesitate to place the federative power [the executive in its external relations] above these other powers, but implied that in this realm the normal constitutional and other limitations did not apply.

[16] A cynic once wrote the following jingle concerning a fictitious Royal Commission on Kissing. It appeared in *Punch* many years ago but may well apply to some more recent Presidential Commissions.

> I never can remember how exactly we began
> But I seem to recollect a case about a clergy-
>   man.
> A mountain was delivered rather strangely by
>   a mouse;
> There were meetings, there were articles, and
>   questions in the House;
> The necessity for action was clear to everyone
> But the view was very general that nothing
>   could be done,
> And the Government courageously decided
>   that the Crown
> Should appoint a score of gentlemen to track
>   the trouble down—
> Which always takes a long, long time.

The Concept of Inherent Powers

Although the Supreme Court of the United States does not quote Locke or go as far as the English philosopher in regarding the federative power as supreme and for practical purposes without constitutional restraint, the Court has said that the powers of the federal government in regulating the external affairs of the nation are not confined to the powers delegated to it in the Constitution. "The investment of the Federal Government," said the Court, "with the powers of external sovereignty did not depend upon the affirmative grants of the Constitution. The powers to declare and wage war, to conclude peace, to make treaties, to maintain diplomatic relations with other sovereignties, *if they had never been mentioned in the Constitution would have vested in the Federal Government as necessary concomitants of nationality. . . ."*[17]

And, says the Court, "in the vast external realm . . . the President alone has the power to speak or listen as a representative of the nation. He [the President] makes treaties with the advice and consent of the Senate, but he alone negotiates. Into the field of negotiation the Senate cannot intrude, and Congress itself is powerless to invade it." Congressmen may talk, congressional committees may investigate, independent administrative agencies may exert great influence, but it is the President, and he alone, who can speak to other nations with authority. In exercising this great federative power, the President is controlled only by his own sense of restraint and responsibility, and by his own knowledge of and respect for the basic American values.

Appointment of Emissaries

The Constitution says the President "shall nominate, and by and with the Advice and Consent of the Senate, shall appoint Ambassadors, other public Ministers and Consuls. . . ." It is through these and other agents, scattered throughout the world in nearly three hundred embassies, ministries, and consulates—and hundreds of other offices, bureaus, or agencies—that the President directs the foreign affairs of the United States. Although the chiefs of these agencies are, as the Constitution says, appointed with the advice and consent of the Senate, the President's nominee is rarely rejected, even though the advice of the Senate may not have been sought save in the most perfunctory way. For the fact is the top-ranking officers who represent the United States abroad do so only as representatives of the President. It is he who appoints them, it is from him that they get their instructions, it is to him that they report, and it is the President who, in the end, can recall them. When they speak, they speak for the President or not at all. It is no breach of etiquette, let alone

[17] *United States* v. *Curtiss-Wright Export Corp.,* 229 U.S. 304 (1936).

of the Constitution, when a President speaks of *my* Ambassador in London, or *my* Minister in Madrid.

If there were any doubt of this, it would be resolved by the long-established right and custom of Presidents to appoint personal agents or ambassadors without even observing the formality of senatorial advice and consent. President Washington established a precedent for this when he sent Gouverneur Morris to England and Colonel David Humphreys to Madrid—as his personal and confidential agents—without as much as a gesture of "by your leave" to the Senate. This custom has been followed by other Presidents. Colonel Edward M. House for many years was President Wilson's private diplomatic adviser whose influence with the President was often a source of resentment to the more formally appointed Secretaries of State and ambassadors. Harry Hopkins, who had served President Franklin Roosevelt in many capacities, ended his career as the President's confidential personal adviser, almost his *alter ego,* on both foreign and domestic policies. When Mr. Hopkins arrived in London, or Moscow, it was he who outranked in power and influence the American ambassadors although he was never formally appointed to those posts. President Johnson used Averell Harriman as a kind of Ambassador at large.

Communication between the President and his agents is in the language of contemporary politics "top secret, secret, restricted, or confidential." Rarely are communications of this kind made public without the prior consent of the President—not even to Congress or to the Courts. "Leaks" do occur—sometimes merely by accident, more often by design to test public reaction—but when they do on matters which the President regards as best kept secret, someone's official head may roll. Again it was President Washington who established a precedent for this when he was asked in March, 1796, by the House of Representatives for certain papers relating to negotiation of the controversial Jay Treaty. The President refused, saying,

> The nature of foreign negotiations requires caution and their success must often depend on secrecy: and even when brought to conclusion, a full disclosure of all the measures, demands or eventual concessions, which may have been proposed or contemplated would be extremely impolitic.

This defense of "secret diplomacy" might well be read and pondered by Congress and formalists who believe in diplomacy by disclosure. Washington well knew the mischief that can be done by overexposure in the delicate and often dangerous field of foreign affairs. This question of when, how, and to what extent intimate diplomatic secrets should be made public poses one of the most difficult problems of democratic government.

The President's power to appoint ambassadors and other public ministers gives him as a corollary power to control the recognition policy of the United States. For the sending, withholding, or withdrawing of an official representative is the most indispensable and in many ways the most tangible evidence of recognition or nonrecognition. This is not the place to review the development of American recognition policy, but it is well to remember that this policy, again, is one that the President largely determines. Thus as a corollary of his power to appoint ambassadors the President may not only extend "recognition," he may also achieve certain substantive goals in the process and prepare the way for further treaty negotiations.

Treaties and Executive Agreements

In the *negotiation* of treaties it is the President and the President alone who is responsible. To be sure, in *making* treaties he must act by and with the advice and consent of the Senate. But here again, he may bypass the Senate and make binding agreements with foreign powers. Presumably the President's power to make such *Executive Agreements* is derived not from any express grant in the Constitution, nor from statutes enacted by Congress, but rather from the powers inherent in the President as the repository of the executive power.[18]

The most successful example of disarmament in American history—and probably in world history—rests upon an Executive Agreement of this kind. The so-called Rush-Bagot Convention of 1817, between the United States and Great Britain, limiting (indeed virtually prohibiting) naval armaments on the Great Lakes was initially embodied in an Executive Agreement, although later embodied in a formal treaty and ratified by the Senate. The Open Door policy in China was defined not by treaty but by Executive Agreements in 1899 and 1900. So too was the so-called "Gentlemen's Agreement" of 1907, regulating Japanese immigration into the United States. The Lansing-Ishii Agreement of 1907, in which the United States formally recognized that Japan had "special" rights and interests in China, was an Executive Agreement.

The constitutionality and the legally binding effect of Executive Agreements have been upheld by the Supreme Court in a number of cases. The so-called Roosevelt-Litvinoff Agreement of 1933 assigned to the United States all claims that Russia had against American nationals. When this was challenged as unconstitutional, it was sustained by the Supreme Court, thus giving to an Executive Agreement the same legally binding effect as a treaty.[19]

Presidential power in the making of treaties is limited by the constitutional provision requiring ratification by a two-thirds vote of the Senate. It is the hazard of this extraordinary majority for ratification that helps explain the increasing use of the Executive Agreement by the Pres-

---

[18] *United States* v. *Curtiss-Wright Export Corp., loc. cit.*
[19] See *United States* v. *Belmont,* 301 U.S. 324 (1937).

ident. But even this hazard can in a measure be circumvented by a President lacking a two-thirds majority in the Senate but having a simple majority in both House and Senate. Instead of a treaty, the President may ask the Congress to ratify an International Agreement by a joint resolution which requires only a simple majority. It was in this way that Texas was annexed in 1845 and Hawaii in 1898. Failure of the Senate to ratify the Treaty of Peace, including the Covenant of a League of Nations, following World War I, made it necessary to conclude peace with the Central powers by joint resolution.

Since World War II, the United States has become inextricably involved in world affairs through the UN, NATO, SEATO, OAS, and literally dozens of multilateral and bilateral Executive Agreements and treaties—all negotiated under the power and the leadership of the President.

Alarmed by this trend Senator John Bricker of Ohio, in 1955, proposed a constitutional amendment to restrain and limit the power of the President to make such agreements. The amendment provided, essentially, that (1) no international agreement "which conflicts with this Constitution, or which is not made in pursuance thereof, shall" be "of any force or effect," (2) all international agreements "shall become effective as internal law in the United States only through legislation valid in the absence of international agreement." The amendment was vigorously debated and was ardently supported by extreme nationalist groups. Fortunately, the combined opposition of the President, the Secretary of State, and a majority of the Congress served to defeat the proposal.[20]

☆ PRESIDENTIAL LEADERSHIP AND PARTY RESPONSIBILITY[21]

In spite of vast powers, the office of the Presidency can become a mere masquerade of power if Congress chooses to make it so. It is not only that many of the powers of the President are derived from acts of Congress, but that what Congress gives, it may also take away. Even those presidential powers derived directly from the Constitution depend for their effectiveness upon congressional cooperation. Without congressional approval of men and money, the President might be Commander in Chief, but only of a phantom force. Even the President's foreign policy requires congressional support, particularly since World War II, when economic

[20] For the text of this so-called Bricker Amendment and the debate *Pro* and *Con*, see Peter Odegard, *American Government, Readings and Documents* (2nd ed.; New York: Harper & Row, 1966), pp. 291–297.

[21] The following discussion was taken from Peter Odegard, "Presidential Leadership and Party Responsibility," *The Annals of the American Academy of Political and Social Science* (September, 1956).

and military assistance to underdeveloped areas and the associated powers of the free world have loomed so large. Thus it is literally true that, while the President proposes, Congress ultimately disposes; hence the importance of good relations between the President and the legislature.

While the President is, as we say, independent of Congress, elected for a term different from that of either house and from a different constituency, Congress is also independent of him. Of all the 537 elected officers of the United States, the President and Vice-President alone are chosen by all of the voters. Senators and Congressmen, on the other hand, are essentially local officers responsible to the voters of a single state or congressional district. Only once in four years do members of the House of Representatives and the President "go to the country" together and even then only one-third of the Senators go with them. At the so-called midterm elections, both Representatives and Senators must in effect "go it alone," without support from the booming guns of a presidential campaign. Obviously such a system places a premium not on party unity but on diversity, not on discipline but on independence—independence not only of the President but also of the party organization of which the President is the formal leader.

Even after his election the relations between a President and his party are largely informal, irregular, and tenuous. As for the party in opposition, we indulge in the fiction that the defeated candidate for the Presidency is its leader. But normally, with no official position either in the government or the party, his "leadership" is but a shadow of that represented by the Leader of the Opposition in Parliament. Even the President's influence as party leader is vitiated by the generally loose character of party organization in this country.

Normally a presidential election will sweep into office not only a President but a majority in Congress of the same party. Under such circumstances, the President can, if he is a strong man and understands the party system, enforce some degree of party unity and discipline on major administration measures. By consultation and cooperation with the Big Four in Congress (the Vice-President, the Speaker of the House, and Majority Leaders in the House and Senate), such a President can often have his way.

But this honeymoon period is normally short-lived, and by the time of the second Congress in a presidential term the familiar pattern of factional conflict reappears and the discipline of pressure groups tends to displace that of the parties.

Party unity falls away because it is enforced as much by a judicious distribution of patronage and party favors as by any basic agreement on matters of policy. With thousands of appointments for which every Congressman has a candidate or two, the President is in a good bargaining position, and he uses patronage to buy support for his legislative program.

Yet even under the best of circumstances it would be easy to exaggerate the influence of presidential patronage in securing support for administration measures. The gradual extension of the merit system, "senatorial courtesy," and an emerging tradition of nonpartisanship even in the appointment of officials not formally covered by civil service rules have had a corrosive effect upon this weapon of presidential leadership. In any case, once the appointments have been made and the favors distributed, Congressmen tend to revert to their local, sectional, or special loyalties.

In this mood, as we have seen, they bargain not so much with the President as party leader as with other members of their own party and even with members of the opposition. We call this process "logrolling" or "back scratching." Thus votes in Congress after the honeymoon rarely show Republicans and Democrats lined up solidly on opposite sides, but rather conservatives of both parties joining against liberals of both parties, or high-tariff representatives, Republican and Democrat, united against those of both parties who seek to reduce or abolish protective rates. So numerous are these various groups and blocs that on most measures party loyalty is meaningless and party discipline nonexistent.

A second reason for the falling off of party unity after the honeymoon is the fact that the term of office of members of the House of Representatives and of one third of the Senators expires midway in the term of the President. This fact compels representatives of the President's own party to give their attention to their local political fences, often to the subordination or disregard of national interests. And of course the midterm elections not infrequently return a Congress controlled not by the President's own partisans but by the opposition. (See Table 14–1.)

Presidential efforts to enforce party discipline under existing conditions have never been conspicuously successful. Nor have the steering committees of the major parties been any more effective in enforcing discipline on matters of policy. As someone has said, "They seldom meet, and never steer." Furthermore, the President has no very effective control over these and other agencies of party government in Congress; indeed those who compose the ruling clique in the House (the Speaker, the Rules Committee, the majority floor leader, the party whip, the chairmen of important standing committees) are less dependent on the President than he is on them.

The complex, almost chaotic, character of American political parties, the intensity of intraparty as well as interparty conflicts, make the President's position as party leader extraordinarily difficult. No President who hopes to see his legislative program succeed can safely rely exclusively upon his own partisans in Congress, not even when they comprise a "safe" majority in both houses. During the honeymoon period the prospect of federal patronage may help to firm the wavering ranks. But what Cleveland once called the "cohesive power of public plunder" is no longer the "big stick" it once was. And even the so-called coattail effect of

TABLE 14-1
Party Line-Up, Congress and Presidency, 1854–1968

Election Year	Congress Elected	House					Senate						Presidency	
		Members Elected			Gains/Losses		Members Elected			Gains/Losses			Elected	Popular Vote Plurality
		Dem.	Rep.	Misc.**	Dem.	Rep.	Dem.	Rep.	Misc.**	Dem.	Rep.			
1854	34th	83	108	43			42	15	5				Pierce (D)	
1856*	35th	131	92	14	+ 48	− 16	39	20	5	− 3	+ 5		Buchanan (D)	493,023
1858	36th	101	113	23	− 30	+ 21	38	26	2	− 1	+ 6			
1860*	37th	42	106	28	− 59	− 7	11	31	7	− 27	+ 5		Lincoln (R)	482,880
1862*	38th	80	103		+ 38	− 3	12	39		+ 1	+ 8			
1864*	39th	46	145		− 34	+ 42	10	42		− 2	+ 3		Lincoln (R)	403,151
1866*	40th	49	143		+ 3	− 2	11	42		+ 1	0		Johnson (R)	
1868*	41st	73	170		+ 24	+ 27	11	61		0	+19		Grant (R)	309,584
1870	42nd	104	139		+ 31	− 31	17	57		+ 6	− 4			
1872*	43rd	88	203	3	− 16	+ 64	19	54	1	+ 2	− 3		Grant (R)	753,279
1874	44th	181	107		+ 93	− 96	29	46		+10	− 8			
1876	45th	156	137	14	− 25	+ 30	36	39		+ 7	− 7		Hayes (R)	−247,448
1878	46th	150	128		− 6	− 9	43	33		+ 7	− 6			
1880*	47th	130	152	11	− 20	+ 24	37	37	2	− 6	+ 4		Garfield (R)	39,213
1882*	48th	200	119	6	+ 70	− 33	36	40		− 1	+ 3		Arthur (R)	
1884	49th	182	140	2	− 18	+ 21	34	41		− 2	+ 1		Cleveland (D)	29,214
1886	50th	170	151	4	− 12	+ 11	37	39		+ 3	− 2			
1888*	51st	156	173	1	− 14	+ 22	37	47		0	+ 8		Harrison (R)	−90,728
1890*	52nd	231	88	14	+ 75	− 85	39	47	2	+ 2	0			
1892*	53rd	220	126	8	− 11	+ 38	44	38	3	+ 5	− 9		Cleveland (D)	372,736
1894*	54th	104	246	7	−116	+120	39	44	5	− 5	+ 6			
1896	55th	134	206	16	+ 30	− 40	34	46	10	− 5	+ 2		McKinley (R)	609,687
1898	56th	163	185	9	+ 29	− 21	26	53	11	− 8	+ 7			

Year	Congress	House Dem	House Rep	House Other	House Dem +/−	House Rep +/−	Senate Dem	Senate Rep	Senate Other	Senate Dem +/−	Senate Rep +/−	President	Plurality (popular vote)
1900	57th	153	198	5	−10	+13	29	56	3	+3	+3	McKinley (R)	861,757
1902*	58th	178	207		+25	+9	32	58		+3	+2	Roosevelt (R)	
1904	59th	136	250		−42	+43	32	58		0	0	Roosevelt (R)	2,544,238
1906	60th	164	222		+28	−28	29	61		−3	+3		
1908*	61st	172	219	1	+8	−3	32	59		+3	−2	Taft (R)	1,263,026
1910	62nd	228	162		+56	−57	42	49		+10	−10		
1912*	63rd	290	127	18	+62	−35	51	44	1	+9	−5	Wilson (D)	2,809,827
1914	64th	231	193	8	−59	+66	56	39	1	+5	−5		
1916	65th	210	216	9	−21	+23	53	42	1	−3	+3	Wilson (D)	605,188
1918	66th	191	237	7	−19	+21	47	48		−6	+6		
1920	67th	132	300	1	−59	+63	37	59	1	−10	+11	Harding (R)	7,013,079
1922	68th	207	225	3	+75	−75	43	51		+6	−8	Coolidge (R)	
1924	69th	183	247	5	−24	+22	40	54	1	−3	+3	Coolidge (R)	7,332,928
1926	70th	195	237	3	+12	−10	47	48	1	+7	−6		
1928	71st	163	267	1	−32	+30	39	56	1	−8	+8	Hoover (R)	6,375,769
1930	72nd	216	218	1	+53	−49	47	48	1	+8	−8		
1932	73rd	313	117	5	+97	−101	59	36	1	+12	−12	Roosevelt (D)	7,050,737
1934	74th	322	103	10	+9	−14	69	25	2	+10	−11		
1936	75th	333	89	13	+11	−14	75	17	4	+6	−8	Roosevelt (D)	11,078,204
1938	76th	262	169	4	−71	+80	69	23	4	−6	+6		
1940	77th	267	162	6	+5	−7	66	28	2	−3	+5	Roosevelt (D)	4,986,801
1942	78th	222	209	4	−45	+47	57	38	1	−9	+10		
1944	79th	243	190	2	+21	−19	57	38	1	0	0	Roosevelt (D)	3,591,840
1946	80th	188	246	1	−55	+56	45	51		−12	+13	Truman	
1948	81st	263	171	1	+75	−75	54	42		+9	−9	Truman (D)	2,135,747
1950	82nd	234	199	2	−29	+28	48	47	1	−6	+5		
1952	83rd	213	221	1	−21	+22	47	48	1	−1	+1	Eisenhower (R)	6,621,242
1954	84th	232	203		+19	−18	48	47	1	+1	−1		
1956	85th	234	201		+2	−2	49	47		+1	0	Eisenhower (R)	9,567,720
1958*	86th	283	154		+49	−47	66	34		+17	−13		

TABLE 14-1 (Continued)

Election Year	Congress Elected	House					Senate					Presidency	
		Members Elected			Gains/Losses		Members Elected			Gains/Losses			Popular Vote
		Dem.	Rep.	Misc.**	Dem.	Rep.	Dem.	Rep.	Misc.**	Dem.	Rep.	Elected	Plurality
1960	87th	263	174		− 20	+ 20	64	36		− 2	+ 2	Kennedy (D)	112,803‡
1962*	88th	259†	176		− 4	+ 2	68††	32††		+ 4	− 4		
1964	89th	295	140		+ 38	− 38	68	32		+ 2	− 2	Johnson (D)	15,951,244
1966	90th	248†††	187		− 47	+ 47	64***	36		− 5	+ 5		
1968	91st	243	192		− 4	+ 4	58	42		− 5	+ 5	Nixon (R)	354,974

* Size of House increased or decreased.
** Miscellaneous totals do not include vacancies.
‡ Includes divided Alabama elector slate votes.
† Figures as of Nov. 7, 1962. Changed to 257–178 in 1964.
†† Figures as of Nov. 7, 1962. Changed to 67–33 on Nov. 30, 1962, and to 66–34 on Sept. 16, 1964.
††† Changed to 247–188 in August, 1968.
*** Changed to 63–37 in September, 1968.

SOURCE: Facts about the Presidents, Joseph Nathan Kane; H. W. Wilson Co., 1959.

SOURCE: Reprinted by permission from Congressional Quarterly *Special Report,* Revised Dec. 15, 1964 (Washington, D.C.: Congressional Quarterly, Inc., 1964), p. 27.

[NOTE: Data since 1964 have been computed by authors of the present book from various figures reported in *The New York Times.*]

presidential leadership in a national campaign, however important it may be, has been weakened. The adoption of the Twenty-second Amendment limiting a President to two terms will inevitably impair this aspect of his leadership during the second term. Moreover, the seniority rule, by awarding key committee posts to members who come from "safe" districts or states, in effect gives control to those who are least dependent on such presidential support.

There are, however, weapons in the presidential arsenal that help to fortify his position. His power to recommend to Congress "such measures as he shall judge necessary and expedient," together with his power to veto measures hostile to his own aims, gives him a control of public policy that no other officer of the government can match. Indeed the mere threat of a veto may serve to stifle opposition measures and prevent them from reaching a vote on the floor. But the veto, as a political instrument, reaches beyond merely stopping "bad" legislation. On important matters of policy it serves as a dramatic device for appealing over the heads of Congress to the people. To be sure, it requires great political "savvy" to use the veto well, for it is a two-edged sword. The opposition can seek to embarrass the President by presenting him with legislation which he can veto only at the cost of offending factions in his own party as well as powerful interest groups upon whose support even his own adherents may depend. Legislation dealing with farm benefits, veterans' pensions, tariff rates, general appropriations, immigration, education, and welfare lends itself to this kind of political maneuver. Nevertheless, an astute President can use his veto power to provide campaign material for himself and his party and to strengthen his own prestige in the country. It is not surprising, under the circumstances, that "political" vetoes are more frequent where the White House and Congress are controlled by rival parties.

Beyond his power to initiate and to veto legislation, the President as a political leader has other sources of strength. As the sole official voice of the nation in foreign affairs he can, particularly in times of crisis, command support even from the opposition. But to do so he must give more than lip service to the belief that "politics stops at the water's edge." The President cannot plead for "nonpartisanship in foreign policy" with one breath and denounce the opposition party as a compound of incompetence, corruption, and disloyalty in the next. The President must himself assume leadership in defining his policies with clarity and firmness and in resisting those who seek to sabotage or subvert not only foreign policies to which he is committed, but the Presidency itself, as the sole official voice in this vast field. One of the most dramatic moves ever made by a President was President Johnson's televised announcement on March 31, 1968, that he would not seek re-election. The announced purpose was to enable the President to devote full time to the great problems facing the nation; the obvious hope was that by withdrawing, the President might help to restore national unity in international affairs and thus perhaps increase the possibility of peace in Vietnam.

On the domestic front also the President enjoys advantages over any opposition leader. He more than any other person in the nation, perhaps in the world, has access to the eyes and ears of the people. The press, radio, and television are, if not at his beck and call, ever alert to report what he says or does or proposes to do. Nowhere is his skill as a political leader more clearly revealed than in the use he makes of communication facilities to mold public opinion.

In final analysis, the President's strength as a party leader derives from his power and prestige as President, and the office of President can exalt a man of character and vision as it can inflate a man of mean dimensions. For weal or woe the American President is the spokesman, sign, and symbol of the American people. He is an image both of what the nation is and of what it aspires to be, and his success as a party leader thus will often depend on his success in rising above party in the service of the nation. As Wilson said:

> Let him once win the admiration and confidence of the country, and no other single force can withstand him, no combination of forces will easily overpower him. His position takes the imagination of the country. He is the representative of no constituency, but of the whole people. . . . He cannot escape being the leader of his party, except by incapacity and lack of personal force, because he is at once the choice of the party and of the nation. He can dominate his party by being spokesman for the real sentiment and purpose of the country. . . . He may be both the leader of his party and the leader of the nation, or he may be one or the other. If he leads the nation, his party can hardly resist him.

These comments, like Cleveland's aphorism that "he serves his party best who serves his country best," are not simply copybook generalities. They harbor political wisdom of a very practical sort. Jackson added to the strength of the Democratic party as much by defying the nullificationists within its ranks as by his war on the Whigs and the Bank. Who can say that the Republican party would not have been better served had Lincoln lived to win his war on the Radicals with their demand for a Draconian peace? The fact is that those Presidents who have translated the slogans of Cleveland and the counsel of Wilson into maxims of practical politics have not only been our great Presidents but also our great party leaders.

To be sure, a President, and still more a presidential candidate, is a creature of his party, for the party nominates and elects him. But if he is shaped by the party as President, he can be the instrument for shaping the party in turn, for leading it, as Walter Lippmann might say, from Drift to Mastery. As President he derives great strength from his position as party leader. But the party can be a source of frustration as well as strength. Lesser party leaders will admonish him, as Professor Rossiter says:

> . . . [to] be careful not to plunge too far ahead or lag too far to the rear of his allies in Congress . . . [to] select his chief lieutenants from [party] ranks, act as "honest broker" among its squabbling wings, and endure silently attacks upon his integrity, by men who roam the outer reaches of party loyalty. In doing all these things for the sake of harmony, and for the sake of victory in the next election, he cannot help losing some of his zest for bold experiment. . . . The party, as we know from the history of a dozen administrations, is more likely to tame him than he is to reshape it. Franklin Roosevelt, supposedly the most dominant of political leaders, felt the drag of his own party through most of his years in office. . . . And even Mr. Eisenhower, who has little taste for adventure, has been hampered rather than invigorated by his leadership of the Republican party.[22]

Most Presidents have not been conspicuously successful as party leaders, being content at best to be party managers and at worst party hacks. For a President to evade his responsibilities as party leader is in effect to abdicate his leadership as President. For neither of our major parties deprived of a strong hand at the helm is fit to govern. Neither is a united party. Both are torn by internal conflict. If they are to offer the voters meaningful alternatives, they need spokesmen who can translate and clarify these issues. If the President fails to do this for the party in power, he will fail in what is probably his most important task.

The Presidency, as Hoover once said, is a "compound hell." To make it less so, a President should make more effective use of the weapons available to him as President and party leader.

1. He should make full use of the big stick of patronage among his own partisans by holding up appointments until major bills are passed.
2. He must make his own position clear on major matters of public policy and not hesitate to use his veto power to stifle or turn back legislation inconsistent with these aims.
3. He must be respectful but firm in dealing with Congress and congressional leaders on policy matters.
4. He dare not abdicate control of foreign policy to anyone, and he must resist congressional intrusion in this field.
5. He must discipline and indoctrinate his own Cabinet members to treat Senators and Representatives with respect if not deference and to clear with him before making public statements on matters of policy.
6. He must never forget that it is he and he alone who speaks for all the people.

No one who shares the American passion for freedom will want a President who can enforce party unity only at the price of uniformity.

---

[22] Clinton L. Rossiter, *The American Presidency* (New York: Harcourt, Brace & World, 1956), p. 44.

The Communist and Fascist parties achieve unity by harsh internal discipline, and those who dissent are destroyed. This is the unity of the slave pens. Yet stable and effective government in these days cries out for greater unity in our major parties. And we must look to the President if it is to be achieved.

☆ *THE NEW VICE-PRESIDENCY*

The American Presidency as an institution includes, of course, the office of Vice-President, a kind of second-class executive without substantial powers, occupying an ambiguous, even shadowy, position. As conceived by the framers, the Vice-President was to be the second choice of the electors in their balloting for President. This plan of election was, of course, changed by the Twelfth Amendment which requires the electors to "name in their ballots the person voted for as President, and in distinct ballots the person voted for as Vice-President. . . ." But the ambiguous position of the Vice-President has remained. He is at the same time a part of the executive branch of government and "President of the Senate," serving thus as a rather weak link between the Presidency and the Congress. As part of the executive establishment, he has no constitutional powers except that "in Case of the Removal of the President from Office, or of his Death, Resignation, or Inability to discharge the Powers and Duties of the said Office, the Same shall devolve on the Vice President." As President of the Senate he is voiceless in debate and voteless in decision making unless the Senators in voting "be equally divided." On rare occasions his parliamentary decisions on disputed points of procedure, if sustained by the Senate, may have an important effect upon policy. But for the most part even his powers as the presiding officer are confined by Jefferson's *Manual of Procedure* and the customs and usages of the Senate. What influence he may have on legislation will be due not to his constitutional powers but to the force of his character and skill as a politician among politicians.

The result of this is that the Vice-President, even though he stands but one step from the Presidency, has been regarded as an empty vessel without power or prestige. Even John Adams, its first incumbent, wise, sedate, and conservative though he was, described the position of Vice-President as "the most insignificant office that ever the invention of man contrived or his imagination conceived." Benjamin Franklin, who opposed any such office in the Constitutional Convention, is said to have suggested as a title "Your Superfluous Excellency." Daniel Webster declined the Whig nomination for Vice-President in 1840, saying "No thank you. I do not propose to be buried until I am really dead." The Vice-Presidency, at least since Jefferson succeeded Adams to the Presidency, has been regarded as a kind of consolation prize for politically ambitious men. Theodore Roosevelt was almost literally forced much against his will to accept the vice-presidential nomination in 1900.[23] And Thomas Platt, the wily Republican boss of New York, congratulated himself on having thus banished into political obscurity a dangerous political rival.

Other strong party leaders with legitimate claims on their party's presidential nomination have more successfully, if unwisely, resisted pressure to accept second place. Senator Hiram Johnson of California, for example, is often cited as an example of a powerful party leader who in 1920 refused his party's vice-presidential nomination. Had he accepted, he, and not Calvin Coolidge, would have succeeded to the Presidency on Harding's death.

The low esteem in which the nomination and the office itself have been held is reflected in the almost offhand manner in which the major parties have selected their vice-presidential candidates. After the major battle for the presidential nomination has been resolved, the convention delegates, exhausted both physically and financially, pick a vice-presidential candidate almost as an afterthought. The presidential nominee, in consultation with party leaders, normally selects someone who has earned some sort of recognition, or someone who can properly "balance" the ticket by giving recognition to some important sectional, economic, or ideological wing of the party. The result is often a combination that to European observers appears strange if not bizarre. Thus in 1840 the Whigs, passing over strong leaders like Webster and Clay, turned to an anti-Jackson Democrat, John Tyler, as the running mate of their presidential candidate General William Henry Harrison. In 1860 the Republicans balanced their ticket by selecting as Lincoln's running mate Senator Hannibal Hamlin from Maine. And in the next election Hamlin was passed over in favor of Andrew Johnson, a Democrat, in an obvious bid for northern Democratic votes. In 1901 conservative Republican William McKinley of Ohio was balanced with liberal Theodore Roosevelt of New York, and in 1932 liberal Democrat Franklin Roosevelt of New York was offset with conservative John Nance Garner of Texas.

It is worth noting that had the original plan of electing the Vice-President been continued, the contrast between President and Vice-President might have been even greater. The first Vice-President, John Adams, shared his chief's general political outlook, so that his succession would have entailed no sharp lift in public policy. But when Thomas Jefferson, having secured the second highest vote for President, became Vice-President under John Adams, the result was an executive establishment divided against itself. Had the Twelfth Amendment not changed the

[23] Theodore Roosevelt himself or persons speaking on his behalf had repeatedly declared that he would not under any circumstances accept the vice-presidential nomination. See *Theodore Roosevelt: An Autobiography* (New York: Macmillan, 1913).

method of electing a Vice-President, the Adams-Jefferson type of combination might well have become the usual pattern. Normally, under our party system the "runner-up" in a presidential election would be the rival party's candidate for the Presidency; Whig and Republican Presidents would have served with Democratic Vice-Presidents or vice versa. It is to avoid situations like this that most students of the Presidency have long urged each major party in nominating its vice-presidential candidate to complete the ticket with a man having a political outlook similar to that of the presidential candidate. As the custom of allowing the presidential nominee to pick his running mate becomes more firmly established, these so-called balanced tickets of disparate candidates may become less common. Otherwise we may repeatedly have a situation like that which occurred in 1841, when Vice-President John Tyler, a renegade Democrat, succeeded to the Presidency on the death of William Harrison, the successful Whig candidate. It was not long until Tyler was at loggerheads with Harrison's Whig Cabinet, and with most of the Whig party's public policies. In effect a Whig President was succeeded by a Democratic Vice-President who had been nominated by a Whig Convention to "balance" the ticket. A similar result occurred in 1849 when President Zachary Taylor was succeeded by Vice-President Fillmore, and, as we have seen, conservative President McKinley was succeeded by the liberal Theodore Roosevelt.

An able Vice-President, in any case, on succeeding to the Presidency, will insist on being his "own man," and if possible, President in his own right by election of the people. Although Lyndon Johnson succeeded to office under the shadow of a martyred and beloved President, and although he pledged himself faithfully to carry out the program of President Kennedy, he was not long in placing his own stamp upon the Presidency. Moreover, with the personality, know-how, and experience of a great majority leader in the Senate, and as a member of that body's phantom "inner club," or power elite, he had advantages in dealing with Congress that his brilliant predecessor had lacked. For these and other reasons he not only succeeded in getting a considerable part of the program through Congress, but soon developed a program of his own. And for the "New Frontier" of Kennedy, the country soon began to hear of the "Great Society" as the goal of Lyndon Johnson.[24]

It is well to remember that of 34 elected Presidents no less than 8 have died in office to be succeeded by their Vice-Presidents. These include:

24 Continuity of the Kennedy-Johnson succession was also emphasized by President Johnson's continued reliance on the Kennedy "team" in the White House; Ted Sorenson. P. Kenneth O'Donnell, Lawrence O'Brien, and David Powers, as special assistants, for example, "carried on" during the first months of the Johnson administration. But these, too, were gradually replaced until, by the beginning of Johnson's term as President "in his own right by election," a wholly new White House staff had been recruited.

	VICE-PRESIDENT
PRESIDENT	WHO SUCCEEDED
Wm. H. Harrison	John Tyler
Zachary Taylor	Millard Fillmore
Abraham Lincoln	Andrew Johnson
James Garfield	Chester Arthur
William McKinley	Theodore Roosevelt
Warren Harding	Calvin Coolidge
Franklin D. Roosevelt	Harry Truman
John F. Kennedy	Lyndon B. Johnson

Moreover, 7 Vice-Presidents, including 4 of the foregoing, have been elected to the Presidency on their own account. They were John Adams, Thomas Jefferson, Martin Van Buren, Theodore Roosevelt, Calvin Coolidge, Harry Truman, and Lyndon Johnson. In general the quality of these men would seem to indicate that in spite of the almost casual manner in which vice-presidential candidates have been selected, the nation has, by and large, been well served by them.

Not all Vice-Presidents have been second-raters, as some critics have too readily assumed, and some of them have been at least as able as the Presidents with whom they were elected. In spite of his stormy term as President, John Tyler cannot reasonably be described as a lesser leader than William Harrison, whom he succeeded. Nor were Millard Fillmore or Chester Arthur demonstrably inferior to Presidents Zachary Taylor or James Garfield, whom they succeeded. Calvin Coolidge was surely not inferior to Warren Harding, and in Theodore Roosevelt, Harry Truman, and Lyndon Johnson, the nation had Vice-Presidents who became by succession Presidents of stature.

The Death of Throttlebottom

The image of Alexander Throttlebottom, the lovable but dumb musical comedy Vice-President in "Of Thee I Sing," is defunct as a model Vice-President. For the office has been upgraded, by statute, custom, and tradition, and by the crushing demands now made on the Presidency.

No one can be sure exactly when the new Vice-Presidency began to emerge, but by 1960 it had ceased to be a graveyard of political ambition or a consolation prize. In 1933, for the first time a President invited the Vice-President to attend and participate in Cabinet meetings. Moreover, during President Roosevelt's early days, Vice-President Garner, who had had vast experience as a legislative leader, became a major pilot of New Deal legislation in Congress. "He was," says an English observer, "not so much the presiding officer of the Senate as FDR's personal lobbyist," even though he did not always share the President's views.[25]

[25] Bernard Crick, "The American Vice-Presidency" in *Time and Tide*, London, June 16, 1956.

Although Henry Wallace, Mr. Roosevelt's second Vice-President, was not conspicuously successful as a leader of the Senate or in his relations with Congress generally, he nevertheless performed important services when he served as the President's emissary in a number of foreign and domestic missions, and as the head of important wartime executive agencies. Harry Truman's term as Vice-President was cut short by his succession to the Presidency, but as President he in turn made Vice-President Barkley a good deal more than a muted symbol of executive impotence. Mr. Barkley was a member of the President's Cabinet, was sent on a variety of foreign missions, headed up a number of important investigations for the President, was a tower of strength for him in Congress where he was well-loved and respected, and became by delegation of the President a major figure in Democratic campaigns, including the dramatic presidential campaign of 1948.

Under Presidents Eisenhower and Kennedy the Vice-Presidency continued to grow in power and prestige. Vice-President Nixon not only attended Cabinet meetings and meetings of the powerful Security Council, but also presided over them in the absence of the President. During President Eisenhower's illnesses, moreover, he was called upon to assume not only additional executive responsibilities but also many of the ceremonial functions of the President. His missions to Moscow and to South America and his reports to the President were important contributions to the administration's foreign policy. Most important, perhaps, of all his assignments, were his indefatigable efforts in behalf of Republican candidates everywhere in the country, in 1954, 1956, and 1958. Serving an essentially nonpolitical President, he became President Eisenhower's *alter ego* as leader of the Republican party. Professor Crick, watching this transformation of the Vice-Presidency under President Eisenhower, has referred to it as "an attempt to make [the] Vice-President something like a Prime Minister."[26]

Under President Kennedy the Vice-President continued to serve as an indispensable member of the executive establishment. As President of the Senate and a powerful voice in Democratic legislative councils, Vice-President Lyndon Johnson was thoroughly at home. His influence in support of the President's legislative program was probably second to none. But his responsibilites were not confined to the Hill. He sat with the Cabinet as by law the Vice-President is now directed to sit with the Security Council. The President gave him special responsibilities as chairman of the National Aeronautics and Space Council, and as chairman of the Committee on Equal Employment Opportunities, for the program to prevent racial discrimination in public employment. He was dispatched on critically important missions to Europe, Asia, and Africa, including a formal visit to crisis-crowded Berlin. And some observers claimed to see Vice-President Johnson's hand in many other administration programs

[26] *Time and Tide,* London, June 16, 1956.

and policies, including important matters of patronage and personnel. Like Nixon, he also assumed a major burden in campaigning for candidates of his own party, and the Vice-Presidency became an effective training ground for the Presidency.

How far the current trend toward a new and more powerful Vice-Presidency will go, no one can predict. Under President Johnson the trend continued as Vice-President Humphrey took on more responsibilities formerly assumed by the President himself. The increasing burdens of the Presidency and the quality of recent incumbents are likely to create greater and greater demands upon the Vice-President. Although it is unlikely that former President Hoover's suggestion for a second Vice-President will be adopted in the near future, one can reasonably expect a continued upgrading of the Vice-President provided for in the Constitution.

There are hazards of course in this development. No President who has regard for the full power and dignity of his office can tolerate the emergence of a rival in his own house. Whatever the Vice-President may be called upon to do, the nature of the Presidency will require that he do so as the subordinate and servant of the President. In any case, the time has long passed when one can say, as was said of Cleveland's Vice-President Adlai Stevenson in 1893, "There goes the Vice-President, with nothing in his mind but the state of the President's health."

☆ **THE PROBLEM OF PRESIDENTIAL SUCCESSION**

"The state of the President's health" raises the difficult problem of presidential disability. The Constitution says that "in Case of . . . [the] Inability [of the President] to discharge the Powers and Duties of [his] Office, the Same shall devolve on the Vice President." The order of presidential succession upon the death of an incumbent can be easily resolved and Congress has done so on several occasions, most recently in 1947. After the Vice-President, the Speaker of the House of Representatives, then the President pro tempore of the Senate, and thereafter the members of the Cabinet in the order in which their departments were created.[27] Whoever succeeds to the Presidency under this law must resign his seat in Congress or his Cabinet post.

[27] This order of succession was provided by an act of Congress of July 18, 1947, when President Truman objected to the "undemocratic" character of the earlier law on the subject. This earlier statute, the Presidential Succession Act of January 19, 1886, provided that in case of the disability or disqualification of both the President and the Vice-President, the Secretary of State should "act as President" provided he possessed the qualifications laid down in Article II, Section 1, clause 5, of the Constitution—i.e., was a natural-born citizen, at least thirty-five years of age, and a resident of the United States for at least fourteen years. After the Secretary of State, the Secretary of the Treasury was to "act as President," and after him other Cabinet officers, in the chronological order in which their departments were established.

The assassination of President Kennedy and the succession of Vice-President Johnson to the Presidency brought the whole problem of presidential succession into sharp focus. Under the so-called Truman Succession Act of 1957, the next in line, should President Johnson have died or been incapacitated, would have been Speaker of the House, McCormick, and thereafter, President pro tempore of the Senate, Carl B. Hayden, both Congressmen of distinction but admittedly aged and lacking in the physical and intellectual vigor required of the Man in the White House. After long study and extended debate, the problem was at last resolved by the Twenty-fifth Amendment, submitted in July, 1965, and ratified on February 10, 1967, which provides, among other things, (1) that a Vice-President on succeeding to the Presidency will become President in his own right, and not merely Acting President;[28] (2) that whenever a vacancy occurs in the Vice-Presidency (by reason of the resignation or death of the Vice-President, or by reason of his having succeeded to the Presidency), the President shall nominate a new Vice-President, and he shall take office when confirmed by a majority vote of both houses of Congress.

Since, under this change, there will be no vacancy in the office of Vice-President, there will be no need to provide for succession beyond that office. Had this amendment been in effect in November, 1963, President Johnson would have nominated his own successor as Vice-President to fill the vacancy in that office occasioned by his own succession to the Presidency.

But short of death, who is to say when the President is no longer able "to discharge the Powers and Duties of [his] Office"? On this important point the Constitution has been silent. Who is to decide when this contingency arises, the nature and degree of the disability, and when the disability ends? To allow Congress to make such a finding, it was argued, would violate the separation of powers and open the door to congressional domination of the Presidency. To allow the Vice-President to do so would make him, as it were, a judge in his own cause, and an unscrupulous Vice-President might conceivably use this power unjustly and unnecessarily to place himself in the Presidency.

The problem was by no means academic. President Garfield lingered between life and death for some eighty days after he was shot by an assassin in 1881. Although some members of the Cabinet wished Vice-President Arthur to act as President, others were fearful lest Garfield recover and be unable constitutionally to re-establish his right to the office. A similar situation occurred in 1919 when Woodrow Wilson,

---

28 This precedent may be said to have been established when John Tyler in 1841 succeeded to the Presidency on the death of President William Harrison. Vice-Presidents Fillmore, Johnson, Arthur, Theodore Roosevelt, Coolidge, and Truman, all became Presidents on this assumption, notwithstanding Professor Corwin's opinion that John Tyler "was wrong in his reading of the original intention of the Constitution." Thus does custom confound even distinguished constitutional lawyers.

having suffered a stroke, was unable to discharge the duties of his office for six weeks, and the powers of the Presidency in fact devolved not upon the Vice-President but upon Mrs. Wilson and the President's physician.

During Mr. Eisenhower's Presidency there were no fewer than three periods during which he was physically incapacitated. By a "clear understanding" with Vice-President Nixon, approved by the Attorney General, the President made provision for Nixon temporarily to exercise the "Powers and Duties of the Presidency." A similar "understanding" was made between President Kennedy and Vice-President Johnson and between Vice-President Humphrey and President Johnson in language identical with the Eisenhower-Nixon agreement. It was as follows:

1. In the event of inability the President would, if possible, so inform the Vice-President and the Vice-President would serve as Acting President . . . until the inability had ended.
2. In the event of an inability which would prevent the President from so communicating with the Vice-President, the Vice-President, after such consultation as seems to him appropriate . . . would decide upon the devolution of the powers and duties of the office, and would serve as Acting President until the inability had ended.
3. The President, in either event, would determine when the inability had ended and at that time would resume the full exercise of the powers and duties of the office.

As if to confirm these "understandings" and to provide a constitutional solution for the problem of "incapacity," the Twenty-fifth Amendment also provides that

1. When the President notifies the Speaker of the House and the President pro tempore of the Senate in writing that he is unable to perform the powers and duties of his office, those powers and duties, but not the office, shall devolve upon the Vice-President, who then becomes Acting President.
2. When the Vice-President and a majority of the Cabinet, or such other body as Congress may establish and designate, declare in writing to the Speaker of the House of Representatives and the President pro tempore of the Senate, that the President is unable to carry out the powers and duties of his office, those processes and duties shall devolve on the Vice-President as Acting President.
3. If in either case the President notifies the Speaker and the President pro tempore, in writing, that he is no longer incapacitated and can resume his office, its powers, and duties, he may do so.
4. The Vice-President, however, with the concurrence of a majority of the Cabinet may, within two days, declare that the President was, in fact, not able to resume his office.
5. In this event Congress has ten days within which to sustain the Vice-President and the Cabinet by a two-thirds vote of both houses. In the absence of a two-thirds majority for the Vice-President, the President would resume office.

15

THE FEDERAL BUREAUCRACY

☆ *MASTER OR SERVANT*

Government in the final analysis is people—people doing a wide variety of things, most of which are indistinguishable from the things done by people in private life. There are accountants and architects and administrators, bookkeepers, blacksmiths, biochemists, engineers, economists, electricians, doctors of medicine and doctors of philosophy, lawyers, librarians and linotype operators. Indeed it would be hard to find an occupation or profession not represented among the 12 million or more civilian employees of federal, state, and local governments whom we describe as public servants. Even in the federal military establishment, which includes another 3 million public servants, one can find men and women representing virtually every kind and degree of skill and training, from astronauts to zoologists. It is to these public servants that we refer in speaking of a "governmental bureaucracy"—a term not unmixed in our culture with resentment and reproach. Yet it is upon these "bureaucrats" that we depend for the increasingly numerous, important, and complex services we demand of our new Leviathan, the modern state. As we have said before, a government without bureaucrats is like a centipede without legs, unable to move, even to save itself, and powerless to accomplish any of the goals for which governments are instituted among men.[1]

---

[1] In the federal bureaucracy there are essentially three types of public officials, depending on their manner of appointment. These are (1) those appointed by the President by and with consent of the Senate, (2) "inferior" officers whose appointment is vested by law in the President alone, the courts of law, or the heads of Departments, and (3) employees appointed by subordinate officials not recognized by the Constitution as capable of being vested by Congress with the appointing power.

Public and Private Employment

Although public servants are engaged in tasks not too different from those in private life, there are nevertheless important differences between public and private employment. Perhaps the most important differences are in their over-all goals and the standards by which they are judged. Private business is driven by a profit motive and can be tested against a profit and loss ledger which can apply to government in only a limited degree. The most important functions of law and order, the administration of justice, the public welfare and safety, sanitation, public health and public education, conservation of resources, recreation, police and fire protection, not to mention national defense are not easily measured by any such objective standard.

To be sure, when government operates a railroad, an electric light plant, a water works, a liquor store or even a housing development, many of the standard tests of business can be applied. But even in these enterprises other goals than economic efficiency are likely to enter—goals of public welfare, health, and safety. The Post Office Department might be operated as a business enterprise at a profit, but fail in its responsibility to promote the communication of information, science, and learning. A good fire department may be reflected in lower insurance rates, an efficient police department may show a lower rate of crime and delinquency, and a good health department, lower rates of mortality. Economists have made considerable progress in developing ways to measure cost-benefit ratios of a number of different public works and services. Power dams, irrigation, and reclamation projects lend themselves to this kind of analysis. On the other hand, the intangible and often remote benefits of flood control, reforestation, and conservation, arising from these projects are not so easily measured. Moreover, most agencies of government are financed not out of fees for services rendered or the sale of goods and services to customers, but out of taxes—compulsory exactions levied by the government. And "taxes," said the late Justice Holmes, "are the price we pay for civilization."

All this is not to say that the goods and services supplied by private business, by private hospitals, schools, and colleges do not also contribute to civilization, or that they do not also promote the public welfare, health, and safety. Contemporary theory, we realize, makes no sharp distinction between large-scale public and private organizations in terms of their motivations, roles played, structure, organization, and management. Organization theory, games theory, and various behavioral models, all emphasize "a mixed package" of motivations, purposes, and goals. "The goals and membership of the corporation are varied," says Hawley Johnson. "The norms and roles of big business include a conglomeration of profits, efficiency, democratic human relations, freedom, and justice. Big business is not cast in the simple molds of profit maximization or of pursuit of public welfare."

But there are also those who take a dim view of these adjurations and insist that private business can best serve the public interest by keeping its eye on its major goal of maximizing profits.[2] In any case, the goal and spirit of business enterprise are substantially different from those of the public service, even though the *private* goals of public servants are for the most part indistinguishable from those of the employees of private business. For government employees, like those in private business, have their private goals—income, social status, security. Indeed a major problem of public administration is to see that these private goals do not come into conflict with the public goals of the government as a whole or the particular agency in which the individual is employed.

The public service differs from private employment in other ways than purpose and motivation. To a much larger degree it functions in a goldfish bowl. Business corporations may have trade and other secrets, but government agencies in a democracy, excepting those deemed vital to national defense, can have no secrets. Their day by day operations, their reports, the coming and going of their officers and employees, their blunders and bloopers as well as (indeed, much more than) their successes are subject to the constant and legitimate scrutiny of Congress, the press, and of every wayward scribe who fancies himself a watchdog of the public interest. "Each employee hired," says Paul Appleby, "each one demoted, transferred, or discharged . . . each change in administrative structure . . . has to be thought about in terms of possible public agitation (or) investigation . . . Any employee who . . . may be discharged is a potentially powerful enemy, for he can reach the press and Congress with whatever charges his knothole perspective may have invited."

Public bureaucrats, moreover, must operate according to a code of conduct which most business executives would find frustrating and restrictive. Rules as to what he can do, whom he can hire, whom he can or cannot fire, the friends he can have and those he must eschew, tie the public bureaucrat in a web from which he can escape only by death or resignation.

Another difference is that public bureaucrats, especially in the higher posts, are less well paid than comparable bureaucrats in private business. This was not always so. In the good old days of the English governing class, or in the early days of the American Republic, public employment often offered a higher income than a comparable position in private business. In 1789 in New York one could live in middle class comfort for $1,000 a year. Cabinet officers with salaries of $5,000 a year

---

2 See Arthur S. Miller (ed.), "The Ethics of Business Enterprise," *The Annals of the American Academy of Political and Social Science* (September, 1962).

were fairly affluent. So, too, were subordinate officials at $1,500 to $3,500. Even a humble government clerk's salary of $600 to $1,500 was better than a comparable job outside the government. A standard of living available to an income of $1,000 in 1792 today will cost $10,000 so that even a minor official in the early days of the Republic was better off than all but those in the highest ranks today. If a ratio of 10–1 measures the differences between 1789 and 1968, the top salaries in government today should run $40,000 to $50,000 a year, a figure that applies only to the President and Vice-President.[3]

One final difference noted some years ago by Professor Leonard White is that public servants enjoy less prestige than those of similar skill and training outside the government. Although the prestige of public employment is considerably higher than when Professor White wrote, it still lags behind private business or the professions, although there are many notable exceptions to this.

Members of the Supreme Court and even of inferior federal courts, members of the White House staff, and those in the higher ranks of agencies within the Executive Office of the President, for example, are held as high or higher in public esteem than any corporation official or comparable leader in private life. Moreover, as the role of government increases in American society, as highly skilled and professional employees replace the old time "political appointees," and as salaries in government approach those in private life, the prestige of the public service will grow.[4]

Some Bureaucratic Myths

In very large measure the relatively low prestige of public employment had its roots in a kind of popular mythology concerning government employees. In 1957 the United States Civil Service Commission, in a pamphlet called *Working for the U.S.A.*, listed some of the popular misconceptions about the federal service. They included such notions as

1. *Government employees are all clerks,* a kind of black-coated proletariat on the Potomac. This, of course, is not true. As we have seen, government officers and employees represent nearly every occupation and profession from nuclear physicists to typists and file clerks.

2. *Most federal employees work in Washington.* Actually only about one-tenth of them do. There are as many federal employees in California as in the District of Columbia. There are about twice as many postal employees scattered from coast to coast and border to border as there are employees working in Washington for all executive agencies.

---

[3] See Edwin Dale's story in *The New York Times,* April 28, 1964, "Top level Government employees find jobs so costly they've gone into debt."

[4] See F. P. Kilpatrick, M. C. Cummings, Jr., and M. K. Jennings, *The Image of the Federal Service;* also Dean Mann, *Federal Political Executives.* Both published by the Brookings Institution, Washington, D.C., 1964.

3. *Government employees have lifetime jobs. Once they get their feet in the public trough, they never quit and they can't be fired.* The fact is that turnover is high, mainly from resignation to accept work elsewhere. In a given year, up to 500,000 federal employees—about 20 percent of the total—will leave their jobs for economy reasons. Approximately half of these will be resignations, many of the remainder will be retirement, deaths, or disabilities, and upwards of 30,000 will be "reductions in force" and outright discharges. "Reduction in force" is a Damoclean sword over a bureaucrat's head. To be "riffed" is an ever-present danger.

4. *To get a government job, write your Congressman because it takes political pull to get into the federal service.* Over 90 percent of federal jobs are filled by competitive examination, not by political "pull." Standards of entry are, in fact, higher than in most private organizations.

5. *Bureaucrats are grafters and crooks.* The fact is that standards of conduct in the public service are as high or higher than in other walks of life, if for no other reason than the constant public scrutiny to which public employees are subject. The whole problem of political corruption poses a serious problem, and it is proper to expect higher standards from public servants than from those in private life. On the whole, that expectation is realized. In the final analysis, however, public morality will reflect the morality of the community the government serves. For every corrupt government official, there is usually someone in private life leading him on. For every bribe taker, there is a bribe giver, and both are happily few. We ought not to allow sensational revelations of graft by a few blind us to the loyalty, integrity, and faithful service of the millions. Nor should we, in our preoccupation with petty peculations—gifts of vicuna coats, refrigerators, or free meals—lose sight of so-called "honest graft," often of massive proportions, masquerading as public policy. Grants of oil, land, and other concessions in the public domain, licenses, franchises, and tax and other favors worth millions often escape public notice.

There is an old English limerick that we do well to remember:

> The law locks up both man and woman
> Who steals the goose from off the common
> But lets the greater felon loose
> Who steals the common from the goose.

One final misconception of the public service is that:

6. *The more employees a federal bureaucrat supervises, the higher his salary and status.* There is thus, so runs the argument, a built-in pressure to expand personnel regardless of need. This is only very vaguely true. Many a federal official with no staff and no employees to supervise has higher status and salary than those having administrative

responsibility for hundreds of subordinates. For instance, a supervisor of a small group of scientific workers will usually have higher status and salary than one who supervises a large number of people doing simple routine work.

Although the notion that bureaucratic status is connected with the number of subordinates an official may supervise is not literally true, a trend toward bureaucratic expansion is nevertheless to be noted in nearly every type of large organization. Indeed Professor C. Northcote Parkinson has formalized this trend in what, with tongue in cheek, he calls "Parkinson's Law." Stated briefly and baldly, this "law" asserts that in large scale organizations "work expands so as to fill the time available for its completion." The trend toward expansion of administrative personnel, says Professor Parkinson, arises from two circumstances or axioms, as he calls them, namely (1) "An official wants to multiply subordinates, not rivals," and (2) "Officials make work for each other."[5]

Other examples might be cited. Without taking "Parkinson's Law" too seriously, one may nevertheless ask whether it is not a natural consequence of our Organization Age and of the Managerial Revolution. Doesn't it apply to business as well as to government? How else can one explain the increase of white-collar workers from 19 percent in 1920 to over 50 percent in 1965? Automation may conceivably work a further Parkinsonian revolution. When and if machines do most of our work, workers may vanish and everyone become an expert or a supervisor of experts. Already a revolution has occurred in the federal service as in the total work force of the nation. It may be well to trace its development briefly.

☆ *ANDREW JACKSON AND THE CIVIL SERVICE*

In his first annual message to Congress, Andrew Jackson said that in his judgment, "The duties of all public officers are, or at least admit of being made, so plain and simple that men of intelligence may readily qualify themselves for their performance. And I cannot but believe that more is lost by the long continuance of men in office than is generally gained by their experience." In line with this policy he proceeded to "clean house" of those officials and employees who were closely identified with the outgoing administration. To Jackson's admirers, this was but the practical operation of the democratic principles of "equality" and rotation in office. To Jackson's critics, it appeared as a brazen application of the cynical doctrine, "to the victor belong the spoils."

We cannot now resolve this controversy. It does, however, have some significance for us in considering the problem of bureaucracy in a demo-

---

[5] See C. N. Parkinson, *Parkinson's Law* (Sentry, 1957).

cratic society. In fairness to Jackson, it should be said that although his political purge was more extensive than those of his predecessors, he cannot be regarded as the inventor of the spoils system.[6] In any case, it is estimated that Jackson replaced not more than 20 percent and not less than 10 percent of the civilian employees of the government. We need to remember that in Jackson's day the functions of government were still largely clerical and political rather than technical or professional, and there was considerable force to Jackson's claim that "men of intelligence might readily qualify themselves for their performance." Today's highly specialized bureaucracy had not yet appeared.

Jackson's election, moreover, marked the triumph of party politics in American government. Prior to his nomination and election, public officials, including the President himself, were selected from narrow elites, strongly influenced by the principle of *noblesse oblige.* Jackson challenged all this by defying the congressional caucus, having his own candidacy sponsored by a national nominating convention, conducting a campaign designed to appeal to the newly enfranchised masses, and by choosing as his Cabinet and administrative officers men who were loyal to him and to the party of which he was the leader. His theory of political leadership had deeper and more far-reaching consequences than the establishment or extension of the spoils system. It helped to make political leadership more responsible to the rank and file of the voters rather than to a comparatively limited number of so-called "people of quality."

Through Jackson, the newly enfranchised masses expressed their resentment at a system which excluded them from access to the seats of power. They resented the tendency to confine public appointments to members of the "best" families, so that those in government service came to represent a kind of aristocracy of wealth and family. They resented the number of sons appointed to succeed fathers in civil posts, making the service more like a caste than a career open to all. Against this system Jackson waged a bloodless revolution, opening the way to the public service for great segments of the population which had formerly been excluded.

But the new system had its seamy side. Not only did it result in the appointment of persons poorly, if at all, qualified to do the jobs for which they were appointed; it made the President a job broker, spending time on patronage that might better have been spent on policy. It encouraged the use of the public service for private gain since government employees had to "make hay" while they were in office before victory of the opposition swept them from the public trough. Some public officials

6 As early as 1795 President Washington wrote to Timothy Pickering, saying: "I shall not whilst I have the honor to administer the government, bring any man into any office of consequence knowingly whose political tenets are adverse to the measures which the general government are pursuing; for this in my opinion would be a sort of political suicide."

paid on a fee basis did quite well for themselves. The system also en-couraged the unnecessary expansion of government jobs in order to re-ward the faithful and to make sure that the burdens of the public service would not seriously interfere with the work of partisan politics. Plunkitt of Tammany Hall, in his discussion of the "curse of civil service reform," put the matter with his inimitable logic: "First, this great and glorious country was built up by political parties; second, parties can't hold together if their workers don't get the offices when they win; third, if the parties go to pieces, the government they built up must go to pieces, too; fourth, then there'll be hell to pay."

☆   CIVIL SERVICE REFORM

As the size, scope, and complexity of government increased, the evils of the spoils system became apparent, and agitation for selection on the basis of character and competence gained force. Bills to provide for some such system were introduced in increasing number after 1863 and civil service reform became almost a synonym for political reform. Progress was slow until the tragic death of President Garfield in 1881 at the hands of a disappointed office-seeker. A sense of outrage swept the country, and, in January, 1883, President Chester Arthur signed the first Civil Service Act (the Pendleton Act) to provide for a public service based on com-petence and character and recruited by competitive examination rather than political pull. To administer the act, a Civil Service Commission was established.

The merit principle having been admitted, the subsequent history of the civil service has been mainly a record of its extension, by statute and executive order, to a larger and larger proportion of the employees in the federal service, and also in state and city government. Today 90 percent of federal civilian employees are included in the classified-competitive service, or in merit systems outside the classified service. (See Figures 15–1 and 15–2.)

The battle for a public service recruited on the basis of tested competence and character has been largely won at the federal level. In state and local governments the merit principle has been admitted and is making rapid progress. A majority of the states now provide for the recruitment of all or nearly all their employees on a merit basis, and in others the principle applies to an ever-growing number of departments. Nearly every major city in the country applies the merit principle and many a small city has its civil service board or commission. To be sure, there are many areas, particularly in county government, where the spoils system in its classic form continues. But, by and large, the fight for a public service based on character and competence is being won.

The political leaders and civic reformers who have brought this

Federal Government Civilian Employees

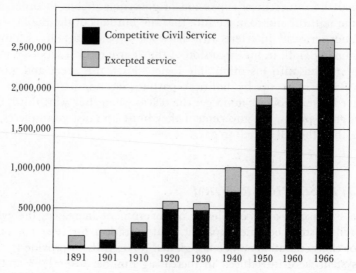

Figure 15–1 Based on data from U.S. Bureau of the Census, *Statistical Abstract of the United States: 1967*. (88th edition.) Washington, D.C., Table 570, p. 407.

about have had some powerful allies. Not the least of these has been the influence of modern science and technology. So long as the major functions of a civil servant were clerical or political, little special competence was required and perhaps no great harm was done in making appointments as a reward for party loyalty. But when government became responsible for services or controls in fields as varied as money and banking,

Occupational Distribution of Federal
White-Collar Workers

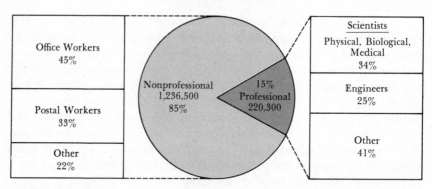

Figue 15–2 Based on data from United States Civil Service Commission.

education, public health, engineering and public works, transportation and communications, soil conservation and reclamation, international trade and commerce, or economic and social planning, the old system was manifestly inadequate. And nowhere has the impact of science and technology been more obvious than in national defense, the largest, most expensive and, perhaps, most important of all governmental functions. This transformation would have spelled death to the old spoils system even if there had been no civil service reform movement.

As a corollary to the impact of science and technology upon the public service, the growth of educational opportunities has made it possible for virtually any American who wishes to do so to qualify for the public service. Thus, the basis has been laid for a civil service open to popular participation without sacrificing the equally important requirements of character and competence. Without mass education, the demands of a modern civil service might have produced a bureaucratic elite, inconsistent with the American spirit of equality.

Historically, the struggle for the career service in the United States has involved a kind of trench warfare between the civil service reformers on the one hand and the political leaders on the other. Step by step, the reformers have pushed the politicians out until, by 1960, over 90 percent of the federal bureaucracy was covered by the so-called merit or "career" system.[7] Demonstrated competence has been substituted for party loyalty, not only in the recruitment of public bureaucrats, but also in their promotion and retirement within the system. So long as the agency for which a civil servant works is provided for by Congress, and so long as the bureaucrat himself does his job with honesty and efficiency, he enjoys security against dismissal except "for cause." The massive turnover of public servants from Cabinet members to clerks and messengers that used to follow each change in control of the White House is a thing of the past.

Moreover, within the government itself faithful service and increasing competence are rewarded by promotion, with correspondingly higher salary, status, and responsibility. And after years of service the modern bureaucrat may look forward to retirement on a modest pension. These principles are the essence of what is called a "career service."

As a corollary or condition of all this the law demands *partisan neutrality* not only in the recruitment and promotion of civil servants but in the day-by-day behavior of the bureaucrats themselves. Partisan assessments or solicitation of party campaign funds within the civil service are forbidden; and under the so-called Hatch Acts (of 1939 and

[7] The major categories in 1965 were (1) the so-called classified service with 18 grades and over 1 million civilian employees; (2) the Postal Field Service with over 500,000; (3) the Foreign Service numbering some 15,000; (4) Veterans Administration (Medicare and Surgery), nearly 22,000; (5) Agricultural and Stabilization Service, about 57,000; (6) the Judicial Branch, about 5,000; and (7) Defense, about 1 million.

1940), civil servants are prohibited from taking an active part in partisan activities. These are laws which apply not only to the federal service but to those state and local officials who are paid in whole or part from federal funds.[8]

☆ AN ELITE CORPS AT THE TOP

By 1965, less than 2 percent of the jobs in the federal service were available for partisan political appointment. Schedules A, B, and C of the Civil Service Rules exempt so-called "policy-making" positions, those having a "personal or confidential" relation with key officials, and those whom it is not practicable to recruit through competitive examination but who may be required to pass noncompetitive qualifying examinations. Ardent civil service reformers have even sought to extend the career system to most of the positions now excluded. They talk also of creating an "elite" corps of top operatives, nonpartisan and nonpolitical —comparable to the so-called Administrative Class in Great Britain.

The most striking contrast between the American career service and the career service of Great Britain (by which the American was originally inspired) is the absence here of an elite corps comparable to the Administrative Class in England. Admission to the Administrative Class is by examination upon graduation from a university; promotion from the lower-status Clerical Class is quite rare, and hence only those who have been in the Administrative Class from youth are likely ever to become permanent secretaries of departments. Since something like the Administrative Class exists in most western European bureaucracies, the absence of such a class in America is quite remarkable. Not surprisingly, civil service reformers have long been agitating for the creation of such a class, but they have not been successful and are not likely to be in the foreseeable future. The notion of a Senior Civil Service or Elite Corps carrying rank in the person rather than in the office is the ultimate in the development of the notion of a career service. Since it runs into direct conflict with the notion of a representative bureaucracy—for a class apart can hardly be representative—it is not surprising that it has made little headway in the United States.

In considering extensions of the career service to include officers now subject to partisan appointment, we need to reflect on the proper role of experts in government. The expert may be a master of *how* something can be done; he is not necessarily a better judge of *why* it should be done at all. The man who wears the shoes may be a better judge of their

[8] It is noteworthy that while employees of state and local governments have increased from 3 million to nearly 8 million, federal civilian employment has remained substantially unchanged between 1942 and 1966.

quality than the shoemaker. One does not have to be a cook to judge the quality of an omelette.

It is on this assumption that the English continue to place confidence in what Anson has called "Government by Amateurs," in which the expert is always on *tap* but never on *top*. It is one thing to insist that those who have responsibility for public health have some knowledge of medical science. It is something else again to say that decisions as to whether the government should do anything at all about the public health ought to be left to the medical profession. In our zeal for competence in the public service, we ought not to confuse means with ends, nor the role of the political leader with that of the technical expert or administrator.

Yet so far had the trend against partisan officials gone that, in 1953, Mrs. Oveta Culp Hobby, upon becoming our first Secretary for Health, Education, and Welfare, found that some of the most important positions in her Department—including the number two job—were under civil service. It was in protest against situations of this kind that President Eisenhower created Schedule "C" to exempt positions of a confidential or policy-determining character from the classified service.

This was done not to increase presidential political patronage but to give some assurance that key positions in the federal bureaucracy could be filled with officials sympathetic and loyal to the President and his policies. Nor is this inconsistent with a sound merit system. The problem here is not mainly one of political patronage against a career service. It has a wider significance, moreover, than merely giving the Chief Executive a weapon of political leadership. As we have seen, some patronage at the disposal of the President can be helpful in mobilizing support from political leaders on whom the success or failure of his administration may depend. But the importance of patronage can easily be exaggerated. Many other factors are more important than a few jobs in the public service, especially jobs subject to the uncertainties of partisan politics. Not the least of these other factors is the personal loyalty and agreement on public policies of a Chief Executive's "team," not only at the executive level but also among legislative and party leaders.

☆ *THE PRESIDENT AND THE BUREAUCRATS*

Under the best circumstances a President has a difficult time moving the vast federal bureaucracy in the direction he believes it should go.

> The Treasury is so large [said F.D.R.] and so far-flung . . . that I find it almost impossible to get the action and results I want, even with Henry Morgenthau there. But the Treasury is not to be compared with the State Department. You should go through the experience of trying to get any

changes in the thinking, policy, and action of the career diplomats. . . .

But the Treasury and the State Departments put together are nothing compared with the Navy. The Admirals are really something to cope with. I should know. To change anything in the Navy is like punching a feather bed. . . .[9]

Presidents Truman, Eisenhower, and Kennedy have made similar complaints.

We ought not to complicate the President's problem by compelling him to keep key officials in top positions who are politically disloyal to him and unsympathetic to his policies. We should therefore not be surprised to learn that when President Eisenhower came to power after thirty years of Democratic rule, a so-called "black list" of federal employees was given to each department and agency head. Those on the black list included (1) officials who had attended Democratic fund-raising dinners; (2) those who were committed to policies, like the Democratic Brannan Plan for Agriculture, which the Eisenhower administration was against.

Nor should we be shocked to learn of a similar "black list" in the first year of any new administration containing the names of officials who had attended fund-raising dinners of the opposition party and those known to be unsympathetic with the policies of the new administration. A bureaucracy which fails to reflect the changing political moods of the nation by a prompt response to changing political moods of the White House is worse than an obstruction—it can be a menace to free and responsible government.

☆   *POLICY AND ADMINISTRATION*

Most students concede that partisan politics is an essential factor in the behavior of top bureaucrats, those who are described as involved in "policy decisions." Hence it is customary to distinguish between *politics*, that is, policy making on the one hand, and *administration*, or the execution of policy, on the other. The distinction is essentially between "ends" and "means." To decide policy is to determine *what* is to be done. Shall the government provide medical care for the aged, or shall the federal government provide support for education? These are questions of *policy*, of *goals*, or of *ends*. Administration, on the other hand, is to decide *how* something is to be done. By what *means* shall the *ends* agreed upon be realized?

This distinction is formally recognized in the Constitution in the principle of separation of powers. "All Legislative Power, herein granted, . . . shall be vested in a Congress," it being assumed that the power to

9 See Richard E. Neustadt, *Presidential Power* (New York: Wiley, 1960).

legislate is the power to determine policy. On the other hand, "The Executive Power," says Article II, . . . "shall be vested in a President." And the President is bound to see that the policies determined by Congress are carried out. To this end he is given extensive administrative powers—to appoint and remove certain executive and administrative officers, "to require the opinion in writing of the heads of departments," and so forth.

The slightest reflection will reveal that this constitutional distinction between policy and administration is by no means neat and clear. Without reviewing all that we have said before, everyone knows that the President not only shares in the legislative power but has become the source of most important legislation. He therefore plays a leading role, indeed, *the* leading role, in making policy decisions. Since he is also the nation's Chief Executive Officer, he unites in a striking fashion both policy and administration.[10]

Finally, Congress, not content with its role as a policy maker intervenes in the administrative process in many ways. It participates in the appointment of top executive and administrative officers, both through formal Senate confirmation and so-called senatorial courtesy, and by determining the qualifications of executive officers. It also determines by legislation the administrative organization of the executive branch, even to the definition of internal structure and administrative procedure. For example, in 1955 Congress required the Secretary of Defense to secure prior consent of the House and Senate Appropriations Committees before separating from his department any function which he thought could be better done by private industry. In 1949 Congress required the Secretary of Air to get the approval of the House and Senate Armed Services Committees before buying any real estate. Obviously such legislation puts Congress into the very heart of the administrative process.

The confusion between policy and administration goes far beyond the formal relations of Congress and the executive. Policy and administration are like Siamese twins—inseparable. As a general proposition, one may say that there is as much *policy* in the process of government as there is discretion, that is, an ability to choose among alternatives. Whenever an official has discretion to decide controversies, he may be said to exercise judicial or quasi-judicial power. When such decisions become precedents for future behavior, they are policy decisions. Whenever an official has power to issue regulations to which penalties for violation are attached, he exercises policy-making authority. Whenever he has power to control conduct by these rules or regulations, he exercises administrative power. Only when all discretion is banished is he wholly free of policy; so long as he is free to choose among alternative courses of action, he is in some measure making policy decisions.

[10] As we shall see later on, the Supreme Court, too, shares in the determination of policy and even in its execution or administration.

In theory, the administrative bureaucrat strives to reduce discretion and to establish routinized if not mechanized modes of behavior. Administration therefore represents a formalized effort to reduce or eliminate the element of choice from official behavior. And since, except for wholly mechanized operations, discretion is never wholly banished, policy and administration are inextricably combined in varying degrees. In the executive branch, discretion is at its maximum in the Presidency and in those who share the responsibility for deciding the goals of the administration.

Congress strives to limit the President's discretion, but the nature and subject matter of modern legislation is such that many important policy decisions must be left to the executive. That is to say, Congress delegates to the President legislative power. And although the Supreme Court has in a few cases held this to be unconstitutional, most such delegations of power have been sustained on the theory that (a) the President is merely filling in the details of a law, or (b) the President is merely deciding when the specific conditions exist to call the law into operation.

In any case, once these decisions are made, subordinate officials, assistant secretaries, bureau chiefs, section heads, and so forth, are bound to carry them into effect. In the higher echelons considerable discretion is likely to remain, especially in the choice of ways and means for best carrying out the policies of the administration. And so intimate is the relation between means and ends that the choice of means may profoundly affect the ends and thus exert an important influence on policy. It is for this reason, among others, that most Presidents have insisted upon a free hand in choosing those officials who sit at the top of the bureaucratic hierarchy.

☆ BUREAUCRACY—THEORY AND PRACTICE

Modern bureaucracy is not an end in itself. It does not exist for the benefit of bureaucrats but for the fulfillment of the great ends for which the government was established, that is, to promote a more perfect union, establish justice, provide for the common defense and welfare, and ensure the blessings of liberty to ourselves and our posterity. It is a basic assumption that the particular policies of Congress and the President are calculated to achieve these goals. It is no part of the role of the bureaucracy to second guess the President and Congress but promptly and faithfully to carry out the policies they have defined.

The classical statement of administrative theory is to be found in Max Weber's essay on *Bureaucracy*. In Peter M. Blau's summary, Weber's principles are outlined as embracing a half dozen axioms or principles including:

1. *The principle of Specialization,* according to which specific tasks are distributed in a fixed way, according to established rules.
2. *The principle of Hierarchy,* according to which each lower office is usually appointed by and under the control and supervision of the one immediately higher—the higher officer being successively responsible *for* the lower as the lower is responsible *to* the higher.
3. *The principle of Regulation,* according to which all operations are governed by a "consistent system of abstract rules" which are applied in a descending order from generalization to particular cases, that is, the lower one goes in the hierarchy, the more specific the rules and the less the discretion.
4. *The principles of Impersonality.* "The ideal official conducts his office . . . in a spirit of formalistic impersonality," without hatred or passion and hence without affection or enthusiasm. This principle is a corollary of the principle of regulation, since it requires "the discharge of business according to rules and 'without regard for persons.' "
5. *The principle of Vocational or Career Commitment.* Administration is regarded as a vocation requiring special training, accessible only on the basis of demonstrated knowledge or skills "which are prerequisites of employment." A corollary of this principle is a "merit" system of recruitment and promotion.
6. *The principle of Security.* Normally bureaucrats are hired for special ability and hence need to be protected from arbitrary dismissal.[11]

One should note, too, that administrative organization implies the concentration of authority at the summit and unquestioning loyalty and obedience from bottom to top. These principles, it is argued, will produce "the highest degree of efficiency," because only in these terms can one achieve the highest measure of rationality and integration in achieving group goals. It is now a commonplace among students of administration that an ideal bureaucratic organization is probably impossible to attain because, for one thing, it fails to take account of certain human traits. An inherent human resistance to both physical and intellectual restraint makes war on most of the classical canons of administrative theory. The model bureaucrat is a cog in a machine—and even at the lowest levels of human intelligence, people resist "cogification" even in the interest of efficiency.

But even if an ideal bureaucracy were attainable, it would be undesirable. Although bureaucratic organization is based on specialized functions and therefore on individual differences, the principle of *impersonality* takes little account of individual differences among those with whom the organization deals. The principle of hierarchy, moreover, tends to produce stratification and blind conformism within the organization. It also tends toward centralization and concentration of decision making. If the greatest possible decentralization of decision making is a sound

[11] See Peter M. Blau, *Bureaucracy in Modern Society* (New York: Random House, 1956).

maxim for a democratic society, bureaucracy in its ideal form is, if not antidemocratic, at least nondemocratic.

Moreover, a decentralized system of decision making is often more flexible, more efficient, and more economical as well as more democratic than one where decisions are made at the top of the pyramid. Many of the advantages of large-scale operations are lost through excessive centralization. What is gained through central control and uniform standards may be lost in rigidities of structure and procedure and the delays that come from the ever-growing mountain of red tape. Hence it is that in many of the most far-flung federal agencies—such as Agriculture, Interior, the Treasury, Health, Education, and Welfare (HEW), and even Defense—devolution of function and decentralization of the administrative process have been recognized as essential features of scientific systems of organization and management. In this respect it is worth noting that devolution and decentralization have been features of recent reorganization plans in private as well as in public administration.

A model administrative state is undesirable, however, not because it is a threat to freedom and to democracy, but because, notwithstanding its bold claims of efficiency and rationality, it tends to be both inefficient and nonrational. It is inefficient simply because its basic principles of specialization, hierarchy, impersonality, and so forth, inevitably generate tension and conflict both within the organization and in its external relations.[12] *Specialization of function,* for example, tends to produce myopic civil servants whose span of interest is so limited that they become robots operating in a maze of bureaucratic rules. The progressive robotization of the civil service is a major threat to administrative efficiency. *Impersonality,* another basic principle, is itself based on the demonstrably false premise that all people with whom the organization deals are not merely equal but identical. To treat individuals with different abilities, responsibilities, needs and circumstances, as identical, is to deny them equality within the democratic meaning of that term. The principle of *hierarchy,* with its corollaries of internal discipline and conformity, must induce in subordinates a reluctance to try out or even to suggest new ideas. Only a rare bureaucrat will venture to "stick his neck out" by experimenting with new techniques of administration or suggesting policy changes to his superiors. The principle of hierarchy thus places a premium upon conformity and "standpatism" at the expense of imagination, initiative, and flexibility.

In short, all those qualities that produce the most distinguished and efficient administrative leadership are held at a discount by classical bureaucratic theory. Even the principles of merit and security can produce *dysfunctions* in the administrative process. A rigid system based on standardized tests and ratings can often produce not a corps of

12 See Robert Merton, *Social Theory and Social Structure* (New York: Free Press, 1949), pp. 21–81.

capable administrators, but a mandarin class, contemptuous of others, capable of passing examinations, but incapable of dealing with the "unprovided case" which is the acid test of good administration. Coupled with the principle of security, a rigid merit system can generate an army of drones, doing what is necessary and no more.

☆ ORGANIZATION AND MANAGEMENT

The bureaucracies in both federal and state governments did not develop according to any consistent plan. Like Topsy, they "just growed." Congress, responding to pressures from business, agriculture, labor, and other organized interest groups and from the executive branch itself, created the various departments and agencies piecemeal. Beginning with three departments (State, War, and Treasury) and an Attorney General in 1789, the number grew until by 1968 there were twelve major departments, something in the neighborhood of fifty so-called independent agencies, and literally hundreds of bureaus, sections, or divisions having more or less distinct functions.[13]

These numerous agencies vary greatly from one another in function, size, and importance. Some, like the Departments of Defense, Agriculture, Health, Education, and Welfare (HEW), and the Post Office Department, are often called "service" agencies, providing services to the country as a whole or to more or less well-defined groups. The services of the Post Office Department are well known. So, too, are those of the Department of Health, Education, and Welfare. The Department of Labor administers the unemployment insurance laws and the fair labor standards act to protect wage earners against the hazards of unemployment and exploitation by enforcing laws establishing minimum wages and maximum hours of work in business engaged in interstate commerce. The Department of Agriculture not only carries on scientific research and education, which have revolutionized American agriculture, but it administers the billion dollar Commodity Credit Corporation, an Agricultural Stabilization and Conservation Service, a Crop Insurance program, Rural Community, Cooperative and Home Administration Services, the far-flung Forest Service, the Rural Electrification Service, and an International Development program. The Department of Commerce aids business and industry by promoting manufacturing and trade, administering grants to the states for interstate highway construction, by maintaining and publishing a more or less continuous census of the population, providing weather reports and accurate statistics concerning nearly every aspect of American life.

Some of the major departments carry on construction work on a

[13] Although regarded as "Cabinet rank" since 1789, the Attorney General did not become the full-fledged Department of Justice until 1870.

The Executive Departments

Agency	Origin	Responsibilities	Headed by	Civil Employees
Department of State	Founded as the Department of Foreign Affairs in 1781, under the Articles of Confederation. Assigned present title in 1789.	Initiates and conducts the foreign policies of the United States under the direction of the President.	Secretary of State	39,000
Department of the Treasury	Established by act of Congress in September, 1789.	Manages the financial affairs of the national government, including the collection and disbursement of monies and the management of the national debt; coins and prints the currency.	Secretary of the Treasury	80,700
Department of Defense	The National Military Establishment was created in 1947 by combining the War and Navy Departments; its name was changed to the Department of Defense in 1949. The War Department had been established by Congress in 1789. The Navy was separated from War and made a department in 1798.	The military forces of the United States are responsible for the security of the nation under the constitutional direction of the President as their Commander in Chief. Strategic defense plans are made, and the armed forces are staffed, equipped, and trained.	Secretary of Defense	1,060,000
Department of Justice	The office of Attorney General was created in 1789, and this officer was ranked as the equivalent of an executive department head. The department as such was established in 1870.	Renders legal advice to the executive branch; investigates and prosecutes violations of federal laws; administers the federal penal institutions.	Attorney General	30,900
Post Office Department	Designated an executive department in 1872. A postal system had existed since at least 1753 under a Postmaster General. This officer was first considered the equal of an executive department head in 1829.	Operates the postal system "for conveying letters and intelligence"; transports parcels; sells postal money orders.	Post master General	580,000

Agency	Origin	Responsibilities	Headed by	Civil Employees
Department of the Interior	Established in 1849 as a consolidation of the General Land Office, Office of Indian Affairs, Pension Office and Patent Office.	Conserves federally owned natural and mineral resources; administers public lands, national parks, United States territories, and Indian Affairs; develops irrigation projects and hydroelectric systems.	Secretary of the Interior	54,000
Department of Agriculture	A Department of Agriculture was established in 1862 under a Commissioner of Agriculture. In 1889 the department was designated an executive department under the Secretary of Agriculture.	Provides a great variety of services for farms and farmers; manages and disposes of surplus agricultural commodities; administers the national forests.	Secretary of Agriculture	91,000
Department of Commerce	The Department of Commerce and Labor was founded in 1903. It became the Department of Commerce in 1913.	Assists, promotes and develops foreign and domestic commerce, including manufacture, trade, and shipping. Among its services are taking census, granting patents, weather forecasting, and grants to states for interstate highways.	Secretary of Commerce	28,500
Department of Labor	A Bureau of Labor was established in the Department of the Interior in 1884. It later became an independent office, and then in 1903, a bureau in the Department of Commerce and Labor. The present executive department was set up in 1913.	Promotes the welfare of wage earners; administers minimum labor standards laws; administers the national unemployment insurance law; collects labor and cost of living statistics.	Secretary of Labor	8,000
Department of Health, Education, and Welfare	The Federal Security Agency was established in 1939. In 1953 it became an executive department under its present title.	Administers the various activities of the public health service and the office of education; makes grants-in-aid for categorical welfare recipients and administers directly the old	Secretary of Health, Education, and Welfare	73,000

Agency	Origin	Responsibilities	Headed by	Civil Employees
		age and survivors insurance program; assists in vocational rehabilitation; administers the pure food and drug laws.		
Department of Housing and Urban Development	In 1965 the department was constituted by merging several agencies, such as the Housing and Home Finance Agency (dating from the 1930s), the Urban Renewal Agency, and the Public Housing Administration.	Includes federal housing administration and other federal activities; community training and development services; urban renewal and planning studies.	Secretary of Housing and Urban Development	14,300
Department of Transportation	In 1966 the Department of Transportation was established by the inclusion of such existing agencies as the Bureau of Public Roads, the Federal Aviation Agency, the Coast Guard, and by taking over the safety functions of the Civil Aeronautics Board and Interstate Commerce Commission.	Promotes safety in transportation; develops a policy for coordinating and improving the national system of transportation; makes recommendations for federal spending in developing transportation facilities.	Secretary of Transportation	· 90,000

large scale, as for example, the Department of Defense, not only in building and maintaining vast defense establishments but through its Corps of Army Engineers in the construction of civilian public works of great variety. The Department of the Interior builds and operates great power dams and irrigation systems, largely through its reclamation service, and in addition, administers millions of acres of public lands and the system of national parks that provide recreation for hundreds of thousands every year. On top of these responsibilities, this "interior" department administers, along with Indian Affairs, the territories of the United States.

Nearly every department has responsibilities for the regulation of some aspect of American life, and for the enforcement of laws, rules, and regulations as different as those establishing "bag limits" for certain migratory birds, licensing the manufacture and sale of narcotics, combating interstate crime and delinquency, smuggling and bootlegging, counterfeiting the currency, licensing and inspecting national banks, and maintaining a free competitive economy by breaking up "combinations" in restraint of interstate trade and commerce. The FBI in the Department of Justice is known to everyone, but not everyone is familiar with the enforcement work of the Immigration and Naturalization Service, the Antitrust Division, the Bureau of Prisons, or the Civil Rights Division within that department. The Department of the Treasury is thought of, and rightly so, as a tax-collecting agency, but few know of the work of the Customs Service, the Intelligence Unit, the Secret Service, the Narcotics Bureau, and the Alcohol Tax Unit, not only in collecting tariffs and taxes, but in combating the crime syndicates who traffic in illegal liquor and narcotics, smuggling and counterfeiting, and whose leaders frequently fail to pay their income taxes and hence run afoul the "T" men. Most people know that the Secret Service guards the President, but few know that it is a Treasury enforcement unit mainly concerned with catching counterfeiters who try to "get rich quick" by actually "making American money." The Department of Health, Education, and Welfare administers a billion dollar Social Security program, the Public Health Service, the Office of Education, a Vocational Rehabilitation program, multiple welfare services, and the Pure Food and Drugs Administration. The new Department of Housing and Urban Development is itself in a developmental period and may well become one of the largest and most important federal agencies.

The Department of State has been called the Department for the Maintenance of Peace, and in many respects it is an apt description. So long as diplomatic talks can continue, just so long will the guns be silent, and it is to this end that the 40,000 employees of this department are committed. The main outlines of its organization reflect the scope of its interests and responsibilities. (See Figure 15–3.)

None of the twelve major departments of the federal government operates alone or in isolation from the rest. The formal exchange of gossip, information, and concern among department heads at Cabinet meetings gives one only the faintest outline of the complex and continuous cooperation that goes on at lower working levels. Not even the formal structure of interdepartmental councils or committees that are so often described and so much deplored can fully describe the intricate and tangled web of interdepartmental "coordination" and cooperation that gives life to what we have come to know as the process of government. The Bureau of Customs in the Department of the Treasury, for example, works closely with the Immigration and Naturalization Service in the Department of Justice, the plant and animal Quarantine activities of the Department of Agriculture, the United States Coast Guard in the Treasury, and the independent Maritime Commission, as well as other agencies involved in the entrance or exit of persons or property from or into the United States. The intimate and interdependent relations of the

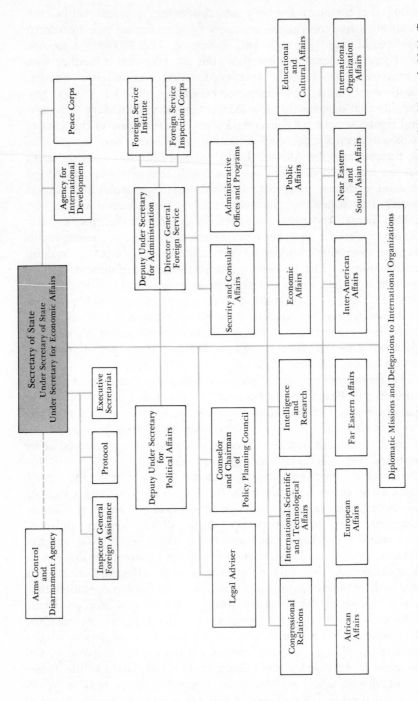

Figure 15–3 Organization of the Department of State. (After *United States Government Organization Manual, 1966–67*, Washington, D.C., Revised June 1, 1966, p. 609.

Department of State, the Department of Defense, the Department of the Treasury, the Atomic Energy Commission, the Aeronautics and Space Administration, the CIA, and the Office of Special Representatives for Trade Negotiations in the Executive Office of the President are but another illustration of how different a government in action is from the static government of formal organization charts.

Even when we have accounted for the twelve great departments that by tradition rather than by law are included in the President's Cabinet, we have only begun to encompass the American federal bureaucracy. For there remains some forty or fifty more or less independent agencies and establishments, and regulatory boards and commissions, with thousands of employees, processes, and responsibilities that often transcend those of the so-called old line departments. To be sure, some of these, such as the American Battle Monuments Commission, and the Small Business Administration, are neither impressive in their power or the role that they play in the process of government. Others, however, such as the Atomic Energy Commission, the Veterans Administration, the National Aeronautics and Space Administration, the Farm Credit Administration, and the Housing and Home Finance Agency, are engaged in large-scale operations which have an impact on American economic and social life that is hard to measure. And there are other so-called independent agencies, such as the TVA., The Panama Canal Company, the St. Lawrence Seaway Development Corporation, the Federal Deposit Insurance Corporation, that operate large-scale, quasi-business, government-owned enterprises. Only slightly different in structure and purpose is the Federal Aviation Agency, which operates systems of air traffic control and air navigation facilities for both civilian and military aircraft.

Other agencies such as the Civil Service Commission and the General Services Administration serve the government itself in the recruitment, promotion, and retirement of its personnel, and in the procurement, management, and conservation of public properties, records, and archives. Finally, among these independent agencies is the United States Information Agency which carries news and information about the United States, its culture, its goals and objectives, and its often mysterious and quixotic behavior to other peoples around the world.

Nor is the story fully told without mention of the so-called independent regulatory boards and commissions. Beginning with the Interstate Commerce Commission in 1887, they now include the Federal Trade Commission, the Federal Reserve System, the Federal Communications Commission, Federal Power Commission, National Labor Relations Board, Securities and Exchange Commission, the Civil Aeronautics Board, and the Federal Maritime Commission. Independent of the President, and for practical purposes, of Congress, too, these boards or commissions, within their respective jurisdictions, make and enforce rules and regulations and hear and decide controversies affecting some of the most critical areas of our economic, intellectual, and social life. The vast network of railroads, trucks and bus lines, domestic water carriers, and petroleum pipe lines operate under license from the ICC and rules and regulations that it makes concerning rates, services, safety, and sanitary devices and facilities. The Civil Aeronautics Board, the Federal Maritime Commission, and the Federal Power Commission exercise a similar control over airlines, off-shore shipping, and the interstate transportation of electric energy and natural gas, respectively. The Power Commission also licenses the construction of power dams on public lands and waterways, and regulates the rates of the electricity generated by them. To a large extent the vast monetary and credit system of the United States is under the surveillance and control of the Federal Reserve Board and the Securities and Exchange Commission. The former, created in 1913, helps to set interest rates, maintain a stable currency, and control the supply of bank credit through the purchase and sale of government securities by its Open Market Committee, and by the issuance of Federal Reserve Notes the latter regulates the stock market by supervising the conditions of the issues and their sales.

To cure some of the ambiguities and uncertainties of the Sherman Antitrust Act, the Federal Trade Commission was established in 1914 to help maintain a competitive economy by preventing unfair trade practices and other acts tending toward monopoly. In recent years it has also been authorized to prevent unfair and deceptive advertising, and dishonest or misleading labeling of certain products. Perhaps the best-known of the so-called New Deal agencies created in the early 1930s is the National Labor Relations Board. Its jurisdiction extends to unfair labor practices of both management and labor, and after elections supervised by the Board, it certifies the appropriate bargaining agency.

The communications industry is under the surveillance and control of the Federal Communications Commission, which also regulates telephone, telegraph, radio and cable rates and services. Although it has no power directly to control the content of television and radio programs, it can, and occasionally does, influence program policies through its power to issue, renew, or revoke the licenses of broadcasting stations.

The foregoing includes only the major executive departments, independent agencies, and commissions of the federal government. Together they represent the hard core of the executive public power structure, with jurisdiction over affairs as seemingly trivial as the analysis of various brands of lipstick, and as important as the life and death problems of war and peace. Yet what we have described represents only an incomplete structural outline. Tucked away within these major agencies are hundreds of bureaus, divisions, and units, variously named, which carry on the work to be done. Some of these subunits or subsystems, such as the Food and Drug Administration, and the Office of Education, the Bureau of Standards in the Department of Commerce, the Reclamation

Service in the Department of the Interior, or the Corps of Engineers in the Department of Defense, have power and responsibilities that help to shape not only the American economy but the public health, education, and culture of the American people.

We have said that executive agencies vary in function, size, and importance. We shall have occasion later on in the present book to talk about the function and importance of some of them. Here we may note some of the striking variations in the size of government agencies, since size raises special problems of organization and management. The major executive departments vary in size from the Department of Labor with about 8,000 employees to the Post Office Department with nearly 600,000 and the Department of Defense with over a million civilians on its rolls. These, along with Agriculture, the Treasury, Transportation, and HEW, each of which has nearly 100,000 employees, are the giants in terms of the size and complexity of their organization. Following them in order of size are the Departments of the Interior, of State, of Justice, of Commerce, of Housing and Urban Development, and of Labor. Among the independent agencies are the Veterans Administration, in a class by itself, with nearly 200,000 employees, the Federal Aviation Agency with nearly 50,000, and General Services with over 30,000. The TVA has nearly 20,000 employees; the Selective Service Administration, about 7,000; the Small Business Administration, under 300; the FDIC, 1,300; the National Science Foundation, 800; Farm Credit Administration, 325; and the St. Lawrence Seaway Corporation, 150. None of the great regulatory boards and commissions has as many as 3,000 employees, although the ICC, with 2,400, comes close. All of these, despite their importance and their great powers, are comparatively modest in the size of their personnel payrolls.

It is interesting to observe that three agencies—the Department of Defense, the Post Office Department, and the Veterans Administration—account for over 75 percent of all civilians employed by the federal government. The Department of Defense alone accounts for nearly half. If one adds to the Department of Defense the Post Office Department and the Veterans Administration, the Departments of Agriculture, of State, and of the Interior, we account for nearly 85 percent of all civilian employees, leaving only 15 percent to fifty or more other agencies.

The size of these great federal agencies, the nature of their services and responsibilities, the skill with which they are administered, and the quality of their political leadership are major factors in their survival and growth. For all must run the gauntlet of objective surveillance by the Bureau of the Budget, committees and subcommittees of Congress, Congress itself, and the President. Important also are the size of the clientele they serve and general public concern in the problems with which they deal or the services they supply. The successful launching of a space satellite and a widespread public concern for health and scientific research can almost literally propel a whole department or one or more of its bureaus from the bottom to the top of committee and congressional approval, with a corresponding increase in its operations personnel and appropriations. On the other hand, a department or bureau, lacking an extensive and interested clientele, not identified with widespread public concern, and/or unable to transcend partisan or interest group opposition is likely to suffer. It is indeed at the point where the bureaucracy meets Congress and its committees that its political mettle meets its most severe test.[14]

As this complex structure grew, it developed (1) overlapping, duplication, and confusion of functions, (2) lack of clear lines of authority and responsibility, and (3) "independent" boards and commissions owing clear responsibility to no one.

In 1925 Herbert Hoover, while Secretary of Commerce, found that public health work was divided among two departments and four different bureaus; conservation of resources was in eight agencies located in five departments; public works was under fourteen agencies in nine departments; the merchant marine was in fourteen agencies in six departments, and government purchasing was in forty different agencies in Washington and thirty-four in other parts of the country. The Bureau of Home Economics was in Agriculture; Public Health was in the Treasury; St. Elizabeth's Hospital in the Department of the Interior; the Children's Bureau was in Labor; the Pure Food and Drugs Administration was in Agriculture; and the Bureau of Fisheries was in Commerce. Nor were these the only administrative anomalies. The War Department had charge of civil affairs in the Philippines, but the administration of Hawaii, Puerto Rico, and the Virgin Islands was under the Department of the Interior. The Bureau of Reclamation was in the Department of the Interior (where it still is) but Soil Conservation was in Agriculture (where it still is). Even today the Improvement of Rivers and Harbors, including flood control (and in some cases power dams) is under the Corps of Army Engineers—but dams built for reclamation and irrigation are in Interior. These arrangements often make for a strange "chain of command" or line of responsibility. For example, the Bonneville Power Administration of the Department of the Interior is the marketing agency for electric power generated at a dozen or more dams on the Columbia, Flathead, Pend Oreille, Yakima, Snake, and Willamette rivers. But administrative management of the dams themselves is divided between the Bureau of Reclamation in the Department of the Interior and the Corps of Army Engineers in the Department of the Army.

All of these arrangements at one time made sense to somebody and presumably to Congress. But for the President who has responsibility for the management of this hydra-headed monster, it often makes little sense and creates administrative headaches of monumental proportions.

14 See Richard Fenno, Jr., *The Power of the Purse* (Boston: Little, Brown, 1966), esp. chaps. 8 and 9.

There have been repeated cries for reform, but reorganization is difficult. Once created, government agencies are almost impossible to alter or abolish. "Nothing approaches immortality in this world," it is said, "as do government bureaus, and they do not practice birth control." Congress, jealous of its powers, has been reluctant to give the President power to deal with the problem.

In December, 1929, President Hoover, in a message to Congress, urged reorganization. "This subject," he said, "has been under consideration over twenty years. It was promised by both political parties. . . . It has been repeatedly examined. . . . The conclusions of these investigations have been unanimous that reorganization is a necessity of sound administration, of economy, of more effective governmental policies, and relief of the citizen from unnecessary harassment in his relations with a multitude of scattered governmental agencies."

Nearly everyone agreed, moreover, that Congress could not itself do the kind of reorganization that was necessary. "This process of reorganizing the fundamental structure," said Senator Vandenburg, "is never in the world going to be achieved by Congressional effort. . . . It is absolutely impossible to get a meeting of minds when there are 531 minds that have got to meet. It must be an executive function."

Accordingly, in 1933, on the eve of leaving office, President Hoover was given power to reorganize the executive branch by executive orders unless the orders were disallowed by either house of Congress within 60 days. The act also forbade the President to abolish any of the ten major departments, although he could transfer, consolidate, and (except for the major departments and agencies) abolish bureaus, services, sections, and divisions. President Hoover submitted eleven executive orders under this act but the Democratic Congress disallowed them all on the ground that executive reorganization ought not to be carried out by a defeated President.

Upon coming to power in 1933, President Franklin Roosevelt joined the battle for reorganization. Under the authority of Appropriation legislation, the President was given power to carry out extensive reorganization by executive orders to take effect within 60 days of their promulgation. A good many transfers and consolidations were made, and some agencies were even abolished. It was evident, however, that a more systematic attack on the problem was necessary. In 1936, therefore, President Roosevelt appointed a Committee on Administrative Management whose report was followed by the Reorganization Act of 1939.[15] Under this act a major reorganization took place not by acts of Congress but by executive orders of the President—subject, as under earlier legislation, to

15 It is interesting to note that this President's Commission was composed of three distinguished political scientists—Louis Brownlow of Washington, D.C.; Charles C. Merriam, of the University of Chicago; and Luther Gulick of the Institute of Public Administration.

congressional veto within 60 days. If Congress (both houses) did not disallow an order within this period, the order became effective without formal action by the Congress. The President's power to reorganize the executive branch has been renewed and extended by Reorganization Acts in 1945, 1949, 1959, and 1961. Upon recommendation of Presidents Truman and Eisenhower, Congress, in 1947 and in 1953, established what came to be known as the First and Second Hoover Commissions on Reorganization of the executive branch of the government.[16]

☆ *PRINCIPLES OF REORGANIZATION*

We cannot here review the details of these various reorganizations. The general problems, however, have been essentially the same as have been the principles governing reorganization. "The only way," said Franklin D. Roosevelt, "in which the President can be relieved of the physically impossible task of directly dealing with thirty to forty major agencies is by reorganization—by the regrouping of agencies according to their major purposes under responsible heads who will report to the President . . . as contemplated by the Reorganization Act of 1939." To this end there was established an Executive Office of the President. As of 1968, the Executive Office of the President included the Bureau of the Budget, the White House Office, the National Security Council, the National Aeronautics and Space Council, the Office of Civil Defense Mobilization, the Office of Economic Opportunity, the Office of Science and Technology, the Office of Emergency Planning, a special Office for Trade Negotiations, and the Council of Economic Advisers. (See Figure 15–4.) These agencies and officials are the "strong right arm" of the President in his role as manager and chief executive of the federal bureaucracy.

"The Second Step (in reorganization)," said President Roosevelt, "is to improve the allocation of departmental activities" on a more unified functional basis. To accomplish this, he created three new agencies, mainly to consolidate bureaus or divisions engaged in similar activities but scattered among a number of departments. Reflecting the continuous process of reorganization, none of these agencies remain in existence.

"The Third Step," said President Roosevelt, "is to improve intradepartmental management . . ." To accomplish this there has been a continuous process of intra-agency reorganization through the years. Since 1959 over 75 reorganization plans have been submitted by Presidents Eisenhower, Truman, Kennedy, and Johnson. For reorganization of the executive branch is not something that can be accomplished in a year or even in a presidential term. It is a continuous process.

[16] The First Hoover Commission (1947) made no fewer than 273 recommendations while the Second Hoover Commission (1953) made well over 300.

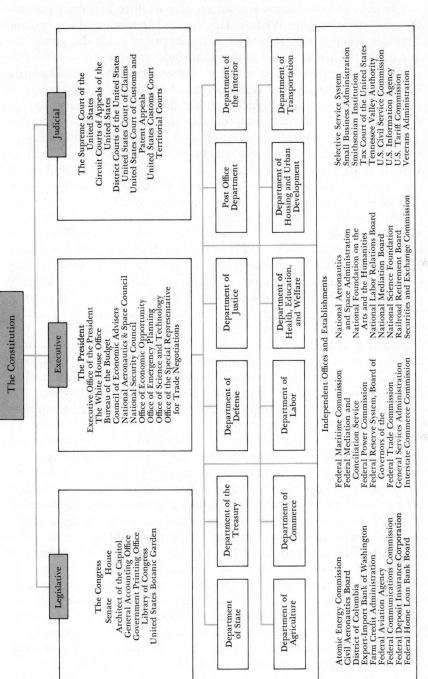

Figure 15–4 Organization of the Government of the United States. (After *United States Government Organization Manual, 1966–67*, Washington, D.C., Revised June 1, 1966, p. 605.)

In spite of vast changes and the creation of three new departments—Health, Education, and Welfare, Housing and Urban Development, and Transportation—the basic problems remain pretty much the same. The findings of the first Hoover Commission would probably be as applicable to the government of 1968 as to the government of 1949. "The Executive Branch," said that report, "is not organized into a workable number of major departments and agencies which the President can effectively direct." A second and recurring problem noted by the commission is that "the line of command and supervision from the President down through his department heads to every employee . . . has been weakened or actually broken in many places and in many ways. A third problem is that "the President and the heads of Departments lack the tools to frame programs and policies and to supervise their execution.[17]

At least we now recognize that problems of organization and management in the federal bureaucracy are continuing problems. The Bureau of the Budget in the Office of the President includes an "Office of Management and Organization" for continuous study of "better agency management and organization . . . ," and to conduct work "to improve government-wide management practices and procedures." No amount of reorganization, however, can "solve" the tremendous problems faced by the President as head of the federal bureaucracy. Even with the best organization in the world, he is going to be confronted with the built-in conservatism, stubbornness, and inflexibility of an extensive bureaucracy. Like F.D.R., he is going to feel, as he tries to move this vast machine in the direction he wants it to go, that he is punching a feather bed. To succeed, he must continue to pull and haul, plead and threaten, wheedle and command, but keep on punching.

Two examples of administrative reorganization in the federal bureaucracy may be cited. Prior to 1947 the administration of national defense was under the two major Departments of War and Navy. Their Secretaries were of Cabinet rank and not only reported directly and independently to the President but, under the President as Commander in Chief, exercised command over the armed forces. To mitigate confusion and interservice rivalry, especially after the establishment of a Department of the Air Force in 1947, a national military establishment was created by the National Security Act of that year. Notwithstanding this tentative move toward unity, the creation of an independent Department of the Air Force threatened not only to increase the burden on the President but to multiply interservice rivalries. Although some coordination was made possible through the Joint Chiefs of Staff, the existence of three more or less independent departments in the chain of command made unified direction difficult.

[17] Notwithstanding a large Democratic majority in both houses, President Kennedy's plans for reorganizing the independent commissions and for creating a new Department of Urban Affairs were defeated or badly mangled in the legislative mill.

Characterizing the so-called Unification Act of 1947 as "little more than a weak confederation of sovereign military units," President Eisenhower in 1958 said, "We cannot allow differing service viewpoints to determine the character of our defenses. Our country's security requirements must not be subordinated to outmoded or single service concepts of war."

Accordingly, National Security Act Amendments in 1949, 1953, and 1958 created a new Department of Defense, with a Secretary of Defense at its head, reporting directly to the President. (See Figure 15–5.) The act also created a Deputy Secretary of Defense, eight Assistant Secretaries, and a Chairman of the Joint Chiefs of Staff. The three Departments of the Army, Navy, and Air Force were made subordinate to the Secretary of Defense. Moreover, an Armed Forces Policy Council was established to include not only the three service secretaries, but the Joint Chiefs of Staff, the Munitions Board, and the Research and Development Board.

Legislation also compelled further unification among the armed services by removing the Secretaries of the Army, Navy, and Air Force from the direct chain of command, placing the Joint Chiefs of Staff directly under the Secretary of Defense, and giving to the Secretary of Defense greater control over defense research and development. As matters now stand, therefore, all defense functions are unified under the Secretary of Defense. "The chain of command runs from the President to the Secretary of Defense through the Joint Chiefs of Staff to the com-

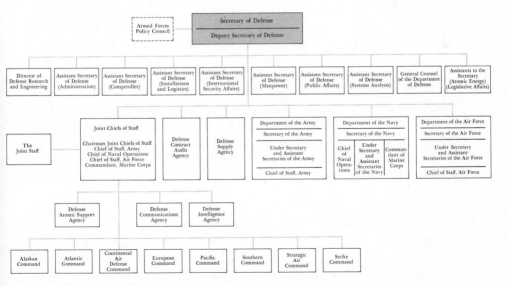

Figure 15–5 Organization of the Department of Defense. (After *United States Government Organization Manual, 1966–67,* Washington, D.C., Revised June 1, 1966, p. 611.)

manders of unified and specified commands. Orders to such commanders are issued by the President, the Secretary of Defense, or by the Joint Chiefs of Staff by authority . . . and direction of the Secretary of Defense.[18]

Another example of administrative reorganization may be cited. For more than 100 years, a variety of agencies had been established in the federal government concerned with problems of health, education, and welfare. Through the years there had emerged a Public Health Service in the Department of the Treasury, a Food and Drug Administration in the Department of Agriculture, a Children's Bureau in the Department of Labor, an Office of Education in the Department of the Interior, and other similar agencies in other departments. With the expansion of federal services in these and other related fields, some administrative unification was essential.

The first major move in this direction was made in 1939 when, under President Franklin Roosevelt's Reorganization Plan I, a Federal Security Agency was established to bring under a single administrator the Office of Education, the Public Health Service, the Social Security Board, the United States Employment Service, Civilian Conservation Corps, and the National Youth Administration. Subsequent legislation transferred still other agencies to the Federal Security Agency.

Although the Federal Security Administrator enjoyed Cabinet rank and regularly attended Cabinet meetings, he lacked the status, dignity, and power associated with a full-fledged departmental secretary. Accordingly one of the first acts of President Eisenhower's administration was to create a new Department of Health, Education, and Welfare under Reorganization Plan I of 1953. (See Figure 15–6.) The Federal Security Agency was abolished and the Social Security Administration, Food and Drug Administration, Office of Education, Office of Vocational Rehabilitation, the Public Health Service, and St. Elizabeth's Hospital were all transferred to the new department to which a Welfare Administration was added in 1963. The creation of the Departments of Defense, of Health, Education, and Welfare, and of Housing and Urban Development serve only to emphasize the continuing problem of administrative organization if government is to respond to its ever-changing environment.

---

[18] See the *United States Government Manual,* 1961–1962, pp. 136 ff.

Many informed students of military organization and management urge further unification, extending even to the abolition of the three separate services with their separate Secretaries for the Army, Navy, and Air Force. A modern defense establishment, they argue, has become so highly technical that the traditional distinctions between Army, Navy, and Air Force have lost much, if not all, of their validity. A defense establishment in which all those in the armed services would wear a common uniform and be subject to a unified command would not only be more flexible and efficient but also more economical.

For the pros and cons of this argument see Roswell L. Gilpatric (former Deputy Defense Secretary) , in *New York Times Magazine,* March 29, 1964.

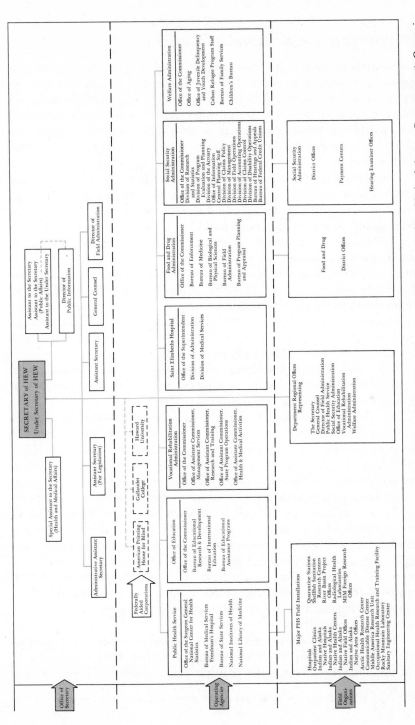

Figure 15–6 Organization of the Department of Health, Education, and Welfare. (After *United States Government Organization Manual, 1965–66,* Washington, D.C., p. 610.)

☆ TOWARD A RESPONSIBLE BUREAUCRACY

A government without bureaucrats, we have said, is like a centipede without legs unable to move. For it is upon the bureaucrats that we depend to see that public policies are realized in practice. Yet there is a widely current notion that bureaucracy and democracy are somehow incompatible—a notion that Professor Friedrich calls "an oratorial slogan which endangers the future of democracy. For a constitutional system which cannot function effectively cannot live."[19]

Nevertheless, the fears expressed pose problems for those who want government to be both effective and democratic. For among the so-called immutable principles of democratic theory is the assumption that power and responsibility must go hand in hand.

A responsible bureaucrat is a man of not one but many responsibilities. He owes a *political responsibility* to those who make policy. He owes both a *political* and an *administrative* responsibility to his superior officers. He owes a *legal* responsibility through the courts when he transgresses the rights of citizens by abusing or exceeding his powers. He owes a *professional* responsibility to his fellow bureaucrats to maintain high standards of integrity and competence. He owes a *moral* responsibility to the state and society in which he lives.

We cannot explore fully these multiple loyalties and responsibilities. It may, nevertheless, be useful to suggest some of the perplexities that occur in thinking about a responsible bureaucracy.

As far as the majority of bureaucrats have any *political* responsibility, it must be vicarious and not direct. In the federal government, the President, in final analysis, must "take the rap" for what is or is not done. The heads of the major departments are political officers appointed by and accountable to him; and as they must answer for the acts of their subordinates, so the President in turn must answer for them. If the President is to be responsible, he must have power to control the behavior of the bureaucrats for whom he is responsible. However, this situation has been confounded by the creation of "independent" boards, commissions, corporations, and authorities, responsible (if they may be so described) not to the President, but to Congress. This so-called "headless fourth branch of the government" has posed problems of administrative organization, management, and responsibility for which no one seems to have found satisfactory solutions.

The President—no less than the Congress—represents the people; and, through him, no less than through Congress, bureaucrats can be held responsible. Although the political responsibility of bureaucrats is

19 Carl J. Friedrich, *Constitutional Government and Democracy* (Boston: Ginn, 1941) , p. 57.

vicarious in either case, in the Presidency it comes to fairly clear focus in a single office, whereas in Congress it appears in fragments and at uneven intervals. And whereas through Congress the bureaucrat's responsibility to his state or local "clients" is emphasized, it is under the President that the bureaucracy can most effectively promote the "general welfare" of all the people.

Not the least of the President's burdens is political responsibility for the conduct of the executive establishment. Insolence, inefficiency, incompetence, and corruption in any executive official or agency are properly chargeable to him. He ought not to escape this responsibility by talk of betrayal by "faithless men in high places." These men are his agents and for better or worse their deeds are his.

In the final analysis political responsibility in a big democracy can be effectively enforced only through well-organized political parties. Hence the search for a more responsible bureaucracy must be sought not merely in administrative reorganization but also through a more responsible party system.

How far up or down the hierarchy of administrative authority the principle of political responsibility should extend has been a subject of prolonged and intense debate. The issue has been confused by failure to distinguish between political responsibility and partisan loyalty. The former is an indispensable characteristic of democratic government and should extend from the outermost reaches of the bureaucracy to the White House. The latter, unless carefully confined to top administrative posts that share with the President in the determination of high policy, can become a mask for the place-seeker and spoilsman. The partisan neutrality of the civil servant is a cardinal principle of the merit system upon which any sound personnel policy must rest. The tradition, now embedded in law, which bars civil servants from active participation in party politics is based on this assumption.

To say that civil servants should not be held to partisan loyalty is not to say that they should also be exempt from political responsibility. Political responsibility in this sense implies that the civil servant carry out to the best of his ability the policies of the administration, of whatever party. As former Prime Minister Attlee once observed, "We always demand from our civil servants a loyalty to the State, and that they should serve the government of the day, whatever its political color."[20] Anyone who cannot give this elementary loyalty cannot justly claim the security and immunity from partisan responsibility that characterizes the permanent civil service.

Bureaucrats have not only political but *legal* responsibility. The legal definition of their powers and responsibilities is the heart of administrative law and an important part of the criminal code. Laws

[20] Hansard, March 25, 1948, quoted in T. A. Critchley, *The Civil Service Today* (London, 1951), p. 60.

against bribery and corruption, fraud and deceit, misfeasance and malfeasance, are, of course, part of the machinery for enforcing this legal
responsibility.

American legal theory and practice have followed the English rather
than the French tradition. Legal responsibility has been enforced
through the ordinary courts, and liability for wrongful acts by civil
servants has attached to the individual and not to the state. Responsibility of the government for breaches of contract has long been recognized,
but a similar responsibility for the torts (personal wrongs) of its agents
has had but a recent and reluctant recognition. Civil and criminal suits
against public officials as individuals, plus resort to the great writs—quo
warranto, mandamus, injunction, prohibition, habeas corpus—have been
the usual remedies for bureaucratic wrong-doing. Proposals to establish a
system of administrative tribunals on the French model have been made,
but so far without success.

There have, however, been significant changes in traditional Anglo-
American practice. The theory that a public officer was individually responsible for damages resulting from his wrongful acts may have helped
to inspire caution and respect for the rights of others, but it was cold
comfort to those actually damaged to know that their only redress was a
damage suit against impecunious bureaucrats. So the *theory* of individual
responsibility has been maintained as the *practice* of publicly reimburs-
ing officials in the amount of the judgments against them has grown.

Significant of the new trend is the Federal Tort Claims Act of 1946,
which modifies the rule of immunity formerly applied to the federal
government. Under this act the United States is made liable "for injury
or loss of property or personal injury or death caused by the negligent or
wrongful act or omission of any employee of the government while acting
within the scope of his office or employment."[21]

A truly responsible bureaucracy will depend as much—perhaps
more—upon its own code of professional ethics as upon external controls.
The growth of professional *esprit,* without which no code of ethics can
have much meaning, has had to wait upon victory over the spoilsman.
Although this victory is yet to be won, it is not too early to make some
conscious effort to create among public servants a greater sense of professional pride and responsibility.

The experience of other professions such as medicine, law, and
teaching can offer stimulus but also a warning. Too often such associations become primarily concerned not with their responsibilities for
better public service, but with the promotion of more selfish ends. Although we have far to go, we can take comfort in the progress that has
been made. No longer has the patronage peddler or the spoilsman the
hold he once had on the federal service. No longer can it be fairly said

[21] 28 U.S.C.A. Sec. 1346, 2672, 2674.

that American city government is a conspicuous failure. No longer can it accurately be said, as George S. Taylor once said of Britain in the eighteenth century, that politics is "the trade of managing the state in the interests of the men in possession and their friends." Standards of character and competence in the public service will stand comparison with those in other walks of life. But it is not enough that they be as good—they should be better. Just as government should be a model employer, so the public servant should be a model for the community.

16
THE SUPREME
COURT

☆ THE ORIGIN OF JUDICIAL REVIEW

Nearly every aspect of the American process of government may involve participation of the Supreme Court. Is a treaty the law of the land? Are executive agreements of the President enforceable at law? May a deputy federal marshal escape prosecution for murder on the ground that he acted under the authority of an executive order which, it was successfully argued, is as much the law of the land as an act of Congress?

May Congress delegate legislative power to the President? Under what conditions may the President on his own volition suspend the writ of habeas corpus, declare martial law, send federal troops into a state to quell domestic violence, or cross an international border to wage war? Does the President's power to appoint imply a power to remove without the consent of the Senate, or for reasons other than those specified by Congress?

These and hundreds of other questions arise and are resolved by American courts and ultimately by the Supreme Court of the United States. For under our constitutional system, the Supreme Court is the arbiter of conflicts of power arising from the separation of powers, the federal system, and the complex system of constitutional limitations designed to preserve the blessings of liberty to ourselves and our posterity.

At least on these great constitutional questions the Court decides until the matter is otherwise resolved by constititional amendment, an act of Congress or the erosion of time and circumstance.

The political power structure of the United States involves both a separation and a sharing of powers between the President and the Congress and between the central government and the several states. It also involves important constitutional limitations upon both the central government and states, designed to insure a pluralistic society and to protect private persons and groups from certain kinds of political constraint. It is as the guardian or arbiter of this complex system that the Supreme Court has become the unique and powerful institution it is today. In playing its role as guardian or arbiter the Court not infrequently finds itself under attack by one or more protagonists who make up the total public and private power structure in the United States. Whereas the remedy for unconstitutional "usurpation" of power by the Congress, the President, or the several states is normally an appeal to the Supreme Court, relief from alleged "usurpation" of power by the Court itself is not so easily found. If we were to diagram the public power structure in the United States it might look as shown in Figure 16–1.

On these crude diagrams the shaded areas are areas of conflict, and it is within these so-called twilight zones that the Supreme Court plays its role. When Congress seeks to invade the constitutional powers of the President, when the President acts beyond the powers conferred upon him by the Constitution, when Congress and the President, acting separately or together, invade the powers reserved to the states, when a state invades the legitimate powers of the central government, when either the central government or a state violates or impairs the constitutional rights of private persons or groups, in all such cases the Supreme Court may, if the matter is properly brought before it, decide the issue.

Not all questions before the Court involve issues of constitutional power. Some, indeed most of them, involve conflicts over the meaning of an act of Congress, an executive order of the President, or a state law as it relates to the rights and obligations of parties in conflict. But on the great issues of constitutional power—"to regulate commerce among the

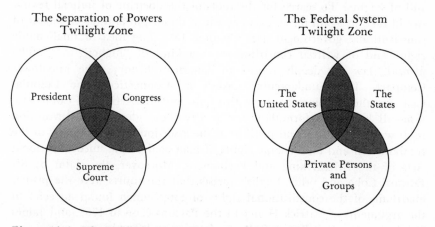

The Separation of Powers
Twilight Zone

President   Congress

Supreme
Court

The Federal System
Twilight Zone

The
United States   The
States

Private Persons
and
Groups

Figure 16–1   The Public Power Structure in the United States.

several states," "to promote the general welfare," "to provide for the common defense,"—and on the meaning of such phrases as "freedom of speech," "equal protection of the law," or "due process of law," the Court is the immediate if not the final arbiter. So central is the Court in the operation of our system that Charles Evans Hughes, when Governor of New York, once said, "We live under a Constitution, but the Constitution is what the judges say it is."

The strategic position of the Supreme Court in our constitutional system has been a subject of great controversy, and its power to declare acts of Congress (and of the several states) unconstitutional has been described as judicial usurpation.

> It has long been my opinion [wrote Thomas Jefferson in 1821] that the germ of dissolution of our Federal Government is in the Constitution of our Judiciary . . . an irrepressible body (for impeachment is scarcely a scarecrow) working like gravity by day and night gaining a little today and a little tomorrow and advancing its noiseless steps like a thief over the field of jurisdiction." In an earlier letter he had said, "The Constitution . . . is a mere thing of wax in the hands of the judiciary which they may twist and shape into any form they please. . . .

On the other hand, the power of the Supreme Court as arbiter of the American power structure has been hailed by the late Chief Justice White as the "Glory and ornament of our system which distinguishes it from every other government on the face of the earth . . . a great and mighty power hovering over the Constitution of the land to which has been delegated the awful responsibility of restraining all the coordinate departments of government within the wall of the . . . fabric which our fathers built for our protection and immunity."

Whence comes this mighty power? By whom or by what has the Court been appointed to be custodian of the Constitution, the arbiter of the separation of powers and the federal system, and the guardian of the Bill of Rights? To search for the roots of the doctrine of judicial review would take us again on an excursion into the origin and development of constitutional government (see Chapter 13). The idea of unalienable rights and of written constitutions as a kind of "higher" or "fundamental" law are deeply rooted in American history. The Mayflower Compact, The Fundamental Orders of Connecticut, the Colonial Charters, the Revolutionary constitutions, and the Articles of Confederation—all helped to formulate and fortify these ideas. The Revolution itself was rationalized and justified as the assertion by the colonists of the fundamental and unalienable rights of man against the unconstitutional Acts of the British king and Parliament. Moreover, the claim by Sir Edward Coke and other English jurists that the courts were the proper guardians of the constitutional rights of Englishmen found an echo in the arguments of Patrick Henry in the Parsons Case in 1764, and James Otis in his *Rights of British Colonies Asserted and Proved.*

The Revolutionary constitutions of New York, Pennsylvania, and New Hampshire provided for Councils of Revision or of Censors (composed largely of judges) "to inquire whether the Constitution has been preserved inviolate in every part." Massachusetts provided for advisory opinions from its supreme court on the constitutionality of pending legislation. Even during the so-called "critical period" when legislatures were nearly everywhere supreme, the supreme courts of Rhode Island, Virginia, and North Carolina asserted their right to declare acts of the state legislature to be unconstitutional and void. According to Charles Beard, at least 17 of the 55 members of the Constitutional Convention expressed themselves as assuming that the Constitution did in fact give to the Court power to pass on the constitutionality of acts of Congress. These 17 members were included among the 25 most influential members of the Convention according to Beard.[1]

"Independent tribunals of justice," said Madison in 1789, "will consider themselves in a peculiar manner the guardians of [the Bill of Rights]; they will be as . . . a bulwark against any assumption of power in the legislative or executive; they will be naturally led to resist every encroachment upon rights expressly stipulated . . . in the Constitution."

Hamilton, too, in article 78 of *The Federalist* had this to say:

The complete independence of the courts of justice is . . . essential to a United Constitution . . . *No legislative Act contrary to the Constitution can be valid.* . . .

The interpretation of the laws is the proper and peculiar function of the Courts, and the Constitution is a fundamental law. It therefore remains for the Courts to determine its meaning as well as the meaning of any particular act proceeding from the legislative body. If there should be an irreconcilable variance between the two, that which has the superior obligation and authority ought of course to be preferred. . . .

And where a statute contravenes the Constitution, it is the duty of the judicial tribunals to adhere to the latter and disregard the former . . . the intention of the people to the intention of their agents. . . .

The long tradition of constitutionalism in the Western world, the more specific traditions of the English common law, the experience of Americans with written Constitutions and with Courts inclined to hold the Constitution as superior to a statute, the debates in the Constitutional Convention, and the candid avowal of the principle of judicial review in the *Federalist* papers should lay the ghost of usurpation that has haunted the Supreme Court for nearly two centuries.

For reasons not too clear, the framers of the Constitution did not write the doctrine of judicial review into the Constitution, not, at least, in so many words. Only in Article VI is there any language from which the power of judicial review can be inferred, and even this is not clear as

[1] See Charles Beard, *The Supreme Court and the Constitution* (New York: Macmillan, 1912) ; also (Englewood Cliffs, N.J.: Prentice-Hall [Spectrum Books, 1962]) , p. 47.

to acts of Congress. "This Constitution," reads Article VI, "and the Laws of the United States which shall be made in pursuance thereof: All Treaties made, or which shall be made under the Authority of the United States, shall be the Supreme Law of the land: and the Judges in every State shall be bound thereby, anything in the Constitution or laws of any State to the contrary notwithstanding."

In establishing the Constitution, the laws and treaties of the United States as the supreme law of the land, the Constitution clearly gives to the Supreme Court power to determine wherein the Constitution or laws of any state are in conflict with the Constitution, laws or treaties of the United States, and in such cases to declare them null and void. Moreover, the language of Section 25 of the Judiciary Act of 1789 leaves no doubt that the Supreme Court is to have this power vis-à-vis the states.

Nor was the Court long in asserting this power. As early as 1797 a state statute was held to be invalid because it was in conflict with a treaty of the United States. The following year the Court sustained a state statute as *not* being an ex-post facto law, but in doing so Justice Wedell commented, "If any Act of a Legislature of a State violates the Constitution, it is unquestionably void."[2]

In the case of *Fletcher* v. *Peck,* decided in 1810, the Court held a state law unconstitutional under the contract clause of the United States Constitution. In *McCulloch* v. *Maryland* (1819) a state law regulating and taxing the Bank of the United States was held unconstitutional. And in the famous case of *Dartmouth College* v. *Woodward* a law of New Hampshire was held unconstitutional under the contract clause of the United States Constitution. These early cases established beyond any doubt the power of the Supreme Court to declare the constitutions or laws of the states in conflict with the Constitution or laws of the United States, to be null and void. Unless this were so the Constitution and laws of the United States might mean one thing in New York and something else in Tennessee.

Although these principles were not established without bitter opposition and occasional open defiance of the Court by state authorities, the net result was to proclaim and establish the United States not as a confederation of sovereign states but as a single sovereignty. "I do not think," said the late Justice Holmes, "the United States would come to an end if we lost our power to declare an Act of Congress void. I do think the Union would be imperilled if we could not make that declaration as to the laws of the several states."

But what about acts of Congress? Section 2 of Article III speaks of cases arising under this Constitution. Article VI speaks of "this Constitution and the Laws which shall be made in pursuance thereof" . . . and of treaties made "under the authority of the United States," as "the Supreme law of the land." But what does the phrase mean? Does this

2 *Calder* v. *Bull,* 3 Dallas 386 (1798).

mean anything more than that the procedure for enacting laws or making treaties, as outlined in the Constitution, shall be followed. Or does it go beyond mere procedure—to say that the substance of the law must be consistent with the spirit and language of the Constitution? If it is merely procedural, then no duly enacted law could be questioned by the Court and the supremacy of Congress and the President would be as clear as the supremacy of Parliament in England. Certainly the bare language of the Constitution admits of such an interpretation, but the history of constitutional government in the United States, the views of the most influential members of the Constitutional Convention, and the spirit if not the letter of the Constitution itself support the view that the Court is bound, in cases where the issue is raised, to ask not only, Has the law been duly enacted as provided in the Constitution? but also, Is the law within the scope of the powers conferred by the Constitution? At any rate this was the view taken by John Marshall and the Supreme Court in *Marbury* v. *Madison,* decided in February, 1803, the first case to declare an act of Congress unconstitutional.

The facts were as follows: The Federalist party, after twelve years in control of the White House under Washington and John Adams, gave way in 1801 to a Republican, or Democrat-Republican, President, Thomas Jefferson. John Marshall, an ardent Federalist, served as Secretary of State from June, 1800, until March, 1801, during the closing months of the Adams administration. But President Adams, intent upon saving as much of the government as possible from control of the incoming Jeffersonians, appointed Marshall to be Chief Justice of the United States Supreme Court to begin January 31, 1801. Thus his term as Chief Justice overlapped by two months his term as Secretary of State. Adams also appointed, under authority of an act of Congress of February 27, 1801, a number of Federalist district judges and court officials. Among these so-called "midnight" appointees was one William Marbury, appointed to be a justice of the peace for the District of Columbia.

For some reason Marshall, who continued to serve as Secretary of State, although he had signed and sealed Marbury's commission of office, had neglected to deliver it to him. Thus, as it turned out, James Madison, Jefferson's new Secretary of State, found Marbury's undelivered commission on his desk when he moved into that office in March, 1801. When Madison failed to deliver the commission, Mr. Marbury asked the Supreme Court, now presided over by John Marshall, for a writ of mandamus to compel him to do so. The legal basis for this action was Section 13 of the Judiciary Act of 1789, which authorized the Supreme Court to issue writs of mandamus, "in cases warranted by the principles and usages of law to any courts appointed or persons holding office under the authority of the United States."

It was a simple enough case to decide. Either the Court could have issued the writ and then faced up to what to do if Madison refused to obey it, or it could have denied the writ by saying that the Court had no jurisdiction in such a case. Marshall did neither. He said that (1) in equity and justice Marbury was entitled to his commission; (2) unfortunately the Court could do nothing about it because (a) Section 13 of the Judiciary Act, giving the Court power to issue writs in such cases, was unconstitutional, since it increased the Court's original jurisdiction as set forth in the Constitution itself; (b) hence the Court did not have jurisdiction. The decision as such was of no importance, but the reason for the decision has probably had more far-reaching effect than any other single decision of the Court.

In his opinion Marshall obviously relied heavily upon the arguments made by Hamilton in *The Federalist,* and much of Marshall's language is word for word the language of Hamilton. Congress, he held, had no power to increase or diminish the original jurisdiction of the Court as provided in the Constitution. In this decision Marshall established the supremacy of the Constitution over the laws of Congress as later decisions were to establish the supremacy of the Constitution and the laws and treaties of the United States over those of the States. In doing so the Court also made itself the guardian and arbiter of the American constitutional system.[3]

☆ JUDICIAL RESTRAINT

In no other system of government in the world do the courts of law play so important a role as they do in the United States. Alexis de Tocqueville, in his *Democracy in America* (1831), described lawyers and judges as the "American Aristocracy."

> The Lawyers, [he said] form the most powerful, if not the only counterpoise to the democratic element. . . . When the American people are intoxicated by passions or carried away by the impetuosity of their ideas, they are checked . . . by the almost invisible influence of their legal counselors. These secretly oppose their aristocratic propensities to the nation's democratic instincts, their superstitious attachment to what is old to [the nation's] love for novelty, their narrow views to its universal designs, and their habitual procrastination to its ardent impatience.

The conservative character of the judicial mind has been a familiar theme of students of history and politics. And this is especially true in the Anglo-American system in which "judge-made law" (the common law) has played so large a role. To the conservatism of the common law one must add in the United States a constitutional system deliberately designed to impose restraints upon what the framers called the "tyranny of the majority" by an elaborate system of countervailing powers and constitutional limitations. In this system it has been a major function of the

[3] For *Marbury* v. *Madison,* see Peter Odegard, *American Government, Readings and Documents* (2nd ed.; New York: Harper & Row, 1966), pp. 326–331.

courts not only to serve as an arbiter among rival public authorities but to ratify, rationalize, and protect the existing power structures against the claims of popular majorities at every level of government. In this context it is easy to understand why critics of our system should refer to it as a "Judicial Oligarchy." Professor Fred Rodell of the Yale Law School said, "The nine men who are the Supreme Court of the United States are at once the most powerful and the most irresponsible of all the men in the world who govern other men."[4]

While there are restraints upon the power of Congress and the President, it is said, and upon the powers of the several states, there are no effective restraints upon the Supreme Court. As Justice Stone said in a famous dissenting opinion, "While unconstitutional exercise of power by executive and legislative branches . . . is subject to judicial restraint, the only check upon our own exercise of power is our own sense of self-restraint."[5] This is, however, not strictly true. There are a good many restraints on the Supreme Court not only in the Constitution, but in the custom and tradition of the Court itself. The size of the Court is determined by Congress, and Congress has from time to time used this power to influence judicial behavior.

The original Judiciary Act of 1789 provided for a Chief Justice and five Associate Justices. The number was gradually increased until it reached ten under the Act of March 6, 1863. As part of its war against President Andrew Johnson the Reconstruction Congress reduced the number to seven, as vacancies should occur, in order to prevent Johnson from appointing any new justices. Actually the number never went below eight, and when President Johnson was succeeded by Grant in the White House, Congress restored the number to nine, where it has remained. President Franklin D. Roosevelt in 1937 tried to increase the number of justices to a maximum of fifteen by giving the President power to appoint a new justice for every justice who, upon reaching the age of 70, declined to retire. The purpose, of course, was to bring the Court into line with the policies of the President. Although Congress after a bitter conflict declined to go along, it could have done so.[6] Congress may also remove a Supreme Court justice by impeachment, and this too has been tried, but only once, in the case of Associate Justice Chase, and then unsuccessfully.

As in the case of other agencies Congress has some control of the Court's budget and, one would think, over the compensation of the justices. But this power is limited by the constitutional provision saying, "The Judges . . . both of the Supreme and Inferior Courts shall . . .

---

4 *Nine Men* (New York: Random House, 1955) , p. 4.

5 *United States* v. *Butler*, 297 U.S. 1, 1936.

6 To guard against such attempts to "pack" the Court conservative members of Congress in 1954 sponsored a constitutional amendment to fix the size of the Court and deny to Congress power to regulate the Court's appellate jurisdiction. This effort was supported by the American Bar Association and approved by the Senate 58 to 19, but it failed in the hurricane generated by *Brown* v. *Board of Education of Topeka*, 347 U.S. 483 (1954) .

receive for their services a compensation, which shall not be diminished during their continuance in office." This provision, incidentally, was applied by the Court for many years to exempt the justices from an income tax on the ground that such a tax would diminish their salaries while in office and hence violate this provision of the Constitution.[7]

Congress has however, a formidable weapon that it can use to restrain the Supreme Court. Section 2 of Article III confines the original jurisdiction of the Court within very narrow limits, to "cases affecting Ambassadors, other public ministers and Consuls, and those in which a State shall be a party."[8] In all other cases the Court has only appellate jurisdiction, which it exercises "with such exceptions, and under such regulations as the Congress shall make." Since the vast bulk of the Court's business comes to it on appeal, congressional control of its appellate jurisdiction is, if Congress wishes to use it, a power almost of life and death. On one occasion Congress used this power to prevent the Court from acting upon a pending case.

The Reconstruction Acts of 1867 and 1868 were bitter medicine for the former Confederate States, and their constitutionality was repeatedly attacked. A Mississippi editor named McCardle was arrested by the military authorities in Mississippi, acting under authority of these Reconstruction Acts. McCardle filed a petition for habeas corpus on the ground that the Reconstruction Acts were unconstitutional. The writ was issued by a circuit court, but after a hearing McCardle was turned back to the custody of the military authorities. He then appealed to the Supreme Court.

The Court agreed to the appeal, heard arguments on the merits of the case, and took the whole matter under advisement. But before a conference could be held and a decision made, Congress, fearful lest the Court declare the Reconstruction Acts unconstitutional, enacted a statute withdrawing appellate jurisdiction from the Court in such cases. The Court then dismissed the appeal for want of jurisdiction.

"Without jurisdiction," said Chief Justice Chase, "the Court cannot proceed at all in any case. Jurisdiction is the power to declare the law, and when it ceases to exist, the only function remaining to the Court is that of announcing the fact and dismissing the Case."[9]

Although Congress has not again acted so dramatically to curb the Court by abolishing its appellate jurisdiction, its power to do so has been repeatedly upheld by the Court itself.[10] And in recent controversies over

---

7 *Evans* v. *Gore*, 253 U.S. 245 (1920) , and *Miles* v. *Graham*, 268 U.S. 501 (1925) . This immunity ended with *O'Malley, Collector of Internal Revenue* v. *Wood*, 307 U.S. 277 (1939) .

8 As we have seen, under the ruling of *Marbury* v. *Madison* Congress is powerless to expand or contract this original jurisdiction.

9 Ex parte *McCardle*, 6 Wall. 318 (1868) ; 7 Wall. 506 (1869) .

10 *R.R. Co.* v. *Grant*, 98 U.S. 398 (1828) ; *King* v. *Moffitt*, 115 U.S. 497 (1888) ; *Cross* v. *Burke*, 146 U.S. 82 (1892) ; *Missouri* v. *Missouri Pac. R.*, 292 U.S. 13 (1934) ; *Stephan* v. *United States*, 319 U.S. 423 (1903) ; *United States* v. *Betty*, U.S. 393 (1908) .

internal security and civil rights decisions, bills have been introduced in Congress to limit the Court's power to hear appeals in such cases.

Decisions of the Supreme Court in which *the meaning of an act of Congress,* rather than its constitutionality, is at issue may of course be overcome or corrected by legislation. Even when the Court has held an act of Congress or of a state unconstitutional, Congress or the state legislature can often "save the Act by appropriate amendment." Finally, of course, decisions of the Court, even on great constitutional issues, can be reversed (a) by the Court itself, (b) by constitutional amendment as in the case of *Chisholm* v. *Georgia,* which was in effect reversed by the Eleventh Amendment. The Sixteenth Amendment, too, was ratified to overcome a decision of the Supreme Court holding a federal tax on incomes to be unconstitutional.

In addition to these more or less formal restraints on the Court a number of other limitations are observed by the Court itself or grow out of the nature of the judicial process. First and most important is the fact that unlike Congress or the President, the Court is essentially inert. It does not legislate or initiate policy, nor does it have its own machinery even to enforce its own decisions. Moreover, the Court does not pass upon the constitutionality of a law "in general" nor will it give advisory opinions as to the validity of legislative measures before or after their promulgation. Only when a case involving a conflict of real interests is properly before the Court will it pass upon the validity of any statute that may be questioned by either party to the case.

As the Court itself has said, it has no "immediate and general supervision" of the constitutionality of legislation. Only when "the validity of any act of any legislature, State or Federal" is called into question by an actual "assertion of rights by one individual against another" will the Court decide on its constitutionality. A friendly suit to test the constitutionality of a law is not enough. A case must involve a real conflict of interests.

The Court has no veto over legislation comparable to the President's veto. The so-called judicial veto of legislation is, wherever possible, narrowly confined to particular provisions or sections of the law and not to the entire statute. By the same token, "An Act of Congress or a State legislature is presumed to be constitutional." That is to say, the burden of proof falls on those who attack the law rather than those who defend it.[11]

The principle that an act is presumed to be constitutional unless proved otherwise "beyond all reasonable doubt" is a little hard for lay-

---

[11] At one time the Court implied that a statute limiting freedom of contract would be presumed to be unconstitutional until proved valid. This rule was never generally applied and is no longer cited. At another time it was said that laws designed to limit freedom of speech, of the press, of religious worship, would be regarded as unconstitutional until proved to be constitutional, i.e., that rights guaranteed in the First Amendment have a "preferred position" in the Constitution. But this doctrine, too, although still defended by Justices Black and Douglas, is no longer applied by the Court.

men to understand as they contemplate the frequency with which the Court divides 5–4. How, they ask, can a margin of one vote remove "all reasonable doubt." What is a layman to think when three such distinguished justices as Stone, Brandeis, and Cardozo say, "The majority opinion hardly rises to the dignity of argument and must lead to absurd consequences."[12] Nevertheless, the presumption of validity which attaches as a principle to legislation challenged before the Court is an important component of what is called "judicial restraint."

Another example of judicial self-restraint is the principle that wherever possible a case will be decided without facing the issue of constitutionality. That is to say, the case will not be decided on broader terms than are necessary, and wherever possible constitutional issues will be avoided. Where they must be faced, the Court concerns itself only with questions of constitutional powers, rights and procedures, and not with the wisdom of the legislation, the motives of the legislators, or with questions of natural justice, immutable principles of government, or the "spirit of the Constitution." As Justice Stone once said, "Courts are concerned only with the power to enact statutes, not with their wisdom. . . . For the removal of unwise laws from the statute books, appeal lies not to the Courts but to the ballot and to the processes of democratic government."[13] This view has been repeatedly expressed by other justices, and especially by the late Justice Frankfurter.

An even more emphatic disavowal of any concern by the Court for the wisdom of a law was made by Justice Roberts: "[T]he judicial branch of the Government has only one duty—to lay the article of the Constitution which is invoked beside the statute which is challenged and to decide whether the latter squares with the former."

It is doubtful that even Justice Roberts believed this highly romantic theory of the judicial process. In deciding constitutional questions the Supreme Court is engaged in something more complex than matching parts of a jigsaw puzzle. No one will seriously contend that the economic, social, and political views of the justices do not play a large part in the decisions of the Court. They may affect the decision only as inarticulate premises, but their influence will be nonetheless real. Nevertheless, the principle that the Court is concerned with questions of power and not of policy no doubt helps to counteract the intrusion of personal bias into the making of judicial decisions.

Although each case before the Court must be decided upon the basis of the law and the facts pertinent to that case alone, the justices are by no means free to decide each case as though it were an isolated or unique event in history. In their judgment they are influenced not only by numerous formal and informal restraints, but also by the legal principle

---

12 *United States* v. *Butler,* 297 U.S. 1 (1936).
13 *United States* v. *Butler,* 297 U.S. 1 (1936).

of *stare decisis* (precedent). The fabric of constitutional law is not an indiscriminate accumulation of disconnected cases, but a more or less continuous series of cases falling within various categories: the Bill of Rights, the commerce clause, the taxing power, and so forth.

In deciding each new case the Supreme Court is guided by its own earlier decisions and by the decisions of other courts in similar cases. One should note, of course, that while the doctrine of *stare decisis* does limit the Court's freedom to decide, it is by no means as important as it is in other courts in which the common law is more rigorously applied.

Although the Court strives to follow precedent, it does not hesitate to reverse its own past decisions when new circumstances, new facts, new faces, and new ideas on the bench indicate this is the right, the constitutional, thing to do. One need not admit that the Constitution is a thing of wax in the hands of the Court to note that the vague, ambiguous language of our fundamental law allows for wide variance in its meaning from time to time.

In an opinion in 1943 which reversed an earlier decision of the Court, Justice Reed cited fourteen other cases between March 27, 1937, and June 14, 1943, in which one or more earlier decisions were reversed. Reversals during the 1930s and the early 1940s were so numerous that Justice Roberts compared Supreme Court decisions to a "railroad ticket, good for this day and train only."[14]

One final restraint upon the Court's power to declare legislation unconstitutional may be described as a political restraint. The Supreme Court as a matter of policy avoids what it calls "political questions," although what they mean by this phrase is not clear. Nevertheless its own decisions through the years reflect the influence of the changing pattern of American politics. The late Finley Peter Dunne's Mr. Dooley put the matter bluntly when he said, "The Supreme Court follows the election returns."

The most dramatic example of this, perhaps, was the sharp shift in the Court's decisions on so-called New Deal legislation, before and after the threat of President Roosevelt's Court Reform Bill and the appearance of some new faces on the bench. Cynics referred to this as "the switch in time that saved nine." But to those who know the history of the Court, it is not an isolated instance.

☆ THE SUPREME COURT AND POLITICS

In the American model of an independent judiciary, politics is usually not only not included, but rigorously excluded. Yet a moment's reflection will indicate that many decisions of the court have important political consequences. This being so, we ought not to be surprised if politics, even

[14] *Smith* v. *Allwright*, 321 U.S. 649 (1944).

partisan politics, occasionally raises its head in the selection and behavior of justices on the Supreme bench. "If partisanship," wrote Charles Beard, "is taken in the narrow sense to mean that judges of the Supreme Court have perverted the Constitution and the law to serve some low interest of party managers, I think it would be true to historical facts to maintain that the Supreme Court has been remarkably free from partisanship."[15]

But politics, even party politics, when it refers to concern over great issues of public policy, has from the beginning been an important factor in the appointment and behavior of Supreme Court judges. In line with this policy Washington's first appointees to the Supreme Court were without exception loyal Federalists.[16] The policy established by Washington was continued by Adams and has been followed with fair consistency by every President since that time. Adams, for example, at the very end of his administration, appointed Marshall as Chief Justice, together with 16 Federalist judges for new courts provided for by the last ditch Judiciary Act of February 27, 1801 (7 days before Jefferson's inauguration). John Randolph at the time made the acid comment that the whole Federal judiciary was "a hospital of decayed politicians." "The Federalists," he said, "have retired into the judiciary as a stronghold. There the remains of Federalism are to be preserved and all the works of Republicanism are to be beaten down and destroyed."

The political battle for control of the judiciary continued under Jefferson, against active opposition of some of the intrenched Federalist judges. Indeed the Jeffersonian Republicans have the distinction, if it be a distinction, of vainly launching impeachment proceedings against the only Supreme Court justice ever to be so assailed—the Federalist Associate Justice Samuel Chase.[17]

For 34 years, from 1801 to 1835, Chief Justice Marshall dominated the Supreme Court. So much was this the case that even Democratic judges appointed by Democratic Presidents came under his abiding influence. This indeed seems to be the fate of most partisan efforts to control the Supreme Court. Even the most loyal partisans find their partisanship attenuated or sterilized by service on that high tribunal. "Thus," says Charles Warren, "judges appointed by Jefferson and Madi-

---

15 *The Republic* (New York: Viking, 1943), pp. 229–234.

16 John Jay, the first Chief Justice, and his four Associate Justices, John Rutledge, William Cushing, James Wilson, and John Blair, were faithful adherents of "the measures which the general government" under Washington was pursuing. To be sure, the Federalist Senate refused to confirm Rutledge when he was nominated to succeed Jay in 1794. But this merely serves to indicate the intensity of partisan feeling on the matter. The Federalist objection to Rutledge was that he had criticized the Jay Treaty on a minor point: its failure to provide compensation for slaves carried off by the British during the Revolution. The Federalist leadership in the Senate could not countenance even this small deviation from the strict party line.

17 One must admit that the attack was not without provocation. Justice Chase, in May, 1803, in speaking to a Baltimore Grand Jury, referred to the "deterioration of our republican Constitution . . . into a mobocracy, the worst of all possible governments."

son did not hesitate to join with Federalists Marshall and Story . . . in flat opposition to Jackson (on the Cherokee case) . . . In every case involving slavery, anti-slavery judges joined with pro-slavery judges," and Republican President Lincoln's legal tender policy was held unconstitutional by a Republican bench. "In fact," says Mr. Warren, "nothing is more striking in the history of the Court than the manner in which the hopes of those who expected a judge to follow the political views of the President appointing him have been destroyed."[18]

But partisan neutrality does not imply political neutrality in the larger sense of public policy. This distinction was clearly in the mind of President Theodore Roosevelt when in writing to Henry Cabot Lodge (September 4, 1906) concerning the nomination of Judge Lurton of Tennessee (a nominal Democrat) to the Supreme Court, he said, "Nothing has been so strongly borne in on me concerning lawyers on the bench as that the *nominal* politics of the man has nothing to do with his actions on the bench. His *real* politics are all important." Explaining what he meant by *real* politics the President said, "In Lurton's case (although a Democrat) . . . He is right on the Negro question; he is right on the power of the Federal Government; he is right on the insular business (Porto Rico, etc.) ; he is right about corporations; he is right about labor. On every question that would come before the bench, he has . . . shown himself to be in much closer touch with the policies in which you and I believe than even White, because he has been right about corporations where White has been wrong."

Lodge replied drily that it would be better to find someone in whom *nominal* and *real* politics coincided. And, as a matter of record, few Presidents have appointed to the Supreme Court men whose nominal politics were different from their own; Democratic Presidents have nominated Democrats and Republican Presidents have nominated Republicans.

There have been some exceptions. President Truman appointed Republican United States Senator Harold Burton in 1945, and President Eisenhower appointed a lifelong Democrat, William Brennan, in 1956, to succeed Justice Minton, a Democrat. Where this happens, however, there are usually other factors operating. It has, for example, come to be traditional that both parties should have representation on the Court. When the President's own party already makes up a majority, he can afford to be generous by appointing a member of the other major party. This was the case with Truman's appointment of Burton to succeed Justice Roberts to a Court which already included six Democrats. Mr. Truman's other appointments were all Democrats; so, too, were the two justices appointed by President Kennedy: Byron White and Arthur Goldberg.

President Eisenhower's appointment of Brennan to succeed Minton

[18] *The Supreme Court in United States History* (Boston: Little, Brown, 1922) , vol. I, pp. 20–23.

was more than matched by his appointment of Justice Harlan, a Republican, to succeed Robert Jackson, a Democrat; Earl Warren, a Republican, to succeed Justice Vinson, a Democrat; and Potter Stewart, a Republican, to succeed Burton, a Republican: four Republicans to one Democrat.

Mr. Hoover's appointment of Benjamin Cardozo to succeed Justice Holmes in 1932 was perhaps the most atypical appointment made by any President. Cardozo was not only a nominal Democrat but he was from New York, and there were already two other justices from that state. Mr. Cardozo was a Jew and there was already a Jew, Louis Brandeis, on the Court. Finally, Cardozo was commonly classified as a liberal, as distinguished from the conservative Hoover. No doubt in making this appointment President Hoover was responding to a virtually unanimous opinion of the knowledgeable bench and bar that Cardozo was a logical if not inevitable choice.

It would, of course, be naïve to assume that the political affiliation of a judge has *no* effect upon his judicial behavior in deciding cases that come before the Court. Professor Stuart Nagel in 1961 published a study of the relation between party affiliation and behavior on the bench of 298 state and federal Supreme Court judges. A careful analysis of their decisions in 15 different kinds of cases showed a significant correlation between partisan affiliation and a judge's voting pattern. Democratic judges tended much more frequently than Republican judges to favor the defense in criminal cases, the government agency in business regulation cases, the claimant in cases involving unemployment compensation, the defendants in cases on civil liberties, the government in tax cases, and the tenant in landlord-tenant cases.[19] It would be too much to say that partisan affiliation was a major factor in the judicial behavior of Supreme Court justices. It would also be too much to say that it was a negligible factor. Otherwise, Republican and Democratic Presidents would not so consistently nominate their own partisans to that high tribunal.

However important politics—nominal or real—may be in determining the composition of the Supreme Court, the Court's decisions often have political consequences as important as an act of Congress or even an amendment to the Constitution. Indeed the Court has been described not only as a court of law, but as a continuous Constitutional Convention. The real meaning of judicial power in the United States, said Max Lerner, "is to be found in the political rather than the legal realm and . . . its concern is more significantly with power politics than with judicial technology."

The allocation of power between Congress and the President, between the central government and the states, and between government at

19 "Political Party Affiliation and Judges' Decisions," *American Political Science Review*, December, 1961, pp. 843–850.

all levels and the private economy has been determined not so much by the language of the Constitution as by the decisions of state and federal courts, of which the Supreme Court is the capstone. It is well to remember, however, that the 100 to 200 decisions of the Supreme Court each year are but a tiny fraction of approximately 160,000 new cases filed each year in lower federal courts, not to mention the state courts. They too help to determine the law and the living Constitution. Notwithstanding the supremacy clause, it may take months, even years, for decisions of the Supreme Court to affect all relevant cases in every part of the country, and by then the situation may have drastically changed, or the Supreme Court may have reversed itself.

"The trial and appellate judges of the country," says John Frank in *Marble Palace: The Supreme Court in American Life*,[20] [do not] carry the teachings of 350 or more volumes of U.S. Supreme Court Reports in their heads, nor do they . . . stand anxiously at the mail box to receive the new wisdom ground out weekly. If a principle is not called to its attention by counsel, the lower court may not know that it exists."

The decisions of the Supreme Court in the School Segregation Cases show that however much the Constitution may be wax in the hands of the Court, as Jefferson said it was, the custom and habits, prejudices and predilections, of the American people are not, or at least are less so. Yet in these decisions the Supreme Court is not only helping to mold the Constitution, but is adding its considerable weight to a revolution in American values and patterns of behavior. They illustrate also how the Constitution may in effect legislate in an area where, for many reasons, Congress is unable or unwilling to act. In general, however, decisions of the Court are seldom very far out of line with Congress or with public opinion. When they are "out of line" for any considerable period they die aborning, are reversed by legislation, by constitutional amendment, by the Court itself—or by civil war.

When all qualifications are made, however, the Supreme Court has been a master force in determining the shape and purpose of American civilization. By *Marbury* v. *Madison* the whole complex system of countervailing powers, of checks and balances, was put to work as a dynamic principle of American government. The decision in *McCulloch* v. *Maryland* (1819) ratified and fortified Alexander Hamilton's program for establishing a national central bank to bolster the credit of the United States, insure a stable and uniform currency, and provide capital for our early economic growth as a nation. But the decision went far beyond these immediate issues, to extend the powers of the central government beyond anything specifically set forth in the naked language of the Constitution. The Constitution, the Court said, was not merely a compact among sovereign states. On the contrary,

20 (New York: Knopf, 1958.)

> The government of the Union . . . is . . . a government of the people.
> In form and substance it emanates from them. Its powers are granted by
> them and for their benefit.

Nor are these limited to specific items set forth in the Constitution. To be
sure, said the Court,

> The government is . . . one of enumerated powers. [And] among the
> enumerated powers one does not find the word "bank" but we do find the
> power to lay and collect taxes, to borrow money on the credit of the United
> States, to pay its debts, provide for the common defense, and promote
> the general welfare. And most important we find the Central Government
> endowed with power to make "all laws which shall be necessary and proper
> for carrying into execution the [enumerated] powers. . . . " Let the means
> be legitimate: let it be within the scope of the Constitution, and all means
> which are appropriate, which are plainly adapted to that end, which are
> not prohibited, but consistent with the letter and spirit of the Constitution,
> are constitutional.

With this decision the necessary and proper clause became a broad
highway for the exercise of power to promote the goals set forth in the
Preamble and in the body of the Constitution, even when not expressly
enumerated. It also erected a legal barrier against the use of state taxes to
burden or impair the instrumentalities of the general government established to carry these great powers into effect.

And to make this declaration of federal supremacy when acting
(within the scope of its constitutional powers) unambiguously clear, the
Court in a subsequent case upheld the power of the federal government
to tax the circulating notes of state banks while denying (as they did in
McCulloch v. *Maryland*) any power in the state to tax those issued by the
United States.[21]

In decision after decision, following *McCulloch* v. *Maryland,* in cases
involving the respective powers of the nation and the states, the Supreme
Court cut away the underbrush of state sovereignty to establish the
supremacy of the Union and the great ends for which it was established.

But the Court has not always been on the side of history and its
decisions have not always helped to promote "a more perfect Union." In
Dred Scott v. *Sanford* (1857), to cite one example, the Court held an act
of Congress, called the Missouri Compromise, unconstitutional. The
Fifth Amendment, said the judges, forbids Congress to deprive any
person of property "without due process of law." Slaves were property.
Therefore the Missouri Compromise, which sought to exclude slavery
from certain territories of the United States, was an unconstitutional
breach of the Fifth Amendment. In thus denying to the central government power to prohibit slavery in the territories, the Court may not have
caused the Civil War, as some have suggested, but it surely did not

---

21 *Veazie Bank* v. *Fenno* (1869) .

contribute to the peaceful solution of the combustible issue of chattel slavery.

One thinks also of *Pollock* v. *Farmers' Loan and Trust Company* (1895), which declared a federal income tax unconstitutional, the Child Labor Cases of 1919–1943, which held the central government powerless to enact legislation forbidding child labor, *Plessy* v. *Ferguson* (1896), which gave constitutional absolution to racial segregation with the doctrine of "separate but equal," and the so-called New Deal Cases (1935–1937), which in rapid succession struck down the National Industrial Recovery Act, the Agricultural Adjustment Act, and Federal Minimum Wage and Welfare laws, as illustrations of the essentially conservative bias of the Court. All aroused political storms that in the end, through constitutional amendment or by the revision or reversal of its own decisions, compelled the Court to submit to the superior decrees of history and public opinion.

On the other hand we should not forget *Marbury* v. *Madison, McCulloch* v. *Maryland,* and *Brown* v. *Board of Education of Topeka* (1954), which outlawed racial segregation in Public Schools; *Baker* v. *Carr, Reynolds* v. *Sims,* and *Wesberry* v. *Sanders* (1964), which are transforming our representative system. Nor should we forget the numerous cases extending the guarantees of the Bill of Rights. All are illustrations of how the Court has often led the nation in determining the shape of things to come.

☆ **THE COURT UNDER FIRE**

It is too much to expect that a tribunal whose decisions touch such tender political nerve endings should be immune from criticism or political assault. And as we know, particular justices and the Court itself have been the object of bitter political attacks.

When President Wilson nominated Louis D. Brandeis to the Court in 1916, the nomination was subjected to extended denunciation and opposition by conservatives generally and the organized bar in particular. Brandeis had come to be known as the "peoples' lawyer" for, among other things, his part in the investigation of the Equitable Life Insurance Company and his successful advocacy of low-cost life insurance through state-owned savings banks in Massachusetts. Known as a foe of big business and as a liberal Democrat, the opposition was fearful (a fear well founded) that he would carry his *real* as well as his *nominal* politics to the bench.

Commenting upon the campaign against confirmation of Mr. Brandeis, the *New Republic* said: "There is no shrinking from the facts, The Court has been dragged into politics, and if at some future time, an appointment is made which is as conspicuously conservative as that of Mr.

Brandeis is conspicuously liberal, it will not be surprising if the radicals, throwing off the restraint they have shown this time, should follow the wretched example set by the conservative enemies of Mr. Brandeis."[22] In the end Mr. Brandeis was confirmed and served with great distinction for 23 years on the Supreme Court.

The prediction of this editorial, however, was not long in being realized. In 1930 the nomination of Charles Evans Hughes as Chief Justice was attacked by liberals because of his long association with big business.[23] "No man in public life," said Senator Norris of Nebraska, "so exemplifies the influence of powerful combinations in the political and financial world as does Mr. Hughes. . . . During the past five years he has appeared in fifty-five cases before the Supreme Court. Almost invariably he has represented corporations of almost untold wealth. . . . His view point is clouded. He looks through glasses contaminated by the influence of monopoly. . . . Such men should not be called upon to sit in final judgment in contests between organized wealth and the ordinary citizen. . . ."

Mr. Hughes was, nonetheless, confirmed and went on as Chief Justice from 1930 to 1941 to confute his critics by becoming not only a great Chief Justice, but a strong defender of civil liberties, freedom of the press, and of orderly social change.

The "liberals" in the country and in the Senate returned to the attack in 1932 when President Hoover's nomination of Judge Parker of North Carolina came under the fire of organized labor and the National Association for the Advancement of Colored People (NAACP). Their opposition was not to his professional qualification, nor to his *nominal* politics (he was a southern Republican), but to his allegedly conservative economic principles, his decision upholding "yellow dog" contracts in labor-management relations, and his identification with the "lily white" faction of the Republican party in North Carolina. Parker's nomination was rejected by the Senate, to the later regret of many who at the time actively opposed his confirmation.

In 1937, amidst nationwide tumult and shouting by conservative newspapers, Congressmen, and Senators, Franklin D. Roosevelt sent to the Senate the name of Senator Hugo Black of Alabama as a nominee to succeed Justice Van Devanter on the Supreme Court. To many conservatives, Senator Black was suspect for his vigorous conduct of a

[22] June 10, 1916.

[23] Hughes had been elected as a liberal Republican governor of New York, 1906–1910, following his vigorous investigation of insurance frauds as counsel for the so-called Armstrong Committee in 1906. President Taft appointed him to the Supreme Court in 1910 and he served as an Associate Justice until 1916 when he resigned to become Republican candidate for President. He was then denounced by some critics for "dragging the Court into politics." He had also served as counsel for large corporate interests and had served as Secretary of State under Harding and Coolidge. When, therefore, President Hoover nominated him in 1930 to return to the Court as Chief Justice, the liberals in both parties were incensed.

Senate investigation of big business, especially the utility business, and his ardent sponsorship of the Public Utility Holding Company Act in 1935. But the campaign against him concentrated not on these matters but on the fact that as a young politician in Alabama, Senator Black, for a brief period, had been an inactive member of the Ku Klux Klan.

Using this item, the conservative opposition could direct its fire at Senator Black behind what can only be described as a smoke screen of ambiguous liberalism. Few if any of the leaders of the campaign against Black's appointment had been conspicuous in their opposition to or criticism of the Ku Klux Klan. Indeed there were some signs that the Klan itself was used to fight Black's appointment on the ground, paradoxically, that even a temporary and inactive membership in that organization would disqualify a man for membership on the Supreme Court. Yet even this most sensational of all campaigns against a Supreme Court nominee failed when Black was confirmed in 1937 to become, along with Justice Douglas, a leader of the liberal, anti-segregation, pro-civil liberties group on the Court.

At the end of the 1967–1968 term of the Court, Chief Justice Warren wrote President Johnson indicating his desire to retire and his intention to do so as soon as a replacement was decided upon. President Johnson almost immediately nominated Justice Fortas to replace Mr. Warren as Chief Justice, and simultaneously nominated Judge Homer Thornberry of the Fifth Circuit Court of Appeals to replace Mr. Fortas as Associate Justice. When the Fortas nomination reached the Senate for confirmation, some southern Democrats joined with a few northern Republicans in a filibuster to prevent the Senate from acting on the Fortas appointment. The arguments against Mr. Justice Fortas's qualification centered on the allegation that he had continued to advise President Johnson on policy questions even after joining the Court and he had been paid a sizable fee for teaching a seminar in a university School of Law during the previous summer. But the critical factor was that the Senate was nearing adjournment prior to the November election, which was an unusually favorable time to give full effect to a filibuster. After a vote on closure failed by a considerable margin to reach the two-thirds majority necessary to cut off debate, it was obvious that the filibuster had succeeded in blocking confirmation, despite the fact that the majority vote necessary to confirm appeared to be relatively easy to attain. The result was that President Johnson reluctantly withdrew the nomination, thereby leaving Chief Justice Warren in office until such time as President Nixon makes his own appointment. Mr. Fortas, of course, continues as Associate Justice.

Many other illustrations could be cited to show that politics, both *real* and *nominal*, have played an important role in determining the composition of the Supreme Court. Once a justice is on the Court, however, one cannot be sure how he will behave: how his past party affiliation, the kind of clients he may have had in private practice, or even his political, social, and economic ideas will affect his decisions. Nevertheless, partisan affiliations and general orientation on matters of public policy are at least partly reliable clues to judicial behavior. Conservatives tend on the whole to remain conservatives on the bench and liberals to follow a liberal line in their decisions. The ambiguous nature of these terms, however, provide a fairly wide margin within which judges may move without sacrificing either a conservative or a liberal label. Any rigid classification is subject to great risks. Nevertheless, judges do differ in their orientation and ideology.

On the one hand there has recently been a liberal "bloc" composed, during the 1967–1968 term, of Chief Justice Warren, Justices Hugo Black, W. O. Douglas, Abe Fortas, and William J. Brennan. A more recent appointee, Justice Thurgood Marshall, probably will join the liberal group on most opinions, although he has been on the Court for too brief a period to categorize with assurance. These justices generally favor pro-civil liberties and pro-social legislation. The conservative bloc, one may suggest, would include Justices Potter Stewart, Byron White, and John Marshall Harlan.

Classification of justices on a liberal-conservative scale is something less than an exact science, and to submit a case to the Supreme Court, or indeed to any court, bears little resemblance to feeding punch cards into a mechanical brain. But it is nevertheless clear that the personality, education, economic and social status, political orientation and ideology of a judge affects his decisions. Otherwise it becomes difficult to explain not only some of the more stable patterns of behavior among the justices but dramatic shifts in judicial decisions.[24]

In 1881, for example, the Court held that an income tax was not a direct tax and hence quite constitutional, even though not apportioned according to population.[25] But in 1895 a Court differently composed, held that a tax on incomes was a direct tax and hence unconstitutional because it was not and could not be apportioned according to population.[26] The Constitution had not changed in the meantime, but a change in the Court had transformed a 6–2 vote in favor of the law to a 5–4 vote against it.

An even more striking example of the mutability of judicial decisions on important constitutional issues is to be seen in the so-called Legal Tender Cases in 1870–1871. To finance the Civil War, Congress authorized the Treasury to issue notes, "greenbacks," which, although

---

[24] See, however, Glendon Schubert, *Quantitative Analysis of Judicial Behavior* (New York: Free Press, 1959) ; also Glendon Schubert (ed.) , *Judicial Decision Making* (New York: Free Press, 1963) ; S. Sidney Ulmer, "Supreme Court Behavior and Civil Rights," *Western Political Quarterly*, June, 1960; also "The Analysis of Behavior Patterns on the Supreme Court," *Journal of Politics*, November, 1960.

[25] *Springer* v. *United States, 102 U.S. 586* (1887) .

[26] *Pollock* v. *Farmers' Loan and Trust Company, 157 U.S. 429* (1895) .

not redeemable in specie (gold or silver), were declared to be legal tender in the payment of private debts. In *Hepburn* v. *Griswold* in 1870 the Supreme Court, by a vote of 4 to 3, said this legal tender legislation was unconstitutional as a violation of an implied obligation of contracts provision, which the majority read into the due process clause of the Fifth Amendment. But on a reargument of the issue the next year, 1871, in the case of *Knox* v. *Lee,* the Court, by a vote of 5 to 4, reversed its earlier decision and held the Legal Tender Acts to be constitutional. Here again it was the judges who changed, not the Constitution. Between the first and second decisions two new justices had been appointed by President Grant to fill vacancies on the Court. Both were known to favor the Legal Tender Acts. Hence the reversal.[27]

In these cases the judges voted as follows:

First Case (1870)

Unconstitutional	*Constitutional*
Chase, Chief Justice	Miller
Nelson	Swayne
Clifford	Davis
Field	

Second Case (1871)

Chase	Swayne
Nelson	Miller
Clifford	Davis
Field	Strong (newly appointed)
	Bradley (newly appointed)

From 1914 to June, 1921, state minimum wage legislation had been sustained in Oregon, Arkansas, Minnesota, Washington, and the District of Columbia, with a total of 29 *yes* votes and 4 *no.* Moreover, at that time six Supreme Court justices were known to regard such legislation as constitutional as against three who believed it to be unconstitutional. The pros were Brandeis, Holmes, Taft, Day, Pitney, and Clark. The antis were McKenna, Van Devanter, and McReynolds. But between June, 1922, and April, 1923, when the District of Columbia minimum wage law was held to be unconstitutional by a vote of 5 to 3, with Brandeis not participating, three pros had been replaced by three antis. Antis Sutherland, Butler, and Sanford succeeded pros Clark, Day, and Pitney, thus transforming a 6–3 vote, or, with Brandeis not voting, a 5–3 vote in favor of the law into a 5–3 vote, with Brandeis not voting, against the law. It is obvious that in this case it was the calendar and the changed complexion

27 Grant's appointments were made possible by action of Congress increasing the number of justices from seven to nine. It will be recalled that the number had been reduced to seven to prevent any appointments by President Johnson. Thus Grant was able, in effect, to "pack the Court" in favor of the Legal Tender Acts.

of the Court and not the Constitution, as such, that defeated minimum wage legislation and delayed it for nearly 15 years, when a still different Court found such laws to be constitutional.[28]

One final illustration of the mutability of the Constitution in the hands of the Supreme Court is the dramatic reversal of the so-called New Deal legislation between 1935 and 1937. One by one the great legislative victories of the New Deal had been struck down by the Court: the National Industrial Recovery Act, 1935; the Railroad Retirement Act, 1934; the Agricultural Adjustment Act, 1935; the Guffey Coal Act, 1935. All went down. Other key laws like the National Labor Relations Act, and the Social Security Act seemed doomed.

It was at this point, following his triumphant re-election in 1936, that President Roosevelt sought to overcome the Court's opposition by an ingenious plan of judicial reorganization. A "Battle of the Century" was waged over this plan. Cries of "Usurpation," "Despotism!" "Rubber Stamp," were heard on all sides. Party lines crumbled. Senator Wheeler, a Democrat, led the fight against the plan. Senator Joseph Robinson, Democratic majority leader, fought for the plan.

On March 9 President Roosevelt, in a Fireside Chat, recounted that the Court had "cast doubt on the ability of the elected Congress to protect us against catastrophe by meeting squarely our modern social and economic conditions." Besides, he said, the Court was overburdened and needed help. Chief Justice Hughes replied that the Court did not need new judges. In the end the Court plan was defeated.

By a combination of circumstances, including the President's impressive victory at the polls in 1936, his Court Reorganization Bill in 1937, and the replacement of Justice Van Devanter by Hugo Black in the same year, the mind of the Court was changed. At any rate, between March 29 and May 18, 1937, the Court sustained the National Labor Relations Act, the Farm Mortgage Moratorium Act, the Social Security Act, and the Washington State Minimum Wage Act. And within four years, between 1937 and 1941, President Roosevelt was able to appoint six justices, including a Chief Justice, and to create what came to be called the New Deal Court.

The puzzlement of all this is not that Courts reverse themselves. The history of the law is full of reversals or "corrections" of earlier opinions. There is, in fact, as Lord Justice Bowen has said, "no such thing as finality about the administration of the law. It changes, it must change, it ought to change, with the broadening wants and requirements of a growing country and with the gradual illumination of the public conscience."

[28] Brandeis did not participate because he had helped to develop the case for such legislation before being appointed to the Supreme Court. The leading cases involved here were *Adkins* v. *Children's Hospital* (1923), which held a District of Columbia minimum wage law to be unconstitutional. In *West Coast Hotel* v. *Parrish*, 300 U.S. 379 (1936), a Washington state law was upheld and the earlier case overturned, thus clearing the way for minimum wage legislation.

Or, as Justice Proskauer of New York once said, "The law does not lead, but follows public opinion. And yet it does constantly readapt itself slowly but surely to those modifications of life and thought which are soundly established."

The puzzlement comes when Courts claim to be applying, not the vague and uncertain standards of the Constitution to a dynamic, changing society, but unchanging, immutable principles to which they and they alone have the key.

Impatience and anger with the Court for its decisions has been a constant factor in American political history. At one time the winds of opposition blow from the left, at another time from the right. And the bitter-end foes of the Court today may well become its great and good defenders tomorrow. Men who were delighted by the Court's anti-New Deal decisions became equally infuriated by its post-1937 rulings on social and economic legislation. Those sectional leaders who were the Court's staunch defenders when it was upholding fugitive slave laws and deciding against Dred Scott became bitter critics when it turned to outlaw racial segregation in the schools. "O Noble Judges! O Wise Judges!" they cry, when the Court is going their way, "A Daniel Come to Judgment." But "A pox upon the bench," and cries of "Usurpation," "Tyranny," and even "Treason" follow when the Court turns a corner and takes another path.

It is not surprising therefore that there have been many plans to curb the Court, to reform it, even to alter and abolish it, crying, as the English Liberals said of the House of Lords, "It must be either mended or ended."

President Roosevelt's plan of February, 1937, would have provided voluntary retirement for judges at full pay at age 70. If a justice on reaching 70 failed to retire, the President could have appointed an additional justice; furthermore, he could have appointed a total of 6 new members if this many justices attained the age of 70 without retiring, thus making the Supreme Court's maximum membership 15. The proposal also provided for 50 new federal judges for other federal courts to relieve crowded dockets and allow the assignment of judges from one district to another to relieve congestion. And it would have required lower federal courts to hear arguments by the Department of Justice before issuing any injunction against an act of Congress alleged to be unconstitutional. After the hue and cry generated by this proposal, it is worth noting that except for the proposal to increase the size of the Court, most of the other provisions have been enacted into law.

In recent years a renewed and bitter campaign has been waged against the Court, stimulated by some of its decisions in desegregation, civil liberties, internal security, and reapportionment cases. In California (and some other states) the highways have been replete with billboards shouting "Impeach Chief Justice Earl Warren," the mails are filled with incendiary literature directed against the Court, and Congress resounds with cries of "Judicial usurpation." "The Supreme Court of the United States," declared Representative John Bell Williams of Mississippi, on January 25, 1956, "through the Segregation decisions, and many previous decisions under the 'commerce,' 'welfare,' and 'supreme law of the land' clauses of the Constitution is completely destroying the fabric of our Republican form of Government."[29]

It is not surprising that such critics of the Court should again be asking that it be curbed in some way. Senator Jenner of Indiana proposed to repeal the Court's appellate jurisdiction in certain cases having to do with congressional investigations, federal security regulations, and state laws against subversive activities.[30] Another proposal by Senator Dirksen of Illinois would forbid the Court to take jurisdiction of cases involving the apportionment of representation in at least one house of state legislatures. Pending amendments to the Constitution would (1) declare that nothing in the Constitution shall limit the power of the States to apportion representation; (2) establish a "Court of the Union" to be composed of the chief justices of the several states with power to review, revise, or reverse any decision of the Supreme Court concerning the rights of the states or of the people; (3) allow the states to propose amendments to the Constitution directly by a two-thirds vote of the states without the intervention of either Congress or a convention—the amendments so proposed to become part of the Constitution when ratified by three-fourths of the state legislatures.

At this writing none of these proposals has been enacted or ratified, but the outcry continues and no doubt will continue as the Supreme Court in its decisions offends now the right and now the left, now the conservatives and now the liberals. This has been its history. This, no doubt, is its destiny.

Most of the proposals to curb the Court would in fact subvert the judicial process and undermine both the separation of powers and the federal system as we have learned to operate them in this country. They are mostly the offspring of passion and anger rather than of reason and mature reflection. They illustrate the kind of legislation that our system of checks and balances, including judicial review, was designed to prevent. The Supreme Court and the American system of judicial review are not only a part of our system of government, they are a part of our culture and civilization. To much of the rest of the world they are a "puzzlement" defying the laws of logic as much as the English queen in Parliament, and the Constitution itself, defy the laws of logic.

29 See reprint of this speech distributed by *Federation for Constitutional Government*, 801 American Bank Bldg., New Orleans, La.

30 For Senator Jenner's proposal and the *Pros* and *Cons* of the protagonists, see Peter Odegard, *American Government, Readings and Documents, op. cit.*

The Constitution [said the late Justice Cardozo] is a constant reminder of the basic values to which American civilization is committed. And the Court with its "restraining power, aloof in the background . . . tends to stabilize and rationalize the legislative judgment to infuse it with the glow of principle . . . for those who must run the race and keep the faith.

The restraining power of the judiciary does not manifest its chief worth in the few cases in which the legislature has gone beyond the . . . limits of [its] discretion. Its chief worth [is] in making . . . audible the ideals that might otherwise be silenced, in giving them continuity of life and expression. . . .

This function should preserve to the courts the power that now belongs to them, if only the power is exercised with insight into social values and with . . . adaptation to changing social needs.[31]

☆ HARD LABOR FOR LIFE

When the Supreme Court moved from its old chambers in the Capitol building to its new "great marble temple" Justice Stone wrote to one of his sons: "The [new] place is almost bombastically pretentious, and thus it seems to me wholly inappropriate for a quiet group of old boys such as the Supreme Court. . . ." The Justices, he said, would look like "nine black beetles in the Temple of Karnak."[32]

Yet these "old boys" or "nine old men" (as they were once called) in their marble temple are both the symbol and the substance of one of the oldest and most noble of all human aspirations: *Equal Justice Under Law.* These words inscribed on the pediment of the Supreme Court building may be said to sum up in a single phrase the basic values of the American Republic.

The building itself with the Court in session seems to embody all those paradoxical qualities that since ancient times have been associated with the quest for equal justice under law. As Anthony Lewis has described the scene it is "grandiose and intimate: ritualistic and informal; austere, yet human."

The late Justice Brandeis was fearful lest the new marble place undermine "the spirit of humility" that should characterize "those whose title to govern rests on the power of reason." But there are few signs that the ornate pillars, the red velvet draperies, the general solemnity of the place have done more than emphasize "the intrinsic strength" of the Court, which comes from what it does and "not from the trappings of power."

[31] *The Nature of the Judicial Process* (New Haven, Conn.: Yale University Press, 1921), pp. 92–94.
[32] A. Lewis, *The New York Times,* October 26, 1958.

What it does can have reverberations throughout the nation and around the world, as did its decision on racial segregation in 1954. And what other Court could compel the head of state, at a time of grave national emergency, to submit to its decree in a matter as momentous as that involved in the steel seizure case? In doing what they do, Supreme Court justices labor long and hard at a job that requires talents unlike those required for any other job in the world.

Legal training and experience are not enough; a knowledge of economics and history, a passion for philosophy and respect for logic, and the acumen of a practicing politician are just as essential. It is often proposed that some prior judicial experience be required as a qualification for appointment to the Supreme Court. Had such a qualification been in force many of our most distinguished justices would have been disqualified. Of the 75 justices who have served up to June, 1965, 30 had no prior judicial service. A requirement of five years' prior judicial service would have ruled out 44 of the 75 justices.

Those with no judicial experience at all include some of the most distinguished members of the Court: James Wilson, Bushrod Washington, John Marshall, Joseph Story, Roger Taney, Charles Evans Hughes, Louis Brandeis, Harlan Stone, Felix Frankfurter, William Douglas, and Earl Warren, to mention some of them. Public service in Congress, in the Cabinet, as District Attorney, or Attorney General may be quite as valuable as prior judicial experience. Justices Holmes and Cardozo, who moved to the Supreme Court, the former after 20 years on the highest court in Massachusetts, the latter after 18 years on the New York Court of Appeals, found themselves (or so they said) like fish out of water during their first years on the Supreme Court of the United States.[33]

John Marshall's experience as a diplomat (the famous XYZ Mission 1797–1798) and as Secretary of State; Roger Taney's experience as a state legislator and as Secretary of the Treasury; Harlan Stone's service as a dean of law and as Attorney General; Charles Evans Hughes' background as governor of New York probably afforded better training for the Supreme Court of the United States than years on a state or inferior federal court. For a Supreme Court judge must be more than a judge in the usual sense. He must combine an inquiring mind with a judicial temper, political wisdom without partisan ardor, and, above all, what the late Max Radin once called a "sense of right . . . [that] perpetual striving to fit doubtful situations into a scheme that moves in the direction of a realized sense of right." It is this *sense* rather than legal lore that the Court must bring to bear on cases as varied as Sunday closing laws, gambling, labor disputes, a giant antitrust suit, or a routine negligence

---

[33] Mr. Cardozo often complained to his friends about being taken from *judicial* work (on the New York Court of Appeals) with which he was familiar to deal with questions on the Supreme Court—political, economic, social, ethical, moral questions—for which his judicial experience was not good preparation.

case involving a defective wrench and an injured foot. Perhaps this "sense of right" develops with age, for one thing is clear, the Supreme Court is not a usual habitat for men under 50.

"I venture to believe," said the late Learned Hand, "that it is as important to a judge called upon to pass on a question of Constitutional law, to have at least a bowing acquaintance with [Lord] Acton and Maitland, Thucydides, Gibbon and Carlyle, with Homer, Dante, Shakespeare and Milton, . . . Plato, Bacon, Hume, and Kant, as with the books which have been specifically written on the subject."[34]

Whatever their background, the justices are a hard-working lot of men. During an average term, extending from October to June, the Supreme Court will have to act on from 1,500 to 2,000 petitions of one kind or another. "Week in and week out," says Anthony Lewis, "during the October to June term, about forty such applications cross each man's desk." Each justice must consider every petition, but it takes a vote of four members to grant review. Out of this avalanche of 1,500 to 2,000 petitions or "cases" the Court will ordinarily accept some 150 to 200 for oral argument, followed by formal opinions.

In the process of winnowing the wheat from the chaff, and in doing the research necessary for preparing his opinions, each justice relies heavily on his law clerks.[35] In the end, however, it is the justice who must decide, and it is he who must assume responsibility for his decision and the reasons given to support it. The number of petitions considered by the Court at its conference is such that according to the late Justice Robert Jackson, "All that saves the Court from being hopelessly bogged down is that many of the items are so frivolous . . . that no one finds them worthy of discussion and they are disposed of by unanimous consent." Having agreed upon the cases to be heard, the Court proceeds to hear oral arguments in the ornate, but impressive, chamber, where a curious public may watch what has been described as the most interesting spectacle in Washington. Court is in session for four hours beginning at

---

[34] Quoted by F. Frankfurter, "Supreme Court in the View of the Justices," *University of Pennsylvania Law Review*, vol. 105 (1957), p. 781.

The 1968 Court included a wide variety of training and experience: *W. O. Douglas*, law teacher, Yale and Columbia, Chairman of SEC, world traveler, writer; *Earl Warren*, District Attorney, Attorney General of California, Republican candidate for Vice-President, three-term Governor of California; *Hugo Black*, United States Senator, police judge and prosecutor in Alabama; *Byron White*, lawyer, Deputy Attorney General, all-American football player; *John Marshall Harlan*, grandson of Justice Harlan, a judge of the U.S. Court of Appeals, 2d Circuit, Rhodes Scholar, Wall Street lawyer; *William J. Brennan, Jr.*, lawyer, and member of New Jersey Supreme Court; *Abe Fortas*, private practice in Washington, D.C., formerly Undersecretary of the Interior and presidential confidant; *Potter Stewart*, City Councilman of Cincinnati, U.S. Circuit Court judge; *Thurgood Marshall*, Civil Rights leader, a judge of the U.S. Court of Appeals, 2d Circuit, U.S. Solicitor General.

[35] In recent days ardent critics of the Court have argued that some of the justices have relied too heavily upon the work of these young law clerks, usually honor graduates of leading law schools, but there is little to indicate that this is so.

10 o'clock four days a week for two weeks in every month from October to June; that is, the Court sits for two weeks and goes into recess for two weeks.

At the top of the room, just under the bench where the justices sit, are tables and chairs reserved for lawyers, staff, and distinguished visitors. Behind the bar, separating those having business with the Court, are the seats for the public. Everyone stands as the justices file in from their robing room to take their places, the Chief Justice in the center, with the Associate Justices arranged on either side in order of seniority. Sitting in this order they look not so much like "black beetles in the Temple of Karnak" as like black-gowned venerable members of some council of Elder Statesmen.

Lawyers for either side are allowed not more than an hour, sometimes only half an hour to present their arguments. A small rostrum is provided just below the Chief Justice at which the lawyer stands to argue his case. A white light tells him when he has five minutes to go and a red light when his time is up.

There was a time in the great days of oratory when arguments in a single case would go on for days—with highly emotional pleas to support an often shaky constitutional position. Arguments today are shorter, more informal, and less given to purple prose. Although quill pens are still provided at the lawyers' tables, and the Solicitor General of the United States and his aides still appear in cutaway coats, the atmosphere is more informal than it used to be.

"The Court," says Rule 44, "looks with disfavor on any oral argument that is read from a prepared text." A lawyer is well advised to remember that his written brief (40 copies) is already in the Court's hands—to be read and studied by the justices. Hence he is encouraged to use his oral argument to highlight, emphasize, and illustrate the points he thinks crucial to his case. Moreover, he must be prepared to be interrupted—even many times—by questions and even arguments from the judges on the bench. "The Court," said the late Justice Frankfurter "is not designed as a dozing audience for the reading of soliloquies, but as a questioning body, using oral arguments as a means for exposing the difficulties of a case with a view to meeting them."[36]

Questions from the bench may be friendly or hostile, inquisitive or argumentative, and the experienced lawyer will be prepared for every kind without losing his composure or the thread of his argument, even when, through their questions, the honorable justices argue with one another from the bench.

---

[36] "Is that all there is to your case?" one lawyer was asked.

"No, sir," he replied.

"Well, as you state it," said the justice, "it's so simple that I'm suspicious. . . . What is the milk in the cocoanut?"

The oral arguments can, and often do, have an important influence on the Court's decision. The Friday conferences, at which cases are at least tentatively decided, follow hard upon the oral arguments and may therefore have a greater impact on the decision than the written brief. It is, incidentally, at these conferences that the Chief Justice displays his talent for leadership or lack of it. "The Chief Justice," says one student of the Court, "shapes the character of the conference by deciding, for example, how long to let debate continue before calling for a vote."

Speaking of Chief Justice Hughes, one justice has said, "To see him preside was like witnessing Toscanini lead an orchestra." This is no mean feat when one recalls that differences among the justices are often heated, occasionally exploding in open court.

Conferences of the justices are carried on in strict secrecy, and the Court has its own printer to insure that decisions are not "leaked" before being officially read or announced. At the weekly conference the Chief Justice calls up the case and says what he has to say about it, and then discussion proceeds, with the Associate Justices speaking in order of their seniority. When they come to vote, the order is reversed, with the newest member voting first and the Chief Justice last. After voting on the case that has been heard, the Chief Justice, if he has voted with the majority, will either reserve the writing of the opinion of the Court to himself or assign it to an Associate Justice on the majority side. Dissenting opinions are assigned by the senior justice on the minority side.

A wise Chief Justice, in assigning responsibility for writing an opinion for the Court, will try to select a justice who can best sum up the reasoning of the majority, since his opinion becomes the official opinion of the Court. Draft opinions are circulated and each justice may suggest changes. Each justice may also write an opinion of his own to concur with the majority, or to dissent. In some cases as many as five or six opinions will be published—where the justices may agree or dissent from the decision, but for different reasons.

Thomas Jefferson believed that each justice in every case should declare his own opinion, so that the President, Congress, and the people could know where he stands on important constitutional issues. There is, of course, a hazard in this. Too great fragmentation of opinions, even where all or a majority agree on the decision, may not only be confusing, but may impair confidence in the Court.

The burden of writing opinions, although not evenly distributed among the justices, is nevertheless not light for any of them. Decisions are, after all, legal documents often with far-reaching consequences and the conscientious justice will not sacrifice legal logic, common sense, and clarity, for literary style. Where, as sometimes happens, all are combined, the product becomes an important part of America's cultural heritage. This has been true of many of the opinions of John Marshall, Roger

Taney, Oliver Wendell Holmes, Louis Brandeis, and Benjamin Cardozo. Others, too, like Taft's opinion in *Myers* v. *United States* or Frankfurter's dissent in *Baker* v. *Carr* rank high in the literature of the Court.

When the Court makes public its decisions, which are read either in whole or in summary, the chamber is likely to be crowded. Until recently Monday was "opinion day," but in 1965 the Court announced that it would not restrict itself to issuing opinions only on Monday. However, after a term of handing down opinions on other days the Court returned informally to its old practice of rendering its decisions on Mondays.

Many years ago Mildred Adanis described an Opinion Monday, which, with a minor change or two, can serve to describe a similar scene today.

> Long before noon the court room was filled. A bloc of lawyers, a pair of nuns, one whole row of awkward men whose shoes squeaked as they filed in, an Oregon bride in an orange sweater, Senators graciously condescending to their constituents, city men, ladies in mink coats, farmers, students, and one active urchin whose cheeks were as red as the apple bulging from his pocket. The people of the United States assembled to watch their highest court hand down its weekly opinions.
>
> The highest court came at 12 o'clock [now 10 o'clock] in a slow line, and the people arose. When all nine of the black-robed figures had sunk into thick black chairs the people sat down. With no more ceremony than that, and the rolling "Oyez, Oyez, Oyez," which opens judicial sessions wherever Anglo-Saxon justice prevails, the Supreme Court of the United States took up the work of public hearings after a two weeks' recess.
>
> The white-haired newest justice at one end of the row sat forward and delivered the opinion of the court in a case that concerned an ancient quarrel between two States. When he finished, the next newest justice at the other end of the row delivered the opinions which had been assigned to him. For almost two hours this went on, the justices speaking one after another in reverse order of seniority. It held the eyes like a kind of grave verbal ballet.
>
> There was no public program and no prompter, but the play moved on. Sometimes it was interesting, sometimes dull, and the dullness or the interest seem to lie in manner even more than in matter. One justice blurred all his words into a sleepy drone, one pounded out every fourth word, but swallowed those that came between. Three leaned forward and took the audience into their confidence, apparently certain that these people were interested, trying to let them hear and understand every word.
>
> Here was no visible drama, yet the people sat as if enthralled. The bloc of lawyers had business with the court, but the spectators in the curving rows of benches along the wall were held by no such necessity. Nor was it any visible force that held them motionless, almost breathless. . . . Except for the voice from the bench, the court room was so still that the proverbial dropped pin would have been noise.
>
> Once only did they stir. Then, as if in grave approval of the Chief

Justice's words, a little ripple ran over the whole audience. "The question," he said, "is not one of public policy which the courts may be considered free to declare, but of the continued efficacy of legislation in the face of controlling action of the people, the source of the power to enact and maintain it."[37]

This, indeed, is the proper role of the Court, not as a House of Lords to decide on the wisdom or unwisdom of public policy, but to uphold the "continued efficacy of legislation in the face of the controlling action of the people, the source of [all] power to enact and maintain it." "I know of no one in the entire governmental establishment," says a distinguished student of the Court, "who has to work under conditions such as these. . . . Were it not for the fiction that judges have only to apply the law—which by hypothesis they already know—no one could possibly do his job."

Yet somehow he does it. In recent years members of both the bench and the bar have worried about this heavy load. Even by working 60 to 70 hours a week, they say, the Court is unable to keep abreast of the cases that keep piling up. Not only are decisions in important cases delayed, but, according to some, the quality of the opinions suffers. Against this argument, however, are some members of the Court itself who say they are not overworked. Justice Douglas, who carries more than his share of the load, has said, "I do not recall any time in my twenty years or more of service on the Court when we had more time for research, debate, or meditation."

On one thing everyone will agree. An appointment to the Supreme Court to serve during good behavior is for the conscientious justice a sentence to hard labor for life.

[37] *The New York Times,* February 18, 1934. © 1934 by The New York Times Company. Reprinted by permission.

THE ADMINISTRATION
OF JUSTICE

☆ *INFERIOR FEDERAL COURTS*

Organization

In the preceding chapter, we examined the significance of the Supreme Court in the American governmental system. Recognition of the Supreme Court's role as a key instrument of government does not, of course, mean that it decides every important judicial question, nor does it mean that whim or caprice may be substituted for the trial record when important questions reach the Supreme Court for decision. This latter point is illustrated by an exchange, during the oral argument of a "sit-in" case, between counsel for the State of Louisiana and Justice Frankfurter. One of the issues in the case was whether the Baton Rouge police had grounds to fear violence when they arrested Negro "sit-in" students. John F. Ward, Jr., representing Louisiana, told the justices, "There's no doubt in my mind that this would have led to violence." "I respect your mind," Justice Frankfurter commented, "but your mind is not in the record."

The so-called inferior courts, the trial and appellate courts, require our attention for at least two reasons: (1) The official record of the trial is often of crucial importance in subsequent review of the case by the Supreme Court. (2) Since only a minute percentage of cases are reviewed by the Supreme Court, the decisions of inferior courts are usually final. The average citizen's typical contact with the judicial system is at the level of the trial court.

Many of the questions likely to involve the average American in a judicial proceeding originate and are resolved in the state courts. Disputes between landlords and tenants, divorce actions, and most crimes fall traditionally within their jurisdiction. Only if there is a question of denial of a right guaranteed by federal law or by the Constitution can such proceedings be reviewed by the United States Supreme Court. In a number of specific situations, the jurisdiction of lower federal courts rather than state courts may be invoked; and it is useful to understand the organization of the federal court system as well as the essentials of civil and criminal procedure that underlie our legal system. (See Figure 17–1.)

Article III of the Constitution provides that

[t]he judicial Power of the United States, shall be vested in one supreme Court, and in such inferior Courts as the Congress may from time to time

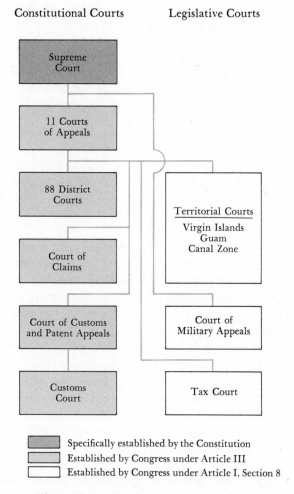

Figure 17–1 The Federal Courts of the United States.

ordain and establish. The Judges, both of the supreme and inferior Courts, shall hold their Offices during good Behavior, and shall, at stated Times, receive for their Services, a Compensation, which shall not be diminished during their Continuance in Office.

The lower federal courts owe their existence to Congress rather than to the Constitution; for Congress is not required to establish any lower courts. Once Congress does create such courts, however, the Constitution provides that the judges shall be appointed for life, subject only to removal for misbehavior. Starting with the Judiciary Act of 1789 Congress has developed a comprehensive inferior court system over the years.

There are 88 federal district courts, which are courts of original jurisdiction, located throughout the United States, including one in the District of Columbia and one in Puerto Rico. There are also territorial district courts in the Canal Zone, Guam, and the Virgin Islands. As a general rule, the smaller states rate one court and the larger states as many as four. Each district court has one or more judges, the number depending upon the amount of business the court must handle. The court for the southern district of New York, which includes New York City, has 24 judges, which is almost double the number of any other district.

District court judgeships are choice plums of federal patronage because of their high prestige. While a judgeship is often a reward for an active political life, once a man becomes a federal judge he normally breaks any close ties to his political party, for his is a lifetime appointment at a salary that can be raised but never can be lowered. An independent, competent, and dispassionate federal judiciary is one of the strongest assets of our governmental system.

The appointments by President Kennedy pursuant to the Omnibus Judgeship Act of May, 1961, offer some interesting illustrations of the interrelations of law and politics. Pressure had been mounting for a decade to enlarge the federal bench, the case loads in many jurisdictions having become so great that delays of up to five years were not unusual. Despite pleas from lawyers' groups to take action, Democratic-controlled Congresses refused to enlarge the judiciary while a Republican President was in the White House. Compromises between Democratic party leaders and President Eisenhower were sought repeatedly but without success. The Democrats expected to capture the White House in 1960, since the unbeatable President Eisenhower could not seek a third term. Even if Nixon were victorious, the Democrats still expected to control Congress; hence they decided to wait until after the election before passing the bill.

Kennedy's victory and continuing Democratic control of Congress meant that the new judgeships would be the exclusive property of the Democratic party. New judgeships, vacancies and resignations authorized the President to appoint 106 judges in all. No other President in history has appointed so many judges in so short a time.

While the judgeships are filled with the consent of the Senate, it is customary for the President to submit the names of potential appointees to the Standing Committee on the Federal Judiciary of the American Bar Association for advice on their competence. The President is not, of course, bound to follow the reports of the committee, but it would be embarrassing for him and for the Bar if he were to submit the names of many persons with less than minimum standards of legal competence.

In his report to the American Bar Association in August, 1961, the Chairman of the Standing Committee on the Federal Judiciary, Bernard G. Segal, pointed out that the Attorney General had requested the committee to render informal reports on 246 persons and formal reports on 49. President Kennedy expressed his appreciation for the important role played by the Bar in a telegram to the Association's President Whitney North Seymour. Kennedy said:

> The administration is aware of its great responsibilities in selecting qualified people for these new positions as well as for other judicial vacancies. The impact of 100 or more new judges could affect the quality of justice in this country for many years to come, and I want to express my personal appreciation for the useful assistance which the judiciary committee of your Association, under the able chairmanship of Bernard Segal, is rendering to the Attorney General in evaluating the qualifications of candidates for judicial appointments. . . .

The telegram did not mention bipartisanship, and Chairman Segal expressed the hope that bipartisanship would be followed in practice.

> If President Kennedy does not break new ground at this time, if he does not introduce a real and convincing bipartisanship into appointments now, when for the first time in our generation, the judges sitting in the federal courts throughout the nation are just about evenly divided as to their preappointment political party affiliation—one-half Democratic, one-half Republican—now, when he has more judges to appoint at one time than in the whole history of the country, then the last best hope of achieving this goal in our generation will have been forfeited.

Despite Segal's plea, of the 128 judges appointed by President Kennedy, 117 were Democrats and only 11 were Republicans. Partisan bias has continued to determine judicial appointments under his successor, although a total tally remains to be made. Nor are Presidents Kennedy and Johnson unique in preferring their own partisans on the bench. Between 1933 and 1945 President Roosevelt appointed 288 judges to various federal courts, of whom all but 19 were Democrats. President Truman's record was 18 Republicans to 160 Democrats, and President Eisenhower's choices fell on only 13 Democrats out of a total of 210 judicial appointments.

Jurisdiction

The jurisdiction of the federal judiciary is discussed in Article III, Section 2 of the Constitution:

> The judicial Power shall extend to all Cases, in Law and Equity, arising under this Constitution, the Laws of the United States, and Treaties made, or which shall be made, under their Authority (*) ;—to all Cases affecting Ambassadors, other public Ministers and Consuls (#) ;—to all Cases of admiralty and maritime Jurisdictions (*) ;—to Controversies to which the United States shall be a Party (#) ;—to Controversies between two or more States (#) ; . . .—between Citizens of different States (#) ;—between Citizens of the same State claiming Lands under Grants of different States (#) and between a State, or the Citizens thereof, and foreign States, Citizens or subjects (#) .

The symbols (*) and (#) indicate that these jurisdictional grants can be classified conveniently into two categories: jurisdiction based upon substantive matter (*), that is, the Constitution, treaties, or laws of the United States; and jurisdiction based upon the parties involved in the litigation (#), that is, where different states or citizens of different states are included. There is no access for anyone to a federal court unless he meets one of these jurisdictional standards.

The Eleventh Amendment removed from the jurisdiction of the federal judiciary "any suit in law or equity, commenced or prosecuted against one of the United States by Citizens of another State, or by Citizens or Subjects of any Foreign State." This amendment was prompted by the Supreme Court's holding in *Chisholm* v. *Georgia* in 1793 that states could be sued by citizens of other states in federal courts.

Jurisdiction of federal courts based on subject matter has grown steadily as the federal government has legislated in areas previously left to the states. Federal laws dealing with antitrust matters, criminal law, and civil rights have materially enlarged the case loads of the district courts. For example, the Civil Rights Act of 1957 confers jurisdiction on the federal district courts to try cases arising out of the act "without regard to whether the party aggrieved shall have exhausted any administrative or other remedies that may be provided by law." The Civil Rights Acts of 1964 and 1965 have added to the responsibilities of federal district courts. This potential case load, added to other responsibilities of federal district courts, places them in an unenviable position, particularly in the southern states. Professor Jack Peltason's study of the task of the southern federal judges, *Fifty-eight Lonely Men,* may well lead one to wonder why anyone would want to be a federal judge. Perhaps the challenging nature of the task is the very factor that makes the position appealing.

Much of the jurisdiction of the federal courts overlaps that of the state courts, since many crimes such as kidnapping and auto theft can be violations of both state and federal law, and Congress has deliberately allowed the state courts to exercise some federal jurisdiction in civil cases. The potential conflict between jurisdictions might have been aggravated if two distinct bodies of law could be applied to the same set of facts in a case. Such conflict was possible under the rule of *Swift* v. *Tyson,* decided in 1842, in which the Supreme Court interpreted the Judiciary Act of 1789 to mean that federal courts were free, in the absence of state statutes, to apply their own conceptions of applicable law.[1] By 1888, there were more than twenty-five kinds of cases, including torts, contracts, wills, and negotiable instruments, in which federal courts could apply different rules than state courts. Litigants were thus encouraged to shop around for the court most likely to be favorable to their interests. Confusion was bound to result.

In 1938, in *Erie Railroad Co.* v. *Tompkins,* the Supreme Court reversed its ruling in the *Tyson* case and thereby helped to restore uniformity to laws applied by federal and state courts within the same state. Tompkins, a citizen of Pennsylvania, had been injured by a passing Erie freight train while walking along the railroad's right of way. Under Pennsylvania common law, the railroad was liable only for wanton or willful negligence since Tompkins was a trespasser. Tompkins sued in the federal court in New York, the state in which the railroad was incorporated, and a district court jury awarded him $30,000. The Court of Appeals affirmed the decision, pointing out that the question of the railroad's duty and liability was one of "general law" on which the federal court was free to exercise its independent judgment.

In reversing the Court of Appeals and overruling the *Tyson* decision, the Supreme Court condemned the *Tyson* doctrine for rendering impossible the equal protection of the laws. "It made rights enjoyed under the unwritten general law vary according to whether enforcement was sought in the state or in the federal courts; and the privilege of selecting the court in which the right should be determined was conferred upon the non-citizen."[2] The *Erie* doctrine, which is the law today, requires that, except in matters governed by the Constitution or federal law, the law to be applied by federal courts is the law of the state in which the court resides. "There is no federal general common law."

In addition to the cases in which federal courts have concurrent jurisdiction with state courts, there are a number of areas in which the federal courts have exclusive jurisdiction. These include all cases in bankruptcy, suits against foreign agents, and patent and copyright actions.

The intermediate appellate courts of the federal system are the eleven United States Courts of Appeals. Their decisions for all practical purposes are final in almost 90 percent of the cases. Appeals are usually

---

[1] *Swift* v. *Tyson,* 16 Peters 1 (1842).
[2] *Erie Railroad Co.* v. *Tompkins,* 304 U.S. 64 (1938).

heard before three judges. They serve both as a kind of judicial filter keeping unnecessary cases from cluttering up the Supreme Court and as a judicial magnet attracting cases of national interest that call for ultimate resolution by the Supreme Court. Although one can never predict with complete accuracy when the Supreme Court will review a case, the likelihood of review is strong when Courts of Appeals of different circuits have reached different conclusions about the same federal statute or constitutional provision. One justice of the Supreme Court is assigned to each circuit and he occasionally sits with the circuit judges. Life tenure for federal judges often has literal meaning. Even after nominal retirement, judges may be called on to preside over cases. The late Learned Hand continued to preside for several years after his retirement, and Stanley Reed, who retired from the Supreme Court in 1957, served on the Court of Appeals in a number of instances thereafter.

State court systems generally include a broad range of special courts, like police courts, domestic relations courts, probate courts, juvenile courts, and the like. In the federal system there are three principal courts of special jurisdiction: the Court of Claims, the Customs Court, and the Court of Customs and Patent Appeals. The first was established in 1855 to deal primarily with claims against the government growing out of contract disputes. It also has power to award damages to persons erroneously convicted and imprisoned by the federal government. The Customs Court decides disputes between private parties and customs officials who determine the value of goods coming into the country in order to assess tariff duties. Appeals from the decisions of this court, as well as from the Patent Office, may be taken to the Court of Customs and Patent Appeals, which, like the Court of Claims, sits in the District of Columbia. Its decisions are appealable to the Supreme Court on the same basis as appeals from any other court. To these one should probably add the United States Tax Court, the United States Court of Military Appeals, and the territorial courts, although they differ markedly, not only from other federal courts, but from one another. The United States Tax Court of 16 members is "actually more of an adjunct of the executive branch, a quasi-administrative agency independent of the Internal Revenue Service, than a Court *per se*." As its name implies, it reviews tax cases in which the United States Commissioner of Internal Revenue is almost always the defendant. Its removal from the executive branch has long been recommended, but thus far no such action has been taken. The United States Court of Military Appeals was created in 1950 to give military personnel an appeal to a civilian court, even though they continue to be subject to military law.

Territorial courts are created by Congress under its power to "make all needful rules and regulations respecting the territories or other property belonging to the United States." Their powers and jurisdiction derive therefore from acts of Congress, and not from Article III of the

Constitution. As legislative courts they exercise a jurisdiction comparable to that of state courts as well as that of federal district courts. Territorial courts operate in the Canal Zone, Guam, Puerto Rico, and the Virgin Islands.[3]

The widespread operations of the federal courts call for at least basic housekeeping functions if minimal efficiency is to be maintained. In 1922 Congress established the Judicial Conference of the United States to be "the governing body for the administration of the federal judicial system as a whole." At yearly conferences, its members—composed of the Chief Justice of the United States, the chief judge of the Court of Claims, the chief judge of each Court of Appeals, and a district judge from each of the eleven circuits—examine the major problems of the federal court system. The conference has substantial administrative powers including the power to approve the annual budget of all federal courts except the Supreme Court, and the power to determine the number and set the salaries of referees in bankruptcy and district court official reporters.

The Director of the Administrative office of the United States Courts works under the supervision of the Judicial Conference. He plays a quiet but efficient role in accumulating comparative data on court dockets, case loads, and personnel. The undramatic but vital function performed by the Director as a co-ordinator of data about the system has led a number of states to establish similar offices for state courts.

Direct responsibility for supervising the administration of individual courts is vested by the Administrative Office Act of 1939 in the judicial council of each circuit, which is made up of the judges of the Courts of Appeals. Reluctance on the part of many a judge to exercise such administrative responsibility, however, has often created administrative vacuums. The judicial conferences held each year in each of the circuits provide lively criticism and commentary about current trends in judicial administration. Circuit judges, district judges, and representatives of the Bar participate in the conferences to examine civil and criminal rules, sentencing procedures, or a host of other matters of concern to bench and bar. These discussions are not simply academic for the Supreme Court, which now has the power to make rules of procedure for the lower federal courts, looks to the judicial conferences for advice and assistance. Not the least of the advantages of such devices is their enhancement of the independence of the judiciary.

☆   THE JUDICIAL PROCESS—CIVIL AND CRIMINAL

What are the procedures by which a judicial decision is reached? How is guilt or innocence determined? In the law's primitive stage, trial by

[3] See Henry J. Abraham, *The Judicial Process* (New York: Oxford University Press, 1962) , pp. 134–138.

ordeal was not unusual. The defendant could submit to the ordeal of boiling water or the hot iron, and if he emerged unscathed, he was innocent. Trial by combat, in which physical victory was deemed the equivalent of legal righteousness, was another early method for determining guilt or innocence. The hallmark of today's Anglo-American legal system is the adversary method for determining truth. It postulates that there are two sides to every legal dispute and that truth can be ascertained only after both sides have been presented in court.

The first step in a judicial proceeding is notification to the defendant of the charge against him and the recovery sought. In a civil proceeding this consists of serving the defendant with a declaration or complaint. In a criminal proceeding this is done by indictment or presentment by the grand jury, or the filing of an "information" by the district attorney and subsequent arraignment of the defendant in open court.

While no law compels a defendant to hire a lawyer, the layman would be foolhardy to appear in court without counsel to represent him. "A man who serves as his own lawyer," says an old aphorism, "has a fool for a client." If he has no money, he can generally obtain help without charge from the Legal Aid Society, he can ask the court to appoint counsel for him, or, in prosecutions in many state courts, he can elect to be represented by the public defender.[4]

In *Johnson* v. *Zerbst* in 1938, the Supreme Court ruled that the Sixth Amendment's guarantee of "assistance of counsel" meant that any defendant in a federal criminal trial who could not afford to hire his own lawyer, and who desired to be represented by counsel, was entitled to have counsel appointed for him by the court before the trial could proceed, and this constitutional guarantee was extended to state criminal trials as well in *Gideon* v. *Wainwright* in 1963.

Once the defendant has been notified of the charge, it is important to determine whether he admits it, denies it, or admits it but denies that it violates any law. The pleadings in the case are designed, in short, to reach an issue or issues of fact which can then be subjected to trial. Decisions in a civil action are based on the "weight of the evidence." In a criminal action there must be "proof beyond a reasonable doubt." Before going to trial, however, two devices of increasing importance may well be utilized, especially in the federal courts. One is "discovery," a procedure for the disclosure of facts, titles, documents, or other things which are in a party's exclusive knowledge or possession and which are necessary to the party seeking the discovery in order to prepare his case. Liberal rules for

---

[4] Nevertheless thousands of poor people annually suffer denial of legal rights because of lack of counsel. To assist these "legally deprived" persons a neighborhood Legal Assistance Foundation has been established with federal assistance. One legal aid society in 1965 handled 7,500 cases. See *San Francisco Chronicle,* September 16, 1966.

use of discovery techniques have been hailed by the Section on Judicial Administration of the American Bar Association as aids in the fundamental search for truth and the elimination of the outmoded "sporting theory of justice."

The importance of discovery in criminal cases was highlighted by the Supreme Court's decision in *Jencks* v. *United States* in 1957. The Court ruled, over strenuous objections from the Department of Justice, that a defendant in a federal court had the right to examine written statements made before the trial by a witness for the prosecution if those statements were related to the witness's testimony. Jencks filed a non-Communist affidavit with the National Labor Relations Board in 1950. In seeking to prove that the affidavit was false, the government presented as witnesses two paid FBI informers who had made oral and written reports to the agency on Communist party activities in which Jencks allegedly participated. Jencks's counsel sought to examine the written reports to compare what the informers had recorded originally with their subsequent testimony at the trial. Needless to say, he was seeking discrepancies or contradictions which could be used to impeach the witnesses' testimony on cross-examination. The district judge denied the request for discovery of the statements, and Jencks was convicted for filing a false affidavit. The Supreme Court reversed the conviction, stressing as "unconscionable" the government's action in first prosecuting Jencks and then depriving him of anything which might be material to his defense.

Soon after this decision, Congress passed the so-called Jencks Act which placed some limitations on the right of defendants to gain access to documents in the prosecution's possession. Pursuant to this statute, the trial judge is supposed to examine the desired documents outside the presence of the parties and to delete "unrelated" matter. In *Campbell* v. *United States* in 1961, the Supreme Court reiterated its position on the importance of the right to discovery when it held that the trial court erred in denying defendant's motions to have the court either order the government to produce pretrial statements of a government witness or strike the witness's testimony at the trial.[5]

The second important device before the actual trial begins is the pretrial conference between the judge and counsel for both sides. The Federal Rules describe the principal functions of the pretrial conference as simplification of the issues, determining the necessity or desirability of amendments to the pleadings, and obtaining admissions about facts and documents so as to avoid unnecessary proof at trial. The tone of such conferences is generally informal, since the object is to get to the heart of the issues without courtroom formalities. One frequent result, though not a principal or stated objective of the conference, is settlement of civil

[5] *Campbell* v. *United States*, 365 U.S. 85 (1961).

cases prior to trial. Reasonable disclosure of the parties' positions in the presence of an impartial judge in an informal meeting often provides encouragement for settlement of disputes.

It must be recognized that the pretrial conference is a relatively recent development, having been introduced in 1929 in the courts of Detroit. Although now used in some forty states and in the federal district courts, there is still some hostility to it on the part of adherents to the sporting theory of justice, who prefer the intricate razzle-dazzle and surprise of courtroom histrionics to quicker but more pallid methods for resolving disputes.

The pleadings, discovery, and the pretrial conference are all part of the quest for the specific issues in dispute. Once the specific issues have been determined, the case may proceed to trial. At the trial stage the adversary process focuses on the rules governing the presentation and evaluation of evidence. To be admissible, evidence must generally meet the tests of relevance, competence, privilege, and opportunity for cross-examination. In the first place, the documents, physical objects, or testimony presented as evidence must bear upon the specific issues of the case. Even when this standard is met, however, evidence may be excluded because some other principle of the law is deemed more important than the principle that all relevant evidence should be introduced. Young children, for example, are usually held to be incompetent as witnesses, not because their testimony is likely to be irrelevant but because they may not understand the difference between truth and falsity.

Even though relevancy of the evidence and competence of the witness may have been established, the concept of privilege may prevent introduction of the evidence. Consider this illustration of the husband-wife privilege, for example, which prevents a spouse from testifying against his or her mate. In *Hawkins* v. *United States* in 1958, the Supreme Court had to decide whether a wife could testify voluntarily against her husband, who had been charged with a federal crime. Hawkins was convicted and sentenced to five years' imprisonment on a charge that he violated the Mann Act by transporting a girl from Arkansas to Oklahoma for immoral purposes. The girl testified that Hawkins had taken her to Tulsa to practice prostitution, together with a woman called "Jane Wilson." Hawkins maintained that he had taken the girl into Oklahoma only as an accommodation incidental to a business trip he was making. The prosecution placed "Jane Wilson" on the stand. She swore that she was Hawkins' wife, and that she was a prostitute before and since her marriage, as well as at the time Hawkins took the other girl to Tulsa.

Hawkins appealed his conviction on the ground that testimony of his wife was improperly admitted. The Supreme Court unanimously reversed the conviction, emphasizing that "the basic reason the law has refused to put wife against husband or husband against wife in a trial where life or liberty is at stake was a belief that such a policy was necessary to foster family peace."[6] It is difficult to see, the Court added, how "family harmony" is less disturbed by a wife's voluntary testimony against her husband than by her compelled testimony. Although the "marriage relation" here might have been for the sole purpose of protecting the husband from effective prosecution, the Court pointed out that the marital privilege served not merely to protect the particular husband and wife involved in the case but was "for the benefit of the public as well." Preserving "family harmony" is thus one principle deemed more important as a matter of law than the introduction of relevant testimony by otherwise competent witnesses.

Similar to the husband-wife privilege are those of confidential communication between priest and parishioner, attorney and client, or doctor and patient. Such privileged relationships are based on certain essential conditions: the communication must have been made in confidence; the relationship ought to be fostered; and injury caused by disregarding the confidence is greater than the benefit conferred through disclosure. The privilege can, of course, be waived, though it is not the priest, lawyer, or doctor who has the power to waive it in order to testify. Reporters have often claimed that data obtained from news sources are privileged, but the claim has been denied by the courts. The privilege against self-incrimination is certainly the most famous as well as perhaps the most controversial of the bases for banning relevant evidence.

It is important to note that the privilege applies only to self-incrimination—to evidence which could expose the witness to punishment. It does not apply to testimony that would disgrace or degrade him; nor can it be invoked in another person's behalf by a witness. The purposes of the privilege are to insure thorough investigation of all circumstances surrounding an offense, to prevent the use of third-degree methods of interrogation, and to avoid false confessions. That it may be waived if the witness begins to testify about the incriminating matter explains why it is so often invoked when even innocent-sounding questions such as "Where do you reside?" are asked.

The late Dean John Henry Wigmore, author of the leading treatise on the law of evidence, believed the right of cross-examination to be the most effective device ever invented for the extraction of truth. In general, testimony which is not subject to cross-examination will not be admitted, even though it meets the other tests of relevance, competence, and privilege; for perjury, slander, and sly innuendo thrive in the absence of cross-examination. The basic assumption of the law is that truth can withstand the most vigorous challenge, whereas falsehood withers before the frontal assault. This is what underlies the "hearsay" rule barring from admission into the record statements of persons other

[6] *Hawkins* v. *United States,* 358 U.S. 74 (1958).

than those testifying at the trial. There are exceptions to this rule, though most of these apply only when there is circumstantial assurance of trustworthiness, as in the case of a declaration of a person made just before he died. Attorneys have greater leeway in their questioning on cross-examination than on direct examination, since the objective of cross-examination is to test the credibility of the witness.

The final stage of the judicial process is concerned with verdict, judgment, and appeal. The pros and cons of trial by jury are discussed in a later section of this chapter. It is helpful to point out here only that the presiding judge has the power in a civil case to "direct" the jury's verdict if he believes that reasonable men could not differ over the overwhelming weight of the evidence. Judgment follows the verdict, though here again the judge has the power to enter a judgment contrary to the verdict if he believes the overwhelming weight of the evidence warrants it. Needless to say, the trial court's judgment does not always end the case. The "double jeopardy" clause of the Constitution prevents the government from appealing an acquittal in a criminal case; but, otherwise, the losing party has the right of appeal, which minimizes the possibility of judicial abuse of discretion.

The foregoing procedures are neither the ultimate solution to our need for an impartial mechanism to resolve conflicts, nor are they a meaningless mass of technicalities to enrich members of the legal profession. They are, to use the late Judge Vanderbilt's language, "a set of workable rules designed to aid in the simple, speedy, and just disposition of controversies between man and man or between a citizen and his government."

☆ FEDERAL LAW ENFORCEMENT—ORGANIZATION AND PROCEDURE

"Is a national police force necessary or advisable? Is there need for further centralization of law enforcement in a state or federal agency? My answer to both of these questions is an unequivocal 'No!' " These remarks of J. Edgar Hoover, Director of the Federal Bureau of Investigation since 1924, typify the opposition of most Americans to consolidation of the police power by the federal government.

Notwithstanding that centralization of police power represents a distinct danger to democratic self-government, the functions and responsibilities of the FBI have greatly increased since its establishment in 1908. Extension of national controls over crimes like kidnapping and bank robbery during the 1930s, over espionage and sabotage during World War II, and over loyalty and security matters in the past 15 years has accounted for most of this increase in FBI activities. Pursuant to the Atomic Energy Act of 1946, for example, the FBI was given responsibility for investigating the character and loyalty of employees of the Atomic Energy Commission and of all other persons seeking access to restricted information about atomic energy. The agency's files, which contain unevaluated "raw data" about millions of Americans, could be a source of grave embarrassment and even blackmail if they fell into the wrong hands. Needless to say, their secrecy is guarded carefully, although there have been instances of leaks of damaging information despite the precautions.

In addition to its responsibilities for investigation and arrest under federal criminal statutes, the FBI performs important service functions for local police agencies. One of the most famous of these is the FBI laboratory, which conducts chemical and physical tests of such evidence as firearms, hairs, fibers, and shoe prints, in criminal cases. Written reports are made, and the FBI's examining technician is available for appearance in court when needed. The FBI's Identification Division offers a national repository of fingerprint records. In a single year more than 10,000 fugitives from justice have been identified through this facility alone. Another FBI service is its training facilities. The agency sponsors law enforcement conferences in which FBI field officers meet with representatives of local, county, and state law enforcement agencies to discuss mutual problems and achieve closer cooperation. The FBI National Academy, established in 1935, helps prepare local, county, and state officers as police executives, administrators, and instructors. "Students" receive intensive training in a wide range of subjects including scientific crime investigation methods, fingerprinting, firearms, constitutional law, and professional standards. Publications like the *FBI Law Enforcement Bulletin* and *Uniform Crime Reports* help publicize new developments in crime detection as well as current trends in crime. The integrity and efficiency of its personnel have won the respect of most Americans, but the continuous expansion of its functions poses a serious challenge to our traditional view that there should be no federal police force.

While the FBI is the best known of the federal law enforcement agencies, it is not the oldest nor does it control all of the vital police function at the federal level. The Secret Service of the Treasury Department, for example, was organized in 1865—more than forty years before the FBI—primarily to suppress counterfeiting. Other departments of the federal government increasingly requested the services of Secret Service agents for investigating violations of other laws. An illustration was the smashing of the Spanish espionage ring during the Spanish-American War by the so-called T-Men of the Secret Service. Responsibility for investigations and arrests in most areas of federal control, other than those under the jurisdiction of the Treasury Department, was shifted to the FBI in 1908. The Secret Service still has exclusive responsibility for protecting the President and members of his immediate family, for protecting the currency and securities of the United States, and for investigating violations of laws enforced by the Treasury Department. Other Treasury enforcement agencies include the Intelligence Unit of the Internal Revenue Service, the Bureau of Narcotics, the Customs Service, and the Coast Guard.

In addition to the FBI and the Treasury agencies, the federal government's law enforcement machinery include the inspectors of the United States Post Office who have responsibility for detection of mail fraud, the detection of dissemination of pornography through the mails, and other violations of the postal laws; inspectors of the Immigration and Naturalization Service who investigate violations of our immigration laws; and inspectors of the Bureau of Customs who have responsibility for the prevention of smuggling.

Prior to 1870 the responsibility for prosecutions of violations of national laws was dispersed as widely as the responsibility for investigations. Although the Attorney General became a member of the Cabinet in 1789, his role until 1870 was predominantly that of chief legal adviser to the President. Establishment of the Department of Justice made him the nation's chief law enforcement official below the President and centralized his authority over the district attorneys and marshals of the United States, who previously had had no clear responsibility to any single government department. The Department of Justice conducts virtually all actions on behalf of the United States government before the Supreme Court and most such actions in the lower federal courts. Through the Solicitor General's office, it determines whether and when cases involving government agencies should be appealed to the Supreme Court. In addition to the prosecuting services it offers to other agencies, the Justice Department has direct responsibility for the enforcement of a number of key statutes ranging from corrupt practices acts to the Sherman Antitrust Act and civil rights legislation. The burden of implementing specific departmental policies generally falls on the district attorneys and marshals in the various judicial districts of the United States. These are patronage, rather than civil service positions; and in practice political considerations may outweigh purely legal considerations in discretionary decisions by these officeholders. There is no problem concerning the prosecution of persons accused of traditional crimes such as murder, bank robbery, and kidnapping; but prosecutions for violations of the antitrust laws and for violations of the civil rights laws are not likely to enhance the popularity of United States attorneys in many judicial districts. Without job security, the prosecutor is likely to think twice before giving his wholehearted support to a case which is unpopular in his district. Pressure will be exerted on the Attorney General, in turn, to "go easy" on prosecutions which may prove embarrassing to the employees of his agency who are beneficiaries of local patronage power. During much of Herbert Brownell, Jr.'s, tenure as Attorney General in the Eisenhower administration, for example, the

Civil Rights Section of the Department of Justice was unable to initiate major tests of the validity of racial discrimination. The reluctance of United States attorneys and FBI investigators to antagonize local officials whose cooperation they needed to enforce the criminal laws helps to explain, though not to justify, the resultant inaction. After elevation of the Civil Rights Section to a Division of the Department of Justice in 1957, and the appointment of William Rogers as Attorney General, the level of enforcement increased materially. "If you can't stand the heat, stay out of the kitchen" seemed to be the advice given to many a recalcitrant United States attorney. Thus while it is as true today, as it was in 1948, when the Report of the President's Commission on Civil Rights was filed, that a civil rights prosecution "often places the United States attorney in the unenviable position of having to take a public stand in court against the ingrained prejudices and mores of his own community," it is also true that more prosecutors are willing to make such stands today than ever before.

A note of caution in evaluating enforcement policies is perhaps appropriate at this point. The number of cases prosecuted is not necessarily the only or even the most important measure of law enforcement. Preventive measures are less dramatic than prosecutions but may be more effective. A sophisticated knowledge of politics may be as helpful as a comprehensive knowledge of the law in taking effective preventive action. Different civil rights officials having an equal sense of dedication and equal legal skills, but living in different parts of the country, may approach civil rights cases quite differently. One whose home is in the South is likely to be more effective in preventing and resolving disputes informally than one whose home is in New York, Chicago, or Los Angeles. To illustrate, high points of success were achieved by the Civil Rights Section under the direction of Turner Smith of Albany, Georgia, and A. B. Caldwell of Little Rock, Arkansas. The dedication of such men to the principle of equal justice, combined with their understanding of southern mores, made possible much significant, albeit undramatic, progress in combating racial discrimination.

When informal techniques of law enforcement are not feasible, formal processes must be invoked. Just as it is important to understand the theory and practice of the adversary system in trial courts, it is necessary to understand also the nature and limits of the major steps in the criminal law process from arrest to trial.

A basic assumption of our legal system is that allowing guilty persons to remain free is preferable to convicting innocent persons. As a result the law imposes strict restraints on exercises of the police power that might lead to punishing the innocent, even though such restraints may interfere with the apprehension and conviction of the guilty.

From an administrative standpoint, we have traditionally organized and staffed our law enforcement agencies so as to emphasize deterrence of crime and rehabilitation of criminals rather than arrest and punishment of every guilty person. The central concern is not the capture and punishment of everyone whose behavior has been defined as socially undesirable, but rather the selection from among them of the particular people to be subjected to the criminal law process. The member of a narcotics ring and the philanderer traveling with his mistress are both guilty of crimes, but law enforcement officers can be expected to focus on capture of the former and generally to ignore the latter. It is not unusual for police to offer immunity from prosecution to lesser criminals in return for information that may help to catch major violators. These are examples of administrative restraints often imposed by limitations of budget and personnel. The legal restraints are more formal and tangible; yet their precise limits are difficult to define. Two cases dealing with the validity of arrests by law enforcement officers help to illustrate the problem.

In *Draper v. United States* in 1959, the Supreme Court was called upon to decide whether a federal narcotics agent could make an arrest without a warrant on the basis of a "tip" from a previously reliable paid informer. An officer may make an arrest without a warrant under the Narcotics Control Act, which has a typical arrest clause, "where the violation is committed in the presence of the person making the arrest or where such person has reasonable grounds to believe that the person to be arrested has committed or is committing such violation." A federal narcotics agent named Marsh, who had twenty-nine years of experience, received reliable tips from a paid informer, Hereford, over a period of about six months. On September 3, 1956, Hereford told Marsh that one James Draper recently had moved to a stated address in Denver and was "peddling narcotics to several addicts" in that city. On September 7, four days later, Hereford told Marsh that Draper had gone to Chicago the day before by train, that "he was going to bring back three ounces of heroin," returning to Denver by train on the morning of September 8 or 9. Hereford described Draper physically and added that he would be carrying "a tan zipper bag" and habitually "walked real fast."

Marsh and a Denver police officer kept watch at the Denver Union Station on September 8 but saw no one meeting the description by Hereford. On the morning of September 9, they saw a person having the precise attributes described by Hereford get off an incoming Chicago train and start walking "fast" toward the exit. He was carrying a tan zipper bag. Marsh arrested him, searched him and found two envelopes containing heroin clutched in his left hand. Did Marsh have "reasonable grounds" and "probable cause" to make the arrest?

In a 6–1 decision, the justices upheld the validity of the arrest.[7] Justice Whittaker stated that Marsh "would have been derelict in his duties" if he had not pursued Hereford's information. Once Marsh had

---

[7] *Draper v. United States,* 358 U.S. 307 (1959).

verified every other bit of Hereford's statement on seeing Draper alight from the train, he had "reasonable grounds" to believe "that the remaining unverified bit of Hereford's information—that Draper would have the heroin with him—was likewise true." The majority opinion emphasized that "probable cause" deals with "probabilities," and that probabilities are not measurable technically. "They are the factual and practical considerations of everyday life on which reasonable and prudent men, not legal technicians, act."

Justice Douglas dissented, pointing out that "if the word of the informer on which the present arrest was made is sufficient to make the arrest legal, his word would also protect the police who, acting on it, hauled the innocent citizen off to jail." He blamed the "education" Americans receive from mystery stories and television detective dramas for creating "a distorted reflection of the constitutional system under which we are supposed to live."

Once a person has been arrested by a federal officer, he must be "taken without unnecessary delay before the nearest available commissioner or before any other nearby officer empowered to commit persons charged with offenses against the laws of the United States." The Federal Rules of Criminal Procedure then require the commissioner "to inform the defendant of the complaint against him, of his right to counsel, and of his right to have a preliminary examination." The purpose of these requirements is to avoid secret interrogation and other "third-degree" practices. In *McNabb* v. *United States* in 1943 the Court had stressed that the rule requiring appearance of an arrested person before a commissioner "without unnecessary delay" was designed to make the police show legal cause for detaining arrested persons.[8] "The awful instruments of the criminal law cannot be entrusted to a single functionary."

But what constitutes "unnecessary delay"? *Mallory* v. *United States,* decided by the Supreme Court in 1957, offers an interesting case in point. Mallory was convicted of rape by the United States District Court and the jury imposed the death sentence. His counsel claimed that Mallory was not arraigned before a commissioner or other committing magistrate "without unnecessary delay," although less than twenty hours had elapsed between Mallory's arrest at 2:30 in the afternoon and his arraignment before a commissioner the following morning. The Court ruled in Mallory's favor and reversed his conviction.

Justice Frankfurter explained that arraignment "without unnecessary delay" does not call for "mechanical or automatic obedience." Circumstances may justify delay in arraignment where, for instance, "the story volunteered by the accused is susceptible of quick verification through third parties." He emphasized, however, that the delay, no matter how brief, "must not be of a nature to give opportunity for the extraction of a confession." The police did not arraign Mallory until

[8] *McNabb* v. *United States,* 318 U.S. 332 (1943) .

after he had confessed, a time when "any judicial caution had lost its purpose."[9]

Once again the major concern here was with police adherence to the standards of the criminal law rather than with the removal from society of a convicted criminal. Such concern, in the eyes of many law enforcement officials, succeeds only in tying the hands of the police. As former Assistant United States Attorney Frank McGarr recently put it, "I am not suggesting as a blood-thirsty prosecutor that everybody is guilty and they should be marched to jail without a trial. But I do suggest to you that we consider how far we have strayed from the proposition that the function of a trial is to send a guilty man to jail and to acquit an innocent man."

Following arraignment before a commissioner under the federal rules of criminal procedure, the defendant may exercise his right to have a preliminary examination. At such a preliminary examination, the magistrate or commissioner hears the evidence known at the time and decides whether or not the accused should be "held over" for the grand jury's consideration. The defendant may cross-examine witnesses against him and may introduce evidence in his own behalf. Any person can, of course, waive the preliminary hearing, and many do.

After the determination of the magistrate or commissioner that "there is probable cause to believe that an offense has been committed and that the defendant has committed it," the next stage is that of formal charging of the defendant by indictment or information. Indictment by a grand jury is not a determination of guilt. As the Supreme Court said in 1906, in *Hale* v. *Henkel*, the grand jury is a mediating force for society between the accused and the prosecutor; it has to consider "whether the charge was founded upon credible testimony or was dictated by malice or personal ill will." The second function of the grand jury indictment is to spell out precisely the charges against the accused so that he may prepare his defense. A vague or nebulous charge is likely to be thrown out of court, as was the charge that Owen Lattimore was a "follower of the Communist line" or "a promoter of Communist interests." The courts have ruled that such phrases have "no meaning about which men of ordinary intellect could agree."

Trial by Jury

One of the most widely disputed features of our legal system is the right to trial by jury. Three separate provisions of the Constitution deal with this topic. Article III, Section 2, provides:

> The Trial of all Crimes, except in Cases of Impeachment, shall be by Jury. . . .

[9] *Mallory* v. *United States*, 354 U.S. 449 (1957).

The Sixth Amendment specifies:

In all criminal prosecutions, the accused shall enjoy the right to a speedy
and public trial, by an impartial jury of the State and district wherein
the crime shall have been committed. . . .

The Seventh Amendment states:

In Suits at common law, where the value in controversy shall exceed
twenty dollars, the right of trial by jury shall be preserved, and no fact
tried by a jury, shall be otherwise re-examined in any court of the United
States, than according to the rules of the common law.

The Constitution says nothing about the common law tradition that a
trial jury should have twelve members, that a grand jury should have
twenty-three members, or that the verdict shall be unanimous in criminal
cases, but the Supreme Court has read these features into the federal jury
system. The right to trial by jury does not extend, however, to equity or
admiralty cases;[10] nor do these provisions of the Constitution apply to
state law and state courts. An accused may, of course, waive his right to
trial by jury in a federal case and elect to be tried by a judge.

Jurors are generally selected at random from voters' lists. The examination of prospective jurors for a particular case is conducted by the
trial judge and counsel for both sides. In federal courts, as well as a
majority of state courts, the initial questioning and the control over
supplemental questioning by counsel are in the hands of the trial judge.
In ten states this so-called *voir dire* (to say the truth) examination of
jurors is conducted by the judge alone, and in nine states it is conducted
by the attorneys alone. Impaneling of alternate jurors to avoid mistrials
resulting from death or disability of a regular juror is practiced in federal
courts and in two-thirds of the state courts.

The attorneys have the opportunity, after questioning, to challenge
a juror *peremptorily* or *for cause*. A peremptory challenge removes the
prospective juror automatically, but each side has only a limited number
of such challenges. Although challenges for cause are unlimited, it is
within the judge's discretion to decide whether sufficient cause for removal has been shown. Examples of reasons for challenges for cause
would be that the juror has already formed an opinion as to guilt because of what he has read in the newspapers; or that the juror might
dislike all members of some minority group to which the defendant belongs. It may take days or weeks to impanel a jury that will have the
requisite traits of impartiality in cases that have attracted newspaper or
TV publicity. Juries are usually called upon to render general verdicts—

---

[10] *Equity* is a branch of law (originally developed in England) which seeks to
provide a remedy in cases in which the common law is not applicable or effective;
usually this involves redress or prevention of a wrongful action. *Admiralty cases* involve
shipping and commerce on the high seas or on navigable waters within the United
States.

guilty or not guilty in criminal cases, and for the plaintiff or the defendant in civil cases. There is no statement or explanation by the jury as to what facts were found, or how they were applied to the law. In a majority of states, "special interrogatories," together with the general verdict, allows the judge to test the consistency of the general verdict with the jury's answers to specific questions of fact.

Critics of the jury system could prepare a powerful brief for the curtailment of jury power. They contend that juries go beyond their function through errors of omission or commission. Under the jury system, no matter what the judges say "the law" is, it is the twelve common people who have the last word in any given dispute. The jury's theoretical role is that of finder of the facts, but this role may in practice become maker of the law.

Critics also claim that juries are ruled by passion rather than by reason. Trial practice manuals often stress courtroom techniques that will evoke the emotions of jurors and suppress rational comprehension. One need only observe some jury trials to appreciate the wide range of histrionics employed by lawyers and witnesses in playing for jurors' support. Not a few commentators have observed that jurors' minds wander during the course of the trial; they become concerned over personal matters or are just bored. It is known that some juries have "decided" on the basis of a flip of a coin, a drawn lot, or as Richard Morris contended in *Fair Trial:*

> . . . it is doubtful if any system can be humanly devised which will
> assure a jury free of deep-seated prejudices and possessed of that measure
> of emotional stability and intellectual discipline essential for rational
> and critical examination of the evidence.[11]

It has been charged, too, that juries are not truly representative, since minority groups have been excluded in effect from some jury panels. The courts have ruled that systematic exclusion of Negroes from juries deprives a Negro defendant of his constitutional right to the "equal protection of the laws." While systematic exclusion may invalidate a conviction, such a declaration of illegality does nothing, in practice, to enhance systematic *inclusion* of minority groups.

The "blue-ribbon" jury, it is charged, carries with it the odious practice of "elitism." Although the constitutionality of such a jury, which imposes qualifications beyond those used for selection of ordinary juries, has been upheld by the Supreme Court, resort to such a device makes a mockery of the concept of trial by one's peers. As the late Justice Murphy said in a dissent in *Moore* v. *New York* in 1948, "such panels are completely at war with the democratic theory of our jury system. . . . One is constitutionally entitled to be judged by a fair sampling of all one's

11 Richard Morris, *Fair Trial* (New York: Knopf, 1952) , p. xi.

neighbors who are qualified, not merely those with superior intelligence or learning."

Supporters of the jury system hail it as an instrument for keeping the law flexible and in step with public opinion. They point out that judges are no better qualified than laymen to pass on many highly technical and scientific issues of fact. Training in law does not qualify a judge to pass on ballistics test results, explanations of the operation of heavy machinery, or the cause-effect relation of a new drug.

Whereas judges are sometimes prejudiced or incompetent, the fact that twelve people are involved collectively in a jury proceeding minimizes the likelihood of such evils. It is also maintained that participation on juries is an excellent education for citizens on the workings of democracy, and that such citizens fulfill their duties conscientiously. Isolated defects in jury selection should not be cited to condemn the entire system. A preoccupation with technical trivia and revering legal abstractions are ailments of the judiciary, whereas a jury seeks out the realities rather than the technicalities of a case. As Judge Bernard Botein has said in *Trial Judge:*

> The thinking of a judge who reviews steadily a passing parade of varied cases may become grooved. He may not bring to each case the eager, fresh consideration of a juror. From long experience, his attitude toward certain types of witnesses and certain types of cases may understandably have become frozen.

On balance, the jury system is neither as ideal as its proponents maintain nor as base as the carping of its critics would indicate. Comprehensive research into its operations by the University of Chicago Law School has developed some pertinent data on this point. One of the questions the Chicago researchers sought to resolve was, What difference would it make if we had no jury trials and all of our trials were bench trials? Five hundred trial judges throughout the United States were asked to say, prior to the rendition of the jury verdicts, how they would have decided the case had there been no jury. Data were received on 1,500 criminal cases and 1,500 personal injury cases.

The judge and jury agreed in 81 percent of the criminal cases. In the cases in which they disagreed, the judges were more prone to convict, and the jury to acquit. Judges and juries saw eye to eye in narcotics cases, but disagreed often in statutory rape cases and first offense drunk driving cases. Several judges commented that they were pleased that the jury had acquitted the first offenders on the drunk driving charges, even though the judges would have had to convict them. In second and third offenses for drunk driving, however, judges and juries were in almost complete agreement.

Judges agreed with juries on questions of liability in 83 percent of the personal injury cases. Judges found for the plaintiff in 57 percent of the cases and juries in 58 percent. Juries found against "wealthy" defendants (corporations, railroads, cities, and states) from 2 percent to 8 percent oftener than judges. In cases in which judges and juries agreed on the liability of the wealthy defendant, jury awards of damages were 10 to 30 percent higher than judges' awards. The percentages of agreement and disagreement showed no significant difference between state and federal courts. The use of written instructions, judicial summaries of the evidence, and judicial comments on the weight of the evidence similarly had no distinct effect on the percentages of agreement between judges and juries.

The moderate position on trial by jury taken by the Section of Judicial Administration of the American Bar Association has much to commend it. The Section maintains that "trial by jury is the best means within our knowledge of keeping the administration of justice in tune with the community." At the same time, the Section notes that "it is highly important that everything be done which can be done to insure the most efficient methods of jury selection and trial procedure." Proposals for improving the jury system include reforming processes of selection, cutting down exemptions from jury service, and improving the treatment of jurors so as to make service on juries more attractive.

☆ CRIME AND PUNISHMENT IN THE UNITED STATES

The attitude of society toward crime changes and evolves, just as the ideas of society change in respect to the government's role in areas such as business, education, and social welfare. A criminal is a social deviant, one whose conduct is contrary to the norms extablished by society, and those norms can and do change.

Under Roman law the emphasis on political crimes such as sedition and treason led to an emphasis on branding, banishment, mutilation, and death as punishments rather than to efforts at rehabilitation. No purpose could be served by striving to reform the criminal, it was believed, since by his actions he had declared war on society and had forfeited his membership in it. Christianity introduced the element of repentance into the treatment of social deviance, and the criminal was viewed as one who must repent before being punished. Torture was often practiced because of a reluctance to execute a criminal who had not confessed and repented his crimes. Religious crimes were common and death was the penalty for heresy.

During the eighteenth century brutality was the instrument used by the police to protect private property. That the death penalty could have been imposed for petty theft strikes us as inconceivable; but it was the harshness and inequality of eighteenth- and nineteenth-century criminal law that inspired demands for reform and led in time to the substitution of rehabilitation for retribution as the principal aim of the criminal law.

Today we can point to progress in the definition and control of crime; but the problems of our own time are far from resolved. The criminal law is not considered an attractive field by the typical young lawyer, and few of us manifest enough concern to demand that something constructive be done about the increasingly troublesome problem of aberrant behavior.

How prevalent is crime in America, and what should we do about it? The Senate Crime Investigating Committee, headed by the late Estes Kefauver, dramatized the seriousness of the condition in 1951. During the course of the committee's investigations, an intricate network of narcotics and gambling activity was discovered to be running efficiently, and often with the help of corruptible local officials. Kefauver, in his book, *Crime in America,* presented several suggestions as to how the "crime syndicate" could be effectively combated. Some of his proposals were (1) to establish a racket squad in the Department of Justice; (2) to step up investigations of possible tax evasions of known gamblers and gangsters; (3) to make illegal the use of interstate communications facilities for gambling purposes; (4) to tighten up immigration laws so as to facilitate deportation of undesirable aliens. Senator Kefauver concluded his book on an optimistic note:

> I look about the country and see the continuing and expanding results of what our committee has started: numerous states are setting up their own legislative committees to dig into intrastate crime along the pattern which our committee developed on a national scale. Local grand juries are joining the anti-crime crusade with zeal. Towns once wide open to vice and gambling are cleaning up, and the crooked officeholders who fattened on the bribes of the lawbreakers are crawling for cover. The new racket and fraud squads of the Justice Department and Internal Revenue Bureau are going into action, and some stirrings are evident from other agencies which have been half asleep for generations. Criminals of the lowest order, who for years have sneered at the law and successfully evaded payment of any penalty for their illegal acts are going to jail.[12]

Events since this statement seem to cast doubt on the accuracy of the Senator's prediction. Congressional concern about stamping out organized crime has not proceeded beyond occasional investigations highlighted by the inevitable invocation of the Fifth Amendment by alleged mobsters summoned to testify. Perhaps the fault lies not so much with congressional indifference as with the dual standard of many Americans. People who are appalled at the suggestion that gambling be legalized may gamble in local clubs that depend upon payoffs to local officials for protection. Respectable citizens who call for wars on vice often begin to

[12] Estes Kefauver, *Crime in America* (Garden City, N.Y.: Doubleday, 1951), p. 174.

bleat that "you're hurting our business" when stringent enforcement by police officials keeps away conventioneers bent on having a good time in the big city. Murder remains a principal weapon of the syndicate in preserving the silence that cloaks its operations, and federal as well as local officials have been stymied in efforts to solve crimes gangland style.

The FBI's Reports on Crime in the United States contain much data to cause concern and little to warrant optimism. We know that crime is on the increase, but we do not know quite what to do about it. The continuing debate over capital punishment may be examined in this context. Critics view it as an act of brute vengeance, whereas proponents claim it is an effective deterrent to the commission of heinous crimes. Critics point out that would-be murderers and rapists are insensitive to the possibility of death as a punishment if caught; they simply do not think about being caught.

Empirical research, as reported in *New Horizons in Criminology,* reveals

> In states where the death penalty has been abolished, the rate of homicide is approximately the same as in states in the same area where the death penalty still persists. In other words, the presence of the death penalty appears to have nothing to do with the amount of homicide. As Professor George B. Vold states, life in Maine is just as secure as life in New Hampshire or Vermont, yet the latter states have capital punishment, while Maine does not. . . .[13]

The run-down condition of many of our correctional facilities offers another illustration, of how we often preach rehabilitation but practice retribution and training, not for a creative life but for careers in crime. In many of our correctional institutions, especially at the local level, we find indiscriminate intermingling of hardened criminals with minor offenders. The Cook County, Illinois, jail offers a sordid but typical example. Designed to house approximately 1,000, the jail has had to accommodate between 1,500 and 2,400 persons on occasion. Small wonder that such prisons function more as educational institutions for crime than for the rehabilitation of criminals.

The federal government has a vast spectrum of specialized institutions: penitentiaries for intractable male offenders (Alcatraz, Calif., recently closed), habitual tractable male offenders (Leavenworth, Kans.), and older improvable male offenders (McNeil Island, Wash.); reformatories for younger improvable male offenders (Englewood, Colo.), and female offenders (Alderson, W. Va.); institutions for male juvenile offenders (National Training School for Boys, D.C.); and for short-term male offenders (Ashland, Ky.); prison camps for minimum-custody improvable male offenders (Florence, Ariz.); medical center for physically and mentally maladjusted male offenders (Springfield, Mo.); and the

13 H. E. Barnes and N. K. Teeters, *New Horizons in Criminology* (Englewood Cliffs, N.J.: Prentice-Hall, 1959), p. 319.

Public Health Service Hospital for narcotic addicts (Lexington, Ky.). Programs in these institutions certainly embody important advances, but public understanding and support are as necessary as the enlightened policies of the federal Bureau of Prisons to achieve the full potentialities of programs for rehabilitation.

Rehabilitation is not likely to be successful with the hardened criminal. Recognition of this fact, combined with the increase in juvenile crime, has led criminologists to study the behavior of juvenile offenders in an effort to discover what factors lead some to reform and others to embark on careers in crime. Some of the research findings to date are as disquieting as the FBI's statistics on current crime. For one thing, an alarming number of youths return to criminal patterns of behavior. The gentle judge who feels that he is helping a juvenile offender by suspending sentence and placing him on probation often finds that he has contributed toward renewed delinquency. Parole supervision is frequently inadequate, and release of the delinquent may encourage him to expect similar treatment the next time he gets into trouble. Release may even be construed as indifference on the part of society toward helping the offender with his problems. A recent study by David Clayson of George Washington University lends support to the notion that early arrest, placement in a rigorous but fair institution such as the National Training School for Boys, and a stay there for an adequate length of time are assets in achieving rehabilitation. Assuming that further studies support these conclusions, there remains the key problem of establishing other treatment centers that come up to the standards of the National Training School.

A similar problem exists with other offenders such as narcotics addicts. Our approach to the narcotics problem has been essentially punitive. Four federal statutes and the Uniform Narcotic Drug Act, which has been adopted in forty-six states, Puerto Rico, and the District of Columbia, apply a wide range of criminal sanctions to violations of the narcotics laws. Critics claim that the "punishment approach" is ineffective in handling the problem of the addict, especially because of the huge profits in narcotic sales, the organization and wealth of international narcotics syndicates, and the nature of opiate addiction. In a major article in the January, 1961, issue of the *Journal of Criminal Law, Criminology and Police Science,* Donald Cantor called for an approach "not placing primary reliance upon the deterrent capabilities of penal laws," but upon "socio-medical" plans that would enlist the professional skills of doctors, biochemists, psychologists, pharmacologists, sociologists, lawyers, legislators, and educators. Such plans would conceivably utilize narcotics clinics at which addicts could obtain medically determined dosages; they would require expert personnel and call for follow-up treatment after the cure. All aspects would have to be administered or closely supervised by some agency of government.

Defenders of the present system argue that punitive measures to control narcotics sales do work. Whatever the number of incurable addicts may now be, it would be several times that number if punishment were restricted or abandoned. As Malachi Harney, a career specialist in narcotics control has put it, "Instead of abandoning hard-won gains, we need to hew to the line and to supplement our already extensive efforts by some additional concentration on taking the addict off the street to give him the benefit of whatever medicine and constructive social work can do to rehabilitate him." We must not, however, he emphasizes, substitute a legalized state instrumentality for the dope peddler.

A New York prosecutor, Richard Kuh, has pointed with concern to the constant rise of narcotics cases, a steady increase of 5 percent a year. He denies that larger budgets for law enforcement can eliminate the profitable narcotics trade. He is also opposed to legalization of narcotics sales to addicts for a number of reasons, including the contention that addiction increases proportionately to the availability of drugs. He proposes a hospitalization plan that can achieve the dual goals of protecting the community against addicts, and of treating addicts humanely during the time they are quarantined for the "cure." The plan, which is "simple but expensive," calls for a series of curative institutions; some might be work camps, others farms, still others in the more conventional hospital atmosphere. "They would not exist for punishment and vengeance but would be dedicated to hope and to encouragement."

The National Institute of Mental Health, in addition to its work in other fields, is developing centers for studies of narcotic and drug abuse, conducting clinical research on this problem, and providing related patient care for addicts at Lexington, Kentucky, and Fort Worth, Texas.

The treatment advocated for juvenile offenders and narcotics addicts might also apply to the treatment of forgers, burglars, prostitutes, and other social deviants. The dollar cost of such treatment is high compared to throwing the offender into a cell and leaving him there to serve out his sentence. Some painful introspection is called for to determine how we shall meet the mounting social and moral costs if the criminal trend of the last decade continues unabated. This is not a problem exclusively for criminologists, penologists, prosecutors, judges, and probation authorities; the control and treatment of crime are as significant for the average citizen as for the specialist, if only because his ultimate security depends upon finding an effective solution to the problem.

18

THE BILL OF RIGHTS:
FREEDOM, DUE PROCESS,
AND EQUAL PROTECTION

☆ BLESSINGS OF LIBERTY

Order and Freedom

Government and politics, it is said, have to do with the authoritative allocation of values in society. Values, however, are likely to be vague and ambiguous. Being so, conflicts arise and decisions must be made as to their meaning in particular cases. To make these decisions is to choose among a variety of both means and ends—and to be able to choose is to be free. For the essence of freedom is the capacity to choose among meaningful alternatives that significantly affect human life. Who makes these decisions, or choices, how are they made, and within what margins of toleration or legitimacy? In the answers given to these questions one can find the major differences among various political systems.

Theoretically freedom is more widespread and secure where each individual is able to make *all* decisions affecting his own life without other restraints than those imposed by nature.[1] But even in a state of nature, the individual soon finds that certain decisions are beyond his own span of control. As society becomes more complex, the number of such decisions increases. Other persons become involved and decision making (choosing) becomes a family, community, national, or even

[1] "The natural liberty of men," wrote John Locke, "is to be free from any supreme power on earth, and not to be under the will or legislative authority of man, but to have only the law of nature for his rule."

Even in a state of nature man was by no means as free as some utopians have dreamed. Mountains and rivers and oceans, a rocky reluctant soil and scarce resources, not to mention the limitations of the human organism itself, set severe limits to the freedom with which even Rousseau's "noble savage" could choose.

international, concern. It is out of such circumstances that political systems emerge for making and enforcing decisions concerning problems beyond the power of individuals, as such, to resolve. Most important are those decisions affecting the order, security, and welfare of the group or community concerned.[2]

To reconcile this need for order, welfare, and security—with freedom for every man to live his own life and choose his own course of conduct— was the supreme goal of the framers in establishing the Constitution of the United States.[3] This they sought to accomplish:

1. By providing for a government of limited powers, leaving most decisions to be made by private individuals or voluntary groups.
2. By dividing power among coordinate branches of the government, and between the central government and the states to make sure that political decisions would reflect wide consensus if not unanimity.
3. By enacting a Bill of Rights to insure civil liberties, including freedom of expression and association, and "equal protection" and "due process of law," to all persons.
4. By providing for limited and indirect participation of the people in the public decision-making process.

Maximum freedom for individuals and voluntary groups to decide their own course of conduct and to participate in making other decisions that insure law and order and promote the general welfare is a central principle of the American political system. Popular participation in making public decisions imposes upon citizens a special obligation to consider not only their own private goals and purposes, but those of the community as well. Since most public decisions, however, have far-reaching and differential effects upon various individuals and groups, this is by no means easy. All may believe in freedom, security, and welfare as goals. But what is freedom or welfare for the sheep may be hunger or starvation for the wolf; freedom for the monopolist may mean bankruptcy or servitude for the small merchant. Labor leaders who hailed the National Labor Relations Act (which guaranteed workers the right to organize and bargain collectively) as a Magna Carta for trade unions denounced

---

[2] Freedom in political society, wrote Locke, is not, as Robert Filmer argued, "a liberty for everyone to do what he lists to live as he pleases . . . (No!) "freedom of men under government is to have a standing rule to live by, common to everyone and made by the legislative power erected in it." [A legislative power based on free, voluntary consent.]

Every individual, according to Locke, should thus be at "liberty to follow [his] own will in all things," which the laws do not forbid, but "not to be subject to the inconstant, uncertain, unknown, arbitrary will of another man. . . ."

[3] The Preamble to the Constitution makes this clear in saying that the overriding goals of the new government were "to form a more perfect Union, establish Justice, insure domestic Tranquility, provide for the common defence, promote the general Welfare and secure the Blessings of Liberty to ourselves and our Posterity."

the Taft-Hartley Act, which limited these rights, as a "Slave Labor Act." Employers, on the other hand, who denounced the National Labor Relations Act as an unconstitutional impairment of their freedom, hailed the Taft-Hartley Act as a necessary step toward their emancipation.

Conflicts of this kind raise basic questions concerning the use of public power to limit the freedom of some, in order, presumably, to safeguard or to expand the freedom and welfare of all. In authoritarian or totalitarian systems these issues are in principle resolved by a ruling elite, with little or no participation by the people, either as individuals or groups.[4] To Rousseau—whose essay in *The Social Contract* has been variously regarded as a formula for a free society, and a model for totalitarian democracy—individual freedom was viewed as congruent, if not identical, with the "general will" of the community. The "real" will of the individual, indeed, was to be found only in strict conformity with the general will. Individuals or groups, therefore, compelled to conform to the general will, are merely being "forced to be free."[5]

The problem of reconciling individual will with the general will, and individual freedom with the general welfare, has been a central problem in every political society. It may also be said that in most political systems what is called public order and welfare have had a higher priority than private interest or individual freedom. *Salus Populi—Suprema Lux* is but one of many historic slogans that embody this idea.

The difficulty in all this, of course, has been how to discover the general will and to define the public welfare to which individual or group freedom must defer in particular cases. Ideally, in democratic societies, the public interest or the general will, and the margins of freedom for individuals or groups, are discovered, even in particular cases, by

---

[4] "The Fascist conception of life," wrote Mussolini, "stresses the importance of the State [that is, the ruling elite] and accepts the individual only in so far as his interests coincide with those of the State. . . . Liberalism denied the State in the name of the individual. Fascism reasserts the rights of the State as expressing the real essence of the individual. . . . The Fascist conception of the State is all-embracing; outside of it no human or spiritual values can exist . . . Thus understood, Fascism is totalitarian . . ."

At the other extreme are the Anarchists. "The goal of anarchism," said Emma Goldman, "is the freest possible expression of all the latent powers of the individual. . . . economic arrangements must consist of voluntary productive and distributive associations. . . . Anarchism (consequently) directs its forces against the . . . greatest foe of all . . . namely the State organized authority . . ."

[5] "The problem," said Rousseau, "is to find a form of association which will defend and protect with the whole common force the person and goods of each associate, and in which each, while uniting himself with all, may still obey himself alone and remain as free as before."

Since the individual's "real" will is identical with the general will, any conflict must be assumed to arise from failure to perceive either the individual's "real" will or a true "general will." "Whoever [therefore] refuses to obey the general will shall be compelled to do so by the whole body. This means nothing less than that he will be forced to be free." See *The Social Contract* (Everyman's edition; New York: Dutton, 1927), pp. 18, 25.

popular vote. Where unanimity is lacking, decisions are made by variable majorities or pluralities, depending upon the issues involved and the time available for making the decision.[6] But most modern democratic systems commonly place certain kinds of individual or group behavior beyond majority control, however great the majority may be. The American system, for example, denies omnipotence to majorities by imposing limits beyond which no government may go in regulating human behavior, and by prescribing procedures to be followed in the administration even of legitimate laws or regulations. The Bill of Rights establishes a "sphere of anarchy" which no majority, however large, may legally enter. In thus placing limits upon public authority, it seeks to safeguard not only certain "unalienable rights" of private individuals and groups, but the essential requirements of the "method of freedom" by which a free society is sustained.

These limitations on the scope of legal or constitutional authority do not, of course, in themselves, insure freedom for all individuals or groups from restraints imposed by custom or tradition, or from inequalities of income or status. Not the least of these unofficial constraints is the pressure of public opinion. Many commentators on American civilization, from Tocqueville to Walter Lippmann, have expressed concern about the unofficial pressures for conformity in a nation committed to political freedom.[7]

It is a paradox of political freedom that the very absence of official restraints on political association and expression often invites agitation by extremist groups whose devotion to the "method of freedom" is limited to those who share their own fevered phobias. One needs only to recall the anti-Catholic agitation of the 1830s and 1840s, the turbulence and intolerance of the proslavery—antislavery agitation of the 1850s, and

---

[6] Except for the social contract itself, wrote Rousseau, "the vote of the majority always binds all the rest . . . but there are several grades of unequal division [that is, of majority] which . . . may be fixed in accordance with the condition and needs of the body politic [the issues to be resolved] . . . For the more grave and important the questions discussed, the nearer should the opinion that is to prevail approach unanimity. Secondly, the more the matter in hand calls for speed, the smaller the prescribed difference in the number of votes may be allowed to become. Where an instant decision has to be resolved, a majority of one vote should be enough."

One thinks in this connection of the special majorities commonly required for constitutional amendments, bond issues, overcoming an executive veto and so on, and of emergency legislation of various kinds.

See *The Social Contract* (Everyman's edition: New York: Dutton, 1927), .p. 84.

[7] "Liberty of thought and opinion in America," said Harriet Martineau in 1835, "is strenuously maintained: in this proud land it has become almost a wearisome cant. . . . But does it, after all, characterize any community among us? . . . On the contrary, is it not a fact, a sad and deplorable fact, that in no land on this earth is the mind more fettered than it is here? That here what we call public opinion has set up a despotism such as exists nowhere else? Public Opinion—a tyrant sitting in the dark, wrapt up in mystification and vague terrors of obscurity, deriving power no one knows from whom; public opinion like an Asian monarch . . . bringing the timid perpetually under an unworthy bondage of mean fear. . . ."

more recently the anti-Communist crusades of the 1950s.[8] Every such period of hysteria and intolerance, however, has produced men and women who, relying on the guarantees of the Bill of Rights, have risked reputations and even personal security to stand against the tide. To protect their right to do so, to protect the right of dissent in general against the pressures to conform is indeed a major responsibility of governments based on what we have called the "method of freedom." For the gravest threat to personal freedom arises when the pressure against dissent is aided and abetted by force of law. And it is against this threat that the Bill of Rights is primarily directed.

The First Amendment

The language of the First Amendment is as categorical and unqualified as it is possible to be. "Congress shall make no law," it states, "respecting the establishment of religion, or prohibiting the free exercise thereof; or abridging the freedom of speech, or of the press; or the right of the people peaceably to assemble, and to petition the Government for a redress of grievances."

The prohibition would seem to be absolute against any official impairment of free speech, the press, religious worship, and assembly. Yet, before the amendment was ten years old, Congress enacted the Alien and Sedition Laws of 1798 which, on their face, did in fact impose restraints upon some of these basic rights. Among other things they authorized punishment for any false, scandalous, and malicious statements against the United States or either house of Congress, or the President, with intent to defame or bring into contempt or stir up the hatred of the people. Under these vague terms some twenty or more persons were arrested for such offenses as denouncing the Alien and Sedition Acts, opposing land taxes, and criticising President Adams and his administration.

Then, as now, these acts of censorship and suppression were de-

---

[8] At one point during this agitation, and to test its scope and intensity, a reporter of the Madison, Wisconsin, *Capital Times,* on the Fourth of July, 1951, circulated a "petition" composed entirely of excerpts from the Declaration of Independence and the Constitution, asking persons if they would sign and thus affirm their faith in the American public philosophy. Of 112 people interviewed, only one was willing to sign. Most of those who refused said they were afraid of the consequences, and 20 persons asked the reporter if he were a Communist. One woman, reading a section from the Preamble of the Declaration of Independence said: "This may be the Russian declaration of Independence, but you can't tell me it is ours." A man referred to the excerpts as "that Communist stuff . . ."; another said, "I see you are using an old Commie trick—putting God's name in a radical petition."

The first man approached said, "You can't get me to sign that—I'm trying to get loyalty clearance for a Government job."

The one man who signed (Wentworth A. Millar, an insurance man) said: "Sure I'll sign the Declaration of Independence and the Bill of Rights. We were never closer to losing the things they stand for."

See the *San Francisco Chronicle,* July 29, 1951.

fended as necessary to national security and public morality.[9] Nevertheless they aroused widespread opposition; and, although never challenged
before the Supreme Court, were widely denounced as unconstitutional.
With Jefferson's inauguration, in 1801, they were repealed or allowed to
expire; and those who had been convicted were pardoned.

From 1802 (the end of the Alien and Sedition Acts) to 1917–1918
(World War I) Congress enacted no other legislation so clearly calculated to limit the rights guaranteed in the First Amendment. During this
period, however, there were numerous incidents in which these rights
were denied or impaired by an impassioned and intolerant public opinion. There were also official acts of the President, most notably President
Lincoln during the Civil War, which raised, or might well have raised,
serious questions both of constitutionality and of wise public policy. As
Commander in Chief he undertook to censor the mails and to close this
channel of communication to persons alleged to be "disloyal," and
thousands of political prisoners were held without regard to the Bill of
Rights or due process of law. And, under an act of Congress, President
Lincoln suspended the privilege of the writ of habeas corpus, one of the
basic guarantees of individual freedom for persons held for interfering
with military operations.[10]

By a sad paradox it was World War I—proclaimed by President
Wilson as a war to "make the world safe for democracy"—that brought

[9] "Are we to be the unresisting spectators of these exertions [efforts] to destroy all
that we hold dear?" said one Congressman. "Are these approaches to revolution and
Jacobin domination to be observed with the eye of meek submission? No Sir! . . .
They are calculated to freeze the very blood in our veins . . . God deliver us from such
liberty [of press and opinion], the liberty of vomiting on the public floods of falsehood
and hatred to everything sacred, human, and divine! If any gentleman doubts the
effects of such a liberty, let me direct his attention across the water; it has there made
slaves of thirty millions of men." See *Annals of Congress*, 5th Cong., 2nd Sess. 2098;
quoted in Carl Brent Swisher, *American Constitutional Development* (New York:
Houghton Mifflin, 1943), p. 92.

[10] Early in the Civil War President Lincoln had authorized the suspension of
habeas corpus "along any military line between Philadelphia and Washington." Chief
Justice Taney denounced this declaration and said that only Congress could authorize
such action. Congress had, therefore, in 1863, declared that "during the present rebellion, the President of the United States, whenever in his judgment the public safety
may require it, is authorized to suspend the writ of habeas corpus in any case throughout the United States or any part of it."

Under congressional authorization President Lincoln, in September, 1863, suspended the writ of habeas corpus and ordered persons held in custody as "spies" and
"abettors of the enemy" to be tried by military commissions. The Supreme Court did
not challenge the law's validity, but objected to such action outside the theater of war
itself. "Martial law," said Chief Justice Taney, "can never exist where the courts are
open and in proper and unobstructed exercise of their jurisdiction."

And in 1946 the Court held a declaration of martial law issued by the Governor of
Hawaii and approved by the President on December 7, 1941, following the Japanese
attack on Pearl Harbor, to be unconstitutional, although "the regime which the
proclamation set up continued with certain abatements until October 24, 1944."

See Ex parte *Merryman*, Taney's Reports, 246 (1861); Ex parte *Milligan*, 4 Wall. 2
(1866); *Duncan* v. *Kahanomoku* 327 U.S. 304 (1946).

with it the first major legislation since the Alien and Sedition Acts to limit the rights guaranteed in the First Amendment. The Espionage Act of 1917 made it a crime to give aid to the enemy by conduct calculated to obstruct recruiting, cause insubordination, disloyalty or refusal of duty in the armed services. It also authorized the Postmaster General to exclude from the mails all materials deemed treasonable or seditious. An amendment added in May, 1918, (known as the Sedition Act) made it a crime "when the U.S. is at war" to "wilfully utter, print, write or publish any disloyal, profane, scurrilous or abusive language about the form of government of the U.S., or the military or naval forces of the U.S., or the uniform of the army or navy of the U.S. or any language intended to bring . . . any of them into contempt, scorn, contumely or disrepute. . . ." The terms of this legislation were broad enough to make almost any criticism of the government or of public officials punishable by heavy fine or imprisonment.[11] Men and women were attacked, sometimes physically, and many were arrested for such remarks as the following:

1. "I cannot see how the government can compel troops to go to France. If it was up to me I'd tell them to go to hell!"
2. "Men conscripted to go to Europe are condemned to death and everybody knows it."
3. "The Attorney General . . . is so busy sending to prison men who don't stand up when the Star Spangled Banner is played . . . he has no time to protect the food supply from gamblers."
4. "This is a poor man's fight and a rich man's war. President Wilson and Congress ought to be assassinated. My boy and I will take to the woods and die there before we go to war."

That such statements should arouse popular anger and resentment in a time of war is, no doubt, to be expected. But how far, in the absence of some overt behavior to sabotage the war effort, should the government be allowed to go in adding its coercive power to the pressures of public opinion? It was inevitable that the Espionage and Sedition Acts, which gave rise to litigation in over 2,000 cases, would be challenged as unconstitutional under the First Amendment. After all, said critics of the legis-

11 Although the Sedition Act was limited to the period of World War I, the Espionage Act continued to serve as the basis for both official and unofficial campaigns against alleged "subversives" and nonconformists even after the war ended. Moreover the clamor for conformity growing out of the fears and tensions of a nation at war were aggravated after 1918 by the Bolshevik Revolution in Russia. Beginning in the fall of 1919 mass arrests of radical political and labor agitators took place under the direction of Attorney General A. Mitchell Palmer. On one day, January 2, 1920, government agents in 33 cities took 2,700 persons into custody. Hundreds of aliens were deported, and the publicity attendant upon all this created a mood of mass panic in many communities. So numerous were the alleged violations of constitutional guarantees of freedom and due process that a group of distinguished lawyers, including the Dean of Harvard Law School, protested against what they called *The Illegal Practices of the Department of Justice*. The peak of the agitation was passed by the spring of 1920, and by May the raids ceased.

lation, the First Amendment says categorically, "Congress shall make *no* law . . . abridging the freedom of speech, or of the press; of the right of the people peaceably to assemble, and to petition for a redress of grievances." How can this language be reconciled with the Espionage Act of 1917 or the Sedition Law of 1918? It was not until the war itself was over that this question reached the Supreme Court in a number of cases, in which the Court not only upheld the laws as constitutional, but upheld the judgments of the trial courts in finding the defendants in these cases guilty of violating the law.

In *Schenck* v. *United States* (March, 1919) the defendants were charged with conspiracy to violate the Espionage Act by publishing material designed to "obstruct the recruiting and enlistment service of the United States."[12] Defendants replied by asserting that the Espionage Act was an unconstitutional abridgment of freedom of speech and press. Speaking for a unanimous Court, Justice Oliver Wendell Holmes in upholding the law, said:

> We admit that in many places and in ordinary times the defendants in saying all that was said in the circular would have been within their constitutional rights. But the character of every act depends upon the circumstances in which it is done. . . . The question in every case is whether the words used are used in such circumstances and are of such a nature as to create a *clear and present danger* that they will bring about the substantive evils that Congress has a right to prevent. . . . When a nation is at war many things that might be said in time of peace are such a hindrance to its effort that their utterance will not be endured so long as men fight and that no Court could regard them as protected by any constitutional right.[13]

Thus was born the so-called "clear and present danger" doctrine by which to test legislative acts allegedly abridging the rights guaranteed in the First Amendment. The test, however, has been more important as a piece of judicial rhetoric than as stating a basic legal rule. Even Justice Holmes, in two subsequent cases involving the Espionage Law, sustained the law and the convictions under it without mentioning the "clear and present danger" test.[14] When, however, he and Justice Brandeis dissented from Justice Clarke's opinion in *Abrams* v. *United States*, uphold-

---

[12] Specifically the defendants had issued pamphlets charging that the Selective Service Act was an unconstitutional breach of the prohibition in the Thirteenth Amendment against "involuntary servitude, i.e., except as a punishment for crime whereof the party shall have been duly convicted." "Do not submit to Intimidation," said one pamphlet. "Assert Your Rights," said another. "If you do not assert . . . your rights you are helping to deny or disparage rights which it is the sovereign duty of all citizens and residents of the United States to retain." It declared also that arguments in support of the draft came from cunning politicians and a mercenary, capitalist President.

[13] *Schenck* v. *United States*, 249 U.S. 47 (1919).

[14] See *Frohwerk* v. *United States*, 249 U.S. 204 (1919); and *Debs* v. *United States*, 249 U.S. 211 (1919).

ing the Sedition Act of 1918, they did so on the ground that the acts for which the defendants were convicted did not constitute "a clear and present danger" such as to justify abridgment of their rights under the First Amendment.

When the nation is at war, it might well be argued that the fact of war itself creates such a clear and present danger as to justify restraints on individual liberties in the interest of national security. There is an old aphorism that "during war the laws are silent," and presumably this might apply to the Constitution itself. Such a doctrine, however, has not been generally admitted in the United States and the Court has said that constitutional guarantees operate in time of war and emergency as well as in time of peace. Yet no one would pretend that constitutional guarantees of freedom and due process are not severely strained in time of war or national emergency. Nor can it be said that the Supreme Court has been a tower of strength in the defense of the Bill of Rights against the claims of a nation at war. For the most part it has sustained both Congress and the President against those who have sought to impose constitutional restraints upon official acts.

In February, 1942, for example, President Roosevelt issued an executive order authorizing military commanders to transport all Japanese-Americans from certain areas in California, Oregon, and Washington to relocation centers where they were to be kept under military surveillance. It would be difficult to find a public policy more clearly calculated to impair the constitutional rights of those affected. Yet when Fred Korematsu, one of 70,000 native-born American citizens involved, refused to obey the order, he was taken into custody by military police, found guilty of violating the exclusion order, and placed on probation for five years. He appealed to the Supreme Court on the ground that he had been deprived of rights guaranteed to him under the Constitution, but he appealed in vain.

It is important to note that neither the executive order of the President nor the act of Congress which ratified that order authorized or included a proclamation of martial law for the military areas affected. There was, therefore, no suspension of habeas corpus, and no impairment of the normal civilian procedures by which persons accused or suspected of crimes are apprehended and tried. Nor did the order of the act of Congress apply to *all* persons in the areas, but only to those of Japanese ancestry, who were taken into custody and transported to relocation centers without regard for what is normally called "due process of law." We are thus confronted with a naked confrontation of the Bill of Rights with the war powers of President and Congress. In the opinion of the Court, delivered in December, 1944, it was made clear that under these circumstances the war power, at least in the judgment of six of the nine judges, enjoyed a higher priority than the Bill of Rights.

Speaking for the Court Justice Black said:

Korematsu was not excluded from the military area because of hostility to him or to his race. He was excluded because we are at war with the Japanese empire, because the properly constituted military authorities decided that . . . all citizens of Japanese ancestry be segregated from the West Coast temporarily, and . . . because Congress . . . determined that they should have the power to do just this. . . . We cannot—by availing ourselves of the calm perspective of hindsight—now say that at that time these actions were unjustified.

Justice Frankfurter, in his concurring opinion, made clear that in his judgment the Bill of Rights might be suspended in time of war. "The validity of action under the war power," he said, "must be judged wholly in the context of war [and] action is not to be stigmatized as lawless because like action in times of peace would be lawless."

Three justices, Roberts, Murphy, and Jackson, declined to accept this view. The exclusion order, said Justice Murphy, "on a plea of military necessity in the absence of martial law, ought not to be approved. Such exclusion goes over the very brink of constitutional power and falls into the ugly abyss of racism."

Admittedly these are difficult decisions. Military commanders or executive officers in time of war or emergency are often compelled to act in situations in which a careful weighing of evidence and a scrupulous regard for the rights of individuals may not be possible. When the nation itself is in mortal danger, the temporary sacrifice of the constitutional rights of some persons may be a small price to pay for the greater good of national security and survival.

As Justice Jackson, in his dissenting opinion, observed: "In the very nature of things military decisions are not susceptible of intelligent judicial appraisal. . . . Hence courts [have no real alternative but to accept] the mere declaration of the authority that issued the order that it was reasonably necessary from a military viewpoint." But, he argued, while the Court cannot, in such cases, "second guess" the military as to the necessity of an order, it can and must pass upon the effect of such an order on constitutional rights. A judicial decision to sustain an unconstitutional order can be "a far more subtle blow to liberty than the promulgation of the order itself. A military order, however unconstitutional, is not apt to last longer than the military emergency. . . .

"But once a judicial opinion rationalizes such an order to show that it conforms to the Constitution, or rather rationalizes the Constitution to show that the Constitution sanctions such an order, the Court for all time [or until it reverses itself] has validated the principle of racial discrimination in criminal procedure and of transplanting American citizens" to concentration camps. That is to say, judicial rationalizations of unconstitutional acts of yesterday may well serve to give legal absolution to unconstitutional acts tomorrow.

To say that the Court, in the Korematsu Case, gives a higher priority to the war powers of the President and Congress than to the Bill of Rights is, perhaps, too harsh a judgment, for the war powers are also embedded in the Constitution. Where legitimate constitutional powers collide with constitutional safeguards against the abuse of power, the Court is placed in the awkward situation of deciding which, under the circumstances, are to prevail. Does one part of the Constitution carry greater weight than another, and, if so, under what circumstances? Some justices, notably the late Chief Justice Stone, and Justices Black and Douglas, have argued that the individual rights guaranteed in the Constitution, and more especially in the First Amendment, enjoy or should enjoy, "a preferred position" in our scheme of constitutional values. In cases where acts of government, "on their face" impose restraints upon such rights, the burden of proof must be placed on the government to establish their legitimacy, and not on those who challenge them. In other cases, it is argued, the burden of proof must be upon those who challenge the legitimacy of governmental acts and not on the government.[15] This doctrine of a "preferred" position for the Bill of Rights, however, has not been generally approved by the Court, although it may seem to be implied in some recent decisions. In the light of decisions involving the war powers of the central government, however, there would seem to be no doubt that, in case of conflict, considerations of national security will enjoy a higher priority than the defense of individual rights.

In the long run the preservation of constitutional liberties will depend upon the respect which Congress, the President, and ultimately the people have for those liberties. Nevertheless, the Supreme Court has a special responsibility to keep the coercive powers of the State within their constitutional limits—in bad times as well as in good times. As Justice Cardozo has said, the great maxims of the Constitution, enshrined in the Bill of Rights, must be "preserved against the assaults of opportunism, the expediency of the passing hour, the erosion of small encroachments. . . ."; otherwise they "may be violated with impunity [and] honored often with lip service which passes easily into irreverence. . . . The restraining power of the judiciary . . . [finds] its chief worth in making vocal and audible the ideals which might otherwise be silenced."

Communism and the Bill of Rights

If in wartime the guarantees of the First Amendment must on occasion yield to considerations of national security, what about civil liberties in time of domestic crisis or cold war? Since the emergence of the USSR as a great power, following World War I, and the triumph of Communist

---

15 See *Herndon* v. *Lowry*, 301 U.S. 242 (1937) ; *United States* v. *Carolene Products Co.*, 304 U.S. 144 (1938) , esp. in the footnotes to Stone's opinion; *Thornhill* v. *Alabama*, 310 U.S. 88 (1940) ; *Cantwell* v. *Connecticut*, 301 U.S. 296 (1940) ; *Kovacs* v. *Cooper*, 336 U.S. 22 (1949) .

governments in Eastern Europe and China, public opinion and official policy in the United States have had, as a major goal, the "containment of Communism." As a product of this policy, domestic campaigns of varying intensity have been launched not only against espionage and sedition, but against individuals and groups thought to be disloyal, subversive, or otherwise "un-American." How such campaigns are to be reconciled with the civil liberties guaranteed in the Constitution has been a major problem of American government and politics for a generation.

As early as 1939 the so-called Hatch Act forbade the employment in the federal government of any member of an organization advocating the overthrow of the government by force and violence. In 1940 the Secretaries of War and Navy were authorized to remove summarily anyone regarded as a security risk, and in 1946 a similar power of summary dismissal was given to the Atomic Energy Commission. In 1942 President Roosevelt issued war-service regulations ordering the exclusion from all civil service positions, of anyone concerning whose loyalty there was a reasonable doubt. President Truman, in 1946, created a Temporary Presidential Commission on Employee Loyalty, and the Department of Justice was asked to prepare a list of subversive organizations, membership in which was in effect proscribed for federal employees. And on March 22, 1947, President Truman issued an executive order establishing a full-scale loyalty check of all federal employees to purge the government service of all disloyal or subversive persons. An elaborate appeals procedure was provided to prevent injustice in individual cases. This was followed by still other executive orders, and by 1956 an elaborate machinery had developed to purge the federal service of persons who might be "security risks."[16]

Even more important than these executive orders was the Alien Registration Act of June, 1940, more commonly called the Smith Act. In addition to requiring all aliens in the United States to register and be fingerprinted, to carry an identification card at all times, and to report annually, the Smith Act outlaws:

1. The teaching or advocating of the overthrow of any government in the United States by force or violence.
2. Organizing any society or group to do any of these things knowingly, or to be a member of any such group.
3. Conspiring to do any of these things.

[16] In 1958 Professor Ralph S. Brown "estimated that 13.5 million employees in the United States—roughly one-fifth of the labor force—were exposed to some form of loyalty or security test. Of these 7.2 millions were in government or military service . . . 4.5 million in manufacturing, construction, transport, and utilities, 1.6 million in professions, including teaching, and the rest in managerial positions." See *Congress and the Nation 1945–1964* (Washington, D.C.: Congressional Quarterly Service, 1965), p. 1646.

Penalties up to $10,000 fine and up to 10 years in jail, or both, are imposed by the act; and no one convicted under the law can be eligible for federal employment during five years following his conviction.

Other legislation of the same genre include:

1. Section 9 of the Taft-Hartley Labor Management Relations Act of 1949, which requires labor union officials to disavow any affiliation with the Communist party and to swear that they are not members of any organization teaching the overthrow of government by force and violence. Unless this is done, the union is barred from access to the United States Labor Relations Board.
2. The Internal Security Act of 1950—the so-called McCarran Act—passed over President Truman's veto, requires the Communist party and Communist-front organizations to register as instruments of a foreign power, prohibits employment of their members in defense work, and authorizes the arrest and detention of persons deemed dangerous or disloyal in time of invasion, war, or insurrection.[17]
3. The Communist Control Act of 1954 declares that the Communist party, although purportedly a political party, is in fact an instrumentality of a conspiracy to overthrow the government of the United States. It is, accordingly, required to register with a Subversive Activity Control Board. It also denies "any of the rights, privileges, or immunities attendant upon legal bodies . . . in the U.S." Anyone who knowingly becomes or remains a member is ineligible for nonelective jobs, or jobs in defense plants, and cannot get a passport. Failure to register carries fines up to $10,000, and five years in jail.
4. The Labor Management Reporting and Disclosures Act of 1959 made it a crime for a member of the Communist party to serve as an officer or (except in clerical or custodial positions) an employee of a labor union.

This is not a complete catalogue of the executive orders and legislative acts aimed at the "containment of Communism" on the domestic front. It does, however, give a fair idea of the nature and scope of such

---

[17] "The net result of the registration provision [of the Internal Security Act]," said President Truman in his veto message, "would probably be an endless chasing of one organization after another with the Communists always able to frustrate the law enforcement agencies. . . .

"Unfortunately these provisions are not only ineffective and unworkable. They represent a clear and present danger to our institutions. . . . the registration requirements [applied] to so-called Communist front organizations can be the greatest danger to freedom of speech, press, and assembly since the Alien and Sedition Acts of 1798. . . . This provision . . . could be used to classify as a Communist-front organization, any organization which [advocates] a single policy or objective which is also being urged by the Communist Party, or by a Communist foreign government. . . . Thus an organization which advocates low-cost housing . . . [or one might add, racial integration or public power] might be classified as a Communist-front organization because the Communists . . . exploit slum conditions as one of their . . . techniques. . . .

"Our position in the vanguard of freedom rests . . . on our demonstration that the free expression of opinion, coupled with government by popular consent, leads to national strength and human advancement. Let us not in cowering and foolish fear, throw away the ideals which are the fundamental basis of our free society."

measures. It was inevitable that they would be challenged in the courts as unconstitutional restraints upon civil liberties.

The first major test of the Smith Act came in 1949, when eleven of the top leaders of the Communist party of the United States were convicted of conspiracy to "advocate and teach" the overthrow of the government of the United States.[18] On appeal to the Supreme Court in 1951, the Communist leaders argued (1) that the Smith Act was an unconstitutional breach of freedom of speech, of the press, and of the right of people to assemble and petition the government for redress of grievances; (2) that even if the act were constitutional, their conviction should be reversed, since no clear and present danger to the government had been shown to exist as a result of their activities and since there was no charge of actual violence or any overt attempt to overthrow the government.

Chief Justice Vinson, speaking for the Court, upheld the act and the conviction, saying that the interest which the government seeks to protect by the Smith Act, that is, the overthrow of the government by force and violence, "is certainly substantial enough to justify some limitation on free speech." As to whether the threat presented in this case constituted a "clear and present danger" which Congress had a right to prevent, the Chief Justice was by no means clear. "In each case," he said, "[courts] must ask whether the gravity of the evil, discounted by its probability, justifies such invasion of free speech as is necessary to avoid the danger."[19] Justice Frankfurter, in a concurring opinion, emphasized the need to weigh carefully the competing values of freedom of speech on the one hand and security on the other, since without security there can be no freedom. "How best to reconcile competing interests," he said, "is the business of legislatures," not the courts, "and the balance they strike is a judgment not to be displaced by ours but to be respected unless outside the pale of fair judgment." Finally Justice Jackson, also in a concurring opinion, declined to apply the clear and present danger test to this case.

> The clear and present danger test [he said] was an innovation by Mr. Justice Holmes in the Schenck case . . . arising before the . . . modernized, revolutionary techniques used by totalitarian parties . . . I would save it . . . for application as a rule of reason in the kind of case for which it was devised . . . when the issue is . . . a hot headed speech on a street corner, or circulation of a few incendiary pamphlets, or parading by some zealots behind a red flag. . . .
>
> Unless we are to hold our Government captive in a judge-made verbal trap, we must approach the problem of a well-organized, nationwide conspiracy . . . as realistically as our predecessors faced the trivialities that were being prosecuted until they were checked . . . with the clear and present danger test.

18 See *Dennis et al.* v. *United States*, 341 U.S. 494 (1951).
19 This is the language not of Justice Holmes, but of Chief Judge Learned Hand, speaking for the U.S. Circuit Court of Appeals in this same case.

Thus the doctrine associated with the late Justice Holmes and invoked in so many cases, should, according to Justice Jackson, be reserved for "trivialities," in which no real danger is present or imminent.

Two dissenting justices, however, Douglas and Black, were unwilling to abandon the clear and present danger test or, in this case, to weight the competing values of freedom and security in favor of a security which they did not believe was in jeopardy.

> The freedom to speak [said Justice Douglas] is not absolute; . . . There comes a time when even speech loses its constitutional immunity. . . . That is the meaning of the clear and present danger test. When conditions are so critical that there will be no time to avoid the evil that the speech threatens it is time to call a halt. . . . [But] The restraint to be constitutional must be based on more than fear. . . . There must be some immediate injury to society that is likely if speech is allowed. . . . [No such conditions are involved in this case.] On the record no one can say that petitioners and their converts are in such a strategic position as to have even the slightest chance of achieving their aims. . . .
>
> The political censor has no place in our public debates. . . . Free speech—the glory of our system of Government—should not be sacrified on anything less than plain and objective proof of danger that the evil advocated is imminent.

Finally Justice Black, who, it will be recalled, wrote the majority opinion in the Korematsu Case, protested vigorously against the judgment of the Court in this case.

> These petitioners [he said] were not charged with an attempt to overthrow the Government. They were not charged with acts of any kind designed to overthrow the Government. They were not even charged with saying anything or writing anything designed to overthrow the Government. . . . The indictment is that they conspired to organize the Communist party and to use speech and newspapers and other publications in the future to teach and advocate the forcible overthrow of the Government. No matter how it is worded, this is a virulent form of prior censorship . . . which I believe the First Amendment forbids. I would hold section 3 of the Smith Act authorizing this prior restraint unconstitutional on its face and as applied.

The issues posed in the Court's opinion in *Dennis* v. *United States* are by no means fully resolved. Nor can one say that the doctrine of clear and present danger, although badly battered, has now been wholly abandoned by the Court or restricted to "trivialities" as Justice Jackson suggested.[20] It is worth noting, however, that legal restraints upon the

---

[20] Writing in 1954, Professor E. S. Corwin has this to say: "It can probably be safely said, on the basis of the Dennis holding, that the 'clear and present danger' formula will never be successfully invoked in behalf of persons shown to have conspired to incite to a breach of Federal law." See *The Constitution and What It Means Today* (Princeton, N.J.: Princeton University Press, 1954), p. 200.

Communist party and upon members of Communist organizations have been upheld in a number of cases, even where no clear and present danger was suggested.[21] In other cases, however, the Court has construed some of the language of the Smith Act and the Internal Security Act in such a way as to temper the severity of its decision in *Dennis* v. *United States*. In the Yates cases, for example, the Court has said that the Smith Act "was aimed at the advocacy and teaching of concrete action for the forcible overthrow of the Government, and not principles divorced from action." There can be no conviction, said the Court, for "advocacy in the realm of ideas." In the Noto Case, decided in 1961, the Court said: "We held in *Yates* and we reiterate now, that the mere abstract teaching of Communist theory, including the teaching of the moral propriety, or even moral necessity for a resort to force and violence, is not the same as preparing a group for violent action . . ."[22]

In 1963 and again in 1965 the Court has held that, although the registration requirements of the Internal Security Act were constitutional, no official or member of the Communist party could be required to register for the party, since to do so would be to require him to testify against himself in violation of the Fifth Amendment. In 1964 the Court held unconstitutional that section of the Subversive Activities Control Act which denied passport privileges to members of the Communist party as a breach of the due process clause of the Fifth Amendment. In 1965, however, it upheld a similar ban on travel to Cuba. And in 1965 the Court held unconstitutional section 504 of the Labor Management Reporting and Disclosures Act of 1959 which made it a crime for a member of the Communist party to serve as an officer or employee of a labor union. Chief Justice Warren, speaking for the Court in a 5 to 4 decision, held that the act was invalid as a bill of attainder, forbidden in Section 9, Article I, of the Constitution. Having decided the issue on this basis, the Court found "it unnecessary to consider the First and Fifth Amendments . . ."[23]

Freedom of Religious Worship, Public Morality, and Public Power

The restraints of the First Amendment against interference by Congress or the President with freedom of speech, press, religious worship, popular

21 (1) In *American Communications Association, the CIO et al.* v. *Douds*, 339 U.S. 328 (1950), the Court upheld Sec. 9 of the Taft-Hartley Act requiring labor leaders to swear that they are not members of the Communist party. (2) In *Communist Party of United States* v. *Subversives Activities Control Board*, 367 U.S. 1 (1961), the Court held that to require the Communist party to register as an organization "substantially dominated or controlled" by the Soviet Union does not violate the First Amendment.

22 See *Yates* v. *United States*, 354 U.S. 298 (1957); *Noto* v. *United States*, 367 U.S. 290 (1961).

23 *Communist Party* v. *United States*, 331 Fed. 2nd (1963). In *Albertson* v. *Subversive Activities Control Board* (1965), the Supreme Court itself took this position. See also *United States* v. *Archie Brown*, 386 U.S. 457 (1965). Also *Aptheker* v. *Secretary of State* 378 U.S. 500 (1964) and *Zemel* v. *Rusk*, 381 U.S. 1 (1965).

assembly, and protest cut a wide swath and raise complex questions of priority and legitimacy among the competing political values. We have seen that the Supreme Court has been reluctant to give priority to the rights of individuals or groups against acts of Congress or of the President deemed essential to public order or national security. Even official acts limiting religious freedom have been sustained as essential to the maintenance of national security, public order, and morality. Thus the Supreme Court has sustained acts of Congress which deny citizenship to applicants whose religious scruples forbade them to declare on oath their willingness to take up arms in defense of the United States.[24]

In 1878 an act of Congress prohibiting polygamy in all territories "over which the United States have exclusive jurisdiction" was upheld by the Court, even though belief in plural marriages was an article of religious faith in the Mormon Church. Subsequent legislation to annul the charter of the Church of Jesus Christ of Latter-Day Saints and to declare its property forfeited to the government was also sustained. "Laws," said the Court, "are made for the Government of actions, and while they cannot interfere with mere religious belief and opinions, they may with practices." Otherwise, the Court said, government would be powerless to prevent crime and corruption or even human sacrifice if committed in the name of religion.[25] Yet in 1944 the Supreme Court set aside a verdict of guilty against a religious sect for using the mails to defraud—"whose founder had at different times identified himself with St. Germain, Jesus, George Washington and Godfre Ray King." The promoters of the sect had been convicted for soliciting money through the mails on the claim that they could heal persons by supernatural means. Their appeal to the Supreme Court had been based on the constitutional guarantee of religious freedom. "The religious views expressed by the respondent," said Justice Douglas for the Court, "might seem incredible, if not preposterous, to most people. But if those doctrines are subject to trial before a jury charged with judging their truth or falsity, then the same can be done with the religious beliefs of any sect." Chief Justice Stone, in a dissenting opinion, observed: "I cannot say that freedom of thought and worship includes freedom to procure money by knowingly making false statements about one's religious experiences."[26]

The First Amendment not only forbids Congress to prohibit the free exercise of religion, it also says "Congress shall make no law respecting the establishment of religion." No one knows exactly what this means, but the Court has, on the whole, been tolerant of official acts by the federal government to assist and even promote certain religious practices,

[24] *United States* v. *Schwimmer,* 279 U.S. 644 (1929); *United States* v. *Macintosh,* 283 U.S. 605 (1931).

[25] See *Reynolds* v. *United States,* 98 U.S. 145 (1879); *Davis* v. *Beason,* 133 U.S. 333 (1890); *The Late Corporation of the Church of Jesus Christ of Latter Day Saints* v. *United States,* 136 U.S. 1 (1890).

[26] *United States* v. *Ballard,* 322 U.S. 78 (1944).

from the appointment of chaplains in the armed services and in Congress to tax exemption and government subsidies for activities and institutions operated by or under the auspices of religious bodies.[27] This tolerance, however, has not always extended to official acts of Congress or of the President which limit individual freedom in order to protect or promote public morality. When, for example, the Postmaster General, under the ambiguous language of an act of Congress, suspended the mailing permit of *Esquire* magazine on the ground that it did not "contribute to the public good and the public welfare," his action was enjoined (prohibited) by the Court. A "requirement," said Justice Douglas, "that literature or art conform to some norm prescribed by an official smacks of an ideology foreign to our system."[28] Again when customs officials forbade the importation of the book *Ulysses,* by James Joyce, on the ground that it was "obscene," within the meaning of a federal law excluding obscene literature, they were overruled by a federal district court and by the U.S. Circuit Court of Appeals.[29]

It is, however, well established that neither libel nor obscenity is protected by the federal Bill of Rights. But what constitutes libel or obscenity, in particular cases, is a question not easily resolved, and the decisions on specific cases are not always consistent. In some cases the so-called English or *Hecklin* test has been applied which established a rigid standard of obscenity based on the "effect of an isolated excerpt upon particularly susceptible persons," including adolescents and teen-agers. Such a test of obscenity would, in effect, reduce the importable or mailable literary fare of adults to standards compatible with those applied to children. A more recent test applies a broader standard, namely "whether to the average person, applying contemporary community standards, the dominant theme of the material taken as a whole appeals to prurient interest." It is this test that the Supreme Court has applied in recent cases—rejecting the still broader test of whether the material in question, when taken as a whole, "is without any literary merit what-

---

27 See, for example, *Bradfield* v. *Roberts,* 175 U.S. 291 (1899). This case involved Providence Hospital in the District of Columbia, incorporated by an act of Congress and supported by federal funds, but operated by a religious order, the Sisters of Charity of Emmetsburg, Maryland, under the auspices of the Roman Catholic Church. The Supreme Court rejected an attack on this arrangement as an unconstitutional act "respecting the establishment of religion." Other examples are federal grants-in-aid to students in parochial schools, and to the building and maintenance of nonreligious physical facilities at such institutions.

28 *Hannegan (Postmaster General)* v. *Esquire, Inc.,* 327 U.S. 146 (1964).

29 *United States* v. *One Book called Ulysses,* 165 Fed. 188. "I am quite aware," said District Judge Wolsey, "that owing to some of its scenes *Ulysses* . . . is a rather strong draught to ask some sensitive persons to take. By my considered judgment, after long reflection, is that whilst in many places the net effect of *Ulysses* . . . is somewhat emetic, nowhere does it tend to be an aphrodisiac. *Ulysses* may therefore be admitted into the United States."

ever."[30] Even the moderately liberal standard recently applied by the Court suggests that published materials, to escape the penalties of federal anti-obscenity laws, must not offend the moral sensibilities of the "average man" or "contemporary community standards." When the Court sustains convictions on the basis of these tests, said Justice Douglas, "we make the legality of a publication turn on the purity of thought which a book or tract instills in the mind of the reader. I do not think we can approve that standard and be faithful to the command of the First Amendment . . ."[31]

We cannot here explore the legal, political, social, or cultural aspects of official acts that limit freedom of speech, press, religion, petition, or assembly. Some of the constitutional issues, as they apply to the federal government, have been indicated in the cases discussed above. Others arise, as we shall see, from the application of the First Amendment to the states.[32] In every case, however, essentially the same problem appears, namely the determination of priorities among different and often competing values: law and order, national defense and security, conventional standards of morality and religious behavior, the public interest or welfare, on the one hand, and the untrammelled freedom of individuals and groups to dissent from or even denounce official acts or "commonly accepted" patterns or standards of conduct, on the other. The task of deciding cases arising under these competing values is essentially a political one and forms the principal business of Congress, the President, and the Supreme Court, as well as of state or local governments.

[30] See *Regina* v. *Hecklin,* L. R., 3b. B 360 (1868); *Roth* v. *United States,* 354 U.S. 476 (1957).

[31] Dissenting opinion in *Roth* v. *United States, supra* (1957).

In several recent cases the Court has upheld two convictions for violation of federal obscenity laws and reversed a state court decision which ordered the suppression of *The Diary of Fanny Hill,* an eighteenth-century "classic" of pornographic literature. In *Ginzburg* v. *United States* the Court held that, although the publications in question were not themselves so obscene as to justify the publisher's convictions for sending obscene matter through the mails, the advertising and promotional literature used to sell them was. Ralph Ginzburg's conviction in the lower court was therefore sustained. So too was the conviction of Edward Mishkin, on similar grounds, for publishing and promoting the sale of paperback books emphasizing sadism, masochism, and homosexuality.

On the other hand, the Massachusetts conviction in the case of "Fanny Hill" was sent back for review and a new trial on the ground that this book, published first in 1749, was not so obscene as to be without social or literary value. In his concurring opinion, Justice Douglas noted, among other things, that the Library of Congress had sought permission to translate "Fanny Hill" into Braille.

See *Ginzburg* v. *United States,* 383 U.S. 463 (1966); *Mishkin* v. *New York,* 383 U.S. 502 (1966); *A Book Named "John Cleland's Memoirs of a Woman of Pleasure"* v. *Attorney General of Massachusetts,* 383 U.S. 413 (1966).

[32] In 1956 the Supreme Court reversed the conviction of a Communist leader under a state law on the ground that by the Smith Act the Federal Government had occupied the field and preempted state legislation against subversive activities directed at the overthrow of the Government of the United States. See *Pennsylvania* v. *Nelson,* 350 U.S. 497 (1956).

In general it may be said that the Bill of Rights, and especially the First Amendment, introduces a constitutional bias in favor of freedom, as against legal censorship and enforced conformity. In this respect it reflects the views of the great philosophical protagonists of libertarian democracy—of John Milton and John Locke, of Blackstone and Voltaire, of Thomas Paine and Thomas Jefferson.

☆ NATIONALIZATION OF THE BILL OF RIGHTS

The First Amendment

The rights guaranteed in the First Amendment—free speech, a free press, the right of peaceable assembly, even religious worship—have always been limited by the demands of public order, public morals, respect for public and private property, and the individual's right to privacy, as well as by laws against fraud, misrepresentation, libel and slander. Moreover, it had long been assumed that the Bill of Rights in the Constitution applied only to the government of the United States and not to those of the several states.[33] This, at least, was the law on the matter for more than a hundred years—from 1789 to 1925. When the proposed amendments, which were to become the Bill of Rights, were under consideration in the First Congress one, among many that were rejected by the Senate, read as follows: "The equal rights of conscience, the freedom of speech or of the press, and the right of trial by jury in criminal cases, shall not be infringed by any State."

Notwithstanding Madison's statement that this proposal was "the most valuable of the whole list," it was not included among the amendments submitted to the states and, accordingly, did not become a part of the Bill of Rights in the federal Constitution. Nevertheless the argument was frequently advanced that the rights guaranteed in the First Ten Amendments should be made applicable to the states—an argument which the Supreme Court consistently rejected. As early as 1833 Chief Justice Marshall declared: "Had the framers of these Amendments intended them to be limitations on the powers of the State Governments they would have expressed that intention."[34] In some twenty or more

[33] "Congress shall make no law . . ." says the First Amendment. The Seventh Amendment refers to "any Court of the United States," presumably meaning the courts of the central government. And the Tenth Amendment says that "powers not delegated to the United States by the Constitution *nor prohibited by it to the States* are reserved to the States respectively or to the people." Presumably the prohibitions referred to here are those in the body of the Constitution (Sec. 9 of Article I and Article IV) and not in the Bill of Rights.

[34] See *Barrow* v. *The Mayor and City of Baltimore,* 7 Peters 243.

cases thereafter, where the issue was raised, the application of the federal Bill of Rights to the states was denied.[35]

The adoption of the Fourteenth Amendment in 1868, however, raised the issue in a more insistent form. "No State," says this amendment, "shall make or enforce any law which shall abridge the privileges and immunities of citizens of the United States; nor shall any State deprive any person of life, liberty, or property without due process of law; nor deny to any person within its jurisdiction the equal protection of the laws."

What, it was repeatedly asked, do these terms mean? Do the "privileges and immunities of citizens of the United States" include the rights guaranteed in the federal Bill of Rights? Are the procedural safeguards in the federal Constitution essential to "due process of law" now to be applied to the States? Does the term "liberty" which the Fourteenth Amendment guarantees against state encroachment include freedom of religious worship, of speech, press, and assembly as guaranteed against federal encroachment in the First Amendment? Until 1925 a negative reply was made to these questions. Except for limitations contained in their own constitutions, the states were free to impose restraints upon the press, public speech, assembly, and even religious worship. As late as 1922 the Supreme Court said: "Neither the 14th Amendment nor any other provision of the Constitution of the U.S. imposes upon the States any restriction about freedom of speech . . ."[36]

In 1923, however, the Court, feeling its way toward a broader interpretation of the term "liberty" as used in the Fourteenth Amendment, held a Nebraska law unconstitutional which forbade the teaching of any subject "in any language other than English" to pupils below the 9th grade, in any school, public or private, in the state. Mr. Meyer had been convicted of teaching the subject of reading in the German language in a parochial school to a 10-year-old child not yet having completed the 8th grade. The Supreme Court reversed this conviction as an unconstitutional interference with the right of a foreign language teacher to teach and of "parents to engage him so to instruct their children." Two years later the Court considered an Oregon law of 1922 requiring all children 8 to 16 years of age to attend public schools, thus in effect outlawing private schools in that state. In a unanimous opinion the Supreme Court declared the law to be an unconstitutional interference with the "liberty of parents and guardians to direct the upbringing and education of children under their control."[37] More significantly, Justice McReynolds, speaking for the Court, said:

35 See Charles Warren, "The New Liberty" Under the 14th Amendment, *Harvard Law Review*, vol. 39 (1926), p. 431.
36 See *Prudential Insurance Co.* v. *Cheek*, 259 U.S. 530.
37 See *Pierce* v. *the Society of Sisters*, 268 U.S. 510 (1925).

As often heretofore pointed out, rights guaranteed by the Constitution
may not be abridged by legislation which has no reasonable relation to
some purpose within the competency of the state. The fundamental
theory of liberty upon which all governments in this Union repose
excludes any general power of the state to standardize its children by
forcing them to accept instruction from public teachers only. The child
is not the mere creature of the state. . . ."

In the same year (1925) the scope of these decisions was vastly
expanded. Benjamin Gitlow had been convicted in New York for the
statutory crime of criminal anarchy, that is, for teaching and advocating
the "necessity and propriety of overthrowing . . . organized governments by force, violence, and unlawful means." Mr. Gitlow's defense was
that the "liberty" protected against state abridgment in the Fourteenth
Amendment includes freedom of speech and press, except in circumstances where some substantive evil resulted. Although the Court sustained the law and Mr. Gitlow's conviction, it said: "For present purposes
we assume that freedom of speech and of the press—which are protected
by the 1st Amendment from abridgment by Congress—are among
the fundamental personal rights and 'liberties' protected by the due process clause of the 14th Amendment from impairment by the States . . ."[38]

The effect of these words was to change the First Amendment to the
Constitution to read: *"Neither* Congress, *nor any state,* shall make any
law respecting an establishment of religion, or prohibiting the free exercise thereof, or abridging the freedom of speech or of the press, or the
right of the people peaceably to assemble or petition the Government for
redress of grievances."

Although the Supreme Court has been reluctant to strike down acts
of Congress under the First Amendment, it has not hesitated to strike
down state laws under this revised version of the Fourteenth Amendment. State laws abridging freedom of speech, freedom of the press, freedom of religious worship, and freedom of peaceable assembly have been
set aside as unconstitutional deprivations of "liberty without due process
of law" under the Fourteenth Amendment. "It is no longer open to
doubt," said Chief Justice Hughes in 1931, "that the liberty of the press
is within the liberty safeguarded by the due process clause of the 14th
Amendment from invasion by State action."[39]

Freedom of Religious Expression

This nationalization of the First Amendment by the Supreme Court has
not followed a straight or altogether consistent line. Nor have the issues

---

[38] See *Gitlow* v. *New York,* 268 U.S. 652 (1925).

[39] See *Near* v. *Minnesota,* 203 U.S. 697 (1931); *Fiske* v. *Kansas,* 274 U.S. 380
(1927); *Cantwell* v. *Connecticut,* 310 U.S. 296 (1940); *DeJonge* v. *Oregon,* 299 U.S. 353
(1937).

posed been neatly distinguishable as affecting free speech, religious worship, the right of assembly and petition, or the prohibition against an establishment of religion. On the contrary, in many cases one or more of these issues tend to merge. Take, for example, some of the cases involving a religious sect calling itself Jehovah's Witnesses. Three members of this sect were convicted in Connecticut "for unlicensed soliciting of funds . . . and on a general charge of breach of the peace by accosting, in a strongly Catholic neighborhood, two communicants of that faith and playing to them a phonograph record which grossly insulted . . . the Catholic Church . . ." There was no evidence of any violent encounter, although the restraint of the two Catholics involved was remarkable and the "Witnesses" left the scene peaceably when told to do so. On appeal to the Supreme Court the conviction of the Jehovah Witnesses was reversed on the ground that the Connecticut legislation requiring a prior license to solicit for religious purposes and the common-law charge of breach of the peace were an unconstitutional breach of freedom of speech as guaranteed in the First Amendment.

> In the realm of religious faith [said Justice Roberts, speaking for the Court] and in that of political belief, sharp differences arise. In both fields the tenets of one man may seem the rankest error to his neighbor. To persuade others to his own point of view, the pleader, as we know, at times resorts to exaggeration, to vilification . . . and even to false statements. But the people of this nation have ordained . . . that in spite of the probability of excesses and abuses, these liberties are . . . essential to enlightened opinion and right conduct on the part of citizens of a democracy.[40]

Two years later, (1942), however, the Supreme Court upheld the conviction of Jehovah Witnesses for selling religious literature in violation of municipal ordinances requiring the payment of annual license fees by peddlers, book agents, street vendors, and transient merchants.[41] The Court rejected the claim that such ordinances were in violation of the guarantees of religious freedom and freedom of speech in the First Amendment. Within a year, however, this decision was reversed in cases holding that "the constitutional rights of those spreading their religious beliefs through the spoken and printed word are not to be judged by standards governing retailers or wholesalers of books."

In 1949 the Court also drew the line at the use of "loud and raucous" sound trucks to blare out religious propaganda on the streets of Trenton, New Jersey, in violation of an ordinance against the use of such trucks. A few years earlier (1944) the Supreme Court upheld the conviction of Jehovah's Witnesses in Massachusetts for violating the state's child labor laws. The fact that the child involved—a girl nine years of

---

[40] *Cantwell* v. *Connecticut,* 310 U.S. 296 (1940).
[41] *Jones* v. *City of Opelika,* 316 U.S. 584 (1942).

age—was used to sell religious literature on the streets did not protect her parents from the law forbidding the use of children "to sell, expose, or offer for sale . . . merchandise of any description . . . in any street or public place. " "Parents," said Justice Rutledge for the Court, "may be free to become martyrs themselves. But it does not follow they are free . . . to make martyrs of their children."[42]

There were vigorous dissents in all of these cases, indicating not only the volatile nature of the issues involved, but the difficulty of assigning differential constitutional values to the competing demands for public order and individual freedom. Under these circumstances it is not surprising to find the Court reversing itself as this problem arises in various ways. In 1940, for example, a badly divided Court sustained an ordinance of Minersville, Pennsylvania, requiring all school children to salute the flag each school day, against the charge that it unconstitutionally interfered with freedom of worship for members of Jehovah's Witnesses. Such an ordinance, said Justice Frankfurter, was a legitimate exercise of the states' police power to instill loyalty and thus promote national unity and security. Three years later, however, this decision was reversed when, with three justices dissenting, the Court declared a similar rule of the West Virginia Board of Education to be unconstitutional.

National unity as an end which officials may foster by persuasion and example is not in question," said Justice Jackson for the majority. "The problem is whether under our Constitution, compulsion as here employed is a permissible means for its achievement. . . . Struggles to exercise uniformity of sentiment have been waged by good as well as evil men. . . . Ultimate futility of such attempts . . . is the lesson of every such effort from the Roman drive to stamp out Christianity . . . to the fast failing efforts of our present totalitarian enemies. . . .

Compulsory unification of opinion achieves only the unanimity of the grave yard.

If there is one fixed star in our constitutional constellation it is that no official, high or petty, can prescribe what shall be orthodox in politics . . . religion or other matters of opinion . . .

We think the action of the local authorities in compelling the flag salute . . . transcends the Constitutional limitations . . . of the 1st Amendment . . .[43]

These cases do not exhaust the issues raised by the extension of the First Amendment to state and local governments. Does the use of state funds to furnish nonsectarian textbooks to children attending parochial schools violate the First Amendment's prohibition against "the establishment of religion"? What about the use of public funds to provide trans-

42 See *Pierce* v. *Commonwealth of Massachusetts,* 321 U.S. 158 (1944); *Kovacs* v. *Cooper,* 336 U.S. 77 (1949).
43 See *Minersville School District* v. *Gobitis,* 310 U.S. 506 (1940); *West Virginia State Board of Education* v. *Barnette,* 319 U.S. 624 (1943).

portation to children attending parochial schools? In these cases the Court has held that where the aid is to the children, and not to the church, it cannot be said to violate the First Amendment.[44] But can a state or local board of education introduce religious instruction into the public schools even where attendance is voluntary and instruction is not given by the regular school faculty but by special teachers supplied by an interdenominational council? The Court has said *no* to this on the ground that such a scheme uses a "tax established and tax supported school system to aid religious groups to spread their faith. . . . This is not separation of Church and State."[45] The Court found no constitutional impediment, however, to a New York law which provided for the release of students, on written request of their parents, to attend religious instruction at religious centers outside the public schools.[46] But official acts providing for nonsectarian prayers to be read or recited in public schools have been held to be in conflict with the First Amendment.[47] Do laws requiring business and other commercial enterprises to close on Sundays violate religious freedom or the First Amendment prohibition against the "establishment of religion"? By majorities varying from 8 to 1 to 5 to 4 the Supreme Court has said that Sunday closing laws do not run afoul the First Amendment.[48]

How issues of free speech, a free press, and religious freedom may merge is illustrated in a recent case involving an Italian motion picture called *The Miracle.* This picture, with English subtitles and licensed by the Motion Picture Division of the New York State Board of Regents, was exhibited in New York City, where mass pickets, organized by the Catholic War Veterans, demanded that its exhibition be prohibited on the ground that it was, among other things, "sacreligious." There were also counter pickets defending the picture, and a considerable agitation resulted as prominent church leaders joined in a campaign for tighter censorship laws. Under this pressure, the State Board of Regents cancelled the license. This action, under challenge, was upheld by the New York Court of Appeals and the exhibitors appealed to the Supreme Court in Washington, on the ground that the New York statute, under which the action to suppress the picture was taken, was unconstitutional. The statute, they argued (1) "violates the Fourteenth Amendment as a prior restraint upon freedom of speech and of the press, (2) is invalid . . . as a violation of the guaranty of separate church and state and . . . the free exercise of religion, (3) that the term 'sacreligious' is so vague and

---

[44] *Bradfield* v. *Roberts,* 175 U.S. 291 (1899) ; *Cochran* v. *Louisiana Board of Education,* 281 U.S. 370 (1930) ; *Everson* v. *Board of Education,* 330 U.S. 1 (1947) .

[45] *McCollum* v. *Board of Education,* 333 U.S. 203 (1948) .

[46] *Zorach* v. *Clauson,* 343 U.S. 306 (1952) .

[47] *Engel* v. *Vitale,* 320 U.S. 421 (1962) ; *School District of Abington Township* v. *Schempp,* 374 U.S. 203 (1963) .

[48] *McGowan* v. *Maryland,* 366 U.S. 420 (1961) ; *Braunfeld* v. *Brown,* 366 U.S. 599 (1961) .

indefinite as to offend due process." Part of the state's argument, in defense of the statute under which *The Miracle* was banned, was that because motion pictures have a "greater capacity for evil, particularly among the youth . . . than other modes of expression" and because the production and distribution of motion pictures "is a large scale business conducted for profit," they cannot claim the protection of the First Amendment.

These arguments the Court rejected, saying that the fact "that books, newspapers and magazines are published and sold for profit does not prevent them from being a form of expression . . . safeguarded by the First Amendment." The Court also declared that "expression by means of motion pictures is included within the free speech and free press guarantees of the First and Fourteenth Amendments." As for banning a picture because it was allegedly "sacreligious," the Supreme Court was equally emphatic. "It is not the business of government in our nation," said Justice Clark, "to suppress real or imagined attacks upon a particular religious doctrine, whether they appear in publications, speeches or motion pictures."[49] In thus extending the scope of the First Amendment to include new forms of mass communication and in rejecting official censorship of material deemed "officially and personally blasphemous" to the censor, the Supreme Court once again gave high priority in our system of values to individual and group freedom of expression.

Privileges and Immunities of Citizens

Not only have the guarantees of the First Amendment been extended to the states, but so too have most of the procedural safeguards provided for in the Fourth, Fifth, and Sixth Amendments. Protection against "unreasonable search and seizures, double jeopardy, and self-incrimination is now afforded against both federal and state governments. More recently, the right "to have the assistance of counsel for one's defense has also become a requirement in both federal and state criminal proceedings. All of this has been done by reading these guarantees into the due process clause of the Fourteenth Amendment. Much the same might have been accomplished by a broader interpretation of another phrase in that amendment. "No state," it says, "shall make or enforce any law which shall abridge the privileges or immunities of citizens of the United States." Substantially the same phrase, it will be recalled, occurs in Article IV of the Constitution where "the citizens of each state are [said to be] entitled to all privileges and immunities of citizens of the several states." The Supreme Court, in construing this phrase, might conceivably have included all the rights guaranteed in the federal Bill of Rights as among the "privileges and immunities of citizens." The Court, however,

49 *Burstyn, Inc.* v. *Wilson,* 343 U.S. 495 (1952) .

did not follow this course. By a process of inclusion and exclusion it restricted the meaning of "privileges and immunities of citizens" to what one authority has called "a practical nullity."[50] Only on a few occasions has this phrase been said to include rights guaranteed in the Bill of Rights of the Constitution.

One such case involved a Jersey City Ordinance requiring a permit for a public assembly which was used to deny the right of certain labor organizers to hold meetings, on the ground that such meetings might lead to riots, disturbances, or disorderly assemblage. Such an ordinance, said the Court, was void upon its face, since the right to assemble peaceably for discussion was a "privilege and immunity of a U.S. citizen" protected against state restraint by the Fourteenth Amendment. Two justices, however, preferred to invoke the due process clause of the Fourteenth Amendment since, they argued, it assured the right of assembly for aliens as well as citizens. "I think," said Justice Stone, [the right] does not depend on . . . citizenship," but applies to all persons whether citizens or not.[51] Another case involved a California law restricting the entry of indigent migrants into that state. The Court held the law to be an unconstitutional burden on interstate commerce. Four justices, however, believed it to be in violation also of the Fourteenth Amendment because, in interfering with the right of citizens to move freely from state to state, it unconstitutionally abridged the "privileges and immunities of citizens of the U.S."[52]

☆ DUE PROCESS OF LAW

Among the rights guaranteed in the Constitution, none is more important than due process of law. Both the Fifth and the Fourteenth Amendments say that neither the central government nor the states may "deprive any person of life, liberty or property, without due process of law." These words recognize that in any civilized society the coercive power of the state may, at times and under certain circumstances, be used to deprive a person of his property, his liberty, or even his life. For these are the deprivations or sanctions which organized governments have always used to enforce the "laws of the land." They comprise, in a few words, the essence of the coercive power of the political state as distinguished from the power of private or voluntary associations. This coercive power to limit or deprive persons of their property, liberty, or lives is almost always present, even when the state assumes its most benevolent posture as patron or protector of life, liberty, and property, when it regulates traffic on streets, enforces health regulations, or the provisions

[50] See Slaughter-House Cases, 16 Wall. 36 (1873).
[51] See *Hague* v. *CIO* 307, U.S. 496 (1939).
[52] See *Edwards* v. *California,* 314 U.S. 160 (1941).

of the building code, as well as when it enforces the criminal law. For what is one man's indulgence may be, or appear to be, another's deprivation. To say to those who feel deprived that they are being forced to be free may serve to rationalize and mitigate their sense of deprivation, but only if they are persuaded that what is done has been by due process of law. It is customary in the United States to think of due process of law as imposing both procedural and substantive limitations upon public authority, but the substance of most private rights is in final analysis dependent upon the procedures by which they are insured.

A catalogue of these procedures as they appear in the Constitution and the Bill of Rights would include immunity from bills of attainder and ex post facto laws, the right to a writ of habeas corpus when held in custody, the right "to be secure . . . against unreasonable searches and seizures," the right to a fair trial in criminal cases, including presentment or indictment by a grand jury, and to "a speedy and public trial by an impartial jury." The catalogue would also include protection against excessive bail, cruel and unusual punishments, protection against being "twice put in jeopardy of life or limb . . . for the same offense," and against being compelled in any criminal case "to be a witness against himself." Nor may "private property be taken for public use without just compensation." In criminal proceedings, moreover, due process requires that the accused "be informed of the nature and cause of the accusation, . . . be confronted with the witnesses against him, . . . [have] compulsory process for obtaining witnesses in his favor, and . . . the assistance of counsel for his defense." The simple phrase, "due process of law," when viewed in the light of these procedural guarantees, may be said to sum up a major distinction between the wilful, arbitrary, and irresponsible rule of a tyrant and the lawful, responsible rule of a representative republic. The history of these guarantees is, in a very real sense, the history of the struggle for human freedom.

Bills of Attainder

Bills of attainder are acts of legislation which inflict punishment (in the past even death) upon individuals for some alleged offense, without a judicial trial. Fortunately we have been generally free of this violation of due process. Yet three acts of Congress have been set aside by the Supreme Court as bills of attainder. In 1862 a Test Oath Act provided that no person should be allowed to practice law in a federal court unless he declared on oath that he had never borne arms against the United States or given aid and comfort to enemies or persons in rebellion against the United States. Because it imposed a penalty without judicial trial, the Supreme Court declared the act to be a bill of attainder and hence unconstitutional.[53] Again, during World War II Congress, by amend-

---

[53] Ex parte *Garland,* 4 Wall. 333 (1867).

ment to a general appropriation act, forbade the payment of compensation to certain federal employees named in the amendment because they had been accused before a committee of Congress of being disloyal, subversive, and generally un-American. Unable to veto this single item in the appropriation act, President Roosevelt, although denouncing the amendment, signed the act but refused to dismiss the employees named, and they continued to perform their duties. In due course they sued for the compensation that Congress had denied them and, on appeal, the Supreme Court upheld their claim on the ground that the amendment denying them compensation was unconstitutional as a bill of attainder.[54] Finally, in 1959 Congress made it a crime for a member of the Communist party to serve as an officer or employee of a labor union. A certain Archie Brown, an avowed Communist, was elected to the Executive Board of Local 10 of the International Longshoremen's and Warehousemen's Union. In 1961 he was convicted and sentenced to six months in jail under the Congressional Act of 1959. This conviction was set aside by the Circuit Court of Appeals, on the ground that the Congressional Act under which Brown was convicted was an unconstitutional breach of the First and Fifth Amendments. The government, thereupon, appealed to the Supreme Court, which affirmed the decision of the Court of Appeals, holding, however, that the law, because it imposed punishment without a judicial trial, was a bill of attainder and hence unconstitutional.[55]

Ex Post Facto Laws

In an early decision the Supreme Court limited this phrase to retroactive criminal legislation that makes an act a crime that was innocent when done, changes the rule of evidence that applied when the act was done, or inflicts a heavier penalty than was provided when the crime was committed. Whether it was the intention of the framers to limit the phrase to criminal legislation is a moot question, since the rule as we have stated it is now an accepted principle of American constitutional law.[56]

Habeas Corpus and the Right to Counsel

"The privilege of the Writ of Habeas Corpus shall not be suspended, unless when in cases of rebellion or invasion the public safety may require it," says Section IX, Article I, of the Constitution. We have seen

54 *United States* v. *Lovett,* 328 U.S. 303 (1946).
55 *United States* v. *Archie Brown,* 381 U.S. 437 (1965).
56 *Calder* v. *Bull,* 3 Dallas 386 (1798); *Hawker* v. *New York,* 170 U.S. 189 (1898); *Graham* v. *West Virginia,* 224 U.S. 616 (1912). See also In re *Yamashita,* 327 U.S. 1 (1946) for a discussion of whether the treaty creating the so-called Nuremburg Court for the trial of war criminals was an ex post facto law, since the crimes for which the Nazi and Japanese leaders were tried were not legally punishable as such at the time they were committed.

how the Supreme Court rebuked President Lincoln in 1867 and the government of Hawaii in 1946 for unconstitutionally suspending this writ, that is, suspending it when the ordinary courts were still open. The right to a writ of habeas corpus under the Constitution applies only to the federal government, but it is almost universally recognized in all the states. Federal courts may also issue the writ to state officials, provided the applicant has exhausted his remedies in the state courts.

The writ of habeas corpus has been called "the greatest of the safeguards of personal liberty embodied in the common law." Its purpose is to compel law enforcement officers to produce persons arrested or detained, before a magistrate to determine why and under what legal authority they are being held. Without some such safeguard an individual might be subjected to arbitrary arrest and imprisonment, held incommunicado without benefit of counsel, and without even knowing why he was being held. Arbitrary and illegal arrests by overzealous enforcement officers, secret confinement without a hearing and without opportunity to communicate with friends or advisers, are the evils against which the writ of habeas corpus is directed. Holding persons under arrest without formal arraignment in order to extract confessions or other statements that can be used against them later in court has been an abuse that American courts have sought to prevent. A confession of a crime, voluntarily made while the individual is in the custody of the police, may, of course, be admitted as evidence at the trial, but confessions made before the arrested person has been arraigned and before he has had a chance to consult his attorney or his friends may, when challenged, be excluded. In 1943, for example, five brothers named McNabb were found guilty of the second degree murder of a revenue officer in the course of a raid on their whiskey still. The Supreme Court reversed the convictions because they were based on statements "obtained by questioning the defendants for prolonged periods in the absence of friends and counsel and without their being brought before a commissioner or judicial officer as required by law."[57]

This so-called McNabb rule has been further extended to prohibit "unnecessary delay in bringing an accused person before a magistrate for arraignment" and before providing him with counsel. Andrew Mallory had been convicted of the brutal rape and murder of a woman in Washington, D.C., on the basis of his own confession, obtained by police after prolonged and intensive interrogation *before* he had been arraigned and before he had an opportunity to consult with a lawyer or with friends. In reversing his conviction the Supreme Court said, "the police may not arrest upon mere suspicion but only on 'probable cause.' The next step . . . is to arraign the arrested person before a judicial officer as quickly as possible so that the issue of probable cause may be promptly

---

[57] McNabb v. *United States,* 318 U.S. 333 (1943).

determined. The arrested person may, of course, be 'booked' . . . by the police. But he is not to be taken to police headquarters in order to carry out a process of inquiry that lends itself . . . to eliciting damaging statements to support the arrest and ultimately his guilt." The Mallory decision was widely denounced by many police officers and other public officials, on the ground that to exclude such confessions as evidence in criminal cases would not only release dangerous criminals upon the public, but would seriously handicap law enforcement officers in their war on crime. Notwithstanding this criticism the Supreme Court has continued doggedly to insist on a scrupulous regard for constitutional due process, including proper arraignment, the right to counsel of persons held in custody, and protection against self-incrimination by enforced confession or evidence illegally obtained.[58]

Right of Counsel

Among the most important of these procedural rights is "the right of persons accused of crime to have assistance of counsel for their defense," a right long recognized in federal courts, but only in recent years extended to the states as well. Without the assistance of a trained lawyer, a person accused of crime may well be intimidated by police officers and official prosecutors or hopelessly lost in a wilderness of legal rules and stratagems. Hence, even where he cannot afford to hire a lawyer for himself, the courts are now required to provide such legal assistance for him in both federal and state jurisdictions. As early as 1932 the Supreme Court held that this right to counsel was essential to due process of law, not only in federal criminal cases, but in state cases involving capital crimes. In *Powell* v. *Alabama*, the Court reversed the conviction of nine Negroes sentenced to death for rape because, among other things, they had not had adequate counsel for their defense. In capital cases, the Court held, where the defendant is unable to employ counsel and is incapable of his own defense because of ignorance, illiteracy, or the like, "it is the duty of the court, whether requested or not, to assign counsel for him as a necessary pre-requisite of due process of law."[59]

Ten years later, however, the Court declined to extend the right to counsel in state cases other than those involving capital crimes. An unemployed farmhand convicted of robbery in Maryland and sentenced to eight years in prison appealed to the Supreme Court on the ground that he had been denied his constitutional right to counsel. Too poor to hire a lawyer he had asked the Maryland court to appoint one for him. His request was denied and he served as his own attorney. His conviction followed. The Supreme Court heard his appeal but refused to reverse the conviction as a violation of due process.

[58] *Mallory* v. *United States*, 354 U.S. 449 (1957).
[59] *Powell* v. *Alabama*, 287 U.S. 45 (1932).

"While want of counsel," said the Court, "in a particular case may result in a conviction lacking in . . . fundamental fairness, we cannot say that the [Fourteenth Amendment] embodies an inexorable command that no trial for any offense, or in any court, can be fairly conducted and justice accorded a defendant who is not represented by counsel." In a dissenting opinion, Justice Black argued: "If this case had come . . . from a Federal court, it is clear we should have to reverse it, because the 6th Amendment makes the right to counsel in criminal cases inviolable by the Federal Government. I believe the 14th Amendment made the 6th applicable to the States."[60]

As sometimes happens, the Court soon reversed itself. In two dramatic cases, in 1963 and 1964, the decision in *Betts* v. *Brady* was overruled and the right "to have assistance of counsel" in all state, as well as federal criminal proceedings, was declared to be an essential component of "due process of law." In *Gideon* v. *Wainwright,* Justice Black, now speaking for a unanimous Court, said: "The Court in *Betts* v. *Brady* departed from the sound wisdom upon which the Court's holding in *Powell* v. *Alabama* rested. . . . Twenty-two states, as friends of the Court, argue that Betts was an anachronism when handed down and that it should now be overruled. We agree." And in 1964 in the case of *Escobedo* v. *Illinois,* the Supreme Court, by a vote of 5 to 4, extended the right to counsel, not only to all criminal proceedings in open court, that is, after a trial has begun, but to the whole process of investigation and interrogation, after an arrest has been made and the accused person is held in custody. "We hold," said the Court, "that when the process shifts from investigatory to accusatory, when the focus is on the accused and its purpose is to elicit a confession, our adversary system begins to operate, and under the circumstances here, the accused must be permitted to consult his lawyer."[61]

Again the Supreme Court was assailed for making the task of law enforcement difficult. It was pointed out that an estimated 60 percent of criminal defendants cannot afford a lawyer, and that some 90 percent of them plead guilty under police interrogation and are sentenced without

[60] The decision in *Betts* v. *Brady* was sharply criticized by two distinguished lawyers—Benjamin V. Cohen of Washington, D.C., and Erwin Griswold, Dean of the Harvard Law School. "Most Americans," they said, "lawyers and laymen alike, before the decision in *Betts* v. *Brady* would have thought that the right of the accused to counsel in a serious criminal case was unquestionably a part of our own Bill of Rights. Certainly the majority of the Supreme Court which rendered the decision in *Betts* v. *Brady* would not wish their decision to be used to discredit the significance of that right and the importance of its observance.

"Yet at a critical period in world history, *Betts* v. *Brady* dangerously tilts the scales against the safeguarding of one of the most precious rights of man. For in a free world no man should be condemned to penal servitude for years without having the right of counsel to defend him. The right to counsel, for the poor, as well as the rich, is an indispensable safeguard of freedom and justice under law."

[61] *Gideon* v. *Wainwright*, 372 U.S. 335 (1963); *Escobedo* v. *Illinois,* 378 U.S. 428 (1964). See Anthony Lewis, *Gideon's Trumpet* (New York: Random House, 1964).

trial. Now, said the critics, the *Escobedo* ruling would make this impossible. Moreover, because thousands of prisoners had been convicted and sentenced without the assistance of counsel, all might appeal for new trials, the jails emptied, and the whole fabric of law and order might be undermined. It is, of course, impossible to predict what, if any, of these consequences will follow as a result of *Escobedo* v. *Illinois*. At the present writing there have been no wholesale appeals, the jails have not been emptied, and the process of law enforcement has not collapsed. As Justice Goldberg said, in speaking for the Court in the Escobedo Case: "A system of law enforcement which comes to depend on the confession will in the long run be less reliable than a system which depends on extrinsic evidence independently secured through skillful investigation. If the exercise of constitutional rights will thwart the effectiveness of a system of law enforcement, then there is something very wrong with that system."

Unreasonable Search and Seizure and Self-incrimination

Among the most important components of due process of law are the guarantees of the Fourth Amendment. "The right of the people," it says, "to be secure in their persons, houses, papers, and effects, against unreasonable searches and seizures, shall not be violated, and no Warrants shall issue, but upon probable cause, supported by Oath or affirmation, and particularly describing the place to be searched, and the persons or things to be seized."

Before the Revolution, American colonists had bitterly denounced the British government for its use of so-called writs of assistance, under which royal customs officers could carry on general searches for evidence of smuggling. "This writ," said James Otis, "is the worst instrument of arbitrary power, the most destructive of English liberty that ever was found in an English law book. . . ." The idea of a fundamental right to privacy—that a man's house is his castle—is a basic attribute of any free society. Only in the most primitive, punitive, and ruthless totalitarian regimes is this elementary right denied. When police or other law enforcement agents, without proper warrant, break in upon the homes, headquarters, or hideaways of crooks·or alleged crooks, many of us are inclined to be indulgent and to forget that the lawless invasion of the rights, even of alleged lawbreakers, may put our own right in jeopardy. It should be emphasized that the Constitution does not prohibit *all* searches and seizures but only those that are unreasonable. What then makes a search reasonable? Alan Barth has summarized the canons of a reasonable search as follows:

1. A search is reasonable only if there is a probable cause to justify it and "the information relied on to justify a search must be sworn to by somebody."

2. To be reasonable, a search must be specific. It cannot be undertaken at random. As the Fourth Amendment says, "no warrants shall issue but upon probable cause supported by oath or affirmation, and particularly describing the place to be searched and the person or things to be seized."
3. To be reasonable, a search must be authorized by some judicial authority. The one exception to this rule is that "a policeman may search an arrested person as an incident to a lawful arrest." And an arrest is lawful when it is made "on the basis of a warrant . . . or on the basis of probable cause for belief that the arrested person has committed" a crime.[62]

These canons of what constitutes a reasonable search are not always scrupulously observed, and, in many cases, the courts have to decide whether evidence allegedly illegally obtained should be admitted or excluded from criminal proceedings. The Court has, for example, held that when a person is lawfully arrested "while committing a crime," officers may, without a warrant, "search the place where the arrest is made in order to find and seize things connected with the crime as its fruits or as the means by which it was committed. . . ."[63]

In 1947 the Court upheld an extensive and prolonged search without a warrant of the four-room apartment of a man under investigation for forging a check and using the mails to defraud. Federal agents "arrested him in the living room of the flat, handcuffed him to a chair and then, for five hours, conducted a . . . search of all four of his rooms. They looked under carpets, stripped the bed, . . . rummaged through closets and bureau drawers. . . ." They found two checks which the suspect (Harris) was thought to have stolen; and, in a sealed envelope labeled "personal papers," they discovered some selective service cards unlawfully in his possession. The suspect was then charged with a new offense, the illegal possession of selective service cards, and he was convicted on the basis of the evidence seized in this general search. In a 5 to 4 decision, the Court held this was not an unreasonable search under the Fourth Amendment. "If," said the Court, "entry upon the premises be authorized and the search which follows be valid, there is nothing in the 4th Amendment which prohibits the seizure by law enforcement agents of government property, the possession of which is a crime, even though the officers are not aware that such property is on the premises when the search is initiated."[64]

In vigorous dissents Justices Frankfurter and Murphy urged return to more rigid standards. "The decision of the Court in this case," said Justice Murphy, "can have but one meaning. . . . It effectively takes away the protection of the 4th Amendment against unreasonable searches and seizures from those . . . placed under arrest in their homes. . . . Under today's decision a warrant of arrest for a particular crime au-

62 See Alan Barth, *The Price of Liberty* (New York: Viking, 1961), ch. V.
63 *Aguello* v. *United States*, 26 U.S. 20 (1925).
64 *Harris* v. *United States*, 331 U.S. 145 (1947).

thorizes an unlimited search of one's home from cellar to attic for evidence of 'anything' that might come to light whether bearing on the crime charged or any other crime."

Obviously there are sharp differences as to what constitutes an "unreasonable" search or seizure, and standards will vary from case to case, depending upon the Court's appraisal of what is "reasonable." Moreover, since the case of *Boyd* v. *United States* in 1886, the prohibition in the Fourth Amendment against unreasonable searches and seizures must be read in conjunction with the provision of the Fifth Amendment which protects the individual in any criminal case against being compelled "to be a witness against himself."

Obviously if a person's private papers, letters, or recorded conversations obtained through illegal search and seizure may be used as evidence against him in a criminal proceeding, he may be thus compelled to testify against himself. The admissibility of such evidence, therefore, is a matter of grave importance. In one notorious case, for example, Los Angeles County officers, acting on a tip that a certain person was selling narcotics, went to his house. Entering through an unlocked door they forced open a bedroom door to find the suspect sitting half-dressed on the bed. On a side table the officers saw two capsules which they suspected to contain narcotics. Before they could seize them the suspect picked them up, put them in his mouth, and swallowed them. Rushed by the deputies to a hospital, a strong emetic was administered, and the suspect regurgitated the capsules. Upon examination these proved to contain morphine, and were later introduced as evidence and became the basis for the suspect's conviction of crime.

Should this evidence have been admitted? A unanimous Court said, *no.* "It is conduct," said Justice Frankfurter, "that shocks the conscience. Illegally breaking into the privacy of the petitioner, the struggle to open his mouth and remove what was there, the forcible extraction of his stomach's contents—this course of proceedings by agents of government to obtain evidence is bound to offend even hardened sensibilities. They are methods too close to the rack and the screw" to be tolerated. "[In criminal prosecutions the Government must] respect certain decencies of civilized conduct. Due process of law . . . precludes . . . convictions . . . brought about by methods that offend 'a sense of justice.' " Justices Black and Douglas agreed with the result but did not agree with the reasons given. In their opinion the Court should set aside state action of this kind not because it "shocks the conscience" or offends a "sense of justice," but because it compels a person in a criminal case to be a witness against himself. [65]

In recent cases the Supreme Court has not hesitated to reverse criminal convictions where evidence was obtained by "unreasonable

[65] *Rochin* v. *California,* 342 U.S. 165 (1952) .

searches and seizures," and also because the admission of such evidence may violate the guarantee in the Fifth Amendment against self-incrimination. To be compelled to be a witness against oneself violates a most important principle of our accusatory system of criminal law; namely that a person be presumed to be innocent until those who accuse him have proved him to be guilty. In a recent case, for example, a conviction for murder in a Connecticut court was reversed by the Supreme Court when it appeared that the confession on which conviction was based resulted from a threat by the police to bring the accused man's wife in for questioning. "Our decisions under [the Fourteenth Amendment]," said the Court, "have made clear that convictions following the admission into evidence of confessions which are involuntary . . . cannot stand. This is so . . . because the methods used to extract them offend an underlying principle . . . of our criminal law: that ours is an accusatorial and not an inquisitional system—a system in which the State must establish guilt by evidence, independently and freely secured, and may not by coercion prove its charge against an accused out of his own mouth."[66]

If a person accused of crime may not be compelled to testify against himself by confession or otherwise, may a *witness* be compelled to give testimony if he claims that to do so would tend to "incriminate him"? In a federal tribunal the answer would be *no,* since to compel such testimony would violate the guarantee against self-incrimination in the Fifth Amendment. But what about a state tribunal? In the case of *Malloy* v. *Hogan,* a witness in a state court-sponsored inquiry refused to answer certain questions relating to gambling on this ground. The Connecticut Supreme Court of Errors ruled that answers to the questions asked would not in fact tend to incriminate the witness and upheld his punishment for contempt for refusing to answer. On appeal to the Supreme Court of the United States this ruling was set aside. "We hold," said the Court, "that the Fourteenth Amendment guarantees the petitioner the protection of the Fifth Amendment's privilege against self-incrimination and that under the applicable Federal standard, the Connecticut Supreme Court of Errors erred in holding that the privilege was not properly invoked."[67] Thus the Court in effect reversed a 1961 decision that "the Fifth Amendment's privilege against self-incrimination" was not applicable to the states.[68]

The Exclusionary Rule

The major deterrent against unreasonable searches and seizures and involuntary self-incrimination has been the exclusion of evidence so ob-

66 *Rogers* v. *Richmond,* 365 U.S. 534 (1961).
67 *Malloy* v. *Hogan,* 378 U.S. 1 (1964).
68 *Cohen* v. *Hurley,* 366 U.S. 117 (1961).

tained from proceedings in criminal trials. If enforcement officers are faced with the prospect of having evidence illegally obtained thrown out of court, they are more likely to respect the constitutional prohibitions against unreasonable searches and seizures and self-incrimination. In 1914 the Supreme Court had held that evidence illegally obtained could not be introduced in federal courts, and this has been reaffirmed and reinforced in more recent cases.[69]

But the application of this so-called exclusionary rule to criminal trials in state courts was not clear. On this point the Supreme Court followed the law of the states where in some cases it was allowed and in others disallowed. The result was confusing and inequitable. It was even possible, under these circumstances, for federal officials legally to receive and to use in Court evidence illegally obtained by state officials and vice versa.[70] By 1966, however, this confused situation was being clarified: first by the states themselves adopting the exclusionary rule, and second by the Supreme Court extending it to criminal trials in state as well as federal courts.[71]

The Supreme Court in recent cases has extended the exclusionary rule to state as well as federal criminal proceedings. As recently as 1949 the Court had held that "in a prosecution in a State Court for a State crime, the Fourteenth Amendment does not forbid the admission of evidence obtained by unreasonable search and seizure."[72] But in 1961 in *Mapp* v. *Ohio,* the Court declared that "all evidence obtained by searches and seizures in violation of the Constitution is . . . inadmissable in a State Court." "We find," the Court continued, "that [the Fourth and Fifth Amendments apply to the states as to the federal government—in order to insure] freedom from unconscionable invasions of privacy. . . . Together the [Fourth and Fifth Amendments] assure . . . that no man is to be convicted on unconstitutional evidence."[73]

How vital this ruling may be to the preservation of freedom and due process of law is emphasized in the remarks of Justice Robert Jackson

---

[69] *Weeks* v. *United States,* 232 U.S. 383 (1914) ; *Olmstead* v. *United States,* 27 U.S. 438 (1928) ; *McNabb* v. *United States,* 318 U.S. 332 (1943) .

[70] In *Feldman* v. *United States,* 322 U.S. 487 (1944) , the Supreme Court upheld the federal conviction of a person on the basis of testimony which a state court extracted under a grant of subsequent immunity by the state. And in an earlier case the Court said that a state could convict a person on the basis of testimony for which he had secured immunity from Federal prosecution. See *United States* v. *Murdock,* 284 U.S. 141 (1931) .

[71] In 1955, for example, the California Supreme Court adopted the federal rule excluding such evidence. "We have been compelled," said the Court, "to reach that conclusion because other remedies have completely failed to secure compliance with the constitutional provisions on the part of police officers with the . . . result that courts . . . have been . . . required to participate in, and in effect condone, the lawless activities of law enforcement officers." See E. L. Barrett, Jr., *California Law Review* (October, 1955) , *People* v. *Cahan,* 44 Cal. 434 (1955) .

[72] *Wolf* v. *Colorado,* 338 U.S. 33 (1949) .

[73] *Mapp* v. *Ohio,* 367 U.S. 643 (1961) .

shortly after his return from the Nuremburg trials of Nazi war criminals. "Uncontrolled search and seizure," he said, "is one of the first and most effective weapons in the arsenal of every arbitrary government. One need only to have dwelt and worked among people . . . deprived of these rights to know that the human personality deteriorates and dignity and self-reliance disappear when homes, persons, and possessions are subject at any hour to unheralded search and seizure by the police."[74]

Technology and the Bill of Rights: Wiretapping

Science and technology have posed new problems for law enforcement officers and for Courts striving to apply the guarantees of the Fourth and Fifth Amendments to the administration of criminal justice. Today anyone intent upon a course of criminal conduct need not write a letter, note, or memorandum to his victims, clients, or confederates. He can pick up the telephone or use some form of electronic recording and communication. Unlike personal papers or effects telephone messages usually leave no tangible evidence, even for the conscientious police officer armed with a valid warrant to search a suspect's premises. And unlike other more pedestrian forms of communication these new electronic devices enable the lawbreaker to extend himself beyond his office or home or hideout without moving from his own bed or easy chair or even sending an emissary on a criminal mission.

How and to what extent are the provisions of the Fourth and Fifth Amendments to apply under these circumstances? The issue was posed as early as 1928 in the case of *Olmstead* v. *United States*. A vast bootleg ring operating in Seattle, Washington, and British Columbia during prohibition had illegal business transactions in the neighborhood of $2 million a year. For many months prohibition agents of the United States tapped the telephone lines of members of this criminal syndicate. The evidence obtained, based on recorded conversations of the conspirators, brought about their arrest, trial, and conviction.

The Supreme Court agreed to review the convictions on the sole question of whether the use of evidence obtained by tapping of telephone lines was a violation of the Fourth and Fifth Amendments. By a vote of 5 to 4 the Court said it was not. "The 4th Amendment," said Chief Justice Taft, "does not forbid what was done here. There was no searching, there was no seizure. . . . There was no entry of the houses or offices of the defendants, the telephone lines beyond his house and messages passing over them are not within the protection of the 4th Amendment. . . ." But, it was argued, wiretapping was illegal in the State of Washington. Could a federal court admit evidence obtained in violation of state law? Yes, said the Court, holding that under the common law the admissibility of evidence was not affected by its having been illegally obtained.

[74] See W. Gellhorn, *American Rights* (New York: Macmillan, 1960), p. 36.

Four Justices dissented. "It is desirable," said Holmes, in his dissent, "that criminals should be detected, and to that end all available evidence should be used. It is also desirable that the Government should not itself foster and pay for other crimes [wiretapping] when they are the means by which the evidence is to be obtained. . . . We have to choose, and for my part I think it a less evil that some criminals should escape than that the government should play an ignoble part." Holmes called all such illegal methods a "dirty business."[75]

Six years after the Olmstead decision, Congress, in the Federal Communications Act of 1934, prohibited wiretapping. "No person," said the act, "not being authorized by the sender, shall intercept any communication and divulge or publish the . . . contents . . . of such intercepted communication to any person. . . ." As matters now stand, wiretapping and the use of "bugging" or other electronic listening devices, except in cases involving national security, are illegal and unconstitutional.[76]

Most law enforcement officers would no doubt like to see some change in the present law which, under proper safeguards, would allow them, in certain types of cases, to tap wires and to use the evidence so obtained, in state and federal courts. As science and technology develop new devices for tapping wires and for eavesdropping in even more subtle and ingenious ways, pressure to authorize their use will mount. It is a development to be watched with great care and a jealous eye. Nothing so symbolizes the police state—the sodden state of George Orwell's novel *1984*—as a police force unrestrained by Congress or the courts in its invasion of the individual's right to privacy.

In this, as in other problems, we are confronted with the establishment of priorities among competing political values. How can we reconcile, in this new electronic age, the demand for law and order, for protection against violence and crime, with the basic rights of freedom, due process, and individual privacy?

Excessive Bail and Cruel and Unusual Punishments

The federal Bill of Rights in the Eighth Amendment declares that "excessive bail shall not be required, nor excessive fines imposed, nor cruel and unusual punishments inflicted." The prohibition against excessive bail is of special importance to poor persons caught in the toils of the criminal law. It is also important to all accused persons in making possible better preparation for their defense. Although only relatively few cases involving excessive bail have been decided by the Supreme Court, they tend to restrict this guarantee to criminal proceedings under federal authority. The Court's standard of what constitutes excessive bail, more-

[75] *Olmstead* v. *United States,* 277 U.S. 438 (1928).
[76] See for a leading case, *Nardonne* v. *United States,* 302 U.S. 379 (1937); *Nardonne* v. *United States,* 308 U.S. 338 (1939).

over, may produce "anomalous results." In 1951, for example, the Court unanimously held that "bail of $50,000 . . . for each of twelve second string Communist leaders was excessive, even though four other leaders indicted earlier had disappeared forfeiting their bail." Later, however, in a 5 to 4 decision, the Court held that five aliens could be refused bail altogether on the basis of "unproved allegations . . . that the aliens were 'security risks,' " and that "deportation is not a criminal proceeding."[77]

Considerably more litigation has reached our highest Court concerning "cruel and unusual punishments," applicable alike to both federal and state authorities. In these cases, also, the meaning of the phrase itself is by no means as clear as crystal. In one of its earliest cases the Supreme Court noted the difficulty of defining "with exactness" the words "cruel and unusual punishments," but said that it would surely include "punishment of torture . . . and all others in the same line of unnecessary cruelty."[78] More specifically, the Court has held that "shooting as a mode of execution" was not cruel and unusual, but that fine and imprisonment of from twelve to twenty years for entering a false statement in a public record, was.[79] In 1962 the Court held that "a State law which imprisons a [narcotic addict] as a criminal, even though he has never touched any narcotic drug within the State or been guilty of any irregular behavior there, inflicts a cruel and unusual punishment in violation of the Fourteenth Amendment."[80] It is precisely in this process of applying the abstract and often ambiguous language of the Constitution to particular cases that the guarantees of the Bill of Rights become meaningful and significant.

Double Jeopardy

Among the few remaining exceptions to the general trend toward nationalization of the federal Bill of Rights is the provision in the Fifth Amendment against double jeopardy. "Nor shall any person," it says, "be subject for the same offense to be twice put in jeopardy of life or limb." In general this guarantee does not protect an individual from being tried separately for the same offense under valid legislation by both state and federal authorities. Nor does it preclude a state or the federal government from prosecuting a person "in separate trials for different offenses growing out of the same action." Thus in *Gore* v. *United States* the accused was punished for three separate offenses which arose out of a single sale of narcotics: illegal sale, a sale of unstamped narcotics, and the

[77] *Stack* v. *Boyle,* 342 U.S. 1 (1956); *Carlson* v. *Landon,* 342 U.S. 524 (1952). See Harold Spaeth, *The Warren Court* (San Francisco: Chandler, 1966), pp. 341–348.

[78] *Wilkerson* v. *Utah,* 99 U.S. 130 (1879).

[79] *Weems* v. *United States,* 217 U.S. 349 (1910).

[80] *Robinson* v. *California,* 370 U.S. 660 (1962).

sale of unlawfully imported drugs.[81] The Supreme Court has held that a person acquitted of a criminal offense in a federal court may not be tried again by the federal government for the same offense. But where an act is a criminal offense under both state and federal laws, a person acquitted in a federal court may be tried again for the same offense in a state court.[82]

Although the due process clause of the Fourteenth Amendment has not been construed by the Supreme Court to include the Fifth Amendment's guarantee against double jeopardy, not a few of the justices would do exactly this. In a recent dissenting opinion by Justice Black and concurred in by Chief Justice Warren and Justice Douglas, he said: "I would hold that a Federal trial following either state acquittal or conviction is barred by the Double Jeopardy clause of the Fifth Amendment. . . . I think double prosecutions for the same offense are so contrary to the spirit of our free country that they violate even the prevailing view of the Fourteenth Amendment expressed in *Palko* v. *Connecticut*. . . ."[83] In this latter case, decided in 1937, the Court applied the principle of "selective incorporation" of the Bill of Rights into the due process clause of the Fourteenth Amendment. In doing so, it distinguished certain "fundamental rights" such as those set forth in the First Amendment from others, presumably less fundamental, set forth in the other Amendments which make up the Federal Bill of Rights. The first it would include; the remainder, only "selectively."[84]

As we have seen, however, this process of "selective incorporation" has gone on apace until all except a few guarantees of the federal Bill of Rights have now been included in the due process clause of the Fourteenth Amendment. Only the guarantees of compulsory process for obtaining witnesses, a jury trial, indictment by a grand jury, and of protection against excessive bail and double jeopardy remain to be included as essential components of due process of law, applicable to both state and federal governments. Yet even in most of these cases, state constitutions already include guarantees similar to those in the federal Bill of Rights. And where these may prove inadequate or ineffective, recent decisions indicate an increasing willingness of the Court to apply them to the states through the Fourteenth Amendment. Step by step, the federal Bill of Rights is becoming a charter of liberties for people in every part of the nation against the misuse of coercive power, whether by state or federal authorities.

81 *Gore* v. *United States*, 357 U.S. 386 (1958). See Harold Spaeth, *The Warren Court* (San Francisco: Chandler, 1966), p. 316.
82 *Bartkus* v. *Illinois*, 359 U.S. 121 (1959); see also *Fox* v. *Ohio*, 5 Howard 410 (1847); *United States* v. *Marigold*, 9 Howard 560 (1850); *Moore* v. *Illinois*, 14 Howard 13 (1852); *United States* v. *Lanza*, 260 U.S. 377 (1922).
83 *Bartkus* v. *Illinois*, 359 U.S. 121 (1959).
84 *Palko* v. *Connecticut*, 302 U.S. 319 (1937).

☆ *EQUAL PROTECTION OF THE LAWS*

If the basic goal of the American Republic could be summed up in a single phrase, it might be described as a continuing quest for freedom and equality. In the final analysis this is what both the Declaration of Independence and the Constitution are all about. Hence it is that the equal protection clause of the Constitution is a logical corollary of the due process clause. And it is no accident that they occur together in Section I of the Fourteenth Amendment. "No state," it says, "shall . . . deprive any person of life, liberty or property, without due process of law; nor deny to any person within its jurisdiction the equal protection of the laws." Neither due process without equal protection, nor equal protection without due process, makes any sense in our scheme of values. For if the procedural or the substantive guarantees of due process of law can be limited in their application to specialized groups, based on class or creed, ethnic or racial origin, they become a mask for injustice and make a mockery of the life, liberty, and property they are designed to protect. By the same token, equal protection of the laws is not only difficult, but impossible, to achieve if the guarantees of due process are denied.

It is important to remember that "equal protection of the laws" is a political or legal, not a psychological, concept. When the Declaration of Independence says that all men are created equal, it does not imply that all men are identical. On the contrary, it means that because individuals differ from one another in interests and aptitudes, in physique and character, they must be afforded an equal opportunity under law to grow and develop, to realize the best that is in them, including an equal opportunity to achieve distinction. In the American system, when poverty, physical handicaps, or other disabilities, arising from nature or a hostile environment, interfere with this equal right to achieve distinction, we strive, both through law and through philanthropy, to restore it in whatever measure we can. For we know that to treat different individuals as though they were the same is to deny them equality of opportunity. Equal justice under law means something more than prohibiting both rich men and poor men from sleeping on the benches in the park. Moreover, laws which deny equality of opportunity because of race or class or creed are at war with both equal justice under law and the integrity or dignity of the individual, which are at the base of the American public philosophy. In that philosophy individuals are to be judged in terms of what they are and do as individuals, and not in terms of who their parents were, their ethnic origin, or the color of their skin. Public policy based on racial, religious, or class differences denies both due process and equal protection of the laws, precisely because it denies recognition of those individual differences that are at the heart of both freedom and equality.

This does not mean that laws must be blind to differences of all kinds and that every law must apply in the same way to every man, woman, and child in the state or nation. This would be to fly in the face of common sense, to confuse identity with equality, and to fail in using law as an active instrument to promote both freedom and equality. Nearly every law is based on classification of some kind. There are laws for doctors and lawyers, for motorists and airplane pilots, and they are not the same. Legal classifications of business and the professions for purposes of regulation and taxation are so numerous and complex that they make your head swim. People are classified for tax purposes, according to the source and size of their incomes and their family or business responsibilities. They are classified for voting and for holding office, for military service and compulsory education.

Classification, as such, does not deny equal protection of the laws. On the contrary, it is essential to equal protection, if we are not to deny equality by treating persons with different needs and aspirations as though they were identical. Legal classification, however, must be reasonable and not arbitrary. In general, classifications based on skill or competence, on age and education, on common needs and interests will normally be regarded as reasonable. These are matters over which individuals themselves may exercise a large measure of control. But legal classifications on the basis of attributes over which the individual has no control, or only slight control at best, or on attitudes and beliefs that touch his private conscience, are looked upon with suspicion. Hence laws based on race or ethnic origin or religion are particularly odious.

It was to prevent such classification or discrimination that the Constitution provides that (1) no religious test for public office shall ever be required; (2) no laws shall be passed respecting the establishment of a religion or prohibiting the free exercise thereof; (3) the right to vote shall not be denied because of race, color, previous condition of servitude, or sex; (4) no state shall deny to any person within its jurisdiction the equal protection of the laws. That is why, in the avalanche of litigation that involves constitutional issues, few laws are set aside as violations of "equal protection," except where classification is on the basis of race, religion, or nationality, or otherwise "unreasonable."

Laws limiting the right to vote and to certain kinds of public employment to citizens have been upheld as not denying equal protection of the laws to aliens. But where such distinctions have been extended by law to private employment, to the ownership of property, to equal access to certain common callings, and to jury service, they have been set aside as a denial of equal protection of the laws.[85]

The most prolific source of conflict and litigation under the equal protection clause has been legislation designed to deny Negroes the right

---

[85] See, for example, *Yick Wo* v. *Hopkins*, 118 U.S. 356 (1886); *Santa Clara County* v. *Southern Pacific Ry. Co.*, 118 U.S. 394 (1886). *Truax* v. *Raich*, 239 U.S. 33 (1915); *Strandis* v. *Virginia*, 100 U.S. 303 (1899).

to vote and to segregate them in their places of residence, in the use of transportation and other public or quasi-public services, and in public schools.[86] Most of such legislation is a part of our unhappy heritage of slavery, the Civil War, and Reconstruction. It is based mainly on ideas of racial superiority and inferiority which are rooted in a primitive xenophobia or a none too subtle rationalization of status hunger on the part of the white population. As a result, partly by law and partly by the force of public opinion, Negroes in many places—both North and South—have been compelled to live in segregated neighborhoods, go to segregated schools, ride in segregated trains, street cars and buses, eat in segregated restaurants, seek recreation in segregated parks and playgrounds, and even worship God in segregated Sunday schools and churches.

The Doctrine of State Action

Not all of this has been accomplished by law, and, in general, the courts have held that only racial segregation provided for, sponsored, or encouraged by law may be challenged under the equal protection clause. The Fourteenth Amendment says, *"No State* shall . . . deny to any person within its jurisdiction the equal protection of the laws." Hence the Court has said it is only racial discrimination accomplished by state action that may be successfully challenged in the courts. Discrimination by private persons, not acting under law or under the color of law, would not fall under the ban of the Fourteenth Amendment.

Following the Civil War, in no less than seven civil rights acts, Congress undertook to protect the legal, political, and civil rights of Negroes. Most important of these acts were (1) the Act of April 9, 1866, when only the Thirteenth Amendment was in effect, to "Protect all persons in the United States in their Civil Rights," (2) the Act of May 31, 1870, following ratification of the Fourteenth and Fifteenth Amendments, to "Enforce the Right of citizens of the United States to vote in the several States of the Union," and (3) the Act of March 1, 1875, to "Protect all Citizens in their Civil and Legal Rights." Although cast in general terms the central purpose of these laws was to protect the civil rights of Negro citizens from interference, not only by state action but by illegal acts of private persons or groups. The first of these was to insure to everyone, regardless of race, the right "to make and enforce contracts, to sue, be parties and give evidence, to inherit, purchase, lease, sell, hold, and convey real and personal property, and to full and equal benefit of all laws and proceedings for the security of persons and property." The second act undertook to protect the right to vote, to provide federal machinery for supervising elections in the states, and to impose penalties for any interference with the exercise of suffrage because of race or color.

[86] See Chapter 7 for a discussion of the Negroes' struggle for the right to vote.

The Civil Rights Act of 1875 declared that "all persons within the juris-diction of the United States shall be entitled to the full and equal en-joyment of . . . public conveyances on land and water, theaters and other places of amusement, subject only to the conditions and limitations established by law and applicable alike to citizens of every race and color. . . ." The act was directed against discriminatory acts, not only by the states, but by private persons.[87]

For many reasons these laws were either stillborn or smothered in the passionate and bitter conflicts of the Reconstruction years. The Su-preme Court helped in this process by holding, in the so-called Slaughter-House and Civil Rights Cases, that Congress had no power to protect Negroes in their right to vote, or from discrimination by private per-sons.[88] The Fourteenth Amendment, the Court said, applies to state action, not action by private persons. "It is state action that is pro-hibited," said the Court. "Individual invasion of individual rights is not the subject matter of the Amendment."

For many years after these decisions the Supreme Court not only refused to extend the equal protection clause to acts of private persons, but gave its imprimatur to state acts *requiring* racial segregation and discrimination. Indeed, in a decision antedating the Civil Rights cases, it frowned upon state action designed to prevent such discrimination. When Louisiana, by statute in 1869, forbade carriers in the state to segregate passengers by race or color, the Supreme Court held it to be an unconstitutional burden on interstate commerce.[89] On the other hand, a Mississippi law which required separate accommodations for Negroes and whites on railroads was upheld by the Court.[90] And in 1896, in *Plessy* v. *Ferguson,* the Court gave its approval to a Louisiana law of 1890 requir-ing separate but equal accommodations for Negroes and whites on rail-roads operating within the State.[91]

This decision furnished constitutional absolution for racial segrega-tion by law for more than 50 years. "The object of the 14th Amend-ment," said the Court, "was undoubtedly to enforce equality of the two races before the law, but in the nature of things it could not have been

[87] See Thomas Emerson and David Haber, *Political and Civil Rights in the United States* (Buffalo, N.Y.: Dennis, 1952) , pp. 12–35.

[88] See *Slaughter-House Cases,* 16 Wall. 36 (1873) ; *Civil Rights Cases,* 109 U.S. 27 (1883) .

[89] *Hall* v. *De Cuir,* 95 U.S. 85 (1878) . See, however, *Morgan* v. *Virginia,* 328 U.S. 373 (1946) , where a Virginia statute requiring segregation of passengers was declared unconstitutional as a burden on interstate commerce.

[90] *Louisville, N.O. and Texas Ry. Co.* v. *Mississippi,* 133 U.S. 587 (1890) .

[91] The Louisiana law provided that "all railway companies carrying passengers in their coaches in this State shall provide equal but separate accommodations for the white and colored races by providing two or more passenger coaches for each passenger train, or by dividing the passenger coaches by a partition so as to secure separate accommodations. . . . No person . . . shall be admitted to occupy seats in coaches other than the area assigned to them on account of the race they belong to." (*sic*) *Plessy* v. *Ferguson,* 163 U.S. 537 (1896) .

intended to abolish distinctions based upon color, or to enforce social, as distinguished from political, equality, or a commingling of the two races upon terms unsatisfactory to either." Racial segregation, said the Court, does not "necessarily imply the inferiority of either race to the other . . . Enforced separation does not stamp the colored race with the badge of inferiority." If it does, the Court said, "it is not by reason of anything found in the Act, but solely because the colored race chooses to put that construction on it." Besides, the Court continued, "legislation is powerless to eradicate racial instincts or to abolish distinctions based upon physical differences, and the attempt to do so can only result in accentuating the difficulties of the present situation."

For these and other similar reasons, the Court held that "a law which authorizes or even requires the separation of the two races in public conveyances" is [not] such an unreasonable or arbitrary classification as to deny to any person equal protection of the laws. Justice Harlan entered a lone dissent to this decision and to this argument. "Our Constitution," he said, "is color blind, and neither knows nor tolerates classes among citizens. In respect of civil rights, all citizens are equal before the law . . . The arbitrary separation of citizens, on the basis of race, is a badge of servitude wholly inconsistent with . . . equality before the law established by the Constitution."

Following *Plessy* v. *Ferguson,* a vast and complex system of social segregation was established by law in many states, not only on railroads, but on cars and buses and other public conveyances, and in public schools and other public facilities as well. Theoretically and legally this system was defended and upheld on the theory that if such facilities for whites and Negroes were *separate but equal,* segregation did not deny equal protection of the laws.

By 1950 twenty-one states and the District of Columbia required or permitted social segregation in schools. Many states' laws also required racial segregation in other public facilities. In fact, of course, facilities were not equal, although they were separate. Appropriations for Negro schools, for Negro parks and playgrounds, for Negro common rooms in railroad and bus stations and other public places, health and hospital facilities, Negro wage rates and job security—both in public and private employment—were poorer than those for whites. Table 18–1 illustrates this inequality.

Judicial Lawmaking

For nearly 75 years following the legal emasculation of its initial Civil Rights Acts, Congress made no serious effort to enact legislation to translate the equal protection clause of the Fourteenth Amendment into a meaningful safeguard against racial segregation and discrimination. Deadlocked by a built-in minority "veto system" and by a compact bloc

TABLE 18–1
Expenditures per White and Negro Pupil in Segregated Schools,
1946 and 1948–1949

	White	Negro		White	Negro
*Alabama	120.50	81.83	*North Carolina	138.85	115.02
*Arkansas	111.15	62.22	*Oklahoma	166.31	175.32
*Delaware	188.35	131.67	*South Carolina	148.48	69.65
Florida	134.76	61.75	Tennessee	80.30	55.44
Georgia	82.57	31.14	Texas	123.14	91.22
Kentucky	90.05	98.35	Virginia	104.29	53.15
Louisiana	136.12	43.81	West Virginia	100.63	111.47
Maryland	130.40	110.66	*District of	281.41	210.42
*Mississippi	122.74	28.81	Columbia		
Missouri	137.68	133.35			

* Figures are for 1948–1949. All other for 1946.

SOURCE: Monroe Berger, *Equality by Statute* (New York: Columbia University Press, 1952) , p. 56. Reprinted by permission of Columbia University Press.

of members from segregationist states and districts, the Congress lapsed into impotence or apathy and ceased even to be an effective forum for debate on civil rights issues. During these years the main struggle was carried on in the courts, and it was in the Supreme Court, after many years of indecision and frustration, that the first victories were won.

It was, however, nearly 60 years before Justice Harlan's dissenting opinion in *Plessy* v. *Ferguson* became the unanimous opinion of the Supreme Court. In 1954 in the case of *Brown* v. *Board of Education of Topeka* a unanimous Court held that "in the field of public education, the doctrine of 'separate but equal' has no place. Separate educational facilities are inherently unequal and hence deprive persons of the equal protection of the laws guaranteed by the 14th Amendment." Unlike other cases, said the Court, "there are findings below that the Negro and white schools involved [here] have been equalized, or are being equalized, with respect to buildings, curricula, qualifications and salaries of teachers and other tangible factors." The decision, therefore, did not turn on any inequality of facilities but on "the effect of segregation itself on public education." Even the Kansas court which had upheld racial segregation in the Topeka schools admitted that:

> Segregation of White and Colored children in public schools has a detrimental effect upon the colored children . . . for the policy of separating the races is usually interpreted as denoting the inferiority of the Negro group. A sense of inferiority affects the motivation of the child to learn. Segregation with the sanction of the law, therefore, has a tendency to retard the education . . . development of Negro children and to deprive them of some of the benefits they would receive in a racially integrated school system.

A storm of rage and abuse followed the decision in this case. There were demands for reform of the Supreme Court and for Chief Justice Warren's impeachment. The Court, and especially the Chief Justice, were denounced as "revolutionaries" who, with a stroke of the pen, were destroying a major pillar of society and a hundred years of established custom and tradition. The fact is, however, that the decision of the Supreme Court, in *Brown* v. *Board of Education of Topeka,* was not the result of a sudden judicial aberration or usurpation of power. Since 1938 there had been many harbingers of some such change in the rule established in *Plessy* v. *Ferguson.* Indeed, as early as 1917 laws providing for racial segregation in residential areas were held unconstitutional as a denial of equal protection of the laws.[92]

Moreover, in subsequent cases it was held that although *private* covenants forbidding the sale of real property to persons of certain race or color were lawful, such restrictions cannot be enforced in the courts. Decisions upholding such racial covenants were a form of state action prohibited by the equal protection and due process clauses of the Fourteenth Amendment.[93] In another series of decisions from 1927 to 1953 the Supreme Court overruled some of the more obvious devices used to deny Negroes the right to vote.[94] In the field of education important cases compelled Missouri, Oklahoma, and Texas to admit Negroes to university law schools and to graduate school, where in fact other facilities of equal quality for Negroes were not available and could not, under a system of racial segregation, be made available. In two of these cases, (*Sweatt* v. *Painter* and *McLaurin* v. *Oklahoma,* decided in 1950) the Court seemed to be feeling its way toward a position close to that announced in *Brown* v. *Board of Education of Topeka* in 1954. In both these cases the Court held that full participation with other students, without regard to race or color, was an essential factor in the learning process. Students could not learn, removed from the interplay of ideas and the exchange of views that characterize full participation in a nonsegregated environment. Moreover, in the Texas case (*Sweatt* v. *Painter*), the Court "expressly reserved decision on the question whether *Plessy* v. *Ferguson* should be held inapplicable to public education."[95]

Aftermath

The decision in *Brown* v. *Board of Education of Topeka* illustrates in a dramatic way the essentially political nature of many Supreme Court

---

[92] *Buchanan* v. *Warley,* 245 U.S. 60 (1917).

[93] *Corregan* v. *Buckley,* 271 U.S. 323 (1926); *Shelly* v. *Kraemer,* 334 U.S. 1 (1948).

[94] See *Nixon* v. *Herndon,* 273 U.S. 536 (1927); *Nixon* v. *Condon,* 286 U.S. 73 (1932); *United States* v. *Classic,* 213 U.S. 209 (1941); *Smith* v. *Allwright,* 321 U.S. 649 (1944); *Terry* v. *Adams,* 345 U.S. 461 (1953). See also Chapter 7 for a discussion of these cases.

[95] *Missouri* ex rel *Gaines* v. *Canada,* 305 U.S. 337 (1938); *McLaurin* v. *Oklahoma Board of Regents,* 339 U.S. (1950); *Sweatt* v. *Painter,* 339 U.S. 629 (1950).

decisions. For all practical purposes the Court was not only deciding a "case or controversy" arising under the equal protection clause but was establishing a new legal norm to govern interracial relations, a role that one usually associates with the legislative branch of government. Although both the President and the Congress had made a number of furtive efforts to deal with other aspects of this problem, little tangible progress had been made. Caught in the cross-currents of interfactional conflict and immobilized by a minority veto system under which control of the legislative process was largely in the hands of leaders unfriendly to civil rights legislation, neither Congress nor the President had been able to act. It was into this power vacuum, so to speak, that the Supreme Court moved to face bitter denunciation not only from White Citizens Councils and the Ku Klux Klan, but also from more conservative leaders who felt that the Court had "gone too far."[96]

In doing so, it set off a political chain reaction of expectation and demand among Negroes and whites and civil rights protagonists that has not yet run its course. A new civil rights movement was launched under the leadership of long-established organizations such as the National Association for the Advancement of Colored People, and the Urban League, and new and more militant groups, including the Southern Christian Leadership Conference, the Congress of Racial Equality

[96] Some civil rights achievements by Presidents and Congress prior to 1954 would include (1) the creation by Attorney General Murphy of a Civil Liberties unit in the Criminal Division of the Department of Justice in 1939; (2) the establishment, by executive order and under pressure from Negro leaders, of a Fair Employment Practices Committee by President Roosevelt in 1941, a committee which died for lack of funds in 1946; (3) the banning of racial discrimination in the armed services and on work done under federal government contracts, by executive order of President Truman, following defeat of an antisegregation amendment to the Selective Service Act in 1948.

For the most part, however, in the long period from the post-Civil War Civil Rights' Acts to 1954, the legislative and executive civil rights output was unimpressive. Although President Roosevelt had accomplished something with his Committee on Fair Employment Practices, he did not even recommend any significant civil rights legislation. On February 2, 1948, President Truman submitted to Congress a civil rights program of legislation to (1) establish a permanent Commission on Civil Rights, a Joint Congressional Committee on Civil Rights, and a Civil Rights Division in the Department of Justice; (2) strengthen existing civil rights statutes; (3) provide federal protection against lynching; (4) provide federal protection of the right to vote; (5) establish a permanent Fair Employment Practices Commission; (6) prohibit segregation and discrimination in interstate transportation facilities.

It was this program that led to the bitter battle over civil rights in the Democratic National Convention in 1948, the bolt of the southern delegates, and the nomination of Strom Thurmond as the party's candidate for President that year. In spite of Mr. Truman's dramatic and surprise re-election, he was never able to get his civil rights program through Congress. President Eisenhower continued the civil rights executive orders of President Truman and added his voice in support of many of his predecessor's recommendations, but they too found Congress unreceptive and unresponsive. In Congress itself during these years virtually all efforts to enact legislation to outlaw lynching, poll taxes, racial discrimination in voting, transportation, and employment failed in the face of opposition from conservative Republican leaders and a Dixiecrat or quasi-Dixiecrat bloc of southern Democrats. See *Congress and the Nation 1945–1964* (Washington, D.C.: Congressional Quarterly Service, 1965), pp. 1596–1642.

(CORE), and the Student Non-Violent Coordinating Committee (SNCC). Within all of these groups there were conservatives, moderates, and militants, and beyond them all were the so-called Black Muslims who talked of Negro superiority and separation from the white population. Demonstrations against both legal and *de facto* racial segregation and discrimination were organized throughout the country: "sit-ins" were organized to protest discrimination in restaurants, motels, hotels, public and private employment; "Freedom Rides," to defy racial segregation in public transportation facilities, mass picketing and buyers strikes against merchants, and other employers who allegedly practiced racial discrimination. Demands for racial integration in the schools, now ratified by the Supreme Court, were followed by demands for open housing, fair employment practices, and access to all public or quasi-public facilities of entertainment and recreation. "Freedom Marches" through racially segregated housing areas, and on state and national capitols, multiplied in nearly every state of the Union. When the militant civil rights demonstrants were met by even more militant official or unofficial segregationists, violence often occurred and the nation faced what many called a third American revolution.[97]

On the legislative front, a so-called Leadership Conference of civil rights groups translated the pressure and turbulence of the streets into demands for official action by both State and Federal authorities to insure equal protection of the laws to all persons, regardless of race, religion, or ethnic origin.[98] We cannot here review the history or evaluate the results of this new civil rights movement beyond noting some of the major official acts that have been taken since 1954. In 1957, on the recommendation of President Eisenhower, Congress adopted the first Civil Rights Act since 1875. This act established the United States Commission on Civil Rights as an independent agency in the Executive Office of the President, and a Civil Rights Division in the Department of Justice. It also gave to the Attorney General power to "file civil suits for injunctions against obstruction or deprivation of civil rights." The act fell short of the demands made by civil rights protagonists, but it marked a hopeful beginning. In February, 1959, President Eisenhower submitted

[97] See William Brink and Louis Harris, *The Negro Revolution in America* (New York: Simon and Schuster, 1964); Hubert Humphrey (ed.), *School Desgregation, Documents and Commentaries* (New York: Crowell, 1964); E. A. Essien-Udom, *Black Nationalism* (New York: Dell, 1962).

[98] Included in this Leadership Conference are The NAACP; National Urban League; Congress of Racial Equality; Southern Christian Leadership Conference; Southern Regional Council; Student Non-Violent Coordinating Committee; Negro American Labor Council; AFL-CIO; eight national religious groups, including National Council of Churches of Christ, Catholic Conference for Inter-racial Justice, National (Jewish) Community Relations Advisory Council, and six other Jewish groups. In addition to these are the Americans for Democratic Action, American Civil Liberties Union, Japanese-American Citizens League, Women's International League for Peace and Freedom, and the American Veterans Committee.

a seven-point program to add new legislation to the Civil Rights Act of 1957 and this bore fruit in the Civil Rights Act of 1960, the main provision of which authorized federal courts to appoint referees to help Negroes to register and vote, and provided criminal penalties for bombings, bomb threats, and mob action to obstruct court orders.

Civil Rights Act of 1964

Not satisfied with these steps toward what they regarded as "full equality" or "first class citizenship" under the law, civil rights leaders intensified their efforts for new legislation and more vigorous enforcement of existing laws and executive orders. By the end of 1963, it was estimated that there had been mass civil rights demonstrations in over 800 cities and towns. And on August 28, more than 200,000 persons joined in a "March on Washington for Jobs and Freedom" to listen to an eloquent appeal by Martin Luther King of the Southern Christian Leadership Conference and other civil rights leaders in the Mall facing the Lincoln Memorial. More specifically, their demands included (1) more effective legislation to protect Negro citizens in their right to vote, (2) federal financial and technical assistance to effect desegregation in public schools, with penalties for failure to desegregate, (3) legislation to guarantee equal access by Negroes to public accommodations, and (4) more effective legislation against racial discrimination in housing and employment.

Most of these demands were incorporated in legislation recommended by President Kennedy in June, 1963, and embodied in the Civil Rights Act of 1964 which was signed into law in July of that year by President Johnson. Described as "the most far-reaching civil rights legislation since the Reconstruction Era," this act provided for

> New [and more drastic measures] to . . . guarantee Negroes the right to vote; [equal] access to public accommodations such as hotels, motels, restaurants and places of amusement; [direct Federal intervention] to sue to desegregate public facilities and schools; new powers and an extended life to the Civil Rights Commission; [denial or withdrawal] of Federal funds . . . where programs [are] administered discriminatorily; [requires] most companies and labor unions to grant equal employment opportunity; [establishment of] a new Community Relations Service to help work out civil rights problems; the Census Bureau to gather voting statistics by race; authorized the Justice Department to enter into pending civil rights cases.[99]

Congress found its authority to pass this most comprehensive of all civil rights acts, not under the equal protection or due process clauses of the Constitution, but under its powers to regulate commerce. The act was immediately challenged and unanimously sustained by the Supreme

---

[99] This summary is from *Congress and the Nation, op. cit.,* p. 1635.

Court in the same year it became a law. "The power of Congress over interstate commerce," said the Court, "is not confined to commerce among the States. It extends to those activities intrastate which so affect interstate commerce . . . as to make regulation of them appropriate means to the attainment of a legitimate end, the exercise of the granted power of Congress to regulate interstate commerce." At the same time, by a 5 to 4 vote, the Court "construed the Civil Rights Act of 1964 retroactively to bar prosecution of sit-in demonstrators who had tried peacefully before the Act's passage to desegregate establishments now covered by the Act."

Besides the Civil Rights Acts of 1957, 1960, and 1964, there were other steps taken to extend equal protection of the laws to the 22 million Negroes living not only in the South but in nearly every state and especially in the great metropolitan centers, both North and South. The Department of Health, Education, and Welfare, for example, made racial desegregation a condition for the receipt of federal funds in so-called "impacted" school districts. President Kennedy, by executive order, barred racial discrimination in federally assisted housing. And in 1964 the Twenty-fourth Amendment was added to the Constitution, prohibiting poll taxes as a requirement for voting in federal elections. Nor was the Supreme Court inactive during this period. In a number of decisions, it continued to insist upon racial desegregation of public schools against the delaying, evasive, and even defiant acts of some state and local authorities. "While giving weight," said the Court, "to [local] public and private considerations, the courts will require . . . a prompt and reasonable start toward full compliance with our May 17, 1954, ruling."[100]

More Recent Action

Notwithstanding the impressive record of legislation and executive action to insure in greater measure equal protection of the laws for colored, as well as white persons, the struggle for civil rights goes on. In the Voting Rights Act of 1965 Congress put real teeth into earlier legislation designed to insure Negroes the right to vote. The intervention of examiners and registrars appointed by the Department of Justice under this act has made it possible for thousands of Negroes, formerly denied, to register and vote.[101] On April 28, 1966, President Johnson again ad-

---

100 See *Brown* v. *Board of Education of Topeka*, 349 U.S. 294 (1955); *Cooper* v. *Aaron*, 358 U.S. 1 (1958); *Griffin* v. *School Board of Prince Edward County*, 377 U.S. 218 (1964); *Heart of Atlanta Motel* v. *United States*, 379 U.S. 241 (1964); *Katzenbach* v. *McClumy*, 379 U.S. 294 (1964); *Hamm* v. *City of Rock Hill*, 379 U.S. 306 (1964). See also Harold H. Spaeth, *The Warren Court, op. cit.*, p. 145.

101 See Peter Odegard, *American Government: Readings and Documents* (New York: Harper & Row, 1966), pp. 88 and 431, for the text of the Court's opinion upholding the Voting Rights Act and Civil Rights Act of 1964.

dressed Congress on the need for additional legislation and proposed the enactment of the Civil Rights Act of 1966. This measure, as proposed, would have prohibited racial discrimination in the selection of both grand and petit juries in both state and federal courts, authorized the Attorney General to bring suit to prevent "official or private intimidation of persons" because of race in schools, colleges, or other facilities owned or operated by state or local authorities, and prohibited "discrimination on the basis of race, color, religion, or national origin in the sale or rental of any house or vacant land intended for housing." Although a modified version of this proposal was passed in the House of Representatives, a Senate filibuster resulted in its death in the upper chamber.

Although President Johnson included requests for open housing legislation in his proposals to Congress at the beginning of both the 1967 and 1968 sessions, prospects for passage did not appear bright in the face of a Ninetieth Congress which was considerably more conservative than the Eighty-ninth. However, the shock of the assassination of the Reverend Dr. Martin Luther King, Jr., in Memphis, Tennessee, on April 4, 1968, led to an immediate congressional response. On April 11 the President was able to sign the 1968 Civil Rights Act which contained the following general provisions:

1. Open Housing—Prohibited refusal to sell or rent a dwelling because of race, color, religion or national origin. Also prohibited discrimination in terms, conditions or privileges of sale or rental of dwellings, in advertising of sales or rentals of dwellings, "blockbusting", misrepresentation of availability of dwellings, and in the conditions of loans or brokerage services. The Act is phrased in such a way that 80 per cent of all housing sold or rented after 1969 will be covered.

2. Civil Rights Protections—Provided criminal penalties for injury, intimidation or interfering with any person because he is voting or campaigning as a candidate in an election, serving on a federal jury, working for a federal agency or participating in a federal program, attending a public school or college, participating in a state or locally administered program, working for state, local or private employer, joining or using the services of a labor union, serving on a state jury, using a common carrier or public accomodations, or, during a riot, with a shopkeeper or other person engaged in business or commerce.

3. Antiriot, Civil Obedience—Provided federal penalties for persons traveling in interstate commerce with the intent to incite, organize, encourage or take part in a riot or to assist others in doing so. Also provided penalties for persons who teach the use, application or making of a firearm or explosive with the knowledge or intent that these instruments would be used in a civil disorder, and for obstruction or interfering with a law enforcement officer or fireman performing official duties during a civil disorder.

4. Rights of Indians—Prohibited tribal governments from making or enforcing laws violating specified constitutional rights, and directed the

Secretary of the Interior to recommend a model code governing the Courts of Indian Offenses on Indian Reservations, authorized the states to assume jurisdiction in certain types of cases in Indian country, and provided for a more rapid approval of agreements for employment of legal counsel for an Indian or Indian tribe.

In 1947 President Truman's Committee on Civil Rights, on the theory that "every human being has an essential dignity and integrity which must be respected and safeguarded," outlined four basic rights which it deemed essential to equal protection of the laws. These were

1. *The right to safety and security of the person,* not alone from mob violence and terror, but from the more subtle insecurity that comes from racial discrimination and condescension.
2. *The right to citizenship and its privileges,* including the right to vote and to hold office without regard to race or class and free from arbitrary literacy tests, poll taxes and other devices designed to keep colored voters from the polls.
3. *The right to freedom of conscience and expression,* including all the rights set forth in the First Amendment. In many communities today, Negroes are not free to speak their minds without fear.
4. *The right to equality of opportunity,* including accesss to education, employment, housing, health, recreation and transportation and to public places with complete disregard for race, color and national origin.

Even though recent legislation and Court decisions have made inroads into these areas of unfulfilled civil rights, to accomplish all this will, no doubt, require new legislation and more vigorous enforcement of present laws. But ultimately it will also require a new outlook—"a climate of public opinion which will outlaw individual abridgment of personal freedom, a climate of opinion as free from racial prejudice as we can make it."

THE STATES IN
THE FEDERAL SYSTEM

To the uninitiated, government at the grass roots in the United States is a complex wilderness of power centers, both public and private, that all but defies analysis. Nobody knows for sure at any given time how many units of government bear allegiance to the Constitution and the Stars and Stripes. Some years ago one careful count found more than 150,000, or one unit of government, for approximately every 700 people. A more recent estimate puts the number closer to 90,000, reflecting the trend toward consolidation at the local level. Included were (1) the government of the United States, (2) fifty state governments, (3) some 3,000 counties, (4) more than 18,000 municipalities, (5) approximately 17,000 towns and townships, (6) nearly 18,000 special districts, and (7) about 30,000 school districts. The total number changes from year to year but will no doubt remain in the neighborhood of 90,000 units for some time to come. Changes in the size, location, and mobility of the population, the steady expansion of governmental services of all kinds, economic and technological change, governmental reorganization and reform, are among the factors involved.[1] The pattern is by no means uniform throughout the country and seems to bear no necessary relation to population density. Thus Nebraska with a population of less than one and a half million in 1964 had more than 5,000 units of government, one for approximately every 300 people, whereas Rhode Island managed its affairs with only 97 units, or one for roughly each 9,000 of population. New York with one unit for each 4,000 people, and North Dakota, with one

---

[1] Most notable has been the decline in the number of school districts, which dropped from 71,000 in 1951–1952 to less than 29,000 in 1964–1965. See *The Book of the States, 1966–1967* (Chicago: The Council of State Governments, 1966), p. 207.

for each 200 people indicate how wide the variation can be from state to state.[2]

☆ *STATE SOVEREIGNTY*

To examine in detail the structure and functions of all governments in the United States is beyond the scope of this volume. Most important of these, below the level of the central government, are the states. In discussions of state government, one encounters two quite different propositions. One is that the "sovereign" states are in a bitter struggle for survival with a political Moloch in Washington called the federal government and that if we are to keep our freedom and save our American way of life, we must restore the powers of the states and stop the centripetal forces that are stripping the states of their sovereignty and independence.

A second argument, which in a strange sort of way complements the first one, is that in an age of jet planes and instantaneous communication, of big business and big labor, the states have lost any real reason for their continued existence. We ought to reorganize our federal system, it is said, on the basis of new administrative and political areas corresponding to geopolitical or demographic regions. Contradictory as they seem at first glance, these two ideas, of the states as sovereign political communities and as unrealistic, outmoded administrative and political areas, have a strange affinity. For both assume that the states are in danger of being swallowed up by a monster known as Uncle Sam.

What about the notion that the states are "sovereign" political communities whose sovereignty is in jeopardy from federal encroachment? In the Articles of Confederation occurs a phrase reading: "Each state retains its sovereignty, freedom, and independence and every power, jurisdiction, and right, which is not by this Confederation expressly delegated to the United States in Congress assembled." The idea of the Confederation as a Union of "sovereign" states persisted and has been asserted even under the Constitution. Yet it is doubtful that at any time before, during, or after the Revolution, the several states were vested with "sovereignty, freedom, and independence." They were not sovereign and independent as colonies under the British Crown. Nor did they become so by the Declaration of Independence. It was not as separate and sovereign states that they cut their ties with the Mother Country, but as "the representatives of the United States of America in General Congress Assembled."

The states were not sovereign during the Revolution, for it was the Congress that carried on the war, made treaties and exercised all the powers of external sovereignty. Although the Articles of Confederation

2 See *Governmental Units in the United States* (Bureau of the Census, 1964).

declared that "each state retains its sovereignty, freedom, and independence," even in that document the states were stripped of all the essential attributes of sovereignty. They were forbidden to conduct foreign relations, to make treaties even among themselves, to wage war or engage in acts of war without the consent of Congress.

The fact is that the states were "sovereign" or "independent" only in a literary and not in a legal sense. Nevertheless the myth of "sovereignty, independence, and freedom" persisted and has been a source of conflict in American constitutional development. Yet there would seem to be no reasonable doubt that the Constitutional Convention sought to establish within the limits of the powers conferred, a single sovereignty in the government of the United States, and not what is known in some circles as plural or divided sovereignty.

The Convention was a victory for those who believed the Revolution was indeed the birth of a nation or, as the Supreme Court described it in 1869 in *Texas* v. *White,* as an "indestructible union of indestructible states."

An examination of the Constitution itself supports this view. To begin with, the Preamble declares that it is "We the People"—not we the confederated representatives of thirteen sovereign states—who "ordain and establish this Constitution for the United States of America."[3] To be sure, the powers of Congress were enumerated and presumably limited by this enumeration. But the powers conferred included virtually all those customarily associated with a unified sovereign state.

The dependent position of the states in the new Union was emphasized by the provision in Article IV that the "central government shall guarantee to every state in this Union a Republican Form of government."

To remove any doubt about the supremacy of the central government, Article VI of the Constitution provides that "This Constitution and the Laws of the United States which shall be made in Pursuance thereof; and all Treaties made or which shall be made under the Authority of the United States, shall be the supreme Law of the Land; and the Judges in every State shall be bound thereby, any Thing in the Constitution or Laws of any State to the Contrary notwithstanding."

The Tenth Amendment has often been cited to support the theory of plural or divided sovereignty. This amendment declares that "the powers not delegated to the United States by the Constitution, nor prohibited by it to the States, are reserved to the States respectively, or to the people." It would take us too far afield to examine the many and diverse interpretations of this amendment. Suffice it to say at this point that it does not constitute a limitation on the sovereign powers of the central government and was not designed to do so. A vain attempt was

[3] In ratifying the Constitution, it was not to the state legislatures but to specially elected conventions that the framers turned.

made in 1923[4] to invalidate federal grants-in-aid on the ground that they unconstitutionally invaded the powers reserved to the states in the Tenth Amendment. The Court gave no support to this contention, nor to a similar argument in 1941 when the Tenth Amendment was cited in an attempt to overthrow the Federal Fair Labor Standards Act of 1938. The Tenth Amendment, the Court has said,

> states but a truism that all is retained which has not been surrendered. There is nothing in the history of its adoption to suggest that it was more than declaratory of the relationship between the national and state governments as it had been established by the Constitution before the amendment or that its purpose was other than to allay fears that the new national government might seek to exercise powers not granted and that the states might not be able to exercise fully their reserved powers. From the beginning . . . the amendment has been construed as not depriving the national government of authority to resort to all means for the exercise of a granted power which are appropriate and plainly adapted to the permitted end.[5]

The point is that the American Federal Union is not based on a compact among independent sovereign states but on a Constitution ratified by "We the people of the United States," united for certain purposes outlined in the Constitution. To achieve these ends we the people have delegated—often in very general tems—broad but limited powers to the central government, reserving other powers "to the States *or to the people.*"

However plausible the argument might be that the Constitution was a compact among the original states, it would be hard to sustain this argument with reference to the 37 states that have entered the Union since 1789. And, since each state, whatever the date of its admission, has all the rights of every other state, it would seem to follow that none has sovereign powers. The fact is that the states admitted since 1789 are not the creators, but the creatures, of the United States. Upon coming into the Union these territories had nothing to delegate since whatever powers they have as states comes from the fact of their admission to the Union.

Once in the Union, to be sure, they enjoy full equality with all other states, although the Constitution does not, in so many words, guarantee this. Section 3 of Article IV merely says: "New States may be admitted by the Congress into this Union. . . ." But this same article includes certain guarantees that "no new State shall be formed . . . within the Jurisdiction of any other (existing) State" and that no state may "be formed by the Junction of two or more States, or Parts of States, without the Consent of the Legislatures of the States concerned as well as of the Congress." And Article V provides that no state "without its consent" can be

4 *Massachusetts v. Mellon,* 262 U.S. 447 (1923).
5 *United States v. Darby,* 312 U.S. 100 (1941).

deprived of its equal suffrage in the Senate. It is, however, only when the state has become a full-fledged member of the Union that these guarantees apply. Prior to statehood the Constitution (Section 3, Article IV) clearly gives Congress power to "dispose of and make all needful Rules and Regulations respecting the Territory or other Property belonging to the United States."

Can Congress, therefore, attach conditions to the admission of a state that would impair its full equality with other states? Apparently not, although Congress has tried to do so.[6] The Joint Resolution of Congress, admitting Texas to the Union in 1845, explicitly provided that the new state was to be admitted on an "equal footing with the original states in all respects whatever. . . ." Did this imply that it might have been admitted conditionally had Congress wished to do so? On several occasions Congress has, in fact, attached conditions to the admission of new states. When Oklahoma was admitted in 1907, Congress stipulated that the state capital be located at Guthrie, a stipulation that was promptly ignored by Oklahoma once it had been admitted to the Union. And in the case of *Coyle* v. *Smith,* the Supreme Court held the congressional stipulation to be unconstitutional. "This Union," said the Court, "was and is a union of states, equal in power, dignity, and authority, each competent to exert that residuum of [power] sovereignty not delegated to the United States by the Constitution itself." In August, 1911, President Taft vetoed the joint resolution of Congress admitting Arizona to the Union. The proposed constitution of Arizona contained a provision for the recall of judges, a practice which the President said would impair the independence of the judiciary. Arizona thereupon removed the offending clause and was admitted (February, 1912), but almost at once restored the obnoxious provision to its constitution; and neither Congress nor the President could do anything about it.

Even valid statutes of Congress regulating a territory of the United States become inapplicable when the territory becomes a state, except when adopted by state law. New states, however, may not claim special rights not enjoyed by other states except by act of Congress. Even rights enjoyed as a territory before admission may have to be surrendered on admission to the Union. Texas, for example, as an independent republic,

---

[6] When Section 3 of Article IV was first reported to the Convention by the Committee on Detail, it read as follows: "New states shall be admitted on the same terms with the original states." But this guarantee of full equality for new states was eliminated, over the objection of James Madison. "The Western states," he said, "neither would nor ought to submit to a union which degraded them from an equal rank with the other states."

Although the Constitution does not expressly guarantee new states full equality with the older states, the Supreme Court has consistently held that "Equality of constitutional right and power is the condition of all the states of the Union, old and new."

See *Escanaba and L. M. Transportation Co.* v. *Chicago,* 107 U.S. 678 (1883).

could claim ownership and control of off-shore oil resources within a three-mile limit of ocean beyond the shoreline. After admission to the Union as a state, however, ownership of these resources was held to have passed to the United States.[7] "Since the original states had been found not to own the soil under the three-mile belt," said the Court, "Texas which [in fact] did own this soil before its annexation to the United States, was held to have surrendered its dominion and sovereignty over it upon entering the Union on terms of equality with the existing states." It required an affirmative act of Congress, therefore, to convey these off-shore oil lands to Texas and the other states having similar lands, an act which presumably Congress could repeal if it were so minded.

☆ THE VARIETY OF STATES

Although the states are equal under the law and the Constitution, they are by no means equal in other ways. Texas has over one hundred times the area of Delaware but is dwarfed by Alaska; and, as we have seen, sheer physical size creates its own problems of government.[8] California stretches for nearly 1,000 miles from Oregon to Mexico; and culturally and politically, northern California and southern California—roughly above and below the Tehachapi Mountains—are two states. Upstate New York and the metropolitan complex around the City of New York present similar contrasts. If Delaware is less than 1/100 the size of Texas, and has only 1/16 as many people as New York, it nevertheless stands near or at the top in terms of per capita income.

States vary in other important respects, too. Iowa has a selective service rejection rate of 32.8, Mississippi 74.2 (1964); in the per 100,000 murder rate (1963), Iowa is 1.3, New York 3.8, Delaware 4.6, and Mississippi and Alabama, over 10; in the percent of population classified as urban, New York has 85.5, California 86.4, and Mississippi only 27.9. States differ from one another in terms of topography, climate, natural resources, and demography—differences that find political expression in sectional or regional loyalties. The tidewater states of the South Atlantic shore are strikingly different in economics, politics, and cultural tradition from the states of the New England or even the Middle Atlantic groups. The states of the Mississippi Valley, of the Great Lakes shoreline, of the Great Plains and the high mountains of the West have fairly distinct interests. States differ in terms of the racial and religious composition of

---

[7] See *United States* v. *Texas,* 339 U.S. 207 (1950).

[8] Two states, California and Texas, embrace over 100 million acres; 11 states, over 50 million; 14, over 20 million; 3, more than 10 million; 4, over 5 million; 3, over 1 million. Alaska with 365 million leads, and Rhode Island with 677,000 is smallest.

their populations and in their political and civic culture.[9] The people of New York, Massachusetts, and Connecticut, for example, differ from those of Maine and Vermont as those of Washington and Oregon differ from the people of Georgia and Alabama. States differ in their *rate of growth* not only in terms of population but also in terms of per capita income and industrialization, as they differ in the age, occupational composition, and degree of union organization of their labor force. In educational expenditures per pupil, New York (1964) reported $790, Alaska $683, Connecticut $600, Arkansas $317, South Carolina $284, and Mississippi $273.

It is this variegated pattern that makes the study of government and politics in the several states so fascinating and so bewildering. It is this variety in Union, this diversity within a basic conformity, that gives significance and vitality to the American federal system. For, in spite of many similarities, the governments, the parties and pressure groups, and the political behavior of the several states are sufficiently different to make generalization risky and at best tentative. How different they can be one item alone may indicate. Per capita tax collections in New York, Delaware, Washington, and Nevada are roughly twice what they are in Virginia, Missouri, South Dakota, and New Hampshire, and nearly three times the rate in Nebraska.

These differences indicate that, within the general value system we call the American way of life, there are also important variations. In the northeastern states local tax support for elementary and secondary education is well established and fairly liberal, along with a strong tradition of private support and control of higher education. Colorado and Wisconsin, on the other hand, spend more than half of their state educational funds on their state universities. In the South, generally, a higher percentage of total state expenditures go for education than in the New England states, although per pupil expenditures are lower in the South. California spends one-third more for welfare than New York, but only 60 percent of what New York spends on public health. At the same time, California and New York spend about the same amount on education, but California spends nearly three times as much on higher education as any other state.

God and nature have not endowed the various states with equal resources of raw materials or of human resources. While the population of the country has more than doubled in the last fifty years, some states have remained stationary, while others—Florida and California, for

---

[9] Daniel Elazar has endeavored to classify states according to what he calls their Dominant Political Culture. Three main types of political culture are recognized, namely Moralistic (M) , Individualistic (I) , and Traditionalistic (T) ; the map on page 97 of his book indicates his classification of each state. See Daniel J. Elazar, *American Federalism: A View from the States* (New York: Crowell, 1966) , chap. 4.

example—have multiplied several times over. Half the people of the country now live in ten states. This differential growth has had a profound effect on the states. Mainly it has been due to internal migration rather than to immigration from abroad or natural increase. The mass movement of people to California and Florida, as well as the migration from farms to cities and from cities to suburbia, has been both cause and effect of dramatic cultural and political changes in every section of the country. Commodity cultures—the cotton belt, the wheat states, the cattle kingdom, the dairy states—have diversified. As new industries multiply and the demand for services increases, the composition of the labor force has changed until white-collar clerical, technical, and professional workers outnumber blue-collar workers. In Florida, Hawaii, Arizona, Nevada, and California, tourism has come to rival citrus fruits, sugar, pineapple, and even oil, corn, and cotton in the economy. Diversification and conformity by a curious paradox go along together. The striking diversity that used to distinguish one-commodity states is giving way to a more uniform economy based, paradoxically, on diversification within these same states and sections.

Not the least of these new forces at work has been government itself. Federal expenditures for national defense, reclamation, conservation, and other public works and services have become a major source of income for many states and for hundreds of local communities. Federal expenditures in 1963 as a percentage of total personal income varied from over 68 percent in Alaska and 42 percent in Utah to 17 percent in Delaware. In 14 states federal expenditures accounted for 20 to 40 percent of total personal income, whereas in 6 states the proportion was less than 20 percent. On a per capita basis, federal expenditure payments in 1963 varied from $1,891 in Alaska, $951 in Hawaii, and $896 in California to $439 in Vermont, $418 in Wisconsin, and $398 in Iowa. In Kansas, Arkansas, Virginia, Maryland, Georgia, Alabama, Mississippi, Oklahoma, New Mexico, Arizona, Wyoming, Washington, California, and Hawaii the percentage was between 30 and 40 percent, and in New York, Delaware, Wisconsin, Michigan, Illinois, and Nevada it was less than 20 percent.[10] Hawaii's three major private industries—sugar, pineapples, and tourists—combined are less than military expenditures in that state. A sudden major shift in the pattern of defense procurement may bring boom or bust to states in which defense industries are concentrated.[11] Many a state that was formerly a fief of some corporate giant has today become a fief of Uncle Sam, and most likely of the Department of Defense. We annually spend on military security alone more than the net income of all United States corporations, and the influence of this is

---

[10] See *Federal Expenditures to States and Regions,* Report of Subcommittee on Intergovernmental Relations of Senate Committee on Government Operations, June 26, 1966. 89th Congress, 2nd Sess.

[11] *The New York Times,* November 24, 1961, p. 15.

felt in every city hall and every state house, but by no means to the same degree or in the same way. Much depends on civic culture of the various communities.[12]

☆ STATES ARE IMPORTANT IN THE SCHEME OF THINGS

Because the states are not sovereign in any meaningful sense of that term, because they are not equal in population and resources, because the influence of the federal government is felt in every state and nearly every village, it does not follow that state and local governments are unimportant. Nor does it follow that they are mere pawns and puppets of Uncle Sam. In those aspects of government which most closely affect the average citizen, it is the states, counties, and cities that loom largest. Total government expenditures for certain public services indicate that state and local governments still account for by far the largest share. In 1962 state and local governments accounted for more than 70 percent of all government expenditures for domestic, nondefense purposes. And it is worth noting that whereas federal expenditures for domestic purposes had increased by some 150 percent between 1902 and 1962, state expenditures for these purposes, exclusive of those by local authorities, had increased by more than 270 percent.[13] Notwithstanding large federal appropriations since 1962 the major costs of education, fire and public protection, crime and correction, public health, parks and recreation, public welfare, and even highways are borne by state and local governments. The importance of state and local governments is revealed also in the figures in Tables 19–1 and 19–2, showing public employment in various public services. Only in national defense, the postal services, and agriculture and natural resources do federal employees exceed those of state and local governments. For other public services the figures as of October, 1964, were as shown in Tables 19–1 and 19–2.

Nor is this the whole story. The licensing and regulation of business, the professions, and other common callings is almost exclusively the re-

---

[12] See Daniel Elazar, *op. cit.*, esp. chap. 4, pp. 79–117.

[13] The same trend is to be seen in the growth of state and local indebtedness in recent years. Between 1946 and 1963 the per capita debt of state and local governments had increased from $120 to 467, or approximately 390 percent, while the per capita federal debt, for all purposes, actually declined from $2,034 in 1946 to $1,646 in 1963, a *decline* of nearly 19 percent. State and local governments now account for 22 percent of the total public debt as against only 5 percent in 1946. In his recent study on *Federalism* Professor William Riker reports that in the following areas state governments in 1964 exercised either exclusive or predominant responsibility: (a) Public Safety, (b) Property Rights, (c) Morality, (d) Utilities, (e) Education.

See Peter Vanderwiken, in the *Wall Street Journal*, February 2, 1964. See also F. Mosher and O. Poland, *The Costs of American Government* (New York: Dodd, Mead, 1964) , chap. 3, pp. 37–60.

TABLE 19–1
Public Employment in Various Public Services
(As of October, 1966)

	Federal	State and Local	State	Local
Education	18,000	4,404,000	866,000	3,538,000
Highways	5,000	589,000	292,000	297,000
Health and hospitals	188,000	861,000	423,000	438,000
Police protection	24,000	413,000	44,000	369,000
Financial administration	84,000	226,000	82,000	143,000
General control	37,000	312,000	37,000	275,000
All others	323,000	1,650,000	335,000	1,315,000

SOURCE: Adapted from Bureau of the Census, Public Employment in 1966.

sponsibility of state and local governments. So, too, are domestic relations, marriage and divorce, and the agencies dedicated to family and child welfare. The vast majority of problems arising in connection with contracts, torts, personal and real property are governed by state and local governments.

It is obvious from all of this that even though the states are not sovereign, neither are they outmoded anachronisms. In the seamless "web of government" that reaches from Washington to Peach Tree Creek, states, counties, and cities are, if anything, more important in 1968 than they were in 1868—if for no other reason than because government at all levels has become vastly more important in American life. From Maine to California the states today are a vital part of American government, and, as we shall see, they do not lack a considerable measure of independence. If, in our highly mobile culture, state loyalties no longer burn with the same incandescent fervor as in 1786 or 1860, nevertheless states are much more than administrative or judicial districts. The central importance of the state has been dramatically revealed in the recent struggles for racial integration and civil rights. More often than not, in this as in other things, the federal government may propose policies, but their success or failure depends on state and local authorities.

☆ STATES–SCOPE AND STRUCTURE OF POWER

If we apply to state constitutions the standards usually used to distinguish a constitution from a statute or ordinary law, we run into a mare's nest of confusion and contradiction.

Most state constitutions do all of the things that constitutional lawyers expect constitutions to do; but they do a lot more. They provide for the form and structure of the government. In general, they follow the

TABLE 19–2

Employment and Payrolls of State and Local Governments, by Function:
October, 1966

Function	All employees (full-time and part-time) (in thousands)			Monthly payroll (in millions of dollars)			Average monthly earnings of full-time employees
	Total	State govern- ments	Local govern- ments	Total	State govern- ments	Local govern- ments	
All functions	8,618	2,211	6,407	3,808.0	975.2	2,832.8	$518
Education	4,404	866	3,538	2,030.0	353.0	1,677.1	558
Local schools	3,436	13	3,423	1,633.7	7.1	1,626.6	544
Instructional personnel	2,229	9	2,219	1,312.4	5.5	1,306.8	625
Other	1,207	4	1,203	321.3	1.5	319.8	339
Institutions of higher education	920	804	116	372.3	321.8	50.5	641
Other education	49	49	. . .	24.1	24.1	. . .	542
Functions other than education	4,214	1,344	2,869	1,777.9	622.2	1,155.7	480
Highways	589	292	297	254.9	139.0	115.9	459
Public welfare	190	70	120	81.3	30.7	50.6	447
Hospitals	752	382	370	277.3	149.4	127.9	384
Health	109	41	68	50.5	19.9	30.6	504
Police protection	413	44	369	201.6	24.4	177.2	557
Local fire protection	246	. . .	246	100.5	. . .	100.5	590
Natural resources	163	130	33	72.0	60.4	11.6	512
Correction	119	74	45	58.2	37.9	20.3	502
Financial administration	226	82	143	89.6	40.3	49.3	474
General control	312	37	275	106.0	21.4	84.6	505
Local utilities	253	. . .	253	139.1	. . .	139.1	570
All other	842	191	651	346.9	98.8	248.0	485

SOURCE: Bureau of the Census, Public Employment in 1966. Statistics for local governments are subject to sampling variation. Because of rounding, detail may not add to totals.

pattern of the United States Constitution in providing for a separation of powers and a check and balance system with three coordinate branches of government. Some do so in express terms, and others by implication by having the three branches chosen independently of one another.[14] Except in Nebraska, all of the state constitutions provide for bicameral

[14] Just as the framers drew heavily on the state constitutions of 1787 in framing a Constitution for the nation, so the states, coming into the Union since 1790, have copied from the framers' work.

legislatures, usually a Senate and a House of Representatives or Assembly. Terms of office are four years for the Senate in 34 states, and two years in 16 states. In all but five states, the House of Representatives or Assembly serves for two years, including the unicameral legislature of Nebraska. In five states both chambers serve for four-year terms.[15] Every state constitution provides for a governor, lieutenant governor, and from three to eight other state-wide executive officers (secretary of state, auditor, controller, treasurer, attorney general, etc.) elected directly by the people.

In 35 states the governor's term (and usually other statewide executives) is four years; in 15 states, it is two years. In 22 states, the governor either cannot succeed himself or is limited by the constitution to two terms. Thus in nearly half of the states, the old colonial suspicion of a strong independent executive lives on. Every constitution provides for a state judiciary, to be selected in a variety of ways. Finally, state constitutions have bills of rights, containing either expressly or by judicial extension, most of the guarantees of the federal Bill of Rights.

But state constitutions differ from the Constitution of the United States in a number of important respects. The national government is a government of delegated powers, whereas the states are governments of reserved powers. Legally a state government may exercise any power not delegated to the United States, nor forbidden by the United States Constitution, or by the constitution of the state. However, there are numerous things the states are expressly forbidden to do. They may not impair the obligation of a contract, make anything but gold and silver a legal tender, lay imposts on imports except as incidental to their inspection laws, deny any person equal protection of the laws, or deprive anyone of property without due process.

Do the powers delegated to the central government leave the states as powerless, empty vessels with the forms but not the substance of power? On the contrary, the residual powers vested in the states are substantial and significant. They include power to frame and to amend their own constitutions or to adopt new ones; power to lay and collect taxes almost without legal limit; power to determine who may vote for members of Congress and for President (subject only to the Fourteenth, Fifteenth, and Nineteenth Amendments); power to enact both criminal and civil laws of all kinds and to prescribe punishments (except for the limitations of the Bill of Rights); power to establish and maintain their own systems of law enforcement; and power to establish political subdivisions and to prescribe their form of government and the scope of their powers.

15 The upper house is known as the Senate everywhere, and the lower house, as the House of Representatives except in California, Nevada, New Jersey, New York, and Wisconsin, where it is known as the Assembly, and in Maryland and Virginia, where it is known as the House of Delegates.

Consider but one item in the foregoing catalogue, the relation of the state government to its political subdivisions, including counties, cities, towns, villages, and all manner of special districts. Unlike the federal government in its relations with the states, the state governments have plenary power over their political subdivisions. State boundaries, state constitutions, equal representation in the Senate, and so forth, are immune from change by the United States without the state's consent. But the boundaries, form of government, rights and powers of cities and other subdivisions are subject to the power of the state unless this power is limited by the state constitution itself. And most important is the fact that the states have what lawyers call a "police power"—power to provide for the health, welfare, safety, and public morals of the community— again limited only by their own constitutions or the Constitution of the United States. The United States has no such police power except (1) in the territories and the District of Columbia, and (2) as it may be in- cidental to the exercise of other powers—to regulate commerce, lay and collect taxes, establish post offices, and so forth.

Under their reserved powers, state governments, up to the middle of the nineteenth century, actively engaged in a wide variety of private or quasi-private enterprises. As the Missouri constitution said: "Internal improvement shall forever be encouraged by the government of this state; it shall be the duty of the general assembly . . . to make provision by law for ascertaining the most proper objects of improvement." To this end, canals, tollroads, and bridges were constructed either directly by the state or by companies acting under special charters. One of the most ambitious of these projects was the Erie Canal, 400 miles long, built and operated by the State of New York. Other states used mixed corporations for a variety of purposes, including the establishment of banks and trans- portation companies. Indeed, in the 1820s bank dividends were a princi- pal source of state revenue in Pennsylvania. And where the state did not act directly, it did so through chosen instruments—corporations specially chartered for a particular purpose. Massachusetts is said to have issued 300 such charters to manufacturing corporations alone.

This revival, or survival, of quasi-mercantilist economic policies soon developed its seamy side. Corruption and bribery appeared as politically influential groups bid for special charters and franchises. By 1860 most states had sold their interests in mixed corporations and were moving away from mercantilism to laissez faire. General incorporation laws re- placed special charters and franchises, so that manufacturing companies, banks, and other business enterprises that could meet these terms were free to organize. Encouraged by these laws, private corporations grew in number and size, as did their influence at state capitals and in city halls, ushering in the period characterized as the "Era of the Robber Barons," an era described by Professor Allan Richards as the era of "Greed, Grab and Gain." Pressure to avoid or evade state regulation brought lobbyists in great numbers to state capitals, and an unholy alliance between political bosses and business tycoons emerged. The ups and downs of the business cycle, added to a mounting wave of moral discontent, led to demands for political reform to break the power of the bosses and an increasing use of the police powers of the states to regulate business enterprise.

The demand for political reform expressed itself in a mounting distrust of state governments, and especially of state legislatures, a distrust reflected in demands for direct primaries for the nomination of candidates, nonpartisan elections, constitutional limitations upon the power of the legislature, plural elective executives, and an increasing use of the initiative and referendum, which not only gave the voters a direct veto on acts of the legislature but, through the initiative, put legislative power in the hands of the people themselves. Between 1898 and 1920 some 1,500 constitutional amendments were proposed and over 900 adopted, and the use of the initiative and referendum to pass upon ordinary legislation as well as to amend state constitutions has continued.

Facilitating this development has been the process for amending state constitutions. Like the Constitution of the United States, state constitutions as a rule are not easy to amend. No less than 39 states authorize the calling of conventions to revise the state constitution, and in 26 of these prior approval of the legislature is required even "before the question of whether a constitutional convention shall be held can be submitted to the voters." In at least 9 states the question of constitutional revision of the document as a whole must be submitted to the voters periodically. In other states the legislature may refer the matter to the voters at its discretion. Thirteen states allow constitutional amendments to be initiated directly by popular petition, and in every state except New Hampshire the legislature can submit constitutional amendments to popular vote. In some states this can be done by simple majority. In others it requires a two-thirds or even a three-fourths vote, and in nine states a resolution to refer a law or amendment to the people must be passed by a majority vote in two successive sessions of the legislature. Ratification of amendments submitted to the people usually requires only a simple majority vote. Connecticut and New Hampshire require ratification in town meetings, and the Delaware legislature can propose an amendment at one session and ratify it at the next. In South Carolina and Mississippi the legislature must approve even after a popular vote has ratified the proposal.

One result of all this has been to transform the constitution of many a state into an *omnium gatherum* of provisions of a purely statutory character. The average state constitution is four times as long as that of the United States. And the constitution of Louisiana, with over 400 amendments, is more than 30 times as long. How detailed this kind of constitutional law can be is illustrated by the California amendment to establish a State Department of Welfare and, at the same time, to name Myrtle Willians, one of its proponents, as the first Welfare Director. It became necessary therefore to amend the constitution again at a subsequent election to take her name out of the fundamental law of the state. A recent report in New York of a Committee to study the state constitution said that out of 54 sections in the constitution, 23 were superfluous. Governor Coleman of Mississippi referred to the constitution of that state as an "ox cart law in a jet age."

Another by-product of state constitutional prolixity has been legislation to hamstring state legislatures in dealing with urgent state problems. State governments are by no means free to exercise all of the plenary powers which they have in theory. Constitutional debt limitations impair the states' capacity to deal with many urgent problems. Those who lament the drift of power to Washington and the increasing dependence of the states on the federal government might want to examine the effect of these limitations on this trend. The financial crisis, for example, which all but immobilized the government of Michigan in 1959, was related to a constitutional debt limit which prevented the state from borrowing to meet its payrolls pending action on new taxes. Also, more than half of the state's annual revenue was set aside by the constitution for particular purposes, and was not available to meet even emergency needs. The California constitution, to take another example, requires state support of local public schools in a specified amount per pupil in average daily attendance during the preceding year. This item accounts for approximately one-quarter of the state's annual budget. Altogether nearly 70 percent of California's total annual expenditures are fixed obligations that the legislature has no power to alter. These limitations are, if anything, a greater source of constraint than the express limitations on the states in the Constitution of the United States.

Many state constitutions impose rigid controls and limitations on the state's capacity to go into debt even for major capital expenditures. Nearly all require special voter approval of state bond issues, some set arbitrary limits on state indebtedness, and a few prohibit any debt whatever. Spurred on as much by the so-called Reapportionment Revolution set in motion by the Supreme Court as by general dissatisfaction, a widespread movement toward constitutional revision is under way. Between July, 1963, and June, 1965, six states held constitutional conventions; a dozen others are pending, with the number taking action increasing each year.

Federal Limitations on State Powers

We cannot examine all federal limitations on state powers, but a few illustrations will suffice to indicate their nature and significance. To restrict the power of the states over contracts was a major goal of the framers. "A violation of contracts," said Madison, "had become familiar in the form of depreciated paper made a legal tender, of property substituted for money, and installment laws [stay laws], [and] the occlusions of courts of justice." Back of Daniel Shays and his tatterdemalion rebels was a bitter conflict between creditors and debtors. The debtors, mainly small farmers, sought relief in all manner of reforms that impaired the obligation of contracts. To protect property owners and creditors against such legislation the framers wrote into the Constitution, in Section 10 of Article I, "No state shall make any law impairing the obligation of contracts." The earliest application of this section came in 1810 in the case of *Fletcher* v. *Peck*.[16] In 1795 the legislature of Georgia had ordered the sale to four land companies of public lands comprising most of what is now Alabama and Mississippi. The sale was accomplished by open bribery, and a new legislature, chosen by an irate electorate, repealed the act of sale at its 1795–1796 session. In the meantime, the companies had disposed of several million acres to speculators and settlers, who, in face of the act revoking the sale, consulted Alexander Hamilton concerning their title to the land. Hamilton assured them of a clear title on the ground that the act repealing the grant violated "the first principles of natural justice and social policy," especially as it was "to the prejudice . . . of third persons . . . innocent of the alleged fraud or corruption." Moreover, he said, "the Constitution declares that no state shall pass a law impairing the obligation of contract. . . ." The case came to the Supreme Court in 1810 and, in an opinion by Chief Justice Marshall, the Court held that a grant of land is an executed contract—"a conveyance—but carries an implied contract not to claim again the thing granted." Hence this act, it was held, violated the Constitution. Georgia, he said, was restrained from passing the law revoking the grant "either by general principles which are common to our free institutions, or by particular provisions of the Constitution of the United States." Presumably, in the Court's opinion a "sovereign" state legislature was powerless to repeal an unjust law, even one passed under color of fraud and corruption, if it adversely affected private contract rights. Two years later the Court held that a grant of tax immunity to certain lands could not be revoked against subsequent purchasers of the land.[17]

Hard on the heels of these decisions came an even more dramatic application of the contract clause as a limitation on the power of a state. Dartmouth College had its charter from the British Crown. In 1816, some thirty years after the Revolution, the New Hampshire legislature altered the royal charter and vested control in a Board of Trustees appointed by the state. The old self-perpetuating board originally appointed by the Crown, protested, saying that this act was unconstitutional because it

16 6 Cranch 87 (1810).
17 *New Jersey* v. *Wilson,* 7 Cranch 164 (1812).

impaired the obligation of a contract. The board brought suit against William H. Woodward, secretary of the new board, for recovery of the seal and charter of the college. The New Hampshire State Supreme Court upheld the legislature, whereupon the Trustees of the old board appealed to the United States Supreme Court. John Marshall, speaking for the Court, held that such a charter was a contract, a living agreement between existent parties, the "considerations of which were the objects for which the corporation was created"—that is, education.

For over one hundred years the doctrine of *Fletcher* v. *Peck* and *Dartmouth College* v. *Woodward* was applied so as to deprive state governments of power fully to regulate private business corporations operating under charter, license, or grant from the state, but not to impair the power of the state to revise or revoke the charters of municipal corporations. Such a charter, said the Court, creates a civil institution for the better "administration of the government," and, as such, could be revised as the legislature saw fit, even when such revision impaired the power of the municipality to control business corporations operating under grants from the city.

For more than a century the contract clause was a major source of litigation in cases involving state legislation and was considered in about 40 percent of the Supreme Court cases involving the states' power to modify special grants or charters to private corporations. But in recent years the doctrine has been modified to hold that a state may reserve the right to "amend, alter, and repeal" a charter as a condition of the original grant. Even when a state fails to reserve this right, it is not without power to control its corporate creatures. "Private corporations," says the Court, "like other private persons are always presumed to be subject to the legislative power of the state." Exemptions from this are treated as exceptions and must be expressly stipulated and strictly construed.

Liberalization of the strict doctrine laid down in the cases of *Fletcher* v. *Peck* and *Dartmouth College* began early, notably in the case of the *Charles River Bridge Company* v. *Warren Bridge Company*.[18] In 1785 the Massachusetts legislature had authorized the former to build and operate a toll bridge over the Charles River, and in 1792 this charter was extended for seventy years, although not as an exclusive privilege. In 1828 the Warren Bridge Company was chartered to build a second bridge a short distance from the first, on condition that the new bridge was to become the property of the state upon recovery of construction costs. The Charles River Bridge Company asked for an injunction against this grant on the ground that the grant to the Warren Bridge Company would be an impairment of the obligation of its contract. The Court, however, rejected this plea, holding that no rights could be implied in a charter from the state beyond the *specific* terms of the grant itself. In the absence

[18] 11 Peters 420 (1837).

of an express grant to an exclusive right, no such right would be implied. Although Justice Story dissented, arguing that he could see no distinction between this and the Dartmouth College Case, the Charles River Bridge Case was the beginning of a more liberal view of state police power.

Strict construction of contract rights where they implied limits on state power was applied to tax exemptions and other claims of privilege. Moreover, the Court has held that certain police powers of the state are inalienable and cannot be the subject of a contract.[19] The contemporary doctrine would seem to be that the contract clause of the United States Constitution "does not prevent the State from exercising such powers as are vested in it for the promotion of the common good or are necessary for the general good of the public, [even] though contracts previously entered into between individuals may thereby be affected. . . ."[20]

War and Emergency

In World War I, New York, declaring a housing emergency to exist, passed a law forbidding landlords to oust their tenants at the expiration of a lease, provided the tenants were able and willing to pay a reasonable rent. The law was upheld under the contract clause on the ground that all "contracts are made subject to the exercise of power by the state . . ." to protect the public health, safety, and welfare.[21] Another emergency arose from the economic depression of the 1930s, when both state and federal governments, under heavy pressure from debtors, enacted relief legislation not unlike that passed in the so-called critical period following the Revolution. In 1933 the Minnesota legislature, citing frequent foreclosure sales, authorized state courts to extend the period of redemption for such additional time as the court deemed just and equitable, although not beyond May 1, 1935. This modern "stay law" left the mortgagor in possession of the property, provided he paid a reasonable rent set by the court. As in other cases this law was assailed as an impairment of the obligation of contracts. The Supreme Court, however, upheld the law.

> It is manifest [said the Court] . . . that there is [need] . . . of finding ground for rational compromise between individual rights and public welfare. Exhaustion of public lands, density of population, complexity and interdependence of economic life have inevitably led to an increased use [of the public power] of society in order to protect the very bases of individual opportunity. Where in early days it was thought that only the

19 Viz., New York City conveyed lands for a church and cemetery, together with a covenant (promise) to assure quiet enjoyment. The City later passed a law forbidding the use of these lands as a cemetery. The State court denied an action against the City for breach of covenant, saying that the State "had no power . . . to make a contract which should control or embarrass their legislative powers and duties."

20 *Marigault* v. *Springs*, 199 U.S. 473 (1905).

21 *Brown (Marcus) Holding Co.* v. *Feldman*, 256 U.S. 242 (1922).

concerns of individuals or of classes were involved, . . . it has later been found that the fundamental interests of the State are directly affected, and . . . the question is no longer merely that of one party to a contract as against another but of the use of reasonable means to safeguard the economic structure upon which the good of all depends . . . the reasonable exercise of the protective power of the States is read into all contracts.[22]

Other laws in Missouri and Arkansas, however, were thrown out as being unreasonable and hence in violation of the contract clause. But as recently as 1945 the Supreme Court upheld an extension of New York's moratorium legislation on the ground that "the sudden termination of the legislation which has dammed up normal liquidation of these mortgages for more than eight years might well result in an emergency more acute than that which the original legislation was intended to alleviate. . . ." In the light of these and other decisions, the contract clause has ceased to be a major restraint upon the power of the state.

Other Restraints on the States

The contract clause, however, is but one of many limitations upon the reserved powers of the states. They are also forbidden to enter "into any Treaty, Alliance, or Confederation," and, unless Congress gives its consent, no state may "enter into any Agreement or Compact with another State or with a foreign Power. . . ." States are also forbidden to "coin Money, emit Bills of Credit, make any Thing but gold and silver Coin a Tender in Payment of Debts, . . . lay any Imposts or Duties on Imports or Exports except what may be absolutely necessary for executing its inspection Laws." If a state levies any fees for this purpose, the "net produce," that is, anything beyond the costs of executing its inspection laws, "shall be for the use of the Treasury of the United States." In any case, "all such Laws shall be subject to the Revision and Control of the Congress." In addition to these limitations, the Constitution forbids states to "pass any Bill of Attainder, ex post facto law, . . . or grant any Title of Nobility." (Section 10, Article I.)

Although the limitations imposed by the Bill of Rights were long held to apply only to the national government, many have been extended to the states by judicial interpretation of the Fourteenth Amendment, which forbids any state to "make or enforce any law which shall abridge the privileges and immunities of citizens of the United States [or] . . . deprive any person of life, liberty, or property without due process of law . . . [or] deny to any person within its jurisdiction the equal protection of the laws." The guarantee of "liberty" has been held to apply many of the guarantees of the federal Bill of Rights to the states, and the due process and equal protection clauses have imposed severe limitations

[22] *Home Building Loan Association* v. *Blaisdell,* 290 U.S. 398 (1934).

upon the powers of state governments over their own citizens. Not only in cases involving civil rights and liberties but in cases involving state economic and welfare legislation, contracts, and property rights, the due process and equal protection provisions of the Fourteenth Amendment have confined state powers to much narrower limits than the naked language of the Tenth Amendment would seem to imply. Even the control of suffrage qualifications has been limited by the Fourteenth, Fifteenth, and Nineteenth Amendments as well as by recent federal legislation and Supreme Court decisions to protect Negroes in their right to vote.[23]

Yet notwithstanding the formal limitations on the powers of the states in the Constitution of the United States, and in the state constitutions themselves, and notwithstanding the meteoric increase in the scope of power exercised by the central government, there remains in American state governments a vast reservoir of political power over many of the most important aspects of American life. Reckless and repeated reports of the decline and even death of state government in the United States are, like the premature reports of Mark Twain's death, grossly exaggerated.

Even the state-imposed limitations on indebtedness can, and are being, cured or by-passed. The use of "revenue bonds" to finance self-liquidating projects and the establishment of special state authorities with more or less independent powers are among the more common devices used. New York, for example, in 1963, had some 25 such "authorities," and Florida, whose constitution prohibits any state debt, has similar state-operated "authorities" with over $600 million of indebtedness in 1963.[24]

☆ THE STATES: LEGISLATURE AND GOVERNOR

It is a common complaint that the structure and process of government at the grass roots in America is woefully inadequate to the job it has to do. And this is especially true of the government of the several states. State legislatures, it is claimed, are unrepresentative of the best forces in society and attract but mediocre talent. Their size, organization, and procedures inhibit honest discussion, obscure responsibility for policy decisions, and invite excessive influence by organized special interests. Part of the problem arises from the inability of the governor to assume responsibility for policy and administration, for he is but one of several elected executive officers.

The drift of power to Washington, it has been argued, is due in part

---

23 It is worth noting also that nearly 34 percent of the total land area of the states is owned by the federal government. In Nevada federal lands account for over 85 percent of the state area; in Idaho 65 percent; in Utah 68 percent; in Arizona 51 percent; and in Alaska 98 percent.

24 See the *Wall Street Journal,* February 18, 1964.

at least to the failure of the states to put their own houses in order so as to meet the challenge of government in the late twentieth century. The low prestige of state governments is not wholly due to competition with the vastly greater, more dramatic and more visible government in Washington. Part of it is due to the fact that, in spite of clichés about "states' rights," the states have lagged behind in the science and art of government. This, in substance, is the burden of the indictment to be heard these days against the states. Their faults, as Caesar might have put it, are not in their stars but in themselves. Instead of bemoaning federal centralization and the loss of power to the Leviathan on the Potomac, they are advised to look inward and homeward.

When the voter confronts the ballot for national officers, he has a comparatively simple task: two candidates for Congress in the off years, and in presidential years, two other candidates for President and Vice-President, and perhaps two candidates for United States Senator—a small number of names to ponder, and these neatly grouped and labeled as Democrats or Republicans. The ballot for federal officers could easily be printed on a postal card with names so arranged as not to tax the time or intellect of the most casual citizen.

Contrast the voter's job as he confronts his ballot for state and local officers. Many times the number of names on a federal ballot are likely to be there, and he is asked to choose, from 10 to 40 candidates, for governor, lieutenant governor, secretary of state, treasurer, comptroller, attorney general, state superintendent of instruction, board of equalization, secretary of agriculture, state representative and senator, judges of the Supreme Court as well as for county and municipal benches, for mayor and city council, for sheriff and county engineer or surveyor, for coroner, district attorney, for county commissioner or supervisor, and, in some places, other medieval survivals like fire warden and fence viewer. A recent Indiana ballot listed 246 candidates for 58 offices, of which 3 were for President, Vice-President, and member of Congress. The ballot measured 2414 square inches—over 16 square feet. No wonder it is called a blanket ballot. And at the bottom appeared this warning: "Each voter is allowed not more than one minute in which to vote."

To be sure, this is an extreme case, but the long ballot is a symptom of the survival of Jacksonian democratic ideas in a day when rotation in office and annual elections of every government official no longer make sense. We Americans like to streamline nearly everything from automobiles to women's hats, but not state and local government. To make confusion worse, in some states (Minnesota and Nebraska) and in many cities where a passion for nonpartisanship prevails, we deny the overburdened voter the elementary guidance that comes from party labels. The result, of course, is that the average citizen, when he votes, votes blind.

A recent Minnesota survey asked a sample of voters to identify two persons: Arthur Hansen and Ancher Nelson. "Four percent knew that Nelson was the Republican candidate for lieutenant governor, but only one percent knew or could identify Hansen as the Democratic nominee for that office." This is low visibility to the point of blindness. "Yet in November," says Professor Hacker, "Nelson and Hansen received between them the votes of almost 1,500,000 Minnesotans."[25]

This, again, is not typical, but it points up the low visibility and complexity of state and local government. This low visibility is reflected also in the generally smaller turnout of voters at state and local elections. From 20 to 25 percent of the voters who express a choice for governor in a presidential year do not bother to vote in the so-called off year. In Michigan, for example, it was found that some 700,000 people who voted for governor in a presidential year failed to vote for governor two years later. If the vote for governor falls off when only state and local offices are at stake, it falls off even more precipitously for other state officials.

The politics of American states is a wilderness of both partisan and nonpartisan factions, a veritable crazy quilt of interests that defy discipline and make stable party organizations difficult or impossible. Minnesota and Nebraska reject partisanship altogether in the election of their legislatures. The result is mainly to force party government underground and to make impossible even the minimal responsibility that Republican and Democratic organizations enforce in other states. This revolt against partisan politics in the interest of what reformers call "good government" usually results in political domination by special interest factions undisciplined by the wider loyalty that major political parties acknowledge to the community as a whole. For this and other reasons, nonpartisanship in state government has not been conspicuously successful, and there is some evidence of increasing respect for the two-party system. The number of nonpartisan states has not increased and the number of one-party states has declined. The built-in conflicts between the legislative and executive branches are aggravated in many states by a system of election and representation that puts legislative and executive leadership in the hands of rival parties. In twelve states with Democratic governors in 1960, at least one house was controlled by the Republicans, and in three, Republicans were in control of both houses. That is, in twenty-two states executive and legislative leadership was in rival hands.

The state system of directly elected plural executives often results in confusion and conflict. Not only is a Republican governor often required to work with a Democratic lieutenant governor, but with from one to half a dozen other independently elected executives of the opposite party. In 1960 nine Republican governors had such split administrations, and

---

[25] *The New York Times,* October 29, 1961.

in four of these, all state executives except the governor were Democrats. Eleven Democratic governors had one or more Republican executive officers on his "team." And in Iowa, a Democratic governor had Republicans as lieutenant governor, secretary of state, state auditor, attorney general, treasurer, and secretary of agriculture. In these circumstances, party responsibility is at a minimum and pressure politics replaces party politics in state legislatures; without strong party backing, legislators and executive officers turn to pressure groups for campaign support.

Most students of state government agree that special interest groups are more powerful at the state level than in Washington. In California, for example, lobbyists outnumber members of the legislature at the state capitol by as much as four to one. It is this situation that helps to account for the low esteem in which state legislatures are held as compared with Congress.

There are, of course, other reasons as well for the low esteem in which state legislatures are held. Membership in the state legislature is a part-time job. Less than half the states have annual sessions (19) and in these, the length of the session is usually limited to 30 or 60 days. Only in 7 states may it exceed 60 days. In most states the legislature meets only every two years (30 states) and even in these states (with 4 exceptions) the session is limited to not more than 60 days. The result is a sudden rush of legislation in the last days of the session, with little time for debate or serious study of the issues involved. Indeed, so little is debate in state legislatures esteemed that no verbatim records are made. Even committee hearings are seldom reported either officially or in the press. The public is poorly informed about what goes on, and suspicion thrives on ignorance.

As part-time workers, state legislators are poorly paid, and few can afford the job. In 13 states members receive less than $2,500 a year, in 23 less than $5,000. In 15 states they receive a per diem allowance limited to the length of the session and ranging from $50 in Georgia and Louisiana to $10 in Kansas and Tennessee and $5 in Rhode Island and North Dakota. In only 5 states do they receive anything like a "decent" wage. Modest travel allowances and expense accounts during the session enable most legislators to make out, but on the whole, it is not a profession at which a person can make a living. Most legislators accordingly depend on income derived from other business or professional activities. Effective "conflict of interest" legislation would play havoc with many legislators whose business or professional commitments are not wholly compatible with a selfless dedication to the public interest. Legal retainers, consulting fees, partnerships, and directorships in corporations, trade associations, and organized interest groups are not uncommon, and many a legislator serves his business clients with greater zeal than he does his political constituents.

Space forbids a detailed discussion of state legislative organization and procedure. In general, however, state legislatures, like Congress, are ruled by their senior members in committees. Seniority plays a large role in the choice of speaker, President pro tem, and other legislative officers, in committee assignments, and general influence on legislation, although not so great as in Congress. Nevertheless some relaxation of the seniority rule might open the way to new and more vigorous leadership. A good deal of lost motion might be saved by more joint committee hearings, the use of a consent calendar to take care of noncontroversial bills, annual sessions without rigid time limits, and the elimination of companion bills (the introduction of identical bills in House and Senate). The larger states might well consider representation in the legislature a full-time occupation with the public servant worthy of his hire. Greater facilities for research, legislative analysis, and drafting and permanent law revision commissions with better staffing would also help. Considerable progress has been made in this respect, and 43 states now have legislative councils, or council-like agencies, for service between sessions. Many other states have research or reference libraries, legislative auditors, advisory commissions, or other such aids. Closer relations with universities has done much to improve sources of information and research. Improvement in the system of apportionment, and a general raising of legislative status and prestige may attract better-trained legislators and may also strengthen the two-party system to a point where power and responsibility can again go together.[26]

In a series of cases beginning with *Baker* v. *Carr* in 1962 the Supreme Court has issued a mandate to the states to remedy the glaring inequalities in the apportionment of representation.[27] Most states have already complied, and the remainder are in process of striving toward a system in which the Court's formula of "one man, one vote" will be applied. Effects of this reapportionment drive are beginning to be felt. In Georgia, for example, the notorious "unit" system had for years made a mockery of majority rule, and the Negro population had gone without direct representation. But the Court's decision outlawing the unit rule and requiring a more equitable apportionment is beginning to change things. Not the least significant of these changes has been the election of eight Negroes to the Georgia legislature, giving Georgia as many Negro members as any other state with the exception of Illinois and Michigan (which have 11 each). Reapportionment under judicial mandate, plus the effects of federal civil rights legislation, plus the pressure of the so-called Negro

26 See Alexander Heard (ed.), *State Legislatures in American Politics* (American Assembly; Englewood, N.J.: Prentice-Hall, 1966), esp. chaps. 2, 5, 6.

27 See *Baker* v. *Carr*, 369 U.S. 186; *Gray* v. *Sanders*, 372 U.S. 1 (1963); *Wesberry* v. *Sanders*, 376 U.S. 1 (1964); *Reynolds* v. *Sims*, 377 U.S. 583 (1964).

See also "GOP State Legislature Gains Aided by Reapportionment," *Congressional Quarterly*, June 7, 1963; also map in Gordon Baker, *Reapportionment Revolution* (New York: Random House, 1966), p. 40.

revolt has worked this change.[28] Reapportionment in Virginia shifted 11 legislative seats from rural to urban areas, and the election of the entire House of Representatives in Illinois, at large, pending a Court-ordered reapportionment, are other examples of how state legislatures are being modernized.[29]

The Governor

The office of governor in a major state has been regarded as a stepping-stone to the Presidency, and his job in many ways resembles that of the President. He is the ceremonial head of the state and a major force in determining public policy, for his recommendations to the legislature—if backed by forceful leadership and strong party support—can shape the policy of a state as the President shapes the policy of the nation. The governor, moreover, in his item veto has a weapon denied the President.

The governor in large states has extensive patronage and great power to shape not only public policy but public administration. In states with a well-developed executive budget the governor can influence if not control the fiscal policies of the state. We do well to remember that governors preside over administrations that spend over 50 billions a year. The governor of a large state such as New York, Illinois, Ohio, or California has powers and responsibilities exceeding those of the chief executives of many a sovereign nation, however much these officials may surpass the American governors in the pomp and pageantry of office. It is not surprising therefore that the governorship of a major state has become a training ground and launching pad for many a presidential career. "Since 1896," reports Paul David, "over half of the presidential nominees and about one-third of the vice-presidential nominees have been Governors or former Governors."[30] Only recently have Senators nudged the governors out of first place in the presidential sweepstakes. Many of our great Presidents have been great governors. One thinks of Thomas Jefferson, Andrew Jackson, Woodrow Wilson, and Franklin Roosevelt. But there have been great governors, too, who have failed to win the grand prize—governors such as Charles Evans Hughes, Alfred Smith, and Thomas Dewey of New York, Adlai Stevenson and Frank Lowden of Illinois, and Earl Warren of California, for example.

[28] This change is the more remarkable when one recalls that in 1962 Negroes were ordered out of the "White Only" section of the gallery in the Georgia House of Representatives. See *News Week,* June 28, 1965.

[29] In the Illinois elections of 1964 "the entire Democratic slate of 116 candidates was elected (leaving) the Republicans with 59 seats." See *The New York Times,* February 2, 1965.

For a definitive rundown on the overall effects of the reapportionment "revolution" both in state legislatures and congressional districts see *Apportionment in the Nineteen Sixties* (New York: National Municipal League, August, 1967).

[30] *The Politics of National Party Conventions* (Washington, D.C.: Brookings Institution, 1960), p. 149.

But, with the best will in the world, it is not easy to be a great governor. The job is beset with difficulties from which even a President is free. In most states the governor is but one among a number of independently elected executive officers. The tidy centralized control that, constitutionally at any rate, the President has over the heads of executive departments and agencies is denied the governor. Not infrequently these officers are men of the opposition party or of rival factions within his own party. Each is likely to have his own political organization and his own political aspirations which do not always stop short of the governor's mansion. A governor with a lieutenant governor of the opposite party might literally be afraid to leave the state lest the latter, as acting governor, obstruct, divert, or defeat his program.

Thomas Desmond, a veteran New York State Senator, described the governor's position a few years ago as a combination of "Roy Rogers chasing the bad guys, . . . a financial wizard [giving maximum service at little or no cost], . . . a political boss to his enemies and leader to his friends, the state's chief tubthumper and public relations director, a one-man chamber of commerce, a friend of every man, a paragon of civic virtue, and a symbol of the conscience of the state. . . ." To be all this under ideal conditions would be difficult, and the average governor's position is far from ideal. He is "shackled with ancient . . . managerial handcuffs that most businessmen would find intolerable. . . ." Typically, a large part of state management is outside his control, although he will be held responsible for anything that goes wrong. His "span of control" is supposed to cover from 50 to 150 departments, boards, commissions and agencies, many of which are independent and hence irresponsible. No wonder the Council of State Governments has said: "Most Governors have a more difficult job than that of the President of the United States in giving effective managerial direction from the top." To master the job would take a long time. "The man doesn't live," said Governor Al Smith, "who can understand the job in his first two years." Yet 22 states limit the governor to one or two terms.

Recently, little Hoover Commissions in nearly every state have recommended: greater concentration of authority in the governor, including a reduction or elimination of other independent executive officers; departmental integration on a functional basis; elimination of independent boards and commissions; greater power and integration in the governor's cabinet; an increase in the governor's power over the state budget, and over appointments and general personnel management.

Some progress has been made in putting these reforms into effect. The new constitutions of Hawaii and Alaska, taking note of earlier reforms in New York and New Jersey, have made the governor not only the ceremonial but the actual head of the state government. The following provisions of the Alaska constitution illustrate the trend:

Sec. 22. All executive and administrative officers, departments, and agencies of the state government and their respective functions, powers, and duties shall be allocated by law among and within not more than twenty principal departments, so as to group them as far as practicable according to major purposes . . .

Sec. 23. The governor may make changes in the organization of the executive branch or in the assignment of functions among its units which he considers necessary for efficient administration. Where these changes require the force of law, they shall be set forth in executive orders. The legislature shall have sixty days of a regular session, or a full session if of shorter duration, to disapprove these executive orders . . .

Sec. 24. Each principal department shall be under the supervision of the governor.

Sec. 25. The head of each principal department shall be a single executive unless otherwise provided by law. He shall be appointed by the governor, subject to confirmation by a majority of the members of the legislature in joint session, and shall serve at the pleasure of the governor . . .

The battle for effective executive leadership in the states is, however, far from won. Arrayed against it are powerful politicians including the independently elected executives who value the patronage and power independence brings; pressure groups that find it convenient to deal with independent boards and commissions which are more friendly and "understanding"; well-meaning reform groups that want to keep education or recreation or conservation or public health independent and "free of politics"; and professional groups—lawyers, engineers, auditors, and so forth—that want autonomy for themselves but strict control for others.

Personnel

Great progress has been made in freeing state government from the worst effects of the "spoils system." A majority of states have a merit system of some kind. But some 20 states still operate with a system under which it is still more important to ask "Whom do you know?" than "What do you know?" in applying for public employment. Yet even where a formal merit system is still engaged in warfare with the spoilsmen, an informal merit system is making headway. Among the factors leading to this are (1) the federal grant-in-aid system, which usually requires that the employees chosen to administer the aided program be selected on the basis of merit, and (2) the technical nature of many state activities which simply make the old spoils system impossible. Engineers, public health officers, foresters, and geologists can no longer be recruited by the catch-as-catch-can methods of the spoils system.

☆ STATE COURTS AND THE ADMINISTRATION OF JUSTICE

We have discussed elsewhere some of the problems arising in the American quest for equal justice under law. We have noted the dual system of federal and state courts, each with its own jurisdiction defined by the Constitution and laws of the United States and of the several states. An essential feature of our federal system is that both federal and state courts within certain limits have jurisdiction over the same people in any given area. Whether a federal or a state court has jurisdiction will depend on the nature of the parties and/or the nature of the legal problem involved.

The ordinary citizen is much more likely to have his "day in court" not in a federal court—and certainly not in the Supreme Court of the United States—but in a court of the state in which he lives. The organization of these courts is by no means uniform from one state to another, but the fifty different systems have much in common. At the bottom of the hierarchy in nearly every state are the justices of the peace. These courts, presided over by a popularly elected justice, have jurisdiction over lesser civil cases, traffic violations, and minor criminal offenses. In civil cases their jurisdiction normally does not extend to controversies involving more than $100. Although they may not try persons accused of felony, they may hold preliminary hearings in such cases. Usually justices of the peace need not be trained as lawyers or judges, and they are frequently paid not a fixed salary but by fees collected as fines from persons hailed before them. Only in a few places do these local justices of the peace, or magistrates, as they are sometimes called, have legal training. Justices of the peace represent an ancient institution and the system responds only slowly to modernization. But in recent years there has been a more or less concerted effort to abolish them and to absorb their jurisdiction in that of municipal or county courts. Ohio did this in 1957, and Connecticut did so in 1959.

Next above the justices of the peace are a number of minor courts having a variety of names: small claims courts, municipal courts, police courts, traffic courts, city courts. Each has a single judge, usually a lawyer popularly elected, serving for a limited term and paid a fixed salary, although in some places the ancient fee system survives. Their jurisdiction is usually confined to civil suits involving no more than a few hundred dollars and criminal cases involving minor infractions of local ordinances. At their best, these minor courts can be fountains of justice and mercy. At their worst, they can be what one writer called "Our Reeking Halls of Justice."[31] Too often they are poorly housed, crowded,

31 See Morton Sontheimer in *Collier's*, April 2, 1949

and poorly staffed, more inclined to "clear the docket" than to see that justice is done. Unfortunately, to tens of thousands of minor miscreants and other bewildered people caught in the toils of the law, these courts present the only image they have of equal justice under the laws.

Above these minor courts are the general trial courts. These, too, are known by a variety of names including county, district, quarter sessions, circuit, common pleas, or superior courts. Often described as the "backbone of the American judicial system," they have both civil and criminal jurisdiction. It is in these courts, presided over by a single professionally trained, popularly elected judge, that criminal cases presented by "information" or "indictment of a grand jury," and prosecuted by the county or district attorney, are tried before a jury of "twelve good men and true." Felonious assault, burglary, mayhem, and murder, civil cases often involving large sums, actions in tort, contracts, and domestic relations are their stock in trade. Their decisions in most cases are final. They frequently hear appeals from minor courts and appeals may be taken from them to higher courts in the judicial hierarchy. For most people, however, this right to appeal is more theoretical than real.

Beyond the county, district, or superior courts, many states have intermediate courts of appeal. Known as District Courts of Appeal, or simply as the Appellate Division of the Superior Courts, their main job is to hear appeals from the county or superior courts. These intermediate courts of appeals are not trial courts in the usual sense and do not use the jury system. Normally they are presided over by from three to nine judges who hear and decide only questions of law. That is, they do not retry the case but only those aspects in which it is claimed an error of law in the lower court deprived either party of a fair trial. When the volume of litigation justifies it, these intermediate courts of appeals are often organized with special divisions devoted to civil or criminal appeals, or appeals in domestic relations cases. Decisions of these courts are final in most cases, made so either by law or by circumstances that make further appeal futile.

At the top of the state's judicial hierarchy are the supreme courts, or, as they are called in New York, Kentucky, and Maryland, the State Courts of Appeals, or in Connecticut, the Supreme Court of Errors. These courts, too, are presided over by from three to nine judges, usually elected and representing the elite of the state's judicial and legal talent. Theirs is solely an appellate jurisdiction to hear appeals from lower courts and from administrative agencies on questions of law. It is here that questions of constitutionality under the state constitution are finally resolved. Questions of constitutionality under the federal Constitution are also considered and usually settled, although in these matters appeal may lie to the Supreme Court of the United States. In some states, the state supreme court may, upon request of the governor or legislature, render an advisory opinion on a pending bill or administrative order, a role consistently declined by the Supreme Court of the United States. Decisions of state supreme courts are final unless an important federal question, arising under the laws or Constitution of the United States, is involved. For the most part, the Supreme Court of the United States accepts the decisions of these state supreme courts.

There are a number of other courts to be found in the states. For example, in New York there are surrogate courts, elsewhere called probate courts, with jurisdiction over the estates of deceased persons and conflicts over wills. Some states provide for special courts of domestic relations in the hope that a specialized court may exert a more constructive influence in troubled domestic affairs. An increasing number of states are making provision for juvenile courts, where the physical surroundings and rules of procedure are likely to be relaxed and informal. Specialized courts of this kind also reflect the growing need for special training of those who deal with people who are in trouble.

Recruitment of Judges

Shortly before his death, the late Judge Arthur Vanderbilt outlined what he called "The Essentials of a Sound Judicial System."[32] Foremost among these essentials, he said, was "a corps of judges, each of them utterly independent and beholden only to the law and to the Constitution, thoroughly grounded in his knowledge of the law and of human nature . . . , experienced at the Bar in either trial or appellate work and preferably in both, of such a temperament that he can hear both sides of a case before making up his mind, devoted to the law and justice, industrious, honest, and, above all, believed to be honest."[33] Assuming that paragons of this calibre exist or are numerous enough to staff our courts, how do we discover them and how do we get them on the bench? Mankind has experimented with an hereditary judiciary, a judiciary recruited by bargain and sale of judicial posts, an appointed judiciary, and an elective judiciary. Rejecting both hereditary judges and those who buy their posts, we are left with recruitment by appointment or election. And if to be appointed or elected, we need to ask, by whom and for how long?

In Great Britain, Canada, and in most of the countries of Europe and Asia, judges are appointed for life either by the titular or active executive, usually on nomination of a select body presumed to be

---

[32] See *Northwestern University Law Review*, March and April, 1953.

[33] Other features of Judge Vanderbilt's model court system were "(1) a simple system of courts, (2) competent judges and jurors; (3) effective use of judicial manpower through the administrative head of the courts; (4) simplified procedures to insure decisions on the merits without delay, technicalities, or surprise; (5) an effective appellate practice."

knowledgeable concerning the qualities that make a good judge. In this same tradition, all judges of federal courts are appointed by the President with the advice and consent of the Senate, and they serve during good behavior.

The states, on the other hand, have employed both appointment and popular election. Although the pattern changes from year to year, and what we say today may not be true tomorrow, the prevailing method is by popular election. In two-thirds of the states this is true, while in five states judges are elected by the legislature. In only nine states are they appointed by the governor with the advice and consent either of the governor's council, as in Massachusetts, or by the state senate elsewhere.

To temper the harsh winds of politics, about half of the states providing for popular election specify that the election shall be nonpartisan. But in others, except in cases of some Supreme Court justices, judges are chosen in strictly partisan campaigns. However, partisanship is often tempered by a gentleman's agreement between the major parties on judicial nominees. In this way the parties not only divide the judicial posts between them but relieve the process of electing judges of some of the brash and raucous tones of partisan conflict. For even where judges are popularly elected, a partisan judiciary is regarded not only as unseemly but as incompatible with equal justice under law.

Thus the American states are almost alone in retaining the ancient custom of choosing judges by direct vote of the people. Not everyone, however, is happy with the prevailing system. "No system," said the late Judge Vanderbilt, "could be worse than popular election on party tickets along with a host of other national, state, and local party candidates. . . . The plain truth is that popular partisan judicial elections would have faded long since were it not for the fact that in state after state about one-third of the judges in office die or resign, giving the governor an opportunity to make ad interim appointments." But the testimony is by no means all on one side. "Any attempt," says Professor William S. Carpenter, "to draw inference in favor of an appointive bench is certain to be subject to notable exceptions. . . . In many states a judiciary of the highest order has been maintained by popular election. . . . The method of selecting judges is perhaps best determined by local conditions. . . . In Wisconsin [for example] the elective judiciary has achieved unusual distinction." Some critics also point out that selection of judges by appointment is no sure guarantee against partisan politics. "Congress today," said *The New York Times* on February 4, 1954, "passed a bill to create thirty new Federal judgeships," giving President Eisenhower his first opportunity to appoint Republicans to a large number of judgeships. And as we have already noted judicial appointments by most Presidents are not conspicuously nonpartisan.

One solution seeks to combine the advantages of appointment with the blessings of popular election. The plan, variously known as the Missouri Plan, the California Plan, or the American Bar Association Plan, is used in these two states and Alaska. It provides that at least supreme court and district judges be appointed for an initial term by the governor upon recommendation of a commission on qualifications or some similar screening body. At the end of his first term the judge must face the voters if he seeks a second term, although no other candidate will appear on the ballot against him. He will, in short, campaign "on his record,"- thus giving the voters a veto on those judges of whom they may disapprove. In case an incumbent judge does not seek a second term, the governor, with the approval of a commission on judicial qualifications, may nominate another candidate—again, without opposition.

A further limitation on the principle of popular election of judges is a longer term for those who serve. Life tenure "during good behavior" is prescribed in the Constitution and the laws for members of the federal judiciary. In the states, life tenure is provided for judges of the higher courts in Massachusetts, Rhode Island, and New Jersey, and in New Hampshire up to the age of 70. In fifteen states the term for the highest court is ten years, and this seems to be an increasingly favorite term. At the other extreme, Vermont limits even its supreme court judges to a two-year term.

Although no special training is required for some minor courts, most states require that judges in courts having general trial or appellate jurisdiction be lawyers. The phrase most commonly used is that aspiring judges must be "learned in the law" without usually specifying just how learned they are to be. Some states require some "legal experience" as well as legal training, one or two require "sobriety of manner," and at least one state requires judges to believe in God.

To attract better legal talent to our courts a radical revision of financial rewards may be necessary. More liberal retirement systems and more professional help might also increase the appeal of a judicial career to outstanding members of the Bar.

As one reflects on the central importance of the courts in our system of government, it is not surprising that popular election, or at least a popular veto, limited terms, and rather liberal qualifications for judicial office should be so widely found. Nor is it surprising in a system where courts pass on important political questions that politics should be an important part of the total judicial environment. If our courts had no power to pass on the constitutionality of legislation or executive orders, the argument for a judiciary wholly immune from political considerations might have greater cogency.

In summary there must be an awakening among the people to the vital importance of state government in the American scheme of things— and a better understanding of the structure of power at the state level. For this understanding we shall need to revitalize our two-party system in the states. Without responsible political parties, to nominate and elect public officials, to discipline special interest factions, and to develop programs of public policy to meet the great responsibilities that the states have, the rank and file of voters cannot find effective guidance and leadership.

20

THE URBAN DRIFT: PROBLEMS OF METROPOLITAN GROWTH

☆ *CITY-STATE: ATHENS AND NEW ENGLAND*

Alexis de Tocqueville, in his *Democracy in America,* saw in the principle of local self government and particularly in the town meeting the heart of American democracy. "Town meetings," he wrote over a hundred years ago, "are to liberty what primary schools are to science. . . . Without municipal institutions [a nation] cannot have the spirit of liberty. . . . A centralized administration is fit only to enervate the nation . . . by diminishing their local spirit."

In more ways than one Tocqueville was *the* philosopher of American democracy and we do well to ponder what he had to say. But we must also ask how relevant his model of a working democracy is to our own day and age. The vitality of the New England town in colonial society has been stressed by other writers. Emerson, writing in 1853, said, "The town is the unit of the Republic. The New England states founded their constitutions on towns and not on [larger] communities which districting leads to. And thus are the politics [of the town] the school of the people, the game which everyone learns to play. . . ."

Lewis Mumford, in his study *The City in History,* has written that "the New England towns added a new feature that has never been sufficiently appreciated nor as widely copied as it deserved: the township. The township is a political organization which encloses a group of towns, villages, or hamlets, along with the open country area that surrounds them; it performs the functions of local government including the provision of schools and the care of local needs without accepting the long established division between town and country." The town or the township, he argues, as distinguished from the county or the municipal corporation or the special district, is more of a living organism. There is a more integral relation between town and country—a recognition of the interdependence of one town with another and of all towns in the township with the countryside from which they draw their sustenance.

The New England town, like the classic Greek city-state, was more than an agglomeration of buildings. It was a community of citizens alert to its needs and active in its affairs.

> What distinguished the Greek polis [city-state] [says Mumford] was the fact that no part of its life was out of sight or out of mind. . . . All that men did was open to inspection, alike in the market, the workshop, the law court, the council, the gymnasium. . . . [nevertheless] not the least of Athens's achievements was its establishment of a golden mean between public and private life. . . . [the citizen] not merely performed military service at call, . . . but he served in the assembly and the law courts, and if he did not become a contestant in one or another of the games, if he did not act in the theater or sing in the chorus, he would at least have a place in . . . the procession. Almost every male Athenian, at one time or another, had to take part in public business. . . . Work now done by executives, permanent secretaries, inspectors and magistrates was done by ordinary Athenians.

It was this full participation by the citizens in the life of the community that made the city-state the shining model we so revere.

In many ways the New England town, subject to the reserve and austerity of a Puritan way of life, was the American prototype of the Athenian model. But both were transformed, as growth in area and population undermined the identity of the citizen with the city. Athens at its height had a population estimated at 40,000 male citizens, plus 150,000 other free people (metics—alien residents who had some citizenship privileges—women, children), plus 100,000 slaves. As economic activities expanded and the burden of public business increased, the gap between citizens and the city grew.

On the one hand the citizens, who treasured the intellectual and aesthetic values of the ancient city, withdrew from full participation in public life. The men of business became increasingly indifferent so long as they were left free to reap the material rewards that came from a brisk and expanding life of trade and commerce. The result was the substitution of the paid civil servant—first introduced by Pericles—for the citizen, in the governance of the city. Gradually political power grew apart from the religious, aesthetic, and economic life. "By failing to turn the businessman into a citizen," says Mumford, "the Greek eventually turned the citizen into a businessman: first the insolent conqueror and exploiter, then the subservient subject, the cringing pedagogue, the cadger and bootlicker, the refined parasite, whose name became a by-word of contempt among the Romans, much as they admired and copied the classic Greeks."

The intimate interpersonal relations that had characterized the ancient city-state gave way to impersonal relations among strangers. Democracy gave way to alternating cycles of oligarchy and tyranny. "Probably the greatest failure of the Greek cities," says Mumford, "was their failure to transform direct democracy into a representative republic, as a solution for the problems of growth and diversity. Not merely was there a hesitation . . . to delegate authority, but the Greeks, in all their large popular assemblies, seemed to try to recapture the appearance at least of a village meeting in which every one took part." The New England town, up to a point, followed the Greek cycle of growth and decay. But its decline was arrested by the principle of representation which enabled it to evolve from the town meeting to the *representative* town meeting, to the mayor and city council, and thus to solve the problem of size and diversity. But many of the evils that plagued the Greek city continue—the alienation of the city from the countryside, the identification of the citizen not with the city but with one or more of the innumerable special interests that grow up in the city, and the substitution of the civil servant for the citizen.

By and large in America, as in ancient Greece, the citizen has become a businessman, a doctor, lawyer, merchant, trade unionist, or teacher who is at best a part-time and indifferent citizen, except where his particular interests are at stake. As cities grew and the preoccupation of citizens with their own private affairs increased, public affairs were left more and more in the hands of professionals who, in the words of George Washington Plunkitt of Tammany, "seen" their opportunities and "took 'em."

The unholy alliance at the state capital between political bosses and spokesmen for special interest groups was matched at City Hall by an alliance between city bosses and those seeking special privileges of one kind or another. The rule of Tom Platt at Albany had its local counterpart in the boss rule of William Marcy Tweed in New York City. As cities grew in size the need for services of all kinds expanded at a geometric ratio. The supply of water, transportation, fire and police protection, created opportunities not only for public service but also for private profit on a vast scale. Special charters and franchises to corporations for street railways, bus lines, and supply of water, gas, and electricity were worth millions. Even those services supplied by public authority—the administration of justice, education, sanitation, garbage disposal, police and fire protection—created a lucrative business for contractors and manufacturers in the building and supply of courthouses, schools, sewers and disposal plants, police stations, fire houses, and even streets. Huge fortunes were made from municipal contracts for the humble but essential service of garbage disposal. Private services like food, housing, recreation, and medical care were necessarily subjected to public regulation. And this opened a way for a corrupt bargain between those seeking special dispensation or exemption from these regulations and venal politicians and public servants willing for a price to look the other way.

Political bossism and corruption were not unknown in rural areas, but their most luxuriant growth occurred in those cities where size and density of population created a maximum demand for public services and a maximum need for regulation. "Living to a great extent on the corporations," wrote a most perceptive student of American politics in 1900, "bossism burst into full bloom in the states where big [corporate] interests were concentrated. . . . But in almost all other places where the machine created the boss . . . he reduced politics to a business . . ." And, one might add, forced business into politics.

"The alliance between the two kinds of privilege, political and financial," wrote Theodore Roosevelt in his autobiography, "was closely cemented. . . . In Pennsylvania the alliance [Roosevelt said] was so far reaching and so corrupt that it is difficult to describe it without seeming to exaggerate." For a decade, before and after 1900, this alliance was exposed and analyzed by a school of writers he described as "muckrakers." Gustavus Myers, *History of Great American Fortunes;* Frank Norris, *The Pit* and *The Octopus;* William D. Howells, *Hazard of New Fortunes;* Edward A. Ross, *Sin and Society;* Tom Lawson, *Frenzied Finance;* and Judge Ben Lindsay's *The System* and *The Beast* are a few titles that had a wide reading. Outstanding among other books of the muckrakers were *Progress and Poverty* by Henry George, and *The Shame of the Cities* by Lincoln Steffens. Even Viscount Bryce, the most eminent English student of American politics, referred to municipal government as our most conspicuous failure. Steffens, in *The Shame of the Cities,* put city after city under a kind of journalistic microscope to produce what can only be described as a study in American political pathology. In Philadelphia, which he described as "corrupt and contented," in Pittsburgh, St. Louis, Minneapolis, and New York, Steffens found the same combination of bossism and special privilege.[1]

Like Lorenzo de Medici in Renaissance Florence, the bosses of the Gilded Age were not wholly lacking in a sense of civic pride and social

[1] For those interested in historical parallels, *The Shame of the Cities* as described by Lincoln Steffens was not too different from the scathing indictment of the government of Florence under the Medici family by Savonarola, in a notable sermon.

"The sermon," according to Ralph Roeder (*Man of the Renaissance*), "was a summary of all the charges levelled against Lorenzo (de Medici) by his enemies—favoritism, financial maladministration, manipulation of the ballot, all the normal corruption . . . by which as a political boss he controlled the machinery of a nominal republic. . . . The Medici had merely anticipated their rivals in acquiring political power to protect their fortune. They identified their interests with those of the city, and both had prospered. Their tyranny rested, in last analysis, on popular consent . . . Studiously respecting the appearances of liberty-[Lorenzo] achieved the substance of it by an invisible dictatorship which substituted order and stability for the factitiousness of Florentine life. . . . Whatever corruption this paternalistic government cost was a small price to pay for its benefits."

responsibility. Under their benevolent tutelage, it is argued, the country prospered, industry grew by leaps and bounds, canals, bridges, railroads and highways were built. Schools and colleges, public parks and playgrounds increased, along with rapid transit, better sanitation and water supply, and improved streets and public buildings. The price may have been high, not only in terms of political corruption but in terms of human exploitation; but, as even Henry George was willing to admit, there was progress as well as poverty.

Nevertheless the writings of the muckrakers shocked the country and contributed to the reforms that followed in the Progressive movement. Reform movements cropped up all over the country: Good Government Leagues, Civic Clubs, Civil Service Reform Associations, Bureaus of Municipal Research, Citizen Unions—their name was legion and their programs as varied as their names.

☆   *MUNICIPAL HOME RULE*

High among the common objectives was municipal home rule. Under our constitutional system, cities, towns, counties, villages, and boroughs, as well as countless special districts are creatures of the states. Legally they are but agents of the state.

In many ways a city, or municipal corporation as it is called, is like a private corporation. Each is an artificial person with power to own property, make contracts, to sue and be sued. But as a public corporation, the city is denied many rights and privileges of private corporations. The private corporation is a voluntary association, organized under general laws, and its charter is a contract protected by a clause of the Constitution. Unlike a private corporation, a municipal corporation may be created without the consent of its members or residents. Its charter is not a contract and hence is "subject to constant involuntary and sometimes arbitrary changes. . . ." Its charter can be revised or revoked by the state without so much as "by your leave" unless the state constitution prohibits this. A private corporation can undertake almost any line of activity that is not forbidden by law, but a municipal corporation's powers are limited to certain public purposes. To expand its activities beyond those authorized in its charter will normally require permission from the state.

Other local governments—unincorporated counties, school districts, special districts, and authorities—are regarded as quasi-corporations acting as administrative agents for the state, for more or less specific purposes: as judicial districts, sewage disposal districts, airport districts, and even mosquito abatement districts.

Because local governments are creatures of the state, courts have generally applied what is called "Dillon's rule" in construing their powers. For a city to establish a parking lot or use the revenue from parking meters for this purpose, it is normally not enough for the mayor and the city council to act; it is not enough that the people approve. Extended hearings before state legislative committees or designated courts will be necessary. And, in the end, if it is a court that decides, the decision will follow Dillon's rule, "if in doubt, the answer is no!"

Even under ideal circumstances this close control of local government by the state would be a source of irritation, frustration, and conflict. But it becomes even more so when the legislature or at least one chamber is dominated by what city folks call the "cow county representatives." American cities, said Senator John F. Kennedy in 1958, "have been held back and hamstrung by antiquated debt limits, patchwork city charters and prehistoric municipal boundaries which uninterested and distrustful legislators balk at altering. Often they have been denied even the right to manage their own affairs." The root of the problem, according to Senator Kennedy, is that "the urban majority is politically a minority, and the rural minority dominates the polls." This situation is being substantially changed as state legislatures, under the impact of recent Supreme Court decisions, are reapportioned to give more equitable representation to the urban population. But the conflict between urban and rural interests remains.

As we have seen, this conflict between the back country and the cities is nothing new. It reaches back to colonial times and was reflected in the struggle between the agrarian rebels of the critical period and the commercial, creditor interests, between the Federalists and the Anti-Federalists in the struggle for ratification of the Constitution. And it is part and parcel of the politics of nearly every major city in every major state even today.

No political principle in America is more hallowed than the principle of "local self government," and Tocqueville's vision of democracy would probably find favor among a large majority even today. Yet since the earliest days of the Republic, "local government" has been under leading strings to the states. For over 100 years there has been active agitation to make the principle of "local self-government" more than a slogan and to translate it into practice. It has even been argued that among the unalienable rights of man is an "inherent right to self-government" on the part of cities and towns.

An important step toward municipal home rule was taken in 1851 when Ohio and Indiana, by constitutional amendment, outlawed all special legislation, including legislation affecting municipalities. If private corporations could organize under general laws, why not municipal corporations? But the first of these general laws prescribed the same form of government, the same powers and the same principles of organization and management, to all cities or towns in the state, a remedy often worse than the special laws they were designed to replace. After all, not all urban communities are alike, not all have the same needs or the same problems. Hence the so-called general act charter applying to all cities was soon abandoned. In one way or another, state constitutions and laws recognized individual differences among urban communities. Cities were classified, usually by population, and a variety of charters or forms of government were made available from which the citizens could choose a mayor-council, commission, or council-manager form. New Jersey laws provide a wide choice from something in the neighborhood of a dozen or more different types of government. Having taken these first steps toward greater local self-government, a good many states have gone still farther by granting power to local units of government to frame, adopt, and amend their own charters, subject only to the Constitution and general laws of the state. Some thirty states have granted home rule of this kind at least to the larger cities and in some cases even to smaller units of government. Approximately two-thirds of the cities having populations of over 200,000 have home rule charters.[2]

It is interesting to note that our two newest states have followed quite different policies in this respect. In Alaska the Constitution vests local governmental authority in the cities and boroughs, the purpose being "to provide a maximum of local self-government with a minimum of local governmental units." Cities and boroughs are classified according to population, geography, economy, transportation, culture, and so forth. First-class cities and organized boroughs have home rule. In unorganized boroughs the state controls. In Hawaii, on the other hand, there are but three counties and seventeen special districts. Control is highly centralized in the state and county governments, with a statewide and state-administered school system under a superintendent of public instruction. The governor appoints the county police and various local commissions including liquor commissions, library boards, and so forth.

Home rule may not necessarily enlarge the scope of power of the local units of government, although in most cases it does. State legislatures retain a large measure of control over the activities in which a city may engage, and over its finances, and general acts of the legislature take precedence over municipal legislation. The tight rein that is kept on our largest cities even in home rule states may be inferred from the fact that special legislation is still the rule in New England and in the South. How far state control may go is illustrated by some of the legislation passed in 1964 by the New York legislature for New York City. Some of the measures involved were to improve the cash position of the Transit Authority to enable it to maintain a 15-cent fare; to require the city to submit any tax proposals to the legislature not later than the third Tuesday in February; to require the city to grant tax relief to food

2 See "Unshackling Local Government," Thirtieth Report, Committee on Government Operations, House of Representatives, 89th Congress, 2nd Sess., June, 1966, esp. pp. 3–32.

wholesalers and processors under certain conditions; to permit Putnam County to divert an additional 2 million gallons daily from New York City's reservoir in order to supply a brewery in that county; to give the New York City Board of Education power to curb excessive earnings of public school custodians; to raise the salaries of the Transit Authority chairman from $35,000 to $40,000 a year, and that of two Authority members from $30,000 to $35,000; to increase pension benefits of a wide range of city employees.[3]

In spite of home rule, the centripetal forces at work in the nation at large are also at work within the states. Such is the nature of our increasingly integrated society that few, if any, of our cities can hope adequately to deal with the major problems that traditionally have been regarded as "local." Education, sanitation, police protection, transportation, parks and recreation, or air pollution are not easily administered or financed on a strictly local basis. More and more, local governments are looking to the larger metropolitan area, the regional authority, the state government, and the federal government for help in meeting the needs of our urbanized and suburbanized society.

It is well to remember also that the balance of political power in the states, as in the nation, is moving toward the metropolitan area. State legislatures formerly dominated by the "cow" counties are becoming more representative of urban areas; the governor and other state officials as well as United States Senators are dependent upon urban votes to win. In the Presidency, which is also increasingly dependent on urban areas, the cities have a powerful ally. Moreover, the organization of suburbia and exurbia and even of the open countryside is creating a new pattern of urban-rural relations.

All of these forces may well revolutionize local government in the next decade or so. By June, 1966, nine states had created agencies "to provide technical assistance to local officials and units of government and to coordinate the entire range of services applicable to community affairs." Known variously as Office of Local Government (New York), Department of Community Affairs (Pennsylvania), Intergovernmental Council on Urban Growth (California), their powers are modest but significant in aiding cities to meet the demands of modern life.

Not least important among these developments was the establishment of a Cabinet level Department of Housing and Urban Development in September, 1965, with an operating budget for fiscal year 1967 exceeding $2 billion. This revolution in government at the grass roots does not invalidate Tocqueville's vision of an American Republic resting on the town meeting or its equivalent. But it does require us to see the problem in a somewhat different framework and from a somewhat different perspective.

☆ *LOCAL GOVERNMENTS*

As we have seen, centripetal forces at work in the nation at large are also at work within the state. The revolution in transportation and communication, in business and industrial organization and management, has had far-reaching effects on government at all levels. The superhighway, the modern shopping center, television and radio, the fabulous increase in the mobility of people, the continuous interchange not only between towns and cities but between town and country, have compelled a reassessment of many time-honored principles of local government.

Literally millions of people move back and forth between our central cities and suburbia or exurbia every day. An estimated 370,000 commute daily to New York City from other communities in New York, New Jersey, and Connecticut. We spend in the neighborhood of $100 billion a year on nonmilitary transportation, of which some $25 billion is for urban and interurban transportation. The progressive urbanization of suburbs and the open country and the reciprocal influence of suburbia upon the city is noticeable in the overall pattern and style of American life. Our culture is becoming homogenized to a degree inconceivable to Alexis de Tocqueville and Ralph Waldo Emerson. The very special style of life in a southern town, a middle western metropolis, or a New England village is giving way to life in which cities and towns are almost as standardized as the interchangeable parts of a typewriter or a sewing machine.

The influences that work to homogenize our culture operate at the same time as both centripetal and centrifugal forces in our political life. On the one hand, they result in the dispersal of population into the suburbs and the open country, at the expense of the central city; and on the other hand, they operate to make it increasingly difficult for local governments as traditionally organized to cope with contemporary problems. The result is a greater reliance on larger, special *ad hoc* districts and authorities, regional or area arrangements, intercity agreements, state, and even federal, agencies. By December, 1965, the federal government was administering over 40 separate programs for urban development in which no less than 13 federal departments and agencies were involved. The programs are of great variety, ranging from Air Pollution to Water Supply, including Education, Health, and Welfare, Housing and Urban Planning.[4]

All of these forces may transform local governments in the next decade or so as they look more and more to the states and the federal

---

[4] See *The Federal System as Seen by Federal Aid Officials*, A Study of the Subcommittee on Intergovernmental Relations of the Senate Committee on Government Operations. 89th Congress, 2nd Sess., December 15, 1965.

government. Connecticut has recently abolished its eight counties as governmental units and the state has taken over their functions. The Indiana legislature abolished the fee system for county sheriffs and justices of the peace and has put them on regular salaries. Ohio has abolished the justices of the peace by creating a system of county courts and extending the jurisdiction of municipal courts. Arizona has authorized the establishment of intercounty flood control districts; Michigan has legalized the work of a six-county intercounty committee, for a variety of purposes; Nebraska has authorized the City of Lincoln to unite Lancaster County to provide for certain joint services. In other states, intermunicipal support of ambulance service, water, conservation, flood control, stream pollution, sewage disposal, library, recreational, and other services have been authorized. In fifteen states there are regional planning commissions to cope with the new problems of our urbanized civilization.

Local governments have justly complained about state restrictions on their power to tax, incur debts, and spend money. But not all state activity in these areas is restrictive. In many cases the state, because of its more extensive jurisdiction and greater power, is able to collect and administer certain taxes more efficiently than can local governments. No small part of the revenues of state governments accordingly are collected on behalf of and disbursed to local governments on a more equitable basis than would be possible for these units acting by themselves. State collection and disbursement can help to equalize services and thus bring those in poorer communities to a level closer to their more affluent neighbors.

In 1962 over 34 percent of all state expenditures (roughly $11 billion) were payments to local governments. In California, more than half its state budget goes to local governments of various kinds for education, welfare, and general governmental support. For many functions local governments would be helpless were it not for state intervention and assistance. However much the ancient conflict between rural and urban interests may persist, it will not do to think of intergovernmental relations within the states solely in these terms. More often than not the relation is not that of adversaries or of rivals but one of mutual aid and cooperation.

Special Districts

The basic structure of local government in America has grown in response to the needs of people settled in a continent of 3 million square miles. Many of the governmental units established were designed literally for the age of the horse and buggy. Now that the horse and buggy have gone, save in Amish country, the governmental structure might well be overhauled. To bring government within the reach of all the people has led to the multiplication of governmental units. Yet it is worth re-membering that over 60 percent of our 90,000 units are school districts or other special districts created not for general purposes but for special and limited functions. This proliferation of special districts reflects, among other things, a desire to remove the function or service in question from "political" control. The theory seems to be that where a particular service is placed under the jurisdiction of the county, city, or town gov-ernment, it will become, as the saying is, "a political football," or it will be lost or neglected in the preoccupation of government with other matters. This has been notoriously true in the case of education, where the independent school district with its elected board of education, or its popularly elected school superintendent has existed from very early times. Literally hundreds of these independent school districts had a school population scarcely large enough to fill a single school. Many of them contained little more than a one-room school taught by one under-paid, overworked teacher. There have indeed been school districts in which there were more school officials than there were children. These were literally "horse and buggy" units of government, made necessary and tolerable in sparsely settled rural areas if education was to be brought within the reach of all children.

With improved transportation and the migration of population to urban areas, literally thousands of these school districts became re-dundant. The consolidated school, and school buses made it possible for one district to serve a larger area and a larger school population. The result has been that between 1942 and 1962 the total number of school districts declined by more than 73,000. (See Table 20–1.)

TABLE 20–1
Local Governments in the United States

Numbers by Types	*1942*	*1952*	*1957*	*1962*
U. S. Government	1	1	1	1
States	48	48	48	50
Counties	3,050	3,052	3,050	3,043
Municipalities	16,220	16,807	17,215	17,997
Townships	18,919	17,202	17,198	17,144
School districts	108,579	67,355	50,454	34,678
Special districts	8,299	12,340	14,424	18,323
Total Local	155,067	116,756	102,341	91,185
Grand total	155,116	116,807	102,392	91,236

SOURCE: U.S. Bureau of the Census, *1962 Census of Governments: Governmental Units in 1962,* Preliminary Report No. 6 (Washington, D.C., December 6, 1962) , p. 1; *Historical Statistics of the United States, 1961,* p. 694.

As the cost of education has increased, the independent or county school district has become less and less able to finance its own schools without state aid. Accordingly, state programs have been developed under which grants from the state establish a "foundation" or minimum appropriation for the schools and thus, in some measure, "equalize" educational opportunity.[5] In 1965 state and federal support of local schools in all the states was approximately 50 percent of total educational expenditures. As state aid increases and the financial viability of the independent district declines, there may be a further reduction in the number of such units. Besides, a serious question may be raised concerning the advisability of setting education off from other governmental functions under an independent agency. Mayors, city managers, city councilmen, and county supervisors speak bitterly about local school boards as "sacred cows."

Other special districts have been established and justified not only to "keep them out of politics" but because it is said they can operate more efficiently, employ more professional help, can more easily be financed by special taxes or fees, and can be more easily "watched" by those most interested in their operations. Moreover, boundaries for irrigation districts, sewage disposal districts, or air pollution districts, it is said, can be drawn to conform more closely to the problem area than is the case with more general units like counties or townships.[6]

In many cases special districts have been established under pressure from organized groups who prefer that these special services be independent of more general local governmental units, which is another way of saying that they prefer not to be responsible to the general voting public. It is interesting to note that whereas the number of independent school districts has declined by about 60 percent since 1942, the number of other special districts has increased by over 100 percent, from around 8,300 to some 18,000. Professor John Bollens, in a recent book *Special District Governments in the United States,* voices the misgiving of most authorities concerning this development. Fear is expressed that control of local government may be passing from the traditional county and city government into the hands of more or less independent agencies not responsible to the wider political community. Altogether, special districts spend more money each year than is spent by all county, township, and town governments, and almost as much as all city governments. How to bring these special districts into some more responsible relation to other local units is a major problem.

Although special districts, including school districts, constitute over half of all governmental units in the United States, the major units of local government in terms of population, income, and expenditures are

---

[5] These state grants are usually so much per child in average daily attendance.

[6] In the case of other special districts, as in the case of the independent school district, state aid has been necessary although in nothing like the same magnitude.

some 18,000 municipalities, 3,000 counties and approximately 17,000 towns or townships. By a perhaps unhappy paradox, the least important of these are the towns or townships so warmly praised by Tocqueville, Jefferson, Emerson, and others. The close integration of town and country which the New England township made possible has largely been lost in the modern municipal corporation and even in the unincorporated towns of rural America. In spite of some efforts at imitation elsewhere, the New England town did not take root outside of New England. Even where it was copied, as in the Middle Atlantic states and in a half-dozen Middle Western states, it never developed the kind of organic relation between town and country where the "town common" and the "town forest" were symbols of the interdependence of the town dweller with the sons of the soil. Even in New England the town meetings have declined in importance as the open meeting gave way to the "representative" meeting, and this in turn to the city council. The town board of selectmen is, in effect, a town council and the moderator is more like a weak mayor. Some towns have hired managers who, with paid civil servants, carry on the work of government, thus divorcing not only the countryman from the town but the town dweller from active participation in the governance of his community.

The County

The county has been called a "dark continent" in American government. Unlike the New England town, most of our 3,000 counties were not an organic growth. With a few exceptions they have been more or less arbitrary areas whose boundaries correspond to no "natural" features of the landscape or of the population. Although they have enclosed both urban and rural areas, sometimes cutting quite arbitrarily across towns and cities, they have not, on the whole, represented a satisfactory integration of town and country.

Most counties, like most school districts, have been "horse and buggy" governments, designed to bring certain public services within physical reach of citizens compelled to travel on foot, on horseback, or in a horse and buggy. In Texas 242 counties were necessary to cover the state; in Connecticut 8; in Hawaii only 3—the average being about 63 per state. Governed by boards of commissioners or supervisors directly elected by the people, they have as a rule had no unified or effective executive leadership. A rather confused direction has been given by a number of independently elected administrative officers; an elective county auditor, treasurer, recorder, sheriff, coroner, surveyor, assessor, clerk, and sometimes superintendent of schools, make even the plural executive of the state governments seem modest by comparison. For a predominantly rural America providing minimal governmental services the county served perhaps as well as any other unit might have done. The county seat, presumably centrally located to enable easy access, was a center for the administration of justice, health and welfare activities, record-keeping (births and deaths), law enforcement (outside the urban areas), road building and maintenance, and sometimes education. The county fair and the circus, the Chautauqua circuit and other cultural attractions of rural America had their focus at the county seat. Most important, politically, the county has been a unit of representation in the state legislature. But with the urban drift of recent decades, in many states, the county has become redundant or at least downgraded in the total web of government.

Fewer than 2.5 percent of the 3,000 counties (about 75) now contain over one-third of our total population. Out of 433 counties in ten middle western states, 381 showed a net decline in population between 1950 and 1960. One-fourth of the counties (some 750 out of 3,000) serve only about 3.5 percent of the population. The entrenched power of county political machines, feeding on archaic systems of personnel management (the spoils system is still widely prevalent) and plural executives, many with fantastic incomes from fees, have made it difficult to reform or to abolish counties even where their redundancy is openly acknowledged.[7]

Nevertheless some progress has been made. Some county governments have been reorganized to provide for a single executive and at least the beginning of a merit system for personnel. A few have adopted a county-manager plan to improve management and to reduce costs. In some places where city and county boundaries more or less correspond, city and county governments have been consolidated. In some states the number of counties has been reduced by law, and in Connecticut they have been abolished. But in the county, as in other areas of American government, we confront something of a paradox. As the problems facing local government increasingly transcend the limits of towns or cities, the county may be a more reasonable area both for policy and administration than the town or city itself. This is especially true as the suburban drift matches or exceeds the urban drift. It could be, therefore, that county government may be on the threshold of a renaissance as public services demand larger areas if they are to serve not only the central cities but the suburbs and the population living on the urban fringe.

Throughout the country there are signs that the role of the county in the total governmental process is increasingly important. This is reflected in the fact that within ten years, 1953–1963, employees of county governments increased by 54 percent (from 498,000 to 764,000), while city payrolls grew by only 27 percent (from 1,175,000 to 1,496,000). County budgets have increased by more than 75 percent. Nor is this surprising when one recalls that two-thirds of the so-called "standard metropolitan

---

[7] Some county officials operate on a "fee for service" basis, and many a county sheriff, purchasing agent, health officer, coroner, or clerk have incomes exceeding those paid to the mayors and city managers of great cities or to the governors of most states.

areas" in the United States lie within the boundaries of a single county. In many of these areas, it is said, "the county is the only unit of government with the broad tax base and unused debt authority needed to organize area-wide services . . . [and] in most of these areas there is no other unit of local government with the geographic jurisdiction to cope with metropolitan problems."[8] Increasingly federal grant programs, especially in metropolitan areas, are being administered on a county basis. A recent study of local governmental administration of federal grants-in-aid programs showed that although less than 20 percent of all such programs were administered on a county level, "44 percent of the metropolitan grant administrators indicated county administration of their grant programs."[9]

However, if there is to be such a renaissance of the county, there must be some pretty drastic changes in its power structure. Counties, like cities, will need a greater measure of home rule. The typical board of county commissioners or supervisors must be transformed into a more representative body. A single responsible elective executive officer must replace the plural executives now common in most counties. This in turn will require a modern system of personnel administration. Where feasible there should be a consolidation of county and city governments, or, in any case, the elimination of overlapping jurisdictions and duplication of services now so prevalent. A redefinition of the area and powers of the county will be needed if it is to conform to modern methods of transportation and communication. There must be closer liaison with state agencies; and, finally, counties that have outlived their usefulness should be abolished.

☆   *THE URBAN COMPLEX*

Both the town and the county have been eclipsed in importance by the incorporated municipality. By 1965 some 70 percent of our population was living within the jurisdiction of incorporated urban communities, and the city had become both the hope and the despair of American democracy.

Among cities as among counties, there are wide differences as to size, structure, and functions. At one end of the scale nearly three-fourths of them (72 percent or 13,000 out of 18,000) have fewer than 2,500 people and include altogether only 5 percent of the total population. Most of these are little more than villages, organized as municipalities. For their residents they often provide a kind of community life reminiscent of the New England town in its heyday. For those who believe with Plato that

---

8 See Mitchell Gordon, "Counties' Comeback," in the *Wall Street Journal,* August 26, 1963.

9 *The Federal System as Seen by Federal Aid Officials,* 1965, *op. cit.,* p. 79.

"there is no greater good in a city than that the citizens should be known to each other," these miniscule municipalities have much to offer. Unfortunately many of them on the fringes of larger cities are not so much communities as dormitories for commuters who work and live in the big city and sleep in the small one, or perhaps more accurately live *off* the city but *in* the suburbs. They are, in effect, urban carpetbaggers whose daily bread comes from the central city but whose hearts belong to Shady Hill.

At the other end of the scale are approximately 300 cities of 50,000 or more, which include over half of our total urban population—that is, fewer than 2 percent of the cities include 50 percent or more of the population. The total urban population of the nation occupies only about 1 percent of the nation's land area, and the basic difference between urban and rural communities is best represented by differing degrees of population density. For places of 1,000,000 or more, the average density is nearly 14,000 per square mile. Cities with 100,000 to 1,000,000 people have an average density of 4,000 to 6,000 per square mile, while cities of 2,500 to 5,000 have a density of 1,400 per square mile. The so-called urban fringe has a density of 1,700 per square mile, and the rural fringe a density of only 15 to the square mile.

But the urban drift is not properly understood solely in these terms. The Bureau of the Census now recognizes a new and complex pattern of urban growth, the so-called standard Metropolitan statistical area. As defined by the Bureau, it consists of an area surrounding a central city of not less than 50,000, the county in which it is located, plus other continuous urbanized nonagricultural areas and with extensive economic and social contacts with the central city. Three-fourths of the population of the Metropolitan Area is engaged in nonagricultural employment. By 1965, the Bureau of the Census had identified over 227 such metropolitan areas in which nearly two-thirds of our total population now lives. Some 24 of these areas contain over 1,000,000 people, five contain 3,000,000 or more, and one has an estimated population of 11,000,000.

Another term for the most extensive and complex of these areas is *megalopolis.*[10] A recent book by Jean Gottman, published by the Twentieth Century Fund, identifies one such megalopolis as an area stretching from New Hampshire to northern Virginia, embracing over 53,000 square miles with a 1960 population of 37,000,000. Other areas, not quite so vast but almost as impressive, are found in the Middle West between the Great Lakes and the Ohio River, and in California from Sacramento to San José. In these areas a number of central cities serve as focal points for a complex structure of smaller towns, suburbs, fringe areas and other urbanized territory.

[10] The term *megalopolis* comes from an ancient Greek city founded in 370 B.C. according to legend, as headquarters for the new anti-Spartan Arcadian League. In the process of building the city, many small towns and villages were absorbed.

These new metropolitan or megalopolitan areas, as they urbanize the surrounding country and suburbanize the central city, may provide a reintegration of the city and the country in a way hitherto unknown, even in ancient Greece or colonial New England. In most of them population density in the central city is over twice that of the fringe areas, although in thirteen of the Standard Metropolitan Areas the density of the fringe area exceeds that of the central city. This new megalopolis poses problems and presents opportunities that we have only begun to explore. In these areas a new kind of culture and civilization is emerging. "Cities that were once dots on the rural landscape," says Wilfred Owen, "may become part of the landscape itself. . . . [Not as] congested areas . . . but interspersed with farms, forests, parks, and recreation lands." The countryside and the city may again join hands. The kinship broken by metropolis will be restored by megalopolis.[11]

The Central City

In projecting the problems of urban America into the broader framework of the metropolitan area, we ought not to overlook the central importance of the central city. Thirteen of the largest contain about 20 percent of the total urban population and provide 23 percent of its nonagricultural employment. Their population per square mile is 23 times that of the rest of the metropolitan areas of which they are the heart and center. Even manufacturing activity, which has been moving to suburbia, is nineteen times as high per acre in the central city as in the rest of the metropolitan area. The central city still serves as the heart which gives and sustains life in the greater metropolitan area.

In one sense the metropolitan area evolved as one means by which the central city has sought to solve some of the most urgent problems of urban America. The central city was running out of space and, between 1950 and 1960, it lost population to suburbia: 43 cities of 100,000 or more lost population in this period. Of five cities with 1,000,000 or more people, all except Los Angeles lost population as did seven of the 16 with 500,000 to 1,000,000. On the other hand, fourteen cities of 25,000 in 1950

11 The Standard Metropolitan Areas present some interesting growth trends. Whereas Standard Metropolitan Areas increased by 23.6 millions or about 26 percent between 1950 and 1960, the country outside Standard Metropolitan Areas increased only 7.1 percent and the country as a whole, only 18 percent. The inc.ease in the Areas was more than twice that of the central cities themselves. There are also significant regional differences in this urban drift. In the Northeast, where the overall population increased by 13 percent, the central cities declined by 3 percent and the suburban ring increased by 34 percent. In the North Central states, SMSA's increased 23.5 percent, and the area outside the SMSA increased 6.6 percent; central cities, 4 percent, and suburbia 56 percent. In the South, SMSA increased 36.2 percent, outside SMSA, 2.7 percent; (i.e., SMSA 13 times as fast) ; central cities increased 25 percent; suburban ring, 50 percent. And in the West, SMSA increased 49 percent; outside SMSA, 19 percent; central cities increased 31 percent; suburbia 66 percent.

had increased by over 100 percent in 1960.[12] As the population of the central cities declines more space may make possible a renovation and renaissance of urban life.

The extent to which America has become a nation of city dwellers or at least residents of urban areas, is a bit startling. In California by 1960 over 80 percent of the population was living in nine metropolitan areas. In New York, Pennsylvania, Illinois, and elsewhere a similar concentration is to be found. And as population increases, the demand for government services and the cost of providing them grow at an even faster rate. Government costs indeed seem to follow a pattern that may be summarized in the formula:

$$\text{Costs} = (\text{Population} \times \text{density} \times \text{mobility})^2.$$

Consequently more people living in less space, and/or moving at an accelerated rate within the city, between cities and between the city and suburbia, mean a greater demand for virtually every kind of public service. Schools, houses, streets, parking lots, sewers, heating, hospitals, parks—everything must be multiplied and multiplied again, at costs that balloon overnight. A city lot or tract for a housing project may cost ten times tomorrow what it costs today as the demand for land burgeons with the population.

In California Governor Brown's Commission on Metropolitan Area Problems reported in 1961 that "each new family arriving in California requires approximately $13,000 of public expenditures to provide for its needs in the local community. Based on an estimated state population of 30 million by 1980, local government in California faces an expenditure for basic public facilities of about $60 billions, in the next twenty years." With inflation and the increased costs that increasing density entails, this figure is probably conservative. Catherine Bauer Wurster, in her report for the President's Commission on National Goals, has projected some of the problems of our urban society up to 1970. Total population, she estimates, will increase by 30 million to approximately 210 million, and the metropolitan areas will get most of this increase. Two-thirds of our people will be living in metropolitan areas, a third in agglomerations of over a million. Most of them, however, will live outside the old central cities, which will continue to lose population to suburbia and exurbia. Racial minorities will increase in metropolitan areas, but will be more evenly distributed among the major cities. By 1970 another bumper crop of babies, as young people marry earlier, will generate an increasing demand for schools, hospitals, parks, and playgrounds—not to mention an increase of some 50 percent in the number of job-seekers under 25.[13]

---

[12] 2 in Arizona; 1 in Ohio; 2 in Texas; 1 in Virginia; 5 in California; 2 in Florida; 1 in New Mexico.

[13] Although the rate of increase may be somewhat reduced by family planning, increased recreational facilities, and other environmental factors, these figures remain fairly constant.

There will also be an increase in the proportion of older workers with their special problems. And, although business services, finance, insurance, real estate, wholesale supply may remain in the central city, manufacturing and a large share of retail trade will move out to the fringe area or the suburb. Indeed, half of American manufacturing is already located outside the central city.

This relocation of business and industry will have a profound effect on the employment pattern. Automation will reduce industrial employment and increase employment for urban white-collar workers. Shorter hours, higher pay, and more leisure will mean a greater demand for recreational facilities, more parks and playgrounds, more adult education, more music, drama, and art centers. In spite of the relocation of business and industry, the commuter problem will increase, and a 40 percent increase in automobiles will not make it any easier to break the traffic congestion.

More specifically these changes will require more and better housing, slum clearance, and urban redevelopment. Over 400 cities by 1962 had renewal programs under way, and others were in the planning stage. "Since 1950 about 15,000 acres of slums and blight have been acquired for redevelopment and public housing," says Mrs. Wurster, "but several hundred thousands of acres should be cleared." About one and a half million substandard houses have been demolished, but an estimated 10 million remain. Racial discrimination and segregation will be inevitable and politically explosive unless public authority is alert and eager to prevent it.[14] In suburbia the multiplication of detached dwellings will create problems of inflated land and building costs, of transportation, education, sanitation, fire and police protection. The taxes paid by the average family may fall short of the civic costs this kind of development entails. Suburban shopping centers, theatres, and restaurants will urbanize the countryside with "fringe centers" to rival the central city.

All of these trends will complicate and magnify the problems of urban government. Take, for example, the problem of intra- and interurban transportation. Americans spend $100 billion a year or more on nonmilitary transportation. About $25 billion of this is transportation in metropolitan areas. Almost as much is spent for this service as for housing. How can megalopolis prevent 40 percent more cars by 1970 from producing strangulation and stagnation? Is the answer to be found in more public mass rapid transit? In the San Francisco Bay Area, for example, it is estimated that such a system, now under construction, will cost over $1 billion. Even then, no one is really sure that commuters will use it. Are more freeways the answer? If so, we will need an increase from

14 The tragic race riots in 1965, 1966, 1967, and 1968 in Los Angeles, Chicago, New York, and other cities of the North as well as in the South are largely the product of failure to solve these basic problems of metropolitan growth.

10,000 to 50,000 miles by 1970, and half of this in urban areas. Can we cut commuting by moving jobs to people rather than people to jobs? Can we at the same time decentralize other things such as the theater, restaurants, schools, and museums which have made the city the center of culture? Are there values in the big city, not transferable to the small town or the suburbs? Will millions of people be willing to sacrifice these things to avoid from one to four hours a day just on the journey to and from work or play? In the face of vanishing open space and spreading pollution, how can we satisfy the demand for outdoor recreation? "There should be at least 30 acres of reasonably convenient parks and/or wilderness per 1,000 people for active recreational use, with further acreage for other kinds of open space," says the President's Commission on National Goals. Yet every increase of 1,000 people will urbanize more than 100 acres of open land and make the rest of it frightfully expensive. A million acres costing $500,000 today will cost several billions in a few years.[15]

Many metropolitan areas will have to make better use of the land they now enclose. In city after city, and in the suburbs, land is held for speculation while developers move in and around it, creating not urban growth but urban sprawls with housing developments that turn into what one writer has characterized as "slurbs"—to indicate suburban slums. In 1960 there were about 6,000,000 acres in state, county and municipal parks. By 1970 this should be increased by at least 5,000,000 acres. What will it be by A.D. 2000? The rate of growth and change is such that, like the Red Queen, urban America must run faster and faster just to stay where it now is.

Structure of City Government

How are cities organized to meet these Promethean problems? In the early years the same fear of a strong executive afflicted our cities as has plagued our state governments. Down to the beginning of this century, the standard municipal government was a city council often elected by wards or other districts and an elective mayor with little more than ceremonial powers. As part of the reform movement following the *Shame of the Cities* and the Progressive crusade, the powers of the mayor were increased. The city council was reduced in size from as many as 50 to 7 or 9, elected at large and on a nonpartisan ballot. Terms of office were increased to a normal four years so that councilmen, part-time public servants, could learn their jobs.

The key to this "strong mayor and council" system which now

[15] In 1960 in San Francisco, for example, Henry Doelger, a mass builder of houses, paid $580,000 for a tract offered for $15,000 in 1948. On Long Island, builders in 1960 were paying $16,000 an acre for land bought for $3,500 in 1950. In South Jersey, a farmer bought 60 acres and a house in 1948 for $20,000; in 1960 he refused to sell the land without the house for $360,000. Land in Orange County selling for $2,000 an acre in 1952 sold for $16,000 an acre in 1960. See *House and Home,* August, 1960.

governs a large majority of American cities, is, as the name implies, a strong mayor. He is normally the only elected executive officer. He appoints the chief administrative officers who are responsible to him. The mayor prepares the budget and is the chief source of major policy recommendations to the council. In some cases a chief administrative officer may be hired as an assistant but subordinate to the mayor. In outline the plan is a good one. Power and responsibility are combined in the mayor, and the decision-making process involves a popularly elected council, large enough to be representative and small enough to discourage the demagogue and to encourage deliberation. The administrative process is sufficiently flexible and responsible to expand with the growing needs of the city. Of course a major problem remains where the state legislature refuses to give the city the power needed to deal with its problems. But a reasonable accommodation of urban-state relations is probably more easily accomplished under the strong mayor-form of government than any other.

Two other forms of government should be mentioned: the so-called commission plan and the council-manager plan. (See Figure 20–1.) The commission plan grew out of the experience of Galveston, Texas, in meeting a municipal crisis resulting from a hurricane in September, 1900. The state legislature suspended local self-government and appointed a temporary government of local businessmen who became the Galveston Commission. Under the plan, which for a time was widely copied, there is no independent mayor and no council as such. A commission of five to seven members is elected at large, usually for 4-year terms with the commissioner getting the highest vote designated as mayor, a more or less honorific job. Commissioners are full-time public servants and they divide responsibility among themselves for the major functions of the city. One will be commissioner of public safety, another of police and fire, a third will be commissioner of public works; a fourth, commissioner of health and welfare, and so on. Other administrative officers report to their respective commissioners and executive responsibility is divided among them. Meeting together, the commissioners serve as a city council (with the honorific mayor in the chair) and decide on policy. Thus in a kind of bizarre imitation of parliamentary government the executive and legislative powers are integrated. Hailed as a "businessman's government," as many as 500 cities had adopted the plan by 1901. But the commission plan has not come up to its advance billing, and the number of cities so organized has steadily declined.

In theory the commission plan puts government in the hands of nonpartisan "businessmen"; concentrates responsibility for particular services in particular men so that you know whom to praise or blame; and simplifies the voter's task by making possible a short ballot. Unfortunately the nonpartisan commissioners are not always able businessmen, or men of vision and civic virtue. Nonpartisan in theory, they are often

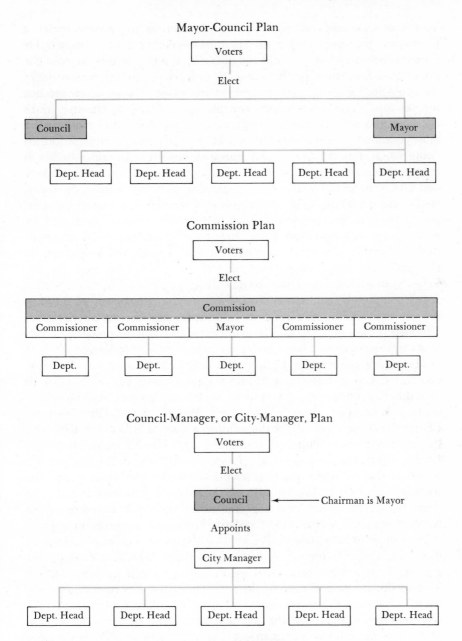

Figure 20–1   The Three Forms of City Government.

nominated by urban factions to whom they owe a fealty not always consistent with the public interest. By placing legislative power in the elected commissioners, the plan quite properly placed responsibility for policy in the hands of amateurs responsible to the people. But by uniting legislative, executive, and administrative leadership in the same hands, it placed an excessive burden on commissioners not always trained for public administration. Nor did the election of men specially trained for police administration, public works, or other specialized functions solve the problem. "Experts," runs a familiar aphorism, "should be on *tap* but not on *top*." The commission plan, moreover, lacks an effective inner check on the administrative bureaucracy by unwisely combining in the same commissioners responsibility for both policy and administration. In doing so, it ignores nearly two hundred years of American political theory and practice. If serious conflict occurs between the commissioner and subordinates in his department, the plan offers no satisfactory way to resolve the conflict or to get any reasonably impartial review as might be gotten from an independent council. Finally, it is generally agreed by students of administration that, except for quasi-legislative or quasi-judicial functions, a committee administrator is weak and ineffective. As Georges Clemenceau once observed: "If the good Lord had left the Creation to a committee, chaos would still reign."

More popular and more effective is the council-manager plan. This, too, is a business form of organization resembling the corporation, although it owes much to the German system of city government to which many reformers turned for a model. In 1908, probably following the lead of Haven Mason, editor of *California Municipalities,* Staunton, Virginia, hired a general manager as a full-time administrator at a high salary to run the city under the government of a weak mayor and bicameral council. The experiment worked well, and a model City Manager Charter soon appeared under the guiding genius of Richard S. Childs of the National Short Ballot Organization and the National Municipal League. The council-manager, or city-manager, plan became the favorite of progressive reformers, political scientists, and business leaders alike. Its basic features may be briefly outlined. A city council of from five to nine members, elected at large for staggered terms, usually of four years, on a nonpartisan basis, serves as the legislative branch of the government. It is large enough to be representative, yet small enough to serve as a board of directors. There is usually a mayor, sometimes popularly elected, but ordinarily chosen by the council to preside at council meetings and to serve as the ceremonial head of the city. The mayor has no real administrative or executive powers, however, since these are concentrated in a city manager, trained for the job and appointed to serve during the pleasure of the council. The manager, like the president of a corporation, is the real executive of the city, reporting and responsible to the council, as the corporation president is responsible to the board of directors. The demonstrable efficiency of this streamlined government and the close analogy to the structure of the corporation made the plan popular with business organizations not otherwise noted for their interest in political reform. By 1965 over 1,700 cities and counties had adopted the plan,

TABLE 20–2
Relative Popularity of the Three Forms of City Government

Population	Mayor-Council	Commission	Council-Manager
Over 500,000	80%	0%	20%
250,000–500,000	43%	17%	40%
100,000–250,000	39%	12%	49%
50,000–100,000	36%	13%	51%
25,000–50,000	35%	13%	52%
10,000–25,000	49%	10%	41%
5,000–10,000	67%	5%	28%
All Cities	54%	9%	37%

including such sizable places as Dallas, Hartford, Des Moines, Oakland, and Berkeley, California. Over 50 percent of the cities of 25,000 or more have city-manager plan governments. (See Table 20–2.) In metropolitan areas it has been less popular, although both Kansas City and Cleveland tried it for a time. An International City Managers Association has promoted the plan and helped develop high professional standards for those who aspire to become city or county managers. Salaries have lagged behind comparable salaries in private business, but somewhat ahead of what cities had formerly paid even for top administrative positions. The profession has attracted men trained in law, engineering, industrial management, business, and public administration. But technical training alone does not produce the most successful city managers, for the job requires the tact of a diplomat, the thoroughness of an efficiency expert, and the patience of Job.

Some 85 percent of the city managers have been recruited from outside the cities they serve, and a tradition has developed of successful managers moving out and upward to positions of increasing opportunity and responsibility. "An experienced outsider with a fresh viewpoint, directed by a council that knows local conditions, can do a better job than a local man hampered by local ties," says one observer.

In some ways the city-manager plan is the apotheosis of the reformer's dream. City government, they say, is essentially a business like any other business. It should be managed in a nonpartisan, objective manner with staff and line personnel appointed on the basis of merit alone and subject only to tests of competence, loyalty, and integrity. The manager is conceived of as being not only nonpartisan but even nonpolitical. Where and how cities under this plan are to get political leadership, no one seems to know. The council as a part-time body of nonpartisan amateurs, or the mayor as the ceremonial officer of the city, cannot supply it. If the plan has an Achilles' heel, this failure to provide for dynamic political leadership may be it.

Beginning in the 1880s our larger cities have adopted merit systems for selecting their administrative personnel. Progress in this respect has been due as much to the changing nature of municipal services as to the municipal reform movement. Traffic engineering, public housing, water supply, public health, sanitation, even modern methods of police and fire protection can no longer be left to catch-as-catch-can personnel methods. The trend in the larger cities toward a strong mayor and a full-time city council has also brought into the municipal legislature a different kind of legislator. The absence of a plural executive and the increased power of an elected chief executive serving full time and more adequately paid has brought into city government men of greater experience and a greater sense of commitment to the public service. More important, and this is particularly true of the strong-mayor type of government, it has again combined power with political responsibility.

"The profile of today's big city mayor, with one difference, is quite similar to that of the chief executive of a large corporation," said *Fortune Magazine* in November, 1952. "Typically the mayor is a college graduate, usually with a legal or business background, and is now in his late fifties. He puts in hard, grinding hours at his desk, sometimes seven days a week. The difference is in salary: he usually makes $20,000 to $25,000. . . ." A comparable corporation executive would get two to four times as much.

There are, of course, other and more profound differences. The mayor is responsible to a wide electorate, the corporation executive to his board of directors. The mayor's job is not to show a profit but to promote the health, welfare, and safety of the city. The mayor cannot pass his job on to his son (as many a corporation executive can), nor can he, without grave political risk, do many other things open to corporation executives. But *Fortune's* analogy is not a bad one.

Not the least of the changes since the days of Steffens and Bryce has been in the character of the cities' population. It is better educated, better paid, more confident and secure in its social and economic life, and hence less susceptible to the kind of "immigrant overlord bossism" that characterized municipal politics in the days of Plunkitt, Tweed, and their confreres. Some graft and peculation is still to be found, ranging from "inside tips" on land speculation to traffic ticket fixing. But standards of ethics in public life will compare favorably with standards in private business or the professions. Although one cannot measure municipal government by profit and loss standards, it is no exaggeration to say that the average citizen buys more for less money with his city tax dollar than with any other dollar he spends.[16]

Metropolitan Government

If we may paraphrase an aphorism, metropolitan America's fault is not in itself but in its stars. The transformation of American life by modern

16 See Edward Banfield (ed.), *Urban Government* (New York: Free Press, 1961); also his *Political Influence* (New York: Free Press, 1962).

electronics, the automobile, TV, and our all but incredible mobility, accelerated by a standard of living that is the envy of most of the world, has simply moved faster than city governments have been able to move or have been allowed to move. The central problem has become not government in the central city, although it bristles with problems of its own, but metropolitan government and ultimately the government of megalopolis. Density and mobility, plus the endless quest for more light and air, have produced not only a population explosion but a problem expansion of even greater dimensions. With the best will in the world, with the strongest mayor, the best city council, the finest civil service, cities as they now operate are powerless to solve the problems of the metropolitan areas. These problems have expanded beyond the legal walls or jurisdiction of the city. The population has spilled into the suburbs, into the adjoining counties, and even across state lines and has carried its problems with it.

In studies of metropolitan area problems in California, New York, Pennsylvania, Massachusetts, and elsewhere there is a striking unanimity in the nature of the problems to be dealt with. They include water and electricity supply, transportation, sewage disposal, flood control, garbage and waste disposal, and air pollution control, as major metropolitan problems that can no longer be dealt with on the basis of separate autonomous towns or cities.[17] Most studies emphasize the need for a strong economic base if metropolitan government is to succeed. Virtually every community will seek to expand its income-producing activities. If this is done by a kind of dog-eat-dog competition for the location of industry, for schools and colleges, streets and highways, the area can become not a community but an array of rival power centers in deadly tribal combat.[18]

"As long as the present system of government exists," says Robert Wood, "the regional economic system . . . functions less effectively. Lacking a mechanism for regional policy-making, the metropolitan political system is unable to use planning, joint redevelopment, and transportation programs to assist the processes of production and distribution."[19]

Since high-value property normally returns more in tax revenue than the cost of the public services it requires, every governmental unit in the great metropolitan areas will try to attract the greatest possible

[17] The Sayre Report on the New York Metropolitan Regional Council includes all of these (except flood control) but adds the provision of recreation space and facilities. Others include police administration and law enforcement, a wider tax base, elimination of overlapping and duplication of services, etc. Most studies also emphasize the need for the conservation of cultural resources, many of which are threatened by the growth of strip cities as well as by the drift to the suburbs.

[18] See *Guiding Metropolitan Growth,* a report of the Committee on Economic Development, 1960.

[19] *Metropolis Against Itself,* Committee on Economic Development, 1959.

amount of such property. And as they succeed individual property values will increase faster than the tax burden, a consummation devoutly wished by prudent investors. On the other hand, as George Duggar points out, low-value property "not only costs the government more in services on a per unit basis than it returns in revenue but also adversely affects the property owners. . . ." These differences of economic opportunity and adversity are reflected in problems of human behavior, in delinquency, family disorganization, and racial conflict. Unless more comprehensive plans are made than are now possible to prevent slums, ghettoes, skid rows, and "slurbs," these signs of urban blight will transform the central city into an asphalt jungle. Metropolitan government can help to prevent this decay. It can also strengthen and enrich the cultural resources of the great city. For government, whether in a town or a metropolitan area, is not an end in itself.

According to the Governor's Commission on Metropolitan Area Problems, "not a single identified metropolitan area in California has a planning function extending over the entire area. . . . In the meantime, in the absence of metropolitan land-use plans, much of the state's best agricultural land is disappearing under subdivisions. The daily increase of 1,500 people in our population is converting 140,000 acres annually to urban use . . . 375 acres a day." By 1980 this will cost the state 3,000,000 acres, about 50 percent of all the top quality farm land in California.

In the meantime other problems multiply. One hundred thousand miles of county roads and city streets must be improved or constructed. Every day 12,500 tons of pollutants are discharged into the air in Los Angeles, and water is already in short supply. Stream, lake, and beach pollution goes on at a dizzy pace. Some measure of the total need is indicated by some figures from California, where in 1960 some $3 billion in bond issues were approved, not including over $1/2 billion more for water and sewer facilities, port improvement, recreation and park facilities, and garbage disposal.

What is to be done, and how? One obvious and apparently easy answer is to create by state law, for each new and burgeoning problem, a special *ad hoc* district or agency, called an authority, commission, board, or corporation: the Port of New York Authority, the Boston Metropolitan District Commission, the East Bay Transit Commission, the Golden Gate Authority, the New Jersey Water Supply District, the Chicago Park District, the New York Triborough Bridge and Tunnel Authority—their names are legion.

The Port of New York Authority, created in 1921 by the legislatures of New York and New Jersey, is a prototype of this device. It is, no doubt, "a convenient way to finance improvements through revenue bonds without interference with the debt structure, fiscal policies and budget procedures of regular governments." It is an autonomous agency with a board of twelve commissioners, six each appointed by the governors of New York and New Jersey for staggered terms of six years. Commissioners serve without pay. Its executive director heads a staff of 4,400 employees responsible for the operation of bridges, tunnels, piers, air, truck, and train terminals. Investments of the Authority are in the neighborhood of a billion dollars.

Special agencies of this kind are no doubt effective devices "to provide competent engineering solutions" to difficult problems, and they have multiplied in recent years. By 1956 there were eleven in California, seven in Illinois, eleven in Ohio, five in Texas, and four in Wisconsin engaged in a wide variety of public services. But the special district, *ad hoc* authority or corporation poses some difficult questions. Their multiplication not only increases the confusion of local government but removes many important problem areas from effective control by the people living in the area.

"The *ad hoc* approach," says Luther Gulick, "makes self-government by the people of the metropolitan area . . . impossible as a practical matter. . . . The *ad hoc* agencies and authorities . . . [are left] floating around in a sort of irresponsible political limbo." As management or administrative agencies, much can be said for them, but not as agencies for making basic policy for a whole metropolitan area. To allow them to do so is to let the tail wag the dog. The *ad hoc* agency is no answer to the main problem of metropolitan government. What is needed is a new kind of urban government competent to deal with the general problems of a metropolitan area. Such a government need not take the same form everywhere, and it may be accomplished in a number of ways. Annexation of fringe areas and suburban communities by the central city is one way. City-county consolidation is another, with the new county becoming the metropolitan government, as has occurred in Boston, San Francisco, New Orleans, and Philadelphia. Still another way is the reallocation and reassignment of functions among existing federal, state, and local governments in the area. Government in metropolitan areas is already a crazy quilt of overlapping and conflicting authorities. In 1962 the 212 metropolitan areas embraced over 18,000 local governments, 310 counties, 4,142 municipalities, 2,575 townships, 6,004 school districts, and over 5,000 special-purpose local governments. The Chicago area alone included over 1,000 local governments; New York included about the same. Not more, but fewer and more responsible, governments are needed.

Finally we might move toward federation. After all, we Americans invented federalism as it is known in the modern world. The model of our federal government adapted to the environment and existing power structure of the metropolitan area, might provide all the advantages of both stability and flexibility, permanence and change. It can combine centralized decision making on problems of metropolitan scope, with decentralized decision making on problems within the competence of the central city, the county, the special district or authority. It could provide for a legislature representing both the people of the area and the various units of government within the area—for both numerical and concurrent majorities. It could provide a single executive to be selected by a metropolitan congress or directly by the people.

Much hopeful experimentation is already under way. The metropolitan area of Toronto, Canada, has become a maze in which some thirteen separate municipalities struggled vainly to deal with area-wide problems. For Toronto to annex the outstanding cities was neither feasible nor desirable. In 1953 the Ontario Municipal Board recommended federation, which was approved for the thirteen municipalities in the area. A municipality of Metropolitan Toronto was created with a council of twenty-four members, twelve from Toronto and twelve from the twelve smaller cities. The Toronto members are the mayor and the two Toronto councillors getting the highest vote at the last city-wide election and the nine aldermen getting the largest vote in the last election. The other cities are represented by their mayors. To the Metropolitan Municipality has been delegated power to legislate for water, sewage, arterial highways, health and welfare, housing and redevelopment, parks, and metropolitan planning. The Metropolitan Council has its own budget and may levy taxes that are added to the aggregate assessment of each municipality.

Neither the Toronto plan of metropolitan federation nor the plan of city-county consolidation (as in Dade County, Florida, or San Francisco) is necessarily a model for other areas to follow. Annexation, consolidation, federation, and even the *ad hoc* agency, each may contribute at various times and places to a solution of the problems of metropolitan government. The road to an ideal solution will be long and rough. State metropolitan councils and the new federal Department of Housing and Urban Development may well give high priority to research on ways and means for adapting America's grass-roots governments to the new world that has grown up around them.

Politics and the City

Many of the municipal reform movements have been characterized not as some have said, by a "headlong flight from power," but by a headlong flight from politics. The upsurge of civic reform at the turn of the century derived its major force from a general revulsion to the spoils system in local government, symbolized by the City Boss and his political machine. To get rid of spoils, the remedy seemed simple—banish partisan politics from municipal government. "More business and less politics" became a slogan. Whatever reservations were made about applying this to state and national government, municipal government, it was said, was a strictly business proposition. "There is no Republican or Democratic way to run a city," it was said. "The lines that divide men in national affairs," wrote Charles Merriam, "do not run in the same direction in local questions, and the attempt to force them to do so has been a conspicuous failure in this country."

On this theory civic reformers hit upon various ways to eliminate politics or at least partisan politics from municipal government. Staggered elections were adopted so that state and municipal elections fell in different years from national elections. Nonpartisanship in local campaigns, with voluntary citizens' committees replacing political parties, was extended. Party designations disappeared at local elections. Nonpartisan primaries were held to cut down on the number of candidates, not to select rival party nominees. The brilliant achievements of the Cincinnati Charter Reform movement, a voluntary nonpartisan organization, gave that city a city manager and transformed it from the "worst governed city in America" to the "best governed city." It is interesting to note that this movement was inspired in no small degree by the so-called Birdless Ballot League dedicated to removing partisan symbols—the Democratic Rooster and the Republican Eagle—from the municipal ballot. There was also a widespread demand for a "short ballot," reducing the number of elective officials, simplifying the voter's task and streamlining the government to provide a greater concentration of power and responsibility. As a corollary of these reforms, and indispensable to their success, was the demand for civil service reform in municipal administration. More controversial but also widely hailed was the proposal for proportional representation not only to make the city council an accurate mirror of the community but to enable reform groups to win a beachhead in local legislative bodies.

The drive for reform along these lines found its focus, its sign, and symbol in new municipal charters to provide for a commission, council-manager, or strong mayor-council form of government. The reform movement's idea of banishing political parties from municipal life contributed immensely to the development of higher standards both of integrity and competence in municipal government. But there have been some unforeseen results of this flight from politics that we need to consider.

Staggered elections and nonpartisanship have contributed to a reduction of voter participation in municipal elections. Not only have they sent the voter to the polls nearly every year, but the off-year elections generally suffer from low visibility when compared with elections held in presidential years. By excluding parties from local elections, moreover, we sacrifice the organizing energies of the regular parties in nominating candidates, in getting out the vote, and in disciplining the various factions which operate at the city as well as at the state and federal level. Municipal candidates are often picked in fact by special factional interests: the chamber of commerce, trade unions, or social and ethnic groups. They do not vie with one another as partisans openly identified, and they owe responsibility not to the political party with its more general interests but to the factions whose candidates they really are. By banishing partisanship we also sacrifice the help of the parties in formulating programs of public policy and in serving as some guide for voters in choosing among candidates. The simple fact is that there are important differences on matters of public policy in the city as in the state and nation. And even the most cursory analysis will show that the lines of cleavage in municipal affairs do, in fact, correspond to those in state and national affairs. In terms of income and social status, education, racial and ethnic origin, and religious affiliation, municipal voters divide as Democrats and Republicans substantially as they do at state and national elections.

Nonpartisanship also cuts municipal government off from its political ties with state and national government at the very time it is becoming more dependent on decisions made at the state capital or in Washington. It may be that in a small town party labels are unnecessary to guide voters in choosing among candidates. But this is hardly true of the great cities and metropolitan areas in which most of us now live. To bring some order into what will otherwise be a wilderness of rival factions, the political party may be indispensable.

All of these considerations have led even some civic reformers to reverse their earlier zeal for nonpartisanship in municipal or at least in metropolitan government. Norman Thomas and Paul Blanshard, for example, in their challenging book *What's the Matter with New York,* say: "Theoretically we might imagine a city of 7,000,000 people voting wisely regardless of party. [But] in practical life the picture is impossible. . . . The more complex the community is, the greater is the need of the unifying influence of the political party. . . . [Metropolitan government] requires government by parties because the citizens are too numerous, too ill-informed and too preoccupied to come together spontaneously to choose the policies and leaders they wish to prevail. Political machinery has to be worked. The parties work it."

However much it may go against the grain to acknowledge it, it is to the politician that we must look for that prophetic leadership without which our democratic megalopolis can find neither direction nor salvation. Our great metropolitan areas, no less than the states and the nation itself, need the kind of leadership of which the President is the prototype. "Without vision," says an old aphorism, "the people perish." It is equally true that without political leadership a nation or a city is at best a confusion of tongues and at the worst a mob. To be a political leader, one must be a politician, a broker of consent, a voice for the voiceless, giving expression to the aspirations of a people caught in the treadmill of daily life. We must therefore restore the politician to his rightful place of honor in the community. It is time that politics ceased being a dirty word, and politician, a term of reproach.[20]

20 See Edward Banfield and James Wilson, *City Politics* (Cambridge, Mass.: Harvard and MIT Presses, 1963) ; Robert Dahl, *Who Governs? Democracy and Power in an American City* (New Haven: Yale University Press, 1961) ; Morris Janowitz, *Community Political Systems* (New York: Free Press, 1962) .

PART **III**

PUBLIC
POLICY IN
AMERICAN
DEMOCRACY

TO PROMOTE
THE GENERAL WELFARE

One of the objects of the Constitution was to promote "the general Welfare." It would be a mistake, however, to assume that the general welfare is separate and apart from the other purposes of the Constitution, such as a more perfect Union, domestic tranquility, the common defense and the blessings of liberty. To examine the relation of these other goals to the general welfare is more than an exercise in semantics. It has been a recurrent issue in American politics and constitutional law.

The phrase "general Welfare" appears not only in the Preamble but also in Section 8 of Article I in which the powers of Congress are enumerated. Among the powers conferred is the power "To lay and collect Taxes, Duties, Imposts and Excises, to pay the Debts and *provide for the common Defence and general Welfare of the United States. . . .*" Neither the Preamble as a whole nor the separate goals listed in it have ever been regarded as affecting the powers of Congress or the central government. The true function of the Preamble, said Justice Joseph Story "is to expound the nature and extent and application of the powers actually conferred by the Constitution, *and not substantially to create them.*"

Section 8 of Article I, on the other hand, is indubitably a grant of powers. But is its reference to the general welfare a separate grant of power or merely a phrase to explain *one* of the general purposes for which taxes may be laid? Thomas Jefferson was of the opinion that "the laying of taxes is the *power,* and the general welfare the *purpose* for which the power is to be exercised. They [Congress] are not to lay taxes *ad libitum* for any purpose they please; but only to pay the debts or provide for the welfare of the union. . . . they are not to do anything they please to provide for the general welfare, but only to lay taxes for that purpose."[1] If this is true of the general welfare clause, it might also be considered true of the phrase referring to the "common Defence," since this occurs in the same context, that is, the power to lay and collect taxes. However, the "common Defence" clause as a grant of power finds additional support elsewhere in the Constitution—notably in the powers to "raise and support Armies," "to provide and maintain a Navy," and "to declare War." No comparable language, it is argued, can be cited to support a case for "the general Welfare" as a grant of power. On the other hand, it can be argued that "the general Welfare" is the basic grant of power, and the power to tax, to pay debts, coin money, establish post offices, regulate commerce, and provide for defense, are particular instances of ways and means for carrying this power into effect.

Jefferson's narrow view of the "general Welfare" clause was shared by Madison and other leaders of the anti-Federalist party. It was, however, most emphatically not shared by Alexander Hamilton and the Federalists. "The phrase [general Welfare]," said Hamilton in 1791, "is as comprehensive as any that could have been used, because it was not fit that the constitutional authority of the Union to appropriate its revenues should have been restricted within narrower limits than the 'general welfare'. . . . It is therefore . . . left to the discretion of the national legislature to pronounce upon the objects which concern the general welfare. . . . And there seems to be no room for doubt that whatever concerns the general interests of learning, of agriculture, of manufactures, and of commerce, are within the sphere of the national councils, as far as regards the application of money."[2] According to this view, the mandate of the Constitution to "provide for . . . the general Welfare" is very broad indeed. Except for express limitations, the scope of congressional power can reasonably be assumed to extend, as Hamilton said, "to whatever concerns the general interests of learning, of agriculture, of manufactures and of commerce. . . ."

Although the Hamiltonian theory was challenged from the beginning and is under continuing challenge today, it has nevertheless prevailed over the narrower, more restrictive Jeffersonian doctrine. Congress has moved steadily into one area after another "to provide for the general Welfare" until many critics, and some friends, of this trend have described the American Republic as a welfare state. Federal aid to education, scientific research and development, pure food and drug legislation, public health and medical care, old-age and survivor's insurance, unemployment insurance, public assistance, hot lunches for school children, public housing and urban redevelopment are but a partial list of the welfare services of the federal government. And if to these we add

[1] *Writings of Thomas Jefferson*, vol. III, pp. 147–149 (Library Edition, 1904) quoted in *The Constitution of the United States, Analysis and Interpretation*, ed. by Edward S. Corwin (Washington, D.C.: U.S. Government Printing Office, 1953), p. 113.

[2] *The Federalist, Nos. 30 and 34.*

similar services provided by state and local governments the variety of government welfare activities become even more impressive. If we were to add together all the budget estimates for fiscal year 1967 which may be classified under the broad rubric of social and welfare activities, the total would exceed $22 billion, not including nearly $25 billion in trust funds earmarked for social security payments.[3] We must, however, content ourselves with describing a few examples.

☆ **AID TO EDUCATION**

Among the earliest "welfare" services of government in the new world was the establishment of public schools. In 1642 Massachusetts required that every child be taught "to read and understand the principles of religion and the capital laws of the country." Five years later every town was required to establish common grammar schools for this purpose. Other colonies followed suit and free public elementary education became a feature of American society even before the Revolution. In 1821 Boston established the first public high school. As with most welfare services, the use of public funds for secondary education was challenged. In 1874 the Supreme Court of Michigan resolved this conflict by holding that both secondary and elementary education was a proper function of government. Under this and other decisions the responsibility of state and local government for education was accepted. In 1870 high school enrollment was less than 100,000 in a total population of 40,000,000. By 1900 more than 500,000 youngsters were in public secondary schools and in 1960 the number exceeded 12,000,000. From one high school student for every 400 of the population in 1870, the number has grown to one for every 15. In 1964 total enrollment in public schools exceeded 40,000,000, or one school child for every 4.5 people in the country. State and local expenditures for public schools have grown from $215 million to nearly $20 billion, exclusive of over $4 billion for higher education. While the total population increased less than two and a half times, expenditures for public elementary and secondary education have grown by seventy times.

The expansion of elementary and secondary education has been accompanied by a corresponding increase in education beyond the high school. Prior to World War I, a college education was a privilege reserved for a tiny minority. In 1900 only 4 percent of the college-age population was enrolled in an institution of higher education. By 1964 over 30 percent of the college-age population was attending college. As in the case of secondary education, what had once been the privilege of a few is fast becoming a right for all qualified young men and women. The total

[3] See *The Budget of the United States Government, Fiscal Year 1967*, pp. 39 and 127.

college student body had grown from less than 250,000 in 1900 to over 4,000,000 by 1964. Expenditures had increased from an estimated $35 million in 1900 to more than $4 billion in 1964. While population increased two and a half times, college enrollment multiplied more than twelve times and expenditures more than a hundred times. In 1965 over 60 percent of the enrollment and expenditures were accounted for by colleges and universities maintained at public expense.[4]

It will be recalled that in the original Northwest Ordinance of 1785 the Congress of the Confederation had allocated "lot No. 16 of every Township for the maintenance of public schools within the said townships." Thus from the beginning of our history as a nation the central government has come to the aid of education. Such grants have been supplemented by grants-in-aid of princely dimensions for a variety of educational projects. In 1917, for example, the Smith-Hughes Act provided for federal aid to assist schools in giving instruction in agriculture, home economics, trade and industrial subjects. In 1936 this was expanded under the George-Deen Act to instruction in certain commercial subjects. Liberal appropriations were also made for educational activities in the Department of Agriculture through the land-grant colleges, agricultural extension, and agricultural research institutes of various kinds. Other programs were either expanded or initiated through the Office of Education in the Department of the Interior. Still other federal funds went to support ROTC and other programs of defense training and research. During the 1930s federal funds were made available to the states not only for school and college construction and maintenance, but to provide for a school lunch program. During and after World War II federal programs under the so-called GI Bill of Rights, the National Defense Education Act, and other legislation, hundreds of millions of federal dollars have been made available as grants or loans for educational projects. Over a billion dollars were spent so that veterans might continue their education. Any serious doubt about the continuing interest of the federal government in education and welfare was laid to rest when Congress in 1953 established as a permanent agency with Cabinet rank a Department of Health, Education, and Welfare. Table 21–1 shows federal expenditures for 1967, with estimates of expenditures for fiscal years 1968 and 1969.

Large as these expenditures are, they fall short of the needs of the nation. With a burgeoning population it becomes increasingly difficult for state and local governments to keep abreast of the needs for educational services. Our increase in population has been accompanied by an even more spectacular increase in school costs. Failure to expand physical

---

4 U.S. Bureau of the Census, *Historical Statistics of the United States, Colonial Times to 1957* (Washington, D.C.: U.S. Government Printing Office, 1960), pp. 211, 213; U.S. Bureau of the Census, *Statistical Abstract of the United States, 1965* (Washington, D.C.: U.S. Government Printing Office, 1965), pp. 106–136.

TABLE 21–1
Federal Expenditures for Education

	(Fiscal years. In millions)			
	Expenditures and Net Lending			Recommended NOA and LA for 1969[a]
Program or Agency	1967 actual	1968 estimate	1969 estimate	
EXPENDITURES:				
Elementary and secondary education:				
Children from low income families	$1,057	$1,070	$1,073	$1,200
Other education of the disadvantaged	67	70	109	154
Special school projects	75	155	169	219
School books, equipment, counseling, and strengthening State education agencies	213	237	155	121
Assistance to schools in federally impacted areas	447	372	416	410
Other (teaching training)		26	9	
Higher education:				
Aid for undergraduate and graduate students	421	597	673	558
Academic facility grants	198	308	213	86
Other aids to higher education	92	153	179	182
Proposed legislation				23
Science education and basic research:				
National Science Foundation				
Basic research and specialized research facilities	209	226	230	244
Grants for institutional science programs	49	72	78	66
Science education	118	115	120	131
Other science activities	39	43	52	59
Other aids to education:				
Training of education manpower	41	13	57	216
Vocational education:				
Present program	250	271	247	257
Proposed legislation			7	15

TABLE 21-1 *(Continued)*

(Fiscal years. In millions)

Program or Agency	Expenditures and Net Lending			Recommended NOA and LA for 1969[a]
	1967 actual	1968 estimate	1969 estimate	
Educational research and development	57	76	99	146
Grants for libraries and community services	57	100	141	149
Indian education services	112	116	153	155
Library of Congress and Smithsonian Institution[c]	62	83	98	100
National Foundation on the Arts and Humanities[c]	10	15	23	24
Other:				
Present programs	37	55	61	66
Proposed legislation for public broadcasting			20	20
Applicable receipts from the public (−)	−11	−15	−16	−16
Subtotal, expenditures	3,602	4,157	4,364	4,585
NET LENDING:				
Elementary and secondary education	−2	[b]	1	1
Higher education	447	383	334	686
Subtotal, net lending	445	384	335	687
Total	4,047	4,541	4,699	5,272

[a] Less than $500 thousand.

[b] Compares with new obligational authority (NOA) and lending authority (LA) for 1967 and 1968, as follows:

NOA: 1967, $4,430 million; 1968, $4,673 million.

LA: 1967, $901 million; 1968, $2,002 million.

[c] Includes both Federal funds and trust funds.

SOURCE: *The Budget of the United States Government, Fiscal Year 1969* (Washington, D.C.: U.S. Government Printing Office, 1968).

plant, teaching staff, and administrative personnel after World War II created something of a crisis in American education. Estimates indicated an overall shortage of 130,000 classrooms in 1960 and an anticipated shortage in 1970 of more than 300,000, not taking account of the need for replacement of outmoded facilities. The teacher shortage appeared to be equally acute, with estimates of additional teachers needed by 1970 running as high as 450,000 or more. Moreover the nation faces increasing costs as the general price level goes up and the costs of both physical plant and teaching staff mount. The $15.5 billion spent on elementary and secondary education in 1960 will probably exceed $30 billion by 1970.[5]

The rather narrow and inflexible tax base upon which state and local governments have had to meet these costs has created a demand for increased federal aid to education at all levels.[6] This demand is strengthened by the wide differences among the states in their ability and will to support education. "Can Mississippi," asked Senator Benton, "with one-third the per capita income of my own state of Connecticut, do justice to the education of its children, or to the American doctrine of equal opportunity for all?" It is the latter consideration that has given impetus to the demand for federal aid.

Congress has responded in a number of ways. But grants of federal funds for general aid to education have come slowly and painfully. In 1959 President Eisenhower recommended modest grants to help local communities finance school construction. The cost would have been about $2 billion over a period of twenty-five or thirty years. The Murray-Metcalf Bill, however, sought to expand federal aid in the unprecedented amount of nearly $4.5 billion per year as outright grants to the states. When both the Eisenhower and the congressional plans failed, the whole problem was projected into the presidential campaign of 1960. Both candidates, Kennedy and Nixon, pledged their support of federal aid, although they differed in the nature and scope of such assistance.

In both his initial State of the Union address and in a special message to Congress, President Kennedy gave high priority to federal aid to education. His program, which during a three-year period would have provided nearly $2.5 billion in federal aid, was characterized as "probably the most important piece of domestic legislation. . . . Our progress as a nation can be no swifter than our progress in education. . . ."

A revised and enlarged program of Federal Aid to Education was enacted by the Eighty-ninth Congress largely on the recommendation of President Johnson in January, 1965. In summary the program involved the appropriation of $1 billion for the fiscal year 1966, to be distributed to school districts in which there were large numbers of needy children. The basis for allocation of these funds is the percentage of children in the school district who come from families with incomes below a certain

[5] *Goals for Americans, The Report of the President's Commission on National Goals* (American Assembly; Englewood Cliffs, N.J.: Prentice-Hall, 1960) , chap. 3.

[6] Of the $15½ billion spent by state and local governments, 50 percent comes from local property taxes, about 34 percent from sales taxes, poll taxes, and income taxes, and 16 percent from borrowing. David D. Lloyd, *Spend and Survive* (Indianapolis: Bobbs-Merrill, 1960) , p. 97.

amount.[7] In addition to this basic appropriation, federal funds are provided to support school libraries and research on instruction methods and materials in regional educational laboratories, Fellowship grants for needy college students, aid to small colleges, and for the support of University Extension programs.

"We are now embarked," said President Johnson, "on another venture to put the American dream to work . . . [And] once again we must start where men who would improve their society must begin with an educational system restudied, reinforced, and revitalized." As the federal government moves into increased support of formal education in the schools, it also is moving toward support of what may be called less formal education in the Arts, that is, drama, dance, painting and sculpture, music and literature. Legislation was passed in the Eighty-ninth Congress to establish an Arts and Humanities Foundation to parallel the already existing National Science Foundation. In asking Congress for an initial appropriation of $10 million for this purpose President Johnson said: "Pursuit of artistic achievement and making the fruits of that achievement available to all its people, is also among the hallmarks of a great society." This program is a renewal, long delayed, of many artistic and literary activities supported by the federal government during the great depression of the 1930s in what was called the WPA program for the Arts.

☆ HEALTH AND WELFARE

Some indication of the extent of government involvement in welfare can be seen in the establishment of the Department of Health, Education, and Welfare as an independent agency with Cabinet rank. The new department brought together under a single head most of the major welfare activities of the federal government. Before 1953 the Public Health Service, the Office of Education, the Social Security Administration, the Office of Vocational Rehabilitation, the Food and Drug Administration and Saint Elizabeth's Hospital were scattered in various other agencies. The regrouping in one department not only improved their status within the government but served notice that it is in fact a major function of government in the United States to "promote the general Welfare." (See Figure 21–1 showing Major Social Welfare Expenditures, 1940 to 1966.)

The oldest of these agencies, the Public Health Service, was created in 1798 as a part of the Treasury Department to administer marine

[7] It has been estimated that in 9 states in the South (North Carolina, South Carolina, Kentucky, Tennessee, Arkansas, Louisiana, Mississippi, Alabama, Georgia) and California, in the West, 20 percent of the children come from homes with family incomes of $2,000 or less; in 17 other states the percentage was more than 10 percent but less than 20 percent; and in the remaining 24 states it was less than 10 percent. Federal grants under the bill, it is estimated, will vary from $75 million to New York and $74 million to Texas; to some $600,000 to Nevada. See *The New York Times,* March 28, 1965.

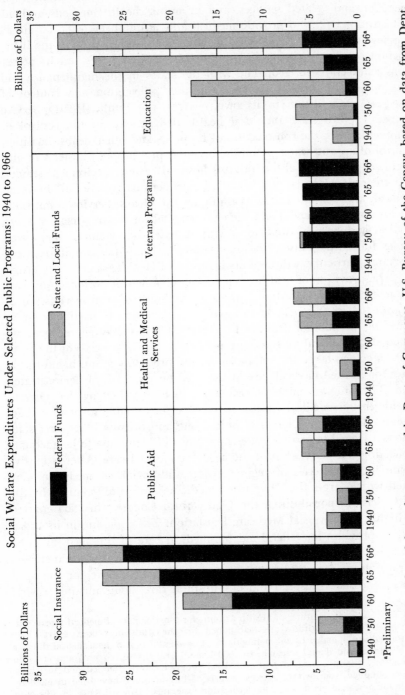

Figure 21–1 Adapted from chart prepared by Dept. of Commerce, U.S. Bureau of the Census, based on data from Dept. of Health, Education, and Welfare, Social Security Administration, in U.S. Bureau of the Census, *Statistical Abstract of the United States: 1967.* (88th edition.) Washington, D.C., 1967, pp. 282, 283.

hospitals for the care of merchant seamen. Since that time its responsibilities have been expanded (1) to include research and training in medicine and related services, and in public health methods and administration; (2) "to provide medical and hospital services . . . aid in the development of the nation's hospitals . . . and to prevent the introduction of communicable diseases into the United States and its possessions"; and (3) "to co-operate with the states in the maintenance and development of health services" and the "prevention and control of diseases.". In addition to its own services, the Public Health Service cooperates with state and local health departments in the control of chronic diseases, the construction of hospitals and other health facilities, control of air and water pollution, accident prevention, disaster aid, and health education. It also maintains hospitals where servicemen, seamen and their dependents, and other eligible persons receive full hospital, medical, and dental care. In Washington the Health Service administers the Freedman's Hospital as a "general hospital for the treatment of acute medical and surgical conditions, with an extensive system of specialized clinics for outpatients." Not the least of its activities are its research programs, particularly through its Institutes of Health.[8]

The provision of health services by government is no longer an issue in American politics, although the size and scope of such services are. A major issue in this field is the extent of government participation in providing prepaid or free medical care. The issue came to focus on proposals for federal assistance in meeting the medical needs of the aged. A first step was taken in 1960 by legislation providing grants-in-aid to the states for limited medical care of the aged on the basis of demonstrated need. The program offers federal funds to be matched by the states to provide certain medical services to aged persons unable to pay for these services. Because the plan is a limited one and because it requires state action, it lagged in getting under way. Nor did it promise to be adequate in meeting the needs even of the aged for medical care. After extensive debate in which cries of regimentation and socialized medicine were mixed with charges that "organized medicine" was indifferent or hostile to its social responsibilities, the Eighty-ninth Congress in 1965 enacted the highly controversial Medicare legislation. The program, in its broad outline, provides for federal aid for medical care of the aged, financed through Social Security taxes. Also included in the program are increased appropriations for child health and mental health. Care for the aged meets the costs of hospital and post-hospital care, home nursing service,

---

[8] The National Institutes of Health account for a major part of medical research in the United States. Institutes are maintained for the study of cancer, allergy and infectious diseases, arthritis and metabolic diseases, mental health, neurological diseases and blindness, and dental research. In 1960 federal health research programs cost $30 million. Mr. Nixon estimated that if federal programs were doubled and matching support obtained from private sources, "nearly $3 billion would have been invested by 1970 in our research facilities and modernization programs." Howard Rusk, in *The New York Times,* October 23, 1960.

and outpatient diagnosis. In addition, a voluntary insurance plan is included which covers 80 percent of physicians' and surgeons' care, mental hospital care, home nursing care, and such health devices as X-rays, laboratory tests, medical equipment, and so forth, after an annual payment in each case of $50 by the patient. Increased appropriations are also provided for the development of regional medical complexes to combat heart disease, cancer, stroke, and other major "man killers." Existing programs of grants and scholarships for training doctors, dentists, nurses, and medical technicians have been expanded, and pure food and drug laws were enacted for the control of habit-forming drugs. Measures requiring better labeling of hazardous products were also enacted. Increased federal aid for medical research, hospital construction, and public health education are part of the total plan.[9]

A related welfare activity is a federal program of vocational rehabilitation. Begun in 1920 as a service to disabled veterans it has become an important permanent service in the Department of Health, Education, and Welfare. It has been estimated that the men and women rehabilitated in one recent year had earnings in excess of $170 million during their first year after training as compared with $28 million a year prior to rehabilitation. Their contribution of more than 130 million man-hours to the nation's productive effort represented a human salvage operation of no mean dimensions. "Within three years," says Dr. Howard Rusk, "through Federal income taxes alone they will repay the Federal Government every dollar spent on their rehabilitation."[10] Thus the government by a modest expenditure contributes not only to an act of compassion but to the economic and social strength of the nation.[11]

☆ SOCIAL SECURITY

The most ambitious of all federal welfare activities is the Social Security program. More than any other federal activity it typifies the so-called

---

[9] Among the most controversial features of this program were proposals, not made by the President, to impose more stringent controls on the manufacture and sale of cosmetics, pharmaceuticals, and cigarettes. The Public Health Service, after years of research, is persuaded that cigarette smoking is a major cause of lung cancer. "In my mind," said Surgeon General Dr. Luther Terry, "there is absolutely no question about the cause and effect relationship between smoking and lung cancer." It was estimated that 125,000 deaths in 1965 could be directly attributed to lung cancer caused by cigarette smoking. It was also pointed out that on the strength of similar research in Great Britain, the British government had taken steps to restrict, and ultimately to ban, cigarette advertising on television. To all this the tobacco industry has replied with a firm "not proved." The importance of tobacco in the economy of several states, and as a source of federal revenue, will no doubt delay any very drastic measures, although an administrative order of the Federal Trade Commission requires cigarette manufacturers to add to their present labels a warning that cigarette smoking may be hazardous to health.

[10] *The New York Times,* December 4, 1960.

[11] Expenditures on this federal program of vocational rehabilitation in 1965 exceeded $137 million. For fiscal year 1967 more than $300 million was needed. See *The Budget of the United States Government, Fiscal Year 1967,* p. 248.

welfare state. This program, begun in 1935 amidst bitter political controversy, has now been accepted even by its former critics as a proper responsibility of government. The Social Security Administration in the Department of Health, Education, and Welfare administers national programs of Old-Age and Survivors Insurance, Public Assistance, Aid to the Blind, Child Welfare, and nonveteran Vocational Rehabilitation. The Department of Labor administers programs of workmen's compensation, unemployment insurance and public employment, industrial safety, regulation of child labor, and minimum wage laws.

The dimensions of these programs are impressive. Over 13 million retired persons in 1963 were receiving pensions of more than $14 billion a year. Under the system about nine out of ten employed persons contribute, under a federal tax plan, to an old-age insurance fund, contributions which are matched by their employers. Over 50 million workers are also protected against unemployment, with weekly payments up to $50 or more for periods up to 26 weeks. Under the unemployment insurance plan the federal government levies a uniform tax on payrolls, but credits to each state in which the tax is collected 90 percent of the total received from employers in the state. To receive these credits, however, the state must establish its own system of unemployment compensation. Although there is considerable variation in the terms of state laws, all must meet certain minimum federal standards to be eligible for the tax credit. Eligibility for compensation must be established by each worker before payments are made. Payments are made through federal-state employment offices at which workers must register for work and to which they must report regularly for possible employment when they are unemployed.

A federal-state program of public assistance extends financial aid to the blind and to persons permanently and totally disabled. Assistance is also available to needy children under certain circumstances, and grants are made to the states to support programs of Maternal Aid and Child Welfare. The social security system provides at least minimum aid to millions of retired, unemployed, and disabled persons and others suffering economic distress.

When the Social Security law was under debate in 1935, it was assailed as un-American, socialistic and even communistic. "Never in the history of the world," said Congressman John Taber of New York, "has any measure been brought in here [Congress] so insidiously designed to prevent business recovery, to enslave workers, and to prevent any possibility of the employer providing work for the people." Few persons today would agree with Mr. Taber, although the debate goes on over the scope of the system and the size of the benefits to be provided. Every Congress is confronted with proposals to extend coverage to classes now excluded and to liberalize the benefits. Against these proposals are those which, without repudiating the program entirely, strive to restrict its scope and limit its benefits.

☆ SOME CONSTITUTIONAL PROBLEMS

The growth of the so-called welfare state has encountered a number of constitutional hurdles. For the most part these have occurred at the state rather than the federal level, but the Congress too has now and again been enjoined by the Supreme Court from entering upon programs of social welfare. It will be remembered that when Congress endeavored to regulate the employment of children in industry, the Supreme Court held the laws to be unconstitutional. Congressional action to protect workers in their right to organize, to regulate conditions of employment, to maintain minimum standards of safety and sanitation, to provide programs of workmen's compensation and employers' liability for injuries sustained in the course of employment, and to establish maximum hours of work and minimum wages have all raised constitutional questions that had to be resolved. As early as 1838 laws were passed and sustained by the Supreme Court to require certain safety devices on steam vessels; and these laws were later extended to railroads and other carriers operating in interstate commerce. In 1907 came a first Hours of Service Act to limit the length of the working day for employees of interstate railroads. This too was upheld by the Court as a safety measure and as a legitimate exercise of federal power to regulate interstate commerce.[12] Even a Federal Employers Liability Act passed in 1908, establishing a system of workmen's compensation for injuries received in the course of employment on interstate railroads, was sustained by the Supreme Court under the commerce clause.

However, when in 1934 Congress sought to establish a system of compulsory retirement insurance for railroad workers, the Supreme Court, by a narrow majority, held the act to be beyond the powers of Congress under the commerce clause of the Constitution. "We feel bound to hold," said Justice Roberts, "that a pension plan thus imposed is in no proper sense a regulation of . . . interstate transportation. It is . . . not a rule or regulation of commerce . . . but . . . an attempt for social ends . . . [to assure] a particular class of employees against old-age dependency."

Chief Justice Hughes in a dissenting opinion stated what has since become the accepted doctrine of both Congress and the Supreme Court. "The fundamental consideration," said Hughes, "which supports this type of legislation is that industry should take care of its human wastage, whether this is due to accident or old age. . . ."[13] When in 1937 the

---

12 *Baltimore & Ohio Railroad Co.* v. *Interstate Commerce Commission,* 221 U.S. 612 (1911).

13 *Railroad Retirement Board* v. *Alton Railroad Co.,* 295 U.S. 330 (1935).

Supreme Court upheld the old-age benefits provision of the Social Security Act of 1935, it said: "The problem is plainly national in area and dimensions. Moreover, laws of the separate states cannot deal with it effectively." As for the powers conferred by the general welfare clause the Court said that these remained largely a matter for congressional decision "unless the choice is clearly wrong, a display of arbitrary power." Nor is the concept of general welfare a static one. "Needs that were narrow or parochial a century ago may be interwoven in our day with the well-being of the nation. What is critical or urgent changes with the times."[14] The decision in *Helvering* v. *Davis* was sharply attacked as late as 1956 by minority members of the President's Commission on Intergovernmental Relations. The effect of this and other decisions, they said, "has been to create a situation under which the Congress may by the expenditure of money enter virtually any sphere of government. . . . These decisions have fundamentally altered the balance of power designed by the architects of the Constitution."

☆ *LEGISLATION AFFECTING ORGANIZED LABOR*

Step by step, the power of Congress to enact welfare legislation has been established against vigorous political opposition and judicial interposition. For example, a major goal of working men and women has been to establish their right to organize and bargain collectively, through agents of their own choosing, concerning wages, hours, and conditions of employment. The old English common-law doctrine of conspiracy was long applied to labor organizations in America. In 1806, 1809, and 1815 workers were convicted of criminal conspiracy for seeking increased wages through organized effort. By 1842, however, following the important case of *Commonwealth* v. *Hunt* in Massachusetts, labor's right to organize was generally recognized, although criminal prosecutions for conspiracy occurred as late as 1890.

Reluctant to recognize labor unions, employers turned from conspiracy charges to court injunctions and antitrust laws. Injunctions were issued not only to restrain violence and intimidation by unions, but in many cases to forbid even peaceful picketing. "Loitering about the premises, inducing . . . any person to abandon employment [to join the strike] by . . . epithets . . . abusive language, intimidation, display of number or force, jeers, entreaties, arguments, persuasion," were prohibited under penalty of prosecution for criminal contempt of court. Professor Edwin Witte reported 508 cases in federal courts and 1,364 cases in state courts in which injunctions were issued prior to May 1, 1931. He also estimated that the unreported cases outnumbered the reported cases

[14] *Helvering* v. *Davis,* 301 U.S. 619 (1937).

in the ratio of five to one.[15] But injunctions were not the only legal weapon used against labor organizations. The Sherman Antitrust Act was also construed by the courts as applying to combinations of workers as well as to business combinations in restraint of trade. Injunctions as a means to enforce the antitrust laws against organized labor became so frequent after 1900 that labor leaders sought relief from Congress in legislation recognizing their right to organize and bargain collectively without harassment of this kind.

An early attempt by Congress to protect the right of railroad workers to organize was declared unconstitutional by the Court. The Erdman Act of 1898 made it a misdemeanor for any interstate railroad to require an employee not to be a member of a trade union as a condition of his employment. Such legislation, the Court held, had no necessary relation to the legitimate power of Congress to regulate interstate and foreign commerce.[16] It was not until the Railway Labor Act of 1926 was sustained by the Court that the "connection between interstate commerce and union membership" was recognized as real and substantial.[17] In the meantime agitation to protect labor's right to organize became more widespread and intense.

In 1908 and again in 1912 the Democratic platform promised legislation to exempt labor unions from the antitrust laws by providing that "labor organizations and their members should not be regarded as illegal organizations in restraint of trade." To carry out this pledge the first Wilson administration succeeded in getting Congress to declare in the Clayton Act that "the labor of a human being is not a commodity or article of commerce," and that labor unions were not "illegal combinations in restraint of trade, under the antitrust laws." The act also sanctioned peaceful picketing, and guaranteed trial by jury in certain contempt cases arising from injunctions issued in labor disputes. The Clayton Act, in practice, proved to be something less than a Magna Charta for labor, but it marked an important step in federal intervention on behalf of organized labor.[18] Notwithstanding the Clayton Act, the courts continued to hold labor unions liable in certain cases, under the antitrust laws. And many employers required their employees to sign so-called yellow-dog contracts, agreeing not to join a union, as a condition of employment.

[15] Edwin E. Witte, *The Government in Labor Disputes* (New York: McGraw-Hill, 1932) ; see, also, J. .P Frey, *The Labor Injunction* (New York: Equity, 1922) ; and Felix Frankfurter and Nathan Greene, *The Labor Injunction* (New York: Macmillan, 1930).

[16] *Adair* v. *United States*, 208 U.S. 161 (1908).

[17] *Texas and N.O.R. Co.* v. *Brotherhood of Railway & S.S. Clerks*, 281 U.S. 548 (1930).

[18] Samuel Gompers, President of the American Federation of Labor, described the Clayton Act as "the most fundamental, the most comprehensive enumeration of freedom found in any legislative act in the history of the world." A.F.L. Convention Proceedings, 1941.

In 1932 labor's campaign for more comprehensive legislation to protect its right to organize and bargain collectively bore fruit in the Norris–La Guardia Anti-Injunction Act. This act outlawed yellow-dog contracts and limited injunctions in labor disputes to acts of violence and direct intimidation. It was followed in 1933 with Section 7-A of the National Industrial Recovery Act which provided:

1. That employees [in interstate commerce] shall have the right to organize and bargain collectively through representatives of their own choosing free from the interference, restraint or coercion of employers of labor or their agents. . . .

2. That no employee and no one seeking employment shall be required as a condition of employment to join any company union or to refrain from forming, organizing or assisting a labor organization of his own choosing. . . .

When the National Recovery Act was declared unconstitutional in 1935, a National Labor Relations Act (the so-called Wagner Act) was passed containing similar guarantees of labor's right to organize, and creating a National Labor Relations Board to enforce the act. The Board can protect workers engaged in interstate commerce in their right to organize and bargain collectively, to hold elections by secret ballot to determine which among competing unions shall be their bargaining agent, and to hold hearings and render decisions concerning complaints of unfair labor practices.

When this act was sustained by the Supreme Court it laid to rest any serious question of the power of Congress to legislate concerning labor relations where interstate commerce is involved.[19] Since few businesses today operate wholly outside the field of interstate commerce the regulation of this aspect of American economic life is for all practical purposes now lodged in Congress. The original act has been amended in many important respects, in 1947 by the Taft-Hartley Act, and again in 1951 and 1959. Most important of these amendments are those which, in addition to forbidding unfair labor practices by employers, also proscribe certain specified unfair practices by trade unions.

For example, unions are forbidden to coerce employees and employers in their choice of bargaining representatives; to cause an employer to discriminate against an employee because of his membership or lack of membership in a labor organization "except under a duly authorized union shop agreement"; to force an employee or "self-employed person" to join any labor organization, or to bargain with a labor organization not recognized by the NLRB, or to assign particular work to employees in a particular labor organization; to require excessive

---

[19] *National Labor Relations Board* v. *Jones & Laughlin Steel Corp.,* 301 U.S. 1 (1937).

initiation fees, or to demand money "or other thing of value" for services not performed.

Legislation Concerning Conditions of Work

In addition to protecting labor's right to organize, Congress has moved to limit the length of the working day and to establish certain minimum wages and labor standards for employers engaged in interstate commerce. Beginning with the Hours of Service Act of 1907, limiting the hours of labor on interstate railroads, Congress has extended these regulations to other industries. After a number of efforts at piecemeal legislation, some of which ran afoul of the Supreme Court, Congress in 1938 enacted a Fair Labor Standards Act applicable to all employers engaged in interstate commerce. Using a formula that had been declared unconstitutional in the original child labor case, the law now prohibits "the shipment in interstate commerce of goods manufactured by employees whose wages are less than the prescribed minimum, or whose weekly hours of labor are greater than the prescribed maximum." Under this act and the Court's liberal interpretation of interstate commerce, a large majority of employees engaged in manufacturing are now covered by federal regulations affecting their hours, wages, and general conditions of employment.[20] The effect of the Court's decision has been, according to former Justice Roberts, "to place the whole matter of wages and hours of persons employed throughout the United States, with slight exceptions, under a single federal regulatory scheme and in this way completely to supersede state exercise of the police power in this field."[21]

☆ STATE WELFARE LEGISLATION

If state regulations have been superseded by federal statutes, other state activities in promoting the general welfare have continued to expand, often with the support of the federal government. It is worthy of note that the constitutional barriers to state welfare legislation have been as great or greater than in the case of federal action in this field. In dealing with state legislation the Court has sought to reconcile three often conflicting principles of American constitutional law: the principle of dual federalism; the principle of substantive due process of law; and the equally ancient principle of the police power.

Under the principle of dual federalism the Supreme Court struck

[20] *United States* v. *Darby*, 312 U.S. 100 (1941), in which the Supreme Court sustained the Fair Labor Standards Act.

[21] Owen Roberts, Jr., *The Court and the Constitution* (Cambridge, Mass.: Harvard University Press, 1951), p. 56.

down many state laws on the ground that they conflicted with powers delegated to the central government. The other side of this coin were decisions restricting federal action to prohibit child labor and to regulate hours and wages, on the ground that these were matters reserved to the states by the Tenth Amendment. In the process of applying constitutional restraints to both federal and state "welfare" legislation the Court was in a fair way to create a constitutional "no man's land" beyond the reach of both the states and the central government. It was to avoid this *impasse* that the Court in recent years has taken a more indulgent view of both federal and state powers to promote the general welfare. State and central governments are now seen not as rivals but as partners in a common endeavor to promote the general welfare.

Under the states' police power and the commerce and taxing powers of the United States a broad highway has been opened for legislation designed to provide for the general welfare. "The public welfare," said Justice Douglas in 1952, "is a broad and inclusive concept. The moral, social, economic, and physical well-being of the community is one part of it; the political well-being another."[22]

In spite of criticism, and often bitter opposition, the trend toward public welfare policies of various kinds continues. Although the proportion of federal expenditures devoted to welfare projects is still small—up to 1966 considerably less than 25 percent of the federal budget—it has been impressive and is more likely to increase than diminish. This increase reflects what President Johnson calls the American quest for the "Great Society," of which federal aid to education and medical care legislation of 1965 are major components.

☆ THE WAR ON POVERTY

Perhaps even more dramatic, if financially less impressive, has been the Johnson administration's "war on poverty." In his first State of the Union message to Congress in January, 1964, President Johnson announced an "unconditional war on poverty in America." The paradox of progress and poverty, of affluence and deprivation, must, he said, be somehow resolved. "Unfortunately many Americans live on the outskirts of hope, some because of their poverty, some because of their color, and all too many, because of both. Our task is to help replace their despair with opportunity."

To this end, the President proposed a multipronged program which, except for medicare and federal aid to education, represented mainly a more effective mobilization of existing federal welfare activities with only modest increases in appropriations:

[22] *Day-Brite Lighting, Inc.* v. *Missouri,* 342 U.S. 421 (1952) .

1. Reduced taxes on both incomes and consumer goods.
2. An extension of federal minimum wage coverage to "two million workers now lacking this basic protection of purchasing power."
3. An increase in unemployment benefits and an extension of the period during which they are to be paid.
4. New youth employment legislation "to put jobless, aimless, hopeless youngsters to work on useful projects."
5. An increase and acceleration of federal housing programs to provide "a decent home for every American family."
6. More hospitals and nursing homes, more doctors and nurses.
7. A National Service Corps "to help the economically handicapped of our own country as the Peace Corps helps those abroad."
8. An extension of the food stamp plan to distribute more food to the needy.
9. A massive effort to provide low-cost transportation, both within and between communities, to facilitate the journey to and from work.
10. A National Commission on Automation to study the effect of technological change upon job opportunities.

"If," said the President, "we have the brain power to invent these machines, we have the brain power to make certain that they are a boon and not a bane to humanity."

In addition to these programs the President asked for an expansion of "our small but successful area redevelopment program," with a "special effort" to be made in the chronically depressed areas in West Virginia, and along the Appalachian mountain chain. This so-called Appalachian program, to redevelop communities whose economic underpinnings have been all but destroyed by technological change became a kind of symbol for this "unconditional war on poverty." Part of the plan was the establishment of a joint federal-state corporation to undertake necessary public works, loans to state and local development groups, and expanded social services.[23]

To integrate these various programs an *Office of Economic Opportunity* was created with Sargent Shriver, Director of the Peace Corps, as its first director. In asking for some $500 million annually for the new Regional Aid Plan, President Johnson summarized the basic policies according to which it was to be administered. "No Federal plan or Federal project," he said, "will be imposed on any regional, state, or local body. No plan will be approved unless it has the approval of state and local authorities. No programs or projects will be originated at the Federal level. The initiative, the ideas, and the request for assistance must all come *to* Washington, not *from* Washington."[24] This, no doubt, is a wise policy, not only to protect the antipoverty program from charges

[23] See the *Wall Street Journal,* January 9, 1964, in which the "War on Poverty" is outlined.
[24] *The New York Times,* March 26, 1965.

of federal dictation or usurpation, but because state and local communities have traditionally assumed responsibility for welfare programs.[25]

Year by year, and from one administration to another, the American government at all levels has become increasingly preoccupied with what we have generally called social, or welfare, problems. The gradual transformation of a laissez-faire economy to a mixed, or compensatory political, economy has been accompanied by the transformation of a laissez-faire state into a welfare state. The trend has been denied, deplored, and bitterly assailed, but it continues. How far and to what end no one can say.[26]

[25] In 1962, for example, 97 percent of total educational expenditures were for state and local governments; 99 percent of public welfare spending; and 71 percent of spending on health and hospitals. Even when some of these funds came from the federal government, it was the state and local governments which assumed responsibility for their expenditure and for the administration of welfare programs.

In New York City's budget of $3.3 billion for the fiscal year 1964–1965, nearly $2 billion was allocated to "schools and colleges, pensions, hospitals and health, and public welfare." This is a conservative estimate, since it does not include substantial proportions of expenditures for sanitation, police and debt service that are properly allocable to general welfare activities.

See F. Mosher and O. Poland, *The Cost of American Government* (New York: Dodd, Mead, 1964), pp. 46–48; also *The New York Times*, April 16, 1964.

[26] Few, even of the sharpest critics of the so-called welfare state, would agree with Senator Goldwater's assertion in 1964 that "youth riots in Oregon," "gang rape in California," and the rising crime rates in American cities were somehow traceable to this "welfare state." "If," he is quoted as saying, "it is entirely proper for the government to take from some to give to others, then won't some be led to believe that they can rightfully take from anyone who has more than they have?" See Charles Mohr, *The New York Times*, September 11, 1964.

GOVERNMENT AND
THE ECONOMY

☆ *LAISSEZ FAIRE IN THEORY AND PRACTICE*

Endless argument goes on about the proper relation of government to the economy. The argument at times seems to assume that they are separate entities, even rivals in an everlasting struggle for power. Government, in fact, is not something apart from and hostile to the national economy, but, rather, an important part of it. So integral is the relation between government and economics that political science and political economy for a long time were synonymous.

When economists estimate the gross national product (GNP—the total value of all goods and services produced in the nation), included in the total are the expenditures of federal, state and local governments. For the year 1965, for example, the Department of Commerce estimated that in a total GNP of over 600 billions the money paid out by federal, state, and local governments amounted to some $200 billion, or nearly a third of the total. Approximately one in every six persons gainfully employed works for some unit of government, that is, in the public sector of the economy.

The purchase of goods and services of all kinds by the government has become an increasingly significant factor in the economic life of the nation as a whole. In some state and local communities government expenditures for defense and related goods and services account for the largest part of their total income and employment. So important have defense and related expenditures become that many people fear that any substantial disarmament, with a radical reduction in arms expenditures, might bring on a major economic depression. Most economists discount this danger, but it illustrates in a striking way the importance of government as a part of the total economy.

The importance of government to the national economy is not to be measured solely in terms of its purchase of goods and services. The character of these goods and services is such that their influence upon our economic and social life is more far reaching and subtle than can be stated in any statistical analysis, however sophisticated. What quantitive standards can reveal, for example, the importance to the economy, not merely of defense expenditures as such, but the national security itself which these expenditures make possible? What, in economic terms, is the value of uniform standards of weights and measures, or a uniform currency to agriculture and labor, commerce, and industry? How can one appraise or describe statistically the economic significance of the American common market, made possible by the Constitution and without which our mass production industries might never have developed on anything like their present scale?

Nearly every type of expenditure in the private sector, no less than in the public sector of the economy, yields both material and psychic returns. A new automobile, a pair of shoes, a phonograph record, a painting, a color TV set, not to mention a house and garden, a public school, hospital, or fire department—all yield psychic satisfactions not easily measured. But the allocation of expenditures within the GNP as a whole and between the public and private sectors of the economy affords a good indication of the nature of a nation's total political economy and for that matter of its culture and civilization.

In a totalitarian state, where no significant private economy exists, the allocation of expenditures between capital goods and consumer goods, between armaments, agriculture and industry, between education and medical care, housing and highways, and so forth, is controlled in a high degree by the central government. Natural resources, raw materials, and manpower are employed according to some central plan. Production and distribution are carried on in state-owned facilities. Quality, quantity, and price of the goods and services supplied are determined by decree, and not by the interplay of demand and supply in a free-market place, although these forces no doubt still play a role in the process.

Under these circumstances political and economic power are combined and the coercive power of the state extends to virtually every economic transaction from the manufacture of space ships to the production and distribution of ham and eggs. Nor are the decrees that govern the economy subject to any extensive control by the general public or its representatives. Normally, decisions of this kind are proposed by "experts"—economists, engineers, technicians—to the central committees of the ruling political party. Theoretically, such a system admits of a high degree of rationality in the allocation of major expenditures in the economy. Less is left to chance and to the vagaries of popular demand expressed in the market place. By the same token, "interests of state" are likely to be paramount and economic decisions are made primarily to serve the state rather than the people as consumers. Since, in such a system, the components of the nation's GNP are determined by planning officers of the state, they tend to reflect the tastes, interests, and general priorities of the ruling oligarchy rather than those of the people at large.

Communist economists and some Socialists argue that such a system can not only yield a large supply of goods and services, but because of central planning and control can direct expenditures into channels that will be more socially useful and culturally elevating. This is one challenge that communism makes to the free world.

In the United States economic decision making is lodged not in the central government, controlled by a single political party, but is widely diffused among millions of private businesses, farms, and professional offices. These include more than 5 million individual proprietorships, corporations, and partnerships, 3 or 4 million commercial farms, and a half million independent professional offices. The dispersal of economic decision making through these private enterprises, in response to the demands of the people as consumers, is a major characteristic of the American economy.

The facilities for economic production and distribution for the most part are privately owned. The allocation of expenditures, the quantity, quality, and price of the various components of the GNP—for investment or for consumer goods and services such as food, housing, recreation, medical care, and to some extent education—are determined, in theory at least, not by any group of experts according to a central plan, but by the action of buyers and sellers in a competitive market. A large and sustained demand for some goods and services, it is assumed, will stimulate increased investment in enterprises for meeting this demand. As demand slackens or is replaced by competing demands for other goods and services, investment in facilities will shift to follow these changes in market demand. Demand in turn will respond to changes in popular needs and desires, and to such other factors as price, quality, and convenience.

This privately owned, competitive system, based on private ownership of the facilities for production and distribution, it is argued, enlists the selfish interests and desires of individuals as producers and consumers who, in the process of satisfying their own desires, are led by an "invisible hand" to meet the needs of society.[1] This system, it is said, also provides continuous stimulation for the development of new and improved goods and services and more efficient ways of production and distribution. By decentralizing decision making and bringing most economic transactions under the discipline of free competition rather than under the coercive

---

[1] As Adam Smith put it, the free market economy makes it possible for each individual by pursuing his own selfish interest to be "led by an invisible hand to promote an end which was no part of his intention."

power of the state, this system of laissez faire expands the area of freedom for the individual. It is, moreover, scientific and progressive, whereas central ownership and control tend to be ideological and stagnant.

This price and market system has been described as

the most efficient system of social organization ever conceived. It makes it possible for huge multitudes to cooperate effectively, multitudes who may hardly know of each other's existence, or whose personal attitudes toward one another may be indifference or hostility. . . . It [also] affords a maximum of individual freedom and a minimum of coercion. And since people can cooperate effectively in production [and distribution] even where their attitudes on other issues are hostile there is no need for unity and conformity in religion, politics . . . and language.[2]

Although a system based on each man's pursuit of his own interest seems at first blush to be completely lacking in rationality, the net result is nevertheless highly rational. For as each man calculates his own best interest, the sum total of these calculations will be the best interest of society. This model of a free enterprise system, moreover, implies a sharp distinction between the private and the public sectors of the national economy. And it tends to regard government at any level as an alien and hostile intruder whenever it seeks to expand the public sector or to intervene in other ways in the private sector of the economy.

The proper role of government in this model system is to maintain law and order, provide for an impartial administration of justice through courts of law, protect private property, enforce contracts, and provide for the common defense against external attack. So far as the economy is concerned, government policy should be laissez faire.

"The best means ever devised," says a recent policy statement of the Republican National Committee, "to plan and organize the production people want is through private initiative exercised in competitive markets. . . . A primary objective of government policy must be to strengthen this unique economic system with its millions of centers of initiative in businesses, farms and professional offices. . . . Government should set the legal framework for private action, serve as the court of last resort and carry on those functions which the private sector cannot do or cannot do as well." When government goes beyond these limits, it is said, it not only threatens the legitimate freedom and interests of private businessmen but of workers and consumers as well. And what is worst of all, it interferes with operation of the "natural laws" of supply and demand.

But the natural laws of supply and demand are by no means self-evident or, at least, not self-evident once one moves from the model of the market place to the market itself. When it is said that "government

2 C. Harland, *Readings in Economics and Politics* (New York: Oxford University Press, 1961) , p. 193.

should do only those things that private business cannot do, or cannot do as well," the statement invites wide differences of opinion as to what these things are. It is from this phrase and from the differences that develop in time between the model and the real market that argument arises as to the proper relation of the government to the economy.

An essential characteristic of classical competition is the lack of power in any individual producer or purchaser to control the supply and the price at which goods and services are sold. In the laissez-faire model, monopoly or combinations to control prices are mortal sins. Like government intervention, they are said to be "artificial" restraints on the law of supply and demand. Classical competition requires a large number of independent producers so that no one of them can significantly affect the price by his own decisions.

Wage rates for labor, it assumes, will be subject to the same laws of supply and demand: when jobs outnumber workers, wages rise; when workers outnumber jobs, wages fall. This highly flexible system, it is argued, will keep prices and costs within reasonable balance, insure an equitable, although not equal, distribution of income, provide for the optimum use of resources, and create continuous pressure for new products and for improved methods of production and distribution. In this way the "invisible hand" will guide self-interest to serve the public interest, without benefit of governmental intervention. Indeed, it is argued, government intervention will prevent the system from working smoothly and efficiently by interfering with the natural laws of supply and demand.

As it turned out, however, there were developments within the system that impaired the working of these natural laws. The appearance of the limited liability corporation as the major unit of business enterprise was one factor. The "representative form" of business organization in the classical model was thought of more as an individual proprietorship or partnership than as an immortal, impersonal, far-flung limited liability corporation. Alfred Marshall, for example, "the last of the great classical economists," thought of an industry "as having hundreds or even thousands" of small enterprises. It was, he said, like a forest, with new, individual trees sprouting, growing, and finally declining, but with new trees to replace the old.

Nor did the classical model anticipate the growth of one or a relatively few great corporations dominating whole industries to the point where they could establish prices by administrative decree, rather than having prices determined by the interplay of supply and demand in the market. Yet, as Gardiner Means has said: "Today, 130 big corporations account for nearly half of manufacturing output in the United States." And Adolf Berle has recently estimated that "about 2/3rds of the economically productive assets of the United States, excluding agriculture, are owned by a group of not more than 500 corporations out of a total of approximately a million. And "within each of [these] . . . a still smaller group has the ultimate decision making power. This is, I think, the highest concentration of economic power in recorded history. . . . "Many of these corporations have budgets, and some of them have payrolls which with their customers, affect a greater number of people than most of the ninety-odd sovereign countries of the world."[3]

In 1958, twenty of the largest corporations together had more employees than the government of the United States. The 500 largest industrial corporations with total sales of approximately $200 billion accounted for about 30 percent of the total sales for all manufacturing and trade concerns, corporate and noncorporate. About one-half of this total was accounted for by 180 corporations.[4] To be sure, there is competition even among these giants. But it is not price competition as the classic model would have it. The steel giants, for example, are meeting heavy competition from the behemoths of aluminum, glass, and cement. This new limited form of competition among industrial giants is referred to as monopolistic, oligopolistic, or simply "imperfect" competition.

Standing like saplings among these 500 giants with their far-flung branches are 2,500,000 small business concerns engaged in marketing their own and the products of the giants and competing for a share of the market. To preserve competition and prevent the giants from starving out the smaller firms altogether has been a major goal of public policy from the enactment of the Sherman Antitrust Act in 1890 to the Supreme Court's decree in 1957 ordering the divorce of DuPont and General Motors.[5]

The limited liability corporation and the corporate giants are only two factors that tend to complicate the smooth working of the classical model of a free competitive market economy. Other complications have been introduced through the organization of trade associations, holding companies, interlocking directorates, trusts and "gentlemen's agreements." Even the classical theorists recognized certain "natural" monopolies, or quasi-monopolies such as railroads, docks and waterfront facilities, street care and bus lines, telephone and telegraph companies, electric utilities, water companies, and so forth. These enterprises, usually operat-

---

[3] *Economic Power and the New Society* (New York: Fund for the Republic, 1957). Adolf Berle has recently estimated that nearly 100 percent of the total supply of automobiles, cigarettes, rubber tires, steel, matches, tin cans and tinware, glass, steam engines, aircraft, photographic equipment, pianos, and petroleum products is produced by twenty or fewer corporations operating in each area.

[4] The trend toward bigness in industry is also characteristic of insurance, banking, and finance. Of 14,000 commercial banks in 1958, the twenty largest—about 1/10th of one percent—accounted for 25 percent of total deposits. Between 1945 and 1958 the number of banks declined from 14,725 to 14,034, while population increased 20 percent and GNP by 33 percent. Twenty insurance companies out of 1,400 held 75 percent of insurance assets.

[5] See *United States* v. *E. I. DuPont de Nemours & Co. et al.*, 353 U.S. 586 (1957).

ing under special charters from federal, state, or local governments, were generally recognized as not subject to the same natural laws of supply and demand, as were other forms of business enterprise. Different power companies, telephone companies, or street car lines might compete in different states or cities or in different parts of the same city, but if many companies were to compete for every potential customer throughout the city, the waste, inconvenience, and inefficiency involved would be intolerable to the community. In the absence of competition as the natural, automatic regulator of these concerns, other forms of "artificial" regulation were deemed necessary to keep services and rates or prices within some reasonable relation to costs. Such enterprises were quite early described as "affected with a public interest" and hence were among the first to be subjected to governmental regulation—regulation, incidentally, that was not merely tolerated, but often welcomed by the enterprises themselves.

There were other areas of economic enterprise where, for a variety of reasons, access was limited, and to which, therefore, the natural laws of supply and demand did not apply. Notable among these were the radio and television industries. To avoid chaos in the air—with multiple stations operating on the same channel or wave length—some authority had to be established to license and allocate channels. Theoretically, this might have been left to the industry itself, but again the "public interest" in these valuable media of communication dictated that responsibility be assumed by a public authority: hence the establishment of the Radio Commission in 1927 and, in 1934, the Federal Communications Commission.

There are still other cases in which limited access to the market invited government intervention. Access to hydroelectric power sites on navigable streams, or to grazing, lumbering, or mining privileges on public lands, could not be controlled or regulated by the ordinary laws of supply and demand, and led inevitably to systems of government license and control. So too did participation in certain activities intimately concerned with national defense, to which access was limited by considerations of national security. National defense policies and programs have always been regarded as a legitimate area of governmental intervention and activity. They have never, or hardly ever, been carried on in a free competitive market, and in recent years have assumed a magnitude unparalleled in our history. Control of these vast undertakings on both sides, in the government and in the private economy, is highly centralized. Upwards of 70 percent of prime defense contract awards to private industry go to a relatively few large corporations. Extensive subcontracting among hundreds or even thousands of smaller companies not only extends the influence of defense expenditures but gives to the giants an added measure of influence over smaller enterprises throughout the country. A relationship resembling a kind of interlocking directorate of industrial and military leaders develops. Retired officers of the armed services in considerable numbers become directors, officers, or consultants of the top defense contractors.

In his final address to the nation on January 19, 1961, President Eisenhower spoke of this "military-industrial" complex. He pointed out that the demands of national security had compelled the United States to "create a permanent armaments industry of vast proportions" and to maintain a defense establishment employing 3.5 million persons, and spending billions of dollars each year. "This . . . immense military establishment and a large arms industry," he said, "is new in American experience. The total influence, economic, political, even spiritual, is felt in every city, every state house, every office of the Federal Government. . . . Our toil, our resources and livelihood are all involved; so is the very structure of our society. ". . . we must be on guard," he continued, "against the acquisition of unwarranted influence . . . by the military industrial complex. . . . Only an alert and knowledgeable citizenry can compel the proper meshing of the huge industrial and military machinery of defense with our peaceful methods and goals, so that security and liberty may prosper together."[6]

The limited liability corporation, the giant corporation or combine, the big banks, insurance companies, and other centralized sources of credit, "natural" monopolies, and areas of limited access are not the only factors that have impaired the classic laissez-faire model of the economy. Even the labor market is no longer free. If big business has substituted the administered price for the competitive price, big labor has substituted the negotiated and administered labor contract for the individual or local labor agreement. By 1965 there were some 150 national and international labor unions with headquarters in the United States. Their combined membership has grown from about 3 1/2 million in 1935 to over 18 million. About 34 percent of all nonagricultural employment is now governed by trade-union agreements of one kind or another. As there are giants among the corporations so too are there giants among labor organizations. The United Automobile Workers, the Steel Workers, the Teamsters, Machinists, Longshoremen, and Electricians are among the giants, with memberships of 250,000 to 1,000,000 or more.

The labor market is no longer a local market, as it used to be. It has become a national market as industry-wide bargaining and industry-wide contracts have replaced contracts covering only the local plant or the shop or chapel within the plant. Nor is the labor contract solely concerned with wages and hours and overtime. It embraces a complex structure of work rules, guarantees of status and seniority, fringe benefits of various kinds including unemployment and disability benefits, separa-

---

[6] For a further exploration of the economic and political problems involved in this development, consult *Congress and the Nation, 1945–1964* (Washington, D.C.: Congressional Quarterly Service, 1965) , pp. 1579–1584.

tion allowances, pensions, and profit-sharing schemes.[7] Wage rates, so far from being established by the natural laws of supply and demand are often based on complex production ratios and cost-of-living indices, with escalation clauses to provide for automatic adjustments to changing conditions. Increasingly government has become a partner and not always a silent partner in regulating this labor market.

Despite the many influences working against an open competitive market, it would be a mistake to assume that competition and the laws of supply and demand are no longer major factors in the control and regulation of our economy. Perhaps the bulk of goods and services are still produced and distributed under conditions comparable, if not exactly corresponding, to the ideal model of a competitive economy envisioned by Adam Smith and the classical economists. The laws of supply and demand still govern, but in a restricted jurisdiction.

Some economists estimate that from 20 to 30 percent of our goods and services are produced and sold under conditions of administered prices and imperfect or monopolistic competition; and from 50 to 60 percent under conditions of fairly intensive competition. The remainder is produced by government or by industries closely controlled or regulated by government. But even in those areas where competition is most intense—perhaps because it is so intense—businessmen have sought to mitigate the rigors of the struggle by calling upon government to limit entry into the field, to establish production controls, standards of fair competition, and fair prices. State boards to license doctors, lawyers, merchants, barbers, realtors, morticians, and literally hundreds of other common callings have been established with the full knowledge and consent, and often pressure from the occupation to be licensed. Although both federal and state legislation to establish standards of quality, purity, and reliability in the manufacture and sale of food and drug products were at first resisted, they too have been largely accepted by the major concerns involved. More recently, and often encouraged by organized business itself, additional legislation has been passed at both federal and state levels to protect consumers against dishonest and fraudulent business practices.

In agriculture, where the natural laws of supply and demand might otherwise operate with greater effect than in any other major industry, both federal and state governments have intervened on a grand scale.

These, then, are some of the factors to keep in mind in any discussion of government and the economy. To see the relations between the public sector of the economy and the private sector solely as a kind of internal cold war between two rival power structures is as misleading as to see our federal system as a continuing conflict between the states and the federal government. And to see in the expansion of the public sector

[7] By 1962 it was estimated that some $60 billion had been accumulated in various union pension plans.

and the increasing intervention of government in the private sector a sign of the decline and fall of our free economy is also to misread the record and to misunderstand what in fact is taking place.

In terms of the quantity as well as the quality of goods and services produced, at prices close to marginal costs; in terms of an equitable distribution of income, and a continuing pressure for new products, new industries, and improved methods of production and distribution, there has been nothing to approach the American economy, not even in the Elysian Utopias of literature.

Communist propagandists would like us to believe the theory of the decline and fall of the American economy. Deriving their image of a capitalist, free-enterprise, system from the gloomy pages of Karl Marx, Henry George, and Charles Dickens, they have failed to see that the capitalism of the nineteenth century is as far removed from the capitalism of the United States in the second half of the twentieth century as the communism of the USSR is from the Twenty-third Psalm or the Sermon on the Mount. The real revolution of our century is not the so-called Communist revolution of 1918 or 1966, but the continuing American Revolution in which this new political economy is a major factor.

☆ OUR POLITICAL ECONOMY

From the earliest days of the American Republic the establishment of proper relations between government and the economy has been a major problem in American politics. On the whole the relationship has been a friendly one. Nevertheless conflict and hostility have not been lacking, not so much between government as a whole on one side and private business on the other, as between competing interests both within government and the private economy seeking to influence public policy, with each side claiming to represent the public welfare.

For example, the agrarian interests in 1789 were by no means as enthusiastic as the banking, business, and manufacturing interests for Alexander Hamilton's Central Bank, protective tariff, and the funding at par of the debts of both federal and state governments. It is well to remember that Hamilton's first Report on Public Credit in 1790 came as the result of memorials, not from farm organizations but from public creditors "praying the aid and interposition of Congress . . . for the punctual payment of the interest of the public debt . . . by the adoption of such . . . means, as . . . shall best promote the public welfare and render justice to the public creditors."

As we have seen, the American Revolution and the Constitution were not only declarations of political independence but of economic independence from a mercantilist system in which the economy was controlled by a central government and certain government-sponsored monopolies. Hamilton, nevertheless, rejected the argument of those who said that government ought not to intervene in economic affairs at all but should leave economic development solely to "the quick-sighted guidance of private interest." Nor did he hesitate, notwithstanding his strong leaning toward laissez faire, to recommend a Central Bank as a mixed corporation, chartered by the government, in which both private investors and the government would participate. The pragmatic course that Hamilton charted has in general been followed ever since in defining the relations of the government to the economy. A strong predilection for laissez faire has not prevented the government from striving to promote, protect, and regulate the private economy or to provide certain goods and services to its citizens, even though this involved its active participation in a variety of economic enterprises.

Protective tariffs and other public policies to encourage various types of private economic endeavor have been a feature of American government from the beginning. The use of public funds or public lands to help in the building of roads and canals, transcontinental highways, railroads, steamship lines, air lines, and airports is well known.[8] Encouragement of this kind has not been confined to the central government. State and local governments too have played a part in the development of the vast transportation system that has transformed a continent into a neighborhood. Federal grants-in-aid have been used both to stimulate and to support state and local activities in these as in other fields. Who can estimate the full economic effects of government efforts to promote agricultural production through education and research, or the revolutionary changes arising from inventions and copyrights promoted and protected by the central government? Although patent laws confer a limited monopoly on the use, manufacture, or sale of an invention, not even laissez-faire economists would propose abolition of the patent system. But the government's part in scientific and technological change is not confined to the granting of patents and copyrights. "The Federal Government today," says Thomas Watson, Jr., of IBM, "plays by far the most significant role in the whole area of technological change. More than 60 percent of all expenditures for research and development are now made through the Department of Defense, A.E.C., National Aeronautics and Space Agency and other federal agencies."[9]

The $2 billion gamble of the United States government in the so-called Manhattan Engineer District, established in 1942 for the develop-

---

[8] A recent report of the United States Bureau of Roads estimates that the 41,000 miles of Interstate Highways under construction will cost in the neighborhood of $47 billion. See Joseph Ingraham, in *The New York Times*, January 14, 1965.

[9] *Goals for Americans, The Report of the President's Commission on National Goals* (American Assembly; Englewood Cliffs, N.J.: Prentice-Hall, 1960) , p. 193.

Between 1961 and fiscal 1965 federal expenditures on research and development jumped from $9.3 billion to $15.3 billion. See the *Wall Street Journal*, February 24, 1964.

ment of atomic energy, may have more far-reaching effects on our economy than even the steam engine or the internal-combustion engine. And who can predict the full consequences for our economy of the $2.5 billion a year now being spent on space research and development?[10] Billions of dollars in direct government subsidies or loans to agriculture, business, labor, home builders, and other components of the American economy are now an accepted feature of our economy.

Government in the United States not only seeks to promote private economic activity, but seeks in a variety of ways to protect the economy and the economic system as a whole. This it does by striving to conserve the nation's land, forests, water, and other natural resources from erosion by wind and rain and flood and fire, and to protect them from devastation and pollution through excessive exploitation and wasteful methods of use and development. It builds giant dams to hold back flood waters, generate power, and provide areas for recreation and reforestation. It experiments in more efficient methods for the conservation, use, and management of irreplaceable natural resources. The TVA, the Bonneville Power Administration in Oregon, the Hoover Dam in Nevada, the Central Valley Project in California, and dozens of other projects of this kind make an incalculable contribution, not merely to the economy of the states or regions in which they are located, but to the national economy as well.

Government has tried to protect the economic system from itself. Much of government intervention in, or regulation of, the economy is designed to protect the free competitive market from practices that, uncontrolled, might seriously impair or destroy it. Government regulation thus undertakes to (1) foster and promote competition, (2) mitigate the rigors of unfair, or antisocial competition, or (3) serve as a substitute when competition fails or is inapplicable.

It was to protect and promote competition that the Sherman Antitrust Act was passed in 1890, following similar legislation in most of the states. Its purpose was "to protect trade and commerce against unlawful restraint and monopolies."

The Clayton Antitrust Act of 1914, the Federal Trade Commission Act of the same year, and the Public Utility Holding Company Act (Wheeler-Rayburn Act) of 1935, and other such legislation, were aimed at preventing monopoly or combinations able to control prices and thus interfere with the operation of the natural laws of supply and demand.

---

[10] Some of the immediate effects are more apparent. For example, the McDonnell Aircraft Corporation, prime contractor for building the capsule used on the 1965 Gemini two-man space flight, reported that more than 3,000 subcontractors in many states had supplied $348,887,143 worth of materials and services "for our part in the program." An additional 1,500 to 1,800 subcontractors had participated in building the launching vehicle under the prime contractor, the Martin Company. See *The New York Times,* March 21, 1965.

In 1938, nearly 50 years after the enactment of the first antitrust law, President Franklin Roosevelt called for a thorough study of the concentration of economic power in the United States. "This concentration," he said, "is severely impairing the economic effectiveness of private enterprise. . . . One of the primary causes of our present difficulties lies in the disappearance of pure competition in many industrial fields. . . ."

Some critics, noting the increase in industrial giantism and the growing concentration of control of the American economy, have been inclined to dismiss this trust-busting policy as futile, if not foolish. Most economists, however, would agree with Professor Sumner Schlichter of Harvard that "Competition in American industry is far more vigorous and pervasive than in the industries of any other advanced industrial country . . . [notwithstanding that] the U.S. has many more huge business enterprises than any other country." "It would be wrong," he continued, "to ascribe the widespread and intense competition in American industry solely to the strong public policy against restraint of trade. [Nevertheless] America's unique and firm public policy against restraints on competition has . . . helped greatly to keep industry strongly competitive."[11]

Governmental regulation has also sought to mitigate the rigors of competition. This it has done, for example, by setting up the Federal Trade Commission in 1914 with power "to prevent persons, partnerships, or corporations . . . from using unfair methods of competition in commerce." And the Clayton Antitrust Act, passed shortly after the Federal Trade Commission Act, undertook to define and to outlaw some specific kinds of "unfair competition": (1) Discrimination in price between different customers; (2) conditional sales which limit the purchaser's freedom to handle goods produced by a competing company; (3) stock ownership by one company in another where the effect would be to lessen competition; (4) interlocking directorates.

To these powers others have been added to prevent false and misleading advertising: (1) to insure truthful labeling, and (2) to prevent discrimination among competing customers in furnishing advertising or promotional services. Under the Robinson-Patman Act of 1936 the commission may also prevent price cutting designed to reduce competition. "The basic objective," says a report of the Federal Trade Commission, "is the maintenance of free competitive enterprise as the keystone of the American economic system. . . . To promote free and fair competition . . . through prevention of price-fixing arrangements, boycotts, combinations in restraint of trade, other unfair methods of competition, and unfair and deceptive practices."

[11] See also Theodore J. Kreps, "An Evaluation of Anti-Trust Policy . . .," Joint Economic Committee (Washington, D.C.: U.S. Government Printing Office), January 30, 1960.

Similar goals have been set for the Securities and Exchange Commission established in 1934. Basically its role is "to protect . . . the public and investors against malpractices in the securities and financial markets." This it does by (1) requiring the disclosure of information concerning securities offered for sale to the public and listed on the exchanges; (2) regulation of the stock exchanges and over-the-counter markets; (3) enforcing sanctions against companies and persons guilty of securities frauds and manipulation in the marketing of securities.

In many states similar legislation has been passed to mitigate the rigors of competition including Fair-Trade, or Fair-Price, laws, which enable producers to set a minimum retail price on their products, and to have state enforcement agencies see that retailers do not fall below the prices set. In theory these laws are to protect small merchants from the rough competition of large producers or distributors, who, by temporarily selling below costs, can drive small businessmen out of the market, thus lessening competition in the long run.

Finally, government regulation often serves as a substitute for competition where the natural laws of supply and demand in a free market do not or cannot operate without grave danger to the public. This has been the case in those areas of the economy dominated by "natural" monopolies, or where unrestrained, free, competition would not be in the public interest. At the federal level the Interstate Commerce Commission, and to a lesser extent the Federal Power Commission, the Federal Communications Commission, and the Federal Aviation Agency illustrate this use of government regulation as a substitute for free competition. The Interstate Commerce Commission, for example, has power to (1) regulate rates, (2) establish standards of service and safety, and (3) authorize or disallow proposed mergers or discontinuance of service by rail, water, and motor carriers operating in interstate commerce or directly affecting interstate commerce. These modes of transportation were deemed to be either natural monopolies, and hence not subject to effective control by free competition, or so affected with a public interest that public regulation was required as a substitute for uncontrolled competition.

The Federal Power Commission also serves as a substitute for free competition by licensing hydroelectric projects on government lands or navigable waters, and by regulating the transmission and sale, at wholesale, of electric energy and natural gas by public utilities engaged in interstate commerce.[12] In similar fashion the Federal Communications Commission has responsibility for regulating interstate and foreign communications by wire and radio (including TV) so as to make available

[12] The Federal Power Commission has recently embarked on a program to reduce rates for electricity by as much as 27 percent by 1980. See *National Power Survey,* Federal Power Commission, 1964. See also report by Gene Smith in *The New York Times,* December 13, 1964.

the most efficient communications service at reasonable charges. It may grant broadcasting licenses for a maximum of three years and may revoke licenses. The basic standard that guides the commission in granting or revoking licenses is the "public interest, convenience and necessity." How far this ambiguous phrase gives power to the FCC to consider, let alone regulate, program content is a matter of great dispute.[13] But the need for some such commission is obvious if competition is not to produce chaos on the air.

The Federal Aviation Agency and the Civil Aeronautics Board between them serve for air transportation the same functions essentially served by the ICC for interstate transportation by land and water.

These substitutes for the free competitive market in regulating important aspects of the nation's economy are matched or supplemented by state boards and commissions having jurisdiction over the intrastate activities of railroads, public utilities, motor carriers, and so forth. They too serve to illustrate how government not only strives to (1) foster and promote competition, (2) mitigate the rigors of competition, and (3) serve as a substitute for free competition.

What is lacking in this system of government intervention, say its critics, is any overall plan for the national economy as a whole. Most of government's relations to the economy, they say, are accidental, incidental, indirect, and indecisive. The individual good citizen is expected to develop some kind of overall plan for himself and his family, for a job, housing, education, health, recreation, and so forth. Private business too is expected to plan; even towns and cities have planning boards. But comprehensive economic planning by government has been regarded as either unnecessary, immoral, or downright subversive.

The central planning of some totalitarian societies has exercised a strange fascination on both friends and foes of economic planning in America. To some it points to the need for more careful and systematic national planning if we are to meet the threat of Communist competition. Others point to central planning as the inherent evil of totalitarian states, and as something to be avoided at all costs. The real issue here would seem to be, Can central planning of our economic and social life be reconciled with a political system and an economy based on individual freedom of choice and democratic decision making?

☆   *ECONOMIC PLANNING IN A FREE SOCIETY*

When one speaks of national economic planning, he opens a Pandora's box of conflicting theories concerning the nature, purpose, and scope of

[13] Note the recent attack on the commission for violating the First Amendment by considering the amount of time devoted to religious broadcasting in deciding whether a station has served the "public interest, convenience and necessity." See *The New York Times,* January 11, 1965.

the planning function in any society. Someone has said that the master plan of the United States is the Constitution, in which the basic goals and the ways and means of reaching these goals are outlined. But the Constitution at best is a plan that requires a lot of planning to carry out. And it is with this process of planning that we are concerned.

It is obvious that economic planning in a free economy and a democratic society is necessarily a different kind of process than it is in a Communist dictatorship or even a Socialist system. Socialist or Communist planning assumes government ownership of basic material resources of the nation and control over manpower. In such systems central planning and control can be direct and coercive. In the United States, with its long tradition of laissez faire, government ownership and operation of economic enterprises has played only a minor role in economic planning. Nevertheless it has not been negligible. Government-owned corporations and authorities operate economic facilities of considerable variety and scope. The Tennessee Valley Authority, the Commodity Credit Corporation, the Bonneville Power Administration, the Virgin Islands Corporation, the Panama Canal with all its varied operations, the Alaska Railway, the Inland Water Ways Corporation, the Federal Deposit Insurance Corporation, and the Post Office Department are but a partial catalogue of large-scale business enterprises carried on by the federal government. Nor does this list include the numerous arsenals, factories, shipyards, and drydocks of the Department of Defense, loan agencies, especially for agriculture and housing, the vast Veterans Administration, systems of insurance against illness, old age, and unemployment, and numerous government-owned restaurants, hotels, and recreation facilities that provide services for the general public. Nor does it include the hundreds of water plants, liquor stores, electric power and transit systems, and other quasi-business operations of state and local governments. Nearly 25 percent of the electric energy produced in the United States is produced in power plants owned and operated by federal, state, and local governments. It is estimated that upwards of $5 billion or $6 billion of local revenues come annually from these and other quasi-business operations.[14]

However much this trend toward government ownership and operation of economic enterprises may be praised or deplored, it does not play a major role in overall economic planning in the United States. With the vast bulk of agriculture, commerce, industry, recreation, and professional services privately owned and operated, planning in the United States must be mainly indirect and persuasive rather than direct and compulsive.[15]

[14] See the Second Hoover Commission Report for a more complete list of government-owned business enterprises.

[15] Both types of planning require a good deal of forecasting and prediction, which in turn require basic information that is relevant and reliable. To realize such basic

The basic instruments used include the best possible estimates of the annual gross national product (GNP), the executive budget, taxes, tariffs and trade policies, debt management, price supports, subsidies of various kinds, licensing and other forms of official regulation and control. To make the best possible use of these instruments Congress has recently taken steps to create central planning agencies in the Executive Office of the President.

Because the executive budget of the federal government is an important instrument in this planning process, the establishment of the Bureau of the Budget in 1921 and its transfer to the White House in 1939 was a first and major step in the direction of a planning agency. In his executive budget the President is able to present to the Congress an overall plan for the government in its relation to the national economy. In addition to the Bureau of the Budget, the President has had, since 1946, a Council of Economic Advisers, composed of two members and a chairman, appointed by the President by and with the advice and consent of the Senate. Describing its work, a recent chairman of the council says: "The Council analyses the national economy; . . . advises the President on economic developments; appraises the economic programs and policies of the Federal Government; recommends to the President policies for economic growth and stability; and assists in the preparation of the economic report of the President to the Congress."

Previous efforts to create a planning agency in the office of the President were not too successful. The Council of Economic Advisers was preceded by a National Resources Board (1933), which became the National Planning Board in 1934, the National Resources Committee in 1935, and the National Resources Planning Board in 1939. Its studies on public works, regionalism, urban government, the structure of the national economy, and population trends were valuable as research and planning tools, but the National Resources Planning Board was never taken seriously as a planning agency. Many members of Congress resented an executive agency that seemed to usurp the policy role of Congress. At any rate, in 1943 Congress refused to vote further funds for the board, and it died.[16] In 1946, however, with the memory of the great depression of the 1930s still vivid, Congress passed a so-called Employment Act, which among other things established the Council of Economic Advisers to the President. The act also authorized the use of deficit

---

objectives as national security, full employment with a rising standard of living at reasonable prices, a reasonable rate of economic growth, optimum use of manpower and resources, and a healthy balance of international payments will require the knowledge and skills of virtually every branch of learning, plus the insights of practical businessmen, politicians, and administrators.

[16] By a kind of irony, the National Resources Planning Board went out of existence about the same time the government embarked upon a vast program of nuclear research under the Manhattan Engineers Project.

financing, public works, and economic controls on whatever scale might be necessary to maintain full employment and avoid another major economic depression. To provide legislative review of the President's Economic Report, a Joint Committee on the Economic Report was established in Congress. In his seventh and Final Economic Report to Congress in January, 1953, President Truman said:

> The Employment Act of 1946 . . . represents the refusal of Americans in all pursuits . . . to accept recurrent depressions as a way of life. . . .
> It has been calculated that the depression cost us some 600 billion dollars of output measured in 1952 dollars. . . .
> The Employment Act stands as a pledge . . . that never again shall any such sacrifice be laid on the altar of [so-called] "natural economic forces."

For those to whom the thought of economic planning by government is redolent of radicalism, it may be some comfort that the threefold goal of the Employment Act of 1946, and the Council of Economic Advisers is to (1) maintain a free enterprise economy, (2) provide reliable and relevant knowledge for the determination of price and employment policies, and (3) keep ultimate responsibility for planning and policy in the President and Congress.

As the President prepares his Budget Message and his Economic Report to the Congress his central concern is with the economic welfare of the nation. President Kennedy, for example, in 1962 outlined a legislative program "to raise our entire economy to a new and higher level of business activity . . . to improve American Education, and technical training . . . expand civilian research and technology . . . [and] step up the development of our natural resources." Most important, he said, it was "to make possible an increase in private consumption and investment demands." This he proposed to do by a cut in federal taxes of some $11 billion to increase consumer purchases and to increase investment incentives. "When consumers purchase more goods," he said, "plants use more of their capacity, men are hired instead of laid off, investment increases and profits are high." In laying major emphasis on tax reduction he de-emphasized other instruments that might have been used and that he was urged to support. These included legislation to establish a 35-hour week to increase employment, a large public works program, an increase in the level of minimum wages in industry, an expansion of credit, and higher tariffs against imports that compete in the American market with American-made goods. When Lyndon Johnson succeeded to the Presidency, he pushed the Kennedy program through the Congress with a tax cut of $11.5 billion as its major feature. Two years later the Financial and Business Editor of *The New York Times* referred to the "historic performance" of the American economy in 1964 and said that "without the tax cut the tempo of business almost certainly would have slowed."[17] In his Budget Message and Economic Report in January, 1965, President Johnson continued to emphasize the importance of tax legislation and government fiscal policies as basic instruments for economic planning, without, however, discounting the importance of public works, wage and hour legislation, and expenditures for education, research, and resources development.

Not the least among the planning instruments available are certain built-in economic stabilizers such as the defense program, social security payments, interest on the public debt, highway trust funds, and veterans' benefits. Added to these stable, one might say inflexible, components of the gross national product are more flexible items such as appropriations for public works and emergency relief. Most important as flexible items are tax rates, credit facilities, and interest rates. Because these are more flexible and require less time to take effect than public works, they have been preferred instruments for economic planning. Reviewing the President's budget for fiscal year 1966, Representative George Mahon of Texas, chairman of the House Appropriations Committee, commented: ". . . the feeling is prevalent . . . that the Federal budget is not so much a recitation of Government programs as it is an instrument for managing the National Economy."[18]

☆ *CONSTITUTIONAL LIMITATIONS ON PLANNING*

In developing programs and policies for the promotion, protection, and regulation of American economic life, no small part of the task requires action by state as well as federal government. And the road toward planning has not been smooth. Not the least of the obstacles has been the limitations imposed by the Supreme Court under certain provisions of the Constitution. Due process of law, for example, has been interpreted to include substantive as well as procedural limitations on action by both federal and state governments. The Constitution also forbids government to take private property for public use without just compensation, and Section 10 of Article I forbids any state to impair the obligation of contracts.

[17] See President Kennedy's address to the Economic Club of New York, December 15, 1962; President Johnson's Economic Report to the Congress, *Wall Street Journal,* January 21, 1964; President Johnson's Budget Message, January 22, 1964; "Trends in the Economy of the United States," by Thomas Mullaney, Financial and Business Editor, *The New York Times,* January 11, 1965.

[18] See *The Budget for 1966: Hearings before the House Appropriations Committee,* 89th Congress, 1st Sess.

Do these provisions establish certain vested rights in property and in contracts that neither federal nor state governments may impair without depriving some person or persons of property or liberty without due process of law? Or to put the matter more concretely, does the guarantee that private property shall not be taken for a public use without just compensation extend not only to government condemnation and purchase of property, but also to the regulation of private property? Can the government, for example, establish maximum rates for a public utility, rates below what it might charge in a free market, without paying compensation? If it does so regulate property without compensation, is this a deprivation of property without due process of law?

Does legislation regulating the use of property, limiting the right of persons to engage in certain businesses, regulating the hours and wages of one's employees, or the conditions of employment in a private business, fall under the constitutional prohibition against depriving a person of liberty or property without due process of law? Are such regulations equivalent to a taking of private property for a public use without just compensation? Does the term *liberty* as used in the Fifth and the Fourteenth Amendments include liberty to enter into contracts, or liberty to do what one wishes with his own property without government regulation or interference? Claims such as these have been made and upheld by the courts against public policies aimed at government regulation and control of the economy. So common did decisions of this kind become after 1890 that a distinguished constitutional lawyer, writing as late as 1952, could say: "Today the due process clause is important chiefly, not as consecrating certain procedures, but as limiting the substantive content of legislation."[19] State legislation, especially, was set aside as unconstitutional on the ground that it deprived corporations, as well as natural persons, of "a reasonable return on their investment," of "liberty of contract," and other vested rights in violation of the constitutional prohibition: "No person . . . shall be deprived of life, liberty, or property, without due process of law." (Fifth Amendment.)

In 1905, for example, a New York law establishing a maximum 10-hour day for workers in bakeries was declared unconstitutional because it deprived both employer and employee of liberty to contract without due process of law.[20] In 1923 the Supreme Court held that an act of Congress prescribing a minimum wage for women in the District of Columbia was also an unconstitutional interference with freedom of contract guaranteed by the due process clause. The Court recognized the power of the state and of Congress in the District of Columbia to legislate, under their general police powers, for the health, safety, and public morals of the community; but it denied that the establishment of maximum hours of

[19] E. S. Corwin, *Constitution of the United States, Annotated* (Washington, D.C.: U.S. Government Printing Office, 1952) , p. 845.
[20] *Lochner* v. *New York*, 198 U.S. 45 (1905) .

employment or minimum wages had any reasonable relation to health or safety or public morals.[21]

The so-called Lochner decision set off a long course of litigation in which state laws affecting working conditions, rates and prices for services of public utilities, rent control, employers' liability, and other social and economic controls, were set aside as violations of the substantive guarantees of the due process clause. The emphasis in all of these cases was upon freedom of private enterprise from political constraint and not upon so-called police power of government to regulate the economy in the interest of public health, welfare, and safety.

There was, however, another line of cases in which regulatory and welfare legislature was sustained because certain businesses or business practices were said to be "affected with a public interest" and hence subject to the "police power" of the state or the power of Congress to regulate interstate and foreign commerce.

Through the years both of these concepts, substantive due process on the one hand and the police power on the other, were used by the Court to strike down or to sustain government intervention in the private sector of the economy.

It would be pointless to review here the history of these two principles as they were applied to particular aspects of our economic life. In summary, it may be said that the doctrine of *substantive* due process has been progressively narrowed, while the "police power," "business affected with a public interest, and interstate commerce concepts have been broadened. That is to say, the Court has increasingly approved of legislation designed to regulate or otherwise intervene in the economic and social life of the nation. By 1934 the Court was, in effect, saying that virtually any business was affected with a public interest if the legislature said it was. In that year the Supreme Court upheld a New York law fixing milk prices and regulating the milk industry against an attack that the milk business was *not* so affected with a public interest as to bring it within the power of the state to regulate. The Court rejected that argument, saying: "There is *no* closed class or category of business affected with a public interest. The function of the Court is . . . to determine whether . . . the . . . regulation . . . [is] a reasonable extension of governmental authority."[22]

This decision was anticipated by a dissenting opinion of Justice Stone in a 1922 case involving the regulation of ticket scalpers. "The proper course for the court," he said, "is to recognize that a state legislature can do whatever it sees fit to do unless it is restrained by some express prohibitions in the Constitution of the United States or of the State. . . . The truth seems to me to be that subject to compensation,

---

[21] *Adkins* v. *Children's Hospital*, 26 U.S. 576 (1923).
[22] *Nebbia* v. *New York*, 291 U.S. 502 (1934).

where compensation is due, the Legislature may forbid or restrict any business when it has sufficient force of public opinion behind it."[23]

Finally, even the contract clause, as a limitation upon the state's power to regulate economic activity, was seriously weakened, when in 1934 the Court upheld a Minnesota law providing for a moratorium on mortgages. "A promise [that is, a contract] engaged between individuals," said Justice Cardozo, "[must] not paralyze the state in its endeavor in times of . . . crisis to keep its life blood flowing." Moreover, he said, "A gospel of *laissez faire* . . . may be inadequate in the great society that we live in to point the way to economic salvation. . . . The State when it acts today by statutes like the one before us is not furthering the selfish good of individuals or classes. . . . It is furthering its own good by maintaining the economic structure on which the good of all depends."[24]

One by one the legal barriers against economic and social planning have come down. A long line of cases which had raised obstacles to government regulation of the economy have been reversed. Just as the commerce clause and the taxing power have endowed the federal government with vast powers over the nation's economic life, so the *police power* has given extensive authority to the states over the social and economic life of their inhabitants.

By 1950 one may say that the long experiment in laissez faire of the classical model, as the automatic and sole governor of our economy, had come to an end. The United States, like Canada, Great Britain, France, Germany, Scandinavia, and most other modern industrial states, had become a *mixed* political economy, with implications for the future that we now only dimly see. At any rate, the great issues of our political economy no longer turn primarily on questions of constitutional power but on questions of policy. For all practical purposes in the economic field, what Congress and the President, state legislatures and governors will to do, they may do. Concerning the wisdom of what they do, only time will tell.

☆   *THE FARM PROBLEMS: A HARDY PERENNIAL*

If one were to seek for the ideal model of the independent, self-reliant, God-fearing American, he would no doubt find him in the American farmer. And if one were to search for an industry operating most faithfully in a free competitive market governed by the natural laws of supply and demand, he would find it in American agriculture before World War I. The image of an independent farmer, cultivating his own broad acres, asking favors from no man, and fearing none, has been so much a

---

23 *Tyson & Bros.—United Theater Offices* v. *Banton*, 273 U.S. 418.
24 *Home Building and Loan Association* v. *Blaisdell*, 290 U.S. 398 (1934).

part of our culture that it is hard to conceive of America without him. "Those who labor in the earth," wrote Thomas Jefferson, "are the chosen people of God, if ever He had a chosen people. . . ." The family farm was the source and repository of most, if not all, the homely virtues celebrated by Parson Weems and McGuffey. To have been born and raised on a farm became almost a requirement for nomination to public office, especially to the Presidency. For the family farm was the cradle of courage, of self-reliance, of industry and thrift—of all the virtues.

By 1930 this model and this image had begun to fade, and by 1960 it had all but vanished. John Fischer, writing in *Harper's Magazine* in 1955, cried out against "The Country Slickers" who, he said, were out to "Take Us Again"—"Us" in this context being the rest of the American People. "Our pampered tyrant, the American farmer, is about to get his boots licked again by both political parties. . . . The record . . . indicates that the farmer is generally eager to sell his vote to the highest bidder, and the city people are too indifferent [or benumbed] to resent this legalized corruption."

There follows a description (or caricature) of the American farmer of the 1950s as an indolent, but scheming, oaf, living on a government dole, with "two new cars, . . . usually brand new Buicks, Oldsmobiles or Cadillacs. . . ." crying out for more and more government largesse. "For," says this literary expert on farm problems, "everybody knows that it is the taxpayer who keeps the farmers living in clover and Cadillacs."[25]

If this is a caricature, it is a caricature that is widely held. Paradoxically, there is still another and contrary image of the contemporary farmer that sees him as an intellectual cretin, dying of rickets, or some other nutritional disease, victimized by drought and flood, and living in poverty while government granaries and warehouses overflow with surplus wheat, cotton, and other crops that other farmers continue to raise only to turn them over to a benevolent Uncle Sam at the expense of the sturdy yeomen of exurbia. As for the family farm, the Rock of Gibraltar of our culture and our economy, it has become an anachronism, or worse, a trap for the unwary, or the road to bankruptcy. "A self-sufficient farm in our time," writes W. A. Griswold, "is more likely to be a haunt of illiteracy and malnutrition than a well-spring of democracy."

There are other images of the American farm and farmer, equally false when generalized, but equally true when narrowly focussed. He is, in one version, a bloated capitalist living in luxury in Mid-Manhattan, San Francisco, or Miami, while his serfs, an army of migratory workers under the lash of poverty, toil at less than subsistence wages to till his vast estates. And when supply exceeds demand and prices fall below costs, he turns the surplus over to the government at guaranteed parity prices and lets the nation, that is, the rest of us, absorb the loss.

[25] *Harper's Magazine,* December, 1955, pp. 21–24.

In this image it is not unusual for single growers to receive adjustment or support payments of tens or even hundreds of thousands of dollars every year. As a gloss upon the picture, there often appears the "gentleman farmer," whose farm is a hobby, a part-time thing, useful for weekends, or as a status symbol, whose cost can be deducted from an otherwise intolerable tax.

Another version of this image shows the farmer as a vassal of a huge and heartless bureaucracy in Washington, compelled to kill his little pigs, plough under his cotton and his corn to satisfy the academic theories of long-haired radicals in the Department of Agriculture.

No matter what the image, most critics seem to see farmers as a well-organized, tightly knit pressure group, overrepresented in Congress and in state legislatures and able, therefore, to work their will in Washington, and in every state capitol in the country. A few others see them as a kind of organized anarchy with the Farmer's Union on the left battling the Farm Bureau Federation on the right, and the National Grange and Patrons of Husbandry in the middle.

How come this transformation of Jefferson's "chosen people of God"? How come these many and contradictory accounts of American agriculture, that last frontier of individual initiative and enterprise where the laws of supply and demand were supposed to be in control?

The easy answer, of course, is to say that all of this is true. Each of these many diverse images is a part of the truth, part of the pattern of American agriculture, an industry, or a way of life, that blankets the continent, reaches into every state and nearly every county, but almost literally has no headquarters, no central office, no board of strategy, no planning board. None, that is, except the government in Washington.

Actually, only a minority of farmers belong to any farm organization. This fact is at the same time both cause and effect of the farmer's plight. He simply is not organized to operate in the highly specialized, interdependent economy that has emerged in contemporary America. In a society of which the Organization Man is the sign and symbol, the unorganized will be outsiders.

But American farmers have become outsiders in another sense and for another reason. Relative to other groups in our society they are and have been, for a century or more, declining. In 1790 some 90 percent of the population lived on farms. By 1965 it was less than 10 percent. The tables had completely turned.

In 1790 some 85 percent of those gainfully employed were farmers; by 1965 the figure was only about 8 percent. Between 1920 and 1959 farm population dropped from 32 million to 20 million, a loss of 12 million, while population grew by nearly 70 million. The number of farms dropped from about 6 1/2 million in 1920 to less than 5 million in 1954 and about 3 1/2 million in 1960. In a single year—April, 1956, to April, 1957—nearly 2 million people abandoned farms for the city.

In 1850 agriculture accounted for 34 percent of the national income. By 1950 it was less than 10 percent, and by 1965, considerably less than that. In these later years farm income includes government parity payments. Except for the war years 1917–1918 and 1942–1945, the money income of farm families has lagged behind the income of workers in other occupations. Wherever one turns, the same picture appears. Here is a report in *The New York Times* for January, 1927, a year of boom. "The farmers," it says, "compose about 27% of the population; but today they get a little over seven percent of the nation's income."

The New York Times for December 11, 1932, had this to say: "Farm income . . . has dropped from $16 billion in 1919 to $11 billion in 1929, to $5 billion in 1932."

If the farmer has become an outsider in the economy, it is not because he has declined or failed as a producer. Within the memory of this generation a silent revolution has occurred in agriculture. American agriculture is one of our most automated industries. Look at these figures:

Energy Source	1910	1963
Horses and Mules	24.2 million	5.6 million
Tractors	1,000	4.4 million

	1940	1953
Combines	190,000	1,000,000
Corn Pickers	110,000	588,000
Hay Balers	25,000	244,000

Better seed and fertilizer, better feed and care of livestock, better breeds of livestock, better knowledge of the weather and its ways, and of the land and its needs have helped to make this miracle. Today a population of 200 million people is better fed and better clothed by 4 million farmers than a population of 40 million in 1870 was by 7 million farmers. Today in the United States, one farmer produces an abundance for over 60 other persons living in towns and cities. In 1870 the ratio was 1 farmer for every 5 1/2 people. Not only is this miracle of farm production unique in history, it is unique even in the contemporary world. While one American farmer produces an abundance of food and fiber for some 60 nonfarmers, the ratio is about 1 to 12 in Europe, and in the USSR, 1 to 6.

In large measure the farmer's unfortunate plight is not because he is highly organized, but precisely because he is not. At least he has never been able to organize his market or to control his production as industry, labor, and the professions have done. Millions of individual farm enterprisers, more than any other group in our economy, more even than several million small merchants and manufacturers, have known the full rigors of an uncontrolled competitive market. The farmer has had to meet competition not only from other farmers in other states but from farmers in Australia, the Argentine, Canada, and other great agricultural producers. Not only have the millions of highly individualistic, isolated farmers not organized to manage their market or their output, but the conditions under which they operate make organization next to impossible.

When a businessman finds himself faced with a glutted market and declining prices, he cuts his production until demand increases. But the nature of agricultural production makes this impossible for the farmer. His buildings, his livestock, his machinery, his land, all are fixed costs whether he produces much or little. They represent a much larger share of his total costs than do the direct expenditures that can be controlled. As prices fall under the impact of increased production, the farmer's impulse is to expand production still more, since at the lower prices he will have to sell more than ever to meet his fixed costs. Moreover, the unpredictable forces of nature make effective planning or control of production difficult. It is simply impossible for the farmer "to arrange sunshine, rain, and frost in such a way" as to adjust production neatly, or even approximately to demand. As experience shows, especially in the case of nondurable or nonstorable food, a small increase in supply may bring a large decrease in prices.

"This inability," says James Hearst, "to control his production leaves the farmer bouncing on an erratic and unstable price level. In national emergencies he is well rewarded as prices shoot up. . . . But in peacetime, when the farmer loses his big customers [the army and our allies, whom he must help to feed], he becomes a poor relation, hat in hand, asking for help."

Under normal circumstances a large part of the American agricultural output is exported, and in an uncontrolled market this export surplus determines the price, both at home and abroad, of some 80 percent of American farm production. Inability to control output, plus the technological revolution in agriculture, results in a kind of paradox of progress and poverty.

In 1926, for example, when government forecasts estimated a cotton crop of 14 million bales, the price of cotton on the market was 24 cents a pound. But this estimate proved to be too low by about 2 million bales—that is, 16 million bales were actually produced. The price immediately dropped to 15 cents. At this low price, farmers had to plant more to keep even. The result was a still larger crop the next year, which forced the price down to 12 cents, a figure that meant bankruptcy for many farmers.[26]

The sharp fluctuation of farm prices in an uncontrolled and unorganized farm market can produce chaos. When the supply of food goes

[26] *The New York Times,* January 2, 1927.

up by as much as 5 percent, farm prices decline by 15 to 20 percent. Even during the great depression the collapse of prices did not result in any comparative cut in output. While farm production fell less than 3 percent, and this mainly because of drought, farm income dropped nearly 60 percent, from $12 billion in 1929 to $5 billion in 1932. Between June, 1928, and June, 1931, wheat prices fell by 61 percent; wool by 68 percent; rye by 64 percent; cotton by 55 percent; corn by 60 percent. From 76 cents a bushel in May, 1931, wheat dropped again to 46 cents in December, 1932; cotton from 10.9 cents to 5.3 cents a pound.

The surplus problem, arising when supplies exceed effective demand, is aggravated by factors other than a surplus of unorganized producers and the forces of nature. The expansion of production to meet war needs in 1914–1919 and 1941–1946 was one. The replacement of nearly 20 million horses and mules by tractors reduced the consumption of hay and feed grains by these animals, and threw on the market supplies that otherwise might have been consumed on the farms. And changes in style, diet, and the development of substitutes for such things as cotton and wool can alter needs for farm products.

Although most branches of agriculture are plagued by surpluses, the heart of the problem is in grain and cotton. And in the case of grains, market prices are so interrelated that the problem cannot be dealt with on a single commodity basis. To expect the individual farmer to adjust his own production to this market is chimerical. Without organized effort and some degree of discipline to insure cooperation, no effective control can be expected. At any rate, since the great depression of the thirties the government has struggled to find some solution that will (1) insure the nation of an adequate supply of food and fiber at reasonable prices to consumers; (2) provide for a sufficient backlog in storage against years in which, because of drought, floods, demands from needy nations abroad, or other circumstance, demand might exceed current supply; (3) provide farmers with an income comparable to that earned by workers and enterprisers in nonagricultural industries.

Many plans have been tried, and all, for one reason or another, have been found wanting. Since 1938 most plans have involved parity payments or loans to insure the farmer a price on certain commodities equal, or nearly equal, to the real price he received in the prosperous years 1910–1914. Parity prices are calculated in terms that will make farm prices today equal in purchasing power for the farmer, to prices in the base period.

If there is no "surplus" and the market price is equal to or above parity, the farmer simply sells his crop and takes his money. If there is a surplus and the market price is below parity, he turns his crop over to the government for storage and receives a loan equal to the parity price established. If, after a year, the market price is still below parity, the government becomes the owner of the crop, the loan is canceled, and the farmer keeps the money. The plan applies only to nonperishable commodities that can be stored. The government may, of course, sell, loan, or give away those surplus foods in storage on which the loans have been canceled.

Under this policy the Federal Commodity Credit Corporation, which administers the program, had advanced loans exceeding $42 billion between 1933 and 1964. In 1964 loans outstanding amounted to nearly $3 billion and inventories of commodities owned by the government were valued at more than $4 billion.[27]

Farm price stabilization is only a part of the total agricultural program of the federal government. Related to it are programs for flood control, irrigation, hydroelectric development, forest conservation, conservation of fish and wildlife resources, extension and improvement of national parks, forests, and outdoor recreational facilities. Included in these operations are the TVA and other such multipurpose projects, designed to conserve and develop the natural resources of the nation.

But the Farm Income Stabilization program is the heart of what is commonly called the farm problem. It is this that engenders endless argument—argument that usually generates more heat than light. It has been attacked on several grounds:

1. It is of little or no help to the majority of small and subsistence farmers who have too little to sell to participate in the program. Less than half of the 3.5 million commercial farmers market 80 percent of the total food and fiber of the nation. Actually the program benefits mostly the more prosperous commercial farmers who need it least. The Department of Agriculture reports that "56 percent of the nation's farm families got just 9 percent of the . . . price support payments in the 1963–64 crop year."[28]

2. So long as the government is willing to buy surpluses, surpluses will continue, and continue to increase, even when as a condition of parity support payments, reductions in acreage are required.

3. In the long run the "farm problems can be solved only (a) by reducing the overproduction of farm products in relation to demand, and (b) by reducing the excess agricultural population by at least another million or more.

The sad fact is that the small farmer, like the small businessman, is a victim of the revolution in organization, technology, and scale of operations that has transformed the American economy. In the process literally millions of farms and farmers have become redundant.[29]

[27] *Statistical Abstract of the United States* (Washington, D.C.: U.S. Government Printing Office, 1965) , p. 635.

[28] See the *Wall Street Journal*, March 10, 1965.

[29] As we watch the small family farm go under to the corporate or commercial farm of 1,000 acres or more, and the independent farmer and his family give way to the migrant worker and the farm laborer, we may well wonder if perhaps something else is going with them? Even the Russians are finding that giant farms tended by hired hands are not necessarily more efficient than farms in which the family finds a way of life.

4. The stabilization program confuses the problem of rural poverty, which is very real, with price stabilization. Of the 2 million commercial farmers (out of a total of 3.5 million) who marketed only 20 percent of the food and fiber, 1.5 million, or 75 percent, of them "sell less than $25 worth of products annually." Many of these are only part-time farmers whose main income is from jobs in rural communities, or as highway workers, truck drivers, and so forth. Economists of the Department of Agriculture estimate that it would require an increase of 169 percent to bring the 1.5 million low-income farmers up to parity of income with the average full-time factory worker.[30]
5. The cost of the program's parity payments, plus storage costs, has reached intolerable levels.

To these criticisms defenders of the program reply:

1. The program has indubitably prevented farm disaster in the case of supported crops.
2. The program has been a major factor in maintaining farm income and thus removing a major cause of economic depression. Farmers are a multibillion dollar market for manufacturing and business. It is estimated that if "price supports . . . were abandoned . . . farm prices and net incomes would fall 30 to 40 percent in the next few years." This could be catastrophic not to farmers alone but to the whole economy.
3. The surpluses now in storage have been and can be not only an important hedge against years of drought and scarcity, but an important factor in an enlightened foreign aid program.

Friends of the farm program also answer critics by pointing out:

1. Farm prices are not the only prices that are supported by government. There are minimum wage laws for workers, and administered prices in many branches of industry often supported by government defense contracts.

   "Do wages fluctuate with supply and demand?" they ask. "Does supply and demand determine the cost of transportation, electric power, telephone service?"

   "In the past 50 years," says Capper's Farmer Magazine, "for every $1000 this country has spent for subsidies the American Farmer has received only $5." One thinks of subsidies to transportation, both surface and by air, shipping, housing, foreign aid, and others.
2. Against the cash cost of the program, one should set the income. The Commodity Credit Corporation's support of major storable crops from 1933 to 1953 showed a 20-year profit of $13 million After all, the food in government warehouses is a great natural resource.[31]

Both critics and defenders of the program generally agree on a few needed "reforms." Among these is (1) a dollar limit on the amount of

[30] *The New York Times,* February 7, 1965.
[31] Expenditures of the Commodity Credit Corporation are estimated at $2.2 billion in fiscal year 1966 with repayments of $2.4 billion. See Budget Hearings, *op. cit.,* p. 22.

federal funds that can be "loaned" to any single farm enterprise for price support purposes; (2) a more liberal policy for the sale or free distribution of surplus foods to low-income families, school children, and the aged; and (3) closer cooperation through the United Nations, especially the Food and Agriculture Organization, to increase the usefulness of our surpluses in underdeveloped countries.[32]

Whatever the end of this argument may be, whatever "reforms" are adopted, the "farm problem" will be with us for many years to come. It was a farm problem that inspired Daniel Shays to rebellion in 1782. It was a farm problem that set off the great Westward movement. It was a farm problem that inspired Lincoln to sign the Homestead law in 1861. It was a farm problem that set the West aflame in the Granger movement of the 1870s, the Populist Revolt of the 1890s, and the Realignment of Parties in the great depression of 1932. It is a farm problem that lies at the root of rebellion and revolution in Asia, Africa, and Latin America and of the unrest in eastern Europe and the USSR.

It was a farm problem over 2000 years ago that made Joseph *de facto* ruler of Egypt. The ever-normal granary was not a New Deal invention.

And in the seven plenteous years, Joseph "gathered up all the food . . . which were in the land of Egypt and laid up the food in the cities. . . ."

"And Joseph gathered corn as the sand of the sea, very much until he left numbering."

And when the seven years of dearth came, "dearth was in all lands; but in all the land of Egypt there was bread."

---

[32] The Swedish economist Gunnar Myrdal has recently pointed out that in terms of the world's food needs there is no surplus problem. On the contrary, the United Nations Food and Agriculture Organization has calculated that world food supplies must be doubled by 1980 and trebled by the year 2000. Under these circumstances the so-called agricultural surplus problem is a purely local phenomenon. This will continue to be true, he says, since the biggest population increases are coming in those nations least able to feed themselves. Perhaps American farm policies point the way to a solution of this basic problem. In 1964 the Department of Agriculture spent $3.2 billion to buy crop surpluses, and in addition to this it gave away or sold for local foreign currencies $2.1 billion worth of food and fiber.

See Donald Janson in *The New York Times*, March 16, 1965; see also J. H. Carmical's story in *The New York Times*, August 14, 1966, describing the virtual disappearance of crop surpluses except cotton. "With surplus stocks, except in cotton, virtually exhausted because of heavy shipments abroad," he writes, "the nation for the first time in more than a decade depends almost entirely on current production, especially in grains, to meet growing domestic and export requirements."

TAXATION:
THEORY AND PRACTICE

We began this volume with a discussion of political analysis and the uses and abuses of political power. We have seen how political power in the American political system has increased. From a few hundred civilian employees and an authorized army of 840 men, the government of the United States has grown into a Leviathan of 2 1/2 million civilian employees with 3 million more in the armed services. This growth has taken place not only in the "old-line" departments but in new departments and agencies that the founding fathers knew not of—even in their dreams. The time-honored and proper functions of government—law and order, the administration of justice, and national defense—have proliferated into dozens of new activities having to do with highways, education, scientific research, public health and welfare, medical care and hospitalization, employment security, and security in old age. Urban renewal, public housing, college housing, community facilities, atomic energy research and development, space research, hospital construction, and dozens of other functions now commonly accepted are relatively new to the federal government.

The expansion of old-line functions and the proliferation of new ones have affected not only the federal government but state and local governments as well. Child care centers, nursery schools, and vast programs for the care and cure of mental disease are comparatively new to state and local government. And of course old-line state and local functions such as highways, police and fire protection, public health and sanitation, education, parks and recreation have expanded beyond limits never contemplated even a generation ago.

And as the health, education, and welfare activities of government have grown, so, too, have its police and regulatory functions. Virtually every occupation is subject to license and control. Business enterprises from the giant holding company to the corner grocer, from the New York Stock Exchange to the dollar limit bookmaker, are subject to surveillance and regulation by government at federal, state, or local level, and often by all three.

As we have seen, government as a supplier of services, as policeman, as regulator, umpire, and defender, has become so inextricably involved with the private sector of the economy that what it does or does not do can send tremors through the whole system and affect prices, profits, interest payments, wages, levels of employment, and the rate of economic growth.

Pity, then, the bureaucrats and politicians who have to make economic policy decisions and find the funds to make them work. For these normal functions are both the ends and the means by which government economic policy is determined and administered. Total government expenditures in the United States will run to more than $200 billion a year, or about 30 percent of the gross national product. If the national government did nothing more than carry on its most traditional functions of national defense, the administration of justice, the Post Office Department, foreign relations, veterans' welfare, and the normal activities of the legislative, executive, and judicial branches, it would nevertheless exert a decisive influence upon the economic life of the nation.

The point is that government expenditures, by their character and their volume, exert an important influence not only upon our economy but upon our civilization. One need not argue, as some folks do, that public expenditures make a richer contribution to our total culture than an equal amount spent by private persons. Nor need one argue that $8 billion or $10 billion spent on tobacco and other billions spent on liquor or at race tracks add more to the good life than equivalent sums spent on public schools and colleges, hospitals, highways, parks, and playgrounds.

In any case, it is from the private sector of the economy that government derives most of the funds which it spends. One of its major roles therefore is to determine the direction as well as the volume of total expenditures in the economy by demanding a share of total private income and expenditures for itself. In this way the private consumer's addiction to alcohol and tobacco yields upwards of $6 billion a year for national defense, education, and the other functions of government. The volume of public expenditures has been steadily upward since the beginning of our history as a nation, not only in absolute figures but in relation to the total economy. That is to say, government expenditures have accounted for an ever increasing percentage of our total GNP. Even when allowance is made for changes in prices, government expenditures have expanded at a rate many times the rate for population increase. In their book *The Costs of Government* Frederick C. Mosher and Orville F. Poland show that "as proportions of GNP, total government expenditures in the United States rose from 7.7 percent in 1902 to . . . 31.8 percent in 1961."[1] These figures, with those of intervening years, are as follows:

	Percent		Percent
1902	7.7	1938	20.9
1913	8.2	1948	21.2
1922	12.5	1954	30.8
1927	11.8	1958	30.4
1932	21.3	1961	31.8

We need not review here the causes for this great expansion of public expenditures. Not the least of the factors at work, and one not always mentioned, has been a change in the tax structure of federal, state, and local governments. For it is from taxes that governments derive their income—not all of it, but most of it.

☆ AN ANCIENT GRUDGE: TAXES

There are, say the cynics, but two things of which a man can be sure: death and taxes. For taxes, unlike other items in the average man's cost of living, are unavoidable compulsory exactions collected under threat of fine and imprisonment. And however much we may appreciate the services the government provides in defense against external aggression, law and order within the country, education for our children, and all the rest, we resent having to pay for them the way we do. Cigarettes and cocktails, bookmakers and beauticians may cost us more, but these, we say, are voluntary costs of life; we can take them or leave them alone. Not so with taxes.

To review the history of tax struggles in the Western world would be to review the political history of Europe and America. It was largely in the conflicts for control of public revenues that constitutional government was born. "No Taxation without Representation" was not a slogan created for the American Revolution. It reaches back to Magna Charta at least and has not yet lost its pertinence.

Almost the first test of strength for the new American government under President Washington was a contest over taxes, in the so-called Whiskey Rebellion. Among taxes levied under Hamilton's leadership was a tax on distilled spirits. Farmers in the mountainous counties of western Pennsylvania who found it easier and more profitable to ship their grain to market as whiskey than as bulk grain bitterly resented the new tax. Several United States marshals were killed in the process of trying to collect it. So widespread and violent was the opposition that Washington mobilized a military force of some 15,000 men to move against the insur-

[1] (New York: Dodd, Mead, 1964) .

rection, which collapsed as two ringleaders were arrested and convicted of treason. Although both were subsequently pardoned, the rebellion made two points clear: (1) Taxation and especially new taxation is bitter medicine, and (2) to maintain order and put down the rebellion that taxes breed requires more taxes still.

The old principle that the King should live off his own, with only an occasional and relatively minor levy for a special purpose, is not unlike public finance as it operates in a fully socialized economy where the state, as owner and operator of virtually all enterprises, derives its income from their earnings. Social services like education, medical care, recreation, and even national defense are provided for out of the earnings of government-owned enterprises that sell goods and services to the people for a price or fee. Virtually all prices and fees are administered, that is, determined not by competition but by official fiat. Only in a small "free trade" sector of the economy are prices determined by competition and the laws of supply and demand.

By adjusting the margin between prices and the costs of goods and services which the Socialist government supplies, it can accumulate the funds necessary to pay for the so-called free or subsidized services and also for capital investment. The rate of economic growth, the supply of consumer goods, and the general standard of living can thus be planned and controlled not only in terms of quantity but also quality. Consumer demands responding to variations in prices can be more or less directed. By putting high prices on clothing, vodka, and luxury items like cosmetics or jewelry, a greater demand can be created for books and radio sets, phonograph records and theater tickets, housing and recreational facilities that are assigned low prices or fees. Taxes—at least direct taxes—can be few and modest. Many a tourist to Soviet Russia comes away with a feeling of some envy for the relatively low taxes on incomes levied in that country. What is not so obvious are the innumerable hidden taxes collected from the Soviet consumer as part of the price he pays for most of the goods or services he buys. These hidden taxes are what we call sales taxes, and they are just as burdensome and just as regressive in the USSR, where they are seldom seen, as they are in the United States, where they are often all too painfully visible.

Governments in mixed economies like England, France, Sweden, Denmark, and Germany also rely in different degrees upon revenue from state-owned and -managed economic enterprise. In these countries railroads and major transport industries, telephone and telegraph systems, the communications industry, electric light and power industries, and a wide variety of other economic enterprises are owned and operated by the government or government-owned corporations. Consumers of goods and services furnished by these concerns often pay a hidden tax in the form of a higher rate or price for the support of other public services.

Even in a relatively free-enterprise system like the United States, a considerable volume of economic activity is carried on directly by the government or by government-owned corporations. This publicly owned sector of the economy does not loom very large in the United States, but it serves to illustrate what may be described as *nontax* sources of government revenue.

☆ NONTAX SOURCES OF REVENUE

During our early history the federal government derived considerable revenue from the sale of public lands. Revenues from this source might have been much greater had the government not given so much of its land away in order to help develop the country. Had American cities been more provident in the use and disposal of their own land, urban life might have had a much more orderly development at much less cost. Today many municipalities are finding it necessary to buy back land for use as parks, housing sites, highways, and so forth, that had been squandered in the "good old days."

A modest nontax source of public revenue is the collection of fees or licenses for special rights or privileges granted by the community. Fees for patents and passports, for example, help to defray the cost of administering the patent and passport laws. A still unexplored source of revenue might be a percentage of royalty payments for the use of patents granted and protected by the government. At the state and local level hunting licenses sometimes help to maintain public game preserves, and dog and pet licenses contribute something to the cost of administering the license laws, as do marriage licenses and licenses to engage in certain occupations or professions.

A federal license to sell narcotics scarcely pays the cost of collection. Its primary purpose is to bring federal law enforcement agencies into the campaign against dope peddlers and drug addiction. Fees for revenue loom a bit larger in other areas. Tuition fees at public colleges and universities often account for a considerable part of the institution's income, thus putting part of the burden on the student and his parents. Fees for public services have been extended to sewage disposal, water consumption, garbage disposal, and even for access to public highways. Indeed, tolls for the use of freeways, bridges, and harbors administered by toll authorities of one kind or another have become a fairly common device for financing this kind of public service.

One of the most irritating of all nontax sources of public revenue are fines for violations of traffic laws, building codes, and a number of other fairly common offenses. But notwithstanding the average motorist's impression to the contrary, traffic fines are not a significant source of public revenue. Some wit once remarked that "if the finance minister were also the administrator of justice . . . the revenue from fines would show a marked increase." Where justices of the peace, sheriffs, and other local officers depend on fees or fines for their income, this happy state of affairs already seems to exist.

One or two other nontax sources of revenue might be mentioned. One of these is the Public Lottery. Sponsored by governments in England, France, Russia, and other countries, official lotteries raise fairly substantial revenues for the government and rich prizes for a few lucky citizens. For reasons not unrelated to our Puritan heritage, this source of public revenue has not been widely employed in the United States, although the State of New Hampshire and the City of New York now have lotteries. Nobody knows what a national lottery in the United States might yield, although it would probably be considerably less than its enthusiastic proponents claim. Although we disapprove of gambling, and in 1963 arrested over 100,000 persons for this offense, it continues to thrive, and not only in Las Vegas and Reno. Some 23 states have legalized betting on horse and dog races, and the governments of these states share in the take of the tracks. Estimated as a billion dollar business, the parimutuel tax on horse racing yields a considerable if not an altogether "respectable" source of revenue. Arguments over the ethics or morality of all this would keep a college bull session going for a semester. So, too, would the argument frequently heard about the "hypocrisy" of the federal government that holds interstate gambling in such low esteem as to make it a crime and yet requires gamblers to report their incomes for tax purposes.

Special Assessments

Moving from *nontaxes* to taxes as sources of public revenue, we pass through a twilight zone of *nontax taxes,* one of which is the special assessment. When a water main or a sewer line is installed or a street is paved in a neighborhood, it is assumed that a special benefit is conferred on that neighborhood—a benefit reflected in increased value of the property. Consequently it is regarded as right that property-owners in the vicinity should pay a "special assessment," that is, a special tax to meet the cost. This practice was upheld in 1898 by the United States Supreme Court in the case of *Norwood* v. *Baker.* "The principle underlying special assessments to meet the cost of public improvements," said the Court, "is that the property on which they are imposed is peculiarly benefitted and therefore the owners do not, in fact, pay anything in excess of what they receive by reason of such improvement." To this general theory no reasonable man can object. But in practice the assessment and the value or size of the increment which the improvement brings to the property assessed does not always show a one-to-one relation. Indeed, the fact of any increment at all is often denied. And in our mobile society the assessment may continue to be collected on property long after the original owner of the improved property has sold it at a price that includes the whole increment or more, leaving his successor with the burden but no special benefit.

Nevertheless, and in spite of many inequities, the special assessment remains as an important source of public revenue for specific purposes. That it is not a true tax is indicated by the fact that although churches and private colleges are normally exempt from property taxes, they often are required to pay these special assessments.

Not unrelated to the principle of the special assessment is the land-increment tax—often called the Single Tax because Henry George proposed it as a tax to end all other taxes. Just as an improved sewer or street adds to the value of nearby property, so, it is argued, the growth of the city itself creates most of the value of the land in or near the city. An acre of ground worth perhaps $100 as a remote piece of farmland becomes an urban building site worth $20,000 as people settle in the neighborhood and build a city. Since, it is said, the community as a whole—its people, traffic, homes, schools and colleges, churches, apartment buildings create this added value—the community as a whole (rather than the owner) should have all or a major part of it. The increased value, said Henry George, is an *unearned increment* which should be recaptured by the community through taxation. Such a tax, he argued, would encourage building and all manner of improvements, since they would not be taxed and there would then be no incentive to hold land for speculation. So great was the total of this unearned increment on land, George insisted, that a proper tax to absorb it all could pay all the costs of a modern urban civilization.[2] We are not disposed to argue the land increment tax issue—not at least as a "single tax," since there are other unearned increments in modern society to which the principle might be applied. But some such tax may be necessary if American state and local governments are to plan for population growth and proper land use in our new emerging metropolitan areas.

[2] A modest form of this land increment tax has been applied in England, Australia, and New Zealand, and has been proposed for the United States.

Under the Town and Country Act in England, which provided for comprehensive planning in urban development, "increments to land value resulting from an approved change of (land) use (i.e., from farm to housing site or shopping center) would go to the government as a developmental charge." Viz: suppose land on the outskirts with a value of $1,000 increases in value to $2,000 before the Act, and as the town develops, it goes to $3,000. The unearned increment is set at $1,000 and this is taken by the government as a developmental charge. If the land were excluded from the urban development, and therefore dropped in value to $1,000, the government would pay the owner $1,000 to restore it to the $2,000 value it had in anticipation of the Act—i.e., compensation for the "floating value."

The plan, however, was too complicated and was abandoned.

☆ KINDS AND PURPOSES OF TAXES

When we move from nontax and twilight tax sources of public revenue to taxes themselves, we enter a wilderness of such awesome complexity as to defy orderly description or analysis. The major items can be classified easily enough, for they appear in hundreds of pie charts showing major sources of revenue for the federal government and for state and local governments. (See Figures 23–1 and 23–2.)

For the fiscal year 1967 slightly more than 52 percent of total federal revenues came from the personal income tax ($61.5 billion out of $116.1 billion); another 29 percent from the tax on corporation income ($33.9 billion out of $116.1 billion); and 12 percent from what are called excise taxes, sometimes referred to as "miscellaneous internal revenue" ($13.7 billion out of $116.1 billion). The remaining 7 percent came from "other" taxes—a catch basket for everything that cannot be otherwise tagged. Not included in these figures are the billions of trust fund income for social insurance (not included in the President's administrative

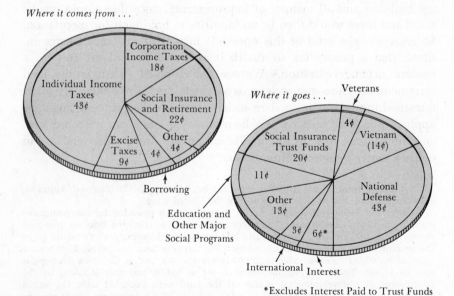

The Federal Government Dollar

Fiscal Year 1969 Estimate

Where it comes from . . .

Individual Income Taxes 43¢

Corporation Income Taxes 18¢

Social Insurance and Retirement 22¢

Excise Taxes 9¢

Other 4¢

↑ Borrowing

Where it goes . . .

Veterans 4¢

Social Insurance Trust Funds 20¢

Vietnam (14¢)

National Defense 43¢

Other 13¢

11¢ ← Education and Other Major Social Programs

3¢ / 6¢*

International Interest

*Excludes Interest Paid to Trust Funds

Figure 23–1 After *The Budget of the United States Government, Fiscal Year 1969*, Washington, D.C., 1968, p. 6.

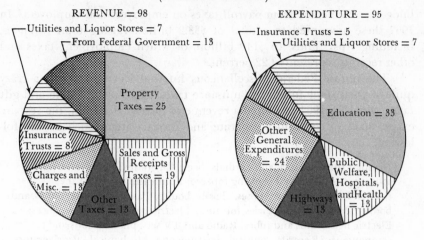

State and Local Government Revenue and Expenditure: 1966
(In billions of dollars)

REVENUE = 98

—Utilities and Liquor Stores = 7
—From Federal Government = 13

Property
Taxes = 25

Insurance
Trusts = 8

Sales and Gross
Receipts
Taxes = 19

Charges and
Misc. = 13

Other
Taxes = 13

EXPENDITURE = 95

—Insurance Trusts = 5
—Utilities and Liquor Stores = 7

Education = 33

Other
General
Expenditures
= 24

Public
Welfare,
Hospitals,
and Health
= 13

Highways
= 13

Governmental Per Capita Tax Revenue, by Level of Government:
1950 to 1966

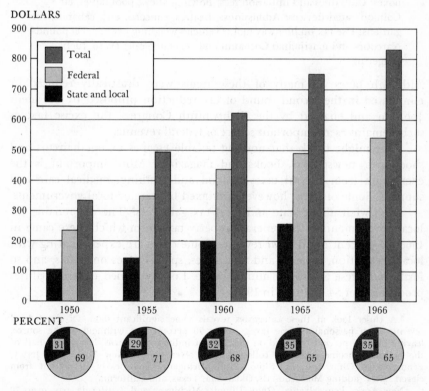

DOLLARS

Total
Federal
State and local

1950 1955 1960 1965 1966

PERCENT

31 / 69   29 / 71   32 / 68   35 / 65   35 / 65

Figure 23–2 After Department of Commerce, U.S. Bureau of the Census, *Statistical Abstract of the United States: 1967*. (88th edition.) Washington, D.C., 1967, p. 415.

budget) which come from payroll taxes on employees and employers.[3] In 1967 these amounted to a total of $33.2 billion raising total revenues, including trust funds, to $149 billion, of which employment taxes and other receipts represented 22 percent.[4]

The phrase Federal Miscellaneous Internal Revenue covers a crazy quilt of what some folks call "nuisance taxes." Except for estate and gift taxes, which in 1967 produced a revenue of nearly $3 billion, the rest are excise taxes on over fifty separate and distinct items such as the following:

> Distilled spirits, wines and cordials, beer; Cigarettes, cigars, and pipe tobacco—also snuff and chewing tobacco; Lubricating oil, gasoline, tires and tubes; Trucks, buses, chassis, bodies; Passenger automobiles and bodies; Parts and accessories for auto; Electric gas and oil appliances; Electric light bulbs and tubes; Radio and TV sets, phonographs and components; Records, musical instruments; Mechanical Refrigerators, air conditioners, freezers; Cameras, lenses, film; Sporting goods, firearms; Furs, jewelry, luggage, toilet preparations; Sugar, long distance and local telephone calls; Transportation of persons and property; Safe deposit boxes; Club dues and initiation fees; Bowling alleys, pool tables, etc.; Coin-operated devices; Admissions: theatres, concerts, etc., cabarets, roof-gardens; Use tax on highway motor vehicles weighing over 25,000 pounds; Narcotics and marijuana; Cocoanut and vegetable oils; Diesel fuel; Wagering.

Although taxes on many of these items were drastically reduced or eliminated in the second round of tax reduction proposed by President Johnson and enacted by the Eighty-ninth Congress, the excise tax, as such, remains as an important source of federal revenue.

One might think that nothing taxable escapes except haircuts and shoeshines, newspapers, books and magazines. More important is the exemption from federal taxes of food and clothing, medical care and supplies. Some of these, however, are taxed by state or local governments.

And what about state and local tax gatherers? The old reliable for local governments is the general property tax—from which there came in 1963, 68 percent of all *local* revenue. Some cities are experimenting with local occupation, income, and sales taxes, special taxes on hotels, and so forth, but these are still a minor source. Locally owned electric utilities produced over $4.5 billion in 1963.

---

[3] A closer look at these categories reveals some significant data. Of the federal revenue from personal income taxes, nearly 70 percent was withheld at the source, leaving only 30 percent collected on the basis of individual returns. Nearly one-half of the personal income taxes are collected from seven states (New York, New Jersey, Pennsylvania, Ohio, Indiana, Illinois, and Michigan); and nearly 70 percent from eleven states (adding Massachusetts, Oklahoma, Texas, and California).

New York, Pennsylvania, Ohio, Illinois, Michigan, and California pay over 70 percent of the corporation tax, and of this 70 percent New York alone pays nearly half.

[4] *The Budget for Fiscal 1969,* Table 2, p. 52.

At the state level, there have been some striking changes. Property taxes, which in 1902 accounted for 46 percent of total state revenue, had shrunk to negligible proportions by 1963. In 1902 state liquor stores yielded $2 million. In 1963 they produced over $10 billion. In 1902 there were no general sales taxes. In 1963 general and collective sales taxes amounted to about $13 billion, or more than half of all state tax revenues. In some states food and medicine are exempt, but nearly everything else is taxed, including many items also taxed by the federal government. License taxes on motor vehicles, corporations, saloons, hunting and fishing, bring in about 12 percent of total state tax collections, and state income taxes, about the same.

☆ THE BASIS FOR TAXATION

How can we make sense of this wilderness of taxes? Is there any rhyme or reason to the patterns that have developed? Are there any canons or principles by which taxes can be rationalized? On this there are two schools of thought, concerning the primary function of taxation. One holds that taxes ought to be levied primarily for the purpose of raising revenues sufficient for the operation of essential government services. A second believes that the tax structure ought to be used primarily as a planning instrument or to effect changes in the social structure of the nation and only secondarily to raise funds for governmental operations.

If one adheres to the first school, he will favor taxes that promise the maximum revenue without regard for other considerations. If one adheres to the second school, he will think mainly of taxes to protect domestic industries against foreign competition, reduce unemployment, eliminate large inheritances, reconstruct the income pattern, change ratios of investment and consumer spending, and promote economic growth.

Most American economists and statesmen would not accept either of these alternatives. Taxes, they would say, ought to yield enough revenue for government operations, and at the same time contribute as much as possible to the smooth, stable, and efficient operation of the total economy, or at least not interfere with it. And as corollaries to this, they would add (1) that taxes ought to contribute to, or at least not interfere with, full employment, maximum use of resources, and a satisfactory rate of economic growth, and (2) ought not to violate the basic goals of freedom and equality for which the nation strives.

It may never be possible to develop a tax system that can conform to these standards, but we ought to try. In the process, we can derive some help from Adam Smith's classic statement of the four canons of taxation in Book V of *The Wealth of Nations:*

1. The subjects of every state ought to contribute toward the support of government as nearly as possible in proportion to their respective abilities: that is, in proportion to the revenues which they respectively enjoy under the protection of the State. [Taxes, in short, should be equitable.]
2. The tax which each individual is bound to pay ought to be certain and not arbitrary. [And the yield should be as certain as possible.]
3. Every tax ought to be levied at the time, or in the manner, in which it is most likely to be convenient for the contributor to pay it.
4. Every tax ought to be so contrived as both to take out and keep out of the pockets of the people as little as possible over and above what it brings into the public treasury. [That is, the cost of tax collection and administration should be as low as possible.][5]

Most political economists accept Adam Smith's canons in the evaluation of tax systems, although some of his principles have not gone unchallenged. Most controversial is the first canon that taxes should be levied according to the taxpayer's ability to pay. Aside from the difficulty of defining "ability to pay," it has been challenged on other grounds. To tax ability, it is said, is to penalize the enterprising, the thrifty, or the creative in favor of the unenterprising, the improvident, and the dullards. If we do this long enough, we will destroy initiative, undermine frugality, and discourage creative minds so that the economy will stagnate, culture lag, and civilization crumble. In the end not only the strong and the able will suffer, but the weak and improvident also.

A better basis for taxation, it is argued, would be the *benefits* which various classes derive from government. This benefit theory, it is said, is less ambiguous and also more just. Those who benefit most from the public schools, parks, playgrounds, hospitals, and housing projects should pay more than those who are less dependent on these public services. And if there is any doubt concerning who benefits and in what proportion, this can be resolved by putting all public services on a fee basis. The father of a family with six children in school benefits more from the public schools than does the father of an only son. Therefore shouldn't he pay more?

However plausible at first glance, the benefit theory breaks down on even the most casual inspection, when one seeks some objective standard by which to measure benefits. Who most enjoys the benefits of government, of police protection, of courts of law, or schools, hospitals, and public health programs, or of armies and navies to protect the nation? To measure benefits is even more difficult than to measure ability to pay, which at least has some relation to an individual's income. One may also

---

[5] In summary, Adam Smith's canons spell the Latin word "Ecce" or "behold."
E stands for Equity or Equality—i.e., ability to pay.
C stands for Certainty—taxes ought not to be arbitrary.
C stands for Convenience—or as much convenience as possible.
E stands for Economy of Collection and Administration.

argue that in the final analysis income is itself the best evidence of benefits received. If this has any validity, the conflict between the benefit theory and the theory of ability to pay disappears, since ability to pay becomes the standard measure of benefits received.

Before considering these and other more subtle questions that arise in applying tax theories to tax policy, perhaps we ought to look at the current tax structure in the light of Adam Smith's four canons of taxation. How, for example, does the general property tax—which is still the mainstay of local government—measure up in terms of Adam Smith's canons? Property for tax purposes falls into two main categories: (1) real estate, and (2) personal property. Real estate, in turn, includes both land and improvements on the land. Personal property includes (1) tangibles like furniture, jewelry, automobiles, and (2) intangibles like stocks and bonds, mortgages, and so forth.

Without examining the complex theoretical problems involved in taxing these various kinds of property, a few generalizations can be made. Personal property is not a good measure either of benefits received or ability to pay. Some of the most expensive automobiles are "owned" (at least they own a bill of sale) by people with very low incomes and low tax-paying ability. The girl with the most elaborate wardrobe, the most impressive costume jewelry, is not necessarily better able to pay taxes than her more frugal and modest sisters. On the contrary, possession of a lot of tangibles may mean, for that very reason, a low capacity to pay taxes.

Not only is personal property a poor measure of ability to pay; it is likely to be expensive to administer. Problems of assessment, difficult enough in the case of real property, are compounded in the case of personal property. Obsolescence and depreciation, plus the relative ease of concealment, make honest assessment almost impossible. And what is true of tangibles, such as furniture, clothing, and jewelry, is also true of intangibles, such as stocks, bonds, and mortgages. On nearly every point of equality, certainty, convenience, and economy, the personal property tax fails.

Nor is real property much better as evidence of ability to pay or of benefit received. Compare these two cases. A is a single, professional man with a net taxable income of $10,000 a year. Under present federal income tax rates, he would pay about $2,000, or 20 percent. B is a single farmer with a farm assessed at $100,000, on which he earns $10,000. He, too, would pay $2,000 under the federal graduated income tax. But under the property tax, this farm, taxed at 4 percent—that is, $4 per $100 of value—would pay a tax of $4,000, or 40 percent of the farmer's income.

Nor is real property necessarily a reliable measure of ability to pay when applied to two farms with the same income. Consider, for example, farmers A and B, both with farms assessed at $100,000. A's farm is free and clear of debt, while B must pay 5 percent interest on a $50,000 mortgage. While B is obviously less able to pay his tax than A, the property tax is blind to such differences.

Aside from difficulties of this kind, property taxes are notorious for the inequities that creep into the process of assessment. The whole process lends itself to conscious bias or favoritism. Two adjoining lots in a city block have been known to be assessed at values as disparate as 10 or even 20 to 1—with lot A assessed at $100,000 and lot B at only $10,000. Instead of being a measure of benefit or ability to pay, a property tax may be a measure of the taxpayer's social status or political influence.[6] Besides, a property tax is costly to collect and to administer. Small wonder that the late E. R. A. Seligman said that "Practically [speaking] the general property tax as actually administered is beyond all doubt one of the worst taxes known in the civilized world."

What about excise or sales taxes that account for some 60 percent of all state tax revenue and about 11 or 12 percent of federal revenue? In terms of ability to pay, a general tax on every sales transaction makes no pretense of measuring either benefits received from government or ability to pay. The relief client who spends his meager check in Seattle's retail establishments pays the same 4 percent tax on everything he buys as the banker whose income runs into six figures. To say that both are taxed equally because both pay the same rate of tax is to make a mockery of the meaning of equality. In fact because he spends a larger proportion of his income on goods subject to sales taxes, the poor man is more heavily taxed than his more affluent neighbor. That is to say, the sales tax is *regressive* not *progressive*. In terms of Adam Smith's first canon of equity, therefore, a sales tax must score nearly zero.

To mitigate the regressive character of general sales taxes, most states exempt certain sales from the tax. Food is commonly exempt. So, in many states, are drugs and medical supplies. But these are at best makeshift compensations for the inequities inherent in a general sales tax. To avoid these inequities, selective sales taxes are sometimes levied on certain goods and services deemed to be luxuries and hence more likely to be purchased by the affluent members of the community. Motor fuels, alcoholic beverages, amusements, musical instruments, and TV sets are in this category. If not luxuries, at least they are not necessities. But few would argue that even selective sales taxes measure ability to pay.

Excise or sales taxes do, however, conform to Adam Smith's canons of certainty and convenience. The tax rate is known, and since the demand for the commodities taxed is comparatively inflexible, the yield of the tax is stable. Sales taxes are also convenient to pay. More often than not, the tax becomes a part of the purchase price and the taxpayer pays it

---

[6] Recent disclosures of property tax "irregularities" in California and Oregon have sent a number of tax assessors to prison. Nor are such incidents confined to western states.

unwittingly and unknowingly. Many a taxpayer who would find it most inconvenient to pay a tax of $160 at one fell swoop will find it no conscious burden to pay the same amount as a 4 percent sales tax on $4,000 of purchases through the year. Even though sales taxes are inequitable and expensive to collect, they are extremely lucrative and yield very substantial revenues.

☆ INCOME TAXES

Corporate Income

The major source of federal tax revenue is the income tax on individuals and corporations. Over 50 percent of federal tax revenues comes from the tax on individual incomes and another 25 or 30 percent from the tax on corporation income. The tax on corporations does no serious violence to the principles of certainty, convenience, and economy. It is levied at a certain time and at established rates so that the corporate taxpayer can make provision for it well in advance of the due date. Because most of the larger corporations are bureaucratically organized with well established accounting procedures, the problem of audit and control by the Internal Revenue Service is relatively simple and inexpensive. Hence the income tax on corporations may be said to be in accord with Smith's canon of economy of administration.

But when tested by the canon of ability to pay, or equality, the corporation tax as administered in the United States is grossly defective. A tax on corporate income is essentially a withholding tax on the income of the corporation's stockholders without any regard for their individual ability to pay.[7] The American tax on corporation income is levied at a flat rate and is not graduated according to the size of the firm or its income, and thus takes almost no account of ability to pay. Moreover even if the tax were so graduated, it would make little sense in terms of ability to pay. A corporation with an income of $1,000,000 may be earning only 1 percent on its capital while another with an income of only $100,000 may be earning anywhere from 10 to 100 percent. Therefore, unless the government wishes to impose a tax penalty solely on the basis of size, a graduated tax on corporate income makes little sense in terms of ability to pay. Since the tax is paid out of earnings and takes no account of the income of individual stockholders, it taxes the small stockholder whose dividends are modest at the same rate as the large stockholder whose dividends may be very large. A corporation with an income of $100,000 with but one stockholder has more relative ability to

---

[7] Incidentally, the American government, unlike the British, allows the stockholder no credit on his own income tax for the tax paid by the corporation out of earnings that might otherwise have been distributed to him.

pay than another corporation with earnings of $1,000,000 but with its stock widely distributed among 1,000 stockholders. Yet both are taxed at the same rate. Apart from its economic effect upon capital accumulation, the corporation income tax operates most inequitably between the large and the small stockholder. In spite of these defects, the tax is certain, convenient, economical, and has a very large annual yield.[8]

The Personal Income Tax

The personal or individual income tax is, as we have seen, the major source of revenue for the federal government, accounting for slightly over 50 percent of the total revenue.[9] More than any other tax in the American fiscal structure, the graduated tax on individual incomes closely apportions the tax burden according to Adam Smith's first canon of ability to pay and equality of sacrifice. The theory is that the measure of a tax burden is not merely in the amount of tax one pays but also in the amount that is left after paying the tax, that is, in "disposable income." Basically this assumes that the higher the income the less will be the value to the individual of each additional dollar he receives. Hence a tax on a small income may entail a greater sacrifice to the taxpayer than a tax on a large income. In general, it is assumed that as one moves from an income of $1,000 to one of $2,000, of $4,000, and progressively on upward to, say, $1,000,000, each succeeding increment of income will have less value to the individual. Consequently, to tax each succeeding increment at a higher rate is necessary if the tax system is even to approximate equality of burden or sacrifice.

This theory bristles with ethical and psychological problems too subtle for examination; but, as a practical matter, as a rough-handed standard of justice, it seems to commend itself to people who value both equality of opportunity and special rewards for talent, initiative, and thrift. This striving for the maximum equality of sacrifice compatible with recognition for initiative, thrift, and talent is reflected also in the rather elaborate system of exemptions, deductions, and allowances that has developed as part of the progressive tax system on individual incomes. In the first place the tax is levied on net or taxable income rather than gross or total income. To tax total income would take no account of individual differences of need, obligation, or responsibility,

---

[8] Our discussion of the corporation tax has focused on the federal tax, although taxes on corporation incomes are levied in over three-fourths of the states as well. As in the federal government, the tax is at a flat rate, although there are meager efforts at graduation of the tax in four states (Arizona, Hawaii, Kentucky, and North Dakota). Several states tax banks or financial corporations at higher rates than business corporations. Rates for business corporations range from 1 percent to 9 percent and for financial corporations, from 4 1/2 percent to over 11 percent.

[9] In terms of the proportion of revenue raised, the graduated tax on individual income occupies about the same position in the federal revenue system as general and selective sales taxes in the state fiscal scheme of things.

and might therefore produce inequalities as great as those which characterize a nonprogressive system. To avoid such inequalities, our tax laws provide for certain exemptions and deductions in determining taxable income as distinguished from gross or total income.

First of all, there are basic exemptions that establish a minimum income on which no tax at all is levied. These exemptions may be justified as necessary (1) to protect a minimum or subsistence standard of living, as, for example, a basic exemption of $1,200 for a man and his wife; (2) to differentiate among taxpayers according to need—as, for example, standard exemptions for children and other dependents of $600 each;[10] (3) to avoid the excessive cost and administrative inconvenience of collecting taxes on small incomes; (4) to help maintain a basic market for consumer goods; (5) to avoid the political hazard of imposing taxes on millions of people having small incomes but many votes.

In addition to what we may call these social and subsistence exemptions, the law also allows for the deduction of certain business and professional expenses. Such expenses to be allowed must, in theory, meet three tests: (1) They must be incurred in the process of earning one's income; (2) they must be ordinary and necessary; (3) they must be operating expenses, as it were, and not outlays of capital. But in applying these tests the tax law and the Internal Revenue Service, in the judgment of many people, have been excessively indulgent. Entertainment of customers and clients, trips to fashionable resorts, elaborate hotel suites, expensive gifts, wining and dining in night clubs and cafes, all have found sanctuary from taxation as business and professional expenses. The expense account aristocracy, as it is sometimes called, has played no small role in the inflation of hotel, restaurant, and entertainment costs in most of our cities. In the judgment of many tax experts a searching review and revision of the laws, policies, and practices affecting both personal exemptions and "business and professional expenses" are long overdue. A beginning was made in the revenue acts of 1963 and 1964, but the problem remains. There are other aspects of the American tax system that need careful restudy. We might ask, for example, whether the policy of exempting interest paid on state and municipal bonds should be continued. Since 1940 the federal government has taxed income derived from interest paid on federal securities. Is the present hidden subsidy granted to state and local governments, by exempting their bonds from federal taxation, in the public interest? Or does the tax-free haven that it provides for some taxpayers create an inequity in the tax system that more than offsets the value of the subsidy to state and local governments?

With all of its imperfections, the federal tax structure more nearly

[10] Those who do not want to figure in detail their other deductions may simply take a blanket deduction of 10 percent of their gross income, up to $1,000. Other exemptions include such things as medical expenses beyond a certain minimum, interest on personal debts, and certain contributions to charitable or religious institutions.

measures up to Adam Smith's canons of taxation than the tax systems of state and local governments—not only in terms of certainty, convenience, and economy, but also of equality.

Whatever disadvantages attach to the increasing importance of federal, as distingusihed from state and local taxation, inequality of burden is not one of them since the federal taxes are on the whole less regressive than state and local taxes.

☆ *TAXATION AND PRIVATE PHILANTHROPY*

Taxes contribute to the general welfare in two ways. First, they provide revenue to support the multifarious activities of government—national defense, education, and all the rest. Second, they represent a major instrument of government for social reform and for the regulation and control of economic activity.

Government fiscal policies can help to encourage education, religion, sobriety, thrift, not merely by providing government with revenue, but also by providing tax incentives for the private support of good works. Churches, independent schools and colleges, cemeteries, charitable trusts and foundations, and all manner of civic organizations and institutions are customarily exempt from most forms of direct taxation. Moreover, gifts for educational and charitable purposes by individuals and corporations are deductible from otherwise taxable income.

Close to $10 billion is contributed annually to charitable, health, welfare, religious, and educational purposes in the United States, and most of it is deductible for income tax purposes. How much of this vast total would have been contributed had the contributions not been deductible, it would be difficult to say. The principle of allowing such gifts to be deducted from income subject to tax, plus the high rate of progression in the personal income tax, has made it possible for large income receivers to make relatively painless gifts to these good causes. A taxpayer in the upper bracket of the federal income tax can make a contribution of this kind at a net cost to himself of less than half the amount of the contribution. The natural tendency of Americans to help one another through private philanthropy is thus encouraged by tax policies.

Many private activities now supported in this way might find it hard to get direct appropriations from government itself. For some purposes, notably for religious institutions, direct government support is forbidden by the Constitution. By exempting churches and other religious institutions from taxation and by providing tax incentives to encourage contributions to them, the government is able to do indirectly what it cannot do directly.

☆ **TAXES AND SOCIAL POLICY**

"No taxation without representation" was not only a revolutionary slogan but, for centuries, embodied a basic principle of republican government—that taxation should also be a condition of representation. The principle of "no representation without taxation" was almost universally applied until near the end of the nineteenth century. To own property on which taxes were paid was a qualification for voting and for public office until fairly recent times. Some remnants of this principle remain in the requirement still quite common that for bond-issue or special tax levies only taxpayers be allowed to vote. Another vestige of this principle was the poll tax as a suffrage requirement, but this, too, has been outlawed in federal elections by constitutional amendment.

If tax policies are designed, on one hand, to encourage good works, they are also used to discourage less desirable forms of conduct. In the days of militant temperance agitation, "high license" taxes on the manufacture and sale of alcoholic beverages were deliberately designed to discourage the traffic. And in many communities "high license" became a synonym for temperance reform. Present policies of levying high taxes on hard liquors as distinguished from beer and soft drinks are not unrelated to the moral purpose of the government to discourage their consumption.

A tax of $2 or more on a fifth of whiskey, plus state levies on the same bottle, can represent a tax of 40 to 50 percent of the retail price. By pushing the cost up, the theory seems to be that we put this beverage out of the reach of men and women of low income, thus protecting them from the evils against which their more affluent neighbors presumably can defend themselves.[11]

At any rate, the federal revenue from taxes on alcoholic beverages is impressive.[12] In 1965 nearly $4 billion of federal revenue came from taxes on alcoholic beverages, that is, some 36 percent of the total excise revenue. How much more this would yield if the tax were reduced and the sale of alcoholic beverages increased as a result of reduced prices, it

[11] As taxes and prices mount, so do the problems of enforcement; and the Alcohol Tax Unit of the Treasury has furnished us with some of our best cherished folklore in the eternal battle between bootleggers, moonshiners, and revenue agents or "revenooers."

[12] Most of the states, moreover, derive a considerable revenue from such taxes. Even in states like Washington and Idaho, which operate their own liquor stores, this is true. What is not clear is whether this basic policy represents a moral purpose or simply a need for more revenue. (State taxes on distilled spirits vary from $3.50 a gallon in Alaska to 80¢ in Missouri.) When these taxes are added to the federal levies, the taxes in the retail price of liquor assume spectacular proportions.

would be hard to say. To do this would of course sacrifice any moral purpose of the tax.

The federal tax of 8 cents a pack on cigarettes was pyramided in some states by state and local taxes varying from 2 cents in Missouri to 8 cents in Louisiana and Montana, and also by city taxes such as the 2-cent a pack levied in New York City. A package of cigarettes may thus bear a tax burden of 10 cents to 16 cents which the consumer pays. It is not easy to say how much of this tax is intended to discourage the use of tobacco and how much for revenue purposes alone. With recently published data indicating a statistical relation between lung cancer and cigarette smoking, the upward trend of tobacco taxes may be accelerated, and the health purpose of the tax may become increasingly important.[13]

How far may the taxing power of government be used for purposes of social reform and regulation? Among the earliest cases to raise this question was the tax designed to protect butter from the competition of oleomargarine. The tax was assailed on the ground that it was not properly a revenue measure but an unconstitutional attempt by Congress to regulate or even prohibit trade under the guise of taxation. The Supreme Court refused to inquire into the motives of Congress and sustained the measure as a legitimate exercise of the federal taxing power.[14] Again, in 1919, when Congress imposed a license tax on the sale of narcotics, solely for the purpose of bringing the traffic under control of the federal government, the Supreme Court sustained the law as within the proper taxing power of the Congress.[15] In still a more recent opinion, the Court has said ". . . a tax does not cease to be valid merely because it regulates, discourages, or even definitely deters the activities taxes. . . . The principle applies even though the revenue obtained is obviously negligible. . . ." Moreover, said the Court, the taxing power may extend in this way to objects and purposes "beyond the constitutional power of the lawmakers" to reach by more direct legislation.[16]

Use of the taxing power for purposes of social reform or economic regulation has generally been upheld by the Supreme Court.[17] An exception was the decision in *Bailey* v. *Drexel Furniture Co.*, which held unconstiutional an act of Congress that imposed a tax on goods produced by child labor and intended for sale in interstate commerce. This was held to be an unconstitutional use of the taxing power to encompass

[13] As matters stood in 1966, however, taxes did not seem to constitute a serious deterrent. Estimated federal revenues from tobacco amounted to over $2 billion, with 95 percent from cigarettes. Taxes on alcoholic beverages and tobacco together accounted for some $6 billion, or more than one-half of revenue from excise taxes.

[14] *McCray* v. *United States,* 195 U.S. 27 (1904).

[15] *United States* v. *Doremus,* 249 U.S. 86 (1919).

[16] See *United States* v. *Sanchez,* 340 U.S. 42 (1950); also *Magnano Co.* v. *Hamilton,* 292 U.S. 40 (1934).

[17] As early as 1869 the Court upheld as a valid use of the taxing power a Federal tax levied with destructive effect on the circulating notes of state banks. *Veazie Bank* v. *Fenno,* 8 Wall. 533 (1869).

social reform otherwise beyond the power of Congress. Few constitutional lawyers today would challenge the right of Congress to use its taxing power for almost any purpose it deemed necessary to promote the general welfare.

What is true of the federal government is, in almost equal measure, true of state governments, within the scope of their constitutional powers. A state, the Supreme Court has said, may adjust "its system of taxation in all proper and reasonable ways. It may, if it chooses, exempt certain classes of property from any taxation at all. . . . It may impose different . . . taxes upon different trades and professions, and may vary the rates of excise upon various products; it may tax visible property . . . ; it may allow deductions for indebtedness or not allow them."[18]

As we have seen, the federal government has used its taxing power to encourage certain kinds of conduct and to discourage others. It has also used its taxing power to induce the states to enact social legislation which they might otherwise have been unwilling or unable to adopt.

Tax Rebates and Inheritance Taxes

Notable among these reforms have been social security laws and inheritance taxes. Levying a tax on payrolls through the country to provide for unemployment compensation, the Congress rebates each state 90 percent of the revenue collected in that state, provided it has an unemployment tax and insurance law. A similar plan is used to encourage states to adopt estate or inheritance taxes. Although some states had inheritance taxes before the federal government moved seriously into this field, in 1916, most shied away from it lest it scare rich men away. The federal law helps to reduce this risk by imposing a graduated tax on the total estate passed on by a deceased person. Estates of less than $60,000 are exempt, but others are taxed at rates ranging from 3 percent to 77 percent. To encourage the states to enact their own estate and inheritance taxes, the federal law allows a taxpayer to pay up to 80 percent of his federal tax with state inheritance tax receipts. A state that has no inheritance tax thus forfeits an important source of revenue because in such cases the whole estate tax must be paid to the federal government.

The state of Florida attacked the federal law in the United States Supreme Court in 1927, charging that it was unconstitutional because (1) it wasn't uniform—that is, states with inheritance tax laws could keep up to 80 percent of the federal tax, while those without such laws got nothing; and (2) it interfered with the freedom of the states to choose their own tax systems. In *Florida* v. *Mellon* the Supreme Court rejected these arguments and sustained the law.[19] Partly on their own

---

18 *Bell's Gap Railway Co.* v. *Pennsylvania*, 134 U.S. 232 (1890).
19 *Florida* v. *Mellon*, 273 U.S. 12 (1927).

initiative, and partly in response to the inducements offered by the federal Estate Tax Law, all the states now levy taxes of this kind.[20]

As a source of revenue, estate or inheritance taxes and gift taxes, combined, do not loom large in the total fiscal resources of either the federal or the state governments, being about 2 percent of the total federal and state revenues in 1966. But the social implications of such taxes are more important than the revenue they produce.

Inheritance taxes are defended as a necessary safeguard against the accumulation of vast fortunes by a few families and the concentration of the nation's wealth in fewer and fewer hands. Not only does an inheritance tax take some of these accumulations for public benefit, but to pay the tax the heirs often are compelled to sell part of their inheritance, thus contributing to a more equitable distribution of wealth. But, it is said, inheritance taxes destroy initiative, discourage saving, and compel the break-up of effective economic units. How much of this is true we cannot say. As for initiative and saving, it is doubtful that inheritance taxes discourage these virtues any more than other forms of taxation. If death duties discourage saving in one generation, they may operate as a stimulus to the next generation which will have to make its own way rather than rely on its forebears.

As for breaking up businesses, this need not occur, although the sale of equities in a firm to pay the inheritance tax may result in a shift in ownership or control. But this could as likely be an advantage as a disadvantage by bringing in new blood and new leadership. One thing seems clear: many of the charitable trusts and foundations, including some of the largest ones, owe their existence to the gentle nudging of estate taxes. This alone might justify some of the disadvantages of these fiscal policies.

Taxes and Economic Growth

A standard complaint against corporation and inheritance taxes and the highly progressive rates of the personal income tax is that they slow down the rate of capital investment in new industries and new equipment, and thus reduce the overall rate of economic growth. Most saving for investment occurs among those in the upper brackets of income and if these incomes are subject to excessively high tax rates, the total volume and rate of investment will decline. Moreover, an excessively high rate of progression, it is said, will undermine the initiative of those industrial leaders on whom the country must rely for new enterprise.

It might, on the contrary, be argued that highly progressive personal income taxes could be a stimulus to new enterprise. They might encour-

[20] In 1963 the states collected about $600 million from death taxes, and the federal government, slightly over $2 billion.

age corporations to allocate more of their earnings to research and development and less to the payment of dividends to stockholders where they are taxed away at highly progressive rates. Moreover, government itself has become such a major factor in scientific research and development that money taken in taxes contributes as much to the research and development on which economic growth depends as does money left in private hands. It is not altogether certain that the retention by private persons of funds that are now taken in taxes by government would, in fact, increase the total being spent for scientific research and development. Moreover, if the reduction in taxes of those in the upper brackets were to increase the tax burden of those in the lower brackets, it might operate to reduce consumer demand upon which most economic enterprise depends. Economists generally agree that one cause of the great depression of the 1930s was not *under*-saving but *over*-saving and *over*-investment by those at the upper income levels and a corresponding failure of effective consumer demand. In any case, it is clear that the rate of taxation on individual incomes is an important factor in maintaining a stable and dynamic economy.

The same is true of the taxation of corporation income. The prevailing tax on corporation income undoubtedly reduces the funds that might otherwise go into new investment and thus contribute to increased productivity, employment, and general prosperity. On the other hand, present laws make provision for the depreciation of new facilities. During the first five years approximately two-thirds of the cost can thus be written off—to enable new investment in more modern plant and equipment. Still other tax stimulants to new investment have been embodied in more recent tax legislation, including a tax credit (a reduction in taxes) for funds invested in new machinery and equipment. Businessmen and some economists believe that even more liberal provisions for accelerated depreciation, if not tax credits for new investment, should be made if the American economy is to grow in competition with other industrial states.[21]

Early in 1961 it was argued that rates of depreciation in West Germany, Japan, France, Italy, Sweden, England, and Canada were higher than in the United States, and that this helped to explain their higher rate of economic growth.[22] A comparison of 1960 industrial production levels in the United States and some other countries, it was argued, showed the effect of their more liberal depreciation allowances. Taking

[21] In September, 1966, however, President Johnson recommended a sharp reduction in these tax credits to business enterprise. Their original enactment in 1963 and 1964 was to stimulate business investment. President Johnson's recommendation that they be reduced or eliminated was to check investment and thus curb inflation.

[22] On a piece of equipment with a life of fifteen years, the United States allows only 13 percent to be depreciated—i.e., written off as a tax deduction during the first year. Japan and England allow over 50 percent, Sweden 40 percent, Italy and Canada, 30 percent or more, and France 20 percent.

1953 as 100, Japan in 1960 showed 258 percent; Italy 181 percent; West Germany 180 percent; France 172 percent; Sweden 134 percent; England 128 percent; Canada 127 percent; and the United States only 119 percent.[23]

How much of the higher rates of economic growth in these countries can be attributed to accelerated depreciation under the tax laws and how much to other factors, it would be hard to say. But the argument for liberal tax credits and depreciation allowances, as well as President Johnson's move to reduce them, again emphasizes the importance of tax policy in national economic planning.

Taxation and public expenditures have thus become major factors in economic stabilization. One school of thought holds that when economic recession threatens, a reduction of taxes would put more money into the hands of consumers and thus help to revive trade, restore jobs, and start the economy moving forward again. It was on this assumption that Presidents Kennedy and Johnson proposed major reductions in federal taxes in 1963, 1964, and 1965. If public expenditures and lower taxes may be used in time of recession to stimulate the economy, so in times of full employment and rising prices, with threats of price inflation, these policies in reverse may help to stabilize the economy. Thus it was that President Johnson proposed a 10 percent surtax on income taxes in 1967. The surtax was put into effect in 1968, initially, at least, on a temporary basis. A reduction in public expenditures and an increase in taxes might help to stop the upward spiral of prices and generally stabilize the economy. Under these circumstances, tax increases all along the line— and especially at the lower income levels and on consumers—might exert a decisive influence in checking the boom.

Unfortunately, when, as has been the case since 1951, 60 percent or more of federal expenditures arise from irreducible defense activities, the possibility of major reductions in federal expenditures is not great. The defense program itself thus becomes a major factor in producing inflation, since the billions paid out for arms production are not matched by goods and services available for consumer purchase. Under these circumstances, only a Draconian policy of taxation can hope to check an upward thrust of prices.

These, then, are but some aspects of government fiscal policy to which students of American government must attend. Death and taxes may both be inevitable and unavoidable. But the one can, by proper care, be postponed, and the other can be mitigated and made more compatible with equality and freedom. For it is in these terms that Americans, at any rate, have come to identify taxes as "the price we pay for Civilization."

[23] *The Wall Street Journal*, April 10, 1961.

24
FOREIGN POLICY

☆ THE EMERGING ONE WORLD

Factors Contributing to the One–World Concept

The United Nations buildings, standing on the East River in New York, extending roughly from 47th Street to 42nd Street, are a symbol of a new world that has come into being since 1945. For the United Nations brings into sharp focus a world in which the dimensions of time and space have so changed that, whether we like it or not, we live in what the late Wendell Willkie called *One World*. It is one world, not because it is a united world; the headlines every day proclaim disunity and discord as pervasive and as bitter as ever in human history. It is one world because jet airplanes and instantaneous communication, among other things, have made Kansas and the Congo neighbors in fact, if not in theory. And what is true of Kansas and the Congo is true of New York and New Delhi, Houston, Texas, and Istanbul, Turkey.

Science and technology have made the nations of our modern world neighbors only in fact; it has not made them all friendly neighbors in the posture they assume toward one another. When they meet as 122 of them do—in almost daily conferences in those majestic buildings along New York's East River—they display the same polite perversities, the same intricate pattern of dealing and double-dealing that characterized the Congress of Vienna in 1815.

In the UN Assembly, in its committees and in its specialized agencies, diplomats move in and out, changing partners, now to the left, now to the right, in patterns as intricate as a Morris Dance. But behind these complex maneuvers the discerning observer knows that the moves are by no means random or meaningless. There is continuity, and even some stability, in the partnerships that emerge—partnerships that become cliques, and cliques that become blocs as they take their positions within or around the United States and the USSR. These partnerships or alignments become more stable, even stolid, in the Security Council, where the great powers sit in judgment on the affairs of the UN—that pale, and some would say, feeble, symbol of that Parliament of Man which poets have extolled.[1]

However much the UN may fall short of the poet's dream, it is nonetheless the symbol of both a new world in being and a new world striving to be born. Not important solely because, as the late Dag Hammarskjold said, it offers an opportunity for new forms of negotiation, for public diplomacy to supplement the private diplomacy that continues among its members. Nor is it important only because it has created a kind of continuing conference on world affairs, or in its Secretariat, an international administrative agency run by international civil servants of whom Dag Hammarskjold, U Thant, and Ralph Bunche are distinguished examples. The UN is important because it underwrites and makes manifest the reality of John Donne's sermon that

> No man is an island, intire of itselfe; everyman is a piece of the Continent: a part of the maine: if a Clod be washed away by the sea, Europe is the lesse . . . any man's deathe diminishes me, because I am involved in Mankind: And therefore, never send to know for whom the bell tolles, It tolls for thee. . . .

This might have been dismissed as mere rhetoric in John Donne's day— or even a hundred years ago. But it is no longer a sentimental sermon, it has come too close to being literally true for that. Am I my brother's keeper? is no longer a question but, rather, a condition of life, of security and of survival.

THE REVOLUTION IN TRAVEL, TRANSPORTATION, AND COMMUNICATIONS. Those who scoff at the reality of all this forget that from the invention of the horse-drawn chariot about 3000 B.C. to the coming of the steam engine in 1698 there had been no great change in travel and communication. An Englishman of A.D. 1700 had few, if any, advantages over an Egyptian of 1700 B.C. Better roads were built, and the Romans became celebrated for their highways, although these were allowed to fall into disrepair during the long twilight of the Middle Ages. In 1872 Jules Verne wrote a fancy tale about one Phineas Fogg, who accomplished the incredible feat of going around the world in 80 days. Compared to Magellan's record of 1,083 days, Mr. Fogg's voyage seemed fantastic. In

---

[1] See Margaret Bell, "Bloc Voting in the General Assembly," *International Organizations,* February, 1951; also Arend Lijphart, "The Analysis of Bloc Voting in the General Assembly: A Critique and a Proposal," *American Political Science Review,* December, 1963.

1929 a German airship went around the world in 20 days and 4 hours. In 1938 Howard Hughes did it in 92 hours; in 1948 it could be done in 43 hours. Today's astronauts go not around the world, but around and outside the earth itself in 90 minutes or so—in a spacecraft moving at 17,000 miles an hour. And in 1962 a land-based plane flew round trip from California to New York in about 4 1/2 hours. In 1790 Pittsburgh was 11 days from Boston—today it is little more than 2 hours by regular commercial plane. Today, Mandalay is closer to New York than New York was to Boston when Thomas Jefferson was President. Moreover, Russia is closer to Moscow, Idaho, in 1962 than either was to villages 100 miles away in 1862.

The revolution has been even more spectacular in the means of communication. Paul Revere's fast mail between Boston and Philadelphia took 11 days for the round trip and the Pony Express of legendary fame was no better. The electric telegraph, the undersea cable, the telephone, radio, television, radar, have changed all this. Eighty million Americans could watch the coronation of a Queen in Westminster Abbey; and both good and bad news travels from Paris or Bombay, London or Lahore, with the speed of light. Even more dramatic has been the development of communication satellites in space which literally make the world a communications community.

"A lie," Mark Twain once said, "can go around the world while the truth is putting on her shoes." In our contemporary world this may still be true, but truth as well as falsehood can travel on the wings of light.

The point of all this is that what obstacles remain to communication and enlightenment, travel and transportation, among the nations and peoples of the world, are no longer physical or geographical, but human —they are man-made. Science and technology have made Wendell Willkie's *One World* no longer merely a political slogan. Whether we like it or not Americans and Englishmen, Frenchmen and Algerians, Chinese and Russians live as neighbors and no amount of tubthumping, wishful thinking, or denigration of our disagreeable neighbors can change this fact. We have in our hands the tools to build a real Parliament of Man, unless in a desperate game of power politics we end in mutual annihilation, for which the tools lie ready and waiting.

THE REVOLUTION IN WEAPONS DEVELOPMENT. "The revolution in weapons development," says John McCloy, the President's advisor on Disarmament, "has resulted in the creation of delivery systems with fantastic rates of speed. Certain missiles that might be used . . . have a speed around 16,000 miles an hour . . . about 1/2 hour between the Soviet Union and the United States: and missile launching submarines will provide no warning time at all."[2]

2 *Foreign Affairs,* April, 1962.

EFFECT OF MODERN INDUSTRY AND TECHNOLOGY ON DOMESTIC AND WORLD
ECONOMICS AND INTERNATIONAL RELATIONSHIPS. If travel, transportation,
and communications—not to mention the ominous implications of thermonuclear missiles—have all but obliterated time and space as barriers
among the nations of the world, the nature of modern industry and
technology has made earlier notions of national self-sufficiency or
autarkie untenable by reasonable men. Today only the most primitive
agrarian economy could hope to survive without some measure of trade
and commerce with the outside world. Industrialization as we have seen
has meant progressive specialization through an elaborate division of
labor. The result has been increasing interdependence not only within
industry itself, and between industries, but between cities, states, and
regions.

A similar trend toward interdependence among nations has long
been apparent. Even the United States of America, perhaps the most
richly endowed nation on earth, simply cannot survive, let alone prosper,
as an industrial civilization without the mutual aid that comes from the
exchange of goods and services with other countries. In the contemporary
world the price of political independence, at least for industrial nations,
is economic, cultural, scientific, and technological interdependence. Paradoxically, the surest way to destroy the freedom and independence of the
so-called sovereign nations of the world is to continue in force those
economic policies, tariffs, quotas, currency restrictions, and embargoes
which have been designed to insure national self-sufficiency and so-called
economic independence.

To think of these policies or for that matter of other policies affecting our economic life—taxes, debt management, labor management
relations, farm subsidies, and so forth—solely in domestic terms is to
ignore their impact upon our foreign relations. Although the line of
distinction between domestic and foreign policy has never been clear, it
has become increasingly indistinct as our involvement in the shrinking
world has grown.

Not only is Central Europe becoming a "common market" for half a
dozen sovereign nations, but economic and cultural "markets" of even
wider scope are beginning to emerge. How far behind this functional
integration, supranational political integration will lag remains to be
seen.

☆ *AMERICAN LEADERSHIP OF THE FREE WORLD*

The interaction of domestic and foreign policy is also reflected in U.S.
policies and attitudes toward civil liberties, religious minorities, and
education and social welfare. In large measure they create an American

image abroad that can profoundly affect our relations with other nations. Moreover, what happens in America is a matter of importance to governments and people around the world. For better or for worse, leadership of the free world, almost against its will, has been thrust upon the United States.

The United Nations not only symbolizes this emerging One World of the late twentieth century—its location in New York serves to symbolize this American leadership. So too does the meteoric growth of international relations in the government and politics of the United States. The modest establishment of the Department of State under Secretaries of State such as Jefferson, Randolph, Pinckney, and Lee stands in sharp contrast to the department under John Foster Dulles or Dean Rusk.

Although the Department of State in those days was responsible for the Mint, the Patent Office, land grants, and the census—as well as for foreign affairs—it employed in 1800 only a dozen or so clerks, interpreters, doorkeepers, and messengers in Washington, and a diplomatic and consular force of 75. Today this department has grown to embrace over 40,000 employees, the vast majority of whom occupy posts outside the United States. Nor do these include thousands of other employees involved in international relations in other agencies such as the CIA, and Export-Import Bank, and other agencies and bureaus in agriculture, commerce, and labor. And to all these one must of course add close to 1 million civilian employees of the Department of Defense, who, along with about 3 million in the armed services, bear major responsibility for our national security.

Reaching outward, the United States has become a party to what both Washington and Jefferson called "entangling alliances" around the world. Among these are the United Nations and its numerous specialized agencies: the Organization of American States embracing most of the Latin American nations; the North Atlantic Treaty Organization (NATO) including some 15 countries of Europe, Canada, and the United Kingdom; the South East Asia Treaty Organization (SEATO) including Australia, France, New Zealand, Pakistan, Philippines, Thailand, and the United Kingdom. The United States is now a party to thousands of international agreements and an ally of 42 nations.

Appropriations to sustain our foreign relations have grown to match our commitments and our responsibilities. So marked have been the changes in the nature and scope of our international relations that comparing costs with pre-World War II expenditures is fruitless and all but meaningless. At no time since 1952 have expenditures for what the Bureau of the Budget calls International Affairs and Finance been less than $2 1/2 billion, and President Johnson's budget for fiscal year 1967 called for expenditures of $4 1/2 billion, exclusive of national defense.

Even these large sums tell only part of the tale. If we include military expenditures as an essential part of total expenditures to implement our foreign policy, the sum grows from $4 1/2 billion to more than $65 billion. Indeed the Bureau of the Budget estimated that nearly 63 percent of total budgeted expenditures for fiscal 1967 of some $112 billion was for national defense, international aid, and space research and development. The impact of these vast and mounting expenditures upon nearly every aspect of American life serves only to emphasize again the intimate relation that exists between domestic and foreign affairs.

☆ THE POPULATION EXPLOSION AND THE REVOLUTION IN RISING EXPECTATIONS

Foreign policy and international relations, like other aspects of government and politics, have to do with people. Not the least of the factors making for conflict and change in this new and shrinking world is the so-called population explosion that has been under way now for a generation or more. In 1900 world population was calculated to be 1.5 billion with about 0.5 billion in Asia. By 1960 that total had approximately doubled to 2.9 billion, with nearly two-thirds in Asia. At the current rate of increase of 1.7 percent a year, the world's population has been projected (extrapolated) to nearly 4 billion by 1975 and over 6 billion by the year 2000, that is, little more than 30 years from now.

This population growth is unprecedented, not only in terms of absolute numbers, but in terms of the rate of increase. According to Professor Kingsley Davis, world population grew by 6 percent in each ten-year period between 1850 and 1900; by 7 percent between 1900 and 1930; 10 percent between 1930 and 1950; and, as estimated, 17 percent between 1950 and 1960. Every year some 50 million people are added to the total world population and soon it may be 75 million, an increase considerably larger than the population of France or of the United Kingdom.

This spectacular increase in the world's population is due almost entirely to a radical reduction in death rates. By spraying with DDT to control malaria in Ceylon, death rates fell by 30 percent in one year. Life expectancy grew from 44 to 53 years of age. It is not more babies but more who stay alive that account for the population explosion. By the same token, the most impressive growth has occurred in the less-developed and underdeveloped countries of the world—in Central and South America, China, India, the Middle East, Australia and New Zealand, Indonesia, Africa, and Canada. All these places have rates of increase substantially above the average increase rate of 1.7 percent. If birth rates continue at present levels, say State Department demographers, "economic expansion must . . . be achieved or death rates will be forced up again. In the long run a country can have low death rates with all that they imply in the way of economic and social well-being, only if a reasonable balance is maintained between population growth and available resources."

Unfortunately, in the less-developed countries, mortality rates have declined "before there has been any . . . substantial improvement in levels of living or . . . in economic and social structure." With more effective economic organization the earth, no doubt, can support a much larger population. But unless economic growth and efficiency accompany population growth, the pressure of population will generate crises until an increased death toll brings production and population into better balance.

The facts seem to show that in spite of revolutionary progress in science and technology—indeed in some measure because of improved knowledge of health and sanitation—the world faces a Malthusian problem vastly greater than even Thomas Malthus posed. And it will be most acute in those areas of Asia, Africa, the Middle East, and Latin America, where the free world and the Communist world are in sharpest conflict for the allegiance of the people. China, with an estimated population of 700 million, India with over 400 million, Africa with nearly 250 million, and South America with 137 million, and with annual rates of increase of 2 to nearly 3 percent a year—these are also areas in which the so-called revolution of rising expectations is most widespread and intense.

The explosive force of burgeoning populations in these areas is accompanied by demands for better standards of living, more education, more of all the good things of life. Above all, they are demanding equality as human beings, to be treated not merely with kindness and toleration but with dignity and respect. Translated into political terms, these demands explain the raucous "new nationalism" of Asia, Africa, and the Middle East, and the revolutionary upsurge in Latin America. Since World War II some 50 new nations have emerged.

By a cruel paradox, the scientific and political revolutions that have produced the new nations and this population explosion have failed, so far, to meet the demands of the people for a better life and an increased measure of human dignity. Despite technological and economic progress, despite national independence and political self-determination, there are probably more hungry people in the world today than there were fifty years ago.

Campaigns of family limitation, which are official policy in Japan and India; step-by-step measures of economic and technical aid; even more important, mass investment in power dams and steel mills, highways and railways, schools, and hospitals may prove inadequate to meet the demands of this revolution in rising expectations. Upon its outcome may well depend the welfare and security, even the survival of our world. Essentially, the goals are the same as the goals the American people set for themselves nearly 200 years ago—equality and freedom, secured by governments which derive their just powers from the consent of the governed.

☆ FOREIGN POLICY IN THE WORLD OF NATION-STATES

In their relations with one another sovereign nations continue to operate in an atmosphere closely approximating the "state of nature" described by Thomas Hobbes over 300 years ago. "Hereby it is manifest," wrote Hobbes, "that during the time men live without a common power to keep them all in awe, they are in that condition which is called war, and such a war, as is of every man against every man. . . . [And in such a state of nature] men live in continuall fear and danger of violent death, and the life of man [is] solitary, poor, nasty, brutish and short."

Not even Thomas Hobbes argued that such a state of nature ever actually existed among human beings. For to live at all, men have had to carve out areas—sometimes as wide as the great empires of history, sometimes as narrow as a single family—in which some semblance of law and order could insure them against external attack and internal disobedience and disorder. In modern times these areas of law and order have been coextensive with the nation-state, sovereign and independent, owing no allegiance to external authority.

The history of modern times has been a history of adjustment, conflict, or cooperation among these sovereign nation-states for the elementary goals of which Hobbes spoke—gain, safety, and prestige. It has been a conflict carried on by diplomacy, mutual espionage, treaty making and treaty breaking, tariffs and embargoes, wars and rumors of war. Looked at from the outside, this world of nation-states looks for all the world like the state of nature described by Hobbes, in which every nation, at one time or another, is pitted against every other nation. Alliances, blocs, ententes, combinations of almost infinite variety are formed, dissolved, and re-formed for purposes of negotiation, to exert political or economic pressure, or to wage war.

Professor Quincy Wright, in his monumental *Study of War,* found not only that war was a common if not continuous part of human experience, but from the founding of the Jamestown colony in 1606 to 1946 there have been no fewer than fifteen wars "in which all the great powers of the world participated," including, incidentally, the American colonies and the United States of America, an average of one world war each 20 or 21 years. And during most of recorded history the stakes of foreign policy have remained pretty much the same: power and prestige, access to raw materials and markets, national security and welfare—the major components of what today we call national interest.[3]

In the conduct of foreign policy, patterns of behavior have emerged in customs and conventions, principles of protocol, treaties, and international law. Unlike domestic law, however, international law lacks the authority that comes from a monopoly of coercive power in a government able to enforce its decrees, put down violence, and maintain the peace. In the international community—in the so-called Society of Nations—"men live," as Hobbes said, "without a common power to keep them all in awe." Until some such common power is created, nations must continue to rely on their own power—alone, or in alliance with others of like mind and interest—to provide for their security and for the welfare of their people. Foreign policy thus becomes the plan by which each nation strives to protect and promote its own safety and welfare and to advance the basic values that give meaning and direction to its life in a world of hostile or potentially hostile states. These values may be said to compose a nation's public philosophy in terms of which both its foreign policy and domestic policy are carried on. One source of international conflict is therefore to be found in differences of public philosophy among nations.

In the struggles between ancient Athens and Sparta, between Greeks and Persians, between Rome and Carthage, between the Axis powers (Nazi Germany, Fascist Italy, and Japan) and the so-called United Nations of World War II and more recently in the cold war between Communist and non-Communist states, more has been at stake than raw materials and markets, or even power and prestige. Basic values, different ways of life, different public philosophies have been involved.

☆ AMERICAN FOREIGN POLICY IN THE PAST

In his book *U. S. Foreign Policy*, published in 1943, Walter Lippmann said that for nearly fifty years (since 1898), the United States "has not had a settled and generally accepted foreign policy. . . . Thus its course of foreign affairs depends . . . not on reflection and choice but on accident and force." It has also been·said that the United States lacks a philosophy or theory of international relations to give drive and direction to its foreign policy. American foreign policy, it is said, has been both pragmatic and sentimental, materialistic and moralistic. On the one hand, it is said, American statesmen indulge in messianic preachments about freedom and democracy, and on the other hand, practice "dollar diplomacy" and Yankee imperialism. Continental isolationism has walked hand in hand with continuous intervention in world affairs; an

---

[3] See Hans Morgenthau, *In Defense of the National Interest* (New York: Knopf, 1951).

insatiable hunger for power and prestige has accompanied a flight from power and its responsibilities.[4]

There is a measure of truth in all these criticisms. The United States has not had a master plan of foreign policy, nor has it followed a straight course toward a predetermined goal. Walter Lippmann is quite right: our international relations—both before 1898 and since—have been carried on largely in response to accident and the force of circumstances. But we *have* had a purpose and we have had foreign policy goals. This purpose and these goals, it may be said, are best expressed in our own Declaration of Independence and in the Preamble to the Constitution. Together these may be described as an American Democratic Manifesto with global implications as clear as those of the Communist Manifesto. To reconcile, if not to identify, this *democratic manifesto* with the aspirations of other nations in Europe, Africa, and Asia, in Latin America, and in the Middle East may well be described as the overriding goal of American foreign policy.

But a statement of national goals and purposes, or of a nation's public philosophy, is not the same as a statement of its foreign policy. For policy moves at a somewhat lower level, within narrower limits of time and circumstance, and is related more intimately with vital national interests as these appear from time to time. It is, therefore, no serious reproach to American foreign policy to say, as Walter Lippmann has said, that it depends "not on reflection and choice but on accident and force." Or to say, on the other hand, that it has always been imbued with a high degree of moralizing and sentimentality. Nor should one be surprised to find apparent contradictions in our day-by-day behavior toward other nations—tactics appearing at one time as Yankee imperialism or power hunger, and at another, as a sentimental flight from power itself.

In the final analysis foreign policies, like domestic policies, must be tested by their success or failure in contributing to the overriding ends for which they are designed—not in the world as we may wish it to be, but in the world as it is. Nor can American foreign policy be understood apart from the physical, political, and cultural context within which the American nation has developed. Our physical and cultural kinship with the North Atlantic Community and the European Continent has had a profound influence in shaping American foreign policy. No less important has been our inescapable involvement in the affairs of the Western Hemisphere.

American continentalism or isolationism is more easily understood if we take account of the vast, virtually uninhabited and unexplored North American continent that lay at our feet to be explored, occupied, and exploited. And if our early external ties were with Europe and the Atlantic Community, American involvement in Asian affairs was in-

[4] See George Kennan, *Realities of American Foreign Policy* (Princeton, N.J.: Princeton University Press, 1954) .

evitable as the line of settlement moved from the Atlantic coast to the Pacific. And not least among the basic factors affecting American foreign policy in more recent times has been the technological revolution that has virtually annihilated time and space and made the natural isolation both impossible and absurd.

Finally, the persistence into our own time of a world made up of sovereign states living in what continues to resemble an international state of nature is an inescapable condition of foreign policy—a condition somewhat mitigated, but not fundamentally changed, by the growth of international law, regional and international associations, and special international agencies of various kinds. "Moralists," said Winston Churchill, "may find it a melancholy thought that peace [in the 1960s] can find no nobler foundations than mutual terror. . . ."

It is in the context of some such combination of time and circumstance, of accident and force that American foreign policy is to be carried on and understood. Foreign relations are conditioned not only by their physical and cultural environment, but also by the organization and processes by which foreign policies are determined and administered. The foreign policy of a government in which power is divided between the President, the Senate, and the House of Representatives and is subject to review by an independent Supreme Court is less likely to appear coherent and consistent, neat and tidy, than the foreign policy of a centralized cabinet system, let alone an authoritarian dictatorship. No small part of the apparent confusion that often seems to characterize American foreign policy may be traced not only to this separation of powers, but also to a political system that invites the participation of public opinion in making decisions.

One need not accept Walter Lippmann's jaundiced view of the impact of mass opinion on foreign policy to recognize that in the United States, where popular loyalties are so often divided along racial, ethnic, or religious lines corresponding to power clusters and conflicts in the outer world, it does present special hazards. Small wonder that American foreign policy appears as a pattern of paradoxes, of cross pressures, confusion, and even contradiction, as the nation strives to adapt itself to a world of continuous and often cataclysmic change. We may note, for example, a historic policy of isolation, continentalism, and neutrality, accompanied by an equally historic policy of continuous intervention and participation in world affairs. Only in this generation has this paradox been resolved by recognition of our inescapable involvement in areas as near as Cuba and the Caribbean and as remote as Antarctica and the China Sea.

This long commitment to the doctrine of isolation and the practice of participation was accompanied by a policy of continental expansion from coast to coast and from the Great Lakes to the Gulf of Mexico. By conquest, purchase, and persuasion we took possession of the Louisiana territory, Florida, Texas, and the Great Southwest, California, Oregon, Alaska, Hawaii, and the Philippines, from France, Spain, Mexico, Great Britain, and Russia, not to mention the Indian tribes, which we displaced. If the Monroe Doctrine marked the end of European colonial expansion in this hemisphere, the so-called Theodore Roosevelt corollary made us the guardian of the republics established there.[5]

It may well be, as some historians say, that we acquired Hawaii and the Philippines in a fit of absent-mindedness. But there were those who were not unmindful of what lay within and beyond these rich and strategic islands. "The Philippines," said Senator Albert Beveridge to the United States Senate on January 9, 1900, "are ours forever. . . . And just beyond the Philippines are China's illimitable markets. We will not abandon our opportunity in the Orient. We will not renounce our part in the mission of our race as trustee under God, of the civilization of the World. . . . He has marked us as his chosen people, henceforth to lead in the regeneration of the World."

This, to be sure, was a large order but not surprising to men who had read and pondered the work of Admiral Alfred T. Mahan, whose books the *Influence of Sea Power upon History, The Moral Aspect of War,* and *The Problem of Asia* argued that "Whether they will or not, Americans must now begin to look outward." And speaking more specifically of America's new role in Asia, he said, "the incorporation of this vast mass of beings, [in China] the fringe of which alone we have as yet touched, into our civilization . . . , is one of the greatest problems that humanity has yet had to solve."[6] There were those, of course, who did not share these grand visions, but by the turn of the century America had become the governor or guardian for an empire reaching from Boston to Manila, and from Maine to Cape Horn.

Like other great empires the American empire, too, was a product of trial and error, wisdom and chance. The road it had followed, and the path it was thereafter to pursue, was by no means as straight as a string. But foreign policy was at no time far from the center of our concern, however much we talked of splendid isolation. Although in more recent times the messianic fervor of an Admiral Mahan or a Senator Beveridge has been considerably tempered, faint echoes of it can be heard in contemporary discussions of America's role as guardian of democracy in South Vietnam, Santo Domingo, Lebanon, and other troubled areas of

[5] In his annual address to Congress, December 6, 1904, President Theodore Roosevelt declared that "chronic wrongdoing or an impotence which results in a general leavening of . . . civilized society, may in America, as elsewhere . . . require the intervention by some civilized nation, and in the Western Hemisphere the adherence of the United States to the Monroe Doctrine may force the United States . . . to the exercise of an international police authority!" Quoted in Richard C. Snyder and Edgar Furniss, Jr., *American Foreign Policy; Formulation, Principles, and Programs* (New York: Holt, Rinehart and Winston, 1955), p. 73.

[6] How the persistence of this vision complicates our present relations with Communist China is a topic too difficult and too subtle for exploration here.

the world. But today as in the past one can also hear the voices of those who in one way or another continue to remind us of the counsel given by Washington and Jefferson, not only against "entangling alliances," but against assuming international responsibilities beyond our political, economic, or military capabilities.

It ought not to be surprising that in the development of the United States as a nation the strategy and tactics of our foreign policy have not always seemed consistent with the grand design of our basic public philosophy. And the critics have not failed to point this out. Although our history began with a revolutionary protest against colonialism and although we have denounced the colonial system and the intervention by great powers in the affairs of weaker states, nevertheless, we, even as they, acquired colonies of our own and intervened in the affairs of other states on many occasions. The Philippines and Puerto Rico, Morocco and Mexico, Hawaii and Haiti, Cuba and the Congo, Nicaragua, China, and Santo Domingo, Lebanon and South Vietnam—these are but a partial list of areas in which American diplomacy has been supported by armed force. But colonialism and shotgun diplomacy are not the only examples of paradox in American foreign policy.

It was the United States, say the critics, that sired and sponsored the League of Nations, only to leave it like an abandoned child on the doorstep of Europe. After World War I we insisted on the payment of war debts by our erstwhile European Allies and at the same time raised our tariff rates to levels that made such payment virtually impossible. While refusing to recognize Japan's conquest of Manchuria and vigorously denouncing Japanese aggression against China, we nevertheless continued to supply the aggressor with oil, scrap metal, and other materials without which Japanese aggression might well have been impossible.

Having helped to beat back German aggression in 1917 and 1918, we declined to give France and Britain military assurances against a similar attack in the future. When World War II began, although our hearts bled for France and Britain, Belgium and Denmark, the Netherlands and Norway, we stood aside until the Japanese at Pearl Harbor brought the war into our own front yard.

There is even more to the indictment. Since World War II, it is said, we have been so preoccupied with the negative goal of containing communism that we have failed to develop an affirmative policy of our own. What Communists support, we oppose; what they oppose, we support, in what has been called a foreign policy of the rebound, which in effect allows the Communist powers to determine policy for us. We seem to know what we *fear*—not what we are *for*.

Almost overnight, the critics continue, we moved from a policy to pastoralize Germany to one of German rearmament, and in the process made Germany the most powerful and prosperous country in Europe. In

Asia, having given the Kuomintang and Chiang Kai-shek up for lost, we continue to pretend that as exiles on Taiwan they nevertheless speak for China. Small wonder, say the critics, that American foreign policy is confused, unable to give drive and direction to the revolution that is sweeping like a hurricane across the face of the earth.

Such is the indictment. Like most indictments, however, it presents but a partial and distorted image. To reproach us with colonialism because of the Philippines, Hawaii, and Puerto Rico is to forget that the Philippines are now an independent republic, Hawaii a free and equal member of our Federal Union, and Puerto Rico a Commonwealth, bound to the United States by trade and tax policies of unexampled generosity. To speak of American colonialism is also to forget the historic policy that has governed our treatment of the new territories acquired in our expansion from the Atlantic to the Pacific. Even during their period of tutelage the new territories were treated, not as colonies or conquered provinces, but as self-governing territories. "And whenever," said the Northwest Ordinance of 1780, "any of the said [territories] shall have sixty thousand free inhabitants therein, such territory shall be admitted . . . into the Congress of the United States on an equal footing with the original states in all respects whatever. . . ." This promise has been kept, from the admission of Vermont in 1791 to that of Alaska and Hawaii in 1960.

America's failure to join the League of Nations no doubt delayed the development of an effective world organization and may have helped to make World War II inevitable. But the failure and demise of the League cannot be laid exclusively at the door of the United States. Members in good standing of that organization—the United Kingdom, France, not to mention Italy and Japan—did quite as much to destroy it from within as the nonparticipation of the United States may have weakened it from without. Although we never joined the League, we participated actively and frequently in its various projects. By 1931 more than 200 Americans had officially represented the United States in over forty League meetings.

Although, it is true, we stood aside in the early years of World War II, we were not wholly disengaged. We were, as the saying was, "neutral" —but we were "neutral against" the Berlin-Rome-Tokyo Axis. And the exchange of 50 destroyers for bases in the West Indies, the Atlantic Charter in 1940, and the Lend-Lease Act (HR 1776) in May, 1941, put us actually, if not officially and formally, on the side of the victims of Nazi aggression.

Nor has our foreign policy been wholly negative since 1945. The United Nations Relief and Rehabilitation Administration established in 1945 provided over $11 billion of aid to countries devastated by war. The Truman Doctrine of March, 1947, was not only a response to Communist threats against the independence and integrity of Greece and Turkey, but it also provided for a major program of economic recovery and reconstruction.

Nor was the revolutionary Marshall Plan for the Economic Recovery of Europe, and the vastly expanded foreign aid programs that have followed, wholly inspired by threats of Communist subversion and conquest. They were also motivated by fairly clear considerations of our own national interest in preventing the collapse of a friendly power structure in Europe. And underlying American intervention in the crises of Guatemala, Cuba, Suez, Lebanon, Korea, and Vietnam is a fairly consistent conception of American national interest.

☆ INTERNATIONAL RELATIONS AND THE ART OF INTERNATIONAL POLITICS

It is however not our purpose or responsibility here to review in detail, defend or deplore, American foreign policy but rather to strive for some understanding of the major factors that condition the conduct of the United States in its external relations with other sovereign states.

The term *international relations* refers to all of those patterns of behavior that involve interaction of independent nation states or political systems with one another. In its broadest sense the term may embrace the interactions of private citizens or groups of different nation-states with or toward one another. At the formal or official level the art of international politics is practiced by thousands of official representatives or agents of more than 100 nation-states which make up the so-called society of nations. But below and behind these formal representatives are other thousands of quasi-official or even private individuals and groups serving as foreign correspondents, attending international conferences of all kinds, participating in the operation and management of international cartels or corporations, teaching in foreign colleges and universities, "seeing the sights" as tourists, or simply living abroad to escape the tensions and anxieties of living at home. All consciously or unconsciously play a role in the conduct of international relations. To explore in all of its ramifications this complex pattern of international interaction is beyond the scope of our discussion here. At best we can but suggest some of the problems confronted by the United States in striving to give form and direction to what is called American foreign policy.

☆ AN ANALYSIS OF AMERICAN FOREIGN POLICY

Analysis of foreign policy involves at least four basic patterns of international relations or behavior that may be described as (1) diplomatic, or more strictly, "political," (2) economic, (3) military, (4) ideological, that is, cultural or "idealistic." It would be foolish to think of these various patterns of behavior as independent of one another. On the contrary, none can function or can be understood wholly apart from the others. Nevertheless, in some such terms we can impose order of a kind upon the historic and contemporary foreign policies of the United States if we remember always that they represent simply different ways of looking at the total process. Nor must we forget the general context (outlined in the preceding section) in which the total process takes place.

Diplomacy and the Art of International Politics

Diplomats, it has been cynically said, are agents sent to "lie abroad" for the good of their country. But diplomats, or at least good ones, do not *lie* although they do traditionally live abroad.

"The art of diplomacy," says a distinguished British diplomat, "like the art of war, has two ingredients. First . . . the formulation of policy, [and] this is the responsibility of the statesmen. Second comes the execution of that policy [which] is generally the task of the diplomats who in every country except the United States are professionals."[7]

This is, of course, too narrow an interpretation of the role of diplomacy and makes an unnecessary distinction between the diplomat and the statesman or politician; for most of the work and many of the traits required in diplomacy are precisely those required of the statesman or politician: communication, negotiation, rationalization, reconciliation, and the successful search for a middle ground when confronted by conflict or contradiction. Although it has been said that diplomats make war, more often than not they become specialists in the art of resolving, not in generating, conflict. Political dogmas or ideologies, *either/or* propositions, *yes* or *no* ultimata are the pitfalls not the tools of diplomacy.[8] "The task of diplomacy," wrote George Kennan, "[is seen] as essentially a menial one, consisting of hovering around the fringes of a process one is powerless to control, tidying up the messes other people have made, attempting to keep small disasters from turning into big ones, moderating the passions of governments and opinionated individuals."[9]

The traits that make a successful diplomat are generally those that make for success in a statesman or politician: (1) Integrity and with it an ability to inspire confidence; (2) knowledge of his own country, its culture and public philosophy and of the nature and background of major sources of conflict; (3) "a sense of reality" that sees diplomacy as the art

7 See Sir Ivone Kirkpatrick, "As a Diplomat Sees the Art of Diplomacy," *The New York Times* Magazine, March 22, 1959.

8 See Francis Neilson, *How Diplomats Make War* (New York: Huebach, 1921).

9 See M. A. Fitzsimons and S. D. Kertesz, eds., "History and Diplomacy as Viewed by a Diplomat," in *Diplomacy in a Changing World* (Notre Dame, Ind.: University of Notre Dame Press, 1959).

of the possible and not the art of building castles in the air or winnng points in a battle of wits; (4) patience and perseverance and a large measure of constancy and consistency.

Diplomats, in this extended view, are both the architects and the administrators of policy. And since they are invariably inheritors of the past, they too are governed by policies, not of their own devising, but within which they must operate until revised, repealed, or repudiated. Successful diplomats are also governed by fairly rigid standards of judgment and discretion. Much of what they do must be done in secret, away from the bright light of publicity, often without public acknowledgment of any kind. "The test of diplomacy is not whether it is dramatic . . . [or] open to public view, or whether a particular ideology prevails. The test is whether there is an effective accommodation of harmonious as well as of conflicting interests."[10] And this is true whether the issue involved is an international trade agreement, a boundary dispute, disarmament and arms control, or a test ban treaty. Cynics may tell how "diplomats make war," but the highest stakes of diplomacy are not those of war but of peace.

The U.S. Foreign Policy Machine

To carry on this important business the United States maintains embassies or legations in well over 100 foreign countries, each under the direction of an ambassador, minister, or chief of legation. From Abidjan in the Ivory Coast to Zomba in Malawi, American diplomats are striving to "represent" the United States in the turbulent political waters of the New Africa. Others find themselves caught in the cross fires of conflicting national interests of Israel's Tel Aviv and Egypt's United Arab Republic with their tangled web of blocs and alliances, both formal and informal. In Asia and Oceania the American presence is made known in embassies, from Nepal's Katmandu and Burma's Rangoon, from New Zealand's Wellington and Australia's Canberra, from Tokyo in Japan and Taipei in Taiwan (Formosa) to India's New Delhi and South Vietnam's Saigon. In the Western Hemisphere, from Ottawa to Buenos Aires and Santiago, Chile, to Rio de Janeiro, American embassies serve as outposts of observation, representation, information concerning matters of vital interest and concern to the United States. And in Europe, from Moscow to Dublin and Oslo to Rome, the security and welfare of the United States are the constant concern of American diplomats. Reflecting the changing pattern of world politics, it is interesting to note that whereas only 25 American embassies now operate in Europe, including a half dozen in Communist countries, no fewer than 28 are maintained in Asia and the Middle East and more than 30 in Africa.

[10] Joseph E. Black and Kenneth W. Thompson, *Foreign Policies in a World of Change* (New York: Harper & Row, 1963) , p. 20.

The American "presence" around the world is maintained not only by ambassadors, ministers, and chiefs of legation in these far-flung embassies. Assisting them are thousands of other Foreign Service officers and employees, including counselors of embassy, attachés, diplomatic secretaries, consuls general, consuls and vice-consuls who play a wide variety of roles in hundreds of cities beyond those that boast an embassy or legation. Other Special Missions, of ambassadorial or quasi-ambassadorial rank, are maintained at the United Nations in New York and its other International Organizations in Switzerland, the Organization of American States in Washington, D.C., the International Civil Aviation Organization in Montreal, Canada, the Berlin Mission in Germany, the European Communities in Belgium and Luxembourg, the International Atomic Energy Agency in Austria, the North Atlantic Treaty Organization, and European Regional Organizations. Nor does this comprise all of the Officials of the United States actively engaged in the conduct of American foreign policy. The Central Intelligence Agency, the United States Arms Control and Disarmament Agency, the United States Information Agency, the Special Representative for Trade Relations, for example, operate under presidential direction, with only tangential relations or responsibility to the Secretary of State.

The assignment of diplomatic and other posts abroad as a reward for partisan political services has, since World War II, become the exception rather than the rule. An integrated and unified Foreign Service based on professional training and experience has not, however, been wholly achieved, although the Rogers Act of 1924, the Moses Linthicum Act of 1931, and the Foreign Service Act of 1946 were important steps in this direction. As recently as 1949 the Hoover Commission reported that no fewer than 46 executive agencies were involved in the conduct of foreign affairs. The Defense, Treasury, Commerce, Agriculture, Justice, and Labor Departments, among others, have representatives of various kinds in many places around the world. Coordination of these agencies to insure a consistent, not to say, integrated foreign policy, has been a major problem. Although responsibility for all of these departments and agencies comes to focus in the White House, the number, variety, and technical nature of the activities involved cast an impossible burden upon the President. To provide better coordination and to enable the President more effectively to control these varied and far-flung affairs, the Congress in 1949 created a National Security Council in the Executive Office of the President. "Its function is to advise the President with respect to the integration of domestic, foreign and military policies relating to the national security."[11]

It is obvious even from this sketchy outline that the foreign policy machine of the United States is a vast, complex and far-flung mechanism.

[11] U.S. Government Organization Manual, *1965–66* (Washington, D.C.: U.S. Government Printing Office) , p. 58.

It is the responsibility of the President to make sure that it operates effectively to provide for the peace, security, and welfare, not only of the United States, but of a world torn by conflict and threatened by nuclear annihilation; for these are the basic goals of American diplomacy. Our recognition policy, our policy of "containment" in what has been called a "cold war against Communist expansion," our tariff policies, the Marshall Plan, the continuing program of foreign economic and military assistance, and our expanding program of international cultural relations are best understood within the context of these basic goals. It is common to summarize these goals as representing American national interest, but such is the nature of the contemporary world that national interests—whether of the United States and Great Britain, or of the USSR and Communist China—require for their realization respect for the common interests of people everywhere in peace, security, freedom, and welfare.

We cannot review or analyze in any detail the contemporary foreign policy of the United States. A brief account however of some of its major political, economic, military, and cultural components may help to clarify how and to what purpose the foreign policy machine operates.[12]

The Recognition Policy of the U.S.

Central to the conduct of foreign relations and a precondition for constructive international politics is the mutual recognition of nation-states by one another. "The recognition of a new state," said Secretary of State Stimson in 1931, "[is] the assurance given to it that it will be permitted to hold its place and rank . . . [as] an independent political organism in the society of nations." In the United States, recognition of foreign states is a presidential prerogative, and legally the accredited ambassador is the President's ambassador. Although his formal appointment requires Senate confirmation, the right to receive ambassadors, to refuse to see them, to request their recall, or to dismiss them are powers subject exclusively to the discretion of the President.

Recognition can and usually does involve more than a formal exchange of ambassadors and official courtesies. Involved also may be economic, cultural, and military arrangements of great importance. Historically a distinction was made between *de facto* and *de jure* recognition. Theoretically *de facto* recognition applied to any government which was recognized as having effective control of the country, whereas *de jure* recognition applied only to governments regarded as "legitimate," that is, which met certain standards as to their origin, organization, competence, morality, or policies. The distinction is one to which modern students of international relations take exception, since it seems to connote a "revival of the now almost forgotten policy of European

12 See Robert E. Elder, *The Policy Machine* (Syracuse, N.Y.: Syracuse University Press, 1960).

monarchial governments of contrasting *de facto* with *de jure divino* states thus stigmatizing all republican or democratic governments" as illegitimate. "This is bad international politics," says Professor Philip Jessup, "and may . . . put the recognizing state in the impossible position of attempting to pass on constitutional provisions of another state."[13]

Conscious of its own revolutionary and hence "illegitimate" origin, the United States from the beginning extended recognition liberally on a *de facto* basis even to the revolutionary governments of Latin America. "It is the established policy of the United States," said President Pierce in 1856, "to recognize all governments without question of their source or their organization, or the means by which the governing persons attain their power provided there be a government *de facto* accepted by the people of the country."[14]

Recognition was extended to any government of which it could be said that it had—

1. Control of the administrative machinery of the state.
2. The general acquiescence of its people.
3. The ability and willingness to discharge its international and conventional obligations.

No inquiry was made concerning its origin, organization, or "legitimacy." As Jefferson said in 1792, "We certainly cannot deny to other nations that principle whereon our own government is founded, that every nation has a right to govern itself internally under what forms it pleases and to change those forms at its own will, and externally to transact business with other nations through whatever organ it chooses whether he be king, convention, president or whatever it be."

But this long-standing policy was significantly modified by President Wilson in 1913 when he refused to recognize the government of the Provisional President of Mexico, General Victoriano Huerta. Huerta had come to power through a *coup d'état* including the murder of President Francisco Madero, who had been elected to that office in 1911 following the revolutionary upheaval of 1910 against the military dictator Porfirio Diaz. "The military *coup d'état* of Victoriano Huerta," says one authority, "nurtured in treason and stained with the blood of the murdered President . . . precipitated between Mexico and the United States the political crisis that was to run an uneasy course for the greater part of the first Wilson administration."[15]

President Wilson withheld recognition of President Huerta's government and in the process proclaimed a new recognition policy for the United States. The President might have simply withheld recognition on

---

[13] See Philip Jessup, *A Modern Law of Nations* (New York: Macmillan, 1948) , p. 57.
[14] See Snyder and Furniss, *op. cit.,* p. 15.
[15] See Frank Tannenbaum, *Mexico, The Struggle for Peace and Bread* (New York: Knopf, 1950) , p. 253.

the ground that the Huerta government lacked effective control of the country and could not therefore be recognized even as the *de facto* government of Mexico. But President Wilson went beyond this to say: "Cooperation [with our sister republics of Central and South America] is possible only when supported at every turn by the orderly processes of just government based upon law, not upon arbitrary or irregular force. We hold . . . that just government rests always upon the consent of the governed, and that there can be no freedom without order based upon law and upon the public conscience and approval. We shall look to make these principles the basis of mutual intercourse . . . between our sister republics and ourselves."

Although President Wilson also declared that thereafter the United States would not use force to support special interests in Mexico or elsewhere, the American government nevertheless supported a counterrevolution to overthrow Huerta with promises of loans to a new government to be based on free elections in which Huerta would not be a candidate. When Huerta refused to resign, President Wilson, early in 1914, took the further step of lifting an embargo on arms shipments to Huerta's opponents and sent naval vessels to blockade the port of Vera Cruz, in order to prevent European supplies from reaching the Huerta government. Moreover American forces were landed in Mexico, and the city of Vera Cruz was bombarded and occupied. Constant political, economic, and military pressure finally forced Huerta to resign on July 15, 1914. He was succeeded by Venustiano Carranza, who on October 19, 1915, was recognized by the United States as *de facto* President. And when in February, 1917, a new constitution for Mexico was proclaimed under which Carranza was duly elected President, the United States extended *de jure* recognition to his government.

President Wilson's revision of our traditional recognition policy serves to point up the complications that can arise when recognition goes beyond an enquiry concerning the *de facto* status of a new government, and the apparent contradiction in American policy vis-à-vis Mexico. On the one hand we insisted upon a "just government based upon law . . . [and consent], not upon arbitrary or irregular force." On the other hand, we did not hesitate to use force and even to invade and occupy a friendly neighboring state to remove a government that we did not approve. Recognition or nonrecognition thereafter became not merely a formal procedure for establishing our relations with new governments but a weapon to be used in promotion of a particular political system or ideology. Couched in moralistic or legalistic terms, it inevitably appeared to other powers as an impudent intrusion of American ideas of political morality in the conduct of international relations.

Republican administrations after 1920 formally "declined to follow the policy of Mr. Wilson, [but instead] followed . . . the former practice of this government since the days of Jefferson. As soon as . . . the new governments in Bolivia, Peru, Argentina, Brazil, and Panama were in control of the administrative machinery of the state, . . . they were recognized by our government."

But the return to the policy of Washington and Jefferson was not complete. By special treaty in 1907 five republics of Central America (Guatemala, Honduras, Salvador, Nicaragua, and Costa Rica) had agreed not to "recognize any other government which may come into power in any of the five republics as a consequence of a *coup d'état* or of a revolution against the recognized government so long as the freely elected representatives of the people thereof have not constitutionally reorganized the country." In 1923 the recognition policy outlined in this treaty was reaffirmed and endorsed by the United States. In 1931 Secretary of State Stimson was able to say that, "Since the adoption . . . in 1923 of the policy of recognition agreed upon by the five republics . . . not one single revolutionary government has been able to maintain itself in any of those five republics. I think that no impartial student can avoid the conclusion that [this special] treaty and the policy which it has established in that locality has been productive of very great good. . . ."[16]

Stimson's evaluation of the new policy may very well be true, but one might also ask whether it may not also have delayed or prevented revolutions in countries where revolution may be the only effective way to achieve political, economic, and social change. By endorsing this policy the United States appeared to put itself in the posture of a counterrevolutionary power at the very time it was proclaiming to all the world the revolutionary precepts of the American Declaration of Independence.

A modified version of the Wilsonian policy of recognition has been followed, more or less, ever since its reaffirmation in 1923. For more than 15 years (1918–1933) we withheld recognition of the Soviet government in Russia, and other Socialist or Communist governments have been denied recognition on grounds that Jefferson and most of his successors up to Wilson would no doubt have disapproved. However pure our motives in pursuing this policy, we pay a price for it. Refusal to extend

---

16 It is important to note that the treaty of 1907 was a joint declaration by five republics in the Caribbean area. It was not a unilateral policy as was Wilson's declaration vis à vis President Huerta or our continuing refusal to recognize Communist China, North Vietnam, and a number of other established governments. Under the League of Nations Covenant, as in the United Nations Charter, admission to membership in the organization may be regarded as a form of joint recognition even though individual members of the organization may not themselves extend recognition to all member governments. Hence the admission of Communist China to the United Nations would not necessarily imply recognition by the United States. But, as Professor Jessup has said, "The traditional practice of unilateral recognition of new states is not consistent with the . . . concept of community interest." See his *Modern Law of Nations* (New York: Macmillan, 1948), p. 44.

A more recent example of joint action in withdrawing recognition from an established government was the action taken by the Organization of American States in January, 1962, expelling Cuba from membership in both the OAS and the Inter-American Defense Board.

de facto recognition to Communist China, for example, has not only cut us off from any official contact or communication with nearly one-third of the human race, but has placed us in the somewhat ambiguous position of treating the Chinese government of Chiang Kai-shek on Taiwan as *the* government of China. Withdrawal of American recognition of the government of Guatemala in 1954 and of the Dominican Republic in 1962, together with other diplomatic, economic, and military sanctions, no doubt contributed to the overthrow of regimes that fell short of our standard of political morality. A similar policy applied to the Castro government of Cuba, however, has thus far failed to put an end to the Castro regime and may have contributed to the disastrous "Bay of Pigs" invasion in April, 1961, and the harrowing missile crisis of October, 1962. In any case, continued nonrecognition of the governments of Cuba, China, and other states that fail to measure up to our standards of political morality and ideology complicates our foreign policy by impairing effective communications with them and by denying our decision makers access to important sources of information and intelligence. Moreover the standards by which in practice we assess the "legitimacy" of such governments are by no means clear or consistent.

When avowed dictatorships like those of Salazar in Portugal, General Franco in Spain, Mussolini in Italy, Hitler in Germany, Batista in Cuba, and Stalin and his successors in Russia are recognized while dictatorships in China, the Dominican Republic in 1962, Guatemala in 1954, and Cuba in 1962 are thrust beyond the pale, objective observers are puzzled. Some critics are led to say that having abandoned the *de facto* policy of recognition without applying consistently the revised policy of Wilson, we have no well-defined recognition policy. The fact, however, would seem to be that in extending or withholding recognition we do so, not because we approve or disapprove particular forms of government, but because of what we conceive to be our national interest. General political, economic, strategic, or military considerations would seem to weigh more heavily in the recognition process than moral or ideological values.

The beginning of what can be a policy of greater candor and consistency, if not of greater wisdom, has been suggested in a State Department release to all United States embassies in August, 1958:

> Despite the emotions engendered and the abhorrence of the American people for the brutality and utter lack of morality of Communist systems, the policy of the U.S. Government toward China has . . . been based on objective considerations of national interest. . . .
>
> Basically the U.S. policy of not extending recognition to the Communist regime in China proceeds from the conviction that such recognition would produce no tangible benefits to the U.S. or to the free world as a whole and would be of material assistance to Chinese Communist attempts to extend Communist dominion throughout Asia.

Whether one agrees with the logic or the wisdom of this policy, it is one that can be understood. Our recognition policy, it says, rests not simply on *de facto* control of the governmental machinery of a state, in line with the practice of Washington and Jefferson. Nor does it rest on legalistic or moralistic judgments concerning the legitimacy of particular governments, but simply and solely on considerations of our own national interest. If it suits our interest we recognize, if not, we do not.[17]

☆   AMERICAN FOREIGN AND DOMESTIC POLICY

Tariff and Trade Policies

"The tariff," said an American politician, "is a local issue." Not just a domestic issue, but a *local* domestic issue at that. This idea, it would seem, reflects the general opinion of the American people for 150 years—that tariff rates ought to be determined solely out of consideration for (1) the needs of the government for revenue, and (2) the effect of tariff rates on our domestic economy. In short, whatever may be the effect of tariff policy on our international relations, the interests of our own farmers, workers, manufacturers, and businessmen were regarded as paramount. Because these effects are not uniform, the politics of tariff making have been almost infinitely complex. Perhaps no other decisions made by the President and Congress exhibit so clearly the cross pressures of rival factional interests as does the tariff. To say that the tariff was not a domestic issue, or even a local issue, would therefore fly in the face of common sense and experience. But the tariff is also an important issue of foreign policy. For tariff policy determines the terms on which goods and services produced abroad may enter American markets, just as the trade and tariff policies of other states determine the terms on which American goods may enter foreign markets.

And as the world grows smaller, more highly industrialized, and hence more interdependent, a nation's tariff and general trade policies become more and more important to its welfare and security. Even in 1789 the men who established the government realized the importance of trade policy in both domestic and foreign relations. They knew that the prosperity of our colonial cities—Boston, New York, Philadelphia, Baltimore—depended in one way or another on foreign trade. The hated tax on tea was a tax on imports; the detested writs of assistance were general search warrants directed against smuggling. The trade and navigation laws that sparked the Revolution were part of an economic foreign policy

17 The United States is not the only great power that uses its recognition policy as an instrument for promoting its national interest. Under the so-called Halstein Doctrine the West German Federal Republic, not only withholds recognition from the so-called East German Democratic Republic, but also from all other governments that do recognize the East German regime.

bitterly resented by American shipbuilders, importers and exporters, and the trades and services that attended them.

Following the Revolution, discriminatory trade regulations, the loss of shipping and shipbuilding contracts, and the dumping of foreign goods on the American market helped to account for the economic depression and disorders of the "critical period" culminating in Shays' Rebellion. Foreign trade declined and the balance of payments (the balance between income from exports and outgo for imports) turned sharply against the infant Republic. In 1784, for example, imports from England were nearly £4,000,000 and exports were but £750,000. At that rate America might soon be drained of specie, her shipping irretrievably lost, and her local infant industries smothered in their cradle. Under these circumstances it was not surprising that the first measure introduced in the new Congress under the Constitution was a bill to aid manufacturers, raise revenue, and improve the nation's balance of payments.

From the very first, then, tariff and trade policies have been an important part of American foreign and domestic policy. These policies, with their differential effect on various regions of the country, were also an important factor in the sectional cleavage that ultimately led to the Civil War. The South and the West, producing raw materials and agricultural commodities for export, saw little or no advantage in trade policies designed to protect northern manufacturers from foreign competition. High tariffs, they quite correctly reasoned, not only raised the prices of imports they had to buy, but also undermined their markets abroad. But tariffs won out and by 1824 Henry Clay was defining the protective tariff as a central pillar of what he called "The American System."

Under Whig and Republican administrations, tariff rates generally went up, and under the Democrats they went down; but up or down the Protective Tariff system became a permanent feature of American domestic and foreign policy. In the Fordney-McCumber Act of 1922 and the Smoot-Hawley Tariff of 1931, rates reached an all time high, raising a Chinese wall against foreign trade and contributing in no small way to the onset of the great depression of the 1930s.[18] American protection invited retaliation from abroad; and as tariffs, trade quotas, embargoes, and other restrictions multiplied around the world, international trade languished, and with it languished prospects for prosperity and peace.

[18] At the same time that we were raising tariff rates to unprecedented levels, we were insisting that our erstwhile European Allies pay the loans advanced by the United States to them in fighting World War I. Since high tariffs made it difficult for these countries to sell their products in America, it became progressively more difficult for them to acquire the dollar reserves required to pay their debts. Thus the American tariff policy stood virtually in contradiction to the American policy on war debts. In the end the debts were scaled down, canceled, or repaid when tariff rates were reduced after 1934.

In an heroic effort to revive foreign trade, Congress in 1934 passed the first Trade Agreement Act, authorizing the President to enter into agreements with other countries for a reciprocal reduction in specific tariff rates by as much as 50 percent. This so-called Reciprocal Trade Agreements Policy has been continued and extended to the present time. The United States has concluded agreements with over 50 nations, accounting for more than 80 percent of our normal foreign trade. Equally important has been the General Agreement on Tariff and Trade (GATT), concluded at Geneva, October 30, 1947. This agreement covered tariff concessions on about two-thirds of the trade items between 28 participating countries.

The resources of the world are no more evenly distributed among the nations of the world than the resources of the American continent are evenly distributed among the several states. New England with its forests and its falling water; Virginia with its deep, rich, alluvial soil; Ohio, Pennsylvania, and West Virginia with their coal deposits; Minnesota with its iron; Texas, Oklahoma, Louisiana, and California with their oil; and other states with special resources of their own had to be brought together to build a viable industrial economy. To accomplish this, that is, to create an American common market, the founding fathers gave the central government power "to regulate commerce with foreign nations and among the several states."

The same logic lies behind efforts to create a common market in Europe and in other regions of the world where the boundaries of political systems bear little or no relation to the distribution of natural and human resources. Moreover the growth of industry has made it more and more difficult for an industrialized political community to maintain itself through the resources and markets within its own borders. The European colonial systems of the eighteenth and nineteenth centuries and our own so-called dollar diplomacy of the early twentieth century were logical end products of this situation. "Before World War II," said Lord Cecil of England, "we imported four-fifths of our cereal, two-thirds of our meat, the whole of our cotton and almost the whole of our wool. If we were blockaded for a month . . . we should have to surrender."

Japan must import one-fourth of the food it eats and 80 percent of its industrial raw materials. For the United States, "To build up tariff walls against Japan," says one authority, "is to tear down our alliance with Japan." American trade and tariff policies with the so-called one-commodity countries of Central and South America can mean the difference between poverty and prosperity, political stability and revolution for them, since the United States is their major market.

Even fabulously rich nations like the United States are dependent on imports to keep their industrial machine operating and to maintain high standards of living. To list our own major imports is to indicate the nature of our dependence: nonferrous metals, paper and paper products, petroleum and petroleum products, coffee, cocoa, cane sugar, rubber, wool.[19] But our dependence is not to be measured solely in terms of imports, for without export markets for goods and services, and for investment capital, which we also produce in abundance, we could not buy the imports we so sorely need. "As ye buy, so must ye sell." To buy over $16 billion of imports in 1964, the United States sold exports of some $26 billion including nearly $4 billion of foodstuffs, $3 billion of cotton, synthetic rubber, wood and wood pulp, soybeans, our metal scrap, over $9 billion in machinery including over $1 1/2 billion in automobiles, about $5 billion of other manufactured products, and more than $2 billion of chemicals and chemical products.

Foreign Loans and Capital Investments

The United States also exported capital in the form of loans and investments exceeding $8 billion in 1964. Yet prior to World War I we were a net importer of investment capital, and an important factor in American industrial development was the capital invested here by Europeans. By the turn of the century, however, the export of American capital began to grow at a dizzy pace as American investors put their money into oil wells, mines, and factories, power plants, railroads, telephone and telegraph companies in Canada, Western Europe, Latin America, the Middle East, Asia, and Africa. By 1960 American private investments in foreign countries were in the neighborhood of $30 billion, of which approximately one-third (nearly $9 billion) was invested in Canada, another one-third ($8.7 billion) in Latin America. By 1966 total American capital investments abroad exceeded $50 billion, plus $20 billion "in stock and other portfolio holdings."[20]

The relation of governments to the private foreign investment of their nationals has been a central and significant aspect of economic foreign policy for 200 years. What, if any, responsibility does a government have to encourage or discourage its nationals to seek investment opportunities abroad or to protect their investments from regulation, cancellation, or confiscation? Can the governments of Latin America, Asia, and Africa, or of Western Europe, hope to attract private investment capital from abroad without giving assurance against burdensome taxation, regulation, or confiscation? To what extent can governments give such assurance without impairing their own welfare, independence, and prestige?

Loans and investments made by foreign investors in what is called

---

[19] Recent estimates indicate that the American economy must rely on imports for 93% of its natural rubber, 67% of its tin, 78% of its manganese, 77% of its hemp, 99% of its industrial diamonds, 69% of its cobalt, and 96% of its chrome.

[20] See Richard J. Barber, "American Business Goes Global," *The New Republic*, April 30, 1966.

"the normal course of business" will require rates of return commensurate with the risks assumed; and where the risks are too great, or the prospect of profit too remote, foreign investment is unlikely. In such circumstances other sources of capital for economic development must be sought either at home or abroad. If at home, the accumulation of capital for industrialization may impose heavy, if not intolerable, burdens upon the people. By forcing reduced standards of living in order to accumulate savings for capital improvement, a government may face political hazards that only a totalitarian dictatorship can withstand. Yet the so-called "revolution of rising expectations" that is sweeping the world makes capital accumulation more and more imperative. For these and other reasons private investment in foreign countries has been supplemented by intergovernmental loans, credits, and grants and payments to finance economic development.

Although other governments have participated in this new pattern of foreign aid or investment, the United States has taken the lead and has accounted for the largest share. Notable have been (1) The United Nations Relief and Rehabilitation Administration (UNRRA) established in 1943 to provide aid to countries devastated by war and striving for economic recovery. Although 44 nations participated, nearly 75 percent of the $11 billion came from the United States. (2) To aid the United Kingdom in the transition from war to peace the United States not only settled its lend-lease and reverse lend-lease accounts on the most generous terms, but in 1946 extended additional credits of $3.7 billion to be repaid at 2 percent interest over a period of 50 years. (3) France, Belgium, Italy, and other countries of Western Europe were in many respects in more dire straits than the United Kingdom. Their transportation systems, mines, and factories were in a state of disrepair approaching ruin. Their dollar resources had been exhausted by the war and they were therefore in no position to buy the needed supplies from us. Unemployment, widespread hunger, and despair threatened to provide a fertile soil for Communist revolutionary agitation.

The Marshall Plan

At this juncture, on June 5, 1947, in a speech at Harvard University, Secretary of State George Marshall announced that the United States would be willing to contribute to the economic recovery of European states if they would determine their most urgent needs and agree to cooperate in the process of recovery. American policy, in this respect, said Marshall, was directed, "not against any country or doctrine, but against hunger, poverty, desperation, and chaos. Its purpose should be the revival of a working economy in the world so as to permit the emergence of political and social conditions in which free institutions can exist." The upshot of this invitation was the establishment in Europe in 1947 of the

Organization for European Economic Cooperation (OEEC) in which 16 nations participated. In the United States an Economic Cooperation Administration (ECA) was established in 1948. The OEEC estimated Europe's needs during four years (up to 1952) at between $16 billion and $22 billion. Between January, 1948, and December 31, 1951, when the European Recovery Plan (as it was called) was replaced by the Mutual Security Program, the United States had made in the neighborhood of $15 billion available in loans and grants to 16 European nations. The European countries had, on their part, supplied another $9 billion in counterpart funds (that is, their own currency) to supplement the American grants. In 1950 this so-called Marshall Plan aid was extended to some countries in Asia.

☆ THE SHIFT FROM ECONOMIC TO MILITARY AID

The termination of the Marshall Plan in December, 1951, did not mark the end of foreign aid as a major factor in American foreign policy, although the name was changed to Mutual Security Program and the emphasis shifted somewhat from economic recovery and development to military assistance. With intensification of the cold war the program has continued with a dual purpose of military assistance and economic aid.

Trade and tariff policies have been important weapons in the American cold war against Communist countries since 1945.

> Exports of strategic items to the Soviet Union and its satellites were cut off, beginning in 1948, under Export Control legislation dating from 1940. All U.S. trade with Communist China and North Korea was prohibited beginning in 1950. With the passage of the Mutual Defense Assistance Control Act of 1951 the U.S. attempted to cut off strategic exports to the Communist bloc from other countries by threatening to withhold American aid. When Cuba's Fidel Castro allied himself with the Communist bloc in 1960 the U.S. cut off imports of Cuban sugar, and in 1962 . . . President Kennedy imposed an almost total embargo on U.S. trade with Cuba.[21]

Although these strict controls have been somewhat mitigated in recent years the use of trade policies as a weapon in the cold war continues.

Between 1946 and 1964 it is estimated that the United States had made available nearly $100 billion in economic and military assistance to foreign governments in virtually every quarter of the globe. Although they cannot be too sharply distinguished, the ratio of military to economic aid has shifted up and down with the years from nine-tenths economic aid in 1949 to nearly two-thirds military aid in 1953, and back

21 See *Congress and the Nation 1945–1964* (Washington, D.C.: Congressional Quarterly Service, 1965) , p. 189.

to about one-third military and two-thirds economic in 1964.[22] President Johnson's budget request for fiscal 1967 called for approximately $2 1/2 billion for the Agency for International Development, plus more than $1 1/2 billion for the so-called Food for Peace Program, exclusive of major grants for military assistance. Nor do these figures include budget requests to support the Export-Import Bank, the International Bank for International Development, the OAS, and the United Nations.

☆ ECONOMIC AID TO LATIN AMERICAN COUNTRIES

In 1961 a greatly expanded program of aid to Latin American countries was launched. Under the terms of the Declaration of Punta del Este of August, 1961, adopted by the United States and 19 other American republics (not including Cuba), the United States agreed to provide the major part of $20 billion for economic development in Latin America. The Latin American countries, on their part, "agree to devote a rapidly increasing share of their own resources to economic and social development." The need for economic development in Latin America and other underdeveloped areas of the world is great. Underlying the revolutionary tensions in Bolivia and Brazil, Paraguay and Peru, Nicaragua and Guatemala are annual per capita incomes of less than $200 a year. In Colombia, one of Latin America's more prosperous states, the GNP increase of about 2.5 percent a year falls behind a population growth rate in excess of 5.5 percent. This production gap is a major cause of poverty in most of South America. Poverty breeds illiteracy as illiteracy perpetuates poverty. Nearly 50 percent of the population in Latin America can neither read nor write. And although most of the people live on the land, more than 70 percent of the land is owned by less than 5 percent of the people. These are components in a situation that is ripe for revolution, a fertile soil for Communist penetration.

What is true in Latin America is, if anything, more vividly true in other underdeveloped areas of the world. With a dim, but dawning, consciousness that poverty is not a necessary evil, not part of the law of nature, people in these areas are coming to believe that economic progress, social justice, personal dignity, and political liberty are as possible for them as for others.

The program of foreign economic aid has now become a major feature of American foreign policy, second only in terms of cost to national defense.

> One of the brightest pages of the world's history [said President Kennedy in his 1962 Foreign Aid Message to Congress] has been the series of programs this nation has devised . . . to help free peoples achieve economic development and the control of their own destinies. . . .

[22] U.S. Department of Commerce, Office of Business Economics.

I realize that there are those who are weary of sustaining this continual effort to help other nations. But I would ask them to look at a map and recognize that many of those whom we help live on the "front lines" of the long twilight struggle for freedom. . . .

. . . All of our armies and atoms combined will be of little avail if these nations fall. . . .

This program [therefore] . . . is vital to the interests of the United States.

☆ AN APPRAISAL OF THE U.S. FOREIGN ECONOMIC AID PROGRAM

This vast program of economic aid has been justified or rationalized as necessary: (1) To check the spread of Communist power on the theory that "hungry nations are sick nations [and hence] prone to heed Communist propaganda." (2) Quite apart from the Communist threat, it is in our interest as a nation to assist underdeveloped countries to achieve economic maturity and viability, on the theory that "free prosperous and healthy nations are our natural allies." (3) To meet the revolution of rising expectations and to bring population growth and economic growth into balance, industrialization, modern methods of transportation and sanitation, improved systems of government and administration, and improved agricultural technology are necessary if we are to avoid violence, revolution, or civil war in these areas. (4) Unless we act, the Communist bloc, which is growing in power and influence, will win these uncommitted underdeveloped lands.

The foreign aid program however has not been without its critics and detractors, who say: (1) Too frequently our aid to underdeveloped countries has gone, not to benefit the people, but to ruling elites or dictators who have thus been saved from the just and righteous wrath of their own people. (2) Foreign aid, and especially aid to Western Europe, has enabled the United Kingdom, France, Italy, and even Germany and Japan, to build new and modern industrial plants and so become our most dangerous competitors. (3) Foreign aid, both economic and military, has not only replenished Europe's dollar resources, but has resulted in a dangerous deficit in the American balance of payments.[23]

---

[23] To American economists who note that, despite an excess of commercial exports over imports the United States faces a severe deficit in its international balance of payments, this charge against the foreign aid program needs particular attention. In this connection it is well to remember that a very large part of foreign aid expenditures are made in the United States in payment for food, raw materials, military matériel, machinery, and even personal services on behalf of foreign recipients of such aid. In his budget message of January 24, 1966, President Johnson emphasized this aspect of foreign aid expenditures. "Continual progress," he said, "is being made in tying

Even critics of foreign aid, however, generally admit that the Marshall Plan was a major factor in European recovery after World War II and probably helped to save Western Europe from falling under Communist control. But not everyone would agree that aid to underdeveloped areas has been equally successful. "I am forced . . . to the conclusion," said Robert Garner, former vice-president of the World Bank, "that economic development or lack of it is primarily due to differences in people . . . in their attitudes, customs, [and] traditions . . ." If "experience, competence, honesty, and organization," are lacking, "large injections of capital into developing countries can cause more harm than good."

Mr. Garner suggested six basic prerequisites for economic development: (1) Law and order, a "government which can govern"; (2) reasonably honest and effective public administration; (3) financial stability; (4) a "sensible plan" of economic development; (5) an honest and effective tax system; (6) avoidance of a "feudal" type of society in which the "wealth and power are in the hands of a few."

"In the less developed nations the drive for rapid advance under forced draft could . . . collapse into frustration and despair," Mr. Garner said. "There are explosive forces in vast pools of unskilled, uprooted, urban laborers, in landless social workers and in a class of intellectuals lacking outlets for their abilities and acutely aware of the disparities between rich nations and poor."[24]

Part of the problem is the compulsion of time and the demand for immediate results. It is well to remember that the industrialization of the Western nations took a long time. It takes time to train technical and managerial talent, to foster proper attitudes and loyalties, and to cope with exploding populations, technological change, and the mounting pressure for a better life.

Whatever balance may be struck in an appraisal of our foreign aid program, it has begun to produce serious complications in the overall foreign policy of the United States. During all except one or two years since the turn of the century the United States has had a favorable balance of foreign trade as measured by an excess of commercial exports over imports. Nevertheless, the United States has had a deficit in its total balance of payments in every year since 1949. How does it happen that a nation with a surplus of income from exports over imports has a deficit in

---

economic assistance programs to the purchase of goods and services in the United States. More than 80% of AID [Agency for International Development] expenditures in 1967 will be for the purchase of U.S. goods and services compared to about 42% in 1960. This minimizes the effects of our assistance program on the U.S. balance of international payments. In addition the foreign aid program assists the long-term *growth* of U.S. exports by stimulating new trade patterns and opportunities." See text of the budget message in *The New York Times,* January 25, 1966.

24 Louis Henkin (ed.), *Arms Control* (American Assembly; Englewood Cliffs, N.J.: Prentice-Hall, 1961), p. 54.

TABLE 24–1

U.S. Balance of International Payments

(In billion of dollars)

	1961	*1963*
Expenditures Abroad:		
Merchandise imports	$ 14.5	$ 17.0
Military expenditures	3.0	2.9
Other services	5.4	6.3
Remittances & pensions	.7	.8
Govt. grants, capital flow	4.1	4.5
U.S. private capital	4.2	4.1
TOTAL expenditures	$ 31.9	$ 35.6
Receipts from Abroad:		
Merchandise exports	$ 19.9	$ 21.9
Services, investments, income, military sales	8.4	9.7
Govt. loans repaid	1.3	1.0
Foreign investments in U.S.	.7	.8
TOTAL receipts	$ 30.3	$ 33.4
Transactions unaccounted for (net receipts, payments)	—.9	—.5
Balance of payments	$—2.4	$—2.7

SOURCE: *Congress and the Nation, 1954–1964* (Washington, D.C.: Congressional Quarterly Service, 1965), p. 191. Reprinted by permission.

its international balance of payments? Table 24–1 suggests part of the answer.

To remedy this deficit the following changes in our foreign policy have been suggested:

I. *A Sharing of the Burden.* Other nations having been restored to economic prosperity should now contribute to the total foreign aid program in amounts commensurate with their economic ability. Increased contributions to the cost of military defense should be made, especially by NATO. This would be particularly helpful, since military costs loom large in our balance-of-payments deficit.

II. A further expansion of American foreign trade by an active association of the United States with the burgeoning Common Market of Europe.

A. A first step in this direction was the ratification on March 23, 1962, of American membership in the Organization for Economic Cooperation and Development. The United States thus became an active member of a 20-nation economic grouping designed to promote policies of economic growth and stability in the free world.

B. A second step is an extension of the Reciprocal Trade Agreements policy to enable the United States to gain access to the European Common Market on terms mutually beneficial to the European members of the Common Market and the United States. To be excluded from this market could mean economic stagnation and political isolation. To have access to it could mean acceleration in our rate of economic growth, a more favorable balance of international payments, and an economic and political union that, in its capacity to produce and to assist in the economic development of the uncommitted countries of the world, could be a vastly more formidable bulwark against the growth of Communist power in the world.

This, in most general summary, is the new economic foreign policy of the United States. In reporting to Congress (March 7, 1962) on the tariff agreements recently reached in Geneva between the United States and the 6-nation European Common Market and 18 other countries, President Kennedy said:

> The European Common Market created in 1957 . . . establishes a giant economic community in Western Europe. It encompasses a market whose imports are greater than those of the U.S. . . . with a growth rate well in excess of the current U.S. growth rate . . . the six member countries of the European Community are rapidly eliminating tariffs within the community and are establishing a common external tariff . . . which will apply generally to products of outside countries including the U.S.
>
> At the same time (they) are merging their separate . . . programs for the protection of . . . agriculture into an integrated community-wide program . . . [to include] . . . a single . . . support price for each of several major agricultural commodities.
>
> In the face of these developments the U.S. objectives in the negotiations were two-fold:
>
> (1) to secure reductions in the common external tariff which would expand trade between the European Economic Community and the U.S.
>
> (2) to ensure that the common agricultural policy took account of the interest of U.S. agricultural exporters.
>
> These objectives were sought in the framework of the long-run U.S. policy of . . . expanding trading relations among free world nations.
>
> To a most encouraging degree, a careful reading of the report will indicate "these results were achieved."

Thus, although we have not come full course in reversing our policy of protective tariffs, we have moved a long step in that direction. There will be resistance to this new policy, and not alone from American interests that may be adversely affected. These can be provided for in a number of ways. The most dangerous resistance may come from those who are afraid to compete or who are sure that America cannot compete in markets open to the world. But as a distinguished American business-man has recently said: "It is a myth that U.S. businesses cannot compete with foreign business. We are competing successfully abroad. We are competing successfully at home. And we know how to compete in both areas in the future."[25]

The price of economic isolation, of trying to hide behind tariff walls or to seek sanctuary in quotas, drawbacks, or embargoes can be high. It can be higher today than in 1934 when Franklin Roosevelt, in inaugurat-ing the first Reciprocal Trade Program, said that declining world trade means "idle hands, still machines, ships tied to their docks, despairing farm households, and hungry industrial families." Moreover a declining world trade can mean a setback, even defeat, for the cause of democratic government in critical areas of the world.

☆ MILITARY POWER AND INTERNATIONAL RELATIONS

The monopoly of violence (of coercive power) which makes for law and order and peace and tranquility *within* the territory of the sovereign nation is lacking in the external relations of nation-states. In the absence of such a common power each nation is compelled to rely upon its own power—alone, or in alliance with other states—to provide for its own security against external attack. The race for supremacy or at least parity in both nuclear and conventional weapons and the negotiation of al-liances and regional defense or security pacts among the great powers are logical consequences of this situation. The Warsaw Pact among the Com-munist states of Eastern Europe, the North Atlantic Treaty Organization (NATO), the South East Asian Treaty Organization (SEATO) and the Organization of American States (OAS) among non-Communist nations of Europe, Asia, and the Americas are the tangible effects of this competi-tion for security through military supremacy. In the case of the United States, bilateral treaties with the Philippines, Japan, South Korea, and Formosa are other forms of security agreements, and in our generous policy of foreign aid mutual security grants loom large.

Although the state of nature among the nations of the world has not been one of perpetual war, it nevertheless has been a condition in which war is an ever-present and recurring fact of life. The roots of interna-tional conflict and war are many and varied and they lie deep in the economic, political, and cultural life of nation-states. Not even the most optimistic pacifist, we believe, anticipates a time when conflict among men and nations will cease. The best that we can hope for is not to banish conflict—presumably the struggle for gain, safety, and prestige

25 See Eric Johnson, *The New York Times,* March 11, 1962.

will go on—but to provide a forum, a congress, or a court in which conflicts *among* nations can be resolved by nonviolent means, just as conflicts among individuals are now normally resolved *within* the nation-state. The human condition being what it is, no such system among nations can hope to be fully successful without that monopoly of coercive power which the governments of nations now possess within their own territorial limits. The perpetual peace of which Immanuel Kant dreamed, therefore, is not likely to be a condition lacking in coercive power, but one in which the instruments of coercion will be controlled by some common power or authority, as Hobbes said, "to keep us all in awe."

Although the UN and the World Court, NATO, SEATO, the OAS, the Moscow Pact, and other regional or bilateral agreements provide for a wider sharing of responsibility for the common defense, no one, we believe, would argue that they do more than mitigate the Hobbesian state of nature within which nations continue to live.

Except for the UN and the World Court, these other institutions are little more than an extension of the system of military alliances that have characterized world politics for a thousand years or more.[26] How deeply and inextricably the United States is involved in all this can be seen in a map of our military alliances and installations around the world. It is a system of agreements and alliances made meaningful by the so-called cold war between Communist powers—the USSR, China, and their allies—and the non-Communist powers. The pattern of United States military arrangements in Europe, Asia, Latin America, and the Middle East reflect the basic American policy, since World War II, of "containing" Communism.[27]

By 1965 power in the world had been not only polarized between Communist and non-Communist states, with the United States at one pole and the USSR and Communist China at the opposite pole, but even this polarized structure had begun to change as the Russo-Chinese conflict emerged and the NATO alliance began to exhibit internal conflicts of major proportions. France finally withdrew from NATO, and the conflict between the USSR and Communist China continues to grow in scope and bitterness. Within these major polarities or alliances are upwards of 50 sovereign states, each with its own complement of force and violence, that is, of military power. Not all of the sovereign states of the world have been caught up in the basic Communist—non-Communist alignment. Among the uncommitted are most of the new nations of Africa, Saudi-Arabia, Iraq, and Afghanistan, in the Middle East; India and Indonesia, in South and South East Asia; Finland, Sweden, and Yugoslavia, in

---

[26] Some would argue that with the continual exclusion of states like Japan, Communist China, and Germany from membership, even the UN may appear to be a military alliance growing out of World War II.

[27] See *Congress and the Nation, op. cit.,* p. 232.

Europe. But the major powers—those whose guns, as it were, speak loudest—are found on one side or the other of a Communist—anti-Communist military alignment.

Although armies and navies have been transformed and the instruments of war revolutionized, and although only a handful of states can hope by their own unaided might to defend themselves against a major attack by a major power—all cling to military power as the sign and symbol, if not the substance, of their sovereignty and their security. Military policy remains, therefore, a central factor, perhaps *the* central factor in the foreign policy of most sovereign states.

How important the armed might of a nation can be was dramatically described by Winston Churchill in his book *The World Crisis*. Mr. Churchill was recalling his first visit to the Portsmouth naval base where the British Navy lay at anchor. His own yacht, he said, was surrounded by the great ships "so vast in themselves, yet so small, so easily lost on the surface of the waters. [Yet] on them floated the might, majesty, dominion, and power of the British Empire. . . . Open the sea-cocks and let them sink beneath the surface, and in a few minutes, half an hour at the most, the whole outlook of the world would be changed. The British Empire would dissolve like a dream. . . . "

As the world is and has been, the hidden and silent partners of every diplomat are the armed forces of the country he represents. The President's powers as Commander in Chief are among his most persuasive arguments as he speaks for the United States in the arena of world politics. Churchill expressed this situation in his phrase "we arm to parley." Cordell Hull, Franklin Roosevelt's Secretary of State, put the matter directly when he said that in negotiations with the Axis dictators, "They would look at me in the face but I soon discovered that they were looking over my shoulder at our Navy and our Army and that our diplomatic strength goes up or down with their estimate of what that [military strength] amounts to."

The history of mankind is full of examples to show how the balance or fulcrum of power can shift from one nation or group of nations to another with the shift in military strength. Military strength will, of course, depend upon many things—strategic location, natural resources, GNP, including the capacity for producing the machines and implements of war, and the size, skill, loyalty, and morale of the population. But military power in being, at any particular time, can be more decisive of a nation's status than military potential. Consider the shift in power reflected in these figures for American and British naval strength:

January 1939 U.K.	1,351,000	tons
" " U.S.A.	1,213,000	"
January 1945 U.K.	1,500,000	"
" " U.S.A.	11,707,000	"

By 1945 the United States had 61,000 naval vessels and the command of the sea had passed from London to Washington.

New weapons and methods of delivery, defense, and detection may also result in a dramatic shift in the power status of nations. The upsurge of American leadership among the great powers during and after World War II was due as much to an increase in its air power, to new explosives, new weapons and delivery systems, and new and radical devices for detecting enemy ships and planes as it was to an increase in naval power.

But even more dramatic in its effect upon the power status of the United States was the atomic bomb. It was America's monopoly of this new weapon, which, according to Churchill, more than anything else kept communism from sweeping over Europe in the first years following World War II. The precipitous demobilization of the Allied armies, and especially of the American army, accompanied by economic paralysis, widespread hunger, and discontent, might have enabled Communist armies, aided by well-organized Communist parties in France and Italy, to overcome the democratic governments of Western Europe.

The Marshall Plan for European Economic Recovery was a major factor in preventing this catastrophe. But the first line of defense, and who knows, maybe the decisive one, was the American Strategic Air Command and the Atomic Bomb. Speaking at MIT, March 31, 1949, Winston Churchill said: "It is certain that Europe would have been Communized like Czechoslovakia, and London would have been under bombardment some time ago but for the deterrent of the atomic bomb in the hands of the U.S." A few days later he told the House of Commons: "The situation [in Europe] is . . . unprecedented and incalculable. Over the whole scene reigns the power of the atomic bomb, ever growing in the hands of the U.S. It is this, in my mind, and this alone that has given us time to take the measures of self-protection and to develop the units which make those measures possible."

No one will ever know whether Mr. Churchill's analysis of the European situation was in fact a correct one. But it illustrates the immense weight that can be attached to military might in the foreign relations of sovereign states. In any case, the explosion of an atomic device by the Soviet Union in August, 1949, changed the situation again. Mr. Churchill was among the first to acknowledge this when on March 16, 1950, he urged "a conference on the highest level . . . between the leading powers without delay. . . . It might be that no hard and fast agreements would be reached, but there might be a general feeling among those gathered that they might do something better than tear the human race . . . into bits."

Problems of International Arms Control and Disarmament

Since it was obviously impossible to put this evil genie back into the bottle, American military policy has sought to bring nuclear weapons under some form of effective international control. In general outline this policy has had four major components.

1. To develop among the so-called nuclear powers (the U.S., the USSR, and the U.K.) some system of international control through the United Nations or otherwise to prevent the proliferation of nuclear weapons among other nation-states.
2. To work not only for arms control but also for disarmament; for a progressive reduction in both atomic and conventional weapons.
3. In the meantime, to exert every effort to maintain our own nuclear superiority by keeping ahead in the race for nuclear stocks, strategic bombers, super-bombs, missiles, and other modern weapons systems.
4. As a corollary of these policies, to strengthen our military alliances and bases in Europe and Asia, without conceding to our allies (except for the British) independent access to American nuclear weapons or know-how.

Within three months of its organization, the UN Assembly created a commission to study the control of atomic energy, and a month later, February 28, 1946, the American State Department issued the Acheson-Lilienthal report on the international control of atomic energy. This report became the basis for the so-called Baruch Plan presented by the American delegate to the UN Atomic Energy Commission. This plan for the international control of atomic weapons—the most ambitious, and, considering the American monopoly of atomic weapons at the time, a most generous plan—was approved in November, 1948, by the UN. In brief, it provided for an International Atomic Development Authority, to which the United States would turn over its atomic bomb secrets under international control and inspection, not subject to veto by any of the great powers. It provided, moreover, that there should be no further manufacture of atomic weapons and that existing stock piles of bombs should be destroyed. The Soviet Union offered a counterplan for outlawing atomic weapons, but with no provision for international control and inspection. In January, 1952, the Russian delegate to the Security Council of the United Nations, Andrei Vishinsky, proposed a plan for international control and inspection under the Security Council and hence subject to great power veto. But this was unacceptable to the United States. Moreover the bitterness engendered during the early 1950s by the Korean War, with Communist China's open intervention in that struggle against the UN forces led by the United States, put an end to any serious discussion of arms control or disarmament.

By 1953 the American monopoly of atomic weapons had given way to an approximate parity of atomic power between the United States and the USSR, resulting in a polarization of power which continues to be the most persistent and ominous fact of contemporary life. With the explosion of new and vastly more destructive hydrogen bombs, and with the development of Intercontinental Missiles bearing atomic warheads, of atomic-powered submarines and Polaris-type atomic missiles that can be fired from beneath the surface of the sea, and of a variety of other weapons systems, by both the United States and the USSR, the stalemate between the two great atomic powers produced a "balance of terror" upon which the peace of the world precariously depends.

Military policy of the great powers today is not so much a policy of defense or offense as it is a policy of deterrence. So terrible are the consequences of all-out war that no nation can contemplate the use of the weapons it spends so much time and treasure to accumulate. To achieve some measure of control over these new weapons systems, to put an end to further research and development of even more fiendish methods of annihilation, to prevent the proliferation of nuclear weapons among other powers, and perhaps some day to achieve a measure of reduction in the burden of all armaments—these are among the goals of American military and foreign policy, with priority second only to the security of the nation and the peace of the world. With the development of atomic weapons by France in 1960 and by Communist China in 1965 and their potential independent development by half a dozen other minor powers, the problems of proliferation and control have become immeasurably more urgent and more complicated.[28]

Problems of arms control and disarmament cannot realistically be solved in the absence of some accommodation of the major political problems that divide the world into rival camps. Armaments are as much an effect as a cause of political conflicts, although it is by no means easy to disentangle one from the other. An armaments race itself raises political problems of grand dimensions. It is possible that a reduction in armaments may contribute as much to a solution of political issues as a solution of political issues can contribute to reduction in armaments. One of the most successful and dramatic disarmament agreements in history was the Rush-Bagot agreement in 1817, which limited British and United States naval forces on the Great Lakes to four armed revenue cutters for each nation. It was negotiated at a time of great tension, in the wake of the War of 1812, and it did not precede but, rather, accompanied and helped to make possible the settlement and accommodation of outstanding political issues between Britain and the United States.

The political issues dividing the United States and the Communist world are of course more complex and difficult. They involve not merely economic, strategic, and political differences in the usual sense, but ideological differences that run deeper than boundary lines or conflicts over markets and resources. It is a conflict that no doubt will go on even in a disarmed and war-less world. Disarmament or arms control will not eliminate this struggle. But in a world freed from fear of nuclear war the ideological struggle may be less intense and in time may yield, as it shows signs of doing now, to new rationalizations more compatible with genu-

28 See "The Bomb: From Hiroshima To . . ."—a feature article in *Newsweek* Magazine, August 9, 1965, quoted in Peter H. Odegard, ed., *American Government: Readings and Documents* (New York: Harper & Row, 1966), pp. 593–597.

ine coexistence and to world peace. Arms control may reduce the fanaticism of fear arising in the USSR and China of encirclement by the United States, and in the United States, of Communist subversion and aggression.

The prospects for arms control and disarmament are not auspicious, although they are by no means hopeless.[29]

Formal organizations, both national and international, for continual discussion and negotiation of the complex issues involved have been established. The UN Atomic Energy Commission appointed in 1946 was in 1952 merged with the UN Commission for Conventional Armaments, which had been set up by the Security Council in 1947. Together these agencies became the UN Disarmament Commission, which, with varying membership, has kept the problems of arms control and disarmament on the agenda of the United Nations. On the theory that any realistic program of arms control or disarmament would require the concurrence of the great powers on the Security Council, the UN Commission included a Sub-Committee of Five composed of Canada, France, the U.K., the U.S., and the USSR. The Sub-Committee of Five, however, seemed forever deadlocked and led a fitful if not wholly fruitless existence from April, 1954, to September, 1957. To meet the Soviet demand for a "balanced" East-West forum, a 10-member Disarmament Committee was established in September, 1959, as advisory to the UN Disarmament Commission. The United States, the U.K., Canada, France, and Italy represented the West, while the USSR, Bulgaria, Czechoslovakia, Poland, and Rumania represented the East. But this too met with scant success and ceased to function in June, 1960, when the Soviet bloc members withdrew. Finally, in December, 1961, there was established an 18-nation Disarmament Committee to include not only the great powers and their satellites or allies but also the so-called "neutral" or noncommitted states. Notwithstanding the withdrawal of France from the committee in March, 1962, and notwithstanding discouraging internal tensions and conflicts, this committee has continued to function. It has, moreover, contributed to the most notable achievement in the field of arms control since World War II: the Nuclear Test Ban Treaty of 1963. It was a 3-nation subcommittee of the 18-nation Disarmament Committee, composed of the U.K., the U.S. and the USSR, that finally agreed to a treaty to ban nuclear explosions in the atmosphere or "in any other environment if such explosion causes radioactive debris to be present outside the territorial limits of the state under whose jurisdiction or control such explosion is conducted." Ratified not only by the major atomic powers (the U.S., the U.K., and the USSR) but by many nonnuclear states, the Test Ban Treaty of 1963, despite its limitations, represents an important step toward international control of nuclear weapons.

Another important advancement toward this end was achieved when, on July 1, 1968, 36 countries, including the United States and the

[29] John McCloy, "Balance Sheet of Disarmament," *Foreign Affairs*, April, 1962.

Soviet Union, signed a Nuclear Non-Proliferation Treaty. Under the terms of the treaty, the United States, the Soviet Union, and Great Britain agreed not to give other countries nuclear weapons, control over these weapons, or assistance in the development of them. The remaining countries who were signatories to the treaty committed themselves not to acquire or develop nuclear weapons.

However, a major problem remains. Both France and Communist China (the other two members of the uneasy nuclear weapons club) have refused to sign both the Test Ban Treaty and the Non-Proliferation Treaty, and both are building their own nuclear arsenal. Nor have the latter two countries been willing to join with other major powers in seeking more effective international control of nuclear weapons. The Test Ban Treaty itself, moreover, is limited to tests in the atmosphere, and each party to the treaty may withdraw "if it decides that extraordinary events related to the subject matter of the treaty have jeopardized the supreme interests of the country." But effective arms control or disarmament will not be achieved overnight. In searching for solutions to these and other problems of foreign policy we must be on guard against the illusion of an apocalyptic peace.

As matters now stand, the nuclear arms race may be arrested and brought under some measure of effective control through international agreements to (1) prevent the proliferation of nuclear weapons to countries which still are not covered by the 1968 treaty, (2) persuade France and Communist China to subscribe to an expanded treaty that will ban underground as well as atmospheric tests, (3) strive for regional agreements to limit nuclear armaments to present levels, and (4) begin serious negotiations for nuclear disarmament "by the actual dismantling or destruction of nuclear weapons and the means of their delivery."[30] Even these modest proposals are beset by monumental difficulties, not the least of which are (1) reasonable guarantees to protect nonnuclear states against nuclear attack by members of the so-called nuclear club, (2) safeguards against indirect access to nuclear weapons by nonnuclear powers through regional security agreements such as NATO and the Warsaw Pact, and (3) an effective system of inspection and control to ensure faithful observance of international agreements concerning nuclear weapons. Only when tangible steps have been taken to surmount these difficulties can we hope realistically to proceed toward nuclear disarmament. A somewhat hopeful sign was run up on the day the Non-Proliferation Treaty was signed, when the United States and the Soviet Union agreed to a series of discussions of limitations of missile systems and other steps toward disarmament. However, both of these promising developments were soon jeopardized when, on August 20, 1968, the Soviet Union and some of its Eastern European satellites militarily occupied Czechoslovakia in order to halt the liberalization of the Com-

[30] See "Halting the Nuclear Arms Race," in *International Affairs*, Report of the American Friends Service Committee, Vol. XIII, No. 1, February 25, 1966.

munist regime in that country. The tensions generated by this military invasion have (at the very least) delayed ratification of the Nuclear Non-Proliferation Treaty by the United States Senate and temporarily disrupted plans for broadened discussions of disarmament.

Although the possibility of nuclear warfare is the darkest cloud upon the international horizon, the problems of arms control and disarmament are not confined to nuclear weapons. So-called conventional weapons have become increasingly "efficient" and hence increasingly dangerous to the peace of the world. The examples of Korea, Suez, and South Vietnam, to name but three of many "hot spots" in the contemporary world, remind us that conventional warfare with conventional weapons remains an ever-present danger where national interests or hostile ideologies clash. And there is the correlative danger that "local wars" or "limited wars" with conventional weapons may escalate into nuclear wars. Moreover the burden of conventional armaments in terms of human as well as financial and economic costs may equal or exceed the burden of nuclear weapons.

Economic and Social Effects of Arms Control and Disarmament

The economic and social effects of the present armaments race—not only for the United States but for every great power—are second only to the ominous implications of nuclear war itself. A recent (1966) estimate of the total annual cost of arms and other defense items for the nations of the world exceeded $130 billions, or more than $40 for every man, woman, and child. In the United States these expenditures amount to nearly 70 percent of the federal budget and account for over 10 percent of our gross national product. Civilian employees of the Department of Defense alone exceed a million persons—nearly 50 percent of the total number of federal employees. To these one must add upwards of 3 million in the armed services—a number greater than the total of *all* civilian employees in *all* federal agencies. And beyond these are literally hundreds of thousands of employees engaged by private industry in the production of defense services and materials of wide variety. Included are thousands of employees and billions of dollars engaged in defense or defense-related scientific research and development.

The social and economic effects of the armaments race and disarmament are staggering and raise questions to which no simple answers are available: To what extent, for example, does our economic prosperity depend upon defense or defense-related activities? What is the effect on our total scientific research of this dependence on defense or defense-related appropriations and activities? Would a comprehensive and effective program of arms control and disarmament result in mass unemployment and economic and scientific stagnation? What alternatives are available to take up the slack "created by a massive reduction in defense expenditures?" Is the gargantuan defense program itself not a drag on the economy, a waste of precious natural and human resources, a major cause of financial inflation and economic instability? Would the American image abroad and our own national security be improved or impaired by a radical reduction in our foreign military aid and a corresponding increase in aid for economic and social development? What are the political effects of what President Eisenhower has called the "military-industrial complex," whose influence, he said, is "felt in every city, every statehouse, every office of the Federal Government"?

The international implications of all this are reflected in the appointment of a UN committee of experts in 1960 to study "the national economic and social consequences of disarmament in countries with different economic systems and at different stages of economic development." When Secretary Dag Hammarskjold later submitted a report titled "Economic and Social Consequences of Disarmament," he summarized the unanimous conclusions of the experts. "All the problems . . . of transition connected with disarmament," he said, "could be met by appropriate national and international measures [and that] there should thus be no doubt that the diversion to peaceful purposes of the resources now in military use could be accomplished to the benefit of all countries and lead to the improvement of world economic and social conditions."[31]

The importance of these and other questions that may be asked concerning arms control and disarmament are not likely to be answered in the immediate future. We can, however, take some comfort in the fact that official agencies of the United Nations, the United States, and other major powers have been established to seek answers to these problems. In addition to participation in the arms control and disarmament agencies of the United Nations, President Eisenhower in 1955 appointed Harold Stassen as Special Assistant to the President on Disarmament. When Mr. Stassen's negotiations with other nations brought him into conflict with the Secretary of State, his office was transferred to the State Department, where it was allowed to expire in 1958. In 1961, however, upon recommendation of President Kennedy, Congress established the United States Arms Control and Disarmament Agency under a director appointed by and responsible to the President. Although primarily a research agency, it plays an important role in the planning and organization of international negotiations on arms control and disarmament.[32] The scope of its responsibilities is reflected in the four major bureaus under which its work is organized: International Relations, Weapons Evaluation and Control, Science and Technology, and Economics. A Senate Committee

---

[31] See Richard Taylor, "Spears into Pruning Hooks: Some Politics of the Peace Race," in Rocco J. Tressolini and Richard T. Frost (eds.), *Cases in American National Government and Politics* (Englewood Cliffs, N.J.: Prentice-Hall, 1966), p. 286.

[32] The director of this agency has led the American delegation to the 18-nation disarmament conference at Geneva.

on Disarmament has also had these matters under study and in December, 1963, President Johnson appointed an interdepartmental Committee on the Impact of Defense and Disarmament.

The systematic search for viable policies that can lead to effective arms control and disarmament has thus been given higher priority than at any other time in our history. Between 1946 and 1961 the United States and the USSR participated in no less than 70 international conferences at which arms control and disarmament were discussed. At one of these, in September, 1961, the great powers agreed upon a joint statement: Principles to Govern Disarmament Talks. These principles included agreement that (1) "disarmament shall be general and complete and war shall no longer be an instrument for settling international problems," and (2) "disarmament shall be accompanied by the establishment of reliable proceedings for the peaceful settlement of disputes . . ." It is, of course, easier to agree on these general principles than it is to put them into practice.

Effective arms control and disarmament must wait upon the resolution of outstanding political issues and the reduction of international tensions among the great powers. Nevertheless there is a growing recognition that the arms race itself is a major source of international tension. Ultimately, no doubt, the final solution will be found in the development of an international police force under the United Nations or some similar world organization to provide for the peaceful resolution of international conflicts and for the prevention or punishment of military aggression. The example of United Nations Security forces in Korea, in the Congo, in Suez, and on Cyprus may prove to be a harbinger of things to come. "Given hostility and dependence on self-help," writes Robert Bowie, "no state will accept or carry out any measures for arms control which it believes will materially affect its relative ability to protect itself."[33] As we have moved in our search for security and peace from a balance of power among nations to a balance of terror in a polycentric world, we may see a balance of regional agreements gradually develop into a security pact to embrace all nations and all mankind. But this happy day lies in a dim and distant future.[34]

☆ THE STRUGGLE FOR THE MINDS OF MEN

"War," it has been said, "begins in the minds of men." So, it is also argued, the foundations of a lasting peace must ultimately rest upon the

[33] See Robert R. Bowie, "Arms Control and United States Foreign Policy," in Louis Henkin (ed.), *Arms Control: Issues for the Public* (American Assembly; Englewood Cliffs, N.J.: Prentice-Hall, 1961), p. 67.

[34] See Bernard Brodie, *Strategy in the Missile Age* (Princeton, N.J.: Princeton University Press, 1959); Herman Kahn, *On Thermonuclear War* (Princeton, N.J.: Princeton University Press, 1960); Donald Brennan (ed.), *Arms Control, Disarmament and National Security* (New York: Braziller, 1961).

ideas, attitudes, and opinions that prevail among ruling elites and the people who look to them for leadership. In the long run the success of diplomatic, economic, and even military, policies will depend upon public opinion, both at home and abroad. This is true of both modern dictatorships and democracies, but it is especially true of the United States, where public opinion, as the saying is, "rules the most." Through the press, radio and television, word-of-mouth conversation among individuals, through schools, churches, trade unions, service clubs, and thousands of organized channels of public communication, the people help to shape foreign policy. Presidents and Congresses, prime ministers and Parliaments, listen intently to what they say, for what they say and do is the best measure of public morale, on which all policy finally depends. From Periclean Athens to Lyndon Johnson's America and from the Ptolemys of Egypt to the tyrants of the late twentieth century, this has been true. Although the relationship between public policy and public opinion has been more direct and obvious in open or democratic societies, it has been a force that even dictators could not ignore.[35]

Commentators, such as Walter Lippmann, and professional diplomats, such as Dean Acheson, may deplore the intrusion of the people in the policy-making process, especially as it relates to foreign affairs; but even they recognize its importance, and as protagonists of particular policies, they too join in seeking to mold and mobilize that fickle and fugitive mistress of all free government: public opinion.

In the good old days, when public opinion was more latent than active, diplomats and their principals—kings, presidents and prime ministers—no doubt had more discretion, more freedom for maneuver. Negotiations were carried on in secret beyond the prying eyes of newsmen, radio commentators, TV cameras, congressional committees, and parliamentary commissions of inquiry. Even the final deals agreed upon, the alliances made, and the treaties formalized remained secret until the ruling elites themselves saw fit to make them public. Indeed it was against this pattern of secret diplomacy that the revolutionary leaders of the eighteenth and nineteenth centuries directed some of their most bitter protests.

Although much contemporary diplomacy is carried on in private conversations, and even formal negotiations are conducted in secret, Woodrow Wilson's plan for "open covenants openly arrived at" is widely

[35] See, for example, Wilhelm Bauer, *Die Öffentliche einung in der Welt Geschichte* (Wildpark, Potsdam, 1930) ; Harold Lasswell, *Propaganda Technique in the World War* (New York: Knopf, 1927) ; Harold Lasswell, *World Revolutionary Propaganda* (New York: Knopf, 1939) ; W. E. Daugherty (ed.) , *Psychological Warfare Case Book* (Baltimore, Md.: Johns Hopkins Press, 1958) ; Robert Blum (ed.) , *Cultural Affairs and Foreign Relations* (American Assembly; Englewood Cliffs, N.J.: Prentice-Hall, 1963) ; Gabriel Almond, *The American People and Foreign Policy* (New York: Harcourt, Brace & World, 1950) ; Wallace Carroll, *Persuade or Perish* (Boston: Houghton Mifflin, 1948) ; Daniel Lerner, *Propaganda in War and Crises* (New York: Stewart, 1951) ; B. L. Smith, Harold Lasswell, and Ralph Casey, *Propaganda, Communication and Public Opinion: A Comprehensive Reference* (Princeton, N.J.: Princeton University Press, 1946) .

observed, perhaps, indeed, too widely observed. However that may be, and however much the practice of "open covenants secretly arrived at" may be preferred by contemporary decision makers, none would deny the central importance of public opinion in the conduct of foreign affairs.

Nor is it only public opinion at home to which presidents and prime ministers, foreign secretaries and ambassadors must give attention. Equally important is public opinion abroad, not only in those countries whose friendship and cooperation we seek, but also in those which we regard as hostile or unfriendly. "Today," said the President's Committee on Information Activities Abroad (1961), "it is recognized that unless governments effectively communicate their policies and actions to all politically influential elements of foreign populations, their programs can be impeded and their security placed in jeopardy."

Conscious efforts to inform, mold, or manipulate public opinion both at home and abroad are of ancient vintage, although the science and art of international public relations or image making is a fairly recent development. Since World War II "propaganda" and "psychological warfare"—despite somewhat sinister implications—have become accepted if not wholly respectable instruments of modern war and diplomacy. George Creel's Committee on Public Information, in World War I, was but an American model of similar organizations operated by nearly every major power—both belligerent and nonbelligerent—during that struggle.[36] With President Wilson as the chief spokesman virtually every channel of communication, both at home and abroad, was used to carry on the war to "make the world safe for democracy." During World War II a vastly expanded Office of War Information (OWI) carried on a similar, if more subtle, campaign to mold and mobilize opinion at home and abroad in support of the Allied war effort and to undermine public morale among soldiers and civilians alike in the Axis countries.

Although formal campaigns of this kind were generally accepted in wartime, they were frowned upon in peacetime. Such activities as were carried on were left to unofficial organizations and to more modest, informal efforts of the President, the Department of State, and the Diplomatic and Consular Corps. After World War I the terms *propaganda* and *psychological warfare* fell into disrepute, and even formal official programs of "public information," "public relations," and "cultural relations," were suspect.

It was not until 1940 that an Office of Cultural Relations in the

---

[36] The French had their famous *Maison de la Presse*, the British their *Crewe House* operation under that arch propagandist, Lord Northcliffe. The Central Powers never quite succeeded in World War I in creating an effective central propaganda organization, although a culture committee of the General Staff and a *Zentralstelle für Aüslandsdienst* tried to meet this need. In World War II the Nazi Propaganda Ministry under Joseph Goebbels compensated—perhaps overcompensated—for German neglect of psychological warfare in World War I. When Dr. Goebbels declared early in that conflict that he was glad the Allies had no one comparable to Woodrow Wilson in World War II, he was paying tribute to a master in the art of international propaganda.

Department of State was established and in 1946 that an Office of Coordinator of Inter-American Affairs (CIAA) was created to promote intercultural relations between the United States and Latin America. An Office of Government Reports and an Office of Facts and Figures were also created about this time, as experiments in the coordination of the widely dispersed information offices of the federal government primarily concerned with domestic affairs. But all of these agencies were absorbed in the global jurisdiction of the Office of War Information, with domestic and overseas divisions, established by executive order of the President in June, 1942. With the liquidation of the OWI in 1945, an Office of International Information and Cultural Affairs in the Department of State was created to continue some of the activities of the more ambitious wartime agency. To provide statutory basis for these new peacetime efforts, a United States Information and Educational Exchange Act was passed by Congress in 1948 to be administered by an International Information Administration in the Department of State. This act (also known as the Smith-Mundt Act) authorized and directed the Secretary of State "to provide for the preparation and dissemination abroad of information about the United States, its people and its policies, through press, radio, motion pictures and other information media and through information centers and instructors abroad."

The new legislation not only put a congressional imprimatur on official overseas information and cultural activities, but more than doubled the funds available for these purposes. Finally, in 1953 the United States Information Agency (USIA), as an independent establishment under the President, was created, to be followed in 1961 by the United States Mutual Educational and Exchange Act, which outlined and authorized a program of information, education, and cultural exchange extending around the globe.

The scope and purpose of the USIA can be seen from the organizational chart (see Figure 24–1) and the official statement of the agency director himself. The purpose of the agency, he said

> is to help achieve U.S. foreign policy objectives by influencing public attitudes in other nations and advising the President, his representatives abroad and the various departments and agencies on the implications of foreign opinion for present and contemplated U.S. policies, programs and official statements. This purpose is carried out by using personal contact, radio broadcasting, libraries, book publication and distribution, press, motion pictures, television, exhibits, English language instruction and other means of communication to encourage public support abroad for U.S. policy objectives, and to unmask and counter hostile attempts to distort or frustrate the objectives and policies of the United States.[37]

This is indeed a broad mandate, and in carrying it into effect the USIA has engaged in virtually every form of communication and per-

[37] *U.S. Government Organization Manual, 1965–1966, op. cit.*, pp. 516 and 637.

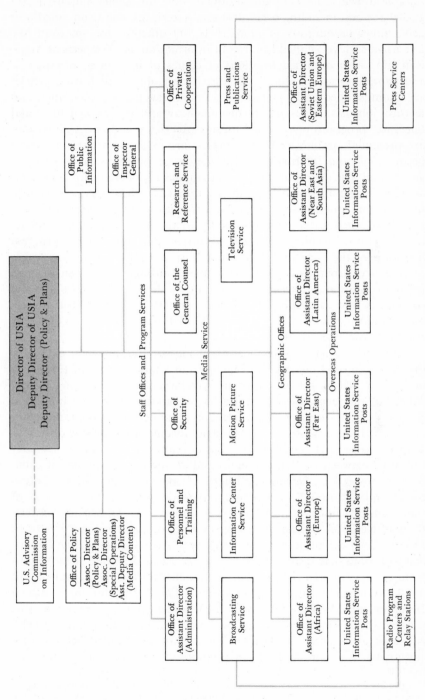

Figure 24-1 Organization of the United States Information Agency (USIA). (After *United States Government Organization Manual, 1966–67*, Washington, D.C., Revised, June 1, 1966, p. 648.)

suasion known to man. By the middle of 1964 the agency employed over 12,000 persons, including over 7,000 non-Americans, and maintained over 200 centers or outposts in more than 100 different foreign countries. Extensive and well-staffed libraries of information on all aspects of American life are maintained; millions of copies of magazines, newspapers, and pamphlets are produced and distributed; news and feature articles are commissioned and "placed" in foreign newspapers, magazines, and learned journals; thousands of documentary and educational films and television programs of recorded music, interviews, and panel discussions are presented; public lectures, concerts, art exhibits, ballets, theatrical productions, and international conferences or institutes are sponsored; and formal instruction in the English language is offered. Not least of its activities is the operation of an international broadcast service known as the Voice of America and beamed to reach not only listening publics in friendly countries, but more especially to those in Communist and so-called neutral, or noncommitted, countries. For nearly 1,000 program hours a week the Voice of America broadcasts in over 35 foreign languages to audiences around the world. How many millions may listen to these programs no one can accurately say, but the bitter jibes of Communist columnists and cartoonists and official protests of Communist governments and their studied efforts to jam VOA broadcasts indicate that they reach a considerable public.[38]

Nor do the activities of the USIA comprise the sum total of American efforts to reach the minds of men. From a modest start in 1938, with one policy officer and one full-time secretary, the Division of Cultural Affairs of the Department of State has expanded to become in 1961 a Bureau of Educational and Cultural Affairs under an Assistant Secretary of State with an extensive staff. With the income from the sale of American surplus property abroad, there has developed a program of scholarly exchange between the United States and an increasing number of countries. Sponsored by Senator Fulbright of Arkansas, the Mutual Educational and Cultural Exchange Act has made possible the exchange of thousands of scholars in nearly every field of human knowledge between the United States and an increasing number of countries. A Director of International Scientific and Technological Affairs, also in the Department of State, has responsibility for an overseas Scientific Attaché program and "serves as a central point of liaison with both Government and non-Government scientific organizations." The Agency for International Development (AID), established in December, 1961, supervises a vast program of nonmilitary foreign assistance reaching around the world. Not least of the State Department agencies is the so-called Peace Corps, authorized by statute in 1961 "to promote world peace and friendship"

---

[38] The frequency with which both friendly and unfriendly demonstrations in foreign capitals focuses on the American Information Agencies may be taken as a more or less subtle tribute to their effectiveness.

by making available to interested countries, men and women of the United States "to help the people of such countries and areas in meeting their needs for trained manpower, and to help promote a better understanding of the American people on the part of the people served and a better understanding of other peoples on the part of the American people."

Beyond the USIA, and the State Department, there are important bureaus or agencies in other departments of the federal government involved in the complex pattern of American foreign relations. A partial listing will indicate something of the nature and variety of these links between the United States and a shrinking, ever more closely integrated world. In addition to the Defense Department's military attachés in American embassies abroad and its military forces on every continent, there is an Assistant Secretary of Defense for International Security Affairs responsible for American military affairs in Africa, Latin America, the Near East, South Asia, and the North Atlantic area, plus Deputy Assistant Secretaries for Arms Control, International Logistics, Negotiations and foreign Military Assistance. The Treasury Department's Assistant Secretary for International Affairs supervises the work of eight Treasury Offices for (1) Latin America, (2) Industrial Nations and Developing Nations, (3) Balance of Payment Programs, (4) Operations and Statistics (overseas), (5) International Financial Policy Coordination and Operations, (6) International Gold and Foreign Exchange Operations, (7) International Economic Affairs, and (8) Administration of the Exchange Stabilization Fund. American participation in the operations of the International Monetary Fund, the International Bank for Reconstruction and Development, the Inter-American Development Bank, and foreign lending and assistance programs come to focus in the Treasury Department.

Nor do these agencies of the Departments of State, Defense and the Treasury exhaust the list of federal agencies concerned with the "nuts and bolts" of foreign policy. A Bureau of International Education and a Cuban Refugees Staff in the Department of Health, Education, and Welfare; a Bureau of International Labor Affairs in the Department of Labor; the United States Travel Service, a Bureau of International Commerce, and an Office of Foreign Commercial Services in the Department of Commerce; and a Foreign Agricultural Service, an International Agricultural Development Service, and an International Organization (or conference) staff in the Department of Agriculture are among other official agencies involved in this intricate web of international relations.

Equally, if not more important, are the innumerable unofficial individuals, groups, and agencies that help to project an image of the United States abroad. Millions of tourists viewing with contempt or condescension the strange ways of their foreign hosts, or with unalloyed admiration and envy their customs and traditions, their political institutions, and their cultural and educational resources, contribute to the American image and become an important factor in our foreign policy. Hundreds of American corporations with their thousands of employees share both credit and responsibility for the American image. Thousands of exchange students and scholars, including both Americans abroad and foreigners in America, newspaper correspondents, and motion picture producers and distributors are partners in the process. Not least of these unofficial channels of communication is the quasi-official Radio Free Europe, supported by voluntary subscription, which broadcasts news and comment and music and entertainment to the USSR and the Communist satellites in Eastern Europe.

However impressive the monumental official program of information, education, economic, and cultural relations may seem, and however much it may contribute to world peace, its total costs constitute no more than one percent of the annual expenditure for national security. And a good deal less than half of the roughly $500 or $600 million these multifarious activities cost is spent on the strictly educational, exchange or cultural components of the total program. An estimated half or more of the total goes for "non-official" (unacknowledged) propaganda, "where attribution to the U.S. Government is considered undesirable." This is not to say that the activities of the Central Intelligence Agency or other "undercover" operational or "intelligence" work is unimportant, but only that the secrecy that enshrouds these activities makes an objective evaluation of the total program difficult.[39] We cannot hope here to resolve the conflict over whether a strictly educational, informational, and cultural program is compatible with programs of policy-oriented propaganda, military "intelligence," espionage and undercover, quasi-military operations. Ideological guerrilla warfare is not generally regarded as an appropriate vehicle for what President Truman in 1950 described as a "campaign of truth" in international affairs. Nor is the struggle for the minds of men likely to be won by applying the simple slogans of commercial advertising to our foreign policy as was suggested by Senator Homer Capehart in 1961. The job of the USIA, he said, was to "sell the United States to the world, just as a sales manager's job is to sell a Buick or a Cadillac or a television set." Much more complex and subtle motivations and many more strongly "structured" attitudes and value systems are involved when nations speak to nations than when commercial salesmen speak to customers. "We are dealing," says Professor Padover "with

---

[39] There are, however, some crude methods for measuring the effectiveness of these programs. Among these are the circulation of magazines such as *America* and other publications in the USSR and other Communist countries, the attendance at art and other exhibits, conferences, lectures, and motion pictures, the number of persons using USIA libraries and information centers, the number of column inches "placed" in foreign newspapers, letters from listeners to the Voice of America or Radio Free Europe, and a number of fragmentary but not insignificant formal surveys of public opinion in foreign countries.

a world revolutionary situation, involving races and cultures and aspirations totally alien to the experience of the average advertising executive."

We ought not to expect too much of any program of education or cultural relations in building the foundations of a peaceful world. Nations, like individuals, are more likely to be judged by what they do than by what they say. The best-conceived and best-administered program of information and cultural relations will have a hard time, unless it is matched by public policies and behavior compatible and consistent with what is said. Words and music, ballet companies and exchange professors, can contribute immensely to a nation's foreign policy, but only, in the long run, if that policy appeals to the aspirations of other nations for independence, security, and welfare. "What you do," someone has said, "speaks so loudly I cannot hear what you're trying to say."

A nation's image in our modern world will depend not on its words alone, but also, and perhaps more significantly, on its deeds. "Ninety per cent of the impression which the United States makes abroad," said USIA Director George E. Allen, "depends upon our policies, and not more than 10 per cent, to make a rough estimate, on how we explain it."

In any case, the image of a nation is a vastly more complex thing than the image of man. The cartoonists' Uncle Sam and John Bull are scarcely adequate, although they may be better than nothing. Yet Uncle Sam—the long, lean, bewhiskered trader and philanthropist—intent on spreading light and learning, commerce and industry, goodness and truth, freedom and equality, can suddenly become Uncle Shylock, exacting a last pound of flesh from impoverished Europeans, or the Yankee freebooter imperialist and warmonger of Vietnam, or Cuba and everywhere else south of the border. John Bull, the jovial combination of Falstaff and Mr. Pickwick, freeing the slaves and transforming a colonial empire into a Commonwealth of Free Nations, can become Colonel Blimp—a snobbish, stupid image of colonialism and conquest or Perfidious Albion, upon whose word no honest man can rely.

The point is that the image of a nation, like the image of man, changes with circumstances and events—with the way its agents behave at various times and in various places, and with the way that behavior is perceived by its own and other people. And the public perception of a nation depends on many things: on knowledge and experience, on communication and contact, on imagination as well as information, on vision and reality.

As a general proposition one may say that the more we know about one another, about our systems of values—our traits of personality and character, our behavior patterns, customs and conventions—the more will the image correspond to reality.

The congruence of image and reality will not necessarily produce better interpersonal or international relations. It certainly cannot guarantee lasting friendships or mutual affection. Full and accurate knowl-

edge of a scoundrel will not make him any less a scoundrel. Full knowledge of the nature, values, and inner dynamics of Hitler and his Storm
Troopers would not have removed or materially reduced the tensions
generated by the conflicting ideologies, purposes, and goals that set us
apart.

But congruence of image and reality can produce understanding and
save us from the pitfalls of misunderstanding—from surprises, disillusionment, false hope, and groundless fears. When facts rather than
fantasy govern both our interpersonal and international relations, we are
less easily victimized or led astray by alternating moods of political
paranoia. We can, in a word, move with greater confidence and hence
with greater security in the world as it is, and not simply as we hope or
imagine it to be. To this extent, understanding (the congruence of our
image or perception of the world and reality) can contribute to the peace
and security of the world.

The gap between image and reality is always greater in relations
among nations than among groups and individuals within nations. As a
general rule we see a nation not as a whole but in fragments rarely tested
by firsthand knowledge and experience. From random bits and pieces of
information, from fortuitous contact and chance experience, we create
images of nations and their people. The image of a nation is thus a
compound of myth and metaphor, in which reality is at best an accidental component. It would, in fact, be more accurate to speak not of one
image, but of many, none of which is in very good focus and all of which
are subject to change without notice. And this is true not only of the
image that is projected by millions of tourists, exchange students, scholars, businessmen, and entertainers, but also by the official image projected by ambassadors and other public ministers and by the professional
image makers of the commercial movies and the USIA and other such
agencies. It requires no little sophistication in a French or English
citizen, let alone a Chinese, Arab, or Vietnamese, to reconcile the image
of America projected by films such as *National Velvet, Rebecca of Sunny-
brook Farm, Fugitive from a Chain Gang, An American Tragedy,* a
typical gangster epic of crime and corruption, and *How the West Was
Won.*

The fact is that life in the United States, as in other countries too,
presents a pattern of such variety, of such contrast and contradiction
that whatever one says about it is probably true of some part or parcel of
it. Hence the image of America held by most foreigners depends upon
those aspects of American life that come within their angle of vision or
experience. In those countries where schools and other communication
media are centrally controlled, where travel is restricted and interpersonal relations are under close and constant scrutiny, the image of the
American can be almost anything the government wants it to be. It will,
accordingly, be more likely to reflect the official posture of the govern-

ment toward the United States and its policies than it will any firm or constant image of America.

Even in those countries where some measure of freedom is allowed, the American image that appears in the mass media is likely to be conditioned by events, by international crises, or by domestic conflict. An exchange of epithets, threats and counterthreats by both official and unofficial spokesmen of the great powers, and news of espionage and counterespionage is likely to get a better "play" than expressions of mutual confidence or news of the friendly adjustment of potential conflict. News of domestic infidelity, of corruption, crime, and vice, of strikes, race riots, and mob violence, of celebrities enmeshed in scandal, of two-headed calves and talking dogs sell more papers than less sensational accounts of life in the United States.

Against this background the wonder is, not that the American image abroad is so bad, but that on the whole it has been so good.

APPENDICES

THE DECLARATION
OF INDEPENDENCE

WHEN, IN THE COURSE of human events, it becomes necessary for one people to dissolve the political bands which have connected them with another, and to assume, among the powers of the earth, the separate and equal station to which the laws of nature and of nature's God entitle them, a decent respect to the opinions of mankind requires that they should declare the causes which impel them to the separation.

We hold these truths to be self-evident: That all men are created equal; that they ·are endowed by their Creator with certain unalienable rights; that among these are life, liberty, and the pursuit of happiness. That, to secure these rights, governments are instituted among men, deriving their just powers from the consent of the governed; that, whenever any form of government becomes destructive of these ends, it is the right of the people to alter or to abolish it, and to institute a new government, laying its foundation on such principles, and organizing its powers in such form, as to them shall seem most likely to effect their safety and happiness. Prudence, indeed, will dictate that governments long established should not be changed for light and transient causes; and accordingly all experience hath shown that mankind are more disposed to suffer while evils are sufferable, than to right themselves by abolishing the forms to which they are accustomed. But when a long train of abuses and usurpations, pursuing invariably the same object, evinces a design to reduce them under absolute despotism, it is their right, it is their duty, to throw off such government, and to provide new guards for their future security. Such has been the patient sufferance of these colonies; and such is now the necessity which constrains them to alter their former systems of government. The history of the present King of Great Britain is a history of repeated injuries and usurpations, all having in direct object the establishment of an absolute tyranny over these states. To prove this, let facts be submitted to a candid world.

He has refused his assent to laws the most wholesome and necessary for the public good.

He has forbidden his governors to pass laws of immediate and pressing importance, unless suspended in their operation till his assent should be obtained; and, when so suspended, he has utterly neglected to attend to them.

He has refused to pass other laws for the accommodation of large districts of people, unless those people would relinquish the right of representation in the legislature,—a right inestimable to them, and formidable to tyrants only.

He has called together legislative bodies at places unusual, uncomfortable, and distant from the depository of their public records, for the sole purpose of fatiguing them into compliance with his measures.

He has dissolved representative houses repeatedly, for opposing, with manly firmness, his invasions on the rights of the people.

He has refused, for a long time after such dissolutions, to cause others to be elected, whereby the legislative powers, incapable of annihilation, have returned to the people at large for their exercise; the state remaining, in the mean time, exposed to all the dangers of invasions from without and convulsions within.

He has endeavored to prevent the population of these states; for that purpose obstructing the laws for the naturalization of foreigners, refusing to pass others to encourage their migration hither, and raising the conditions of new appropriations of lands.

He has obstructed the administration of justice, by refusing his assent to laws for establishing judiciary powers.

He has made judges dependent on his will alone for the tenure of their offices, and the amount and payment of their salaries.

He has erected a multitude of new offices, and sent hither swarms of officers to harass our people and eat out their substance.

He has kept among us in times of peace standing armies, without the consent of our legislatures.

He has affected to render the military independent of, and superior to, the civil power.

He has combined with others to subject us to a jurisdiction foreign to our constitutions and unacknowledged by our laws, giving his assent to their acts of pretended legislation:

For quartering large bodies of armed troops among us;

For protecting them, by a mock trial, from punishment for any murders which they should commit on the inhabitants of these states;

For cutting off our trade with all parts of the world;

For imposing taxes on us without our consent;

For depriving us, in many cases, of the benefits of trial by jury;

For transporting us beyond seas, to be tried for pretended offenses;

For abolishing the free system of English laws in a neighboring province, establishing therein an arbitrary government, and enlarging its boundaries, so as to render it at once an example and fit instrument for introducing the same absolute rule into these colonies;

For taking away our charters, abolishing our most valuable laws, and altering, fundamentally, the forms of our governments;

For suspending our own legislatures, and declaring themselves invested with power to legislate for us in all cases whatsoever.

He has abdicated government here, by declaring us out of his protection and waging war against us.

He has plundered our seas, ravaged our coasts, burned our towns, and destroyed the lives of our people.

He is at this time transporting large armies of foreign mercenaries to complete the works of death, desolation, and tyranny already begun with circumstances of cruelty and perfidy scarcely paralleled in the most barbarous ages, and totally unworthy the head of a civilized nation.

He has constrained our fellow-citizens, taken captive on the high seas, to bear arms against their country, to become the executioners of their friends and brethren, or to fall themselves by their hands.

He has excited domestic insurrection among us, and has endeavored to bring on the inhabitants of our frontiers the merciless Indian savages, whose known rule of warfare is an undistinguished destruction of all ages, sexes, and conditions.

In every stage of these oppressions we have petitioned for redress in the most humble terms; our repeated petitions have been answered only by repeated injury.

A prince whose character is thus marked by every act which may define a tyrant is unfit to be the ruler of a free people.

Nor have we been wanting in our attentions to our British brethren. We have warned them, from time to time, of attempts by their legislature to extend an unwarrantable jurisdiction over us. We have reminded them of the circumstances of our emigration and settlement here. We have appealed to their native justice and magnanimity; and we have conjured them, by the ties of our common kindred, to disavow these usurpations, which would inevitably interrupt our connections and correspondence. They, too, have been deaf to the voice of justice and consanguinity. We must, therefore, acquiesce in the necessity which denounces our separation, and hold them, as we hold the rest of mankind, enemies in war, in peace friends.

We, therefore, the representatives of the United States of America, in General Congress assembled, appealing to the Supreme Judge of the world for the rectitude of our intentions, do, in the name and by the authority of the good people of these colonies, solemnly publish and declare, That these united colonies are, and of right ought to be, free and independent states; that they are absolved from all allegiance to the British Crown, and that all political connection between them and the state of Great Britain is, and ought to be, totally dissolved; and that, as free and independent states, they have full power to levy war, conclude peace, contract alliances, establish commerce, and do all other acts and things which independent states may of right do. And, for the support of this declaration, with a firm reliance on the protection of Divine Providence, we mutually pledge to each other our lives, our fortunes, and our sacred honor.

THE CONSTITUTION
OF THE UNITED STATES

PREAMBLE. *We the people of the United States, in order to form a more perfect union, establish justice, insure domestic tranquility, provide for the common defense, promote the general welfare, and secure the blessings of liberty to ourselves and our posterity, do ordain and establish this Constitution for the United States of America.*

ARTICLE I *(Legislative Department)*

SECTION I *(Congress)*

All legislative powers herein granted shall be vested in a Congress of the United States, which shall consist of a Senate and a House of Representatives.

SECTION II *(House of Representatives)*

1 The House of Representatives shall be composed of members chosen every second year by the people of the several States, and the electors in each State shall have the qualifications requisite for electors of the most numerous branch of the State Legislature.

2 No person shall be a Representative who shall not have attained to the age of twenty-five years, and been seven years a citizen of the United States, and who shall not, when elected, be an inhabitant of that State in which he shall be chosen.

3 Representatives and direct taxes shall be apportioned among the several States which may be included within this Union, according to their respective numbers, which shall be determined by adding to the whole number of free persons, including those bound to service for a term of years, and excluding Indians not taxed, three fifths of all other persons. The actual enumeration shall be made within three years after the first meeting of the Congress of the United States, and within every subsequent term of ten years, in such manner as they shall by law direct. The number of Representatives shall not exceed one for every thirty thousand, but each State shall have at least one representative; and until such enumeration shall be made, the State of New Hampshire shall be entitled to choose three, Massachusetts eight, Rhode Island and Providence Plantations one, Connecticut five, New York six, New Jersey four, Pennsylvania eight, Delaware one, Maryland six, Virginia ten, North Carolina five, South Carolina five, and Georgia three.

4 When vacancies happen in the representation from any State, the Executive authority thereof shall issue writs of election to fill such vacancies.

5 The House of Representatives shall choose their Speaker and other officers; and shall have the sole power of impeachment.

SECTION III (Senate)

1 The Senate of the United States shall be composed of two Senators from each State, chosen by the legislature thereof, for six years; and each Senator shall have one vote.

2 Immediately after they shall be assembled in consequence of the first election, they shall be divided as equally as may be into three classes. The seats of the Senators of the first class shall be vacated at the expiration of the second year, of the second class at the expiration of the fourth year, and of the third class at the expiration of the sixth year, so that one third may be chosen every second year; and if vacancies happen by resignation or otherwise, during the recess of the legislature of any State, the Executive thereof may make temporary appointments until the next meeting of the legislature, which shall then fill such vacancies.

3 No person shall be a Senator who shall not have attained the age of thirty years, and been nine years a citizen of the United States, and who shall not, when elected, be an inhabitant of that State for which he shall be chosen.

4 The Vice-President of the United States shall be President of the Senate, but shall have no vote, unless they be equally divided.

5 The Senate shall choose their other officers, and also a President *pro tempore,* in the absence of the Vice-President, or when he shall exercise the office of President of the United States.

6 The Senate shall have the sole power to try all impeachments.

When sitting for that purpose, they shall be on oath or affirmation. When the President of the United States is tried, the Chief Justice shall preside: and no person shall be convicted without the concurrence of two thirds of the members present.

7 Judgment in cases of impeachment shall not extend further than to removal from office, and disqualification to hold and enjoy any office of honor, trust or profit under the United States: but the party convicted shall nevertheless be liable and subject to indictment, trial, judgment and punishment, according to law.

SECTION IV *(Election and Meetings of Congress)*

1 The times, places and manner of holding elections for Senators and Representatives shall be prescribed in each State by the legislature thereof; but the Congress may at any time by law make or alter such regulations, except as to the places of choosing Senators.

2 The Congress shall assemble at least once in every year, and such meeting shall be on the first Monday in December, unless they shall by law appoint a different day.

SECTION V *(Organization and Rules of the Houses)*

1 Each house shall be the judge of the elections, returns and qualifications of its own members, and a majority of each shall constitute a quorum to do business; but a smaller number may adjourn from day to day, and may be authorized to compel the attendance of absent members, in such manner, and under such penalties, as each house may provide.

2 Each house may determine the rules of its proceedings, punish its members for disorderly behavior, and with the concurrence of two thirds, expel a member.

3 Each house shall keep a journal of its proceedings, and from time to time publish the same, excepting such parts as may in their judgment require secrecy; and the yeas and nays of the members of either house on any question shall, at the desire of one fifth of those present, be entered on the journal.

4 Neither house, during the session of Congress, shall, without the consent of the other, adjourn for more than three days, nor to any other place than that in which the two houses shall be sitting.

SECTION VI *(Privileges and Prohibitions upon Congressmen)*

1 The Senators and Representatives shall receive a compensation for their services, to be ascertained by law and paid out of the treasury of

the United States. They shall in all cases except treason, felony and breach of the peace, be privileged from arrest during their attendance at the session of their respective houses, and in going to and returning from the same; and for any speech or debate in either house, they shall not be questioned in any other place.

2 No Senator or Representative shall, during the time for which he was elected, be appointed to any civil office under the authority of the United States, which shall have been created, or the emoluments whereof shall have been increased, during such time; and no person holding any office under the United States shall be a member of either house during his continuance in office.

SECTION VII (*Method of Making Laws*)

1 All bills for raising revenue shall originate in the House of Representatives; but the Senate may propose or concur with amendments as on other bills.

2 Every bill which shall have passed the House of Representatives and the Senate, shall, before it become a law, be presented to the President of the United States; if he approve he shall sign it, but if not he shall return it with his objections to that house in which it shall have originated, who shall enter the objections at large on their journal, and proceed to reconsider it. If after such reconsideration two-thirds of that house shall agree to pass the bill, it shall be sent, together with the objections, to the other house, by which it shall likewise be reconsidered, and, if approved by two thirds of that house, it shall become a law. But in all such cases the votes of both houses shall be determined by yeas and nays, and the names of the persons voting for and against the bill shall be entered on the journal of each house respectively. If any bill shall not be returned by the President within ten days (Sundays excepted) after it shall have been presented to him, the same shall be a law, in like manner as if he had signed it, unless the Congress by their adjournment prevent its return, in which case it shall not be a law.

3 Every order, resolution, or vote to which the concurrence of the Senate and House of Representatives may be necessary (except on a question of adjournment) shall be presented to the President of the United States; and before the same shall take effect, shall be approved by him, or being disapproved by him, shall be repassed by two thirds of the Senate and House of Representatives, according to the rules and limitations prescribed in the case of a bill.

SECTION VIII (*Powers Granted to Congress*)

1 The Congress shall have power to lay and collect taxes, duties, imports, and excises, to pay the debts and provide for the common defence and general welfare of the United States; but all duties, imposts and excises shall be uniform throughout the United States;

2   To borrow money on the credit of the United States;

3   To regulate commerce with foreign nations, and among the several States, and with the Indian tribes;

4   To establish an uniform rule of naturalization, and uniform laws on the subject of bankruptcies throughout the United States;

5   To coin money, regulate the value thereof, and of foreign coin, and fix the standard of weights and measures;

6   To provide for the punishment of counterfeiting the securities and current coin of the United States;

7   To establish post offices and post roads;

8   To promote the progress of science and useful arts by securing for limited times to authors and inventors the exclusive right to their respective writings and discoveries;

9   To constitute tribunals inferior to the Supreme Court;

10   To define and punish piracies and felonies committed on the high seas and offences against the law of nations;

11   To declare war, grant letters of marque and reprisal, and make rules concerning captures on land and water.

12   To raise and support armies, but no appropriation of money to that use shall be for a longer term than two years.

13   To provide and maintain a navy;

14   To make rules for the government and regulation of the land and naval forces;

15   To provide for calling forth the militia to execute the laws of the Union, suppress insurrections, and repel invasions;

16   To provide for organizing, arming and disciplining the militia, and for governing such part of them as may be employed in the service of the United States, reserving to the States respectively the appointment of the officers, and the authority of training the militia according to the discipline prescribed by Congress;

17   To exercise exclusive legislation in all cases whatsoever, over such district (not exceeding ten miles square) as may, by cession of particular States, and the acceptance of Congress, become the seat of government of the United States, and to exercise like authority over all places purchased by the consent of the legislature of the State, in which the same shall be, for the erection of forts, magazines, arsenals, dock-yards, and other needful buildings;—And

18   To make all laws which shall be necessary and proper for carrying into execution the foregoing powers, and all other powers vested by this Constitution in the government of the United States, or in any department or office thereof.

SECTION IX (*Restrictions on the United States*)

1   The migration or importation of such persons as any of the States now existing shall think proper to admit shall not be prohibited by

the Congress prior to the year 1808; but a tax or duty may be imposed on such importation, not exceeding $10 for each person.

2 The privilege of the writ of *habeas corpus* shall not be suspended, unless when in cases of rebellion or invasion the public safety may require it.

3 No bill of attainder or *ex post facto* law shall be passed.

4 No capitation, or other direct, tax shall be laid, unless in proportion to the census or enumeration herein before directed to be taken.

5 No tax or duty shall be laid on articles exported from any State.

6 No preference shall be given by any regulation of commerce or revenue to the ports of one State over those of another: nor shall vessels bound to, or from, one State, be obliged to enter, clear, or pay duties in another.

7 No money shall be drawn from the treasury, but in consequence of appropriations made by law; and a regular statement and account of the receipts and expenditures of all public money shall be published from time to time.

8 No title of nobility shall be granted by the United States: and no person holding any office of profit or trust under them, shall, without the consent of the Congress, accept of any present, emolument, office, or title, of any kind whatever, from any king, prince, or foreign state.

SECTION X *(Restrictions on the States)*

1 No State shall enter into any treaty, alliance, or confederation; grant letters of marque and reprisal; coin money; emit bills of credit; make anything but gold and silver coin a tender in payment of debts; pass any bill of attainder, *ex post facto* law, or law impairing the obligation of contracts, or grant any title of nobility.

2 No State shall, without the consent of the Congress, lay any imposts or duties on imports or exports, except what may be absolutely necessary for executing its inspection laws: and the net produce of all duties and imposts, laid by any State on imports or exports, shall be for the use of the treasury of the United States; and all such laws shall be subject to the revision and control of the Congress.

3 No State shall, without the consent of Congress, lay any duty of tonnage, keep troops or ships of war in time of peace, enter into any agreement or compact with another State, or with a foreign power, or engage in war, unless actually invaded, or in such imminent danger as will not admit of delay.

ARTICLE II *(Executive Department)*

SECTION I *(President and Vice-President)*

1 The executive power shall be vested in a President of the United States of America. He shall hold his office during the term of four

years, and together with the Vice-President, chosen for the same term, be elected as follows:

2 Each State shall appoint, in such manner as the legislature thereof may direct, a number of electors, equal to the whole number of Senators and Representatives to which the State may be entitled in the Congress; but no Senator or Representative, or person holding an office of trust or profit under the United States, shall be appointed an elector.

3 The electors shall meet in their respective States, and vote by ballot for two persons, of whom one at least shall not be an inhabitant of the same State with themselves. And they shall make a list of all the persons voted for, and of the number of votes for each; which list they shall sign and certify, and transmit sealed to the seat of government of the United States, directed to the President of the Senate. The President of the Senate shall, in the presence of the Senate and House of Representatives, open all the certificates, and the votes shall then be counted. The person having the greatest number of votes shall be the President, if such number be a majority of the whole number of electors appointed; and if there be more than one who have such majority, and have an equal number of votes, then the House of Representatives shall immediately choose by ballot one of them for President; and if no person have a majority, then from the five highest on the list the said house shall in like manner choose the President. But in choosing the President the votes shall be taken by States, the representation from each State having one vote; a quorum for this purpose shall consist of a member or members from two thirds of the States, and a majority of all the States shall be necessary to a choice. In every case, after the choice of the President, the person having the greatest number of votes of the electors shall be the Vice-President. But if there should remain two or more who have equal votes, the Senate shall choose from them by ballot the Vice-President.

4 The Congress may determine the time of choosing the electors and the day on which they shall give their votes; which day shall be the same throughout the United States.

5 No person except a natural-born citizen, or a citizen of the United States, at the time of the adoption of this Constitution, shall be eligible to the office of President; neither shall any person be eligible to that office who shall not have attained to the age of thirty-five years, and been fourteen years a resident within the United States.

6 In case of the removal of the President from office or of his death, resignation, or inability to discharge the powers and duties of the said office, the same shall devolve on the Vice-President, and the Congress may by law provide for the case of removal, death, resignation, or inability, both of the President and Vice-President, declaring what officer shall then act as President, and such officer shall act accordingly, until the disability be removed, or a President shall be elected.

7 The President shall, at stated times, receive for his services a compensation, which shall neither be increased nor diminished during

the period for which he shall have been elected, and he shall not receive within that period any other emolument from the United States, or any of them.

8   Before he enter on the execution of his office, he shall take the following oath of affirmation:—"I do solemnly swear (or affirm) that I will faithfully execute the office of President of the United States, and will to the best of my ability preserve, protect and defend the Constitution of the United States."

SECTION II (*Powers of the President*)

1   The President shall be commander in chief of the army and navy of the United States, and of the militia of the several States, when called into the actual service of the United States; he may require the opinion, in writing, of the principal officer in each of the executive departments, upon any subject relating to the duties of their respective offices, and he shall have power to grant reprieves and pardons for offences against the United States, except in cases of impeachment.

2   He shall have power, by and with the advice and consent of the Senate, to 'make treaties, provided two thirds of the Senators present concur.

And he shall nominate, and by and with the advice and consent of the Senate, shall appoint ambassadors, other public ministers and consuls, judges of the Supreme Court, and all other officers of the United States, whose appointments are not herein otherwise provided for, and which shall be established by law: but the Congress may by law vest the appointment of such inferior officers, as they think proper, in the President alone, in the courts of law, or in the heads of departments.

3   The President shall have power to fill up all vacancies that may happen during the recess of the Senate, by granting commissions which shall expire at the end of their next session.

SECTION III (*Other Powers and Duties of the President*)

He shall from time to time give to the Congress information of the state of the Union, and recommend to their consideration such measures as he shall judge necessary and expedient; he may, on extraordinary occasions, convene both houses, or either of them, and in case of disagreement between them, with respect to the time of adjournment, he may adjourn them to such time as he shall think proper; he shall receive ambassadors and other public ministers; he shall take care that the laws be faithfully executed, and shall commission all the officers of the United States.

SECTION IV (Impeachment)

The President, Vice-President and all civil officers of the United States shall be removed from office on impeachment for, and on conviction of, treason, bribery, or other high crimes and misdemeanors.

ARTICLE III (Judicial Department)

SECTION I (Federal Courts)

The judicial power of the United States shall be vested in one Supreme Court, and in such inferior courts as Congress may from time to time ordain and establish. The judges, both of the Supreme and inferior courts, shall hold their offices during good behavior, and shall, at stated times, receive for their services a compensation which shall not be diminished during their continuance in office.

SECTION II (Jurisdiction of Federal Courts)

1   The judicial power shall extend to all cases, in law and equity, arising under this Constitution, the laws of the United States, and treaties made or which shall be made, under their authority;—to all cases affecting ambassadors, other public ministers and consuls;—to all cases of admiralty and maritime jurisdiction;—to controversies to which the United States shall be a party;—to controversies between two or more States;—between a State and citizens of another State;—between citizens of different States;—between citizens of the same State claiming lands under grants of different States, and between a State, or the citizens thereof, and foreign states, citizens or subjects.

2   In all cases affecting ambassadors, other public ministers and consuls, and those in which a State shall be a party, the Supreme Court shall have original jurisdiction. In all other cases before mentioned, the Supreme Court shall have appellate jurisdiction, both as to law and fact, with such exceptions and under such regulations as the Congress shall make.

3   The trial of all crimes, except in cases of impeachment, shall be by jury; and such trial shall be held in the State where the said crimes shall have been committed; but when not committed within any State, the trial shall be at such place or places as the Congress may by law have directed.

SECTION III (Treason)

1   Treason against the United States shall consist only in levying war against them, or in adhering to their enemies, giving them aid and

comfort. No person shall be convicted of treason unless on the testimony of two witnesses to the same overt act, or on confession in open court.

2 The Congress shall have power to declare the punishment of treason, but no attainder of treason shall work corruption of blood, or forfeiture except during the life of the person attainted.

ARTICLE IV *(Relations of the States to One Another)*

SECTION I *(Credit to Acts, Records, and Court Proceedings)*

Full faith and credit shall be given in each State to the public acts, records, and judicial proceedings of every other State. And the Congress may by general laws prescribe the manner in which such acts, records, and proceedings shall be proved, and the effect thereof.

SECTION II *(Duties of States to States)*

1 The citizens of each State shall be entitled to all privileges and immunities of citizens in the several States.

2 A person charged in any State with treason, felony, or other crime, who shall flee from justice, and be found in another State, shall on demand of the executive authority of the State from which he fled, be delivered up, to be removed to the State having jurisdiction of the crime.

3 No person held to service or labor in one State, under the laws thereof, escaping into another, shall, in consequence of any law or regulation therein, be discharged from such service or labor, but shall be delivered up on claim of the party to whom such service or labor may be due.

SECTION III *(New States and Territories)*

1 New States may be admitted by the Congress into this Union; but no new State shall be formed or erected within the jurisdiction of any other State; nor any State be formed by the junction of two or more States, or parts of States, without the consent of the legislatures of the States concerned as well as of the Congress.

2 The Congress shall have power to dispose of and make all needful rules and regulations respecting the territory or other property belonging to the United States; and nothing in this Constitution shall be so construed as to prejudice any claims of the United States, or of any particular State.

SECTION IV *(Protection to the States)*

The United States shall guarantee to every state in this Union a republican form of government, and shall protect each of them against invasion; and on application of the legislature, or of the executive (when the legislature cannot be convened) against domestic violence.

ARTICLE V (*The Process of Amendment*)

The Congress, whenever two thirds of both houses shall deem it necessary, shall propose amendments to this Constitution, or, on the application of the legislatures of two thirds of the several States, shall call a convention for proposing amendments, which in either case shall be valid to all intents and purposes, as part of this Constitution, when ratified by the legislatures of three fourths of the several States, or by conventions in three fourths thereof, as the one or the other mode of ratification may be proposed by the Congress; provided that no amendments which may be made prior to the year one thousand eight hundred and eight shall in any manner affect the first and fourth clauses in the ninth section of the first article; and that no State, without its consent, shall be deprived of its equal suffrage in the Senate.

ARTICLE VI (*General Provisions*)

1   All debts contracted and engagements entered into, before the adoption of this Constitution, shall be as valid against the United States under this Constitution, as under the Confederation.

2   This Constitution, and the laws of the United States which shall be made in pursuance thereof; and all treaties made, or which shall be made, under the authority of the United States, shall be the supreme law of the land; and the judges in every State shall be bound thereby, anything in the Constitution or laws of any State to the contrary notwithstanding.

3   The Senators and Representatives before mentioned, and the members of the several State legislatures, and all executive and judicial officers, both of the United States and of the several States, shall be bound by oath or affirmation to support this Constitution; but no religious test shall ever be required as a qualification to any office or public trust under the United States.

ARTICLE VII (*Ratification of the Constitution*)

The ratification of the conventions of nine States shall be sufficient for the establishment of this Constitution between the States so ratifying the same.

AMENDMENTS TO
THE CONSTITUTION

AMENDMENT 1 *(Religious and Political Freedom)*

Congress shall make no law respecting an establishment of religion, or prohibiting the free exercise thereof; or abridging the freedom of speech, or of the press; or the right of the people peaceably to assemble, and to petition the government for a redress of grievances.

AMENDMENT 2 *(Right to Bear Arms)*

A well-regulated militia being necessary to the security of a free State, the right of the people to keep and bear arms shall not be infringed.

AMENDMENT 3 *(Quartering of Troops)*

No soldier shall, in time of peace, be quartered in any house without the consent of the owner, nor in time of war, but in a manner to be prescribed by law.

AMENDMENT 4 *(Searches and Seizures)*

The right of the people to be secure in their persons, houses, papers, and effects, against unreasonable searches and seizures, shall not be violated, and no warrants shall issue but upon probable cause, supported by oath or affirmation, and particularly describing the place to be searched, and the persons or things to be seized.

AMENDMENT 5 (*Right to Life, Liberty, and Property*)

No person shall be held to answer for a capital, or otherwise infamous crime, unless on a presentment or indictment of a grand jury except in cases arising in the land or naval forces, or in the militia, when in actual service in time of war or public danger; nor shall any person be subject for the same offence to be twice put in jeopardy of life or limb; nor shall be compelled in any criminal case to be a witness against himself, nor be deprived of live, liberty, or property, without due process of law; nor shall private property be taken for public use without just compensation.

AMENDMENT 6 (*Procedures in Criminal Trials*)

In all criminal prosecutions the accused shall enjoy the right to a speedy and public trial, by an impartial jury of the State and district wherein the crime shall have been committed, which district shall have been previously ascertained by law, and to be informed of the nature and cause of the accusation; to be confronted with the witnesses against him; to have compulsory process for obtaining witnesses in his favor, and to have the assistance of counsel for his defence.

AMENDMENT 7 (*Suits at Common Law*)

In suits at common law, where the value in controversy shall exceed twenty dollars, the right of trial by jury shall be preserved, and no fact tried by a jury shall be otherwise re-examined in any court of the United States, than according to the rules of the common law.

AMENDMENT 8 (*Bail and Punishments*)

Excessive bail shall not be required, nor excessive fines imposed, nor cruel and unusual punishments inflicted.

AMENDMENT 9 (*Concerning Rights Not Enumerated*)

The enumeration in the Constitution of certain rights shall not be construed to deny or disparage others retained by the people.

AMENDMENT 10 (*Powers Reserved to the States and to the People*)

The powers not delegated to the United States by the Constitution, nor prohibited by it to the States, are reserved to the States respectively, or to the people.

AMENDMENT 11 *(Suits Against a State)*

The judicial power of the United States shall not be construed to extend to any suit in law or equity, commenced or prosecuted against one of the United States by citizens of another State, or by citizens or subjects of any foreign state. [*Adopted in 1798.*]

AMENDMENT 12 *(Election of President and Vice-President)*

1 The electors shall meet in their respective States, and vote by ballot for President and Vice-President, one of whom, at least, shall not be an inhabitant of the same State with themselves; they shall name in their ballots the person voted for as President, and in distinct ballots the person voted for as Vice-President, and they shall make distinct lists of all persons voted for as President, and of all persons voted for as Vice-President, and of the number of votes for each, which lists they shall sign and certify, and transmit sealed to the seat of government of the United States, directed to the President of the Senate:—the President of the Senate shall, in the presence of the Senate and House of Representatives, open all the certificates and the votes shall then be counted;—the person having the greatest number of votes for President shall be the President, if such number be a majority of the whole number of electors appointed; and if no person have such majority, then from the persons having the highest numbers not exceeding three on the list of those voted for as President, the House of Representatives shall choose immediately, by ballot, the President. But in choosing the President, the votes shall be taken by States, the representation from each State having one vote; a quorum for this purpose shall consist of a member or members from two thirds of the States, and a majority of all the States shall be necessary to a choice. And if the House of Representatives shall not choose a President whenever the right of choice shall devolve upon them, before the fourth day of March next following, then the Vice-President shall act as President, as in the case of the death or other constitutional disability of the President.

2 The person having the greatest number of votes as Vice-President shall be the Vice-President, if such number be a majority of the whole number of electors appointed; and if no person have a majority, then from the two highest numbers on the list the Senate shall choose the Vice-President; a quorum for the purpose shall consist of two thirds of the whole number of Senators, and a majority of the whole number shall be necessary to a choice. But no person constitutionally ineligible to the office of President shall be eligible to that of Vice-President of the United States. [*Adopted in 1804.*]

AMENDMENT 13 *(Slavery Abolished)*

1 Neither slavery nor involuntary servitude, except as a punishment for crime whereof the party shall have been duly convicted, shall exist within the United States, or any place subject to their jurisdiction.

2 Congress shall have power to enforce this article by appropriate legislation. [*Adopted in 1865.*]

AMENDMENT 14 *(Citizenship and Limitations on the States)*

1 All persons born or naturalized in the United States, and subject to the jurisdiction thereof, are citizens of the United States and of the State wherein they reside. No State shall make or enforce any law which shall abridge the privileges or immunities of citizens of the United States; nor shall any State deprive any person of life, liberty, or property, without due process of law; nor deny to any person within its jurisdiction the equal protection of the laws.

2 Representatives shall be apportioned among the several States according to their respective numbers, counting the whole number of persons in each State, excluding Indians not taxed. But when the right to vote at any election for the choice of Electors for President and Vice-President of the United States, Representatives in Congress, the executive and judicial officers of a State, or the members of the legislature thereof, is denied to any of the male inhabitants of such State, being twenty-one years of age and citizens of the United States, or in any way abridged, except for participation in rebellion, or other crime, the basis of representation therein shall be reduced in the proportion which the number of such male citizens shall bear to the whole number of male citizens twenty-one years of age in such State.

3 No person shall be a Senator or Representative in Congress, or Elector of President and Vice-President, or hold any office, civil or military, under the United States, or under any State, who, having previously taken an oath, as a member of Congress, or as an officer of the United States, or as a member of any State legislature, or as an executive or judicial officer of any State, to support the Constitution of the United States, shall have engaged in insurrection or rebellion against the same, or given aid or comfort to the enemies thereof. But Congress may, by a vote of two thirds of each house, remove such disability.

4 The validity of the public debt of the United States, authorized by law, including debts incurred for payment of pensions and bounties for services in suppressing insurrection or rebellion, shall not be questioned. But neither the United States nor any State shall assume or pay any debt or obligation incurred in aid of insurrection or rebellion against the United States, or any claim for the loss or emancipation of

any slave; but all such debts, obligations, and claims shall be held illegal and void.

5   The Congress shall have power to enforce by appropriate legislation the provisions of this article. [*Adopted in 1868.*]

AMENDMENT 15   (*The Right to Vote*)

1   The right of citizens of the United States to vote shall not be denied or abridged by the United States or any State on account of race, color, or previous condition of servitude.

2   The Congress shall have power to enforce this article by appropriate legislation. [*Adopted in 1870.*]

AMENDMENT 16   (*Income Taxes*)

The Congress shall have power to lay and collect taxes on incomes, from whatever source derived, without apportionment among the several States, and without regard to any census or enumeration. [*Adopted in 1913.*]

AMENDMENT 17   (*Direct Election of Senators*)

1   The Senate of the United States shall be composed of two Senators from each State, elected by the people thereof, for six years; and each Senator shall have one vote. The electors in each State shall have the qualifications requisite for electors of the most numerous branch of the State legislatures.

2   When vacancies happen in the representation of any State in the Senate, the executive authority of such State shall issue writs of election to fill such vacancies: Provided that the Legislature of any State may empower the executive thereof to make temporary appointment until the people fill the vacancies by election as the Legislature may direct.

3   This amendment shall not be so construed as to affect the election or term of any Senator chosen before it becomes valid as part of the Constitution. [*Adopted in 1913.*]

AMENDMENT 18   (*National Prohibition*)

1   After one year from the ratification of this article the manufacture, sale, or transportation of intoxicating liquors within, the importation thereof into, or the exportation thereof from, the United States and all territory subject to the jurisdiction thereof, for beverage purposes, is hereby prohibited.

2   The Congress and the several States shall have concurrent power to enforce this article by appropriate legislation.

3   This article shall be inoperative unless it shall have been ratified as an amendment to the Constitution by the legislatures of the several States, as provided by the Constitution, within seven years from the date of the submission thereof to the States by the Congress. [*Adopted in 1919.*]

AMENDMENT 19 (*Woman Suffrage*)

1   The right of citizens of the United States to vote shall not be denied or abridged by the United States or by any State on account of sex.

2   The Congress shall have power to enforce this article by appropriate legislation. [*Adopted in 1920.*]

AMENDMENT 20 (*Presidential and Congressional Terms*)

1   The terms of the President and Vice-President shall end at noon on the 20th day of January and the terms of Senators and Representatives at noon on the 3d day of January, of the years in which such terms would have ended if this article had not been ratified; and the terms of their successors shall then begin.

2   The Congress shall assemble at least once in every year, and such meeting shall begin at noon on the 3d day of January, unless they shall by law appoint a different day.

3   If, at the time fixed for the beginning of the term of the President, the President-elect shall have died, the Vice-President-elect shall become President. If a President shall not have been chosen before the time fixed for the beginning of his term, or if the President-elect shall have failed to qualify, then the Vice-President-elect shall act as President until a President shall have qualified; and the Congress may by law provide for the case wherein neither a President-elect nor a Vice-President-elect shall have qualified, declaring who shall then act as President, or the manner in which one who is to act shall be selected, and such persons shall act accordingly until a President or Vice-President shall have qualified.

4   The Congress may by law provide for the case of the death of any of the persons from whom the House of Representatives may choose a President whenever the right of choice shall have devolved upon them, and for the case of the death of any of the persons from whom the Senate may choose a Vice-President whenever the right of choice shall have devolved upon them.

5   Sections 1 and 2 shall take effect on the 15th day of October following the ratification of this article.

6   This article shall be inoperative unless it shall have been ratified as an amendment to the Constitution by the Legislatures of three fourths

of the several States within seven years from the date of its submission. [*Adopted in 1933.*]

AMENDMENT 21 (*Repeal of National Prohibition*)

1   The eighteenth article of amendment to the Constitution of the United States is hereby repealed.

2   The transportation or importation into any State, Territory, or Possession of the United States for delivery or use therein of intoxicating liquors, in violation of the laws thereof is hereby prohibited.

3   This article shall be inoperative unless it shall have been ratified as an amendment to the Constitution by conventions in the several States, as provided in the Constitution, within seven years from the date of the submission thereof to the States by the Congress. [*Adopted in 1933*]

AMENDMENT 22 (*Length of Time a President May Serve*)

1   No person shall be elected to the office of the President more than twice, and no person who has held the office of President, or acted as President, for more than two years of the term to which some other person was elected President shall be elected to the office of the President more than once. But this Article shall not apply to any person holding the office of President when this Article was proposed by the Congress, and shall not prevent any person who may be holding the office of President, or acting as President, during the term within which this Article becomes operative from holding the office of President or acting as President during the remainder of such term.

2   This Article shall be inoperative unless it shall have been ratified as an amendment to the Constitution by the legislatures of three-fourths of the several States within seven years from the date of his submission to the States by the Congress. [*Adopted in 1951.*]

AMENDMENT 23 (*District of Columbia Suffrage in Presidential Elections*)

1   The District constituting the seat of Government of the United States shall appoint in such manner as the Congress may direct:

A number of electors of President and Vice-President equal to the whole number of Senators and Representatives in Congress to which the District would be entitled if it were a State, but in no event more than the least populous State; they shall be in addition to those appointed by the States, but they shall be considered, for the purposes of the election of President and Vice-President, to be electors appointed by a State; and they shall meet in the District and perform such duties as provided by the twelfth article of amendment.

2 The Congress shall have power to enforce this article by appropriate legislation. [*Adopted in 1961.*]

AMENDMENT 24 (*Poll Tax Barred in Federal Elections*)

1 The right of citizens of the United States to vote in any primary or other election for President or Vice-President, for electors for President or Vice-President, or for Senator or Representative in Congress, shall not be denied or abridged by the United States or any State by reason of failure to pay any poll tax or other tax.

2 The Congress shall have power to enforce this article by appropriate legislation. [*Adopted in 1964.*]

AMENDMENT 25 (*Presidential Succession*)

1 In case of the removal of the President from office or of his death or resignation, the Vice-President shall become President.

2 Whenever there is a vacancy in the office of the Vice-President, the President shall nominate a Vice-President who shall take office upon confirmation by a majority vote of both Houses of Congress.

3 Whenever the President transmits to the President pro tempore of the Senate and the Speaker of the House of Representatives his written declaration that he is unable to discharge the powers and duties of his office, and until he transmits to them a written declaration to the contrary, such powers and duties shall be discharged by the Vice-President as Acting President.

4 Whenever the Vice-President and a majority of either the principal officers of the executive departments or of such other body as Congress may by law provide, transmit to the President pro tempore of the Senate and the Speaker of the House of Representatives their written declaration that the President is unable to discharge the powers and duties of his office, the Vice-President shall immediately assume the powers and duties of the office as Acting President.

Thereafter, when the President transmits to the President pro tempore of the Senate and the Speaker of the House of Representatives his written declaration that no inability exists, he shall resume the powers and duties of his office unless the Vice-President and a majority of either the principal officers of the executive department or of such other body as Congress may by law provide, transmit within four days to the President pro tempore of the Senate and the Speaker of the House of Representatives their written declaration that the President is unable to discharge the powers and duties of his office. Thereupon Congress shall decide the issue, assembling within forty-eight hours for that purpose if not in session. If the Congress, within twenty-one days after receipt of the latter written declaration, or, if Congress is not in session, within twenty-one days after Congress is required to assemble, determines by two-thirds vote of both Houses that the President is unable to discharge the powers and duties of his office, the Vice-President shall continue to discharge the same as Acting President; otherwise, the President shall resume the powers and duties of his office. [*Adopted in 1967.*]

SELECTIVE BIBLIOGRAPHY

* Indicates paperback edition available. See issues of *Paperbound Books in Print* for names of publishers.

CHAPTER 1
Analysis of Political Systems

Dahl, Robert A. *Modern Political Analysis.** Englewood Cliffs, N.J.: Prentice-Hall, 1963.

De Jouvenal, Bertrand. *On Power.** Boston: Beacon Press, 1949.

Easton, David. *The Political System.* New York: Knopf, 1953.

Friedrich, Carl J. *Man and His Government.* New York: McGraw-Hill, 1963.

Hyneman, Charles S. *The Study of Politics.* Urbana: University of Illinois Press, 1959.

Lasswell, H., and A. Kaplan. *Power and Society.** New Haven, Conn.: Yale University Press, 1952.

MacIver, Robert M. *The Web of Government,* (rev. ed.).* New York: Free Press, 1965.

Ranney, Austin (ed.). *Essays on the Behavorial Study of Politics.* Urbana: University of Illinois Press, 1962.

Storing, Herbert J. (ed.). *Essays on the Scientific Study of Politics.* New York: Holt, Rinehart and Winston, 1962.

Van Dyke, Vernon. *Political Science: A Philosophical Analysis.** Palo Alto, Calif.: Stanford University Press, 1960.

Voegelin, Eric. *The New Science of Politics.** Chicago: Chicago University Press, 1952.

CHAPTER 2
Democratic Government in Theory and Practice

Bryce, James. *Modern Democracies.* New York: Macmillan, 1921.

Dahl, Robert A. *A Preface to Democratic Theory.** Chicago: University of Chicago Press, 1956.

Downs, Anthony. *An Economic Theory of Democracy.** New York: Harper & Row, 1957.

Hallowell, John M. *The Moral Foundation of Democracy.* Chicago: University of Chicago Press, 1954.

Lindsay, A. D. *The Modern Democratic State.** New York: Oxford University Press, 1947.

Mayo, Henry B. *An Introduction to Democratic Theory.** New York: Oxford University Press, 1960.

Riemer, Neal. *The Revival of Democratic Theory.** New York: Appleton-Century-Crofts, 1961.

Spitz, David. *Democracy and the Challenge of Power.* New York: Columbia University Press, 1958.

Thorson, Thomas L. *The Logic of Democracy.** New York: Holt, Rinehart and Winston, 1962.

Tocqueville, Alexis de. *Democracy in America.** New York: Knopf, 1945.

CHAPTER 3
Foundations of Constitutional Government

Corwin, Edward S. *The "Higher Law" Background of American Constitutional Law.** Ithaca, N.Y.: Cornell University Press, 1955.

Friedrich, Carl J. *Constitutional Government and Democracy* (3rd ed.) . Boston: Ginn, 1964.

Hartz, Louis. *The Liberal Tradition in America.** New York: Harcourt, Brace & World, 1955.

Jameson, J. Franklin. *The American Revolution Considered as a Social Movement.** Boston: Beacon Press, 1956.

McIlwain, Charles H. *Constitutionalism: Ancient and Modern.** Ithaca, N.Y.: Cornell University Press, 1940.

Neumann, Franz. *The Democratic and the Authoritarian State: Essays in Political and Legal Theory.** New York: Free Press, 1957.

Parrington, Vernon L. *Main Currents in American Thought* (3 vols.) .* New York: Harcourt, Brace & World, 1927.

Rossiter, Clinton. *Seedtime of the Republic* (Pts. I–III) .* New York: Harcourt, Brace & World, 1953.

Sutherland, Arthur E. *Constitutionalism in America: The Origin and Evolution of Its Fundamental Laws.* New York: Blaisdell, 1965.

Wormuth, Francis D. *The Origins of Modern Constitutionalism.* New York: Harper & Row, 1949.

CHAPTER 4
Framing and Ratification of the American Constitution

Beard, Charles A. *An Economic Interpretation of the Constitution of the United States.** New York: Macmillan, 1913.

Becker, Carl L. *The Declaration of Independence—A Study in the History of Political Ideas.** New York: Random House, 1958.

Brown, Robert E. *Charles Beard and the American Constitution.** Princeton, N.J.: Princeton University Press, 1956.

Elliott, Jonathan (ed.). *Debates in the Several State Conventions on the Adoption of the Federal Constitution* (4 vols., 2nd ed.). Philadelphia: Lippincott, 1901.

Farrand, Max. *The Framing of the Constitution of the United States.** New Haven, Conn.: Yale University Press, 1913.

Farrand, Max (ed.). *The Records of the Federal Convention of 1787* (4 vols.).* New Haven, Conn.: Yale University Press, 1923.

Hamilton, Alexander, James Madison, and John Jay. *The Federalist.* Available in numerous editions.

Jenson, Merrill. *The New Nation—A History of the United States During the Confederation.** New York: Knopf, 1950.

McDonald, Forrest. *We the People—The Economic Origins of the Constitution.** Chicago: University of Chicago Press, 1958.

Main, Jackson Turner. *The Antifederalists—Critics of the Constitution, 1781–1788.** Chapel Hill: University of North Carolina Press, 1961.

Rossiter, Clinton. *1787: The Grand Convention.* New York: Macmillan, 1966.

Smith, David G. *The Convention and the Constitution.** New York: St. Martin's Press, 1965.

CHAPTER 5
The Separation of Powers

Bock, Edwin A., and Alan K. Campbell (eds.). *Case Studies in American Government.* Englewood Cliffs, N.J.: Prentice-Hall, 1962.

Finer, Herman. *Theory and Practice of Modern Government.* New York: Holt, Rinehart and Winston, 1949.

Montesquieu, Baron de. *The Spirit of the Laws.** New York: Hafner.

Odegard, Peter, and Victor Rosenblum. *The Power to Govern.* New York: Fund for Adult Education, 1957.

Vile, M. J. C. *Constitutionalism and the Separation of Powers.* Oxford: Clarendon Press, 1967.

Wilson, Francis G. *The Elements of Modern Politics.* New York: McGraw-Hill, 1936.

Wilson, Woodrow. *Congressional Government.** Boston: Houghton Mifflin, 1885.

CHAPTER 6
The Federal System

Anderson, William. *The Nation and the States, Rivals or Partners?* Minneapolis: University of Minnesota Press, 1955.

Elazar, Daniel J. *American Federalism: A View from the States.** New York: Crowell-Collier, 1966.

Grodzins, Morton. *The American System: A New View of Government in the United States.* Chicago: Rand McNally, 1966.

MacMahon, Arthur W. *Federalism: Mature and Emergent.* Garden City, N.Y.: Doubleday, 1955.

Riker, William H. *Federalism: Origin, Operation, and Significance.** Boston: Little, Brown, 1964.

Rockefeller, Nelson A. *The Future of Federalism.** Cambridge, Mass.: Harvard University Press, 1962.

Vile, M. J. C. *The Structure of American Federalism.* New York: Oxford University Press, 1962.

Wheare, K. C. *Federal Government.** London: Oxford University Press, 1951.

White, Leonard D. *The States and the Nation.* Baton Rouge: Louisiana State University Press, 1953.

Wildavsky, Aaron. *American Federalism in Perspective.** Boston: Little, Brown, 1967.

CHAPTER 7
Public Opinion and Suffrage

Campbell, Angus, Philip E. Converse, Warren E. Miller, and Donald E. Stokes. *The American Voter.** New York: Wiley, 1960.

Hennessy, Bernard C. *Public Opinion.* Belmont, Calif.: Wadsworth, 1965.

Key, V. O., Jr. *Public Opinion and American Democracy.* New York: Knopf, 1961.

Klapper, Joseph T. *The Effect of Mass Communication.* New York: Free Press, 1961.

Lane, Robert E., and David O. Sears. *Public Opinion.** Englewood Cliffs, N.J.: Prentice-Hall, 1964.

Lazarsfeld, Paul, Bernard Berelson, and Hazel Gaudet. *The People's Choice.* New York: Columbia University Press, 1948.

Lippmann, Walter. *Public Opinion.** New York: Macmillan, 1922.

Lowell, A. Lawrence. *Public Opinion and Popular Government.* New York: McKay, 1913.

Milbrath, Lester W. *Political Participation: How and Why Do People Get Involved in Politics?** Chicago: Rand McNally, 1965.

Porter, Kirk H. *A History of Suffrage in the United States.* Chicago: University of Chicago Press, 1918.

Rogers, Lindsay. *The Pollsters.* New York: Knopf, 1949.

Sanders, Marion K. *The Lady and the Vote.* Boston: Houghton Mifflin, 1956.

Schattschneider, E. E. *The Semisovereign People.** New York: Holt, Rinehart and Winston, 1960.

Watters, Pat, and Reese Cleghorn. *Climbing Jacob's Ladder.* New York: Harcourt, Brace & World, 1967.

CHAPTER 8
The American Party System

Binkley, Wilfred E. *American Political Parties, Their Natural History* (3rd ed.). New York: Knopf, 1958.

Bone, Hugh. *Party Committees and National Politics.* Seattle: University of Washington Press, 1958.

Chambers, William N. *Political Parties in a New Nation: The American Experience, 1776–1809.** New York: Oxford University Press, 1963.

Duverger, Maurice. *Political Parties: Their Organization and Activity in the Modern State.** New York: Wiley, 1961.

Eldersveld, Samuel J. *Political Parties: A Behavioral Analysis.* Chicago: Rand McNally, 1964.

Fenton, John H. *People and Parties in Politics.* Chicago: Scott, Foresman, 1966.

Key, V. O., Jr. *Politics, Parties, and Pressure Groups* (5th ed.). New York: Crowell-Collier, 1964.

Michels, Robert. *Political Parties.** Gloucester, Mass.: Peter Smith, 1960.

Ranney, Austin, and Willmoore Kendall. *Democracy and the American Party System.* New York: Harcourt, Brace & World, 1956.

Rossiter, Clinton. *Parties and Politics in America.** Ithaca, N.Y.: Cornell University Press, 1960.

CHAPTER 9
The Politics of Political Parties: Choosing the Candidates

Brogan, D. W. *An Introduction to American Politics.* London: Hamish Hamilton, 1954.

Brown, W. Burlie. *The People's Choice.* Baton Rouge: Louisiana State University Press, 1960.

David, Paul T., Malcolm Moos, and Ralph M. Goldman (eds.). *Presidential Nominating Politics,* 5 vols. Baltimore: Johns Hopkins Press, 1954.

David, Paul T., Ralph M. Goldman, and Richard C. Bain. *The Politics of National Party Conventions.** Washington, D.C.: Brookings Institution, 1960.

Heard, Alexander. *The Costs of Democracy.** Chapel Hill: University of North Carolina Press, 1960.

O'Connor, Edwin. *The Last Hurrah.** New York: Bantam Books.

Roseboom, Eugene H. *A Short History of Presidential Elections.* New York: Macmillan, 1957.

Van Riper, Paul. *Handbook of Practical Politics,* 3rd. ed.* New York: Harper & Row, 1960.

White, Theodore H. *The Making of the President, 1964.** New York: Atheneum, 1965.

White, Theodore H. *The Making of the President, 1960.** New York: Atheneum, 1961.

CHAPTER 10
Party Politics and the Process of Government

Acheson, Dean. *A Democrat Looks at His Party.* New York: Harper & Row, 1959.

Bailey, Stephen. *The Condition of Our National Parties.* New York: The Fund for the Republic, 1959.

Burns, James M. *The Deadlock of Democracy: Four Party Politics in America.** Englewood Cliffs, N.J.: Prentice-Hall, 1963.

Herring, E. Pendleton. *The Politics of Democracy: American Parties in Action.** New York: Norton, 1965.

Larson, Arthur. *A Republican Looks at His Party.* New York: Harper & Row, 1956.

Lubell, Samuel. *The Future of American Politics.** New York: Harper & Row, 1951.

Mayhew, David R. *Party Loyalty Among Congressmen.* Cambridge, Mass.: Harvard University Press, 1966.

Ranney, Austin. *The Doctrine of Responsible Party Government.** Chicago: University of Chicago Press, 1954.

Schattschneider, E. E. *Party Government.** New York: Holt, Rinehart and Winston, 1942.

Truman, David B. *The Congressional Party.* New York: Wiley, 1959.

CHAPTER 11
Interest Groups and Pressure Politics

Blaisdell, Donald C. *Democracy Under Pressure.* New York: Ronald Press, 1957.

Brady, Robert A. *Business as a System of Power.* New York: Columbia University Press, 1943.

Cater, Douglas. *Power in Washington.** New York: Random House, 1964.

Garceau, Oliver. *The Political Life of the American Medical Association.* Cambridge, Mass.: Harvard University Press, 1941.

Hardin, Charles M. *The Politics of Agriculture.* New York: Free Press, 1952.

Holtzman, Abraham. *Interest Groups and Lobbying.** New York: Macmillan, 1966.

McConnell, Grant. *Private Power and American Democracy.* New York: Knopf, 1966.

Milbrath, Lester W. *The Washington Lobbyists.* Chicago: Rand McNally, 1963.

Odegard, Peter H. *Religion and Politics.* Dobbs Ferry, N.Y.: Oceana, 1960.

Truman, David B. *The Governmental Process.* New York: Knopf, 1951.

Ziegler, Harmon. *Interest Groups in American Society.* Englewood Cliffs, N.J.: Prentice-Hall, 1964.

CHAPTER 12
Congress and the Committee System

Acheson, Dean. *A Citizen Looks at Congress.* New York: Harper & Row, 1957.

Bailey, Stephen K. *Congress Makes a Law.** New York: Columbia University Press, 1950.

Bailey, Stephen K. *The New Congress.** New York: St. Martin's Press, 1966.

Berman, Daniel M. *A Bill Becomes a Law: Congress Enacts Civil Rights Legislation.** New York: Macmillan, 1962.

Berman, Daniel M. *In Congress Assembled: The Legislative Process in National Government.* New York: Macmillan, 1964.

Clapp, Charles L. *The Congressman: His Work as He Sees It.** Washington, D.C.: Brookings Institution, 1963.

Fenno, Richard F. *The Power of the Purse.* Boston: Little, Brown, 1966.

Galloway, George B. *The Legislative Process in Congress.* New York: Crowell-Collier, 1953.

Harris, Joseph P. *The Advice and Consent of the Senate.* Berkeley: University of California Press, 1953.

Jewell, Malcolm E., and Samuel C. Patterson. *The Legislative Process in the United States.* New York: Random House, 1966.

MacNeil, Neil. *Forge of Democracy: The House of Representatives.** New York: McKay, 1963.

Matthews, Donald. *U.S. Senators and Their World.* Chapel Hill: University of North Carolina Press, 1960.

Taylor, Telford. *Grand Inquest.* New York: Simon and Schuster, 1955.

White, William S. *Citadel: The Story of the U.S. Senate.* New York: Harper & Row, 1957.

CHAPTER 13
The Presidency

Binkley, Wilfred E. *President and Congress.** New York: Knopf, 1947.

Burns, James M. *Presidential Government.** Boston: Houghton Mifflin, 1966.

Corwin, Edward S. *The President: Office and Powers* (4th rev. ed.) .** New York: New York University Press, 1957.

Hyman, Sidney. *The American President.* New York: Harper & Row, 1954.

Kallenbach, Joseph E. *The American Chief Executive: The Presidency and the Governorship.* New York: Harper & Row, 1966.

Koenig, Louis W. *The Chief Executive.* New York: Harcourt, Brace & World, 1964.

McConnell, Grant. *The Modern Presidency.** New York: St. Martin's Press, 1967.

Neustadt, Richard E. *Presidential Power.** New York: Wiley, 1960.

Rossiter, Clinton. *The American Presidency.** New York: Harcourt, Brace & World, 1964.

CHAPTER 14
Presidential Policy and Administration

Burns, James M. *Roosevelt: The Lion and the Fox.** New York: Harcourt, Brace & World, 1956.

Evans, Rowland, and Robert Novak. *Lyndon B. Johnson: The Exercise of Power.* New York: New American Library, 1966.

Fenno, Richard F., Jr. *The President's Cabinet.** Cambridge, Mass.: Harvard University Press, 1959.

Hobbs, Edward H. *Behind the President.* Washington, D.C.: Public Affairs Press, 1954.

Hughes, Emmet John. *The Ordeal of Power.* New York: Atheneum, 1963.

Koenig, Louis W. *The Invisible Presidency.* New York: Holt, Rinehart and Winston, 1960.

May, Ernest R. (ed.) . *The Ultimate Decision: The President as Commander in Chief.* New York: Braziller, 1960.

Rossiter, Clinton. *The Chief Executive.* New York: Harcourt, Brace & World, 1964.

Schlesinger, Arthur M. *A Thousand Days.** Boston: Houghton Mifflin, 1965.

Sorensen, Theodore C. *Decision-Making in the White House.** New York: Columbia University Press, 1963.

Warren, Sidney. *The President as World Leader.** New York: McGraw-Hill, 1964.

Williams, Irving G. *The American Vice-Presidency: New Look.** New York: Random House, 1954.

CHAPTER 15
The Federal Bureaucracy

Appleby, Paul H. *Big Democracy*. New York: Knopf, 1945.

Bernstein, Marver. *The Job of the Federal Executive*. Washington, D.C.: Brookings Institution, 1958.

Blau, Peter M. *Bureaucracy in Modern Society.** New York: Random House, 1956.

Boyer, William. *Bureaucracy on Trial: Policy Making by Government Agencies.** Indianapolis: Bobbs-Merrill, 1964.

David, Paul T., and Ross Pollock. *Executives for Government.** Washington, D.C.: Brookings Institution, 1957.

Downs, Anthony. *Inside Bureaucracy.** Boston: Little, Brown, 1967.

Hyneman, Charles. *Bureaucracy in a Democracy*. New York: Harper & Row, 1950.

Sayre, Wallace S. *The Federal Government Service* (2nd ed.) .** Englewood Cliffs, N.J.: Prentice-Hall, 1965.

Simon, Herbert A. *Administrative Behavior* (2nd ed.) .** New York: Macmillan, 1957.

Van Riper, Paul P. *History of the United States Civil Service*. New York: Harper & Row, 1958.

Woll, Peter. *American Bureaucracy.** New York: Norton, 1963.

CHAPTER 16
The Supreme Court

Beth, Loren P. *Politics, the Constitution, and the Supreme Court: An Introduction to the Study of Constitutional Law.** New York: Harper & Row, 1962.

Bickel, Alexander M. *The Least Dangerous Branch: The Supreme Court at the Bar of Politics.** Indianapolis: Bobbs-Merrill, 1962.

Danelski, David J. *A Supreme Court Justice Is Appointed.** New York: Random House, 1964.

Hyneman, Charles. *The Supreme Court on Trial*. New York: Atherton, 1963.

McCloskey, Robert G. *The American Supreme Court.** Chicago: University of Chicago Press, 1960.

Mendelson, Wallace. *The Constitution and the Supreme Court* (2nd ed.) . New York: Dodd, Mead, 1965.

Murphy, Walter F. *Elements of Judicial Strategy*. Chicago: University of Chicago Press, 1964.

Schmidhauser, John R. *The Supreme Court as Final Arbiter in Federal-State Relations*. Chapel Hill: University of North Carolina Press, 1958.

Schubert, Glendon. *The Judicial Mind: The Attitudes and Ideologies of Supreme Court Justices, 1946–1963*. Evanston, Ill.: Northwestern University Press, 1965.

Swisher, Carl Brent. *The Supreme Court in Modern Role* (rev. ed.).* New York: New York University Press, 1965.

CHAPTER 17
The Administration of Justice

Abraham, Henry J. *Courts and Judges.* New York: Oxford University Press, 1959.
Cardozo, Benjamin. *The Nature of the Judicial Process.** New Haven, Conn.: Yale University Press, 1921.
Fellman, David. *The Defendant's Rights.* New York: Holt, Rinehart and Winston, 1958.
Frank, Jerome. *Courts on Trial.** Princeton, N.J.: Princeton University Press, 1950.
Holmes, Oliver Wendell. *The Common Law.** Boston: Little, Brown, 1881.
Hurst, Willard. *The Growth of American Law.* Boston: Little, Brown, 1950.
Jacob, Herbert. *Justice in America: Courts, Lawyers, and the Judicial Process.** Boston: Little, Brown, 1965.
Peltason, Jack W. *Fifty-eight Lonely Men.* New York: Harcourt, Brace & World, 1961.
Roche, John P. *Courts and Rights: The American Judiciary in Action* (rev. ed.).* New York: Random House, 1961.
Vanderbilt, Arthur T. *Judges and Jurors.* Boston: Boston University Press, 1956.
Westin, Alan F. *The Anatomy of a Constitutional Law Case.** New York: Macmillan, 1958.

CHAPTER 18
The Bill of Rights: Freedom, Due Process, and Equal Protection

Berns, Walter. *Freedom, Virtue, and the First Amendment.** Baton Rouge: Louisiana State University Press, 1957.
Brant, Irving. *The Bill of Rights: Its Origin and Meaning.** Indianapolis: Bobbs-Merrill, 1965.
Brown, Ralph S., Jr. *Loyalty and Security.* New Haven, Conn.: Yale University Press, 1958.
Gellhorn, Walter. *American Rights.* New York: Macmillan, 1960.
Harris, Robert. *The Quest for Equality.* Baton Rouge: Louisiana State University Press, 1960.
Lewis, Anthony. *Gideon's Trumpet.** New York: Random House, 1964.
Lewis, Anthony. *Portrait of a Decade: The Second American Revolution.** New York: Random House, 1964.
Miller, Loren. *The Petitioners: The Story of the Supreme Court of the United States and the Negro.** New York: Pantheon, 1966.
Pfeffer, Leo. *Church, State, and Freedom* (rev. ed.). Boston: Beacon Press, 1966.
Spicer, George W. *The Supreme Court and Fundamental Freedoms* (rev. ed.).* New York: Appleton-Century-Crofts, 1967.
Westin, Alan F. *Privacy and Freedom.* New York: Atheneum, 1967.
Wood, Virginia. *Due Process of Law, 1932–1949.* Baton Rouge: Louisiana State University Press, 1951.

CHAPTER 19
The States in the Federal System

Adrian, Charles. *State and Local Government: A Study in the Political Process.* New York: McGraw-Hill, 1960.

Allen, R. S. (ed.). *Our Sovereign States.* New York: Vanguard Press, 1949.

American Assembly. *The Forty-eight States.* New York: Columbia University Press, 1955.

Baker, Gordon E. *The Reapportionment Revolution: Representation, Political Power, and the Supreme Court.* New York: Random House, 1966.

Graves, W. Brooke. *American State Government* (4th ed.). Boston: Heath, 1953.

Heard, Alexander (ed.). *State Legislatures in American Politics.* Englewood Cliffs, N.J.: Prentice-Hall, 1966.

Jacob, Herbert, and Kenneth N. Vines (eds.). *Politics in the American States: A Comparative Analysis.* Boston: Little, Brown, 1965.

Jewell, Malcolm E. *The State Legislature: Politics and Practice.* New York: Random House, 1962.

Key, V. O., Jr. *American State Politics: An Introduction.* New York: Knopf, 1956.

Ransome, Coleman B., Jr. *The Office of Governor in the United States.* University, Alabama: University of Alabama Press, 1956.

CHAPTER 20
The Urban Drift: Problems of Metropolitan Growth

Abrams, Charles. *The City Is the Frontier.* New York: Harper & Row, 1965.

Banfield, Edward C., and James Q. Wilson. *City Politics.* Cambridge, Mass.: Harvard University Press and Massachusetts Institute of Technology Press, 1963.

Bollens, John C., and Henry J. Schmandt. *The Metropolis.* New York: Harper & Row, 1965.

Dahl, Robert A. *Who Governs: Democracy and Power in American City.* New Haven, Conn.: Yale University Press, 1961.

Fiser, Webb. *Mastery of Metropolis.* Englewood Cliffs, N.J.: Prentice-Hall, 1962.

Gottman, Jean. *Megalopolis: The Urbanized Northeastern Seaboard.* New York: The Twentieth Century Fund, 1961.

Greer, Scott. *Governing the Metropolis.* New York: Wiley, 1962.

Hunter, Floyd. *Community Power Structure.* Chapel Hill: University of North Carolina Press, 1953.

Martin, Roscoe C. *The Cities and the Federal System.* New York: Atherton Press, 1965.

Mumford, Lewis. *The City in History.* New York: Harcourt, Brace & World, 1961.

Sayre, Wallace S., and Herbert Kaufman. *Governing New York City.* New York: Russell Sage Foundation, 1960.

Wood, Robert C. *Suburbia: Its People and Their Politics.** Boston: Houghton Mifflin, 1958.

CHAPTER 21
To Promote the General Welfare

Altmeyer, Arthur. *The Formative Years of Social Security.** Madison: University of Wisconsin Press, 1966.

Banfield, Edward C., and Morton Grodzins. *Government and Housing in Metropolitan Areas.* New York: McGraw-Hill, 1958.

Burns, Eveline M. *Social Security and Public Policy.* New York: McGraw-Hill, 1956.

Feingold, Eugene (ed.) . *Medicare: Policy and Politics.** San Francisco: Chandler, 1966.

Harrington, Michael. *The Other America.** New York: Macmillan, 1962.

Price, Don K. *Government and Science.** New York: New York University Press, 1954.

Rivlin, Alice M. *The Role of the Federal Government in Financing Higher Education.** Washington, D.C.: Brookings Institution, 1962.

Seligman, Ben B. *Permanent Poverty—An American Syndrome.* Chicago: Quadrangle, 1968.

Somers, Herman M., and Anne R. Somers. *Workmen's Compensation.* New York: Wiley, 1954.

Wengert, Norman. *Natural Resources and the Political Struggle.** New York: Random House, 1962.

CHAPTER 22
Government and the Economy

Berle, Adolph A., Jr. *Power Without Property: A New Development in American Political Economy.** New York: Harcourt, Brace & World, 1959.

Bernstein, Marver H. *Regulating Business by Independent Commission.** Princeton, N.J.: Princeton University Press, 1955.

Dahl, Robert A., and Charles E. Lindblom. *Politics, Economics, and Welfare: Planning and Politico-Economic Systems Resolved into Basic Social Processes.** New York: Harper & Row, 1953.

Fabricant, Solomon. *The Trend of Government Activity in the U.S. Since 1900.* Princeton, N.J.: Princeton University Press, 1952.

Fainsod, Merle, Lincoln Gordon, and Joseph C. Palamountain, Jr. *Government and the American Economy.* New York: Norton, 1959.

Galbraith, John K. *The Great Crash, Nineteen Twenty Nine.** Boston: Houghton Mifflin, 1955.

Musolf, Lloyd D. *Government and the Economy.** Chicago: Scott, Foresman, 1965.

Reagan, Michael D. *The Managed Economy.** New York: Oxford University Press, 1963.

CHAPTER 23
Taxation: Theory and Practice

Burkhead, Jesse. *Government Budgeting*. New York: Wiley, 1956.

Doris, Lilian (ed.). *The American Way in Taxation: Internal Revenue 1862–1963*. Englewood Cliffs, N.J.: Prentice-Hall, 1963.

Groves, Harold M. *Financing Government* (5th ed.). New York: Holt, Rinehart and Winston, 1958.

Heilbroner, Robert L., and Peter L. Bernstein. *A Primer on Government Spending.** New York: Random House, 1963.

Paul, Randolph E. *Taxation in the United States*. Boston: Little, Brown, 1954.

Rolf, Earl R., and George F. Break. *Public Finance*. New York: Ronald Press, 1961.

Sievers, Allan M. *Revolution, Evolution, and the Economic Order.** Englewood Cliffs, N.J.: Prentice-Hall, 1961.

Strayer, Paul J. *Fiscal Policy and Politics*. New York: Harper & Row, 1958.

Wildavsky, Aaron. *The Politics of the Budgetary Process.** Boston: Little, Brown, 1964.

CHAPTER 24
Foreign Policy

Almond, Gabriel. *The American People and Foreign Policy.** New York: Harcourt, Brace & World, 1956.

Claude, Inis L. *Swords into Plow-shares* (2nd ed.). New York: Random House, 1959.

Crabb, Cecil V., Jr. *American Foreign Policy in the Nuclear Age* (2nd ed.). New York: Harper & Row, 1965.

Emerson, Rupert. *From Empire to Nation: The Rise to Self-Assertion of Asian and African Peoples.** Cambridge, Mass.: Harvard University Press, 1960.

Fairbank, John K. *The United States and China.** Cambridge, Mass.: Harvard University Press, 1958.

Fliess, Peter J. *International Relations in the Bipolar World*. New York: Random House, 1968.

Goldwin, Robert A. (ed.). *America Armed: Essays on United States Military Policy.** Chicago: Rand McNally, 1963.

Kennan, George F. *American Diplomacy: 1900–1950.** Chicago: University of Chicago Press, 1951.

Kissinger, Henry A. *Nuclear Weapons and Foreign Policy*. Garden City, N.Y.: Doubleday, 1957.

Montgomery, John D. *The Politics of Foreign Aid*. New York: Praeger, 1962.

Perkins, Dexter. *The United States and Latin America*. Baton Rouge: Louisiana State University Press, 1961.

Sapin, Burton M. *The Making of United States Foreign Policy.** Washington, D.C.: Brookings Institution, 1966.

Stebbins, Richard P. *The United States in World Affairs.** New York: Harper & Row, 1967.

Thompson, Kenneth W. *Political Realism and the Crisis of World Politics.* *
Princeton, N.J.: Princeton University Press, 1960.

Thorp, Willard (ed.). *United States and the Far East.* (2nd ed.). Englewood
Cliffs, N.J.: Prentice-Hall, 1962.

Westerfield, H. Bradford. *The Instruments of America's Foreign Policy.* New
York: Crowell, 1963.

69 70 71 7 6 5 4 3 2 1